P9-AQK-753

Educational Research

Planning, Conducting, and Evaluating Quantitative and Qualitative Research

THIRD EDITION

John W. Creswell
University of Nebraska-Lincoln

Upper Saddle River, New Jersey
Columbus, Ohio

Library of Congress Cataloging-in-Publication Data

Creswell, John W.
Educational research : planning, conducting, and evaluating quantitative and qualitative research / John W. Creswell. — 3rd ed.
p. cm.
Includes bibliographical references and index.
ISBN-13: 978-0-13-613550-0 (casebound)
ISBN-10: 0-13-613550-1 (casebound)
1. Education—Research—Methodology. I. Title.
LB1028.C742 2008
370.7'2—dc22

2007013087

Vice President and Executive Publisher: Jeffery W. Johnston
Publisher: Kevin M. Davis
Development Editors: Autumn Crisp Benson, Christina Robb
Editorial Assistant: Sarah N. Kenoyer
Production Editor: Mary Harlan
Production Coordination: Thistle Hill Publishing Services, LLC
Design Coordinator: Diane C. Lorenzo
Text Design and Illustrations: Integra
Cover Design: Ali Mohrman
Cover Image: SuperStock
Production Manager: Laura Messerly
Director of Marketing: David Gesell
Marketing Manager: Autumn Purdy
Marketing Coordinator: Brian Mounts

This book was set in Garamond by Integra. It was printed and bound by Edwards Brothers, Inc. The cover was printed by Phoenix Color Corp.

Pearson Education Ltd.
Pearson Education Singapore Pte. Ltd.
Pearson Education Canada, Ltd.
Pearson Education–Japan
Pearson Education Australia Pty. Limited
Pearson Education North Asia Ltd.
Pearson Educación de Mexico, S.A. de C.V.
Pearson Education Malaysia Pte. Ltd.

10 9 8 7 6 5 4 3 2
ISBN-13: 978-0-13-613550-0
ISBN-10: 0-13-613550-1

This text is dedicated to Karen, who provided caring editorial help and support through three editions of this book. You have been my inspiration and thoughtful advocate throughout this project. Thanks for standing beside me.

Preface

The philosophy that guided the development of this text is twofold. First, research involves a process of interrelated activities rather than the application of isolated, unrelated concepts and ideas. Educators practice research following a general sequence of procedures—from the initial identification of a research problem to the final report of research. This means that understanding the sequence or flow of activities is central to inquiry. Thus, the text begins with specific chapters devoted to each step in the process of research and the inclusion of concepts and ideas within this process.

Second, the educational researcher today needs a large toolbox of approaches to study the complex educational issues in our society. No longer can we, as educators, use only experiments or surveys to address our research problems. Educators in this new century—whether conducting research or reading research to self-inform—need to know about both quantitative and qualitative approaches to inquiry and to have an in-depth understanding of the multiple research designs and procedures used in our studies today. In each step in the process of research, this text will introduce you to both quantitative and qualitative approaches. Throughout the text, you will learn about the differences and similarities of qualitative and quantitative research. In the last section of the text, you will be introduced to eight distinct quantitative and qualitative research designs or procedures that comprise the repertoire of the educational researcher in the quantitative, qualitative, and combined applications of research.

KEY FEATURES

This text is the first introduction to educational research text to offer a truly balanced, inclusive, and integrated overview of the field as it currently stands. As you will see from the table of contents, the book's coverage is unique in its balanced presentation of quantitative and qualitative research. Moreover, it consistently examines foundational issues of research—for example, determining how to approach a project and understanding what constitutes data and how to analyze them—from both quantitative and qualitative perspectives. This approach helps students understand fundamental differences *and* similarities of these approaches. This text has three main purposes:

- It provides balanced coverage of quantitative and qualitative research.
- It helps students learn how to begin to conduct research.
- It helps students learn how to read and evaluate research studies.

Let's look at each of these in detail to see how each can help you achieve your course objectives.

Balances Coverage of Quantitative and Qualitative Research

This text provides balanced coverage of all types of research designs. This provides readers with a complete picture of educational research as it is currently practiced. The text begins with an overview in part I of the general nature of educational research and the specific quantitative and qualitative approaches to educational research. Next, in part II, chapters 3 through 10, the book examines in depth the steps in the research process:

1. Identifying a research problem
2. Reviewing the literature
3. Specifying a purpose and research questions or hypotheses
4. Collecting either quantitative or qualitative data
5. Analyzing and interpreting either quantitative or qualitative data
6. Reporting and evaluating the research

Looking at the process simultaneously from both quantitative and qualitative perspectives helps students understand what choices a researcher has available and what meaning exists for a particular choice.

After this discussion, in part III, students will learn the procedures for conducting specific types of quantitative, qualitative, and mixed-methods studies. Chapters 11 through 18 provide balanced coverage and examples of each of these types of educational research designs: experimental, correlational, survey, grounded theory, ethnographic, narrative, mixed methods, and action research.

Helps Students Learn How to Begin to Do Research

Both the research process and design chapters offer the researcher step-by-step guidance in the basic aspects of planning, conducting, and evaluating research. A number of features guide readers through the steps and procedures of research. For example, a fictional beginning researcher, Maria, who is also a high school teacher and new graduate student, is followed throughout part II and part III to illustrate one researcher's efforts and to provide students with a realistic perspective of the process of research and the selection of specific research designs. Other features include, but are not limited to:

- Tips on planning and conducting research in "Useful Information for Producers of Research"
- Checklists that summarize key points such as evaluation criteria used to assess the quality of a quantitative or qualitative study
- In-text examples of actual and hypothetical studies that illustrate the correct and incorrect ways of reporting research
- Follow-up activities in "Understanding Concepts and Evaluating Research Studies" to help students apply the concepts they've just learned
- A "Think Aloud" feature that describes practices the author has found useful

Helps Students Learn How to Read and Evaluate Research Studies

Direct guidance on reading research is offered throughout the text. To further help students become more skilled at interpreting and evaluating research, the text offers a number of features. Most important among these are the many articles included in the text and the "Useful Information for Consumers of Research" feature.

- The text provides annotated research articles in each of the design chapters in part III. Two other articles—one qualitative, one quantitative—appear at the end of chapter 1. All of these complete articles (there are numerous other, shorter article excerpts in the book) include highlighted marginal annotations that help students understand the structure of articles and the key issues with which a reader should be concerned when evaluating the quality and the applicable scope of each particular piece of research.
- The "Useful Information for Consumers of Research" feature appears at the end of every chapter and offers concrete guidance in interpreting and evaluating research.

CHANGES IN THE THIRD EDITION

You will find several key changes included in this third edition:

- Many concepts have been clarified and simplified in the discussion of quantitative data collection and analysis. For example, information about quantitative validity has been expanded to include multiple forms of criterion-related validity, and new content analyzes the relationship between reliability and validity. Clarifications are made about the interpretations of scales as either ordinal or interval. Topics such as hypothesis testing, commonly used statistical tests, and various procedures for calculating effect sizes have been both clarified and developed further in this third edition.
- Quantitative and qualitative research approaches are no longer seen as two completely separate approaches but as forms of research that lie along a continuum. The discussion about characteristics of both quantitative and qualitative research now reflects more of a continuum than polar approaches. Often in educational research, the studies are not entirely either quantitative or qualitative but contain some elements of both approaches. The design chapters on mixed methods and action research reinforce this emerging trend in research.
- Ethical issues have been expanded to include discussions on deceptive practices, the disclosure of the purpose of studies, respect for research sites, and issues of ethics unique to qualitative interviewing. Ethical discussions now frame our introduction to research, and they become an important consideration in both quantitative and qualitative data collection.
- New articles are included to update the sample articles. The new quantitative article used as an example through chapters 1–10 reflects the current issue in education of the involvement of parents in the education of their adolescents. A new article on experimental research in chapter 11 provides a recent research report on factors that influence students' reading motivation and competence. Many articles that were included in the last edition are retained because they still serve as good illustrations of both the strengths and pitfalls of conducting research.
- A more balanced perspective is given to the use of many different computer databases that readers can access to review the literature. Computerized databases are continually revised and updated, and this edition provides a balanced view of such databases as EBSCO, ERIC, and PsycInfo.

- As with the second edition, an attempt has been made to update references and other materials throughout the text, update the sources of information that readers can use in their courses or as reference materials and other material, and streamline the text so that it can be easily accessed and read by students with both an interest in conducting research as well as reading and using research.

SUPPLEMENTARY MATERIALS

A number of ancillaries are available to complement the text. For students, a Study Guide and a Companion Website are available to reinforce and extend learning. Instructors may use the online Instructor's Manual and Test Bank, a Computerized Test Bank, customized online PowerPoint slides, and WebCT, and Blackboard Cartridges.

Student Study Guide The *Student Study Guide* (0-13-159296-3) has been designed to assist students in identifying the important concepts of each chapter, applying the ideas in practice activities, and testing understanding of the concepts. Each chapter in the Study Guide has Chapter Learning Objectives, Practice in Understanding Key Concepts, and Practice Test Items with an Answer Key. The Study Guide also includes sample studies and reviews of the research designs.

Six complete educational research studies are provided in the *Student Study Guide*. These articles represent a range of educational topics (music education, children with Asperger syndrome, eating disorders, preservice teaching, study abroad programs, and leadership), participant types, and approaches to research.

In Part III on Research Designs, the *Student Study Guide* includes brief reviews for the Quantitative, Qualitative, and Combined research designs. These reviews ask students to summarize what they have learned across multiple chapters and give them an opportunity to compare and contrast the different designs.

Companion Website You can find the Companion Website at **www.prenhall.com/creswell**. This free online learning site helps students master course content with essay and multiple-choice questions, interactive Building Research Skills exercises, and Internet links to explore related topics.

Test Bank A Test Bank is available online for this text. It contains various types of items—multiple choice, matching, short essay, and fill in the blank—for each chapter. Questions ask students to identify and describe research processes and design characteristics they have learned about and to classify and evaluate quantitative and qualitative studies and research situations. The Test Bank is available on the Instructor's Resource Center at **http://www.prenhall.com**.

TestGen TestGen (0–13–233949–8), a computerized test bank, is available on disk for Windows and Macintosh.

PowerPoint Slides. PowerPoint slides are available on the Instructor's Resource Center at **http://prenhall.com**.

OneKey Course Management OneKey is Prentice Hall's exclusive resource for instructors and students. OneKey is an integrated online course management resource featuring everything students and instructors need for work in or outside of the classroom. OneKey is available in WebCT (0-13-233946-3) and Blackboard (0-13-233947-1).

ACKNOWLEDGMENTS

This book is a culmination of 30 years of experience in conducting both quantitative and qualitative research in education and the social sciences. It could not have been written without the capable assistance of numerous individuals such as graduate students, research assistants, and colleagues at the University of Nebraska–Lincoln. Dr. Dana Miller assisted in a timely and thorough review of many chapters. Vicki Plano Clark provided editorial assistance and a key conceptual eye for missing details. Amanda Garrett has provided invaluable assistance in locating up-to-date materials and in conceptualizing ideas. Dr. Ron Shope developed the initial PowerPoint presentation and has revised it extensively for this third edition. Others have been helpful as well. Dong Dong Zhang provided inspiration for many applied ideas and support at critical phases of the project. Other graduate students offered useful ideas, including Michael Toland, Kathy Shapely, and many other students in my graduate program area, quantitative and qualitative methods of education, as did students in my classes on the foundations of educational research. Dr. Bill Mickelson served as a statistics consultant and quantitative analysis reviewer.

I am also indebted to Kevin Davis at Prentice Hall/Merrill for initiating this book and providing the vision to launch it as the "next-generation" research methods text in education. Autumn Benson, my excellent development editor at Prentice Hall/Merrill, provided patience, support, and useful insights throughout the project.

Numerous reviewers helped to shape this book. They include Rick Brigham, George Mason University; David A. Gilman, Indiana State University; David Pugalee, University of North Carolina, Charlotte; Linda Shepard, Indiana University–Bloomington; Wendy G. Troxel, Illinois State University; Belinda M. Wholeben, Rockford College; and Brent E. Wholeben, Northern Illinois University.

Research Navigator: Research Made Simple!

www.ResearchNavigator.com

Merrill Education is pleased to introduce Research Navigator—a one-stop research solution for students that simplifies and streamlines the entire research process. At **www.researchnavigator.com**, students will find extensive resources to enhance their understanding of the research process so they can effectively complete research assignments. In addition, Research Navigator has three exclusive databases of credible and reliable source content to help students focus their research efforts and begin the research process.

HOW WILL RESEARCH NAVIGATOR ENHANCE YOUR COURSE?

- Extensive content helps students understand the research process, including writing, Internet research, and citing sources.
- Step-by-step tutorial guides students through the entire research process from selecting a topic to revising a rough draft.
- Research Writing in the Disciplines section details the differences in research across disciplines.
- Three exclusive databases—EBSCO's ContentSelect Academic Journal Database, *The New York Times* Search by Subject Archive, and "Best of the Web" Link Library—allow students to easily find journal articles and sources.

WHAT'S THE COST?

A subscription to Research Navigator is $7.50 but is available at no additional cost when ordered in conjunction with this textbook. To obtain free passcodes for your students, simply contact your local Merrill/Prentice Hall sales representative, and your representative will send you the Evaluating Online Resource Guide, which contains the code to access Research Navigator as well as tips on how to use Research Navigator and how to evaluate research. To preview the value of this website to your students, please go to **www.educatorlearningcenter.com** and use the Login Name "Research" and the password "Demo."

Brief Contents

Contents

Chapter 18 *Action Research Designs 596*

NOTE: Every effort has been made to provide accurate and current Internet information in this book. However, the Internet and information posted on it are constantly changing, so it is inevitable that some of the Internet addresses listed in this textbook will change.

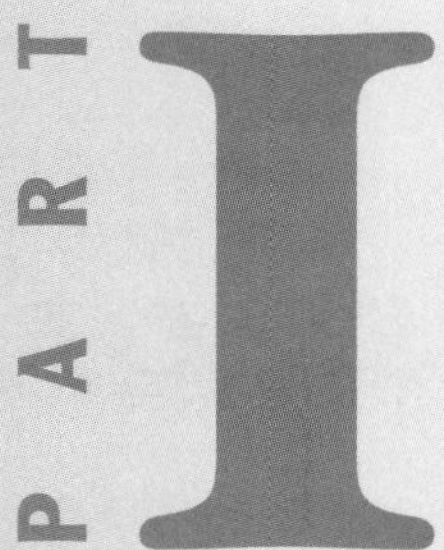

An Introduction to Educational Research

Consider research your personal journey. It will be challenging but also exciting. Pack along for your journey a toolkit. In chapter 1 you will be introduced to the basic supplies. In your pack place a solid understanding of "research." Also include a map—the six steps in the process of conducting research. Realize that on this journey you need to respect people and the places you visit. Enjoy the process using your natural skills such as the ability to solve puzzles, use library resources, and write.

In chapter 2, with these basics in place, you will explore each section of a "research" map as you cross its terrain. Each of the six steps of research will unfold, showing you that educational research uses different paths. We will focus on two major paths—quantitative and qualitative research—and see how both of these paths take you to the end of the journey but in different ways.

Let us begin.

CHAPTER 1

The Process of Conducting Research

What is research? Research is a process in which you engage in a small set of logical steps. In this chapter, we define research, discuss why it is important, advance six steps for conducting research, and identify how you can conduct research ethically by employing skills that you already have.

By the end of this chapter, you should be able to:

- ◆ Define educational research.
- ◆ Identify three reasons for the importance of research.
- ◆ Name the six steps typically undertaken by researchers in the process of research.
- ◆ Identify important ethical issues in conducting research.
- ◆ Reflect on the skills you bring to the research process.

Maria, a teacher with 10 years of experience, teaches English at a midsized metropolitan high school. Lately, a number of incidents in the school district have involved students possessing weapons:

- ◆ A teacher found a 10th grader hiding a knife in his locker.
- ◆ A 12th-grade student threatened another student, telling him "he wouldn't see the light of day" unless he stopped harassing her.
- ◆ At a nearby high school, a student pointed a handgun at another student outside the school.

These incidents alarm district officials, school administrators, and teachers. The principal forms a committee made up of administrators and teachers to develop guidelines about how the school should respond to these situations. In response to a call for teachers to serve on this committee, Maria volunteers immediately.

Maria sees the school committee assignment and her graduate program's research study requirement as mutual opportunities to research school violence and weapon possession. Where does she begin?

Maria's situation of balancing the dual roles of professional and graduate student may be familiar to you. Let's assess her present research situation:

- Maria recognizes the need to closely examine an important issue—school violence and weapons at school—although she is new to research. However, she is not a stranger to looking up topics in libraries or to searching the Internet when she has a question about something. She has occasionally looked at a few research journals, such as the *High School Journal,* the *Journal of Educational Research,* and *Theory into Practice,* in her school library and has overheard other teachers talking about research studies on the subject of school violence. Although she has no research background, she expects that research will yield important findings for her school committee and also help her fulfill the requirement to conduct a small-scale research study for her graduate degree.
- To complete the required research for her graduate program, Maria must overcome her fears about planning and conducting a study. To do this, she needs to think about research not as a large, formidable task, but as a series of small, manageable steps. Knowing these smaller steps is key to the success of planning and completing her research.

Your situation may be similar to Maria's. At this stage, your concerns may start with the question "What is research?"

WHAT IS RESEARCH?

Research is a process of steps used to collect and analyze information to increase our understanding of a topic or issue. At a general level, research consists of three steps:

1. Pose a question.
2. Collect data to answer the question.
3. Present an answer to the question.

This should be a familiar process. You engage in solving problems every day and you start with a question, collect some information, and then form an answer. Although there are a few more steps in research than these three, this is the overall framework for research. When you examine a published study, or conduct your own study, you will find these three parts as the core elements.

WHY IS RESEARCH IMPORTANT?

Not all educators have an understanding and appreciation of research. For some, research may seem like something that is important only for faculty members in the ivory tower of colleges and universities. Although it is true that college and university faculty members value and conduct research, personnel in other educational settings also read and use research, such as school psychologists, principals, school board members, adult educators, college administrators, and graduate students. Research is important for three reasons.

Research Adds to Our Knowledge

Educators strive for continual improvement. This requires addressing problems or issues and searching for potential solutions. **Adding to knowledge** means that educators undertake research to contribute to existing information about issues. We are all aware of pressing educational issues being debated today, such as the integration of AIDS education into the school curriculum.

Research plays a vital role in addressing these issues. Through research we develop results that help to answer questions, and as we accumulate these results, we gain a deeper understanding of the problems. In this way, researchers are much like bricklayers who build a wall brick by brick, continually adding to the wall and, in the process, creating a stronger structure.

How can research specifically add to the knowledge base and existing literature? A research report might provide a study that has not been conducted and thereby fill a void in existing knowledge. It can also provide additional results to confirm or disconfirm results of prior studies. It can help add to the literature about practices that work or advance better practices that educators might try in their educational setting. It can provide information about people and places that have not been previously studied. In chapter 3, we will discuss these contributions in more depth and review them again as good reasons for studying a topic or research issue.

Suppose that you decide to research how elementary schoolchildren learn social skills. If you study how children develop social skills, and past research has not examined this topic, your research study addresses a gap in knowledge. If your study explores how African American children use social skills on their way home from school, your study would replicate past studies but would test results with new participants at a new research site. If your study examines how children use social skills when at play, not on the school ground, but on the way home from school, the study would contribute to knowledge by expanding our understanding of the topic. If your study examines female children on the way home from school, your study would add female voices seldom heard in the research. If your study has implications for how to teach social skills to students, it has practical value.

Research Improves Practice

Research is also important because it *suggests improvements* for practice. Armed with research results, teachers and other educators become more effective professionals. This effectiveness translates into better learning for kids. For instance, through research, personnel involved in teacher-education programs in schools of education know much more about training teachers today than they did 20 years ago. Zeichner (1999) summarized the impact of research on teacher training during this period (see Table 1.1). Teacher trainers today know about the academic capabilities of students, the characteristics of good teacher-training programs, the recurring practices in teacher-training programs, the need to challenge student beliefs and worldviews, and the tensions teacher educators face within their institutions. But before these research results can impact teacher training or any other aspect of education, individuals in educational settings need to be aware of results from investigations, to know how to read research studies, to locate useful conclusions from them, and to apply the findings to their own unique situations. Educators using research may be teachers in preschool through Grade 12, superintendents in school district offices, school psychologists working with children with behavioral problems, or adult educators who teach English as a second language. Research may help these individuals improve their practices on the job.

TABLE 1.1

Zeichner's (1999) Summary of Major Research Results in Teacher Education

Research Conducted	What Researchers Have Learned
Surveys about students in teacher education programs	• From academic, social class, racial, ethnic, and gender characteristics of both teacher educators and their students, the research has challenged the misconception that students who go into teaching are academically inferior to those who go into other fields. • Despite changing U.S. demographics, teacher education programs admit mostly students who are white, monolingual English speakers.
Specific case studies of individual teacher education programs	• Successful teacher education programs have a coherent vision of good teaching and close links to local schools. • Researchers need to spend time living in teacher education programs to understand them.
Conceptual and historical research on teacher education programs	• Teacher education programs differ in their approaches, such as the importance of disciplinary knowledge versus students learning versus critiquing societal inequalities in schooling practices. • Programs throughout the 20th century have emphasized recurring practices such as performance-based teacher education.
Studies of learning to teach in different settings	• It is difficult to change the tacit beliefs, understandings, and worldviews that students bring to teacher education programs. • The impact of a program on students can be increased through cohort groups, portfolio development, case studies, and narratives in which they examine their beliefs.
The nature and impact of teacher education activities and self-studies	• Despite the sometimes unfavorable structural conditions of teacher educators' work, their voices are being heard. • Teachers, in these self-studies, describe the tensions and contradictions involved in being a teacher educator.

Research offers practicing educators *new ideas* to consider as they go about their jobs. From reading research studies, educators can learn about new practices that have been tried in other settings or situations. For example, the adult educator working with immigrants may find that small-group interaction that focuses on using cultural objects from the various homelands may increase the rate at which immigrants learn the English language.

Research also helps practitioners *evaluate approaches* that they hope will work with individuals in educational settings. This process involves sifting through research to determine which results will be most useful. This process is demonstrated in Figure 1.1, which focuses on three steps that a classroom teacher might use (Connelly, Dukacz, & Quinlan, 1980). As shown in Figure 1.1, a teacher first decides what needs to be implemented in the classroom, then examines alternative lines of research, and finally decides which line of research might help accomplish what needs to be done.

For example, a reading teacher decides to incorporate more information about cultural perspectives into the classroom. Research suggests that this may be done with classroom interactions by inviting speakers to the room (line A) or by having the children consider and think (cognitively) about different cultural perspectives by talking with individuals at a local cultural center (line B). It may also be accomplished by having the children inquire into cultural messages embedded within advertisements (line C) or identify the cultural

FIGURE 1.1

Lines of Research and Your Decision Making

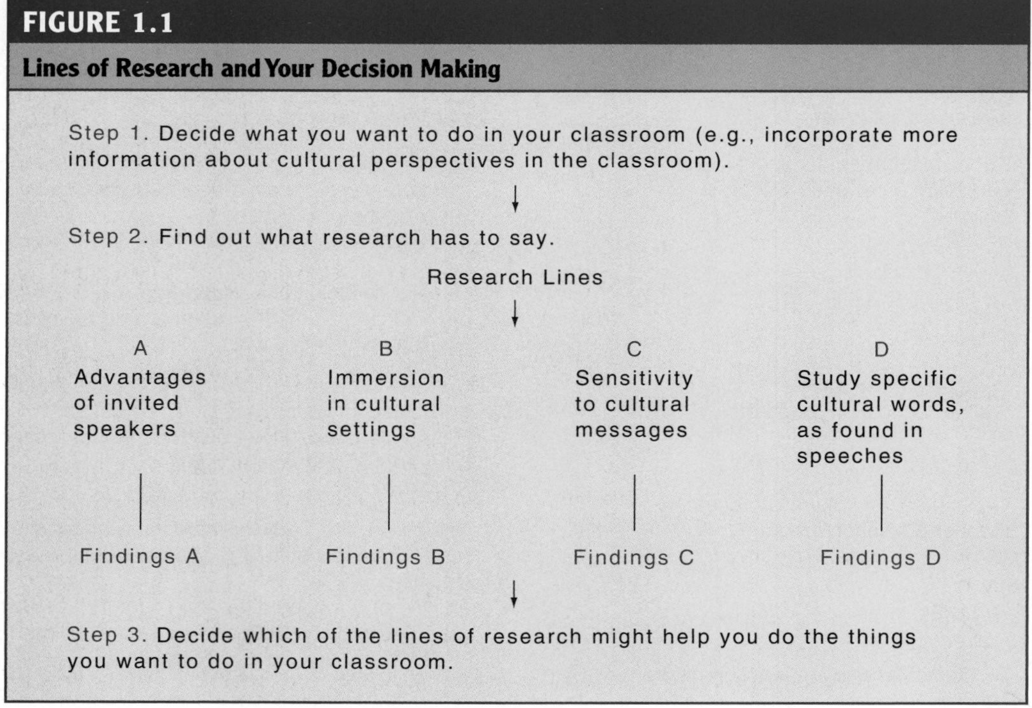

Source: Adapted from Connelly, Dukacz, & Quinlan, 1980.

subject matter of speeches of famous Americans (line D). A line of research is then chosen that helps the teacher to accomplish classroom goals. This teacher might be Maria, our teacher conducting research on weapon possession in schools and its potential for violence. Maria hopes to present options for dealing with this issue to her committee and needs to identify useful research lines and consider approaches taken by other schools.

At a broader level, research helps the practicing educator *build connections* with other educators who are trying out similar ideas in different locations. Special-education teachers, for example, may establish connections at research conferences where individuals report on topics of mutual interest, such as using small-group strategies for discipline management in classrooms.

Research Informs Policy Debates

In addition to helping educators become better practitioners, research also creates conversations about important issues when policy makers debate educational topics. Policy makers may range from federal government employees and state workers to local school board members and administrators, and they discuss and take positions on educational issues important to constituencies. For these individuals, research offers results that can help them weigh various perspectives. When policy makers read research on issues, they are informed about current debates and stances taken by other public officials. To be useful, research needs to have clear results, be summarized in a concise fashion, and include data-based evidence. For example, research useful to policy makers might summarize the alternatives on:

- Welfare and its effect on children's schooling among lower income families
- School choice and the arguments proposed by opponents and proponents

SEVERAL PROBLEMS WITH RESEARCH TODAY

Despite the importance of research, we need to realistically evaluate its contributions. Sometimes the results show only contradictory or vague findings. An education aide to the Education and Labor Committee of the U.S. House of Representatives for 27 years expressed this confusion: "I read through every single evaluation . . . looking for a hard sentence—a declarative sentence—something that I could put into the legislation, and there were very few" (Viadero, 1999, p. 36). Not only are policy makers looking for a clear "declarative sentence," many readers of educational research search for some evidence that makes a direct statement about an educational issue. On balance, however, research accumulates slowly, and what may seem contradictory comes together to make sense in time. Based on the information known, for example, it took more than 4 years to identify the most rudimentary factors about how chairpersons help faculty become better researchers (Creswell, Wheeler, Seagren, Egly, & Beyer, 1990).

Another problem with research is the issue of questionable data. The author of a particular research report may not have gathered information from people who are able to understand and address the problem. The number of participants may also be dismally low, which can cause problems in drawing appropriate statistical conclusions. The survey used in a study may contain questions that are ambiguous and vague. At a technical level, the researcher may have chosen an inappropriate statistic for analyzing the data. Just because research is published in a well-known journal does not automatically make it "good" research.

To these issues we could add unclear statements about the intent of the study, the lack of full disclosure of data-collection procedures, or inarticulate statements of the research problem that drives the inquiry. Research has limits, and you need to know how to decipher research studies because researchers may not write them as clearly and accurately as you would like. We cannot erase all "poor" research reported in the educational field. We can, however, as responsible inquirers, seek to reconcile different findings and employ sound procedures to collect and analyze data and to provide clear direction for our own research.

WHAT ARE THE STEPS IN CONDUCTING RESEARCH?

When researchers conduct a study, they proceed through a distinct set of steps. Years ago these steps were identified as the "scientific method" of inquiry (Kerlinger, 1972; Leedy & Ormrod, 2001). Using a "scientific method," researchers:

- Identify a problem that defines the goal of research
- Make a prediction that, if confirmed, resolves the problem
- Gather data relevant to this prediction
- Analyze and interpret the data to see if it supports the prediction and resolves the question that initiated the research

Applied today, these steps provide the foundation for educational research. Although not all studies include predictions, you engage in these steps whenever you undertake a research study. As shown in Figure 1.2, the **process of research** consists of six steps:

1. Identifying a research problem
2. Reviewing the literature
3. Specifying a purpose for research
4. Collecting data

FIGURE 1.2

The Research Process Cycle

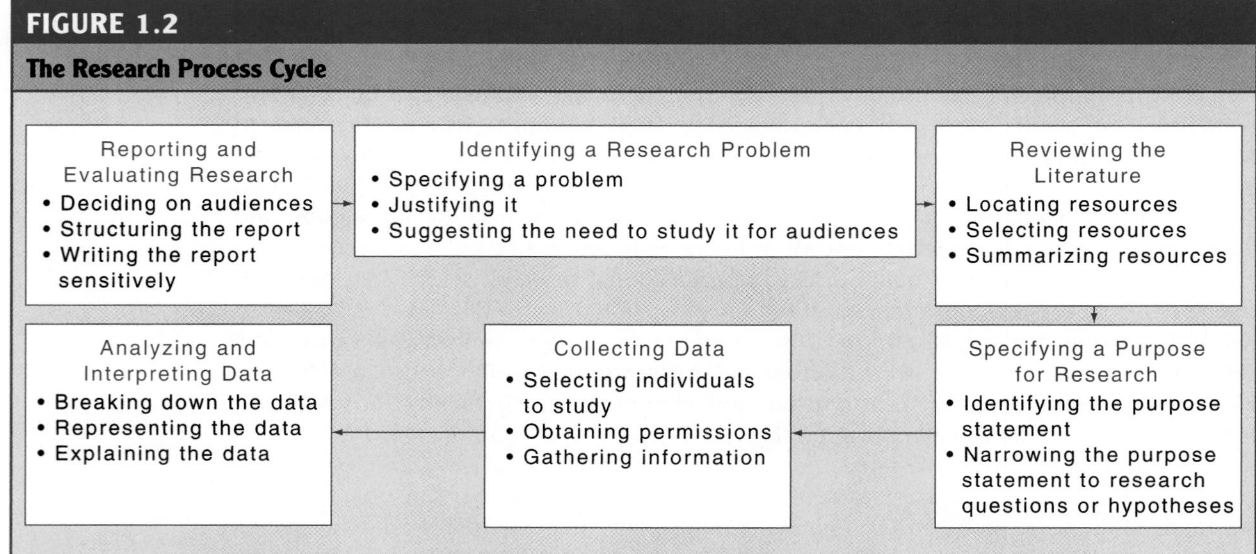

5. Analyzing and interpreting the data
6. Reporting and evaluating research

Each of these steps will be discussed in detail in chapters 3 through 10, but we introduce them here.

Identifying a Research Problem

You begin a research study by identifying a topic to study—typically an issue or problem in education that needs to be resolved. **Identifying a research problem** consists of specifying an issue to study, developing a justification for studying it, and suggesting the importance of the study for select audiences that will read the report. By specifying a "problem," you limit the subject matter and focus attention on a specific aspect of study. Consider the following "problems," each of which merits research:

- Teens are not learning how to connect to others in their communities.
- Teenage smoking will lead to many premature deaths.

These needs, issues, or controversies arise out of an educational need expressed by teachers, schools, policy makers, or researchers, and we refer to them as *research problems.* You will state them in introductory sections of a research report and provide a rationale for their importance. In a formal sense, these problems are part of a larger written section called the "statement of the problem," and this section includes the topic, the problem, a justification for the problem, and the importance of studying it for specific audiences such as teachers, administrators, or researchers.

Let's examine Maria's research to see how she will specify her study's research problem.

> Maria plans to study school violence and weapon possession in schools. She starts with a problem: escalating weapon possession among students in high schools. She needs to justify the problem by providing evidence about the importance of this problem and documenting how her study will provide new insight into the problem.

To identify and justify the research problem, Maria will follow steps such as those described in chapter 3, "Identifying a Research Problem."

Reviewing the Literature

It is important to know who has studied the research problem you plan to examine. You may fear that you will initiate and conduct a study that merely replicates prior research. However, faculty and advisors often fear that you will plan a study that does not build on existing knowledge and does not add to the accumulation of findings on a topic. Because of these concerns, reviewing the literature is an important step in the research process. **Reviewing the literature** means locating summaries, books, journals, and indexed publications on a topic; selectively choosing which literature to include in your review; and then summarizing the literature in a written report.

Your skills required for reviewing the literature develop over time and with practice. You can learn how to locate journal articles and books in an academic library, access computerized databases, choose and evaluate the quality of research on your topic, and summarize it in a review. Library resources can be overwhelming, so having a strategy for searching the literature and writing the review is important. Let's examine Maria's approach to reviewing the literature.

> To inform her committee about the latest literature on school violence and to plan her own research, Maria needs to conduct a literature review. This process will involve becoming familiar with the university library holdings, spending time reviewing resources and making decisions about what literature to use, and writing a formal summary of the literature on school violence. She consults the library catalog at her university and plans to search the computerized databases.

The types of procedures Maria will need to follow are described in chapter 4, "Reviewing the Literature."

Specifying a Purpose for Research

If your research problem covers a broad topic of concern, you need to focus it so that you can study it. A focused restatement of the problem is the *purpose statement*. This statement conveys the overall objective or intent of your research. As such, it is the most important statement in your research study. It introduces the entire study, signals the procedures you will use to collect data, and indicates the types of results you hope to find.

The **purpose for research** consists of identifying the major intent or objective for a study and narrowing it into specific research questions or hypotheses. The purpose statement contains the major focus of the study, the participants in the study, and the location or site of the inquiry. This purpose statement is then narrowed to research questions or predictions that you plan to answer in your research study. Let's check again with Maria to see how she will write a purpose statement and research questions.

> Maria now needs to write down the purpose of her study and formulate the questions she will ask of the individuals selected for her study. In draft after draft she sketches this purpose statement, recognizing that it will provide major direction for her study and help keep her focused on the primary aim of her study. From this broad purpose, Maria now needs to narrow her study to specific questions or statements that she would like her participants to answer.

Chapter 5, "Specifying a Purpose and Research Questions or Hypotheses," provides information about the elements that go into writing good purpose statements, research questions, and hypotheses.

Collecting Data

Evidence helps provide answers to your research questions and hypotheses. To get these answers, you engage in the step of collecting or gathering data. **Collecting data** means identifying and selecting individuals for a study, obtaining their permission to study them, and gathering information by asking people questions or observing their behaviors. Of paramount concern in this process is the need to obtain accurate data from individuals and places. This step will produce a collection of numbers (test scores, frequency of behaviors) or words (responses, opinions, quotes). Once you identify these individuals and places, you write *method* or *procedure sections* into your research studies. These sections offer detailed, technical discussions about the mechanics and administration of data collection. Many decisions, however, go into creating a good data-collection procedure. Let's see how Maria will address data collection.

> At this point in the research process, Maria needs to think about where she will conduct her study of school violence and weapon possession, who will participate in the study, how she will obtain permission to study them, what data she will collect, and how she will gather the data. She needs to decide whether she will have students fill out forms or talk to them directly to gather data to answer her research questions. Whichever course she chooses, she will need permission from the high school students and, because the students are minors, from their parents.

Chapter 6, "Collecting Quantitative Data," and chapter 8, "Collecting Qualitative Data," describe the types of procedures Maria will need to follow in her study.

Analyzing and Interpreting the Data

During or immediately after data collection, you need to make sense of the information supplied by individuals in the study. Analysis consists of "taking the data apart" to determine individual responses and then "putting it together" to summarize it. **Analyzing and interpreting the data** involves drawing conclusions about it; representing it in tables, figures, and pictures to summarize it; and explaining the conclusions in words to provide answers to your research questions. You report analysis and interpretation in sections of a research report usually titled *Results, Findings,* or *Discussions*. How will Maria analyze and interpret the data in her research?

> If Maria collects information on a written questionnaire from students across the school district, she will need to enter the questionnaire responses into a computer program, choose a statistical procedure, conduct the analyses, report the results in tables, and draw conclusions about (or interpret) whether the data confirm or disconfirm her expected trends or predictions. If she conducts face-to-face interviews, she will collect audiotapes of students talking about weapon possession at school and transcribe these tapes to obtain a written record. With her transcriptions, she will engage in making sense of student comments by selecting specific sentences and paragraphs and by identifying themes of information. From these themes, she will interpret the meaning of student comments in light of her own personal stance and the suggestions found in past studies.

For help in the data analysis and interpretation phase of her study, Maria will need to understand the research procedures described in chapter 7, "Analyzing and Interpreting Quantitative Data," and in chapter 9, "Analyzing and Interpreting Qualitative Data."

Reporting and Evaluating Research

After conducting your research, you will develop a written report and distribute it to select audiences (such as fellow teachers, administrators, parents, students) that can use your information. **Reporting research** involves deciding on audiences, structuring the report in a format acceptable to these audiences, and then writing the report in a manner that is sensitive to all readers. The audiences for research will vary from academic researchers who contribute and read journal articles, to faculty advisors and committees that review master's theses and dissertations, to personnel in educational agencies and school districts who look for reports of research on timely topics. Your structure for the research report will vary for each audience, from a formal format for theses and dissertations to a more informal document for in-house school reports. In all types of reports, however, researchers need to be respectful and to avoid language that discriminates on the basis of gender, sexual orientation, race, or ethnic group.

The audience for your report will have its own standards for judging the quality and utility of the research. **Evaluating research** involves assessing the quality of a study using standards advanced by individuals in education. Unfortunately, there are no ironclad standards for evaluating educational research in the academic research community; in school districts; or in local, state, or federal agencies. Still, we need some means of determining the quality of studies, especially published research or reports presented to practitioner audiences. Let's look at how Maria thinks about organizing her research report.

> Maria thinks about how she will organize her final report to her school committee and to her university graduate committee. Her graduate committee likely has a structure in mind for her graduate research study, and she needs to consult her faculty advisor about the format that students typically use. She should have a general idea about what the major sections of the study will be, but the contents of the specific paragraphs and ideas will take shape as her data analysis and interpretation progress.
>
> Her school report will likely be different from her research report. The school report will be informative and concise, will offer recommendations, and will include minimal discussions about methods and procedures. Whatever the audience and structure for her report, it must be respectful of the audience and be devoid of discriminatory language.

Chapter 10, "Reporting and Evaluating Research," focuses on strategies that Maria might find helpful as she writes her final reports.

WHAT ETHICAL PRACTICES SHOULD YOU OBSERVE?

Respect for audiences and the use of nondiscriminatory language are ethical issues that Maria must observe. In all steps of the research process, you need to engage in ethical practices. You will be introduced to ethical issues as they arise in later chapters. At this stage in your introduction to research, you might think about them as they relate to respecting the rights of participants, to honoring research sites that you visit, and to reporting research fully and honestly.

Respecting the Rights of Participants

Ethical standards to use in research are available from professional associations. Examples of professional associations that offer helpful guidelines include the American Educational

Research Association (AERA; *Ethical Standards of the American Educational Research Association,* Strike et al., 2002), the American Psychological Association (APA; *Ethical Principles of Psychologists and Code of Conduct,* 2003), the American Anthropological Association (AAA; *Code of Ethics,* 1998), and the Joint Committee on Standards for Educational Evaluation (*Program Evaluation Standards,* adopted November 21, 1980; amended through September 20, 1995).

According to these guidelines, individuals who participate in a study have certain rights. Before participating in research, individuals need to know the purpose and aims of the study, how the results will be used, and the likely social consequences the study will have on their lives. They also have the right to refuse to participate in a study and to withdraw at any time. When they participate and provide information, their anonymity is protected and guaranteed by the researcher. Individuals are not to be offered excessive financial inducements to participate in a project. Participants also have the right to gain something from a study. Researchers need to actively look for ways to "give back" (or reciprocate) to participants in a study because the participants have freely provided their time. For example, in one study involving individuals with HIV, the author shared book royalties with the participants in the study. In another study, a researcher volunteered to help supervise lunchroom activities in exchange for information from students in the school.

Honoring Research Sites

It is important to respect the site in which the research takes place. This respect should be shown by gaining permission before entering a site, by disturbing the site as little as possible during a study, and by viewing oneself as a "guest" at the place of study. Lincoln Public Schools (n.d.) in Lincoln, Nebraska, provides illustrative guidelines to follow for conducting research with minimal disruption to a school district. Their guidelines list several reasons why a project may not be approved. Disapproved projects are those that take away considerable amounts of instructional time; require large amounts of teacher, administrator, or office time (the district may ask to be reimbursed for the costs of compiling information, staff time, or materials); interfere with district data collection or the work of current research projects; are planned for the first or last month of the school year; or are received too late in the year to be adequately reviewed.

Another strategy for respecting the research site with minimal disruption is to gain access through gatekeepers. Researchers may need to consult with different gatekeepers at multiple levels in an organization. For example, in a study in one high school classroom, the researcher sought permission from several individuals, including the school board responsible for ensuring that the rights of human participants were protected, the research official in the school district, the principal of the school, the teacher in a government class, and the actual students who participated in the study and their parents.

Reporting Research Fully and Honestly

You need to show respect to audiences who read and use information from studies. Data should be reported honestly, without changing or altering the findings to satisfy certain predictions or interest groups. It may, however, be appropriate for the primary investigator to provide those at the research site with a preliminary copy of any publications. In addition, studies completed by others should not be plagiarized, and credit should be given for material quoted from other studies. This credit involves citing the authors and the date of the publication, and listing the publication in the reference section of the study. In addition, research should be free of jargon and be understandable to those being studied. As ethical educators, we need to make every effort to communicate the practical significance of our research to the community of researchers and practitioners so inquiry will be encouraged and used.

Ethical Context

Practicing ethics is a complex matter that involves much more than merely following a set of static guidelines such as those from professional associations mentioned earlier. Ethically conducting research requires researchers to actively interpret these principles for their individual projects, tailoring these ethical guidelines to suit the unique contexts of their research. Additionally, ethics should be a primary consideration rather than an after-thought. Researchers should reflect on ethical issues throughout the research process, from defining the problem to advancing research questions to collecting and analyzing data to writing the final report. Ethics should, at all times, be at the forefront of the researcher's agenda (Hesse-Bieber & Leavy, 2006).

WHAT ARE THE SKILLS NEEDED FOR RESEARCH?

As a new researcher, you may wonder whether you have the ability to read, evaluate, and actually conduct research. Knowing the process of research, you may say, does not guarantee an adequate research study. Certainly Maria, who is new to research, has these concerns.

Let me set your mind at ease. You have already learned valuable research skills through your life experiences. These skills include solving puzzles, employing a long attention span, using a library, and, of course, writing out your thoughts.

Solving Puzzles

Researchers look at problems as puzzles to solve. The steps in the research process are viewed as a series of puzzle pieces that the inquirer assembles. You already have skills in solving puzzles. You fit together the debits and credits to balance your checkbook. As a parent, you engage in multiple roles during the day that require juggling of different tasks. These are puzzles that we work out by breaking them down into manageable parts ("What will be the demands on my time today?"), setting obtainable objectives ("I will have a busy day at work, so I will focus on my job today"), and possibly writing them down ("I need to make a list of what I must accomplish today"). As you examine research studies or engage in the process of inquiry, assembling these parts of the puzzle—such as first working on a research problem and then specifying a purpose for a study—will require that all of the pieces fit together, as with the many puzzles that we solve in daily living.

Lengthening Your Attention Span

Although we generally make time to complete the tasks we love, our attention span certainly varies from task to task. The process of research involves six steps that may span a period of 6 months or more. To read through a journal article and identify each of these steps, for example, requires patience as well as knowledge about what to look for. We all bring attention spans of varying lengths to the process of research. But if we consider the tasks we love and the amount of time we devote to them, we can see that we have already developed an attention span long enough to spend considerable time at research.

Using Library Resources

The step in the research process that requires you to review the literature means spending time in an academic library. For most of us, going to the library probably began in grade school with trips to the school library. Engaging in research requires spending time with library resources, a process that is facilitated by home computers and Internet connections to library catalogs. But the process of research requires that you use skills in locating studies, summarizing them, and writing a review of the literature. These skills are developed during research, if you do not already have them. They develop from our comfort level with a library and with experiences that began early in our schooling and continue today.

Writing, Editing, and More Writing

Researchers cannot escape the ever-present aspect of writing as a key facet of research. As writers, we work through numerous drafts, receive reactions from others, and develop new drafts. Research involves writing the study for an audience. Do you enjoy writing and communicating your thoughts? Do you like to write in a journal or a diary? Do you get satisfaction from completing projects? You have probably written several essays in college already or worked on a research report with other students or a faculty member. In short, you have experience in writing. As you know, writing is more than recording ideas on paper or in a computer file. It is also organizing ideas, preparing interview questions, jotting down notes during an observation, and writing for permission to use someone else's questions or articles. Writing exists in all phases of the creative process of planning and in conducting research.

APPLYING THE RESEARCH PROCESS TO ACTUAL STUDIES

In this book, especially in chapters 2 through 10, we will refer to two journal articles that provide specific application of the steps in the research process. At this time, read carefully the two articles at the end of this chapter. They are:

- Deslandes, R., & Bertrand, R. (2005). Motivation of parent involvement in secondary-level schooling. *Journal of Educational Research, 98*(3), 164–175.
- Asmussen, K. J., & Creswell, J. W. (1995). Campus response to a student gunman. *Journal of Higher Education, 66*, 575–591.

Read these journal articles, on pages 17 and 33, *before* beginning chapter 2, "Quantitative and Qualitative Approaches." As you read these articles, note the marginal annotations in the articles that parallel the steps of the research process covered in this chapter. Also, these annotations signal the major characteristics of both *quantitative* and *qualitative* research to be discussed in chapter 2. In chapter 2 we will reflect back on these two articles frequently to demonstrate the authors' use of those characteristics.

Also, as you read the articles, please bear in mind that they may seem difficult to read and understand. You are new to research. Reading research studies will become easier in time because you will understand the basic features of good research. In addition, here are a few tips that will facilitate your reading.

Look for cues about the major ideas by studying the major headings. Also, remember that research is a process consisting of several steps. Look for the major parts of the research process: problem, literature, purpose, data collection, data analysis, and overall structure of the report. Examining the abstract may or may not be helpful in locating these parts; abstracts vary considerably in their quality and their inclusion of the major parts of research. The statistics and data analysis may be difficult to understand. To obtain a general sense of what you can learn from the data analysis, look for the research questions at the beginning of the study and then ask yourself how the researchers addressed or answered them. Look for the most important statement in the study, the purpose statement, which typically begins with a phrase such as "The purpose of this study is," "The intent of the study is," or "The objective of this study is." Titles may not always be helpful in understanding the article. Titles are often short and may not contain all of the information you need to understand the direction of the study. Instead, look at the purpose statement, research questions, or hypotheses for this information.

KEY IDEAS IN THE CHAPTER

Research involves asking a question, collecting data, and analyzing data to determine the answer to the question. It helps educators understand problems or issues through the accumulation of knowledge. It can assist educators in improving practice, and it focuses attention on important policy issues being discussed and debated by decision makers. Also, engaging in research provides valuable conceptual, writing, and presenting skills for students. Despite these strengths, however, *some* research today provides poor answers to our questions. Research can be contradictory, vague, based on questionable data, unclear in its intent, and written poorly.

Six steps are followed when conducting a research study. The study begins with identifying a research problem or issue of study. It then consists of reviewing the literature; advancing direction through research questions and statements; and then collecting, analyzing, and interpreting the data. This process culminates in a research report presented, evaluated, and potentially used by the educational community.

When using these steps, researchers should engage good ethical practices. They should respect the rights of participants, honor research sites, and be honest in reporting results to audiences. Using these steps also involves skills that many individuals already possess, such as solving puzzles, focusing attention on topics, using the library, and writing.

USEFUL INFORMATION FOR PRODUCERS OF RESEARCH

- As you plan and conduct a study, keep in mind that research needs to be valuable to educators. Include comments in your study that convey the value to specific educational audiences.
- Use the general framework of the six steps for thinking about your plans and the conduct of research. These six steps make research manageable, help ensure that you conduct thorough inquiries, and provide a useful strategy for the design and writing of the research.
- Be ethical in conducting research. Respect the rights of participants, research sites, and individuals who will be readers of your study.
- Consider the skills that you need to develop to be a researcher. You may already have developed the skills of reading and writing, using library resources, solving puzzles, and focusing in on a topic of interest.

Useful Information for Consumers of Research

- As you examine a study, recognize that authors emphasize different reasons for undertaking their study. Look for suggestions by the author for practical applications of a study.
- Recognize that researchers proceed through a process of research and then construct sections of a study that reflect different steps in this process. For the research problem, examine the "introduction" to a study; for the literature review, explore the "literature review" section. For the data-collection discussion, visit the "method" or "procedure" section, and for the data analysis and interpretation, see the "results" or "findings" as well as the "discussion" sections.
- Look for statements in the study where the researcher discusses respect for participants and sites.

Understanding Concepts and Evaluating Research Studies

1. What preconceptions do you bring to the study of research? List three advantages and three disadvantages of conducting research.
2. Assume that you are Maria in the introductory scenario in this chapter. List three steps that you might take to begin your research study.
3. Again consider Maria's situation. If she gathers data from students in her school, what ethical issues does she need to be sensitive to? List two issues.

Conducting Your Research

What skills do you bring to research? What skills do you still need to learn? List three skills that you bring and three that you will develop as you learn about research.

Go to our Companion Website at **www.prenhall.com/creswell** to:

- assess your understanding of chapter content with Multiple-Choice Questions,
- apply what you've learned with Essay Questions,
- practice your research skills with interactive Building Research Skills exercises, and
- broaden your knowledge of research with Web Links to research topics on the Internet.

Motivation of Parent Involvement in Secondary-Level Schooling

Steps in the Research Process

Quantitative Characteristics

Rollande Deslandes
Université du Québec à Trois-Rivières, Canada
Richard Bertrand
Université Laval, Quebec, Canada

Abstract

Inspired by K. V. Hoover-Dempsey and H. M. Sandler's (1995, 1997) model of the parent involvement process, the authors examined 4 psychological constructs of parent involvement: (a) relative strength of parents' role construction, (b) parents' self-efficacy for helping adolescents succeed in school, (c) parents' perceptions of teacher invitations to become involved, and (d) parents' perceptions of students' invitations to become involved. The authors obtained survey responses from 770 parents of adolescents in 5 Quebec secondary schools—354 parents of 7th graders, 231 parents of 8th graders, and 185 parents of 9th graders. Results emphasize that it is important that researchers distinguish parent involvement at home and at school when examining the predictive power of the 4 psychological constructs. Findings also provide evidence of grade-level differences in the predictive models of parent involvement at home and at school. Parents' perceptions of students' invitations was the most powerful predictor of parent involvement at home models across the 3 grade levels. Parents' role construction made important contributions to the prediction of their involvement at Grades 7 and 9; parents' perceptions of teacher invitations were associated with parent involvement at school across the 3 grade levels. Whether at home or at school, parents became involved if they perceived that teachers and students expected or desired their involvement.

Key words: parent involvement, parent motivation, secondary schools

Reviewing the literature

(01) In past decades, a wealth of studies showed that parent involvement is essential in children's educational process and outcomes (Henderson & Mapp, 2002). Parent involvement refers to parents' roles in educating their children at home and in school (Christenson & Sheridan, 2001). Involvement can take different forms, including discussions about school, help with homework, or volunteering at school. Parent involvement appears to have lasting benefits even through high school. When parents are involved, secondary students tend to earn higher grades (Deslandes, Royer, Turcotte, & Bertrand, 1997; Dornbusch & Ritter, 1988; Lee, 1994; Steinberg, Lamborn, Dornbusch; & Darling, 1992), show higher aspirations (Trusty, 1996), and have fewer disciplinary problems (Deslandes & Royer, 1997; Eccles, Early, Frasier, Belansky, & McCarthy, 1997).

Identifying a research problem

(02) Even though the benefits associated with parent involvement at the secondary level seem to be well understood, educators still know little about what factors lead parents to decide to become involved in their adolescents' schooling. In the present study, we explored how the psychological constructs, as defined in Hoover-Dempsey and Sandler's model (1995, 1997), influence the parent involvement process at the secondary level, and more precisely, at the first three grade levels in Quebec secondary schools. We addressed the following research question: What are the relative contributions of parents' (a) role construction, (b) self-efficacy, (c) perception of teacher invitations, and (d) perception of adolescent invitations to predict

---

Address correspondence to Rollande Deslandes, Education Department, Université du Québec à Trois-Riviéres, C.P. 500, Trois-Riviéres, Québec, Canada, G9A 5H7. (E-mail: Rollande_Deslandes@uqtr.ca)

parent involvement at home and at school in Grades 7, 8, and 9? (Because the invitation for parents to become involved is presented by teachers and students, we considered, as did Walker, Hoover-Dempsey, Reed, and Jones [2000], teacher invitations and student invitations as two difference constructs, thus leading to four psychological constructs related to parent involvement.) Previous research on the evolution of adolescents' autonomy and parent involvement in secondary schools led us to expect some differences across grade levels in the predictive models of parent involvement at home and at school (Deslandes, 2003).

Influences on Parent Involvement

(03) Jordan, Orozco, and Averett (2001) identified factors that influence levels and aspects of parent involvement. Family (e.g., education level, family structure, family size, parent gender, work outside the home) and child characteristics (e.g., age, gender, grade level, academic performance) are of particular relevance in this study. Research has shown that undereducated parents and single parents are less involved in certain types of involvement activities. For instance, Deslandes, Potvin, and Leclerc (1999) found that adolescents from traditional families and well-educated parents report more affective support (parent encouragement and praise, help with homework, frequent discussions about school, and attendence at school performances or sports events) than do adolescents from nontraditional families and less educated parents. Astone and McLanahan (1991) also indicated that adolescents who live with single parents or stepparents report that their homework is monitored less than the homework of adolescents from traditional families. Deslandes and Cloutier (2000) reported that mothers are more involved with homework than are fathers. Dauber and Epstein (1989) argued that well-educated parents and those who do not work outside the home (Eccles & Harold, 1996) are more likely to be involved at school. Eccles and Harold concluded that parents with fewer children provide more help with homework than do parents with more children.

(04) Child characteristics also may influence parent involvement. For example, Deslandes and Potvin (1999) observed that mothers of adolescent boys communicated with teachers more often than did mothers of adolescent girls. Parents tend to become more involved when their children experience their first learning or behavior difficulties. According to Eccles and Harold (1996), parents of high-achieving children tend to participate more in school activities than do parents of low-achieving children. Epstein (2001) showed that parent involvement decreases dramatically as children move into secondary school. When Deslandes (2003) compared parent involvement in Grades 8, 9, and 10, he found a steady decline in parent involvement, but a steady increase in adolescent autonomy.

Parents' Role Construction

(05) Parents need to understand their roles because that understanding identifies the activities that they believe are necessary and part of their responsibilities as parents. In other words, parents are more likely to become involved if they view their participation as a requirement of parenting. Hoover-Dempsey, Jones, and Reed (1999) hypothesized three components of role construction, depending on whether parents focused responsibility for children's education on themselves as parents, on the school, or on parent-school partnerships.

Parents' Self-efficacy for Helping Children Succeed in School

(06) Parent self-efficacy is rooted in Bandura's (1997) self-efficacy theory and suggests that parents are more likely to be involved if they believe that they

have the skills and knowledge to help their children. In other words, parents become involved if they believe that their actions will improve learning and academic performance (Hoover-Dempsey, Bassler, & Brissie, 1992; Stevenson, Chen, & Uttal, 1990). Prior research has indicated that parents believe that they will have more influence over their children's schooling when their children are in the elementary grades than they will when their children are in the upper grades (Freedman-Doan, Arbreton, Harold, & Eccles, 1993). In general, the stronger their self-efficacy, the more persistence parents exhibit in their involvement (Hoover-Dempsey et al., 2001).

Parents' Perceptions of Teacher Invitations

(07) Research also has shown that teachers' demands and opportunities for involvement, coupled with an inviting school climate, are related significantly to level of parent involvement (Comer & Haynes, 1991; Dauber & Epstein, 1993; Eccles & Harrold, 1996; Epstein, 1986). Parents tend to be more involved if they perceive that teachers and students both want and expect their involvement (Hoover-Dempsey et al., 2001).

The quantitative literature plays a major role

Parents' Perceptions of Student Invitations

(08) Parents will become involved if they perceive that their young children or adolescents want them to do so. Students' invitations are either implicit or explicit and emerge as a function of their age, their press for independence, and their performance level (Hoover-Dempsey et al., 2001; Walker & Hoover-Dempsey, 2001; Walker et al., 2000). For instance, when young children or adolescents ask for help with homework, they are expressing explicit invitations. On the other hand, if they express the desire to work alone, parents might respond by reducing their involvement. If children bring a poor report card home, they might be conveying implicit invitations. Seeking parental help does not necessarily mean that young children or adolescents are having academic difficulties. For example, Zimmerman and Martinez-Pons (1986) found that high-achieving students wanted more parental assistance than did low-achieving students.

The quantitative literature justifies the research problem and provides direction for the study

(09) Reflecting on three of the four psychological constructs to involvement cited in the preceding paragraphs (i.e., parents' role construction, self-efficacy, and perceptions of teacher invitations), Reed, Jones, Walker, and Hoover-Dempsey (2000) found that parents' role construction, self-efficacy for helping the child succeed in school, and perceptions of teacher invitations represent motivators of parents' involvement in their children's education at the elementary level. Role construction was the first predictor of parent involvement; perception of teachers' invitations was the second predictor. Parent self-efficacy seemed less influential. The authors suggested that role construction may be a mediator of efficacy's influence on involvement (Reed et al.).

(10) In a study that compared 5th, 8th, and 11th graders' self-reported invitations to parent involvement in homework, Walker and Hoover-Dempsey (2001) revealed decreased levels of parent homework involvement across adolescence. Across the three age groups, students' invitations for parents' homework involvement was steady, but the authors found that parents of younger students tend to help without being asked.

(11) Investigations are needed to better understand what motivates parents to become involved in their young children's education and, more particularly, in their adolescents' educational process. Researchers need to examine differences in parents' motivation to become involved across secondary-grade levels. To our knowledge, no study has yet examined the individual and combined contributions of Hoover-Dempsey and Sandler's (1995, 1997)

four psychological constructs to predict parent involvement decisions across secondary-grade levels.

(12) We targeted adolescents in the first 3 years of secondary school in Quebec (equivalent to Grades 7, 8, and 9 in the American school system). Prior work (Deslandes, 2003) showed that parent involvement is significantly lower, and adolescent autonomy level is significantly higher, in the fourth year of secondary school in Quebec (Grade 10 in the American school system) than in the second and third years of secondary school).

(13) To examine how the four psychological constructs influence parent-involvement decisions across the three secondary grade levels, we posed the following research question: What are the relative contributions of parents' role construction, self-efficacy, perceptions of teacher invitations, and perceptions of adolescent invitations to predict parent involvement at home and at school in Grades 7, 8, and 9?

Specifying a purpose

The quantitative purpose statement, research questions, or hypotheses are specific and narrow

Method

Participants

(14) Participants were 770 parents of secondary-level students attending five public schools located in urban and rural areas in the Mauricie and Centre du Quebec and Monteregie regions. The regions are representative of the general Quebec population. Forty-six percent (354) of the participants were parents of Secondary I students (equivalent to Grade 7 students in the American school system), 30% (231) were parents of Secondary II students (equivalent to Grade 8 students in the American system), and 24% (185) were parents of Secondary III students (equivalent to Grade 9 students in the American system). Nearly 51% of the students were girls and 49% were boys. Forty-seven percent of the students were first born in their family, 37% second born, 13% third born, and 3% fourth and fifth born, respectively.

Collecting data

(15) The demographics of the sample were as follows: Approximately 84% of the respondents were mothers, and 13% were fathers. The other respondents were either stepmothers or stepfathers, or others. Seventy percent of the participants were employed outside of the home. Seventy percent lived in a traditional family, and 30% lived in a nontraditional one, which corresponds exactly to what is being reported in the Quebec population in general (Quebec Statistics Institute, 2001). The majority of the families (37%) had two children, 25% had one child, 21% had three children, and the remainder of the sample (17%) had four or more children. About 3% of the respondents had less than a high school education, 65% had a high school diploma or a secondary-level trade formation, and 32% had a college or university education. Seventy-two percent of the participants had a job outside the home environment. Table 1 presents the characteristics of the whole sample and of the three subsamples.

Measures

(16) Among the eight constructs that we used, parents' role construction, self-efficacy, perception of teacher invitations, and reports of parent practices of involvement were adapted from the Sharing the Dream! Parent Questionnaire (Jones, Gould, Brown, Young, & The Peabody Family School Partnership Lab of Vanderbilt University, 2000). They are grounded in Hoover-Dempsey and Sandler's (1995, 1997) model of the parent-involvement process. The parents' perceptions of student invitations and their reports of involvement activities include items from questionnaires designed by Epstein and her colleagues (Epstein, Connors, & Salinas, 1993; Epstein, Connors-Tadros, Horsey, & Simon, 1996). The items have been translated in French, adapted in the Quebec context, and used in previous studies on the basis of adolescents'

The quantitative purpose statement, research questions or hypotheses seek measureable, observable data on variables

TABLE I
Demographic Characteristics of the Sample and Subsamples (in Percentages)

Characteristic	*N*	Grade 7	Grade 8	Grade 9
Adolescent gender	Female (51)	Female (44)	Female (52)	Female (60)
	Male (49)	Male (56)	Male (48)	Male (40)
Rank in family	1 (47)	1 (46)	1 (46)	1 (49)
	2 (37)	2 (36)	2 (39)	2 (36)
	3 (13)	3 (13)	3 (13)	3 (12)
	Others (3)	Others (5)	Others (2)	Others (3)
Participant gender	Mothers (84)	Mothers (84)	Mothers (83)	Mothers (87)
	Fathers (13)	Fathers (12)	Fathers (15)	Fathers (13)
	Others (3)	Others (4)	Others (2)	Others (0)
Participant education level				
Primary level	3	2	2	3
High school or equivalent	65	63	68	65
College or university	32	35	30	32
Participant outside work	Yes (73)	Yes (76)	Yes (69)	Yes (69)
	No (27)	No (24)	No (31)	No (31)
Family structure				
Traditional	70	68	71	74
Nontraditional	30	32	29	26
Family size				
One child	25	31	26	27
Two children	37	33	37	43
Three children	21	23	23	17
Four or more children	17	13	15	13

perceptions (Deslandes, 2000; Deslandes & Cloutier, 2002; Deslandes et al., 1997; Deslandes & Potvin, 1999).

(17) We used classical item analysis and factor analysis to evaluate the psychometric properties of the eight constructs (see the list of constructs presented as the predictors and the outcomes with the control variables in Table 2). The final decision of keeping or rejecting some of the items was based mostly on the eigenvalues greater than 1 criterion and on the scree test. For all the analyses, we used only those items loaded at least 30 on the factor to interpret the factors. We computed Cronbach's alpha reliability coefficient for each scale. We obtained all scores by calculating the mean score of the items of the same constructs, which are described in the following paragraphs.

TABLE 2
Control Variables, Predictors, and Outcome Measures

Control variable	Predictor	Outcome
Participant gender	Parents' role constructions	Parent involvement at home.
Participant outside work	Parents' self-efficacy for helping adolescents succeed in school	Parent involvement at school
Participant education level		
Family size	Relative parent influence	
Family structure	Impact of parent efforts	
Adolescent gender	Parents' perceptions of teacher invitations	
Rank in family		
Results in French	Parents' perceptions of adolescent invitations	
	Invitations in academic domain	
	Invitations in social domain	

Parents' role construction.

(18) This construct measured the extent to which parents believed that it is their responsibility to help the school educate their adolescent (Hoover-Dempsey & Sandler, 1995, 1997). We based the construct on Hoover-Dempsey's work that suggests three types of parent role construction: parent focused (six items), school focused (five items), and partnership focused (six items; Hoover-Dempsey et al., 1999; Reed et al., 2000). Principal axis factor analysis revealed a single-factor solution that corresponded to a combination of the three types of role construction with a predominance of items related to the partnership-focused role construction. We used a construct that comprised 10 items (α = .72) that measure behaviors that are parent focused, school focused, and mainly partnership focused in accordance with the adolescents' education. The parents had to respond to items, for example, "It's important that I let someone at school know about things that concern my teenager," and "I make it my business to stay on top of things at school") by using a 6-point, Likert-type scale that ranged from (1) *disagree very strongly* to (6) *agree very strongly*. One possible explanation for obtaining only one scale instead of three could be a cultural one. Another explanation could be associated with the fact that Hoover-Dempsey and her colleagues developed the constructs on the basis of pilot work with a small sample of 50 parents of elementary school children, reported in Reed et al. (2000).

Quantitative data collection involves studying a large number of individuals

Quantitative data collection involves gathering numeric data

Quantitative data collection is based on using instruments identified prior to the study

Parents' self-efficacy for helping adolescents succeed in school.

(19) We assessed this construct with Hoover-Dempsey and colleagues' scale after adaptations for parents of high school students (Jones et al., 2000). Factor analysis revealed a two-factor solution that accounted for 49% of the total variance in parents' self-efficacy for helping adolescents succeed in school. The first factor, relative parent influence, contained four items (α = .68) and measured the extent to which parents believed that they could help their adolescent succeed in school compared with other sources of influence (e.g., "Other adolescents have more influence on my adolescent's motivation to do well in school than I do"). The second factor, impact of parent efforts, estimated the level of influence that parents' perceptions had on their adolescents' education. We assessed perceptions with five items (α = .63; e.g., "I feel successful about my efforts to help my adolescent learn"). Participants used a 6-point, Likert-type scale that ranged from 1 (*disagree very strongly*) to 6 (*agree very strongly*).

Parents' perceptions of teacher invitations.

(20) This construct provided an assessment of parents' perceptions of teacher invitations to become involved in their adolescents' schooling at home. We based the measure on an eight-item scale created by Hoover-Dempsey and her colleagues (Jones et al., 2000; Reed et al., 2000). In the present study, principal axis factoring analysis yielded a one-factor solution that was composed of four items (α = .70; e.g., "One or more of my teenager's teachers has spoken with me about homework"). We asked parents to rate the frequency of teachers' invitations on a 6-point, Likert-type scale that ranged from 1 (*never*) to 6 (*once or more per week*).

Parents' perceptions of student invitations.

(21) This construct is a modification of a similar construct for adolescents (Deslandes & Cloutier, 2002) that we derived from Epstein et al., (1993) and Epstein et al. (1996). Principal axis factor analysis revealed the presence of two factors that explained 50% of the total variance in parents' perceptions of student invitations. The first factor, invitations in the academic domain,

included five items (α = .79; e.g., "My adolescent has asked me to . . . listen to him/her read something he/she wrote"). The second factor, invitations in the social domain, consisted of four items (α = .71; e.g., "My adolescent has asked me to . . . talk with me about current events"). All items were answered on a 6-point, Likert-type scale that ranged from 1 (*disagree very strongly*) to 6 (*agree very strongly*).

Parent reports of involvement activities.

Analyzing the data

(22) This measure was a modified version of the questionnaires elaborated by Epstein and colleagues (1993; 1996) and used in prior studies on the basis of adolescents' perceptions (e.g., Deslandes, 2000; Deslandes & Cloutier, 2002; Deslandes et al., 1997) and those designed by Hoover-Dempsey and her colleagues (e.g., Jones et al., 2000). Principal axis factoring analysis followed by varimax rotation revealed a two-factor solution that accounted for 35% of the total variance. The first factor, parent involvement at home, was composed of 16 items and assessed how often parents get involved in educational activities at home with their adolescents (α = .87; sample items: ". . . encourage my adolescent about school," ". . . help my adolescent study before a test"). The second factor, parent involvement in school, included eight items and measured how often parents were at school and how often they interacted with their adolescents at school and with the teachers (α = .67; sample items: ". . . go to school to attend an extracurricular event," ". . . have a conference with one or more of my adolescent's teachers"). Parents were asked to answer on a 6-point, Likert-type scale that ranged from 1 (*never*) to 6 (*once or more per week*).

Demographics.

(23) We collected information on family and student individual characteristics from the parents. Participants reported on their gender (mother, father, or other), education level (primary, secondary, college or university levels), family structure (traditional, nontraditional), family size (number of children living at home), and outside work (yes/no). They also provided information on their adolescents' gender (female, male), rank in the family, grade level (7, 8, or 9), and grades in French, their mother tongue, as reported in the last report card (see Table 2).

Procedures

(24) We collected all the data from survey respondents by means of questionnaires in late spring 2001. Following the school principals' acceptance to participate in the study, we mailed nearly 2,560 parent questionnaires to the schools. Forty-five classroom teachers from five schools volunteered to send the questionnaires to 1,500 parents via the students. The package included a letter that explained the purpose of the study and requested voluntary participation. The participation rate was approximately 51% (770 parents accepted from the 1,500 questionnaires that were sent home). The classroom council received a token payment of thanks ($1) for each returned questionnaire, and the classroom teachers received a token payment of thanks ($10) for their collaboration and support. (The token payments were considered as costs associated with the collaboration and were paid through the research grant.)

Results

Predicting Parent Involvement

(25) The primary question in the study focused on the relative strength of parents' role construction, self-efficacy, and perceived teacher and

TABLE 3
Means and Standard Deviations for all Predictors and Outcome Measures

Variable	Grade 7 (n=246)		Grade 8 (n=156)		Grade 9 (n=112)	
	M	*SD*	*M*	*SD*	*M*	*SD*
Parents' role constructions	4.52	.56	4.40	.59	4.30	.67
Parents' self-efficacy for helping adolescents succeed in school						
Relative parent influence	4.14	.87	4.13	.94	4.14	.90
Impact of parent efforts	4.41	.66	4.32	.71	4.19	.73
Parents' perceptions of teacher invitations	1.55	.61	1.40	.52	1.31	.48
Parents' perceptions of adolescent invitations						
Invitations in academic domain	3.96	1.06	3.82	1.04	3.39	1.04
Invitations in social domain	3.80	1.06	3.61	1.0	3.65	1.0
Parent involvement at home	4.67	.73	4.45	.83	4.13	.87
Parent involvement at school	2.28	.70	2.12	.71	2.00	.66

student invitation measures for predicting parent involvement at home and at school. We performed separate stepwise regression analyses to examine the best predictive models at Grades 7, 8, and 9 in Quebec secondary schools. We computed Mallow's C(P) statistic[1] for each final model and grade level. Descriptive statistics of the measures are illustrated in Table 3.

Quantitative data analysis consists of statistical analysis

Parent Involvement at Home for Seventh-Grade Students

(26) First, eight family and individual adolescent characteristics,[2] used as control variables, were introduced as a block and forced into the regression equation. Together, the control variables explained 4% of the variance in parent involvement at home. After the introduction of the control variables, the analyses yielded a final five-variable model that explained an additional 42% (total R^2 = 46%; total R^2 adj. = 42.5%) of the variance in parent involvement at home, $F(13,232) = 15.47$, $p < .001$ (see Table 4). The variable corresponding to parents' perception of student invitations in the academic domain was the best predictor of parent involvement in schooling at home, $\Delta R^2 = .28$; $\beta = .31$, $p < .001$. The variable was followed by parents' role construction, $\Delta R^2 = .07$; $\beta = .18$, $p < .001$, parents' perceptions of student invitations in the social domain, $\Delta R^2 = .04$; $\beta = .25$, $p < .001$, and parents' self-efficacy, that is, perceived impact of efforts, $\Delta R^2 = .02$; $\beta = .15$, $p < .01$, and perceived relative influence $\Delta R^2 = .01$; $\beta = .12$, $p < .05$.

Quantitative data analysis consists of describing trends, comparing groups, or relating variables

Parent Involvement at Home for Eighth-Grade Students

(27) We observed a somewhat different pattern of relations in analyses conducted at the eighth-grade level; control variables explained 10% of the variance. Regression analysis revealed a three-variable model that accounted for an additional 38% of the total variance (total R^2 = 48%; total R^2 adj. = 43%) in the level of parent involvement at home, $F(11, 144) = 11.69$, $p < .001$. Parents' perceptions of students' invitations in the social domain was the most powerful predictor; it accounted for an additional

TABLE 4
Final Regression Models for Each Grade Level Predicting Parent Involvement at Home

Variable	ΔR^2	β
Grade 7		
Control variables	.04	
Parents' perceptions of adolescent invitations in the academic domain	.28	.31***
Parents' role constructions	.07	.18***
Parents' perceptions of adolescent invitations in the social domain	.04	.25***
Parents' self-efficacy		
Impact of parent efforts	.02	.15**
Impact of parent influence	.01	.12*
Grade 8		
Control variables	.10	
Parents' perceptions of adolescent invitations in social domain	.28	.35***
Parents' perceptions of adolescent invitations in academic domain	.07	.26**
Parents' self-efficacy		
Impact of parent efforts	.03	.19**
Grade 9		
Control variables	.11	
Parents' perceptions of student invitations in academic domain	.26	.44***
Parents' perceptions of student invitations in social domain	.03	.20*

Note: $\Delta R^2 = R^2$ change. Grade 7: Mallow's C(P) = 14.385; P = 14 (independent variables, including constant); Grade 8: Mallow's C(P) =10.335; P = 12 (independent variables, including constant): Grade 9: Mallow's C(P) = 9.769; P = 11 (independent variables, including constant).
$^*p < .05$. $^{**}p < .01$. $^{***}p < .001$.

28% of the variance (b =.35, $p < .001$). Parents' perceptions of student invitation in the academic domain was the second strongest predictor, $\Delta R^2 = .07$; $\beta = .26$, $p < .01$, followed by parents' self-efficacy, that is, impact of efforts ($\Delta R^2 = .03$; $\beta = .19$, $p < .01$).

Parent Involvement at Home for Ninth-Grade Students

(28) The control variables accounted for 11% of the variance in the first step. A two-variable model explained an additional 30% of the variance (total R^2 = 41%; total R^2 adj. = 34%) in the level of parent involvement at home, $F(10,101) = 6.81$, $p < .001$. Parents' perceptions of student invitations in the academic domain emerged as the first predictor in the final model, accounting for 26% of the variance ($\beta = .44$, $p < .001$); parents' perception of student invitation in the social domain was the second predictor, explaining 3% of the variance ($\beta = .20$, $p < .05$).

Parent Involvement at School for Seventh-Grade Students

(29) As shown in Table 5, control variables explained 9% of the variance in parent involvement at school. A three variable model explained an additional 17% of the variance (total R^2 = 26%; total R^2 adj. = .23%) for level of parent involvement at school, $F(11, 234) = 7.51$, $p < .001$. Parents' role construction explained the greatest part of the variance, $\Delta R^2 = .13$, $\beta = .31$, $p < .001$. Parents' perceptions of teacher invitations ($\beta = .14$, $p < .05$) and parents' perceptions of student invitations in the social domain explained an additional 2% of the variance ($\beta = .15$, $p < .01$).

Parent Involvement at School for Eighth-Grade Students

(30) For eighth-grade students, introducing the demongraphic variables resulted in a small contribution to the model ($\Delta R^2 = .05$). Parents' perceptions of

TABLE 5
Final Regression Models for Each Grade Level Predicting Parent Involvement at School

Varible	ΔR	β
Grade 7		
Control variables	.09	
Parents' role constructions	.13	.31***
Parents' perceptions of teacher invitations	.02	.14*
Parents' perceptions of student invitations in the social domain	.02	.15**
Grade 8		
Control variables	.05	
Parents' perceptions of teacher invitations	.12	.31***
Parents' perceptions of student invitations in the social domain	.08	.29***
Grade 9		
Control variables	.09	
Parents' role constructions	.22	.36***
Parents' perceptions of teacher invitations	.08	.31***

Note. $\Delta R^2 = R^2$ change. Grade 7: Mallow's C(P) = 12.199: P =12 (independent variables, including constant): Grade 8: Mallow's C(P) = 12.845: P = 11 (independent variables, including constant): Grade 9: Mallow's C(P) = 8.138: P = 11 (independent variables, including constant). *$p <.05$. **$p <.01$. ***$p < .001$.

teacher invitations (ΔR^2 = .12; β = .31, $p < .001$), and parents' perceptions of student invitations in the social domain, ΔsR^2 = .08; β = .29, $p < .001$, added significance to the final model (total R^2 = 25% total R^2 adj. = 19%), $F(10, 145) = 4.61$, $p < .001$.

Parent Involvement at School for Ninth-Grade Students

(31) For ninth-grade students, the control variables first introduced explained 9% of the variance in parent involvement at school. Subsequently, parents' role construction appeared as the stronger predictor of parent involvement at school (b = .36, p < .001), accounting for 22% of the variance. The second predictor was parents' perceptions of teacher invitations, explaining an additional 8% of the variance, which resulted in a final model (total R^2 = 39% total R^2 adj. = 33%), $F(10, 101) = 6.48$, $p < .001$.

Discussion

(32) We investigated the contribution of Hoover-Dempsey and Sandler's (1995, 1997) four psychological constructs—parents' role construction, self-efficacy, perceived student invitations, and perceived teacher invitations—to predict parent involvement at home and at school. We addressed whether predictive models might differ across the first three grade levels in Quebec secondary schools. The following paragraphs summarize the overall results.

(33) Of great importance were our findings that extended beyond family and adolescent characteristics—two different models that predicted secondary-level parent involvement at home and parent involvement at school. In similar research conducted with 1,227 parents of elementary students, Deslandes and Bertrand (2003) also reported two different parent involvement models—a home-based model and a school-based model.

Parent Involvement at Home

(34) With respect to seventh-grade students, after we controlled for family and individual characteristics, our findings showed that parents decided to become involved at home mostly because of their adolescents' specific

academic invitations, such as asking (a) for ideas for a story or a project, (b) that a parent listen to the student read an original writing, (c) that a parent observe something learned or done well, or (d) for help to study or practice for a test. When personally invited by the adolescents, parents tended to perceive their involvement as expected and desired. Also predictive at a much lesser degree were parent beliefs that their responsibility was for example, to closely watch their adolescents' progress and to keep abreast of activities at school (parents' role construction). Similarly, adolescents' personal invitations in the social domain, like talking with a parent about a TV show or current events or interviewing a parent for information or opinions, contributed to parent involvement at home. Contributing to a much lesser extent were significant parents' beliefs that their involvement could make a difference in their adolescents' school performance and that their help was better than any other sources of influence (parents' self-efficacy). Parents subsequently responded with high levels of involvement at home manifested by their help with homework when asked, discussions about school, future plans, course options, and so forth. Findings at the seventh-grade level supported a five-variable, predictive model of parent involvement at home that explained a significant portion of the variance (42.5%).

(35) Concerning eighth-grade students, the full model comprised three variables that included, as the major predictors, (a) parents' perceptions of student invitations in the social domain (i.e., ask for opinion or information, discuss current events exchange information on trends during parents' youth), (b) parents' perception of student invitations in the academic domain, and (c) parents' self-efficacy. One especially striking result in our prediction of parent involvement at home was the importance of adolescents' personal invitations in the social domain, such as talking with a parent about a TV show or current event or interviewing a parent for information or opinions. Those findings suggest that positive parent–adolescent interactions might contribute to adolescents' personal invitations to parents to become involved, which is related to subsequent parent involvement at home.

(36) According to Belsky (1981) and Sameroff's (1975) transactional model, our results highlight the importance of reciprocal influences in the parent–adolescent relationship regarding schooling. Obviously, the quality of parent-adolescent relationships is key to a better understanding of parent involvement at home for secondary-level students. The quality of those relationships seems to be of paramount importance for eighth-grade students. The results are consistent with those of previous studies conducted in Quebec that provide evidence of the positive relation between authoritative parenting style characterized by high levels of warmth, supervision, and psychological autonomy (Steinberg, Elmen, & Mounts, 1989; Steinberg, Lamborn, Darling, Mounts, & Dornbusch, 1994), parent involvement in schooling (Epstein et al., 1993), perceived autonomy (Greenberger, Josselson, Knerr, & Knerr, 1975), and adolescent school grades (Deslandes et al., 1997; Deslandes, 2000; Deslandes & Potvin, 1999). Similarly, Deslandes and Cloutier (2002) found with a sample of 872 eighth-grade students in Quebec that specific invitations to involve parents requires that the adolescents are willing and open to work and exchange ideas with parents. The authors concluded that adolescents with a high level of autonomy, and more precisely, those who are highly work oriented and self-confident are more likely than adolescents without these traits to invite parent involvement.

Quantitative researchers report in an objective and unbiased approach

(37) Concerning ninth-grade students, analyses revealed a two-variable predictive model: (a) Parent perception of student invitations in the academic domain made the most significant contribution and (b) parent

perception of student invitations in the social domain was a less powerful predictor. Whether parents believe that their involvement will have a positive impact on their adolescents' school performance is not significant at Grade 9. Rather, parents wait for their adolescents' invitations before they become involved at home. One possible explanation is that parents may consider that Grade 9 students have developed self-responsible behaviors toward school and schoolwork (see Xu & Corno, 2003). Consequently, parents rely on the adolescents to initiate the requests for parent involvement at home. That behavior somewhat reinforces the perspective that differences in adolescent autonomy modulate the degree of parent involvement at home (Deslandes, 2000).

(38) At the Grade 7 level, after the introduction of controlled variables, the addition of the four psychological constructs resulted in a three-variable model that predicted parent involvement at school. Across various family and individual characteristics, the more that parents of Grade 7 students believed their involvement was part of their parenting responsibilities (e.g., teacher conferences are helpful to parents; parents should call the school with concerns about their adolescents' progress), the more they perceived invitations from the teachers (e.g., one of the teachers spoke with them about homework; a school employee has asked the parents to have a conference about their adolescent) and the more they perceived invitations from their adolescents in the social domain (e.g., interview parents for information or opinions), the more they reported involvement at school (e.g., having a conference with one or more of their adolescents' teachers, attending an extracurricular event at school). Noteworthy is the more significant contribution of parents' role construction to the predictive model at the Grade 7 level. Parents reported that they would be more involved at school if they believed that it is their duty.

(39) **Interpreting the data**

Once we controlled for demographics, regression analyses yielded a two-variable predictive model at the Grade 8 level. Parents of Grade 8 students are involved at school if they perceive invitations from the teachers and from their adolescents in the social domain. The question of whether parents of Grade 8 students are involved at school seems to be primarily an issue of relations and parent–teacher and parent–adolescent relationships. We think of the development of trust in teachers (Adams & Christenson, 2000) and of positive parent–adolescent interactions as prerequisites to parents' decisions to become involved at school, and more important, at the Grade 8 level (see Christenson & Sheridan, 2001).

(40) For Grade 9, adding the four psychological constructs yielded a two-variable model that contributed significantly to the prediction of parent involvement at school. Parents' understanding that involvement at school is part of their responsibilities (parents' role construction) was by far the best predictor, followed by parents' perceptions of teacher invitations.

(41) To summarize, our findings clearly identify two categories of predictive models: (a) parent involvement at home and (b) parent involvement at school. Contrary to Hoover-Dempsey and Sandler's (1995) measures, parents' self-efficacy in its francophone version comprised two factors: (a) relative parent influence and (b) impact of parent efforts, whereas parents' role construction consisted of only one factor. Our findings confirmed the relevance of Hoover-Dempsey and Sandler's model mainly for the seventh graders' parent involvement at home model, in which perceived teacher invitations was the only missing construct (one of four). Parents' role construction contributed more significantly to seventh and ninth graders' parent involvement at school models. Parents' self-efficacy contributed significantly only in the seventh and eighth graders' parent involvement at home models, and its overall contribution was marginal.

(42) Of major interest in this study is the powerful contribution exerted by parents' perception of student invitations in the models of parent involvement at home at the three secondary-grade levels. As adolescents mature, parent involvement at home becomes more a question of parent–adolescent relationships, which is particularly important at the eighth-grade level. Parents of students in Grades 7, 8, and 9 appear to be involved more proactively (e.g., in reponse to invitations) than reactively (e.g., in reaction to prior school grades, adolescent gender). The links between perceived adolescents' invitations and parent involvement at home are robust across various individual and family characteristics.

(43) Two notable patterns stand out in our results regarding parent involvement at school. The most outstanding pattern is the greater influence of parents' role construction. Parents must comprehend that parent involvement at school is part of their responsibilities before they decide to become involved. Also of interest in this study are the perceived invitations from the teachers to motivate parents to become involved at school.

Implications and Limitations

(44) The main implication derived from this study relates to the two identified categories of parent involvement predictive models. First, if the objective of the school interventions is to enhance parent involvement at home, the findings suggest the need to work directly with adolescents. That effort could be undertaken by (a) sensitizing adolescents to the importance of their inviting parents to become involved at home and by (b) coaching them on how to involve a family member in homework; discussions, or other tasks (Balli, Demo, & Wedman, 1998). For example, adolescents could ask their families to offer feedback about the assignments. Evidently, if parent involvement at home is the objective of school interventions, the involvement should focus on increased adolescent acceptance of and openness to developmentally appropriate parent involvement in schooling activities. Our findings also suggest that parent education programs should enhance parents' skills and self-efficacy. Parents should be aware of the importance of sustained parent–adolescent communication about schooling, and career and work planning over time. Parents could regularly attend workshops or meetings (e.g., parenting classes) to increase their parenting skills and their knowledge of different types of parent involvement, including less intensive involvement.

(45) Second, if the objective is increased parent involvement at school, the implications are fairly straightforward: school interventions should first focus on individualized contacts that teachers initiate with parents. Our finding regarding perceived invitations involved specific requests from teachers, such as "One or more of my teenager's teachers has spoken with me about homework," ". . . has asked me to encourage my teenager to read," and so forth. Parents responded to teachers' specific invitations by attending an extracurricular event, by volunteering at school, and so forth. The findings call attention to the value of personal teacher–parent contacts for building trusting relationships that will be manifested subsequently by parent involvement activities at school and by other forms of parents' willingness to help. Those results suggest that preservice and inservice teachers could benefit from training programs that offer the opportunity to develop knowledge and skills needed to initiate first contacts with parents and foster parent involvement (Hiatt-Michael, 2001; Shartrand, Weiss, Kreider, & Lopez, 1997).

(46) There are limitations of this study that suggest directions for future investigations. First, the sample used in our investigation included only students in Grades 7, 8, and 9, and the subsamples were of various sizes. Future investigations need to expand across the secondary levels. We collected data only from parents of adolescents. Past research focused primarily on

adolescents' perceptions; researchers should endeavor to use both adolescent and parent reports.

(47) Research findings indicate the need for further research on parent–adolescent and parent–teacher relationships to better understand parents' decision to become involved at home and at school. In addition, more research is needed on the relationship between parents' self-efficacy, role construction, and involvement. Some issues remain unclear. For instance, what is the explanation for the marginal contribution of parents' self-efficacy in the parent involvement at home model? As Hoover-Dempsey and colleagues (2000) suggested, is it possible that parents' self-efficacy is distal to parents' involvement decisions, whereas parents' role construction and perceived teacher and student invitations are more proximal? Researchers need to replicate this study in other settings by comparing different age categories to determine greater "generaliablity" of the findings. Longitudinal research would help clarify the extent to which each of the studied psychological constructs changes over time and in different settings. To fully understand parents' motivation to become involved, educators need more qualitative studies that focus on the subject.

Reporting the research

Conclusions

(48) The results of this study highlight the importance of researchers considering parent involvement at home and parent involvement at school separately as opposed to their examining parent involvement in terms of global involvement. For example, parents' perception of student invitations in the academic domain made a significant contribution to the prediction of parent involvement at home but did not appear as a predictor of parent involvement at school. In addition, parents' perceived teacher invitations were associated with parent involvement at school, but not with parent involvement at home. Thus, the findings would have been missed had parent involvement been assessed in global terms. Obviously, the different models obtained in this study require more research that examines the influences on parent involvement at home and at school separetely. In terms of practical implications, our research suggests that use of one of the psychological constructs should depend on whether parent involvement at home or parent involvement at school is the target. To enhance parent involvement at home, school administrators and teachers should work mainly with adolescents. To improve parent involvement at school, the results suggest the importance of sensitizing parents to their duties and responsibilities and of regarding the role of the school and the teachers when motivating parents to become involved.

Quantitative interpretations compare results with predictions

(49) The results of this study provide evidence of grade-level differences in the predictive models of parent involvement at home and at school. For instance, at Grade 7, the parent involvement at home predictive model included three constructs: (a) perceived student invitations, (b) parents' role construction, and (c) parents' self-efficacy. At Grade 9, only one construct made a significant contribution—perceived student invitations. Regarding parent involvement at school, the predictive power of parents' role construction at Grade 9 was nearly twice as important as that at Grade 7. Overall, the pattern of results differs to some extent by grade levels. Analogous to those results, one might focus on the specific influences of each grade level that seem to be used in parents' involvement decisions. Further longitudinal research is needed to test changes in the models across all secondary grade levels.

Quantitative research reports use standard, fixed structures and evaluation criteria

Notes

This research was supporred by grants to the first author from the Fonds québécois de la recherche sur la sociétéet la culture (FQRSC) and to both authors from the Centre de Recherche et d'Intervention sur la Réussite Scolaire (CRIRES).

1 One can use Mallow's C(P) statistic to evaluare the amount of mean square error (bias and random error) in the model. We sought values of C(P) near or below p (number of independent variables in the model; Neter, Wasserman, & Kutner, 1990, p. 448). We obtained all statistics with SPSS 11.0 (e.g., the stepwise regression method and the SELECTION keyword [for the Mallow's staistic]).

2 Merging the 770 parents' file with the students' file totaled 514 cases.

References

Adams, K. S., & Christenson, S. L. (2000). Trust and the family-school relationship examination of parent-teacher differences in elementary and secondary grades. *Journal of School Psychology, 38,* 477–497.

Astone, N. M., & McLanaban, S. S. (1991). Family structure, parent practices and high school completion. *American Sociological Review,* 56, 309–320.

Balli, S. J., Demo, D. H., & Wedman, J. F. (1998). Family involvement with children's homework: An intervention in the middle grades. *Family Relations, 47,* 142–146.

Bandura, A.(1997). *Self-efficacy in changing societies.* New York: Freeman.

Belskv, J. (1981). Early human experience: A family perspective. *Developmental, Psychology, 17,* 2–23.

Christenson, S. L., & Sheridan, S. M. *(2001). Schools and families: Creating essential connections for learning.* New York: Guilford Press.

Comer, J. P., & Haynes, N. M. (1991). Parent involvement in schools: An ecological approach.*The Elemantary School Journal, 91,* 271–277.

Dauber, S. L., & Epstein, J. L.(1989). *Parents' attitudes and practices of involvement in inner-city elementary and middle schools* (CREMS Report 33). Baltimore: Johns Hopkins University, Center for Research on Elementary and Middle Schools.

Dauber, S. L., & Epstein, J. L (1993). Parents' attitudes and practices of involvement in inner-city elementary and middle school. In N. F. Chavkin (Ed.), *Families and schools in a pluralistic society* (pp. 53–71). Albany: State University of New York Press.

Deslandes, R. (2000, April). *Direction of influence between parenting style and parent involvement in schooling practices, and students autonomy: A short-term longitudinal design.* Paper presented at the 10th International Roundtable on School, Family, and Community Partnerships, New Orleans, LA. (ERIC Document Reproduction Service No. ED441586)

Deslandes, R. (2003). Evolution of parenting and parent involvement in schooling practices and Candian adolescents' autonomy over a three year span. In S. Castelli, M. Mendel, & B. Ravns (Eds.), *School, family, and community partnerships in a world of differences and change* (pp. 89–104). Poland: Gdansk University.

Deslandes, R., & Bertrand R. (2003). *Raisons qui motivent les parents a participer au suivi scolaire de leur enfant du primaire.* [Reasons that motivate parents to be involved in their child's schooling at the elementary level]. Manuscript submitted for publication.

Deslandes, R., & Cloutier, R. (2000). Engagement parent dans l' accompagnement scolaire et réussite des adolescents à l'école [Parent involvement in their adosescent's schooling and success in school]. *Bulletin de psychologie Scolaire et d'Orientation, 2,*1–21.

Deslandes, R., & Cloutier, R. (2002). Adolescents' perception of parent-school involvement. *School Psychology International, 23* (2), 220–232.

Deslandes, R., & Potgin, P. (1999, April). *Autonomy, parenting, parent involvement in schooling and school achievement: Perception of Quebec adolescents.* Paper presented at the annual meeting of the American Educational Research Association, Montreal, Canada. (ERIC Document Reproduction Service No. ED430697)

Deslandes, R., Potvin, P., & Leclerc, D. (1999). Family characteristics predictors of school achievement: Parent involvement as a mediator. *McGill Journal of Education, 34*(2), 133–151.

Deslandes, R., & Royer, E. (1997). Family-related variables and school disciplinary events at the secondary level. *Behavioral Disorders, 23 (1), 18–28.*

Deslandes, R., Royer, E., Turcotte, D., & Bertrand, R. (1997). School achievement at the secondary level: Influence of parenting style and parent involvement in schooling. *McGill Journal of Education, 32*(3), 191–208.

Dornbusch, S. M., & Ritter, P. L. (1988). Parents of high school students: A neglected resource. *Educational Horizons, 66*(2), 75–77.

Eccles, J. S., Early, D., Frasier, K., Belansky, E., & McCarthy, K. (1997). The relation of connection, regulation, and support for autonomy to adolescents' functioning, *Journal of Adolescent Research, 12,* 263–286.

Eccles, J. S., & Harold, R. D. (1996). Family involvement in children's and adolescents' schooling. In A. Booth & J. Dunn (Eds.), *Family–school links: How do they affect educational outcomes?* Hillsdale, NJ: Erlbaum.

Epstein, J. L. (1986). Parents' reactions to teacher practices of parent involvement. *Elementary School Journal, 86,* 277–294.

Epstein, J. L. (2001). *School, family, and community partnerships: Preparing educators and improving schools.* Boulder, CO: Westview Press.

Epstein J. L., Connors-Tadros, L., Horsey, C. S., & Simon, B. S. (1996). *A report from the School, Family & Community Partnership Project.* Baltimore: Johns Hopkins University, Center on Families, Communities, Schools and Children's Learning.

Epstein, J. L., Connors, L. J., & Salinas, K. C. (1993). *High school and family partnerships: Questionnaires for teachers, parents, and students.* Baltimore: Johns Hopkins University, Center on Families, Communities, Schools and Children's Learning.

Freedman-Doan, C., Arbreton, A. J., Harold, R. D., & Eccles, J. S. (1993). Looking forward to adolescence: Mothers' and fathers' expectations for affective and behavioral change. *Journal of Early Adolescence, 13,* 472–502.

Greenberger, E., Josselson, R., Knerr, C., & Knerr, B. (1975). The measurement and structure of psychosocial maturity. *Journal of Youth and Adolescence, 4,* 127–143.

Henderson. A. T., & Mupp, K. L. (2002). *A new wave of evidence. The impact of school, family, and community connections on student achievement. Annual synthesis.* Austin, TX: National Center for Family & Community Connections with Schools. Southwest Educational Development Laboratory. Retrieved from www.sedl.org/connections

Hiatt-Michael, D. (Ed). (2001). *Promising practices for family involvement in school.* Greenwich, CT: Information Age Publishing, Inc.

Hoover-Dempsey, K. V., Bassler. O.C., & Brissie. J. S. (1992). Explorations in parent–school relations. *The Journal of Educational Research, 85,* 287–294.

Hoover-Dempsey, K. V., Battiato, A. C., Walker, J. M. T., Reed, R. P., DeJong, J. M., & Jones, K. P. (2001). Parent involvement in homework, *Educational Psychologist, 36,* 195–209.

Hoover-Dempsey, K. V., Jones. K. P., & Reed. R. (1999, April). *"I wish I were a bird in the window": The voices of parents seeking children's school success.* Paper presented at the annual meeting of the American Educational Research Association, Montreal, Canada.

Hoover-Dempsey, K. V., & Sandler, H. M. (1995). Parent involvement in childrens's education: Why does it make a difference? *Teachers College Record, 95,* 310–331.

Hoover-Dempsey, K. V., & Sandler, H. M. (1997). Why do parents become involved in their children's education? *Review of Educational Research, 67,* 3–42.

Jones, K., Gould, D., Brown, A., Young, J., & The Peabody Family School Partnership Lab of Vanderbilt University. (2000). *"Sharing the dream" parent questionnaire.* Retrieved from www.Vanderbilt.edu/Peabody/family.school

Jordan, C., Orozco, E., & Averett, A. (2001). Emerging issues in school, family, & community connections. Austin, TX: National Center for Family & Community Connections with Schools. Southwest Educational Development Laboratory. Retrieved from www.sedl.org/connections

Lee, S. (1994). *Family-school conncections and students' education: Continuity and change of family involvement from the middle grades to high school.* Unpublished doctoral dissertation, Johns Hopkins University, Baltimore, MD.

Neter, J., Wasserman, W., & Kutner. M. H. (1990). *Applied linear statistical models.* Honnewood., IL: Irwin.

Quebec Statistics Institute. (2001). *Portrait social du Québec. Données et analysis.* Quebec, Canada: Publications governmentales du Québec.

Reed, R. P., Jones, K. P., Walker, J. M., & Hoover-Dempsey, K. V. (2000, April). *Parents' motivations for involvement in children's education: Testing a theoretical model.* Paper presented at the annual meeting of the American Educational Research Association, New Orleans, LA.

Sameroff, A. J. (1975). Early influences on development: Fact or fancy. *Merrill-palmer Quarterly, 21,* 267–294.

Shartrand, A. M., , Weiss, H. B. Kreider, H. M., & Lopez, M. E. (1997). *New skills for new schools: Preparing teachers in family involvement.* Harvard Family Resarch Project. Cambridge, MA: Harvard Graduate School of Education. Retrieved from http:gov//www.ed./pubs/New Skills

Steinberg, L., Elmen., J. D., & Mounts, N. S (1989). Authoritative parenting, psychosocial maturity, and academic success among adolescents. *Child Development, 60,* 1424–1436.

Steinberg, L., Lamborn, S. D., Darling, N., Mounts, N. S., & Dornbusch, S. M. (1994). Over-time changes in adjustment and competence among adolescents from authoritative, authoritarian, indulgent, and neglectful families. *Child Development, 65,* 754–770.

Steinberg, L., Lamborn, S. D., Dornbusch, S. M., & Darling, N. (1992). Impact of parenting practices on adolescent achievemént: Authoritative parenting, school involvement, and encouragement to succeed. *Child Development, 63,* 1266–1281.

Stevenson, H. W., Chen, C., & Uttal, D. H. (1990). Reliefs and achievement. A study of Black, White, and Hispanic children. *Child Development, 6,* 508–523.

Trusty, J. (1996). Relationship of parent involvement in teens' career development to teens' attitudes, perceptions, and behavior, *Journal of Research and Development in Education, 30,* 317–323.

Walker, J. M. T., & Hoover-Dempsey K. V. (2001, April). *Age-related patterns in student invitations to parent involvement in homework.* Paper presented at the annual meeting of the American Educational Research Association, Seattle, WA.

Walker, J. M., Hoover-Dempsey, K. V., Reed, R. P., & Jones, K. P. (2000, April). *"Can you help me with my homework?" Elementary school children's invitations and perspectives on parent involvement.* Paper presented at the annual meeting of the American Educational Research Association, New Orleans, LA.

Xu, J. & Corno, L., (2003). Family help and homework management reported by middle school students. *The Elementary School Journal, 103,* 503–536.

Zimmerman, B. J., & Martinez-Pons, M. P. (1986). Development of a structured interview for assessing interview student use of self-regulated learning strategies. *American Educational Research Journal, 23,* 614–628.

Campus Response to a Student Gunman

Kelly J. Asmussen
John W. Creswell

Steps in the Research Process | **Qualitative Characteristic**

Identifying a research problem — **A qualitative problem requires exploration and understanding**

(1) With increasingly frequent incidents of campus violence, a small, growing scholarly literature about the subject is emerging. For instance, authors have reported on racial [12], courtship and sexually coercive [3, 7, 8], and hazing violence [24]. For the American College Personnel Association, Roark [24] and Roark and Roark [25] reviewed the forms of physical, sexual, and psychological violence on college campuses and suggested guidelines for prevention strategies. Roark [23] has also suggested criteria that high-school students might use to assess the level of violence on college campuses they seek to attend. At the national level, President Bush, in November 1989, signed into law the "Student Right-to-Know and Campus Security Act" (P.L. 101–542), which requires colleges and universities to make available to students, employees, and applicants an annual report on security policies and campus crime statistics [13].

Reviewing the literature — **The qualitative literature plays a major role**

(2) One form of escalating campus violence that has received little attention is student gun violence. Recent campus reports indicate that violent crimes from thefts and burglaries to assaults and homicides are on the rise at colleges and universities [13]. College campuses have been shocked by killings such as those at The University of Iowa [16], The University of Florida [13], Concordia University in Montreal, and the University of Montreal—Ecole Polytechnique [22]. Incidents such as these raise critical concerns, such as psychological trauma, campus safety, and disruption of campus life. Aside from an occasional newspaper report, the postsecondary literature is silent on campus reactions to these tragedies; to understand them one must turn to studies about gun violence in the public school literature. This literature addresses strategies for school intervention [21, 23], provides case studies of incidents in individual schools [6, 14, 15], and discusses the problem of students who carry weapons to school [1] and the psychological trauma that results from homicides [32].

The qualitative literature justifies the research problem

Specifying a purpose and research questions — **The qualitative purpose statement and research question are broad and general**

(3) A need exists to study campus reactions to violence in order to build conceptual models for future study as well as to identify campus strategies and protocols for reaction. We need to understand better the psychological dimensions and organizational issues of constituents involved in and affected by these incidents. An in-depth qualitative case study exploring the context of an incident can illuminate such conceptual and pragmatic understandings. The study presented in this article is a qualitative case analysis [31] that describes and interprets a campus response to a gun incident. We asked the following exploratory research questions: What happened? Who was involved in response to the incident? What themes of response emerged during the eight-month period that followed this incident? What theoretical constructs helped us understand the campus response, and what constructs were unique to this case?

The qualitative purpose statement and research question seek participants' experiences

---

Kelly J. Asmussen is a professor of criminal justice at Peru State College, and John W. Creswell is professor of educational psychology at the University of Nebraska–Lincoln.

From "Campus Response to a Student Gunman" by Kelly J. Asmussen and John W. Creswell, *The Journal of Higher Education,* Volume 66, Number 5 (Sept/Oct 1995).

The Incident and Response

Analyzing the data

Qualitative data analysis consists of describing information and developing themes

(4) The incident occurred on the campus of a large public university in a Midwestern city. A decade ago, this city had been designated an "all-American city," but more recently, its normally tranquil environment has been disturbed by an increasing number of assaults and homicides. Some of these violent incidents have involved students at the university.*

(5) The incident that provoked this study occurred on a Monday in October. A forty-three-year-old graduate student, enrolled in a senior-level actuarial science class, arrived a few minutes before class, armed with a vintage Korean War military semiautomatic rifle loaded with a thirty-round clip of thirty caliber ammunition. He carried another thirty-round clip in his pocket. Twenty of the thirty-four students in the class had already gathered for class, and most of them were quietly reading the student newspaper. The instructor was en route to class.

(6) The gunman pointed the rifle at the students, swept it across the room, and pulled the trigger. The gun jammed. Trying to unlock the rifle, he hit the butt of it on the instructor's desk and quickly tried firing it again. Again it did not fire. By this time, most students realized what was happening and dropped to the floor, overturned their desks, and tried to hide behind them. After about twenty seconds, one of the students shoved a desk into the gunman, and students ran past him out into the hall and out of the building. The gunman hastily departed the room and went out of the building to his parked car, which he had left running. He was captured by police within the hour in a nearby small town, where he lived. Although he remains incarcerated at this time, awaiting trial, the motivations for his actions are unknown.

(7) Campus police and campus administrators were the first to react to the incident. Campus police arrived within three minutes after they had received a telephone call for help. They spent several anxious minutes outside the building interviewing students to obtain an accurate description of the gunman. Campus administrators responded by calling a news conference for 4:00 P.M. the same day, approximately four hours after the incident. The police chief as well as the vice-chancellor of Student Affairs and two students described the incident at the news conference. That same afternoon, the Student Affairs office contacted Student Health and Employee Assistance Program (EAP) counselors and instructed them to be available for any student or staff requesting assistance. The Student Affairs office also arranged for a new location, where this class could meet for the rest of the semester. The Office of Judicial Affairs suspended the gunman from the university. The next day, the incident was discussed by campus administrators at a regularly scheduled campuswide cabinet meeting. Throughout the week, Student Affairs received several calls from students and from a faculty member about "disturbed" students or unsettling student relations. A counselor of the Employee Assistance Program consulted a psychologist with a specialty in dealing with trauma and responding to educational crises. Only one student immediately set up an appointment with the student health counselors. The campus and local newspapers continued to carry stories about the incident.

(8) When the actuarial science class met for regularly scheduled classes two and four days later, the students and the instructor were visited by two county attorneys, the police chief, and two student mental health counselors who conducted "debriefing" sessions. These sessions focused on keeping

students fully informed about the judicial process and having the students and the instructor, one by one, talk about their experiences and explore their feelings about the incident. By one week after the incident, the students in the class had returned to their standard class format. During this time, a few students, women who were concerned about violence in general, saw Student Health Center counselors. These counselors also fielded questions from several dozen parents who inquired about the counseling services and the level of safety on campus. Some parents also called the campus administration to ask about safety procedures.

(9) In the weeks following the incident, the faculty and staff campus newsletter carried articles about post-trauma fears and psychological trauma. The campus administration wrote a letter that provided facts about the incident to the board of the university. The administration also mailed campus staff and students information about crime prevention. At least one college dean sent out a memo to staff about "aberrant student behavior," and one academic department chair requested and held an educational group session with counselors and staff on identifying and dealing with "aberrant behavior" of students.

(10) Three distinctly different staff groups sought counseling services at the Employee Assistant Program, a program for faculty and staff, during the next several weeks. The first group had had some direct involvement with the assailant, either by seeing him the day of the gun incident or because they had known him personally. This group was concerned about securing professional help, either for the students or for those in the group who were personally experiencing effects of the trauma. The second group consisted of the "silent connection," individuals who were indirectly involved and yet emotionally traumatized. This group recognized that their fears were a result of the gunman incident, and they wanted to deal with these fears before they escalated. The third group consisted of staff who had previously experienced a trauma, and this incident had retriggered their fears. Several employees were seen by the EAP throughout the next month, but no new groups or delayed stress cases were reported. The EAP counselors stated that each group's reactions were normal responses. Within a month, although public discussion of the incident had subsided, the EAP and Student Health counselors began expressing the need for a coordinated campus plan to deal with the current as well as any future violent incident.

The Research Study

(11) We began our study two days after the incident. Our first step was to draft a research protocol for approval by the university administration and the Institutional Review Board. We made explicit that we would not become involved in the investigation of the gunman or in the therapy to students or staff who had sought assistance from counselors. We also limited our study to the reactions of groups on campus rather than expand it to include off-campus groups (for example, television and newspaper coverage). This bounding of the study was consistent with an exploratory qualitative case study design [31], which was chosen because models and variables were not available for assessing a campus reaction to a gun incident in higher education. In the constructionist tradition, this study incorporated the paradigm assumptions of an emerging design, a context-dependent inquiry, and an inductive data analysis [10]. We also bounded the study by time (eight months) and by a single case (the campus community). Consistent with case study design [17, 31], we identified campus administrators and student newspaper reporters as multiple sources of information for initial interviews. Later

Collecting data

Qualitative researchers take a reflexive and biased approach

Qualitative data collection involves studying a small number of individuals or sites

Qualitative data collection is based on using protocols developed during the study

TABLE 1
Data Collection Matrix—Type of Information by Source

Information/Information Source	Interviews	Observations	Documents	Audio-Visual Materials
Students involved	Yes		Yes	
Students at large	Yes			
Central administration	Yes		Yes	
Campus police	Yes	Yes		
Faculty	Yes	Yes	Yes	
Staff	Yes			
Physical plant		Yes	Yes	
News reporters/papers/T.V.	Yes		Yes	Yes
Student health counselors	Yes			
Employee Assistance Program counselors	Yes			
Trauma expert	Yes		Yes	Yes
Campus businesses			Yes	
Board members			Yes	

Qualitative data collection involves gathering text or image data

we expanded interviews to include a wide array of campus informants, using a semistructured interview protocol that consisted of five questions: What has been your role in the incident? What has happened since the event that you have been involved in? What has been the impact of this incident on the university community? What larger ramifications, if any, exist from the incident? To whom should we talk to find out more about the campus reaction to the incident? We also gathered observational data, documents, and visual materials (see Table 1 for types of information and sources).

Qualitative data analysis consists of text analysis

(12) The narrative structure was a "realist" tale [28], describing details, incorporating edited quotes from informants, and stating our interpretations of events, especially an interpretation within the framework of organizational and psychological issues. We verified the description and interpretation by taking a preliminary draft of the case to select informants for feedback and later incorporating their comments into the final study [17,18]. We gathered this feedback in a group interview where we asked: Is our description of the incident and the reaction accurate? Are the themes and constructs we have identified consistent with your experiences? Are there some themes and constructs we have missed? Is a campus plan needed? If so, what form should it take?

Analyzing the data

Qualitative data analysis consists of describing information and developing themes

Themes

Denial

(13) Several weeks later we returned to the classroom where the incident occurred. Instead of finding the desks overturned, we found them to be neatly in order; the room was ready for a lecture or discussion class. The hallway outside the room was narrow, and we visualized how students, on that Monday in October, had quickly left the building, unaware that the gunman, too, was exiting through this same passageway. Many of the students in the hallway during the incident had seemed unaware of what was going on until they saw or heard that there was a gunman in the building. Ironically though, the students had seemed to ignore or deny their dangerous situation. After exiting the building, instead of seeking a hiding place that would be safe, they had huddled together just outside the building. None of the students had barricaded themselves in classrooms or offices or had exited at a safe distance from the scene in anticipation that the gunman might return. "People wanted to stand their ground and stick

around," claimed a campus police officer. Failing to respond to the potential danger, the class members had huddled together outside the building, talking nervously. A few had been openly emotional and crying. When asked about their mood, one of the students had said, "Most of us were kidding about it." Their conversations had led one to believe that they were dismissing the incident as though it were trivial and as though no one had actually been in danger. An investigating campus police officer was not surprised by the students' behavior:

> It is not unusual to see people standing around after one of these types of incidents. The American people want to see excitement and have a morbid curiosity. That is why you see spectators hanging around bad accidents. They do not seem to understand the potential danger they are in and do not want to leave until they are injured.

(14) This description corroborates the response reported by mental health counselors: an initial surrealistic first reaction. In the debriefing by counselors, one female student had commented, "I thought the gunman would shoot out a little flag that would say 'bang.' " For her, the event had been like a dream. In this atmosphere no one from the targeted class had called the campus mental health center in the first twenty-four hours following the incident, although they knew that services were available. Instead, students described how they had visited with friends or had gone to bars; the severity of the situation had dawned on them later. One student commented that he had felt fearful and angry only after he had seen the television newscast with pictures of the classroom the evening of the incident.

(15) Though some parents had expressed concern by phoning counselors, the students' denial may have been reinforced by parent comments. One student reported that his parents had made comments like, "I am not surprised you were involved in this. You are always getting yourself into things like this!" or "You did not get hurt. What is the big deal? Just let it drop!" One student expressed how much more traumatized he had been as a result of his mother's dismissal of the event. He had wanted to have someone whom he trusted willing to sit down and listen to him.

Fear

(16) Our visit to the classroom suggested a second theme: the response of fear. Still posted on the door several weeks after the incident, we saw the sign announcing that the class was being moved to another undisclosed building and that students were to check with a secretary in an adjoining room about the new location. It was in this undisclosed classroom, two days after the incident, that two student mental health counselors, the campus police chief, and two county attorneys had met with students in the class to discuss fears, reactions, and thoughts. Reactions of fear had begun to surface in this first "debriefing" session and continued to emerge in a second session.

(17) The immediate fear for most students centered around the thought that the alleged assailant would be able to make bail. Students felt that the assailant might have harbored resentment toward certain students and that he would seek retribution if he made bail. "I think I am going to be afraid when I go back to class. They can change the rooms, but there is nothing stopping him from finding out where we are!" said one student. At the first debriefing session the campus police chief was able to dispel some of this fear by announcing that during the initial hearing the judge had denied bail. This announcement helped to reassure some students about their safety. The campus police chief thought it necessary to keep the students informed of the gunman's status, because several students had called his office to say that they feared for their safety if the gunman were released.

(18) During the second debriefing session, another fear surfaced: the possibility that a different assailant could attack the class. One student reacted so severely to this potential threat that, according to one counselor, since the October incident, "he had caught himself walking into class and sitting at a desk with a clear shot to the door. He was beginning to see each classroom as a 'battlefield.' " In this second session students had sounded angry, they expressed feeling violated, and finally began to admit that they felt unsafe. Yet only one female student immediately accessed the available mental health services, even though an announcement had been made that any student could obtain free counseling.

(19) The fear students expressed during the "debriefing" sessions mirrored a more general concern on campus about increasingly frequent violent acts in the metropolitan area. Prior to this gun incident, three young females and a male had been kidnapped and had later been found dead in a nearby city. A university football player who experienced a psychotic episode had severely beaten a woman. He had later suffered a relapse and was shot by police in a scuffle. Just three weeks prior to the October gun incident, a female university student had been abducted and brutally murdered, and several other homicides had occurred in the city. As a student news reporter commented, "This whole semester has been a violent one."

Safety

(20) The violence in the city that involved university students and the subsequent gun incident that occurred in a campus classroom shocked the typically tranquil campus. A counselor aptly summed up the feelings of many: "When the students walked out of that classroom, their world had become very chaotic; it had become very random, something had happened that robbed them of their sense of safety." Concern for safety became a central reaction for many informants.

(21) When the chief student affairs officer described the administration's reaction to the incident, he listed the safety of students in the classroom as his primary goal, followed by the needs of the news media for details about the case, helping all students with psychological stress, and providing public information on safety. As he talked about the safety issue and the presence of guns on campus, he mentioned that a policy was under consideration for the storage of guns used by students for hunting. Within four hours after the incident, a press conference was called during which the press was briefed not only on the details of the incident, but also on the need to ensure the safety of the campus. Soon thereafter the university administration initiated an informational campaign on campus safety. A letter, describing the incident, was sent to the university board members. (One board member asked, "How could such an incident happen at this university?") The Student Affairs Office sent a letter to all students in which it advised them of the various dimensions of the campus security office and of the types of services it provided. The Counseling and Psychological Services of the Student Health Center promoted their services in a colorful brochure, which was mailed to students in the following week. It emphasized that services were "confidential, accessible, and professional." The Student Judiciary Office advised academic departments on various methods of dealing with students who exhibited abnormal behavior in class. The weekly faculty newsletter stressed that staff needed to respond quickly to any post-trauma fears associated with this incident. The campus newspaper quoted a professor as saying, "I'm totally shocked that in this environment, something like this would happen." Responding to the concerns about disruptive students or employees, the campus police

department sent plainclothes officers to sit outside offices whenever faculty and staff indicated concerns.

(22) An emergency phone system, Code Blue, was installed on campus only ten days after the incident. These thirty-six ten-foot-tall emergency phones, with bright blue flashing lights, had previously been approved, and specific spots had already been identified from an earlier study. "The phones will be quite an attention getter," the director of the Telecommunications Center commented. "We hope they will also be a big detractor [to crime]." Soon afterwards, in response to calls from concerned students, trees and shrubbery in poorly lit areas of campus were trimmed.

(23) Students and parents also responded to these safety concerns. At least twenty-five parents called the Student Health Center, the university police, and the Student Affairs Office during the first week after the incident to inquire what kind of services were available for their students. Many parents had been traumatized by the news of the event and immediately demanded answers from the university. They wanted assurances that this type of incident would not happen again and that their child was safe on the campus. Undoubtedly, many parents also called their children during the weeks immediately following the incident. The students on campus responded to these safety concerns by forming groups of volunteers who would escort anyone on campus, male or female, during the evening hours.

(24) Local businesses profited by exploiting the commercial aspects of the safety needs created by this incident. Various advertisements for self-defense classes and protection devices inundated the newspapers for several weeks. Campus and local clubs who offered self-defense classes filled quickly, and new classes were formed in response to numerous additional requests. The campus bookstore's supply of pocket mace and whistles was quickly depleted. The campus police received several inquiries by students who wanted to purchase handguns to carry for protection. None were approved, but one wonders whether some guns were not purchased by students anyway. The purchase of cellular telephones from local vendors increased sharply. Most of these purchases were made by females; however, some males also sought out these items for their safety and protection. Not unexpectedly, the price of some products was raised as much as 40 percent to capitalize on the newly created demand. Student conversations centered around the purchase of these safety products: how much they cost, how to use them correctly, how accessible they would be if students should need to use them, and whether they were really necessary.

Retriggering

(25) In our original protocol, which we designed to seek approval from the campus administration and the Institutional Review Board, we had outlined a study that would last only three months—a reasonable time, we thought, for this incident to run its course. But during early interviews with counselors, we were referred to a psychologist who specialized in dealing with "trauma" in educational settings. It was this psychologist who mentioned the theme of "retriggering." Now, eight months later, we begin to understand how, through "retriggering," that October incident could have a long-term effect on this campus.

(26) This psychologist explained retriggering as a process by which new incidents of violence would cause individuals to relive the feelings of fear, denial, and threats to personal safety that they had experienced in connection with the original event. The counseling staffs and violence expert also stated that one should expect to see such feelings retriggered at a later point in time, for example, on the anniversary date of the attack or

whenever newspapers or television broadcasts mentioned the incident again. They added that a drawn-out judicial process, during which a case was "kept alive" through legal maneuvering, could cause a long period of retriggering and thereby greatly thwart the healing process. The fairness of the judgment of the court as seen by each victim, we were told, would also influence the amount of healing and resolution of feelings that could occur.

(27) As of this writing, it is difficult to detect specific evidence of retriggering from the October incident, but we discovered the potential consequences of this process firsthand by observing the effects of a nearly identical violent gun incident that had happened some eighteen years earlier. A graduate student carrying a rifle had entered a campus building with the intention of shooting the department chairman. The student was seeking revenge, because several years earlier he had flunked a course taught by this professor. This attempted attack followed several years of legal maneuvers to arrest, prosecute, and incarcerate this student, who, on more than one occasion, had tried to carry out his plan but each time had been thwarted by quick-thinking staff members who would not reveal the professor's whereabouts. Fortunately, no shots were ever fired, and the student was finally apprehended and arrested.

(28) The professor who was the target of these threats on his life was seriously traumatized not only during the period of these repeated incidents, but his trauma continued even after the attacker's arrest. The complex processes of the criminal justice system, which, he believed, did not work as it should have, resulted in his feeling further victimized. To this day, the feelings aroused by the original trauma are retriggered each time a gun incident is reported in the news. He was not offered professional help from the university at any time; the counseling services he did receive were secured through his own initiative. Eighteen years later his entire department is still affected in that unwritten rules for dealing with disgruntled students and for protecting this particular professor's schedule have been established.

Campus Planning

(29) The question of campus preparedness surfaced during discussions with the psychologist about the process of "debriefing" individuals who had been involved in the October incident [19]. Considering how many diverse groups and individuals had been affected by this incident, a final theme that emerged from our data was the need for a campuswide plan. A counselor remarked, "We would have been inundated had there been twenty-five to thirty deaths. We need a mobilized plan of communication. It would be a wonderful addition to the campus considering the nature of today's violent world." It became apparent during our interviews that better communication could have occurred among the constituents who responded to this incident. Of course, one campus police officer noted, "We can't have an officer in every building all day long!" But the theme of being prepared across the whole campus was mentioned by several individuals.

(30) The lack of a formal plan to deal with such gun incidents was surprising, given the existence of formal written plans on campus that addressed various other emergencies: bomb threats, chemical spills, fires, earthquakes, explosions, electrical storms, radiation accidents, tornadoes, hazardous material spills, snow storms, and numerous medical emergencies. Moreover, we found that specific campus units had their own protocols that had actually been used during the October gun incident. For example, the police had a procedure and used that procedure for dealing with the gunman and the students at the scene; the EAP counselors debriefed staff and

TABLE 2
Evidence from the Case, Questions for a Campus Plan, and References

Evidence from the Case	Question for the Plan	References Useful
Need expressed by counselors	Why should a plan be developed?	Walker (1990); Bird et al. (1991)
Multiple constituents reacting to incident	Who should be involved in developing the plan?	Roark & Roark (1987); Walker (1990)
Leadership found in units with their own protocols	Should the leadership for coordinating be identified within one office?	Roark & Roark (1987)
Several unit protocols being used in incident	Should campus units be allowed their own protocols?	Roark & Roark (1987)
Questions raised by students reacting to case	What types of violence should be covered in the plan?	Roark (1987); Jones (1990)
Groups/individuals surface during our interviews	How are those likely to be affected by the incident to be identified?	Walker (1990); Bromet (1990);
Comments from campus police, central administration	What provisions are made for the immediate safety of those in the incident?	
Campus environment changed after incident	How should the physical environment be made safer?	Roark & Roark (1987)
Comments from central administration	How will the external publics (e.g., press, businesses) be appraised of the incident?	Poland & Pitcher (1990)
Issue raised by counselors and trauma specialist	What are the likely sequelae of psychological events for victims?	Bromet (1990); Mitchell (1983)
Issue raised by trauma specialist	What long-term impact will the incident have on victims?	Zelikoff (1987)
Procedure used by Student Health counselors	How will the victims be debriefed?	Mitchell (1983); Walker (1990)

faculty; the Student Health counselors used a "debriefing process" when they visited the students twice in the classroom following the incident. The question that concerned us was, what would a campuswide plan consist of, and how would it be developed and evaluated?

(31) As shown in Table 2, using evidence gathered in our case, we assembled the basic questions to be addressed in a plan and cross-referenced these questions to the literature about post-trauma stress, campus violence and the disaster literature (for a similar list drawn from the public school literature, see Poland and Pitcher [21]). Basic elements of a campus plan to enhance communication across units should include determining what the rationale for the plan is; who should be involved in its development; how it should be coordinated; how it should be staffed; and what specific procedures should be followed. These procedures might include responding to an immediate crisis, making the campus safe, dealing with external groups, and providing for the psychological welfare of victims.

Discussion

(32) The themes of denial, fear, safety, retriggering, and developing a campuswide plan might further be grouped into two categories, an organizational and a psychological or social-psychological response of the campus community to the gunman incident. Organizationally, the campus units responding to the crisis exhibited both a loose coupling [30] and an interdependent communication. Issues such as leadership, communication, and authority emerged during the case analysis. Also, an environmental response developed, because the campus was transformed into a safer place for students and staff. The need for centralized planning, while

allowing for autonomous operation of units in response to a crisis, called for organizational change that would require cooperation and coordination among units.

(33) Sherrill [27] provides models of response to campus violence that reinforce as well as depart from the evidence in our case. As mentioned by Sherrill, the disciplinary action taken against a perpetrator, the group counseling of victims, and the use of safety education for the campus community were all factors apparent in our case. However, Sherrill raises issues about responses that were not discussed by our informants, such as developing procedures for individuals who are first to arrive on the scene, dealing with non-students who might be perpetrators or victims, keeping records and documents about incidents, varying responses based on the size and nature of the institution, and relating incidents to substance abuse such as drugs and alcohol.

Qualitative interpretations situate findings within larger meanings

(34) Also, some of the issues that we had expected after reading the literature about organizational response did not emerge. Aside from occasional newspaper reports (focused mainly on the gunman), there was little campus administrative response to the incident, which was contrary to what we had expected from Roark and Roark [25]. No mention was made of establishing a campus unit to manage future incidents—for example, a campus violence resource center—reporting of violent incidents [25], or conducting annual safety audits [20]. Aside from the campus police mentioning that the State Health Department would have been prepared to send a team of trained trauma experts to help emergency personnel cope with the tragedy, no discussion was reported about formal linkages with community agencies that might assist in the event of a tragedy [3]. We also did not hear directly about establishing a "command center" [14] or a crisis coordinator [21], two actions recommended by specialists on crisis situations.

Interpreting the data

(35) On a psychological and social-psychological level, the campus response was to react to the psychological needs of the students who had been directly involved in the incident as well as to students and staff who had been indirectly affected by the incident. Not only did signs of psychological issues, such as denial, fear, and retriggering, emerge, as expected [15], gender and cultural group issues were also mentioned, though they were not discussed enough to be considered basic themes in our analysis. Contrary to assertions in the literature that violent behavior is often accepted in our culture, we found informants in our study to voice concern and fear about escalating violence on campus and in the community.

(36) Faculty on campus were conspicuously silent on the incident, including the faculty senate, though we had expected this governing body to take up the issue of aberrant student or faculty behavior in their classrooms [25]. Some informants speculated that the faculty might have been passive about this issue because they were unconcerned, but another explanation might be that they were passive because they were unsure of what to do or whom to ask for assistance. From the students we failed to hear that they responded to their post-traumatic stress with "coping" strategies, such as relaxation, physical activity, and the establishment of normal routines [29]. Although the issues of gender and race surfaced in early conversations with informants, we did not find a direct discussion of these issues. As Bromet [5] comments, the sociocultural needs of populations with different mores must be considered when individuals assess reactions to trauma. In regard to the issue of gender, we did hear

that females were the first students to seek out counseling at the Student Health Center. Perhaps our "near-miss" case was unique. We do not know what the reaction of the campus might have been, had a death (or multiple deaths) occurred; although, according to the trauma psychologist, "the trauma of no deaths is as great as if deaths had occurred." Moreover, as with any exploratory case analysis, this case has limited generalizability [17], although thematic generalizability is certainly a possibility. The fact that our information was self-reported and that we were unable to interview all students who had been directly affected by the incident so as to not intervene in student therapy or the investigation also poses a problem.

(37) Despite these limitations, our research provides a detailed account of a campus reaction to a violent incident with the potential for making a contribution to the literature. Events emerged during the process of reaction that could be "critical incidents" in future studies, such as the victim response, media reporting, the debriefing process, campus changes, and the evolution of a campus plan. With the scarcity of literature on campus violence related to gun incidents, this study breaks new ground by identifying themes and conceptual frameworks that could be examined in future cases. On a practical level, it can benefit campus administrators who are looking for a plan to respond to campus violence, and it focuses attention on questions that need to be addressed in such a plan. The large number of different groups of people who were affected by this particular gunman incident shows the complexity of responding to a campus crisis and should alert college personnel to the need for preparedness.

Epilogue

Qualitative researchers take a reflexive and biased approach

(38) As we conducted this study, we asked ourselves whether we would have had access to informants if someone had been killed. This "near miss" incident provided a unique research opportunity, which could, however, only approximate an event in which a fatality had actually occurred. Our involvement in this study was serendipitous, for one of us had been employed by a correctional facility and therefore had direct experience with gunmen such as the individual in our case; the other was a University of Iowa graduate and thus familiar with the setting and circumstances surrounding another violent incident there in 1992. These experiences obviously affected our assessment of this case by drawing our attention to the campus response in the first plan and to psychological reactions like fear and denial. At the time of this writing, campus discussions have been held about adapting the in-place campus emergency preparedness plan to a critical incident management team concept. Counselors have met to discuss coordinating the activities of different units in the event of another incident, and the police are working with faculty members and department staff to help identify potentially violence-prone students. We have the impression that, as a result of this case study, campus personnel see the inter-relatedness and the large number of units that may be involved in a single incident. The anniversary date passed without incident or acknowledgment in the campus newspaper. As for the gunman, he is still incarcerated awaiting trial, and we wonder, as do some of the students he threatened, if he will seek retribution against us for writing up this case if he is released. The campus response to the October incident continues.

Qualitative research reports use flexible and emerging structures and evaluation criteria

Reporting the research

References

Asmussen, K. J. "Weapon Possession in Public High Schools." *School Safety* (Fall 1992), 28–30.

Bird, G. W., S. M. Stith, and J. Schladale. "Psychological Resources, Coping Strategies, and Negotiation Styles as Discriminators of Violence in Dating Relationships." *Family Relations,* 40 (1991), 45–50.

Bogal-Allbritten, R., and W. Allbritten. "Courtship Violence on Campus: A Nationwide Survey of Student Affairs Professionals." *NASPA Journal,* 28 (1991), 312–18.

Boothe, J. W., T. M. Flick, S. P. Kirk, L. H. Bradley, and K. E. Keough. "The Violence at Your Door," *Executive Educator* (February 1993), 16–22.

Bromet, E. J. "Methodological Issues in the Assessment of Traumatic Events." *Journal of Applied Social Psychology,* 20 (1990), 1719–24.

Bushweller, K. "Guards with Guns." *The American School Board Journal* (January 1993), 34–36.

Copenhaver, S., and E. Grauerholz. "Sexual Victimization among Sorority Women." *Sex Roles: A Journal of Research,* 24 (1991), 31–41.

Follingstad, D., S. Wright, S. Lloyd, and J. Sebastian. "Sex Differences in Motivations and Effects in Dating Violence." *Family Relations,* 40 (1991), 51–57.

Gordon, M. T., and S. Riger. *The Female Fear,* Urbana and Chicago: University of Illinois Press, 1991.

Guba, E., and Y. Lincoln. "Do Inquiry Paradigms Imply Inquiry Methodologies?" In *Qualitative Approaches to Evaluation in Education,* edited by D. M. Fetterman. New York: Praeger, 1988.

Johnson, K. "The Tip of the Iceberg." *School Safety,* (Fall 1992), 24–26.

Jones, D. J. "The College Campus as a Microcosm of U.S. Society. The Issue of Racially Motivated Violence." *The Urban League Review,* 13 (1990), 129–39.

Legislative Update. "Campuses Must Tell Crime Rates." *School Safety* (Winter 1991), 31.

Long, N. J. "Managing a Shooting Incident." *Journal of Emotional and Behavioral Problems,* 1 (1992), 23–26.

Lowe, J. A. "What We Learned: Some Generalizations in Dealing with a Traumatic Event at Cokeville." Paper presented at the Annual Meeting of the National School Boards Association, San Francisco, Calif., April 4–7, 1987.

Mann, J. *Los Angeles Times Magazine,* 2 June 1992, pp. 26–27, 32, 46–47.

Merriam, S. B. *Case Study, Research in Education: A Qualitative Approach.* San Francisco: Jossey-Bass, 1988.

Miles, M. B., and A. M. Huberman. *Qualitative Data Analysis: A Sourcebook of New Methods.* Beverly Hills, Calif.: Sage Publications, 1984.

Mitchell, J. "When Disaster Strikes." *Journal of Emergency Medical Services* (January 1983), 36–39.

NSSC Report on School Safety. "Preparing Schools for Terroristic Attacks." *School Safety* (Winter 1991), 18–19.

Poland, S., and G. Pitcher. *Crisis Intervention in the Schools.* New York: Guilford Press, 1992.

Quimet, M. "The Polytechnique Incident and Imitative Violence against Women," *SSR,* 76 (1992), 45–47.

Roark, M. L. "Helping High School Students Assess Campus Safety." *The School Counselor,* 39 (1992), 251–56.

———. "Preventing Violence on College Campuses." *Journal of Counseling and Development,* 65 (1987), 367–70.

Roark, M. L., and E. W. Roark. "Administrative Responses to Campus Violence." Paper presented at the Annual Meeting of the American College Personnel Association/National Association of Student Personnel Administrators. Chicago, 15–18 March 1987.

"School Crisis: Under Control" (1991). (1/2" VHS cassette tape) National School Safety Center, A partnership of Pepperdine University and the United States Departments of Justice and Education.

Sherill, J. M., and D. G. Seigel (eds.). *Responding to Violence on Campus.* New Directions for Student Services, No. 47. San Francisco: Jossey-Bass, Fall 1989.

Van Maanen, J. *Tales of the Field.* Chicago and London: The University of Chicago Press, 1988.

Walker, G. "Crisis-Care in Critical Incident Debriefing." *Death Studies,* 14 (1990), 121–33.

Weick, K. E. "Educational Organizations as Loosely Coupled Systems." *Administrative Science Quarterly,* 21 (1976), 1–19.

Yin, R. K. *Case Study Research, Design and Methods,* Newbury Park, Calif.: Sage Publications, 1989.

Zelikoff, W. L., and I. A. Hyman. "Psychological Trauma in the Schools: A Retrospective Study." Paper presented at the Annual Meeting of the National Association of School Psychologists, New Orleans, La., 4–8 March 1987.

CHAPTER 2

Quantitative and Qualitative Approaches

You have now learned that research consists of six steps. Let's add a second idea: You can approach research in two ways—through a quantitative study or a qualitative study—depending on the type of problem you need to research. Your choice of one of these approaches will shape the procedures you use in each of the six steps of research. In this chapter, we explore the many ways these two approaches are similar and different.

By the end of this chapter, you should be able to:

- Define quantitative and qualitative research.
- Explain the major ideas that have influenced the development of quantitative and qualitative research.
- Identify characteristics that distinguish and are similar for quantitative and qualitative research in each of the six steps of research.
- Identify the types of research designs used as procedures in quantitative, qualitative, or combined (or mixed) approaches.
- Identify three factors useful in deciding whether quantitative or qualitative research is best for conducting a study.

Maria weighs what approach she should take for her research project at the university. She hears about a new approach called *qualitative research* and learns that several new faculty members are strong proponents of this approach. However, she also realizes that several faculty members in her program have strong beliefs about the importance of collecting "hard" quantitative data instead of "soft" qualitative data. Maria asks herself, "How do I choose between quantitative and qualitative research?"

As part of making an informed choice, Maria needs to understand the differences between quantitative and qualitative research. Of course, the way in which she frames her research problem will largely determine which approach she uses for her study. However, it is crucial that Maria and other researchers understand the differences and similarities between quantitative and qualitative approaches because the selection of either approach determines how research is conducted along the way.

WHAT DOES IT MEAN TO CONDUCT QUANTITATIVE AND QUALITATIVE RESEARCH?

To understand these differences and similarities, we need to consider definitions of the terms *quantitative* and *qualitative research*. **Quantitative research** is a type of educational research in which the researcher decides what to study; asks specific, narrow questions; collects quantifiable data from participants; analyzes these numbers using statistics; and conducts the inquiry in an unbiased, objective manner. **Qualitative research** is a type of educational research in which the researcher relies on the views of participants; asks broad, general questions; collects data consisting largely of words (or text) from participants; describes and analyzes these words for themes; and conducts the inquiry in a subjective, biased manner.

You may begin to see some differences and similarities in these two definitions. They will become more apparent as we proceed through the six steps of research and discuss how the quantitative and qualitative research will employ each step. But first, the similarities and differences will become clearer if we explore briefly the historical high points in the development of each approach.

HOW DID QUANTITATIVE AND QUALITATIVE RESEARCH DEVELOP?

The 20th century began with one major approach to educational research—quantitative research—and ended with two major approaches—quantitative and qualitative research. The development of the two approaches is not a case of one approach replacing the other; instead, it reflects the addition of qualitative inquiry to the traditional quantitative approach. Today, both approaches are legitimate modes of educational research. However, in practice, rarely is quantitative and qualitative research purely quantitative or qualitative (as discussed by Firestone, 1987, and Smith, 1983); rather, in any given study, a researcher *tends* to frame the study more from one approach than the other approach. Research lies somewhere on the continuum from quantitative to qualitative research (Reichardt & Cook, 1979). For example, in Maria's study, she can collect quantitative data to indicate the frequency with which students bring weapons to school, *and* gather interview data that includes words (or text) of students as they describe their experiences. This example illustrates how a study can consist of both quantitative and qualitative elements, although you may place greater emphasis on quantitative research rather than qualitative research or vice versa.

A Brief History of Quantitative Research

Quantitative research began in the late 19th century and dominated educational inquiry for most of the 20th century (see De Landsheere, 1988, and Travers, 1992, for an expanded discussion). It is remarkable how similar quantitative research is today with its beginnings during the late 19th and early 20th centuries.

The initial ideas for quantitative research came from the physical sciences, such as physics and chemistry. Just as atoms and molecules were subject to predictable laws and axioms, so also were patterns of children's behaviors in schools. Following this line of logic, early quantitative researchers began identifying educational patterns by assessing or measuring individual abilities, collecting scores (or numbers) from individuals, and employing procedures of psychological experiments and large-scale surveys. In the history of the development of quantitative research, three historical trends are present: statistical procedures, test and measurement practices, and research designs. A chronology of these trends is shown in Table 2.1.

In statistics, quantitative research has emerged from 19th-century ideas of correlating and relating two or more ideas. Soon examining related ideas expanded into studying groups, and in the early 20th century, researchers compared the average scores of groups of individuals in educational settings. These two initial ideas—relating ideas and comparing groups—were the origin of common statistics used today. Over time, these elementary

TABLE 2.1

Select Historical Developments in Quantitative Research

Statistical Procedures	Tests and Measurement Practices	Research Designs
• 1980s—challenging traditional approaches to statistical testing by examining the magnitude of relation among variables, called *effect size estimates*	• 1980s—using standardized testing cutoff scores for children in schools	• 1990s—focusing on the sensitivity and power of experiments (Lipsey, 1990)
• 1970s—developing techniques for pooling data across several studies, called *meta-analysis*	• 1970s—developing standards for psychological and educational testing	• 1970s—elaborating the types of validity by Cook and Campbell (1979)
• 1970s—identifying models that examine causal relations among variables, called *structural equation modeling*	• 1960s—developing a theory that explains how items on an instrument differ in difficulty and discrimination, called *item response theory*	• 1960s—identifying types of quantitative research designs by Kerlinger (1964)
• 1970s—specifying models for studying the relation among variables that are categorical, called *log-linear models*	• 1950s—inventing machinery for scoring tests	• 1960s—specifying the types of experiments available to researchers by D.T. Campbell and Stanley (1963)
• 1920s—using procedures for drawing conclusions about a population from a sample, called *inferential statistics*	• 1940s—using tests for selecting personnel during WWII	• 1930s—conducting a study over time by the Progressive Education Association
• 1900s—using comparisons of differences between group means, called t-*tests*	• 1930s—developing first achievement tests	• 1930s—identifying procedures for conducting experiments (Fisher, 1935)
• 1900s—applying procedures for reducing a large number of variables to a smaller set, called *factor analysis*	• 1930s—founding of the Buros Institute for Mental Measurement	• 1910s—using special designs for experiments, such as Thorndike's Latin Square designs
• 1890s—identifying the ability to predict scores using information from correlations, called a *regression line*	• 1920s—administrating the first Scholastic Aptitude Test (SAT)	• 1900s—surveying school dropouts by Thorndike
• 1880s—being able to associate or correlate two variables, called *correlation analysis*	• 1910s—using tests by the Army during WWI	• 1900s—comparing groups in experiments by Schuyten
	• 1890s—developing the first mental tests	• 1880s—studying children by G. Stanley Hall

Sources: Abelson, 1995; De Landsheere, 1998; Vogt, 1999.

statistical ideas have grown into complex models interrelating numerous variables and test cause-and-effect or stimulus-response relationships. For example, does time on task cause better grades? Does depression relate to tobacco use among students?

In measurement, the concept of testing the mental ability of individuals originated in the late 19th century. With the advent of both world wars, the government employed researchers with knowledge of testing and measurement because of the military's need to select individuals and determine their readiness for combat. Also during the early 20th century, the idea of measuring an individual's performance or achievement developed. Standardized tests such as the Scholastic Aptitude Test (SAT) enabled college admissions personnel to predict an individual's future academic performance. By midcentury, measurement specialists were testing and using scoring machinery to facilitate scoring exams. Today, assessment debates surround the use of standardized performance assessments for children in subjects such as math and science. For example, schools use the results of these assessments to allow children to advance to the next grade, or to permit their inclusion in a gifted education program.

When compared with research designs today, the early approaches were simple and uncomplicated. Surveys of educational issues in the community began in the late 19th century. By the early 20th century, researchers were conducting educational experiments, drawing on the lessons learned from psychology. The idea of comparing the attitudes or performance of two groups, the basic concept behind experimental research, also took hold in the early 20th century. Researchers soon developed these early models of design into more complicated designs involving multiple groups and multiple tests. By 1935, various forms of experiments became a mainstay for research. During the 20th century, experimental researchers identified the types of experiments, their strengths and weaknesses, and expanded quantitative approaches to include correlational studies and survey research (D.T. Campbell & Stanley, 1963; Kerlinger, 1964).

These developments contributed to a major presence of quantitative research in education. Today, you can assess its stature by assessing the numerous quantitative projects funded by federal agencies such as the Department of Education and the National Institutes of Health. Similarly, state agencies and private foundations support many quantitative projects. You can also assess this stature by identifying educational journals devoted to publishing quantitative research, such as the the *Journal of Educational Research,* the *Journal of Experimental Education,* the *Journal of Applied Measurement,* and the *Journal of Learning Disabilities* as well as the numerous Web sites devoted to providing resources on statistics and measurement.

These historical trends have led to characteristics of quantitative research that we see today:

- An emphasis on collecting and analyzing information in the form of numbers
- An emphasis on collecting scores that measure distinct attributes of individuals and organizations
- An emphasis on the procedures of comparing groups or relating factors about individuals or groups in experiments, correlational studies, and surveys

A Brief History of Qualitative Research

Today, qualitative research presents an alternative to the traditional form of quantitative research. However, its historical use in education is more recent than that of quantitative research. The ideas for qualitative research developed in the late 1800s and early 1900s in fields other than education. For example, qualitative studies of the poor in Great Britain and Europe, anthropological reports about indigenous cultures, and the fieldwork of sociologists in inner-city Chicago and with immigrants all appear in social science research up through the 1930s and 1940s (Bogdan & Biklen, 1998). However, the actual use of qualitative research in education is most apparent during the last 30 years, and a chronology of events in this brief history appears in Table 2.2. As seen in this table, three themes shape its history in education: philosophical ideas, procedural developments, and participatory and advocacy practices. Current studies today typically exhibit one or more of these themes.

By the late 1960s, philosophers of education called for an alternative to the traditional quantitative approach (e.g., Guba & Lincoln, 1988). The traditional approach, they felt, relied too much on the researcher's view of education and less on the research participant's view.

TABLE 2.2

Select Recent Historical Developments in Qualitative Research

Philosophical Ideas	Procedural Developments	Participatory and Advocacy Practices
• 2000s—clarifying the controversies, contradictions, and confluences among paradigms or worldviews (Denzin & Lincoln, 2005) • 1980s—identifying differences between naturalistic and traditional research (Lincoln & Guba, 1985) • 1980s—distinguishing between two philosophical approaches of idealism and realism (Smith, 1983) • 1970s—advocating an alternative approach, the naturalistic paradigm, to traditional research (Guba, 1978)	• 1990s—advancing a framework for conducting narrative research (Clandinin & Connelly, 2000) • 1990s—distinguishing among five different approaches to qualitative inquiry (Creswell, 2007) • 1990s—advancing alternative inquiry approaches (Denzin & Lincoln, 1994) • 1990s—presenting approaches to designing qualitative studies (Maxwell, 1996) • 1990s—advancing procedures for conducting grounded theory qualitative research (Strauss & Corbin, 1990) • 1990s—introducing a basic overview of qualitative research (Glesne & Peshkin, 1992) • 1990s—advancing ideas about ethnographic research (LeCompte, Millroy, & Preissle, 1992; Wolcott, 1994) • 1980s—introducing the design of qualitative research (Marshall & Rossman, 1989) • 1980s—presenting detailed procedures for qualitative data analysis (Miles & Huberman, 1984) • 1980s—introducing all aspects of designing a study (Bogdan & Biklen, 1982)	• 2000s—using collaborative, participatory approaches to research (Kemmis & McTaggart, 2000) • 1990—exploring issues about racial and cultural identity (Delgado & Stefancic, 1997) • 1990s—examining a sensitivity to gay issues (Tierney, 1997) • 1990s—advancing perspectives about inequality and marginalization (Carspecken, 1995) • 1990s—advocating for a need to better understand racial identity (Sleeter, 1996) • 1990s—examining feminist perspectives about qualitative research (Lather, 1991)

Traditional investigations created a contrived situation in which the research participant was "taken out" of context and placed within an experimental situation far removed from his or her personal experiences. To counter these traditional approaches, philosophers of education suggested an alternative form of research, called *naturalistic inquiry* or *constructivism,* to remedy these deficiencies (Lincoln & Guba, 1985). The central perspective of these new approaches emphasized the importance of the participant's view, stressed the setting or context (e.g., a classroom) in which the participants expressed the views, and highlighted the meaning people personally held about educational issues. This thinking positioned qualitative research as an alternative—at times adversarial—perspective to traditional research.

Another theme developed in qualitative research during the 1980s and early 1990s that softened this perspective. Several writers focused on the procedures of conducting qualitative research rather than on challenging quantitative research. Procedures such as writing general qualitative research questions, conducting on-site interviews and observations, and analyzing data for themes occupied writers' attention (Creswell, 2003, 2007; Glesne & Peshkin, 1992; Miles & Huberman, 1994; Tesch, 1990). Specific books constructed templates for planning qualitative dissertation and master's theses (Creswell, 2003; Marshall & Rossman, 1995). Along with these efforts arose a discussion about "types" of qualitative research designs, such as case studies, grounded theory research, and narrative inquiry (e.g., Creswell, 2007; Stake, 1995; Strauss & Corbin, 1990), and the emergence of qualitative computer software programs for data analysis (e.g., Weitzman & Miles, 1995).

In the last decade, we have seen an emergence of a third theme in educational qualitative research: participatory and advocacy practices. This theme developed from an impassioned concern for the inequity and needs of individuals in lower social classes, of women, and of members of certain racial groups such as African Americans and Hispanics (e.g., Carspecken, 1995). Denzin and Lincoln (2005) summarized the following advocacy position: Advocacy researchers are not objective, authoritative, or politically neutral. Advocacy researchers see qualitative research as a civic responsibility, a "moral dialogue" (Denzin & Lincoln, 2005, p. 1049), and as a means for bringing needed change to our society.

Ideas such as these challenged traditional research that held firm to a neutral and objective stance. It also called for the inquirers to report in their studies their own personal biases, values, and assumptions. It cast research into politics in which it considered the rights of women, gays, lesbians, racial groups, and different classes in our society, and honored different viewpoints during both the writing and the reading of qualitative reports. It also spoke about qualitative data-collection procedures in which inquirers were sensitive to participants, actively collaborated with them (rather than studying them), and respected the dignity of each individual who offered data for research.

One interesting facet of these three themes has been how they coalesce to shape qualitative research today. Proponents of all three themes form a sizable contingent of educational researchers. This diverse group makes many presentations at meetings of professional associations such as AERA and at conferences specifically devoted to qualitative research. Major handbooks are available now, creating the broad landscape of qualitative research in education and in the social sciences (e.g., Denzin & Lincoln, 2005). With increasing frequency, funding agencies at the federal, state, and private levels support qualitative research projects. Major journals today also address qualitative research. Although many social science and education journals are open to publishing qualitative studies, several scholarly journals also publish qualitative research, such as the *International Journal of Qualitative Studies in Education, Qualitative Inquiry, Anthropological and Education Quarterly, Qualitative Research Elementary School Journal,* and the *Journal of Counseling and Development*. An online journal dedicated to qualitative research since 1990, the *Qualitative Report* lists dozens of sites addressing all aspects of qualitative research.

These historical developments have led to characteristics of qualitative research that we recognize today:

- A recognition that as researchers we need to listen to the views of participants in our studies
- A recognition that we need to ask general, open questions and collect data in places where people live and work
- A recognition that research has a role in advocating for change and bettering the lives of individuals

WHAT CHARACTERISTICS DISTINGUISH AND ARE COMMON TO QUANTITATIVE AND QUALITATIVE RESEARCH IN EACH OF THE SIX STEPS?

With different historic origins, it is little wonder that quantitative and qualitative research have dissimilar characteristics. Relating each approach to the six steps in the process of research helps us to understand the distinctive characteristics of each approach. By closely examining each step, you will see that researchers tend to apply the two approaches differently at each step. Look closely at Figure 2.1. It is an important figure in this book. It displays a continuum, with the endpoints denoting a quantitative or qualitative study, and the major characteristics of each approach at these endpoints. Quantitative studies are often characterized by the elements on the left, and qualitative, by elements on the right. Not all quantitative studies have all of the characteristics listed, nor do all qualitative studies have all of the characteristics listed. Thus, it is best to view the differences between quantitative and qualitative research on a continuum rather than a rigid dichotomy. It is helpful, however, to understand the characteristics associated with each endpoint so that you can identify quantitative and qualitative studies when you see them in publications, find them cited in reports, or conduct your own research study. Right now, however, you do not need to master each of these characteristics; in later chapters (chapters 3–10) we will elaborate on them in greater detail.

Identifying a Research Problem

Quantitative **research tends to address research problems requiring:**

- A description of trends or an explanation of the relationship among variables

Qualitative **research tends to address research problems requiring:**

- An exploration in which little is known about the problem
- A detailed understanding of a central phenomenon

In *quantitative* research, describing a trend means that the research problem can be answered best by a study in which the researcher seeks to establish the overall tendency of responses from individuals and to note how this tendency varies among people. For example, you might seek to learn how voters describe their attitudes toward a bond issue. Results from this study can inform how a large population views an issue and the diversity of these views.

However, some quantitative research problems require that you explain how one variable affects another. *Variables* are an attribute (e.g., attitude toward the school bond

FIGURE 2.1

Characteristics of Quantitative and Qualitative Research on a Continuum in the Process of Research

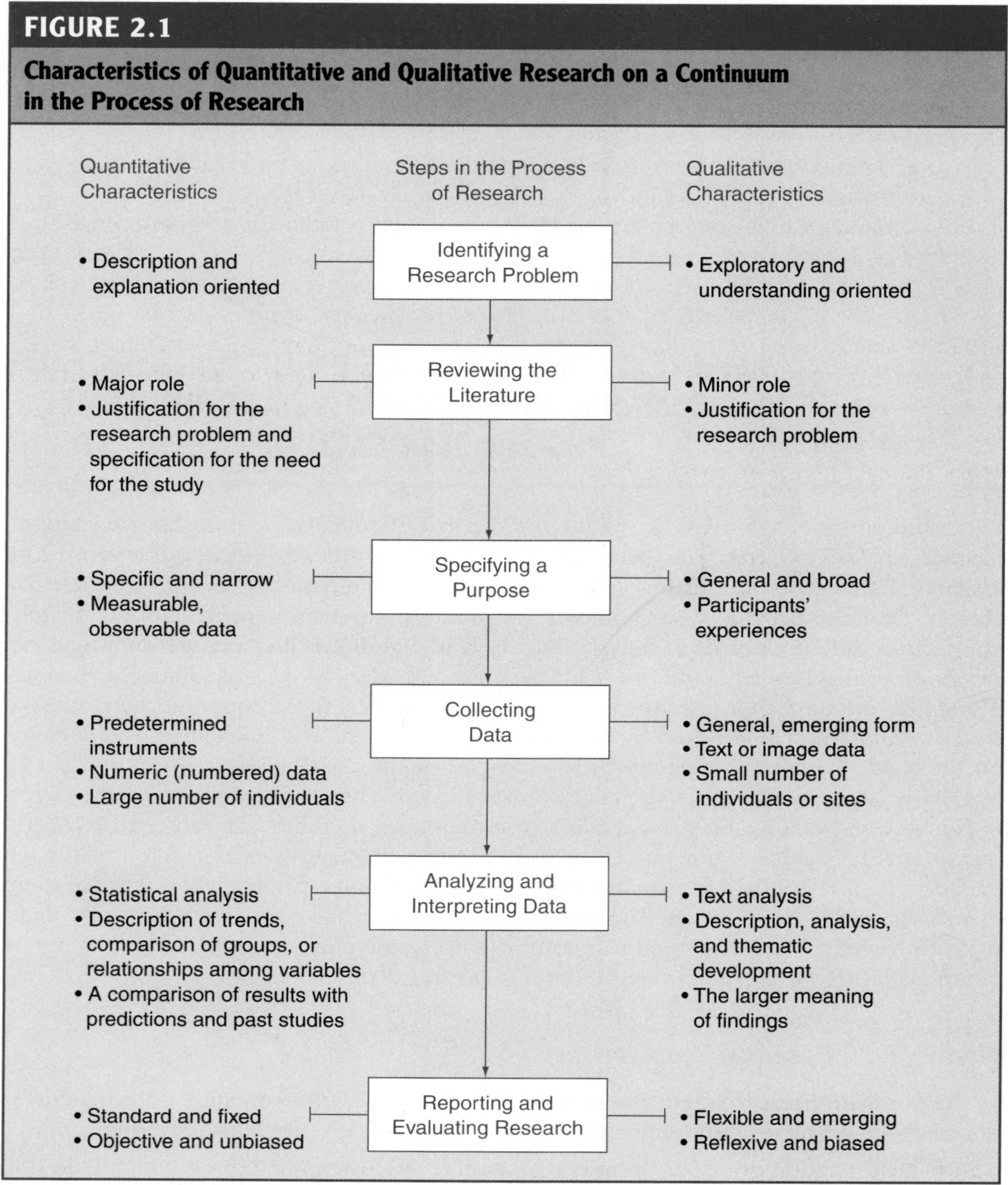

issue) or characteristic of individuals (e.g., gender) that researchers study. By explaining a relation among variables, you are interested in determining whether one or more variables might influence another variable. For example, quantitative researchers may seek to know why certain voters voted against the school bond issue. The variables, gender and attitude toward the quality of the schools, may influence individual votes on the bond issue.

The authors in the parent involvement study (Deslandes & Bertrand, 2005) of chapter 1 are less interested in describing the level of parent involvement in secondary-level schooling and more interested in examining the relationship between four factors—parents' role construction, self-efficacy, perceptions of teacher invitations, and perceptions of adolescent invitations—as predictors of parent involvement at home and at school (see Paragraph 02). To examine this relation, they collect survey data from 770 parents of children in Grades 7, 8, and 9 (American system equivalents to Canadian schools; see Paragraph 14). Thus, the problem being addressed (see Paragraph 02) is that we know little about what factors relate to parental involvement in secondary-level schooling. Assessing whether certain factors predict an outcome is best suited to quantitative research.

Qualitative research, however, is best suited for research problems in which you do not know the variables and need to explore. The literature might yield little information about the phenomenon of study, and you need to learn more from participants through exploration. For example, the literature may not adequately address the use of sign language in distance education courses. A qualitative research study is needed to explore this phenomenon from the perspective of distance education students. Unquestionably, using sign languge in such courses is complex and may not have been examined in the prior literature. A *central phenomenon* is the key concept, idea, or process studied in qualitative research. Thus, the research problem of the difficulty in teaching children who are deaf requires both an exploration (because we do not know how to teach these children) as well as an understanding (because of its complexity) of the process of teaching and learning.

In the gunman case study (Asmussen & Creswell, 1995) of chapter 1, you see both exploration and understanding. In this qualitative research study, the authors are not interested in explaining the incident; rather, they seek to explore and gain a deeper understanding of how those on campus reacted to the incident (see Paragraph 03). They map the process in all of its complexity as it unfolds during an 8-month period following the incident.

Reviewing the Literature

In *quantitative* research, the literature tends to:

- Provide a major role through suggesting the research questions to be asked
- Justify the research problem and create a need for the direction (purpose statement and research questions or hypotheses) of the study

In *qualitative* research, the literature tends to:

- Play a minor role in suggesting a specific research question to be asked
- Justify the importance of studying the research problem

In *quantitative* research, you will typically see a substantial literature review at the beginning of the study. Thus, the literature plays a major role in two ways: justifying the need for the research problem and suggesting potential purposes and research questions for the study. Justifying the research problem means that you use the literature to document the importance of the issue examined in the study. To accomplish this, you search the literature, locate studies that identify the problem as important to examine, and then cite this literature in the opening sections of a research report.

The literature also creates a need for the study, as expressed specifically in the purpose statement and the research questions or hypotheses. You identify in the literature key variables, relation, and trends, and use these to provide direction for your research questions and hypotheses. A literature review on college students, for example, may show that we know little about the problem of binge drinking. Existing literature, however, may identify the importance of peer groups and styles of interacting among student peer groups. Thus, important research questions might address how peers and their interaction styles influence binge drinking on college campuses. In this way, the literature in a quantitative study both documents the need to study the problem and provides direction for the research questions.

In the quantitative parent involvement study (Deslandes & Bertrand, 2005), the authors cite extensive literature at the beginning of the article (Paragraphs 03–10). In these paragraphs, the authors rely on the model of the parent involvement process cited in Paragraph 02, and they discuss the literature surrounding each of the four major factors that are expected to influence parental involvement. They begin by reviewing the literature about the demographic or personal factors such as family size and educational level (see Paragraph 03), then they proceed to review the literature about the major factors in the study that they predict will influence parental involvement—parents' role construction (Paragraph 05), parents' self-efficacy (Paragraph 06), parents' perceptions of teacher invitations (Paragraph 07), and parents' perceptions of student invitations (Paragraphs 08–10). In this way, the introduction establishes the research that has been reported in the literature on each of the four factors in the study (see Paragraph 13) and foreshadows the research questions that will be addressed in the study.

In *qualitative* research, the literature review plays a less substantial role at the beginning of the study. Although you may review the literature to justify the need to study the research problem, the literature does not provide major direction for the research questions. The reason for this is that qualitative research relies on the views of participants in the study and less on the direction identified in the literature by the researcher. Thus, to use the literature to foreshadow or specify the direction for the study is inconsistent with the qualitative approach of learning from participants. For example, one qualitative researcher who studied bullying in the schools cited several studies at the beginning of the research to provide evidence for the problem but did not use the literature to specify the research questions. Instead, this researcher attempted to answer in the research the most general, open question possible, "What is bullying?," to learn how students constructed their view of this experience.

In a similar way, the literature plays a minor role in the qualitative gunman incident study (Asmussen & Creswell, 1995). The article opens with references that support the importance of the problem of campus violence (see Paragraph 01). But in the next section of the study (Paragraph 04), the authors describe the incident, and the literature does not reappear until the final passages in the study, in which the authors describe the need for campus planning. From reading this article, you can see much less literature "up front." The literature justifies the research problem, but it does not lead to the questions asked in the study. The questions are general, allowing the participants to help construct answers. Thus, in a qualitative study, the literature is of secondary importance whereas the views of the participants are of primary importance.

Specifying a Purpose for Research

In *quantitative* research, the purpose statement, research questions, and hypotheses tend to:

- Be specific and narrow
- Seek measurable, observable data on variables

In *qualitative* research, the purpose statement and research questions tend to:

- Be general and broad
- Seek to understand the participants' experiences

In *quantitative* research, you ask specific, narrow questions to obtain measurable and observable data on variables. The major statements and questions of direction in a study—the purpose statement, the research questions, and the hypotheses—are specific and narrow because you identify only a few variables to study. From a study of these variables, you obtain measures or assessments on an instrument or record scores on a scale from observations. For example, in a study of adolescent career choices, the variable, the role of the school counselor, narrows the study to a specific variable from among many variables that might be studied (e.g., role of parents, personal investment by student). To examine the impact of the school counselor on adolescent career choices, data must be obtained from the students.

In the quantitative parent involvement study (Deslandes & Bertrand, 2005), the authors narrow and select a few factors that they predict will explain parental involvement. They state their purpose of the study and the major research questions in Paragraph 13. They say that they will examine four factors that influence parental involvement at home and at school, and then they identify the four factors that they predict will influence this involvement. Thus, their research questions are specific to four factors, and later in the method section, they explain how they will measure these factors (Paragraphs 18–23).

In *qualitative* research, the purpose is much more open ended than in quantitative research. You ask general, broad questions so that you can best learn from participants. You research a single phenomenon of interest and state this phenomenon in a purpose statement. A qualitative study that examines the "professionalism" of teachers, for example, asks high school teachers, "What does it mean to be a professional?" This question focuses on understanding a single idea—being a professional—and the responses to it will yield qualitative data such as quotations.

In the qualitative gunman case study (Asmussen & Creswell, 1995), the authors start with broad, open-ended questions to obtain participants' views about the incident (Paragraph 03). This questioning focuses on understanding the process of the campus reaction to the gunman incident. The researchers' intent is to allow the participants to talk openly about their experiences. For example, examine the authors' first general, broad question: "What happened?" (Paragraph 03).

Collecting Data

In *quantitative* research, the data collection tends to consist of:

- Collecting data using instruments with preset questions and responses
- Gathering quantifiable (numeric) data
- Collecting information from a large number of individuals

In *qualitative* research, the data collection tends to consist of:

- Collecting data using forms with general, emerging questions to permit the participant to generate responses
- Gathering word (text) or image (picture) data
- Collecting information from a small number of individuals or sites

In *quantitative* research, you use an instrument to measure the variables in the study. An *instrument* is a tool for measuring, observing, or documenting quantitative data. It contains specific questions and response possibilities that you establish or develop in advance of the study. Examples of instruments are survey questionnaires, standardized tests, and checklists that you might use to observe a student's or teacher's behaviors. You administer this instrument to participants and collect data in the form of numbers. For instance, you might collect responses based on students' checking boxes on a form, or from checklists you complete as you watch a student perform a task in the classroom. The intent of this process is to apply the results (called *generalizing the results*) from a small number of people to a large number. The larger the number of individuals studied, the stronger the case for applying the results to a large number of people. For example, on a survey sent to 500 parents in a school district, the researcher seeks information about parents' attitudes toward the educational needs of pregnant teenagers in the schools. The researcher selects an instrument, "Attitudes Toward Education of Pregnant Teenagers," found through a search of library resources. The 500 parents who receive this instrument represent a cross section of people from all socioeconomic levels in the school district. After collecting and analyzing this data, the investigator will draw conclusions about all parents in this school district based on the representative sample studied.

Data collection is also an integral part of the quantitative parent-involvement study (Deslandes & Bertrand, 2005). The authors study a large number of parents (i.e., 770) of children in Grades 7, 8, and 9. They survey parents using an adaptation of the instrument, "Sharing the Dream! Parent Questionnaire" (Paragraph 16) as well as items on a questionnaire designed by other researchers to assess parents' perceptions of student invitations. The survey items are translated into French to fit the Quebec context, and they gather quantifiable data (scores) on the survey (Paragraph 17). They discuss the scales used to collect the data and how they are scored (i.e., from 1 = *disagree very strongly* to 6 = *agree very strongly*).

In *qualitative* research, you do not begin data collection with a preestablished instrument to measure distinct variables. Instead, you seek to learn from the participants in the study, and develop forms, called *protocols,* for recording data as the study proceeds. These forms pose general questions so that the participants can provide answers to the questions. Often questions on these forms will change and emerge during data collection. Examples of these forms include an *interview protocol,* which consists of four or five questions, and an *observational protocol,* in which the researcher records notes about the behavior of participants. Moreover, you gather text (word) or image (picture) data. Transcribed audio recordings form a database composed of words. Observing participants in their work or family setting, you take notes that will become a qualitative database. When researchers ask young children to write their thoughts in a diary, these diary entries, too, become a text database. With each form of data, you will gather as much information as possible to collect detailed accounts for a final research report.

In the qualitative gunman case study (Asmussen & Creswell, 1995), the authors collect data from a few individuals on campus representing different constituents (e.g., administrators, counselors, "experts"; paragraph 11). They do not use instruments constructed by other researchers; instead, they develop their own forms for recording information—an interview protocol—during the project (see Paragraph 11). This form contains general questions so that the constituents can provide their own responses to the questions. They also take observational notes about the classroom in which the incident occurred and collect campus newspaper reactions to the crisis.

Analyzing and Interpreting Data

In *quantitative* research, the

- Data analysis tends to consist of statistical analysis
- Data analysis tends to involve describing trends, comparing group differences, or relating variables
- Interpretation tends to consist of comparing results with prior predictions and past research

In *qualitative* research, the

- Data analysis tends to consist of text analysis
- Data analysis tends to involve developing a description and themes
- Interpretation tends to consist of stating the larger meaning of the findings

In *quantitative* research, you analyze the data using mathematical procedures, called *statistics*. These analyses consist of breaking down the data into parts to answer the research questions. Statistical procedures such as comparing groups or relating scores for individuals provide information to address the research questions or hypotheses. You then interpret the results of this analysis in light of initial predictions or prior studies. This interpretation is an explanation as to why the results turned out the way they did, and often you will explain how the results either support or refute the expected predictions in the study.

For example, in the parent involvement study (Deslandes & Bertrand, 2005), the authors collect responses from the parents of secondary-level students who provide scores on the survey instrument. The survey has questions relating to each of the eight factors (or constructs) and the outcome measures as shown in Table 2. To examine the relation of factors to parental involvement, the researchers do not use all of the items on the survey because some were not good measures of the factors. As discussed in Paragraph 17, they use a statistical program (i.e., factor analysis) to help them identify the most important questions for each of the four scales composed of items (or factors) in the study. With this reduced set of questions for each of the four factors in the study, they then conduct descriptive analysis (i.e., means and standard deviations as shown in Table 3), and use the statistical program of regression statistical analysis to predict whether the control or personal items or four predictors best explain the variation in scores for parent involvement. From Tables 4 and 5, we see what variables best explain the variation for each grade level (7, 8, 9) and for the two outcome measures of parent involvement at home and parent involvement at school. In short, the authors use statistical analysis consisting of three phases: factor analysis, descriptive analysis, and regression analysis. The ultimate goal was to relate variables to see what predictors (demographics or the four factors) best explain parental involvement. Then, in the implication section of the article (Paragraphs 44–45), the authors discuss the main results of the study and compare their results with those found in other studies in the literature.

In *qualitative* research, because the data consists of words or pictures, a different approach exists for data analysis. Typically, you gather a text database, so the analysis of text consists of dividing it into groups of sentences, called *text segments,* and determining the meaning of each group of sentences. Rather than using statistics, you analyze words or pictures to describe the central phenomenon under study. The result may be a description of individual people or places. In some qualitative studies, the entire report is mostly a long description of several individuals. The result may also include themes or broad categories that represent your findings. In qualitative studies in which you both describe individuals and identify themes, a rich, complex picture emerges. From this complex picture, you make an interpretation of the meaning of the data by reflecting on how the findings relate to existing research; by stating a personal reflection about the significance of the lessons learned during the study; or by drawing out larger, more abstract meanings.

The authors of the qualitative gunman case study use these analysis and interpretation procedures (Asmussen & Creswell, 1995). They review their text data consisting of transcripts from interviews, written notes from observations, and documents, including newspaper accounts. They also have a videotape of a news conference filmed immediately after the incident (see Paragraph 11 for data sources). From this data (both words and images), the authors first describe chronologically the events for 2 weeks following the incident (Paragraphs 04–10). They then identify themes or categories such as "Denial" (Paragraph 13). Other themes mentioned were safety and campus planning. Finally, in the discussion at the end of the article, the authors interpret the broader meaning of their description and themes (Paragraph 35), mentioning that the theme fits into larger psychological and social-psychological social science perspectives. In the epilogue (Paragraph 38), the authors introduce themselves into the study by commenting about the personal meaning of the incident. Qualitative researchers typically bring themselves directly into the written report in some way, such as writing an epilogue, writing about their experiences when they discuss the procedures, or weaving their personal experiences into the conclusion.

Reporting and Evaluating Research

In *quantitative* research, the:

- Research reports tend to use standard, fixed structures and evaluative criteria
- Researchers tend to take an objective and unbiased approach

In *qualitative* research, the:

- Research reports tend to use flexible, emerging structure and evaluative criteria
- Researchers tend to take a subjective (reflexive) and biased approach

In *quantitative* research, the overall format for a study follows a predictable pattern: introduction, review of the literature, methods, results, and discussion. This form creates a standardized structure for quantitative studies. In addition, it also leads to specific criteria that you might use to judge the quality of a quantitative research report. For example, you examine a quantitative study to see if it has an extensive literature review; tests good research questions and hypotheses; uses rigorous, impartial data-collection procedures; applies appropriate statistical procedures; and forms interpretations that naturally follow from the data.

In quantitative research, you also use procedures to ensure that your own personal biases and values do not influence the results. You use instruments that have proven value and that have reliable and valid scores from past uses of the instruments. You design studies to control for all variables that might introduce bias into a study. Finally, you report research without referring to yourself or your personal reaction.

In the quantitative parent-involvement study (Deslandes & Bertrand, 2005), the authors subdivide the research into standard sections typically found in quantitative studies. The study begins with an introduction that includes the literature review and purpose statement and research questions (see Paragraphs 01–13), the methods (see Paragraphs 14–24), the results (see Paragraphs 25–31), the discussion (see Paragraphs 32–43), and, finally, the implications and limitations (see Paragraphs 44–49). The entire study conveys an impersonal, objective tone, and they do not bring either their biases or their personal opinions into the study. They use proven instruments to measure variables (e.g., Paragraphs 18–19), and they employ multiple statistical procedures (see Paragraphs 17, 25) to build objectivity into the study.

However, in *qualitative* research, you employ a wide range of formats to report your studies. Although the overall general form follows the standard steps in the process of research, the sequence of these "parts" of research tends to vary from one qualitative report to another. A study may begin with a long, personal narrative told in story form or with a more objective, scientific report that resembles quantitative research. With such variability, it is not surprising that the standards for evaluating qualitative research also are flexible. Good qualitative reports, however, need to be realistic and persuasive to convince the reader that the study is an accurate and credible account. Qualitative reports typically contain extensive data collection to convey the complexity of the phenomenon or process. The data analysis reflects description and themes as well as the interrelation of themes. In addition, you will discuss your role or position in a research study, called *being reflexive* (**reflexivity** means that the researchers reflect on their own biases, values, and assumptions and actively write them into their research). This may involve discussing personal experiences and identifying how you collaborated with participants during phases of the project. You may also discuss how your experiences and cultural backgrounds (e.g., Asian American perspectives) affect the interpretations and conclusions drawn in the study.

In the case of the gunman incident (Asmussen & Creswell, 1995), the authors use a structure that is more scientific than storytelling. However, they do not order the scientific "parts" in the sequence typically found in quantitative inquiry. The authors introduce "findings" early in the study when they chronicle the events following the incident

(Paragraphs 04–10), rather than report them late in the study. They also end with an epilogue consisting of personal views by both authors about their experiences with violence and guns (Paragraph 38). In addition, throughout the study the authors use personal pronouns referring to themselves frequently (e.g., "we"). The extensive use of quotes from individuals also accentuates the personal approach in this study.

At this point, you may be asking how quantitative and qualitative research are similar:

- Both forms of research follow the six steps in the process of research.
- In the section on the research problem—found in the introduction to a study—both quantitative and qualitative research can be similar in the topics addressed, such as conveying a problem, pointing out the lack of literature on this problem, and justifying a need to study the problem. This does not mean that the type of problem is the same, only the format for reporting the problem.
- In both quantitative and qualitative research, you collect data using interviews, observations, and documents. However, later we shall see a difference between the *types* of interviews or observations used in these two approaches.

WHAT ARE THE RESEARCH DESIGNS ASSOCIATED WITH QUANTITATIVE AND QUALITATIVE RESEARCH?

It is not enough to know the steps in the process of research, and that quantitative and qualitative procedures differ at each step. In this text, we will also go into detailed procedures involved in quantitative, qualitative, and combined research. **Research designs** are the specific procedures involved in the last three steps of the research process: data collection, data analysis, and report writing, as shown in Figure 2.2. These research

FIGURE 2.2

Three Components to Educational Research

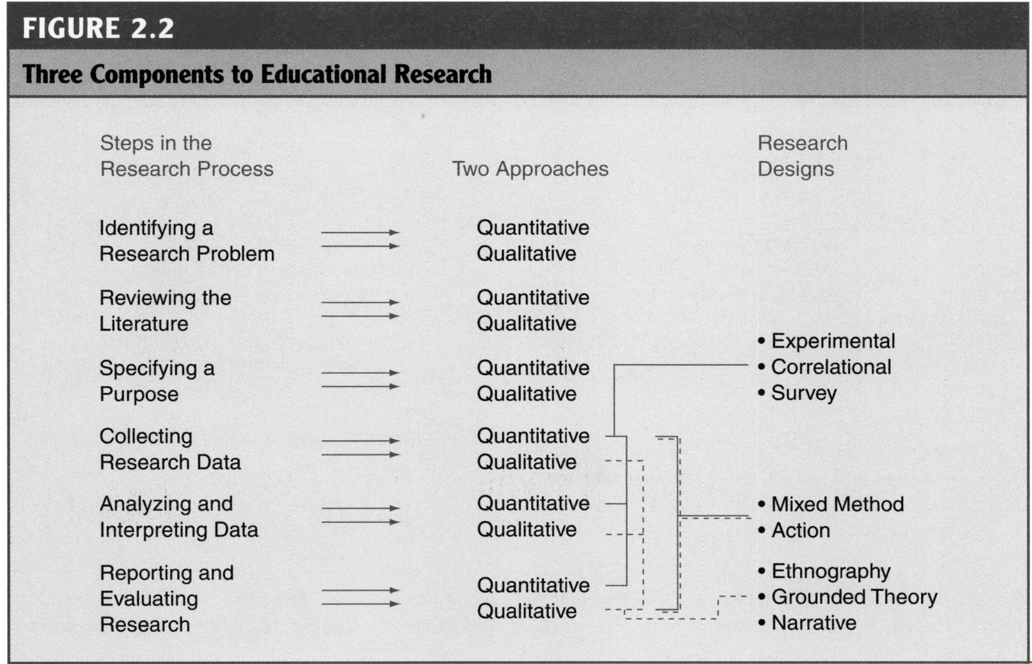

designs differ for quantitative, qualitative, and combined research. Although part III of this text contains chapters on eight specific research designs, this chapter provides a brief overview of each design. Use Figure 2.3 as a general guide to the differences among these designs as we discuss each design.

Experimental Designs

Some quantitative researchers seek to test whether an educational practice or idea makes a difference for individuals. Experimental research procedures are ideally suited for this study. *Experimental designs* (also called intervention studies or group comparison studies) are procedures in quantitative research in which the investigator determines whether an activity or materials make a difference in results for participants. You assess this impact by giving one group one set of activities (called an *intervention*) and withholding the set from another group. In chapter 11, you will learn more about the nature of experiments and the procedures for conducting them.

Correlational Designs

In some studies, you may be unable to provide an intervention or to assign individuals to groups. Moreover, you focus more on examining the association or relation of one or more variables than in testing the impact of activities or materials. *Correlational designs* are procedures in quantitative research in which investigators measure the degree of association (or relation) between two or more variables using the statistical procedure of correlational analysis. This degree of association, expressed as a number, indicates whether the two variables are related or whether one can predict another. To accomplish this, you study a single group of individuals rather than two or more groups as in an experiment. Chapter 12 will detail the procedures for conducting correlational research.

FIGURE 2.3

Types of Quantitative and Qualitative Research Designs and Their Primary Uses

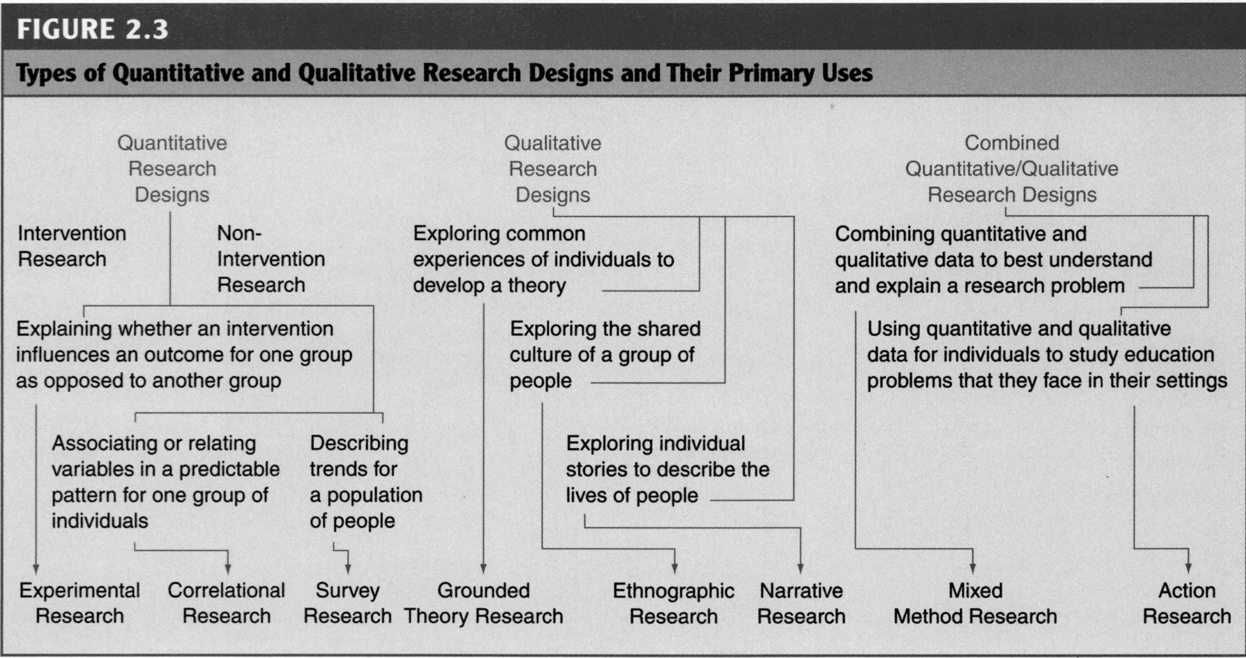

Survey Designs

In another form of quantitative research, you may not want to test an activity or materials or may not be interested in the association among variables. Instead, you seek to describe trends in a large population of individuals. In this case, a survey is a good procedure to use. *Survey designs* are procedures in quantitative research in which you administer a survey or questionnaire to a small group of people (called the *sample*) to identify trends in attitudes, opinions, behaviors, or characteristics of a large group of people (called the *population*). Chapter 13 discusses the purpose and the design of survey research.

Grounded Theory Designs

Instead of studying a single group, you might examine a number of individuals who have all experienced an action, interaction, or process. *Grounded theory designs* are systematic, qualitative procedures that researchers use to generate a general explanation (called a *grounded theory*) that explains a process, action, or interaction among people. The procedures for developing this theory include collecting primarily interview data, developing and relating categories (or themes) of information, and composing a figure or visual model that portrays the general explanation. In this way, the explanation is "grounded" in the data from participants. From this explanation, you construct predictive statements about the experiences of individuals. Chapter 14 discusses how to design and conduct grounded theory research.

Ethnographic Designs

You may be interested in studying one group of individuals, in examining them in the setting where they live and work, and in developing a portrait of how they interact. An ethnographic study is well suited for this purpose. *Ethnographic designs* are qualitative procedures for describing, analyzing, and interpreting a cultural group's shared patterns of behavior, beliefs, and language that develop over time. In ethnography, the researcher provides a detailed picture of the culture-sharing group, drawing on various sources of information. The ethnographer also describes the group within its setting, explores themes or issues that develop over time as the group interacts, and details a portrait of the group. Chapter 15 identifies the procedures involved in conducting an ethnographic research design.

Narrative Research Designs

You may not be interested in describing and interpreting group behavior or ideas, or in developing an explanation grounded in the experiences of many individuals. Instead, you wish to tell the stories of one or two individuals. *Narrative research designs* are qualitative procedures in which researchers describe the lives of individuals, collect and tell stories about these individuals' lives, and write narratives about their experiences. In education, these stories often relate to school classroom experiences or activities in schools. The procedures involved in conducting a narrative study will be addressed in chapter 16.

Mixed Methods Designs

You decide to collect both quantitative data (i.e., quantifiable data) as well as qualitative data (i.e., text or images). The core argument for a mixed methods design is that the combination of both forms of data provides a better understanding of a research problem than either quantitative or qualitative data by itself. *Mixed methods designs* are procedures for collecting, analyzing, and mixing both quantitative and qualitative data in a single study or in a multiphase series of studies. In this process, you need to decide on the emphasis you will give to each form of data (priority), which form of data you will collect first (concurrent or sequential), how you will "mix" the data (integrating or connecting), and whether you will use an advocacy lens (e.g., feminist or class theories) to guide your study. Chapter 17 will review current mixed methods designs.

Action Research Designs

Like mixed methods research, action research often utilizes both quantitative and qualitative data, but it focuses more on procedures useful in addressing practical problems in schools and the classrooms. *Action research designs* are systematic procedures used by teachers (or other individuals in an educational setting) to gather quantitative and qualitative data to address improvements in their educational setting, their teaching, and the learning of their students. In some action research, you seek to address and solve local, practical problems, such as a classroom-discipline issue for a teacher. In other studies, your objective might be to empower, transform, and emancipate individuals in educational settings. Chapter 18 will identify procedures used in conducting action research.

HOW DO YOU CHOOSE WHETHER TO USE THE QUANTITATIVE OR QUALITATIVE APPROACH?

With the differences and similarities of quantitative and qualitative research in mind, as well as the different procedures or designs used to conduct research, how do you decide whether to use a quantitative or qualitative (or some combination) approach? Consider three factors.

Match Your Approach to Your Research Problem

The most important factor that should go into your decision is to match your quantitative or qualitative approach to your research problem. Remember that the problems best suited for quantitative research are those in which trends or explanations need to be made. For qualitative research, the problems need to be explored to obtain a deep understanding. A combined design seeks both trends or explanations and exploration or a deep understanding.

In the parent involvement study (Deslandes & Bertrand, 2005), the authors' interest grows out of a need to better explain what factors lead parents to decide to become involved in their adolescents' schooling. When prediction is involved, researchers use quantitative research. Alternatively, in the qualitative gunman case study (Asmussen & Creswell, 1995), the researchers seek to understand how campus personnel respond to the incident during the 8 months following the incident. When an exploration is needed, and one in which all of the complexity of a situation must be explored, researchers use qualitative research. To explore is at a different end of the research continuum (see Figure 2.1) from explaining the impact of known predictors and measuring their impact.

Fit the Approach to Your Audience

A second factor that goes into your decision involves the audience for whom you are writing the research report. Educators write for several audiences, such as policy makers, faculty and graduate committees, editors and review boards, evaluators of grant proposals, and individuals in schools or educational settings who will read and possibly use the findings from a study. It is important that the audience(s) be familiar with the approach used in a study. Quantitative research may be more familiar to educators today who are trained in experimental research, survey designs, and statistical procedures. However, qualitative research now draws a substantial following, and through books, articles, conferences, and workshops, educators can obtain a much firmer grasp of qualitative inquiry than they could a few years ago. When students choose to use qualitative research, they may need to educate readers about the basic characteristics of a qualitative study. If such education is needed, it can occur through lengthy method discussions in the study (or in a presentation to the audience), or through references to key qualitative readings in the research report. However, the need to do this is occurring less frequently.

Relate the Approach to Your Experiences

Choose your approach based on your personal experiences and training. Conducting research in either quantitative or qualitative research requires skills in conceptualizing research, conducting research, and writing the study. A quantitative researcher typically has taken some courses or training in measurement, statistics, and quantitative data-collection approaches, such as experimental, correlational, or survey techniques. Qualitative researchers need experience in field studies in which they practice gathering information in a setting and learn the skills of observing or interviewing individuals. Course work or experience in analyzing text data is also helpful. Thus, the choice of approach must relate to the personal skills, training, and experiences of the researcher.

EXAMINING THE PARENT INVOLVEMENT AND GUNMAN INCIDENT STUDIES

Let's review by returning to the parent involvement study (Deslandes & Bertrand, 2005) and the gunman incident study (Asmussen & Creswell, 1995).

Let's first summarize the overall intent of the *quantitative* parent involvement study (Deslandes & Bertrand, 2005). The authors start with a model from the literature of factors likely to influence parental involvement with adolescents in secondary-level schooling. They focus on four factors and adapt instruments to measure each of the four factors as well as parental involvement. They then collect data on their instrument from a large sample of parents. Before they analyze the impact of each of the four factors (and background variables), they reduce the number of questions about each of the four factors and then provide a description of the sample. They then discuss the results about which predictors are best at explaining two types of parental involvement—involvement at home and involvement at school. With these results in hand, they then compare the results with other research studies to show how their findings were both similar and dissimilar to prior research. This study illustrates quantitative research.

Let's turn to a *qualitative study,* the gunman case study (Asmussen & Creswell, 1995). The impact of potential violence on a college campus is the focus of this qualitative study.

This study explores a campus reaction to a gunman incident in which a student attempts to fire a gun at his classmates in a university classroom. Fortunately, the gun jams and the gunman panics and leaves the classroom. Police later catch the gunman in a small town 12 miles south of the university. This study traces how the campus reacts to this event over an 8-month period, and it explores the diverse perspectives of students, faculty, psychologists, health center personnel, media, and administrators. From this data, the authors report five themes about the campus response to the incident, and end the article with a discussion about implications for safety on college campuses. This study displays qualitative research.

Do you think that these studies illustrate two different approaches to research? Certainly, the two studies differ in their content: One focuses on parents and the other on a situation on a college campus. Consider how they differ in *research*. Make a list of the different ways the two studies differ.

Here is my list:

In the parent-involvement *quantitative* study, the researchers:

- Predict that four factors will influence parent involvement with their adolescents at school and at home
- Ask specific, narrow questions
- Collect data consisting of numbers (i.e., scores from parents on an instrument)
- Analyze these numbers using mathematical procedures (i.e., statistics)
- Remain invisible (unbiased) in the written report (i.e., do not mention themselves)

In the gunman-incident *qualitative* research study, the researchers:

- Make no prediction about the campus response but rely on participants to shape what they report
- Ask broad, general questions
- Collect data consisting of words (i.e., text from participants during interviews)
- Analyze these words by describing events and deriving themes
- Remain visible, present, and biased in the written report (i.e., mention themselves)

How does this list match your list? You may not have all five of these differences identified, but perhaps two or three. For example, it is easy to see that the quantitative study (the parent involvement study) bases its results on numbers whereas the qualitative study (the gunman-incident study) uses quotes of words from individuals who experienced the incident.

KEY IDEAS IN THE CHAPTER

Educators use quantitative, qualitative, or some combination of approaches during each phase of the research process. Depending on the approach used, you will conduct research differently. Quantitative research is a type of educational research in which the researcher decides what to study; asks specific, narrow questions; collects numeric (numbered) data from participants; analyzes these numbers using statistics; and conducts the inquiry in an unbiased, objective manner. Qualitative research is a type of educational research in which the researcher relies on the views of participants; asks broad, general questions; collects data consisting largely of words (or text) from participants; describes and analyzes these words for themes; and conducts the inquiry in a subjective, biased manner.

Quantitative research began with the development of statistical procedures in the late 19th century. Many developments have occurred since then, not only in statistics but also in measurement and testing and in the types of research designs. Qualitative research also has its antecedents in late 19th-century and early 20th-century history. However, only in the last 30 years has qualitative research played a major role in educational research. During this time, three discernible trends developed: the philosophical movement prior to the 1980s, the push toward procedures and rigor that began in the mid-1980s, and the more recent emphasis in the 1990s on advocacy and participatory research to address the needs of individuals in our society.

To examine the differences and similarities between the quantitative and qualitative approaches, turn to the six-step research process. Quantitative and qualitative characteristics reside on a continuum—any one study may not have all of the characteristics of either quantitative or qualitative research, but studies tend toward one end of the continuum or the other. The types of problems studied, as well as how the literature is used, tend to differ within each approach. The purpose and research questions also vary in scope, and the data collection is clearly distinguishable, with numbers and statistical analysis used in quantitative research, and words and images in qualitative research. Because of the different types of data used, data analysis is also different. Different structures and approaches exist for writing the research report. Similarities between the two approaches are that they both use the six-step research process, have similar introductions in their studies, and use similar data-collection procedures.

Researchers tend to employ specific procedures for data collection, analysis, and report writing within the quantitative and qualitative approaches. This text emphasizes eight research designs: experimental, correlational, survey, grounded theory, ethnographic, narrative, mixed method, and action research designs. A researcher's choice of a design or an approach depends on several factors: the type of research problem, the audience for the research report, and personal experiences and training.

Useful Information for Producers of Research

- As you plan and conduct a study, discuss specifically the characteristics of the approach you are using. Refer to Figure 2.1 for words to describe your approach. By including these characteristics, you will demonstrate your knowledge of the research and help establish the credibility of your inquiry.
- Recognize that research is not either all quantitative or all qualitative, but tends toward one or the other (on a continuum).
- Use of qualitative research is a recent phenomenon in education. This means that individuals reviewing your qualitative plan for research may not be as familiar with qualitative characteristics. You will need to inform readers by sharing with them the characteristics described in this chapter.
- At each step in the research process, the arguments, words, and points you make will differ depending on whether you are conducting a quantitative or qualitative study.

Useful Information for Consumers of Research

- Examine the characteristics of Figure 2.1 to determine if a published study is quantitative or qualitative.
- Because qualitative research came on to the research scene more recently than quantitative research, it may be harder to evaluate. The structure used in the report, as seen in headings, will be more flexible or varied.
- Expect that a quantitative study and a qualitative study will not look the same, because they differ in many steps of the research process. At the same time, they use the same general steps of the process.

Understanding Concepts and Evaluating Research Studies

1. How would the parent involvement study (Deslandes & Bertrand, 2005) be different if you presented it as a *qualitative* study? How would the gunman case study (Asmussen & Creswell, 1995) be different if it were a *quantitative* study?
2. Discuss the developments in quantitative and qualitative research today.

Go to our Companion Website at **www.prenhall.com/creswell** to:

- assess your understanding of chapter content with Multiple-Choice Questions,
- apply what you've learned with Essay Questions,
- practice your research skills with interactive Building Research Skills exercises, and
- broaden your knowledge of research with Web Links to research topics on the Internet.

PART II

The Steps in the Process of Research

Now that you have the general road map for your journey, we will start the trip and proceed through each step. Not all researchers go through each step in the order presented here, but many do. By proceeding down the research path, step by step, you will enhance your ability to read, evaluate, and conduct research using both the quantitative and qualitative approaches.

The chapters in Part II are:

- Chapter 3 Identifying a Research Problem
- Chapter 4 Reviewing the Literature
- Chapter 5 Specifying a Purpose and Research Questions or Hypotheses
- Chapter 6 Collecting Quantitative Data
- Chapter 7 Analyzing and Interpreting Quantitative Data
- Chapter 8 Collecting Qualitative Data
- Chapter 9 Analyzing and Interpreting Qualitative Data
- Chapter 10 Reporting and Evaluating Research

Identifying a Research Problem

Researchers begin a study by identifying a research problem that they need to address. They write about this "problem" in the opening passages of their study and, in effect, give you as a reader the rationale for why the study is important and why you need to read their study. In this chapter, you will learn about specifying a research problem and positioning it within a section that introduces a study, the "statement of the problem" section.

By the end of this chapter, you should be able to:

- Define and identify a research problem and explain its importance to a study.
- Distinguish between a research problem, the topic, the purpose, and the research questions.
- Identify criteria for deciding whether you can or should study a research problem.
- Describe how quantitative and qualitative research problems differ.
- Describe the five elements that comprise a "statement of the problem" section.
- Identify strategies useful in writing a "statement of the problem" section.

Maria begins her research project required for her graduate program. Where does she start? She starts by posing several questions and then writing down short answers to them.

- *"What is the specific controversy or issue that I need to address?"* Escalating violence in the schools
- *"Why is this problem important?"* Schools need to reduce the violence; students will learn better if violence is less a part of their lives, etc.
- *"How will my study add to what we already know about this problem?"* We really don't have many school plans for addressing this escalating violence
- *"Who will benefit from what I learn about this problem?"* Schools, anybody interested in learning how schools can respond to escalating violence (the body of literature, administrators, teachers, etc.)

For a beginning researcher, the difficulty is not developing answers to questions, but coming up with the questions to ask yourself. To do this, we need to learn how to write an introduction or "statement of the problem" section for a research study.

WHAT IS A RESEARCH PROBLEM AND WHY IS IT IMPORTANT?

One of the most challenging aspects of conducting research is to clearly identify the "problem" that leads to a need for your study. Individuals do not seem to give enough attention to why they are conducting their studies. **Research problems** are the educational issues, controversies, or concerns that guide the need for conducting a study. Good research problems can be found in our educational settings, such as:

- The disruptions caused by at-risk students in classrooms
- The increase in violence on college campuses
- The lack of parental involvement in schools for students with challenging behaviors

These problems concern personnel in our schools, classrooms, and college campuses. In writing about the research problem, authors state it as a single sentence or several sentences in a research report. To locate the research problem in a study, ask yourself:

- What was the issue, problem, or controversy that the researcher wanted to address?
- What controversy leads to a need for this study?
- What was the concern being addressed "behind" this study?
- Is there a sentence like "The problem addressed in this study is . . ."?

You can find "problems" in the introduction to a study. They are included in a passage called the "statement of the problem" section. You can locate this passage in the opening, introductory paragraphs of a research report.

We study research problems so we can assist policy makers when they make decisions, help teachers and school officials solve practical problems, and provide researchers with a deeper understanding of educational issues. From a research standpoint, specifying a research problem in your study is important because it sets the stage for the entire study. Without knowing the research problem, readers do not know why the study is important and why they should read the study. What are some educational issues that you might research? Write down these issues.

Although you are aware of many educational problems, it is challenging to write them into a research report. This may be due to a lack of understanding about how to write them or identify them for your study.

HOW DOES THE RESEARCH PROBLEM DIFFER FROM OTHER PARTS OF RESEARCH?

To better understand research problems, you might distinguish them from other parts of the research process. The research problem is distinct from the *topic* of the study (to be addressed later in this chapter), the *purpose* or intent of the study (to be considered in chapter 5 on purpose statements), and specific *research questions* (also discussed in chapter 5). The research problem needs to stand on its own and be recognized as a distinct step because it represents the problem addressed in the study.

In the brief definitions that follow, consider the differences among these parts of research:

- A *research topic* is the broad subject matter addressed by the study. Maria, for example, seeks to study weapon possession by students in schools.
- A *research problem* is a general educational issue, concern, or controversy addressed in research that narrows the topic. The problem Maria addresses is the escalating violence in schools due, in part, to students possessing weapons.
- A *purpose* is the major intent or objective of the study used to address the problem. Maria might state the purpose of her study as follows: "The purpose of my study will be to identify factors that influence the extent to which students carry weapons in high schools."
- *Research questions* narrow the purpose into specific questions that the researcher would like answered or addressed in the study. Maria might ask, "Do peers influence students to carry weapons?"

Looking at these differences, you can see that they differ in terms of breadth from broad (topic) to narrow (specific research questions). Let's examine another example, as shown in Figure 3.1, to make this point. In this example, a researcher begins with a broad topic, distance learning. The inquirer then seeks to learn about a problem related to this topic: the lack of students enrolled in distance education classes. To study this problem, our educator then reformulates the problem into a statement of intent (the purpose statement): to study why students do not attend distance education classes at one community college. Examining this statement requires that our investigator narrow the intent to specific questions, one of which is "Does the use of Web site technology in the classroom deter students from enrolling in distance education classes?" The process involves narrowing a broad topic to specific questions. In this process, the "research problem" becomes a distinct step that needs to be identified to help readers clearly see the issue.

FIGURE 3.1

Distinguishing Among the Topic, Research Problem, Purpose, and Research Questions

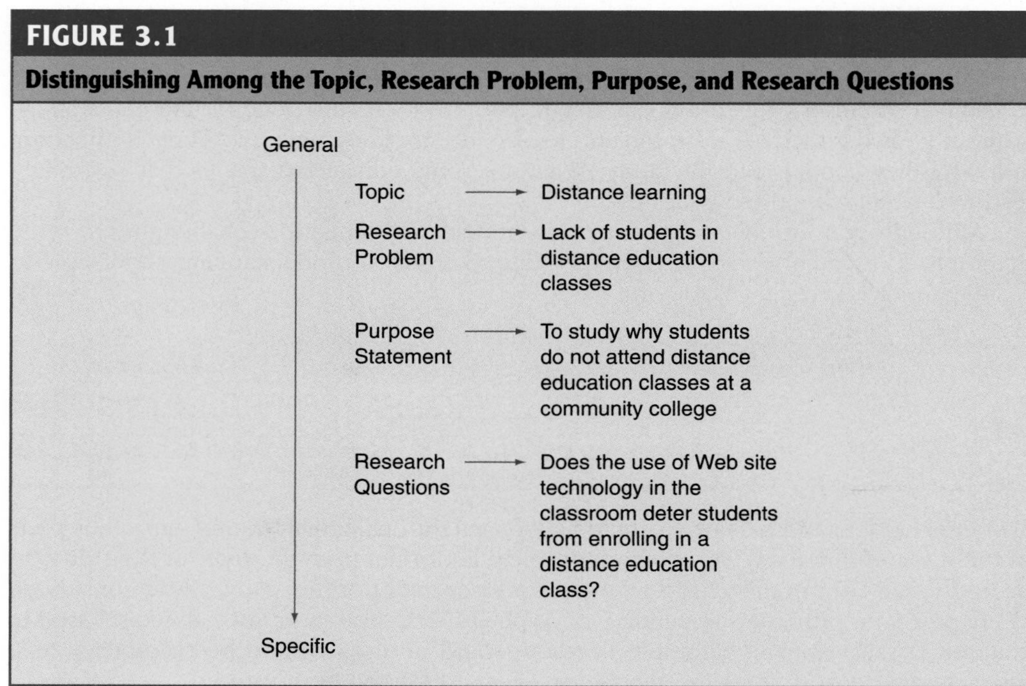

A common error is stating research problems as the purpose of the study or as the research question. The following examples show how you might reshape a purpose or a research question as a research problem.

> ***Poor model.*** The researcher intends to identify the research problem but instead presents it as a *purpose statement:* The purpose of this study is to examine the education of women in Third World countries.
>
> ***Improved model.*** A revision of it as a *research problem:* Women in Third World countries are restricted from attending universities and colleges because of the culturally oriented, patriarchal norms of their societies.
>
> ***Poor model.*** A researcher intends to write about the research problem but instead identifies the *research question:* The research question in this study is "What factors influence homesickness in college students?"
>
> ***Improved model.*** An improved version as a *research problem:* Homesickness is a major issue on college campuses today. When students get homesick, they leave school or start missing classes, leading to student attrition or poor achievement in classes during their first semester of college.

As you design and conduct a study, make sure that you are clear about the distinctions among these parts of research and that your written material differentiates among a topic, the research problem, the purpose, and your research questions.

CAN AND SHOULD PROBLEMS BE RESEARCHED?

Just because a problem exists and an author can clearly identify the issue does not mean that the researcher *can* or *should* investigate it. You *can* research a problem if you have access to participants and research sites as well as time, resources, and skills needed to study the issue. You *should* research a problem if the study of it potentially contributes to educational knowledge or adds to the effectiveness of practice.

Can You Gain Access to People and Sites?

To research a problem, investigators need to gain permission to enter a site and to involve people at the location of the study (e.g., gaining access to an elementary school to study children who are minors). This access often requires multiple levels of approval from schools, such as district administrators, principals, teachers, parents, and students. In addition, projects conducted by educational agencies receiving federal funding (most colleges and universities) need to have institutional review approval to ensure that researchers protect the rights of their participants. Your ability to gain access to people and sites can help determine if you can research the issue.

Can You Find Time, Locate Resources, and Use Your Skills?

Even if you can gain access to the people and sites needed for your study, your ability to research the problem also depends on time, resources, and your research skills.

Time

When planning a study, investigators should anticipate the time required for data collection and data analysis. Qualitative studies typically take more time than quantitative studies because of the lengthy process of collecting data at research sites and the detailed process of analyzing sentences and words. Regardless of the approach used, you can gauge the amount of time needed for data collection by examining similar studies, contacting the authors, or asking researchers who are more experienced. Developing a timeline for a study helps you assess whether you can reasonably complete the study within the time available.

Resources

Investigators need resources such as funds for equipment, for participants, and for individuals to transcribe interviews. Researchers need to create a budget and obtain advice from other, experienced researchers about whether the anticipated expenses are realistic. Other resources may be needed as well, such as mailing labels, postage, statistical programs, or audiovisual equipment. Dependent on these resource requirements, investigators may need to limit the scope of a project, explore funding available to support the project, or research the project in stages as funds become available.

Skills

The skills of the researcher also affect the overall assessment of whether the study of a problem is realistic. Investigators need to have acquired certain research skills to effectively study a problem—skills gained through courses, training, and prior research experiences. For those engaged in quantitative studies, these skills require using computers, employing statistical programs, or creating tables for presenting information. The skills needed for qualitative researchers consist of the ability to write detailed passages, to synthesize information into broad themes, and to use computer programs for entering and analyzing words from participants in the study.

Should the Problem Be Researched?

A positive answer to this question lies in whether your study will contribute to knowledge and practice. One important reason for engaging in research, as we addressed briefly in chapter 1, is to add to existing information and to inform our educational practices. In chapter 1, you saw the ways research adds to knowledge. Now let's examine these ways in more detail as you think about the research problem in one of your studies.

There are five ways to assess whether you should research a problem:

1. *Study the problem if your study will fill a gap or void in the existing literature.* A study fills a void by covering topics not addressed in the published literature. For example, assume that a researcher examines the literature on the ethical climate on college campuses and finds that past research has examined the perceptions of students, but not of faculty. This is a void or gap in the body of research about this issue. Conducting a study about faculty perceptions of the ethical climate would address a topic not studied in the current literature.

2. *Study the problem if your study replicates a past study but examines different participants and different research sites.* The value of research increases when results can apply broadly to many people and places rather than to only the setting where the initial research occurred. This type of study is especially important in quantitative experiments. In a quantitative study of ethical climate, for example, past research conducted in a liberal arts college can be tested (or replicated) at other sites, such as a community college or major research university. Information from such a study will provide new knowledge.

3. *Study the problem if your study extends past research or examines the topic more thoroughly.* A good research problem to study is one in which you extend the research into a new topic or area, or simply conduct more research at a deeper, more thorough level to understand the topic. For example, in our illustration on ethical climate, although research exists on ethical climates, it now needs to be extended to the situation in which students take exams, because taking exams poses many ethical dilemmas for students. In this way, you extend the research to new topics. This extension is different from replication because you extend the research to these topics rather than participants and research sites.

4. *Study the problem if your study gives voice to people silenced, not heard, or rejected in society.* Your research adds to knowledge by presenting the ideas and the words of marginalized (e.g., the homeless, women, racial groups) individuals. For example, although past studies on ethical climate have addressed students on predominantly white campuses, we have not heard the voices of Native Americans on this topic. A study of this type would report and give voice to Native Americans.

5. *Study the problem if your study informs practice.* By examining the problem, your research may lead to the identification of new techniques or technologies, the recognition of the value of historical or current practice, or the necessity of changing current teaching practice. Individuals who benefit from practical knowledge may be policy makers, teachers, or learners. For example, a study of ethical issues in a college setting may lead to a new honor code, new policies about cheating on exams, or new approaches to administering tests.

HOW DOES THE RESEARCH PROBLEM DIFFER IN QUANTITATIVE AND QUALITATIVE RESEARCH?

After you identify a research problem, you should also consider if it better fits a quantitative or qualitative approach. Because the two approaches differ in their essential characteristics (as discussed in chapter 2), there should be a match between your problem and the approach you use. What factors are important in determining this match? What type of research problem is best suited for quantitative research and what type for qualitative research?

Let's look once again at the parent involvement study (Deslandes & Bertrand, 2005) and the gunman incident case study (Asmussen & Creswell, 1995) from chapter 1. We can see that each study addresses a different type of problem. In the quantitative parent involvement study, the researchers make a case that we know little about what factors lead parents to decide to (or to *explain why they*) become involved in their adolescents' schooling. Why would such a lack of involvement be important? The authors cite literature suggesting that involvement means fewer disciplinary problems and higher grades. Explaining or predicting relations among variables is an important characteristic of *quantitative* research, as we learned in chapter 2. Alternatively, in the qualitative gunman incident case study, the authors sought to *explore* campus reaction without preconceived ideas about what they would find. In chapter 2, we learned that exploring a problem is a characteristic of *qualitative* research.

These two factors—explanation and exploration—provide a standard you can use to determine whether your research problem is best suited for a quantitative or qualitative study. Chapter 2 discussed additional characteristics of both quantitative and qualitative research, and from these characteristics, we can identify helpful information to direct our approach to research. Here are some additional factors to consider:

Use *quantitative research* if your research problem requires you to:

- Measure variables
- Assess the impact of these variables on an outcome
- Test theories or broad explanations
- Apply results to a large number of people

Use *qualitative research* if your research problem requires you to:

- Learn about the views of individuals
- Assess a process over time
- Generate theories based on participant perspectives
- Obtain detailed information about a few people or research sites

HOW DO YOU WRITE A "STATEMENT OF THE PROBLEM" SECTION?

After you have identified your research problem, determined that it can and should be researched, and specified either the quantitative or qualitative approach, it is time to begin writing about the "problem" in a statement of the problem section that introduces your research study.

The **statement of the problem** section includes the actual research problem as well as four other aspects:

1. The topic
2. The research problem
3. A justification of the importance of the problem as found in the past research and in practice
4. The deficiencies in our existing knowledge about the problem
5. The audiences that will benefit from a study of the problem

By identifying these five elements, you can easily understand introductions to research studies and write good introductions for your own research reports.

The Topic

The opening sentences of a "statement of the problem" section need to encourage readers to continue reading, to generate interest in the study, and to provide an initial frame of reference for understanding the entire research topic. Given these factors, it makes sense to start with a broad topic that readers can easily understand. In this way, you bring readers into a study slowly and encourage them to read beyond the first page.

An **educational topic** is the broad subject matter that a researcher wishes to address in a study and that creates initial interest for the reader. As shown in Figure 3.2, researchers state the topic in the title and introduce it in the first sentences. Note that the authors ease into the study with general ideas that most readers can understand (standardized tests, the education of Native Americans, the problem-solving mode of teaching elementary science). For example, assume that an author begins the topic discussion with comments about plagiarism on college campuses. This approach may unnecessarily narrow the topic too soon and lose readers who have not studied or read about plagiarism. Instead, writers might begin with the broader topic of dishonesty on campus and the need to explore the values students learn during their college years.

Let's examine the first sentence. We call it a **narrative hook**. It serves the important function of drawing the reader into a study. Good narrative hooks have these

FIGURE 3.2

Select Topics and First Sentences of Research Studies Reported in Educational Journals

The Impact of Mandated Standardized Testing on Minority Students

Richard G. Lomax, Mary Maxwell West, Maryellen C. Harmon, Katherine A. Viator, & George F. Madaus, 1995

One of the original reasons for the introduction of mandated standardized tests was to reduce the effects of patronage and thereby open educational opportunities and a range of occupations to a wider population of students (Madaus, 1991). However,. . .

Inhibitors to Implementing a Problem-Solving Approach to Teaching Elementary Science: Case Study of a Teacher in Change

Mary Lee Martens, 1992

The problem-solving mode of teaching elementary science now recommended in many states implies change for many groups of professionals including teachers, administrators, and other individuals charged with implementing educational policy. Teachers, however,. . .

Living and Working in Two Worlds
Case Studies of Five American Indian Women Teachers

BRENDA HILL, COURTNEY VAUGHN, AND SHARON BROOKS HARRISON, 1995

The Euro-American education of American Indians began under the auspices of missionaries and a few lay educators, with the ongoing purpose of remaking American Indians into the Euro-American image. In. . .

characteristics: cause the reader to pay attention, elicit emotional or attitudinal responses, spark interest, and encourage the reader to continue reading.

A convincing narrative hook might include one or more of the following types of information:

1. Statistical data (e.g., "More than 50% of the adult population experiences depression today.")
2. A provocative question (e.g., "Why are school policies that ban smoking in high schools not being enforced?")
3. A clear need for research (e.g., "School suspension is drawing increased attention among scholars in teacher education.")
4. The intent or purpose of the study (e.g., "The intent of this study is to examine how clients construe the therapist–client relationship.")

Although all of these represent possibilities for you to use, the key idea is that a study begins with an introduction to a topic that the reader can easily understand and with a first sentence that creates reader interest. Examine once again Figure 3.2 and assess whether the first sentence in these three studies captures your interest and encourages you to continue reading. Evaluate each based on the four types of information for a good narrative hook listed above.

The Research Problem

After stating the topic in the opening discussion, you then narrow the topic to a specific research problem or issue. Recall that a **research problem** is an educational issue, concern, or controversy that the researcher investigates. As illustrated earlier, authors may present it as a single sentence or as a couple of short sentences (e.g., see Asmussen & Creswell, 1995). Also, authors may frame the problem as a deficiency in the literature, such as we know little about the factors that lead parents to be involved in their adolescents' schooling (Deslandes & Bertrand, 2005).

What types of research problems do you study? Sometimes research problems come from issues or concerns found in schools or other educational settings. We will call these **practical research problems**. For example, can you see the practical issue in the following research problem posed about the Chinese policy toward single-child families?

> Since the late 1970s a single-child policy has been implemented by the Chinese government to control the largest population in the world. Selective abortion to choose a boy could inevitably skew the Chinese gender distribution, and is clearly prohibited by the government. As a result, although boys were valued higher than girls in traditional Chinese culture, many parents eventually have a girl as their single child. (Wang & Staver, 1997, p. 252)

The practical problem in this study was that boys were valued more than girls and the policy controls people in the population.

In other research studies the "problem" will be based on a need for further research because a gap exists or we need to extend the research into other areas. It might also be based on conflicting evidence in the literature. This type of problem is a **research-based research problem**. For example, see how the author in the next example calls for additional research that connects developmentally appropriate reading practices and teachers' approaches:

> Although both teacher beliefs about developmentally appropriate practices with young children and teacher theoretical orientation to early reading instruction have been previously studied, there is a lack of research that connects the two areas. (Ketner, Smith, & Parnell, 1997, p. 212)

The "problem" in this case is based on a research need for more information.

In some research, you can take both a practical and a research-based approach to the problem and state both types of problems. For example, consider how both play into this statement: "There is a need to better explain reading progress (the practical approach) as well as make up for a lack of research about developmentally appropriate practices and teacher orientation (the research-based approach)."

Whether you find the research problem in a practical setting, find it as a need in the research literature, or both, the point is to state it clearly in a sentence or two in the statement of the problem section. The reader simply needs to know the issue or concern that leads to a need for your study.

Justification of the Importance of the Problem

It is not enough to state the problem or issue. You also need to provide several reasons that explain why this issue is important. **Justifying a research problem** means presenting reasons for the importance of studying the issue or concern. This justification occurs in several paragraphs in an introduction in which you provide evidence to document the need to study the problem. As shown in Figure 3.3, you can justify the importance of your problem by citing evidence from:

- Other researchers and experts as reported in the literature
- Experiences others have had in the workplace
- Personal experiences

These justifications draw from different sources, are used in different types of approaches (i.e., quantitative or qualitative), and typically find expression in select research designs

FIGURE 3.3

The Process of Justifying a Research Problem

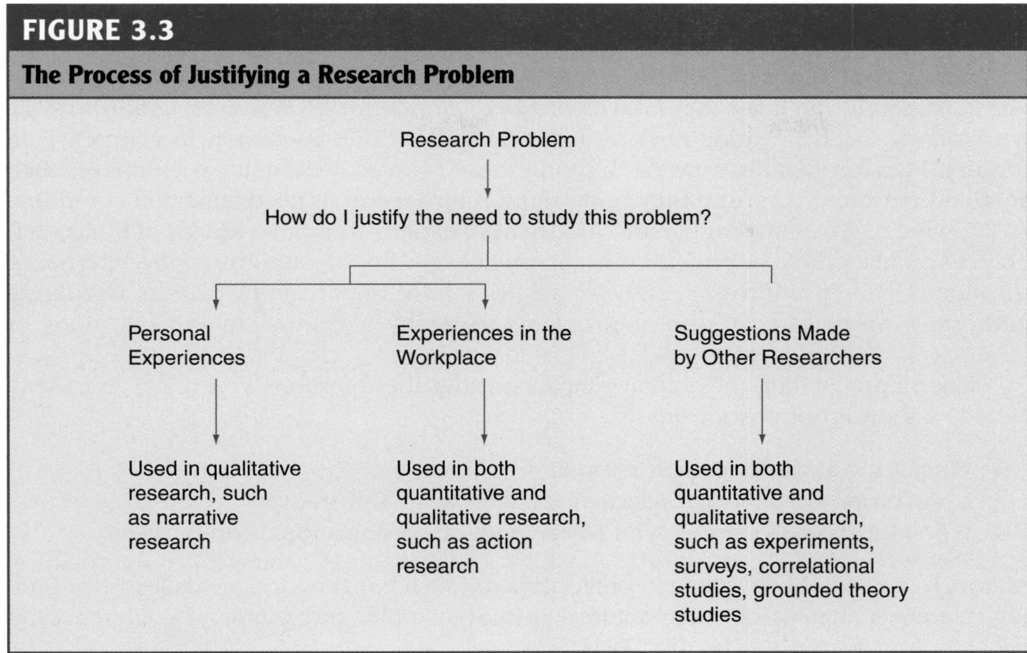

such as experiments, action research, or narrative research (to be addressed more specifically in the research design chapters in part III).

Justification in the Literature Based on Other Researchers and Experts

We will begin with the most scholarly justification—suggestions from other researchers that the problem needs to be studied. Authors often cite research problems that require further study in the conclusions of the literature such as journal articles. For example, note the suggestions for future research in the concluding paragraph in the gunman incident case study (Asmussen & Creswell, 1995):

> Events emerged during the process of reaction that could be "critical incidents" in future studies, such as the victim response, media reporting, the debriefing process, campus changes, and the evolution of a campus plan. (Paragraph 37)

Using this example, you might cite Asmussen and Creswell (1995) and use this information as justification for the need to explore campus plans. Another justification from the literature consists of advancing a need for the study based on an incomplete model or theory that explains the relation among elements of the model or theory. A theory, for example, may be incomplete because it does not address important factors that need to be considered. Thus, a leadership theory may identify the traits of the leader, the characteristics of the follower, and the elements operating in the leadership situation (e.g., congenial environment), but be lacking the element of the daily interactions that occur between the leader and the follower. A research study is needed to account for these interactions and more fully complete the model. Researchers could cite other researchers and experts who have also stated this conclusion but have not followed up on it with a research study.

Cite experts as justification for your research problem. Where do you find references to other researchers or experts who have indicated a need for a study? Often, authors of conference papers, research syntheses, or encyclopedias that report the latest research, such as the *Encyclopedia of Educational Research* (Alkin, 1992), mention the need for additional research on topics. The discussion in chapter 4 on locating literature details steps for locating these sources. Research experts have often studied topics for years, and they understand future research needs that will contribute to knowledge. You can identify and locate these experts through a search of library references, contact them at professional conferences, or find them through the Internet or through Web site addresses. Individuals who have spent entire careers becoming authorities on research topics or problems generally welcome student questions or requests.

When approaching these individuals, consider the questions you might ask them. Here is a short list of possibilities:

- What are you working on at present?
- Is my proposed topic and research problem worthy of study?
- Who else should I contact who has recently studied this topic and problem?

Although you may be hesitant to contact experts, such conversation yields leads for finding references, names of others interested in your topic, and names of conferences at which your research may be discussed.

Another authority on a particular research problem may be your graduate faculty advisor or your graduate committee members. Your advisor may have a long-term research agenda of examining an educational issue through a series of studies. By participating in the faculty member's research, you can learn about other studies and locate useful research to use as justification for your own research problems.

Justification Based on Workplace or Personal Experiences

You can justify your research problem based on evidence from your workplace or your personal experiences. This is the case for Maria, who based her justification for the study of students possessing weapons on the increased use of weapons in high schools in her school (or workplace) in the district.

Issues arise in educational workplaces that you can address in your research. For example, policy makers need to decide whether to mandate state standards of assessment, or principals and teachers must develop approaches to classroom discipline. Closely related are the personal experiences of our lives that provide sources for researchable problems. These personal experiences may arise from intense personal school experiences or experiences drawn from our childhood or family situations. Personal experiences provide justification especially in those studies with a practical orientation, such as solving a particular classroom dilemma in an action research study (see chapter 18). They are also apparent in studies in which the researcher is the object of study, such as in narrative research (see chapter 16). Researchers citing their own personal experiences as justification for a research problem need to be forewarned that some individuals (such as those trained in quantitative research) may feel that such experiences should not be the sole justification for a study. This is a fair warning, and you might consider including not only your own personal experiences, but some of the other reasons mentioned for justifying a research problem.

Consider the following two examples of researchers introducing their own experiences as justification for studying a research problem. One researcher justifies the need to study students in a multiage middle school by referring to her own experiences in school. The study begins:

> In the spring of 1992, the opportunity to conduct classroom action research was offered to Madison, Wisconsin teachers. Though my daily schedule was already full, I was drawn to this opportunity because of its emphasis on practical, classroom-based research. . . . For me, multicultural curricula, cooperative learning, computer technology, and thematic education were exciting developments in classroom teaching. (Kester, 1994, p. 63)

Another researcher justifies the need for studying the ostracism of African American students in schools by tracing personal family experiences. The study starts:

> When I was growing up, there was never a thought in my mind about whether or not I would go to school. It was given that I was going to go to school every day as long as my parents were alive and the Lord woke me up in good health. (Jeffries, 1993, p. 427)

Now consider Maria's justification based on her school experiences. Provide three reasons why a need exists for research on students possessing weapons in school. As a hint, consider how the school, the teachers, and the students themselves might benefit from a better understanding of this problem.

Deficiencies in What We Know

In the "statement of the problem" section, you next need to summarize how our present state of knowledge—both from research and from practice—is deficient. Although a deficiency in the literature may be part of the justification for a research problem, it is useful to enumerate on several deficiencies in the existing literature or practice. A **deficiency in the evidence** means that the past literature or practical experiences of the researchers does not adequately address the research problem. For example, deficiencies in the research may require a need to extend the research, replicate a study, explore a topic, lift the voices of marginalized people, or add to practice. A deficiency in practice means that educators have not yet identified good and workable solutions for schools or other educational settings. As you summarize these deficiencies, identify two or three reasons why existing research and practice are deficient in addressing the research problem, and state these reasons toward the end of the introduction to the study. In the following example, a researcher indicates weaknesses in past research and reflects on personal experiences:

> The past research does not address the cultural differences of children in preschools. It also does not consider the multiple factors that explain teacher interactions with these students. From observing preschools, the need further exists to better understand how teachers interact with preschool children from different cultures.

In Maria's situation, in what areas would her school committee lack information to help them address the problem of weapons in the schools? They might not know how frequently students actually carry weapons, what types they are, and the places where they hide the weapons. State at least two other deficiencies in knowledge the school committee might have.

The Audience

The **audience** in a "statement of the problem" section needs to be identified. It consists of individuals and groups who will read and potentially benefit from the information provided in your research study. These audiences will vary depending on the nature of your study, but several often considered by educators include researchers, practitioners, policy makers, and individuals participating in the studies. One author, for example, in ending an introduction section, commented about the importance of the study for school administrators:

> By exploring the need for athletic trainers in high schools, school administrators can identify potential issues that arise when trainers are not present, and coaches can better understand the circumstances in which trainers are most needed at athletic events.

As this example illustrates, authors often enumerate multiple audiences. Passages such as these are typically found in the concluding passage in the introduction or the "statement of the problem" section and explain the importance of addressing the problem for each audience. Like the narrative hook, this information continues to draw the reader into the study and it personalizes the research so that readers can see that the study will potentially provide meaningful information. When researchers include comments about the importance of the study for audiences, they also remind themselves about the need to report useful results.

WHAT ARE SOME STRATEGIES FOR WRITING THE "STATEMENT OF THE PROBLEM" SECTION?

Writing the introduction or "statement of the problem" section as an opening passage in your research report sets the stage for readers to understand your project and appreciate the strong research orientation of your report. Several writing strategies can help you craft this section.

A Template

One strategy you can use as you write your "statement of the problem" section is to visualize this section as five paragraphs, with each paragraph addressing one of the five aspects of the section. Take sections in order beginning with the topic, the research problem, the justification, the deficiencies, and the audience. Examine the flow of ideas as shown in Figure 3.4. This figure shows that a "statement of the problem" section has five elements, and it provides a brief definition for each element and an example to illustrate the element. The researcher begins with the topic of ethical issues in colleges and narrows it to a specific problem: potential ethical violations among college football recruiters. Since this is a sensitive topic and could be difficult to study (is it researchable, then?), the topic merits a research study. Also, from practical experiences on campuses, the researcher claims that violations are being reported in the news but not openly to campus officials. The evidence, therefore, is deficient in describing these potential violations, and a study of this problem can help determine if violations occur, assist recruiters who seek to engage in ethical behavior, and aid athletes who need to be aware of ethical behavior on college campuses.

Other Writing Strategies

Another writing strategy is to use frequent references to the literature throughout this introductory passage. Multiple references add a scholarly tone to your writing and provide evidence from others, rather than relying on your own personal opinion. The use of references in your study will build credibility for your work. A third strategy is to provide references from statistical trends to support the importance of studying the research problem. How many teenagers smoke? How many individuals are HIV positive? This form of

FIGURE 3.4

Flow of Ideas in a "Statement of the Problem" Section

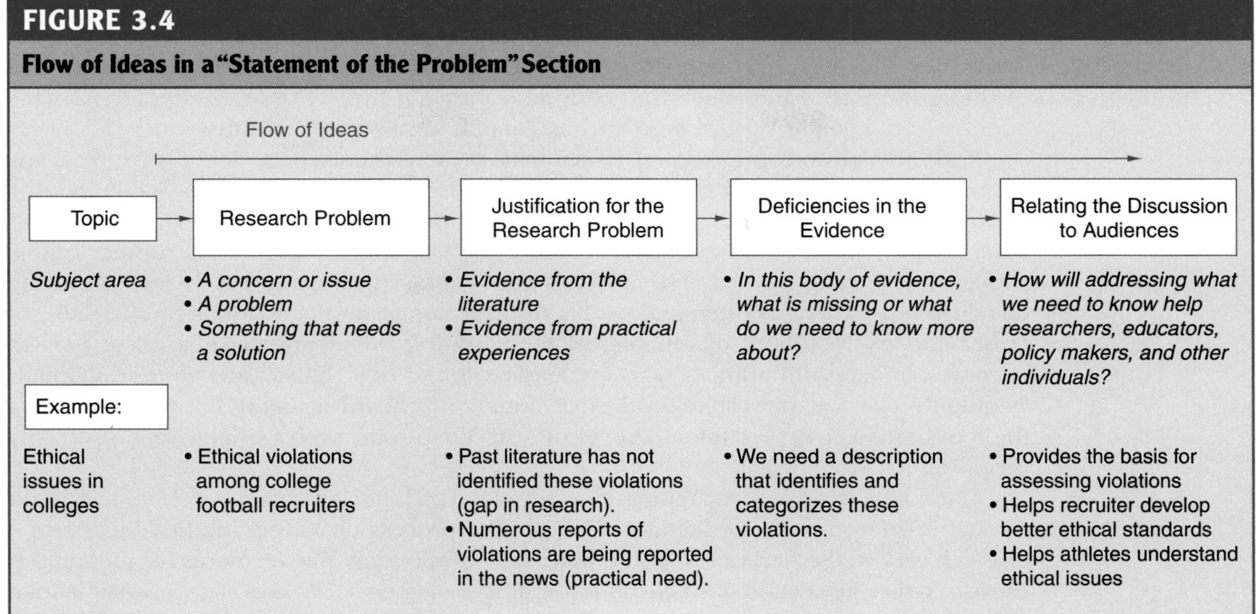

evidence is especially popular in quantitative studies. Another writing strategy is to use quotes from participants in a study or from notes obtained from observing participants to begin your "statement of the problem" introduction. This approach is popular and frequently used in qualitative studies. Finally, be cautious about using quotes from the literature to begin a study, especially in the first sentence. Readers may not extract the same meaning from a quote as the researcher does. The quotes are often too narrow to be appropriate for an introductory section in which you seek to establish a research problem and provide justification for it. To use quotes effectively, readers often need to be led "into" as well as "out of" the quote. We will discuss specific writing strategies in more depth as we discuss writing the research report in chapter 10.

Think-Aloud About Writing a "Statement of the Problem"

I will model how I would write a "statement of the problem" to illustrate the actual practice of research. My approach applies the five-step model regardless of whether the study is quantitative or qualitative. However, close inspection of the research problem indicates a different emphasis in the two approaches. In quantitative research, an emphasis will be on the need for an *explanation* of outcomes, whereas in qualitative research, I will explore a *process, event,* or *phenomenon.*

My introduction begins with a general discussion about the topic of the research. I try to present the first sentence as a good "narrative hook" so that readers will be encouraged to read the report. The writing of this first sentence is difficult, and I may draft numerous revisions before I am satisfied that it will be general, timely, and understandable. I think about the wide range of students in my class who have varied backgrounds and majors, and whether they would understand and relate to my first sentence. I find it helpful to think about my audiences as a diverse group when I write the opening sentence of this passage.

As I've said, the opening paragraph needs to gently lead the reader into the study. My analogy for this is lowering a bucket into a well to get water. I hope to gently lower the bucket rather than drop it suddenly into the depths of the well. With this example in mind, I introduce the study in a paragraph or two and focus the reader's attention on a single subject area and its general importance in education.

With any given topic, several issues may present themselves. Some arise from my experiences in a school or from a review of the past research on a topic. While reading about my topic in research articles (typically in journal articles), I am open to issues that need to be studied, and am most interested in specific issues that other authors suggest need to be studied. These issues are located in future research sections at the conclusion of articles. I often make a list of these suggestions for research on a piece of paper and try to follow up on one of them. When reviewing these studies, I try to become familiar with authors who are leaders in the field. These are often individuals frequently cited in published studies or commonly heard at conferences. Because of their expertise, I may contact these authors by phone or by e-mail to discuss my proposed study.

Once I have an understanding of a problem and can adequately justify studying it through evidence from the literature, I begin the process of writing the first section of a research report, the "statement of the problem." I follow my five elements for writing this section, write the section, and check it for all five elements. My goal is to present a solid rationale for why my study is needed, and I support this need with several arguments using multiple forms of evidence. I extensively cite references in the introductory passage of my study. To ensure that the importance of the study is clear to the audience, I end the "statement of the problem" section with comments about the utility of the study for several audiences.

EXAMPLES OF "STATEMENT OF THE PROBLEM" SECTIONS

An example of a "statement of the problem" section is shown in Figure 3.5. This is from my study about teenage smoking in high schools. I introduce the topic and research problem in the first paragraph. This shows how the topic and the research problem can sometimes blend. I then cite evidence for this problem in the second paragraph. Note that I am not discussing any study in detail here in the introduction; in many of my studies, specific reference to individual studies will appear later in the literature review section. Following the evidence for the problem, I mention in the fourth paragraph the "deficiencies" in past studies and the need for extending past research. In the final paragraph, I appeal to various audiences (i.e., researchers, administrators, and teachers) to read and use this study.

You can learn how to write "statement of the problem" sections from reading introductions to studies, looking for the five elements, and noting sentences that capture the research problem. Examine the following two additional examples to see how an author of a *qualitative* study and an author of a *quantitative* study wrote introductory sections for their studies. Both followed the template, but the type of problem is more exploratory in the qualitative and more explanatory in the quantitative. Following each example, we will relate the passages to each of the five elements of a "statement of the problem" section. The first example is a qualitative study by Brown (1998) on distance learning in higher education, and this passage presents the entire introduction to her study.

FIGURE 3.5

Sample "Statement of the Problem" Section

Statement of the Problem Elements	Exploring the Conceptions and Misconceptions of Teen Smoking in High Schools: A Multiple Case Analysis
The Topic The Research Problem	Tobacco use is a leading cause of cancer in American society (McGinnis & Foefe, 1993). Although smoking among adults has declined in recent years, it has actually increased for adolescents. The Center for Disease Control and Prevention reported that smoking among high school students had risen from 27.5 percent in 1991 to 34.8 percent in 1995 (USDHHS 1996). Unless this trend is dramatically reversed, an estimated 5 million of our nation's children will ultimately die a premature death (Center for Disease Control, 1996).
Evidence Justifying the Research Problem	Previous research on adolescent tobacco use has focused on four primary topics. Several studies have examined the question of the initiation of smoking by young people, noting that tobacco use initiation begins as early as junior high school (e.g., Heishman et al., 1997). Other studies have focused on the prevention of smoking and tobacco use in schools. This research has led to numerous school-based prevention programs and intervention (e.g., Sussman, Dent, Burton, Stacy, & Flay, 1995). Fewer studies have examined "quit attempts" or cessation of smoking behaviors among adolescents, a distinct contrast to the extensive investigations into adult cessation attempts (Heishman et al., 1997).
	Of interest as well to researchers studying adolescent tobacco use has been the social context and social influence of smoking (Fearnow, Chassin, & Presson, 1998). For example, adolescent smoking may occur in work-related situations, at home where one or more parents or caretakers smoke, at teen social events or at areas designated as "safe" smoking places near high schools (McVea et al., in press).
Deficiencies in Evidence	Minimal research attention has been directed toward the social context of high schools as a site for examining adolescent tobacco use. During high school students form peer groups which may contibute to adolescent smoking. Often peers become a strong social influence for behavior in general and belonging to an athletic team, a music group, or the "grunge" crowd can impact thinking about smoking (McVea et al., in press). Schools are also places where adolescents spend most of their day (Fibkins, 1993) and are available research subjects. Schools provide a setting for teachers and administrators to be role models for abstaining from tobacco use and enforcing policies about tobacco use (O'Hara et al., 1999).
	Existing studies of adolescent tobacco use are primarily quantitative with a focus on outcomes and transtheoretical models (Pallonen, 1998). Qualitative investigations, however, provide detailed views of students in their own words, complex analyses of multiple perspectives, and specific school contexts of different high schools that shape student experiences with tobacco (Creswell, in press). Moreover, qualitative inquiry offers the opportunity to involve high school students as co-researchers, a data collection procedure that can enhance the validity of student views uncontaminated by adult perspectives.
The Audience	By examining these multiple school contexts, using qualitative approaches and involving students as co-researchers, we can better understand the conceptions and misconceptions adolescents hold about tobacco use in high schools. With this understanding, researchers can better isolate variables and develop models about smoking behavior. Administrators and teachers can plan interventions to prevent or change attitudes toward smoking, and school officials can assist with smoking cessation or intervention programs.

> Distance learning is an increasingly important aspect of higher education because it meets the needs of an expanding pool of nontraditional students who find education necessary for jobs in today's information age. Distance learning provides a flexible manageable alternative for this developing segment of society. However, students in distance classes work at computers miles apart at varying times of the day and night. This feeling of being alone is overcome when students join in a community of learners who support one another (Eastmond, 1995). The process of forming a community of learners is an important issue in distance learning because it can affect student satisfaction, retention, and learning (Gabelnick, MacGregor, Matthews, & Smith, 1990c; Kember, 1989; Kowch & Schwier, 1997; Powers & Mitchell, 1997). It may even affect faculty evaluations, which tend to be lower in distance education courses (Cordover, 1996).
>
> In reviewing the literature on distance learning for adults and nontraditional students in higher education, I found a decided lack of research about community-building within the class and within the institution. However, other research has paved the way for the exploration of this topic. Studies discussed the need for institutional support (Dillon, Gunawardena, & Parker, 1989) and for student/student and student/faculty interaction (Hiltz, 1986, 1996; Powers & Mitchell, 1997) which appear to be steps in building a community of distance learners. (Brown, 1998, p. 2)

In this example, Brown opens with a comment about distance learning and its importance today (the topic). She then argues that there are several problems facing distance education: Students feel alone (evidence from practice) and faculty evaluations are low (evidence from past research). Next she assesses a shortcoming in past research: the need to explore community-building (a deficiency in past research). Brown does not end the passage with implications for a specific audience, although she might have discussed the importance of addressing community-building in distance learning for the student, teacher, or college personnel. Overall, Brown's "statement of the problem" section contains four of the five elements.

Next you will read the complete "statement of the problem" introducing a quantitative study by Davis et al. (1997) that was reported in a journal article. The study deals with the topic of tobacco use among high school students.

> Adolescent use of all tobacco products is increasing (3–6). By age 18 years, approximately two-thirds of United States teenagers have tried smoking and approximately one-fourth have smoked in the last 30 days (3). In addition, more than 20 percent of white adolescent males use smokeless tobacco products (4). Adolescent tobacco use has been reported by race/ethnicity, gender, and grade level (5); however, the relationship between sports intensity, race, and tobacco use has not been studied to the best of our knowledge. (Davis et al., 1997, pp. 97–98)

This example models the elements of the "statement of the problem" section. Contained within two opening paragraphs in a journal article, it begins with a discussion about the prevalence of smoking in high school (the topic). The authors then advance the issue of the high rate of smokeless tobacco use among athletes (the research problem) and provide evidence for this issue drawing on past studies and statistical trends (evidence from past research documenting this as a problem). Following this, the authors indicate that sports intensity (defined later in the study), race, and tobacco use have not been studied (a deficiency). They seek an explanation for the influence of sports intensity and race on tobacco use. Although the authors do not comment about the audience that will profit from this study, the intended audience is likely students, teachers, schools, coaches, and researchers who study high school students and adolescent tobacco use.

REEXAMINING THE PARENT INVOLVEMENT AND THE GUNMAN INCIDENT STUDIES

Let's revisit the quantitative parent involvement study (Deslandes & Bertrand, 2005) and the qualitative gunman case study (Asmussen & Creswell, 1995) to examine the "statement of the problem" introductory sections to the studies. In the parent involvement study (Deslandes & Bertrand, 2005), the authors introduce the problem and integrate the literature review in the first 12 paragraphs (01–12). They mention the problem in Paragraph 02 by framing it within the existing literature; we know little about the factors that influence parents' involvement in adolescent schooling. A close reading of Paragraphs 01 and 02 shows that the authors do not present the issue strongly as a "problem," instead they talk about the positive advantages of parent involvement. Then they review the literature about the four factors that influence parent involvement (Paragraphs 03–08). Paragraphs 09–10 continue to review the literature about the four factors, but in Paragraph 11, they state the deficiencies of the literature and establish a need for their study. They mention that investigations are needed (i.e., the literature is deficient) to better understand what motivates parents to become involved and that the combined contribution of the four factors has not been studied across secondary-grade levels. In this opening passage, the authors do not mention the audiences who will profit from this study. However, in the concluding sections of the article (Paragraphs 48 and 49), the authors mention the benefits of the study for researchers, school administrators, and teachers.

The qualitative gunman case study (Asmussen & Creswell, 1995) also begins with the authors introducing the research topic: frequent incidents of campus violence (Paragraph 01). More specifically, the problem of gun violence has escalated (Paragraph 02), with the result that individuals have killed students on several campuses (Paragraph 02). A deficiency in our understanding of these practical problems is that we know little about how campuses react to this escalating violence (Paragraph 02). By addressing this problem, audiences could benefit, such as researchers who could develop conceptual models (Paragraph 03), and campus personnel who could devise campus strategies and protocols for reaction (Paragraph 03).

KEY IDEAS IN THE CHAPTER

A research problem is an educational issue, concern, or controversy that the investigator presents and justifies in a research study. In a research report, the investigator introduces this problem in the opening paragraphs of a study in a section called the "statement of the problem." It may consist of a single sentence or several sentences. It is distinct from the topic of a study, the purpose, and the research questions.

Before designing and writing about the problem, researchers need to consider whether it can and should be studied. The researcher must have access to people and sites and possess the time, resources, and skills to study the problem. The study needs to contribute to knowledge and practice. There also needs to be a match between the research problem and the approach—quantitative or qualitative—chosen for the study. Research problems best studied using the quantitative approach are those in which the issue needs to be explained; problems best addressed by the qualitative approach are those that need to be explored.

The "statement of the problem" section or the introduction to a study includes five elements: the educational topic, the research problem, a justification for the problem based on past research and practice, deficiencies or shortcomings of past research or practice, and the importance of addressing the problem for diverse audiences. Several writing strategies assist in this process of designing and writing a "statement of the problem" section. These strategies include writing the elements of this section in order using a template as a guide, using ample citations to the literature, and including references to statistical information in quantitative studies and quotes in qualitative studies.

Useful Information for Producers of Research

- Assess whether a problem can and should be researched. Apply three criteria: (a) Can the participants and sites be studied? (b) Can the problem be researched given the researcher's time, resources, and skills? (c) Will a study of the issue contribute to knowledge and practice?
- Identify and write a distinct research problem. Make it separate from the topic, the purpose of the study, and the research questions.
- Position the research problem in the "statement of the problem" section, and present it as the opening passage of a study.
- When writing the "statement of the problem," introduce the reader to the topic, convey the research problem, justify the need to study the research problem, identify deficiencies in the evidence, and target audiences who will benefit from the study.
- Consider writing the "statement of the problem" section in five distinct paragraphs to ensure inclusion of all elements. Use extensive references, cite statistics for a quantitative study, and include quotes from participants for a qualitative study.

Useful Information for Consumers of Research

- The actual "problem" in a study may be hidden in the opening paragraphs. Look for the issue or concern leading to the study. Ask yourself what educational "problem" is addressed by the study.
- Recognize that not all research problems should and can be researched. A problem *can* be researched if the inquirer has access to people and sites and if the investigator has the time, resources, and skills to adequately study the problem. A problem *should* be researched if the investigator can claim that studying it will add to knowledge or practice.
- Look for five elements in the introduction to a study: the topic, the research problem, the justification for this problem, the deficiencies in this evidence, and the importance of the study for audiences. This structure can help you understand the opening passages of a study and the author's intent.

Understanding Concepts and Evaluating Research Studies

You can test your knowledge of the content of this chapter by answering the following questions that relate to the parent involvement study and the gunman case study. Answers to questions are found in appendix A so that you can assess your progress.

1. Examine the first sentence—the narrative hook—for each study as stated below. Evaluate whether it is an effective narrative hook.

   a. In past decades, a wealth of studies have showed that parent involvement is essential in children's educational process and outcomes (Deslandes & Bertrand, 2005).
   b. With increasingly frequent incidents of campus violence, a small, growing scholarly literature about the subject is emerging (Asmussen & Creswell, 1995).
2. Review the research problem found in Paragraphs 01–12 in the parent involvement study and in Paragraph 02 in the gunman study. Why is the problem for the parent involvement study best suited for a quantitative approach and the problem for the gunman case study best suited for a qualitative approach?
3. A research problem should be researched if it contributes to educational knowledge or practice. Listed below are five ways a study might contribute to knowledge:
   a. Fills a void or extends existing research
   b. Replicates a study with new participants or at new sites
   c. Studies a problem that has not been studied or is understudied
   d. Gives voice to people not heard
   e. Informs practice

   Identify for both the parent involvement study and the gunman study how a study of the problem contributes to knowledge.
4. In the parent involvement study, the researchers base their justification for studying the problem on past research (i.e., a need to understand the four factors that influence parent involvement). Alternatively, in the gunman case study, the authors justify the study of their problem based on practice (i.e., the escalation of violence and deaths of students). If the authors of both studies included a justification based on personal experiences, what would that justification be? Explain these in writing.
5. If multiple references add a scholarly tone to a "statement of the problem" section, which article, the parent involvement study or the gunman case study, introduces a better scholarly introduction to their study? Why?
6. For an educational topic of your choice, write down the topic, the research problem, your justification for the problem based on practice or research, potential deficiencies in the knowledge about the problem, and the audiences that will benefit from your study.

Conducting Your Research

Write a "statement of the problem" section for a research study you would like to conduct. Identify the topic, the research problem, justification for the problem, the deficiencies in knowledge about the problem, and the audience that will benefit from studying the problem.

Go to our Companion Website at **www.prenhall.com/creswell** to:

- assess your understanding of chapter content with Multiple-Choice Questions,
- apply what you've learned with Essay Questions,
- practice your research skills with interactive Building Research Skills exercises, and
- broaden your knowledge of research with Web Links to research topics on the Internet.

Reviewing the Literature

With so much information available, searching and locating good literature on your topic can be challenging. This chapter introduces you to five logical steps in reviewing the literature so that you can locate useful resources and write them into a literature review section of a research report.

By the end of this chapter, you should be able to:

- Define what it means to review the literature and explain its importance.
- List the differences in a literature review for quantitative and qualitative research.
- Identify the five steps in conducting a literature review.
- Write a literature review.

Maria needs to find and review the literature for her study on the possession of weapons by students in high schools. Because she has not spent much time in the university library, she compiles a list of questions for her advisor:

1. What is a literature review?
2. Where do I begin in conducting a literature review?
3. What are the best materials to include in my review and how do I locate them?
4. Is it worth my time to search the Internet for the literature?
5. Are there any shortcuts for identifying journal articles on my topic?
6. Should I gather and summarize both quantitative and qualitative studies?
7. How long should my literature review be?
8. Do you have an example of a literature review that I might examine?

As you begin to think about reviewing the literature for a research study, you may have questions similar to Maria's.

WHAT IS A LITERATURE REVIEW?

A **literature review** is a written summary of journal articles, books, and other documents that describes the past and current state of information; organizes the literature into topics; and documents a need for a proposed study. In the most rigorous form of research, educators base this review mainly on research reported in journal articles. (Recall from chapter 1 that research consists of posing a question, gathering data, and developing answers to the question.) A good review, however, might also contain other information drawn from conference papers, books, and government documents. Regardless of the sources of information, all researchers conduct a literature review as a step in the research process.

Why is this review necessary? Many reasons exist. You conduct a literature review to document how your study adds to the existing literature. A study will not add to the literature if it duplicates research already available. Like Maria, you conduct a literature review to convince your graduate committee that you know the literature on your topic and that you can summarize it. You also complete a literature review to provide evidence that educators need your study (see the chapter 3 section on "What Is a Research Problem and Why Is It Important?"). You may base this need on learning new ideas, sharing the latest findings with others (like Maria and her school committee), or identifying practices that might improve learning in your classroom. Conducting a literature review also builds your research skills of using the library and being an investigator who follows leads in the literature, all useful experiences to have as a researcher. Reading the literature also helps you learn how other educators compose their research studies and helps you find useful examples and models in the literature for your own research. By conducting a literature search using computer databases, you develop skills in locating needed materials in a timely manner.

WHAT ARE THE DIFFERENCES BETWEEN A LITERATURE REVIEW FOR A QUANTITATIVE STUDY AND FOR A QUALITATIVE STUDY?

In a literature review, you may select research articles to summarize that use quantitative or qualitative approaches. Both are acceptable. However, the use of the literature in quantitative and qualitative research differs. You learned about the major differences in chapter 2. Here we will go into more detail. Table 4.1 identifies three primary differences: the amount of literature cited at the beginning of the study, the use it serves at the beginning, and its use at the end of a study.

In a quantitative study, researchers discuss the literature extensively at the beginning of a study (see Deslandes & Bertrand, 2005). This serves two major purposes: It justifies the importance of the research problem, and it provides a rationale for (and foreshadows) the purpose of the study and research questions or hypotheses. In many quantitative studies, the authors include the literature in a separate section titled "Review of the Literature" to highlight the important role it plays. The authors also incorporate the literature into the end of the study, comparing the results with prior predictions or expectations made at the beginning of the study.

In a qualitative study, the literature serves a slightly different purpose. Similar to quantitative research, the authors mention the literature at the beginning of the study to document or justify the importance of the research problem (e.g., Asmussen & Creswell, 1995). However, authors do not discuss the literature extensively at the beginning of a study. This

TABLE 4.1

Differences in Extent and Use of Literature in Quantitative and Qualitative Research

Differences	Quantitative Research	Qualitative Research
Amount of literature cited at the beginning of the study	Substantial	Minimal
Use of literature at the beginning of the study	Justifies or documents the need for the study	Justifies or documents the need for the study
	Provides a rationale for the direction of the study (i.e., purpose statement and research questions or hypotheses)	
Use of literature at the end of the study	Confirms or disconfirms prior predictions from the literature	Supports or modifies existing findings in the literature

allows the views of the participants to emerge without being constrained by the views of others from the literature. In some qualitative studies, researchers use the literature to support the findings. Nevertheless, in many qualitative projects, researchers often cite the literature at the end of the study as a contrast or comparison with the major findings in the study. This contrast and comparison is not the same as prediction in quantitative research. In qualitative inquiry, researchers do not make predictions about findings. They are more interested in whether the findings of a study support or modify existing ideas and practices advanced in the literature, as shown in the gunman incident qualitative study (Asmussen & Creswell, 1995).

WHAT ARE THE FIVE STEPS IN CONDUCTING A LITERATURE REVIEW?

Regardless of whether the study is quantitative or qualitative, common steps can be used to conduct a literature review. Knowing these steps helps you read and understand a research study. If you conduct your own research study, knowing the steps in the process will give you a place to start and the ability to recognize when you have successfully completed the review.

Although conducting a literature review follows no prescribed path, if you plan to design and conduct a study, you will typically go through five interrelated steps. If you are simply looking for literature on a topic for your own personal use or for some practical application (such as for Maria's school committee), only the first four steps will apply. However, learning all five steps will provide a sense of how researchers proceed in reviewing the literature. These steps are:

1. *Identify key terms* to use in your search for literature.
2. *Locate literature* about a topic by consulting several types of materials and databases, including those available at an academic library and on the Internet at Web sites.
3. *Critically evaluate and select the literature* for your review.

4. *Organize the literature* you have selected by abstracting or taking notes on the literature and developing a visual diagram of it.
5. *Write a literature review* that reports summaries of the literature for inclusion in your research report.

Identify Key Terms

Begin your search of the literature by narrowing your topic to a few key terms using one or two words or short phrases. You should choose these carefully because they are important for initially locating literature in a library or through an Internet search. To identify these terms, you can use several strategies, outlined below:

- Write a preliminary "working title" for a project and select two to three keywords in the title that capture the central idea of your study. Although some researchers write the title last, a working title keeps you focused on the key ideas of the study. Because it is a "working" title, you can revise it at regular intervals if necessary during the research (Glesne & Peshkin, 1992).
- Pose a short, general research question that you would like answered in the study. Select the two or three words in this question that best summarize the primary direction of the study.
- Use words that authors report in the literature. In some quantitative research studies, educators test a prediction for what they expect to find from the data. This prediction is an explanation for what researchers hope to find. Researchers use the term *theory* for these explanations, and they might be a theory of "social support" or "learning styles" of students. The actual words of the theory (e.g., "social support" or "learning styles") become the words to use in your search.
- Look in a catalog of terms to find words that match your topic. Visit online databases that are typically available in college or university libraries. For example, one database is the **ERIC database** (see Educational Resources Information Center (ERIC), 1991; **www.eric.ed.gov/**). ERIC provides free access to more than 1.2 million bibliographic records of journal articles and other education-related materials and, if available, includes links to full text. ERIC is sponsored by the U.S. Department of Education, Institute of Education Sciences (IES).
- Go to the bookshelves in a college or university library, scan the table of contents of education journals from the last 7 to 10 years, and look for key terms in titles to the articles. You can also examine the electronic database called *Ingenta* at your academic library. Ingenta supplies access to full-text online publications and journal publications. Especially helpful is the "browse publications" feature, in which you enter the name of the journal you wish to examine, and obtain a list of the titles of articles from that journal for select years.

Maria needs to identify key terms to help her locate literature on weapon possession by high school students. After thinking about how she might get started, she writes down a working title, "Weapon Possession by High School Students." She begins by going to the ERIC Web site (**www.eric.ed.gov/**) and enters the words *weapon possession* in the search terms procedure. She examines the articles identified in her search and feels that narrowing her search to high school students will provide more targeted references in the literature. She then uses the feature of searching within results and adds the additional terms, *high school students*. She has now sufficiently narrowed her search and will closely examine the references in the literature that her search has yielded. Now try duplicating Maria's procedure yourself. Locate the ERIC Web site and insert Maria's terms into the ERIC database.

Locate Literature

Having identified key terms, you can now begin the search for relevant literature. You might be tempted to begin your search from a home computer by accessing Web sites and exploring the electronic literature available on a topic. Although this process may be convenient, not all literature posted on the Internet is dependable. Sometimes individuals post articles that have not passed through standards of external reviews. With increasing frequency, however, full-text documents are becoming available on the Internet and their quality is undoubtedly improving.

You might also begin your search by asking faculty or students to recommend good articles and studies to review. This approach may be helpful, but it lacks the systematic process found in searching library resources.

Use Academic Libraries

A sound approach is to begin your search in an academic library. By physically searching the stacks, reviewing microfiche, and accessing the computerized databases, you will save time because you will find comprehensive holdings not available through other sources. Although a town or city library may yield some useful literature, an academic library typically offers the largest collection of materials, especially research studies.

Academic library resources have changed considerably in recent years as they have moved toward more online journals for easy computer access and more computerized databases, such as ERIC (Ferguson & Bunge, 1997). Academic libraries typically have online catalogs of their holdings so that you can search the library materials easily. In addition, from any location, you can search the online library holdings of many large academic libraries (e.g., University of Michigan or University of California–Berkeley) to see what books are available on your topic. Another useful library to search is the Library of Congress, which contains most published books (**http://catalog.loc.gov**).

When using academic libraries, two challenges face the beginning researcher. First, the researcher needs to locate material—a task often made difficult because of the large and complex holdings in a library, such as journals or periodicals (recent and bound), government documents, the microfiche collection, and indexes. To help locate material, you might use the services of a reference librarian or search through library holdings using a computer. A second challenge is overcoming the frustration that arises when other library users have checked out materials you need, making them unavailable for use. When this occurs, researchers can use an interlibrary loan service as a means of obtaining the literature; however, this process takes time and requires patience.

Use Both Primary and Secondary Sources

Literature reviews often contain both primary and secondary source materials. **Primary source literature** consists of literature reported by the individual(s) who actually conducted the research or who originated the ideas. Research articles published by educational journals are an example of this type of source. **Secondary source literature**, however, is literature that summarizes primary sources. It does not represent material published by the original researcher or the creator of the idea. Examples of secondary sources are handbooks, encyclopedias, and select journals that summarize research, such as the *Review of Educational Research*. Typically, you will locate both primary and secondary sources, but it is best to report mostly primary sources. Primary sources present the literature in the original state and present the viewpoint of the original author. Primary sources also provide the details of original research better than do secondary sources. Secondary sources are helpful as you begin your review, to explore and determine the range of materials on a topic.

For example, you might look for meta-analysis studies on your topic as a type of secondary source material. These are popular in quantitative research. **Meta-analysis** is a type of research report in which the author integrates the findings of many (primary source) research studies by evaluating the results of individual studies and deriving an overall numeric index of the magnitude of results. The intent of this research is to summarize the results of many studies.

The process for conducting a meta-analysis follows systematic steps. The researcher locates studies on a single topic and notes the results for all of the studies. Then the researcher calculates an overall result for all of the studies and reports this information. By using this process, the investigator synthesizes the literature, providing a secondary source of primary research reports.

An illustration of a meta-analysis study as well as the difference between a primary and secondary source of information is seen in Figure 4.1. In the top section we see the first page of a *primary source* research report, an investigation by Smetana and Asquith (1994). They examine the types of parent authority and ratings of adolescent–parent conflict for 68 sixth, eighth, and tenth graders and their parents.

In the bottom section of Figure 4.1, we see that the original research by Smetana and Asquith (1994) is included as one of 27 studies reported in a *secondary source*, a meta-analysis published by Laursen, Coy, and Collins (1998). The 27 studies shown in the table integrated research examining parent–child conflict changes during early, mid-, and late adolescence. Overall, the authors conclude from the meta-analysis that little support exists for the commonly held view that parent–child conflict rises and then falls across adolescence. Because the primary source research report by Smetana and Asquith (1994) shows only a small positive change in parent–child conflict during early and mid-adolescence, relying on this single study would present false conclusions.

Historically, the division into primary and secondary sources has been a useful classification for literature in law and history (Barzun & Graff, 1985) and in combining results from a number of studies in meta-analysis. Today, it is helpful to think about the literature in an academic library using a broader classification of different types of literature.

Search Different Types of Literature

Figure 4.2 provides a useful classification system of the literature that you might consider. Modified from a classification originally developed by Libutti and Blandy (1995), the figure is a guide to resources as well as a framework for getting started in a literature search.

Using this framework, you might begin your search at the bottom of the triangle by consulting summaries of research that synthesize numerous studies on a topic (secondary sources of information). From these broad summaries, you can work your way up to journal articles (primary sources) and up to "early stage" literature found at the top. For many beginning researchers, starting with summaries is a good idea because summaries give an overview of topics at an entry-level discussion. Summaries also have a longer "life" from the initial idea stage, and they have undergone reviews for quality.

FIGURE 4.1

Example of a Primary Source (Journal Article) and a Secondary Source (Meta-Analysis)

Adolescents' and Parents' Conceptions of Parental Authority and Personal Autonomy

Judith G. Smetana and Pamela Asquith
University of Rochester

SMETANA, JUDITH G., and ASQUITH, PAMELA. *Adolescents' and Parents' Conceptions of Parental Authority and Personal Autonomy*. CHILD DEVELOPMENT, 1994, **65**, 1147–1162. Conceptions of parental authority and ratings of adolescent-parent conflict were assessed in 68 sixth, eighth, and tenth graders and their parents. Boundaries of adolescent personal jurisdiction and conflict over these boundaries were examined. Participants judged the legitimacy of parental authority and rated the frequency and intensity of conflict regarding 24 hypothetical moral, conventional, personal, multifaceted (e.g., containing conventional and personal components), prudential, and friendship issues. Adolescents and parents agreed that parents should retain authority regarding moral and conventional issues. Parents treated multifaceted, friendship, prudential, and personal issues as more contingent on parental authority than did adolescents, based on conventional, prudential, and psychological reasons, whereas adolescents treated these issues as under personal jurisdiction, based on personal concerns. Personal reasoning and judgments increased with age. Multifaceted issues were discussed more than all other issues, but moral and conventional conflicts were more intense than all other conflicts. The findings are discussed in terms of previous research on parental authority and adolescent-parent conflict during adolescence.

← The original article as a primary source of information (Smetana & Asquith, 1994)

Table 2 Parent-Adolescent Conflict Effect Size Estimates for Samples Included in Age Meta-Analyses

	Effect Size Estimates											
	Early and Mid-adolescence				Mid- and Late Adolescence				Early and Late Adolescence			
Study	*n*	Total *r*	Rate *r*	Affect *r*	*n*	Total *r*	Rate *r*	Affect *r*	*n*	Total *r*	Rate *r*	Affect *r*
Blase (1989)	63	.05	.00	.10	77	.08	.00	.15	52	−.02	.00	−.04
Block (1937)	352	−.56	−.56		440	.33	.33		264	−.82	−.82	
Carlton-Ford & Collins (1988)	40	−.08	−.08		40	.08	.08		40	−.08	−.08	
Connor et al. (1954)					119	.31	.31					
Flannery et al. (1991)	85	.22		.22								
Furman & Buhrmester (1992)	250	−.01	−.01		337	.14	.14		355	−.15	−.15	
Galambos & Almeida (1992)	66	−.09		−.09								
Greene & Grimsley (1990)	72	.13		.13								
Hagan et al. (1992)[a]	138	-.08	−.14	.09								
Inoff-Germain et al. (1988)	60	.00	−.04	.04								
Johnstone (1975)					1,317	−.01	−.01					
Kahlbaugh (1992)	20	.07	.04	.11								
Kahlbaugh et al. (1994)	41	.04	.11	−.04								
Khatri et al. (1993)	171	.29	.29									
Laursen (1993)					685	.00	.00	.00				
Lempers & Clark-Lempers (1992)	799	−.16	−.16		760	.06	.06		619	−.23	−.23	
Noack (1993)					38	.06	.06					
Papini et al. (1989)	193	.00		.00	201	.07		.07	164	−.08		−.08
Rajalu (1991)					365	−.05	−.05					
Schoenleber (1988)	44	−.22	−.22		44	.00	.00		44	−.22	−.22	
Sidhu & Singh (1987)					64	.03	.03					
Smetana (1989)	52	−.16	−.16		50	.19	.19		50	−.32	−.32	
Smetana (1991)	180	.07	.00	.15	158	.16	.16	.16	172	−.08	−.15	.00
→ Smetana & Asquith (1994)	68	.09	.12	.00								
Smetana et al. (1991)	28	.00	.00	.00								
Wierson et al. (1990)	122	.00	.00	.00								
Wierson & Forehand (1992)	184	.14		.14								

Note: n = participants included in effect size estimates. r = effect size estimate. Positive r values in contrasts of early adolescence and mid-adolescence, and in contrasts of mid-adolescence and late adolescence indicate greater conflict during mid-adolescence. Positive r values in contrasts of early adolescence and late adolescence indicate greater conflict during late adolescence.

[a] The number of participants reported for conflict rate and conflict affect differed; values reported here are averages.

A meta-analysis as a secondary source of information (Laursen, Coy, & Collins, 1998)

Source: From "Reconsidering Changes in Parent-Child Conflict Across Adolescence: A Meta-Analysis," by B. Laursen, K. C. Coy, & W. A. Collins, 1998, *Child Development*, 69, p.823. Reprinted with permission of S.R.C.D.

FIGURE 4.2

A Classification of Sources of Literature Review Materials from Summaries to Early Stage Materials

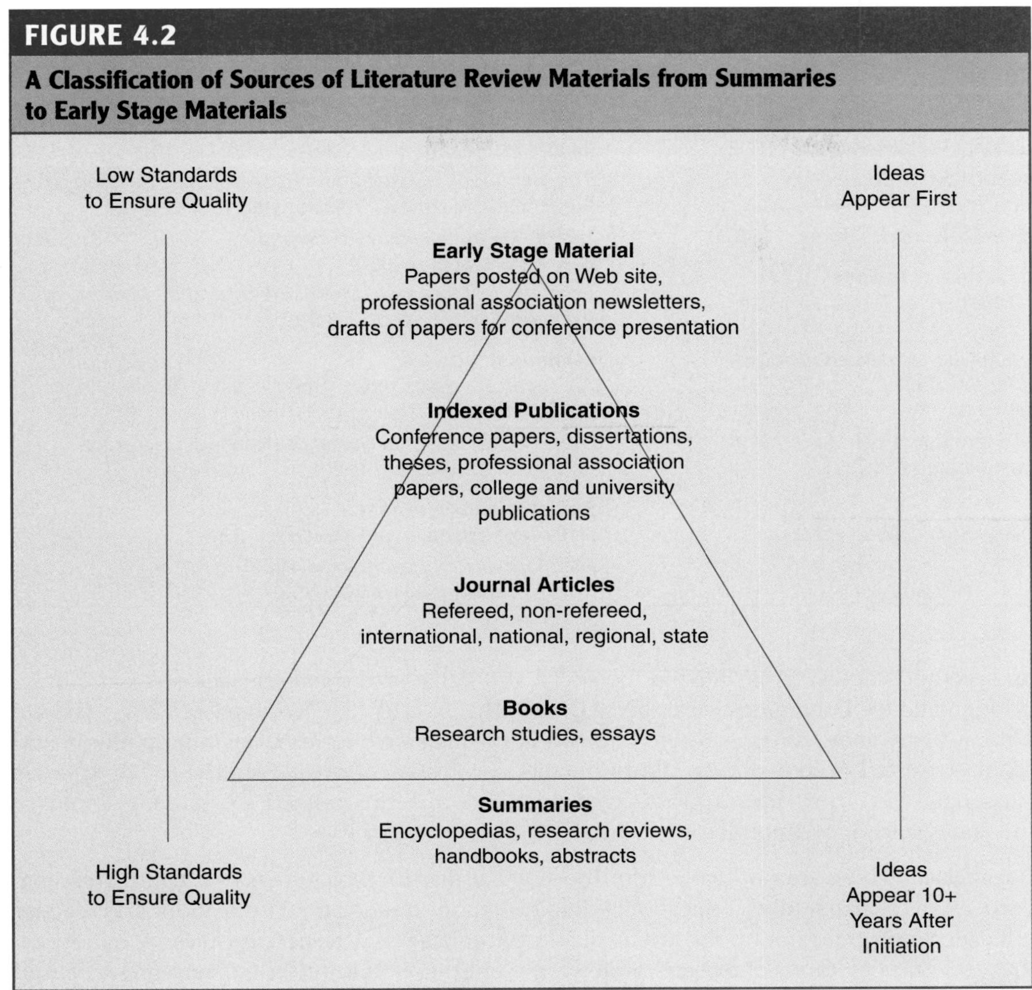

Summaries **Summaries** provide overviews of the literature and research on timely issues in education. A list of available summaries is shown in Table 4.2. These sources include encyclopedias, dictionaries and glossaries of terms, handbooks, statistical indexes, and reviews and syntheses. These summaries introduce a beginning researcher to a problem area, and they help you locate key references and identify current issues. Leading specialists in the field of education write these summaries.

Encyclopedias A good place to start when you know little about a topic is an **encyclopedia**, such as the *Encyclopedia of Educational Research* (Alkin, 1992). Sponsored by AERA, this encyclopedia provides research under 16 broad topics, including the curriculum of elementary and secondary education, education of exceptional persons, and the organizational structure and governance of education. The appendix on "Doing Library Research in Education" is especially useful (Alkin, 1992, p. 1543).

Dictionaries and Glossaries of Terms Other useful tools in the literature review and overall research process are **dictionaries and glossaries** of terms. These dictionaries contain most of the recent educational terms. For example, the *Dictionary of Statistics and Methodology: A Nontechnical Guide for the Social Sciences,* second edition (Vogt, 1999), defines statistical

TABLE 4.2

Types of Summaries Available in Academic Libraries with Examples

Encyclopedias
Encyclopedia of Educational Research (Alkin, 1992)
The International Encyclopedia of Education (Husen & Postlethwaithe, 1994)
Encyclopedia of American Education (Unger, 1996)

Dictionaries and Glossaries of Terms
Qualitative Inquiry: A Dictionary of Terms (Schwandt, 2001)
Dictionary of Terms in Statistics and Methodology: A Nontechnical Guide for the Social Sciences (Vogt, 1999)
Glossary of postmodern terms, in *Post-Modernism and the Social Sciences* (Rosenau, 1992)

Handbooks
Handbook of Research on Multicultural Education (Banks & Banks, 1995)
Handbook of Research on Teacher Education (Houston, Haberman, & Sikula, 1990)
The Handbook of Qualitative Research in Education (LeCompte, Millroy, & Preissle, 1992)
Handbook of Qualitative Research (Denzin & Lincoln, 2000)
Educational Research, Methodology and Measurement: An International Handbook (Keeves, 1988)

Statistical Indexes
American Statistics Index (Congressional Information Service, 1973–)
Digest of Educational Statistics (National Center for Educational Statistics, 1997)

Reviews and Syntheses
Review of Educational Research (1931–)
Anual Review of Psychology (1950–)

and methodological terms used in the social and behavioral sciences; such terms are often problematic for beginning researchers. *Qualitative Inquiry: A Dictionary of Terms*, second edition (Schwandt, 2001), is a reference book of qualitative terms containing multiple and often contested points of view about definitions. *Post-Modernism and the Social Sciences* (Rosenau, 1992) provides a glossary of postmodern terms related to studying issues of inequality and oppression in our society.

Handbooks There are numerous **handbooks** that discuss topics such as teaching, reading, curriculum, social studies, educational administration, multicultural education, and teacher education. Several handbooks are available on educational research topics. A handbook that addresses methods of research inquiry, the utilization of knowledge, measurement, and statistics is *Educational Research, Methodology, and Measurement: An International Handbook* (Keeves, 1988). Two recent handbooks are also available on topics in qualitative research: *The Handbook of Qualitative Research in Education* (LeCompte, Millroy, & Preissle, 1992) and the *Handbook of Qualitative Research* (Denzin & Lincoln, 2000). In quantitative research, handbooks are available as well, such as the *Handbook of Applied Social Research Methods* (Bickman & Rog, 2000). For research that combines both the quantitative and qualitative research approach, you might want to refer to the *Handbook of Mixed Methods in the Social and Behavioral Sciences* (Tashakkori & Teddlie, 2003).

Statistical Indexes **Statistical indexes** such as the annual *Digest of Educational Statistics* (National Center for Educational Statistics [NCES], 1997) report educational trends useful in writing problem statements or literature reviews. The *Digest*, issued since 1933 by the U.S. government, compiles statistical information covering the broad field of American education from kindergarten through graduate school. It also reports information from many sources, including the surveys and activities carried out by the NCES.

Reviews and Syntheses A final summary source on topics consists of timely **reviews and syntheses** in education, psychology, and the social sciences. For example, the *Review of Educational Research* (1931–) is a quarterly journal of AERA that publishes lengthy articles synthesizing educational research on various topics.

Books Academic libraries have extensive collections of books on a broad range of educational topics. The books most useful in reviewing the literature will be those that summarize research studies or report conceptual discussions on educational topics. Textbooks used in classes are less useful because they typically do not contain reports of single research studies, but they contain summaries of the literature and useful references. The *Subject Guide to Books in Print* (1957–) and the *Core List of Books and Journals in Education* (O'Brien & Fabiano, 1990) are guides that might also be helpful in your literature search.

Journals, Indexed Publications, and Electronic Sources Journal (or periodical) articles and conference papers that report research are prime sources for a literature review. As shown in Table 4.3, numerous journals publish research in education. For those looking for journals in which to report research, Table 4.3 lists them based on their emphasis on the quantitative approach, the qualitative approach, or both. This classification is a rough guide because journal preferences shift over time and with appointments of new editors and editorial boards. However, a classification such as this highlights the numerous publication outlets for both quantitative and qualitative research in education. To locate articles in journals, consider searching an abstract series, indexes to journals, or the diverse databases in education and the social sciences.

Abstract Series Abstract series, which allow for a broad search of journal articles by subject area, are available in many fields. In educational administration, for example, you might examine the *Educational Administration Abstracts* (University Council for Educational Administration, 1966–), or in early childhood development, look at the *Child Development Abstracts and Bibliography* (Society for Research in Child Development, 1945–). You can usually find these abstracts by accessing the online library catalog and using key words such as *abstracts*, and the subject field or topic to determine if the library contains a specific abstract series. Another place to search for journal publications are indexes such as the *Education Index* (Wilson, 1929/32–), an index devoted primarily to periodicals and organized into subject areas and fields.

Databases The most likely place to find journal articles is in databases that index journal articles both in print form and on CD-ROMs. A Google search can also often lead to timely articles and discussions on educational topics. A more careful and monitored approach is to examine one of the many literature databases. By examining these databases, you can easily access hundreds of journal articles on educational topics. Computerized databases also facilitate searching the literature for conference papers and miscellaneous publications, such as papers from professional associations or education agencies. You might start a computerized search of the databases with the education data, followed by the psychological and sociological sources of information. Six important databases offer easy retrieval of journal articles and other documents related to education:

1. ERIC (1991) is a national system of information in education established in 1966 by the U.S. Department of Education and the National Library of Education (NLE). Because public monies supported the development of ERIC, you can search the ERIC database free of charge. You can search this extensive database in the following three ways:

- On the Internet
- On CD-ROMs available at many academic libraries, usually installed on library computers for your use
- In print, available on the bookshelves of academic libraries

Education documents allowed into the ERIC database are selected mainly by reviewers at 16 subcontent clearinghouses (e.g., Adult, Career, and Vocational Education; Assessment and Evaluation). Individuals at these clearinghouses examine the educational

TABLE 4.3

Select Education and Social Sciences Journals that Emphasize Quantitative and Qualitative Research

Journals Emphasizing Quantitative Research	Journals Emphasizing Qualitative Research	Journals Emphasizing Both Quantitative and Qualitative Research
Educational and Psychological Measurement (Educational and Psychological Measurement)	*Anthropology and Education Quarterly* (Council on Anthropology and Education)	*Harvard Educational Review* (Harvard University)
Journal of Educational Research (American Educational Research Association)	*International Journal of Qualitative Studies in Education* (Falmer Press)	*American Educational Research Journal* (American Educational Research Association)
Journal of Educational Measurement (National Council on Measurement in Education)	*Journal of Contemporary Ethnography* (Sage)	*The Elementary School Journal* (University of Chicago Press)
Journal of Educational Psychology (American Psychological Association)	*Journal of Narrative and Life History* (Lawrence Erlbaum Associates)	*Educational Administration Quarterly* (University Council on Educational Administration)
Journal of Experimental Education (HELDREF Publications)	*Qualitative Family Research* (National Council on Family Relations)	*Reading Research Quarterly* (International Reading Association)
Journal of Psychology (Journal Press)	*Qualitative Health Research* (Sage)	*Research in the Teaching of English* (National Council of Teachers of English)
Journal of School Psychology (Behavioral Publications)	*Qualitative Sociology* (Human Sciences Press)	*Theory and Research in Social Education* (National Council for Social Studies)
Journal of Social Psychology (Journal Press)	*Qualitative Inquiry* (Sage)	*Theory into Practice* (Ohio State University)
Psychological Bulletin (American Psychological Association)	*Studies in Qualitative Methodology* (JAI Press)	*Journal of Adolescent Research* (Sage)
Psychological Review (American Psychological Association)	*Symbolic Interaction* (Society for the Study of Symbolic Interaction with JAI Press)	*Journal of Counseling and Development* (Counseling Association)
Research Quarterly for Exercise and Sport (American Alliance for Health, Physical Education and Recreation)	*Qualitative Research* (Sage)	*Journal of Research in Mathematics Education* (National Council of Teachers of Mathematics)
Research in Higher Education (Human Sciences Press)		*Journal of Research in Music Education* (Music Educators National Conference)
Applied Measurement in Education (National Council for Measurement in Education)		*Journal of Research in Science Teaching* (John Wiley and Sons)
		Review of Higher Education (Johns Hopkins Press)

Sources: Adapted from Fraenkel & Wallen (2000) and Preissle (1996).

FIGURE 4.3

Sample ERIC Journal Article Resume

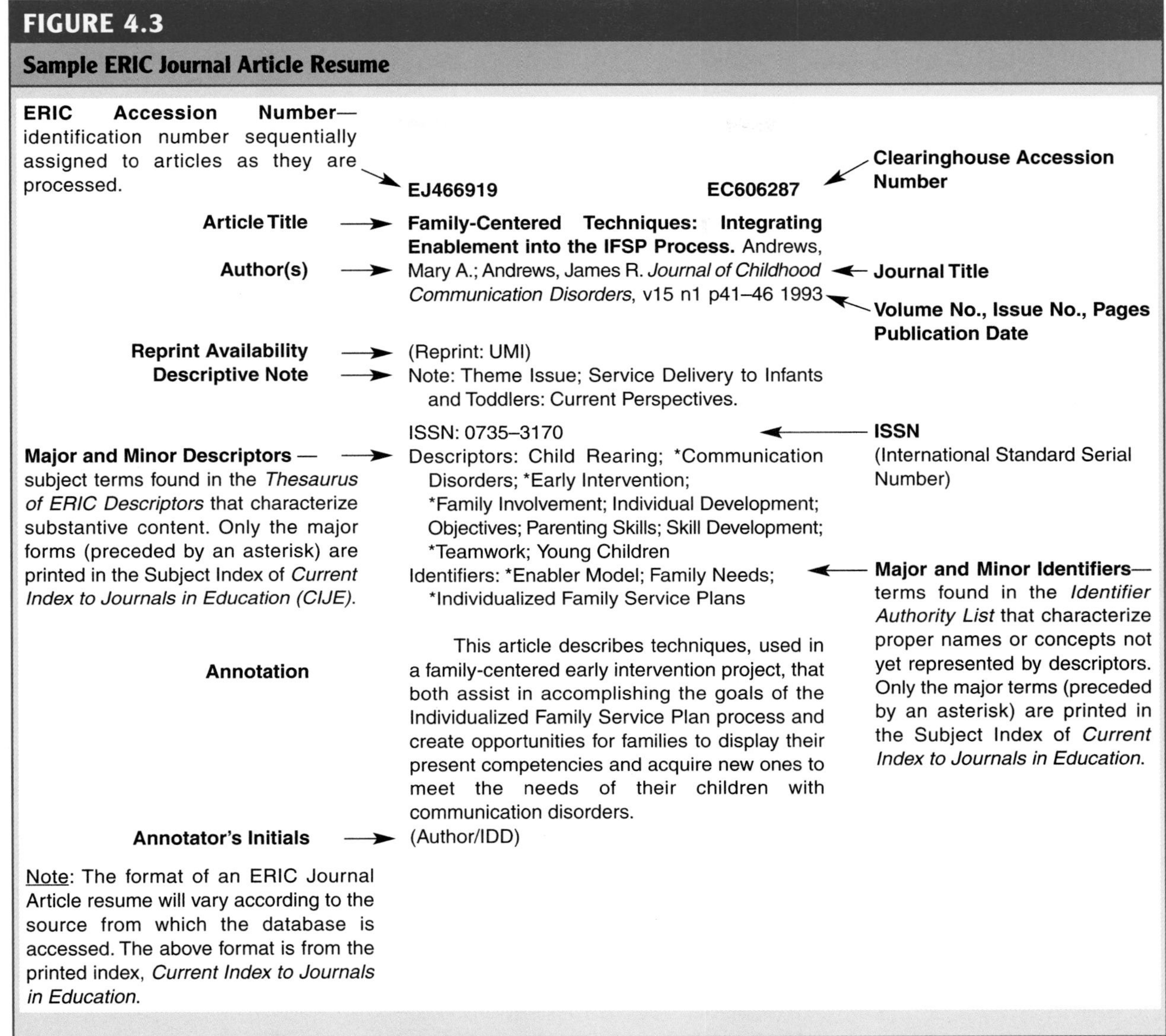

ERIC Accession Number—identification number sequentially assigned to articles as they are processed. → EJ466919

EC606287 ← **Clearinghouse Accession Number**

Article Title → **Family-Centered Techniques: Integrating Enablement into the IFSP Process.**

Author(s) → Andrews, Mary A.; Andrews, James R.

Journal of Childhood Communication Disorders ← **Journal Title**

v15 n1 p41–46 1993 ← **Volume No., Issue No., Pages Publication Date**

Reprint Availability → (Reprint: UMI)

Descriptive Note → Note: Theme Issue; Service Delivery to Infants and Toddlers: Current Perspectives.

ISSN: 0735–3170 ← **ISSN** (International Standard Serial Number)

Major and Minor Descriptors — subject terms found in the *Thesaurus of ERIC Descriptors* that characterize substantive content. Only the major forms (preceded by an asterisk) are printed in the Subject Index of *Current Index to Journals in Education (CIJE).* → Descriptors: Child Rearing; *Communication Disorders; *Early Intervention; *Family Involvement; Individual Development; Objectives; Parenting Skills; Skill Development; *Teamwork; Young Children

Identifiers: *Enabler Model; Family Needs; *Individualized Family Service Plans ← **Major and Minor Identifiers**—terms found in the *Identifier Authority List* that characterize proper names or concepts not yet represented by descriptors. Only the major terms (preceded by an asterisk) are printed in the Subject Index of *Current Index to Journals in Education.*

Annotation

This article describes techniques, used in a family-centered early intervention project, that both assist in accomplishing the goals of the Individualized Family Service Plan process and create opportunities for families to display their present competencies and acquire new ones to meet the needs of their children with communication disorders.

Annotator's Initials → (Author/IDD)

Note: The format of an ERIC Journal Article resume will vary according to the source from which the database is accessed. The above format is from the printed index, *Current Index to Journals in Education.*

material, write abstracts, and assign terms or *descriptors* from the ERIC vocabulary to identify each source of information. The literature that goes into ERIC is not peer reviewed for quality, but reviewers at the clearinghouses do select it for inclusion in the database.

The ERIC database consists of two parts: journals, located in the *Current Index to Journals in Education* (CIJE; ERIC, 1969–), and documents, found in *Resources in Education* (RIE; ERIC, 1966–). *CIJE* is a monthly and cumulative index to information located in approximately 980 major educational and education-related journals. It provides a subject index, an author index, and abstracts of specific studies. *RIE* is a monthly and cumulative index to current research findings, project and technical reports, speeches, unpublished manuscripts, and books. It indexes education information by subject, personal author, institution, and publication type.

A sample ERIC journal article (CIJE) summary (or resume) and a sample ERIC document (RIE) resume are shown in Figures 4.3 and 4.4. You will find these on the ERIC

FIGURE 4.4

Sample ERIC Document Resume

ERIC Accession Number—identification number sequentially assigned to articles as they are processed. →	**ED359626** **EA025062**	← **Clearinghouse Accession Number**
Author(s) →	*Fuhrman.-Susan H. Ed.*	
Title →	**Designing Coherent Education Policy; Improving the System.**	
Institution. (Organization where document originated.) →	Corporate Source—Consortium for Policy Research in Education, New Brunswick, NJ. Sponsoring Agency—Office of Educational Research and Improvement (ED), Washington, DC.	← **Sponsoring Agency**—agency responsible for initiating, funding, and managing the research project.
Contract or Grant Number →	Contract Nos.–R117G10007; R117G10039	
Date Published →	Pub Date—1993	
ISBN (International Standard Book Number) →	ISBN-1-55542-536-4	
	Available from—Jossey-Bass Publishers, 350 Sansome Street, San Francisco, CA 94104.	← **Alternate source for obtaining document.**
	None-370 p.	← **Descriptive Note** (pagination first).
ERIC Document Reproduction Service (EDRS) Avaliabiity—"MF" means microfiche: "PC" means reproduced paper copy. When describes as "Document Not Available from EDRS," alternate sources are cited above. Prices are subject to change. For latest price code schedule see section on "How to Order ERIC Documents," in the most recent issue of *Resources in Education*, or call EDRS at 1-800-443-3742 for price information. →	EDRS Price—MF01/PC15 Plus Postage.	
	Pub Type—Books (010)—Collected Works-General (020)—Guides–Non-Classroom (055)	← **Publication Type**—broad categories indicating the form or organization of the document, as contrasted to its subject matter. The category name is followed by the category code
	Descriptors—Educational Change; Elementary Secondary Education; Governance; Politics of Education; Standards; *Educational Objectives; *Education Policy; *Instructional Improvement; *Policy Formation; *Public Education	← **Descriptors**—subject terms found in the *Thesaurus of ERIC Descriptors* that characterize substantive content. Only the major terms (proceeded by an asterisk) are printed in the Subject Index of *Resources in Education.*
Abstract	This book examines issues in designing coherent education policy for public elementary and secondary schools. It seeks to expand the policy discussion by refining the definition of coherence and considering a number of complex questions raised by the notion of coherent policy. The book offers an indepth look at systemic school reform and offers a variety of ideas as to how educators at the district, state, and federal levels may coordinate the various elements of policy infrastructure around a new set of ambitious, common goals for student achievement. Chapters include the following: (1) "The Politics of Coherence" (Susan H. Fuhrman); (2) "Policy and Practice: The Relations between Governance and Instruction" (David K. Cohen and James P. Spillanc); (3) "The Role of Local School Disctricts in Instructional Improvement" (Richard F. Elmore); (4) "Systemic Educational Policy: A Conceptual Framework" (William H. Clune); (5) "Student Incentives and Academic Standards: Independent Schools as a Coherent System" (Arthur G. Powell); (6) "New Directions for Early Childhood Care and Education Policy" (W. Steven Barnett); (7) "How the World of Students and Teachers Challenges Policy Coherence" (Milbrey W. McLaughlin and Joan E. Talbert); (8) "Systemic Reform and Educational Opportunity" (Jennifer A. O'Day and Marshall S. Smith); and (9) "Conclusion: Can Policy Lead the Way?" (Susan H. Fuhrman). References accompany each chapter. (LMI)	← **Abstractor's Initials**

Note: The format of an ERIC Document resume will vary according to the source from which the database is accessed. The above format is from the printed index, *Resources in Education.*

Web site. Read through the marginal notations that explain the information about the document. This summary contains an accession number (*EJ* for journal and *ED* for documents). It also displays the author, the title, the major and minor descriptors assigned to the article, and a brief annotation describing the article.

2. *Psychological Abstracts* (APA, 1927–) and the CD-ROM versions, *PsycLit* (SilverPlatter Information, Inc., 1986) and *PsycINFO* (**www.apa.org**), are important sources for locating research articles on topics broadly related to psychology. In October 2000, PsycLit and PsycINFO consolidated into one database to provide a comprehensive source of psychological literature from 1887 to the present. This database is available in a print version, on CD-ROM, and on a Web site. These databases are available in libraries or through online versions leased by the libraries and networked through campus computers.

These databases index more than 850 journals in 16 categories. They provide bibliographic citations, abstracts for psychological journal articles, dissertations, technical reports, books, and book chapters published worldwide. The print version has a 3-year cumulative index. An example of a journal record from PsycINFO is shown in Figure 4.5. Similar to an ERIC record, this summary from PsycINFO includes key phrase *identifiers*, as well as the author, title, the source, and a brief abstract of the article.

3. *Sociological Abstracts* (Sociological Abstracts, Inc., 1953–) is available in a print version, on CD-ROM (*Sociofile,* SilverPlatter Information, Inc., 1974/86–), and in a library-leased Web version available to computers networked to the library. Available from Cambridge Scientific Abstracts, this database provides access to the world's literature in sociology and related disciplines. The database contains abstracts of journal articles selected from more than 2,500 journals, abstracts of conference papers presented at sociological association meetings, dissertations, and books and book reviews from 1963 to the present.

4. The *Social Science Citation Index* (SSCI; Institute for Scientific Information [ISI], 1969–) and the CD-ROM version, *Social Sciences Citation Index* (ISI, 1989–), provide a database of cited references to journal articles. The citation index allows you to look up a reference to a work to find journal articles that have cited the work. SSCI covers 5,700 journals, representing virtually every discipline in the social sciences.

5. EBSCO Information Services (**www.ebsco.com/**) is a worldwide information service that provides print and electronic subscription services, research database development and production, and online access to more than 150 databases and thousands of e-journals. Academic libraries purchase the services of EBSCO or individuals can purchase articles of interest through the pay-per-view feature. Using EBSCO, the educational researcher can view tables of contents for journals, abstracts to articles, and link directly to full text from over 8,000 titles. Researchers can also receive e-mails of the tables of contents for their favorite journals as soon as they are published.

6. *Dissertation Abstracts* (University Microfilms International [UMI], 1938–1965/66) and the CD-ROM version *Dissertation Abstracts Ondisc (Computer File;* UMI, 1987–), provide guides to doctoral dissertations submitted by nearly 500 participating institutions throughout the world. It is published in three sections: Section A, The Humanities and Social Sciences; Section B, The Sciences and Engineering; and Section C, Worldwide. Examining these sections, a researcher finds abstracts (350-word summaries) of dissertations. A comprehensive index permits easy access to titles, authors, and subject areas.

Early Stage Literature The final major category of literature to review (see Figure 4.2) comprises materials at an early stage of development that reviewers (e.g., journal editors or book publishers) have probably not screened for quality. Such early stage literature consists of newsletters, studies posted to Web sites, professional-association newsletters, and drafts of studies available from authors. For example, electronic journals and research studies posted to Web sites and available on the Internet represent a growing source of research

FIGURE 4.5

Sample Journal Record from PsycINFO Database (www.apa.org/psychinfo/about/sample.html#journal)

Sample Records from the PsycINFO Database

The values in each field below vary from record to record. For a complete list of possible values for each field, plus a description of each field, please visit our Database Field Guide.

- View a Journal Record
- View a Book Record
- View a Book Chapter Record
- Review sample records representing non-article data

Sample Journal Record

Accession Number
2000-15980-004
Author
Dubois, Michel; Vial, I.
Affiliation
U Pierre Mendes, Lab de Psychologie Sociale, Grenoble, France
Title
Multimedia design: The effects of relating multimodal information.
Source
Journal of Computer Assisted Learning. 2000 Jun Vol 16(2) 157-165
ISSN/ISBN
0266-4909
Language
English
UMI
URL
DOI
Release Date
20000628
Abstract
The are few models that describe learner behaviour during the simultaneous processing of several types of information, yet this is the defining characteristic of the use of multimedia tools, which bring together media in different informational formats (fixed or moving images, sound, text). Following studies in cognitive psychology concerning the increase in the ability to form mental images of words, this article aims at defining how different multimedia presentation modes affect the learning of foreign language vocabulary (Russian). 60 college students learned Russian phrases and then participated in a recall experiment where the multimedia presentation of the phrases was varied. An effect was observed on word memorisation in the different information presentation modes, suggesting better processing when there is co-referencing of the different sources, especially when the encoding and tests modes are the same. In addition to these experimental results, some principles for the design of multimodal learning tools are discussed. (PsycINFO Database Record (c) 2000 APA, all rights reserved)
Key Concepts
information presentation method, recall of foreign language phrases, college students
Keywords (Thesaurus Terms)
*Foreign Language Learning; *Instructional Media; *Recall (Learning); *Visual Display
Classification Codes
2343 Learning & Memory
Population
10 Human; 300 Adulthood (18 yrs & older)
Population Location
France
Form/Content Type
0800 Empirical Study
Table of Contents (Book Records only)
Publication Year
2000

Source: Reprinted with permission of the American Psychological Association, publisher of the PsycINFO Database © 2004, all rights reserved.

TABLE 4.4

Advantages and Disadvantages of Using the Internet as a Resource for a Literature Review

Advantages	Disadvantages
• There is easy access to material since the researcher can search any time of the day.	• Research posted to Web sites is not reviewed for quality by "experts".
• Web sites have a breadth of information on most topics.	• The research found on Web sites may have been plagiarized without the searcher's knowledge.
• Web sites provide a network that researchers can contact about their topic and research problem.	• Research studies may be difficult to find and time consuming to locate.
• Research posted to Web sites is typically current information.	• Web site literature may not be organized or summarized in a way that is useful.
• Web sites can be searched easily using a search engine and key words.	• Full-text electronic journals available on the Web are new and few in number.
• Select research studies can be printed immediately from Web sites.	

information. These materials need to be evaluated carefully. Anyone can put anything up on the Internet, and it is sometimes difficult to discern information about the item (e.g., author, how it got there). Also, it may not be original (e.g., quoted out of context, altered), and it has likely not gone through a filtering or review process. Some of the advantages and disadvantages of using these materials from the Internet appear in Table 4.4.

Unquestionably, the easy ability to access and capture this material makes it attractive; however, because reviewers may not have evaluated the quality of this information, you need to be cautious about whether it represents rigorous, thoughtful, and systematic research for use in a literature review. Ways to determine the credibility of the material include the following:

- See if it is a study reported in an online journal with a peer review board to oversee the quality of publications.
- Determine if you recognize the authors because they have published materials in quality journals or books.
- See if the Web site has standards for accepting the research studies and reporting them.
- Ask a faculty member in your graduate program if he or she feels that the article is of sufficient quality to be included in your literature review.

Critically Evaluate and Select the Literature

Let's return to the major steps in conducting a literature review. The process began with identifying keywords and locating resources. Once you locate the literature, you need to determine if it is a good source to use and whether it is relevant to your particular research.

Is It a Good, Accurate Source?

It sometimes comes as a shock to beginning researchers that even though a study has been published, it may not be worthy of including in a literature review. Some guidelines are helpful to make a careful selection of the literature. Remember, as mentioned in Figure 4.2, there are different types of literature.

- Rely as much as possible on journal articles published in national journals. Typically, a panel of editors (two or three editorial board members plus a general editor) reviews and critically evaluates a manuscript before it is accepted for publication. If the journal lists reviewers or editorial board members from around the country, consider it to be high quality because it is a refereed, national journal.
- Use a priority system for searching the literature. Start with refereed journal articles; then proceed to nonrefereed journal articles; then books; then conference papers, dissertations, and theses; and finally nonreviewed articles posted to Web sites. This order reflects the extent of external review of materials from a high level of review to minimal or no review. If you are using full-text articles from Web sites, review the quality of the material. Use articles reported in national online journals that have undergone a review through editorial boards. Information about the journals and their review process can be obtained online. Material obtained from Web sites not in national, refereed journals needs to be carefully screened to determine the qualifications of the author, the quality of the writing, and the scope and rigor of data collection and analysis.
- Look for "research" studies to include in your literature review. Good research follows the definition of research that we learned in chapter 1, in which research consists of posing questions, collecting data, and forming results or conclusions from the data. Also, the claims made by authors in their results need to be justified and supported based on the data collected.
- Include both quantitative and qualitative research studies in your review, regardless of the approach you might use in your own study. Each form of research has advantages and provides insight for our knowledge base in education.

Is It Relevant?

Whether a source is high quality and worthy of inclusion in a literature review is one consideration. An entirely separate question is whether the literature is relevant to use. You might read the literature you have selected, noting the titles of articles, the contents of abstracts at the beginning of the material (if they are present), and major headings in the study. This review helps determine if the information is relevant to use in a review. Relevance has several dimensions, and you might consider the following criteria when selecting literature for a review:

- Topic relevance. Does the literature focus on the same topic as your proposed study?
- Individual and site relevance. Does the literature examine the same individuals or sites that you want to study?
- Problem and question relevance. Does the literature examine the same research problem that you propose to study? Does it address the same research question you plan to address?
- Accessibility relevance. Is the literature available in your library or can you download it from a Web site? Can you obtain it easily from the library or a Web site?

If you answer yes to these questions, then the literature is relevant for your literature review.

Organize the Literature

Once you have located the literature, assessed its quality, and checked it for relevance, the next step is to organize it for a literature review. This process involves photocopying and filing the literature. At this time you might quickly read it, take notes on it, and determine how it fits into the overall literature. Constructing a visual picture of the literature—a literature map—helps to organize it, positions your study within the literature, and provides a framework for presenting research to audiences about your topic.

Photocopying, Downloading, and Filing

After locating books, journal articles, and miscellaneous documents (such as the education documents in ERIC available on microfiche) in a library, you should make copies of the articles or download the articles (as .html or .pdf files) and develop some system to easily retrieve the information. Copyright laws permit the duplication of only one complete article without the permission of the author. Placing the articles in file folders alphabetized by author may be the most convenient way to organize the materials. Alternatively, you might organize the literature by sources, topic, or keywords. However, using an author index may be the most convenient method because topics and keywords you use in your literature review may shift as you work through drafts of the review.

Taking Notes and Abstracting Studies

During the process of reading the literature, researchers take notes on the information so that a summary of the literature is available for a written review. This note taking is often an informal procedure in which the researcher identifies important ideas about the article or material and writes rough notes on each source of information. This process may involve a citation to the article (see "Using a Style Manual" section later in this chapter) and a brief summary of the major points of the article. These points may generally include (a) the questions being addressed, (b) data collection, and (c) major results (see additional criteria for writing an abstract, in chapter 10).

Instead of this informal approach, a preferred strategy is to systematically record information about each source so that you can easily insert it into a written review of the literature. This process yields useful information so that you can remember the details of the studies.

A systematic approach for summarizing each source of information is to develop an abstract for each one. An **abstract** is a summary of the major aspects of a study or article, conveyed in a concise way (for this purpose, often no more than 350 words) and including specific components that describe the information. Be careful not to use the abstracts available at the beginning of journal articles. They may be too brief to use because of word or space limitations imposed by journal editors. Also, if you use such an abstract, you need to reference it so that you do not plagiarize someone else's work. Instead, write your own abstracts of articles and materials. This calls for identifying the topics that you need to abstract from the study.

The first step is to think about the type of literature you will be abstracting. Researchers typically abstract and include in the literature review only research studies, rather than essays or opinion papers (although you probably need to cite important essays or opinions if authors widely cite them).

To abstract elements for a *quantitative research* study such as a journal article, conference paper, or dissertation or thesis, you might identify the:

- Research problem
- Research questions or hypotheses
- Data collection procedure
- Results of the study

A complete abstract reporting these four elements for a quantitative survey study by Metzner (1989) is shown in Figure 4.6. Notice in this abstract that the summaries of each

FIGURE 4.6

Sample Abstract for a Quantitative Research Study

Metzner, B. (1989). Perceived quality of academic advising: The effect on freshman attrition. *American Educational Research Journal, 26*(3), 422–442.*

Research Problem:

Colleges and universities place emphasis on student retention, and academic advising positively intervenes to reduce dropout. However, surveys show extensive dissatisfaction with advisement. Empirical investigations of this relationship have provided equivocal results. Some studies show a positive relationship between retention and quality of advising; others have failed to discover an association.

Research Questions or Hypotheses:

No specific research questions or hypotheses were raised, but this reader can deduce them from the purpose statement. The general question was: Does the quality of advisement influence student attrition? The specific questions are: Is better advising associated with lower attrition than poor advising? Do changes in quality of advising (from good, poor, or no advising) affect retention differently?

Data Collection Procedure:

Freshmen at a public university were asked about the quality of advising they received, their intent to leave the institution, and their general satisfaction with the college experience. One thousand and thirty-three students completed questionnaires in their English Composition courses late in the fall semester of 1982.

Results:

In response to the question, "Is better advising associated with lower attrition than poor advising?", the results (of regression analysis) showed that good advising reduced dropout while poor advising failed to have any effect. Thus, levels of advising quality did impact freshman attrition differently. In response to the next question: "Do changes in the quality of advising (good, poor, none) affect retention differently?", the results showed that yes, the impact was different. Good advising helped to lower dropout more than no advising, and poor advising lowered dropout more than no advising. The implications of these results is that the best strategy for improving retention is to offer good advising to students who receive no advising.

**Source:* Abstracted with the assistance of Beth Caughlin, Bob Mann, Chad Abresch, Qian Geng, and Ling-Mean Heng from Education 800, University of Nebraska, Lincoln, Fall 1998.

element are short and that a complete reference to the work is listed at the top so that each abstract is fully documented. (Reference format will be addressed later in this chapter.)

For a *qualitative research* study, the topics are the same as those used in a quantitative study, but the headings reflect terms commonly used in qualitative research. Instead of using hypotheses and questions, qualitative researchers state only questions. Instead of *results, findings* is a more acceptable qualitative term.

When abstracting a qualitative research study, you might identify the:

- ◆ Research problem
- ◆ Research questions
- ◆ Data-collection procedure
- ◆ Findings

These elements were used to abstract a qualitative study by Creswell and Brown (1992), shown in Figure 4.7. This study explores the role of academic chairpersons in enhancing faculty research. Again, there is a brief summary of each element and a complete reference to the article at the top of the abstract.

The elements abstracted in both the quantitative and qualitative examples illustrate typical information extracted from research studies. In other forms of abstracting, you may include additional information in which you critique or assess the strengths and weaknesses of the research.

FIGURE 4.7

Sample Abstract for a Qualitative Research Study

Creswell, J. W., & Brown, M. L. (1992). How chairpersons enhance faculty research: A grounded theory study. *The Review of Higher Education, 16*(1), 41–62.

Research Problem:

The authors mention that past research has addressed the correlates of scientific achievement and the research performance of faculty. However, an unexplored correlate is the role of the chairperson in influencing faculty scholarly performance. Since chairs are in a position to enhance and facilitate faculty scholarship, the role of the chair needs clarification.

Research Questions:

The central research question is implied in the title to the study: "How do chairpersons enhance faculty research?" More specifically, the authors asked chairs to discuss an Issue involved in assisting faculty members in the department in his or her professional development. They were also asked to specify actions or roles in performing this assistance, identify reasons for assistance, note signs that the individual needed assistance, and indicate the outcomes of assistance for the individual.

Data Collection Procedure:

The authors collected semi-structured interview data from 33 chairpersons located in a variety of disciplines and types of institutions of higher education. Chief academic officers and faculty development personnel on the campuses nominated these chairs for the study. The authors used the procedures of grounded theory.

Findings:

The authors identified from the interviews seven major categories of roles engaged in by the chairpersons: provider, enabler, advocate, mentor, encourager, collaborator, and challenger. Further analysis then led to understanding how these roles played out for faculty at different stages of their careers. Four levels of faculty were used to illustrate their chair roles: beginning faculty, pre-tenured faculty, post-tenured faculty, and senior faculty. From these profiles, the authors identified a theoretical model of the chair's role and advanced propositions (or hypotheses) for future testing. These propositions related to the type of issue the faculty member experienced, the career stage issue of the faculty member, and the strategies employed by the chairperson.

Constructing a Literature Map

As you organize and take notes or abstract articles, you will begin to understand the content of your literature review. In other words, a conceptual picture will begin to emerge. Having a diagram or visual picture of this conceptualization allows you to organize the literature in your mind, identify where your study fits into this literature, and convince others of the importance of your study.

This visual picture results in a literature map, literally a map of the literature you have found. A **literature map** is a figure or drawing that displays the research literature (e.g., studies, essays, books, chapters, and summaries) on a topic. This visual rendering helps you see overlaps in information or major topics in the literature and can help you determine how a proposed study adds to or extends the existing literature rather than duplicates past studies. As a communication device, a map helps you convey to others, such as faculty committee members or an audience at a conference, the current picture of the literature on a topic.

The actual design of this map can take several forms. Figure 4.8 shows a chart in which the researcher organized the literature hierarchically. Organized in top-down fashion, this chart portrays the literature that Hovater (2000) found on the topic of preservice training for teachers on multicultural topics. At the top of the figure he lists the topic: the need for teacher education programs to train culturally responsive teachers. Next, below the top level, he identifies the two programs available, study abroad

FIGURE 4.8

A Literature Map, Hierarchical Design

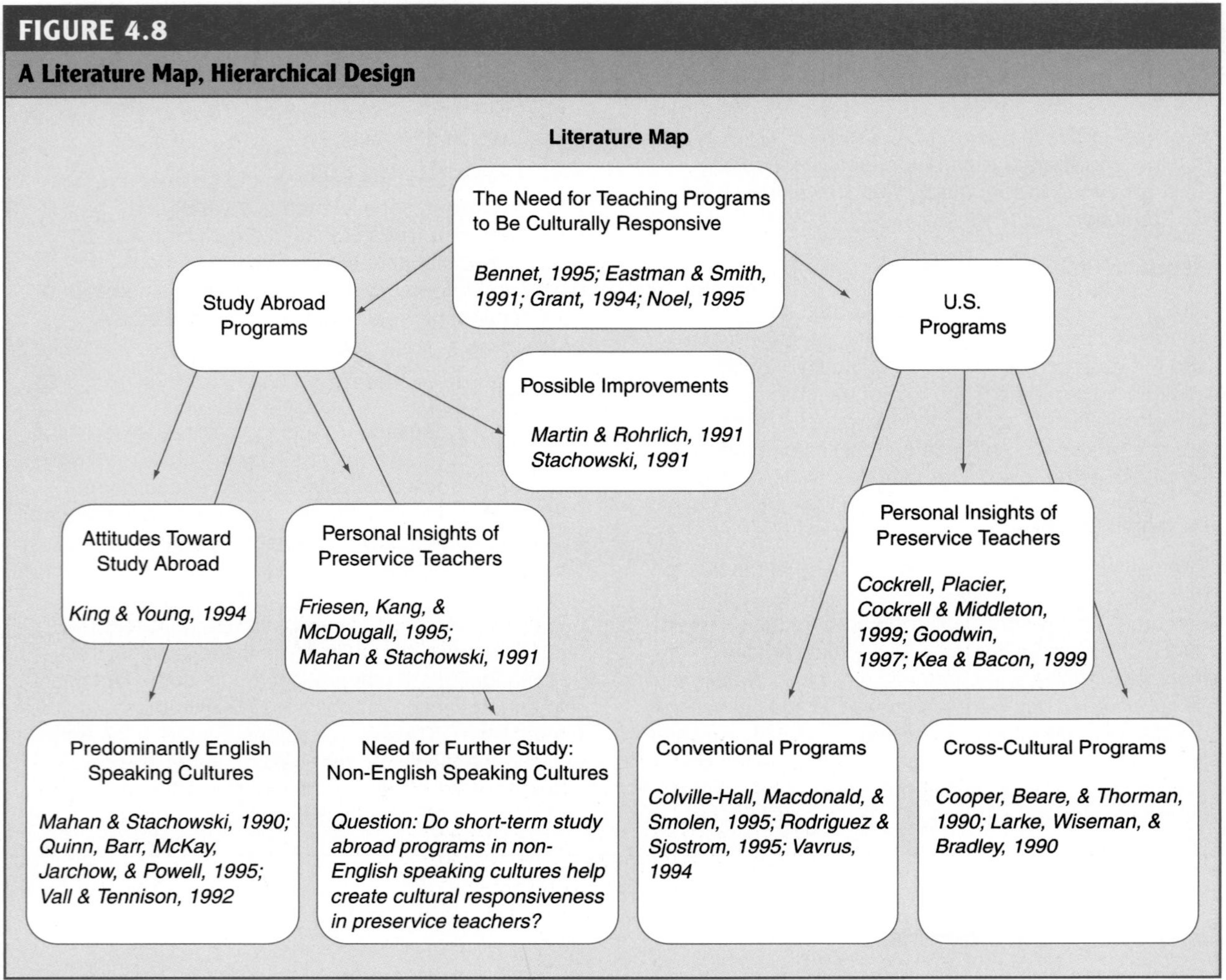

Source: Used by permission of Scott Hovater, 2000.

programs and U.S. programs, and below that, specific studies that address these two types of programs. These studies relate to attitudes of students, personal insights of teachers, and possible improvements in training. At the lower left-center of the map, Hovater advances his proposed study: to extend the literature addressing the question, "Do short-term study abroad programs in non-English-speaking cultures help create cultural responsiveness in preservice teachers?"

Hovater's (2000) literature map includes several useful design features that you can include in a literature map. Here are some guidelines to follow when constructing your own literature map:

- Identify the key terms for your topic and place them at the top of the map. As discussed earlier, these key terms are found in draft titles, questions, or ERIC resources.
- Take the information for your map and sort it into groups of related topical areas or "families of studies." Think in terms of three or four groupings because these groups will likely result in major sections in a written literature review.

- Provide a label for each box (later this label is useful as a heading in your literature review). Also, in each box, include key sources you found in your literature search that fit the label of the box.
- Develop the literature map on as many levels as possible. Some branches in the drawing will be more developed than others because of the extent of the literature. In some cases, you may develop one branch in detail because it is the primary area of focus of your research topic.
- Indicate your proposed study that will extend or add to the literature. Draw a box at the bottom of the figure that says "my proposed study," "a proposed study," or "my study." In this box, you could state a proposed title, a research question, or the problem you wish to study. An extremely important step is to draw lines *connecting* your proposed study to other branches (boxes) of the literature. In this way, you establish how your study adds to or extends the existing literature. The map in Figure 4.8 shows a hierarchical design. Other designs, such as a circular design of interconnecting circles or a sequential design to show the literature narrowing and focusing into a proposed study, can also be used. We can see a circular design by shifting and changing Hovater's (2000) hierarchically designed map into a circular map, as shown in Figure 4.9.

FIGURE 4.9

A Literature Map, Circular Design

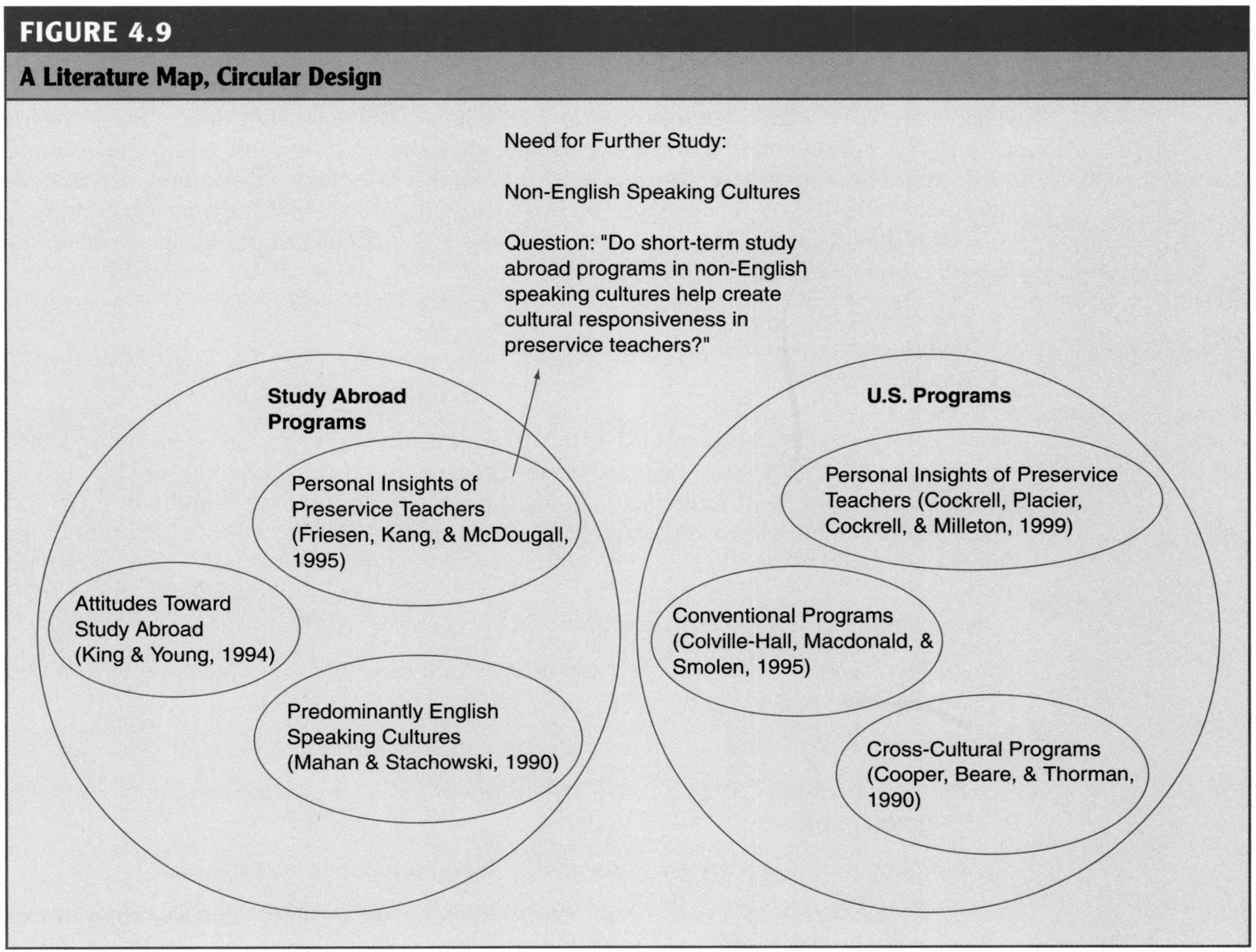

Write a Literature Review

Now that you have scanned the literature to determine its relevance, abstracted it, and organized it into a literature map, it's time to construct the actual written summary of the literature. For the most part, this literature consists of journal articles and research reports found in library resources. Researchers use procedures for summarizing each study, providing a clear reference to it, and writing the literature review. This writing requires pulling together all aspects of the review to this point, such as:

- Using an appropriate style to write complete references for these summaries (for a list at the end of your research report) and to develop headings for the literature review
- Employing specific writing strategies related to the extent of the review, the type of review, and the concluding statements in a review

Using a Style Manual

We have already seen how abstracts can include a complete reference (or citation) to the information in the literature (see Figures 4.7 and 4.8). In writing these references, you should use an accepted style manual. Headings, tables, figures, and the overall format also require use of a specific style manual. A **style manual** provides a structure for citing references, labeling headings, and constructing tables and figures for a scholarly research report. When you use a style manual, the research (and the literature review) will have a consistent format for readers and other researchers, and this format will facilitate their understanding of the study.

The *Publication Manual of the American Psychological Association,* 5th edition (APA, 2001), style manual is the most popular style guide in educational research. Other guides available are the *Chicago Manual of Style,* 15th edition (University of Chicago Press, 2003), *A Manual for Writers of Term Papers, Theses, and Dissertations,* 6th edition (Turabian, 1996), and *Form and Style: Theses, Reports, and Term Papers,* 8th edition (Campbell, Ballou, & Slade, 1990). These style manuals provide a consistent format for writing a research report. Three of the most frequently used approaches found in the *Publication Manual of the American Psychological Association* (APA, 2001) will be emphasized here:

- End-of-text references
- Within-text references
- Headings

End-of-Text References **End-of-text references** are the references listed at the end of a research report. In APA form, they are double spaced and listed alphabetically by author. Include in the end-of-text reference list only the references mentioned in the body of the paper. The APA manual provides examples of end-of-text references for 76 different types of documents. Below are illustrations of three common types of references in appropriate APA form.

An example of a *journal article* end-of-text reference in APA form is:

Elam, S. M. (1989). The second Phi Delta Kappa poll of teachers' attitudes toward public schools. *Phi Delta Kappan, 70*(3), 785–798.

An example of a *book* end-of-text reference in APA form is:

Shertzer, B., & Stone, S. C. (1981). *Fundamentals of guidance* (4th ed.). Boston: Houghton Mifflin.

An example of a *conference paper* end-of-text reference in APA form is:

Zedexk, S., & Baker, H. T. (1971, May). *Evaluation of behavioral expectation scales.* Paper presented at the meeting of the Midwestern Psychological Association, Detroit, MI.

As these examples show, the first line is left adjusted and the second line is indented. We call this a *hanging indent*. Also, observe the use of all lowercase letters (noncapitals) in the titles of the articles. In the journal article example, we capitalize all words in the journal title. In the book example, we capitalize only the first word in the title of the book, the first word following a colon in the title, and proper nouns.

Within-Text References **Within-text references** are references cited in a brief format within the body of the text to provide credit to authors. APA style lists several conventions for citing these in-text references. The following examples illustrate the appropriate use of APA style when you cite both single and multiple authors.

An example of a within-text reference in APA style in which the author refers to a single reference is:

> Rogers (1994) compared reaction times for athletes and nonathletes in middle schools. . . .

As this reference shows, APA style requires that you use only the author's last name for within-text citations, unless first initials are needed to distinguish between authors with identical surnames. This reference also includes information about the year of the publication. These references may also appear anywhere in the sentence.

An example of a within-text reference in APA style in which the author refers to multiple references is:

> Past studies of reaction times (Gogel, 1984; Rogers, 1994; Smith, 1989) showed. . . . Entire groups of studies have addressed the difficulty of test taking and reaction times (Gogel, 1984; Happenstance, 1995; Lucky, 1994; Smith, 1989).

As illustrated by this example, semicolons separate the different studies. Also, the authors are listed in alphabetical order, as in end-of-text references, rather than in chronological order based on the date of publication.

An example of a multiple-author reference for two or more authors when first mentioned in the research is:

> The difficulty of test taking and reaction times has been examined by Smith, Paralli, John, and Langor (1994).

When an author mentions these individuals at subsequent times in the manuscript, only the first author's name is given, and it is followed by "et al."

> The study of test taking and reaction times (Smith et al., 1994)

Finally, good scholarly writing requires that authors cite original sources—where the information came from originally—rather than cite a book or article that contains the reference. For example, an inadequate model would be:

> Smith (1994), as reported in Theobald (1997), said that. . . .

> An improved model, using the original source, would be:

> Smith (1994) said that. . . .

Levels of Headings As you write a literature review, consider the number of topics or subdivisions in your review. **Levels of headings** in a scholarly study and literature review provide logical subdivisions of the text. Headings provide important clues for readers that help them understand a study. They also divide the material in the same way as topics in an outline.

In APA style, the maximum number of heading levels is five. As shown in Figure 4.10, these five headings differ in their use of upper- and lowercase letters; in centered, left-adjusted, and indented words; and in italics. Most educational studies include either two or three levels of headings. Authors seldom use fourth or fifth-level headings because their research lacks the detail needed for many subdivisions. For some books, five levels of headings may be appropriate, but typically two to four levels of headings will suffice for most educational research studies.

The choice of heading levels in a literature review depends on the number of subdivisions of topics you use. Regardless of subdivisions, APA style requires that you use certain types of headings for a two-, three-, and four-level heading format. The following examples illustrate these three popular forms.

When you have only two levels in a research report, use Levels 1 and 3. Thus, the levels are *not* consecutive (i.e., 1, 2) when using only two levels. An example of a *two-level heading* in APA form that uses first (centered, uppercase and lowercase) and third levels (flush left, italicized, uppercase and lowercase) is:

Review of the Literature (Level 1)

Introduction (Level 3)
Social Support Research (Level 3)

If you have three levels in your research, use Levels 1 (centered uppercase and lowercase), 3 (flush left, italicized, uppercase and lowercase), and 4 (indented, italicized, first word uppercase, all other words lowercase, ending with a period, the first sentence continues on right after the period). Again, the levels are not consecutive (e.g., 1, 2, 3). An example of a *three-level heading* in APA form is:

Review of the Literature (Level 1)

Introduction (Level 3)
Social support. People band together in work units. . . . (Level 4)

You will often see Level 5 (centered and uppercase) in titles to research studies, regardless of the levels of headings in the study. Also, in journal articles, the Level 1 heading "Introduction" is often deleted and the text moves from the title into the discussion. In more formal research reports such as theses and dissertations, the first heading is often a Level 1 "Introduction" head. (See chapter 10 section on "What Are the Types of Research Reports?" for more detail about the forms of reports.) In sum, headings are not easy to describe, and they need to be short—typically two or three words—and state exactly and succinctly the content of the passage that follows.

FIGURE 4.10

Headings in APA Fifth Edition Style

CENTERED UPPERCASE HEADING (Level 5)

Centered Uppercase and Lowercase Heading (Level 1)

Centered, Italicized, Uppercase and Lowercase Heading (Level 2)

Flush left, Italicized, Uppercase and Lowercase Side Heading (Level 3)

Indented, italicized, lowercase paragraph heading ending with a period (Level 4)

Writing Strategies

As you write a literature review, several additional elements will need your attention: the extent of the review, the type of review, and the concluding statement of the review.

Extent of the Review One question Maria asked her advisor was "How long should my literature review be?" There is no easy answer to this question, but you can begin by considering the type of research report you are writing (see chapter 10 section on "What Are the Types of Research Reports?"). For dissertations and theses, you need an extensive review of the literature, which often comprehensively includes all sources of information identified in the classification of resources in Figure 4.2. For research plans or proposals, a less than comprehensive literature review may suffice. The literature review in proposals or plans for a study establishes the framework for a study and documents the importance of the research problem. Typically, literature reviews for proposals run from 10 to 30 pages in length, although this can vary. A proposal literature review summarizes the citations obtained from searching databases such as ERIC, PsycINFO, EBSCO, and Sociofile. For a journal article, the extent of the literature review varies, depending on its use and role in the study (as noted earlier).

Also related to the *extent* of the literature review is the question "How far back in the literature do my references need to go?" When completing a dissertation or thesis, the search covers most published literature and the author examines sources back to the inception of the research topic. For research proposals and journal articles (and preliminary reviews), use as a rough guide the last 10 years, focusing on the more recent studies. An exception is to cite an earlier, classical study because it substantially influences subsequent literature published in the last decade.

Types of Literature Reviews At this point you will need to determine how to actually structure the summaries or notes taken on the articles and studies in the literature. The organization of the summaries varies depending on the type of research report and the traditions for literature reviews on different campuses. When writing a literature review for a dissertation or thesis, you might visit with an advisor to determine the appropriate format to use. However, the two models presented here—the thematic review and the study-by-study review—will serve you well. (See Cooper, 1984, and Cooper & Lindsay, 1998, for additional approaches.)

In a **thematic review of the literature,** the researcher identifies a theme and briefly cites literature to document this theme. In this approach, the author discusses only the major ideas or results from studies rather than the detail of any single study. Authors use this approach frequently in journal articles, but students also use it for dissertations and theses in graduate programs. You can identify this form by locating a theme and noting the references (typically multiple references) to the literature used to support the theme.

For example, in a study by Brown, Parham, and Yonker (1996), the authors reviewed the literature about racial identity development of White counselors-in-training in a course on racial identity attitudes of White women and men. This passage, appearing in an early section in the study, illustrates a thematic approach:

> Among other things, racial identity is a sense of group belonging based on the perception of a shared racial heritage with a specific group and, as such, it has an impact on personal feelings and attitudes concerning distinguishable racial groups (Helms, 1990; 1994; Mitchell & Dell, 1992). Researchers agree that White Americans generally are not challenged to ask themselves, "What does it mean to be White?" (Pope-Davis & Ottavi, 1994). . . . (p. 511)

In this case, the authors review the literature about the theme "racial identity" and briefly mention references to support the theme. The authors do not discuss each reference separately and in detail.

In contrast to a thematic review, the **study-by-study review of the literature** provides a detailed summary of each study grouped under a broad theme. This detailed summary includes the elements of an abstract shown in Figures 4.6 and 4.7. This form of review typically appears in journal articles that summarize the literature and in dissertations and theses. When presenting a study-by-study review, authors link summaries (or abstracts) by using transitional sentences, and they organize the summaries under subheadings that reflect themes and major divisions. Using the literature map concept discussed earlier in this chapter, these themes are the topics identified in boxes in the map (see Figure 4.8).

The following review of the literature about cross-cultural competency and multicultural education in the journal *Review of Educational Research* by McAllister and Irvine (2000) illustrates a study-by-study review. Here, the authors discuss the research one study at a time that addresses Helms's racial identity model.

> S. P. Brown, Parham, and Yonker (1996) employed the White Racial Identity Scale to measure change in the white racial identity of thirty-five white graduate students who participated in a sixteen-week multicultural course. Eighty percent of the participants had previous multicultural training and most of them had had experiences with people from at least two different racial backgrounds, though the nature of these experiences is not defined. The authors designed the course based on three areas—acquisition of self knowledge, cultural knowledge, and cross-cultural skills—and they used a variety of teaching methods such as lectures, talks by guest speakers, and simulations. Results indicated that at the end of the course women endorsed more items than men did in the pseudo-independence stage on the White Racial Identity Scale, and men endorsed more items than women did in the autonomy stage. The authors draw a causal relationship between the course and those changes found in the group.
>
> Neville, Heppner, Louie, and Thompson (1996) also examined the change in White racial identity as well. . . . (p. 8)

In this example, the authors first described the study by S. P. Brown et al. (1996) in some detail, then they described the study by Neville et al. (1996). In this way, they discussed one study at a time. They also provided a detailed description of the study to include the research problem (whether the scale measures change), an implied question (whether men and women differ on the scale), the data collection (i.e., 35 participants in the study), and a summary of the results (men and women endorse items differently depending on their stage of development).

Concluding Statement of the Review How do you end a literature review section in a study? The concluding statement of a literature review serves several purposes. It summarizes the major themes found in the literature and it provides a rationale for the need for your study or the importance of the research problem.

First, summarize the major themes. Ask yourself, "What are the major results and findings from all of the studies I have reviewed?" Your answer to this question will result in the identification of three or four themes that summarize the literature. Then, briefly summarize each theme. The summaries should emphasize the major ideas under each major heading in the literature review and highlight what the reader needs to remember from the summary of the review.

Besides stating the major themes in a review, you also need to suggest reasons why the current literature is deficient and why educators need additional research on your topic. These reasons address ways the proposed study will add to knowledge, and they justify the importance of the research problem. Typically, writers mention three or four reasons that play a significant role in research because they often lead into the purpose statement, research questions, and hypotheses (to be addressed in the next chapter).

The example below illustrates both the summary of themes and the author's justification of the need for additional research.

> The factors influencing faculty to be productive researchers found in the literature suggest three themes: early productivity (Did faculty begin publishing early in their careers?); mentoring (Did faculty apprentice under a distinguished researcher?); and support systems (Did faculty have adequate funding for their research?). These factors, although important, do not address the time faculty need to conduct research. When faculty have allotted time for scientific investigations and inquiries, it helps to focus their attention, offers sustained momentum for research, and removes distracting activities that may draw their attention away from research.

In this example, the author states three themes and, from these themes, identifies an area for future research: faculty time. Then, the author identifies three reasons for the importance of the study of faculty time.

REEXAMINING THE PARENT INVOLVEMENT AND THE GUNMAN CASE STUDIES

In both the quantitative parent involvement study (Deslandes & Bertrand, 2005) and the qualitative gunman incident study (Asmussen & Creswell, 1995), the authors begin their articles by citing literature from other studies. As you have learned in this chapter, you can identify this literature by noting when the researchers cite an author and a year. For example, see the reference to "Henderson & Mapp, 2002" (Paragraph 01) in the parent involvement study or an author and number indicating a reference at the end of the article, such as "Roark [24] and Roark and Roark [25]" in the gunman case study (Paragraph 01). Let's take a closer look at the two studies and examine their use of the literature.

Literature Review Analysis in a Quantitative Study

In the *quantitative* parent involvement study (Deslandes & Bertrand, 2005), the citations to the literature cluster around the beginning and the end of the article. In the opening, Paragraph 01, the authors cite studies to document the importance of the problem: the need for parent involvement in their children's educational processes at home and at school. Then, in Paragraph 02, the authors explain that a model exists in the literature that might explain parent involvement —the Hoover-Dempsey and Sandler model. They also present research questions consistent with factors in this model that are expected to influence parent involvement: parents' role construction, parents' self-efficacy, perceptions of teacher invitations, and perceptions of adolescent invitations. You need to see how the authors identify, earlier in the article, the four primary factors that will be the focus of the study. The paragraphs to follow (03–10), merely summarize the literature on each of these four factors. Paragraph 03 begins with an overview of many possible factors that might influence parent involvement. Then Paragraphs 04–08 review the literature on each of the four factors. In Paragraph 09, the authors reflect on the relative importance of each of the four factors when measured together, and Paragraph 10 introduces the idea that grade level will influence parent outcomes and thereby anticipates this element being introduced into the study. Then, when you see Paragraph 13, which is the intent or purpose of the study, it makes sense because we now know that four factors and grade level will be of primary importance in this study. Finally, the authors return again to the literature in Paragraphs 34–43, in which they first state their major results and then compare their results to findings suggested by authors in the literature as well as the theory mentioned at the beginning of the article.

In summary, the literature in the parent involvement study:

- Documents the importance of the research problem at the beginning of the study
- Provides evidence for important components of the model to be tested
- Provides evidence for the research questions
- Provides an explanation for the results at the end of the study by citing other studies and by returning to the theoretical predictions

Literature Review Analysis in a Qualitative Study

Now let's turn to a qualitative study to see the role of the literature. In the *qualitative* gunman case study (Asmussen & Creswell, 1995), the literature serves some of the same purposes and some different purposes than did the literature in the quantitative study. Like the parent involvemant study, the authors also begin their article by citing literature to document the research problem of campus violence. They use the literature sparingly, however, citing only 10 references in the first two paragraphs (see Paragraphs 01 and 02). Literature in qualitative research is used much less than in quantitative research, which is rather typical. Their research questions at the end of the introduction (Paragraph 03) did not follow from this literature. Rather, the questions are general and open ended so the researchers can learn from the participants in the study. Then, they cite the literature again in the "Discussion" section at the end of the article (see Paragraphs 32–36). At this point, the authors use literature to discuss how their themes both reinforce and depart from findings in past research (Paragraph 33), a procedure commonly used in qualitative research.

In summary, the literature in the qualitative gunman case study:

- Documents the importance of the research problem at the beginning of the study
- Does not foreshadow the research questions (which are broad in scope to encourage participants to provide their views)
- Is used to compare and contrast with other studies at the end of the study

KEY IDEAS IN THE CHAPTER

A literature review is a written summary of articles, books, and other documents that describes the past and current state of knowledge about a topic, organizes the literature into topics, and documents a need for a proposed study. This review serves the purpose of providing a need for a study and demonstrating that other studies have not addressed the same topic in exactly the same way. It also indicates to audiences that the researcher is knowledgeable about studies related to a topic.

Literature reviews are different in quantitative and qualitative research. In quantitative research, investigators provide a detailed review of the literature to justify the major purpose and research questions of a study. In qualitative research, the inquirers use a limited amount of literature in the beginning of the study to allow participant views, rather than perspectives from the literature, to play a major role in the study. The literature is cited again at the end of studies in both quantitative and qualitative research, but its use is again different. In quantitative research, the literature at the end compares results with prior predictions made at the beginning of the research. In qualitative research, researchers use the literature at the end to compare and contrast findings in the study with past literature.

Designing and conducting a literature review involves five interrelated steps. First, researchers identify key terms to use in their search of the literature. They look for these terms in titles, research questions, or the ERIC *Thesaurus*. Next, researchers locate literature in library resources such as summaries, books, journal publications and electronic sources, and early stage literature.

After locating the literature, the researcher then critically evaluates the materials and makes a determination of its relevance for use. Criteria for evaluating materials consist of assessing the quality of the publications and the rigor of the research as well as examining the relevance of the topic for a study.

Researchers next obtain the literature, take notes or create abstracts of it, and organize it into a visual rendering of the literature, called a literature map. This map helps to organize past literature as well as portray how a proposed study fits into the overall literature.

The final step is actually writing the literature review. Writing strategies at this point include using appropriate style manual formats and developing headings for the written literature review. Researchers need to consider the extent or length of the review for different types of research reports. The type of review will also vary, depending on the type of report. For journal articles, dissertations, and theses, a thematic literature review summarizes the literature by themes. For reviews of literature on topics for some journals and for dissertations and theses, a study-by-study approach presents each study in detail, highlighting the major elements of each one.

Researchers conclude a literature review by summarizing major themes and presenting reasons for a proposed study or the importance of studying a research problem. These reasons lead to a rationale for a study that builds naturally into the purpose statement and research questions or hypotheses.

Useful Information for Producers of Research

- Use the five-step process explained in this chapter for designing and conducting a literature review.
- Consider the different strategies for selecting key terms: choosing words from the project's title, selecting words from a brief question asked in the study, and using online databases.
- Begin a search of the literature with the most easily accessible material, such as published research studies reported in journals. Use the CD-ROMs in the library or the ERIC system or other database Web sites to search for literature.
- Begin with the ERIC database before using other databases to locate useful educational literature.
- Develop some means for organizing the literature you find, such as a filing system or a graphic rendering of the literature into groupings on a literature map.
- Realize that not every source you locate may provide relevant information for your literature review. To determine which to use, remember these four criteria: the relevance of the topic, the individuals or sites, the problem, and the accessibility of the information.
- Abstract studies before you begin to write the literature review. These abstracts provide a useful summary of studies and can be included in your review. Be sure to include all of the elements that go into a good abstract. (Refer back to Figures 4.6 and 4.7 for models.)
- Use an accepted style manual such as the APA *Publication Manual,* fifth edition, for the end-of-text and within-text references as well as for the headings in your literature review. Avoid the temptation to jot down a citation any old way.

Writing citations in APA-accepted form will save you many hours of extra work later. For most educational research reports, a two- or three-level heading format will suffice.

- Keep your literature review succinct and short. Decide whether a thematic or a study-by-study review is appropriate for your research report. Consider the type of review typically used by audiences for your report.
- Conclude your literature review with a summary of the major themes. Also, discuss how the literature is deficient and how your study adds to the literature.

Useful Information for Consumers of Research

- Recognize that a literature review in a research report will contain many types of literature. Literature syntheses provide a broad summary of research. Books are less valuable as research guides, but they may report useful research. The most popular sources for literature reviews are journal articles. Other research literature is available in publications from conferences. Of less value is research posted to Web sites because reviewers may not have evaluated it for quality.
- Do not assume that all literature cited by an author in a report contains good and valid information. Researchers need to choose the literature to include in a review selectively. Apply the evaluation criteria for relevance found in this chapter to determine whether an author used relevant literature.
- As you evaluate a study, consider whether the author has made a good case that the study adds to existing knowledge. The study should explicitly specify how and in what way it adds to knowledge. A visual literature map of sources of information helps to convey the author's case.
- A research study should employ a consistent form for reporting references to the literature, both in the text as well as at the end of the report. In addition, the headings should be easy to identify and be descriptive of the passage that follows.

Understanding Concepts and Evaluating Research Studies

1. Assume that you wish to conduct a literature review on the topic of the increasing incidence of teenage pregnancies in high schools today. What two or three words would you use to search for research on this topic using the ERIC database?
2. Run a search on your topic using one of the online databases (e.g., ERIC, PsycINFO, EBSCO). What criteria would you use to examine the quality of the articles that you find in your search?
3. Using a reference that emerged from your online database search in #2, write a correct APA (fifth edition) end-of-text reference for the literature citation.

Conducting Your Research

Practice conducting a literature review using the educational topic you chose in chapter 3. Go through the five steps in conducting a literature review, ending with a brief literature review of one or two articles: (a) *Identify key terms* to use in your search for literature; (b) *Locate literature* about a topic by consulting several types of materials and databases, including those available at an academic library and on the Internet; (c) *Critically evaluate and select* the literature for your review; (d) *Organize the literature* you have selected by abstracting or taking notes on the literature and developing a visual diagram of it; and (e) *Write a review* that reports summaries of the literature.

Go to our Companion Website at **www.prenhall.com/creswell** to:

- assess your understanding of chapter content with Multiple-Choice Questions,
- apply what you've learned with Essay Questions,
- practice your research skills with interactive Building Research Skills exercises, and
- broaden your knowledge of research with Web Links to research topics on the Internet.

CHAPTER 5

Specifying a Purpose and Research Questions or Hypotheses

Purpose statements, research questions, and hypotheses provide critical information to readers about the direction of a research study. They also raise questions that the research will answer through the data-collection process. As such, they deserve special attention. In this chapter you will learn about purpose statements, research questions, and hypotheses and how to write them for both quantitative and qualitative research.

By the end of this chapter, you should be able to:

- Distinguish among purpose statements, research questions, hypotheses, and objectives.
- Define the nature of a variable and the types of variables in quantitative research.
- Define a theory and its test using variables.
- Write quantitative purpose statements, research questions, and hypotheses.
- Identify similarities and differences between quantitative and qualitative purpose statements and research questions.
- Define a central phenomenon in qualitative research.
- Describe the emerging design process in qualitative research.
- Write qualitative purpose statements and research questions.

Maria completes her literature review on school violence and writes down a statement that represents the central direction of her study: "I would like to study the reasons why students carry weapons in high schools." This is an example of a quantitative research statement. Alternatively, she could write a qualitative statement: "I would like to study students' experiences with weapons in high school." For her research study at the university, Maria needs to write a statement that advances the overall intent of her study, a purpose statement, as well as research questions. The form of her purpose statement and her questions will reflect her decision to engage in quantitative or qualitative research.

WHAT ARE PURPOSE STATEMENTS, RESEARCH QUESTIONS, HYPOTHESES, AND OBJECTIVES?

Let's begin by defining four terms used in research to convey the intent of a study: *purpose statements, research questions, research hypotheses,* and *research objectives.* These forms differ in intent (their role in research), form (their appearance in studies), use (their application in quantitative and qualitative approaches), and placement (their location) in research reports. Knowing these differences can help you design, write, and evaluate them. Figure 5.1 illustrates the differences among these forms.

The Purpose Statement

The **purpose statement** is a statement that advances the overall direction or focus for the study. Researchers describe the purpose of a study in one or more succinctly formed sentences. It is used both in quantitative and qualitative research and is typically found in the "statement of the problem" section as discussed in chapter 3. It often appears as the last sentence of an introduction. You can recognize it because researchers typically state it beginning with the phrase "The purpose of this study is. . . ." A *quantitative* version of this purpose statement addressing teacher–parent communications and student achievement follows:

> The purpose of this study is to examine the relationship between use of Internet communication between teachers and parents in a Midwestern school district and student achievement on tests in high school social studies.

A *qualitative* version might be:

> The purpose of this study is to explore parent stories regarding Internet communications with teachers about their students in one Midwestern school district.

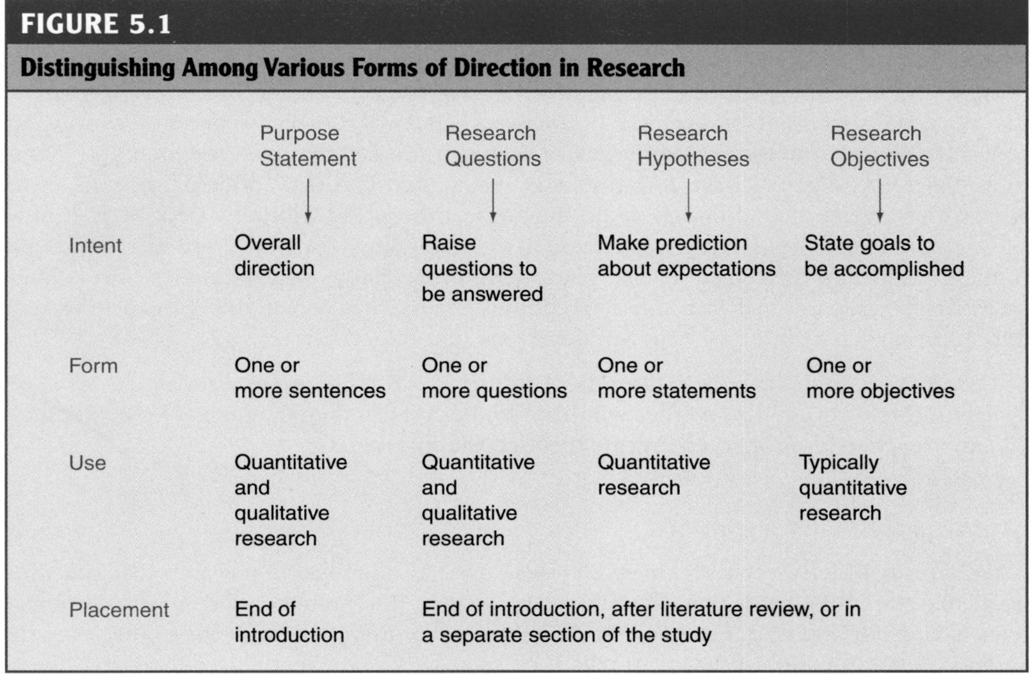

FIGURE 5.1

Distinguishing Among Various Forms of Direction in Research

	Purpose Statement	Research Questions	Research Hypotheses	Research Objectives
Intent	Overall direction	Raise questions to be answered	Make prediction about expectations	State goals to be accomplished
Form	One or more sentences	One or more questions	One or more statements	One or more objectives
Use	Quantitative and qualitative research	Quantitative and qualitative research	Quantitative research	Typically quantitative research
Placement	End of introduction	End of introduction, after literature review, or in a separate section of the study		

Research Questions

Research questions are questions in quantitative or qualitative research that narrow the purpose statement to specific questions that researchers seek to answer. Researchers typically develop them before identifying the methods of the study (i.e., the types of data to be collected, analyzed, and interpreted in a study). Unlike the single statement found in a purpose statement, researchers typically state multiple research questions so that they can fully explore a topic. Research questions are found in both quantitative and qualitative research, but their elements differ depending on the type of research you are conducting.

In quantitative research, the questions relate attributes or characteristics of individuals or organizations. Later in the chapter you will learn that these are called *variables*. In qualitative research, the questions include the central concept being explored. You will learn that this central concept is called a *central phenomenon*. In some studies, both research questions and purpose statements appear—a good presentation style to clarify both the general and specific directions of a study. The research questions are typically at the end of the introduction of the "statement of the problem" section or immediately following the review of the literature. To locate research questions, you might look for opening passages in which authors identify the research questions they are addressing (e.g., Paragraph 02, Deslandes & Bertrand, 2005). For example, a *quantitative* research question would be:

> Do parent–teacher Internet communications affect student performance in the classroom?

A *qualitative* research question is:

> What types of Internet experiences do parents have with teachers about the performance of the parents' children?

Hypotheses

Hypotheses are statements in quantitative research in which the investigator makes a prediction or a conjecture about the outcome of a relationship among attributes or characteristics. Traditionally used in experiments, they serve, like research questions, to narrow the purpose statement to specific predictions. These predictions are not simply an "educated guess." Rather, researchers base them on results from past research and literature where investigators have found certain results and can now offer predictions as to what other investigators will find when they repeat the study with new people or at new sites. You will find these hypotheses stated at the beginning of a study, typically at the end of the introduction. Investigators also place them immediately after the review of the literature or in a separate section titled "Hypotheses." Usually researchers advance several hypotheses, such as three or four. An illustration of a hypothesis is:

> Students in high schools in the school district in which parents and teachers communicate through the Internet will have higher grades than students whose parents and teachers do not communicate through the Internet.

Research Objectives

A **research objective** is a statement of intent used in quantitative research that specifies goals that the investigator plans to achieve in a study. Researchers often subdivide objectives into major and minor objectives. They appear frequently in survey or questionnaire studies or in evaluation research in which investigators have clearly identified objectives.

Like hypotheses and research questions, objectives are found at the end of the "statement of the problem" section, after the literature review, or in a separate section of the study. You can identify objectives by looking for phrases such as "The objectives in this study are. . . ." For instance, the following represent objectives for a study:

1. To describe the frequency of Internet communication between parents and teachers regarding the parents' children in high school social studies classes
2. To describe the types (or categories) of Internet communication between parents and teachers
3. To relate (a) frequency and (b) types of communication to student achievement in the class as measured by performance on tests

Because of the limited use of research objectives in educational research today, our focus in this chapter is on hypotheses and research questions as a means of narrowing and focusing purpose statements.

WHY ARE THESE STATEMENTS AND QUESTIONS IMPORTANT?

These statements are signposts similar to a thesis statement or objectives in term papers you may have written. Without clear signposts, the readers will be lost throughout your study. They simply will not know the central ideas addressed in your study. You can also identify the most appropriate methods for collecting data from the purpose and the questions. They also provide key components for understanding the results of a project. Good research links the purpose statement and questions to major results. To write good purpose statements and research questions, we will begin with some concepts that you need to know, and then begin to establish the building blocks for writing these statements and questions into a study.

HOW DO YOU DESIGN QUANTITATIVE PURPOSE STATEMENTS, RESEARCH QUESTIONS, AND HYPOTHESES?

To write quantitative purpose statements, research questions, and hypotheses, you need to understand the importance and use of variables. We start with their definition, talk about the various types used in quantitative research, and then discuss their use in broad theories or explanations.

Specify Variables

A **variable** is a characteristic or attribute of an individual or an organization that (a) researchers can measure or observe and (b) varies among individuals or organizations studied (see Figure 5.2). They are key ideas that researchers seek to collect information on to address the purpose of their study.

Consider the following examples of variables typically studied in educational research:

- Leadership style (by administrators)
- Achievement in science (by students)
- Interpersonal communication skills (of counselors)

Let's break this definition down for close inspection.

FIGURE 5.2

A Variable Can Be Measured, and it Varies Among Individuals

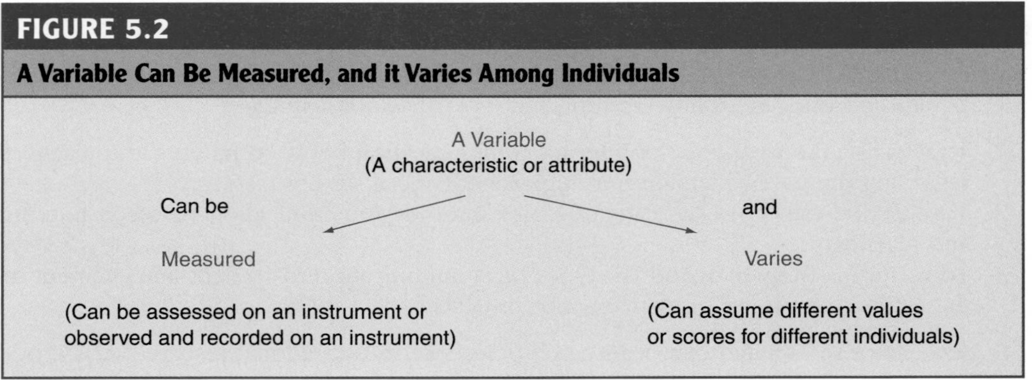

Characteristics of individuals refer to personal aspects about them, such as their grade level, age, or income level. An attribute, however, represents how an individual or individuals in an organization feel, behave, or think. For example, individuals have self-esteem, engage in smoking, or display the leadership behavior of being well organized. You can measure these attributes in a study. To practice, you might take out a sheet of paper and write down three personal characteristics and three attributes about your favorite teacher.

Next, consider what it means to "measure" these attributes or characteristics. **Measurement** means that the researcher records information from individuals in one of two ways:

- Asking them to answer questions on a questionnaire (e.g., a student completes questions on a survey asking about self-esteem)
- Observing an individual and recording scores on a log or checklist (e.g., a researcher watches a student playing basketball and records scores on dribbling techniques)

In either case, student scores will probably *vary,* (hence the name *variable*). When variables vary, it means that scores will assume different values depending on the type of variable being measured. For example,

- Gender varies by two possible scores: female = 2 and male = 1.
- Self-esteem varies by three possible scores: positive = 3, neither positive nor negative = 2, and negative = 1.

In the quantitative parent involvement study (Deslandes & Bertrand, 2005), the authors, for example, measured parents' role construction (see Paragraph 18), the extent to which parents believed that it was their responsibility to help the school educate their adolescent. The authors asked parents to rate on a 6-point scale from "disagree very strongly" to "agree very strongly" statements such as "It's important that I let someone at school know about things that concern my teenager" (p. 167).

Distinguish Between Variables Measured as Categories and as Continuous Scores

When participants in a study complete a question, the researcher assigns a score to their response (e.g., 5 for *strongly agree*). This score is a value for the variable being measured, and investigators measure variables using continuous and categorical scores. Knowing this classification will help you understand the different types of variables and their use in purpose statements, research questions, and hypotheses.

Researchers score variables by grouping them into a limited number of categories or by using them to represent a value of some degree on a continuum, ranging from low to high levels (Gall, Borg, & Gall, 1996; Vogt, 1999). A **variable measured in categories** is a variable measured by the researcher as a small number of groups or categories. In research, authors sometimes call this type of measure a *discrete* or *nominal* score, and it is illustrated by these examples:

- *Groups of students:* males (1) and females (2), or low ability (1) and high ability (2)
- *Types of instruction:* groups of students who experience lectures (1), groups of students who experience discussion (2), and groups of students who experience classroom activities (3)

A second type of score is based on measuring scores along a continuum. A **variable measured as continuous** is a variable measured by the researcher on a point along a continuum of scores, from low to high scores. Sometimes authors call this type of scoring an *interval,* a *rating,* or a *scaled* score. The most typical example of a continuous score would be age (e.g., from 25 years old to 65 years old) or height (e.g., from 5 feet to 6 feet tall). Often, continuous scores indicate the extent to which individuals agree or disagree with an idea or rate the level of importance of an issue.

Distinguish Variables from Constructs

Some attributes, such as "socialization," cannot be measured because they are too abstract. Some characteristics, such as "whether the children engage in thinking in the classroom," do not vary among people. Certainly all children think; what varies is how they think differently, such as when they engage in the activity of writing. A **construct** is an attribute or characteristic expressed in an abstract, general way; a variable is an attribute or characteristic stated in a specific, applied way. For example, student achievement is a construct, while the more specific term *grade point average* is a variable. The trend in educational research is to use variables rather than constructs in purpose statements, research questions, and hypotheses. In this text we will use variables.

The Family of Variables

With these definitions in mind, we can now discuss the different types of variables incorporated into quantitative purpose statements, research questions, and hypotheses. Understanding the "family of variables" requires learning the definition of each type of variable and understanding its role in providing direction for a study.

This "family" is shown in Figure 5.3. In this discussion you will learn about each type of variable listed in this figure, starting with the most important variables: the dependent, independent, and intervening variables. As shown in this figure, a useful way to think about organizing these variables is to consider them in a cause-and-effect relationship (Tuckman, 1999). What variables influence outcomes? Ask yourself:

1. What outcomes in my study am I trying to explain? (the dependent variables)
2. What variables or factors influence the outcomes? (the independent variables)
3. What variables do I need to also measure (i.e., control) so that I can make sure that my major factors influence outcomes and not other factors? (the control variables and the mediating variables)
4. What variables might influence the outcomes but cannot or will not be measured? (the confounding variables)

FIGURE 5.3

The Family of Variables in Quantitative Studies

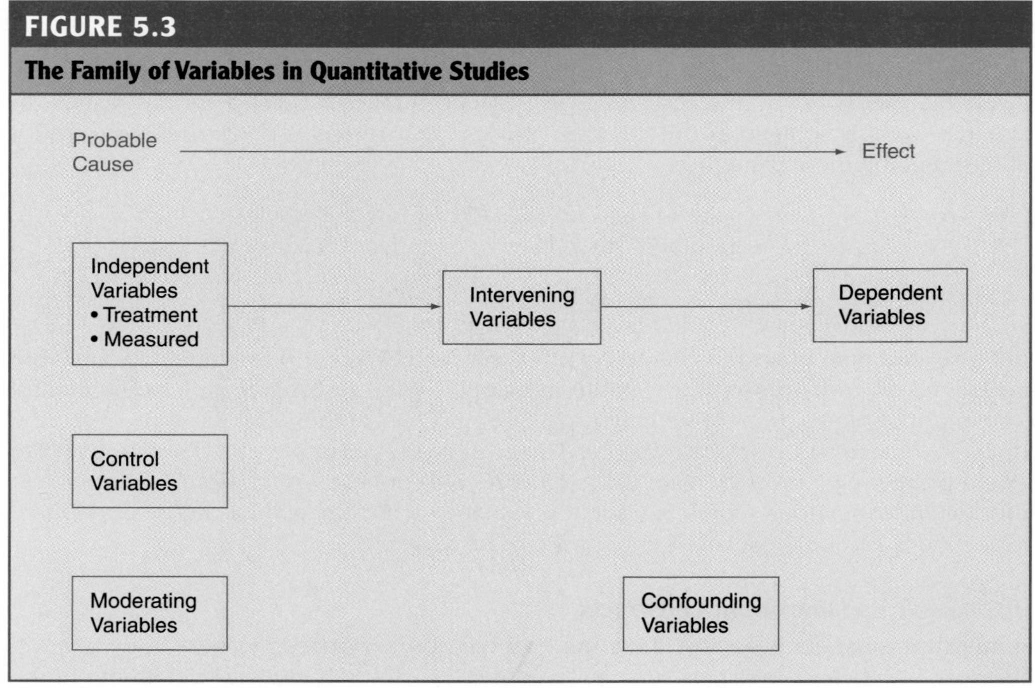

Consider a fender bender car accident as an example. The outcome (dependent variable) was that you hit another car at a stop sign—rammed right into the back of it. You caused this fender bender because you were talking on your cell phone (independent variable). It might have been caused by the slick pavement (control variable), but the skies were sunny and it had not rained for days. The fact that you had daydreamed might have caused the accident (confounding variable), but this fact would be difficult to measure after the accident. See how this works? Now take another situation in your life this last week, and list the dependent, independent, control, and confounding variables in your own cause-and-effect situation.

Dependent Variables

Now we will go into variables in some more depth. Look at Figure 5.3. On the right-hand side are the dependent variables. A **dependent variable** is an attribute or characteristic that is dependent on or influenced by the independent variable. You may find them labeled in the literature as the *outcome, effect, criterion,* or *consequence variables.* Researchers typically investigate multiple dependent variables in a single study (e.g., you hit another car, the other car hit the car in front of it, and so forth), although in many studies, one of the dependent variables is typically of central interest. Dependent variables can be measured using continuous or categorical scores.

Examples of dependent variables in education are achievement scores on a test, the organizational climate of a junior high school, the leadership skills of principals, or the cost effectiveness of student affairs programs in colleges. To locate dependent variables in a study, examine purpose statements, research questions, and hypotheses for outcomes that the researcher wishes to predict or explain. Ask yourself, "What is the outcome in this study?"

Independent Variables

On the left side of Figure 5.3 are the independent variables. An **independent variable** is an attribute or characteristic that influences or affects an outcome or dependent variable. In Figure 5.3, the arrows show how the independent variable influences the dependent variable through the intervening variable. Sometimes an intervening variable exists in a research study, and sometimes it does not. In research studies, you will find the independent variables called *factors, treatments, predictors, determinants,* or *antecedent variables.* Regardless of name, researchers measure this type of variable distinctly (or independently) from the dependent variable, and they identify these variables as worthy of study because they expect them to influence the outcomes.

Researchers study independent variables to see what effect or influence they have on the outcome. For instance, consider this research question:

> Do students who spend more instructional time in class on math have higher math scores than students who spend less time?
>
> Independent variable: Time on math instruction
> Dependent variable: Math scores

As shown in Table 5.1, there are four types of independent variables, and each serves a slightly different purpose.

TABLE 5.1

Four Types of Independent Variables

	Measured Variable	Control Variable	Treatment Variable	Moderating Variable
Definition	An independent variable that is measured in a study	A special type of independent variable that is of secondary interest and is neutralized through statistical or design procedures	An independent variable manipulated by the researcher	A special type of independent variable that is of secondary interest and combines with another independent variable to influence the dependent variable
Type of Variable Measurement	A categorical or continuous variable that is measured or observed in the study	A variable not directly measured but controlled through statistical or research design procedures	A categorical variable actively manipulated by the researcher and composed of two or more groups	A categorical or continuous variable measured or observed as it interacts with other variables
Use in	Experiments, surveys	Experiments, correlational studies	Experiments	Experiments
Examples	Age of a child; performance on a test; attitudes assessed on a survey	Often demographic variables such as age, gender, race socioeconomic level	Classroom learning: one group receives standard lecture and one group receives discussion; researcher assigns students to groups and thus manipulates group membership	Demographic variable such as age, gender, race, or socioeconomic level, a measured variable such as performance or attitude, or a manipulated variable such as classroom instruction

Measured Variables The standard independent variable influences the outcome and is measured by the researcher. A **measured variable** is an independent variable that is measured or observed by the researcher and consists of a range of continuous or categorical scores. For example, consider the following research question:

> How does math ability influence achievement on the final quiz in the classroom?

The independent variable is a measured variable indicating math ability scores assessed by results on an ability test.

Control Variables A control variable is another type of independent variable that researchers measure for the purposes of eliminating it as a possibility, but it is not a central variable of concern in explaining the dependent variables or outcomes. A **control variable** is a variable that is important to consider and "neutralize" (Tuckman, 1999, p. 100) because it potentially influences the dependent variable. Typically, control variables are personal demographic attributes or characteristics (Tuckman, 1999) such as:

- Gender
- Socioeconomic status
- Intelligence
- Race

These variables are typically controlled through statistical procedures. Later we will learn that these variables are called *covariates* and they are statistically adjusted for their effects (see chapter 7 section "Select a Statistical Program").

Treatment Variables Two other specific types of independent variables can be introduced here because they will be used in educational experiments. In an experiment, a researcher treats one group of participants to specific activities and withholds them from another group. The question is whether the group that receives the activities scores differently on the dependent variable than the group without the activities. Because researchers assign individuals to these two groups, the groups are "treated" or "manipulated" by the researcher. A **treatment variable** is measured in categories (received or denied activities) to determine its effect on an outcome. In the literature you will find these variables labeled as *manipulated* variables or variables with *levels*. Experimental researchers refer to these groups as *levels* (i.e., Group 1, Group 2).

In the following example, the treatment variable is the type of instruction used by the teacher in an elementary math classroom:

> In a study of student achievement outcomes in an elementary math classroom, the researcher gives one group small-group discussion (Level 1) and another traditional group lecture (Level 2) to assess the independent variable, type of instruction.
>
> Independent treatment variable: Type of instruction is considered a treatment variable because the researcher intervenes with one group, Level 1.

Moderating Variables Moderating variables deserve our attention because they, too, are often used in educational experiments. **Moderating variables** are new variables constructed by the researcher by taking one variable times another to determine the joint impact of both variables together. This impact is called an *interaction effect* and you will learn more about it in chapter 11. For now, recognize that interaction effects are a special form of independent variable. A moderating variable can be illustrated in this quantitative hypothesis:

> Small-group discussion for students with high prior test scores contributes to higher math quiz results than lecture discussion for students with low prior test scores.

To test this statement, the researcher takes prior test scores (independent variable) times type of discussion (small group or lecture) to determine the joint effects of both variables on math quiz results.

Locating Independent Variables Independent variables are located in purpose statements, research questions, and hypotheses. To find them, look for the variable that exercises influence or predicts an outcome. They may be described in categories or on a continuous scale of scores. They may also be of primary interest (measured variables), controlled in a study (control variables), or have specific application to experiments (treatment variables and moderating variables).

Intervening Variables

Intervening variables are different from dependent variables or any of the types of independent variables. Look at Figure 5.3 one more time. Using cause-and-effect thinking, factors sometime intervene between the independent variable and the dependent one to influence the outcomes. An **intervening variable** is an attribute or characteristic that "stands between" the independent and dependent variables and exercises an influence on the dependent variable apart from the independent variable. Intervening variables transmit (or mediate) the effects of the independent variable on the dependent variable. Thus, they are also called *mediating variables*. In some quantitative studies, intervening variables are controlled using statistical procedures.

To demonstrate how intervening variables work, consider the logic of the sequence of variables shown in Figure 5.4. In this illustration, we first see that convenient office hours for students influences whether students will seek help from faculty (Step 1). However, this situation on most college campuses is too basic. Many factors besides office hours influence student visits with faculty. Convenient office hours convey an open attitude toward students, and they show that faculty members care about their students. They also encourage shy and reserved students who are unable to speak up in class to visit privately with faculty. Students are willing to take risks by visiting with faculty privately in their offices (Step 2). What began as a single factor explaining the help students seek from faculty has now become more complex. When faculty members offer

FIGURE 5.4

Intervening Variables "Stand Between" Independent and Dependent Variables

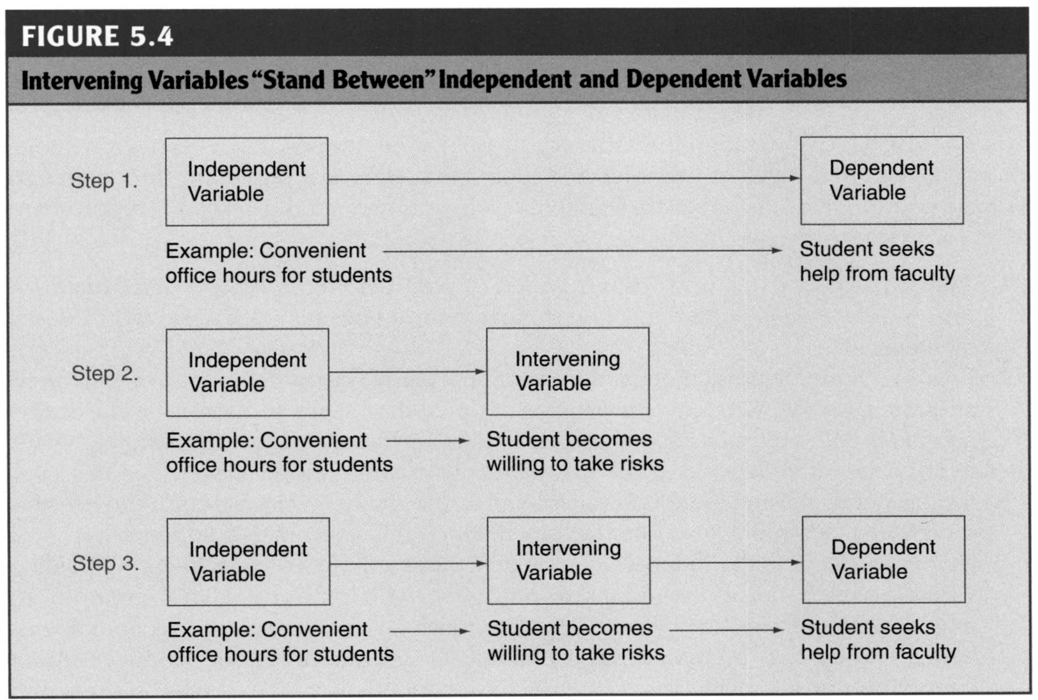

convenient office hours, students become willing to take risks, and they seek help from faculty (Step 3). As an intervening variable, a willingness to take risks is influenced by convenient office hours, and this, in turn, influences whether that student will seek help from a faculty member.

To locate mediating variables in purpose statements, research hypotheses, or questions:

- Ask yourself if any variables stand between the independent and dependent variables in a left-to-right sequence of events.
- In these statements or questions, look for the words *mediate* or *intervene*. These words provide a cue that the researcher intends to consider them as important influences on the dependent variable.
- Go into the "Results" section and look at the statistical analysis of the data to determine if the researcher statistically controls for variables that may stand between the independent and dependent variables.

Confounding Variables

The final variable listed in Figure 5.3 is the confounding variable. In this illustration, confounding variables are not directly in the probable cause-and-effect sequence but are extraneous or uncontrolled variables. **Confounding variables** (sometimes called *spurious variables*) are attributes or characteristics that the researcher cannot directly measure because their effects cannot be easily separated from those of other variables, even though they may influence the relation between the independent and the dependent variable. For example, for a high school student it may be impossible to separate an individual's race and prior discriminatory experiences as predictors of attitudes toward school. Thus, researchers measure the variables they can easily identify (e.g., race) and explain a limitation on their results (e.g., race was so interconnected with discriminatory experiences that it could not be easily separated as an independent measure).

Think-Aloud About Identifying Variables

It is not always easy to identify variables in published studies, even with knowledge about the different types of variables and their roles. Here is a procedure I recommend to help you identify and organize variables to best understand a research report or to plan your own study.

1. Take a piece of paper and write from left to right the words *independent, intervening,* and *dependent variables.* Draw straight vertical lines between these words down the page.
2. Begin with the dependent variable. Examine a study (or consider your own project) and ask yourself: What are the outcomes the author seeks to explain in the study? Look at the title, purpose statement, questions, or hypotheses for this variable. Place the dependent variable(s) under that particular column on the sheet.
3. Next identify the independent variable(s) in the study. What factors influence this outcome? Does more than one factor influence this outcome? If so, what types of factors are they? Is the independent variable assessed as two or more groups? Is it a variable where the author plans to intervene with one group and withhold an intervention with another group? Is some trait or characteristic of the participants being studied that influences the outcome? Does the author use language about controlling for a specific variable? List the independent variables on the sheet and

write the type of independent variable in parentheses after each one (e.g., treatment, measured, or controlled).

4. Locate any intervening variables that may be used by the author. Are there any factors that mediate the influence between the independent and dependent variables in a cause-and-effect sequence? List these variables on your sheet.

With this process, you have compiled a list of major variables in the study. As a picture, this rendering will help reduce a complex study into a simple, understandable model of the research. It can help you identify and plan the variables for your own study, and it provides a useful visual for conveying the major direction of a research report to audiences such as faculty committees and conference attendees.

Theories and Testing of Variables

We need to learn one more idea that is important before we proceed directly into quantitative purpose statements, research questions, and hypotheses. Look at Figure 5.3 again and see that arrows connect the independent variable to the dependent variable. In quantitative research we seek to test whether the independent variable *influences* the outcome or dependent variable. We make this test because we have found past research that suggests that this relationship exists. Some researchers in education go one step further. They have found a theory that predicts the likely impact of the independent variable on the dependent variable. They seek to test a theory. But because this theory deals with humans in unpredictable situations, we say that the independent variable "probably causes" the dependent variable. The idea of **probable causation** is that researchers attempt to establish a likely cause-and-effect relationship between variables, rather than *prove* the relationship.

A **theory in quantitative research** explains and predicts the probable relationship between independent and dependent variables. For example, researchers test the relationship between peer groups' influence and adolescents. This relationship is tested over and over, such as with the Boy Scouts, in church groups, in middle schools, in high schools, and in other settings. Repeatedly the relationship of a positive effect holds true. Then someone comes along, calls this relationship a theory, and assigns a name to it. Smith's theory of peer influence is born, reported in the literature, and tested by other researchers. Thus, as shown in Figure 5.5, you might think about a theory as a bridge that connects the independent and dependent variables. Theories are no more than broad explanations for what we would expect to find when we relate variables.

In quantitative research, investigators locate a theory in the literature, examine the predicted relationship among variables in the theory, and then test the relationships with new participants or at new sites. To test the theory, researchers write purpose statements, research questions, and hypotheses that advance the predicted relationships. For example, a theory of leadership might predict that when principals use consensus-building decision styles, their teachers feel more supported.

Examples of theories include a theory about how students learn, a theory about what motivates people, a theory about how adults learn, a theory about leadership styles, and a theory about personality.

Not all quantitative studies employ a theory to test, but doing so represents the most rigorous form of quantitative research. It is certainly better than basing variables on your own personal hunches that are subject to challenge by other students and professors.

FIGURE 5.5

Theories as Bridges Between Independent and Dependent Variables

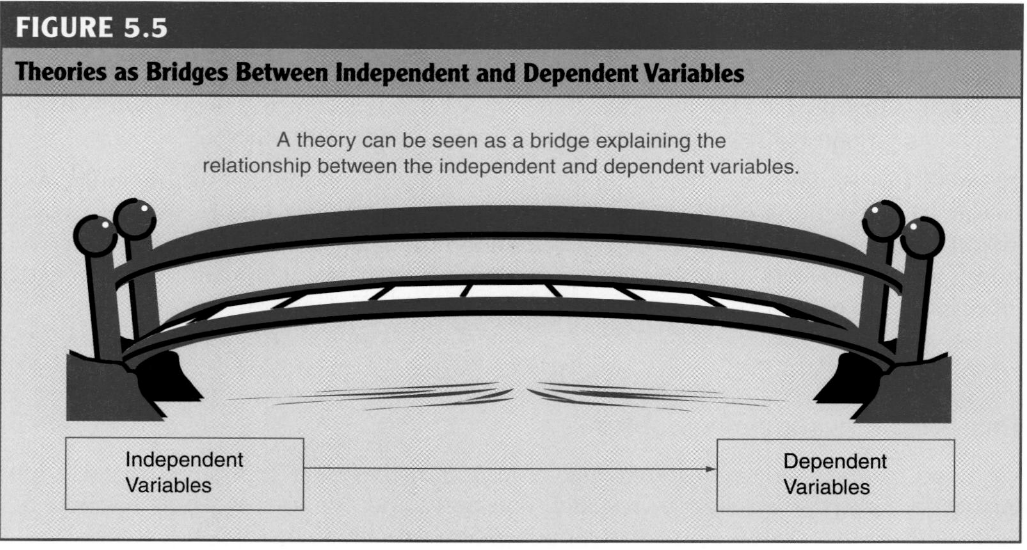

You might think about the test of a theory as the top of a list of reasons for studying the relationship among your variables. Look at Figure 5.6. Assume that several researchers explore the relationship between teacher respect for cultural values (the independent variable) and student performance (the dependent variable) in elementary school. In working from the bottom of the figure to the top, notice how each situation

FIGURE 5.6

Different Types of Explanations in Quantitative Research

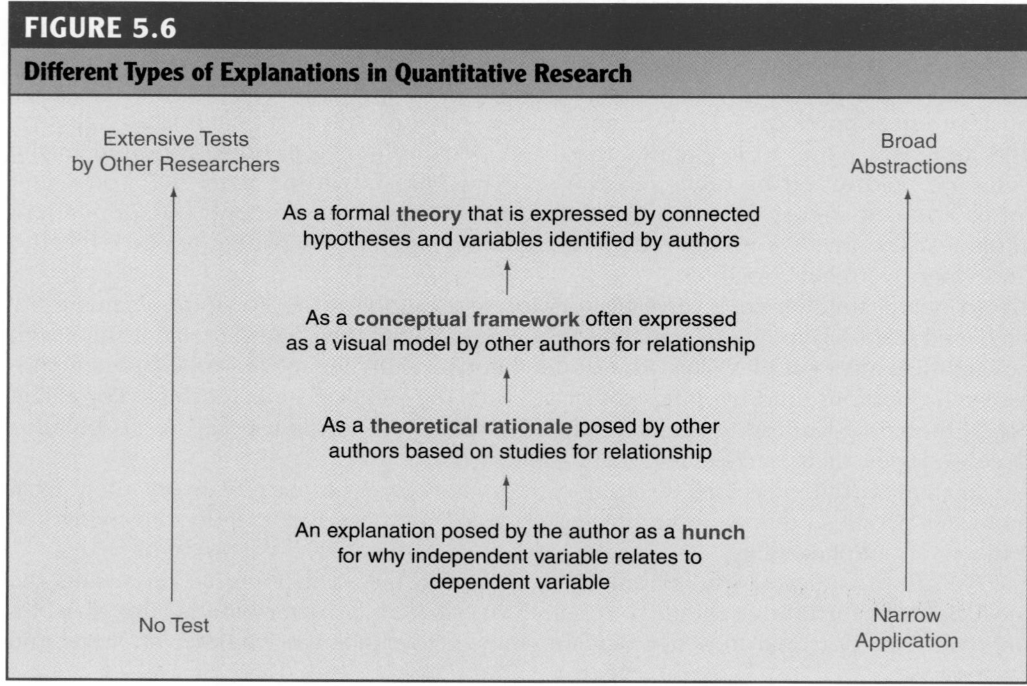

involves an increasing number of tests of studies, from a personal hunch to a sophisticated theory.

1. Some researchers have *hunches* or educated guesses as to why two variables might be related. For example, from personal experience, one researcher might feel that Hispanic children succeed in elementary school because the teacher is sensitive to cultural issues (e.g., the recognition and celebration of Hispanic holidays). Researchers have not tested this hunch, and it represents an unsophisticated approach based on the experiences of the researcher.
2. At a more rigorous level, educators can draw on a *theoretical rationale*—a logical statement for relating the variables—mentioned by authors in other studies. Assume that Jones, for example, found that Hispanic students learned best when teachers celebrated Hispanic holidays in class. With this theoretical rationale, we probably have more confidence in understanding the relationship between cultural sensitivity and performance in class (e.g., learning best).
3. Moving to an even more sophisticated level, assume that five different authors have studied this relationship and found cultural sensitivity to relate to performance. Smith, for instance, developed a *conceptual framework* (e.g., see Figure 5.6) predicting this relationship to hold true. Fox, Davis, Abel, and Sandoz tested this relationship. All found the relationship to hold true for different groups of Hispanic children. Now we have more confidence in the relationship because researchers have tested it multiple times with different Hispanic children.
4. Finally, assume that the relationship between cultural sensitivity and student performance is tested with many groups of *different* cultural orientations (e.g., Asian Americans, Native Americans, African Americans). In all of these situations, a positive relationship exists between teacher sensitivity and student performance. We now have a *theory,* a broad explanation of student performance based on cultural orientations.

What would a theory discussion look like? Here is an example, using "if . . . then" logic. *If* certain conditions are true, *then* the variables will be related. For example,

> Smith's (2000) theory of gender achievement predicts that if achievement in math is gender related, and girls are socialized to be better at math than boys, then girls will perform better in math than boys.

Where are theories located in a quantitative research report? Typically they are located in the literature review section or in the section on research questions or hypotheses. They may be called the *theoretical rationale* or a *theory-base* for the study. A good example of a theoretically driven study is the study of parent involvement by Deslandes and Bertrand (2005). In the opening paragraph of the study (Paragraph 02), they report how they will use the psychological constructs found in the Hoover-Dempsey and Sandler model as independent variables expected to influence the dependent variable, parent involvement.

Writing Quantitative Purpose Statements

With this background about variables and theory, you are ready to design and write a quantitative purpose statement, research questions, and hypotheses. To do this, first specify the elements that go into a good purpose statement, display a script that you can complete to help you design this statement, and illustrate the use of this script using examples.

Guidelines

A **quantitative purpose statement** identifies the variables, their relationship, and the participants and site for research. Several guidelines can help you prepare good purpose statements:

- Write the purpose statement in a single sentence.
- Begin the statement with key identifier words, such as "The purpose of this study," to clearly signal readers.
- If you plan to use a theory, introduce it in this statement by stating that you plan to "test a theory."
- Three options exist for using variables in this statement: You seek to relate two or more variables, to compare a variable composed of two or more groups in terms of the dependent variable, or to describe one variable. Use the words *relate* or *compare* or *describe* to indicate whether variables will be related, groups will be compared, or variables will be described.
- If variables are related or groups compared, specify the independent and dependent variables and any control or intervening variables.
- State the independent variable first (first position in the sentence), followed by the dependent variable (second position in the sentence). If control or mediating variables are used, state them last (in the third position in the sentence). The placement of these variables in this sentence is important because quantitative researchers often view variables as related from left to right, as shown in Figure 5.3.
- Identify the participants to be studied and the research site at which they will be studied.

Sample Scripts

To apply these guidelines, consider completing the following script by filling in the blanks:

> The purpose of this study is to test (the theory) by relating (the independent variable) to (the dependent variable) for (participants) at (the research site).

or

> by comparing (independent variable) with (group 1) and (group 2) in terms of (dependent variable) for (participants) at (the research site).

To apply this script, examine the following example for the case in which the researcher *relates* variables:

> The purpose of this study is to test Fines' theory (1996) by relating leadership style (independent variable) to autonomy (dependent variable) for teachers (participants) in high schools in State X (research site).

The next example illustrates the use of the script in which the researcher *compares* two groups (on an independent variable) in terms of one dependent variable:

> The purpose of this study is to test Smart's theory (1999) by comparing autocratic leaders (group 1) with consensus-building leaders (group 2) in terms of the satisfaction of teachers (dependent variable) in colleges in State X (research site).

Both examples begin with the phrase "The purpose of" to signal the reader. The independent variables precede the dependent variables in the statements. Also in both illustrations, the authors found theories to test, and they mentioned them at the beginning of the sentence. In other studies, a researcher may have only a hunch or a rationale and may not formally include a theory.

Maria, the high school teacher interested in studying weapon possession among high school students, might write the purpose statement with control variables in the third position:

> The purpose of this study is to relate student misbehavior factors (i.e., fighting) (independent variable—*position 1*) to attitudes toward weapon possession (dependent variable—*position 2*) for students in the district's high schools (participants—site), controlling for gender, grade level, and race (*position 3*).

In this example, the variables gender, grade level, and race will be eliminated as factors influencing weapon possession using statistical procedures.

Writing Quantitative Research Questions

Because research questions narrow and focus the purpose statement, they serve to restate the purpose in specific questions that the researcher seeks to answer. Research questions describe the participants' reactions to a single variable, compare groups on an outcome, or relate to variables. Research questions are found in all designs in quantitative research, such as in experiments, correlational studies, and surveys.

Guidelines

The basic steps in forming a research question are:

- Pose a question.
- Begin with "how," "what," or "why."
- Specify the independent, dependent, and mediating or control variables.
- Use the words *describe, compare,* or *relate* to indicate the action or connection among the variables.
- Indicate the participants and the research site for the study.

Three popular forms are available in quantitative research: descriptive questions, relationship questions, and comparison questions.

Descriptive Questions

Researchers use a **descriptive question** to identify participants' responses to a single variable or question. This single variable may be an independent, a dependent, or an intervening variable. The following is a script for writing a descriptive question:

> How frequently do (<u>participants</u>) (<u>variable</u>) at (<u>research site</u>)?

An application of this script might be:

> How frequently do African Americans feel isolated on college campuses?

Relationship Questions

In most research studies, investigators seek to learn more than responses to single variables. They may examine the relationship between two or more variables. **Relationship questions** seek to answer the degree and magnitude of the relationship between two or more variables. These questions often relate different types of variables in a study, such as independent variables to dependent variables or dependent variables to control variables. The most common case occurs when researchers relate the independent variable to the dependent variable. The following is a script for writing a relationship question:

> How does (independent variable) relate to (dependent variable) for (participants) at (research site)?

As applied to the relationship between isolation and ethnic identity, the script suggests:

> How do feelings of isolation relate to (or influence) the ethnic identity of African Americans in the United States?

Comparison Questions

Researchers might ask a **comparison question** to find out how two or more groups on an independent variable differ in terms of one or more outcome variables. Experiments employ comparison questions, and, in these studies, the researcher provides some intervention to one group and withholds it from the second group. A script for writing a comparison question would be:

> How does (group 1) differ from (group 2) in terms of (dependent variable) for (participants) at (research site)?

When this script is applied in a comparison of African Americans and Euro Americans, we get:

> How do African Americans and Euro Americans compare in their perceptions of ethnic identity?

Writing Quantitative Hypotheses

Similar to research questions, hypotheses narrow the purpose statement in quantitative research, but hypotheses advance a *prediction* about what the researcher expects to find. Because hypotheses are more formal than questions, researchers typically use questions rather than hypotheses. Also, as predictions between variables, hypotheses are not used to describe a single variable as in research questions.

Researchers narrow the focus of the study to at least one hypothesis that provides a prediction about the outcome of the study. A prediction that Maria might make would be:

> The more students feel alienated, the more likely they are to carry weapons to school.

Can you think of other predictions about school violence that Maria might make?

Guidelines

Hypotheses need to include specific components. Guidelines for writing them are:

- State the variables in this order: independent (first position), dependent (second position), and control (third position).
- If you compare groups in your hypothesis, explicitly state the groups; if variables are related, specify the relationship among the variables.
- Make a prediction about changes you expect in your groups, such as less or more favorable or no changes (e.g., no difference). You will then test this prediction using statistical procedures (to be discussed in more detail in chapter 7).
- You may state information about the participants and the site of the study, but this information may not be necessary if it repeats information stated in your purpose statement.

TABLE 5.2
The Null and Alternative Hypotheses

Type of Hypothesis	Null Hypothesis	Alternative Hypothesis
Purpose	To test in the general population that there is no change, no relationship, no difference	The hypothesis that may be true if the null is rejected, it suggests a change, a relationship, or a difference
Specific Language Found in the Hypothesis	There is no difference (or relationship) between . . .	Magnitude statements such as higher, lower, more positive, more favorable
How Researchers Test the Hypothesis	A test of the hypothesis (see chapter 7)	A test of the hypothesis (see chapter 7)

There are two types of hypotheses: the null and the alternative to the null. You need both types in a research study, but authors generally write only one or the other into their reports. The basic characteristics of these two forms are shown in Table 5.2.

Null Hypotheses

The null hypothesis is the most traditional form of writing a hypothesis. **Null hypotheses** make predictions that of all possible people whom researchers might study (i.e., called the general *population*), there is no relationship between independent and dependent variables or no difference between groups of an independent variable or a dependent variable. To study this hypothesis, you would select a sample of all possible people and draw conclusions from the statistical analysis of this sample for the population. A null hypothesis might begin with the phrase "There is no difference between" groups or "There is no relationship between (or among)" variables.

To write a hypothesis, you can complete the following script, which employs the language "no difference":

> There is no difference between (independent variable, group 1) and (independent variable, group 2) in terms of (dependent variable) for (participants) at (research site).

An example of the application of this script might be:

> There is no difference between at-risk and non-at-risk students in terms of student achievement on math test scores for third-grade students in a Midwest school district.
>
> Independent variable: at-risk students (members and nonmembers)
> Dependent variable: student achievement test scores
> Participants: third-grade students
> Site: X school district
> Form and language: null indicating no difference

Alternative Hypotheses

In contrast to the null hypothesis, you may write an alternative hypothesis. You will use an alternative hypothesis if you think there will be a difference based on results from past research or an explanation or theory reported in the literature.

The two types of alternative hypotheses are directional and nondirectional. In a **directional alternative hypothesis**, the researcher predicts the direction of a change, a difference, or a relationship for variables in the total population of people. A researcher selects a sample of people from a population and predicts that the scores will be higher, better, or changed in some way. This typical form for writing hypotheses is encountered in the literature more than any other type of hypothesis. Later (chapter 7) we will discuss the directional alternative hypothesis tested by a one-tailed statistical test.

A script for a directional alternative hypothesis is:

> (group 1, independent variable) at (research site) will have (some difference, such as higher, lower, greater, lesser) on (dependent variable) than (group 2 of independent variable).

An example of this script is:

> Students who participate in direct learning in four elementary schools will have higher achievement scores than students who participate in whole-language learning.
>
> Independent variable: learning (direct and whole language)
> Dependent variable: achievement test scores
> Participants: third-grade students
> Research site: four elementary schools
> Key indicator: directional, a prediction is implied

A variation on the directional hypothesis is the nondirectional hypothesis. In a **nondirectional alternative hypothesis** the researcher predicts a change, a difference, or a relationship for variables in a population but does not indicate whether the direction of this prediction will be positive or negative, or greater or less. The nondirectional alternative is not as popular as the directional alternative because the researcher does not take a stand about the direction of the relationship of the variables. A script for a nondirectional alternative hypothesis is:

> There is a difference between (group 1, independent variable) and (group 2, independent variable) in terms of (dependent variable).

An illustration of this script would be:

> There is a difference between varsity athletes in high school who smoke and those who do not smoke in terms of athletic accomplishments.

In this example, the author does not state whether the difference will be positive or negative. Later (chapter 7) we will discuss testing this form of hypotheses using a two-tailed statistical test. An analysis of the variables in this statement shows:

> Independent variable: use of tobacco (smokers and nonsmokers)
>
> Dependent variable: athletic accomplishments
>
> Participants: varsity athletes
>
> Sites: high schools
>
> Key indicator: the words "a difference," but the direction is not specified

HOW DO YOU DESIGN QUALITATIVE PURPOSE STATEMENTS AND RESEARCH QUESTIONS?

The components of good purpose statements and research questions differ for quantitative and qualitative research. Before we learn how to write *qualitative* purpose statements and research questions, we need to understand how *qualitative* research is both similar and different from *quantitative* research.

Differentiating Between Quantitative and Qualitative Purpose Statements and Research Questions

In both forms of research, inquirers use purpose statements and research questions. These statements become major signposts to alert readers to the major direction of the study. You need to write them carefully and incorporate the major elements of design into the statements of intent in your research.

However, the application differs depending on whether you conduct quantitative or qualitative research:

- In *quantitative* research, hypotheses are used. In *qualitative* research, hypotheses are not used; instead, inquirers use only research questions. Because researchers test hypotheses using statistics, and statistics are not used in qualitative research, hypotheses in qualitative research are not appropriate.
- In *quantitative* research, the investigator identifies multiple variables and seeks to measure them. In *qualitative* research, the term *variable* is not used, and instead the inquirer seeks to gather information on a single concept—a central phenomenon—a concept we discuss later in this chapter.
- In *quantitative* research, researchers often test theories, broad explanations that predict the results from relating variables. In *qualitative* research, theories are typically not tested. Instead, the inquirer asks participants in a study to share ideas and build general themes based on those ideas.
- In *quantitative* research, the investigator employs a close-ended stance by identifying variables and selecting instruments to collect data *before* the study begins. Quantitative research questions and hypotheses do not change during the study. In *qualitative* research, the inquirer uses more of an open-ended stance and often changes the phenomenon being studied or at least allows it to emerge during the study. The research questions may change based on the responses of the participants. This makes *quantitative* research more deductive and *qualitative* more inductive.
- In *quantitative* research, the investigator seeks to measure differences and the magnitude of those differences among two or more groups or measure changes over time in individuals. In *qualitative* research, inquirers do not compare groups or relate variables. Instead, the researcher seeks a deep understanding of the views of one group or single individuals.

These factors all influence how we write qualitative purpose statements and research questions. Before we proceed, however, we need to understand two concepts in qualitative research in more detail: the central phenomenon and the emerging process.

The Central Phenomenon in Qualitative Research

A central component of both the purpose statement and the research questions in qualitative research is the central phenomenon. The **central phenomenon** is the concept or a process explored in qualitative research. For example, as a concept, it could be:

- The ethnic identity of Chinese American immigrants

As a process it might be:

- The process of negotiation by a female superintendent with her principals

These examples illustrate the expression of the central phenomenon in a few words. They also show a focus on a single concept or process rather than relating two or more

FIGURE 5.7

How Researchers Explain or Predict Variables versus Exploring or Understanding a Central Phenomenon

Quantitative

Explaining or Predicting Variables
$X \longrightarrow Y$

The independent variable (X) influences a dependent variable (Y)

Qualitative

Understanding or Exploring a Central Phenomenon

Y

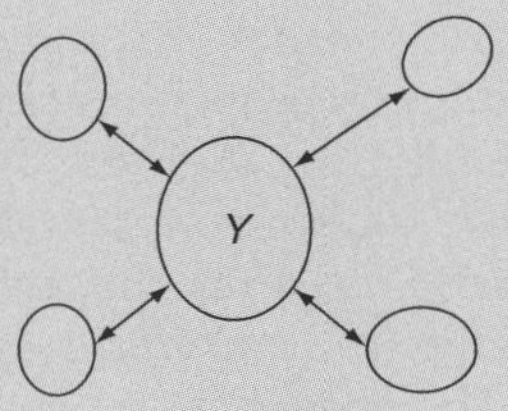

In-depth understanding of Y; external forces shape and are shaped by Y

ideas as found in quantitative research (e.g., "How do alienation and isolation relate for the female superintendent?") or comparing groups (e.g., "How do female principals and superintendents compare in their alienation?"). This comment is not to suggest that researchers may not explore comparisons or relationships in qualitative inquiry. Comparisons and relationships may emerge as the data analysis proceeds (e.g., as in grounded theory, the relating of categories of information to form propositions or hypotheses, as discussed in chapter 14), but the qualitative inquirer *begins* with a single idea, focus, or concept to explore before gathering data.

A picture might best express the differences between explaining and predicting variables in quantitative research and exploring a central phenomenon in qualitative research. As shown in Figure 5.7, one way to visualize this difference is by contrasting the explanation of an outcome (or dependent variable) by an independent variable (on the left of the figure) with the different image for a central phenomenon (on the right side of the figure). Rather than using cause-and-effect logic as in quantitative research, the qualitative researcher seeks to *explore* and *understand* one single phenomenon, and to do so requires considering all of the multiple external forces that shape this phenomenon. At the beginning of a study, the qualitative researcher cannot predict the nature of external forces (i.e., Which ones will be important? How will they exercise influence?). The arrows about forces shaping the central phenomenon are multidirectional. If it is helpful for you to understand the differences better from a *quantitative* perspective, consider the central phenomenon in qualitative research to be a single variable that you would like to explore.

Emerging Processes in Qualitative Research

Another central component about purpose statements and research questions in qualitative inquiry is that these statements and questions may change during the research process. Qualitative research is an emerging design. An **emerging process** indicates that the intent or purpose of a study and the questions asked by the researcher may change during the process of inquiry based on feedback or responses from participants. Questions and purposes may change because the qualitative inquirer allows the participants to set the direction, and in doing so, the researcher learns the participants' views rather than imposing his or her own view on the research situation. One question often asked is if this means that you will be asking different questions of different people in your study. This may well be the case in qualitative research. Remember that the intent of qualitative research is to understand and explore the central phenomenon, not to develop a consensus of opinion from the people you study.

An illustration of the emerging process is shown in Figure 5.8. As you can see, the process of asking questions is a dynamic process. Researchers may start with initial questions, shape them during initial data collection, and further change them because of multiple visits to the field to gather data. Revisions may continue throughout both data collection and analysis in a qualitative project. During this process, the overall direction of the study will change, and authors will rewrite their purpose statement and research questions.

In the example illustrated by Figure 5.8, the researcher may begin with the general question about the experiences high school students have with smoking tobacco. During the initial interviews, the students may discuss locations where they often smoke, such as in front of the apartment complex across the street from the school or in the neighborhood park adjacent to the school. The researcher then focuses direction by asking questions that are more detailed about where students smoke. Then through more in-depth questioning, some students begin discussing their attempts to quit smoking and how friends aide or thwart these attempts in the neighborhood park near the school. The questions change as the researcher delves deeper into the central phenomenon of high school students and smoking. Recall from chapter 2 that the intent of qualitative research is to establish the detailed meaning of information rather than to generalize the results and standardize the responses from all participants in research.

FIGURE 5.8
Emerging Questions in Qualitative Research

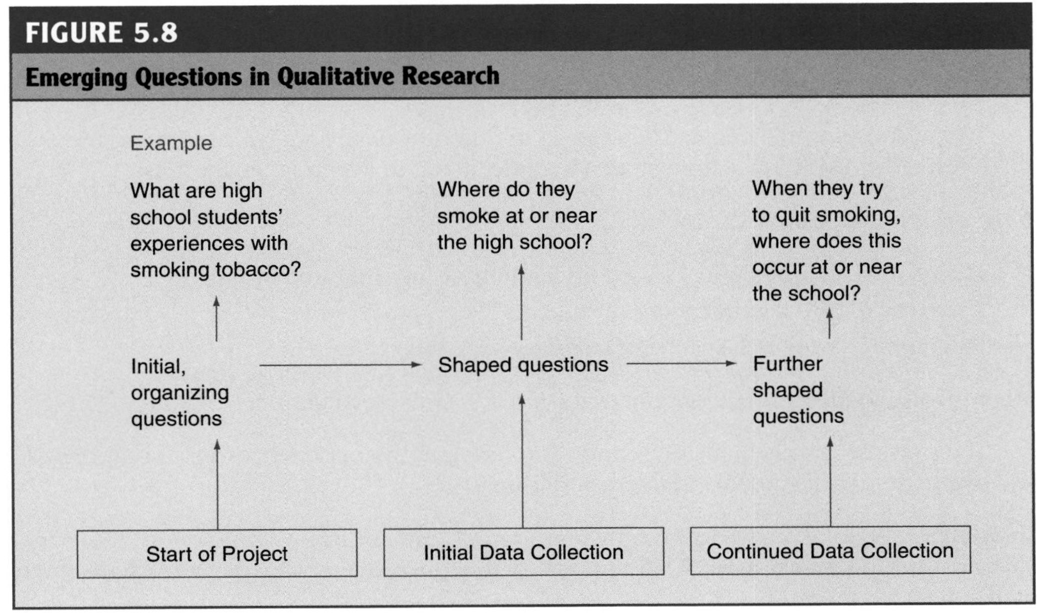

Writing Qualitative Purpose Statements

Inquirers reflect both the nature of an emerging process and the central phenomenon in qualitative purpose statements and research questions. As a major signpost in a study, care needs to be given to writing a good purpose statement that reflects the direction of the study.

A **purpose statement in qualitative research** indicates the intent to explore or understand the central phenomenon with specific individuals at a certain research site. In quantitative research, inquirers write this purpose statement as a single sentence and typically include it in a study at the end of the introduction.

Guidelines

As you design this statement, be sure to:

- Use key identifier words to signal the reader, such as "The purpose of this study is. . . ."
- Consider mentioning that the study is "qualitative" since audiences may not be familiar with qualitative research.
- Become familiar with qualitative research designs (see chapters 14, 15, and 16), and indicate the type of research design you plan to use in your study.
- State the central phenomenon you plan to explore.
- Use words that convey intent about the exploration, such as *explore, discover, understand,* and *describe.*
- Mention the participants in the study.
- Refer to the research site where you will study the participants.

Sample Script

You can use these elements in a script for writing a qualitative purpose statement. A script for a qualitative purpose statement is:

> The purpose of this qualitative study will be to (explore/discover/understand/describe) (the central phenomenon) for (participants) at (research site).

If we apply this script in the study of Internet classroom learning, we get:

> The purpose of this qualitative study is to describe classroom learning using the Internet for five high-school students participating in a sign language class.

If we analyze this example, we find:

> The central phenomenon: classroom learning using the Internet
>
> The participants: five high-school students
>
> The research site: a class in sign language at X high school

What would be the purpose statement for Maria's study? It might be:

> The purpose of this qualitative study is to explore the experiences with weapons of five high school students in the school district.

Look at this statement carefully. Can you identify the central phenomenon, the participants, and the research site? Write these down on a sheet of paper and share them with others.

Writing Qualitative Research Questions

Research questions in qualitative research help narrow the purpose of a study into specific questions. **Qualitative research questions** are open-ended, general questions that the researcher would like answered during the study.

Guidelines

The following general guidelines can help you design and write these questions (also, see Creswell, 1998, 2003):

- Expect your qualitative questions to change and to emerge during a study to reflect the participants' views of the central phenomenon and your growing (and deeper) understanding of it.
- Ask only a few, general questions. Five to seven questions are enough to permit the participants to share information. A few questions places emphasis on learning information from participants, rather than learning what the researcher seeks to know.
- Ask questions that use neutral, exploratory language and refrain from conveying an expected direction (or nondirectional outcome if you are thinking like a quantitative researcher). For example, use action verbs such as *generate, discover, understand, describe,* and *explore* instead of words conveying cause-and-effect relationships, such as *affect, relate, compare, determine, cause,* and *influence.*
- Design and write two types of qualitative research questions: the central question and subquestions.

The Central Question

The **central question** is the overarching question you explore in a research study. To arrive at this question, consider stating the most general question you can ask. The intent of this approach is to open up the research for participants to provide their perspectives and not to narrow the study to your perspective. When you write this question, place it at the end of the introduction to your study, and state it as a brief question. If you are more comfortable thinking about this question from a quantitative perspective, consider it as a single, descriptive question, such as a single dependent variable.

When designing and writing this central question, several strategies may be helpful:

- Begin with the word *how* or *what* rather than *why* so that you do not suggest probable cause-and-effect relationships as in *quantitative research* (i.e., "why" something influences something) but instead suggest exploration in *qualitative research.*
- Specify the central phenomenon you plan to explore.
- Identify the participants in the study.
- Mention the research site for the study.

Because the participants may have already been mentioned in your purpose statement, you do not need to repeat this information for your central question when you include both a purpose statement and a central question in a study.

A Sample Script

A script for a central research question that combines these elements is:

What is (the central phenomenon) for (participants) at (research site)?

The following example illustrates the application of this script to the study of creativity:

What is creativity for five students at Roosevelt High School?

Beginning word: "What"
Central phenomenon: creativity
Participants: five students
Research site: Roosevelt High School

Now consider Maria's research study. Write down the central question she might use in her study incorporating the three major elements: a central phenomenon, participants, and the research site.

Let's visit some of the challenges inherent in writing the central question. You may need to educate others about this question, especially if they are quantitative researchers and trained to "narrow down" questions and not to think in the exact opposite direction of stating the most general question possible. Also, you need to write the central question in such a way that it provides some direction for the study but does not leave the direction wide open. When a central question is too open, readers and audiences for a study will not have enough information to understand the project. Alternatively, when the central question is too specific or too laden with assumptions, it does not offer enough latitude for participants to express themselves, and it can shape too dramatically the views of participants in one direction or another.

In Table 5.3, several specific examples illustrate central questions stated in terms that are too general, too focused, or too laden with assumptions. First a poor example is given, followed by a better, improved version. In the first example, the author states a central question so broadly that readers and audiences do not understand the central phenomenon under study. This situation often occurs when qualitative researchers take too literally the concept of open-ended questions to mean "anything goes."

In the second example, the author focuses the question too much. By asking about specific activities on a committee, the researcher may miss the larger process at work in the committee and lose important information for the research report. In the final example, the researcher starts with the assumption that the committee is "alienated" from the college administration. Although this may be the case, the specification of a *direction* may limit too much what the inquirer can learn from a situation. To open the situation by asking about the "role of the college administration" includes the possibility that the role may be alienating, supportive, or may serve some in-between role.

TABLE 5.3

Problems Typically Found in Central Questions in Qualitative Research

Problems	Poor Example of a Central Question	Better Example of a Central Question
Too general	What is going on here?	What is the process being used by the general education committee at the liberal arts school?
Too focused	How did the committee make a curriculum decision about a course on the environment?	What is the process of the curriculum committee in making decisions about courses?
Too laden with assumptions	How did the curriculum committee address its alienation from the college administration?	What was the role of the college administration in the curriculum committee's deliberations?

Subquestions

In addition to a central question, qualitative researchers pose subquestions. These **subquestions** refine the central question into subquestions to be addressed in the research. These subquestions possess the same qualities as central questions (i.e., open ended, emerging, neutral in language, and few in number), but they provide greater specificity to the questions in the study. Preliminary conversations or interviews with your participants can provide useful leads for these subquestions. Writers refer to these subquestions as issue and procedural subquestions (Creswell, 1998; Stake, 1995), as shown in Table 5.4.

Issue Subquestions **Issue subquestions** are questions that narrow the focus of the central question into specific questions (or issues) the researcher seeks to learn from participants in a study. A script for an issue subquestion is:

> What is (the subquestion issue) for (participants—optional information) at (research site—optional information).

If you state the participants and research site in the central question or purpose statement, you do not need to repeat them in the subquestions. You would state the subquestions immediately after the central question as follows:

> What is self-esteem for high school students? (central question)
>
> What is self-esteem as seen through friends? (subquestion)
>
> What is self-esteem for the participant's family? (subquestion)
>
> What is self-esteem as experienced in extracurricular activities in school? (subquestion)

As these examples illustrate, the central phenomenon, self-esteem, is divided into three topical areas that the researcher explores.

Procedural Subquestions As an alternative form of writing subquestions, **procedural subquestions** indicate the steps to be used in analyzing the data in a qualitative study. Researchers use this form of writing subquestions less frequently than issue questions

TABLE 5.4

Types of Subquestions in Qualitative Research

	Issue Subquestions	**Procedural Subquestions**
Intent	To subdivide the central question into detailed questions	To subdivide the central question into steps for data collection during the study
Example	*Central Question:* What does it mean to be a professional teacher? *Issue Subquestions:* What do professional teachers do? What is difficult/easy about being a professional educator? When did the teacher first become aware of being a professional?	*Central Question:* What is the change process in the revision of a general education curriculum on a college campus? *Procedural Subquestions:* How did the process unfold? Who were the people involved? What events occurred? What was the outcome?

because the procedures for a qualitative study will evolve during a study. To write them, the researcher needs to know what these steps of analysis will be (a topic to be addressed in more detail in chapter 9).

However, if the researcher knows the general steps to be taken later in the analysis, procedural subquestions can be written. They provide those reviewing a study with a more precise understanding of the steps than do issue subquestions. A script for writing procedural subquestions is:

> To study this central question, the following questions will be addressed in order in this study:
>
> (What question will be answered first?)
> (What question will be answered second?)
> (What question will be answered third?)

To illustrate this script, assume for a moment that the steps in the process of data analysis will consist of first developing a description of events, followed by the specification of themes and broad dimensions for understanding the phenomenon. Let's use the familiar example of Maria. Maria's research questions might be:

> What are students' experiences with weapons in high schools? (central question)
>
> What are the categories of experiences of students? (subquestion)
>
> What process occurs that reflects these experiences? (subquestion)
>
> What propositions or hypotheses reflect the relationship among the categories? (subquestion)

These three subquestions trace a procedure for analyzing the data, from identifying categories to tracing a process that students experience to advancing some hypotheses that test this process. (These steps are discussed later in chapter 14.) Procedural subquestions help readers visualize the steps to be taken in data analysis, but they do not provide specific material for interview or observation questions.

Distinguishing Qualitative Research Questions from Data-Collection Questions

Are the types of questions asked during data collection (e.g., conducting interviews or when observing) the same questions as the subquestions? Yes, the core questions you ask might be the *issue* subquestions in your study. You would not ask your central question because that is the overall question you seek to answer with your research. Also, you would not limit your data-collection questions to only *issue* subquestions. There are two additional sets of questions that you need to ask, especially in qualitative interviews. Ask the participants about themselves as your opening question. In this way you break the ice and encourage them to answer your questions. Also, when you conclude the interview, you might ask them to suggest individuals that you might visit with to gather additional data. One of our final interview questions in the gunman case study (Asmussen & Creswell, 1995) was "To whom should we talk to find out more about the campus reaction to the incident?"

REEXAMINING THE PARENT INVOLVEMENT AND THE GUNMAN INCIDENT STUDIES

In both the parent involvement and the gunman incident studies, the authors use purpose statements and research questions to provide the focus and central direction for the studies. In the quantitative parent involvement study, Deslandes and Bertrand (2005) advanced both the purpose statement and the guiding research question in one succinct paragraph (Paragraph 13). They say:

> To examine how the four psychological contructs influence parent-involvement decisions across the three secondary grade levels, we posed the following research question: What are the relative contributions of parents' role construction, self-efficacy, perceptions of teacher invitations, and perceptions of adolescent invitations to predict parent involvement at home and at school in Grades 7, 8, and 9? (p. 166)

Although the authors implied the site to be studied (i.e., secondary schools), the purpose statement clearly conveys the intent of the study. The research question immediately follows the purpose statement and it serves to narrow the broad purpose into a narrower perspective by mentioning the four constructs to be examined. The question also provides more insight about the dependent variable, parent involvement, and the specific grade levels of students to be assessed. We now see in this research question that parent involvement will be measured in two ways, involvement at home and at school, and that the authors are interested in learning (and comparing) parent involvement across seventh, eighth, and ninth grades.

The qualitative gunman case study (Asmussen & Creswell, 1995) also includes both a purpose statement and research questions. At the end of the opening section, the authors mention the purpose statement in one sentence and then introduce five questions they seek to answer in the research:

> The study presented in this article is a qualitative case analysis [3] that describes and interprets a campus response to a gun incident. (Paragraph 03)
> We asked the following questions: What happened? Who was involved in response to the incident? What themes of response emerged during the eight-month period that followed this incident? What theoretical constructs helped us understand the campus response, and what constructs were unique to this case? (Paragraph 03) (p. 576)

As in the parent involvement study, the gunman study also needs to include in the purpose statement the site for the research. However, most of the elements we would expect to find are in place in the purpose statement. The open-ended, exploratory research questions seem to invite the campus personnel to tell their stories.

KEY IDEAS IN THE CHAPTER

The primary reason for purpose statements, research hypotheses, and research questions is to signal the major direction or intent of a study. They are the most important elements in a study. A purpose statement is a sentence in an educational study that states the overall direction or objective of the study. Research questions are questions that focus the purpose of the study into specific areas of inquiry. Hypotheses are statements that narrow the purpose statement into specific predictions about the relationship among variables.

To write quantitative purpose statements, research questions, and hypotheses, you need to understand the nature and types of variables. The three primary types of variables are dependent, independent, and intervening. Types of independent variables are measured, control, treatment, and moderating variables. In quantitative research, investigators often test the relationship among variables using theories.

In qualitative research, inquirers seek to explore a central phenomenon and engage in an emerging process of research. These two elements help inform the writing of qualitative purpose statements and research questions. A good qualitative purpose statement includes the central phenomenon, the participants, and the site of the study. Researchers then narrow the purpose statement to two types of qualitative questions: a central question and subquestions. In the central question the researcher asks the most general question that can be asked in a study. This central question is then subdivided into subquestions called issue or procedural subquestions. These questions either subdivide the central question into topics or they indicate the steps used in analyzing and reporting the data.

USEFUL INFORMATION FOR PRODUCERS OF RESEARCH

- Write both a purpose statement and either hypotheses or research questions into your research study.
- For a quantitative study, know the differences among the types of variables. Be able to identify clearly the independent and dependent variables that you plan to study.
- Locate and identify a theory to test that will provide an explanation for the relationship among variables in your research questions and hypotheses.
- Write a purpose statement that includes the major elements advanced in this chapter.
- Write either hypotheses or research questions, but not both.
- If you write hypotheses, consider whether your statements are directional or nondirectional. Directional hypotheses are more popular today and reflect a prediction about the expected results of a study.
- If you write research questions, use the elements advanced in this chapter.
- Consider in your questions whether you are trying to describe a single variable, to relate variables, or to compare groups on a variable.
- For a qualitative study, know the significance of a central phenomenon and be able to identify the phenomenon in your study.
- Write one central question and several subquestions using the elements advanced in this chapter.
- Clearly identify your subquestions as either issue or procedural subquestions and know the difference between the two types.

USEFUL INFORMATION FOR CONSUMERS OF RESEARCH

- Look for a purpose statement at the end of an introduction to a study. Phrases such as "the purpose of" should signal this statement. Alternative phrases might be "the objective of" or "the intent of."
- In a quantitative purpose statement (or hypotheses or questions), the independent variable should be stated in the first position, followed by the dependent variable in the second position. As you examine a study, ask yourself: What outcome is being predicted in this study? What factors are advanced that might explain this outcome?
- Look for hypotheses or research questions at the end of the introductory section of a study.
- An explanation for how and why the variables are related in hypotheses or research questions is called a *theory* or a *theoretical rationale*. This passage should advance researchers' predictions about what they expect to find.
- In a qualitative study, look for the central phenomenon that provides a focus for the inquiry. Authors should state this phenomenon in a few words and it should represent the focus that the inquirer wants to understand.
- Qualitative researchers often pose one central question as the overriding general issue they wish to explore. Then they advance a small number of subquestions that either narrow the focus to specific topics or advance procedural steps to be used in their data analysis.

Understanding Concepts and Evaluating Research Studies

1. You have just learned how to identify independent and dependent variables in *quantitative* purpose statements, research questions, and hypotheses. For each of the examples below, specify the independent variable(s) (IV) and the dependent variable(s) (DV) by writing the initials above the words:
   a. What is the relation between parental involvement in education and student reading performance?
   b. Our purpose in this study was to isolate the elements of accountability in a mastery learning program and determine if students' knowledge of accountability relates to changes in attitudes toward learning.
   c. Low degrees of mutuality, comprehensiveness, gender sensitivity, and congruence lead to functional mentoring relationships.
2. Show that you can identify the central phenomenon in *qualitative* purpose statements and research questions. In the following examples, place the initials "CP" over the words indicating the central phenomenon.
   a. How are these conceptions of reading played out, or not played out, in the sixth-grade classroom?
   b. In this article, I rely on critical views of culture and power to highlight aspects of sorority life that contribute to the marginalization and potential victimization of men.
   c. What are the major sources of academic change in a community college? What are the major processes through which change occurs?
3. Label each of the following hypotheses as "directional," "nondirectional," or "null."
   a. Students in a supportive environment are more likely to express willingness to seek help from the instructor than are students in a nonsupportive environment.
   b. There is no significant difference between students in a supportive environment and students in a nonsupportive environment in terms of their willingness to seek help from an instructor.

Conducting Your Research

For the educational project you have chosen to design in earlier chapters, write a quantitative purpose statement and research hypotheses. Also, turn the study into a qualitative project and write a qualitative purpose statement and central question.

Go to our Companion Website at **www.prenhall.com/creswell** to:

- assess your understanding of chapter content with Multiple-Choice Questions,
- apply what you've learned with Essay Questions,
- practice your research skills with interactive Building Research Skills exercises, and
- broaden your knowledge of research with Web Links to research topics on the Internet.

CHAPTER 6

Collecting Quantitative Data

The process of collecting quantitative data consists of more than simply collecting data. You decide on what participants you will study. Then you obtain their permission to be studied. You identify the types of measures that will answer your research question, and you locate instruments to use. Then, you can begin collecting data. This chapter discusses these five steps.

By the end of this chapter, you should be able to:

- Identify five steps in the process of quantitative data collection.
- Define different approaches used to sample participants for a quantitative study.
- Describe the process of obtaining permissions to study individuals and research sites.
- List different options for types of data often collected in quantitative research.
- Identify how to locate, select, and assess an instrument(s) for use in data collection.
- Describe procedures for administering quantitative data collection.

Maria decides to study the quantitative research question "Why do students carry weapons in high school?" Maria wonders, "Who can provide this information? Even if I locate some students, will they come forward with information?" Then Maria expresses concern to her graduate advisor about the need to find "a way to obtain this information from students," and she expresses fear that students may not be willing to participate because it is such a volatile topic. Maria digs herself deeper and deeper into complex questions that she needs to sort out so that she can proceed simply and logically through the process of data collection. How does she start?

WHOM WILL YOU STUDY?

The first step in the process of collecting quantitative data is to identify the people and places you plan to study. This involves determining whether you will study individuals or entire organizations (e.g., schools) or some combination. If you select either individuals or organizations, you need to decide what type of people or organizations you will actually study and how many you will need for your research. These decisions require that you decide on a unit of analysis, the group and individuals you will study, the procedure for selecting these individuals, and assessing the numbers of people needed for your data analysis.

Identify Your Unit of Analysis

Who can supply the information that you will use to answer your quantitative research questions or hypotheses? Some possibilities might be students, teachers, parents, adults, some combination of these individuals, or entire schools. At this early stage in data collection, you must decide at what level (e.g., individual, family, school, school district) the data needs to be gathered. This level is referred to as the **unit of analysis**. In some research studies, educators gather data from multiple levels (e.g., individuals and schools), whereas other studies involve collecting data from only one level (e.g., principals in schools). This decision depends on the questions or hypotheses that you seek to answer. Also, the data for measuring the independent variable may differ from the unit for assessing the dependent variable. For example, in the study of the impact of adolescent aggression on school climate, a researcher would measure the independent variable, adolescent aggression, by collecting data from individuals while measuring the dependent variable, school climate, based on data from entire schools and their overall climates (e.g., whether students and teachers believe the school curriculum supports learning).

If Maria wants to answer the question "Why do students carry weapons in high school?" what unit of analysis will she study? Alternatively, if she wanted to compare answers to the question "Why do students carry weapons in rural high schools and urban high schools?" what two types of unit of analysis will she study?

Specify the Population and Sample

If you select an entire school to study or a small number of individuals, you need to consider what individuals or schools you will study. In some educational situations, you will select individuals for your research based on who volunteers to participate or who is available (e.g., a specific classroom of students). However, those individuals may not be similar (in personal characteristics or performance or attitudes) to all individuals who could be studied.

A more advanced research process is to select individuals or schools who are representative of the entire group of individuals or schools. **Representative** refers to the selection of individuals from a sample of a population such that the individuals selected are typical of the population under study, enabling you to draw conclusions from the sample about the population as a whole. This definition is loaded with terms, and we will sort them so that you can see alternative procedures for deciding what individuals or organizations to study.

A **population** is a group of individuals who have the same characteristic. For example, all teachers would make up the population of teachers, and all high school administrators in a school district would comprise the population of administrators. As these

FIGURE 6.1

Populations and Samples

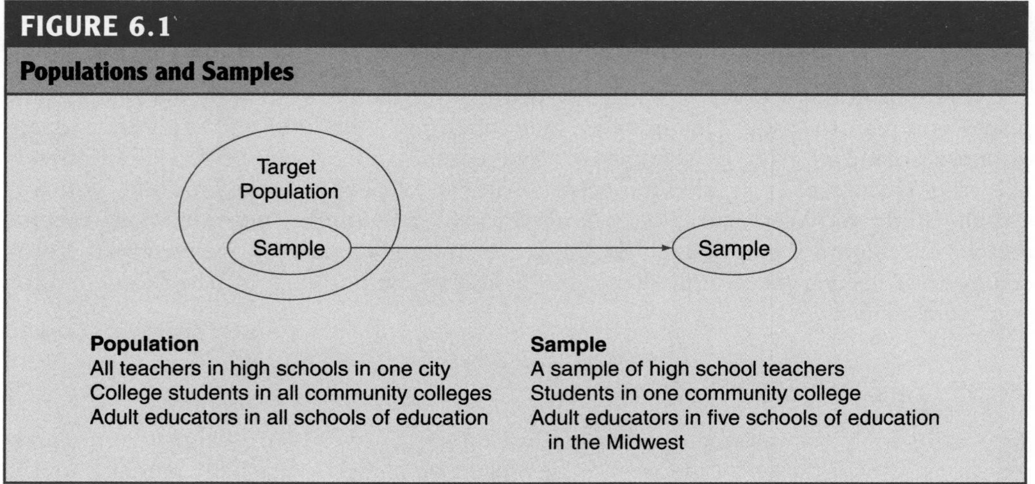

examples illustrate, populations can be small or large. You need to decide what group you would like to study.

In practice, quantitative researchers sample from lists and people available. A **target population** (or the *sampling frame*) is a group of individuals (or a group of organizations) with some common defining characteristic that the researcher can identify and study.

Within this target population, researchers then select a sample for study. A **sample** is a subgroup of the target population that the researcher plans to study for generalizing about the target population. In an ideal situation, you can select a sample of individuals who are representative of the entire population. For instance, as shown in Figure 6.1, you might select a sample of high school teachers (the sample) from the population of all teachers in high schools in one city (the population). Alternatively, you might be able to study only biology teachers in two schools in the city. The first scenario represents rigorous, systematic sampling called *probability sampling* and the second, unsystematic *nonprobability sampling.*

Probabilistic and Nonprobabilistic Sampling

Researchers employ either probability or nonprobability sampling approaches. As shown in Figure 6.2, several types of both approaches are available. Researchers decide which type of sampling to use in their study based on such factors as the amount of rigor they

FIGURE 6.2

Types of Quantitative Sampling Strategies

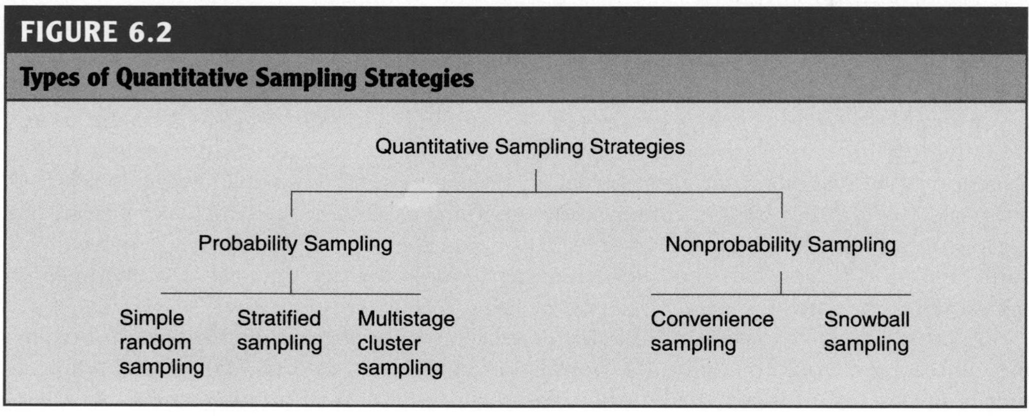

seek for their studies, the characteristics of the target population, and the availability of participants.

In **probability sampling**, the researcher selects individuals from the population who are representative of that population. This is the most rigorous form of sampling in quantitative research because the investigator can claim that the sample is representative of the population and, as such, can make generalizations to the population.

Simple Random Sampling The most popular and rigorous form of probability sampling from a population is simple random sampling. In **simple random sampling**, the researcher selects participants (or units, such as schools) for the sample so that any individual has an equal probability of being selected from the population. The intent of simple random sampling is to choose individuals to be sampled who will be representative of the population. Any bias in the population will be equally distributed among the people chosen. However, equal distribution is not always possible, as was seen during the Vietnam War when officials did not sufficiently turn the drum with names of potential draftees enough times to result in random selection (Wilkinson & the Task Force on Statistical Inference, 1999).

The typical procedure used in simple random sampling is to assign a number to each individual (or site) in the population and then use a random numbers table, available in many statistics books, to select the individuals (or sites) for the sample. For this procedure, you need a list of members in the target population and a number must be assigned to each individual.

An example of a random numbers table is shown in Table 6.1. To use this table, first assign unique numbers to all individuals in the population (say, a population of 100 first graders). Then, starting anywhere in the random numbers table, match the numbers on your list to the numbers in the table. Start at the upper left of Table 6.1 and go down the column. You might choose the first six first graders from the population of 100, having the numbers 52, 31, 44, 84, 71, and 42. This would continue down the column until you have chosen the number of children needed for your sample (later in the "Sample Size" section, we will consider how many first graders you would need).

Systematic Sampling A slight variation of the simple random sampling procedure is to use **systematic sampling**. In this procedure, you choose every *n*th individual or site in the population until you reach your desired sample size. This procedure is not as precise and rigorous as using the random numbers table, but it may be more convenient because

TABLE 6.1

Excerpt from a Random Numbers Table

52	13	44	91	39	85	22	33	04	29	52	06
31	52	65	63	88	78	21	35	28	22	91	84
44	38	76	99	38	67	60	95	67	68	17	18
84	47	44	04	67	22	89	78	44	84	66	15
71	50	78	48	65	74	21	24	02	23	65	94
42	47	97	81	10	99	40	15	63	77	89	10
03	70	75	49	90	92	62	00	47	90	78	63
31	06	46	39	27	93	81	79	100	94	43	39

Source: Adapted from Kerlinger, 1972, p. 714.

individuals do not have to be numbered and it does not require a random numbers table. To illustrate systematic sampling, assume a school district administrator wants to study parent satisfaction with the schools in the district. Using systematic sampling, the administrator would first study a percentage of the parents (e.g., 20%). If there were 1,000 parents in the school district, the administrator would select 200 (or 20%) for the study. The administrator uses an interval of five (200/1,000, or 1 out of 5) to select parents from the mailing list (or target population list). Therefore, this administrator sends every fifth parent on the list a survey.

Stratified Sampling Another type of probability sampling is stratified sampling. In **stratified sampling**, researchers divide (stratify) the population on some specific characteristic (e.g., gender) and then, using simple random sampling, sample from each subgroup (stratum) of the population (e.g., females and males). This guarantees that the sample will include specific characteristics that the researcher wants included in the sample.

When do you use stratification? You use stratification when the population reflects an imbalance on a characteristic of a sample. Assume that there are more males than females in a population. A simple random sample from this population would likely result in the selection of more males than females or maybe even no females. In either case, the male views on questions would be the dominant or exclusive view. To correct for this, researchers use stratified sampling. Stratification ensures that the stratum desired (females) will be represented in the sample in proportion to that existence in the population.

Stratification is also used when a simple random sampling procedure would yield fewer participants in a specific category (e.g., females) than you need for rigorous statistical analysis. Having few females in a population, for example, would result in the likelihood of randomly selecting only a few females. This could possibly result in having numbers too small to analyze statistically.

The procedure for selecting a stratified random sample consists of (a) dividing the population by the stratum (e.g., men and women) and (b) sampling within each group in the stratum (e.g., women first and then men) so that the individuals selected are proportional to their representation in the total population. Let's look at an example of how this procedure is applied.

> Looking at Figure 6.3, we can see that of the 9,000 Native American children in the state, 3,000 are girls and 6,000 are boys. A researcher decides to choose a sample of 300 from this population of 9,000 children. A simple random sample results in the

FIGURE 6.3

Proportional Stratification Sampling Approach

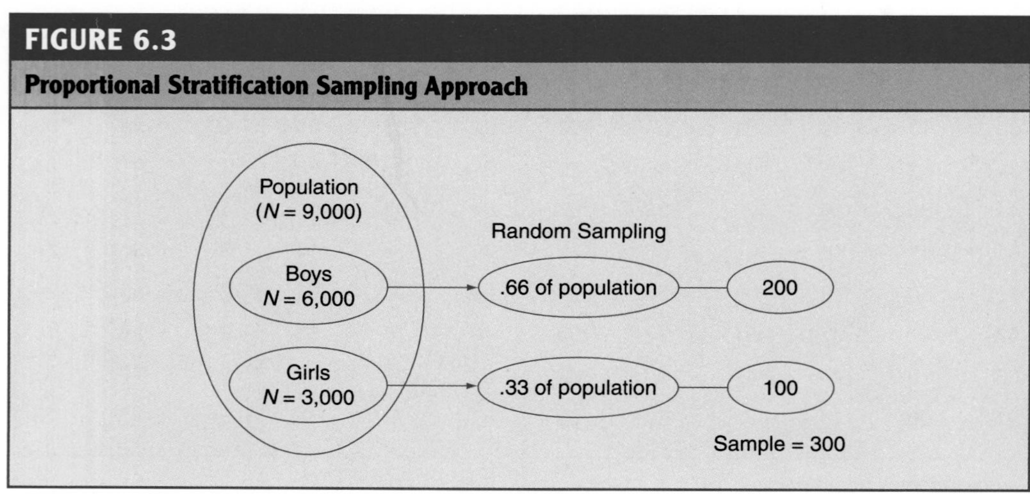

selection of mostly boys because there are more boys than girls in the population. To make sure that the researcher selects boys in proportion to their representation in the population, she divides the list of 9,000 children into boys and girls. Then one third (3,000/9,000) of the sample is chosen to be girls, and two thirds (6,000/9,000), boys. The stratification procedure consists of stratifying by the population into boys and girls and selecting individuals in proportion to their representation in the total population, resulting in 200 boys and 100 girls.

Multistage Cluster Sampling A fourth form of probability sampling is multistage cluster sampling. In **multistage cluster sampling**, the researcher chooses a sample in two or more stages because either the researchers cannot easily identify the population or the population is extremely large. If this is the case, it can be difficult to obtain a complete list of the members of the population. However, getting a complete list of groups or clusters in the population might be possible (Vogt, 1999). For example, the population of all at-risk students in the United States may be difficult to identify, but a researcher can obtain a list of the at-risk kids in select school districts. Using multistage cluster sampling, the researcher randomly selects school districts in the United States and obtains a list of the at-risk students in each of those school districts. Then the researcher randomly samples within each district. Breaking down the process like this makes it easier to identify groups and locate lists. However, with several stages to this design, it is complex and highly dependent on the characteristics of the population (Babbie, 1998).

It is not always possible to use probability sampling in educational research. Instead, a researcher can use nonprobability sampling. In **nonprobability sampling**, the researcher selects individuals because they are available, convenient, and represent some characteristic the investigator seeks to study. In some situations, you may need to involve participants who volunteer and who agree to be studied. Further, you may not be interested in generalizing findings to a population, but only in describing a small group of participants in a study. It may be appropriate to calculate descriptive statistics on these samples and to compare them with the larger population to make inferences from the sample to the population. Researchers use two popular approaches in nonprobability sampling: convenience and snowball sampling approaches.

Convenience Sampling In **convenience sampling** the researcher selects participants because they are willing and available to be studied. In this case, the researcher cannot say with confidence that the individuals are representative of the population. However, the sample can provide useful information for answering questions and hypotheses. Let's look at an example of convenience sampling.

> A researcher conducting a study involving Native American students finds that a large percentage of students in one school are Native Americans. The researcher decides to study this group at this one school because they are available and because the researcher has the permission of the principal and can gain consent from the Native American students to participate in the study. This is a convenience sample because the participants are convenient to the researcher and are available for the study.

Snowball Sampling An alternative to convenience sampling is snowball sampling. In **snowball sampling**, the researcher asks participants to identify others to become members of the sample. For example, you might send surveys to a school superintendent and ask that the superintendent forward copies to the principals of schools in that school district. These principals then become members of the sample. This form of sampling has the advantage of recruiting large numbers of participants for the study. By using this process, however, you give up knowing exactly what individuals will be in your sample.

It also eliminates the possibility of identifying individuals who did not return the survey, and those responding may not be representative of the population you seek to study. For example, participants who received the survey (e.g., principals who attended the Monday morning meeting with the superintendent) may not be representative of all individuals in the population (in this case, all principals in the school district).

Sample Size

When selecting participants for a study, it is important to determine the size of the sample you will need. A general rule of thumb is to select as large a sample as possible from the population. The larger the sample, the less the potential error that the sample will be different from the population. This difference between the sample estimate and the true population score is called **sampling error**. If you were to select one sample after another, the average score of each sample would likely differ from the true average score for the entire population. For example, if we could obtain scores from sixth graders across the country about the importance of student–parent relationships, the average score might be a 30 on a 50-point scale. Of course, we cannot study *every* sixth grader, so instead we obtain a sample from one school district and get an average score of 35 on the scale. The next time we might obtain a score of 33, and the next time a 36, because our sample will change from one school district to another. This means that our average score is five points, three points, and one point, respectively, away from the "true" population average. This difference between the sample estimate and the true population score is sampling error. Therefore, since you usually cannot know the true population score, it is important to select as large a sample as possible from the population to minimize sampling error.

In some studies, you may have a limited number of participants who are conveniently available to study. In other cases, factors such as access, funding, the overall size of the population, and the number of variables will also influence the size of the samples.

One way to determine the sample size is to select a sufficient number of participants for the statistical procedures you plan to use. This presumes that you have identified the statistic to use in analysis. As a rough estimate, an educational researcher needs:

- Approximately 15 participants in each group in an experiment (see chapter 11)
- Approximately 30 participants for a correlational study that relates variables (see chapter 12)
- Approximately 350 individuals for a survey study, but this size will vary depending on several factors (see chapter 13).

These numbers are estimates based on the size needed for statistical procedures so that the sample is likely to be a good estimate of the characteristics of the population. They do not provide a precise estimate of the sample size available through sample size formulas.

Sample size formulas provide the means for calculating the size of your sample based on several factors. Use of a formula takes the guesswork out of determining the number of individuals to study and provides a precise estimate of your sample size. The formulas take into consideration several factors important in determining size, such as confidence in the statistical test and sampling error. Further, you need not calculate the sample size using a formula. With minimal information, you can identify the sample size using tables available to researchers.

Two formulas used are the sampling error formula for surveys (see Fink & Kosekoff, 1985; Fowler, 1988) and a power analysis formula for experiments (Cohen, 1977; Lipsey, 1990; Murphy & Myors, 1998). Appendix B at the end of the text provides factors that you can insert into these formulas to determine the number of participants for your study.

WHAT PERMISSIONS WILL YOU NEED?

After identifying and selecting participants for your study, you next need to obtain their permission to be studied. This permission will ensure that they cooperate in your study and provide data. Besides cooperation, their permission also acknowledges that they understand the purpose of your study and that you will treat them ethically. Federal legislation requires that you guarantee them certain rights and that you request their permission to be involved in your study.

Obtain Different Types of Permissions

In most educational studies, you need to obtain permissions from several individuals and groups before you can gather data. Permissions may be required from:

- Institutions or organizations (e.g., school district)
- Specific sites (e.g., the secondary school)
- A participant or group of participants
- Parents of participants (e.g., 10th graders' parents)
- The campus on which you conduct the research (i.e., permission from your university or college institutional review board)

Permission is often necessary before you can enter a site and collect data. This approval usually comes from leaders or persons of authority in organizations. Obtaining permissions from organizational personnel requires contacting them before the start of a study and obtaining their permission to enter and to study their setting.

The best way to seek permission from the necessary individuals or groups is to ask for it formally in a letter. Include the purpose of the study, the amount of time you will be at the site collecting data, the time required of participants, and how you will use the data or results. Also, state the specific activities you will conduct, the benefits to the organization or individual because of the study, and the provisions you have made to protect the anonymity of study participants. By providing this information, you will show a concern for the potential intrusion of the study into their workplaces and lives and set the stage for realistic expectations on their part.

Obtain Informed Consent

It is important to protect the privacy and confidentiality of individuals who participate in the study. In contrast to early research in education and the social sciences, investigators today are sensitive to the potential harm that participants may experience because of research.

Review Board Approval

In the last 30 years, colleges and universities have required that researchers guarantee to participants that their research will cause minimal risk to participants. In turn, participants consent to participation in research.

In the 1970s, the federal government created legislation to monitor campus-based research because of human abuses in experiments (e.g., Nazi medical experiments, atomic bomb blast tests, and syphilis experiments on African Americans). This legislation mandated that colleges and universities create institutional review boards to approve student and faculty research. An **institutional review board** is a committee made up of faculty members who review and approve research so that the research protects the rights of the participants. The creation of these boards represents the one instance where research done on college and university campuses has been regulated (Howe & Dougherty, 1993).

Process of Obtaining Approval from Review Boards

Institutional review boards implement guidelines developed by the Federal Drug Administration based on three ethical principles: respect for persons (their consent, their right to privacy, and anonymity), beneficence (weighing the benefits of research versus the risks to individuals), and justice (equity for participation in a study). By following the guidelines, researchers guarantee that participants retain their autonomy and judge for themselves what risks are worth taking for the purposes of research (Howe & Dougherty, 1993).

To obtain approval from a campus institutional review board, you are required to summarize the procedures in your research and supply evidence that your research procedures will offer certain protections to participants.

The exact process of gaining approval from an institutional review board varies from campus to campus. However, there are some basic steps that both student and faculty researchers complete when seeking approval. Understanding this process will help you evaluate the ethics of a published study and determine if you are proceeding ethically in your study.

1. *Start by finding out about the review process used by the institutional review board on your campus.* Identify individuals responsible for reviewing projects, locate the forms required for the review, and become familiar with the overall approval procedure. Campus review boards may have a brochure that describes this process.

2. *Determine what information the review board needs about your project.* The extent of the review and the concern of the institutional review board will relate to two factors (e.g., see University of Nebraska at Lincoln [1997] guidelines). The first is the level of risk that your participants will likely experience in the study (e.g., psychological, physical, emotional, legal, social, or economic). Is this risk less than minimal—no known risk? Is it minimal—risks encountered in daily life? Is it greater than minimal—risks beyond those ordinarily encountered in daily life? The higher the risk, the more detailed your project description needs to be, and the more closely the institutional review board will scrutinize your project.

The second factor that affects the extent of the review is whether you are studying a sensitive population considered to be of high risk. These populations include children under the age of 19, who need their own and their parents' consent to participate; mentally incompetent participants, victims, or persons with neurological impairments; pregnant women or fetuses; prisoners; and individuals with AIDS. Also included in this category are studies involving confidential records and/or pathological specimens and HIV testing.

If your study involves a sensitive population, your project will have at least minimal or greater than minimal risk (as opposed to no known risk) and the institutional review board will subsequently scrutinize it closely. Because many educational studies involve children under 19, these studies will require extensive review by the institutional review boards.

3. *Develop an informed consent form for participants to sign before they participate in the study.* Obtain written consent from participants even if your project poses minimal risk to the participants. An exception would be if the return of a questionnaire or instrument implies consent.

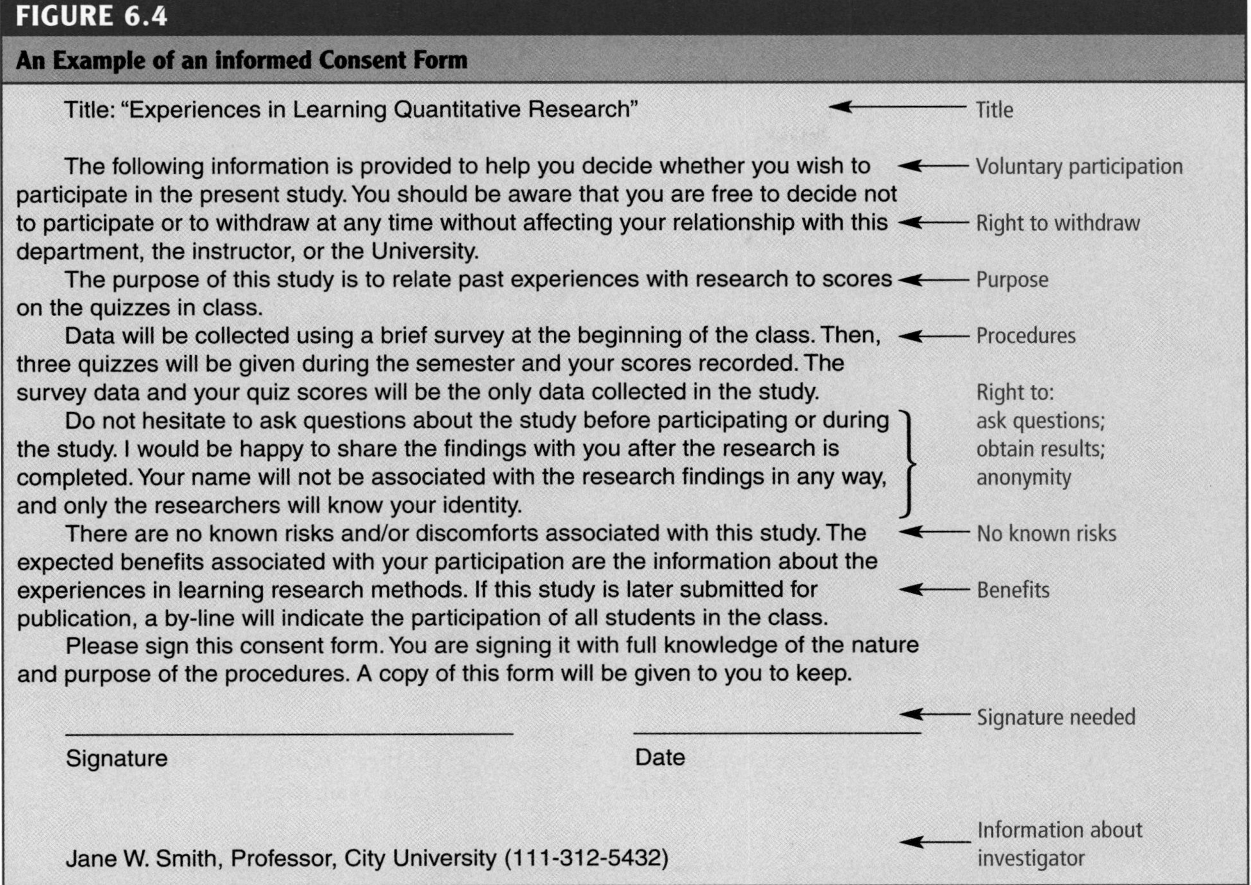

FIGURE 6.4

An Example of an informed Consent Form

Title: "Experiences in Learning Quantitative Research" ← Title

The following information is provided to help you decide whether you wish to participate in the present study. You should be aware that you are free to decide not to participate or to withdraw at any time without affecting your relationship with this department, the instructor, or the University. ← Voluntary participation ← Right to withdraw

The purpose of this study is to relate past experiences with research to scores on the quizzes in class. ← Purpose

Data will be collected using a brief survey at the beginning of the class. Then, three quizzes will be given during the semester and your scores recorded. The survey data and your quiz scores will be the only data collected in the study. ← Procedures

Do not hesitate to ask questions about the study before participating or during the study. I would be happy to share the findings with you after the research is completed. Your name will not be associated with the research findings in any way, and only the researchers will know your identity. } Right to: ask questions; obtain results; anonymity

There are no known risks and/or discomforts associated with this study. The expected benefits associated with your participation are the information about the experiences in learning research methods. If this study is later submitted for publication, a by-line will indicate the participation of all students in the class. ← No known risks ← Benefits

Please sign this consent form. You are signing it with full knowledge of the nature and purpose of the procedures. A copy of this form will be given to you to keep.

______________________ ______________________ ← Signature needed

Signature Date

Jane W. Smith, Professor, City University (111-312-5432) ← Information about investigator

An **informed consent form** is a statement that participants sign before they participate in research. This form should state that you will guarantee them certain rights, and that when they sign the form, they are agreeing to be involved in the study and acknowledge the protection of their rights.

Figure 6.4 shows a typical consent form outlining the participants' rights, including their right to withdraw at any time from the study, their voluntary participation in the project, and their right to know the purpose of the study.

You might try writing a sample informed consent form for use in a research project. In your consent form, include the aspects identified in the right column in Figure 6.4 so that it contains the essential information required by a review board.

4. *Submit a description of your proposed study to the institutional review board.* This description includes the purpose of the study, the data-collection process, the guarantees for protecting the participants, and a sample consent form.

After you have completed the steps listed above, the review board will evaluate your project and determine whether you have guaranteed the protection of participants. If approved, you can proceed with the study. If denied, you will need to visit with the board representative to determine why it did not approve the study and what you need to change in your project description or procedures to get approval.

WHAT INFORMATION WILL YOU COLLECT?

With the identification of participants and a procedure for gaining permission, you next turn to the specific forms of data that will help you answer your research questions or address your research hypotheses. This step involves identifying the variables in your questions and hypotheses, finding definitions for these variables, and considering types of information that will help you assess these variables, a process outlined in Figure 6.5 using the variable *self-efficacy*.

Specify Variables from Research Questions and Hypotheses

As discussed in chapter 5, research questions and hypotheses contain variables. To determine what data need to be collected, you need to identify clearly the variables in your study. This will include independent, dependent, and control variables. A useful strategy is to make a list of the variables so that you can determine what variables are operating in a study, as described in the "Think-Aloud" feature in chapter 5.

Operationally Define Each Variable

Many definitions of variables are possible, such as a dictionary definition, but researchers use an operational definition. An **operational definition** is the specification of how you will define and measure the variable in your study. You can find definitions in published research studies on your topic. Sometimes published studies have sections titled "Definition of Terms." Alternatively, you might examine definitions in research summaries such as handbooks or encyclopedias (discussed in chapter 4). In some situations, a clear, applied definition suitable for finding a measure is not available, and you will need to

FIGURE 6.5

The Flow of Activities in Collecting Data

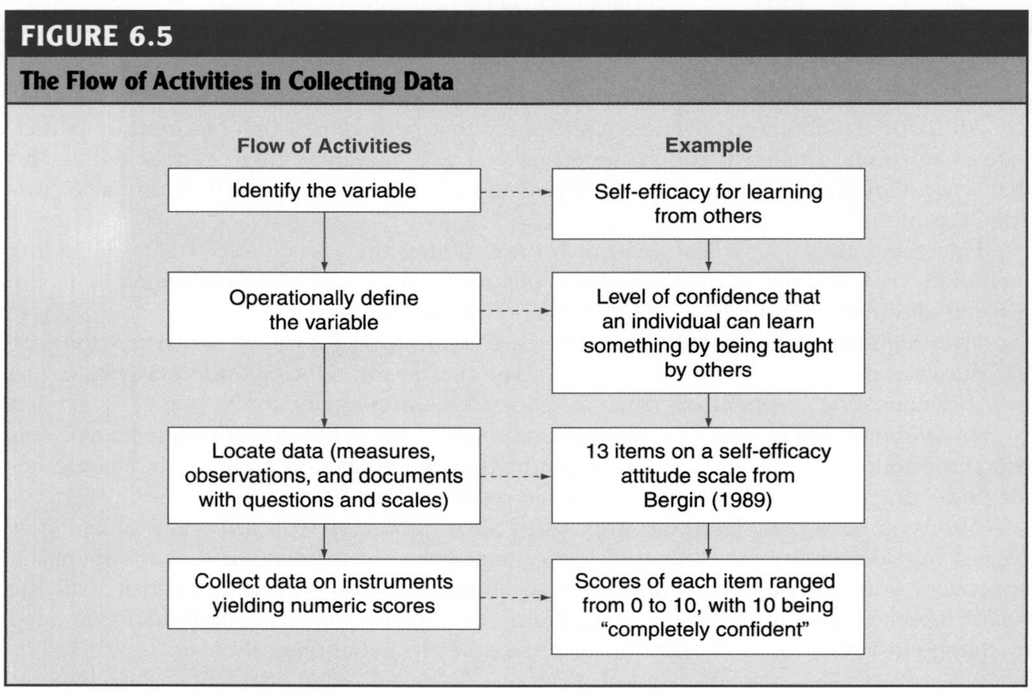

construct your own definition. If this is the case, you should test it with other students or individuals knowledgeable about your topic and variable before you use it in your research. A dictionary definition might be used as well, but remember that such a definition often reflects more common usage of a term rather than a research application.

Consider the variable *weapon possession* that Maria needs to define operationally. Write down two or three possible definitions for this variable, such as "a student who has been discovered carrying a knife to school." What other definitions might you use that will help Maria measure the extent to which high school students possess weapons at school? (*Hint:* Think about what happens when a teacher or administrator finds students with weapons in their possession.)

Choose Types of Data and Measures

With operational definitions for your variables, you next need to identify types of data that will measure your variables. Researchers collect data on instruments. An **instrument** is a tool for measuring, observing, or documenting quantitative data. Identified before the researchers collect data, the instrument may be a test, questionnaire, tally sheet, log, observational checklist, inventory, or assessment instrument. Researchers use instruments to measure achievement, assess individual ability, observe behavior, develop a psychological profile of an individual, or interview a person. In quantitative research, four major types of information are gathered, as shown in Table 6.2. Definitions and examples in this table should help you apply your understanding of different forms of quantitative measures.

Performance Measures

You collect **performance measures** to assess an individual's ability to perform on an achievement test, intelligence test, aptitude test, interest inventory, or personality assessment inventory. Participants take tests that measure their achievement (e.g., the Iowa Test of Basic Skills), their intelligence (e.g., Wechsler), or their aptitude (e.g., Stanford–Binet). In addition, you could gather data that measures an individual's career interests or assesses personality traits. These measures are all available through instruments reported in the literature. Through past research, researchers have developed "norms" for these tests (conducted the tests with a number of individuals, averaged their scores, and looked at the differences in their scores) so that they can compare individual scores with typical scores for people who have taken the test. However, one drawback of performance data is that it does not measure individual attitudes, and performance data may be costly, time consuming to gather, and potentially biased toward specific cultural groups.

Attitudinal Measures

Alternatively, you can measure attitudes of individuals, a popular form of quantitative data for surveys, correlational studies, and experiments. Researchers use **attitudinal measures** when they measure feelings toward educational topics (e.g., assessing positive or negative attitudes toward giving students a choice of school to attend). To develop attitudinal measures, researchers often write their own questions or they find an instrument to use that measures the attitudes. Regardless of the approach, these measures need to contain unbiased questions (e.g., not "Should students carry weapons to schools?" Instead ask, "How do you feel about students carrying weapons to school?") and to encourage participants to answer questions honestly. One drawback of attitudinal measures is that they do not provide direct evidence of specific behaviors (e.g., whether or not students actually carry a weapon to school).

Let's examine a research instrument used to gather attitudinal information. Examine the first few questions (out of 74 on the instrument) on the "Student Adaptation to College

TABLE 6.2

Types of Quantitative Data and Measures

Types of Data	Types of Tests, instruments, or Documents to Collect Data	Definition of the Type of Test, Instrument, or Document	Example of the Specific Tests, Instruments, or Source of Information
Measures of Individual Performance	Achievement Test: Norm-referenced tests	A test where the individual's grade is a measure of how well he or she did in comparison with a large group of test takers (Vogt, 1999)	Iowa Test of Basic Skills
	Criterion-referenced tests	A test where the individual's grade is a measure of how well he or she did in comparison to a criterion or score	General Educational Development or GED Test Metropolitan Achievement Test Series on Reading
	Intelligence test	A test that measures an individual's intellectual ability	Wechsler Intelligence Scale for Children
	Aptitude test	A test to measure a person's ability to estimate how they will perform at some time in the future or in a different situation	Cognitive Ability: Binet-Simon Scale to identify a child's mental level General Ability: Stanford-Blnet IQ Scale
	Interest Inventory	A test that provides information about an individual's interest and helps them make career choices	Strong Interest Inventory
	Personality assessment	A test that helps a person identify and measure human characteristics that help predict or explain behavior over time and across situations (Thorndike, 1997b)	Minnesota Multiphasic Personality Inventory
Measures of Individual Attitude	Affective Scale	An instrument that measures positive or negative affect for or against a topic	Attitudes Toward Self-Esteem Scale Adaptive Behavior Scales
Observation of Individual Behavior	Behavioral Checklist	An instrument used to record observations about individual behavior	Flander's Interaction Analysis Behavioral Checklist in Reading Vineland Adaptive Behavior Scale
Factual Information	Public Documents or School Records	Information from public sources that provides data about a sample or population	Census data School grade reports School attendance reports

Questionnaire" available commercially from Western Psychological Services (Baker & Siryk, 1989) in Figure 6.6. This questionnaire begins with personal information questions (e.g., sex, date of birth, current academic standing, and ethnic background) and then asks students to indicate their attitude toward adapting to college on questions using a 9-point

FIGURE 6.6

Example of an Instrument that Measures Attitudes

Student Adaptation to College Questionnaire (SACQ)

Robert W. Baker, Ph.D. and Bohdan Siryk, M.A.

Published by

wps WESTERN PSYCHOLOGICAL SERVICES Publishers and Distributors 12031 Maple Boulevard Los Angeles, California 90023

Name:________ Date:________

ID Number:________ Sex: ☐F ☐M Date of Birth:________

Current Academic Standing: ☐Freshman ☐Sophomore ☐Junior ☐Senior

Semester: ☐1 ☐2 ☐Summer *or* Quarter: ☐1 ☐2 ☐3 ☐Summer

Ethnic Background (optional): ☐Asian ☐Black ☐Hispanic ☐Native American ☐White ☐Other

Directions

Please provide the identifying information requested on the right.

The 67 items on the front and back of this form are statements that describe college experiences. Read each one and decide how well it applies to you at the present time (within the past few days). For each item, circle the asterisk at the point in the continuum that best represents how closely the statement applies to you. Circle only one asterisk for each item. To change an answer, draw an *X* through the incorrect response and circle the desired response. Be sure to use a hard-tipped pen or pencil and press very firmly. Do not erase.

In the example on the right, Item A applied very closely, and Item B was changed from "doesn't apply at all" to "applies somewhat."

Example

A. * * * * * * * * *

B. * * * * * * * * *

Applies Very Closely to Me ← → Doesn't Apply to Me at All

1. I feel that I fit in well as part of the college environment........ * * * * * * * * *
2. I have been feeling tense or nervous lately........ * * * * * * * * *
3. I have been keeping up to date on my academic work........ * * * * * * * * *
4. I am meeting as many people, and making as many friends as I would like in college........ * * * * * * * * *
5. I know why I'm in college and what I want out of it........ * * * * * * * * *
6. I am finding academic work at college difficult........ * * * * * * * * *
7. Lately I have been feeling blue and moody a lot........ * * * * * * * * *
8. I am very involved with social activities in college........ * * * * * * * * *
9. I am adjusting well to college........ * * * * * * * * *
10. I have not been functioning well during examinations........ * * * * * * * * *
11. I have felt tired much of the time lately........ * * * * * * * * *
12. Being on my own, taking responsibility for myself, has not been easy........ * * * * * * * * *
13. I am satisfied with the level at which I am performing academically........ * * * * * * * * *
14. I have had informal, personal contacts with college professors........ * * * * * * * * *
15. I am pleased now about my decision to go to college........ * * * * * * * * *

Source: Partial sample from the *Student Adaptation to College Questionnaire* copyright © 1989 by Western Psychological Services. Reprinted by permission of the publisher, Western Psychological Services, 12031 Wilshire Boulevard, Los Angeles, California, 90025, U. S. A. Not to be reprinted in whole or in part for any additional purpose without the expressed, written permission of the publisher. All rights reserved.

scale from "applies very closely to me" to "doesn't apply to me at all." Overall, the questions focus on the quality of the student's adjustment to the college environment (e.g., whether the student fits in well, feels tense, keeps up to date on academic work, makes friends, attends class, is satisfied with social life). To analyze these questions, the researcher groups these questions into four scales (called *subscales*): Academic Adjustment (24 questions), Social Adjustment (20 questions), Emotional Adjustment (15 questions), and Goal Commitment–Institutional Attachment (15 questions). Then the analyst sums the scores to the questions on each scale (see chapter 7 section on "Summed Scores") to identify an individual's score on each scale. Dahmus, Bernardin, and Bernardin (1992) provided a review of these procedures and background about this questionnaire.

Behavioral Observations

To collect data on specific behaviors, you can observe behavior and record scores on a checklist or scoring sheet. **Behavioral observations** are made by selecting an instrument (or using a behavioral protocol) on which to record a behavior, observing individuals for that behavior, and checking points on a scale that reflect the behavior (behavioral checklists). The advantage of this form of data is that you can identify an individual's actual behavior, rather than simply record his or her views or perceptions. However, behaviors may be difficult to score, and gathering them is a time-consuming form of data collection. Further, if more than one observer gathers data for a study, you need to train observers to provide consistent procedures and periodically check that the observers apply consistent scoring.

An example of a behavioral checklist is the Measurement of Inappropriate and Disruptive Interactions (MIDI) developed and used in the Saber-Tooth Project, which studied physical education curriculum changes in one middle school and two comparison schools (Ward, 1999) as shown in Figure 6.7. The investigators used this checklist in a

FIGURE 6.7

Example of an Observational Scoring Sheet with Fictitious Data

Social Skills Assessment

Teacher Alis Grade Level 08 Observer JC Date 2/3 Content Area Lacross School School A

	1	2	3	4	5	6	7	8	9	10	11	12	13	14	15	16	17	18	19	20	21	22	23	24	25
C	G	C	C	I	I	I	G	G	G	G	G	M	M	M	G										
B	I	O	V	I	I	I	I	I	I	T	T	I	I	I	T										
E	I	S	I	I	I	I	S	S	S	S	I	I	I	I	S										

	26	27	28	29	30	31	32	33	34	35	36	37	38	39	40	41	42	43	44	45	46	47	48	49	50
C																									
B																									
E																									

	51	52	53	54	55	56	57	58	59	60	61	62	63	64	65	66	67	68	69	70	71	72	73	74	75
C																									
B																									
E																									

	76	77	78	79	80	81	82	83	84	85	86	87	88	89	90	91	92	93	94	95	96	97	98	99	100
C																									
B																									
E																									

	101	102	103	104	105	106	107	108	109	110	111	112	113	114	115	116	117	118	119	120	121	122	123	124	125
C																									
B																									
E																									

	126	127	128	129	130	131	132	133	134	135	136	137	138	139	140	141	142	143	144	145	146	147	148	149	150
C																									
B																									
E																									

	151	152	153	154	155	156	157	158	159	160	161	162	163	164	165	166	167	168	169	170	171	172	173	174	175
C																									
B																									
E																									

C																									
B																									
E																									

C																									
B																									
E																									

Context Categories	Inappropriate Behaviors	Extent of Misbehavior:
Game:	Talking out/Noise:	Class: (15 or more students)
Practice:	Inactive:	Small Group: (4 or more students up to 15)
Cognitive:	Off-task:	Individual/s (less that 3 students)
Instruction:	Non-compliance:	
Management/Other:	Verbal offense:	

Source: Ward, P., Barrett, T. M., Evans, S. A., Doutis, P., Nguyen, P. T., & Johnson, M. K. (1999). Chapter 5: Curriculum effects in eighth-grade Lacrosse. *Journal of Teaching in Physical Education, 18,* 428–443. Reprinted with permission of the authors.

study of four classes in which the teachers provided an instructional unit on lacrosse to eighth-grade students (Ward et al., 1999). During this classroom unit, the researchers observed the students and scored student behaviors using the MIDI scoring sheet in each class portrayed in Figure 6.7.

The legend for this scoring sheet, located at the bottom, lists the codes that observers recorded in each cell. These codes were the first letter of the appropriate word used to describe the context or focus of the lesson in which the behavior occurs (i.e., game, practice, cognitive, instruction, or management/other). The observers also recorded the type of inappropriate behavior during the primary event that involved the most students during the interval (i.e., talking out/noise, inactive, off-task, noncompliance, verbal offense). Finally, observers indicated who was engaged in the disruption (i.e., class, small group, individual) to assess the extent of misbehavior in the class. Numbers at the top of each column on the scoring sheet represent students (e.g., 1, 2, 3, and so forth through 115). Data were collected on-site using this scoring sheet as the instrument, and three observers in the classes recorded their observations (identified by the column numbers) at an interval of 6-second observations. The investigators trained the observers in their scoring procedures so that they would score the behavior consistently. An audiotape recording cued the observers as to when they would mark their observations on the checklist sheet. For example, in the fictitious data shown in Figure 6.7 for student 1, the observer records on the rows:

Context = Game (G)
Inappropriate Behavior = Inactive (I)
Extent of Misbehavior = Individual/s (less than 3 students) (I)

After recording scores for all students, the observers analyzed the differences among students in their disruptive behaviors.

Factual Information

Quantitative, numeric data is also available in public educational records. **Factual information** or personal documents consist of numeric, individual data available in public records. Examples of these types of data include grade reports, school attendance records, student demographic data, and census information. As long as these documents are available in the public domain, researchers can access and use them. Some documents, such as health information about students, cannot be easily accessed by investigators because federal regulations protect the privacy of individuals. Also, researchers need to scrutinize the public documents carefully to determine if they represent accurate data. The availability of public documents does not infer that researchers have collected the data carefully, with an eye toward accuracy.

Web-Based Electronic Data Collection

With the use of Web sites and the Internet, electronic data collection in quantitative research is popular. At this time, use of Web sites and the Internet for data collection consists of administering surveys (Solomon, 2001), gathering interview data (Persichitte, Young, & Tharp, 1997), or using existing databases for analysis (e.g., Texas Lotto, U.S. Census Bureau, Louis Harris Pool; Pachnowski, Newman, & Jurczyk, 1997). Survey applications might consist of optically scanning an instrument and placing it up on a Web site for participants to complete. Another form is computer-assisted self-interviewing (Babbie, 1998). In this approach, the participant in a study logs on to a computer, downloads a questionnaire from the Internet, completes the questionnaire, and sends the completed questionnaire back to the researcher. Other approaches using electronic questionnaires include voice recognition using the telephone keypad, and computerized self-administered questionnaires (Babbie, 1998). Electronic data collection provides an easy, quick form of data collection. However, use of the Internet may be limited because of (a) limitations involving the use of listservs and obtaining of e-mail addresses, (b) limitations of the technology itself, (c) lack of a population list, and (d) the questionable representativeness of the sample data (Mertler, 2001). Not all participants have access to computers or are comfortable using the Internet.

How to Decide What Types to Choose

Confronted by these many options for collecting quantitative data, which one or ones will you use? To select your data sources, ask yourself the following questions:

- *What am I trying to learn about participants from my research questions and hypotheses?* If you are trying to learn about individual behaviors of parents at a student–parent conference meeting, then you could use a behavioral checklist and record observations. If you are trying to measure the attitudes of teachers toward a bond issue, attitudinal questions or an attitudinal instrument will be required.
- *What information can you realistically collect?* Some types of data may not be collectible in a study because individuals are unwilling to supply it. For example, precise data on the frequency of substance abuse in middle schools may be difficult to collect; identifying the number of student suspensions for substance abuse is much more realistic.
- *How do the advantages of the data collection compare with its disadvantages?* In our discussion of each data source, we have talked about the ideal situations for data collection. Given the ease or difficulty of collecting data, each type needs to be assessed.

How would you now advise that Maria collect her data? Assume that she now seeks to answer the general quantitative research question "Why do students carry weapons in high school?" and the following subquestions:

a. "How frequently do students feel weapons are carried into high school?"
b. "What general attitudes do high school students hold toward the possession of weapons in the schools?"
c. "Does participation in extracurricular activities at school influence attitudes of students toward possession of weapons?"
d. "Are student suspensions for possession of weapons on the increase in high schools?"

Before looking at the answers provided, list the type of information that Maria might collect for subquestions a through d.

To answer these subquestions, Maria first needs to locate or develop a questionnaire to send out to a sample of high school students in the school district. Her data collection will consist mainly of attitudinal data. This questionnaire will measure student *attitudes* toward frequency of weapon possession (question a); assess student *attitudes* toward possession of weapons (question b); and gather *factual data* about the students (question c), such as age, level of education, race, gender, and extent of participation in extracurricular activities. To answer question d, she will contact the school officials of several high schools and ask if she can obtain reports on student suspensions—school documents that report quantitative data. In summary, she will collect both attitudinal and factual information.

WHAT INSTRUMENT WILL YOU USE TO COLLECT DATA?

Let's assume that you will collect performance, attitudinal, or observational data. These forms of data collection all involve using an instrument. What instruments will you use to collect your data? Do you find one to use or develop one yourself? If you search for one to use, how will you locate this instrument? Once you find the instrument, what criteria will you use to determine if it is a good instrument to use?

Locate or Develop an Instrument

Three options exist for obtaining an instrument to use: You can develop one yourself, locate one and modify it, or locate one and use it in its entirety. Of these choices, locating one to use (either modifying it or using it in its original form) represents the easiest approach. It is more difficult to develop an instrument than to locate one and modify it for use in a study. **Modifying an instrument** means locating an existing instrument, obtaining permission to change it, and making changes in it to fit your requirements. Typically, authors of the original instrument will ask for a copy of your modified version and the results from your study in exchange for your use of their instrument.

An instrument to measure the variables in your study may not be available in the literature or commercially. If this is the case, you will have to develop your own instrument, which is a long and arduous process. Developing an instrument consists of several steps, such as identifying the purpose of the instrument, reviewing the literature, writing the questions, and testing the questions with individuals similar to those you plan to study. The four phases of development, recommended by Benson and Clark (1983) and shown in Figure 6.8, illustrate the rigorous steps of planning, constructing, evaluating, and checking to see if the questions work (i.e., validating an instrument). In this process, the basic steps consist of reviewing the literature, presenting general questions to a target group, constructing questions for the item pool, and pilot testing the items. The statistical

FIGURE 6.8

Steps in Developing or Constructing an Instrument

Phase I: Planning
- State purpose of test and target groups
- Identify and define domain of test
- Review literature on construct or variable of interest
- Give open-ended questions to target group
- Interpret open-ended comments
- Write objectives
- Select item format

Phase II: Construction
- Develop table of specifications
- Hire and train item writers
- Write pool items
- Validate content
- Have judges complete qualitative evaluation
- Develop new or revise items

Phase III: Quantitative Evaluation
- Prepare instrument for first pilot test
- Administer first pilot test
- Debrief subjects
- Calculate reliability
- Run item analysis
- Revise instrument
- Prepare for second pilot test

Phase IV: Validation
- Administer second pilot test
- Run item analysis
- Repeat steps of revision, pilot administration, and item analysis
- Begin validation
- Administer for validation data
- Continue validation

Source: Adapted from a flowchart provided by Benson & Clark, 1983

procedures of calculating reliability and item analysis are available in computer software programs and discussed in more detail in chapter 7.

Search for an Instrument

If you decide to use an existing instrument, the publisher or author will typically charge you a fee for use of the instrument. Finding a good instrument that measures your independent, dependent, and control variables is not easy. In fact, you may need to assemble a new instrument that consists of parts of existing instruments. Whether you search for one instrument or several to use, several strategies can aid in your search:

- *Look in published journal articles.* Often authors of journal articles will report instruments and provide a few sample items so that you can see the basic content included in the instrument. Examine references in published journal articles that cite specific instruments and contact the authors for inspection copies. Before you use the instrument, seek permission from the author. With limited space in journals, authors are including fewer examples of their items or copies of their instruments.
- *Run an ERIC search.* Use the term *instruments* and the topic of the study to search the ERIC system for instruments. Use the online search process of the ERIC database (see chapter 4). Use the same search procedure to locate abstracts to articles where the authors mention instruments that they have used in their studies.
- *Examine guides to tests and instruments that are available commercially.* Examine the *Mental Measurements Yearbook* (MMY; Impara & Plake, 1999) or the *Tests in Print* (TIP; Murphy, Impara, & Plake, 1999), both of which are available from the Buros Institute of Mental Measurements (**www.unl.edu/buros/**). More than 400 commercial firms develop instruments that are available for sale to individuals and institutions. Published since 1938, these guides contain extensive information about tests and measures available for educational research use. You can locate reviews and descriptions of English-language commercially published tests in the MMY, which is available on CD-ROM databases in many academic libraries.

Criteria for Choosing a Good Instrument

Once you find an instrument, several criteria can be used to assess whether it is a good instrument to use. Ask yourself:

- Have authors developed the instrument recently, and can you obtain the most recent version? With knowledge expanding in educational research, instruments over 5 years old might be outdated. To stay current, authors update their instruments periodically, and you need to find the most recent copy of an instrument.
- Is the instrument widely cited by other authors? Frequent use by other researchers will provide some indication of its endorsement by others. Use by other researchers may provide some evidence about whether the questions on the instrument provide good and consistent measures.
- Are reviews available for the instrument? Look for published reviews about the instrument in the MMY or in journals such as *Measurement and Evaluation in Counseling and Development*. If reviews exist, it means that other researchers have taken the instrument seriously and seek to document its worth.
- Is there information about the reliability and validity of scores from past uses of the instrument?

- Does the procedure for recording data fit the research questions/hypotheses in your study?
- Does the instrument contain accepted scales of measurement?

Because of the importance of the last three criteria—reliability and validity, recording information, and scales of measurement—a discussion will explore these ideas in more depth.

Are Scores on Past Use of the Instrument Reliable and Valid?

You want to select an instrument that reports individual scores that are reliable and valid. **Reliability** means that scores from an instrument are stable and consistent. Scores should be nearly the same when researchers administer the instrument multiple times at different times. Also, scores need to be consistent. When an individual answers certain questions one way, the individual should consistently answer closely related questions in the same way. **Validity**, however, means that the individual's scores from an instrument make sense, are meaningful, and enable you, as the researcher, to draw good conclusions from the sample you are studying to the population. This definition is consistent with the *Standards for Educational and Psychological Testing* jointly formulated by AERA, the APA, and the National Council on Measurement in Education (1999).

Reliability and validity are bound together in complex ways. These two terms sometimes overlap and at other times are mutually exclusive. Validity can be thought of as the larger, more encompassing term when you assess the choice of an instrument. Reliability is generally easier to understand as it is a measure of consistency. To comprehend these concepts more fully, it may be necessary to untangle their relationship. If scores are not reliable, they are not valid; scores need to be stable and consistent first before they can be meaningful. Additionally, the more reliable the scores from an instrument, the more valid the scores may be (however, scores may still not measure the particular construct and may remain invalid). The ideal situation exists when scores are both reliable and valid. Of the two concepts, reliability and validity, reliability is easier to understand and we will begin by identifying the form of testing for stability and consistency. In addition, the more reliable the scores from an instrument, the more valid the scores will be. Scores need to be stable and consistent before they can be meaningful. In this way, validity is the larger, more encompassing term when you assess the choice of an instrument.

Reliability A goal of good research is to have measures or observations that are reliable. Several factors can result in unreliable data, including when:

- Questions on instruments are ambiguous and unclear
- Procedures of test administration vary and are not standardized
- Participants are fatigued, are nervous, misinterpret questions, or guess on tests (Rudner, 1993).

Researchers can use any one or more of five available procedures to examine an instrument's reliability, as shown in Table 6.3. You can distinguish these procedures by the number of times the instrument is administered, the number of versions of the instrument administered by researchers, and the number of individuals who make an assessment of information.

The **test–retest reliability** procedure examines the extent to which scores from one sample are stable over time from one test administration to another. To determine this form of reliability, the researcher administers the test at two different times to the same participants at a sufficient time interval. If the scores are reliable, then they will relate (or will correlate) at a positive, reasonably high level, such as .6 (see the correlation statistical test in chapter 7, "Selecting a Statistical Program"). This approach has the

TABLE 6.3
Types of Reliability

Form of Reliability	Number of Times Instrument Administered	Number of Different Versions of the Instrument	Number of Individuals Who Provide Information
Test–retest reliability	Twice at different time intervals	One version of the instrument	Each participant in the study completes the instrument twice.
Alternate forms reliability	Each instrument administered once	Two different versions of the same concept or variable	Each participant in the study completes each instrument.
Alternate forms and test–retest reliability	Twice at different time intervals	Two different versions of the same concept or variable	Each participant in the study completes each instrument.
Interrater reliability	Instrument administered once	One version of the instrument	More than one individual observes behavior of the participants.
Internal consistency reliability	Instrument administered once	One version of the instrument	Each participant in the study completes the instrument.

advantage of requiring only one form of the instrument; however, an individual's scores on the first administration of the instrument may influence the scores on the second administration. Consider this example:

> A researcher measures a stable characteristic, such as creativity, for sixth graders at the beginning of the year. Measured again at the end of the year, the researcher assumes that the scores will be stable during the sixth-grade experience. If scores at the beginning and the end of the year relate, there is evidence for test–retest reliability.

Another approach is **alternative forms reliability**. This involves using two instruments, both measuring the same variables and relating (or correlating) the scores for the same group of individuals to the two instruments. In practice, both instruments need to be similar, such as the same content, same level of difficulty, and same types of scales. Thus, the items for both instruments represent the same universe or population of items. The advantage of this approach is that it allows you to see if the scores from one instrument are equivalent to scores from another instrument, for two instruments intended to measure the same variables. The difficulty, of course, is whether the two instruments are equivalent in the first place. Assuming that they are, the researchers relate or correlate the items from the one instrument with its equivalent instrument. Examine this example:

> An instrument with 45 vocabulary items yields scores from first graders. The researcher compares these scores with those from another instrument that also measures a similar set of 45 vocabulary items. Both instruments contain items of approximately equal difficulty. When the researcher finds the items to relate positively, we have confidence in the accuracy or reliability of the scores from the first instrument.

The **alternate forms and test–retest reliability** approach is simply a variety of the two previous types of reliability. In this approach, the researcher administers the test twice *and* uses an alternate form of the test from the first administration to the second.

This type of reliability has the advantages of both examining the stability of scores over time as well as having the equivalence of items from the potential universe of items. It also has all of the disadvantages of both test–retest and alternate forms of reliability. Scores may reflect differences in content or difficulty or in changes over time. An example follows:

> The researcher administers the 45 vocabulary items to first graders twice at two different times, and the actual tests are equivalent in content and level of difficulty. The researcher correlates or relates scores to both tests and finds that they correlate positively and highly. The scores to the initial instrument are reliable.

Interrater reliability is a procedure used when making observations of behavior. It involves observations made by two or more individuals of an individual's or several individuals' behavior. The observers record their scores of the behavior and then compare scores to see if their scores are similar or different. Because this method obtains observational scores from two or more individuals, it has the advantage of negating any bias that any one individual might bring to scoring. It has the disadvantages of requiring the researcher to train the observers and requiring the observers to negotiate outcomes and reconcile differences in their observations, something that may not be easy to do. Here is an example:

> Two observers view preschool children at play in their activity center. They observe the spatial skills of the children and record on a checklist the number of times each child builds something in the activity center. After the observations, the observers compare their checklists to determine how close their scores were during the observation. Assuming that their scores were close, they can average their scores and conclude that their assessment demonstrates interrater reliability.

Scores from an instrument are reliable and accurate if an individual's scores are **internally consistent** across the items on the instrument. If someone completes items at the beginning of the instrument one way (e.g., positive about negative effects of tobacco), then they should answer the questions later in the instrument in a similar way (e.g., positive about the health effects of tobacco).

The consistency of responses can be examined in several ways. One way is to split the test in half and relate or correlate the items. This test is called the **Kuder–Richardson split half test** (KR–20, KR–21) and it is used when (a) the items on an instrument are scored right or wrong as categorical scores, (b) the responses are not influenced by speed, and (c) the items measure a common factor. Since the split half test relies on information from only half of the instrument, a modification in this procedure is to use the **Spearman–Brown formula**, which estimates full-length test reliability using all questions on an instrument. This is important because the reliability of an instrument increases as researchers add more items to the instrument. Finally, the **coefficient alpha** is used to test for internal consistency (Cronbach, 1984). If the items are scored as continuous variables (e.g., *strongly agree* to *strongly disagree*), the alpha provides a coefficient to estimate consistency of scores on an instrument. Calculations for the Kuder–Richardson split half, Spearman–Brown prophecy formula, and coefficient alpha are available in Thorndike (1997b).

Validity In addition to reliability, you should examine whether the instrument you select for use has reported scores that are valid. Do authors report assessments of validity? A study may have invalid scores because of:

- A poorly designed study
- Participant fatigue, stress, and misunderstanding of questions on the instrument
- Inability to make useful predictions from scores

TABLE 6.4
Types of Validity

Types of Validity	What is Measured?	What Evidence is Obtained to Substantiate it?
Content Validity	How well do the questions represent all of the possibilities of questions available?	Ask experts if the questions are representative of the area of interest.
Criterion-related	How well do the scores on the instrument relate to an outcome?	Select an outcome and correlate or relate the scores to it.
	How well do the scores on the instrument predict a future outcome?	Select a future outcome and correlate the scores with it.
Construct Validity	What do the scores on the instrument mean or signify?	Use statistical procedures, such as correlating scores with other scores; examine the correlation among questions on an instrument; or test a theory against the scores.
	What is the intended purpose or use for the scores from the instrument? Can we safely generalize from them?	Use nonstatistical procedures, such as examining the values inherent in the interpretation of the scores; assess the relevance of the scores for the purpose of the study; or consider the likely social consequences.

- Poorly designed questions or measures of variables
- Information that has little use and application

Researchers might report different forms of validity, as shown in Table 6.4. The traditional perspective on validity is to discuss three forms: content, criterion-referenced, and construct validity. More recently, measurement specialists have begun to view validity as a unitary concept (Thorndike, 1997b) and advocate that scores are valid if they have use and they result in positive social consequences (Hubley & Zumbo, 1996; Messick, 1980). The following discussion will address both the traditional and the current conceptions of validity.

Content validity is the extent to which the questions on the instrument and the scores from these questions are representative of all the possible questions that a researcher could ask about the content or skills. Researchers evaluate content validity by examining the plan and the procedures used in constructing the instrument. They examine the information about the objectives of the instrument, the content areas, and the level of difficulty of the questions. Typically researchers go to a panel of judges or experts and have them identify whether the questions are valid. This form of validity is useful when the possibilities of questions (e.g., achievement tests in science education) are well known and easily identifiable. It is less useful in assessing personality or aptitude scores (e.g., on the Stanford–Binet IQ test), when the universe of questions is less certain.

Instead of examining the specific questions on an instrument, another form of validity is to see if the scores predict an outcome you would expect them to predict. **Criterion-related validity** determines whether the scores from an instrument are a good predictor of some outcome (or criterion) they are expected to predict. There are two types of criterion-related validity, predictive and concurrent (Thorndike, 2005). Predictive validity uses test scores on an instrument to predict outcomes. The test is implemented before the criterion information is gathered. An example of a predictive validity measure is the Graduate Record Examination (GRE). Scores from this assessment should predict the criterion—performance in graduate school. As another example, a portfolio assessment and a pencil-and-paper test should both predict a student's ability to understand the content of an English methods class (the outcome). In both cases, a researcher would relate the scores on the instrument in the study to the outcome (criterion) to determine if they are related. A high correlation of .6 or above indicates a positive relationship. This form of validity is especially useful for predicting outcomes, but it requires that the researcher clearly identify appropriate outcomes.

Concurrent validity is similar to predictive; however, both the test and criterion measures are collected at the same time (Mertens, 2005) as opposed to the criterion (or outcomes) collected at a later point in time. Researchers measuring this type of validity want to assess current information (knowledge, skills, interests, or personality characteristics). Concurrent validity can be used to assess whether shortened instruments or new instruments are valid. To reduce costs or simplify testing procedures, researchers may test the concurrent validity of an abbreviated instrument with that of a longer instrument measuring the same constructs. Researchers can calculate the concurrent validity of these two sets of scores by correlating the two; high correlations indicate concurrent validity. Additionally, researchers could test the concurrent validity of a new instrument by correlating scores on this instrument with scores on existing instruments.

A third form of validity, construct validity, is the most complicated because it is assessed using both statistics and practical procedures. **Construct validity** is established by determining if the scores from an instrument are significant, meaningful, useful, and have a purpose. In short, are they a good measure, and can you use them to understand a sample from a population? To answer these questions, you need to assess the scores statistically and practically. Through statistical procedures you can:

- See if scores to items are related in a way that is expected (e.g., examine the relationship of a question on a "student depression instrument" to see if it relates to the overall scale measuring depression)
- Test a theory and see if the scores, as expected, support the theory (e.g., test a theory of depression and see if the evidence or data supports the relationships in the theory)
- Correlate the scores statistically with other variables or scales that should be similar (called *convergent validity*) or dissimilar (called *discriminant validity;* Messick, 1980; e.g., see if scores to questions on one student depression instrument relate positively to items on another depression instrument or have little relation to items on an instrument measuring anxiety)

You can also use practical procedures to assess the interpretation (making sense of test scores) and use (application of test scores; Hubley & Zumbo, 1996), such as:

- Examining the consequences of interpreting test scores in terms of values (e.g., when student scores indicate "high depression," does this mean that depression is normal, abnormal, positive, negative, or realistic?)
- Examining the relevance and use of test scores (e.g., are the student scores on "depression" useful for screening? Are they useful for at-risk students more than normal achievers?)
- Examining the consequences of using test scores (e.g., are the scores useful for policy decisions by the school? By teachers?)

After reviewing the forms of reliability and validity, we can now step back and review what questions you should ask when selecting or evaluating an instrument. A short list of questions, provided in Figure 6.9, should aid in this process.

FIGURE 6.9

Validity and Reliability Questions for Selecting/Evaluating a Test or Instrument

When selecting or evaluating an instrument, look for:

Reliability	Validity
1. Did the author check for it?	1. Did the author check for it?
2. If so, what form of reliability was reported?	2. If so, what type of validity was reported?
3. Was an appropriate type used?	3. Was more than one type reported?
4. Were the reliability values (coefficients) reported?	4. Were the values (coefficients) reported?
5. Were they positive, high coefficients?	5. Were they positive, high coefficients?

To practice applying these questions, consider the choice of an instrument by Maria. She finds an instrument titled "Attitudes Toward Possession of Weapons in Schools." An author reports this instrument in a published journal article. What might be two forms of reliability and two forms of validity that she could look for in the author's discussion about this instrument? Write down these forms of reliability and validity.

Do the Instrument's Data Recording Procedures Fit the Research Questions/Hypotheses?

Returning to our question of criteria for assessing a good instrument to use, another criterion was that instruments contain recording procedures that fit the data you need to answer the research questions or hypotheses. Who records the data on the instruments or checklists? Data may be self-reported; that is, the participants provide the information, such as on achievement tests or on attitudinal questionnaires. Alternatively, the researcher may record the data on forms by observing, interviewing, or collecting documents. Having participants supply the data is less time consuming for the researcher. However, when the researcher records the data, he or she becomes familiar with how the participants respond and hence can control for a higher level of quality of the data.

Are Adequate Scales of Measurement Used?

Another criterion is that the instrument should contain good response options to the questions. In chapter 5, we introduced the idea that variables could be measured as categories or on a continuous range of scores. Now it is helpful to assess instruments that you might use in research in terms of the adequacy of their scales of measurement. For example, for a study of student attitudes toward the use of wireless laptops in a college classroom, a researcher might ask the *question* "To what extent does the wireless laptop help you learn in the classroom?" The student might answer this question using a *categorical scale* such as the following:

___________ To a great extent
___________ Somewhat
___________ To a less extent

The easiest way to think about the types of scales of measurement is to remember that there are two basic types: categorical and continuous scales. Categorical scales have two types: nominal and ordinal scales. Continuous scales (often called *scale scores* in

TABLE 6.5

Types of Scales Used in Quantitative Research

Type of Scale	Examples of Questions Using the Scale
Nominal scale (uses categories)	How much education have you completed? _______ No college _______ Some college _______ Bachelor degree _______ Graduate or professional work What is your class rank? _______ Freshman _______ Sophomore _______ Junior _______ Senior
Ordinal scale (uses categories implied or expressed rank order)	Has your advisor helped you select courses? _______ Not at all _______ To a small extent _______ To some extent _______ To a great extent _______ To a very great extent Rank your preference for type of graduate-level instruction from 1 to 4 _______ activity-based learning _______ lecture _______ small-group learning _______ discussion
Quasi-interval or Interval/ratio scale (uses continuous equal intervals)	School is a place where I am thought of as a person who matters. _______ Strongly agree _______ Agree _______ Undecided _______ Disagree _______ Strongly disagree Colleges and universities should conduct research to solve economic problems of cities. _______ Strongly agree _______ Agree _______ Undecided _______ Disagree _______ Strongly disagree

computer data analysis programs) also have two types: interval/quasi-interval and ratio scales. These types of scales are shown in Table 6.5.

Scales of measurement are response options to questions that measure (or observe) variables in categorical or continuous units. It is important to understand scales of measurement to assess the quality of an instrument and to determine the appropriate statistics to use in data analysis.

Nominal Scales Researchers use **nominal scales** (or categorical scales) to provide response options where participants check one or more categories that describe their traits, attributes, or characteristics. These scales do not have any order. An example of a nominal scale would be gender, divided into the two categories of male and female (either one could be listed first as a response option). Another form of a nominal scale would be a checklist of "yes" or "no" responses. A semantic differential scale, popular in psychological research, is another type of nominal scale. This scale consists of bipolar adjectives that the participant uses to check his or her position. For example, in a psychological study of talented teenagers, researchers were interested in studying the teenagers' emotional responses to their everyday activities (Csikszentmihalyi, Rathunde, Whalen, & Wong, 1993). The researchers used a semantic differential scale for teenagers to record their mood on several adjectives at certain times of the day. The researchers used a beeping device (p. 52) and the participants were asked to describe their mood as they were beeped, using the following scale:

	very	quite	some	neither	some	quite	very	
alert	0	0	·	–	·	0	0	drowsy

Although the researchers summed scores of teenagers across several questions such as this one, the response scale to each question was nominal or categorical.

Ordinal Scales Researchers use **ordinal scales** (or ranking scales or categorical scales) to provide response options where participants rank from best or most important to worst or least important some trait, attribute, or characteristic. These scales have an implied intrinsic order. For example, a researcher might record individual performance in a race for each runner from first to last place. Many attitudinal measures imply an ordinal scale because they ask participants to rank order the importance ("highly important" to "of no importance") or the extent ("to a great extent" to "a little extent") of topics. As this example illustrates, the information is categorical in a ranked order.

Interval/Ratio Scales

Another popular scale researchers use is an interval or rating scale. **Interval scales** (or rating scales or continuous scales) provide "continuous" response options to questions with assumed equal distances between options. These scales may have three, four, or more response options. The popular Likert scale ("strongly agree" to "strongly disagree") illustrates a scale with theoretically equal intervals among responses. Although an ordinal scale, such as "highly important" to "of no importance," may seem like an interval scale, we have no guarantee that the intervals are equal, as in the well-tested Likert scale. An achievement test such as the Iowa Test of Basic Skills is assumed to be an interval scale because researchers have substantiated that the response choices are of equal distance from each other.

The popular Likert scale (*strongly agree* to *strongly disagree*) illustrates a scale with theoretically equal intervals among responses. It has become common practice to treat this scale as a rating scale and assume that the equal intervals hold between the response categories (Blaikie, 2003). However, we have no guarantee that we have equal intervals. Hence, often the Likert scale (*strongly agree* to *strongly disagree*) is treated as both ordinal and interval data in educational research (hence the term *quasi-interval* in Table 6.5). How researchers consider this scale (or a similar scale, such as "highly important" to "of no importance") is critical in the choice of statistic to use to analyze the data. Ordinal scales require nonparametric statistical tests whereas interval scales require parametric (see chapter 7, "Conduct Inferential Analysis"). Some researchers stress the importance of viewing Likert scales as ordinal data (Jamieson, 2004). Others indicate that the errors for treating the Likert scale results as interval data are minimal (Jaccard & Wan, 1996). In order to consider treating Likert data on an interval scale, researchers should develop multiple categories or choices in their scale, determine whether their data are normally distributed, and establish whether the distance between each value on the scale is equal. If this cannot be done, then you should treat the Likert scale and scales like "extent of importance" or "degree of agreement" as ordinal scales for purposes of data analysis.

Finally, a **ratio scale** (or true zero scale) is a response scale in which participants check a response option with a true zero and equal distances between units. Although educational researchers seldom use this type of scale, examples of it are the height of individuals (e.g., 50 inches, 60 inches) and income levels (from zero dollars to $50,000 in increments of $10,000).

Combined Scales In educational research, quantitative investigators often use a combination of categorical and continuous scales. Of these, interval scales provide the most variation of responses and lend themselves to stronger statistical analysis. The best rule of thumb is that if you do not know in advance what statistical analysis you will use, create an interval or continuous scale. Continuous scales can always be converted into ordinal or nominal scales (Tuckman, 1999), but not vice versa.

Think-Aloud About Finding and Selecting an Instrument

Often I find beginning researchers developing their own instruments rather than taking the time to locate an existing instrument suitable for their study. Unquestionably, developing your own instrument requires knowledge about item or question construction, scale development, format, and length. Although some campuses may have courses that teach this information, most students develop instruments with little feedback from advisors or consultants about how to design the instrument.

Instead of developing your own instrument, I would encourage you to locate or modify an existing instrument. An example can illustrate how you might find this instrument. In Figure 6.6, I showed you an instrument that I had found on students' attitudes toward adaptation to college. How did I find this instrument?

I knew that I wanted to measure the variable "student adjustment to college" because I had formed a general quantitative research question: "What factors influence how freshman students adjust to college?" I began by searching the ERIC database for an instrument using the descriptors of "students" and "college" and "adjustment" in my online keyword search. Although I found several good journal articles on the topic, none included a useful instrument. Examining the references in these articles still did not net an instrument that would work.

I turned to two books in our academic library that index available instruments, the Buros Institute of Mental Measurements books, *Tests in Print* and the *Mental Measurements Yearbook*. You may recall from earlier in this chapter that the TIP and MMY publications contain information about commercially available tests and instruments, including attitudinal instruments. Although our library contains book copies of the TIP and MMY, I could have used the CD-ROM version of these books available in our library or visited the Buros Web site at **www.unl.edu/buros/**.

I located the latest book copy of the TIP (Murphy et al., 1999) and looked under the alphabetized listing of tests, searching for any instruments that related to students, especially college students. After trying out several words, I found the Student Adaptation to College Questionnaire (SACQ). Reading through this brief description of the SACQ I learned basic information about the instrument, such as its purpose, the population for its use (i.e., college freshman), publication date (1989), and scales. This review also contained price information ($89.50 for 25 hand-scorable questionnaires and a manual), the time required to administer it (20 minutes), authors, publishers, and a cross reference to a review of the instrument to be found in the MMY, 11th edition (Kramer & Conoley, 1992).

Next I was curious about whether scores reported on this instrument were both valid and reliable, so I looked up the instrument in the 11th edition of the MMY (Kramer & Conoley, 1992) and found a review of it by E. Jack Asher, Jr., Professor Emeritus of Psychology, Western Michigan University, Kalamazoo. I also searched the ERIC database and located a review article by Dahmus et al. (1992) reported in the journal *Measurement and Evaluation in Counseling and Development*.

Focusing mainly on the Asher review, I found that it addressed:

- The purpose of the questionnaire
- The subscales on the questionnaire
- Norms on the questionnaire obtained by the authors by administering it from 1980 through 1984

- Evidence for validity of the scores from the instrument (i.e., criterion-related and construct validity)
- Evidence for reliability of the scores based on coefficients of internal consistency
- The value of the manual, especially the inclusion of potential ethical issues in using the instrument
- The overall value of the instrument for college counselors and research applications
- The limitations of the instrument

After reviewing all of these topics about the questionnaire, Asher concluded by summarizing an overall positive reaction to the instrument. Although somewhat dated (1989), the instrument has been widely used and positively reviewed. I decided it would be a good instrument to survey college students.

I next contacted the publisher, Western Psychological Services in Los Angeles, California, for permission to use the instrument and to obtain copies for my study. Using an instrument already developed by someone else, finding one with good validity and reliability scores, and locating a manual for using the instrument led to the early identification of means for collecting my data. You may not be as fortunate in locating an instrument as quickly as I did, but certainly, this process is better than developing numerous versions of your own instrument that might have questionable validity and reliability.

HOW WILL YOU ADMINISTER THE DATA COLLECTION?

The actual process of collecting data differs depending on the data and the instruments or documents you use. However, two aspects are standard across all forms of data and they deserve attention: the use of standard procedures and ethical practices.

Standardization

Performance measures, attitudinal measures, and observations rely on instruments. These instruments may consist of questionnaires that researchers mail to participants or hand out individually to people, surveys often administered in person or over the telephone, and observational checklists that researchers complete. Quantitative investigators also use instruments when they conduct face-to-face interviews with individuals or for a group of individuals.

In all of these cases, it is important to use standard procedures. When procedures vary, you introduce bias into the study and the data for individuals may not be comparable for analysis. Written procedures help keep you, as well as other data collectors assisting in the process, on track. For interviewing using an instrument, you apply the same procedures to each individual. Instructions provided on the interview form will help ensure that you follow a standard process. If others help in interviewing, you will need to train them so that the procedures used by all interviewers are consistent. This training might involve a demonstration interview, followed by a trial interview and a critique of the trial so that all trainees follow the same procedures.

In collecting observational data, training must occur first so that the researchers can collect data using standard procedures. A process similar to the one used in interviewing—demonstration, trial run, and a critique—might be used.

Researchers also collect public documents by obtaining permission to access this information and then taking notes or recording the information in a computer file. Establishing a database of categories of information helps to organize this information. This organization is especially important when you combine data from several sources into one file for analysis (e.g., enrollment data and suspension data for students in high schools).

Ethical Issues

Data collection should be ethical and it should respect individuals and sites. Obtaining permission before starting to collect data is not only a part of the informed consent process but is also an ethical practice. Protecting the anonymity of individuals by assigning numbers to returned instruments and keeping the identity of individuals confidential offers privacy to participants. During data collection, you must view the data as confidential and not share it with other participants or individuals outside of the project. You need to respect the wishes of individuals who choose not to participate in your study. Even when they consent to participate, people may back out or not show up for an observation or interview. Attempts to reschedule may be futile and you may need to select another person for data collection rather than force an individual to participate.

In terms of the research site, you need to recognize that all researchers disrupt the site they are studying, however minimally it might be. Observing in a classroom, for example, may disturb learning by distracting teachers and students, especially when you observe them closely and write down observations about their behavior on checklists. By obtaining permissions and clearly communicating the purpose of the study *before* you collect data, you can lessen the reservations some individuals may have about your presence in their educational setting.

REEXAMINING THE QUANTITATIVE PARENT INVOLVEMENT STUDY

We can turn to the parent involvement study (Deslandes & Bertrand, 2005) to see data-collection procedures in action. Examine once again the authors' "Method" section. We can assume that the authors had institutional review board consent letters signed from each of the parents they surveyed in Quebec. They may also have had permission from officials at the five public secondary schools they studied to obtain the names of the parents of children attending the schools.

The authors do not indicate in their method discussion the sampling strategy used to select the parents (see Paragraph 14). We do know that they selected schools representative of the general Quebec population and then identified 770 parents of students in seventh, eighth, and ninth grades. This procedure would illustrate multistage sampling. We do not know if the parents represented the entire population of parents or a sample of the parents. We also do not know if the parents were selected randomly or nonrandomly. In terms of the data they reported (see Table 3 and their limitation, Paragraph 46), the actual number of parents representative of each grade level was different, raising a question about whether these differences influenced the results in the study.

The authors then collected data from the parents on several instruments, including the Sharing the Dream! Parent Questionnaire, a questionnaire designed by other authors (see Paragraph 16), and demographic data (Paragraph 23). The questions on the instruments utilized a Likert-type scale that ranged from 1 (*disagree very strongly*) to 6 (*agree very strongly*) (see Paragraph 21, for example). They treated scores on these scales as interval-level scales and used parametric statistics to analyze the data (see chapter 7 on inferential analysis). We do know that the authors selected these instruments to measure the concepts of the model of the parent involvement process. We do not have information about the validity of the scores from past uses of these instruments, although the authors checked for reliability (Cronbach alpha) of questions that would measure each of the factors in the study. We also do not have information about whether the researchers used standard procedures during their data collection or about the potential ethical issues that might have developed in the study.

KEY IDEAS IN THE CHAPTER

The process of data collection involves more than simply gathering information; it includes five interrelated steps. The first step is to select participants for the study. This selection involves specifying the population and sample, determining how you will choose the participants, and deciding on an appropriate sample size.

The second step is to obtain permission from the participants to be involved in your study. Permissions may be needed from leaders of institutions or organizations, individuals at specific sites, participants (and their parents, for minor children), and a campus institutional review board.

The third step is to decide what type or types of data to collect. This decision begins with specifying the variables in your research questions or hypotheses, defining these variables, and seeking measures that operationalize these definitions. Typical quantitative data consists of measures of performance and attitudes, observations of behavior, and records and documents.

The fourth step is to locate, modify, or develop instruments that provide these measures. The easiest procedure is to use an existing instrument or modify one rather than develop your own instrument. Procedures exist for searching for an instrument, and when you find one that may be satisfactory, consider whether scores from past uses of it are reliable and valid, whether the procedure for recording information fits your research questions/hypotheses, and whether the scales will measure either categorical or continuous data.

The final step involves actually collecting the data. Your procedures need to be standard so that there is a uniform procedure for data collection. Also, as with all phases in research, the data-collection process needs to be conducted in a way that is ethical to individuals and to research sites.

USEFUL INFORMATION FOR PRODUCERS OF RESEARCH

- When collecting data for a study, plan to engage in five steps: selecting participants, obtaining permissions, selecting types of data, identifying instruments, and administering data collection.
- Identify the population and sample for a study. There are several types of probability and nonprobability sampling. The most rigorous sampling will be simple random sampling. However, the research circumstances may dictate a form of nonprobability sampling.
- Select as large a sample as possible. Use sampling formulas to be systematic in selecting the size of the sample.
- Obtain permission to conduct a study. A research study often requires multiple levels of permission, ranging from campus institutional review boards to organizational and site leaders to individual participants. The process of seeking approval from a campus institutional review board may consist of several steps.
- Consider the provisions that need to be included in a consent form, such as that shown in Figure 6.4.
- Consider how the research questions or hypotheses will be answered when deciding on what data type(s) to use. Then identify your variables, operationally define them, and select measures (e.g., performance and attitudes, observations of behavior, and factual and personal data) that fit the operational definitions.
- Decide whether to develop your own instrument or to use or modify an existing instrument for your research. Locating instruments is the easiest choice, and several library references provide good access to them.

- Consider the types of scales you plan to use on your instruments. These scales will affect the types of statistics to be used in analyzing the data. Make sure they relate to your questions.
- Before deciding on an instrument to use, make sure that the scores from past uses of it are reliable and valid. There are several forms of reliability and of validity.
- Determine whether the administration procedure will provide self-reported data or researcher-reported data. This will depend on the type of data to be collected.

Useful Information for Consumers of Research

- In evaluating a study, determine if the researcher fully disclosed the data collection. Look in a "Method" section for information about data collection.
- Look for studies in which researchers use the most rigorous form of sampling—simple random, probabilistic sampling.
- A rigorous quantitative study often requires multiple types of quantitative data. A research study should provide detailed information about each and all forms of data collected during the investigation.
- If researchers use instruments in their data collection, they need to report whether the scores from the past use of instruments are both valid and reliable. Look for high, positive coefficients (e.g., .6 or above).

Understanding Concepts and Evaluating Research Studies

1. Consider the parent involvement study (Deslandes & Bertrand, 2005). In Paragraph 18, the authors mention that they formed a variable (or construct) on parents' role construction that comprised 10 items with an alpha = .72. Explain what type of reliability they may have used and what it means.
2. If the authors of the parent involvement study (Deslandes & Bertrand, 2005) had mentioned the permissions they might have obtained, who would they cite as providing permission for them to conduct the study in the five schools?
3. Assume you seek to measure the variable of parents' role construction (as did the authors in the parent involvement study). Describe the process you would go through to locate an instrument that might measure this variable.
4. Suppose you are assisting Maria with the design of her study. Discuss the five steps of quantitative data collection and identify the decisions that she needs to make to answer her quantitative research questions.

Conducting Your Research

Design a quantitative data-collection procedure for a study of your choice. Specify the population and sample, the permissions that you will need, the types of quantitative information you will collect, whether you will develop or locate an instrument, the criteria you will set for your instrument, and the administration procedures that will ensure standardization and ethical practices.

Go to our Companion Website at **www.prenhall.com/creswell** to:

- assess your understanding of chapter content with Multiple-Choice Questions,
- apply what you've learned with Essay Questions,
- practice your research skills with interactive Building Research Skills exercises, and
- broaden your knowledge of research with Web Links to research topics on the Internet.

CHAPTER 7

Analyzing and Interpreting Quantitative Data

Statistics can be challenging. However, calculating statistics is only one step in the process of analyzing data. Analysis also involves preparing your data for analysis, running the analysis, reporting results, and discussing them.

By the end of this chapter, you should be able to:

- Describe the process of preparing and organizing your data for analysis.
- Identify the procedures for analyzing your descriptive research questions.
- Identify the procedures for analyzing your inferential research questions or hypotheses.
- Recognize how to design and present results in tables, figures, and a results section.
- Describe a discussion section of a research report that interprets the results.

Maria has always struggled with math. So when she needs to analyze the data from her questionnaire, she wonders, *Will I be able to analyze my data?* She visits with her introductory statistics professor to learn how to proceed. She expects her professor to talk about what statistics Maria will use. Instead, the professor asks these questions: *How do you plan to organize your data before you analyze it? What questions do you hope to answer with your data analysis? How will you present your results in your paper? How will you structure the interpretation of your results?* Maria now realizes that data analysis consists of several steps.

HOW DO YOU PREPARE THE DATA FOR ANALYSIS?

The first step for you will be to organize data for analysis. **Preparing and organizing data for analysis** in quantitative research consists of scoring the data and creating a codebook, determining the types of scores to use, selecting a computer program, inputting the data into the program for analysis, and clearing the data.

Score the Data

When you collect data on an instrument or a checklist, you will need some system for scoring the data. **Scoring data** means that the researcher assigns a numeric score (or value) to each response category for each question on the instruments used to collect data.

For instance, assume that parents respond to a survey asking them to indicate their attitudes about choice of a school for children in the school district. One question might be:

Please check the appropriate response to this statement:

"Students should be given an opportunity to select a school of their choice."
___________ Strongly agree
___________ Agree
___________ Undecided
___________ Disagree
___________ Strongly disagree

Assume that a parent checks "Agree." What numeric score would you assign to the response so that you will assign the same score to each person who checks "Agree"? To analyze the data, you will need to assign scores to responses such as 5 = strongly agree, 4 = agree, 3 = undecided, 2 = disagree, and 1 = strongly disagree. Based on these assigned numbers, the parent who checks "Agree" would receive a score of 4.

Several guidelines can help in assigning numbers to response options:

- For continuous scales (see chapter 6, assuming the scale is interval), you should consistently score each question in this scale using the same numbering system. In the above example, you should consistently score a scale such as "Strongly agree" to "Strongly disagree" as a "5" to a "1."
- For categorical scales such as "What level do you teach? ___________ high school, ___________ middle school, ___________ elementary," you can arbitrarily assign numbers that make sense, such as 3 = high school, 2 = middle school, and 1 = elementary. A good rule to follow, however, is that the more positive the response or the higher or more advanced the categories of information, the higher the assigned number.
- To make scoring easy, you can preassign numbers on the instrument to each response option, such as in this example:

Please respond to this question:

"Fourth graders should be tested for math proficiency."
___________ (5) Strongly agree
___________ (4) Agree
___________ (3) Undecided
___________ (2) Disagree
___________ (1) Strongly disagree

FIGURE 7.1

Codebook for High School Smoking Project

Variable 1.	ID—identification number assigned to each student, from 1–50
Variable 2.	Gender—sex of the student; 1 = Male, 2 = Female
Variable 3.	Grade—grade level of the student; 10 = 10th grade, 11 = 11th grade, 12 = 12th grade
Variable 4.	Parents—parents' marital status; 1 = married, 2 = divorced, 3 = separated
Variable 5.	Smoke—whether the student smokes or not; 1 = no; 2 = yes
Variable 6.	Chewer—whether student chews tobacco; 1 = no; 2 = yes
Variable 7.	Ability—academic ability based on grade point average last semester; 1 = below 2.0; 2 = 2.0–2.9; 3 = 3.0–3.5; 4 = 3.6–4.0
Variable 8.	Peers—peer group student most closely identifies with at school; 1 = athletes; 2 = singers; 3 = punkers; 4 = other
Variable 9.	Depression—total depression score for all items on an instrument measuring depression; scores from 20 to 100

Here you can see that the numbers are already preassigned and you know how to score each response. Sometimes you can have participants fill in circles for responses on "bubble sheets" such as those used to aid in scoring when evaluating teachers in college classrooms. When students darken circles on these sheets, you can optically scan their responses for analysis. If you use a commercially available instrument, the company will often supply scoring manuals to describe how to score the instrument.

- One procedure that can aid you in assigning scores to responses is to create a codebook. A **codebook** is a list of variables or questions that indicates how the researcher will code or score responses from instruments or checklists. An example of a codebook is shown in Figure 7.1. Notice that each variable is given a name (i.e., Grade), a brief definition of the variable (i.e., grade level of the student) is given, and numbers are assigned to each response option (i.e., 10 = 10th grade, 11 = 11th grade, 12 = 12th grade).

Determine the Types of Scores to Analyze

Look again at Figure 7.1. Variable 9, Depression, consists of a score based on adding all items on an instrument. Before conducting an analysis of scores, researchers consider what types of scores to use from their instruments. This is important because the type of score will affect how you enter data into a computer file for analysis.

Table 7.1 presents three types of scores for six students: single-item scores, summed scores on a scale, and net or difference scores.

Single-Item Scores

For a research study, you may wish to examine a single-item score. A **single-item score** is an individual score assigned to each question for each participant in your

TABLE 7.1

Types of Scores Used in Quantitative Analysis

	Single-Item Scores*		
	Question 1 Score	**Question 2 Score**	**Question 3 Score**
Jane	5	4	3
Jim	4	3	4
John	2	1	2
Jean	4	5	4
Julie	4	3	4
Johanna	5	4	5

	Summed Score or Scale*					
	Question 1	**Question 2**	**Question 3**	**Question 4**	**Question 5**	**Summed Scores**
Jane	5	4	3	4	4	20
Jim	4	3	4	4	3	18
John	2	1	2	2	3	10

	Net or Difference Scores		
	Pretest Math Score	**Post-test Math Score**	**Net-Difference Score**
Jane	80	85	+5
Jim	76	77	+1
John	65	75	+10
Jean	95	97	+2
Julie	91	94	+3
Johanna	93	95	+2

*Question response scale is 5 = strongly agree; 4 = agree; 3 = undecided; 2 = disagree; and 1 = strongly disagree.

study. These scores provide a detailed analysis of each person's response to each question on an instrument. In one study, researchers asked individuals at a local school district meeting, "Will you vote yes or no for the tax levy in the election next Tuesday?" In scoring the data, the researcher would assign a value of 1 to a "no" response and a value of 2 to a "yes" response and have a record of how each individual responded to each question. In Table 7.1, all six participants have individual scores for questions 1, 2, and 3.

Summed Scores

In other cases, we may need to sum responses to all of the questions on the instrument, such as in the response scale scores of Table 7.1. This summing occurs because individual items may not completely capture a participant's perspective. Also, participants may misunderstand a single question or the author may have worded the question so that it biases results. In short, responses to single questions may not be reliable and may not accurately reflect an individual's score (as discussed in chapter 6). One solution to these problems is to form scales based on responses to single questions. **Summed scores** are the scores of an individual added over several questions that measure the same variable. Researchers add the individual items to compute an overall score for a variable. As shown in Table 7.1, the three participants—Jane, Jim, and John—have provided responses to five questions. The researcher sums scores for each individual to provide a single score for a variable representing all five questions.

Difference Scores

Summed scores for individuals are used to develop an overall test score that can be compared from one time period to another. **Net or difference scores** are scores in a quantitative study that represent a difference or change for each individual. Some gains may be more meaningful than others. A small change in high scores may be more useful than a larger change in small scores. For example, the small gain in moving from 98 to 99 on a 100-point scale may be more meaningful than the large change of going from 46 to 66 on the same scale. In experiments, researchers often gather scores on instruments before the study begins (Time 1) and after it ends (Time 2). The researcher collects these scores on pretests and posttests, which are typical measures collected during experimental research. In Table 7.1, for each of the 6 participants, we see a pretest math score, a summed score over all items on the test before a unit on math is taught. We also see for each participant a posttest math score, a summed score at the end of the unit that represents the overall score on a final test. The net score shows how each participant's performance improved, in all six cases, between the pre- and posttest.

Select a Statistical Program

After scoring the data, researchers select a computer program to analyze their data. Academic researchers generally use statistical programs on the campus mainframe computer or programs available for microcomputers. With the availability and low cost of software programs for microcomputers, you can conveniently conduct analysis from a home computer. The hardest part is deciding which software package to use. Here are some guidelines to follow when selecting a statistical program. (See Leedy & Ormrod, 2001, for additional suggestions.)

- Find a program with documentation about how to use the program. Programs often have tutorials so that you can easily learn the key features and practice them using sample data sets. Free tutorials are often available from Web sites.
- Ease of use is an important factor when selecting a program. Pull-down menus and easy data entry make a program easy to use.
- Look for a program that includes the types of statistics that you will use to answer your research questions and hypotheses.
- Make sure that the program can analyze the amount of data in your database. Consider how many participants and the maximum number of variables that you will need in your analysis. A program should adequately accommodate missing data and provide some provisions for handling the situation where some data are missing for a participant. Look for a program that has flexibility for data handling, can read data in many formats (e.g., numbers and letters), and can read files imported from spreadsheets or databases.
- Locate a program with the capability to output graphs and tables that you can use in your research reports.

- If you need to purchase the software program, weigh the costs of the various programs. Student versions of programs are available (although they may have limited statistical tests) at minimal cost.
- Select a program that your campus uses so that you can find assistance to answer questions when they arise. Some programs may provide technical support to help answer questions, but it may be time consuming and costly.

With these criteria in mind, what are the most frequently used statistical programs available? Web sites contain detailed information about the various statistical analysis computer programs available. Some of the more frequently used programs are:

- *Minitabl3* (**www.minitab.com**). This is an interactive software statistical package available from Minitab Inc., 3081 Enterprise Drive, State College, PA 16801–3008.
- *StatView* (**www.statview.com**). This is another popular software program available from SAS Institute, Inc., SAS Campus Drive, Cary, NC 27513–2414.
- *SYSTAT* (**www.spssscience.com**). This is a comprehensive interactive statistical package available from SPSS Science, Inc., 233 S. Wacker Drive, 11th Floor, Chicago, IL 60606–6307.
- *SAS/STAT* (**www.sas.com**). This is a statistical program with tools as an integral component of the SAS system of products available from SAS Institute, Inc., SAS Campus Drive, Cary, NC 27513–2414.
- *Statistical Package for the Social Sciences (SPSS) Student Version 11.0 for Windows and Version 6.0 for Macintosh* (**www.spss.com**). This is an affordable, professional analysis program for students based on the professional version of the program, available from SPSS Science, Inc., 233 S. Wacker Drive, 11th Floor, Chicago, IL 60606–6307.

Input Data

After choosing a statistical program, your next step is to enter the data from your instruments or checklists into the computer program. **Inputting the data** occurs when the researcher transfers the data from the responses on instruments to a computer file for analysis. For those new to this process, this grid is similar to a spreadsheet table used in many popular software packages (e.g., Excel). Table 7.2 shows a small database for 50 high school students participating in a study on tobacco use in schools. You have already seen the variables in this database in the codebook presented in Figure 7.1. A close inspection of Table 7.2 shows that the grid contains cells in rows and columns into which the researcher inputs data for analysis. You see displayed in the first column the number of each participant followed by an ID number assigned to each of the 50 students. In the other columns are variables that the researcher is measuring (i.e., gender, grade, parents, and so forth). Using the codebook, the researcher assigns a number to each response that reflects a score on each variable. At the bottom of the sheet is coding information (found in the codebook) that provides an association between the numbers and the responses on the instrument. The names for the variables are short and simple but descriptive (no more than eight characters in SPSS, such as "gender," "smoke," or "chewer").

The actual process of inputting data into this grid (George & Mallery, 2001) to create an SPSS database is as follows:

- Enter the data from scores on the instruments in the cells of the grid by selecting a cell and typing the appropriate value. Enter the data by rows for each individual and use the columns for the values of each variable. **Values** are the numbers assigned to response options for a variable (e.g., 1 = male, 2 = female).

TABLE 7.2

Sample Data Grid for Inputting Information

	id	gender	grade	parents	smoke	chewer	ability	peers	depression
1	1.00	1.00	10.00	1.00	1.00	2.00	1.00	2.00	70.00
2	2.00	1.00	11.00	1.00	1.00	2.00	3.00	1.00	75.00
3	3.00	2.00	12.00	2.00	2.00	1.00	2.00	3.00	80.00
4	4.00	1.00	11.00	3.00	2.00	1.00	4.00	2.00	75.00
5	5.00	2.00	10.00	3.00	1.00	1.00	3.00	4.00	60.00
6	6.00	2.00	12.00	2.00	1.00	1.00	2.00	4.00	70.00
7	7.00	2.00	12.00	1.00	1.00	1.00	1.00	3.00	75.00
8	8.00	1.00	11.00	2.00	2.00	1.00	4.00	2.00	78.00
9	9.00	2.00	11.00	2.00	2.00	2.00	3.00	1.00	81.00
10	10.00	2.00	10.00	3.00	1.00	1.00	3.00	2.00	60.00
11	11.00	1.00	11.00	3.00	2.00	1.00	4.00	3.00	75.00
12	12.00	2.00	12.00	2.00	1.00	1.00	2.00	1.00	76.00
13	13.00	1.00	10.00	1.00	2.00	1.00	4.00	4.00	81.00
14	14.00	2.00	10.00	3.00	1.00	1.00	3.00	4.00	76.00
15	15.00	1.00	12.00	2.00	2.00	2.00	3.00	3.00	84.00
16	16.00	2.00	12.00	1.00	1.00	1.00	3.00	3.00	78.00
17	17.00	2.00	11.00	2.00	2.00	1.00	2.00	2.00	80.00
18	18.00	1.00	11.00	3.00	1.00	1.00	1.00	2.00	70.00
19	19.00	2.00	10.00	1.00	2.00	1.00	2.00	1.00	82.00
20	20.00	2.00	11.00	1.00	1.00	1.00	3.00	1.00	70.00
21	21.00	1.00	12.00	1.00	2.00	1.00	4.00	4.00	85.00
22	22.00	1.00	10.00	2.00	2.00	2.00	3.00	2.00	70.00
23	23.00	2.00	11.00	2.00	2.00	1.00	2.00	3.00	75.00
24	24.00	1.00	12.00	1.00	2.00	2.00	3.00	1.00	80.00
25	25.00	2.00	10.00	2.00	2.00	2.00	1.00	2.00	76.00
26	26.00	1.00	11.00	1.00	2.00	1.00	2.00	3.00	82.00
27	27.00	2.00	11.00	2.00	2.00	1.00	4.00	1.00	79.00
28	28.00	1.00	12.00	1.00	2.00	1.00	2.00	2.00	81.00
29	29.00	2.00	12.00	2.00	2.00	1.00	3.00	3.00	75.00
30	30.00	1.00	10.00	2.00	1.00	1.00	3.00	1.00	68.00
31	31.00	2.00	10.00	1.00	1.00	1.00	3.00	2.00	60.00
32	32.00	1.00	12.00	2.00	1.00	2.00	1.00	4.00	61.00
33	33.00	2.00	11.00	1.00	1.00	1.00	1.00	3.00	76.00
34	34.00	1.00	12.00	2.00	1.00	1.00	2.00	2.00	88.00
35	35.00	2.00	12.00	1.00	1.00	1.00	4.00	1.00	70.00
36	36.00	2.00	12.00	2.00	1.00	1.00	4.00	3.00	71.00
37	37.00	2.00	10.00	1.00	1.00	1.00	4.00	4.00	78.00
38	38.00	1.00	10.00	2.00	1.00	1.00	3.00	1.00	69.00
39	39.00	1.00	10.00	1.00	2.00	1.00	3.00	4.00	82.00
40	40.00	1.00	10.00	2.00	2.00	1.00	3.00	4.00	84.00
41	41.00	2.00	12.00	1.00	1.00	1.00	2.00	3.00	75.00
42	42.00	1.00	12.00	3.00	2.00	2.00	2.00	2.00	79.00
43	43.00	2.00	11.00	3.00	1.00	2.00	1.00	1.00	68.00
44	44.00	1.00	12.00	1.00	2.00	2.00	2.00	4.00	88.00
45	45.00	2.00	11.00	2.00	2.00	1.00	3.00	3.00	81.00
46	46.00	1.00	12.00	2.00	2.00	1.00	4.00	2.00	82.00
47	47.00	2.00	11.00	1.00	1.00	1.00	2.00	1.00	70.00
48	48.00	1.00	12.00	1.00	1.00	1.00	4.00	4.00	70.00
49	49.00	2.00	10.00	1.00	1.00	1.00	3.00	3.00	65.00
50	50.00	1.00	11.00	1.00	1.00	1.00	1.00	2.00	57.00

Gender: 1 = male; 2 = female
Grade: 10 = 10th grade; 11 = 11th grade; 12 = 12th grade
Parents: Parent status 1 = married; 2 = divorced; 3 = separated
Smoke: Do you smoke cigarettes?: 1 = no; 2 = yes
Chewer: Do you chew tobacco?: 1 = no; 2 = yes
Ability (academic, based on grade point average in last semester): 1 = below 2.0; 2 = 2.1–2.9; 3 = 3.0–3.5; 4 = 3.6–4.0
Peers (peer group student most closely identifies with at school): 1 = athletes; 2 = singers; 3 = punkers; 4 = other
Depression = total score on an instrument measuring depression (scores from 20 to 100)

- Assign an identification number to each participant and place this number in the first column or use the predetermined numbers assigned in column 1 by SPSS (i.e., 001, 002, 003, or 343, 344, 345). Your own numbers may reflect the last three digits in the individual's social security number (e.g., 343, 344, 345) or some other identifying number.
- In SPSS, you will see column heads listed as variables: var001, var002, var003, and so forth. Rather than use these headers, replace them with names of your variables (e.g., "var002" could be replaced by "gender").
- You can also assign names to both values and variables so that your printout contains these names and provides an easy way to identify your information. You can assign names to your variables, such as "parents," as well as values for this variable, such as "married," "divorced," and "separated."

Clean and Account for Missing Data

After entering data into the computer grid, you need to determine if there are errors in the data or missing data. Errors occur when participants in your study provide scores outside the range for variables or you input wrong numbers into the data grid. Missing data may result when instrument data is lost, individuals skip questions, participants are absent when you collect observational data, or individuals refuse to complete a sensitive question. For ethical reasons, you report how you handled missing data so that readers can accurately interpret the results (George & Mallery, 2001). Because these problems may occur, you need to clean the data and decide how to treat missing data.

Cleaning the Database

Cleaning the data is the process of inspecting the data for scores (or values) that are outside the accepted range. One way to accomplish this is by visually inspecting the data grid. For large databases, a frequency distribution (discussed shortly) will provide the range of scores to detect responses outside of acceptable ranges. For example, participants may provide a "6" for a "strongly agree" to "strongly disagree" scale when there are only five response options. Alternatively, the researcher might type a score for a participant as "3" for gender, when the only legitimate values are "1" for females and "2" for males.

Another procedure is to use SPSS and have the program "sort cases" in ascending order for each variable. This process arranges the values of a variable from the smallest number to the largest, enabling you to easily spot out-of-range or misnumbered cases. Whatever the procedure, a visual inspection of data helps to clean the data and free it from visible errors before you begin the data analysis.

Assessing the Database for Missing Data

You need to examine your database for missing data. Missing data will yield fewer individuals to be included in the data analysis, and because we want as many people included in the analysis as possible, you need to correct as much as possible for missing data. **Missing data** are data missing in the database because participants do not supply it.

How should you handle missing data? The most obvious approach is to have a good instrument that individuals want to complete and are capable of answering so that missing data will not occur. In some research situations, you can contact individuals to determine why they did not respond. When individuals do not respond, something is wrong with your data collection, which may indicate faulty planning in your design.

You can expect, however, that questions will be omitted or some participants will not supply information, for whatever reason. In this case, you have a couple of options:

- You can eliminate participants with missing scores from the data analysis and include only those participants for which complete data exist. This practice, in effect, may severely reduce the number of overall participants for data analysis.
- You can substitute numbers for missing data in the database for individuals. When the variable is categorical, this means substituting a value, such as "–9," for all missing values in the data grid. When the variable is continuous (i.e., based on an interval scale), the process is more complex. Using SPSS, the researcher can have the computer program substitute a value for each missing score, such as an average number for the question for all study participants. You can substitute up to 15% of the missing data with scores without altering the overall statistical findings (George & Mallery, 2001). More advanced statistical procedures are also available for identifying substitute numbers for missing data (see Gall, Borg, & Gall, 1996).

HOW DO YOU ANALYZE THE DATA?

After you prepare and organize the data, you are ready to analyze it. You analyze the data to address each one of your research questions or hypotheses. Think back to the types of research questions and hypotheses presented in chapter 5. Questions or hypotheses in quantitative research require that you:

- Describe trends in the data to a single variable or question on your instrument (e.g., "What is the self-esteem of middle school students?"). To answer this question, we need **descriptive statistics** that indicate general tendencies in the data (mean, mode, median), the spread of scores (variance, standard deviation, and range), or a comparison of how one score relates to all others (z scores, percentile rank). We might seek to describe any of our variables: independent, dependent, control, or mediating.
- Compare two or more groups on the independent variable in terms of the dependent variable (e.g., "How do boys and girls compare in their self-esteem?"). To answer this question, we need **inferential statistics** in which we analyze data from a sample to draw conclusions about an unknown population. We assess whether the differences of groups (their means) or the relationship among variables is much greater or less than what we would expect for the total population, if we could study the entire population.
- Relate two or more variables (e.g., "Does self-esteem relate to an optimistic attitude?"). To answer this question, we also use inferential statistics.
- Test hypotheses about the differences in the groups or the relationships of variables (e.g., "Boys have higher self-esteem than girls" or "Self-esteem predicts an optimistic attitude among middle school children"). To answer either of these questions, inferential statistics are also used.

Thus, we describe results to a single variable or question or we infer results from a sample to a population. In all quantitative research questions or hypotheses, we study individuals sampled from a population. However, in descriptive questions, we study only a single variable one at a time; in inferential analysis, we analyze multiple variables at the same time. Also from comparing groups or relating variables, we can make predictions about the variables. We can test hypotheses that make predictions comparing groups or relating variables.

Conduct Descriptive Analysis

How do we analyze the data to describe trends? You use **statistics**, the calculations of values based on numbers. Many helpful books provide details about different statistics, their computation, and assumptions (e.g., Abelson, 1995; Gravetter & Wallnau, 2000; Wright, 1997). We focus here on the statistics typically used in educational research.

Choosing a Descriptive Statistics Test

Descriptive statistics will help you summarize the overall trends or tendencies in your data, provide an understanding of how varied your scores might be, and provide insight into where one score stands in comparison with others. These three ideas are the central tendency, variability, and relative standing. Figure 7.2 portrays the statistical procedures that you can use to provide this information.

Measures of Central Tendency **Measures of central tendency** are summary numbers that represent a single value in a distribution of scores (Vogt, 1999). They are expressed as an average score (the mean), the middle of a set of scores (the median), or the most frequently occurring score (the mode). In quantitative studies, researchers typically report

FIGURE 7.2

Examples of the Family of Statistics in Educational Research

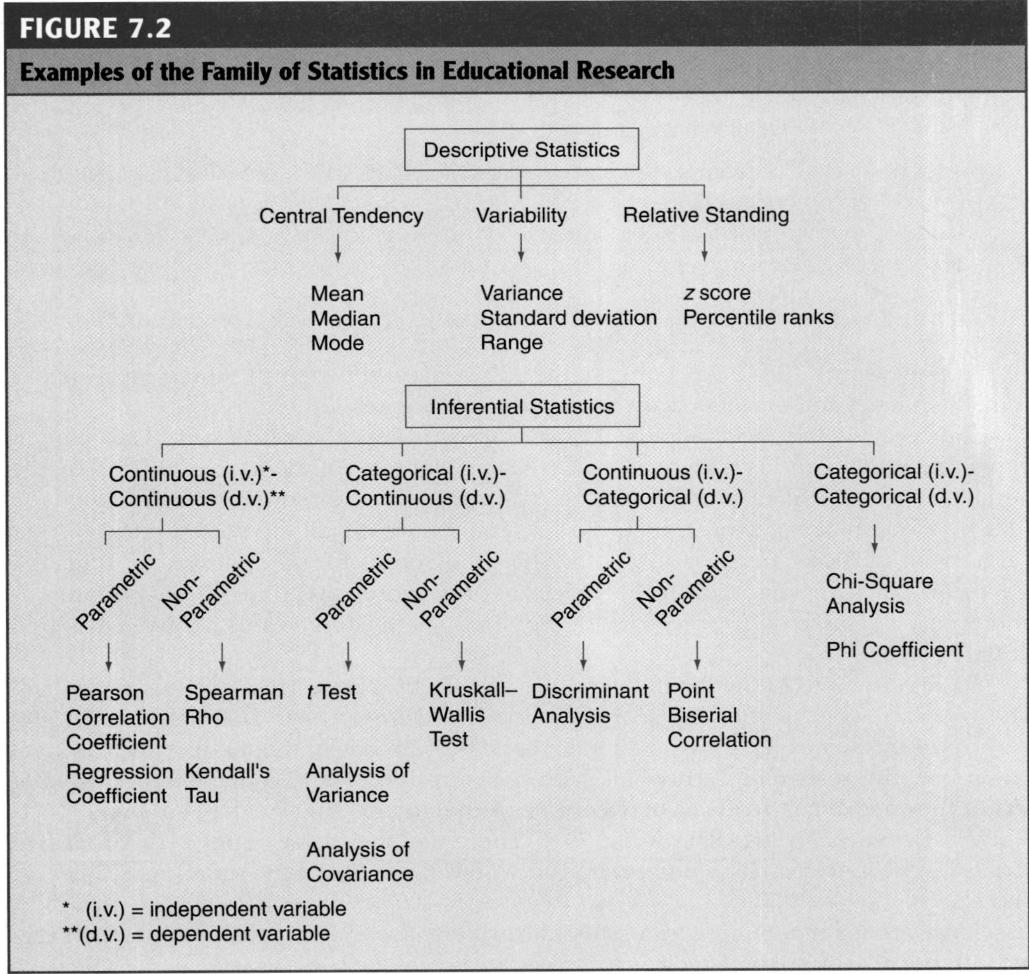

TABLE 7.3

Descriptive Statistics for Depression Scores

Raw Scores	z Score	Rank
60	−1.57	10.0
64	−1.28	20.0
75	− .49	30.0
76	− .42	50.0
76	− .42	50.0
83	+ .09	60.0
93	+ .81	70.0
94	+ .92	80.0
98	+1.22	90.0
99	+1.24	100.0

Sum = 818
Mode (76)
Median (79.5)
Mean (81.8)

$$\text{Variance } (SD^2) = \sum \frac{(\text{raw score} - M)^2}{N}$$

Variance = 173.96

Standard deviation (SD) = $\sqrt{\text{variance}}$

Standard deviation = 13.18

z score = raw score − mean/SD

Range: minimum = 60; maximum = 99

all three measures. Table 7.3 portrays the differences between the three measures of central tendency for 10 students for whom we have depression scores.

The mean is the most popular statistic used to describe responses of all participants to items on an instrument. A **mean (*M*)** is the total of the scores divided by the number of scores. To calculate the mean, you sum all of the scores and then divide the sum by the number of scores. In Table 7.3, you would divide the sum of 818 by 10 to get a mean of 81.80. In calculating other types of scores for other advanced statistics, the mean plays an important role. Notice that the scores in Table 7.3 are continuous and report a sample of 10 scores for depression. The mean gives us an average for all of the scores.

We may want to know the middle score among all scores. This score is the median. The **median** score divides the scores, rank-ordered from top to bottom, in half. Fifty percent of the scores lie above the median and 50% lie below the median. To calculate this score, the researcher arrays all scores in rank order and then determines what score, the median, is halfway between all of the scores. The median in Table 7.3 is halfway between 76 and 83, giving 79.5. There are five scores above 79.5 and five scores below it. Researchers often report the median score, but the score's usefulness is limited.

However, the mode provides useful information. The **mode** is the score that appears most frequently in a list of scores. It is used when researchers want to know the most

TABLE 7.4

Descriptive Statistics for the Categorical Variable, "Peer Group Affiliation"

		Peer Group Affiliation			
		Frequency	**Percent**	**Valid Percent**	**Cumulative Percent**
Valid	athletes	12	24.0	24.0	24.0
	singers	14	28.0	28.0	52.0
	punkers	13	26.0	26.0	78.0
	other	11	22.0	22.0	100.0
	Total	50	100.0	100.0	

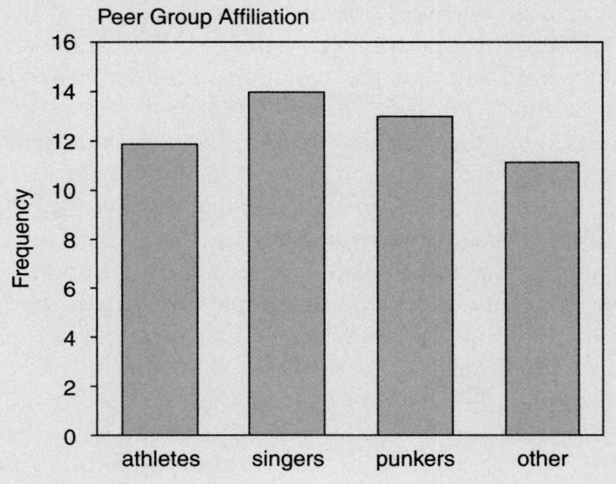

common score in an array of scores on a variable. In Table 7.3, the most frequently reported score was 76, and it was a score for 2 people in the sample of 10. Researchers use the mode for reporting variables with categorical variables. Examine Table 7.4. Here is a categorical variable about the peer group affiliation of students. From looking at this table we can see that the "singers" were more numerous than any other group ($N = 14$). The mode would be the "singers" because they are represented more than any other category. Reporting the mean would report meaningless information. If we assigned numbers to each group (athletes = 4, singers = 3, punkers = 2, and other = 1) and calculated a mean score, 137/50 = 2.74, it would not mean anything because no group is assigned this number. Thus, when we have categorical information, the mode reports meaningful information but the mean does not.

Measures of Variability Variability indicates the spread of the scores in a distribution. Range, variance, and standard deviation all indicate the amount of variability in a distribution of scores. This information helps us see how dispersed the responses are to items on an instrument. Variability also plays an important role in many advanced statistical calculations.

We can see how variable the scores are by looking at the range of scores. The **range of scores** is the difference between the highest and the lowest scores to items on an instrument. In Table 7.3, we see that the scores range from a low of 60 to a high of 99, a range of 39 points.

The **variance** indicates the dispersion of scores around the mean. To calculate this score is easy:

- Find the difference between the mean and the raw score for each individual.
- Square this value for each individual.
- Sum these squared scores for all individuals.
- Divide by the total number of individuals.

In our example, Table 7.3, the variance equals 173.96. This information, by itself, does not mean much, but it is a useful number when calculating statistics that are more advanced. The square root of the variance, the **standard deviation (*SD*)**, does provide useful information, and we look at it as an indicator of the dispersion or spread of the scores. In Table 7.3, the standard deviation is 13.90. If the scores had a standard deviation of 7.30, we would say that the variation around the mean is less than if the standard deviation is 13.18.

The meaning of the standard deviation becomes evident when we graph a theoretical distribution of scores, as shown in Figure 7.3. If we collected sample after sample of scores and plotted them on a graph, they would look like a bell-shaped curve as shown in Figure 7.3. This is called a **normal distribution or normal probability curve**. In reality, the actual scores may not simulate the normal distribrution (e.g., a distribution of salaries), but if we plotted the means of many samples, a normal curve would result. If, for example, we generated 5,000 random samples and calculated a mean salary for each sample, then plotted these 5,000 means, the distribution would reflect a normal distribution. Looking again at Figure 7.3, the shaded areas indicate the percentage of scores likely to fall within each standard deviation from the mean. For example, 68% of the scores fall between +1 (34%) and − 1 (34%) standard deviations from the mean: 95% between +2 (13.5% + 34%) and −2 (13.5% + 34%). You can also associate percentile scores, *z* scores, and *t* scores with each standard deviation.

Percentiles provide another type of descriptive statistic. **Measures of relative standing** are statistics that describe one score relative to a group of scores. In Figure 7.3, 2.28% of the scores fall more than two standard deviations below the mean, and 97.72% of the scores are below the value two standard deviations above the mean. Knowing where a

FIGURE 7.3

The Normal Curve

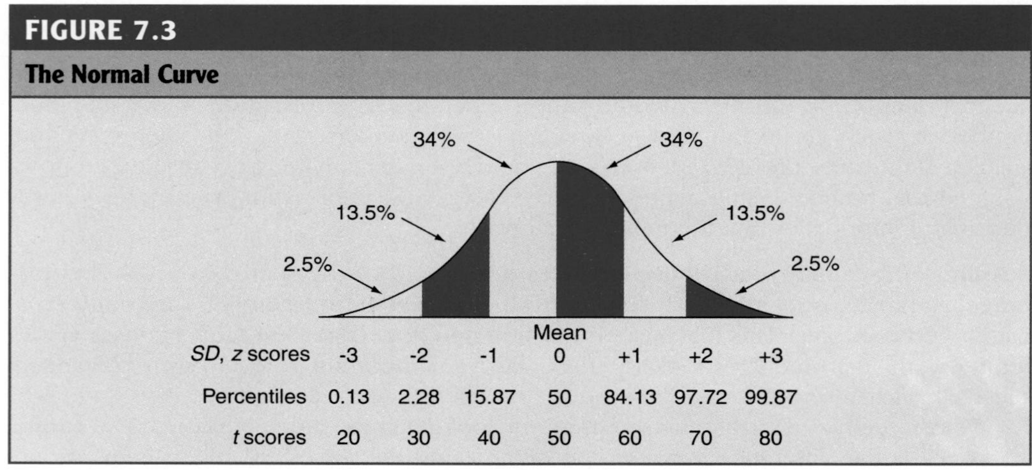

score falls in this distribution is a key factor in testing hypotheses. Two frequently used statistics are the percentile rank and the *z* score.

A measure of relative standing is the percentile rank. A **percentile rank** of a particular score is the percentage of participants in the distribution with scores at or below a particular score. You use it to determine where in a distribution of scores an individual's score lies in comparison with other scores. In Table 7.3, we see that an individual with a score of 94 is at the 80th percentile, with 20% of the participants having scores above this individual, and 80% of the participants having scores at or below this individual.

Another measure of relative standing is the standard score. A **standard score** is a calculated score that enables a researcher to compare scores from different scales. It involves the transformation of a raw score into a score with relative meaning. A ***z* score** is a popular form of the standard score, and it has a mean of 0 and a standard deviation of 1. This yields a *z* score, or a standard score that has the advantage of enabling you to compare scores from one instrument to scores from another instrument. Using standardized scores is also central to calculating many statistics. The procedure is to take a score, subtract it from the mean, and divide it by the standard deviation. In Table 7.3, we see that a person with a score of 60 has a *z* score of −1.57, or a score that is more than one and a half standard deviations below the average (or mean).

Conduct Inferential Analysis

Descriptive statistics help you analyze descriptive questions. However, when you compare groups or relate two or more variables, inferential analysis comes into play. The basic idea is to look at scores from a sample and use the results to draw inferences or make predictions about the population. Recall from chapter 6 that you often cannot study the entire population because of size and cost, so we instead examine a sample that has been carefully chosen from the population.

When you study this sample and obtain scores, several approaches exist for determining if the sample scores you receive are a good estimate of the population scores (see Vogt, 2005). Ask yourself:

1. Is the sample score (e.g., the mean difference between two groups) probably a *wrong* estimate of the population mean? The procedure you use to examine this question is hypothesis testing. **Hypothesis testing** is a procedure for making decisions about results by comparing an observed value of a sample with a population value to determine if no difference or relationship exists between the values. This is the traditional way to test whether the sample mean is a good estimate of the population mean. It provides a yes–no answer: Either the sample mean is a good estimate or it is not. Because we can never absolutely prove that the sample is a good estimate, we try to establish whether it is a *wrong* estimate.

2. How confident are you that your sample score is right? This is the confidence interval approach. A **confidence interval or interval estimate** is the range of upper and lower statistical values that is consistent with observed data and is likely to contain the actual population mean. In this approach, you determine an interval or range in which your population score would likely fall. In this sense, confidence intervals give us more flexibility than the yes–no options of hypothesis testing.

3. Does the sample score or differences between two groups make practical sense? This is the effect size approach. **Effect size** is a means for identifying the practical strength of the conclusions about group differences or about the relationship among variables in a quantitative study. Effect sizes tell us how different the sample values are and allow us to make a judgment as to whether this is significant based on our knowledge of measures, the participants, and the data-collection effort.

The reason we have more than one approach is that recently some researchers have felt that a yes–no hypothesis testing answer to our quantitative questions and hypotheses leads to misinterpretations and errors (Finch, Cumming, & Thomason, 2001). Confidence intervals and effect sizes provide a more practical reading of results. In reporting research today, it is useful to report all three estimates of your population: hypothesis testing, the confidence interval, and the effect size (Wilkinson & Task Force on Statistical Inference, 1999).

Hypothesis Testing

There are five steps in hypothesis testing: (a) identify a null and alternative hypothesis; (b) set the level of significance, or alpha level; (c) collect data; (d) compute the sample statistic; and (e) make a decision about rejecting or failing to reject the null hypothesis.

1. *Identify your null and alternative hypothesis.* As you may recall from chapter 5, the null hypothesis is a prediction about the population and is typically stated using the language of "no difference" (or "no relationship" or "no association"). The alternative hypothesis, however, indicates a difference (or relationship or association), and the direction of this difference may be positive or negative (alternative directional hypotheses) or *either* positive or negative (alternative nondirectional hypotheses).

Returning to the data for high school students in Table 7.2, you may state a null and alternative hypothesis as follows:

Null Hypothesis:

There is no difference between smokers and nonsmokers on depression scores.

Alternative Hypothesis (nondirectional and directional):

There is a difference between smokers and nonsmokers on depression scores.

(Or, written another way):

Smokers are more depressed than nonsmokers.

2. *Set the level of significance, or alpha level, for rejecting the null hypothesis.* If we were to collect a large number of sample means, and if the null hypothesis is true ("no difference"), the theoretical distribution would approximate a normal or bell-shaped curve, as illustrated in Figure 7.4. In this figure, we see a normal curve illustrating the distribution of sample means of all possible outcomes if the null hypothesis is true. We would expect most of our sample means to fall in the center of the curve if the hypothesis is true, but a small number would fall at the extremes. In other words, we would expect to find that, for any sample of smokers and nonsmokers, their depression scores are similar, but in a small percentage of cases, you might actually find them to be different. As you can see, there are shaded areas at each end of this curve. We would expect there to be an extremely low probability that a score would fall within these areas.

A standard is needed for these low probability areas for precisely marking them on this curve. This is called setting a significance level. A **significance level (or alpha level)** is a probability level that reflects the maximum risk you are willing to take that any observed differences are due to chance. It is typically set at .01 (1 out of 100 times the sample score will be due to chance) or .05 (5 out of 100 times it will be due to chance). This means that 1 out of 100 times (or 5 out of 100 times) an extremely low probability value will actually be observed if the null hypothesis is true. In some situations, it is important to set the alpha level even stricter than .01 or .05. Assume that a researcher is testing the effects of a drug that has severe side effects. The alpha level might be set at a stricter level for rejection, say .001, if the drug might have damaging side effects for cancer patients rather than a less conservative level of .05 if the drug would have less damaging side effects for individuals with acne.

FIGURE 7.4

The Normal Curve Distribution of Mean Differences of All Possible Outcomes if the Null Hypothesis Is True

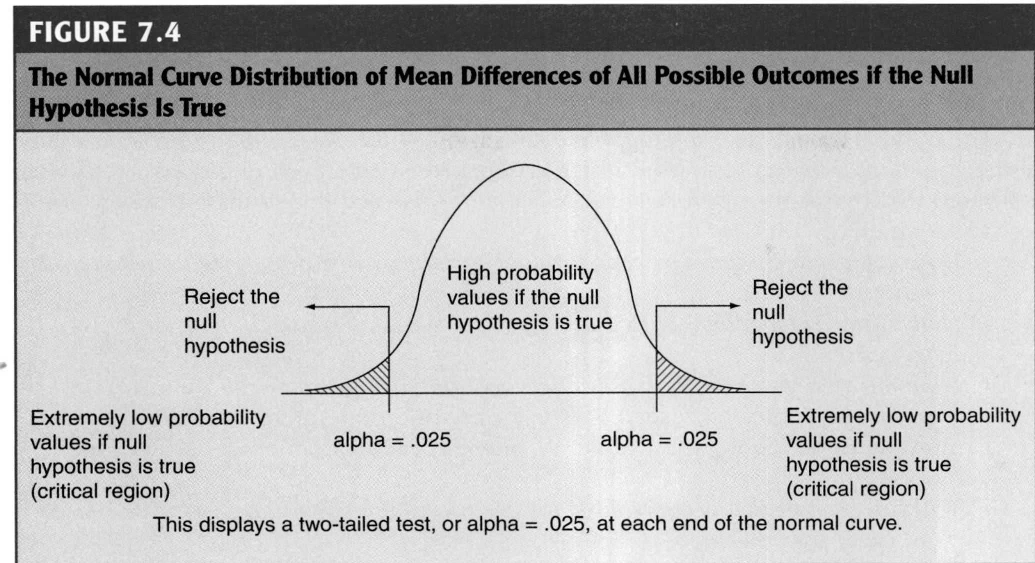

Source: Adapted from Cravetter & Wallnau, 2000.

The area on the normal curve for low probability values if the null hypothesis is true is called the **critical region**. If sample data (i.e., the difference between smokers and nonsmokers on depression) falls into the critical region, the null hypothesis is rejected. This means that instead of "there is no difference" as stated in the null hypothesis, we find the alternative to probably be true: "there is a difference."

Also notice in Figure 7.4 that this critical region marked by a significance level occurs at *both* ends of the normal curve. When the critical region for rejection of the null hypothesis is divided into two areas at the tails of the sampling distribution, we have a **two-tailed test of significance** (Vogt, 1999). However, if we place the region at only one end for rejection of the null hypothesis, we have a **one-tailed test of significance**. You use one-tailed tests when previous research indicates a probable direction (e.g., a directional, alternative hypothesis). In contrast, a two-tailed test of significance is more conservative, or demanding, because the area of rejection at either end of the curve is less than that of a one-tailed test. We say that a one-tailed test has more power, which means that we are more likely to reject the null hypothesis.

3. *Collect data.* You collect data by administering an instrument or recording behaviors on a check sheet for participants. Then, as discussed earlier in this chapter, you code the data and input it into a computer file for analysis.

4. *Compute the sample statistic.* Next, using a computer program, you compute a statistic or *p* value and determine if it falls inside or outside of the critical region. A **p value** is the probability (*p*) that a result could have been produced by chance if the null hypothesis were true. After calculating the *p* value, we compare it with a value in a table located in the back of major statistics books (e.g., Gravetter & Wallnau, 2000) related to the statistical test by finding the value given our significant level (e.g., .01), whether our test is one tailed or two tailed, and the degrees of freedom for our statistical test (or examine the printout for this value). **Degrees of freedom (df)** used in a statistical test is usually one less than the number of scores. For a sample of scores, $df = n-1$. The degrees of freedom establish the number of scores in a sample that are independent and

free to vary because the sample mean places a restriction on sample variability. In a sample of scores, when the value of the mean is known, all scores but one can vary (i.e., be independent of each other and have any values), because one score is restricted by the sample mean (Gravetter & Wallnau, 2007).

The difficult part is determining what statistical test to use. Table 7.5 presents many of the common statistical tests used in educational research. Seven questions need to be answered to arrive at the appropriate statistical test (also see Rudestam & Newton, 1992, for similar criteria):

- *Do you plan to compare groups or relate variables in your hypotheses or research questions?*
- *How many independent variables do you have in one research question or hypothesis?*
- *How many dependent variables do you have in one research question or hypothesis?* Typically, researchers use only one dependent variable, or if multiple dependent variables are of interest, each variable is analyzed one by one.
- *Will you be statistically controlling for covariates in your analysis of the research question or hypothesis?*
- *How will your independent variable(s) be measured?* Recall from chapter 6 that there are two types of scales: categorical (nominal and ordinal) and continuous (interval/ratio).
- *How will your dependent variable(s) be measured?* As with your independent variables, identify whether the dependent variables are categorical or continuous variables.
- *Are the scores on your variables normally distributed; that is, could you assume a normal curve if the scores were plotted on a graph?* Certain statistics have been designed to work best with normally distributed data and others with nonnormally distributed data. (See appendix C for additional information about nonnormal distributions.)

Given these seven questions, what statistical test would you use to study these null hypotheses?

"*There is no difference between smokers and nonsmokers on depression scores.*"

"*There is no difference between smokers and nonsmokers and peer group affiliation.*"

For the first hypothesis, you would select a *t* test, and for the second, the chi-square statistic. Can you identify the decisions that went into selecting both tests based on the seven criteria?

5. *Make a decision about rejecting or failing to reject the null hypothesis.* Let's assume that you have now computed the statistical test for the two hypotheses using the data reported earlier in Table 7.2. Assume that you have used SPSS Version 14.0 and have printouts as shown in Table 7.6. In Table 7.6, you compare smokers and nonsmokers in terms of their scores on depression. The statistical test you computed was a *t*-test analysis and it indicated that the 26 nonsmokers have a mean of 69.77 on the depression scale, whereas the 24 smokers have a mean of 79.79, a difference of 10.02 points between the two groups. The two-tailed significance test indicates a $t = -7.49$ with 48 degrees of freedom, resulting in a two-tailed p value of .00 ($p = .00$). This p value is statistically significant because it is less than alpha = .05. If the p value is less than alpha, you reject the null hypothesis; if it is greater than alpha, you accept the hypothesis. Our overall conclusion, then, is that there *is* a difference between nonsmokers and smokers and their depression, and we reject the null hypothesis (there is no difference) and accept the alternative (there is a difference).

TABLE 7.5

Statistical Tests and Statistics Frequently Used in Educational Research and Criteria for Choosing the Statistic for Hypothesis Testing

Statistical Test	Type of Hypothesis/ Question	Number of Independent Variables	Number of Dependent Variables	Number of Covariates	Continuous or Categorical Independent Variable	Continuous or Categorical Dependent Variable	Type of Distribution of Scores
t test (independent samples)	Group comparison	1	1	0	Categorical	Continuous	Normal distribution
Analysis of variance	Group comparison	1 or more	1	0	Categorical	Continuous	Normal distribution
Analysis of covariance	Group comparison	1 or more	1	1	Categorical	Continuous	Normal distribution
Multiple analysis of variance	Group comparison	1 or more	2 or more	0	Categorical	Continuous	Normal distribution
Mann–Whitney U test	Group comparison	1	1	0	Categorical	Continuous	Nonnormal distribution
Kruskall–Wallis test	Group comparison	1 or more	1 or more	0	Categorical	Continuous	Nonnormal distribution
Friedman's Chi-square test	Group comparison	2 or more	2 or more	0	Categorical	Continuous	Nonnormal distribution
Chi-square	Category within group comparison	1	1	0	Categorical	Categorical	Nonnormal distribution
Pearson product momen correlation	Relate variables	1	1	0	Continuous	Continuous	Normal distribution
Multiple regression	Relate variables	2 or more	1	0	Continuous	Continuous	Normal distribution
Spearman rank-order correlation	Relate variables	1	1 or more	0	Categorical	Categorical	Nonnormal distribution
Point-biserial correlation	Relate variables	1	1	0	Categorical	Continuous	Nonnormal distribution
Phi coefficient	Relate variables	1	1	0	Categorical	Categorical	Nonnormal distribution

TABLE 7.6

t test for Independent Samples for Smoking (Not a smoker, Smoker) on Depression

Variable	Number of Cases	Mean	Standard Deviation	SE of Mean
Depression score				
Nonsmoker	26	69.77	5.33	1.05
Smoker	24	79.79	3.97	.81
Mean difference = −10.02				
Leverne's Test for Equality of Variance: F = 1.26, Significance = 0.27 ← Test if the variances are equal for the two groups				

Variances	*t* value	*df*	2-Tail Significance	SE of Difference	95% Confidence Interval	Effect Size
Equal	−7.49	48	.00	1.34	Lower: −12.71 Upper: −7.33	2.154
	↑ *t* test statistic		↑ Observed *p* value		↑ Confidence interval	↑ Effect size

In making this statement, we followed this procedure:

1. Look at the value of the statistical test and its associated *p* value. You can find this *p* value on your printout.

2. Determine if the observed *p* value is less than or greater than the value obtained from a distribution of scores for the statistic (with certain degrees of freedom and with either a one- or two-tailed test at a significance level). You can determine this table *p* value by hand by comparing the value of the test statistic with the value in a distribution table for the statistic. Alternatively, you can let the computer program identify the observed *p* value, and you can interpret whether it is greater or less than your alpha value.

3. Decide to reject or fail to reject the null hypothesis. We need to next decide if our *p* value is statistically significant to reject or fail to reject the null hypothesis. **Statistical significance** is when p value of the observed scores is less than the predetermined alpha level set by the researcher.

Another example using the chi-square statistic is shown in Table 7.7. This test examines whether nonsmokers and smokers are different in terms of their peer group affiliation. The top table shows cells containing information about the observed count in each cell and an expected count. For example, for athletes, we expected 6.2 individuals to be nonsmokers, and instead we found 8. The Pearson chi-square test = 1.71, with df = 3, resulted in a *p* value (or significance level) of .635. At p = .05, .635 is not statistically significant, and our conclusion is to fail to reject the null hypothesis. We conclude that there is no detectable difference between smokers and nonsmokers and peer group affiliation. Although we might have anticipated that the "punkers" group had more smokers than nonsmokers or that the "athletes"

TABLE 7.7

Chi-Square Analysis, Smoking by Peer Group Affiliation

Smoke Cigarettes? Peer Group Affiliation Crosstabulation

			Peer Group Affiliation				
			athletes	**singers**	**punkers**	**other**	**Total**
Smoke Cigarettes?	No	Count	8	6	6	6	26
		Expected Count	6.2	7.3	6.8	5.7	26.0
		Residual	1.8	−1.3	−8	0.3	
	Yes	Count	4	8	7	5	24
		Expected Count	5.8	6.7	6.2	5.3	24.0
		Residual	−1.8	1.3	0.8	−3	
Total		Count	12	14	13	11	50
		Expected Count	12.0	14.0	13.0	11.0	50.0

Chi-square test statistic ↙

	Value	***df***	**Asymptotic Sig. (2-sided)**	
Pearson chi-square	1.710	3	.635	←Observed *p* value
Likelihood ratio	1.734	3	.629	
Linear-by-linear	.258	1	.611	
N of valid cases	50			

Symmetric Measures

		Value	**Approx. Sig.**
Nominal by	Phi	.185	.635
Nominal	Cramer's V	.185	.635
N of Valid Cases		50	

group had more nonsmokers than smokers, our statistical test did not find these results to be present.

Potential Errors in Outcomes

In both examples, the *t* test and the chi-square test, our results might have been in error. Let's consider four possible outcomes that could occur during hypothesis testing. These possibilities are outlined in Table 7.8. The columns in this table represent the two actual states of affairs in the population: There is no difference between smokers and nonsmokers on depression scores (said another way, smokers and nonsmokers are equally depressed), or there really is a difference between smokers and nonsmokers on depression scores. The information in the rows shows the two decisions that

TABLE 7.8

Possible Outcomes in Hypothesis Testing

	State of Affairs in the Population	
Decision Made by the Researchers Based on the Statistical Test Value	No Effect: Null True	Effect Exists: Null False
Reject the null hypothesis	**Type I error** (false positive) (probability = alpha)	Correctly rejected: no error (probability = power)
Fail to reject the null hypothesis	Correctly not rejected: no error	**Type II error** (false negative) (probability = beta)

Source: Adapted from Tuckman, 1999; Wright, 1997.

researchers make based on actual data they receive: to reject the null hypothesis or to fail to reject the null.

Given these factors, we have four possible outcomes—two possible errors that may occur and two possible positive outcomes in hypothesis testing:

1. The researcher can reject the null hypothesis (i.e., there is a difference) when the population values are truly such that there is no effect. A **Type I error** occurs when the null hypothesis is rejected by the researcher when it is actually true. The probability of this error rate is alpha.
2. The researcher can commit an error by failing to reject the null hypothesis. A **Type II error** occurs when the researcher fails to reject the null hypothesis when an effect actually occurs in the population. The probability of this error rate is called *beta*. In practical terms, a Type II error is typically considered less of a problem than a Type I error, because failing to reject (finding no difference) is less misleading than rejecting (finding a difference). In educational research, we need to be cautious about saying "there is a difference" when one actually does not exist.
3. The researcher can reject the null hypothesis when it should be rejected because an effect exists. This is a correct decision and, therefore, no error is committed. The **power** in quantitative hypothesis testing is the probability of correctly rejecting a false null hypothesis.
4. The researcher can fail to reject the null hypothesis when it should not be rejected because there was no effect.

Estimating Using Confidence Intervals

In Tables 7.6 and 7.7, we have two inferential statistical tests, with one rejecting the null hypothesis and the other failing to reject the null hypothesis. Although the decision to reject or fail to reject provides useful information, it does not indicate the magnitude of differences in mean scores, especially in the case when the null hypothesis is rejected (as in our *t*-test example). Thus, we turn to confidence intervals to help us decide how large the difference actually might be and to estimate a range of acceptable values.

Confidence intervals provide additional information about our hypothesis test. A confidence interval or interval estimate is the range of upper and lower statistical values that is consistent with observed data and is likely to contain the actual population mean. Because means are only estimates of population values, they can never be precise, and sample means indicate a *point estimate* of the population mean. It is helpful, then, to consider a range of values around the sample mean that it could take given the multiple collection of samples. Researchers set a confidence interval around this mean value of the sample to illustrate the potential range of scores that are likely to occur. Moreover, this occurrence is framed as a percent, such as 95% of the time (95 out of 100), the population value will be within the range of the interval. Moreover, this interval can be identified by upper and lower limits, the values that define the range of the interval.

Turning to Table 7.6 again, the computer program reports a 95% confidence interval for the differences between the means of the two groups. If you draw a large number of samples from the population, 95% of the mean differences would fall between the lower and the upper values reported in the statistics for a t test. This conveys that if we could collect a large number of samples of high school students, we might estimate that 95% of the scores for depression would fall between -12.71 and -7.33, around the difference of -10.02 for the mean scores between nonsmokers and smokers ($69.77 - 79.79 = -10.02$). To know this range provides a more accurate estimate of the population values, and it provides additional information about the results of hypothesis testing.

Determining Effect Size

It is important to know whether the statistical test was significant (through p values) and the possible range of acceptable scores (confidence interval), but also to quantify the strength of the difference between two means or two variables. A practical measure of whether means differ is simply to look at the differences and determine whether the difference is meaningful in a practical sense. This is the procedure of calculating effect size. Effect size identifies the strength of the conclusions about group differences or about the relationship among variables in a quantitative study. The calculation of this coefficient differs for statistical tests. For analysis of variance (ANOVA), for example, effect size (eta^2) is measured using the percentage of the variance due to the variable under study. Phi, as used with the chi-square test, is a measure of association of strength. Other measures for effect size for other statistics employ different procedures for calculations, such as omega^2 or Cohen's D (APA, 2001). When examining the mean scores for two groups, however, an effect size of .5 (or one half of an SD) or above is often a standard to use.

We can calculate effect size between groups in our high school smoking example. A researcher, for example, could examine the means in Table 7.6 and see that the mean scores were 10.02 points apart, a sizable difference on a 100-point scale. More precisely, we calculate effect sizes and report them in terms of standard deviation units. For the t-test statistic, the effect size (ES) can be calculated with the equation:

$$\text{ES} = \text{Mean}_{\text{smokers}} - \text{Mean}_{\text{nonsmokers}} \, / \, \text{Standard Deviation}_{\text{weighted}}$$

where the standard $\text{deviation}_{\text{weighted}}$ can be obtained by averaging the standard deviations for the smokers and nonsmokers, taking into account the size of the groups.

Using this equation, we see in Table 7.6 an effect size reported of 2.154. This means that the average smoker would be over two standard deviations higher than a nonsmoker in terms of depression. This is a large difference, in a practical sense.

Turning to our second illustration, as shown in the chi-square analysis of Table 7.7, we see the effect size phi coefficient with a value of .185 and an approximate significance of .635. Using the phi coefficient is a measure of the strength of the association between two categorical variables (two nominal variables). A value of .185 indicates a weak association, and we have additional evidence that smokers and nonsmokers do not differ in terms of their peer group affiliation.

HOW DO YOU REPORT THE RESULTS?

When researchers conclude the statistical testing, they next turn to representing the results in tables and figures and reporting results in a discussion. You might include these results in a section labeled "Results." Several points might aid in your construction of this section and help you understand the contents of a published results section.

This section should address or respond to each research question or hypothesis. A typical approach is to respond to each question or hypothesis one by one in the order in which they were introduced earlier in the study. In reporting the results, the researcher also stays close to the statistical findings without drawing broader implications or meaning from them. Further, this section includes summaries of the data rather than the raw data (e.g., the actual scores for individuals). A results section includes:

- Tables that summarize statistical information
- Figures (charts, pictures, drawings) that portray variables and their relationships
- Detailed explanations about the statistical results

Tables

Researchers display data in tables that summarize statistical results to research questions or hypotheses. A **table** is a summary of quantitative data organized into rows and columns (see Tables 7.6 and 7.7). Typically, tables for reporting results contain quantitative information, but they might contain text information such as summaries of key studies found in the literature (and incorporated earlier in a study, before the results). One advantage of using tables is that they can summarize a large amount of data in a small amount of space. Below are some guidelines for creating tables.

- Although you can present multiple statistical tests in one table, a general guideline is to present one table for each statistical test. Sometimes, however, you can combine data from different statistical analyses into a single table. For example, all descriptive data to questions (*M*, *SD*, and range) can be combined into a single table. However, you should present each inferential test in an individual table.
- Readers should be able to grasp easily the meaning of a table. Tables should organize data into rows and columns with simple and clear headings. Also, the title for the table should accurately represent the information contained in the table and be as complete a description as possible.
- It is important to know the level of statistical detail for descriptive and inferential statistics to report in tables. An examination of tables in scholarly journals typically provides models to use for the level of detail required for each type of statistical test. In addition, the *Publication Manual of the American Psychological Association* (APA, 2001) provides examples of the level of detail to be reported in descriptive tables (e.g., *M*, *SD*, and *N*, or number of participants) and inferential tables (e.g., correlation, ANOVA, and regression). As an additional aid, you might view the typical output for statistical tests using SPSS (e.g., George & Mallery, 2001).
- Authors typically report notes that qualify, explain, or provide additional information in the tables, which can be helpful to readers. Often, these notes include information about the size of the sample reported in the study, the probability values used in hypothesis testing, and the actual significance levels of the statistical test.

Figures

Discerning the difference between tables and figures is not always clear cut. A table includes a summary of quantitative data, whereas a figure presents information in graphs or in visual pictures (APA, 2001). Thus, a **figure** is a summary of quantitative information presented as a chart, graph, or picture that shows relations among scores or variables. Tables are preferred to figures (APA, 2001) because tables convey more information in a simple form.

Figures are suitable for visually presenting information in graphs and pictures in results sections of studies. The *Publication Manual of the American Psychological Association* (APA, 2001) suggests several standards for designing a good figure. A good figure:

- Augments, rather than duplicates, the text
- Conveys only essential facts
- Omits visually distracting detail
- Is easy to read and understand
- Is consistent with and is prepared in the same style as similar figures in the same article
- Is carefully planned and prepared (p. 177)

Various types of figures are found in educational research studies:

- **Bar charts**, which depict trends and distributions of data (see the figure in Table 7.4).
- **Scatterplots**, which illustrate the comparison of two different scores and how the scores regress or differ from the mean (see Figure 12.1). This information is useful for identifying outliers and upper or lower ceiling effects of scores.
- **Line graphs**, which display the interaction between two variables in an experiment (see Figure 11.6).
- **Charts**, which portray the complex relationships among variables in correlational research designs (see Figure 12.3).

The *Publication Manual of the American Psychological Association* (APA, 2001) provides illustrations of a line graph, a bar graph, a scatterplot, and a correlational chart path model. In all of these examples, the figure caption is placed at the bottom of the figure. This is different from table titles, which are placed at the top of the table.

Present Results

Although tables and figures summarize information from statistical tests, the researcher needs to describe in detail the results of the statistical tests. In a **presentation of results**, the researcher presents detailed information about the specific results of the descriptive and inferential statistical analyses. This process requires explaining the central results of each statistical test and presenting this information using language acceptable to quantitative researchers.

For the results to each statistical test, the investigator summarizes the findings in one or two sentences. These sentences should include sufficient statistics to provide a complete picture of the results. They should also include information necessary for reporting results to each statistical test. What represents "sufficient" information depends on the specific type of test. At a minimum:

- Report whether the hypothesis test was significant or not
- Provide important information about the statistical test, given the statistics
- Include language typically used in reporting statistical results

The information about the statistical test, for example, might include a report on degrees of freedom and sample size for the chi-square statistic, and means and standard deviations for descriptive statistics (APA, 2001).

Figure 7.5 shows examples of results statements for both descriptive and inferential statistics. For descriptive statistics, the means, standard deviations, and the range of scores show useful information about results. For inferential statistics, information such as the alpha level used, the actual *p* value, the critical region of rejection, the test statistic results, the degrees of freedom, and effect size should be reported. Confidence intervals should also be reported (Wilkinson & Task Force on Statistical Inference, 1999).

FIGURE 7.5

Examples of Results Statements Using an Analysis of Variance Test

Descriptive Statistics

The students who received questions averaged $M = 4.5$ with a $SD = .98$ on math scores.

Inferential Statistics

Standard Statement

The means and standard deviations for each treatment group are presented in Table 2. The analysis of variance revealed a statistically significant difference between the groups, $F(3,8) = 8.98$, $p = 0.0001$.

Effect Size Added

The means and standard deviations for each treatment group are presented in Table 2. The analysis of variance revealed a significant difference among the groups, $F(3,8) = 8.98$, $p < .05$, effect size = .93 *SD.*

Alpha and Actual p Value Indicated

The means and standard deviations for each treatment group are presented in Table 2. At an alpha of .05, the analysis of variance revealed a significant difference among the groups, $F(3,8) = 8.98$, $p = .0001$.

Ideal Model

Mean score Standard Deviation Significance Level

The scores varied for the three groups (questions only—$M = 4.5$, $SD = .98$; lecture only—$M = 3.4$, $SD = .88$; in-class discussion—$M = 4.8$, $SD = .90$). At an alpha of .05, the analysis indicated a statistically significant difference among the groups, $F(3,8) = 8.98$, $p = .034$, effect size = .93 *SD.*

Effect size | Results of hypothesis test | Statistical test | Degrees of freedom for *F* test | Value of test statistic | Probability value of test statistic

HOW DO YOU DISCUSS THE RESULTS?

After reporting and explaining the detailed results, researchers conclude a study by summarizing key findings, developing explanations for results, suggesting limitations in the research, and making recommendations for future inquiries.

Summarize the Major Results

In the process of interpreting results, researchers first summarize the major findings and present the broader implications of the research for distinct audiences. A **summary** is a statement that reviews the major conclusions to each of the research questions or hypotheses. This summary is different from the results: It represents general, rather than specific, conclusions. Specific conclusions in the results would include detail about statistical tests, significance levels, and effect sizes. General conclusions state overall whether the hypothesis was rejected or whether the research question was supported or not supported.

The research ends with statements by researchers about positive implications of the study. **Implications** are those suggestions for the importance of the study for different audiences. They elaborate on the significance for audiences presented initially in the statement of the problem section (see chapter 3). In effect, now that the study has been completed, the researcher is in a position to reflect (and remark) on the importance of the study.

Explain Why the Results Occurred

After this summary, researchers explain why their results turned out the way they did. Often this explanation is based on returning to predictions made from a theory or conceptual framework that guided the development of research questions or hypotheses. In addition, these explanations may include discussing the existing literature and indicating how the results either confirmed or disconfirmed prior studies. Thus, you will frequently find past research studies being presented by authors in this passage. A concluding passage may contrast and compare results with theories or bodies of literature.

Advance Limitations

Researchers also advance limitations or weaknesses of their study that may have affected the results. **Limitations** are potential weaknesses or problems with the study identified by the researcher. These weaknesses are enumerated one by one, and they often relate to inadequate measures of variables, loss or lack of participants, small sample sizes, errors in measurement, and other factors typically related to data collection and analysis. These limitations are useful to other potential researchers who may choose to conduct a similar or replication study. Advancing these limitations provides a useful bridge for recommending future studies. Limitations also help readers judge to what extent the findings can or cannot be generalized to other people and situations.

Suggest Future Research

Researchers next advance future research directions based on the results of the present study. **Future research directions** are suggestions made by the researcher about additional studies that need to be conducted based on the results of the present research. These suggestions are a natural link to the limitations of a study, and they provide useful direction for new researchers and readers who are interested in exploring needed areas of inquiry or applying results to educational practice. These educators often need an "angle" to pursue to add to the existing knowledge, and future research suggestions, typically found at the conclusion of a research study, provide this direction. For those reading a study, future research directions highlight areas that are unknown and provide boundaries for using information from a specific study.

REEXAMINING DATA ANALYSIS AND INTERPRETATION IN THE PARENT INVOLVEMENT STUDY

To obtain an overview of the process of quantitative data analysis and interpretation, we can turn once again to the parent involvement study by Deslandes and Bertrand (2005). With some advanced statistics used by the authors, it is easy to focus on statistics and miss the overall picture of analysis and interpretation unfolding in this study.

The authors surveyed 770 parents of secondary-level students attending five public schools in Quebec. These parents completed several instruments. To look closely at the data analysis used by the authors, it is helpful to reflect on the question the authors sought to answer and then examine the statistical analysis they used to obtain answers to the question. The key question can be found in Paragraph 13: "What are the relative contributions of parents' role construction, self-efficacy, perceptions of teacher invitations, and perceptions of adolescent invitations to predict parent involvement at home and at school in Grades 7, 8, and 9" (p. 166). In this question, "relative contribution" means what independent variables best explain the two outcomes, parent involvement at home and parent involvement at school. Next, let's scan the tables of statistical information the authors presented. Table 1 shows demographic, descriptive statistics (percentages) about the parent participants in the study. Table 2 simply lists the major predictor (independent) variables, the variables controlled in the data analysis, and the two outcome (dependent) variables. This is a helpful table to use to think about the data analysis and the statistical procedures. Table 3 shows descriptive statistics (means, standard deviations) on the four independent variables and the two dependent variables. Tables 4 and 5 show inferential, multiple regression analyses for the independent variables and the demographic control variables for the parent involvement at home and the parent involvement at school dependent variables respectively. So, from the research question, we know that this study will build toward an understanding of the importance of the four factors in explaining parent involvement. Looking again at Table 7.5, we know that when we have two or more independent variables (four constructs and several control variables in this study) measured with continuous scales (1 = disagree very strongly to 6 = agree very strongly) and one dependent variable (either home or school) measured separately as continuous scales, we will use multiple regression as a statistical procedure. We can look at the two regression tables (Table 4 and Table 5) and see that some of the variables were statistically significant at the $p < .05$, $p < .01$, and $p < .001$ levels (as shown by * markings) as seen in the notes at the bottom of the two tables. Unfortunately, we did not learn about effect sizes in Table 4 or Table 5. But in terms of data analysis, in Table 4 we can see that "parents' perceptions of student invitations in academic domain" strongly predicted parent involvement at home (beta = .44). Then we can read the "Results" section to see the more detailed findings. So our thinking about the major forms of analysis of data in this journal article went from thinking about the research question, exploring the tables, recognizing the major types of statistics and using Table 7.5 in this chapter to assessing why the statistic was chosen and then looking closely at the results presented in the tables as well as in the results discussion.

The Discussion section (starting at Paragraph 32) provides a general summary of the results presented by grade level and for each of the dependent measures, parent involvement at home and parent involvement at school. Note that throughout this discussion, the authors are introducing references to other studies that highlight similar findings (see, e.g., Paragraph 36). Also, the article ends with a discussion of implications for school interventions and for increased parental involvement, and of the importance of teacher–parent contacts. The final section identifies some of the limitations of the study in terms of sampling (Paragraph 46), advances ideas for further research (Paragraph 47), and then ends on a positive note about the final importance of the results of the study (Paragraph 49).

KEY IDEAS IN THE CHAPTER

After collecting numeric scores on instruments or through observations, quantitative researchers need to prepare and organize their data for statistical analysis. This process consists of assigning numeric scores to each response option on instruments (if the instrument does not already include this information); determining whether single-item, net, or difference scores will be used in the analysis; and selecting a computer software program to analyze the data. Next, the investigator enters the data into a computer file by building a data grid consisting of variables and their values. With the data set built, the researcher begins the process of analyzing the data to address the research questions or hypotheses. Some questions may call for describing trends in the data, and the researcher uses descriptive analysis such as measures of central tendency, the spread of the scores, and the relative ranking of the scores.

Other research questions and hypotheses call for inferential analysis in which the researcher studies a sample and draws inferences from the sample to a population. To conduct inferential analysis, three procedures might be used: (a) Conduct hypothesis testing by using statistical tests and calculating p values that are determined to be significant or nonsignificant, and suggest that the sample mean is or is not a good estimate of the population mean; (b) set a confidence interval to identify a range of scores that is likely to include the population mean; (c) calculate an effect size that examines the strength of the differences and the practical meaning of these differences for group comparisons or relating variables.

Whether the analysis consists of descriptive or inferential analysis, or both, the researcher presents results in tables, figures, and in a detailed discussion of the results. Finally, investigators conclude their research by summarizing the detailed results in general statements. They also provide explanations for their findings based on prior predictions made in the literature or in theories, and they contrast their results with past research. It is also important in concluding a study to advance limitations to the research, noting potential weaknesses that might have affected the results. These limitations build directly into suggestions for future research that will improve the weaknesses and further contribute to the literature on a topic.

USEFUL INFORMATION FOR PRODUCERS OF RESEARCH

- As you design or plan quantitative research, consider the broad processes of analyzing and interpreting the data as discussed in this chapter, such as preparing and organizing your data, analyzing it descriptively and inferentially, summarizing the results visually and in a discussion, and concluding a study by summarizing and explaining the results. These topics could be headings in your plan for a study or in the final report.
- In quantitative research, score your data and then input it into a computer program using a grid.
- Choose a computer program that offers a large number of statistical procedures.
- Run a descriptive analysis to answer descriptive questions.
- Conduct inferential analysis to address your group comparison and relationship questions or hypotheses.
- For your inferential analysis, report p values of hypothesis testing, confidence intervals, and effect sizes.
- Represent data in tables and figures using the format of the APA style manual.

USEFUL INFORMATION FOR CONSUMERS OF RESEARCH

- To best understand the statistics presented in a research report, ask yourself what the research questions were that the investigator sought to answer and look for a discussion of results that match these research questions.
- Understand that the selection of statistics by a researcher needs to be based on specific criteria. Examine the data collected to determine if the right decision was made based on the seven factors identified in Table 7.5.
- When researchers compare groups, look for not only a report of the statistical test but also information about confidence intervals and effect sizes for interpreting the magnitude of group differences.

UNDERSTANDING CONCEPTS AND EVALUATING RESEARCH STUDIES

1. Assume that you wish to analyze the following hypothesis:

   > "There is no significant difference between lectures, small-group discussions, and large-group discussions in terms of math achievement scores for sixth graders."

   Using Table 7.5 as your guide, determine the appropriate statistical test to use to analyze this question. Work with the assumption that your sampling distribution is normal. Answer these questions to determine your statistical test:
   - Is the hypothesis a comparison of groups or the relationship of variables?
   - How many independent variables do you have? Dependent variables?
   - Are there any covariates being controlled?
   - Is the independent variable categorical or continuous?
   - Is the dependent variable categorical or continuous?

2. Five individuals respond to five questions using the Likert scale of 5 (*strongly agree*), 4 (*agree*), 3 (*undecided*), 2 (*disagree*), and 1 (*strongly disagree*). You have input the data into an SPSS database and it looks like this:

   5 5 5 6 4
   3 2 1 3 3
   4 3 1 2
   3 5 8 2 4
   2 1 1 1 1

   Your task is to look over this small database and clean it up. What do you fix?
3. In the parent involvement study (Deslandes & Bertrand, 2005), the authors reported results for parent involvement at home for ninth-grade students. They say that the statistical analysis of the independent variables and the level of parent involvement at home was $F(10, 101) = 6.81$, $p < .001$. Discuss the meaning of this statement. What does F stand for? What is 101? What is 6.81? What does $p < .001$ mean?

Conducting Your Research

For your educational project, design the steps you would take in conducting a quantitative analysis. Discuss how you would score the data, select a statistical program, input the data, and clean and account for missing data. Then describe how you would analyze your data descriptively and inferentially to answer your research questions or hypotheses. Discuss how you would select the appropriate statistic to use. Finally, identify the types of figures and tables you would use and the steps you would use to discuss the results.

Go to our Companion Website at **www.prenhall.com/creswell** to:

- assess your understanding of chapter content with Multiple-Choice Questions,
- apply what you've learned with Essay Questions,
- practice your research skills with interactive Building Research Skills exercises, and
- broaden your knowledge of research with Web Links to research topics on the Internet.

CHAPTER 8

Collecting Qualitative Data

Qualitative data collection is more than simply deciding on whether you will observe or interview people. Five steps comprise the process of collecting qualitative data. You need to identify your participants and sites, gain access, determine the types of data to collect, develop data collection forms, and administer the process in an ethical manner.

By the end of this chapter, you should be able to:

- Identify different approaches to selecting participants and sites.
- Know the levels of permissions required to gain access to participants and sites.
- Identify and weigh the alternative types of qualitative data you can collect.
- Identify the procedures for recording qualitative data.
- Recognize the administrative and ethical considerations involved in collecting qualitative data.

Maria is comfortable talking with students and teachers in her high school. She does not mind asking them open-ended research questions such as "What are your (student and teacher) experiences with students carrying weapons in our high school?" She also knows the challenges involved in obtaining their views. She needs to listen without injecting her own opinions, and she needs to take notes or tape-record what people have to say. This phase requires time, but Maria enjoys talking with people and listening to their ideas. Maria is a natural qualitative researcher.

WHAT IS THE PROCESS OF QUALITATIVE DATA COLL

From chapter 2 we know that qualitative data collection consists of collectir forms with general, emerging questions to permit the participant to genera gathering word (text) or image (picture) data; and collecting information number of individuals or sites. Thinking more specifically now,

- In *quantitative* research we systematically identify our participants ar through random sampling; in *qualitative* research, we identify our pa sites based on places and people that can best help us understand o phenomenon.
- In both *quantitative* and *qualitative* research, we need permissions to begin our study, but in *qualitative* research, we need greater access to the site because we will typically go to the site and interview people or observe them. This process requires a greater level of participation from the site than does the *quantitative* research process.
- In both approaches, we also collect data such as interviews, observations, and documents. In *qualitative* research, our approach relies on general interviews or observations so that we do not restrict the views of participants. We will not use someone else's instrument as in quantitative research and gather closed-ended information; we will instead collect data with a few open-ended questions.
- In both approaches, we need to record the information supplied by the participants. Rather than using predesigned instruments from someone else or instruments that we design, in qualitative research we will record information on self-designed protocols that help us organize information reported by participants to each question.
- Finally, we will administer our procedures of *qualitative* data collection with sensitivity to the challenges and ethical issues of gathering information face-to-face and often in people's homes or workplaces. Studying people in their own environment creates challenges for the qualitative researcher that may not be present in *quantitative* research when investigators mail out anonymous questionnaires or bring individuals into the experimental laboratory.

WHAT PARTICIPANTS AND SITES WILL YOU STUDY?

In qualitative inquiry, the intent is not to generalize to a population, but to develop an in-depth exploration of a central phenomenon (see chapter 2 section on "Identifying a Research Problem"). Thus, to best understand this phenomenon, the qualitative researcher purposefully or intentionally selects individuals and sites. This distinction between quantitative "random sampling" and qualitative "purposeful sampling" is portrayed in Figure 8.1. In quantitative research, the focus is on random sampling, selecting representative individuals, and then generalizing from these individuals to a population. Often this process results in testing "theories" that explain the population. However, in qualitative research, you select people or sites that can best help you understand the central phenomenon. This understanding emerges through a detailed understanding of the people or site. It can lead to information that allows individuals to "learn" about the phenomenon, or to an understanding that provides voice to individuals who may not be heard otherwise.

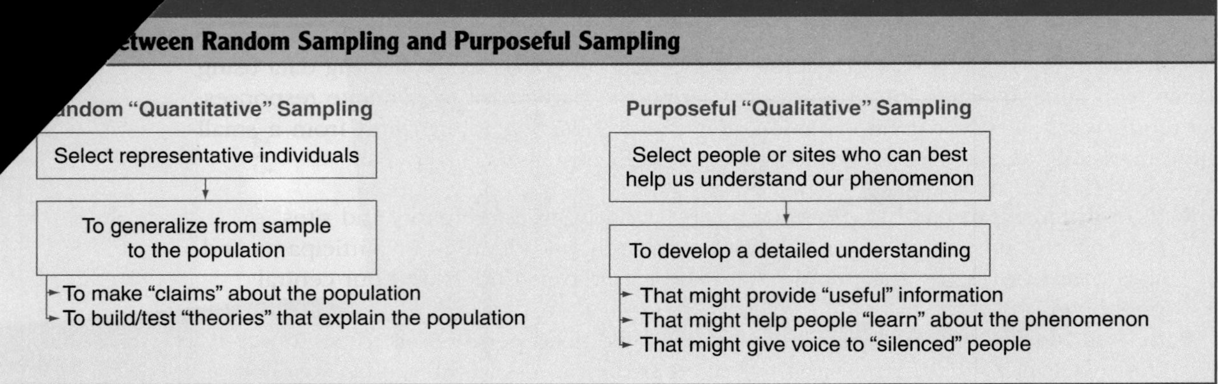

Purposeful Sampling

The research term used for qualitative sampling is *purposeful sampling*. In **purposeful sampling**, researchers intentionally select individuals and sites to learn or understand the central phenomenon. The standard used in choosing participants and sites is whether they are "information rich" (Patton, 1990, p. 169). In any given qualitative study, you may decide to study a site (e.g., one college campus), several sites (three small liberal arts campuses), individuals or groups (freshman students), or some combination (two liberal arts campuses and several freshman students on those campuses). Purposeful sampling thus applies to both individuals and sites.

If you conduct your own study and use purposeful sampling, you need to identify your sampling strategy and be able to defend its use. The literature identifies several qualitative sampling strategies (see, e.g., Miles & Huberman, 1994; Patton, 1990). As seen in Figure 8.2, you have a choice of selecting from one of nine strategies that educators frequently use. These strategies are differentiated in terms of whether they are employed before data collection begins or after data collection has started (an approach consistent with an emerging design). Further, each has a different intent, depending on the research problem and questions you would like answered in a study. All strategies apply to sampling a single time or multiple times during a study, and you can use them to sample from individuals, groups, or entire organizations and sites. (See Patton, 1990, for further discussion of these types.)

Maximal Variation Sampling

One characteristic of qualitative research is to present multiple perspectives of individuals to represent the complexity of our world (see chapter 2 section on "Identifying a Research Problem"). Thus, one sampling strategy is to build that complexity into the research when sampling participants or sites. **Maximal variation sampling** is a purposeful sampling strategy in which the researcher samples cases or individuals that differ on some characteristic or trait (e.g., different age groups). This procedure requires that you identify the characteristic and then find sites or individuals that display different dimensions of that characteristic. For example, a researcher might first identify the characteristic of racial composition of high schools, and then purposefully sample three high schools that differ on this characteristic, such as a primarily Hispanic high school, a predominantly white high school, and a racially diverse high school.

FIGURE 8.2

Types of Purposeful Sampling

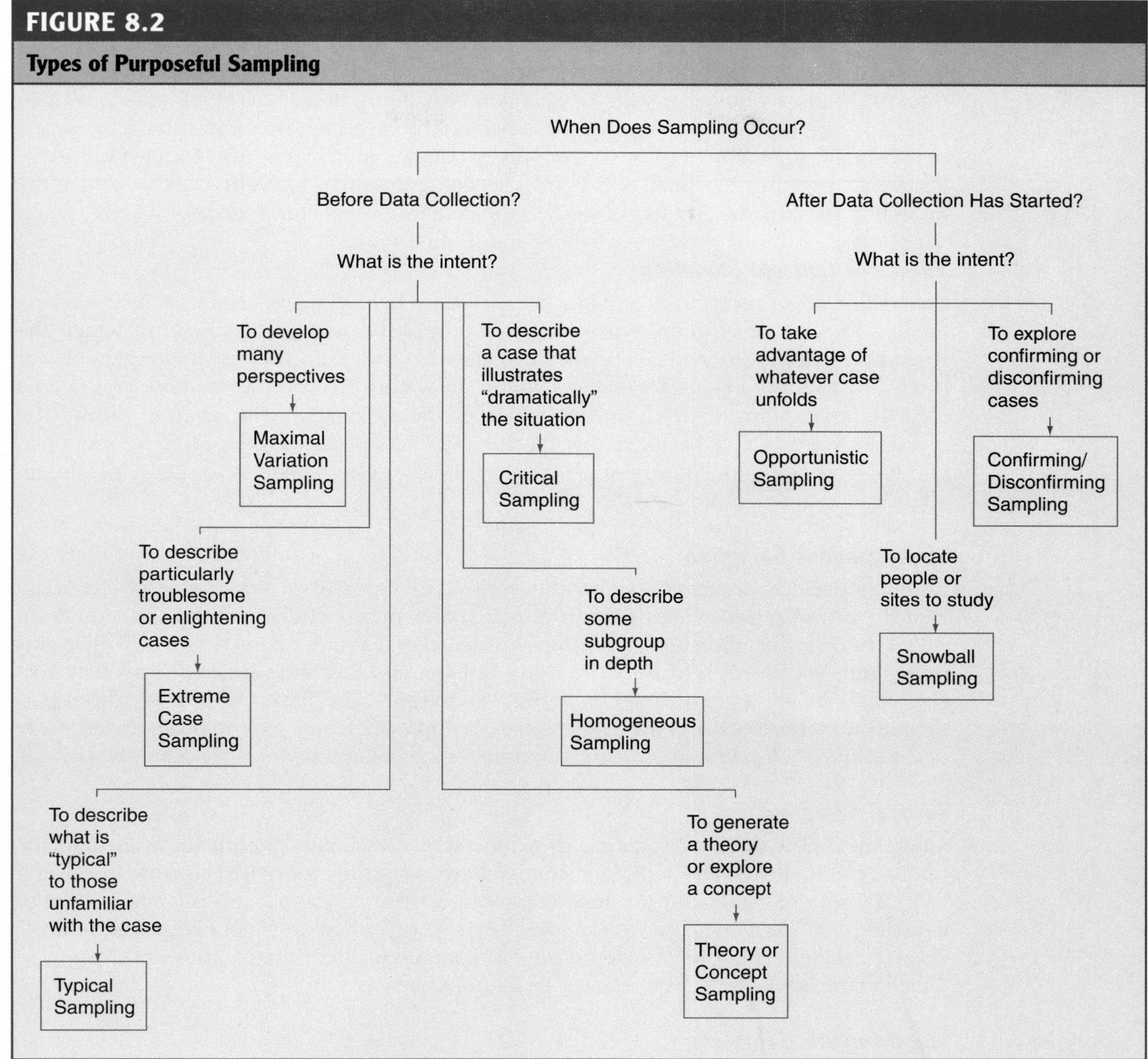

Extreme Case Sampling

Sometimes you are more interested in learning about a case that is particularly troublesome or enlightening, or a case that is noticeable for its success or failure (Patton, 1990). **Extreme case sampling** is a form of purposeful sampling in which you study an outlier case or one that displays extreme characteristics. Researchers identify these cases by locating persons or organizations that others have cited for achievements or distinguishing characteristics (e.g., certain elementary schools targeted for federal assistance). An autistic education program in elementary education that has received awards may be an outstanding case to purposefully sample.

Typical Sampling

Some research questions address "What is normal?" or "What is typical?" **Typical sampling** is a form of purposeful sampling in which the researcher studies a person or site that is "typical" to those unfamiliar with the situation. What constitutes typical, of course, is open to interpretation. However, you might ask persons at a research site or even select a typical case by collecting demographic data or survey data about all cases. You could study a typical faculty member at a small liberal arts college because that individual has worked at the institution for 20 years and has embodied the cultural norms of the school.

Theory or Concept Sampling

You might select individuals or sites because they help you understand a concept or a theory. **Theory or concept sampling** is a purposeful sampling strategy in which the researcher samples individuals or sites because they can help the researcher generate or discover a theory or specific concepts within the theory. To use this method, you need a clear understanding of the concept or larger theory expected to emerge during the research. In a study of five sites that have experienced distance education, for example, you have chosen these sites because study of them can help generate a theory of student attitudes toward distance learning.

Homogeneous Sampling

You might select certain sites or people because they possess a similar trait or characteristic. In **homogeneous sampling** the researcher purposefully samples individuals or sites based on membership in a subgroup that has defining characteristics. To use this procedure, you need to identify the characteristics and find individuals or sites that possess it. For example, in a rural community, all parents who have children in school participate in a parent program. You choose members of this parent program to study because they belong to a common subgroup in the community.

Critical Sampling

Sometimes individuals or research sites represent the central phenomenon in dramatic terms (Patton, 1990). The sampling strategy here is to study a **critical sample** because it is an exceptional case and the researcher can learn much about the phenomenon. For example, you study teenage violence in a high school where a student with a gun threatened a teacher. This situation represents a dramatic incident that portrays the extent to which some adolescents may engage in school violence.

Opportunistic Sampling

After data collection begins, you may find that you need to collect new information to best answer your research questions. **Opportunistic sampling** is purposeful sampling undertaken after the research begins, to take advantage of unfolding events that will help answer research questions. In this process, the sample emerges during the inquiry. Researchers need to be cautious about engaging in this form of sampling because it might divert attention away from the original aims of the research. However, it captures the developing or emerging nature of qualitative research nicely and can lead to novel ideas and surprising findings. For example, you begin a study with maximal variation sampling of different pregnant teenagers in high schools. During this process you find a pregnant teenager who plans to bring her baby to school each day. Because a study of this teenager would provide new insights about balancing children and school, you study her activities during her pregnancy at the school and in the months after the birth of her child.

Snowball Sampling

In certain research situations, you may not know the best people to study because of the unfamiliarity of the topic or the complexity of events. As in quantitative research, qualitative snowball sampling is a form of purposeful sampling that typically proceeds after a study begins and occurs when the researcher asks participants to recommend other individuals to study. Researchers may pose this request as a question during an interview or through informal conversations with individuals at a research site. For example, in the gunman case study (Asmussen & Creswell, 1995), the authors asked interviewees if they could recommend other individuals to interview who might have a reaction to the incident. This procedure led to purposeful sampling of individuals that had not been anticipated when the project began. Interviewing the "expert" psychologist brought to the campus to help individuals through the crisis is an example of this.

Confirming and Disconfirming Sampling

A final form of purposeful sampling, also used after studies begin, is to sample individuals or sites to confirm or disconfirm preliminary findings. **Confirming and disconfirming sampling** is a purposeful strategy used during a study to follow up on specific cases to test or explore further specific findings. Although this sampling serves to verify the accuracy of the findings throughout a study, it also represents a sampling procedure used during a study. For example, you find out that academic department chairs support faculty in their development as teachers by serving as mentors. After initially interviewing chairs, you further confirm the mentoring role by sampling and studying chairs who have received praise from faculty as "good" mentors.

Sample Size or Number of Research Sites

The number of people and sites sampled vary from one qualitative study to the next. You might examine some published qualitative studies and see what numbers of sites or participants researchers used. Here are some general guidelines:

- It is typical in qualitative research to study a few individuals or a few cases. This is because the overall ability of a researcher to provide an in-depth picture diminishes with the addition of each new individual or site. One objective of qualitative research is to present the complexity of a site or of the information provided by individuals.
- In some cases, you might study a single individual or a single site. In other cases, the number may be several, ranging from 1 or 2 to 30 or 40. Because of the need to report details about each individual or site, the larger number of cases can become unwieldy and result in superficial perspectives. Moreover, collecting qualitative data and analyzing it takes considerable time, and the addition of each individual or site only lengthens that time.
- In part III, we will discuss several specific designs (i.e., ethnography, case study, grounded theory, and narrative research) for conducting qualitative research. Once you have selected the procedure or design for your study, the approach will suggest the numbers of individuals you need to study. This may range from studying one individual to studying an entire group of people.

Let's look at some specific examples to see how many individuals and sites were used. Qualitative researchers may collect data from single individuals. For example, in the qualitative case study of Basil McGee, a second-year middle school science teacher, Brickhouse and Bodner (1992) explored his beliefs about science and science teaching and how his beliefs shaped classroom instruction. Elsewhere, several individuals participated in a qualitative grounded theory study. The researchers examined 20 parents of children labeled as ADHD (Reid, Hertzog, & Snyder, 1996). More extensive data collection was used in a qualitative ethnographic study of the culture of fraternity life and the exploitation and victimization of women. Rhoads (1995) conducted 12 formal interviews and 18 informal interviews, made observations, and collected numerous documents.

If you were Maria, and you sought to answer the question "What are the students' experiences with carrying weapons in the high school?" what purposeful sampling strategy would you use? Before you look at the answers I provide, write down at least two possibilities on a sheet of paper.

Let's create some options depending on the students that Maria has available to her to study.

- One option would be to use *maximal variation sampling* and interview several students who vary in the type of weapon infraction they committed in the school. For instance, one student may have threatened another student. Another student may have actually used a knife in a fight. Another student may have kept a knife in a locker and a teacher discovered it. These three students represent different types of weapon possession in the school, and each will likely provide different views on students having knives in the school.
- Another option would be to use *critical sampling*. You might interview a student who actually used a knife during a fight. This is an example of a public use of a weapon, and it represents a dramatic action worthy of study by itself.
- Can you think of other approaches to sampling that you might use? Also, how many students would you study and what is the reason for your choice?

HOW WILL YOU GAIN ACCESS TO THE PEOPLE AND SITES?

Similar to quantitative research, gaining access to the site or individual(s) in qualitative inquiry involves obtaining permissions at different levels, such as the organization, the site, the individuals, and the campus institutional review boards. Of special importance is negotiating approval with campus review boards and locating individuals at a site who can facilitate the collection of qualitative data.

Seek Institutional Review Board Approval

Researchers applying for permission to study individuals in a qualitative project must go through the approval process of a campus institutional review board as outlined in chapter 6. These steps include seeking permission from the board, developing a description of the project, designing an informed consent form, and having the project reviewed. Because *qualitative* data collection consists of lengthy periods of gathering information directly involving people and recording detailed personal views from individuals, you will need to provide a detailed description of your procedures to the institutional review board. This detail is needed because the board may not be familiar with the qualitative approach to educational research and because you will spend time in people's homes, workplaces, or sites in which you gather data.

Several strategies might prove useful when negotiating qualitative research through the institutional review board process:

- Determine if individuals reviewing proposals on the review board are familiar with qualitative inquiry. Look for those individuals who have experience in conducting qualitative research. This requires a careful assessment of the membership of the review board.
- Develop detailed descriptions of the procedures so that reviewers have a full disclosure of the potential risks to people and sites in the study.
- Detail ways you will protect the anonymity of participants. These might be by masking names of individuals, assigning pseudonyms to individuals and their organizations, or choosing to withhold descriptors that would lead to the identification of participants and sites.
- Discuss the need to respect the research site and to disturb or disrupt it as little as possible. When you gain permission to enter the site, you need to be respectful of property and refrain from introducing issues that may cause participants to question their group or organization. Doing this requires keeping a delicate balance between exploring a phenomenon in depth and respecting individuals and property at the research site.
- Detail how the study will provide opportunities to "give back" or reciprocate in some way to those individuals you study (e.g., you might donate services at the site, become an advocate for the needs of those studied, or share with them any monetary rewards you may receive from your study).
- Acknowledge that during your prolonged interaction with participants, you may adopt their beliefs and even become an advocate for their ideas.
- Specify potential power imbalances that may occur between yourself and the participants, and how your study will address these imbalances. For example, a power imbalance occurs when a researcher studies his or her own employer or employees in the workplace. If this is your situation, consider researching sites where you do not have an interest or try to collect data in a way that minimizes a power inequality between yourself and participants (e.g., observing rather than interviewing).
- Detail how much time you will spend at the research site. This detail might include the anticipated number of days, the length of each visit, and the times when visits will take place.
- Include in the project description a list of the interview questions so reviewers on the institutional board can determine how sensitive the questions may be. Typically, qualitative interview questions are open ended and general, lending support to a noninvasive stance by the researcher.

Gatekeepers

In qualitative research, you often need to seek and obtain permissions from individuals and sites at many levels. Because of the in-depth nature of extensive and multiple interviews with participants, it might be helpful for you to identify and make use of a gatekeeper. A **gatekeeper** is an individual who has an official or unofficial role at the site, provides entrance to a site, helps researchers locate people, and assists in the identification of places to study (Hammersley & Atkinson, 1995). For example, this individual may be a teacher, a principal, a group leader, or the informal leader of a special program, and usually has "insider" status at the site the researchers plan to study. Identifying a gatekeeper at a research site and winning his or her support and trust may take time. You might be required to submit written information about the project to proceed. Such information might include:

- Why their site was chosen for study
- What will be accomplished at the site during the research study (i.e., time and resources required by participants and yourself)
- How much time you will spend at the site
- What potential there is for your presence to be disruptive
- How you will use and report the results
- What the individuals at the site will gain from the study (Bogdan & Biklen, 1998)

Let's look at an example of using a gatekeeper in a qualitative study.

> While conducting a qualitative study exploring the behavior of informal student cliques that may display violent behavior, a researcher talks to many high-school personnel. Ultimately, the social studies coordinator emerges as a good gatekeeper. She suggests the researcher use the school cafeteria as an important site to see school cliques in action. She also points out specific student leaders of cliques (e.g., the punk group) who might help the researcher understand student behavior.

WHAT INFORMATION WILL YOU COLLECT?

Another aspect of qualitative data collection is to identify the types of data that will address your research questions. In qualitative research you pose general, broad questions to participants and allow them to share their views relatively unconstrained by your perspective. In addition, you collect multiple types of information, and you may add new forms of data during the study to answer your questions. Further, you engage in extensive data collection, spending a great deal of time at the site where people work, play, or engage in the phenomenon you wish to study. At the site, you will gather detailed information to establish the complexity of the central phenomenon.

We can see the varied nature of qualitative forms of data when they are placed into the following categories:

- Observations
- Interviews and questionnaires
- Documents
- Audiovisual materials

Specific examples of types of data in these four categories are shown in Figure 8.3. Variations on data collection in all four areas are emerging continuously. Most recently, videotapes, student classroom portfolios, and the use of e-mails are attracting increasing attention as forms of data. Table 8.1 shows each category of data collection listed, the type of data it yields, and a definition for that type of data. Now let's take a closer look at each of the four categories and their strengths and weaknesses.

Observations

When educators think about qualitative research, they often have in mind the process of collecting observational data in a specific school setting. Unquestionably, observations represent a frequently used form of data collection, with the researcher able to assume different roles in the process (Spradley, 1980a).

FIGURE 8.3

A Compendium of Data Collection Approaches in Qualitative Research

Observations

Gather fieldnotes by:

- Conducting an observation as a participant
- Conducting an observation as an observer
- Spending more time as a participant than observer
- Spending more time as an observer than a participant
- First observing as an "outsider," then participating in the setting and observing as an "insider"

Interviews and Questionnaires

Conduct an unstructured, open-ended interview and take interview notes.

Conduct an unstructured, open-ended interview; audiotape the interview and transcribe it.

Conduct a semistructured interview; audiotape the interview and transcribe it.

Conduct focus group interviews; audiotape the interviews and transcribe them.

Collect open-ended responses to an electronic interview or questionnaire.

Gather open-ended responses to questions on a questionnaire.

Documents

Keep a journal during the research study.

Have a participant keep a journal or diary during the research study.

Collect personal letters from participants.

Analyze public documents (e.g., official memos, minutes of meetings, records or archival material).

Analyze school documents (e.g., attendance reports, retention rates, dropout rates, or discipline referrals).

Examine autobiographies and biographies.

Collect or draw maps and seating charts.

Examine portfolios or less formal examples of students' work.

Collect e-mails or electronic data.

Audiovisual Materials

Examine physical trace evidence (e.g., footprints in the snow).

Videotape a social situation of an individual or group.

Examine photographs or videotapes.

Collect sounds (e.g., musical sounds, a child's laughter, or car horns honking).

Examine possessions or ritual objects.

Have participants take photos or videotapes.

Sources: Creswell, 2007; Mills, 2000.

Observation is the process of gathering open-ended, firsthand information by observing people and places at a research site. As a form of data collection, observation has both advantages and disadvantages. Advantages include the opportunity to record information as it occurs in a setting, to study actual behavior, and to study individuals

TABLE 8.1

Forms of Qualitative Data Collection

Forms of Data Collection	Type of Data	Definition of Type of Data
Observations	Fieldnotes and drawings	Unstructured text data and pictures taken during observations by the researcher
Interviews and questionnaires	Transcriptions of open-ended interviews or open-ended questions on questionnaires	Unstructured text data obtained from transcribing audiotapes of interviews or by transcribing open-ended responses to questions on questionnaires
Documents	Hand-recorded notes about documents or optically scanned documents	Public (e.g., notes from meetings) and private (e.g., journals) records available to the researcher
Audiovisual materials	Pictures, photographs, videotapes, objects, sounds	Audiovisual materials consisting of images or sounds of people or places recorded by the researcher or someone else

who have difficulty verbalizing their ideas (e.g., preschool children). Some of the disadvantages of observations are that you will be limited to those sites and situations where you can gain access, and in those sites, you may have difficulty developing rapport with individuals. This can occur if the individuals are unaccustomed to formal research (e.g., a nonuniversity setting). Observing in a setting requires good listening skills and careful attention to visual detail. It also requires management of issues such as the potential deception by people being observed and the initial awkwardness of being an "outsider" without initial personal support in a setting (Hammersley & Atkinson, 1995).

Observational Roles

Despite these potential difficulties, observation continues to be a well-accepted form of qualitative data collection. Using it requires that you adopt a particular role as an observer. No one role is suited for all situations; observational roles vary depending on your comfort at the site, your rapport with participants, and how best you can collect data to understand the central phenomenon. Although many roles exist (see Spradley, 1980a), you might consider one of three popular roles.

Role of a Participant Observer To truly learn about a situation, you can become involved in activities at the research site. This offers excellent opportunities to see experiences from the views of participants. A **participant observer** is an observational role adopted by researchers when they take part in activities in the setting they observe. As a participant, you assume the role of an "inside" observer who actually engages in activities at the study site. At the same time that you are participating in activities, you record information. This role requires seeking permission to participate in activities and assuming a comfortable role as observer in the setting. It is difficult to take notes while participating, and you may need to wait to write down observations until after you have left the research site.

Role of a Nonparticipant Observer In some situations, you may not be familiar enough with the site and people to participate in the activities. A **nonparticipant observer** is an observer who visits a site and records notes without becoming involved in the activities of the participants. The nonparticipant observer is an "outsider" who sits on the periphery or some advantageous place to watch and record the phenomenon under study (i.e., the back of the classroom). This role requires less access than the participant role, and gatekeepers and individuals at a research site may be more comfortable with it. However, by not actively participating, you will remove yourself from actual experiences, and the observations you make may not be as concrete as if you had participated in the activities.

Changing Observational Roles In many observational situations, it is advantageous to shift or change roles, making it difficult to classify your role as strictly participatory or nonparticipatory. A **changing observational role** is one where researchers adapt their role to the situation. For example, you might first enter a site and observe as a nonparticipant, simply needing to "look around" in the early phases of research. Then you slowly become involved as a participant. Sometimes the reverse happens, and a participant becomes a nonparticipant. However, entering a site as a nonparticipant is a frequently used approach. After a short time, when rapport is developed, you switch to being a participant in the setting. Engaging in both roles permits you to be subjectively involved in the setting as well as to see the setting more objectively.

Here is an illustration in which a researcher began as a nonparticipant and changed into a participant during the process of observing:

> One researcher studying the use of wireless laptop computers in a multicultural education methods class spent the first three visits to the class observing from the back row. He sought to learn the process involved in teaching the course, the instructor's interaction with students, and the instructor's overall approach to teaching. Then, on his fourth visit, students began using the laptop computers and the observer became a participant by teaming with a student who used the laptop from her desk to interact with the instructor's Web site.

The Process of Observing

As we just saw in the discussion of different observational roles, the qualitative inquirer engages in a process of observing, regardless of the role. This general process is outlined in the following steps:

1. *Select a site to be observed that can help you best understand the central phenomenon.* Obtain the required permissions needed to gain access to the site.
2. *Ease into the site slowly by looking around; getting a general sense of the site; and taking limited notes, at least initially.* Conduct brief observations at first, because you will likely be overwhelmed with all of the activities taking place. This slow entry helps to build rapport with individuals at the site and helps you assimilate the large amount of information.
3. *At the site, identify who or what to observe, when to observe, and how long to observe.* Gatekeepers can provide guidance as you make these decisions. The practical requirements of the situation, such as the length of a class period or the duration of the activity, will limit your participation.
4. *Determine, initially, your role as an observer.* Select from the roles of participant or nonparticipant during your first few observations. Consider whether it would be advantageous to change roles during the process to learn best about the individuals or site. Regardless of whether you change roles, consider what role you will use and your reasons for it.
5. *Conduct multiple observations over time to obtain the best understanding of the site and the individuals.* Engage in broad observation at first, noting the general landscape of activities and events. As you become familiar with the setting, you can begin to narrow your observations to specific aspects (e.g., a small group of children interacting during

reading time). A broad-to-narrow perspective is a useful strategy because of the amount of information available in an observation.

6. *Design some means for recording notes during an observation.* The data recorded during an observation are called *fieldnotes.* **Fieldnotes** are text (words) recorded by the researcher during an observation in a qualitative study. Examine the sample fieldnotes shown in Figure 8.4. In this example, the student–observer engaged in participant observation when the instructor asked the class to spend 20 minutes observing an art object that had been brought into the classroom. This object was not familiar to the students in the class. It was from Indonesia and had a square, bamboo base and a horsehair top. It was probably used for some religious activities. This was a good object to use for an observational activity because it could not be easily recognized or described. The instructor asked students to observe the object and record fieldnotes describing the object and reflecting on their insights, hunches, and themes that emerged during the observation.

As we see in Figure 8.4, one student recorded the senses—touch, sight, sound, and smell—of the object, recording thoughts every 5 minutes or so. Notice that the student's fieldnotes show complete sentences and notations about quotes from other students. The notes in the right column indicate that this student is beginning to reflect on the larger ideas learned from the experiences and to note how other students in the class are reacting to the object. The heading at the top of the fieldnotes records essential information about the time, place, and activities observed.

FIGURE 8.4

Sample Fieldnotes from a Student's Observation of an Art Object

Observational Fieldnotes —Art Object in the Classroom
Setting: Classroom 306
Observer: J
Role of Observer: Observer of object
Time: 4:30 p.m., March 9, 2004
Length of Observation: 20 minutes

	Description of Object	*Reflective Notes (insights, hunches, themes)*
4:35 p.m	*Touch J taps on the base. Gritty wood, pieced together unevenly. The object's top feels like a cheap wig. The base was moved and the caning was tight. The wicker feels smooth.*	*–Many students touch the object—most walk up slowly, cautiously.* *–Several good analogies come to mind.*
4:40	*Sight The object stands on four pegs that holds a square base. The base is decorated with scalloped carvings. The wood is a light, natural color and sanded smooth and finished. Jt is in the shape of a pyramid, cropped close at the bottom on the underside.*	*–This object is really hard to describe—perhaps J should use dimensions? But it has several parts.*
4:50	*Sound Students comment as they touched the object, "Oh, that's hair?" Js it securely fastened?" A slight rustling is heard from brushing the bristles . . ."*	*–Pickup on good quotes from the students.* *–"Sounds" could definitely be one of my themes!*
5:02	*The object smells like roof-dry slate. Jt is odorless. But it has a musty, dusty scent to the top half, and no one wants to sniff it.*	*–This object seems to change smells the more J am around it—probably a dusty scent fits it best.*

7. *Consider what information you will record during an observation.* For example, this information might include portraits of the participants, the physical setting, particular events and activities, and personal reactions (Bogdan & Biklen, 1998). In observing a classroom, for example, you may record activities by the teacher, the students, the interactions between the students and teacher, and the student-to-student conversations.

8. *Record descriptive and reflective fieldnotes.* **Descriptive fieldnotes** record a description of the events, activities, and people (e.g., what happened). **Reflective fieldnotes** record personal thoughts that researchers have that relate to their insights, hunches, or broad ideas or themes that emerge during the observation (e.g., what sense you made of the site, people, and situation).

9. *Make yourself known, but remain unobtrusive.* During the observation, be introduced by someone if you are an "outsider" or new to the setting or people. Be passive, be friendly, and be respectful of the people and site.

10. *After observing, slowly withdraw from the site.* Thank the participants and inform them of the use of the data and the availability of a summary of results when you complete the study.

Figure 8.5 summarizes the steps listed above in a checklist you might use to assess whether you are prepared to conduct an observation. The questions on this checklist represent roughly the order in which you might consider them before, during, and after the observation, but you can check off each question as you complete it.

Interviews

Equally popular to observation in qualitative research is interviewing. A qualitative **interview** occurs when researchers ask one or more participants general, open-ended questions and record their answers. The researcher then transcribes and types the data into a computer file for analysis.

In *qualitative* research, you ask **open-ended questions** so that the participants can best voice their experiences unconstrained by any perspectives of the researcher or past research findings. An **open-ended response** to a question allows the participant to create the options for responding. For example, in a qualitative interview of athletes in high schools, you might ask, "How do you balance participation in athletics with your schoolwork?" The

FIGURE 8.5

An Observational Checklist

_____ Did you gain permission to study the site?

_____ Do you know your role as an observer?

_____ Do you have a means for recording fieldnotes, such as an observational protocol?

_____ Do you know what you will observe first?

_____ Will you enter and leave the site slowly, so as not to disturb the setting?

_____ Will you make multiple observations over time?

_____ Will you develop rapport with individuals at the site?

_____ Will your observations change from broad to narrow?

_____ Will you take limited notes at first?

_____ Will you take both descriptive as well as reflective notes?

_____ Will you describe in complete sentences so that you have detailed fieldnotes?

_____ Did you thank your participants at the site?

athlete then creates a response to this question without being forced into response possibilities. The researcher often audiotapes the conversation and transcribes the information into words for analysis.

Interviews in qualitative research have both advantages and disadvantages. Some advantages are that they provide useful information when you cannot directly observe participants, and they permit participants to describe detailed personal information. Compared to the observer, the interviewer also has better control over the types of information received, because the interviewer can ask specific questions to elicit this information.

Some disadvantages are that interviews provide only information "filtered" through the views of the interviewers (i.e., the researcher summarizes the participants' views in the research report). Also, similar to observations, interview data may be deceptive and provide the perspective the interviewee wants the researcher to hear. Another disadvantage is that the presence of the researcher may affect how the interviewee responds. Interviewee responses also may not be articulate, perceptive, or clear. In addition, equipment issues may be a problem, and you need to organize recording and transcribing equipment (if used) in advance of the interview. Also during the interview, you need to give some attention to the conversation with the participants. This attention may require saying little, handling emotional outbursts, and using icebreakers to encourage individuals to talk. With all of these issues to balance, it is little wonder inexperienced researchers express surprise about the difficulty of conducting interviews.

Types of Interviews and Open-Ended Questions on Questionnaires

Once you decide to collect qualitative interviews, you next consider what form of interviewing will best help you understand the central phenomenon and answer the questions in your study. There are a number of approaches to interviewing and using open-ended questions on questionnaires. Which interview approach to use will ultimately depend on the accessibility of individuals, the cost, and the amount of time available.

One-on-One Interviews The most time-consuming and costly approach is to conduct individual interviews. A popular approach in educational research, the **one-on-one interview** is a data-collection process in which the researcher asks questions to and records answers from only one participant in the study at a time. In a qualitative project, you may use several one-on-one interviews, such as asking administrators and student health counselors to provide their impressions of the gunman incident (see Asmussen & Creswell, 1995). One-on-one interviews are ideal for interviewing participants who are not hesitant to speak, are articulate, and who can share ideas comfortably.

Focus Group Interviews Focus groups can be used to collect shared understanding from several individuals as well as to get views from specific people. A **focus group interview** is the process of collecting data through interviews with a group of people, typically four to six. The researcher asks a small number of general questions and elicits responses from all individuals in the group. Focus groups are advantageous when the interaction among interviewees will likely yield the best information and when interviewees are similar to and cooperative with each other. They are also useful when the time to collect information is limited and individuals are hesitant to provide information (although some individuals may be reluctant to provide information in any type of interview).

When conducting a focus group interview, encourage all participants to talk and to take their turns talking. A focus group can be challenging for the interviewer who lacks control over the interview discussion. Also, when focus groups are audiotaped, the transcriptionist may have difficulty discriminating among the voices of individuals in the group. Another problem with conducting focus group interviews is that the researcher often has difficulty taking notes because so much is occurring.

Let's consider an example of a focus group interview procedure:

> High school students, with the sponsorship of a university team of researchers, conducted focus group interviews with other students about the use of tobacco in several high schools (Plano Clark et al., 2001). In several interviews, two student interviewers—one to ask questions and one to record responses—selected six students to interview in a focus group. These focus group interviews lasted one-half hour and the interviewers tape-recorded the interview and took notes during the interview. Because the groups were small, the transcriptionist did not have difficulty transcribing the interview and identifying individual voices. Each student at the beginning of the interview said his or her first name.

Telephone Interviews It may not be possible for you to gather groups of individuals for an interview or to visit one-on-one with single individuals. The participants in a study may be geographically dispersed and unable to come to a central location for an interview. In this situation, you can conduct telephone interviews. Conducting a **telephone interview** is the process of gathering data using the telephone and asking a small number of general questions. A telephone interview requires that the researcher use a telephone adaptor that plugs into both the phone and a tape recorder for a clear recording of the interview. One drawback of this kind of interviewing is that the researcher does not have direct contact with the participant. This causes limited communication that may affect the researcher's ability to understand the interviewee's perceptions of the phenomenon. Also, the process may involve substantial costs for telephone expenses. Let's look at an example of a telephone interview procedure:

> In a study of academic department chairpersons in colleges and universities, Creswell et al. (1990) conducted open-ended telephone interviews lasting 45 minutes each with 200 chairpersons located on campuses in the United States. They first obtained the permission of these chairpersons to participate in an interview through contacting them by letter. They also scheduled a time that would be convenient for the interviewee to participate in a telephone interview. Next, they purchased tape recorders and adaptors to conduct the interviews from office telephones. They asked open-ended questions such as "How did you prepare for your position?" The interviews yielded about 3,000 transcript pages. Analysis of these pages resulted in a report about how chairpersons enhance the professional development of faculty in their departments.

Electronic E-Mail Interviews Another type of interview is useful in collecting qualitative data quickly from a geographically dispersed group of people. **E-mail interviews** consist of collecting open-ended data through interviews with individuals using computers and the Internet to do so. If you can obtain e-mail lists or addresses, this form of interviewing provides rapid access to large numbers of people and a detailed, rich text database for qualitative analysis. It can also promote a conversation between yourself as the researcher and the participants, so that through follow-up conversations, you can extend your understanding of the topic or central phenomenon being studied.

However, e-mail interviewing raises complex ethical issues, such as whether you have permission for individuals to participate in your interview, and whether you will protect the privacy of responses. In addition, it may be difficult, under some circumstances, to obtain good lists of e-mail addresses that are current or the names of individuals who will be well suited to answer your questions. For example, how do you locate e-mail addresses for children under the age of 10, who probably do not have such an address? Despite these potential shortcomings, e-mail interviewing as a form of collecting data will probably increase due to the expanding possibilities of technology. Consider this example of an open-ended e-mail survey:

> Four researchers combined resources to develop an e-mail list of faculty who might be teaching courses in mixed method research (Creswell, Tashakkori, Jensen, & Shapely, 2003). They began with an e-mail list of 31 faculty and sent an open-ended interview to these faculty, inquiring about their teaching practices. They asked, for example, "Have you ever taught a course with a content of mixed methods research?" "Why do you think students enroll in a mixed method course?" and "What is your general assessment of mixed methods teaching?" After receiving the e-mail survey, the participants answered each question by writing about their experiences, and sent the survey back using the "reply" feature of their e-mail program. This procedure led to a qualitative text database of open-ended responses from a large number of individuals who had experienced mixed method research.

Open-Ended Questions on Questionnaires On questionnaires, you may ask some questions that are closed ended and some that are open ended. The advantage of this type of questioning is that your predetermined closed-ended responses can net useful information to support theories and concepts in the literature. The open-ended responses, however, permit you to explore reasons for the closed-ended responses and identify any comments people might have that are beyond the responses to the closed-ended questions. The drawback of this approach is that you will have many responses—some short and some long—to analyze. Typically, qualitative researchers look for overlapping themes in the open-ended data and some researchers count the number of themes or the number of times that the participants mention the themes. For example, a researcher might ask a closed-ended question followed by an open-ended question:

> Please tell me the extent of your agreement or disagreement with this statement:
>
> "Student policies governing binge drinking on campus should be more strict."
>
> ___________ Do you strongly agree?
> ___________ Do you agree?
> ___________ Are you undecided?
> ___________ Do you disagree?
> ___________ Do you strongly disagree?
>
> Please explain your response in more detail.

In this example, the researcher started with a closed-ended question and five predetermined response categories and followed it with an open-ended question in which the participants indicate reasons for their responses.

Conducting Interviews

In all of the various forms of interviewing, several general steps are involved in conducting interviews or constructing open-ended questionnaires:

1. *Identify the interviewees.* Use one of the purposeful sampling strategies discussed earlier in this chapter.
2. *Determine the type of interview you will use.* Choose the one that will allow you to best learn the participants' views and answer each research question. Consider a telephone interview, a focus group interview, a one-on-one interview, an e-mail interview, a questionnaire, or some combination of these forms.
3. *During the interview, audiotape the questions and responses.* This will give you an accurate record of the conversation. Use adequate recording procedures, such as lapel

microphone equipment (small microphones that are hooked onto a shirt or collar) for one-on-one interviewing, and a suitable directional microphone (one that picks up sounds in all directions) for focus group interviewing. Have an adequate tape recorder and telephone adapter for telephone interviews, and understand thoroughly mail programs for e-mail interviewing.

4. *Take brief notes during the interview.* Although it is sound practice to audiotape the interview, take notes in the event the tape recorder malfunctions. You record these notes on a form called an *interview protocol*, discussed later in this chapter. Recognize that notes taken during the interview may be incomplete because of the difficulty of asking questions and writing answers at the same time. An abbreviated form for writing notes (e.g., short phrases followed by a dash) may speed up the process.

5. *Locate a quiet, suitable place for conducting the interview.* If possible, interview at a location free from distractions and choose a physical setting that lends itself to audiotaping. This means, for example, that a busy teachers' or faculty lounge may not be the best place for interviewing because of the noise and the interruptions that may occur.

6. *Obtain consent from the interviewee to participate in the study.* Obtain consent by having interviewees complete an informed consent form when you first arrive. Before starting the interview, convey to the participants the purpose of the study, the time the interview will take to complete, the plans for using the results from the interview, and the availability of a summary of the study when the research is completed.

7. *Have a plan, but be flexible.* During the interview, stick with the questions, but be flexible enough to follow the conversation of the interviewee. Complete the questions within the time specified (if possible) to respect and be courteous of the participants. Recognize that a key to good interviewing is to be a good listener.

8. *Use probes to obtain additional information.* **Probes** are subquestions under each question that the researcher asks to elicit more information. Use them to clarify points or to have the interviewee expand on ideas. These probes vary from exploring the content in more depth (elaborating) to asking the interviewee to explain the answer in more detail (clarifying). Table 8.2 shows these two types of probes. The table uses a specific illustration from the gunman case study to convey examples of both clarifying and elaborating probes.

9. *Be courteous and professional when the interview is over.* Complete the interview by thanking the participant, assuring him or her of the confidentiality of the responses, and asking if he or she would like a summary of the results of the study.

TABLE 8.2

Types of Probes Used in Qualitative Interviewing

	Examples	
	Clarifying Probes	**Elaborating Probes**
A question in the gunman case study asks, "What has happened since the event that you have been involved in?" Assume that the interviewee says, "Not much" or simply does not answer.	Probe Areas *Comments to other students:* "Tell me about discussions you had with other students." *Role of parents:* "Did you talk with your parents?" *Role of news media:* "Did you talk with any media personnel?"	"Tell me more." "Could you explain your response more?" "I need more detail." "What does 'not much' mean?"

FIGURE 8.6

A Checklist for Interviewing

_____ Who will participate in your interviews?
_____ What type of interviews are best to conduct?
_____ Is the setting for your interview comfortable and quiet?
_____ If you are audiotaping, have you prepared and tested the equipment?
_____ Did you obtain consent from the participant to participate in the interview?
_____ Did you listen more and talk less during the interview?
_____ Did you probe during the interview? (ask to clarify and elaborate)
_____ Did you avoid leading questions and ask open-ended questions?
_____ Did you keep participants focused and ask for concrete details?
_____ Did you withhold judgments and refrain from debating with participants about their views?
_____ Were you courteous and did you thank the participant after concluding the interview?

Source: Adapted from Gay & Airasian, 2003.

Figure 8.6 summarizes good interviewing procedures in a checklist adapted from Gay and Airasian (2003). The questions on the checklist represent the order in which you might consider them before, during, and after the interview.

Let's return to Maria, who needs to decide what data-collection procedure to use. Because she has experience talking with students and fellow teachers, she decides interviewing would be best. She proceeds to conduct five interviews with students and five with teachers in her high school. After obtaining permission from the school district and the principal of her school, she must obtain permission from the students (and their parents or guardians) and the teachers. To select these individuals, she will purposefully sample individuals who can speak from different perspectives (maximal variation sampling). She realizes there are different groups in the school, such as the "athletes," the "singers," the "punkers," the "class officers," and the "cheerleaders." She identifies one student from each group, realizing that she will likely obtain diverse perspectives representing complex views on the topic of weapon possession.

Next, she selects five teachers, each representing different subject areas, such as social studies, science, physical education, music, and drama. After that, she develops five open-ended questions, such as "How do weapons come into our school?" and "What types of weapons are in our school?" She needs to schedule interviews, conduct them, record information on audiotapes, take notes, and respect the views and rights of the students and faculty participating in the interviews.

As you read this procedure, what are its strengths and its limitations? List these strengths and weaknesses.

Documents

A valuable source of information in qualitative research can be documents. **Documents** consist of public and private records that qualitative researchers obtain about a site or participants in a study, and they can include newspapers, minutes of meetings, personal journals, and letters. These sources provide valuable information in helping researchers understand central phenomena in qualitative studies. They represent public and private documents. Examples of public documents are minutes from meetings, official memos, records in the public domain, and archival material in libraries. Private documents consist of personal journals and diaries, letters, personal notes, and jottings individuals write to themselves. Materials such as e-mail comments and Web site data illustrate both public and private documents, and they represent a growing data source for qualitative researchers.

Documents represent a good source for text (word) data for a qualitative study. They provide the advantage of being in the language and words of the participants, who have usually given thoughtful attention to them. They are also ready for analysis without the necessary transcription that is required with observational or interview data.

On the negative side, documents are sometimes difficult to locate and obtain. Information may not be available to the public. Information may be located in distant archives, requiring the researcher to travel, which takes time and can be expensive. Further, the documents may be incomplete, inauthentic, or inaccurate. For example, not all minutes from school board meetings are accurate, because board members may not review them for accuracy. In personal documents such as diaries or letters, the handwriting may be hard to read, making it difficult to decipher the information.

Collecting Documents

With so much variation in the types of documents, there are many procedures for collecting them. Here are several useful guidelines for collecting documents in qualitative research:

1. Identify the types of documents that can provide useful information to answer your qualitative research questions.
2. Consider both public (e.g., school board minutes) and private documents (e.g., personal diaries) as sources of information for your research.
3. Once the documents are located, seek permission to use them from the appropriate individuals in charge of the materials.
4. If you ask participants to keep a journal, provide specific instructions about the procedure. These guidelines might include what topics and format to use, the length of journal entries, and the importance of writing their thoughts legibly.
5. Once you have permission to use documents, examine them for accuracy, completeness, and usefulness in answering the research questions in your study.
6. Record information from the documents. This process can take several forms, including taking notes about the documents or, if possible, optically scanning them so a text (or word) file is created for each document. You can easily scan newspaper stories (e.g., on speeches by presidential candidates) to form a qualitative text database.

Collecting personal documents can provide a researcher with a rich source of information. For example, consider a study that used journals prepared by several women:

> An important source for learning about women in superintendent positions is for them to keep a personal journal or diary of their experiences. A researcher asked three women superintendents to keep a diary for 6 months and record their reactions to being a woman in their capacity of conducting official meetings comprised primarily of men.

These journals were useful for learning about the working lives of women in educational settings.

Audiovisual Materials

The final type of qualitative data to collect is visual images. **Audiovisual materials** consist of images or sounds that researchers collect to help them understand the central phenomenon under study. Used with increasing frequency in qualitative research, images or visual materials such as photographs, videotapes, digital images, paintings and pictures, and unobtrusive measures (e.g., evidence deduced from a setting, such as physical traces of images such as footsteps in the snow; see Webb's [1966] discussion about unobtrusive measures) are all sources of information for qualitative inquiry. One approach in using photography is the technique of photo elicitation. In this approach, participants are shown pictures (their own or those taken by the researcher) and asked to discuss the contents. These pictures might be personal photographs or albums of historical photographs (see Ziller, 1990).

The advantage of using visual materials is that people easily relate to images because they are so pervasive in our society. Images provide an opportunity for the participant to share directly their perceptions of reality. Images such as videotapes and films, for example, provide extensive data about real life as people visualize it. A potential disadvantage of using images is that they are difficult to analyze because of the rich information (e.g., how do you make sense of all of the aspects apparent in 50 drawings by pre-service teachers of what it is like to be a science teacher?). Also, you as a researcher may influence the data collected. In selecting the photo album to examine or requesting that a certain type of drawing be sketched, you may impose your meaning of the phenomenon on participants, rather than obtain the participants' views. When videotaping, you face the issues of what to tape, where to place the camera, and the need to be sensitive with camera-shy individuals.

Collecting Audiovisual Materials

Despite these potential problems, visual material is becoming more popular in qualitative research, especially with recent advances in technology. The steps involved in collecting visual material are similar to the steps involved in collecting documents:

1. Determine what visual material can provide information to answer research questions and how that material might augment existing forms of data, such as interviews and observations.
2. Identify the visual material available and obtain permission to use it. This permission might require asking all students in a classroom, for example, to sign informed consent forms and to have their parents sign them also.
3. Check the accuracy and authenticity of the visual material if you do not record it yourself. One way to check for accuracy is to contact and interview the photographer or the individuals represented in the pictures.
4. Collect the data and organize it. You can optically scan the data for easy storage and retrieval.

To illustrate the use of visual material, look at an example in which the researcher distributed cameras to obtain photographs:

> A researcher gives Polaroid cameras to 40 male and 40 female fourth graders in a science unit to record their meaning of the environment. The participants are asked to take pictures of images that represent attempts to preserve the environment in our society. As a result, the researcher obtains 24 pictures from each child that can be used to understand how young people look at the environment. Understandably, photos of squirrels and outside pets dominate the collection of pictures in this database.

HOW DO YOU RECORD DATA?

An essential process in qualitative research is recording data (Lofland & Lofland, 1995). This process involves recording information through research protocols, administering data collection so that you can anticipate potential problems in data collection, and bringing a sensitivity to ethical issues that may affect the quality of the data.

Using Protocols

As already discussed, for documents and visual materials, the process of recording information may be informal (taking notes) or formal (optically scanning the material to develop a complete computer text file). For observations and interviews, qualitative inquirers use specially designed protocols. **Data recording protocols** are forms designed and used by qualitative researchers to record information during observations and interviews.

An Interview Protocol

During interviewing, it is important to have some means for structuring the interview and taking careful notes. As already mentioned, audiotaping of interviews provides a detailed record of the interview. As a backup, you need to take notes during the interview and have the questions ready to be asked. An interview protocol serves the purpose of reminding you of the questions and it provides a means for recording notes. An **interview protocol** is a form designed by the researcher that contains instructions for the process of the interview, the questions to be asked, and space to take notes of responses from the interviewee.

Development and Design of an Interview Protocol To best understand the design and appearance of this form, examine the qualitative interview protocol used during the gunman case study (Asmussen & Creswell, 1995), shown in Figure 8.7. This figure is a reduced version of the actual protocol; in the original protocol, more space was provided between the questions to record answers. Figure 8.7 illustrates the components that you might design into an interview protocol.

- It contains a header to record essential information about the interview, statements about the purpose of the study, a reminder that participants need to sign the consent form, and a suggestion to make preliminary tests of the recording equipment. Other information you might include in the header would be the organization or work affiliation of the interviewees; their educational background and position; the number of years they have been in the position; and the date, time, and location of the interview.
- Following this header are five brief open-ended questions that allow participants maximum flexibility for responding to the questions. The first question serves the purpose of an icebreaker (sometimes called the "grand tour" question), to relax the interviewees and motivate them to talk. This question should be easy to understand and cause the participants to reflect on experiences that they can easily discuss, such as "Please describe your role in the incident." The final question on this particular instrument helps the researcher locate additional people to study.
- The core questions, 2 through 4, address major research questions in the study. For those new to qualitative research, you might ask more than four questions, to help elicit more discussion from interviewees and move through awkward moments when no one is talking. However, the more questions you ask, the more you are

FIGURE 8.7

Sample Interview Protocol

Interview Protocol

Project: University Reaction to a Gunman Incident

Time of Interview:
Date:
Place:
Interviewer:
Interviewee:
Position of Interviewee:

[Describe here the project, telling the interviewee about the (a) purpose of the study, (b) individuals and sources of data being collected, (c) what will be done with the data to protect the confidentiality of the interviewee, and (d) how long the interview will take.]
[Have the interviewee read and sign the consent form.]
[Turn on the tape recorder and test it.]

Questions:

1. Please describe your role in the incident.

2. What has happened since the event that you have been involved in?

3. What has been the impact on the University community of this incident?

4. What larger ramifications, if any, exist from the incident?

5. Who should we talk to to find out more about campus reaction to the incident?

(Thank the individuals for their cooperation and participation in this interview. Assure them of the confidentiality of the responses and the potential for future interviews.)

Source: Asmussen & Creswell, 1995.

examining what you seek to learn rather than learning from the participant. There is often a fine line between your questions being too detailed or too general. A pilot test of them on a few participants can usually help you decide which ones to use.

- In addition to the five questions, you might use probes to encourage participants to clarify what they are saying and to urge them to elaborate on their ideas.
- You provide space between the questions so that the researcher can take short notes about comments made by interviewees. Your notes should be brief and you can develop an abbreviated form for stating them. The style for recording these notes varies from researcher to researcher.
- It is helpful for you to memorize the wording and the order of the questions to minimize losing eye contact. Provide appropriate verbal transitions from one

question to the next. Recognize that individuals do not always respond directly to the question you ask: When you ask Question 2, for example, they may jump ahead and respond to Question 4.

- Closing comments remind you to thank the participants and assure them of the confidentiality of the responses. This section may also include a note to ask the interviewees if they have any questions, and a reminder to discuss the use of the data and the dissemination of information from the study.

An Observational Protocol

You use an observational protocol to record information during an observation, just as in interviewing. This protocol applies to all of the observational roles mentioned earlier. An **observational protocol** is a form designed by the researcher before data collection that is used for taking fieldnotes during an observation. On this form, researchers record a chronology of events, a detailed portrait of an individual or individuals, a picture or map of the setting, or verbatim quotes of individuals. As with interview protocols, the design and development of observational protocols will ensure that you have an organized means for recording and keeping observational fieldnotes.

Development and Design of an Observational Protocol You have already seen a sample observational protocol in Figure 8.4, in which the student took notes about the art object in class. An observational protocol such as that one permits qualitative researchers to record information they see at the observation site. This information is both a description of activities in the setting and a reflection about themes and personal insights noted during the observation. For example, examine again the sample observational protocol shown in Figure 8.4. This sample protocol illustrates the components typically found on a recording form in an observation:

- The protocol contains a header where you record information about the time, place, setting, and your observational role.
- You write in two columns following the header. These columns divide the page for recording into two types of data: a description of activities and a reflection about themes, quotes, and personal experiences of the researcher.
- The exact nature of this description may vary. Figure 8.4 illustrates possible topics for description. For example, you may include a description of the chronological order of events. This description is especially useful if the observer is examining a process or event. You may also describe the individuals, physical setting, events, and activities (Bogdan & Biklen, 1998). You may also sketch a picture of the site to facilitate remembering details of the setting for the final written report.
- Reflective notes record your experiences as a researcher, such as your hunches about important results and insights or emerging themes for later analysis.

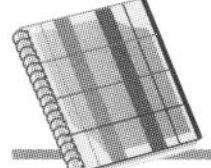

Think-Aloud About Observing

I typically ask my graduate students to practice gathering qualitative data by observing a setting. One of my favorite settings is the campus recreational center, where they can watch students learn how to climb the "wall." The "wall" is an artificial wall created so that students can learn how to rock climb. At this site, we typically find students who are learning how to climb the wall, and an instructor who is giving climbing lessons. The wall itself is about 50 feet high and has strategically located handholds to assist the climbers. The wall contains several colored banners positioned for climbers to use to scale the wall. The objective is for a student to climb to the top of the wall and then rappel down.

Before the observation, my students always ask what they should observe. Here are the instructions that I give them:

- Design an observational protocol using Figure 8.4 as a guide.
- Go to the recreational center and to the base of the wall. Find a comfortable place to sit on one of the benches in front of the wall, and then observe for about 10 minutes without recording information. Initially, simply observe and become acclimated to the setting.
- After these 10 minutes, start focusing on one activity at the site. It may be a student receiving instructions about how to put on the climbing gear, students actually scaling the wall, or other students waiting their turn to climb.
- Start recording descriptive fieldnotes. Consider a chronology of events, portraits of individuals, or a sketch of the site. To provide a creative twist to this exercise, I ask students to describe information about two of the following four senses: sight, sound, touch, or smell.
- Also record reflective notes during the observation.
- After 30 minutes, the observational period ends, and I ask students to write a brief qualitative passage about what they observed, incorporating both their descriptive and their reflective fieldnotes. This final request combines data collection (observing), data analysis (making sense of their notes), and report writing (trying to compose a brief qualitative research narrative).

HOW DO YOU ADMINISTER DATA COLLECTION?

When collecting data, researchers who engage in qualitative studies typically face issues that they need to resolve. Also, because qualitative research typically involves going to the research sites of the participants, staying a considerable time, and asking detailed questions, ethical issues are likely to arise that need to be anticipated.

Field Issues

Prior to a study, anticipate potential issues that might arise during data collection. Figure 8.8 lists issues and categorizes them according to the type of data you will be collecting. These issues include access to site problems, observations, interviews, document research, journals, and the use of audiovisual materials.

- *Access.* Anticipate the amount of time it will take to recruit participants to your study and the difficulty of recruitment. Some useful strategies include providing a small financial incentive for individuals to participate. Also, remind participants a day or two before data collection of the exact time and day when you will observe or interview them. Stage the data collection so that they will feel comfortable responding, and schedule it at a time that is most convenient for their schedules. Be realistic about the amount of time the data collection will take, and convey this time to the participants.
- *Observing.* You need to know your observational role (e.g., participant, nonparticipant) and clearly convey this role to your participants. Try not to take in everything the first time you observe; form general impressions first and then narrow your scope of observation (i.e., funnel approach). Take time to record your notes immediately after you observe so that you do not forget important details (e.g., quotes).

FIGURE 8.8

Field Issues in Qualitative Research

Access

- gaining access to the site and individuals
- getting people to respond to requests for information
- deciding whether to collect information in the natural site
- determining whether one has sufficient "distance" to site

Observations

- determining whether fieldnotes are credible
- writing down "jottings"
- incorporating "quotes" into fieldnotes
- assuming an observer role and how to change roles
- learning how to best collect information from early field visits in case studies
- learning how to "funnel" from broad observations to narrow ones

Interviews

- saying little during interview
- having tapes that will work in the transcribing machine
- scheduling a time for all to participate in a group interview
- matching the level of questions to the ability of informants
- realizing the costliness and lengthy process of transcribing data
- using an appropriate level of questioning at the beginning of the interview
- interruptions during an interview
- difficulty scheduling an interview
- having confidence in interviewing skills
- having difficulty taking notes while interviewing
- conducting interviews with two or more individuals
- encouraging all participants to talk in a group interview
- asking appropriate questions
- learning to listen rather than talk in interviews
- handling emotional outbursts
- addressing participants who do not want to be audiotaped
- finding a transcriptionist and the right type of equipment in a case study and grounded theory project
- moving from icebreakers to questions in the interview
- addressing when interviewees stray from the questions
- giving the interview questions to participants before the interview
- working with the logistics of the tape-recording equipment
- "bracketing" personal bias
- focusing the questions to ask in a group interview

Documents

- having difficulty locating materials
- having difficulty obtaining permission to use materials
- questioning the value of materials

Journals

- having people write complete journal entries
- having difficulty reading handwritten journals
- having informants express the difficulty of journaling
- having informants ask questions about how one might journal

Audiovisual Materials

- having disruptive room sounds
- having problems videotaping in a small room
- having difficulties focusing and positioning the camera

Source: Adapted from Creswell, 2007.

- *Interviews.* Prepare your equipment adequately. Check the functioning of your equipment prior to your interview. During the actual interview, use icebreakers to open the conversation, keep your opinions to yourself, and be prepared to keep the interviewee on track. Interviewees may not answer each question in order, but make sure that they answer each of your questions. Schedule your time so that you cover all of the questions on your interview protocol. Recognize that transcribing audiotape recordings takes substantial time, and schedule for it in your research plan.
- *Documents.* Anticipate the amount of time that may be required to locate, obtain permission for, and secure both public and private documents for your research. Always maintain a critical eye toward the documents you obtain. As much as possible, check them out to make sure they are credible and accurate. If you ask participants to keep a journal, provide clear instructions about the topics to be included in their journals. Recognize that younger children need more specific instructions than older children do. Ask participants to write as legibly as possible in their journals.
- *Audiovisual materials.* When you videotape, plan ahead to keep the room as quiet as possible, place the camera where it will be least obtrusive, and openly discuss with the participants whether they are comfortable being videotaped. If you plan to collect photographs from participants, give clear instructions about what they need to photograph or the nature of the photographs you will be collecting from them. Similar to documents, if you collect artifacts, drawings, or relics, check their authenticity as a useful record for your qualitative research.

ETHICAL ISSUES IN DATA COLLECTION

In gathering data for a qualitative project, a researcher seeks an in-depth description of a phenomena. Participants may be asked to discuss private details of their life experiences over a period of time. This process requires a sufficient level of trust based on a high level of participant disclosure. Because of the nature of this research, **ethical issues** may arise. This discussion offers some ethical issues and guidelines to be anticipated when conducting qualitative research. It begins with the identification of some guidelines for ethical practices, and then reviews key issues likely to arise, such as informing participants of the purpose of the study, refraining from deceptive practices, sharing information with participants (including your role as a researcher), being respectful of the research site, reciprocity, using ethical interview practices, maintaining confidentiality, and collaborating with participants.

Research methodologists and professional associations offer comprehensive but not exhaustive lists of ethical principles that may guide researchers in conducting ethical studies. Patton (2002) offered a checklist of general ethical issues to consider, such as reciprocity, assessment of risk, confidentiality, informed consent, and data access and ownership. The criteria of the AAA (see Glesne & Peshkin, 1992) reflect appropriate standards. For example, researchers need to protect the anonymity of the participants by assigning numbers or aliases to them to use in the process of analyzing and reporting data. In some qualitative studies, to protect the anonymity of participants, you may need to develop a composite picture of the group rather than focus on any single individual.

Further, to gain support from participants, you need to convey to participants that they are participating in a study and inform them of the purpose of the study. A researcher must also not engage in deception about the nature of the study. What if the study is on a sensitive topic, and the participants would not want to be involved if they were aware of the topic? This issue, disclosure of the purpose of the research, is widely discussed in cultural anthropology, and you can address it by presenting general information about the study rather than specific details. Deception is also an issue in observational research. Scholars and researchers possess a variety of opinions, ranging from utter opposition to complete acceptance, about whether it is ethical to conduct covert observations (Patton, 2002). Professional associations and institutional review boards are cautious and skeptical about approving covert observations. Blatant examples of deceptive practices in the past serve as reminders of the importance of ethical guidelines. For example, Stanley Milgram conducted experiments in which he asked participants to apply a shock treatment (which was actually fictitious) to other individuals to assess obedience to a higher authority. Researchers studied Massachusetts schoolchildren who were fed breakfast cereal laced with radioactive isotopes, and investigators tested new drug treatments on prisoners in Philadelphia (Patton, 2002). These are all instances in which deceptive practices were used, and today they would not be approved for research studies. Also, especially vulnerable populations (children, incarcerated individuals, people of color, those from lower socioeconomic classes, and those with limited education) represent high-risk populations and are carefully reviewed as participants by institutional review boards. The researchers' quest for information should be tempered by proper ethical constraints aimed at protecting the participants.

Another issue likely to develop is when the participant shares information "off the record." Although in most instances this information would be omitted from analysis, the issue becomes a problem if *not* disclosing this information would actually harm individuals. For example, when a researcher studying incarcerated Native Americans learned about a potential breakout during one of the interviews, she concluded that it would be a breach of faith with the participant if she reported the matter, and she kept quiet. Fortunately, the breakout was not attempted.

Another ethical issue likely to arise is whether you should share your experiences with participants in an interview setting, such as when, during a study about adolescent smoking behavior with middle school children, a researcher admits his own struggles with smoking. Alternatively, researchers may "go native" and adopt practices of the individuals they are studying—a problem if the study participants are engaging in risky or inappropriate behavior. Along this same line, it may be necessary to clearly define your role as a researcher (not a therapist offering advice or a judge evaluating the circumstances) because of the deep personal relationships that can form through the qualitative research process (Patton, 2002). Boundaries may need to be established to define the research relationship for the investigator and the participants and to determine when or if the relationship will terminate when the project ends (Hatch, 2002). Dealing with contradictory information may be a problem as well. Hopefully, over time, repeated interviews or observations will provide insight about patterns and lead to findings that are less contradictory. Of course, reporting contradictory findings may reflect the situation as accurately as possible in some qualitative studies.

Issues likely to arise about the research site are whether you will disrupt the individuals or groups at the site (e.g., cause a gym class to run overtime because of observations). You may cause permanent, unwelcome changes by your presence, such as taking sides during a focus group interview or disclosing names during e-mail interviewing. You may also act in an inappropriate way that reflects badly on all researchers (e.g., being rude to gatekeepers or failing to view your role as a guest) at the site.

Participants give a great deal when they choose to participate in qualitative research projects, often revealing intimate details and experiences of their lives. How should researchers reward participants for their insights and time? Do these incentives affect the responses or participation in qualitative studies? Researchers may attempt some form of reciprocity as a small reward for their participants. Payments may be cash or may consist of alternate forms of payment, such as gift certificates or vouchers or items derived directly from the study, such as transcripts, publications, or copies of video/audio recordings.

The interview process may also raise ethical issues. Participants may disclose sensitive and potentially distressing information in the course of the interview. Qualitative researchers must be aware of the potential for their own emotional turmoil in processing this information. Debriefing sessions (where researchers can discuss with others what they felt and experienced) and support groups may be useful in allowing researchers to come to terms with the information covered in the interviews.

Participant confidentiality is of utmost importance. The traditions of research in place today remind us that the lives and experiences of participants should be told, but the individuals from which the research was gleaned must be concealed. Or must their identities be kept private? A new wave of research is emerging in which the participants collaborate with researchers to tell their stories (Patton, 2002). In this research, participants may act as coresearchers who help create and approve of the accuracy of the research. In cases such as these, participants may also wish to use their own name instead of a pseudonym. If the participants choose to use their names and have carefully weighed the consequences, can the researcher (or institutional review board) require the coresearchers to conceal their identity? Thus, there are new ethical dilemmas arising that may contradict the ethical guidelines currently in place. Researchers must be vigilant in maintaining high ethical standards while making appropriate accommodations for the changing nature of research and their particular project.

REVISITING THE QUALITATIVE GUNMAN INCIDENT STUDY

Let's use the gunman case study to illustrate the steps used in the process of qualitative data collection (Asmussen & Creswell, 1995). In "The Research Study" section (Paragraph 11), the authors discuss the steps used to obtain permission to conduct the study from the university administration and the institutional review board. Unlike the television violence study, the authors collect information from a small number of sources and do not use instruments that measure variables. They develop their own interview guide to collect reactions. Posing only five questions during their interviews, the researchers allow room for participants to share their views. They record data on an interview protocol, a data-recording instrument the authors designed (Paragraph 11).

They also mentioned that they guaranteed that they would not become involved in the gunman investigation or in the therapy of the students (Paragraph 11). In short, their data-collection procedures—gathering data from a few people, using broad questions, recording data on their own protocols, and gathering data ethically—reflect the steps in the qualitative data-collection process.

KEY IDEAS IN THE CHAPTER

The process of collecting qualitative data follows steps similar to those in quantitative data collection. The researcher selects participants and sites, gains permission to conduct the study, decides on the types of data to collect, develops means for recording information, and administers the data collection. The selection of participants and research sites is intentional and purposeful to understand best the central phenomenon under study. Researchers often seek out gatekeepers to gain access to individuals and sites to study. In gaining permission, qualitative researchers are sensitive to the potentially intrusive nature of their research, and are mindful of respecting individuals and sites, potential power imbalances, and "giving back," or reciprocating.

Researchers collect one or more of the four basic categories of qualitative data: observations, interviews, documents, and audiovisual materials. In choosing the type of data to collect, researchers need to gather information that will answer their research questions, and then weigh the advantages and disadvantages of each form of data. After deciding on the type(s) of data to collect, the inquirer develops means for recording information that might include informal notes or optical scanning of documents. The design of protocols can provide a structured means for collecting data. Once the data-collection procedures are in place, the qualitative inquirer collects data. Prior attention to field issues that may occur will facilitate this process. The data also need to be collected ethically, with sensitivity to individuals and research sites.

Useful Information for Producers of Research

- Plan five phases when designing qualitative data collection: selecting participants, gaining permissions, selecting and weighing different data types, designing recording protocols, and administering data collection.
- Use a purposeful sampling strategy that matches your intent for the study. The intent will vary from one qualitative project to another. Consider using sampling at different levels (e.g., organization, site, individual, parent).
- It is better to select a few, rather than many, individuals or sites to study, to provide an in-depth understanding of the phenomenon.
- Recognize that the campus institutional review board may need extra detail about your qualitative field procedures, such as protecting the anonymity of participants, respecting field sites, and providing reciprocity to participants.
- To obtain access to a field site, locate a gatekeeper on the "inside" who can provide needed permissions and access to people and places.
- Weigh the advantages and disadvantages of each major form of qualitative data and each subtype (i.e., observations, interviews, documents, and audiovisual material) before selecting the type(s) to use in your study. Also consider what type of data will best address your research questions.
- Use the process steps for conducting an observation, interviewing, and collecting documents and visual material, as presented in this chapter.
- Consider how you will record information during data collection. Use interview and observational protocols to structure the data collection as well as to record information.

Useful Information for Consumers of Research

- When evaluating a qualitative data-collection procedure, look for comments by the author about selecting participants, gaining permissions, selecting data types, and developing recording protocols.
- Examine the reasons why researchers select participants for a study. They should detail the reasons that they selected the participants.
- Look for extensive data collection in a qualitative study. It is usual for qualitative inquirers to collect different forms of data in a single study.
- Look for a systematic procedure for the recording of qualitative data. Researchers should discuss their use of protocols, such as interview and observational protocols. Providing a sample protocol as an appendix to a study is helpful in understanding the questions asked.

UNDERSTANDING CONCEPTS AND EVALUATING RESEARCH STUDIES

1. Look at the purposeful sampling strategies in Figure 8.2. If you were to identify one type of sampling that occurred in the gunman incident case study, what would that sampling be? Consider only the procedure for sampling the individuals who participated in the interviews.
2. The researchers in the gunman case study mentioned that they were sensitive to the needs of participants because they obtained consent from participants (in accord with the institutional review board) and because they agreed not to interfere with the investigation or to talk with students in therapy. Using the discussion about ethical issues in this chapter, state three additional ethical issues they might have addressed.
3. In the gunman case study, the authors collected multiple types of data, as shown in Table 8.1. What would collecting both interviews and observations yield? What would collecting documents provide?
4. Assume that you are recruiting participants for interviews in the gunman case study. What four strategies would you use to encourage them to participate in your 30-minute, tape-recorded interview?

CONDUCTING YOUR RESEARCH

Design a qualitative data-collection procedure for your educational project. Determine the people and research sites you will study and the type of purposeful sampling you will use. Next, list the steps you would take to gain permissions to enter and study the people and the site. Identify the types of qualitative data you will collect and the forms for recording the information. Finally, list the anticipated field and ethical issues that you need to consider before you conduct your data collection.

Go to our Companion Website at **www.prenhall.com/creswell** to:

- assess your understanding of chapter content with Multiple-Choice Questions,
- apply what you've learned with Essay Questions,
- practice your research skills with interactive Building Research Skills exercises, and
- broaden your knowledge of research with Web Links to research topics on the Internet.

CHAPTER

Analyzing and Interpreting Qualitative Data

Analyzing qualitative data requires understanding how to make sense of text and images so that you can form answers to your research questions. In this chapter, you will learn about the six steps involved in analyzing and interpreting qualitative data: preparing and organizing the data, exploring and coding the database, describing findings and forming themes, representing and reporting findings, interpreting the meaning of the findings, and validating the accuracy of the findings.

By the end of this chapter, you should be able to:

- Name the steps involved in conducting an analysis of qualitative data.
- Describe how to organize and transcribe qualitative data.
- Read through and form initial impressions of text data.
- Conduct coding of a transcript or text file.
- Develop a detailed qualitative description.
- Generate a qualitative theme.
- Create a visual image that represents your data.
- Write a paragraph describing a theme.
- Make a qualitative interpretation from your data.
- Check the accuracy of your findings and interpretation.

After completing her first interview with a student, Maria starts the process of analyzing her qualitative data. She first transcribes the audiotapes from the interview. She ends up with a 20-page transcript. As she reads the transcript, she writes some notes in the margins. These notes record her first impressions, such as "students need to protect themselves with weapons" or "everyone carries weapons." Reading the transcript again, Maria asks herself, *What are the students saying that answers my research questions?* She learns that they are describing places in the school in which students likely carry weapons. Also, she learns that certain themes or patterns emerge in their responses. She groups the student responses into five themes about the experiences of students carrying weapons in school: self-protection, common practice, hiding places, fear of being caught, and sanctions if caught. She develops a table that summarizes these themes, and she writes down how these themes reflect or differ from experiences reported by other researchers in the literature. She also takes the themes back to a few students in a focus group and asks them whether she accurately identifies their experiences.

HOW DO YOU ANALYZE QUALITATIVE DATA?

Maria has proceeded through the six steps commonly used in analyzing qualitative data. You can visualize the first major steps in this process by examining the "bottom-up" approach to analysis in Figure 9.1. As shown in the figure, qualitative researchers first collect data and then prepare it for data analysis. This analysis initially consists of developing a general sense of the data, and then coding description and themes about the central phenomenon. Let's look at some of the features of this process in more detail.

- It is inductive in form, going from the particular or the detailed data (e.g., transcriptions or typed notes from interviews) to the general codes and themes. Keeping this in mind helps you understand how qualitative researchers produce broad

FIGURE 9.1

The Qualitative Process of Data Analysis

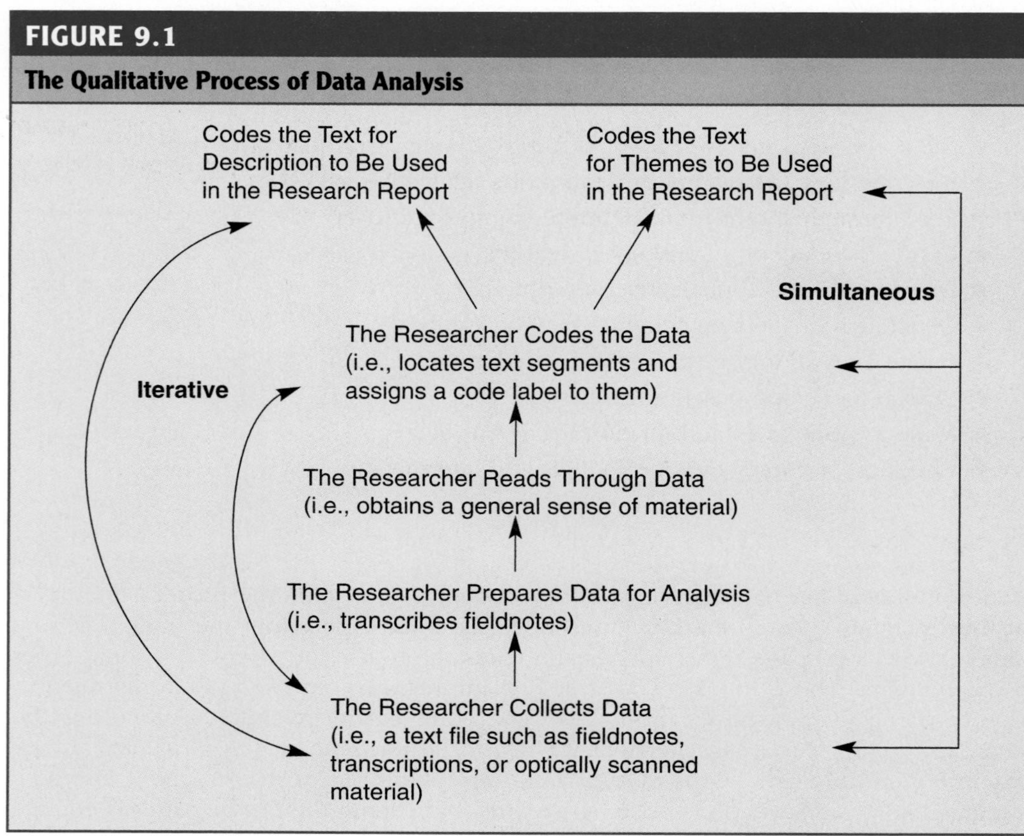

themes or categories from diverse detailed databases. Although the initial analysis consists of subdividing the data (later we will discuss *coding* the data), the final goal is to generate a larger, consolidated picture (Tesch, 1990).

- It involves a simultaneous process of analyzing while you are also collecting data. In qualitative research, the data collection and analysis (and perhaps the report writing) are simultaneous activities. When you are collecting data, you may also be analyzing other information previously collected, looking for major ideas. This procedure differs from traditional approaches in *quantitative* research, in which data collection occurs first, followed by data analysis.
- The phases are also iterative, meaning you cycle back and forth between data collection and analysis. In qualitative research, you might collect stories from individuals and return for more information to fill in gaps in their stories as your analysis of their stories proceeds.
- Qualitative researchers analyze their data by reading it several times and conducting an analysis each time. Each time you read your database, you develop a deeper understanding about the information supplied by your participants.
- There is no single, accepted approach to analyzing qualitative data, although several guidelines exist for this process (see Dey, 1993; Miles & Huberman, 1994). It is an eclectic process.
- Qualitative research is "interpretive" research, in which you make a personal assessment as to a description that fits the situation or themes that capture the major categories of information. The interpretation that you make of a transcript, for example, differs from the interpretation that someone else makes. This does not mean that your interpretation is better or more accurate; it simply means that you bring your own perspective to your interpretation.

HOW DO YOU PREPARE AND ORGANIZE THE DATA FOR ANALYSIS?

Initial preparation of the data for analysis requires organizing the vast amount of information, transferring it from spoken or written words to a typed file and making decisions about whether to analyze the data by hand or by computer.

Organize Data

At an early stage in qualitative analysis, you organize data into file folders or computer files or onto index cards. Organization of data is critical in qualitative research because of the large amount of information gathered during a study. The extensive data that an interview yields often surprises new researchers. For example, a 30-minute interview will often result in about 20 pages of single-spaced transcription. With this sizable amount of data, the transcribing and organizing of information requires a system of organization, which could take several forms, such as:

- Developing a matrix or a table of sources that can be used to help organize the material (see the table in the gunman incident qualitative study, Asmussen & Creswell, 1995)
- Organizing the materials by type: all interviews, all observations, all documents, and all photographs or other visual materials; as an alternative, you might consider organizing the materials by participant, site, location, or some combination of these approaches
- Keeping duplicate copies of all forms of data

Transcribe Data

You might remember from chapter 8 that you obtain words through interviewing participants or by writing fieldnotes during observations. You need to convert these words to a computer file for analysis. Alternatively, you might listen to the tapes or read your fieldnotes to begin the process of analysis. When time is short or funds are scarce, you may be able to have only a few interviews or a few observational notes transcribed. The most complete procedure, however, is to have all interviews and all observational notes transcribed. As a general rule of thumb, it takes approximately 4 hours to transcribe 1 hour of tape (Dana Miller, personal communication, April 11, 2000). Hence, the process of transcription is labor intensive and you will need to allow adequate time for it.

Transcription is the process of converting audiotape recordings or fieldnotes into text data. Figure 9.2 lists suggestions for conducting a taped interview from the transcriptionist's point of view. You may use a transcriptionist to type your text files or you can transcribe the information yourself. In either case, for interview data, transcriptionists need special equipment to help create the transcript. This equipment consists of a machine that enables the transcriber to start and stop tape recordings or to play them at a speed so that the transcriber can easily follow them. Here are a few more guidelines to facilitate transcription:

- Create 2-inch margins on each side of the text document so you can jot down notes in the margins during data analysis.
- Leave extra space on the page between the interviewer's comments and the interviewee's comments. This enables you to distinguish clearly between speakers during data analysis.
- Highlight or mark in some way the questions asked by the interviewer. You will not analyze your questions, but identifying them clearly indicates where one question ends and another begins. Often, you will analyze all answers to a single question.
- Use complete, detailed headers that contain information about the interview or observational session. The headers in the interview and observational protocols in chapter 8 show the type of content to be included in a transcription.
- Transcribe all words, and type the word "[*pause*]" to indicate when interviewees take a lengthy break in their comments. These pauses may provide useful information about times when interviewees cannot or will not respond to a question. You can also record other actions occurring during an interview. For example, type "[*laughter*]" when the interviewee laughs, "[*telephone rings*]" to indicate a phone call that interrupts the interview, or "[*inaudible*]" to mark when the transcriptionist cannot determine what is being said. As a general approach, transcribing all words will provide data that captures the details of an interview.

Analyze by Hand or Computer

With the popularity of computers, researchers have a choice about whether to hand-analyze data or to use a computer. The **hand analysis of qualitative data** means that researchers read the data, mark it by hand, and divide it into parts. Traditionally, analyzing text data involves using color coding to mark parts of the text or cutting and pasting text sentences onto cards. Some qualitative researchers like to hand analyze all of their data. A hand analysis may be preferred when you:

- Are analyzing a small database (e.g., less than 500 pages of transcripts or fieldnotes) and can easily keep track of files and locate text passages

FIGURE 9.2

Hints for Transcribing Audiotaped Interviews

Hints for Taped Interviews: The Transcriptionist's View
Donald Callen Freed
Word Processing Center at
Teachers College, University of Nebraska at Lincoln

The following suggestions are a result of several years of experience transcribing research interview tapes. They are offered for your consideration in order that your transcription may be easier and less time consuming. These suggestions were originally developed for persons who have their tapes professionally transcribed, although many are applicable to those who transcribe their own tapes.

1. Please use an external microphone. This places voices closer to the microphone, and away from the noise of the tape recorder itself. If you must use a machine with an internal microphone, place it as close to *both* interviewer and interviewee as possible. High quality tape recorders also ensure better results and reduce background noise, especially if an external microphone is not available. (Most electronic supply shops have external microphones, which are very inexpensive.)
2. For telephone interviews, please use a telephone pick-up device.
3. Please keep the microphone and/or tape recorder away from possible loud-noise interference—electronic devices, the telephone on a desk, coffee cups or glasses that might be set on the same table as the microphone, etc. An important word or phrase can be lost with the interference of one loud noise.
4. Interviewers: Try to induce slower, more distinct speech by speaking calmly yourself. Try asking questions slowly and distinctly, so that the interviewee will respond in a like manner. Practice keeping your voice up all the way to the end of the sentence, using clear diction. Important questions or probes are sometimes lost because the interviewer trails off or speaks less distinctly at the end of the sentence.
5. Use *new, high-quality* tapes and good, well-maintained recording equipment. If you must rely on previously used tapes, make sure they have been used only once or twice. Older tapes often have bleed-over from previous recordings, and are more likely to jam in a machine. In general, transcription equipment works best with 60-minute tapes. Standard-size cassette tapes work much better than micro- or mini-cassettes, and are more easily turned over in an interview.
6. Think clearly about the format you want for your printed transcription. Consider the margin size and the amount of space you want left for comments, double or triple spacing, large margins for coding purposes, etc.

Following these steps can ensure better quality for your research transcriptions, making research easier and your results more accurate. A transcriptionist can only type what he or she can hear. A small amount of forethought and attention to detail on the interviewer's part can result in a better interview tape and transcription.

Source: Adapted from the January 1990 "Words" newsletter, Teachers College Word Processing Center, University of Nebraska-Lincoln, Marlene Starr and Donald C. Freed, editors.

- ◆ Are not comfortable using computers or have not learned a qualitative computer software program
- ◆ Want to be close to the data and have a hands-on feel for it without the intrusion of a machine
- ◆ Have time to commit to a hand analysis, since it is a labor-intensive activity to manually sort, organize, and locate words in a text database

For others with a greater interest in technology and with the time to learn a computer program, a computer analysis is ideal. **A computer analysis of qualitative data** means that researchers use a qualitative computer program to facilitate the process of storing, analyzing, and sorting the data. With the development of these computer programs, you have a choice as to whether to use hand coding or a computer analysis. You might base your decision on several factors. Use a computer program when you:

- Are analyzing a large database (e.g., more than 500 pages of transcripts or fieldnotes) and need to organize and keep track of extensive information
- Are adequately trained in using the program and are comfortable using computers
- Have resources to purchase a program or can locate one to use
- Need a close inspection of every word and sentence to capture specific quotes or meanings of passages

Use Qualitative Computer Programs

Qualitative computer programs do not analyze the data for you. However, they do provide several convenient features that facilitate your data analysis. A **qualitative data analysis computer program** is a program that stores data, organizes your data, enables you to assign labels or codes to your data, and facilitates searching through your data and locating specific text or words.

Procedures for Using Software Programs

The general procedures for using a software program are as follows:

1. Convert a word processing file into a text file or import the word processing file directly into the computer program. The word processing file will be a transcribed interview, a set of fieldnotes, or other text, such as a scanned document.
2. Select a computer program to use. This program should have the features of storing data, organizing data, assigning labels or codes, and searching the data.
3. Enter a file into the program and give it a name.
4. Go through the file and mark sentences or paragraphs of ideas that pertain to what the participant is saying in the text.
5. Provide a code label for the blocked text. Continue this process of marking text and providing code labels for the entire text file.
6. After blocking and assigning labels to text, search for all text matching each code, and print out a file of these text passages.
7. Collapse these code labels into a few broad themes, or categories, and include evidence for each category.

Basic Features of Software Programs

Many commercial, qualitative data analysis software programs are available today. A recent review of software programs analyzed their features based on eight major dimensions, as shown in Figure 9.3 (Creswell & Maietta, 2002). Using information from this figure, your basic considerations are to find a program that is easy to use, that will accept both your text files (from transcripts) and your images (from pictures), that allows you to read and review text and categorize it, and that sorts and finds text or image passages easily for your qualitative report. Less frequently, you may be interested in merging analyses compiled by different researchers (such as when a research team analyzes the data) or importing or exporting your analyses to other software programs (such as exporting to SPSS or importing from a spreadsheet).

Specific Programs Available

To choose a software program, you need to examine the specific features available in the program. A good sampling of commercially available qualitative data analysis software

FIGURE 9.3

Features to Consider When Comparing Qualitative Data Analysis Software

Ease of Integration in Using the Program
- Windows or Macintosh compatible?
- Is it easy to use in getting started?
- Can you easily work through a document?

Type of Data Program Will Accept
- Will it handle text data?
- WIll it handle multimedia (image) data?

Reading and Reviewing Text
- Can it highlight and connect quotations?
- Can it search for specific text passages?

Memo Writing
- Does it have the capability for you to add notes or memos?
- Can you easily access the memos you write?

Categorization
- Can you develop codes?
- Can you easily apply codes to text or images?
- Can you easily display codes?
- Can you easily review and make changes in the codes?

Analysis Inventory and Assessment
- Can you sort for specific codes?
- Can you combine codes in a search?
- Can you develop a concept map with the codes?
- Can you make demographic comparisons with the codes?

Quantitative Data
- Can you import a quantitative database (e.g., SPSS)?
- Can you export a word or image qualitative database to a quantitative program?

Merging Project
- Can more than one researcher analyze the data and merge analyses from these researchers?

Source: Adapted from Creswell & Maietta, 2002.

products and links is available at **www.sagepub.com**. A brief summary of major programs follows:

- *Atlas.ti*. This Windows PC program enables you to organize your text, graphic, audio, and visual data files, along with your coding, memos, and findings, into a project. Further, you can code, annotate, and compare segments of information. You can rapidly search, retrieve, and browse all data segments and notes relevant to an idea and, importantly, build unique networks that allow you to connect visually selected passages, memos, and codes in a concept map. This program is described and available from Scientific Software Development (**www.atlasti.com**).
- *Ethnograph*. Ethnograph for Windows PCs only is a versatile computer program designed to make the analysis of data collected during qualitative research easier, more efficient, and more effective. Ethnograph helps you search and note segments of interest in your data, mark them with code words, and run analyses that can be retrieved for inclusion in reports or further analysis. Ethnograph will handle your project data files and documents whether your data comes in the form of interview transcripts, fieldnotes, open-ended survey responses, or other text-based documents. This program is described and available from Qualis Research, **www.qualisresearch.com**.

- *HyperRESEARCH™*. This program is available for Windows or Macintosh. It is an easy-to-use qualitative software package that enables you to code and retrieve, build theories, and conduct analyses of your data. Now with advanced multimedia capabilities, HyperRESEARCH allows you to work with text, graphics, audio, and video sources, making it a valuable research analysis tool. HyperRESEARCH is a solid code-and-retrieve data analysis program, with additional theory-building features provided by the Hypothesis Tester. This program, developed by Research Ware, is described and available at **www.scolari.com**.
- *MAXqda*. This Windows PC program is a powerful tool for text analysis that you can use for grounded theory-oriented "code and retrieve" analysis as well as for more sophisticated text analysis. It enables you to combine both qualitative and quantitative procedures. The program has a simple, easy-to-use interface of four main windows showing imported texts, codes, the coded text segments, and the text itself. A unique feature is that you can weight the codes to give a measure of the significance of a piece of coding. You can easily copy, merge, split, or delete codes. Data matrices can be imported and exported between SPSS, SAS, and other statistical packages. This program, developed by Udo Kuckartz of Germany, is described and available at **www.maxqda.com**.
- *NVivo*. This software program is also available for Windows PC. It combines efficient management of nonnumerical, unstructured data with powerful processes of indexing, searching, and theorizing. Designed for researchers making sense of complex data, NVivo offers a complete toolkit for rapid coding, thorough exploration, and rigorous management and analysis. Especially valuable is the ability of the program to create text data matrixes for comparisons. It also provides for visually mapping categories identified in your analysis. NVivo is available at **www.qsrinternational.com**.

HOW DO YOU EXPLORE AND CODE THE DATA IN ANALYSIS?

After you have organized and transcribed your data and decided whether to hand or computer analyze it, it is time to begin data analysis. This consists of exploring the data and developing codes as first steps in analysis.

Explore the General Sense of the Data

The first step in data analysis is to explore the data. A **preliminary exploratory analysis** in qualitative research consists of exploring the data to obtain a general sense of the data, memoing ideas, thinking about the organization of the data, and considering whether you need more data. For example, Agar (1980) suggested you ". . . read the transcripts in their entirety several times. Immerse yourself in the details, trying to get a sense of the interview as a whole before breaking it into parts" (p. 103). Writing memos in the margins of fieldnotes, transcripts, or under photographs helps in this initial process of exploring the data. These memos are short phrases, ideas, concepts, or hunches that occur to you.

In the qualitative gunman incident study, Asmussen and Creswell (1995) collected many forms of data as displayed in their Table 1 matrix of data-collection types and sources (see Paragraph 11). To begin making sense of this diverse information, they spent time reviewing all of the documents and transcriptions. Although they might have specifically reported this process (e.g., in Paragraph 12), they looked over fieldnotes from observations, interview data, newspapers, and videotapes of the television coverage to obtain an initial reading of the campus reaction to the incident.

Code the Data

The further process of analyzing text (or images) in qualitative research begins when you code the data. Coding is the process of segmenting and labeling text to form descriptions and broad themes in the data. Although there are no set guidelines for coding data, some general procedures exist (see Creswell, 2003; Tesch, 1990).

Using a visual model like the one in Figure 9.4 will help you learn this procedure. The object of the **coding process** is to make sense out of text data, divide it into text or image segments, label the segments with codes, examine codes for overlap and redundancy, and collapse these codes into broad themes. Thus, this is an inductive process of narrowing data into a few themes (J. David Creswell, personal communication, January 1, 2001). Also, in this process you will select specific data to use and disregard other data that do not specifically provide evidence for your themes.

Several steps are involved in coding data. Although there is no definite procedure, Tesch (1990) and Creswell (2003) recommend the following steps:

1. Get a sense of the whole. Read all of the transcriptions carefully. Jot down in the margins some ideas as they come to mind.
2. Pick one document (e.g., one interview, one fieldnote). Choose the most interesting, the shortest, or the one on the top of the pile. Go through it, asking the question "What is this person talking about?" Consider the underlying meaning and write it down in the margin in two or three words, drawing a box around it.
3. Begin the process of coding the document. This process involves identifying text segments, placing a bracket around them, and assigning a code word or phrase that accurately describes the meaning of the text segment. Sentences or paragraphs that all relate to a single code are called a **text segment**. **Codes** are labels used to describe a segment of text or an image. Codes can address many different topics, such as those listed here (see also Bogdan & Biklen, 1998):
   - Setting and context (e.g., classroom)
   - Perspectives held by participants (poor learners)

FIGURE 9.4

A Visual Model of the Coding Process in Qualitative Research

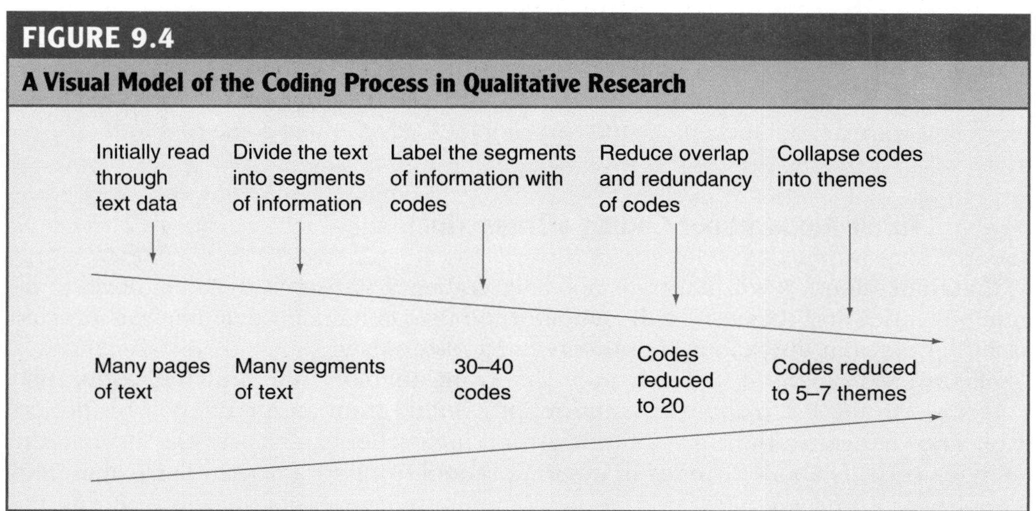

- Participants' ways of thinking about people and objects (problem children)
- Processes (disruptions during the class)
- Activities (student sitting quietly)
- Strategies (teacher giving time-out)
- Relationship and social structure (students talking to each other)

As seen in these examples, you can state codes in the participant's actual words (i.e., a student's perspective about other students, such as "poor learners"), which are called ***in vivo* codes**. They can also be phrased in standard educational terms (a researcher referring to "a classroom") or expressed in your own language (a statement about "students talking to each other"). You do not need to code each sentence or provide multiple codes for each sentence. Instead, use the idea of **lean coding**, in which, the first time through a manuscript, you assign only a few codes. For example, for a 20-page manuscript, you might insert only 10 to 15 codes the first time you analyze it. In this way, you can reduce a smaller number of codes to broad themes rather than work with an unwieldy set of codes.

4. After coding an entire text, make a list of all code words. Group similar codes and look for redundant codes. Your objective is to reduce a list of codes to a smaller, more manageable number, such as 25 to 30. It is best not to overcode the data because, in the end, you will need to reduce the codes to a small number of themes.

5. Take this list and go back to the data. Try out this preliminary organizing scheme to see whether new codes emerge. Circle specific quotes from participants that support the codes.

6. Reduce the list of codes to get five to seven themes or descriptions of the setting or participants. **Themes** (also called *categories*) are similar codes aggregated together to form a major idea in the database. Identify the five to seven themes by examining codes that the participants discuss most frequently, are unique or surprising, have the most evidence to support them, or are those you might expect to find when studying the phenomenon. The reason for the small number of themes is that it is best to write a qualitative report providing detailed information about a few themes rather than general information about many themes. A **description** is a detailed rendering of people, places, or events in a setting in qualitative research. You might use codes such as "seating arrangements," "teaching approach," or "physical layout of the room" to describe a classroom where instruction takes place.

If you were Maria, what are some likely codes that you might describe about the school in a study of students carrying weapons in school? If you are analyzing data about students carrying weapons, one part of that analysis might be to describe the locations where students carry weapons on the school grounds. You might list a few of these, beginning with "school lockers" or the "parking lot." What others come to mind?

Think-Aloud About Coding a Transcript

In this think-aloud, I will illustrate not only coding a transcript but also developing multiple codes and themes. I will also illustrate the preliminary data analysis process of jotting notes in the margin in a first reading of the data.

Figure 9.5 shows a sample transcript from an interview and the codes that I recorded in the left margin. This transcript resulted from an interview for a project exploring changes in the curriculum in a rural high school (Jones, 1999). Overall, the interviewee talks about changes in the high school from a traditional curriculum to a school based on service-learning in the community. Jones asks questions during the

FIGURE 9.5

Coding a Page from a Sample Interview Transcript

The Process of Reconstructing Curriculum in a Rural High School Setting

Codes Here		Themes (and Other Ideas) Here
	JJ: One thing, Lucy, that I've heard talked about was the fact that schools reflect the strengths of communities. What do you perceive as strengths of Greenfield as a community and how that relates to schools?	
Close-knit community	LU: Well, I think Greenfield is a fairly close-knit community. I think people are interested in what goes on. And because of that, they have a sense of ownership in the schools. We like to keep track of what our kids are doing and feel a connection to them because of that. The downside of that perhaps is that kids can feel that we are looking TOO close. But most of the time, that is the nurturing environment that we do provide an atmosphere of concern and	Potential theme: The community Idea: getting a good sense here for the community and its values
Health of community or community values	care. To back up, you said the health of the community itself is reflected in schools. A lot of times communities look at schools and say they are not doing this or they aren't doing that, or we're missing something in our schools. I think perhaps we look at the school and see, this is probably a pretty conservative community overall, and look to make sure that what is being talked about in the schools really carries out the community's values. There is a	
	little bit of an idealization I think, perhaps in terms of what we thought of "basic education." [And I think there might be a tendency to hold back a little bit too much because of that idealization of "you know, we learned the basics, the reading, the	A good quote
Change is threatening	writing and the arithmetic."] So you know, any change is threatening. And I think that goes for the community as well as what we see reflected at the school. Sometimes that can get in the way of trying to do different things. I think, again, idealization, older members of the community forget some of the immaturity that they experienced when they were in school and forgetting that kids are kids. So there is a little bit too much of that mental attitude. But for the most part, I think there is a sense of we're all in this together, and concern for the kids.	
	JJ: In terms of looking at leadership strengths in the community, where does Greenfield set in a continuum there with planning process, understanding the need to plan, forward-thinking, visionary people. You talked about that a little bit before.	Potential theme: Leaders
Visionary skills of talented people	LU: I think there are people that have wonderful visionary skills. I would say that the community as a whole would be . . . would not reflect that. I think there are people who are driving the process, but the rest of the community may be lagging behind a little bit. I think we have some incredibly talented people who become frustrated when they try to implement what they see as their . . .	Idea: returns to description of community again

Source: Reprinted with permission of Jean Jones, Ph.D.

interview and "LU," the interviewee, provides responses. Look over the codes on the left and other ideas recorded in the margins in this figure. I will take you through my thinking as I coded this transcript.

- Notice that the margins on the left and right are extra wide so I could jot down my ideas there.
- On the left side I inserted codes; on the right side, ideas and emerging themes. These features could have been reversed (e.g., codes on the right), but I prefer this organization.
- For codes, I used two or three words as labels. These were the actual words used by the participant, "LU." Sometimes I listed codes as possible alternatives.
- I placed boxes around keywords that I wanted to use as codes or broad ideas or themes.
- By bracketing (drawing a bracket around sentences in the left margin) I identified sentences that seem to "fit together" to describe one idea, my text segments. Notice that I did not bracket all sentences. I did not use all of the data because I needed to reduce it to five to seven themes for my final research report. I asked myself, "What are they talking about here?" drew a bracket around key sentences that related to a code, and assigned a code label.
- On the right, I listed potential themes in the transcript. Also on the right you will see my early jottings (e.g., "getting a good sense here for the community and its values"), and I highlighted a good quote that I might use in my final research report.

The process now, beyond this single page, will be to continue my coding and theme development so that I can construct a description of the community and write about themes relating to this curriculum change in a rural high school setting.

HOW DO YOU USE CODES TO BUILD DESCRIPTION AND THEMES?

From Figure 9.5, you can see that I began thinking about broad themes that emerged from my data. In a qualitative research study, you need to analyze the data to form answers to your research questions. This process involves examining the data in detail to describe what you learned, and developing themes or broad categories of ideas from the data. **Describing and developing themes from the data** consists of answering the major research questions and forming an in-depth understanding of the central phenomenon through description and thematic development. Not all qualitative projects include both description and themes, but all studies include at least themes. Beginning with description, we can explore what it attempts to accomplish, how you might use it, and how it appears in a research report.

Description

Because description is a detailed rendering of people, places, or events in a setting in qualitative research, it is easiest to start the analysis after the initial reading and coding of the data. In some forms of qualitative research design, such as in ethnography or in case studies, the researcher provides a considerable description of the setting. Developing detail is important, and the researcher analyzes data from all sources (e.g., interviews, observations, documents) to build a portrait of individuals or events. To describe an event, the analyst might ask, "What occurred in this setting?" as in the gunman case study

(Asmussen & Creswell, 1995). Alternatively, the researcher might describe an individual by asking "What is this person like?" For describing a place, the question might be "What is this place like?" or "Where in the school do students carry weapons?"

In providing detailed information, description can transport the reader to a research site or help the reader visualize a person. It takes experience and practice to describe the detail in a setting. For example, examine these two illustrations and note the differences in level of detail.

- *Poor example:* The workers built the education building with three floors.
- *Better example:* As the education building developed, iron beams crossed and connected it together. A giant crane lifted these beams into place with a line secured tightly around each beam. A worker underneath the beam fastened it into place. As we watched, the beam tipped back and forth, leading us to wonder if the crane operator had securely fastened it. One slip and disaster would follow, but the beam landed securely in place.

Another good example is the following passage from a short story by Budnitz (2000). The author was writing about the common process of preparing pancakes.

> He was mixing stuff up in a bowl; flour slopped over the edges and sprinkled on the counter and the floor. I'll have to clean that up, I thought. . . . There was butter bubbling and crackling in the frying pan. . . . He poured in the batter, it was thick and pale yellow; and the hissing butter shut up for a while. . . . There were two large lumpy mounds there, side by side, bubbling inside as if they were alive, turning brown on the edges. He turned them over and I saw the crispy undersides with patterns on them like the moon; and then he pressed them down with the spatula, pressed them flat and the butter sputtered and hissed. (pp. 91–92)

By reading vivid short stories or examining qualitative studies, you can find illustrations where writers used detail to take an ordinary experience (like pancake making) and transport you to the setting so that you can almost feel (or taste) the situation.

Let's take an illustration that you have already read—the descriptive passage in the gunman case study (Asmussen & Creswell, 1995). Figure 9.6 reports the events that happened 2 weeks following the gunman incident on campus. The discussion of these events illustrates several features of description that you might include in your own qualitative description or note in a published research report. The labels indicate that:

- The passage starts broadly with the Midwestern city and narrows to the campus, then the classroom, and finally the incident. This broad-to-narrow description helps the reader understand the context or place of the incident and provides a sense of a "real" place where this near-tragedy occurred.
- The authors attempt to use vivid details to create the description. We know, for example, that the rifle was a "Korean War military semiautomatic" and exactly how many "clips" or rounds could be loaded into this weapon.
- The action comes alive in this description with the use of action verbs and movement-oriented modifiers and adjectives. The gunman did not walk out of the building but "hastily departed."
- The authors do not make an interpretation or evaluate the situation—they simply report the "facts" as they heard about them from data sources. Times (e.g., 4:00 p.m.) illustrate detail about the specific occurrence of events.
- The passage includes quotes to provide emphasis and realism in the account. These quotes are short, even one word (e.g., "disturbed"). They may be longer, such as a short phrase or a sentence, but in a brief journal article, writers need to be concerned about space available for the narrative and generally keep the quotes as short as possible.

FIGURE 9.6

Elements of Description in a Narrative Passage

	The Incident and Response
Description builds from broad to narrow; Situate the reader in the place or context	The incident occurred on the campus of a large public university in a Midwestern city. A decade ago, this city had been designated an "all-American city," but more recently, its normally tranquil environment has been disturbed by an increasing number of assaults and homicides. Some of these violent incidents have involved students at the university.
Provide details	The incident that provoked this study occurred on a Monday in October. A forty-three-year-old graduate student, enrolled in a senior-level actuarial science class, arrived a few minutes before class, armed with a vintage Korean War military semiautomatic rifle loaded with a thirty-round clip of thirty caliber ammunition. He carried another thirty-round clip in his pocket. Twenty of the thirty-four students in the class had already gathered for class, and most of them were quietly reading the student newspaper. The instructor was en route to class.
Detail to create a sense of "being there"; Use of action verbs and vivid modifiers and adjectives	The gunman pointed the rifle at the students, swept it across the room, and pulled the trigger. The gun jammed. Trying to unlock the rifle, he hit the butt of it on the instructor's desk and quickly tried firing it again. Again it did not fire. By this time, most students realized what was happening and dropped to the floor, overturned their desks, and tried to hide behind them. After about twenty seconds, one of the students <u>shoved</u> a desk into the gunman, and students ran past him out into the hall and out of the building. The gunman <u>hastily departed</u> the room and went out of the building to his parked car, which he had left running. He was captured by police within the hour in a nearby small town, where he lived. Although he remains incarcerated at this time, awaiting trial, the motivations for his actions are unknown.
Just describe the "facts," do not interpret situation; Use of quotes or italics to emphasize ideas or "reflective" comments	Campus police and campus administrators were the first to react to the incident. Campus police arrived within three minutes after they had received a telephone call for help. They spent several <u>anxious</u> minutes outside the building interviewing students to obtain an accurate description of the gunman. Campus administrators responded by calling a news conference for 4:00 P.M. the same day, approximately four hours after the incident. The police chief as well as the vice-chancellor of Student Affairs and two students described the incident at the news conference. That same afternoon, the Student Affairs office contacted Student Health and Employee Assistance Program (EAP) counselors and instructed them to be available for any student or staff requesting assistance. The Student Affairs office also arranged for a new location, where this class could meet for the rest of the semester. The Office of Judicial Affairs suspended the gunman from the university. The next day, the incident was discussed by campus administrators at a regularly scheduled campuswide cabinet meeting. Throughout the week, Student Affairs received several calls from students and from a faculty member about "disturbed" students or unsettling student relations. A counselor of the Employee Assistance Program consulted a psychologist with a specialty in dealing with trauma and responding to educational crises. Only one student immediately set up an appointment with the student health counselors. The campus and local newspapers continued to carry stories about the incident.

Source: Asmussen & Creswell, 1995, pp, 576–577.

Themes

In addition to description, the use of themes is another way to analyze qualitative data. Because themes are similar codes aggregated together to form a major idea in the database, they form a core element in qualitative data analysis. Like codes, themes have labels that typically consist of no more than two to four words (e.g., "denial," "campus planning").

Through initial data analyses, you may find 30 to 50 codes. In subsequent analyses, you reduce these codes to five to seven major themes through the process of eliminating redundancies. There are several types of themes, and authors typically identify them as follows:

- *Ordinary themes:* themes that a researcher might expect to find (e.g., "exposure to tobacco at school").
- *Unexpected themes:* themes that are surprises and not expected to surface during a study (e.g., "unenforced school tobacco use policies").
- *Hard-to-classify themes:* themes that contain ideas that do not easily fit into one theme or that overlap with several themes (e.g., "students gather in the park").
- *Major and minor themes:* themes that represent the major ideas and the minor, secondary ideas in a database. For example, a major theme might be "attempts to quit smoking." Minor themes might be "physical reaction", "peer pressure to continue smoking", or "starts and stops".

It might be helpful to examine themes that emerged during data analysis. Figure 9.7 is a portion of the discussion of the "safety" theme found in the gunman incident study (Asmussen & Creswell, 1995). The marginal annotations mark elements that are included in the theme. You might consider "safety" to be an ordinary theme because we might expect it to occur on campus. Several participants mention this theme, so the authors selected it and used participants' exact wording. The authors analyzed their data for multiple perspectives on this theme of "safety." The term **multiple perspectives** means that you provide several viewpoints from different individuals and sources of data as evidence for a theme. Multiple perspectives, as you may recall from chapter 2, are important when conveying the complexity of the phenomenon in qualitative research. In this passage, for example, the authors report the perspectives of:

- The chief student affairs officer
- University board members
- Campus security officers
- The counseling and psychological services office
- A professor on campus

It is also useful to see that the authors have one major theme and several minor themes subsumed under the major theme. Diagrammed, this thematic development would be:

Major theme: safety

Minor themes (or subthemes): safety of students in the classroom; types of services

Finally, to add realism to this passage, the authors include short quotes from their interviews and newspaper accounts.

This passage does not include one further element of theme development. A realistic presentation of information does not present only one side or the other. In an attempt to capture the complexity of situations, qualitative researchers analyze data for contrary evidence. **Contrary evidence** is information that does not support or confirm the themes and provides contradictory information about a theme. What would this theme be? Had the authors of the gunman case study searched for this evidence, they might have found that some students actually felt "safe" rather than concerned because the gunman left quickly or because they could outnumber the gunman.

One final point to note about developing themes is that you will reach a point where themes are fully developed and new evidence will not provide additional themes. **Saturation** is the point where you have identified the major themes and no new information can add to your list of themes or to the detail for existing themes. When you

FIGURE 9.7

Elements of Theme Development in a Narrative Passage

Safety

The violence in the city that involved university students and the subsequent gun incident that occurred in a campus classroom shocked the typically tranquil campus. A counselor aptly summed up the feelings of many: "When the students walked out of that classroom, their world had become very chaotic; it had become very random, something had happened that robbed them of their sense of safety." Concern for safety became a central reaction for many informants.

When the chief student affairs officer described the administration's reaction to the incident, he listed the safety of students in the classroom as his primary goal, followed by the needs of the news media for details about the case, helping all students with psychological stress, and providing public information on safety. As he talked about the safety issue and the presence of guns on campus, he mentioned that a policy was under consideration for the storage of guns used by students for hunting. Within 4 hours after the incident, a press conference was called during which the press was briefed not only on the details of the incident, but also on the need to ensure the safety of the campus. Soon thereafter the university administration initiated an informational campaign on campus safety. A letter, describing the incident, was sent to the university board members. (One board member asked, "How could such an incident happen at this university?") The Student Affairs Office sent a letter to all students in which it advised them of the various dimensions of the campus security office and of the types of service it provided. The Counseling and Psychological Services of the Student Health Center promoted their services in a colorful brochure, which was mailed to students in the following week. It emphasized that services were "confidential, accessible, and professional." The Student Judiciary Office advised academic departments on various methods of dealing with students who exhibited abnormal behavior in class. The weekly faculty newsletter stressed that staff needed to respond quickly to any post-trauma fears associated with this incident. The campus newspaper quoted a professor as saying, "I'm totally shocked that in this environment, something like this would happen." Responding to the concerns about disruptive students or employees, the campus police department sent plainclothes officers to sit outside offices whenever faculty and staff indicated concerns.

An emergency phone system, Code Blue, was installed on campus only 10 days after the incident. These 36 ten-foot-tall emergency phones, with bright blue flashing lights, had previously been approved, and specific spots had already been identified from an earlier study. "The phones will be quite an attention getter," the director of the Telecommunications Center commented. "We hope they will also be a big detractor [to crime]." Soon afterwards, in response to calls from concerned students, trees and shrubbery in poorly lit areas of campus were trimmed.

Source: Asmussen & Creswell, 1995, pp. 582–583.

reach this point is a subjective assessment, but most qualitative researchers realize when it occurs. In the development of the theme of "quit attempts in smoking," the researchers drew on their extensive interviews with high school students. They found evidence through specific examples and quotes to illustrate the theme, and when they returned to the interview transcriptions, no new information surfaced during their reading and rereading of the transcripts. They concluded that they had reached saturation on this theme. A check with participants (see the discussion on validating the accuracy of findings later in this chapter) confirmed that they had adequately specified this theme.

Layering and Interrelating Themes

You will see many qualitative studies that stop at reporting description and themes. However, you can add additional rigor and insight into your study by layering themes or interconnecting them.

Layering Themes

Layering themes builds on the idea of major and minor themes but organizes the themes into layers from basic elementary themes to more sophisticated ones. **Layering the analysis** (also called first- and second-order abstractions) means representing the data using interconnected levels of themes. You subsume minor themes within major themes and include major themes within broader themes. The entire analysis becomes more and more complex as the researcher works *upward* toward broader and broader levels of abstraction. The number of layers may vary from two to four or five, and recognizing these layers will help you understand the use of themes in layered qualitative analysis.

Some layering occurred, for example, in the gunman incident study (Asmussen & Creswell, 1995), although the authors did not specifically refer to this analysis procedure. Examine Figure 9.8. This figure shows that the authors used four layers, including the database as one layer. The authors collected data from several sources (Layer 1) and analyzed it to develop a description of events (Layer 2). From this description they then formed five themes (Layer 3) and combined these themes into two broad perspectives (Layer 4). Knowing how layering works will help you see how the authors began with the details and worked their way up to the more general themes in their analysis.

Interrelating Themes

A second thematic analysis approach interconnects the themes. **Interconnecting themes** means that the researcher connects the themes to display a chronology or sequence of events, such as when qualitative researchers generate a theoretical and conceptual model. For example, look at Figure 9.9. Here we see a sample chart used in a qualitative grounded

FIGURE 9.8

Layers in the Qualitative Gunman incident Study

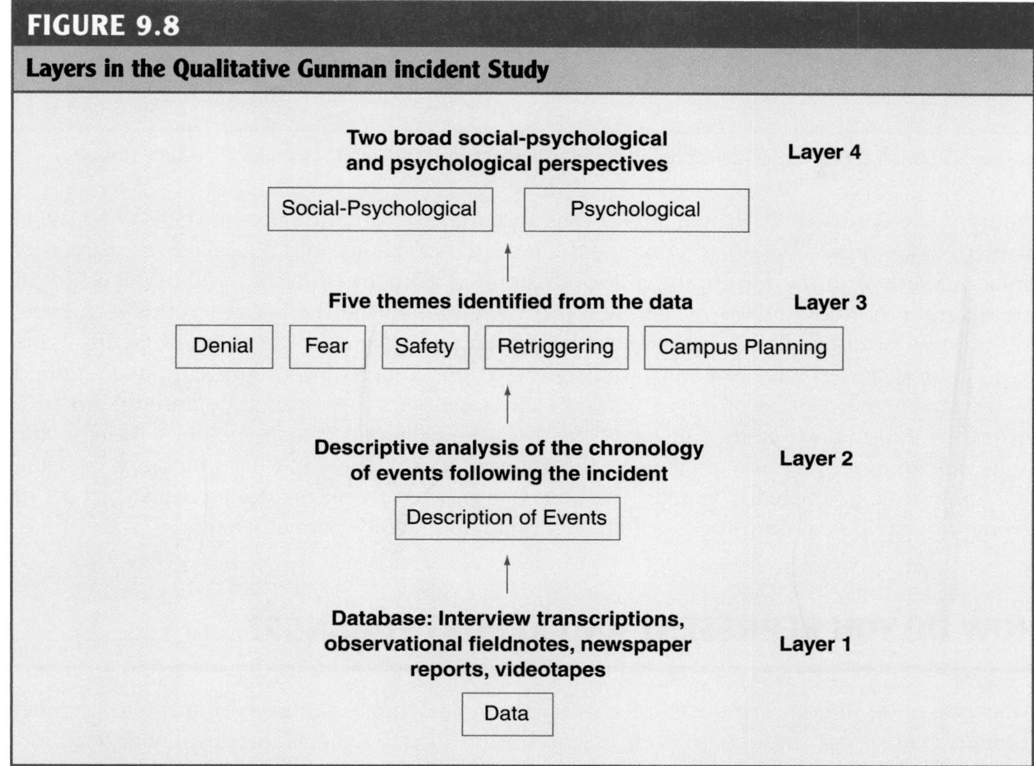

Source: Adapted from Asmussen & Creswell, 1995.

FIGURE 9.9

Interconnecting Themes or Categories in a Qualitative Study

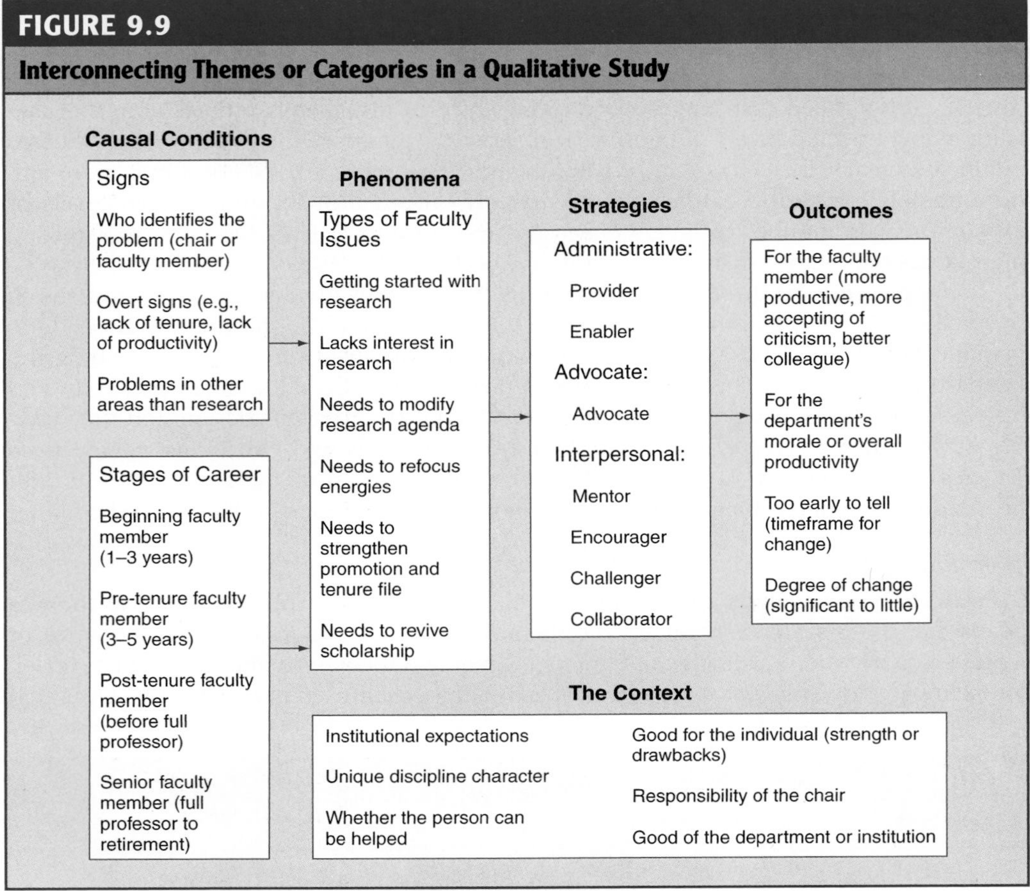

Source: Creswell & Brown, 1992. Reprinted by arrangement with The Johns Hopkins University Press.

theory study (Creswell & Brown, 1992). The researchers examined the practices used by 33 academic department chairs to enhance the research of faculty in their college or university units. As shown in the figure, the authors identified numerous themes within each box in the diagram. In addition, arrows show the connection among the boxes. In this sequence, the process of enhancing faculty research performance relates to the type of faculty issue (e.g., getting started with research), the signs that this issue is important (e.g., as identified by the chair), the context of stages of the faculty member's career (e.g., beginning), and the larger institutional context (e.g., good for the department). It also includes the specific strategies employed by the chair (e.g., the chair as a provider), and the outcomes of using that strategy (e.g., too early to tell). In short, this process displays an interconnected set of events or activities in the process of chairs enhancing faculty performances.

HOW DO YOU REPRESENT AND REPORT FINDINGS?

After you code the data, analyze it for description and themes, and layer and interconnect themes, you report findings to your research questions. This calls for displaying findings in tables and figures and constructing a narrative to explain what you have found in response to your research questions.

Representing Findings

Qualitative researchers often display their findings visually (Miles & Huberman, 1994) by using figures or pictures that augment the discussion. Different ways to display data are listed here:

- *Create a comparison table.* Create a visual image of the information in the form of a comparison table (see Spradley, 1980b) or a matrix, a table that compares groups on one of the themes (e.g., men and women in terms of "safety"; see Miles & Huberman, 1994, for additional examples). In a qualitative study of the meaning of "professionalism," a researcher collected statements from both women and men teachers in a school. Statements from these teachers, shown in Table 9.1, are included in a comparison table to show that females and males can differ in their approaches to professionalism.
- *Develop a hierarchical tree diagram.* This diagram visually represents themes and their interconnections (see again Figure 9.8 for the gunman incident case study, Asmussen & Creswell, 1995).
- *Present figures.* Figures with boxes show the connections among themes (see again Figure 9.9 from the grounded theory study by Creswell & Brown, 1992).
- *Draw a map.* Depict the physical layout of the setting. As shown in Figure 9.10, Miller, Creswell, and Olander (1998) displayed the physical setting of a soup kitchen in their study. The authors provided this diagram so that readers could visualize where different activities happened.
- *Develop a demographic table.* Describe personal or demographic information for each person or site in the research. In a study of the types of technology used by instructors in college classrooms, the researcher described each instructor and his or her primary delivery style in a demographic table, shown in Table 9.2. The six individuals studied in this qualitative study displayed different personal characteristics as well as diverse approaches to using technology. This table provides readers with various demographic information for each instructor, such as number of years teaching, gender, class level of instruction, instructional approach used in the class, and his or her primary form of technology use.

TABLE 9.1

A Sample Comparison Table Used to Represent Information in a Qualitative Study

Female Statements About "Professionalism"	Male Statements About "Professionalism"
• Helping fellow teachers is part of my day. • When another teacher asks for advice, I am generally a good listener. • It is important, once I achieve a certain level of experience, that I become a mentor to other teachers, especially new ones. • Caring about how other teachers employ high standards in their classroom is a sign of my own professionalism.	• Being concerned about following the coordinator's advice about curriculum shows a high level of professionalism. • It is important to be in charge in the classroom and to be aware of student off-task behavior. • I set standards for myself, and try to achieve these goals each year. • It is necessary that each teacher "pull" his or her weight in this school—a sure sign of professionalism.

FIGURE 9.10

Sample Diagram of the Physical Layout in a Qualitative Study

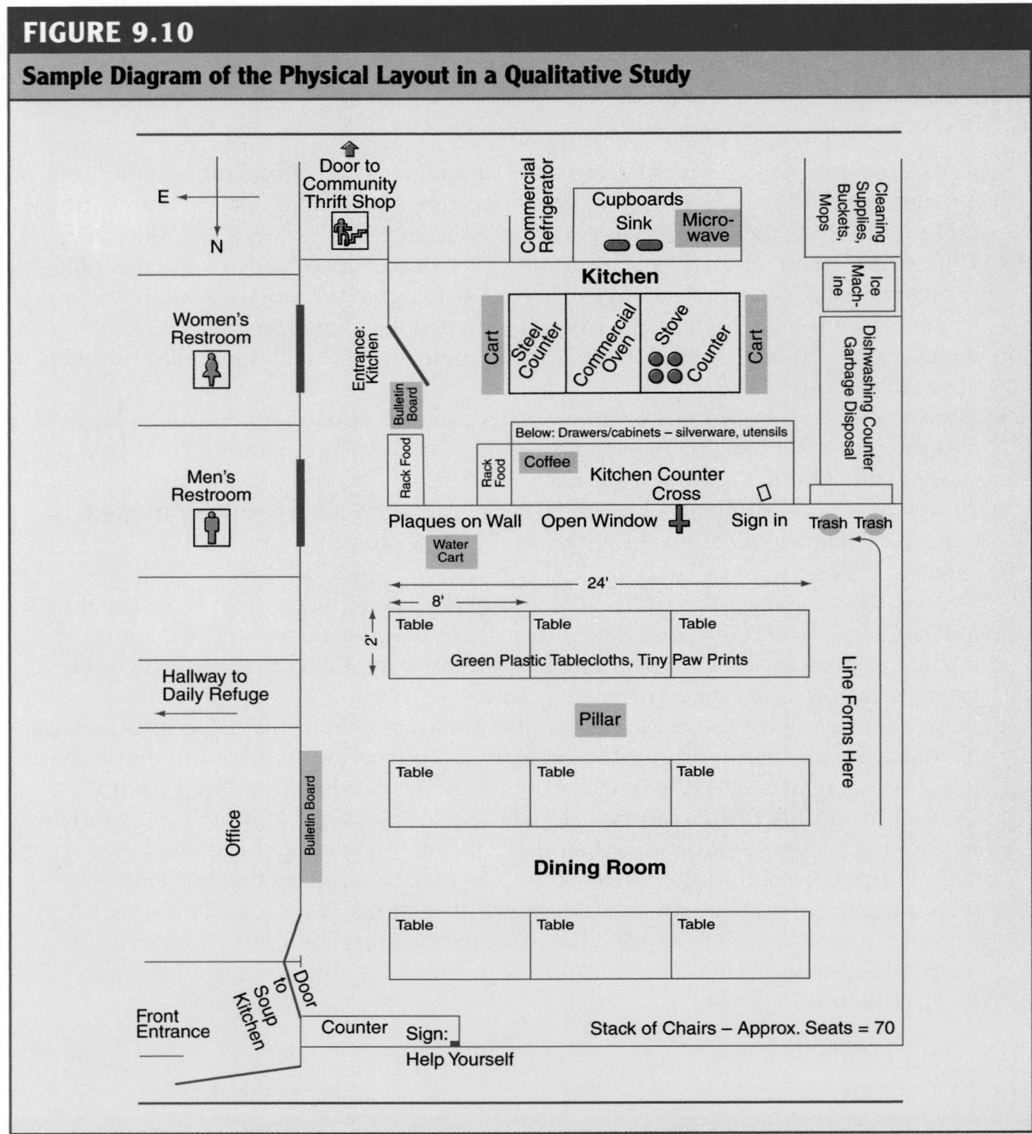

Source: Miller, D. M., Creswell, J. W., & Olander, L. S. (1998). Writing and retelling multiple ethnographic tales of a soup kitchen for the homeless. *Qualitative Inquiry, 4*(4), 475. Copyright © 1998 by Sage Publications. Reprinted by permission of Sage Publications, Inc.

Reporting Findings

The primary form for representing and reporting findings in qualitative research is a narrative discussion. A **narrative discussion** is a written passage in a qualitative study in which authors summarize, in detail, the findings from their data analysis. There is no set form for this narrative, which can vary widely from one study to another. However, it is helpful to identify some frequently used forms, as shown in Table 9.3. Several of these forms have already been discussed, such as developing description, themes, or interconnecting themes. Others are important, too, especially in advocacy and participatory forms of qualitative inquiry, such as raising questions, challenging assumptions based on

TABLE 9.2

A Sample Demographic Table in a Qualitative Study

Name	Years Teaching	Gender	Class Level of Instruction	Instructional Approach in the Classroom	Primary Form of Technology in the Classroom
Rosa	25	Female	12	Discussion	Internet
Harry	20	Male	11	Critique	Not used
Joan	18	Female	11	Discussion	Website and Internet
Ray	20	Male	12	Interactive	Website, Internet, wireless laptops
Jamal	15	Male	11	Discussion	Not used
Yun	36	Male	10	Lecture	Internet

evidence supplied by participants, or reflecting on how participants changed (e.g., became empowered, became advocates, became involved) during the research. Your decision about which form or forms to use depends on the purpose of your research and the type of data you have analyzed for your findings.

TABLE 9.3

Forms of a Narrative Discussion in Qualitative Research

Forms of Narrative Discussion	Examples
A discussion that presents a chronology	The chronology of a teacher's experiences with her special education coordinator leading to her resignation from the school
A discussion that describes events and setting (context)	A description of adolescents reading "teen" magazines
A discussion of themes	A discussion about the theme of the "in-classroom" landscape of a teacher
A discussion of a figure	A figure presenting a model of the process of art therapy with clients
A discussion about layering or interconnecting themes	A discussion about the levels of complexity in a campus response to a gunman incident
A discussion incorporating past literature and research studies	A discussion incorporating past literature of efforts to develop campus plans for avoiding potential violence
A discussion raising further questions that need to be addressed	A discussion that raises questions about the equality and fair treatment of women
A discussion using participants' views to challenge accepted or hidden assumptions	A discussion that probes practices of discrimination in our schools
A discussion about how participants are empowered or change	A discussion about how a teacher, by sharing her story, felt empowered

Consider also the narrative elements that go into a report of your findings. As you make multiple passes through your database, looking for description and themes, consider these useful hints:

- *Include dialogue that provides support for themes.* For example, in a study about reading disabilities of four middle school students, Kos (1991) provided this dialogue about the theme "reading-related stress" for a student named Karen. (Kos's comments are labeled "R"; Karen's comments are labeled "K.")

  K: I feel that it's very difficult for me.
  R: Mm hmm.
  K: And sometimes I can read a book and some books are kind of difficult. And um, my mom said that you have to read or . . . you won't get nowhere.
  R: What do you think about that?
  K: Um, I think, I think it's sad. And um, like Mom says, that you, you might be having a night job picking up trash and sweeping.
  R: Mm hmm.
  K: And you wouldn't have a regular job like my mom and make some money.
  R: Mm. But somebody has to pick up the trash.
  K: *Yeah, somebody. But I don't know who!* (pp. 885–886)

- *State the dialogue in the participants' native language or in the regional or ethnic dialect.* A study that examines the life histories of African American women by Nelson (1990) included examples of *code-switching* of African American dialect to convey the novel metaphors of casual kitchen-table discourse:

  I'm trying to communicate a shoe box full when you only give them (the words) a matchbox. I'm trying to relate the spiritual meaning. (p. 151)

- *Use metaphors and analogies.* In reporting on the competition and concerns surfacing during the implementation of distance education in the state of Maine, Epper (1997) wrote metaphorically about how student and citizen support is a "political football" game:

  As the bickering went on, many students stood by watching their education dreams tossed around like a political football. Some were not content to sit on the sidelines. From the islands, valleys, backwoods, and far reaches of the state came letters to the faculty senates, legislators, and newspapers. (p. 566)

- *Report quotes from interview data or from observations of individuals.* These quotes can capture feelings, emotions, and ways people talk about their experiences.
- *Report multiple perspectives and contrary evidence.* Identify these perspectives based on different individuals, sources of information, or multiple views held by one person.
- *Write in vivid detail.* Find good descriptions of an individual, event, or activity.
- *Specify tensions and contradictions in individual experiences.* For example, Huber and Whelan (1999) report the personal stories of a female teacher who experiences a lack of support about a special education student in the classroom. They discuss the tension this teacher feels between being in control in her classroom and the out-of-class pressure that she experiences from her school coordinator.

HOW DO YOU INTERPRET FINDINGS?

Interpretation involves making sense of the data, or the "lessons learned," as described by Lincoln and Guba (1985). **Interpretation** in qualitative research means that the researcher steps back and forms some larger meaning about the phenomenon based on personal views, comparisons with past studies, or both. Qualitative research is interpretive research, and you will need to make sense of the findings. You will find this interpretation in a final section of a study under headings such as "Discussion," "Conclusions," "Interpretations," or "Implications." This section includes:

- A review of the major findings and how the research questions were answered
- Personal reflections of the researcher about the meaning of the data
- Personal views compared or contrasted with the literature
- Limitations of the study
- Suggestions for future research

Summarize Findings

A typical "Discussion" section begins with a general recap of the major findings. Sometimes you will state each individual research question again and provide findings for each question. The overall intent of this passage is to provide readers with an overview of the findings to complement the more detailed results in the description and theme passages.

Convey Personal Reflections

Because qualitative researchers believe that your personal views can never be kept separate from interpretations, personal reflections about the meaning of the data are included in the research study. You base these personal interpretations on hunches, insights, and intuition. Because you may have been to the field and visited personally at great length with individuals, you are in a good position to reflect and remark on the larger meaning of the data. The two examples that follow illustrate the diversity of personal reflections found in qualitative studies.

In the classic ethnography of the "sneaky kid," Wolcott (1983) reflected about the meaning of learning for Brad:

> Learning—in the broad enculturative sense of coming to understand what one needs to know to be competent in the roles one may expect to fulfill in society, rather than in the narrow sense of learning-done-at-school—is an ongoing process in which each human engages throughout a lifetime. (p. 24)

The next example shows how researchers can offer interpretative commentary about new questions that need to be answered. In the discussion by Tierney (1993), who spoke with a 40-year-old African American who had AIDS on a university campus, the researcher left the interview with unanswered questions:

> How do we create understandings across differences so that we are able to acknowledge and honor one another, rather than bring into question one another's legitimacy? It is incumbent on me as the author, then, to present these voices as fully and carefully as possible; at the same time, it is necessary for the reader or methodologist or administrator who does not understand these realities to try to come to terms with them. (p. 27)

Make Comparisons to the Literature

Interpretation may also contain references to the literature and past studies. Similar to quantitative research, the qualitative inquirer interprets the data in view of this past research, showing how the findings may support or contradict prior studies, or both. This interpretation may compare qualitative findings with reported views of a social science concept found in the literature, or it may combine personal views with an educational or social science term or idea. In a qualitative study of sibling interaction between a young man with Down syndrome and his three brothers, Harry, Day, and Quist (1998) concluded with interpretive comments about the inclusion of "Raul" in situations outside of the family setting. They relate their own views to those in the literature:

> We strongly believe, as does much literature on the topic (Hurley-Geffner, 1995; Schnorr, 1990), that the first requirement must be an inclusive and continuous school structure that keeps students with disabilities with their community and family peers from elementary school right through high school. (p. 297)

Offer Limitations and Suggestions for Future Research

Also similar to quantitative research, the qualitative researcher suggests possible limitations or weaknesses of the study and makes recommendations for future research. These limitations may address problems in data collection, unanswered questions by participants, or better selection of purposeful sampling of individuals or sites for the study. Implications for future research may include the use of the findings for practice (e.g., classrooms, schools, or with certain people such as adults or teenagers) or the need for further research (e.g., by gathering more extensive data or by asking additional questions of participants). You might also state implications for decision making, such as planning for new practices (e.g., better campus planning about how to handle violent incidents) or for the audience you identified in the introduction to your study.

HOW DO YOU VALIDATE THE ACCURACY OF YOUR FINDINGS?

Throughout the process of data collection and analysis, you need to make sure that your findings and interpretations are accurate. **Validating findings** means that the researcher determines the accuracy or credibility of the findings through strategies such as member checking or triangulation. Several qualitative researchers have addressed this idea (e.g., Creswell & Miller, 2000; Lincoln & Guba, 1985). Qualitative researchers do not typically use the word *bias* in research; they will say that all research is interpretive and that the researcher should be self-reflective about his or her role in the research, how he or she is interpreting the findings, and his or her personal and political history that shapes his or her interpretation (Creswell, 2007). Thus, accuracy or credibility of the findings is of upmost importance. There are varied terms that qualitative researchers use to describe this accuracy or credibility (e.g., see *authenticity* and *trustworthiness* in Lincoln & Guba, 1985), and the strategies used to validate qualitative accounts vary in number (see eight forms in Creswell & Miller, 2000). Our attention here will be on three primary forms typically used by qualitative researchers: triangulation, member checking, and auditing.

- Qualitative inquirers triangulate among different data sources to enhance the accuracy of a study. **Triangulation** is the process of corroborating evidence from different individuals (e.g., a principal and a student), types of data (e.g., observational fieldnotes and interviews), or methods of data collection (e.g., documents and interviews) in descriptions and themes in qualitative research. The inquirer examines each information source and finds evidence to support a theme. This ensures that the study will be accurate because the information draws on multiple sources of information, individuals, or processes. In this way, it encourages the researcher to develop a report that is both accurate and credible.

- Researchers also check their findings with participants in the study to determine if their findings are accurate. **Member checking** is a process in which the researcher asks one or more participants in the study to check the accuracy of the account. This check involves taking the findings back to participants and asking them (in writing or in an interview) about the accuracy of the report. You ask participants about many aspects of the study, such as whether the description is complete and realistic, if the themes are accurate to include, and if the interpretations are fair and representative.
- Researchers may also ask a person *outside* the project to conduct a thorough review of the study and report back, in writing, the strengths and weaknesses of the project. This is the process of conducting an **external audit**, in which a researcher hires or obtains the services of an individual outside the study to review different aspects of the research. The auditor reviews the project and writes or communicates an evaluation of the study. This audit may occur both during and at the conclusion of a study, and auditors typically ask questions such as those mentioned by Schwandt and Halpern (1988):
  - Are the findings grounded in the data?
  - Are inferences logical?
  - Are the themes appropriate?
  - Can inquiry decisions and methodological shifts be justified?
  - What is the degree of researcher bias?
  - What strategies are used for increasing credibility?

Let's return to Maria, who reflects on whether her own interpretation is "right." You may recall that Maria realizes that the interpretation of her findings includes her own perspectives drawn from personal experiences. As a Latino, she is aware of the marginalization that some of the kids she interviews about weapon possession feel. She realizes, as well, that family support or lack of support plays a prominent role in Latino families, and that her interpretation of themes (e.g., "student alienation" or "right to protect myself") will reflect her own concerns about these issues. How can Maria separate herself from her findings? Of course, the qualitative answer is that any interpretation *must* include the researcher's personal stance. The larger question is whether Maria's report is both accurate and credible to those she studies. Maria can validate her report by convening a small group of students and teachers she interviewed and having them read the narrative of her themes. During this process, the group will openly discuss whether the themes reflect their experiences, and then Maria can make additions or changes to her thematic discussion to report accurately and credibly on student and teacher experiences.

As you think about Maria checking the accuracy of her findings, what other approaches might she use?

REEXAMINING QUALITATIVE DATA ANALYSIS IN THE GUNMAN CASE STUDY

In the gunman qualitative study (Asmussen & Creswell, 1995), the authors briefly discuss data analysis procedures in Paragraph 12. They tell about describing details, incorporating quotes, and interpreting events. In addition, they provide both a description and thematic development of their findings. They chronicle the events for 2 weeks following the incident, providing a detailed description of those events (Paragraphs 04–10). They also analyze the data to generate themes, such as the five they present in Paragraphs 13–31.

In the final section of the article, they interpret the larger meaning of the study by considering two broad perspectives—the psychological and the social-psychological—to explain the significance of the study (see Paragraph 35). Finally, they briefly discuss their approach to validating the accuracy and credibility of their account. They do this by taking the case study back to select participants for feedback and by incorporating participants' comments into the final report (see Paragraph 12).

KEY IDEAS IN THE CHAPTER

In a qualitative study, initial data management consists of organizing the data, transcribing interviews and typing fieldnotes, and making the decision to analyze the data by hand or by computer. Qualitative researchers conduct a preliminary analysis of the data by reading through it to obtain a general sense of the data. Major analysis of qualitative data consists of coding the data. The process of coding is one of reducing a text or image database to descriptions and themes of people, places, or events. It also involves using the codes to develop themes about the central phenomenon. In addition, qualitative researchers layer their analysis and interconnect themes to present the complexity of the phenomenon.

Qualitative researchers represent their findings in visual displays that may include figures, diagrams, comparison tables, and demographic tables. They report findings in narrative discussions comprising many formats, such as a chronology, questions, or commentary about any changes that the participants experience. From this reporting and representing of findings, qualitative researchers make an interpretation of the meaning of the research. This interpretation consists of advancing personal views, making comparisons between the findings and the literature, and suggesting limitations and future research. To check the accuracy of their research, qualitative inquirers often employ validation procedures such as member checking, triangulation, and auditing.

USEFUL INFORMATION FOR PRODUCERS OF RESEARCH

- As you analyze and interpret data, keep in mind that the picture you assemble will be inductive—that is, you will organize and report findings beginning with the details and working up to a general picture.
- Realize the extensive time that transcribing takes. If you plan to transcribe your interviews or fieldnotes yourself, use the guidelines recommended in this chapter.
- Consider using a computer program if you are analyzing a large database consisting of more than 500 pages of text. A computer analysis of your data has both advantages and disadvantages.
- If you decide to use a computer program, weigh the features of the program you plan to purchase. Try out the tutorials and explore the features of programs available from Web sites before you purchase a program.
- Take the time to read all of your data to obtain a general sense of it before you conduct a detailed analysis.
- When you code your text data, use the steps in the process identified in this chapter. Try not to overcode the material, and remember that the final report will typically include only five to seven themes.
- Use the coding model shown in Figure 9.5 for procedures on how to segment text, assign labels, identify themes, and jot down useful ideas on a transcript.
- If you code for description, look for vivid detail that will transport a reader into the setting and events in your narrative.

- Consider the different types of themes you can identify during coding. Unexpected themes offer surprising findings that spark reader interest, but ordinary, hard-to-classify, and major and minor themes also add complexity to a study.
- Design a qualitative study with thematic complexity. Use layering and interconnecting themes as well as a combination of description and themes.
- Many possibilities exist for constructing a narrative about the findings. Consider the recommended strategies in this chapter, such as using dialogue, metaphors, analogies, tensions, and contradictions.
- To augment your narrative discussion about findings, consider visual displays such as comparison tables, charts with boxes, and descriptive tables.
- Include your own views in your interpretation of findings because you can never completely remove yourself from interpretation and personal experiences.
- Consider using at least two validation strategies when you conduct qualitative research. The most frequently used strategies are member checking and triangulation.

Useful Information for Consumers of Research

- As you read a qualitative study, remember that the researcher will be presenting information inductively from the narrower themes to the broader themes. Throughout the study, the narrative will likely build from the specific (e.g., database) to the general (e.g., broad themes).
- Look to see if an author mentions all of the steps in the data analysis process mentioned in this chapter (e.g., a preliminary reading, the coding, description, thematic development, representation, and interpretation). In well-developed qualitative studies, most of these aspects will be included.
- As you look for findings in a study, first examine the research to determine if the authors describe an event or the setting and then search for the themes in their study. Look for the headings as a clue for description and themes.
- To see the complexity and make sense of themes, identify multiple perspectives mentioned by different individuals or cited from different sources.
- Because qualitative researchers report findings in the form of a narrative discussion, examine qualitative research for these discussions and realize that discussions may take many forms.
- Data displays augment the narrative discussion. They should be easy to understand and clearly related to themes or description.
- Realize that the "Discussion," "Conclusions," "Interpretations," or "Implications" sections of qualitative research typically include the researcher's personal views. This inclusion acknowledges that all research is biased.
- Check if the author uses validation strategies so that you can become confident in the accuracy of the findings.

Understanding Concepts and Evaluating Research Studies

1. In the gunman case study, identify the passages in which the authors reported their "description" of the incident. Identify several details that they included in these passages.
2. Look at Figure 9.5, which shows an example of a transcript page marked for codes and themes. If you were to write about one theme from the coding analysis on this page, what would that theme be?
3. Look at the gunman case study. Are there themes that you would consider to be "unexpected" themes?
4. In the final section of the gunman case study, the authors refer to the psychological and social-psychological level in Paragraph 35. These two dimensions are their larger meaning of the case—its interpretation. On what basis do they form this interpretation?
5. Find one page of a transcript of an interview. Using Figure 9.5, code the page by writing code words and brackets around sentences in the left margin. In the right margin list two or three potential themes emerging from the data.
6. Log on to a qualitative computer software program Web site and download a tutorial for one of the programs. Complete the tutorial to learn about the major features of the software program.
7. Locate a qualitative journal article in which the author provides a description of an event, activity, or process. Use the headings to help you locate this description. Then, using the marginal annotations provided in Figure 9.6, identify descriptive features such as (a) the context, (b) broad-to-narrow description, (c) use of action verbs and vivid modifiers, and (d) quotes.
8. Examine a theme in a published journal article. Use the marginal annotations provided in Figure 9.7 to identify (a) the name of the theme, (b) evidence for multiple perspectives on the theme, (c) subthemes, and (d) quotes.

Conducting Your Research

For your educational project, design your qualitative data analysis and interpretation. Include the preparation for analysis and the exploration and coding of data, code both for description and themes, represent findings in figures and discussion, and include the interpretation of your data.

Go to our Companion Website at **www.prenhall.com/creswell** to:

- assess your understanding of chapter content with Multiple-Choice Questions,
- apply what you've learned with Essay Questions,
- practice your research skills with interactive Building Research Skills exercises, and
- broaden your knowledge of research with Web Links to research topics on the Internet.

CHAPTER 10 Reporting and Evaluating Research

Research culminates in a report in different forms. This chapter addresses how to write and compose a research report and how to evaluate the quality of this report. It emphasizes the importance of audience, structuring your report for your audience, writing in a nondiscriminatory and scholarly way, and using accepted evaluation criteria to assess the quality of your report.

By the end of this chapter, you should be able to:

- Define the purpose of a research report.
- Identify factors important in writing for audiences.
- Distinguish among the different types of research reports and proposals: dissertations or theses, journal articles, conference papers, and policy and school-oriented reports.
- Describe the physical structure of quantitative and qualitative research reports.
- Identify discriminatory language in a research report.
- Use scholarly writing strategies to help readers understand your research.
- List criteria for evaluating a research report.

Maria presents her completed research to her school committee and her faculty advisor in her graduate program. She will write her report differently for these two audiences. For the school committee, she will emphasize the results, downplay the methods, and highlight practical implications. For her faculty advisor, Maria will emphasize the research and her careful attention to data collection and analysis to generate thoughtful answers to her research questions. Writing with a focus on audience is central to Maria's approach, as is her emphasis on being sensitive to the students and teachers included in her study. In the end, both the school committee and her advisor will evaluate her research. She now needs to talk over with both of them the criteria they will use to assess the quality of her research.

WHAT IS A RESEARCH REPORT?

The steps in the process of research end with the development of a written report of your research. A **research report** is a completed study that reports an investigation or exploration of a problem; identifies questions to be addressed; and includes data collected, analyzed, and interpreted by the researcher. It is composed for audiences, varies in length and format, and differs for quantitative and qualitative research.

What Audience Will Receive the Report?

For groups and individuals to understand and potentially use findings from research, you write the research report in a way that is acceptable to the intended audiences. Thus, a cardinal rule for writing is to write for the audience. Unquestionably, different audiences employ varied standards, as shown in Table 10.1.

Rules and procedures in place at colleges and universities govern the criteria used by faculty advisors and committees. Journal reviewers and journal editors employ criteria presented once a year (typically) in their journals and often on the journal's Web page. These criteria set forth, at least in general terms, the standards they use in reviewing a study submitted for publication, the types of research they seek to publish, and guidelines for authors to follow when submitting manuscripts. Policy makers and practicing educators

TABLE 10.1
Audiences for Research

Audiences	Standards
Faculty (advisor/committees)	• Standards used in the past in program area • Standards traditionally used by each individual faculty member • Standards used at the college or university
Journal reviewers	• Use of published standards printed typically once for each volume • Separate standards may be published for quantitative and qualitative research • Editor must reconcile differing opinions among reviewers
Policy makers	• Ease of understanding results • Immediate application of results • Clarity and brevity of ideas
Practicing educators in the field	• Relevance of problem or issue being studied • Ease of identifying results • Practical suggestions from a research study
Conference paper reviewer	• Whether the researcher has submitted the proper materials • Whether the proposal fits the conference theme or the priorities for the conference • Whether the project summary is clearly written, organized, and addresses the guidelines for a summary
The researcher	• Standards of the outlet for the study (e.g., faculty, journal, practitioners, conferences) • Standards related to the five elements and the seven phases in the process of research • Standards related to quantitative and qualitative criteria

FIGURE 10.1

Maria's Notes About Audiences for Her Report

Notes to myself:

1. *What will be the interests of the people on my school committee?*
   Owen (school administrator and chair) wants data and needs to know how we will use findings
   Ray (finance director) wants "numbers"
   Dana (English teacher) wants "rich" stories
   Deb (social studies teacher) wants good "visuals"
   Carolbel (music teacher) wants it to "sing out" to the public
   Isabel (parent) wants to know what this means for her 5 kids in school
2. *What will my advisor and faculty at the university want for my graduate research paper?*
   Harry (chair) wants high "scholarly" standards and insightful questions and findings
   Joan (member of committee) wants to see that I know the literature
   Howard (member of committee) wants to know if people in the "field" can use results
3. *What do I need to do now?*
   a. *ask for past reports from school to see how reports have been written*
   b. *obtain from Harry past research studies to study their format*
   c. *learn from Harry about timetable for submitting and receiving approval of my research*

in schools and other educational settings evaluate studies in terms of their clarity, simplicity, and utility for practice. Conference paper reviewers often use specific guidelines for reviewing proposals submitted for presentation. In short, researchers need to consider the audience for the study and use both general standards available in the literature and specific standards for quantitative and qualitative research.

Maria needs to consider how she will write her research reports for both her school committee and for her graduate advisor. Look at Maria's notes, shown in Figure 10.1. She considers the interests of each member of the school committee so that she can include some practical implications for each. As for her graduate advisor, she recognizes that he has high standards, has supervised many theses before, and probably has a format in mind for her final thesis report. She also creates a to-do list to remind herself to get the information she needs before she proceeds with this phase of the process.

If you were Maria and needed to write a report as a requirement for your graduate degree, how would you write it? How would you write a report for your school committee? List two or three writing strategies you would use. Then turn to the next sections and read about the types of research reports and their overall structures.

What Are the Types of Research Reports?

Students prepare dissertations and theses as a requirement for their doctoral and master's programs. After completing the dissertation or thesis, researchers often condense it into a journal article for submission to an educational journal. Alternatively, they may present an abbreviated version of the dissertation or thesis at a national, regional, or state conference or to individuals in their school setting. After receiving comments from these audiences and making revisions based on these comments, they might submit the research to a journal for possible publication or file it with a school or school district.

Dissertations and Theses

Dissertations and theses are the doctoral and master's research reports prepared for faculty and graduate committees. The length of a dissertation or thesis can vary, depending on the tradition in a school or department. Faculty advisors and committees may prefer different approaches, which could affect which form is used. The doctoral dissertation might range from the shorter dissertation of 100 pages to more than 400 pages. These dissertations, conducted by doctoral graduate students, are usually longer than master's theses. Master's theses may run from 50 to 100 pages. In general, qualitative studies are much longer than quantitative studies. Qualitative researchers often report many quotes and present multiple perspectives on themes.

The process of preparing a dissertation or thesis involves planning the study (i.e., writing the proposal) and presenting it to an advisor and a faculty committee (see appendix D for strategies for defending a research proposal). After receiving approval to conduct the study, the student completes the study and defends it before a faculty committee.

Dissertation and Thesis Proposals

A **dissertation or thesis proposal** is a plan for a research report, initiated and developed before the research actually begins. We will not discuss proposals for external funding here because other writers have adequately covered them (see Locke, Spirduso, & Silverman, 1999), and they are beyond the scope of this text. Before discussing research proposals, however, it is helpful to distinguish them from research reports.

One essential difference between proposals and reports is that you will write a proposal before conducting the research. In a proposal, the researcher writes about what *will* take place; in the final study, the investigator writes about what *has* taken place. This means that a proposal will likely be written using a future verb tense (i.e., *will*) to describe the action. In a final study, the past verb tense (i.e., *was*) describes what has already occurred. However, when the proposal contains a pilot or preliminary study, you need to describe it as an action that has already occurred.

Another distinction between a proposal and the final study is in the report of results and future research. In a proposal, you have not compiled results, nor have you identified future research needs. Thus, the proposal stops with the methods or procedure. A completed study, however, incorporates results and future research directions because you have already collected and analyzed the data.

To develop a dissertation or thesis, you first create a proposal, which is a formal description of a plan to investigate a research problem. This process begins by considering what topics to include in a plan so that readers can fully understand the project. The next step is to organize and format the plan to be consistent with quantitative or qualitative research. This initial planning process ends with a presentation of your proposal to a committee.

Proposing research is a major step in conducting research for a graduate program. The skills used in writing a proposal are the same skills needed for seeking external funding from public and private funding sources and for writing a plan for conducting a small-scale research study in school districts or other educational settings. Whether educators conduct their own research or evaluate someone else's plan, knowing the importance of a proposal and the elements that go into it is important.

The **purpose of a proposal** is to help an investigator think through all aspects of the study and anticipate problems. A proposal also provides a written document that faculty and advisors can read, evaluate, and critique to improve a study. The research plan or proposal becomes a document to *sell* the study—a written narrative that must convince the faculty of the need, importance, and value of the proposed study. A well-defined proposal:

- Facilitates the process of obtaining permissions to study a site or educational setting.
- Provides information to gatekeepers and those in authority so that they can determine the likely impact of a study at their site.
- Provides criteria to assess the quality of a project. Those evaluating and reviewing a study use these criteria. Knowing the proper elements of a good proposal permits evaluators to examine projects for these elements, and to determine, once you complete a project, whether it fulfills its goals.

Quantitative and Qualitative Dissertation and Thesis Proposals

Figure 10.2 illustrates typical quantitative and qualitative proposal formats for both dissertation and thesis reports. The topics in both formats address the major ideas faculty often seek to know about a project. In the format for a quantitative proposal, most of the plan is included in three major sections: the "Introduction," the "Review of the Literature," and the "Methods." In the format for a qualitative proposal, you will find a less standardized structure. By allowing the study to emerge and to be based on the views of participants, qualitative researchers support a flexible and open format for a proposal. Still, it is important for qualitative researchers to convey enough information to the readers to convince them of the merits of the study.

Recognizing the need for flexibility, recent authors have advanced several formats for a qualitative proposal (e.g., Creswell, 2003; Marshall & Rossman, 1999) to provide guidance for students. Their recommendations, however, are flexible enough to allow a study to emerge and to evolve based on what the researcher learns from participants in the field.

As seen in Figure 10.2, the overall format for a qualitative proposal contains only two major sections: the introduction and the procedure. You will notice that the

FIGURE 10.2

Format Quantitative and a Qualitative Proposal

Quantitative Format	Qualitative Format
Title Page	Title Page
Abstract	Abstract
Introduction	Introduction
Statement of the Problem	Statement of the Problem
Purpose and Research Questions or Hypotheses	The Purpose and Research Question
Theoretical Perspective	Delimitations and Limitations
Definition of Terms	Procedure
Delimitations and Limitations of the Study	Qualitative Methodology and Design
Review of the Literature	Research Site and Purposeful Sampling
Methods	Data Analysis Procedures
Study Design	Researcher's Role and Potential Ethical Issues
Procedures, Instruments, Reliability, Validity	Methods of Validation
Data Analysis	Preliminary Findings
Preliminary Results	Anticipated Outcomes of the Study and Tentative Literature Review (Optional)
Potential Ethical Issues	Timeline, Budget, and Preliminary Chapter Outline
Timeline, Budget, and Preliminary Chapter Outline	References
References	Appendices
Appendices	

qualitative proposal format does not contain a separate section on literature review. Instead, you combine the literature with a discussion on the anticipated outcomes of the study, position it near the end of the proposal, and characterize it as optional. As mentioned in chapter 2, the literature review in qualitative research documents the need to study the problem, but it does not lead to the research questions, as it does in quantitative research. In defending this position to faculty unfamiliar with qualitative research, you would provide this rationale for not including a separate literature review section in your proposal. However, if faculty request that you include a complete literature review in a proposal, it is wise to comply with the request. Still, at the end of the review, you might state that the review is tentative and that it will be developed or completed later, after learning about the participants' views. This stance would be consistent with good qualitative research.

Turning again to Figure 10.2, the qualitative proposal includes a "Procedure" section, in which you present the major characteristics of qualitative research and design as well as information about sampling and data analysis. The final section presents a preliminary investigation of your topic, if you have completed such a study. This preliminary study might include interviews with a couple of individuals or field observations of short duration. The chief advantage of such an approach is to test whether you can collect and analyze data from participants and see if your overall design is workable in the field before receiving approval from your faculty committee.

Journal Articles

You prepare a journal article for readers of scholarly publications as well as for the editor and individuals who review the study. A **journal article** is a polished, shorter research report that you send to an editor of a journal. The editor arranges for two to three reviewers to provide comments about the study. The editor then makes a decision based on the reviewers comments, which typically falls into one of three categories: accept, revise and resubmit, or reject. Usually, when the reviewers accept the manuscript provisionally, they do so based on their anticipation of successful revisions by the author. If the article is accepted, the editor publishes it in an issue of the journal.

A journal article is much shorter than a thesis or dissertation because of page limitations imposed by publishers and editors of journals. Still, qualitative journal articles are much longer than quantitative articles because of the extensive quotes and the lengthy discussions of descriptions and themes. The format of quantitative and qualitative journal articles varies from one journal to another.

Conference Papers and Proposals

A norm of research is that individuals publicly share their research reports so that information is accessible to the general education community. One way to do this is by presenting a paper at a professional association conference.

A **conference paper** is a research report presented to an audience at a state, regional, national, or international conference typically sponsored by a professional association (e.g., AERA, American Association of Teacher Educators). Developing and presenting a conference paper from a research study helps to publicize the study, provides a research entry for a résumé, helps to advance the work of the author within the educational research community, and builds knowledge among researchers exploring the topic. The audiences for conferences may be researchers, practitioners, or policy makers. Researchers prepare conference papers for audiences who attend the conference as well as for individuals who review and accept the papers for presentation. Typically, the length of a conference paper is about the same as a journal article—about 25 pages plus tables, figures, and appendices.

A **conference proposal** is a brief proposal to present a study at a conference. Typically, these proposals run about three pages long, and reviewers use them to determine whether they will accept the authors' research for presentation at the conference. A conference proposal needs to conform to the guidelines provided by the conference association.

During or after the completion of a study, the process of presenting a conference paper begins. A researcher sends a proposal to the conference organizers, who have issued a "Call for Proposals" several months in advance of the conference. This call invites researchers to submit proposals about their research for possible presentation at the conference. In response to this call, authors develop a brief proposal about the study and submit it for review. If the proposal is accepted, the author is obligated to attend the conference and present the paper based on the proposal. Following acceptance, the author develops a completed paper, presents it at the conference, and distributes it to conference participants. At the conference, conference organizers often group three or four research papers into a single session and each author has about 15 to 20 minutes to present his or her study. Alternatively, organizers may offer symposia as a format for presenting research papers. This format consists of several research papers from different individuals addressing the same theme.

Sample Guidelines for Proposals

To illustrate the process of developing a proposal for a conference paper, we will examine the AERA "Call for Proposals" that is printed each year in the *Educational Researcher* journal. The format of paper presentations at AERA has changed in recent years to allow for more innovative forms of presentations, such as interactive paper sessions, performances, and town meetings. The most common form of presenting a single research study, called a paper session, requires that an author submit materials by a set deadline. You need to provide a summary about your research that includes:

- Objectives or purposes
- Perspective(s) or theoretical framework
- Methods, techniques, or modes of inquiry
- Data sources or evidence
- Results and/or conclusions/point of view
- Educational or scientific importance of the study (AERA, 1999, p. 33).

You send this summary to a program coordinator for one of AERA's topical divisions or numerous special interest groups (SIGs). To decide what division to send your material to, you might contact the AERA central office (**www.aera.net**). Two to three reviewers who do not know your identity will review your proposal. The review process may take 2 to 3 months, at which time the conference coordinators will inform you as to whether your proposal has been accepted or rejected for presentation.

Report for Policy Makers or School Personnel

A final type of research report is one that you present to practitioners who are in positions of responsibility in education. These individuals may be policy makers in state and federal governments or leaders in schools, such as superintendents, principals, curriculum directors, and teachers. The research report presented to these individuals might follow these guidelines (see Muffo, 1986):

- *The timing is most important.* The topic of the research needs to be timely and provide suggestions for practice. Identify in your research study the suggestions found in the "Implication" section and share these in your research report with practitioners.
- *Report specific results from your research.* You might summarize these results using bullets to highlight the key findings. You should probably not frame the

results in statistical terms in quantitative research or in the many perspectives of qualitative research. Focus on the outcome of the quantitative statistical tests or on the qualitative perspective that most frequently occurred in your database.

- *Present the results simply and clearly.* This means that your report should be short, highlight key findings, and include an abstract that provides an overview of the results. A dramatic graph or a table can bring together many findings.
- *Include a one-page executive summary at the beginning of your research report.* This summary should not dwell on the research or the methods of your study but on the key findings and their implications for practice. You might highlight the problem studied, the question you asked, the data collection, and the major results and implications for practice.
- *Obtain clearance from key individuals to present your research.* You need to have permission from leaders to present and disseminate your research. Share with these individuals the executive summary prior to your presentation or distribution of the report.

Consider Maria's situation. She needs to present her research to the *school committee.* Following the suggestions above, write down the steps Maria should follow to:

1. Make sure that she has approval to present her research
2. Include an executive summary
3. Report specific results simply and clearly
4. Get the results to the committee in a timely fashion

HOW SHOULD YOU STRUCTURE YOUR REPORT?

A study with a clear structure is easy to understand and easy to read, even though the subject matter may be complex. A nationally known author on the subject of writing, Natalie Goldberg (2000), has stressed the importance of understanding the physical structure of a writing project. The **physical structure of a study** is the underlying organization of topics that forms a structure for a research report. Think about a journal article that you have recently read. Was it difficult or easy to understand? Were you able to read it quickly, or did you labor?

Look at the Physical Structure of Research Reports

Being able to identify the underlying structure of a research report will help you write a study as well as understand one. This is not always easy, but the following four techniques can help:

1. The easiest approach is to examine the different levels of headings used in a study. These headings are road signs used by an author to convey major points in a study. Although some headings are better descriptors of content than others are, examining them helps you identify the structure of a study.
2. Look for the six steps in the research process introduced first in chapter 1. All reports, whether quantitative or qualitative, should contain a research problem, literature, a purpose statement and questions or hypotheses, data collection, data analysis and interpretation, and a reporting format.
3. Look for the research questions (or hypotheses) and the answers researchers develop to these questions (or hypotheses). For every question asked, researchers should

pose an answer. Start with the introductory passages (i.e., "Introduction") and then look at the end of the report (i.e., the "Results" or "Discussion") to see how the authors answered the questions.
4. Finally, become familiar with the structures of different types of reports, especially approaches using quantitative and qualitative research.

Design an Appropriate Quantitative Structure

The structure of a quantitative report is shown in Figure 10.3. The topics in this figure should be familiar because they reflect the ideas advanced in prior chapters of this book.

The body of the paper comprises five major sections. These are the same five sections typically found in published quantitative reports. Knowing this structure will help you read studies and understand where to look for information. For journal articles, the front matter and the back matter sections are limited because of space constraints. For a dissertation or thesis, the researcher includes more front matter to help the reader understand the organization of the study. One front matter section, the abstract, is optional in reports, but, if you write it in a complete form to include the elements of an abstract as mentioned in chapter 4, it helps the reader identify the major parts of a study.

Another part of the body of the paper is the "Method" discussion. This section is likely to vary from one research report to another because of the different procedures authors use for their research designs. (See chapters 11 through 13 for the quantitative research designs.)

FIGURE 10.3

The Front, Body, and Back Matter of a Quantitative Study

Front Matter
Title page
Abstract of the study (optional)

Body of the Paper
Introduction
- Statement of the problem
- Purpose statement
- Research questions or hypotheses
- Theoretical or conceptual explanation

Review of the Literature
- Review of the previous research
- Summary of major themes
- How present study will extend literature

Methods
- Sample and site
- Access and permissions
- Instruments and their reliability and validity
- Interventions (if used)
- Procedures of data collection
- Analysis of the data

Results
- Descriptive analysis of all data
- Inferential analysis to address questions/hypotheses
- Tables and figures to display the data

Discussion
- Summary of major results
- Relationship of results to existing studies
- Limitations of the study
- Implications for future research
- Overall significance of the study

Back Matter
References
Appendices (e.g., instruments, key questions)

Design an Appropriate Qualitative Structure

For a qualitative dissertation, thesis, and journal article, the structure varies considerably. The standard five-section structure seen in Figure 10.3 may not be appropriate for a qualitative study. For a qualitative report, such as a dissertation or thesis, authors may include six to eight chapters. For example, Miller (1992) conducted a qualitative ethnography case study of the experiences of a first-year president. She included the following 11 chapters:

Chapter 1 Introduction to the Study
Chapter 2 Path to the Presidency
Chapter 3 Early Surprises and Challenges
Chapter 4 Building Relationships
Chapter 5 Presidential Roles
Chapter 6 Providing Vision and Leadership
Chapter 7 Initiating Change
Chapter 8 External Constituents
Chapter 9 Struggles and Difficulties
Chapter 10 The Spouse's Role
Chapter 11 Summary, Conclusions, and Implications

The 11-chapter structure places emphasis on themes that emerged during the study. It does not include a separate chapter on the literature review or the specific procedures of the study.

You can see the flexible structure found in Miller's dissertation also in qualitative journal articles and conference papers. Just as there are multiple perspectives from participants in a study, there are also many variations in how researchers report their findings. Some forms of qualitative reports will emphasize description, whereas others will focus on themes or personal interpretations of findings by the author. This flexible format for reporting undoubtedly makes reading qualitative research difficult for those new to the approach. Although the structures for reporting continue to emerge, knowing several prominent variations will help you begin to see the focus of authors as they report their research.

Consider these alternative forms for writing qualitative research:

- A *scientific approach* is similar to a quantitative study in which all or most of the five sections ("Introduction", "Review of the Literature", "Methods", "Results", and "Discussion") are present.
- A *storytelling approach* can have varied structure. The author uses literary devices (e.g., metaphors, analogies, plot, climax) and persuasive, creative writing to present the study.
- A *thematic approach* includes extensive discussion about the major themes that arise from analyzing a qualitative database. Often, this approach uses extensive quotes and rich details to support the themes.
- A *descriptive approach* incorporates a detailed description of people and places to carry the narrative. A study in this mode might convey "a typical day in the life" of an individual.
- A *theoretical approach* is when the author either starts with a theory (e.g., a theoretically oriented case study), ends with a theory (e.g., grounded theory), or modifies an existing theory based on views of participants.

- An *experimental, alternative,* or *performance approach* may include a report of qualitative research in the form of a poem, a fictional story, a drama, or a highly personalized account, called an *auto-ethnography* (see Denzin, 1997, or Richardson, 2000). For example, rather than writing a standard research report, the qualitative inquirer develops a play that captures the "unruly, multi-sited, and emotionally laden" subject matter better than standard writing (Richardson, 2000, p. 934).

Although qualitative reports vary from the traditional theory-scientific approach to the more experimental, it is helpful to look at two broad structural approaches called the scientific and the storytelling approaches. Figures 10.4 and 10.5 present these two approaches. As you can see, the formats differ in the basic topics included and in the headings used to convey the topics. Both differ, as well, from the quantitative structure.

In a **qualitative scientific structure** the researcher includes detailed procedures of inquiry and follows a traditional form for reporting research that includes the introduction, the procedures, the findings, and a discussion. However, a scientific qualitative report does differ from a standard quantitative format. In the qualitative scientific approach, you refer to *procedures* instead of methods, and *findings* instead of results. In addition, Figure 10.4 shows that the format includes a rationale for qualitative research, a description of the site or individuals, and an analysis of themes. You find this structural approach in qualitative designs such as case studies and in grounded theory studies.

Figure 10.5 displays the less recognizable qualitative format, the storytelling structure. A **qualitative storytelling structure** is a flexible approach to writing a qualitative report. The meaning of the study unfolds through descriptions, the author's reflection on the meaning of the data, a larger understanding of the phenomenon, and a return to the author's stance on the topic. Figure 10.5 begins with a description or vignette of an individual and brings the *procedures* into the study at the midpoint. It ends with the meaning of the phenomenon, and presents this meaning in terms of the larger understandings,

FIGURE 10.4

The Front, Body, and Back Matter of a Scientific Quantitative Structure

Front Matter
Title page
Preface and acknowledgments (optional)
Table of contents (optional)
List of tables (optional)
List of figures (optional)
Abstract of the study (optional)

Body of the Paper
Introduction
- Statement of the problem
- Purpose statement
- Research questions

Procedures
- Rationale for qualitative approach
- Sample and site
- Access and permissions
- Data gathering strategies
- Data analysis approach

Findings
- Description of site or individuals
- Analysis of themes

Discussion
- Major findings
- Comparison of findings with existing studies
- Limitations
- Implications for future research
- Overall significance of the study

Back Matter
References
Appendices (e.g., figures, interview, or observational protocols)

FIGURE 10.5

The Front, Body, and Back Matter of a Qualitative Storytelling Structure

Front Matter
Title page
Preface and acknowledgments (optional)
Table of contents (optional)
List of tables (optional)
List of figures (optional)
Abstract of the study (optional)

Body of the Paper
Specific Description of Individual of Interest in the Study
Author's Relation or Connection to the Participant
The Data Collected During the Study
A Specific Incident to Understand the Individual's Life
The Meaning of the Incident
Larger Understanding of the Group of People to Which the Individual Belongs
A Comparison of the Meaning with Published Studies
Return to Author's Personal Meaning of the Individual and Events

Back Matter
References

a comparison with published studies, and the author's own experiences. You find this format in qualitative research designs such as ethnographies and narrative research.

Think-Aloud About the Structure of a Study

Having discussed the structure of various forms of research reports, I want to return now to an approach for examining the structure of research regardless of these forms. I think of a research report as two parallel railroad tracks. The researcher proceeds ahead on both tracks at the same time. One of the tracks represents the *subject matter* of the study. In every study, the writer addresses a topic and the results unfold about this topic. The second track is the *research* track. This track consists of steps in the process of research and the specific procedures within each step. Knowing that the research exists as well as the subject matter enables me to understand the underlying research process of a published study, to determine what findings I should identify, and to evaluate whether the research is rigorous enough to use in my own study. We need to know that the research track exists so that we can see the author's underlying research procedures at work.

As I examine the structure of a research report:

- I use the analogy of two railroad tracks going in the same direction to help visualize the structure of a study.
- I look at the study and examine the headings closely to learn about the structure. They are good road signs to help me understand the research.
- Realizing that researchers compose all educational studies with six process steps, I search for a research problem, a question, data collection, data analysis, and interpretation.

- When reading a study I could give emphasis to both, to learn about the results or findings in a study as well as to *see* the research procedures so that I could critically evaluate the study.

Not all studies are perfect examples of research. Editors of journals make choices about what to publish. Sometimes editors publish an article because the research problem is a timely issue or the issue has not been studied using rigorous procedures. In other cases, the methods are strong, and they cause the editor to accept an article for publication. I am not discouraged if the author only minimally addresses one of the six steps. As a developing researcher, you need to understand both the research and subject matter tracks to comprehend fully the structure of a research report.

HOW DO YOU WRITE IN A SENSITIVE AND SCHOLARLY WAY?

In addition to understanding the structure of a study, researchers engage in good writing practices when they compose a research report. They:

- Are sensitive to individuals and do not discriminate against individuals in their writing
- Use appropriate research terms
- employ a point of view consistent with quantitative and qualitative approaches
- Balance research and content
- Interconnect parts of a study
- Use computer aids
- Write a concise title and abstract

Use Nondiscriminatory Language

A research report needs to be sensitive and respectful of people and places. Your study submitted to a dissertation or thesis committee, to a journal, or to a conference will be rejected if you are insensitive to individuals or cultural groups.

The APA has compiled information and developed guidelines about the use of nondiscriminatory language for research reports (APA, 2001). These guidelines state that using nondiscriminatory language means avoiding demeaning attitudes, including biased assumptions, and awkward constructions that suggest bias because of gender, sexual orientation, racial or ethnic group, disability, or age. One helpful suggestion, developed by Maggio (1991), is to test your written research report for discriminatory language by:

- Substituting your own group for groups being discussed
- Imagining that you are a member of the group
- Revising your material if you feel excluded or offended

Another approach is to spend time studying examples of nondiscriminatory language constructions. Determine how these constructions are inclusive and sensitive. You might also examine three guidelines for reducing bias in language recommended in the *APA Style Manual* (APA, 2001):

1. *Describe individuals at an appropriate level of specificity.* This means that you need to use specific terms for persons that are accurate, clear, and free of bias. For example:

- Be specific:

Poor: man or woman	**Preferred:** men and women
Poor: over 62	**Preferred:** ages 63–70

2. *Be sensitive to labels for individuals or groups.* This means calling people names they prefer and acknowledging that preferences for names change over time. Writers should not use their own group as the standard against which to judge others. For example:

- Use adjectival forms.
  Poor: the gays **Preferred**: gay men
- Put "people" first, followed by a descriptive phrase.
  Poor: schizophrenics **Preferred**: people diagnosed with schizophrenia
- Use parallel cultural standards, rather than labels.
  Poor: husband and wife **Preferred**: man and woman

3. *Acknowledge participation of people in a study.* You need to specifically identify participants based on the language they use. For example:

- Use impersonal terms.
  Poor: subjects **Preferred**: participants
  Poor: informants **Preferred**: participants
- Use nonstereotypical and unbiased adjectives.
  Poor: woman doctor **Preferred**: doctor
  Poor: nonaggressive women **Preferred**: nonaggressive participants
- Use specific cultural identity.
  Poor: American Indians **Preferred**: Cherokees
- Put people first, not their disability.
  Poor: mentally ill person **Preferred**: person with mental illness

Encode Scholarly Terms into Your Research

As these nondiscriminatory guidelines suggest, certain terms are preferred over others for referring to participants in a study. Likewise, in the field of research, certain terms need to be included to convey your understanding of research. Others will partly judge your research based on the appropriate use of standard quantitative and qualitative terms. For example, to call the sampling "random" instead of "purposeful" in qualitative research shows your lack of understanding of the basic differences between the two approaches. When you read a research report, you can examine the level of the author's research understanding through the choice of words. The glossary at the end of this text and the key terms (words in bold type) throughout the chapters provide useful words to use in your research report.

Here are some additional ideas that might be helpful in building your vocabulary and using research words:

- ◆ As you write your study, consult the dictionaries of terms mentioned in chapter 4, such as the quantitative dictionary of terms by Vogt (1999) and the qualitative dictionary of terms by Schwandt (2001).
- ◆ When writing a research report, encode your writing with the language of research. In this case, **encoding** is the intentional use by an author of specific terms to convey ideas. This practice will enhance the acceptability of your research to graduate committees, publishers, and conference attendees. For example, in chapter 5 on writing purpose statements, the terms *compare* and *relate* are good words to use in quantitative research, and the terms *explore* and *discover* are good terms to use in qualitative research.

Use an Appropriate Point of View

The presence of the researcher in the study varies between quantitative and qualitative research. In *quantitative* research, the investigator is in the background narrating the study—an omniscient third person. For example, the researcher *reports* the results of the study and *explains* their importance. The first-person pronoun *I* is not used, and instead the writer uses the impersonal point of view. This form of writing also includes the use of past tense to create distance between the report and the writer. Use passive constructions sparingly. For example, in a quantitative report, you might find the following passive construction:

> ***Passive Construction:*** The results were reported at a significance level of $p = .01$.
>
> ***Active Construction:*** The researcher reported results at the significance level of $p = .01$.

Also, a quantitative writer seldom mentions the first names of individuals in a study and also emphasizes objectivity of the results.

In *qualitative* research, however, the researcher is typically present and in the foreground in the narrative report of the study. This is seen in the use of the first-person pronoun *I* (or the collective *we*) and in the personal experiences of the author that are written directly into the report (e.g., the author's difficulty in collecting data, the reflection on themes derived from the data). The author may present sidebars that interpret the personal meaning of themes or personal statements about experiences, such as the "Epilogue" in the gunman case study (Asmussen & Creswell, 1995). The qualitative researcher also seeks to present a persuasive story and often writes in a lively manner using metaphors, analogies, contradictions, and ironies. The study may end with questions that remain unanswered, much like many novels or short stories. Further, qualitative inquirers mention first names of participants (typically using aliases to protect the identity of individuals), and the level of detail, especially in the description, brings the writer and the reader close together.

Balance Your Research and Content

Some researchers feel that their report must demonstrate their knowledge of research more than the content or subject matter of their studies. Other researchers feel just the opposite. Regardless of emphasis, scholarly writing includes a balance between conveying knowledge about research and knowledge about the subject matter of the study (remember the two tracks of the railroad mentioned earlier). When researchers overemphasize methods, they may feel a need to convince faculty, graduate committee members, or journal editors of their knowledge of research methods. However, an underemphasis may indicate that the person lacks skills or knowledge about research. A good research report contains a balance between a discussion about research and the actual content of the study. This balance is in roughly a 50–50 proportion. For example, compare the following two models of a methods discussion about surveying department chairpersons.

> ***Poor Model Displaying an Overemphasis on Method:*** In this project, survey random sampling will be used so that each department chair has an equal probability of being selected. Moreover, it is important to use stratification procedures so individuals in the sample are selected in proportion to which they are represented in the population. . . .
>
> ***Better Model Displaying Balance:*** In this project, 400 academic chairpersons were randomly sampled so that results could be generalized to the population of academic chairpersons in Research I institutions of higher education ($N = 2{,}000$ chairs). Moreover, the 400 chairpersons represented both men and women chairs in proportion to which they were represented in the total population (300 males; 100 females).

The good model includes comments by the researcher that not only convey an understanding of adequate survey research methods but also inform the reader about the subject matter (the study of chairpersons) of the actual study.

Interconnect Sections for Consistency

Another writing strategy used in research is to interconnect the sections of your research report so that you provide a consistent discussion to readers. One way to establish this interconnection is by using key concepts as linking devices. **Linking devices** are words or phrases that tie together sections of a research report.

In a quantitative report, stating the *variables* and using their exact name each time you mention them can help connect the parts. Consider the many times that researchers refer to the variables in their studies. The title specifies the variables in a study; they are also included in the purpose statement and research questions. Researchers operationally define them in the method section. When researchers use the exact same terms each time they mention the variables, they provide a useful linkage among parts of a report.

Another linking device in a quantitative study is to *use the same research questions or hypotheses* wherever they appear in the research report. A slight change in wording can throw readers off and convey different meanings in your research. When you introduce research questions or hypotheses early in the study (as they often appear), include the *exact same words* when you return to them in the results of your study.

In a qualitative study, *state the same central phenomenon* each time you introduce it. You may introduce the phenomenon in the title, in the statement of the problem section, in the purpose statement, in the research questions, and in your findings. For example, the phenomenon "campus response" appears consistently as a phrase several times throughout the gunman case study (Asmussen & Creswell, 1995), such as in the title, the purpose, and the conclusions.

In both quantitative and qualitative projects, *repeat the problem* throughout the study. This binds the entire proposal or report together. You present the research problem in the introductory part of a proposal and emphasize its importance during the discussion about research questions or hypotheses. You discuss it again during the data collection and analysis as the investigators provide results to address the problem. It may also appear in the future research section at the end of a study, when you talk about the need for additional research.

Use Computer Aids

Tools for writing consist of online dictionaries, grammar programs, and features that come with standard word processing programs (Ross-Larson, 2003). The *Merriam-Webster Collegiate Dictionary* can be found online at **www.m-w.com**. Two tools for good writing can be found at **www.clearwriter.com**. This is an online system of tools, training, and resources that improves business and professional writing. A program at the **www.clearedits.com** site searches your prose for problems and suggests solutions. The site also has a plug-in for Microsoft Word, ClearEdits, that searches your drafts for problems and suggests hundreds of helpful edits.

You can also use the spell checker and the grammar-checking tools available on many word processing programs. On your Word program, go to TOOLS>OPTIONS>SPELLING & GRAMMAR>SETTINGS and turn on all of your grammar style options. Finally, you can also use the outline view to check the structure of your manuscript.

Write a Concise Title and Abstract

Two components of a scholarly manuscript deserve special attention because they are of major importance: the title and the abstract. Information from the APA (2001) style manual reviews the components of both a good title and an abstract for writing a scholarly paper.

The purpose of a title is to summarize the major idea of the paper in a concise and clear manner. The title should be 10–12 words in length and should avoid superfluous words such as "a study of" or "an investigation of." It should be able to stand alone in clarity and be self-expanatory. This means that all words should be clear to a reader without definition. A concisely stated title will enable a researcher to compress it into a "header" that can be placed on each page of the manuscript, and this "header" will provide key words for use by indexing services (e.g., ERIC) to catalog the article. In addition to these components mentioned in the APA (2001) manual, you might also consider what elements go into a good title from both a quantitative and a qualitative perspective. A good quantitative title would contain:

- The major independent and dependent variables in a study, typically listed in order from independent to dependent
- The participants in a study
- The reseach site or location for the study

For a qualitative title, the components would be:

- The central phenomenon being studied
- The participants in the study
- The research site or location for the study

An abstract is another key part of a scholarly manuscript to carefully consider. Chapter 4 introduced the idea of writing an abstract for a study. When writing an abstract at the beginning of a manuscript, its purpose is to briefly summarize the major features of a research study. An abstract is important in research because it is the first contact that readers have with a study, indexed in databases, and the information that researchers often retrieve and read to understand journal articles. Further, readers often decide whether they will examine an article based on an abstract (APA, 2001). Thus, it is important to write a concise and accurate abstract for a research report. This abstract should reflect only information also present in the body of the paper, be self-contained so that the reader does not need to decipher abbreviations or terms, be free of quotes (use paraphrased information), and have a strong leading sentence (APA, 2001). A good abstract is typically 120 words or less (it may be more words for dissertations and theses), and it needs to contain key elements. An abstract for a qualitative study would reflect:

- The research problem
- The research central question
- The data collection procedures
- The findings, and the significance of the findings

An abstract for a quantitative study would reflect:

- The research problem
- The research question or hypothesis
- The data-collection procedures
- The results, and the significance of the results

HOW DO YOU EVALUATE THE QUALITY OF YOUR RESEARCH?

Both during the process of conducting a study as well as at its conclusion, you need to be mindful of the quality of the research. The improvement of practice, the quality of policy debates, and the advancement of knowledge, as mentioned in chapter 1, all call for high-quality educational research. It becomes important, then, to consider the evaluation of research by asking "What criteria should I use?"

Employ Appropriate Standards

Because the quantitative and qualitative approaches to research are different, each merits its own criteria for evaluation. However, both approaches reflect the broader research process (i.e., the six steps in the research process), and some common elements should play into the evaluative criteria as well. Also, the audiences for research, mentioned earlier in this chapter, will employ criteria such as:

- Does the research meet the standards for publication?
- Will the research be useful in our school?
- Will the research advance policy discussions in our region?
- Will the research add to our scholarly knowledge about a topic or research problem?
- Will the research help address some pressing educational problem?

These are important questions, and the answers will shape how we evaluate a research report. Because of the various audiences involved, we have no single standard for research. Moreover, standards for quantitative and qualitative research differ because the two approaches to research differ.

Quantitative Standards

In a study by Hall, Ward, and Comer (1988), the authors had a panel of judges rate 128 educational *quantitative* articles. The specific shortcomings of these articles, in order of their importance, were:

- Lack of validity and reliability in data-gathering procedures
- Weaknesses in the research designs
- Limitations of the study were not stated
- Research design not appropriate for the problem
- Inappropriate sampling
- Results of analysis not clearly reported
- Inappropriate methods used to analyze data
- Unclear writing
- Assumptions not clearly stated
- Data-gathering methods not clearly described

As you can see, quantitative evaluators were most concerned about aspects related to the data collection, the analysis, and the reporting of results of a study—the research design phase of the projects.

Another perspective on evaluating the quality of quantitative research is available from Tuckman (1999). As shown in Table 10.2, the standards follow the research process with an emphasis on the quality of the hypotheses and variables, the control of extraneous variables, and the importance of the discussion and its implications for research and practice.

Qualitative Standards

Turning to qualitative research, the criteria for a good research report vary depending on your emphasis as a researcher. In chapter 2, we discussed the major ideas in three themes in educational research: philosophy, procedures, and participation/advocacy. When we examine current perspectives about judging qualitative research, ideas within

TABLE 10.2

Quantitative Criteria for Evaluating Quantitative Research

Research Problem:
- Is it stated?
- Is it clear?
- Is it complete and accurate?
- Does it offer theoretical and practical value?

The Literature Review:
- Is it clear, relevant, recent, based on studies reporting numbers?
- Are the citations and references accurate?

Hypotheses and Variables:
- What are the hypotheses and what types are they?
- Does the study indicate the independent, dependent, intervening moderator, and control variables?
- Were operational definitions given for the variables?
- Were extraneous effects controlled in the study so that bias did not have an effect on the participants, their experiences, or the generalization of the results?
- Were certain variables manipulated?

Design:
- Was the study design identified?
- Were the scores from the measures valid and reliable?
- Were the statistics the right choice?

Findings and Discussion:
- Did the findings fit the problem?
- How significant and important were the findings?
- Did the discussion section report conclusions and were they consistent with the study's results?
- Did the discussion section offer reasonable interpretations of why results did and did not match expectations?
- Did the discussion section suggest reasonable implications about what readers should do with the results?

Soruce: Adapted from Tuckman, 1999.

each of the three themes combine to form our evaluation criteria. For example, as one interested in the philosophical ideas behind qualitative research, you might draw from perspectives about what constitutes knowledge (e.g., an evolving design) or reality (e.g, subjective experiences). As a procedural researcher, you might emphasize the importance of rigorous data collection (e.g., multiple forms of data) and analysis (e.g., multiple levels of analysis). As a participatory/advocacy writer, you might stress the importance of collaboration (e.g., researcher collaborates on equal terms with participants) and persuasive writing (e.g., does it seem true to participants?).

Let's examine three sets of criteria for evaluating qualitative research developed by three authors within a 6-year time frame. As seen in Table 10.3, the standards reflect both overlap and differences. They all speak to the importance of the participant in the research study, as well as standards set within research communities. Writing persuasively and with respect for participants is also paramount in all three standards. Writing from a point of self-awareness and being sensitive to reciprocity and the impact of the study (e.g., emotionally and intellectually) on readers differs. In combination, they all offer philosophical, procedural, and reflexive standards for you to use in evaluating qualitative inquiry.

Evaluate with a Process Approach

Our discussion of evaluation would not be complete without relating evaluation to the steps of the *process of research* addressed in this book. The steps in this process are

TABLE 10.3

Three Sets of Standards for Evaluating the Quality of Qualitative Research

Lincoln's (1995) Philosophical Criteria:	Creswell's (1998) Procedural Criteria	Richardson's (2000) Participatory and Advocacy Criteria
• Standards set in the inquiry community such as guidelines for publication. • Positionality: The "text" should display honesty or authenticity about its own stance and about the position of the author. • Community: All research takes place in, is addressed to, and serves the purposes of the community in which it was carried out. • Voice: Participants' voices must not be silenced, disengaged, or marginalized. • Critical subjectivity: Researchers need to have heightened self-awareness in the research process and create personal and social transformation. • Reciprocity: Reciprocity must exist between the researcher and those being researched. • Sacredness of relationships: The researcher respects the sacredness of the relationships and collaborates on equal terms with participants. • Sharing privileges: The researcher shares rewards with persons whose lives they portray.	• It employs rigorous data collection, which involves multiple forms of data, extensive data, and a long period in the field collecting data. • It is consistent with the philosophical assumptions and characteristics of a qualitative approach to research. These include an evolving design, the presentation of multiple perspectives, the researcher as an instrument of data collection, and the focus on participants' views. • It employs a tradition of inquiry, such as case study, ethnography, grounded theory, or narrative inquiry as a procedural guide for the study. • It starts with a single focus on a central phenomenon rather than a comparison or relationship (as in quantitative research). • It is written persuasively so that the reader experiences *being there.* • Analysis consists of multiple levels of analysis to portray the complexity of the central phenomena. • The narrative engages the reader because of unexpected ideas and believable and realistic information. • It includes strategies to confirm the accuracy of the study.	• Substantive contribution: Does this piece contribute to our understanding of social life? • Aesthetic merit: Does this piece succeed aesthetically? Does the use of practices open up the text and invite interpretive responses? Is the text artistically shaped, satisfying, complex, and not boring? • Reflexivity: How did the author come to write this text? Is there adequate self-awareness and self-exposure for the reader to make judgements about the point of view? • Impact: Does this affect me? Emotionally? Intellectually? Move me to write? Move me to try new research practices? Move me to action? • Expression of a reality: Does this text embody a fleshed out sense of lived experiences? Does it seem "true"?

Source: Lincoin, 1995; Creswell, 2007; Richardson, 2000.

presented to illustrate complete, rigorous quantitative and qualitative research. Because evaluation will differ depending on whether the study is quantitative or qualitative, Figures 10.6 and 10.7 provide criteria specifically related to the six steps introduced in chapter 1. These lists enable you to assess the quality of your own study or to evaluate the quality of a research report.

FIGURE 10.6

Checklist for Evaluating the Process of a Quantitative Study

Title for the Study
_____ Does it reflect the major independent and dependent variables?
_____ Does it express either a comparison among groups or a relationship among variables?
_____ Does it convey the participants and site for the study?

Problem Statement
_____ Does it indicate an educational issue to study?
_____ Has the author provided evidence that this issue is important?
_____ Is there some indication that the author located this issue through a search of past literature or from personal experiences?
_____ Does the research problem fit a quantitative approach?
_____ Are the assumptions of the study consistent with an approach?

Review of the Literature
_____ Are the studies about the independent and dependent variables clearly reviewed?
_____ Does the review end with how the author will extend or expand the current body of literature?
_____ Does the study follow APA style?

Purpose, Hypotheses, and Research Questions
_____ Does the author specify a purpose statement?
_____ Is the purpose statement clear, and does it indicate the variables, their relationship, and the people and site to be studied?
_____ Are either hypotheses or research questions written?
_____ Do these hypotheses or questions indicate the major variables and the participants in a study?
_____ Do the purpose statement and hypotheses or research questions contain the major components that will help a reader understand the study?
_____ Has the author identified a theory or explanation for the hypotheses or questions?

Data Collection
_____ Does the author mention the steps taken to obtain access to people and sites?
_____ Is a rigorous probability sampling strategy used?
_____ Has the author identified good, valid, and reliable instruments to use to measure the variables?
_____ Are the instruments administered so that bias and error are not introduced into the study?

Data Analysis and Results
_____ Are the statistics chosen for analysis consistent with the research questions, hypotheses, variables, and scales of measurement?
_____ Is the unit of analysis appropriate to address the research problem?
_____ Are the data adequately represented in tables and figures?
_____ Do the results answer the research questions and address the research problem?
_____ Are the results substantiated by the evidence?
_____ Are generalizations from the results limited to the population of participants in the study?

Writing
_____ Is the structure of the overall study consistent with the topics addressed in a quantitative study?
_____ Are educational and social science terms carefully defined?
_____ Are variables labeled in a consistent way throughout the study?
_____ Is the study written using extensive references?
_____ Is the study written using an impersonal point of view?
_____ Is the study written appropriately for intended audience(s)?

FIGURE 10.7

Checklist for Evaluating the Process of a Qualitative Study

Title for the Study

_____ Does it reflect the central phenomenon being studied?
_____ Does it reflect the people and site being studied?

Problem Statement

_____ Does it indicate an educational issue to study?
_____ Has the author provided evidence that this issue is important?
_____ Is there some indication that the author located this issue through a search of past literature or from personal experience?
_____ Does the research problem fit a qualitative approach?
_____ Are the assumptions of the study consistent with a qualitative approach?

Review of the Literature

_____ Has the author provided a literature review of the research problem under study?
_____ Has the author signaled that the literature review is preliminary or tentatively based on the findings in the study?
_____ Does the study follow APA style?

Purpose and Research Questions

_____ Does the author specify both a purpose statement and a central research question?
_____ Do the purpose statement and central question indicate the central phenomenon of study and the people and place where the study will occur?
_____ Are subquestions written to narrow the central question to topic areas or foreshadow the steps in data analysis?

Data Collection

_____ Has the author taken steps to obtain access to people and sites?
_____ Has the author chosen a specific purposeful sampling strategy for individuals or sites?
_____ Is the data collection clearly specified and is it extensive?
_____ Is there evidence that the author has used a protocol for recording data?

Data Analysis and Findings

____ Were appropriate steps taken to analyze the text or visual data into themes, perspectives, or categories?
_____ Was sufficient evidence obtained (including quotes) to support each theme or category?
_____ Were multiple-layer themes or categories derived?
_____ Did the findings answer the research questions?
_____ Were the findings realistic and accurate? Were steps taken to support this conclusion through verification?
_____ Were the findings represented in the themes or categories so that multiple perspectives can be easily seen?
_____ Were the findings represented in narrative discussions or in visuals?

Writing

_____ Was the account written persuasively and convincingly?
_____ Was the overall account consistent with one of the many forms for presenting qualitative research?
_____ Was the account written to include literacy approaches, such as the use of metaphor, surprises, detail, dialogue, and complexity?
_____ Was it written using a personal point of view?
_____ Is the study written appropriately for intended audience(s)?

REEXAMINING THE PARENT INVOLVEMENT AND GUNMAN INCIDENT STUDIES

Let's examine one final time the parent involvement study (Deslandes & Bertrand, 2005) and the gunman incident case study (Asmussen & Creswell, 1995). Both of these studies are actual reports of research found in journal articles. This means that as research studies, they address problems or issues, raise questions, and portray the collection of data to answer the questions. Further, as is apparent to you by now, they both reflect the six-step research process introduced in this text. They include a research problem, the use of literature, the collection and analysis of data, interpretation of the meaning of the data, and a format for writing the report. This process constitutes a structure (or organization) for each study. Looking at the headings, you can see this structure. This structure provides a road map to the article and helps you to read, understand, and potentially use the findings.

In addition to having an underlying structure, in the gunman case study, the authors discuss how they respect the rights of the gunman and the students undergoing counseling by not talking with either the gunman or the students in counseling (see Paragraph 11). Both articles illustrate scholarly writing. The authors write using a point of view consistent with a quantitative approach (e.g., impersonal, with the researchers in the background) and a qualitative approach (e.g., personal). In the parent involvement study, the researchers report results in an objective way and remain largely in the background of the study. They do, however, use the personal pronoun "we" (see Paragraph 24) as they talk about their data collection and discuss the major results (see Paragraph 32). Still, after reading this article, we do not know if the authors had children in the seventh, eighth, or ninth grades or had past experiences with being a parent to adolescents at home or in helping with their schoolwork. We also did not learn how they felt about parent involvement on a personal level. In short, the study is written in a quantitative way, with objective reporting by the authors. A different approach is used in the gunman study. In that study, the authors refer to themselves occasionally, and they include an epilogue in they convey their personal experiences with violence on college campuses (Paragraph 38). Also found in the gunman incident study are literary strategies such as a detailed description of the events (Paragraphs 04–10). Finally, a strategy used by the authors in each study is to balance discussing their *procedures* with conveying *content* about what they learned. In the end, readers such as school committees, faculty advisors, and other educators will read these studies, form an impression of them, and potentially use the findings.

KEY IDEAS IN THE CHAPTER

Researchers write their reports with their audiences in mind. The audiences differ for six types of research reports. These reports are dissertations and theses, dissertation and thesis proposals, journal articles, conference papers, conference paper proposals, and policy or school reports. Reports vary in purpose, length, and format. Researchers also structure these reports differently. A good structure facilitates the reading, understanding, and composing of a research study. The structure of a study can be determined by examining the headings and by looking for the process steps of research. Readers can also search for answers researchers provide to questions (or hypotheses) and become familiar with typical structures used in educational research studies. The structure of a quantitative report follows a standard format: introduction, review of the literature, methods, results, and discussion. Several models of presentation are available in qualitative research: scientific, storytelling, thematic, descriptive, theoretical, and experimental.

When writing a scholarly study or proposal, use nondiscriminatory language. Language should avoid demeaning attitudes, biased assumptions, and awkward constructions that suggest bias because of gender, sexual orientation, racial or ethnic group, disability, or age. The language of research can be specific, be sensitive to stereotyped labels, and acknowledge participation of people in a study. Incorporate into research reports standard research terms such as those found in glossaries, encode reports with appropriate language, and frame them within either a quantitative or qualitative approach. The point of view of a study for a quantitative project tends to be the omniscient third-person style of writing. For qualitative research, inquirers express a first-person or collective point of view. In a qualitative study, the writer tends to be more in the foreground than in a quantitative study.

Writers need to balance content about their subject matter with good research discussions. The sections of a report need to interrelate so that a proposal or a final study is an integrated set of ideas. Linking devices such as variables, hypotheses or research questions, key concepts or a phenomenon, and the problem of the study interconnect sections in a research report. Consider using computer tools to aid in your research. These consist of tools to help you check grammar and spelling.

The criteria for evaluating the quality of a study differ depending on the evaluator. Evaluators may be faculty, journal editors and reviewers, policy makers and practicing educators, and conference paper reviewers. Evaluators look for different characteristics of a good quantitative or qualitative study. Although no set standards exist, several general guidelines are available that researchers might use to evaluate a study. Quantitative evaluators are most concerned about aspects related to data collection, analysis, and the reporting of results. Qualitative researchers are concerned about data collection as well, but also about the persuasiveness of the study and the self-awareness of the researcher.

Useful Information for Producers of Research

- Write in a way that meets the needs of your audiences.
- Design and write your research report following the appropriate structure for the type of report advanced in this chapter.
- Write quantitative research to include an introduction, a review of the literature, a method, results, and discussion.
- Write qualitative research using either a scientific or storytelling structure. Also consider the other structural variations presented in this chapter.
- When you design a proposal for a doctoral dissertation or thesis, consider that the structure will vary depending on whether the proposal is for quantitative or qualitative research.
- If you plan a paper for a scholarly conference, follow the guidelines provided by the professional association sponsoring the conference.
- Write your report sensitively, following the three guidelines for reducing bias advanced by the APA.
- To make your research scholarly and easy to read, write your report using research words, advancing a consistent standpoint, and employing consistent style for references and headings.
- Interrelate sections of a study. Consider how words can provide linking devices for all parts of a study.

- Use computer tools to strengthen your writing.
- After writing *your project,* evaluate it using the standards for quantitative and qualitative research advanced in this chapter.

USEFUL INFORMATION FOR CONSUMERS OF RESEARCH

- To identify how a research report is structured, examine headings, look for the research process steps used in this book, search for results that answer the questions or hypotheses, and become familiar with the varied structures for dissertations, theses, journal articles, proposals, and conference papers.
- It is sometimes difficult to identify the structure of a qualitative study because of the variations that exist. Consider looking first for whether the study conforms to a scientific approach or a storytelling approach.
- Research reports should be free of language that presents demeaning attitudes, bias, and awkward constructions that suggest bias because of gender, sexual orientation, racial or ethnic group, disability, or age.
- This chapter offers separate checklists for evaluating the quality of quantitative and qualitative research. Use these checklists to assess the overall quality of a study.

UNDERSTANDING CONCEPTS AND EVALUATING RESEARCH STUDIES

1. If you were to prepare a research report for your faculty advisor, what three standards might this advisor use to assess the quality of your research?
2. Assume that you come across the following sentences in research reports that employ discriminatory language. Write an improved, nondiscriminatory version of each sentence.
   a. Teachers under 25 adopt an open learning environment for students.
   b. The at-risk students scored below the average in math.
   c. The homeless used the school shelter at night.
3. Did you find the gunman qualitative case study to be structured more as a quantitative approach or a storytelling approach? Why?
4. If you were to develop a research report to be presented to the school district based on the parent involvement study, what topics would you include in a list of bulleted points for your one-page executive summary?
5. Find a journal article and develop an outline of the major elements. Use the four suggestions for identifying the structure advanced in this chapter as a guide.
6. Find a journal article and identify the point of view used by the author. Discuss whether the author uses the first person, the collective, or the omniscient point of view. Provide specific examples to document one or more voices in the study.
7. Change the point of view of the author in the journal article you read for Question 6. Discuss specifically how you would change the words to reflect an alternative point of view.
8. Identify the words in a journal article the author uses to convey a research sense of the study. Also discuss where the author uses these words and how they are either good quantitative or qualitative words.
9. Select either a quantitative or a qualitative study published in an educational journal and critique it. Using the checklist in this chapter (Figure 10.6 or 10.7), discuss the strengths and the weaknesses of the article.

CONDUCTING YOUR RESEARCH

For an educational research study of your choice, provide an outline of the structure of your quantitative or qualitative study. For this type of report, indicate the audience(s) that will receive the report, and discuss writing strategies that you plan to use to make the report acceptable to that audience. List the approaches you will use to enhance the scholarly language of your report if your audience consists of individuals on college and university campuses.

Go to our Companion Website at **www.prenhall.com/creswell** to:

- assess your understanding of chapter content with Multiple-Choice Questions,
- apply what you've learned with Essay Questions,
- practice your research skills with interactive Building Research Skills exercises, and
- broaden your knowledge of research with Web Links to research topics on the Internet.

PART III

Research Designs

To understand educational research, you now have the map (the six steps that exist in the process of research) and the different paths you can take (quantitative and qualitative). Now we will explore some distinguishing features along the two paths. These features are the **research designs** you can use to collect, analyze, and interpret data using quantitative and qualitative research. Some of the research designs may be familiar; others may be new, such as how these paths can converge with two designs called mixed methods research and action research.

The discussion of designs will provide a more advanced understanding of educational research on your journey. In each chapter to follow, you will learn about each design: its definition, its historical development, its key characteristics, and the steps and procedures of conducting and evaluating a study. At the end of each chapter is a complete journal article using the design that you can use to apply and check your knowledge about the design.

Chapters 11 through 18 address eight different research designs frequently used in educational research. The first three are quantitative, the next three are qualitative, and the final two combine quantitative and qualitative approaches.

The chapters in this section are:

- Chapter 11: Experimental Designs
- Chapter 12: Correlational Designs
- Chapter 13: Survey Designs
- Chapter 14: Grounded Theory Designs
- Chapter 15: Ethnographic Designs
- Chapter 16: Narrative Research Designs
- Chapter 17: Mixed Method Designs
- Chapter 18: Action Research Designs

CHAPTER 11

Experimental Designs

An experimental design is the traditional approach to conducting quantitative research. This chapter defines experimental research, identifies when you use it, assesses the key characteristics of it, and advances the steps in conducting and evaluating this design.

By the end of this chapter, you should be able to:

- Define the purpose of an experiment and identify when you use experimental research.
- Describe the reasons for random assignment in experiments.
- Identify the types of procedures used to control for extraneous factors in an experiment.
- Describe how experimental researchers manipulate the treatment condition.
- Define an outcome variable in an experiment.
- Explain how researchers compare groups in an experiment.
- Define the types of internal and external validity threats in an experiment.
- Distinguish between between-group and within-group experiments.
- Describe steps in conducting an experimental or quasi-experimental study.
- Identify criteria for evaluating an experimental study.

Maria decides to conduct an experiment. She studies the question, "Do students who receive in-class instruction about the dangers of weapons in high school have different attitudes toward weapons than do students who do not receive instruction about the dangers?" Using two health classes to participate in her experiment, she gives one class the standard health curriculum, and the other class a standard curriculum plus a series of classes about the dangers of weapons among teenagers. At the end of the semester, she administers a survey measuring attitudes toward weapons in schools. Maria finds that the students who experienced the curriculum plus the classes about the dangers of weapons were more negative toward weapons in schools than the students who had the standard health curriculum.

WHAT IS AN EXPERIMENT?

In an **experiment**, you test an idea (or practice or procedure) to determine whether it influences an outcome or dependent variable. You first decide on an idea with which to "experiment," assign individuals to experience it (and have some individuals experience something different), and then determine whether those who experienced the idea (or practice or procedure) performed better on some outcome than those who did not experience it. In Maria's experiment, she tested whether the special health curriculum changed student's attitudes toward weapons in schools.

When Do You Use an Experiment?

You use an experiment when you want to establish possible cause and effect between your independent and dependent variables. This means that you attempt to control all variables that influence the outcome except for the independent variable. Then, when the independent variable *influences* the dependent variable, we can say the independent variable "caused" or "probably caused" the dependent variable. Because experiments are controlled, they are the best of the quantitative designs to use to establish probable cause and effect. (We introduced the idea of probable cause and effect in chapter 5.) For example, if you compare one group that experiences a lecture and another group that experiences discussion, you control all of the factors that might influence the outcome of "high scores on a quiz." You make sure that personal abilities and test conditions are the same for both groups, and you give both groups the same questions. You control for all variables that might influence the outcome except for the difference in types of instruction (lecture or discussion). You also use an experiment when you have two or more groups to study, as in this lecture versus discussion example.

When Did Experiments Develop?

Experimental research began in the late 19th and early 20th centuries, with psychological experiments. By 1903, Schuyler used experimental and control groups, and his use became so commonplace that he felt no need to provide a rationale for them. Then in 1916, McCall advanced the idea of randomly assigning individuals to groups (Campbell & Stanley, 1963). Authoring a major book in 1925, *How to Conduct an Experiment*, McCall firmly established the procedure of comparing groups. In addition, by 1936, Fisher's book *Statistical Methods for Research Workers* discussed statistical procedures useful in experiments in psychology and agriculture. In this book, Fisher advanced the concept of randomly assigning individuals to groups before starting an experiment. Other developments in statistical procedures at this time (e.g., chi-square goodness of fit and critical values) and the testing of the significance of differences (e.g., Fisher's 1935 *The Design of Experiments*) enhanced experimental research in education. Between 1926 and 1963, five sets of textbooks on statistics had undergone multiple editions (Huberty, 1993).

By 1963, Campbell and Stanley had identified the major types of experimental designs. They specified 15 different types and evaluated each design in terms of potential threats to validity. These designs are still popular today. Then, in 1979, Cook and Campbell elaborated on the types of designs, expanding the discussion about validity threats. These two books—Campbell and Stanley and Cook and Campbell—established the basic designs, the notation, the visual representation, the potential threats to designs, and the statistical procedures of educational experiments.

Since the 1980s, experiments have grown in sophistication and complexity, largely because of computers and improved statistical procedures. Researchers now employ multiple independent and dependent variables, compare more than two groups, and study different types of experimental units of analysis, such as entire organizations, groups, and individuals (Boruch, 1998; W. L. Neuman, 2000). Procedural refinements represent the latest development in experiments, and a number of "how to" books (e.g., Bausell, 1994) are available for the educational researcher. Also, books that link statistical procedures with experimental design in terms of designing sensitive experiments (e.g., Lipsey, 1990) represent new ideas about strengthening procedures in experimental studies.

WHAT ARE KEY CHARACTERISTICS OF EXPERIMENTS?

Before you consider how to conduct an experiment, you will find it helpful to understand in more depth several key ideas central to experimental research. These ideas are:

- Random assignment
- Control over extraneous variables
- Manipulation of the treatment conditions
- Outcome measures
- Group comparisons
- Threats to validity

To make this discussion as applied as possible, we will use an educational example to illustrate these ideas. A researcher seeks to study ways to encourage adolescents to reduce or stop smoking. A high school has an in-house program to treat individuals caught smoking on school grounds. In this large metropolitan high school, many students smoke, and the smoking infractions each year are numerous. Students caught take a special civics class (all students are required to take civics anyway) in which the teacher introduces a special unit on the health hazards of smoking. In this unit, the teacher discusses health issues, uses images and pictures of the damaged lungs of smokers, and has students write about their experiences as smokers. This instructor offers several civics classes during a semester, and we will refer to this experimental situation as the "civics–smoking experiment."

Random Assignment

As an experimental researcher, you will assign individuals to groups. The most rigorous approach is to randomly assign individuals to the treatments. **Random assignment** is the process of assigning individuals at random to groups or to different groups in an experiment. The random assignment of individuals to groups (or conditions within a group) distinguishes a rigorous, "true" experiment from an adequate, but less-than-rigorous, "quasi-experiment" (to be discussed later in the chapter).

You use random assignment so that any bias in the personal characteristics of individuals in the experiment is distributed equally among the groups. By randomization, you provide *control* for extraneous characteristics of the participants that might influence the outcome (e.g., student ability, attention span, motivation). The experimental term for this process is "equating" the groups. **Equating the groups** means that the researcher randomly assigns individuals to groups and equally distributes any variability of individuals between or among the groups or conditions in the experiment. In practice, personal factors that participants bring to an experiment can never be totally controlled—some bias or error will always affect the outcome of a study. However, by systematically distributing this potential error among groups, the researcher theoretically distributes the bias randomly. In our civics–smoking experiment, the researcher can take the list of offender smokers in the school and randomly assign them to one of two special civics classes.

You should not confuse random assignment with **random selection**. Both are important in quantitative research, but they serve different purposes. As mentioned in chapter 6, quantitative researchers randomly select a sample from a population. In this way, the sample is representative of the population and you can generalize results obtained during the study to the population.

Experiments often do not include random selection of participants for several reasons. Participants often are individuals who are available to take part in the experiment or who volunteer to participate. Although random selection is important in experiments, it may not be logistically possible. However, the most sophisticated type of experiment involves random assignment.

In the civics–smoking experiment, you may randomly select individuals from the population of offender smokers (especially if there are too many for the special civics classes). However, you will most likely place all of the offenders in the special civics classes, giving you control over random assignment rather than random selection.

Control Over Extraneous Variables

In randomly assigning individuals, we say that we are controlling for extraneous variables that might influence the relationship between the new practice (e.g., discussions on health hazards) and the outcome (e.g., frequency of smoking). **Extraneous factors** are any influences in the selection of participants, the procedures, the statistics, or the design likely to affect the outcome and provide an alternative explanation for our results than what we expected. All experiments have some random error (where the scores do not reflect the "true" scores of the population) that you cannot control, but you can try to control extraneous factors as much as possible. Random assignment is a decision made by the investigator *before* the experiment begins. Other control procedures you can use both before and during the experiment are pretests, covariates, matching of participants, homogeneous samples, and blocking variables.

Pretests and Posttests

To "equate" the characteristics of the groups, experimental researchers may use a pretest. Assume that we are interested in whether the special civics class affects students' attitudes toward smoking. In this experiment, we could measure attitudes before the treatment (i.e., by discussing health hazards) and after, to see if the discussion has an effect on student attitudes. In this experiment, we need a pretest to measure students' attitudes.

A **pretest** provides a measure on some attribute or characteristic that you assess for participants in an experiment *before* they receive a treatment. After the treatment, you take another reading on the attribute or characteristic. A **posttest** is a measure on some attribute or characteristic that is assessed for participants in an experiment *after* a treatment. In our example, this would be assessing students' attitudes toward smoking at the end of the semester after the experimental treatment. A pretest–posttest comparison of attitudes toward smoking would provide a clearer reading on actual smoking behavior than using the posttest measure alone would.

Pretests have advantages as well as disadvantages. They take time and effort to administer (e.g., students have to fill out an instrument early in the semester). They can also raise the participants' expectations about the outcome (e.g., students might anticipate questions later about their smoking attitudes and inflate or deflate their responses later in the semester). The pretest may influence the experimental treatment (e.g., students may ask questions about the treatment because of the pretest on attitudes toward smoking). When attitudinal or achievement tests are used as pretests, the scores may also affect posttest scores because participants can anticipate the questions on the posttest based on their experiences with the pretest.

Covariates

Because pretests may affect aspects of the experiment, they are often statistically controlled for by using the procedure of covariance rather than by simply comparing them with posttest scores. **Covariates** are variables that the researcher controls for using statistics and that relate to the dependent variable but that do not relate to the independent variable. The researcher needs to control for these variables, which have the potential to covary with the dependent variable. Often, these variables are scores on a pretest, but they might be any variables correlated with the dependent variable. The statistical procedure of analysis of covariance adjusts the scores on the dependent variable to account for the covariance. This procedure becomes another means for equating the groups and controlling for potential influences that might affect the dependent variable.

An illustration related to our civics–smoking example shows how the researcher removes the variance between a covariate and a dependent variable to assess the variance between the independent and dependent variable. Examine Figure 11.1, which portrays two sets of circles. The left side shows two variables, an independent variable and a dependent variable, without a covariate. The darkened area indicates the variability in rates of smoking by type of instruction; the unexplained variability (called error) is shown with a hatch mark. On the right side of Figure 11.1, we introduce a covariate: parents who smoke. Now we can see that the explained variance increases, and the total amount of unexplained variability (error) actually decreases because we explain more variance. By adding a covariate related to parents who smoke, the researcher increases the amount of explained variance in rates of smoking and decreases the unexplained variance. The statistical procedure of covariance (see chapter 7) removes the variance shared by the covariate and the dependent variable, so that the variance between the independent and dependent variable (plus error) is all that remains. This test allows the researcher to assess accurately the relationship between the treatment and the outcome (i.e., rate of smoking) because of a reduction in the amount of error.

Matching of Participants

Another procedure used for control in an experiment is to match participants on one or more personal characteristics. **Matching** is the process of identifying one or more personal characteristics that influence the outcome and assigning individuals with that characteristic equally to the experimental and control groups. Typically, experimental researchers match on one or two of the following characteristics: gender, pretest scores, or individual abilities.

For example, examine Figure 11.2, which displays matching individuals (say, 10 girls and boys) on gender to the experimental and control groups. Returning to our high school civics–smoking experiment, we might assign the student smokers equally to two special civics classes (assuming that one class receives the treatment and the other does not) based on gender. In this way, our prior knowledge, for example, that boys may smoke more than girls, controls for the potential influence of gender on frequency of smoking. Procedurally, this matching process means assigning the first boy to the control group, the second to the experimental, the third to the control, and so forth.

FIGURE 11.1

Controlling for Covariate

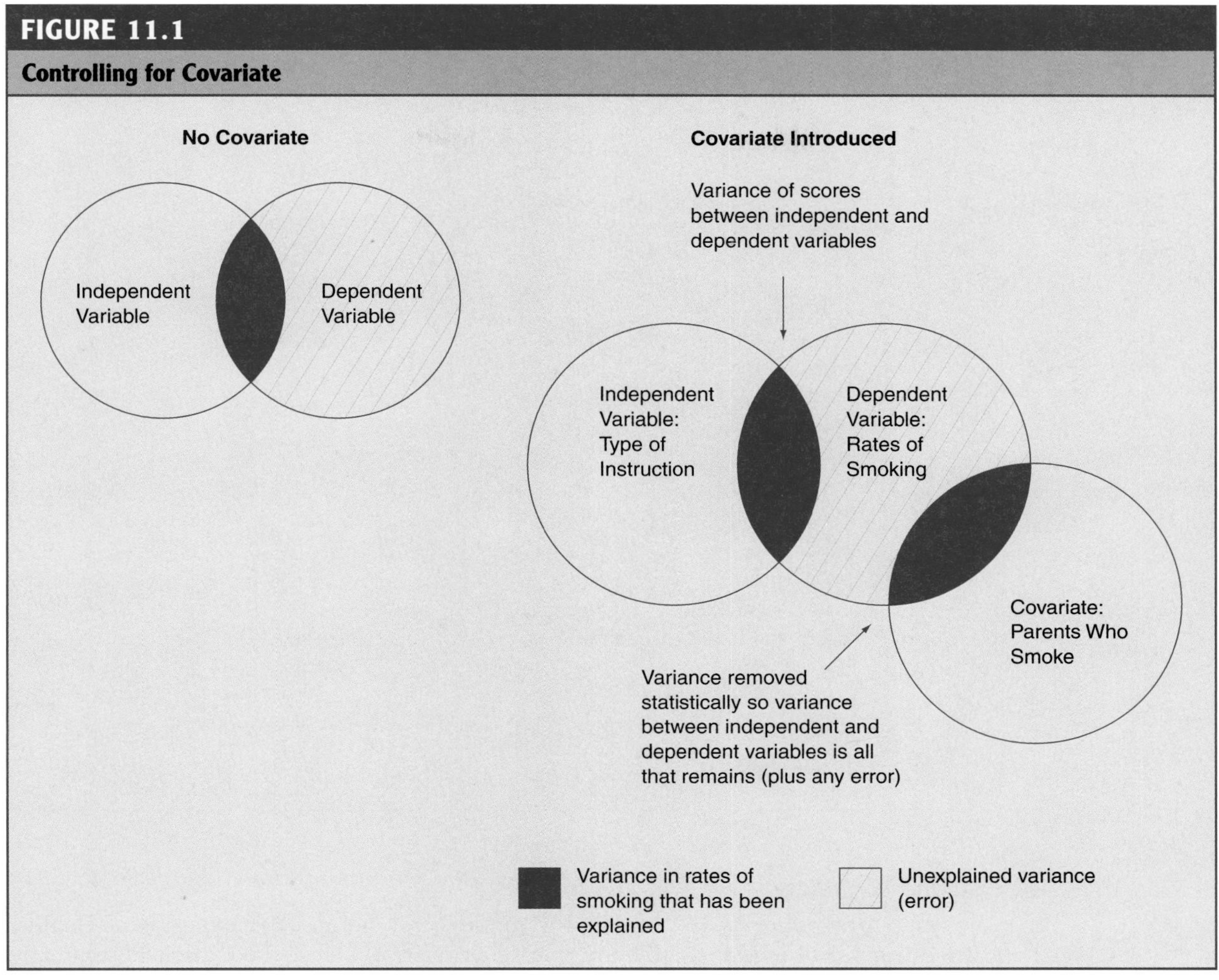

The researcher repeats this process for girls. By using this procedure, we control before the experiment begins for the potential extraneous factor of gender in the experiment.

Homogeneous Samples

Another approach used to make the groups comparable is to choose **homogeneous samples** by selecting people who vary little in their personal characteristics. For example, we might assume that the students in the two civics classes (one receives the lecture on "health hazards" and the second does not) are similar in terms of characteristics that students bring to the experiment, such as their academic grade point average, gender, racial group (e.g., Caucasian, African American), or prior abilities in civics. When the experimenter assigns students to the two classes, the more similar they are in personal characteristics or attributes, the more these characteristics or attributes are controlled in the experiment. For example, if all of the smokers assigned to the two civics classes were juniors, then class level would be controlled in the experiment. Unfortunately, this situation is unlikely to occur in our civics–smoking study, and the researcher may need to use other procedures to control for individuals belonging to different grade levels.

FIGURE 11.2

The Matching Process Based on Gender

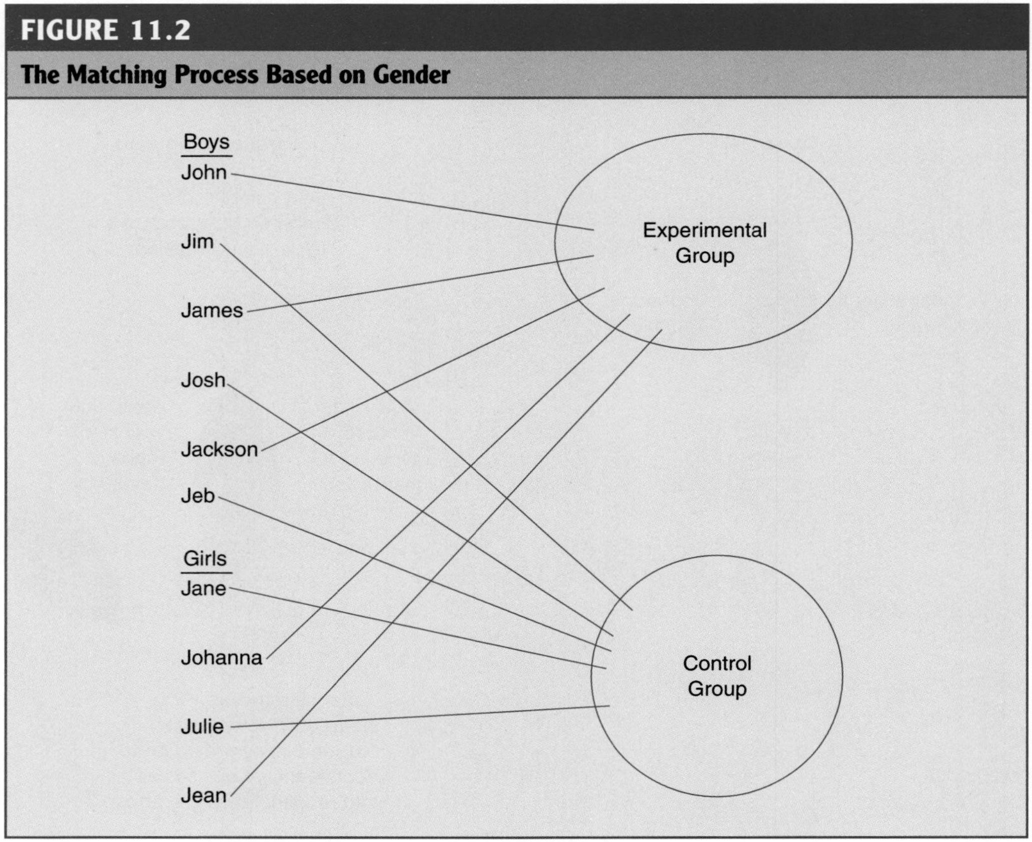

Blocking Variables

One such procedure is to "block" for grade level before the experiment begins. A **blocking variable** is a variable the researcher controls before the experiment starts by dividing (or "blocking") the participants into subgroups (or categories) and analyzing the impact of each subgroup on the outcome. The variable (e.g., gender) can be blocked into males and females; similarly, high school grade level can be blocked into four categories: freshmen, sophomores, juniors, and seniors. In this procedure, the researcher forms homogeneous subgroups by choosing a characteristic common to all participants in the study (e.g., gender or different age categories). Then the investigator randomly assigns individuals to the control and experimental groups using each category of the variable. For example, if the students who participate in the experiment are 15 and 16 years old, you assign an equal number of 15- and 16-year-olds to the control and experimental groups.

Manipulating Treatment Conditions

Once you select participants, you randomly assign them to either a treatment condition or the experimental group. In **experimental treatment**, the researcher physically intervenes to alter the conditions experienced by the experimental unit (e.g., a reward for good spelling performance or a special type of classroom instruction, such as small-group discussion).

In our example, the researcher in the high school example would manipulate one form of instruction in the special civics class—providing activities on the health hazards of smoking. Specifically, the procedure would be:

Identify a treatment variable: type of classroom instruction in the civics class

Identify the conditions (or levels) of the variable: classroom instruction can be (a) regular topics or (b) topics related to the health hazards of smoking

Manipulate the treatment conditions: provide special activities on health hazards of smoking to one class and withhold them from another class

These procedures introduce several new concepts that we will discuss using specific examples so that you can see how they work.

Treatment Variables

In experiments, you need to focus on the independent variable. Remember from chapter 5 that these variables influence or affect the dependent variable in a quantitative study. Recall as well that the two major types of independent variables were *treatment* and *measured* variables. In experiments, treatment variables are independent variables that the researcher manipulates to determine their effect on the outcome, or dependent variable. Treatment variables are categorical variables measured using categorical scales, as discussed in chapter 6. For example, treatment independent variables used in educational experiments might be:

- Type of instruction (small group, large group)
- Type of reading group (phonics readers, whole-language readers)

Conditions

In both of these examples, we have two categories within each treatment variable. In experiments, treatment variables need to have two or more categories, or levels. In an experiment, **levels** are categories of a treatment variable. For example, you might divide type of instruction into (a) standard civics lecture, (b) standard civics lecture plus discussion about health hazards, and (c) standard civics lecture plus discussion about health hazards and slides of damaged lungs. In this example, we have a three-level treatment variable.

Intervening in the Treatment Conditions

The experimental researcher manipulates one or more of the treatment variable conditions. In other words, in an experiment, the researcher physically intervenes (or manipulates with **interventions**) in one or more condition so that individuals experience something different in the experimental conditions than in the control condition. This means that to conduct an experiment, you need to be able to manipulate at least one condition of an independent variable. It is easy to identify some situations in which you might measure an independent variable and obtain categorical data but not be able to manipulate one of the conditions. As shown in Figure 11.3, the researcher measures three independent variables—age, gender, and type of instruction—but only type of instruction (more specifically, two conditions within it) is manipulated. The treatment variable—type of instruction—is a categorical variable with three conditions (or levels). Some students can receive a lecture—the traditional form of instruction in the class (the control group). Others receive something new, such as a lecture plus the health-hazards discussion (a comparison group) or lecture plus the health-hazards discussion plus slides of lungs damaged by smoking (another comparison group). In summary, experimental researchers manipulate or intervene with one or more conditions of a treatment variable.

FIGURE 11.3

The Experimental Manipulation of a Treatment Condition

Independent Variables	*Dependent Variable*
1. Age (cannot manipulate) 2. Gender (cannot manipulate) 3. Types of instruction (can manipulate) a. Some receive lecture (control) b. Some receive lecture plus health-hazard discussion (comparison) c. Some receive lecture plus health-hazard discussion plus slides of lungs damaged by smoking (experimental)	Frequency of Smoking

OUTCOMES MEASURES

In all experimental situations, you assess whether a treatment condition influences an outcome or dependent variable, such as a reduced rate of smoking or achievement on tests. In experiments, the **outcome** (or *response, criterion,* or *posttest*) is the dependent variable that is the presumed effect of the treatment variable. It is also the effect predicted in a hypothesis in the cause-and-effect equation. Examples of dependent variables in experiments might be:

- Achievement scores on a criterion-referenced test
- Test scores on an aptitude test

Good outcome measures are sensitive to treatments in that they respond to the smallest amount of intervention. Outcome measures (as well as treatment variables) also need to be valid so that experimental researchers can draw valid inferences from them.

Group Comparisons

In an experiment, you also compare scores for different treatments on an outcome. A **group comparison** is the process of a researcher obtaining scores for individuals or groups on the dependent variable and comparing the means and variance both within the group and between the groups. (See Keppel, 1991, for detailed statistical procedures for this process.)

To visualize this process, let's consider some actual data from an experiment by Gettinger (1993), who sought to determine the effects of an error correction procedure on the spelling of third graders. As shown in Figure 11.4, we visualize Gettinger's experiment in three ways. Gettinger examined whether the error correction procedure related positively to spelling accuracy (Phase 1). She then created three groups of students: Class A, Class B, and Class C. Class A (the control group) received regular spelling practice on 15 words, consisting of workbook exercises, writing sentences containing each word, and studying words on their own. Class B (the comparison group) had the same experience except that they studied a reduced number of words on a list—three sets of five words each. Class C (the experimental group) used an error-and-correction practice procedure consisting of correcting their own tests, noting incorrect words, and writing both the incorrect and correct spelling for each word. As shown in Phase 2, all three groups received the same spelling practice for 6 weeks, then the experimental group received the error correction procedure for 6 weeks, and after a third 6 weeks, all three groups

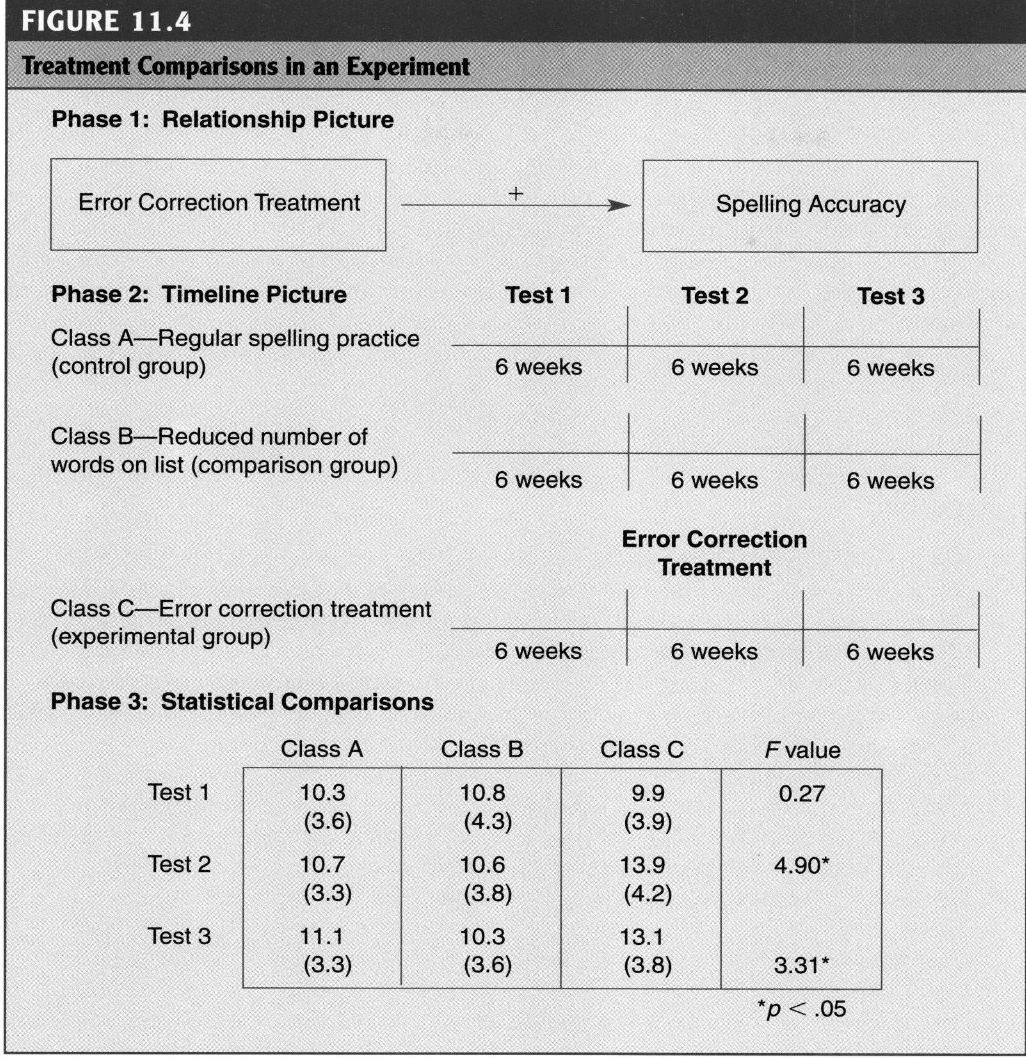

	Class A	Class B	Class C	*F* value
Test 1	10.3 (3.6)	10.8 (4.3)	9.9 (3.9)	0.27
Test 2	10.7 (3.3)	10.6 (3.8)	13.9 (4.2)	4.90*
Test 3	11.1 (3.3)	10.3 (3.6)	13.1 (3.8)	3.31*

*$p < .05$

FIGURE 11.4
Treatment Comparisons in an Experiment

Source: Based on Gettinger, 1993.

were tested. Phase 3 shows the statistical comparisons made among the three groups on each of the three tests. Class A improved slightly (from 10.3 on Test 1 to 11.1 on Test 3), whereas Class B's scores decreased over the three tests. Class C, the experimental group, improved considerably. *F*-test values showed that the scores varied significantly on Test 2 and Test 3 when the researcher compared the groups. These statistical comparisons took into consideration both the mean scores and the variation between and within each group to arrive at statistical significance at $p < .05$.

Threats to Validity

A final idea in experiments is to design them so that you minimize compromises in drawing good conclusions from the scores you obtain in the experiment. A **threat to validity** means that design issues may threaten the experiment so that the conclusions reached from data may provide a false reading about probable cause and effect between the treatment and the outcome. Although authors identify threats such as not having good measures or using inappropriate statistics, two commonly discussed threats of internal validity and external validity will be our focus (Bracht & Glass, 1968; Campbell & Stanley, 1963; Cook & Campbell, 1979).

Threats to Internal Validity

A number of threats to drawing appropriate inferences relate to the actual design and procedures used in an experiment. **Threats to internal validity** are problems that threaten our abitity to draw correct cause-and-effect inferences that arise because of the experimental procedures or the experiences of participants. Of all of the threats to validity, these are the most severe because they can compromise an otherwise good experiment. The following threats to internal validity and recommended procedures to address them are widely discussed in the literature about experimental designs (see Cook & Campbell, 1979; Reichardt & Mark, 1998; Tuckman, 1999). To make each potential threat as realistic as possible, we illustrate them using the hypothetical situation of the civics–smoking experiment.

The first category addresses threats *related to participants* in the study and their experiences:

- *History:* Time passes between the beginning of the experiment and the end, and events may occur (e.g., additional discussions about the hazards of smoking besides the treatment lecture) between the pretest and posttest that influence the outcome. In educational experiments, it is impossible to have a tightly controlled environment and monitor all events. However, the researcher can have the control and experimental groups experience the same activities (except for the treatment) during the experiment.
- *Maturation:* Individuals develop or change during the experiment (i.e., become older, wiser, stronger, and more experienced), and these changes may affect their scores between the pretest and posttest. A careful selection of participants who mature or develop in a similar way (e.g., individuals at the same grade level) for both the control and experimental groups helps guard against this problem.
- *Regression:* When researchers select individuals for a group based on extreme scores, they will naturally do better (or worse) on the posttest than the pretest regardless of the treatment. Scores from individuals, over time, regress toward the mean. For example, the selection of heavy smokers for an experiment will probably contribute to lower rates of smoking after treatment because the teens selected started with high rates at the beginning of the experiment. The selection of individuals who do not have extreme scores on entering characteristics (e.g., moderate smokers or average scores on pretests) may help solve this problem.
- *Selection:* "People factors" may introduce threats that influence the outcome, such as selecting individuals who are brighter, more receptive to a treatment, or more familiar with a treatment (e.g., teen smokers ready to quit) for the experimental group. Random selection may partly address this threat.
- *Mortality:* When individuals drop out during the experiment for any number of reasons (e.g., time, interest, money, friends, parents who do not want them participating in an experiment about smoking), drawing conclusions from scores may be difficult. Researchers need to choose a large sample and compare those who drop out with those who remain in the experiment on the outcome measure.
- *Interactions with selection:* Several of the threats mentioned thus far can interact (or relate) with the selection of participants to add additional threats to an experiment. Individuals selected may mature at different rates (e.g., 16-year-old boys and girls may mature at different rates during the study). Historical events may interact with selection because individuals in different groups come from different settings. For instance,

vastly different socioeconomic backgrounds of students in the teen smoking experiment may introduce uncontrolled historical factors into the selection of student participants. The selection of participants may also influence the instrument scores, especially when different groups score at different mean positions on a test whose intervals are not equal. If the scale for measuring number of cigarettes is ambiguous (e.g., number of cigarettes per week or per day?) groups are likely to interpret the scale differently.

The next category addresses threats *related to treatments* used in the study:

- *Diffusion of treatments:* When the experimental and control groups can communicate with each other, the control group may learn from the experimental group information about the treatment and create a threat to internal validity. The diffusion of treatments (experimental and nonexperimental) for the control and experimental groups needs to be different. As much as possible, experimental researchers need to keep the two groups separate in an experiment (e.g., have two different civic classes participate in the experiment). This may be difficult when, for example, two civic classes of students in the same grade in the same high school are involved in an experiment about teen smoking.
- *Compensatory equalization:* When only the experimental group receives a treatment, an inequality exists that may threaten the validity of the study. The benefits (i.e., the goods or services believed to be desirable) of the experimental treatment need to be equally distributed among the groups in the study. To counter this problem, researchers use comparison groups (e.g., one group receives the health-hazard lecture, whereas the other receives a handout about the problems of teen smoking) so that all groups receive some benefits during an experiment.
- *Compensatory rivalry:* If you publicly announce assignments to the control and experimental groups, compensatory rivalry may develop between the groups because the control group feels that it is the "underdog." Researchers can try to avoid this threat by attempting to reduce the awareness and expectations of the presumed benefits of the experimental treatment.
- *Resentful demoralization:* When a control group is used, individuals in this group may become resentful and demoralized because they perceive that they receive a less desirable treatment than other groups. One remedy to this threat is for experimental researchers to provide a treatment to this group after the experiment has concluded (e.g., after the experiment, all classes receive the lecture on the health hazards of smoking). Researchers may also provide services equally attractive to the experimental treatment but not directed toward the same outcome as the treatment (e.g., a class discussion about the hazards of teen driving with friends).

The following category addresses threats that typically occur during an experiment and *relate to the procedures* of the study:

- *Testing:* A potential threat to internal validity is that participants may become familiar with the outcome measures and remember responses for later testing. During some experiments, the outcome is measured more than one time, such as in pretests (e.g., repeated measures of number of cigarettes smoked). To remedy this situation, experimental researchers measure the outcome less frequently and use different items on the posttest than those used during earlier testing.
- *Instrumentation:* Between the administration of a pretest and a posttest, the instrument may change, introducing a potential threat to the internal validity of the experiment. For example, observers may become more experienced during the time between a pretest and the posttest and change their scoring procedures (e.g., observers change the location to observe teen smoking). Less frequently, the

measuring instrument may change so that the scales used on a pretest and a posttest are dissimilar. To correct for this potential problem, you standardize procedures so that you use the same observational scales or instrument throughout the experiment.

Threats to External Validity

By ruling out extraneous factors and assuming that the treatment influences an outcome, researchers make claims about the generalizability of the results. **Threats to external validity** are problems that threaten our ability to draw correct inferences from the sample data to other persons, settings, and past and future situations. According to Cook and Campbell (1979), three threats may affect this generalizability:

- *Interaction of selection and treatment:* This threat to external validity involves the inability to generalize beyond the groups in the experiment, such as other racial, social, geographical, age, gender, or personality groups. One strategy researchers use to increase generalizability is to make participation in the experiment as convenient as possible for all individuals in a population.
- *Interaction of setting and treatment:* This threat to external validity arises from the inability to generalize from the setting where the experiment occurred to another setting. For example, private high schools may be different from public high schools, and the results from our civics experiment on smoking may not apply outside the public high school where the researcher conducts the experiment. This threat may also result from trying to generalize results from one level in an organization to another. For example, you cannot generalize treatment effects you obtain from studying entire school districts to specific high schools. The practical solution to an interaction of setting and treatment is for the researcher to analyze the effect of a treatment for each type of setting.
- *Interaction of history and treatment:* This threat to external validity develops when the researcher tries to generalize findings to past and future situations. Experiments may take place at a special time (e.g., at the beginning of the school year) and may not produce similar results if conducted earlier (e.g., students attending school in the summer may be different from students attending school during the regular year) or later (e.g., during semester break). One solution is to replicate the study at a later time rather than trying to generalize results to other times.

In our civics–smoking experiment, the researcher needs to be cautious about generalizing results to other high schools, other students in civics classes, and other situations where discussions about the hazards of smoking take place. The behavior of adolescents who smoke may change due to factors associated with the cost of cigarettes, parental disapproval, and advertising. Because of these factors, it is difficult to generalize the results from our civics experiment to other situations.

WHAT ARE THE TYPES OF EXPERIMENTAL DESIGNS?

Although all experiments have common characteristics, their use and applications vary depending on the type of design used. The most common designs you will find in educational research are:

- Between-Group Designs
    - True experiments (pre- and posttest, posttest only)
    - Quasi-experiments (pre- and posttest, posttest only)
    - Factorial designs

- Within-Group or Individual Designs
  - Time series experiments (interrupted, equivalent)
  - Repeated measures experiments
  - Single-subject experiments

Being able to identify these types of designs and their major characteristics will help you choose a suitable design for your study or permit a thoughtful evaluation of an experimental design used in a published study.

A basic set of criteria for differentiating among types of experimental designs is shown in Table 11.1. As we discuss each of the designs, keep these criteria in mind to help you distinguish among them. The designs are differentiated by several characteristics, as shown in the first column in Table 11.1:

- The random assignment of participants to groups
- The number of groups or individuals being compared
- The number of interventions used by the researcher
- The number of times the dependent variable is measured or observed
- The control of extraneous variables

For each design discussed in the following pages, you will be introduced to the major characteristics of the design and its advantages and disadvantages. Among the disadvantages are its potential threats to internal validity—an idea already introduced—but now related specifically to each design. Table 11.2 presents a summary of the internal validity threats for each design.

Remember that Maria studied two health classes for her experiment. She gave one class the standard health curriculum and provided the other class the standard curriculum plus a

TABLE 11.1

Types of Experimental Designs

	True Experiment	**Quasi-Experiment**	**Factorial**	**Time Series**	**Repeated Measures**	**Single Subject**
Random assignment?	Yes	No	May be used	No	No	No
Number of groups/ individuals compared?	Two or more	Two or more	Two or more	One group	One group	One individual studied at a time
Number of interventions used?	One or more interventions	One or more interventions	Two or more interventions	One or more interventions	Two or more interventions	One or more interventions
Number of times the dependent variables measured/ observed?	Once	Once	Once	After each intervention	After each intervention	Multiple points
Controls typically used?	Pretest, matching, blocking, covariates	Pretest, matching, blocking, covariates	Pretest, matching, blocking, covariates	Group becomes its own control	Covariates	Individuals become their own controls

TABLE 11.2

Threats to Internal Validity in Types of Experimental Designs

	True Experiment	Quasi-Experiment	Factorial	Time Series	Repeated Measures	Single Subject
To Participants:						
History	Controlled	Potential threat	Controlled, if random assignment	May be a threat if short intervals not used	May be a threat if short intervals not used	Potential threat
Maturation	Controlled	Potential threat	Controlled, random assignment	Can be controlled if pattern detected	Controlled	Controlled
Regression	Controlled	Potential threat	Controlled, random assignment	Can be controlled if unusual, scores noted	Controlled	Controlled
Selection	Controlled	Potential threat	Controlled, if random assignment	Controlled	Controlled	Controlled
Mortality	Controlled	Potential threat	Controlled, if random assignment	Can be controlled if dropouts noted	Controlled	Controlled
Interaction of selection and maturation, history, and instrumentation	Controlled	Potential threat	Controlled, if random assignment	Controlled	Controlled	Controlled
To Procedures:						
Testing	Potential threat if pre- and posttest used	Potential threat if pre- and posttest used	Potential threat if a pre- and posttest used	With repeated measures and observations before (interrupted design), likely to diminish over time	Potential threat if pre- and posttest used	Controlled
Instrumentation	Potential threat if instrument or observational procedures change	Potential threat if instrument or observational procedures change	Potential threat if instrument or observational procedures change	Can be controlled if procedures monitored	Can be controlled if procedures monitored	May be a threat if multiple interventions used

series of classes about the dangers of weapons among teenagers. What type of experimental design should she use? Maria has a between-group design (a quasi-experiment) without random assignment because she uses two intact classes in her experiment. As you read the discussion about a between-group design, see how you would come to this same decision.

Between-Group Designs

The most frequently used designs in education are those where the researcher compares two or more groups. Illustrations throughout this chapter underscore the importance of these designs. We will begin with the most rigorous between-group design available to the educational researcher, the true experiment.

True Experiments

True experiments comprise the most rigorous and strong experimental designs because of equating the groups through random assignment. The procedure for conducting major forms of true experiments and quasi-experiments, viewing them in terms of activities from the beginning of the experiment to the end, is shown in Table 11.3. In **true experiments**, the researcher randomly assigns participants to different conditions of the experimental variable. Individuals in the experimental group receive the experimental treatment, whereas those in the control group do not. After investigators administer the treatment, they compile average (or mean) scores on a posttest. One variation on this design is to obtain pretest as well as posttest measures or observations. When experimenters collect pretest scores, they may compare net scores (the differences between the pre- and posttests). Alternatively, investigators may relate the pretest scores for the control and experimental groups to see if they are statistically similar, and then compare the two posttest group scores. In many experiments, the pretest is a covariate and is statistically controlled by the researcher.

Because you randomly assign individuals to the groups, most of the threats to internal validity do not arise. Randomization or equating of the groups minimizes the possibility of history, maturation, selection, and the interactions between selection and other threats. Treatment threats such as diffusion, rivalry, resentful demoralization, and compensatory equalization are all possibilities in a between-group design because two or more groups exist in the design. When true experiments include only a posttest, it reduces the threats of testing, instrumentation, and regression because you do not use a pretest. If a pretest is used, it introduces all of these factors as possible threats to validity. Instrumentation exists as a potential threat in most experiments, but if researchers use the same or similar instrument for the pre- and posttest or enact standard procedures during the study, you hold instrumentation threats to a minimum.

Quasi-Experiments

In education, many experimental situations occur in which researchers need to use intact groups. This might happen because of the availability of the participants or because the setting prohibits forming artificial groups. **Quasi-experiments** include assignment, but not random assignment of participants to groups. This is because the experimenter cannot artificially create groups for the experiment. For example, studying a new math program may require using existing fourth-grade classes and designating one as the experimental group and one as the control group. Randomly assigning students to the two groups would disrupt classroom learning. Because educators often use intact groups (schools, colleges, or school districts) in experiments, quasi-experimental designs are frequently used.

Returning to Table 11.3, we can apply the pre- and posttest design approach to a quasi-experimental design. The researcher assigns intact groups the experimental and control treatments, administers a pretest to both groups, conducts experimental treatment

TABLE 11.3

Types of Between-Group Designs

True Experimental Designs

Pre- and Posttest Design — Time →

Random assignment	Control Group	Pretest	No Treatment	Posttest
Random assignment	Experimental Group	Pretest	Experimental Treatment	Posttest

Posttest-Only Design — Time →

Random assignment	Control Group	No Treatment	Posttest
Random assignment	Experimental Group	Experimental Treatment	Posttest

Quasi-Experimental Designs

Pre- and Posttest Design — Time →

Select Control Group	Pretest	No Treatment	Posttest
Select Experimental Group	Pretest	Experimental Treatment	Posttest

Posttest-Only Design — Time →

Select Control Group	No Treatment	Posttest
Select Experimental Group	Experimental Treatment	Posttest

activities with the experimental group only, and then administers a posttest to assess the differences between the two groups. A variation on this approach, similar to the true experiment, uses only a posttest in the design.

The quasi-experimental approach introduces considerably more threats to internal validity than the true experiment. Because the investigator does not randomly assign participants to groups, the potential threats of maturation, selection, mortality, and the interaction of selection with other threats are possibilities. Individuals assigned to the two groups may have selection factors that go uncontrolled in the experiment. Because we compare two groups, the treatment threats may also be present. In addition, when the pretest–posttest design is used, additional threats of history, testing, instrumentation, and regression also may occur. While the quasi–experimental design has the advantage of utilizing existing groups in educational settings, it introduces many threats that you need to address in the design of the experiment.

Factorial Designs In some experimental situations, it is not enough to know the effect of a single treatment on an outcome; several treatments may, in fact, provide a better explanation for the outcome. **Factorial designs** represent a modification of the between-group design in which the researcher studies two or more categorical, independent variables, each examined at two or more levels (Vogt, 1999). The purpose of this design is to study the independent and simultaneous effects of two or more independent treatment variables on an outcome.

For example, in our civics–smoking experiment, the researcher may want to examine more than the effect of the type of instruction (i.e., lecture on health hazards of smoking versus standard lecture) on frequency of smoking. Assume that the experimenter wishes to examine the combined influence of type of instruction and level of depression in students (e.g., high, medium, and low scores on a depression scale) on rates of smoking (as the posttest). Assume further that the investigator has reason to believe that depression is an important factor in rates of teen smoking, but its "interaction" or combination with type of smoking is unknown. The study of this research problem requires a factorial design. Thus, "depression" is a blocking or moderating variable and the researcher makes random assignment of each "block" (high, medium, and low) to each treatment instructional group. This design has the advantage of a high level of control in the experiment. It allows the investigator to examine the combination or interaction of independent variables to better understand the results of the experiment. If only a posttest is used, internal validity threats of testing and instrumentation do not exist. If you randomly assign individuals to groups, you minimize the threats related to participants and their experiences (history, maturation, regression, selection, mortality, and interaction of selection and other factors).

However, with multiple independent variables in a factorial design, the statistical procedures become more complex and the actual results become more difficult to understand. What does it mean, for example, that depression and type of instruction interact to influence smoking rates among teens? Which independent variable is more important and why? As researchers manipulate additional independent variables, more participants are needed in each group for statistical tests, and the interpretation of results becomes more complex. Because of this complexity, factorial designs typically include at most three independent variables manipulated by the researcher.

Let's examine more closely the steps in the process of conducting a factorial design. The researcher identifies a research question that includes two independent variables and one dependent variable, such as "Do rates of smoking vary under different combinations of type of instruction and levels of depression?"

To answer this question, the experimenter identifies the levels of each factor or independent variable:

- *Factor 1*—types of instruction
  - Level 1—a health-hazards lecture in civics class
  - Level 2—a standard lecture in civics class
- *Factor 2*—levels of depression
  - Level 1—high
  - Level 2—medium
  - Level 3—low

Because you measure two levels of instruction and three levels of depression, the design is called a *two by three* factorial design. It is written as "2 × 3" to indicate the levels involved in each independent variable. With three independent variables, the design might be a "2 × 3 × 4" design, with the third variable consisting of four levels.

In the 2 × 3 design, the investigator then assigns participants to six groups so that all groups receive each level on one independent variable (e.g., type of instruction) and each level on the second independent variable (e.g., level of depression). Table 11.4 shows the formation of the six groups and the assignment of participants to each group based on the three levels (i.e., low, medium, and high) of depression and the two levels (i.e., health-hazards lecture, standard lecture) of instruction.

In this process, the researcher creates six groups and assigns student smokers to each group. All students first complete the instrument measuring their level of depression. The researcher scores the instrument and divides the students into low, medium, and high groups based on their depression scores. Further, remember that our study is being conducted in two special civics classes; in one class, the students receive a lecture on the health hazards of smoking, and in the second class, the teacher provides standard lectures on civics topics. Thus, in our factorial design, three groups will receive the health lecture in one civics class and the other three groups will receive the standard lectures in the other civics class. This procedure uses quasi-experimental research in which the investigator uses intact classes for the experiment (two high school civics classes).

At the conclusion of the experiment, the investigator asks all participants to complete a posttest. This posttest will measure the rate of smoking for individuals in the experiment. The means of the posttest scores are organized into six cells to visually portray their differences, as shown in Figure 11.5. A *cell* represents each group in an experiment, and it contains the mean scores for individuals in each group. Once you compute the mean scores, you compare the scores to determine whether they are statistically different. The null hypothesis would be that the means are not different, whereas the alternative would be that they are different.

Let's add one more element into this statistical portrait of scores arrayed in cells as shown in Figure 11.5. Using the parametric statistic of ANOVA, as discussed in chapter 7,

TABLE 11.4

Factorial Design Groups Assigned to Two Conditions

	Extent of Depression	Type of Instruction	Dependent Variable
Group 1	Low depression scores	Receives health-hazards lecture	Posttest (scores on instrument measuring smoking)
Group 2	Medium depression scores	Receives health-hazards lecture	Posttest (scores on instrument measuring smoking)
Group 3	High depression scores	Receives health-hazards lecture	Posttest (scores on instrument measuring smoking)
Group 4	Low depression scores	Receives standard lecture	Posttest (scores on instrument measuring smoking)
Group 5	Medium depression scores	Receives standard lecture	Posttest (scores on instrument measuring smoking)
Group 6	High depression scores	Receives standard lecture	Posttest (scores on instrument measuring smoking)

FIGURE 11.5

Means and Main Effects of the Six Groups in the Factorial Design

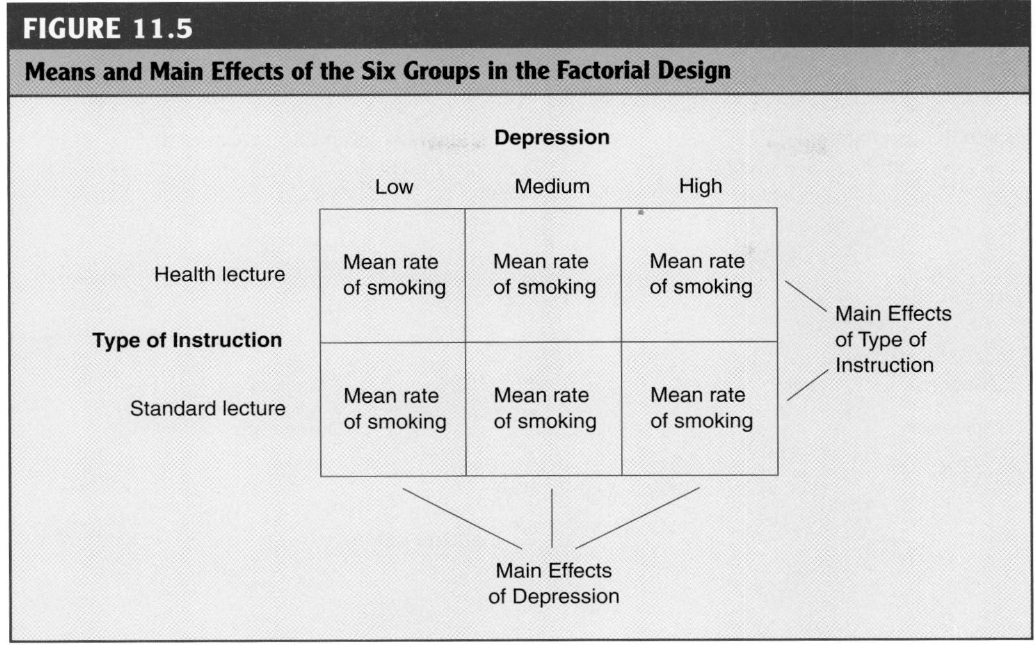

the researcher examines the effect of each independent variable separately and in combination with the dependent variable. Using a statistical software program, analysis of variance will produce statistical results for main effects and interaction effects. **Main effects** are the influence of each independent variable (e.g., type of instruction or extent of depression) on the outcome (e.g., the dependent variable, rate of smoking) in an experiment. **Interaction effects** exist when the influence on one independent variable depends on (or covaries with) the other independent variable in an experiment.

Researchers often graph the main and the interaction effects to help readers visualize them. The graphs in Figure 11.6 portray possible main effects and interaction effects in our hypothetical civics–smoking experiment. Graph (a) displays the results of scores on the posttest (i.e., rate of smoking) and the three factors of depression. The researcher graphs scores for both the groups who receive the health-hazards lecture and the standard lecture in the civics class. As seen in this graph, the extent of smoking for both groups increases with the level of depression. Because the lines are parallel and do not cross, an interaction effect is not present.

However, the results of the experiment could be different, as shown in graphs (b) and (c). In graph (b), the smoking rates for the groups receiving the standard lecture increase as depression increases. Alternatively, smoking rates for students who experience the health-hazards lecture are constant for each level of depression. When these scores are plotted, the lines crossed, showing an interaction effect. In graph (c), the lines again are not parallel, displaying an interaction effect. Typically, in factorial designs, the investigator graphs these trends and explains the meaning of the combination of independent variables.

Within-Group or Individual Designs

In any given experiment, the number of participants may be limited and it may not be possible to involve more than one group. In these cases, researchers study a single group using a **within-group experimental design**. Also, the experimenter might examine

FIGURE 11.6

Graphs of Scores Showing Main Effects and the Interaction Effects

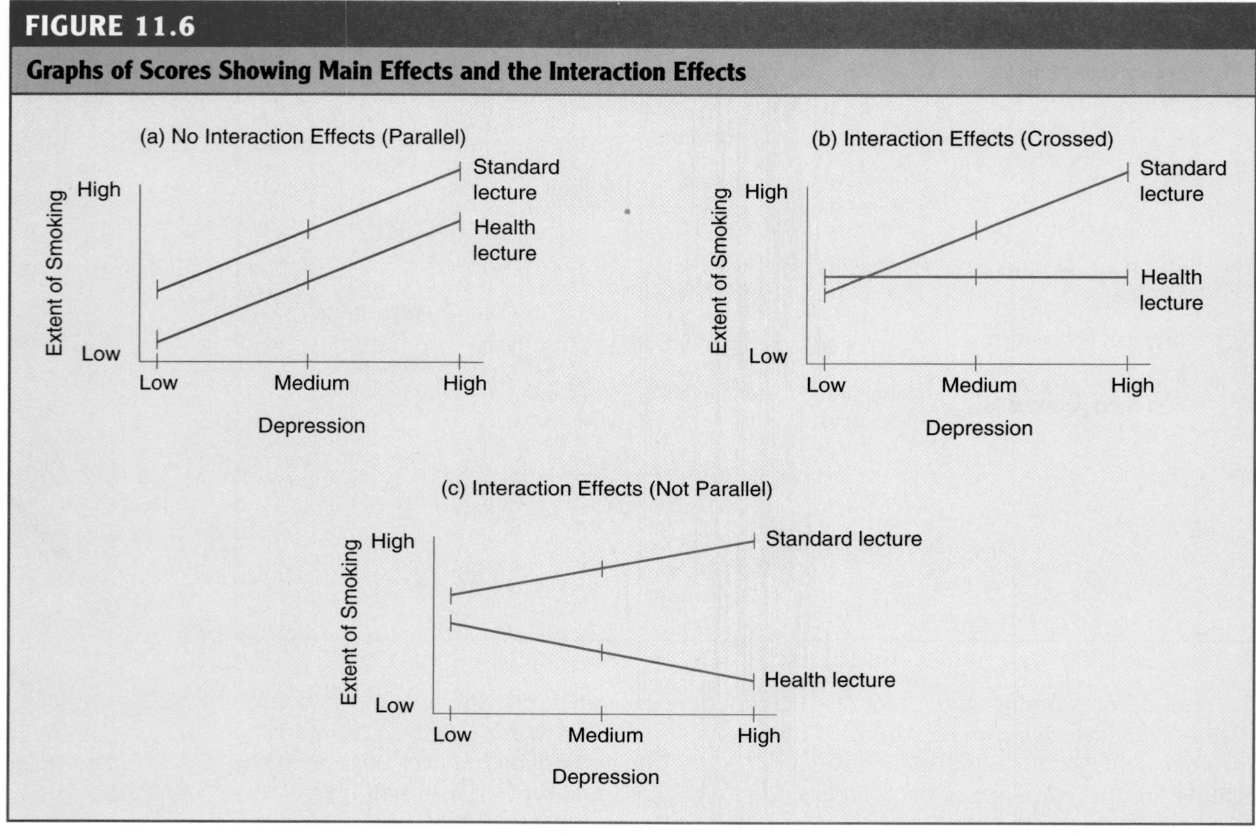

single individuals **(within-individual design)**. This type of design assumes several forms: time series, repeated measures, and single-subject designs.

Time Series

When an experimental researcher has access to only one group and can study them over a period, a time series design is a good experimental approach. A **time series** design consists of studying one group, over time, with multiple pretest and posttest measures or observations made by the researcher. This design does not require access to large numbers of participants, and it requires only one group for the study. It is ideal for examining change in an entire system (e.g., a school district) where it would be difficult to find a control group or system willing to cooperate. However, this design is labor intensive because the researcher needs to gather multiple measures.

These multiple measures are seen in two important variations of this design. As shown in Table 11.5, the first is the **interrupted time series** design. This procedure consists of studying one group, obtaining multiple pretest measures for a period of time, administering an intervention (or interrupting the activities), and then measuring outcomes (or posttests) several times. Data analysis in this example consists of examining difference scores between the pretests and posttests or posttest-only scores and using the pretests as covariates. A variation, also seen in Table 11.5, uses an **equivalent time series** design, in which the investigator alternates a treatment with a posttest measure. The data analysis then consists of comparing posttest measures or plotting them to discern patterns in the data over time.

TABLE 11.5

Time Series Experimental Designs

Interruped Time Series Design

Time →

Select Participants for Group	Pretest Measure or Observation	Pretest Measure or Observation	Pretest Measure or Observation	Intervention	Posttest Measure or Observation	Posttest Measure or Observation	Posttest Measure or Observation

Equivalent Time Series Design

Time →

Select Participants for Group	Measure or Observation	Intervention	Measure or Observation	Intervention	Measure or Observation	Intervention	Measure or Observation

The time series design permits significant control over threats to internal validity. The effects of history are not always clear-cut. History effects are minimized by the short time intervals between measures and observations. However, threats to validity may occur because of the overall length of data collection in this design. The maturation of participants may be a problem, although the researcher can estimate changes in maturation by studying them and removing them statistically in the design. To control for statistical regression, researchers can also observe the scores on the pretests and control for unusually high or low scores. Because only one group is studied, the issues of selection and treatment are not relevant, although individuals can choose to drop out of the study. Testing may be a problem, but the repeated measures or observations over time may diminish the effects of testing. When researchers change the instrument during multiple testing administrations, they may also introduce threats to validity.

In our hypothetical experiment in the high school civics class, our examples thus far consist of studying two civics classes (presumably taught by the same instructor). If only *one* class is available, we could use a time series design that would involve collecting multiple measures of smoking behavior among smokers as pretests. Then the teacher would introduce the intervention "health-hazards discussion," followed by multiple measures of smoking behavior on posttests. A plot of this pretest and posttest data would reveal whether the health lecture contributed to reduced smoking among the students in the class.

Repeated Measures

Another experimental design that has the advantage of employing only a single group is a repeated measures design. In a **repeated measures design**, all participants in a single group participate in all experimental treatments, with each group becoming its own control. The researcher compares a group's performance under one experimental treatment with its performance under another experimental treatment. The experimenter decides on multiple treatments (as in factorial designs) but administers each separately to only one group. After each administration, the researcher obtains a measure or observation. The steps in this design are shown in Table 11.6.

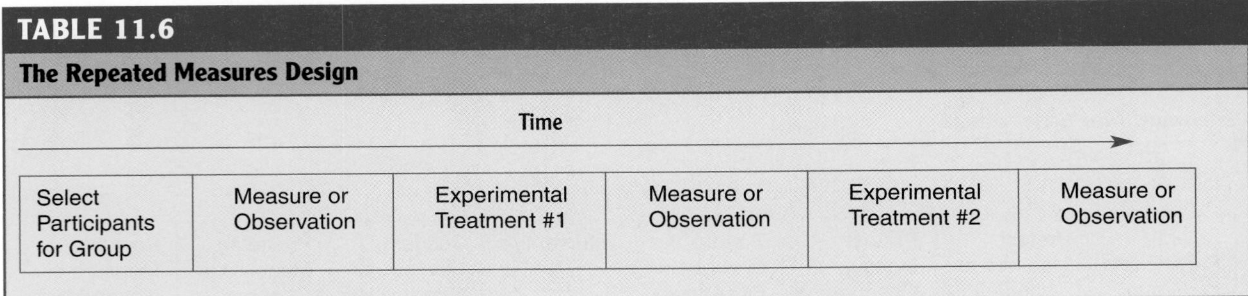

TABLE 11.6

The Repeated Measures Design

Time →

Select Participants for Group	Measure or Observation	Experimental Treatment #1	Measure or Observation	Experimental Treatment #2	Measure or Observation

After selecting participants, the researcher decides on different experimental treatments to determine the effect of each on one or more outcomes. An outcome measure or observation follows the first experimental treatment, and then a second outcome measure or observation is taken following the second experimental treatment. Variations in outcome measures are then assessed for differences from treatment to treatment.

In terms of threats to internal validity, this design is not affected by threats related to comparing groups (i.e., selection, treatments, regression, mortality, maturation, or interactions with selection). Without use of a pretest, testing and instrumentation are not threats in this design. History is a potential problem in that events may occur during the experiment that raise the potential for extraneous influences to affect the outcome measure. One experimental treatment may influence the next treatment, and researchers need to make the treatments as distinct as possible.

Applying this design to our civics–smoking experiment, assume that the investigator has access to only one civics class and can employ several interventions: a lecture on health hazards, cartoons that depict "bad breath" between couples when one individual smokes, and a handout about the rising cost of a pack of cigarettes. Notice in this example that the three treatments all address teen smoking issues, but they are distinct concerns (i.e., health, relationships, and cost). During the semester, the researcher asks the teacher to introduce each intervention separately, and the investigator measures the rate of smoking after each intervention.

Single-Subject Designs

In your experiment, assume that you seek to learn about the behavior of single individuals rather than groups. You also have an opportunity to observe their behavior over time. In these situations, single-subject experimental designs are ideal. **Single-subject research** (also called *N of 1 research, behavior analysis,* or *within-subjects research*) involves the study of single individuals, their observation over a baseline period, and the administration of an intervention. This is followed by another observation after the intervention to determine if the treatment affects the outcome. For example, in one single-subject study, the researcher tested whether elementary students with learning disabilities achieve better if they monitor their own on-task behavior (Kellogg, 1997).

Without random assignment, this design is a quasi-experimental rather than an experimental design. The researcher studies the behaviors of *single* individuals (one or more) rather than a group of subjects, with the subject becoming its own control in the experiment (see Cooper, Heron, & Heward, 1987; Neuman & McCormick, 1995).

The investigator seeks to determine if an intervention impacts the behavior of a participant by observing the individual over a prolonged period of time and recording the behavior before and after the intervention. The researcher assesses whether there is a relationship between the treatment and the target behavior or outcome. The key characteristics of a single-subject study are as follows:

- Prior to administering the intervention, the researcher establishes a stable baseline of information about the individual's behavior. A *stable baseline* means that behavior for an individual varies little over several sessions or days. A behavior is stable if (a) variability over time is minimal, and (b) there is no upward or downward trend in performance over time (Poling & Grossett, 1986).
- The researcher repeatedly and frequently measures behavior (i.e., the outcome) throughout the experiment based on making observations and recording scores for each individual.
- After administering the intervention, the researcher notes the patterns of behavior and plots them on a graph. This pattern may be ascending, descending, flat, or variable. Data are typically analyzed by visually inspecting the data rather than by using statistical analysis. In particular, the researcher notes how the behavior of the individual has changed after the intervention, after withdrawing the intervention, or during multiple interventions.
- In a graphic analysis of the data, the single-subject researcher plots behaviors for specific individuals on a graph. On this graph, the vertical axis records percentages or counts of the behavior being studied. Alternatively, the horizontal axis displays the days or sessions in which the observations occur. The plot can show data for several individuals or multiple dependent variables for a single individual.

Single-subject research has the advantage of providing data on single individuals, such as the learning and behaviors of children with disabilities, where a person-by-person analysis is needed. It also controls for many threats to internal validity. Because only one individual is studied at a time, groups are not involved and the threats to selection, treatments, mortality, maturation, regression, and interactions with selection are not relevant. Assuming that observers use the same standard procedures, instrumentation may not be a problem. When multiple treatments are used, the learning from one intervention may affect the second intervention, and history may be an issue since the experiment takes place over time.

A/B Design Because single-subject studies employ different research designs, the best way to understand them is to examine graphs that show the monitoring of behavior and the administration of an intervention. The simplest design is the A/B design. An **A/B design** consists of observing and measuring behavior during a trial period (A), administering an intervention, and observing and measuring the behavior after the intervention (B). This design is shown in Figure 11.7 for a study about elementary children and their achievement in solving math problems. In this study, the researcher observes baseline behavior and then employs an intervention of feedback to the students about their performance in math.

A variation on this design is an *A/B/A*, or a *reversal, design*, in which the researcher establishes a baseline behavior, administers an intervention, and then withdraws the intervention and determines if the behavior returned to the baseline level. Another variation is an *A/B/A withdrawal design*. In this design, researchers may implement one or more treatments. The disadvantage of this type of design is that in some studies, the withdrawing of the intervention may have serious effects on the participants in the study,

FIGURE 11.7
A/B Single Design

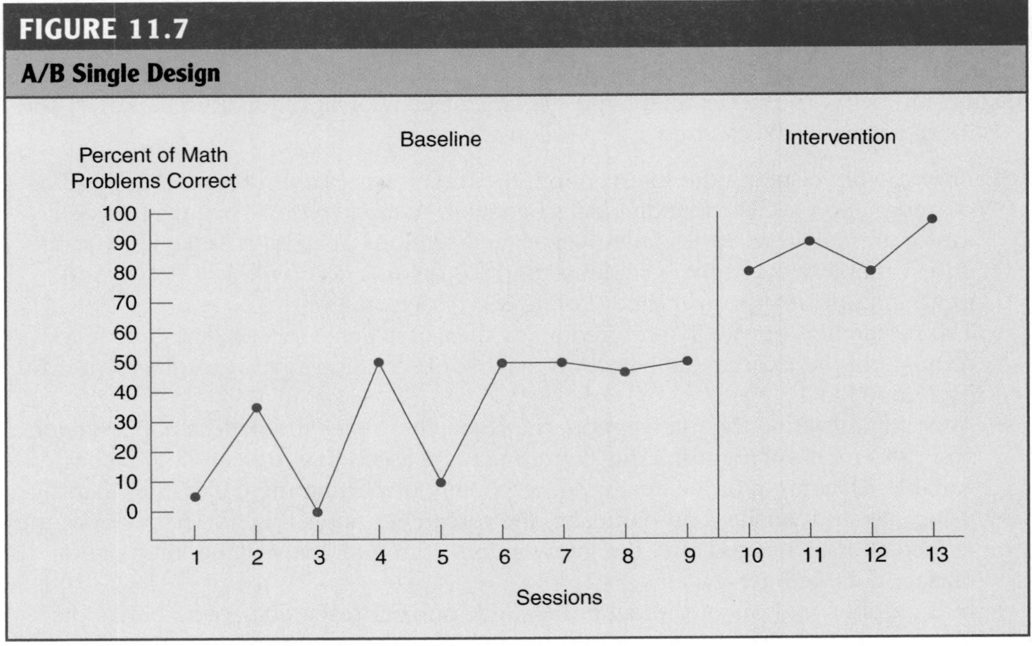

raising an ethical issue for the researcher. This design may also introduce negative irreversible effects, and it requires numerous sessions or observational periods because of the use of multiple interventions.

Multiple Baseline Design A frequently used single-subject design is the **multiple baseline design**, as shown in Figure 11.8. In this design, each participant receives an experimental treatment at a different time (hence, multiple baselines exist) so that treatment diffusion will not occur among participants. Researchers choose this design when the treatment (e.g., skill or strategy being taught) cannot be reversed and doing so would be unethical or injurious to participants. In the example shown in Figure 11.8, five individuals participate in the study and the behavior of each is plotted. Variations on this approach could involve different types of behaviors for the participants or behaviors for participants in different settings. The results of this design may be less convincing than the reversal design and it may introduce negative consequences if the treatment is withheld for an extended period.

Alternating Treatments A final type of single-subject design is the alternating treatment. An **alternating treatment design** is a single-subject design in which the researcher examines the relative effects of two or more interventions and determines which intervention is the more effective treatment on the outcome. As shown in Figure 11.9, four elementary students participated in the experiment on solving math problems. This study had two treatment conditions: practice with feedback from the teacher and practice with a student "coach" in the class. After establishing a baseline of behavior, the researcher implemented the two different experimental treatments and plotted behavior after the treatments. In this type of design, potential problems with threats to internal validity from treatment diffusion may result, but the design permits a test of multiple treatments simultaneously to determine their effect on outcomes.

FIGURE 11.8

Multiple Baseline Single-Subject Design

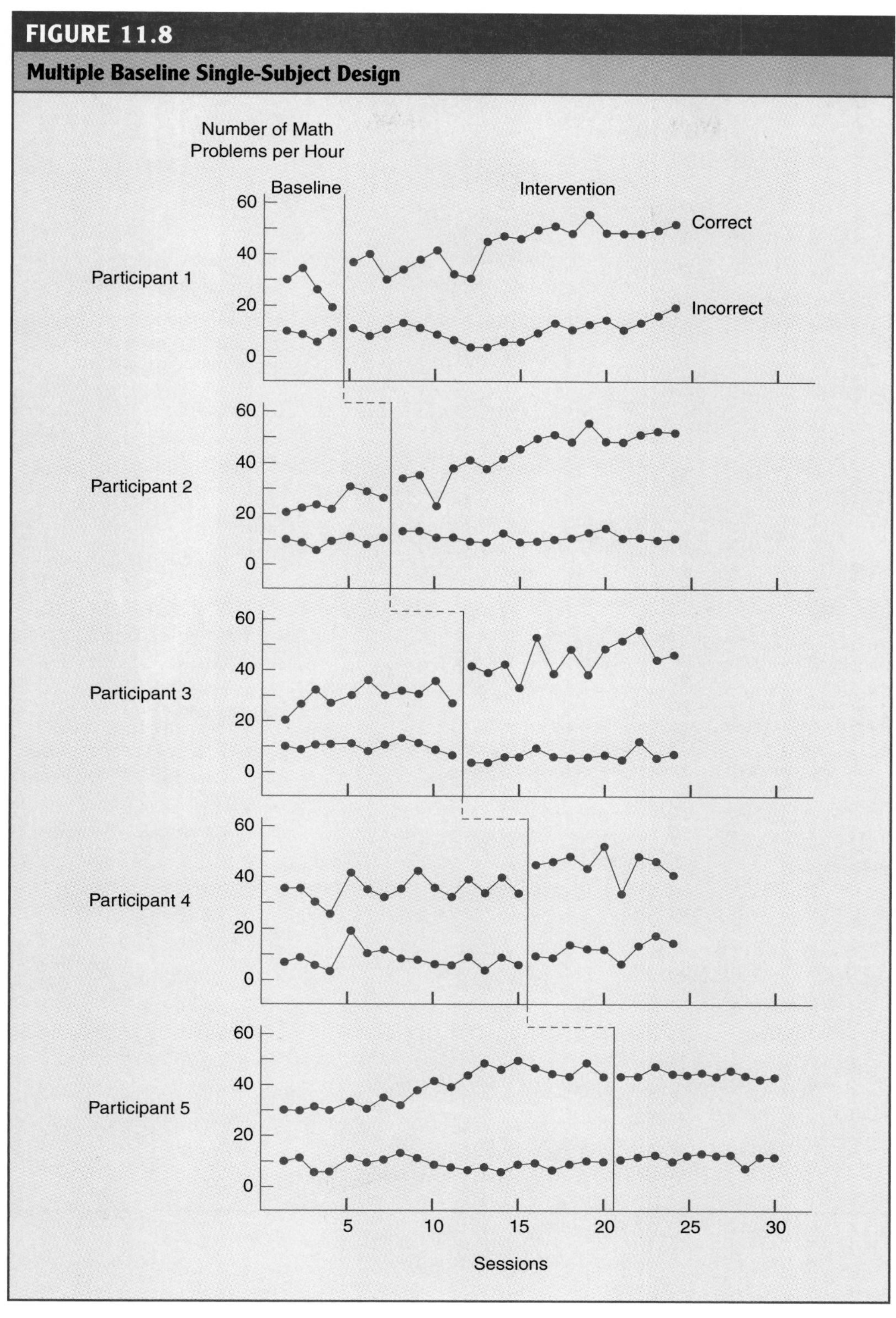

FIGURE 11.9

Alternating Treatments Single-Subject Design

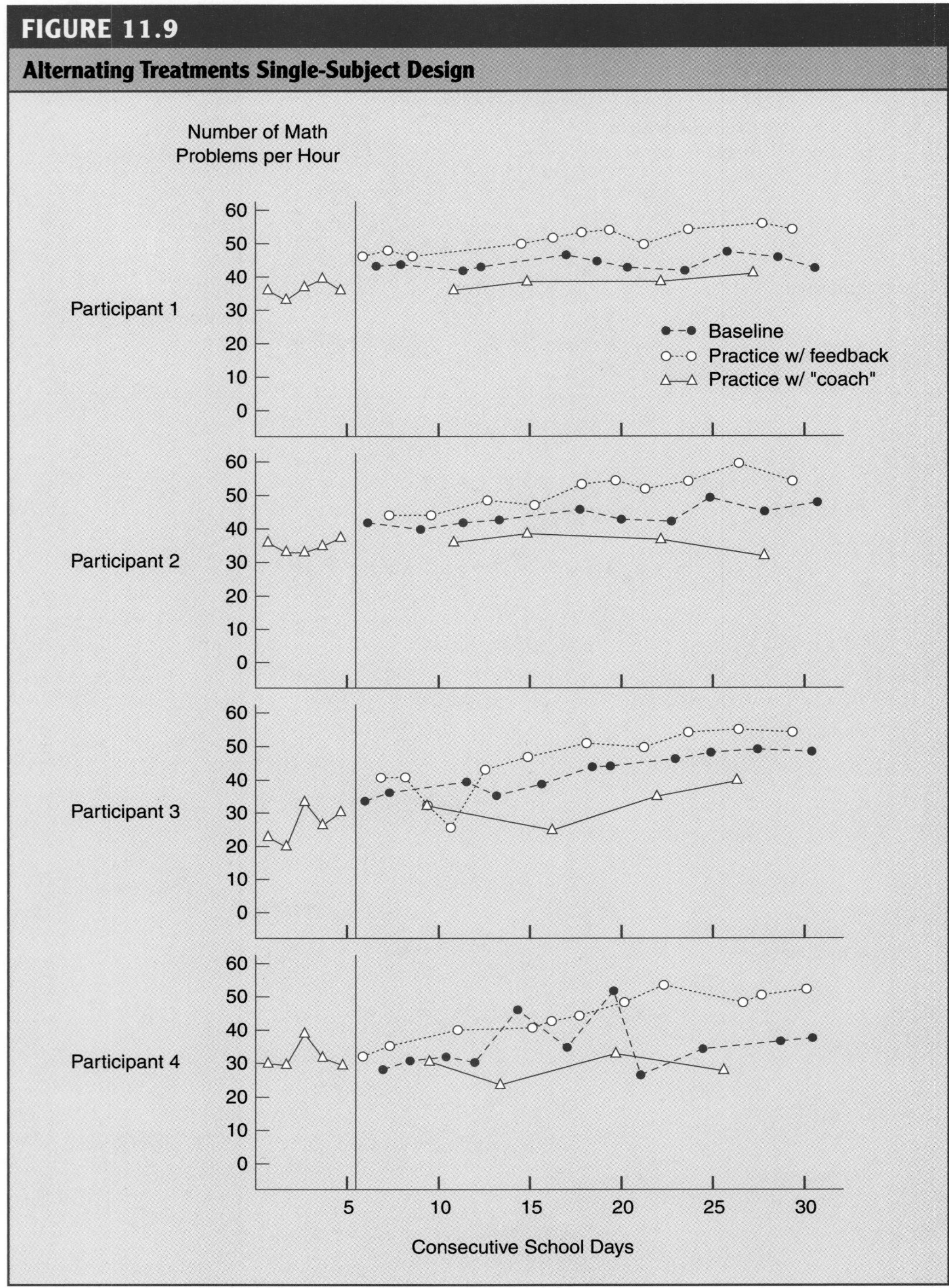

WHAT ARE THE STEPS IN CONDUCTING EXPERIMENTAL RESEARCH?

As we have learned about the different types of experimental designs, we have also begun to understand some of the procedures involved in conducting an experiment. Although there is no set procedure for conducting an experiment, it is helpful to understand the general process before you begin.

Step 1. Decide If an Experiment Addresses Your Research Problem

The type of issue studied by experimenters is the need to know whether a new practice influences an outcome. Of all designs in education, it is the best design to use to study cause-and-effect relationships. However, to study these issues, you must be able to control the setting of the experiment as well as manipulate one level of the independent variable. An experiment is not the best choice when the problem calls for generalizing results to a population or when you cannot manipulate the conditions of the experiment.

Step 2. Form Hypotheses to Test Cause-and-Effect Relationships

A hypothesis, you will recall from chapter 5, advances a prediction about outcomes. The experimenter establishes this prediction (in the form of a null or alternative hypothesis) and then collects data to test the hypothesis. Hypotheses are typically used in experimental research more than are research questions, but both can be used. When stating experimental hypotheses, follow these guidelines:

- Independent variables should contain at least one variable with multiple levels, and the researcher needs to manipulate one of the levels. Dependent variables are outcomes, and experimenters often study multiple outcomes (e.g., student learning and attitudes).
- Variables are measured on an instrument or recorded as observations. They need to produce valid and reliable scores. You need to give special attention to choosing measures that will result in scores with high construct validity.

Hypotheses are often based on relationships found in studies by past researchers or contained within theories that are being tested and continually revised. An example of several hypotheses was included in a study about college students' willingness to seek help from faculty:

> (a) Students would be more likely to express willingness to seek help from the instructor in the supportive statement condition than in the neutral statement condition; (b) younger students would be less likely to express willingness to seek help from an instructor than would older students, independent of support condition; and (c) students would be more likely to express willingness to seek help from an instructor when the class size is small than when it is large, independent of support condition. (Perrine, Lisle, & Tucker, 1996, pp. 44–45)

In these hypotheses, the researchers establish predictions about what they will find in their study. They compared two groups: the experimental group, which received supportive statements from the professor, and the control group, which received no supportive statements. The students in both groups then rated the likelihood that they would seek help from the instructor for six academic problems. The first hypothesis directly tests this group comparison. The second and third hypotheses control for the age of the student and the size of the class.

Step 3. Select an Experimental Unit and Identify Study Participants

One of the first steps in conducting an experiment is to decide on your experimental unit. An **experimental unit of analysis** is the smallest unit treated by the researcher during an experiment. When we use the term *treated,* we are referring to the experimental treatment. You may collect data from individuals, but the experimental unit actually treated differs from one experiment to another. The experimental unit receiving a treatment may be a single individual, several individuals, a group, several groups, or an entire organization.

Who will participate in your experiment? Participants in an experimental study are those individuals tested by the researcher to determine if the intervention made a difference in one or more outcomes. Investigators may choose participants because they volunteered or they agreed to be involved. Alternatively, the researcher may select participants who are available in well-defined, intact groups that are easily studied. For example, a study of third-grade reading may require that the researcher use existing classes of third-grade students. Regardless of the participants, investigators must be careful about the ethical issue of not disadvantaging some participants by withholding a beneficial treatment and advantaging others by giving them the treatment.

How many people will you study? In an ideal experiment, the researcher forms at least one control and one experimental group (Bausell, 1994). In many experiments, the size of the overall number of participants (and participants per group) is dictated by practical issues of the number of volunteers who enroll for the study or the individuals available to the researcher. The researcher also uses statistics to analyze the data, and these statistics call for minimum numbers of participants (see chapter 6).

How should the participants be chosen? If possible, you should randomly select individuals for the experiment from the study population so that inferences can be made from the results to the population. This selection is accomplished through numbering the individuals in the population and randomly selecting participants using a random numbers table. In practice, this procedure may not always be possible because the population cannot be easily identified or you may not have access to all people in the population. However, because a basic premise of all quantitative research is that the findings will be generalized, random selection enables an investigator to make inferences about the population. When random selection cannot be done, an alternative is to conduct multiple experiments with different participants from the population so that some inference of generalizability or external validity can be made.

How should the individuals be assigned to groups? An optimal situation is to randomly assign the individuals to groups, but this procedure may not always be feasible. Also, to provide added control over extraneous factors, matching, blocking, selecting of homogeneous groups, and the use of covariates are recommended.

Step 4. Select an Experimental Treatment and Introduce It

The key to any experimental design is to set levels of treatment and apply one level to each group, such as one level to an experimental group and another level to a control group. Then the groups are compared on one or more outcomes. Interventions may consist of programs or activities organized by the researcher. In deciding what intervention to use, you might consider several factors:

- The experimental researcher should select an intervention of adequate "dosage" (Lipsey, 1998). This means that the intervention must last long enough and be strong enough to actually have an impact on the outcome.

- A good intervention is one that has been used by other researchers and it should predict a change in the outcome. The review of the literature and an assessment of past theories as predictions for relationships help researchers locate an intervention that should predict change.
- Experimental researchers should choose an intervention that can be implemented with as little intrusion in the setting and on the participants as possible. This means that the researcher needs to respect the school or nonschool setting being studied and gain the cooperation of sponsors at the site and of the participants in the study.
- Choose an intervention based on a small pilot test. Select a group of participants in the population and provide the intervention to them. This approach may be a preexperimental design with a single group (to facilitate ease of implementation) or an intervention of a short duration. It may involve as few as five or six subjects (Bausell, 1994). From this pilot, you can draw conclusions about the potential impact of the intervention for the final experiment.

Step 5. Choose a Type of Experimental Design

One aspect of preparing for the experiment is choosing the design and providing a visual diagram of it. You need to make several decisions based on your experience with experiments, the availability of participants for the study, and your ability to practically control for extraneous influences in the project before choosing a design. The criteria given earlier in Table 11.1 will help lead to the selection of a design.

Step 6. Conduct the Experiment

Conducting the experiment involves procedural steps consistent with the design selected. It may involve:

- Administering a pretest, if you plan to use one
- Introducing the experimental treatment to the experimental group or relevant groups
- Monitoring the process closely so that the threats to internal validity are minimized
- Gathering posttest measures (the outcome or dependent variable measures)
- Using ethical practices by debriefing the participants by informing them of the purpose and reasons for the experiment, such as asking them what they thought was occurring (Neuman, 2000)

Step 7. Organize and Analyze the Data

Three major activities are required at the conclusion of the experiment: coding the data, analyzing the data, and writing the experimental report. Coding the data means that the researcher needs to take the information from the measures and set up a computer file for data analysis. This procedure begins with cleaning the data to make sure that those who complete the instruments do not enter unusual data in the computer file through keystroke errors or errant mistakes. You can explore the database for these errors by running a descriptive analysis of it using a statistical analysis program and noting variables for which unusual data exist. This descriptive analysis can provide the first review of the outcomes of the study, and scanning the results can provide an understanding of the responses of all participants to the outcome measures. This step becomes the first phase of the data analysis.

After a descriptive analysis of all participants, the researcher begins the analysis of comparing groups in terms of the outcomes. This is the heart of an experimental analysis, and it provides useful information to answer the hypotheses or research questions in the study. The statistic of choice is a group comparison statistic, such as the *t* test or the family of parametric analysis of variance statistics (e.g., ANOVA, analysis of covariance [ANCOVA]).

Step 8. Develop an Experimental Research Report

The experimental report follows a standard format. In the "Methods" or "Procedures" section of an experiment, the researcher typically includes information about:

- Participants and their assignment
- The experimental design
- The intervention and materials
- Control over extraneous variables
- Dependent measures or observations

As in a quantitative study, you write this report using standard terms for research (e.g., intervention, control, experimental group, pre- and posttest) and an objective, impartial point of view.

HOW DO YOU EVALUATE EXPERIMENTAL RESEARCH?

The key characteristics and the procedures form a basis for evaluating an experimental study. The following list, adapted from Bausell (1994), presents criteria useful in this evaluation. For a good experiment, you would answer yes to each question:

- Does the experiment have a powerful intervention?
- Does it employ few treatment groups (e.g., only two)?
- Will participants gain from the intervention?
- Did the researcher derive the number of participants per group some systematic way?
- Were an adequate number of participants used in the study?
- Were valid, reliable, and sensitive measures or observations used?
- Did the study control for extraneous factors?
- Did the researcher control for threats to internal validity?

APPLYING WHAT YOU HAVE LEARNED: AN EXPERIMENTAL STUDY

Read the experimental study by Guthrie et al. (2006) at the end of this chapter and apply the ideas discussed in this chapter. The strength of this article lies in its use of clearly identified procedures. Note the marginal annotations that identify characteristics of quantitative research *and* experimental research. As you review this article, look for elements of the research process:

- The research problem and use of quantitative research
- Use of the literature
- The purpose statement and research hypotheses or questions
- Types and procedures of experimental data collection
- Types and procedures of experimental data analysis and interpretation
- The overall report structure

The Research Problem and Use of Quantitative Research

The research problem—see Paragraphs 12 and 15

Characteristics of quantitative research—see the annotations on the left side of the page

The authors base the research problem on deficiencies in the past research. They say that the use of stimulating tasks to arouse interest in reading has "received little attention." A few paragraphs later (Paragraph 15) they extend the discussion about gaps in the literature by narrowing the type of stimulating tasks to hands-on acitivites, and they make the point that these activities "have not been studied experimentally." Thus, they clearly set the research problem into a discussion about gaps in the past literature rather than a "problem" that surfaces from inadequate practices in classroom reading instruction.

The article contains key characteristics of a quantitative study:

- Predicting that the larger the number of stimulating tasks, the greater the students' comprehension in reading and higher reading motivation and that stimulating tasks would influence motivation, which, in turn, would influence reading comprehension (Paragraph 24)
- Focusing on variables and their relationships (Paragraph 24)
- Providing substantial literature at the beginning of the study to set the stage to examine factors that influence student teaching behavior (Paragraphs 02–21)
- Collecting information from a sizable number of individuals (N = 98; Paragraph 25)
- Using existing instruments to collect data (Paragraphs 49–50)
- Collecting numeric scores (e.g., Paragraph 41)
- Statistically analyzing the data (e.g., Table 2)
- Analyzing whether the group variable related to the outcome (e.g., Paragraph 59)
- Writing objectively (e.g., Paragraph 56)
- Making interpretations based on comparing the results with initial predictions (Paragraph 64)
- Using a report structure typically found in quantitative research (see headings such as "Method," "Results," and "Discussion").

Use of the Literature

Literature used to justify the problem—starting Paragraph 02

Literature used to justify the intervention—Paragraph 12

Literature used to explain their results—e.g., Paragraph 65

In this experimental study, we find substantial literature, especially past studies, documenting the importance of the intervention—the use of hands-on stimulating tasks to enhance reading (Paragraph 15). Although we do not see a separate literature review section, the literature at the beginning is used to justify the problem and to foreshadow the purpose of the study. At the end of the study, the authors return to the literature to discuss explanations for their results based on past studies.

The Purpose Statement and Research Questions

Purpose Statement—see Paragraph 24

In Paragraph 24, we find the statement of the purpose of the study as well as the three major hypotheses or predictions of the authors. The first sentence conveys the purpose statement and begins, "We tested. . . ." Notice how the mediating variable (motivation) is stated first, the independent variable (stimulating tasks,) second, and the outcome variable (reading comprehension), third. It might also have been stated following the flow of outcomes in Figure 1—number of stimulating tasks influence motivation, which influences reading comprehension. The questions are stated as directional hypotheses or predictions as to what the researchers would hope to find, and the three major hypotheses are listed. One aspect that makes this article of high quality is that in the "Results" section, the authors return to each of these hypotheses and report the results for each, one at a time.

Data Collection Procedures in an Experiment

Participants—Paragraph 25

Measures used—Paragraphs 41–50

Numeric data—e.g., Paragraph 41

The strength of this articles lies in the detailed procedures about the instructions given and in the measures. Four classes were involved in the experiment: two that received from their teachers a high number of stimulating tasks related to reading, and two that received a low number of stimulating tasks related to reading. All four classes then participated in one to four science investigations that focused on the survival of owls in their habitats and predatory diving bugs. The differences between the high-stimulating and the low-stimulating classes were in the number of observations, number of questions, number of hypotheses, tables and graphs, and the number of conclusions (see Table 1). The teachers were provided professional development to help them implement their interventions (Paragraph 37). Data for stimulating tasks consisted of student portfolios that they kept throughout the intervention. The researchers developed a coding rubric to analyze the student information (e.g., the graph was coded on a 2-point scale). The variables of reading comprehension and reading motivation were measured using reading comprehension and motivation tests available in the literature.

Data Analysis and Interpretation Procedures in an Experiment

Data analysis procedures—Paragraphs 52–62

Interpretation—paragraphs 63–75

In Table 1, the authors report descriptive statistics—the number in each group, means, standard deviation, and standard error of measurement. In Table 2, they correlated all of these variables—independent, mediating, and dependent. In Table 3, they presented descriptive statistics for the low-stimulating group and the high-stimulating group. Then in Table 4, they turned their attention to analyzing all of the variables together, and they used the statistical procedure of multiple regression. For each run, they changed the configuration of variables that entered the equation. In some analyses, reading comprehension was the outcome (Analysis 1, 2, 5, 6), and in other analyses, motivation was the dependent variable (Analysis 2, 4). Using this procedure, they could determine which variables were statistically significant ($p < .05$, $p < .01$) in explaining motivation and reading comprehension. They did report effect sizes (see Paragraph 56). In terms of interpretation, the authors presented this material in the "Discussion" section. They summarized their overall findings (Paragraph 63) and referred readers to Figure 1. They then explained Figure 1, and followed this by discussing how their results were consistent with the research of others. They end by stating important conclusions about the role of stimulating tasks and its practical implications, and advancing needs for future research.

The Overall Reporting Structure

Quantitative structure—Paragraphs 01–49

This report of research falls within standard guidelines for writing quantitative investigations. It begins with a problem and purpose, moves on toward methods and results, and ends with a discussion. This format is standard in a quantitative study. Also, consistent with quantitative research, the authors did not talk about themselves and their role in the study, but remained in the background, reporting results.

KEY IDEAS IN THE CHAPTER

Experimental researchers test an idea (or practice or procedure) to determine its effect on an outcome. Researchers decide on an idea with which to "experiment," assign individuals to experience it (and have some individuals experience something different), and then determine whether those who experienced the idea or practice performed better on some outcome than those who did not experience it.

The ideas used in experiments today were mostly in place by the first few decades of the 20th century. The procedures of comparing groups, assigning individuals to treatments, and statistically analyzing group comparisons had been developed by 1940. During the 1960s, the types of experimental designs were identified and the strengths (e.g., control over potential threats) of these designs specified by 1980. Since 1980, computers, improved statistical procedures, and more complex designs have advanced experimental research.

Today, several key characteristics help us understand and read experimental research. Experimental researchers randomly assign participants to groups or other units. They provide control over extraneous variables to isolate the effects of the independent variable on the outcomes. They physically manipulate the treatment conditions for one or more groups. They then measure the outcomes for the groups to determine if the experimental treatment had a different effect than the nonexperimental treatment. This is accomplished by statistically comparing the groups. Overall, they design an experiment to reduce the threats to internal validity and external validity.

Various aspects of these characteristics are included in types of experimental designs. There are several types of between-group designs. A "true" experiment involves random assignment of participants to groups or units. This form of an experiment is the most rigorous and controlled of all types. A quasi-experimental design involves the use of an intervention, but not random assignment of participants to groups. A factorial design also involves two or more groups, but the researcher tests for the interaction of two or more independent variables.

Another type of design involves a within-group or within-individual procedure in which a single group or single individuals are studied. A time series design involves studying a single group and collecting typically more than one outcome measure. A repeated measures experiment also involves only one group, but the researcher tests more than one intervention with this group by alternating administrations of the experimental treatment. A single-subject design examines one individual at a time by establishing a baseline of behavior for the individual, administering the intervention, and determining the long-term impact of the intervention on behavior when it is withdrawn.

The steps in experimental research involve deciding if an experiment is the best design, forming hypotheses, and selecting the experimental unit and participants to be involved in the experiment. The researchers might randomly assign individuals to groups. They then administer the intervention by conducting the experiment, and they analyze and report results. To evaluate the success of this process, the experimenter assesses the groups, intervention, measures or observations, and extraneous factors and control over threats to validity.

Useful Information for Producers of Research

- When you design an experimental study, use the six characteristics as major features of your "Methods" discussion: random assignment, controlover extraneous variables, manipulation of the treatment conditions, outcomes, measures, comparison groups, and threats to validity.
- Use random assignment of participants to groups whenever possible. This equating of groups removes many potential threats to validity in drawing inferences from scores.
- When designing and writing an experiment, distinguish between random selection and random assignment in your discussion—they serve two different purposes in research.
- Consider how you will control for extraneous factors in an experiment. Use pretests, statistically control for covariates, match participants, or select homogeneous samples to better control for characteristics of participants that might influence the relationship between the independent and dependent variables.
- In designing your study, distinguish in the "Methods" section the treatment variable, your intervention, and the actual treatment condition you manipulate.
- Also in designing your study, clarify the experimental outcome (the dependent variable) you seek to measure.
- Select a type of experimental design based on Table 11.1, and identify the potential threats to internal validity that typically relate to this design.
- In most experimental research, the statistical test of choice is a group comparison statistic, such as the *t* test, ANOVA, or ANCOVA.
- In planning your experiment, it might be helpful to draw a visual picture of the flow of procedures in your experiment, such as is shown in Table 11.3.
- When designing and conducting your experiment, follow the eight-step process as a general guide for your procedures.

Useful Information for Consumers of Research

- In reviewing an experimental study, recognize that researchers study different experimental units, such as individuals, groups, or entire organizations.
- When you read an experiment, realize that the researcher may not have randomly assigned individuals to groups because of practical limitations in the experimental situation. These experiments, called quasi-experiments, are still valuable, but they do not have the same rigor as true experiments.
- Recognize that all types of experiments involve an intervention where the investigator manipulates a treatment variable. Ask yourself as you read an experimental study, "What variable does the researcher physically manipulate?"
- Researchers should identify the type of experimental design they use in a research report. If this is unclear, use Table 11.1 and the criteria differentiating the designs as a guide to determine the type they use.
- Also useful in determining the type of experimental design in a study is to recognize that there are two broad types: between-group (in which the researcher compares several groups) and within-group (in which the researcher compares only one group or its variation, a within-individual design).

Additional Resources You Might Examine

For additional detailed discussions about types of experiments and validity issues in experiments (internal, external, construct, statistical conclusion), see:

Bracht, G. H., & Glass, G. V. (1968). The external validity of experiments. *American Educational Research Journal, 4,* 73–81.

Campbell, D. T., & Stanley, J. C. (1963). Experimental and quasi-experimental designs for research. In N. L. Gage (Ed.), *Handbook on research in teaching* (pp. 1–80). Chicago: Rand-McNally.

Cook, T. D., & Campbell, D. T. (1979). *Quasi-experimentation: Design and analysis issues for field settings.* Boston: Houghton Mifflin.

McCall, W. A., & Crabbs, L. M. (1925). *Manual of directions for the Standard test lessons in reading.* New York, N.Y.: [s.n.].

For resources on experimental designs, see:

Bausell, R. B. (1994). *Conducting meaningful experiments.* Thousand Oaks, CA: Sage.

Boruch, R. F. (1998). Randomized controlled experiments for evaluation and planning. In L. Bickman & D. J. Rog (Eds.), *Handbook of applied social research methods* (pp. 161–191). Thousand Oaks, CA: Sage.

Reichardt, C. S., & Mark, M. M. (1998). Quasi-experimentation. In L. Bickman & D. J. Rog (Eds.), *Handbook of applied social research methods* (pp. 193–228). Thousand Oaks, CA: Sage.

For designing sensitive experiments, power analysis, and statistical procedures, see:

Keppel, G. (1991). *Design and analysis: A researcher's handbook.* Upper Saddle River, NJ: Prentice Hall.

Lipsey, M. W. (1990). *Design sensitivity: Statistical power for experimental research.* Newbury Park, CA: Sage.

Go to our Companion Website at **www.prenhall.com/creswell** to:

- assess your understanding of chapter content with Multiple-Choice Questions,
- apply what you've learned with Essay Questions,
- practice your research skills with interactive Building Research Skills exercises, and
- broaden your knowledge of research with Web Links to research topics on the Internet.

Influences of Stimulating Tasks on Reading Motivation and Comprehension

Quantitative Characteristics

Experimental Research Characteristics

John T. Guthrie
Allan Wigfield
Nicole M. Humenick
University of Maryland
Kathleen C. Perencevich
Ana Taboada
Pedro Barbosa
University of Maryland

Abstract

One theoretical approach for increasing intrinsic motivation for reading consists of teachers using situational interest to encourage the development of long-term individual interest in reading. The authors investigated that possibility by using stimulating tasks, such as hands-on science observations and experiments, to increase situational interest. Concurrently, the authors provided books on the topics of the stimulating tasks and teacher guidance for reading to satisfy curiosities aroused from the tasks. Students with a high number of stimulating tasks increased their reading comprehension after controlling for initial comprehension more than did students in comparable intervention classrooms with fewer stimulating tasks. Students' motivation predicted their level of reading comprehension after controlling for initial comprehension. The number of stimulating tasks did not increase reading comprehension on a standardized test when motivation was controlled, suggesting that motivation mediated the effect of stimulating tasks on reading comprehension. Apparently, stimulating tasks in reading increased situational interest, which increased longer term intrinsic motivation and reading comprehension.

Key words: intrinsic motivation, reading motivation and comprehension, stimulating tasks

(01) Motivation for reading is an important contributor to students' reading achievement and school success. Researchers have shown that, especially for students in Grades 3–5, motivation for reading predicts reading achievement on standardized tests (Gottfried, 1985) and school grades (Sweet, Guthrie, & Ng, 1998). In those grades, motivation for reading is differentiated from motivation for other subjects, such as science, social studies, or mathematics, and reading motivation is not easily subsumed into motivation for schooling.

(02) Although reading motivation contributes directly to reading comprehension independent of its influence on children's amount and breadth of reading (Wang & Guthrie, 2004), Wigfield and Guthrie (1997) documented that reading motivation correlates with students' amount of reading. That finding is important because students' self-initiated reading, which also has been called *print exposure*, predicts their knowledge about such topics as history, science, and literature (West & Stanovich, 1995), as well as their proficiency in vocabulary and reading comprehension when background variables of past achievement and parent income are controlled (Cunningham & Stanovich, 1998; Guthrie, Schafer, & Huang, 2001;

Source: Reprinted with permission from the *Journal of Educational Research.*
Address correspondence to John Guthrie, 3304 Benjamin, University of Maryland, College Park, MD 20742. (E-mail: jguthrie@umd.edu)

Stanovich & Cunningham, 1993). Therefore, we investigated whether classroom practices and education programs can influence reading motivation and thereby increase reading comprehension.

(03) The engagement perspective on reading comprehension by Guthrie and Wigfield (2000) provided the broad theoretical framework for this study. They proposed that engagement in reading involves interactions with text that are motivated and strategic. They reviewed evidence showing that when students are engaged in reading, they comprehend better and have stronger reading outcomes than when they are not engaged. Guthrie and Wigfield also presented evidence that reading motivation predicts children's amount of reading, which, in turn, predicts reading comprehension (e.g., Guthrie, Wigfield, Metsala, & Cox, 1999), findings that show the important role of reading motivation in reading comprehension. Finally, the authors discussed instructional practices that can increase reading motivation and reading comprehension and focused on the following practices: (a) providing content goals for reading, (b) supporting student autonomy, (c) providing interesting texts, (d) facilitating social interactions related to reading, (e) maintaining warm relations between teachers and students, and (f) using hands-on activities to spark interest. We focused on the relationship of hands-on activities to reading engagement.

The quantitative literature justifies the research problem and provides direction for the study.

(04) An expanding body of research is shedding light on instructional practices that increase elementary and secondary school students' motivation to read. Drawing on a meta-analysis of 22 investigations (Guthrie & Humenick, 2004), book-length treatments of that issue (Stipek, 2002), qualitative studies of motivating teachers (Dolezal, Welsh, Pressley, & Vincent, 2003), and the synthesis of research on characteristics of engaging schools (Stipek, 2004), we identified seven major instructional practices that increase motivation for reading and reading comprehension.

(05) 1. Using content goals for reading instruction expands students' interest and motivation. Interested students focus on gaining meaning, building knowledge, and understanding deeply, rather than on learning skills or gaining rewards. For example, when fifth graders received content-learning goals for reading, they increased their reading, comprehension more than when they received performance goals of scoring well on tests (Grolnick & Ryan, 1987).

(06) 2. Affording students choices in the classroom is a well-supported motivational practice. When students can choose (a) the texts they read, (b) the tasks they perform with the texts, or (c) their partners during instruction, their intrinsic motivation for reading increases (Reynolds & Symons, 2001), as well as their time spent on reading activities (McLloyd, 1979).

(07) 3. Properties of texts increase interest. When a topic is rated as interesting (Schiefele, 1999), when the format is appealing to students (Schraw, Bruning, & Svoboda, 1995), and when materials are relevant to students' purposes in knowledge-development activities (Schraw & Dennison, 1994), interest and motivation increase.

(08) 4. Social goals or cooperative-learning structures in reading activities improve students' motivation and achievement (Isaac, Sansone, & Smith, 1999; Wentzel, 1993).

(09) 5. Teacher involvement, which refers to students' perception that the teacher understands them and cares about their progress, is associated with intrinsic motivation for academic activities (Skinner, Wellborn, & Connell, 1990; Wentzel, 1993).

(10) 6. Extrinsic rewards and praise include such activities as reading for Pizza Hut prizes or working for recognition in reading (Nolen & Nichols,

1994). Extrinsic rewards for reading are controversial, and, under some circumstances, undermine intrinsic motivation, which energizes long-term reading activities.

(11) 7. Emphasizing mastery goals in the classroom is a practice supported by most motivation theorists (Ames, 1992). When students read for mastery, they seek to (a) gain knowledge from text, (b) understand stories fully, and (c) grasp the essence of literary texts, such as legends or poetry. When teachers emphasize such goals, students internalize them and become more self-determining learners, which increases their achievement in the long term (Ryan & Deci, 2000).

A quantitative research problem requires description or explanation.

(12) A motivation-enhancing instructional practice that has received little research attention is the use of stimulating tasks to arouse interest. In an extended literature review, Hidi and Harackiewicz (2000) argued that educators should attempt to increase motivation for academic activities through increased situational interest. They started that "situational interest is generated by certain conditions and/or stimuli in the environment that focus attention and that represent the more immediate affective reaction that may or may not last" (p. 152). The authors suggested that "by focusing on the enhancement of situational interest in classrooms, educators can find ways to foster students' involvement in specific content areas and increase levels of academic motivation" (p. 153). They proposed further that "creating environments that stimulate situational interest is one way for schools to motivate students and help them make cognitive gains in areas that initially hold little interest for them" (p. 156). If we accept the recommendations of Hidi and Harackiewicz, then our next issues of concern are "(1) identifying educational interventions that can trigger situational interest and (2) identifying interventions that will promote maintenance of situational interest over time" (p. 156). Our challenge is to identify classroom practices or activities or both that will evoke situational interest related to reading.

(13) To garner insight into classroom practice that may influence situational interest, several investigators have surveyed teachers. In an assessment of 178 elementary school teachers, Nolen and Nichols (1994) found that the teachers rated use of stimulating tasks as the best way to maintain student motivation. The teachers also reported that providing stimulating tasks was among the most highly rated practices that increased motivation for unmotivated students. The meaning of "stimulating tasks" was not clearly defined by Nolen and Nichols, but it referred generally to teachers giving students tasks that stimulated them to think in new ways. According to elementary and secondary school teachers, a stimulating task consisted of providing a hands-on activity.

(14) In a survey in which 65 teachers composed extended essays about their motivational practices, they all chose hands-on activities as the most popular practice (Zahorik, 1996). According to Zahorik, *hands-on activities* consisted of a range of interactions in which students used manipulatives, role-played, or engaged in projects such as growing seedlings in science or making television commercials in Spanish. A majority of Grade 8 teachers concurred by noting that providing hands-on experiences and projects resulting in the creation of concrete products was their principal practice for motivating students to learn (Hootstein, 1995). Consistent with those findings was a survey of 68 teachers in Grades 3–6, who reported that motivational activities related to reading comprehension instruction were needed more often for unmotivated students than for motivated students. The teachers reported that the motivation of low-achieving students increased when books were connected to activities in which these

students participated and enabled the students to read about a specialized extracurricular activity (Sweet et al., 1998).

(15) One prominent type of stimulating task is the hands-on activity. However, that practice has not been studied experimentally for an examination of its effect on students' reading motivation or reading comprehension. Although Hidi and Harackiewicz (2000) suggested that the practice appears to be promising for increased situational interest, the question arises of how the stimulating task of hands-on activities can be transferred from the immediate, temporary effect of arousing interest to long-term, lasting effects on reading motivation and reading comprehension.

(16) Our theoretical perspective on the relationship between situational interest and reading comprehension is that for stimulating tasks to have lasting effects on motivation and comprehension, they must be connected conceptually to further knowledge. That view is illustrated in the following scenario:

Event 1: The teacher enables students to perform a stimulating task, such as a hands-on interaction in the classroom.

Event 2: The stimulating task arouses situational interest in the students.

Event 3: Immediately following the performance of the stimulating task, and during the occurrence of situational interest, the students read texts and gain knowledge that is intimately related to the stimulating task.

In this scenario, Events 1–3 may be termed an interest-based reading episode. We propose that the frequent occurrence of such episodes is related to improved reading comprehension. Next, we describe each of the three phases and their relationships in detail.

(17) Our conceptual framework contains the phrase *stimulating task*, proposed by Nolen and Nichols (1994), to refer to a classroom activity that elicits situational interest from students. Stimulating tasks may serve the function of increasing situational interest; one task that teachers use frequently is a hands-on activity. Zahorik (1996) and others suggested that hands-on activities consist of students physically interacting with a concrete object or event. That activity might include students dissecting an owl pellet, observing and drawing the moon, performing a reenactment of early explorers, building a model of colonial life, or experimenting with aquatic bugs. In all cases, the students are using multiple senses of hearing, seeing, touching, and smelling to describe an object (e.g., the moon) or an event (e.g., the Vikings discovering North America).

The quantitative literature plays a major role.

(18) During such hands-on interactions, students are not passive; the teacher expects them to actively address such questions as, "What is it? What are its parts? How are they related to each other? Can I draw this? Can I explain how it is related to the conceptual theme?" Although a hands-on activity may increase situational interest, it might not be associated with a longer term conceptual theme and series of content goals for learning, and, thus, will not lead to increased reading comprehension. For example, dissecting an owl pellet is exciting because students may find the skulls of mice or voles. If the owl pellet is linked to the ecology of birds, the hands-on activity will be meaningful and may lead to increased reading comprehension. However, if the owl peller dissection is not a manifestation of a major phenomenon in the network of knowledge that students need to learn, it will not promote deep conceptual learning.

(19) If the stimulating task is provided in the context of an extended conceptual theme in a subject, one can assume that situational interest will occur for a majority of students. The occurrence of such situational interest

refers to several affective and cognitive processes. Usually high, positive affect is accompanied by focused attention and curiosity (Schiefele, 1999). In a situational-interest activity, several important cognitive processes also occur. Students are highly attentive to the object or event and will spontaneously express their background knowledge. If they observe and draw the moon during the day, students often will recall other times that they have seen the moon and how it looked. Coincident with the priming of background knowledge is the occurrence of spontaneous questioning (Ross, 1988).

(20) After students' situational interest has been elicited by the stimulating task of performing hands-on interactions, the next step is for students to connect directly the situational interest to deeper knowledge and conceptual themes. An approach to achieve that outcome is for students to read texts on the objects or the events in the hands-on activity with some teacher guidance. For example, after dissecting an owl pellet, students should read intently to learn about owls and their survival. After building a model of a colonial New England house, they should read closely about houses or life in different colonies. Schiefele (1999) showed that students process information in text deeply if they possess a high level of situational interest for the topic of the text. Reading comprehension of text is relatively high when students are curious or excited about the topic because of situational interest generated from performing a stimulating task, such as a hands-on activity. Book reading often will expand the background knowledge that the stimulating task primed or address questions that developed when the students performed the task. Thus, the third phase of the interest-based reading episode fostered relatively effective reading comprehension for texts in that topic domain.

(21) An important assumption for the third phase is that books are accessible and that teachers provide support for reading the books in conjunction with a hands-on activity. Without books that are accessible, topically related to the hands-on interaction, and pitched at an appropriate difficulty, the book-reading phase of the interest-based reading episode cannot occur.

(22) It is possible to view the interest-based reading episode as an individual difference variable. Such an interest-based reading episode is an individual difference variable because some students may experience more episodes than others during a specified period of time in a classroom. For example, a student may dissect one owl pellet, be interested in it, and read about it briefly. Another student may dissect two owl pellets that differ in place of origin, be interested in both of them, and read about the survival of owls in both regions. The second student experienced two interest-based reading episodes, whereas the first student experienced one episode. Our expectation is that students who experience more interest-based reading episodes will have a greater increase in reading comprehension than will students who experience fewer interest-based reading episodes. In other words, interest-based reading episodes may be viewed as an individual difference variable that one expects to influence reading comprehension.

(23) Inherent within the interest-based reading episode is an expectation. We expect that the interest-based reading episode, as an individual difference variable, will correlate with students' development of generalized motivation for reading. As students experience situational interest more frequently, in ways that are associated with book reading, their intrinsic motivation for book reading is likely to be enhanced. For instance, students who experience 25 interest-based reading episodes in a classroom during a 2-week period will likely have a higher rate of motivation than will students who experience 1 interest-based reading episode during that period. If those

The quantitative purpose statement, research questions, or hypotheses are specific and narrow.

The quantitative purpose statement, research questions, or hypotheses seek measurable, observable data on variables.

motivation processes do not increase, then students will not be likely to improve their reading comprehension. In other words, students' reading motivation is a mediator that links the interest-based reading episode to the outcome of improve reading comprehension.

(24) We tested whether motivation mediates the effect of stimulating tasks on reading comprehension. Our hypotheses were that (a) students who were given a high number of stimulating tasks related to reading would have higher reading comprehension scores than would students given a low number of stimulating tasks related to reading, controlling for prior comprehension and quality of task performance; (b) students who were given a high number of stimulating tasks related to reading would have higher reading motivation scores than would students who were given a lower number of stimulating tasks; and (c) the effect of reading-related stimulating tasks on reading comprehension would be mediated by students' reading motivation.

Method

Participants

Quantitative data collection involves studying a large number of individuals.

(25) Participants included 98 students in Grade 3 of an elementary school in a mid-Atlantic state. The students were located in four classrooms of two Title 1 schools; 53% were boys and 47% were girls. The students' ethnicity was 53% Caucasian, 24% African American, 6% Asian, 6% Hispanic, and 11% Other. Eighteen percent qualified for special education, and 3% were enrolled in English-as-a-second-language classes. The two intervention groups compared in this study were students in classrooms that provided a high number of stimulating reading activities and students in classrooms that had a low number of stimulating reading activities. The two groups did not differ significantly on any demographic variables.

Instruction Conditions

Experimental researchers select participants and assign them to groups.

(26) We identified two instruction groups. Two teachers provided a high number of stimulating tasks related to reading, and two teachers presented a low number of stimulating tasks related to reading. The teachers from four different, self-contained classrooms in two schools participated and showed natural variations in the number of stimulating tasks that they afforded their students. All four classrooms participated in an intervention intended to increase reading comprehension in Grades 3–5. In the intervention, known as Concept-Oriented Reading Instruction (CORI), teachers linked reading fiction and nonfiction books to science activities (Guthrie, Wigfield, & Perencevich, 2004). Science observations and experiments provided hands-on interactions that were exciting to students. The number of stimulating activities, in the form of hands-on interactions, varied between the four classes participating in the intervention, allowing us to create two groups of classes within the larger intervention.

(27) All classes participated in one to four science investigations that included an owl pellet dissection, observation of guppy behavior, an experiment on guppy defense, and an observation of a predatory diving bug. Differences between the high- and low-stimulating task groups were the number and variety of observations, drawings, questions, hypothesis formations, and interpretations of findings. The two groups worked toward the same content goals from a science inquiry that focused on survival of animals in their habitats, especially owls in a terrestrial biome and predatory diving bugs in a freshwater, aquatic biome. In the science inquiry, both groups posed questions based on background knowledge,

formulated hypotheses, observed the phenomenon (the owl pellet or the diving bug), designed an investigation, identified important variables, collected data, represented data in tables and graphs, and drew conclusions accompanied by explanations containing survival concepts. The science processes were highly similar to those used in a variety of science education studies (Linn & Thier, 1975; Smith & Welliver, 1990).

(28) The teacher initiated the owl pellet investigation by introducing students to a diversity of biomes throughout the world and by taking a habitat walk near the school to experience a sample of woodland in a temperate zone. Students read and discussed how birds survive in various habitats and biomes. The teacher emphasized the ecological processes of feeding, predation, defense, locomotion, reproduction, communication, respiration, competition, niche, adjustment to habitat, and habitat conservation. After discussing owls briefly, students observed an owl pellet, made drawings of it, formed predictions about its contents, and wrote related questions. Then they dissected the owl pellet and used charts to classify the bones and other contents of the pellet. The questioning, dissecting, and classifying took place over 1 week. Students simultaneously read about owls, their habitats, and their survival processes. Furthermore, they read stories such as *Owl Moon* (Yolen, 1987) and native North American legends about owls. Continuing their science inquiry, they created tables and graphs to describe their findings from the owl pellet dissection and drew conclusions about the feeding and predation of owls in comparison with other birds in a temperate forest. The high-stimulating task group observed more owl pellets, wrote more questions, formed more classifications of the contents, and drew more conclusions from their findings than did the group in the low-stimulating task condition.

(29) In the predatory diving bug investigation, students studied adaptations to aquatic environments that the teacher initiated by a field trip to a local pond. They made observations, drew pictures, and posed questions about what lives in a pond. In addition to collecting pond insects, students observed guppies and a predatory diving bug. They wrote questions and hypotheses about when the bug would hunt and how fish (guppies) would defend themselves by hiding in grasses or by forming groups. Students designed an experiment to test a hypothesis and to collect data; they used tables and graphs to represent their data. Finally, they drew conclusions that explained their results of the diving bug predation experiment with concepts of ecological processes. The high-stimulating task group performed approximately twice as many of those activities, including more observations, questions, and experiments than did the low-stimulating task group, and they drew more conclusions than did the low-stimulating task group. The teachers provided an ample supply of books on aquatic plants and animals and the ways that they survive in ponds and lakes. The reading material included nonfiction books in a variety of grade levels appropriate to the students, narrative stories, and chapter books relevant to the theme of survival in wetland environments.

Instructional Context

(30) All teachers and students in both intervention groups participated in a program that included the same reading goals, text materials, strategy instruction, and support for reading motivation and engagement. The time of instruction in all classrooms was 90 min daily for 12 weeks, and it was constant across the two intervention groups. All teachers participated in the same professional development activities in preparation for the instruction (see Guthrie, Wigfield, Barbosa, et al., 2004).

(31) The group with the high number of stimulating tasks in the form of science processes participated in more activities of each type of science process than did the group that experienced the low number of stimulating tasks related to science processes connected to reading.

(32) Table 1 shows that the high-stimulating task group performed a mean of 6.38 observations per student (as indicated by the number of drawings of the science objects); the low-stimulating task group had a mean of 3.64 observations (as indicated by the number of drawings of science objects). The number of science questions posed by the high-stimulating task group was higher (M = 20.10) than was the number of science questions asked by the low-stimulating task group (M = 13.23). The high-stimulating task group (M = 3.02) posed a larger number of hypotheses than did the low-stimulating task group (M = 1.21). Furthermore, the high-stimulating task group (M = 4.56) drew more tables and graphs to represent their data than did the low-stimulating task group (M = 2.02). Each of those differences was statistically significant.

(33) In addition, the total average number of stimulating tasks performed by the high group was 34.20, whereas the number of tasks performed by the low group averaged 20.44, which was a statistically significant difference with an effect size of 1.74. Although the nature of the tasks was identical for both groups, the high-stimulating task group performed tasks under the teacher's guidance. That is, the high-stimulating group performed more science observations, asked more questions, drew more graphic representations of their data, and more actively used their sensory systems of seeing, touching, and manipulating the science object (e.g., an owl pellet) or the science event (e.g., the predatory diving bug hunting for fish and snails in an aquarium).

(34) *Reading goals and materials.* For both groups, the reading goals emphasized comprehension of information text and literary text. Teachers provided support for students' reading fluency in 15-min sessions every other day, and they provided explicit vocabulary instruction daily. However, the emphasis was on gaining content knowledge from information texts and increasing literary understanding from narrative texts and poetry. All classes used the same texts, which included information books on the conceptual theme of animal survival habitats and the subthemes of "Birds Around the World" and "Life in Freshwater Habitats." Approximately 48 information

TABLE 1
Numbers of Tasks Performed by High and Low Groups

Variable	Group	*n*	*M*	*SD*	*SEM*
Number of observations	LST	47	3.64	1.82	.27
	HST	42	6.38	3.50	.54
Number of questions	LST	47	13.23	6.04	.88
	HST	41	20.10	6.75	1.05
Number of hypotheses	LST	47	1.21	.88	.13
	HST	41	3.02	.91	.14
Number of tables and graphs	LST	46	2.02	1.36	.20
	HST	41	4.56	1.91	.30
Number of conclusions	LST	34	5.47	.71	.12
	HST	39	6.13	1.08	.17
Total number of stimulating tasks	LST	46	20.44	7.86	1.16
	HST	40	34.20	9.41	1.49

Note. HST = high number of stimulating tasks: LST = low number of stimulating tasks.

books on the conceptual theme were available, and the majority of students read approximately 4 fiction chapter books.

(35) *Strategy instruction.* To facilitate development of reading comprehension, teachers provided explicit instruction in six comprehension strategies that have been emphasized by the National Reading Panel (2000) and other sources (Block & Pressley, 2002; Duke & Pearson, 2002). Those cognitive strategies for reading comprehension include activating background knowledge, questioning, searching for information, summarizing, organizing graphically, and structuring stories. The teachers emphasized each strategy for 1 week during the first 6 weeks. Then they systematically integrated the strategies and combined them during the second 6 weeks of the 12-week intervention. The instruction enabled students to gain command of strategies and use them actively in conjunction with each other. The strategies facilitate deep processing of text and the integration of text with prior knowledge and experience (see Taboada & Guthrie, 2004).

(36) *Support for reading motivation.* For the majority of students, improving reading comprehension requires effort and persistence. That cognitive engagement requires motivational support, which the teachers explicitly provided in several ways (see Guthrie, Wigfield, & Perencevich, 2004). The teachers afforded students a certain amount of autonomy over the topics of study and the specific texts that the students used to learn information on the conceptual theme. Such choices facilitate investment in gaining knowledge and in comprehending text (Guthrie & Humenick, 2004). Teachers provided support for students' collaborative activities in learning from text by employing reading in pairs and writing chapter books on the conceptual theme in teams of 4–6 students. In addition, teachers provided the hands-on activities of science observations and experiments related to the conceptual theme of "Survival of Life on Land and Water," which generated situational interest and curiosity for reading.

Professional Development for Teachers

(37) All teachers in both intervention groups received the same professional development activities to help them implement their interventions. The professional development workshop consisted of 10 days during the summer and half-day follow-up sessions from early September to early December during the program's implementation. To determine the quality of the program's implementation, we videotaped each teacher for two 1-hr lessons and interviewed the teachers as they viewed the tape to establish their rationale for their classroom practices. We coded the tapes and interviews to determine the level of stimulating tasks in the form of hands-on activities in the science portion of the intervention. (For a description of the quality of implementation monitoring, see Guthrie, Wigfield, & Barbosa, 2004)

(38) We described teacher practices in terms of the extent to which they showed high quality and quantity of instructional support for students' performing stimulating tasks in the form of hands-on science activities. The scale was 1 (*low*) to 4 (*high*). For the use of stimulating tasks, the low-stimulating task classrooms had a mean of 2.5, and the high-stimulating task classrooms had a mean of 4.0, showing a clear distinction between the two groups on the extent that the teacher supported a large number of stimulating activities. Four additional teaching practices described in the quality implementation included (a) use of knowledge goals for reading instruction, (b) use of interesting texts for reading instruction, (c) support for students' learning choice, and (d) support for collaboration in learning

from text. Teachers in the high- and low-stimulating task groups were highly similar on those practices. The high-stimulating task group had a mean of 3.25, and the low-stimulating task group had a mean of 3.37; these were highly comparable. Therefore, the motivational practices of using content goals for reading instruction, drawing on interesting texts in language arts instruction, providing choice, and supporting students' collaborative activities were similar across the two groups. However, the use of stimulating tasks was more evident in the high group than in the low group.

(39) The teachers expected students in both groups to complete portfolios throughout the intervention to provide records of their participation in stimulating tasks related to reading. We collected the portfolios during the middle and end of the 12-week intervention period, and then photocopied and returned them to the teachers for redistribution to the students. We coded the portfolios for the quantity and quality of a set of science processes, including (a) observations, (b) questions, (c) hypotheses, (d) table and graphic representation, and (e) conclusions. Researchers have found that those processes are empirically valid indicators of children's expertise in the scientific method.

(40) For example, Allen (1973) and Smith and Welliver (1990) reported that drawing observations is a sensitive measure that predicts general science achievement. Questioning about a science phenomenon is viewed widely as integral to the science process (Allen; Davis, Raymond, Rawls, & Jordan, 1976). According to many science educators, forming hypotheses to test is a central, measurable process (Davis et al.; Linn & Thier, 1975; Smith & Welliver). Especially important is identifying variables in experimental or observational designs (Bowyer & Linn, 1978; Burns, Okey, & Wise, 1985; Linn & Thier; Smith & Welliver). Representing data with tables and graphics is a science process (Bowyer & Linn; Burns et al.; Smith & Welliver). Finally, drawing conclusions from data and explaining results are often merged (Bowyer & Linn; Burns et al.; Smith & Welliver). Three coders evaluated the portfolios using a coding rubric that is described in the following paragraphs.

Measures

(41) *Coding rubric for the drawings.* We first analyzed student portfolio drawings to determine whether they were science drawings, which were drawings that were generated either as the result of an observation before or during an experiment or to display science knowledge. Drawings that were created for illustrating a book were not considered in this analysis. Once we determined that a drawing served a scientific purpose, we coded it in terms of two dimensions features and quality. We gave each science drawing a feature score ranging from 1 to 3, on the basis of the extent of the labeling of the features in the drawing. A drawing that had a minimum of zero-labeled features and a maximum of one-labeled feature was given a feature score of 1. Drawings that contained 2 to 5 labeled features were given feature scores of 2. Drawings that had six or more labeled features received a feature score of 3. Each drawing also received a quality score from −1 to 1, which was based on the accuracy of the representation of the object being drawn. We summed the feature and the quality scores for each drawing to create a single final score for each drawing, ranging from 0 to 4, which we recoded to range from 1 to 5.

Quantitative data collection involves gathering numeric data.

(42) *Rubric for questions.* We initially categorized student questions found in the portfolios as either a science or a reading question; only science

questions were coded. Science questions were then separated into either science process questions or science reading questions. Science process questions were questions generated from an observation, a science experiment, or another hands-on classroom activity. Science reading questions addressed animals or aspects of animals that were prompted by a text. We coded samplings of one third of the science process questions for each student.

We coded each science process question with a four-level questioning rubric (Taboada & Guthrie, 2004). We coded simple science process questions that requested factual or trivial information as Level 1 questions. Level 2 questions requested global information about a general ecological concept or an aspect of survival. Questions that probed for a more elaborated explanation about a specific ecological concept and contained evidence of an animal survival trait or characteristic were Level 3 questions. Level 4 questions inquired about the complex interactions among multiple survival-concepts or across multiple organisms.

(43) *Rubric for hypotheses.* We first sorted student hypotheses into four categories according to the type of science activity for which we created each hypothesis. We coded hypotheses associated with three types of science investigations (guppy behavior observation, guppy defense experiment, predatory diving bug experiment) according to one rubric. We coded hypotheses for the fourth science activity, the owl pellet investigation, according to a slightly different rubric because students expressed them as predictions.

(44) We coded all hypotheses in terms of the presence or absence of two components of hypotheses: (a) identification of the variables and (b) description of the expected response of the organism or the object to the variable. With respect to the first component, the identification of variables, each hypothesis received a score of 0 or 1. A score of 1 indicated that the student had identified the variable in the experiment and had generated a description of the two different environmental conditions that were to be contrasted as a result of the variable; otherwise, the student received a 0.

(45) We coded the second component, the response of the organism or the object to the variable, on a 5-point scale, ranging from 0 to 4. The code for that component was based on the description of the response that was expected to occur in the organism and the evidence given to support this claim with ecological concepts. For example, we gave a score of 1 to a hypothesis that simplistically described the change the student expected to occur in the organism, without giving an explanation. We gave a score of 4 to an elaborated description of the expected effect with a reason consisting of the core survival concepts taught in the CORI classroom. For the owl pellet, we gave a score of 1 to a hypothesis that included one or two items that were reasonable expectations and a score of 4 to an owl pellet hypothesis that included a conceptual explanation. In each type of hypothesis, we summed the scores for each of the two components, resulting in a final score with a minimum of 0 and a maximum of 5.

(46) *Rubric for tables and graphs.* We coded each table and graph in the students' portfolios on a 2-point scale. On the basis of the analysis of the teacher-given or task-specific instructions, we gave a score of 2 to a table or a graph that appeared to be complete. We considered tables that were missing data and graphs that were missing elements to be incomplete, and we gave them a score of 1.

(47) *Rubric for conclusions.* Student conclusions were available for the guppy experiment and were coded on scale, in terms of four components: (a) a qualitative or quantitative representation of the experiment's results (Scale 1–3), (b) an explanation of results by means of variables (Scale 1–4), (c) a description of a cause-and-effect relationship between the variables (Scale 1–2), and (d) an elaboration of any aforementioned component (Scale 1–2). Each conclusion received a total score that resulted from totaling the scores from each of the four components. Conclusion scores ranged from a minimum of 4 to a maximum of 11.

(48) The high and low-stimulating task groups differed significantly on each task that we measured from the portfolios. The tasks included number of observations, questions, hypotheses, tables and graphs, and total number of stimulating tasks (see Table 1). Data confirmed that the high-stimulating task group participated in a larger number of hands-on activities in the science inquiry aspect of the intervention than did the low-stimulating task group. The data also confirmed the design intended to contrast the two groups and the videotape coding of the extent that teachers provided stimulating tasks in the classrooms.

Quantitative data collection is based on using instruments identified prior to the study.

(49) *Reading comprehension.* We used two measures of reading comprehension: (a) a comprehension measure developed for this project and (b) the Gates-MacGinitie Reading Comprehension Test. In September, students received a reading comprehension pretest. Classrooms were randomly assigned a 1,000-word passage on one of four animals (bat, shark, polar bear, or wolf). After reading the passage on the life and survival of one of the four animals, the students performed a rating task to show their text comprehension. The response format of the assessment consisted of rating the relatedness of key words and terms in the text. For example, in the polar bear text, students rated the relatedness of hunt and seal (highly related), as well as hunt and fur (less highly related) to show their understanding of key concepts and relationships in the text. Researchers have shown that this task has high reliability (Cronbach's $\alpha > .85$) and correlates significantly with standardized achievement tests and experimental reading comprehension tasks. The reading comprehension measure administered in September correlated significantly with the standardized test (Gates-MacGinitie) administered in December, $r(82) = .25$, $p < .02$. The comprehension section of the Gates-MacGinitie test (Form S) given in December required 45 min; reliability exceeded .90.

(50) *Reading motivation.* We used two measures of reading motivation: (a) student self-report measure and (b) teachers' ratings of student motivation. The Motivation for Reading Questionnaire (MRQ; Wigfield & Guthrie, 1997), which teachers administered as a preassessment in September and as a posttest assessment in December, required children to respond to Likert-type items on a 4-point scale. The MRQ measures intrinsic reading motivation, extrinsic reading motivation, and reading self-efficacy (Wigfield & Guthrie). We combined the intrinsic motivation subscales of curiosity, involvement, and preference for challenge to form an intrinsic motivation composite for this investigation (Cronbach's $\alpha = .76$). Table 2 shows that the intrinsic motivation composite administered in December correlated significantly with teachers' ratings of intrinsic motivation in December, $\tau(85) = .26$, $p < .02$, but not teachers' ratings of extrinsic motivation, which indicates convergent and discriminate validity for this measure.

Experimental researchers design experiments to address potential threats to validity.

(51) In December, teachers rated the students individually with regard to their intrinsic motivation, extrinsic motivation, and self-efficacy for reading.

TABLE 2
Correlations Among Variables in Study of Stimulating Tasks for Reading

Variable	1	2	3	4	5	6	7	8
1. Reading comprehension posttest[a]								
2. Motivation (teacher ratings) posttest	.66**							
3. Motivation (self-rating) posttest	.19	.26*						
4. Science process number	.47**	.61**	.24*					
5. Science process quality	.38**	.46**	.03	.65**				
6. Reading comprehension pretest	.23**	.16	−.08	.17	.19			
7. Motivation (self-rating) pretest	.00	−.06	.46**	.05	−.05	−.35**		
8. Instruction groups[b]	.36**	.36**	.15	.63**	.30**	.02	.13	

[a]The standardized test was Gates-MacGinitie (ESS: extended scale score) given after the intervention. [b] The instruction groups were: 2 = *high-stimulating activities* and 1 = *low-stimulating activities*. *p = .05. **p = .01.

Quantitative data analysis consists of statistical analysis.

We gave the teachers a definition of each construct and asked them to rate all their students. We summed the intrinsic motivation and the self-efficacy ratings to form a composite motivation variable because they correlated significantly.

Results

(52) The means and standard deviations of all variables entering regressions are shown in Table 1, and the correlations among variables are given in Table 2. An instructional condition consisting of a high or low number of stimulating tasks in the form of hands-on science activities correlated with all of the outcome variables with which it was theoretically expected to be associated, including reading comprehension, $r(81) = .36$, $p < .01$, and motivation (teacher rating), $r(86) = .36$, $p < .01$.

(53) The correlation of the instructional group variable and number of stimulating tasks was significant, $r(86) = .63$, $p < .01$. That correlation signifies that the instruction group that we expected would have a high number of stimulating tasks was provided a higher number of hands-on activities, according to the students' portfolio records. The mean for the low-stimulating tasks group was 20.44, and the mean for the high-stimulating tasks group was 34.20, which provides partial confirmation of the efficacy of the instructional conditions.

Researchers measure the outcomes for both groups at the end of the experiment.

(54) The variable of number of stimulating tasks, based on portfolios, also correlated with the expected outcome variables of reading comprehension, $r(79) = .47$, $p < .01$, intrinsic motivation (teacher rating), $r(84) = .61$, $p < .01$, and intrinsic motivation (self-report), $r(75) = .24$, $p < .05$. (See Table 3.) Those correlations are slightly higher than the correlations of the instructional group and the outcome variables because there were within-classroom contributions to the associations, as well as between-classroom contributions.

TABLE 3
Means and Standard Deviations of Low-Stimulating Task and High-Stimulating Task Groups

	Low-stimulating task group				High-stimulating task group				Total			
Variable	***n***	***M***	***SD***	***SE***	***n***	***M***	***SD***	***SE***	***n***	***M***	***SD***	***SE***
Gates-MacGinite grade equivalent	41	3.90	2.02	3.15	40	5.28	1.96	.31	81	4.58	2.09	2.33
Gates-MacGinite extended scale	41	467.51	41.17	6.43	40	495.75	32.44	5.13	81	481.46	39.53	4.39
Motivation posttest	46	7.17	2.39	.35	40	8.73	1.60	.25	86	7.90	2.19	.24
Motivation pretest	45	26.36	5.54	.83	39	27.64	4.65	.74	84	26.95	5.15	.56
Reading comprehension pretest	45	.19	.35	5.16	38	.20	.28	4.60	83	.19	.32	3.48
Science process quality	47	11.34	3.98	.58	42	13.60	3.33	.51	89	12.41	3.84	.41

(55) The reading comprehension pretest significantly correlated with the outcome variable of reading comprehension, $\tau(76) = .23$, $p < .01$. Because the correlation was positive, we used reading comprehension as a controlling variable in the regression analyses. Entering the reading comprehension pretest as the first variable reduced preexisting differences in reading comprehension before we examined the effects of the variables of instruction groups or number of stimulating activities on reading comprehension. The variable of science process quality also correlated significantly with the reading comprehension posttest, $\tau(81) = .38$, $p < .01$. Therefore, we used science process quality as a controlling variable to examine the effect of number of stimulating tasks (science processes) on reading comprehension.

Quantitative data analysis consists of describing trends, comparing groups, or relating variables.

(56) Our first hypothesis was that the instruction group with the high number of stimulating activities related to reading would show higher reading comprehension than would the instruction group with the low number of stimulating activities related to reading. We tested that hypothesis (Analysis 1, Table 4) in a multiple regression with reading comprehension by using the Gates-MacGinitie comprehension test (extended scale score) as the dependent variable. We entered the reading comprehension pretest first, the science process quality score second, and the instructional group variable third. Results shown in Table 4 were that the first variable, the reading comprehension pretest, was significant, $F_{change}(1, 74) = 4.14$, $p < .04$, the science process quality was significant, $F_{change}(1, 73) = 8.60$, $p < .004$, and the instructional group's variable was significant, $F_{change}(1, 72) = 5.56$, $p < .02$. The mean of the reading comprehension posttest for the low-stimulating task group was 467.51, and the mean for the group with high-stimulating tasks was 495.75, with an effect size of .71. Therefore, the first hypothesis was confirmed, according to those measures.

(57) In another procedure for testing Hypothesis 1 (Analysis 2, Table 4), we used the variable of number of stimulating tasks measured at the individual level, rather than the instructional group as the independent variable. That alternate way to operationally define the independent variable captures individual differences in number of stimulating tasks performed related to reading, but it is less realistic as a representation of educational contexts than is the instructional grouping as a definition of the variable. We conducted a multiple regression with the Gates-MacGinitie comprehension test (extended scale score) as the dependent variable. The reading comprehension pretest entered first as an independent variable; science process quality entered second as an independent variable; and number of stimulating tasks was the third independent variable. Results showed that the three variables were significant: for the first variable, $F_{change}(1, 73) = 3.99$, $p < .05$; for the second variable, $F_{change}(1, 72) = 8.32$, $p < .005$; and for the third variable, $F_{change}(1, 71) = 12.12$, $p < .001$. The number of stimulating tasks accounted for 27% of the variance in reading comprehension after accounting for the students' pretest comprehension, which confirmed the first hypothesis with these measures.

Experimental researchers statistically compare the groups to determine if they differ on the dependent variables.

(58) Our second hypothesis was that the instruction group with the high number of stimulating tasks related to reading would show higher motivation in reading than would the instruction group with the low number of stimulating tasks related to reading. The first test (Analysis 3, Table 4) was a multiple regression with motivation (teachers' ratings) as the dependent variable. The first controlling variable was the students self-reported motivations in the pretest, which we entered to reduce any differences attributable to motivation prior to instruction. The second controlling variable was the science process quality, and the third variable was the instructional condition of stimulating tasks. The first variable was not

TABLE 4
Multiple Regression Analyses for Stimulating Tasks, Motivation, and Reading Comprehension

Variable		R	R^2	R^2_{change}	F_{change}	Significance F_{change}	Final β
Analysis 1							
Dependent:	Reading comprehension (posttest)[a]						
Controlling:	Reading comprehension (pretest)	.23	.05	.05	4.14	.04	.17
Controlling:	Science process quality	.39	.17	.10	8.60	.004	.22
Independent:	Instruction condition[b]	.46	.22	.06	5.66	.02	.27*
Analysis 2							
Dependent:	Reading comprehension (posttest)[a]						
Controlling:	Reading comprehension (pretest)	.23	.05	.05	3.99	.05	.15
Controlling:	Science process quality	.39	.15	.10	8.32	.005	.09
Independent:	Science process number	.52	.27	.12	12.12	.001	.42**
Analysis 3							
Dependent:	Motivation[c]						
Controlling:	Motivation (pretest)[d]	.06	.00	.00	.32	*ns*	−.07
Controlling:	Science process quality	.46	.21	.21	20.49	.000	.37**
Independent:	Instruction condition[b]	.51	.26	.05	4.62	.03	.23*
Analysis 4							
Dependent:	Motivation[c]						
Controlling:	Motivation (pretest)[d]	.07	.00	.00	.42	*ns*	−.10
Controlling:	Science process quality	.46	.21	.20	19.67	.000	.08
Independent:	Instruction condition[b]	.65	.40	.21	28.55	.000	.60**
Analysis 5							
Dependent:	Reading comprehension (posttest)[a]						
Controlling:	Reading comprehension (pretest)	.23	.05	.05	4.14	.04	.17
Controlling:	Science process quality	.39	.15	.10	8.60	.004	.22
Controlling:	Motivation	.67	.44	.29	37.78	.000	−.56**
Independent:	Instruction condition[b]	.68	.46	.02	2.69	*ns*	.16
Analysis 6							
Dependent:	Reading comprehension (posttest)[a]						
Controlling:	Reading comprehension (pretest)	.23	.05	.05	3.99	.05	.10
Controlling:	Science process quality	.31	.09	.04	3.35	*ns*	.08
Controlling:	Motivation[c]	.66	.44	.35	44.45	.000	.53**
Independent:	Science process number	.67	.45	.01	1.47	*ns*	.14

Note. [a] Gates-MacGinitie. [b] Total number of stimulating tasks. [c]Teachers' rating of intrinsic motivation. [d]Student self-report of intrinsic motivation.
$^*p < .05$. $^{**}p < .01$.

statistically significant, but science process quality was significant, F_{change} (1, 78) = 20.49, $p < .001$, and the treatment variable had a significant effect on motivation, F_{change} (1, 77) = 4.62, $p < .03$. The mean for the high number of stimulating tasks group was 8.72, and the mean for the low group was 7.17, with an effect size of .71.

(59) We further tested the second hypothesis with the variable of number of stimulating tasks measured at the individual level, rather than the instructional group as the independent variable. We conducted a multiple regression (Analysis 4, Table 4) with motivation (teachers' ratings) as the dependent variable, the student motivation prescore as the first independent variable, science process quality as the second variable, and number of stimulating tasks as the third independent variable. Results showed that the first independent variable, initial motivation, was not significant but that the second variable, science process quality, was significant, F_{change} (1, 77) = 19.67, $p < .001$, and the number of stimulating tasks had a significant effect on motivation, F_{change} (1, 76) = 28.55, $p < .001$. Number of stimulating tasks accounted for 22% of the variance in students' motivation

after accounting for students' initial motivation and science process quality. That method of analysis also confirmed Hypothesis 2.

(60) We expected that students' motivation for reading would be associated with their reading comprehension, making it consistent with other research (Gottfried, 1990; Wang & Guthrie, 2004). That finding was shown in Table 2 (teachers' ratings) where motivation correlated significantly with the reading comprehension posttest, $\tau(81) = .66$, $p < .01$, and the instructional condition was correlated with motivation, $\tau(86) = .36$, $p < .01$. Therefore, one can reasonably ask whether the effect of stimulating tasks on reading comprehension is mediated fully or partially by students' motivation.

(61) To examine that issue, we conducted a multiple regression with reading comprehension as the dependent variable (Analysis 5, Table 4). The first independent variable was the pretest of reading comprehension. The second independent variable was the science process quality, and the third variable was students' motivation (teachers' ratings) at the end of the intervention. The fourth independent variable was the instruction groups of high-stimulating tasks or low-stimulating tasks. If the effect of stimulating tasks on reading comprehension is mediated by motivation, then there will be a lower contribution of stimulating tasks to reading comprehension after the contribution of motivation to reading comprehension is accounted for. We found that the first variable of the comprehension pretest had a significant effect, $F_{change}(1, 74) = 4.14$, $p < .04$, the second variable of science process quality was significant, $F_{change}(1, 73) = 8.60$, $p < .004$, and motivation had a significant effect, $F_{change}(1, 72) = 37.78$, $p < .001$. The variable of instruction groups did not have a significant effect.

(62) To examine the issue using a different representation of the independent variable, for example, the number of stimulating tasks, we conducted a multiple regression with reading comprehension as the dependent variable (Analysis 6, Table 4). The first independent variable was the pretest of reading comprehension. The second independent variable was science process quality, and the third variable was students' motivation (teachers' ratings) at the end of the intervention. The fourth independent variable was the number of high-stimulating tasks measured at the individual level. Results were that the first variable of the comprehension pretest had a significant effect, $F_{change}(1, 73) = 3.99$, $p < .05$; the second variable, science process quality, had no significant effect; but motivation had a significant effect, $F_{change}(1, 71) = 44.45$, $p < .001$. The instruction groups variable had no significant effect. The results confirm the previous analysis that stimulating tasks did not increase reading comprehension directly after we accounted for student motivation.

Discussion

(63) Our findings can be summarized by referring to Figure 1. As the figure depicts, the instructional conditions consisted of the number of stimulating tasks related to reading that teachers provided in the classroom. Two classrooms provided a relatively high number of stimulating tasks related to reading, and two classrooms provided a relatively low number of stimulating tasks related to reading during 12 weeks of integrated reading and science instruction for Grade 3 students. As an independent variable, number of stimulating tasks increased students' motivation at the conclusion of instruction when student motivating at the outset of instruction was controlled statistically.

(64) As Figure 1 shows, the motivation variable predicted students' reading comprehension on the Gates-MacGinitie test when their reading comprehension at the beginning of the year was statistically controlled. When the two pathways are combined, it is evident that number of stimulating tasks

increased motivation for reading, which was associated with increased reading comprehension on the standardized test. That result indicates an indirect effect of number of stimulating tasks on reading comprehension but no direct effect of number of stimulating tasks on students' reading motivation. Figure 1 also shows that number of stimulating tasks did not influence reading comprehension at the end of the intervention when students' motivation and quality of their science processes were controlled. The main mediator was motivation, which accounted for a high amount of variance in reading comprehension. The number of stimulating tasks measured at the individual level had a stronger effect on comprehension than at the class level as "operationalized" in instructional groups, which we discuss later in this section. Therefore, we confirmed the basic expectations of this study—that a high number of stimulating tasks would increase motivation and that motivation would increase reading comprehension.

Quantitative interpretations compare results with predictions.

(65) Our findings are consistent with suggestions from previous investigators regarding the development of interest and the acquisition of intrinsic motivation. For example, Hidi and Harackewicz (2000) proposed that *situational interest*, which refers to positive but temporary affective responses to a stimulus or activity, can expand into *individual interest*, which refers to a more permanent, strong predisposition for participation in activities or for pursuit of certain goals. Hidi and Harackewicz suggested that two sets of conditions are important to their formulation: (a) Conditions needed to evoke situational interest should be established and (b) conditions required to enable situational interest to be transformed into individual interest should be specified and established.

(66) Mitchell (1993) said that environmental conditions necessary to catch the students' interest should be identified, as well as the conditions required to hold the students' interest. However, Hidi and Harackewicz (2000) did not specify characteristics of those conditions and examples of variables that represent the conditions in classroom settings. Therefore, their model proposed phases of change in interest, but not in environmental conditions

FIGURE 1
Model of effects of stimulating activities on motivation and reading comprehension

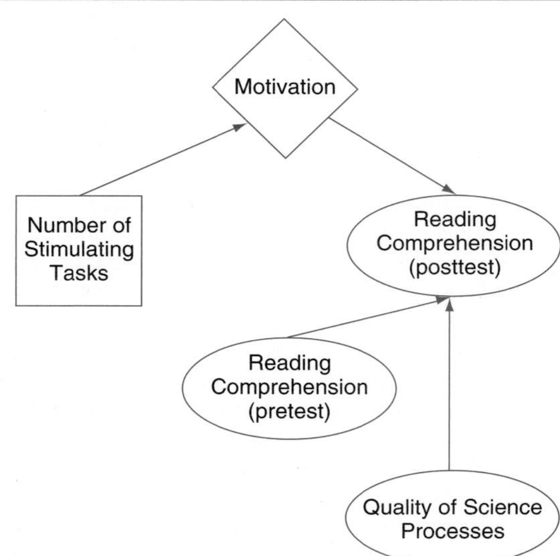

Quantitative researchers take an objective and unbiased approach.

or processes necessary for the change to occur. Expanding on that view, Krapp (2002) suggested that "the central psychological mechanisms that support [the change from situational interest to individual interest] are internalization and identification" (p. 398). He said that "this means that the person has identified with the goals, actions, and topics related to this interest and, therefore, will not change his/her penchants easily and develop an entirely new pattern of personal interest from one day to the next" (p. 400). Krapp continued by suggesting that

> With respect to interest development, the need-related qualities of experience are important because they provide permanent, emotional feedback on the micro level of behavior regulation . . . and that a person will only engage continuously in certain tasks if he/she assesses these engagements as sufficiently . . . important, and if she experiences the course of interactions as positive and emotionally satisfactory. (p. 403)

Krapp said that environmental supports for competence, autonomy, and social relatedness, as described by Ryan and Deci (2000), represent conditions for internalization and identification that enable a situational interest to become transformed into an individual interest. However, Krapp did not present empirical evidence to test his hypothesis or present other empirical support.

(67) To investigate empirically how situational interest occurs and expands to become individual interest, four specifications must be made beyond those provided by previous theorists. The first specification refers to the nature of the interest. In the present investigation, we examine the phenomenon of interest in reading. That is of special significance because we are further dedicated to examining whether the interest in reading leads to improvements in reading comprehension. Consequently, we are interested in situational interest in reading, such as the situational interest that could be evoked by a book. A particular book with a magnificent cover, lavish illustrations, and appealing text may entice a young student. The child's attraction to a specific book does not mean that he or she is motivated for reading in general nor even that he or she will read the entire book. However, the attraction represents a temporary, positive affective response to a text, which we describe as situational interest in reading.

(68) We propose that situational interest in reading also could be evoked or increased by offering stimulating tasks related to the particular text being considered. For example, in the present investigation, students dissected owl pellets as a science activity. The owl pellet was arousing and commanded students' attention. They enjoyed looking at it, manipulating it, and dissecting it. When the stimulating task of dissecting an owl pellet is intimately related to a book on owls, owl pellets, and owl survival, the students' situational interest in reading this book is high. The book may contain pictures of owl pellets, photographs of owls, and text about the uniqueness of owls and their predatory behaviors, which are fascinating to children. Therefore, we propose that a stimulating task (e.g., dissecting an owl pellet or observing a stuffed owl), combined with the presence and accessibility of an interesting book on the identical topic, evokes situational interest in reading that book. The student's interest in reading is limited to that book, at that time, on that topic, and is not automatically generalized to other books and topics. We suggest that the source of situational interest, in this case the stimulating task, is an important specification to this study and to theoretical considerations surrounding development of interest.

(69) Specifying environmental conditions that facilitate the development of interest from situational interest to individual interest also is valuable. The engagement perspective that provides the theoretical framework for this study gives such specifications. Classroom practices that foster the development of students' perceived competence, autonomy, and positive relations with others associated with a specific interest facilitate the development of intrinsic motivation related to this interest (Krapp, 2002; Skinner, Zimmer-Gembeck, & Connell, 1998). According to our classroom observations, as students read a book that evoked situational interest, in this case a book on owls, they may have become identified with reading about owls. As students formulated their questions for further reading (e.g., Why do owls hunt at night?), they became invested in finding the answer to their question. If the answer was available through text interaction, the students became identified with the answer, as well as the question. The took pride in the reading required to generate their new knowledge.

(70) As students gained knowledge about the owls' locomotion, predation, competition, communication, and other survival processes that were initiated by reading about the owl pellet, they gained a sense of competence as experts on owls. In the classrooms in which we conducted this research, students received support for their competence, autonomy, and relatedness during reading instruction (see Guthrie, Wigfield, & Perencevich, 2004). The support linked to the situational interest in reading and the stimulating tasks afforded by the science observations of owl pellets. Therefore, the conditions suggested by Krapp (2002) as valuable for transforming situational interest to individual interest were present within the classrooms of this investigation.

(71) There is an additional, important specification in our formulation of the development of interest in reading. We define the process of increasing interest in reading as dependent on the frequency of experiencing situational interest in reading in a context that continually facilitates long-term intrinsic motivation (or individual interest) in reading. It seems obvious that one 20-min experience of situational interest in reading a particular book is not sufficient to enable a student to become an intrinsically motivated reader. Multiple experiences of situational interest that are supported with multiple classroom practices to facilitate motivation are needed. When students experience multiple situational interests in reading, accompanied by perceived competence, autonomy, or relatedness in reading activities, then students increase their intrinsic reading motivation.

(72) Likewise, students who have fewer experiences of situational interest in reading will have fewer opportunities for experiencing competence in gaining valued information, fewer occasions for directing their learning, and fewer interactions with peers. Consequently, the number of occasions in which students perform stimulating tasks related to reading will be a major contributing variable that influences their acquisition of intrinsic motivation for reading. The mechanism for change from situational interest to individual interest is specified as the frequency of experiencing situational interest in an engagement-supporting environment with an emphasis on knowledge goals, hands-on activities, choice, interesting texts, and collaboration.

(73) The role of stimulating tasks for the development of reading interest has several important characteristics. Although researchers have hypothesized that stimulating tasks could lead to long-term motivation, they have not provided empirical support for the hypothesis nor specified the nature of the stimulating tasks (Hidi & Harackewicz, 2000; Nolen & Nichols, 1994; Pintrich, 2003). We suggest that the stimulating task must be intimately associated with the psychological process being developed. Hootstein (1995) noted that many classrooms contain stimulating tasks that are not

academically significant, and, consequently, do not lead to enhanced motivation for academic activities or competencies. If the educator's goal is to increase motivation for solving mathematics problems, then the stimulating task must necessarily be a part of the mathematical problem-definition or problem-solving process.

(74) Similarly in reading, to facilitate interest development, stimulating tasks must be integrally connected to the contents of texts and the students' activities to derive meaning from texts. In our investigation, texts contained pictures of owl pellets, illustrations of the contents of owl pellets (such as shrew skulls), and illustrations of owls with detailed information about owl predation, feeding, and reproduction. Therefore, the object of the reading (learning about owls) and the purpose of performing the stimulating task (learning about owls) contained many common elements that enabled students to identify the stimulating task with the target educational activity; in this case, developing conceptual understanding about owls. Under those conditions, the stimulating task must not be too time consuming, distract from the mainstream curriculum, or be restricted to a limited number of students.

Quantative research reports use standards, fixed structures, and evaluation criteria.

(75) From an educational perspective, stimulating tasks are egalitarian. All students in the classroom can perform the stimulating task, connect it immediately to books, and experience situational interest for reading. Stimulating tasks are proactive because teachers do not need to seek the preexisting interest of each child in the classroom and attempt to tailor literacy activities in myriad ways to all individuals, which often is impractical. Even for students with low initial interest in reading, participation in a stimulating task will foster reading interest, and the teacher can actively promote reading interest rather than wait for motivation to occur.

(76) Additional research into the nature and type of stimulating tasks that are most effective and efficient in facilitating interest development is needed. The types of teacher support for competence, autonomy, and motivation that facilitate long-term interest among students who have experienced situational interest in reading should be studied. Finally, researchers should continue to explore reading comprehension and reading interest to identify their reciprocal relationships.

Notes

Support for this study was provided by Grant 0089225 from the National Science Foundation, through the Interagency Educational Research Initiative, to John T. Guthrie, Allan Wigfield, and Pedro Barbosa.

We thank the participating school district for their collaboration on this project, and the Reading Engagement Project team members for their assistance.

References

Allen, L. R. (1973). An evaluation of children's performance on certain cognitive, affective, and motivational aspects of the system and sub-systems unit of the science curriculum improvement study elementary science program. *Journal of Research in Science Teaching, 10,* 125–134.

Ames, C. (1992). Achievement goals and the classroom motivational climate. In D. Schunk & J. Meece (Eds.), *Student perceptions in the classroom* (pp. 327–349). Hillsdale, NJ: Erlbaum.

Block, C. C., & Pressley, M. (Eds.). (2002). *Comprehension instruction: Research-based best practices*. New York: Guilford Press.

Bowyer, J. B., & Linn, M. C. (1978). Effectiveness of the science curriculum improvement study in teaching scientific literacy. *Journal of Research in Science Teaching, 15,* 209–219.

Burns, J. C., Okey, J. R., & Wise, K. C. (1985). Development of an integrated process skill test: Tips II. *Journal of Research in Science Teaching, 22,* 169–177.

Cunningham, A. E., & Stanovich, K. E. (1998). The impact of print exposure on word recognition. In J. L. Metsala & L. Ehri (Eds.), *Word recognition in beginning reading*. Hillsdale, NJ: Erlbaum.

Davis, T., Raymond, A., Rawls, C. M., & Jordan, J. (1976). A comparison of achievement and creativity of elementary school students using project vs. textbook programs. *Journal of Research in Science Teaching, 13,* 205–212.

Dolezal, S. E., Welsh, L. M., Pressley, M., & Vincent, M. M. (2003). How nine third-grade teachers motivate student academic engagement. *Elementary School Journal, 103,* 239–267.

Duke, N., & Pearson, D. (2002). Effective practices for developing reading comprehension. In A. Farstrup & S. J. Samuels (Eds.), *What research has to say about reading instruction*. Newark, DE: International Reading Association.

Gottfried, A. E. (1985). Academic intrinsic motivation in elementary and junior high school students. *Journal of Educational Psychology, 77*, 631–645.

Gottfried, A. E. (1990). Academic intrinsic motivation in young elementary school children. *Journal of Educational Psychology, 82*, 525–538.

Gtolnick, W. S., & Ryan, R. M. (1987). Autonomy in children's learning: An experimental and individual difference investigation. *Journal of Personality and Social Psychology, 52*, 890–898.

Guthrie, J. T., & Humenick, N. M. (2004). Motivating students to read: Evidence for classroom practices that increase reading motivation and achievement. In P. McCardle & V. Chhabra (Eds.), *The voice of evidence in reading research* (pp. 329–354). Baltimore: Brookes.

Guthrie, J. T., Schafer, W. D., & Huang, C. (2001). Benefits of opportunity to read and balanced instruction on the NAEP. *The Journal of Educational Research,* 96, 145–162.

Guthrie, J. T., & Wigfield, A. (2000). Engagement and motivation in reading. In M. L. Kamil, P. B. Mosenthal, P. D. Pearson, & R. Barr (Eds.), *Reading research handbook* (Vol. III, pp. 403–424). Mahwah, NJ: Erlbaum.

Guthrie, J. T., Wigfield, A., Barbosa, P., Perencevich, K. C., Taboada, A., & Davis, M. H. et al. (2004). Increasing reading comprehension and engagement through Concept-Oriented Reading Instruction. *Journal of Educational Psychology, 96*, 403–423.

Guthrie, J. T., Wigfield, A., Mersala, J. L., & Cox, K. E. (1999). Motivational and cognitive predictors of text comprehension and reading amount. *Scientific Studies of Reading, 3*, 231–256.

Guthrie, J. T., Wigfield, A., & Perencevich, K. C. (Eds.). (2004). *Motivating reading comprehension: Concept-Oriented Reading Instruction.* Mahwah, NJ: Erlbaum.

Hidi, S., & Harackiewicz, J. M. (2000). Motivating the academically unmotivated: A critical issue for the 21st century. *Review of Education at Research, 70*, 151–179.

Hootstein, H. (1995). Motivational strategies of middle school social studies reachers. *Social Education, 59*, 23–26.

Isaac, J. D., Sansone, C., & Smith, J. L. (1999). Other people as a source of interest in an activity. *Journal of Experimental Social Psychology, 35*, 239–265.

Krapp, A. (2002). Structural and dynamic aspects of interest development: Theoretical considerations from an ontogenetic perspective. *Learning and Instruction, 12*, 383–409.

Linn, M. C., & Thier, H. D. (1975). The effect of experiential science on development of logical thinking in children. *Journal of Research in Science Teaching, 12*(1), 49–62.

McLloyd, V. (1979). The effects on extrinsic rewards of differential value on high and low intrinsic interest. *Child Development, 50*, 1010–1019.

Mitchell, M. (1993). Situational interest: Its multifacered structure in the secondary school mathematics classroom. *Journal of Educational Psychology, 85*, 424–436.

National Reading Panel. (2000). *Teaching children to read: An evidence-based assessment of the scientific research literature on reading and its implications for reading instruction* (NIH Publication No. 00.4769). Washington, DC: U.S. Government Printing Office.

Nolen, S. B., & Nichols, J. G. (1994). A place to begin (again) in research on student motivation: Teachers' beliefs. *Teaching and Teacher Education, 10*, 57–69.

Pintrich, P. R. (2003). A motivational science perspective on the role of student motivation in learning and teaching contexts. *Journal of Educational Psychology, 95*, 667–686.

Reynolds, P. L., & Symons, S. (2001). Motivational variables and children's text search. *Journal of Educational Psychology, 93*(1), 14–23.

Ross. J. A. (1988). Controlling variables: A meta-analysis of training studies. *Review of Educational Research, 58*, 405–437.

Ryan, R. M., & Deci, E. L. (2000). Intrinsic and extrinsic motivations: Classic definitions and new directions. *Contemporary Educational Psychology, 25*, 54–67.

Schiefele, U. (1999). Interest and learning from text. *Scientific Studies of Reading, 3*, 257–279.

Schraw, G., Bruning, R., & Svoboda, C. (1995). Sources of situational interest: *Journal of Reading Behavior, 27*, 1–17.

Schraw, G., & Dennison, R. S. (1994). The effect of reader purpose on interest and recall. *Journal of Reading Behavior, 26*(1), 1–18.

Skinner, E. A., Wellborn, J. G., & Connell, J. P. (1990). What it takes to do well in school and whether I've got it: A process model of perceived control and children's engagement and achievement in school. *Journal of Educational Psychology, 82*(1), 22–32.

Skinner, E., Zimmer-Gembeck, M., & Connell, J. (1998). Individual differences and the development of perceived control. *Monographs of the Society for Research in Child Development, 63*(2–3, Serial No. 254).

Smith, K. A., & Welliver, P. W. (1990). The development of a science process assessment for fourth-grade students. *Journal of Research in Science Teaching, 27*, 727–738.

Stanovich, K. E., & Cunningham, A. E. (1993). Where does knowledge come from? Specific associations between print exposure and information acquisition. *Journal of Educational Psychology, 85*, 211–229.

Stipek, D. (2002). Good instruction is motivating. In A. Wigfield & J. S. Eccles (Eds.), *Development of achievement motivation* (pp. 309–332). San Diego, CA: Academic Press.

Stipek, D. (2004). *Engaging schools: Fostering high school students' motivation to learn.* Washington, DC: National Academies Press.

Sweet, A. P., Guthrie, J. T., & Ng, M. (1998). Teacher perceptions and student reading motivation. *Journal of Educational Psychology, 90*, 210–224.

Taboada, A., & Guthrie, J. T. (2004). Growth of cognitive strategies for reading comprehension. In J. T. Guthrie, A. Wigfield, & K. C. Perencevich (Eds.), *Motivating reading comprehension: Concept-Oriented Reading Instruction* (pp. 273–306). Mahwah, NJ: Erlbaum.

Wang, J. H. Y., & Guthrie, J. T. (2004). Modeling the effects of intrinsic motivation, extrinsic motivation, amount of reading, and past reading achievement on text comprehension between U.S. and Chinese students. *Reading Research Quarterly, 39*, 162–186.

Wentzel, K. R. (1993). Motivation and achievement in early adolescence: The role of multiple classroom goals. *Journal of Early Adolescence, 13*(1), 4–20.

West, R. F., & Stanovich, K. (1995). Knowledge growth and maintenance across the life span: The role of print exposure. *Developmental Psychology, 31*, 811–826.

Wigfield A., & Guthrie, J. T. (1997). Motivation for reading: Individual, home, textual, and classroom perspective. *Educational Psychologist, 32*, 57–135.

Yolen, J. (1987). *Owl moon*. New York: Philomel Books.

Zahorik, J. (1996). Elementary and secondary teachers' reports of how they make learning interesting. *Elementary School Journal, 96*, 551–564.

CHAPTER 12

Correlational Designs

In educational research, your objective may be to relate variables rather than manipulate the independent variable, as in an experiment. If so, your design is correlational research. Although it is not as rigorous as an experiment, you can use it for relating variables or predicting outcomes. This chapter defines correlational research, identifies when you use it, assesses the key characteristics of it, and advances the steps in conducting and evaluating this design.

By the end of this chapter, you should be able to:

- Define the purpose and use of correlational research.
- Distinguish between the explanatory and prediction correlational designs.
- Draw a scatterplot of scores and create a correlation matrix of scores.
- Analyze correlation coefficients for two sets of scores in terms of direction, form, degree, and the strength of the association.
- Explain the reasons for using partial correlations and multiple regression in correlational research.
- Identify steps in conducting a correlation study.
- List the criteria for evaluating a correlational study.

Maria chooses a quantitative correlational design for her graduate school research project. This is her research question: "Is the use of alcohol by students related to suspensions for weapon possession?" In other words, does use of alcohol predict whether a person will receive suspension for possessing weapons in the school? Maria accesses school records for individuals cited for possession of alcohol and the records for weapon possession. She relates these two variables using the correlation statistic. She finds that the two variables are positively related: If a person has been cited for alcohol, he or she is likely to be suspended for weapon possession as well. Maria conducts a correlation research study.

WHAT IS CORRELATIONAL RESEARCH?

Correlational designs provide an opportunity for you to predict scores and explain the relationship among variables. In **correlational research designs**, investigators use the correlation statistical test to describe and measure the degree of association (or relationship) between two or more variables or sets of scores. In this design, the researchers do not attempt to control or manipulate the variables as in an experiment; instead they relate, using the correlation statistic, two or more scores for each individual (e.g., a student motivation and a student achievement score for each individual).

A **correlation** is a statistical test to determine the tendency or pattern for two (or more) variables or two sets of data to vary consistently. In the case of only two variables, this means that two variables share common variance, or they co-vary together. To say that two variables co-vary has a somewhat complicated mathematical basis. **Co-vary** means that we can predict a score on one variable with knowledge about the individual's score on another variable. A simple example might illustrate this point. Assume that scores on a math quiz for fourth-grade students range from 30 to 90. We are interested in whether scores on an in-class exercise in math (one variable) can predict the student's math quiz scores (another variable). If the scores on the exercise do not explain the scores on the math quiz, then we cannot predict anyone's score except to say that it might range from 30 to 90. If the exercise could explain the variance in all of the math quiz scores, then we could predict the math scores perfectly. This situation is seldom achieved; instead, we might find that 40% of the variance in math quiz scores is explained by scores on the exercise. This narrows our prediction on math quiz scores from 30 to 90 to something less, such as 40 to 60. The idea is that as variance increases, we are better able to predict scores from the independent to the dependent variable (Gall, Borg, & Gall, 1996).

The statistic that expresses a correlation statistic as a linear relationship is the **product-moment correlation coefficient**. It is also called the *bivariate correlation, zero-order correlation*, or simply *r*, and it is indicated by an "r" for its notation. The statistic is calculated for two variables (r_{xy}) by multiplying the *z* scores on *X* and *Y* for each case and then dividing by the number of cases minus one (e.g., see the detailed steps in Vockell & Ashner, 1995). The mathematical calculations are illustrated in many introductory statistics books.

When Do You Use Correlational Research?

You use this design when you seek to relate two or more variables to see if they influence each other, such as the relationship between teachers who endorse developmentally appropriate practices and their use of the whole-language approach to reading instruction (Ketner, Smith, & Parnell, 1997). This design allows you to predict an outcome, such as the prediction that ability, quality of schooling, student motivation, and academic coursework influence student achievement (Anderson & Keith, 1997). You also use this design when you know and can apply statistical knowledge based on calculating the correlation statistical test.

How Did Correlational Research Develop?

The history of correlational research draws on the themes of the origin and development of the correlation statistical test and the procedures for using and interpreting the statistical test. Statisticians first developed the procedures for calculating the correlation statistics in the late 19th century (Cowles, 1989). Although British biometricians articulated the basic ideas of "co-relation" during the last half of the 1800s, Karl Pearson presented the familiar correlation formula we know today in a paper before the Royal Society in England in November 1895 (Cowles, 1989). Interestingly, Pearson used illustrations from Darwin's theory of evolution and Sir Francis Galton's ideas on heredity and natural inheritance to advance his ideas about correlation. For example, one idea Pearson explored was to study Galton's idea of the relationship between the left cubit (the distance between the elbow of the bent left arm and the tip of the middle finger) and stature for adult males (Cowles, 1989).

In presenting ideas about correlations, Pearson not only articulated the formula for a correlation, but he also presented concepts familiar to quantitative researchers today, such as the importance of sample size, the value of precise measurement, and the use of unbiased samples. However, Pearson was only one of several British biometricians around the turn of the century who refined and extended ideas about correlations (De Landsheere, 1988). In 1897, Yule (Pearson's student) developed solutions for correlating two, three, and four variables. With Pearson, Yule also advanced the theory of regression and the ability to predict scores using information based on correlating correlation coefficients. By 1904, Spearman published ideas about a correlation matrix to display the coefficients, and he advanced a formula (Spearman's rho) for data that did not fit a normal, bell-shaped distribution.

After the turn of the 20th century, and for almost 50 years, refinements in educational research design centered on experimental procedures rather than correlational designs. However, during this time, Fisher (1935) pioneered significance testing and ANOVA, important statistical ideas for studying the difference between observed and predicted scores in correlational analysis. It was not until 1963 that Campbell and Stanley provided new impetus to correlational research, with their classical treatise on experimental and quasi-experimental designs. In this discussion, they included correlational research as one of the designs, although they saw it as a less rigorous and valid design than experiments. In using correlational research, they encouraged investigators to both recognize and specify the extensive threats to validity inherent in this form of research.

During the 1970s and 1980s, with the advent of computers, improved knowledge about measurement scales, and the need to study complex associations among many variables, quantitative researchers initiated correlational studies. Instead of the physical control available to experimental researchers through techniques such as randomization and matching, correlational researchers sought control through statistical procedures. With computers, they could statistically remove the effects of a large number of variables to examine the relationship among a small set of variables. They could explore the combination of variables (e.g., age, gender, and SAT scores) and an outcome (e.g., college grade point average). From simple regression—the analysis of the variability of a single dependent variable by a single independent variable—the technique of using multiple regression to analyze the collective and separate effects of two or more independent variables on a dependent variable emerged (Pedhazur, 1997). Taking regression to the next step by advancing a theoretical model, collecting data, and estimating the fit of the data to the model led researchers to advanced correlational techniques of path analysis (Kline, 1998). Today, researchers test elaborate models containing many variables (Kline, 1998).

WHAT ARE THE TYPES OF CORRELATIONAL DESIGNS?

Years ago, research method writers specified correlational research as one of the quantitative "designs" (e.g., see Campbell & Stanley, 1963). With the sophisticated applications and explicit procedures of correlations, correlational research can rightfully take its place among our designs in quantitative research. The two primary correlation designs are explanation and prediction.

The Explanatory Design

Various authors refer to explanatory correlational research as "relational" research (Cohen & Manion, 1994, p. 123), "accounting-for-variance studies" (Punch, 1998, p. 78), or "explanatory" research (Fraenkel & Wallen, 2000, p. 360). Because one basic objective of this form of correlational research is to explain the association between or among variables, we will use the term *explanatory research* in this discussion. An **explanatory research design** is a correlational design in which the researcher is interested in the extent to which two variables (or more) co-vary, that is, where changes in one variable are reflected in changes in the other. Explanatory designs consist of a simple association between two variables (e.g., sense of humor and performance in drama) or more than two (e.g., pressure from friends or feelings of isolation that contribute to binge drinking).

When examining a study reported in the literature, how would you identify it as an explanatory correlational study? Look for the following characteristics, which are common in this type of study.

- *The investigators correlate two or more variables.* They report the correlation statistical test and mention the use of multiple variables. Readers find these variables specifically mentioned in the purpose statement, the research questions, or the tables reporting the statistical procedures.
- *The researchers collect data at one point in time.* Evidence for this procedure will be found in the administration of instruments "in one sitting" to students. In explanatory correlational research, the investigators are not interested in either past or future performance of participants.
- *The investigator analyzes all participants as a single group.* Compared to an experiment that involves multiple groups or treatment conditions, the researcher collects scores from only one group and does not divide the group into categories (or factors). Unlike experimental research, all levels of information from the group are used. Rather than divide scores on self-esteem into "high" and "low" categories of scores, as would be done in experimental research, a correlational researcher uses all scores on a continuum, such as from 10 to 90.
- *The researcher obtains at least two scores for each individual in the group—one for each variable.* In the method discussion, the correlational investigator will mention how many scores were collected from each participant. For example, for each individual in a study of optimism and appropriate health behaviors, the researcher would collect two scores: an optimism score and a health behavior score.
- *The researcher reports the use of the correlation statistical test (or an extension of it) in the data analysis.* This is the basic feature of this type of research. In addition, the researcher includes reports about the strength and the direction of the correlational test to provide additional information.
- *Finally, the researcher makes interpretations or draws conclusions from the statistical test results.* It is important to note that the conclusions do not establish a probable cause-and-effect (or causal inference) relationship because the researcher can use only statistical control (e.g., control over variables using statistical procedures) rather than the more rigorous control of physically altering the conditions (i.e., such as in experiments). In correlational research, the investigator "takes the participants as they are," without experimental intervention. Thus, authors of a correlational study often use the phrase "degree of association between two variables" (Thorndike, 1997a, p. 1107), a connotation that conveys a general co-occurrence between variables rather than probable causality. It also accounts for why correlational writers sometimes refrain from using the terms *independent variable* and

dependent variable and instead refer to the correlation of two *variables*, a meaning consistent with something less than the independent variable influencing the dependent variable. They also employ the word *relationship* about correlations among variables.

Let's turn to an explanatory correlational study by Anderson and Keith (1997) to illustrate this type of design. Despite gains in achievement test scores, African American, Hispanic, and low-income students typically achieve below the levels of Caucasian, Asian, and high-income students. African American and Hispanic students also drop out of school at higher rates than do their Caucasian peers. To understand the factors that explain academic success of these at-risk students, Anderson and Keith conducted a correlational study. They proposed a model composed of eight variables (family socioeconomic status, ethnicity, gender, ability, quality of schooling, parental involvement, motivation, and academic coursework) and one outcome variable (academic achievement). They studied one group comprising sophomores in high school who indicated they were of non-Asian minority origin and who had Socio-economic Status (SES) composite scores within the bottom quartile of the SES range. The data collection involved gathering information during the base year (1980) and 2 years later (1982), but for purposes of analysis, the researchers analyzed data together from both years as if they were collected at one point in time. For each participant (N = 7,355), they collected measures on each variable and correlated all variables. They found that each of the variables except parental involvement explained a significant amount of variance in academic achievement.

The Prediction Design

Instead of simply relating variables—two variables at a time or a complex set such as in our last example—in a prediction design, researchers seek to anticipate outcomes by using certain variables as predictors. For example, superintendents and principals need to identify teachers who will be successful in their schools. To select teachers who have a good chance of success, the administrators can identify predictors of success using correlational research. Prediction studies, therefore, are useful because they help anticipate or forecast future behavior.

The purpose of a **prediction research design** is to identify variables that will predict an outcome or criterion. In this form of research, the investigator identifies one or more predictor variable and a criterion (or outcome) variable. A **predictor variable** is the variable used to make a forecast about an outcome in correlational research. In the case of predicting teacher success in a school, the predictor may be "mentoring" during teacher training or "years of experience teaching." In much prediction research, investigators often use more than one predictor variable.

The outcome being predicted in correlational research, however, is called the **criterion variable**. In our example, teacher success is the criterion variable. Although more than one outcome can be predicted, the typical educational study includes only one criterion variable.

To identify a prediction study, look for the following characteristics.

- *The authors typically include the word* prediction *in the title.* It might also be in the purpose statement or research questions.
- *The researchers typically measure the predictor variable(s) at one point in time and the criterion variable at a later point in time.* Therefore, you should examine a study to determine if the researchers build a "time" dimension into the design. For example, the predictor of teacher success, "mentoring," is measured during

a student's teacher training program, whereas "success" is measured later, after the students have performed as teachers.

- *The authors forecast future performance.* They usually state this intent in the purpose statement or in the research questions. In the justification of the research problem, writers also mention their intent to "predict" some outcome.

A prediction study will report correlations using the correlation statistical test, but it may include advanced statistical procedures. For example, the author may be interested in several predictors that help explain the criterion. Although simple linear regression (explained later) addresses this interest, multiple regression (also addressed later) provides a more complex formula.

Let's view a prediction study to see the procedures the researchers used. Royal and Rossi (1999) were concerned about the problem of teacher isolation and sought to identify the factors that predict a better sense of community for high school teachers. Their study included several predictors and one overall criterion (sense of community). They collected data from three large high schools and gathered several measures. They measured sense of community using an 85-item instrument that included a student-related measure of community, a coworker measure, and a school-related measure. Predictors were time-related variables (e.g., tenure in the school), work arrangements (e.g., mentoring, teaching teams), and school organization variables (e.g., innovation in the school). In this configuration of variables, the researchers assumed that the predictor variables operated earlier in time than the criterion (e.g., after the initiation of innovation, teachers developed a sense of community). The investigators correlated these predictors and the outcome variables and conducted a multiple regression to find that the predictors had different effects on each criterion variable. Overall, school tenure, student interaction, and innovation were the best predictors of the measures of a sense of community in the schools.

WHAT ARE THE KEY CHARACTERISTICS OF CORRELATIONAL DESIGNS?

As suggested by the explanatory and prediction designs, correlation research includes specific characteristics:

- Displays of scores (scatterplots and matrices)
- Associations between scores (direction, form, and strength)
- Multiple variable analysis (partial correlations and multiple regression)

Displays of Scores

If you have two scores, in correlation research you can plot these scores on a graph (or scatterplot) or present them in a table (or correlation matrix).

Scatterplots

Researchers plot scores for two variables on a graph to provide a visual picture of the form of the scores. This allows researchers to identify the type of association among variables and locate extreme scores. Most importantly, this plot can provide useful information about the form of the association—whether the scores are linear (follow a straight line) or curvilinear (follow a U-shaped form). It also indicates the direction of the association (e.g., one score goes up and the other goes up as well) and the degree of the association (whether the relationship is perfect, with a correlation of 1.0, or less than perfect).

A plot helps to assess this association between two scores for participants. A **scatterplot** (or **scatter diagram**) is a pictorial image displayed on a graph of two sets of scores for participants. These scores are typically identified as *X* and *Y*, with *X* values represented on the horizontal axis, and *Y* values represented on the vertical axis. A single point indicates where the *X* and *Y* scores intersect for one individual.

Using scales on the horizontal (abscissa) axis and on the vertical (ordinate) axis, the investigator plots points on a graph for each participant. Examine the scatterplot of scores in Figure 12.1, which shows both a small data set for 10 students and a visual plot of their scores. Assume that the correlation researcher seeks to study whether the use of the Internet by high school students relates to their level of depression. (We can assume that students who use the Internet excessively are also depressed individuals because they are trying to escape and not cope with present situations.) From past research, we would predict this situation to be the case. We measure scores on the use of the Internet by asking the students how many hours per week they spend searching the Internet. We measure individual depression scores on an instrument with proven valid and reliable scores. Assume that there are 15 questions about depression on the instrument with a rating scale from 1 (*strongly disagree*) to 5 (*strongly agree*). This means that the summed scores will range from 15 to 45.

As shown in Figure 12.1, hypothetical scores for 10 students are collected and plotted on the graph. Several aspects about this graph will help you understand it:

- The "hours of Internet use" variable is plotted on the *X* axis, the horizontal axis.
- The "depression" variable is plotted on the *Y* axis, the vertical axis.

FIGURE 12.1

Example of a Scatterplot

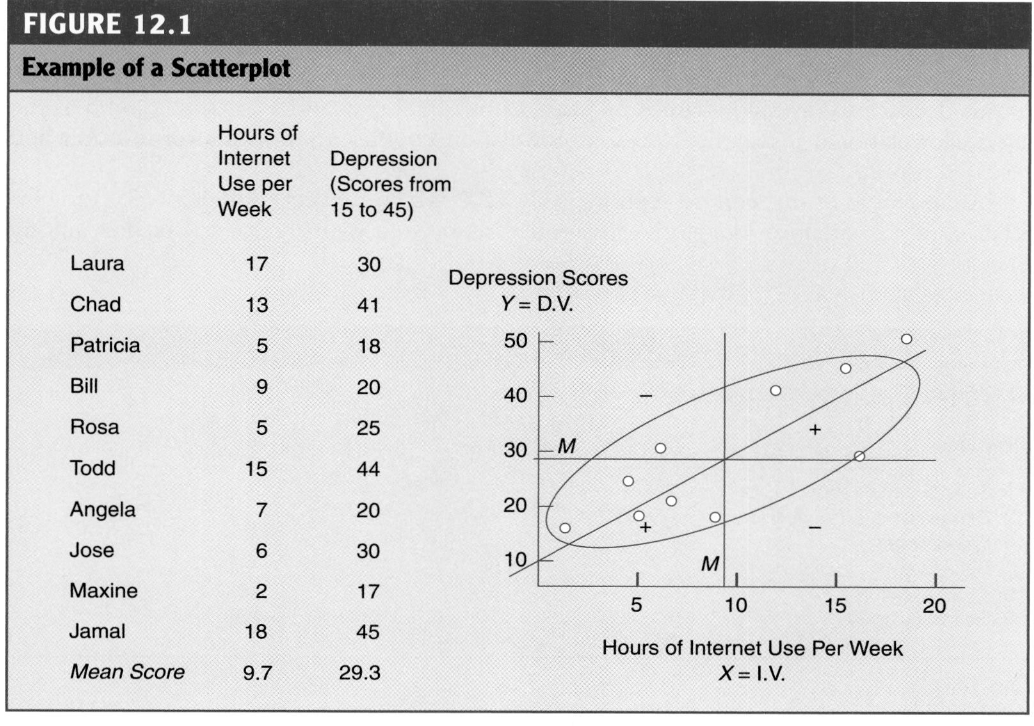

	Hours of Internet Use per Week	Depression (Scores from 15 to 45)
Laura	17	30
Chad	13	41
Patricia	5	18
Bill	9	20
Rosa	5	25
Todd	15	44
Angela	7	20
Jose	6	30
Maxine	2	17
Jamal	18	45
Mean Score	9.7	29.3

- Each student in the study has two scores: one for hours per week of Internet use and one for depression.
- A mark (or point) on the graph indicates the score for each individual on depression and hours of Internet use each week. There are 10 scores (points) on the graph, one for each participant in the study.

The mean scores (*M*) on each variable are also plotted on the graph. The students used the Internet for an average of 9.7 hours per week, and their average depression score was 29.3. Drawing vertical and horizontal lines on the graph that relate to the mean scores (*M*), we can divide the plot into four quadrants and assign a minus (−) to quadrants where scores are "negative" and a plus (+) to quadrants where the scores are "positive." In our example, to have a depression score below 29.3 (*M*) is positive because that suggests that the students with such a score have less depression. To score above 29.3 (*M*) indicates more severe depression, and this is "negative." Alternatively, to use the Internet less than 9.7 (*M*) hours per week is "positive" (i.e., because students can then spend more time on homework), whereas to spend more time than 9.7 hours is "negative" (i.e., overuse of Internet searching is at the expense of something else). To be both highly depressed (above 29.3 on depression) and to use the Internet frequently (above 9.7 on Internet use) is what we might have predicted based on past literature.

Note three important aspects about the scores on this plot. First, the direction of scores shows that when *X* increases, *Y* increases as well, indicating a positive association. Second, the points on the scatterplot tend to form a straight line. Third, the points would be reasonably close to a straight line if we were to draw a line through all of them. These three ideas relate to direction, form of the association, and the degree of relationship that we can learn from studying this scatterplot. We will use this information later when we discuss the association between scores in correlation research.

A Correlation Matrix

Correlation researchers typically display correlation coefficients in a matrix. A **correlation matrix** presents a visual display of the correlation coefficients for all variables in a study. In this display, we list all variables on both a horizontal row and a vertical column in the table. Correlational researchers present correlation coefficients in a matrix in published research reports.

An example of this can be seen in Table 12.1, which reports coefficients for the correlation of six variables in a study of variables associated with school satisfaction among

TABLE 12.1

Example of a Correlation Matrix

Variables	1	2	3	4	5	6
1. School satisfaction	—					
2. Extra-curricular activities	−.33**	—				
3. Friendships	.24*	−.03	—			
4. Self-esteem	−.17	.65**	.24*	—		
5. Pride in school	−.09	−.02	.49**	.16	—	
6. Self-awareness	.29**	−.10	.39**	.03	.22	—

*$p < .05$
**$p < .01$

middle school students. Notice that all six variables are listed in both the horizontal rows and the vertical columns. To simplify the table, the authors assigned numbers to the variables and included only the numbers in the column headings. Coefficients ranging between $-.33$ and $+.65$ are reported in cells in the table. We fill only the lower half of the cells because the half of the cells above the diagonal would simply repeat the same information. Finally, the asterisks indicate whether the coefficient statistics are statistically significantly correlated at the $p < .05$ and $p < .01$ levels.

Associations Between Scores

After correlation researchers graph scores and produce a correlation matrix, they can then interpret the meaning of the association between scores. This calls for understanding the direction of the association, the form of the distribution, the degree of association, and its strength.

What Is the Direction of the Association?

When examining a graph, it is important to identify if the points where the scores intersect move in the same or opposite directions. In a **positive correlation** (indicated by a “1” correlation coefficient) the points move in the same direction; that is, when *X* increases, so does *Y* or, alternatively, if *X* decreases, so does *Y*. In a **negative correlation** (indicated by a “−” correlation coefficient), the points move in the opposite direction; that is, when *X* increases, *Y* decreases, and when *X* decreases, *Y* increases. If scores on one variable do not relate in any pattern on the other variable, then no linear association exists.

What Is the Form of the Association?

Correlational researchers identify the form of the plotted scores as linear or nonlinear. In the Internet and depression example (Figure 12.1), we found a positive, linear relationship. This type of relationship is only one of several possibilities that might result from actual data. In reality, the relationship might assume any one of the forms shown in Figure 12.2.

Linear Relationship Part (a) of Figure 12.2 depicts a **positive linear relationship** of scores, where low (or high) scores on one variable relate to low (or high) scores on a second variable. In our example, low scores on depression are associated with low scores on number of hours using the Internet per week.

Part (b) of Figure 12.2 depicts a **negative linear relationship** result, where low scores on one variable relate to high scores on the other variable. Low scores on depression, for example, might be associated with high scores on use of the Internet, suggesting a negative relationship.

Uncorrelated and Nonlinear Relationships In part (c) of Figure 12.2, we see an **uncorrelated relationship** of scores. In this distribution, the variables are independent of each other. A particular score on one variable does not predict or tell us any information about the possible score on the other variable. In our example, a plot of the scores for depression and the scores for Internet use would be irregular, without any particular pattern.

A **curvilinear distribution** (or nonlinear relationship) shows a U-shaped relationship in scores. This distribution in part (d) of Figure 12.2 shows an increase, plateau, and decline in the *Y*-axis variable with increasing values of the *X*-axis variable. The distribution in part (e) of Figure 12.2 indicates a decrease, plateau, and increase in the *Y*-axis variable, with increasing values of the *X*-axis variable. For example, it is possible that as Internet use increases, so does depression, up to a point at which the Internet actually becomes a coping mechanism for stress, and depression begins to decrease (as illustrated in part [d]).

FIGURE 12.2

Patterns of Association Between Two Variables

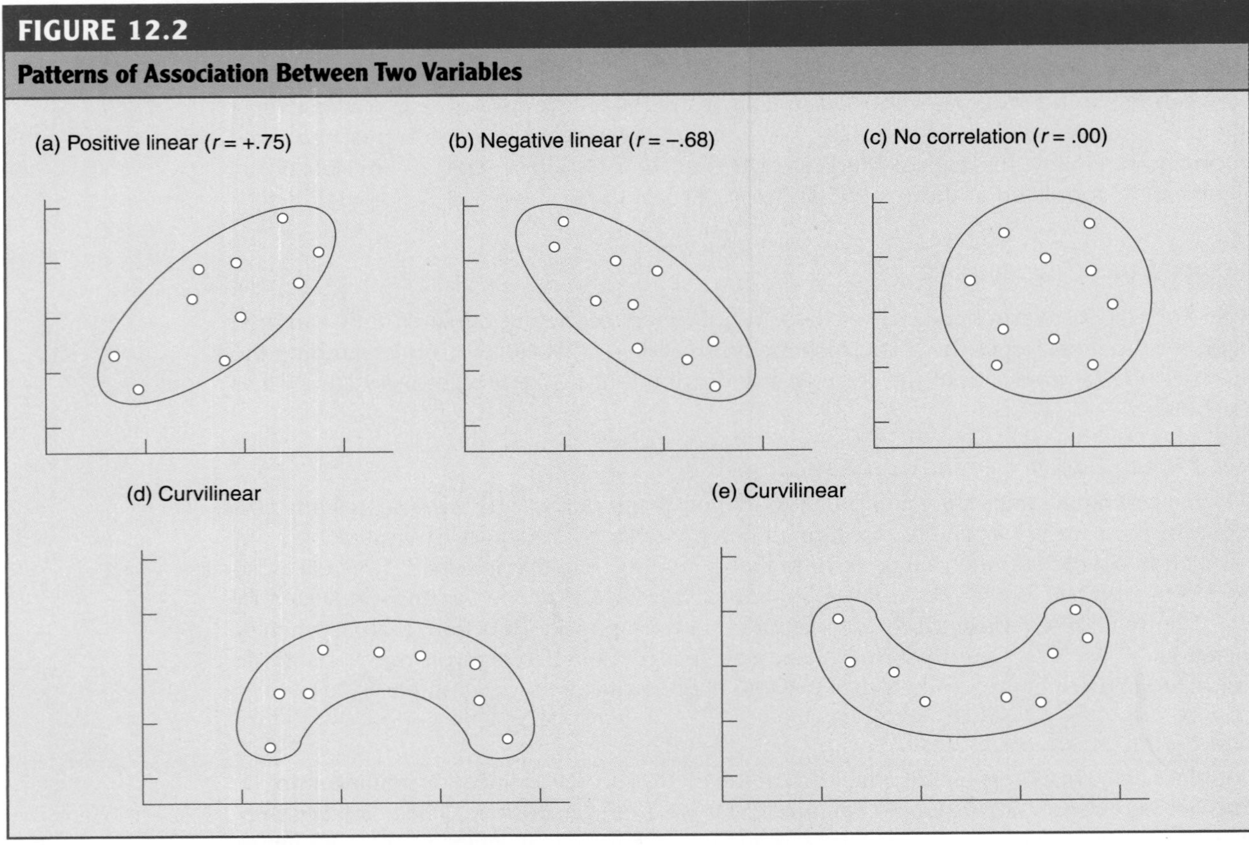

Another example of this form of distribution would be the relationship between anxiety and points scored in a tennis match. With low anxiety initially, a tennis player might score many points, but this may decline as anxiety sets in. As the match progresses, however, anxiety actually helps keep the tennis player alert, and as anxiety builds, performance actually goes up. In short, a plot of anxiety and points scored would show a curvilinear relationship (such as in part [e] of Figure 12.2).

The correlation coefficient is useful for describing and measuring the association between two variables *if the association is linear.* As shown in the patterns of association in Figure 12.2, the association may be curvilinear (or nonlinear). If an r is used to estimate a curvilinear association, it would provide an underestimate of the correlation. Therefore, researchers use different statistics than the r to calculate the relationship between variables for a curvilinear distribution and for relating ranked data.

Instead of the r coefficient, researchers use the **Spearman rho (r_s)** correlation coefficient for nonlinear data and for other types of data measured on categorical (rank-ordered) scales. When you measure one variable on a continuous (interval or ratio) scale and the other is a categorical, dichotomous scale, the correlation statistic should not be the r but the **point-biserial correlation**. Assume that a researcher correlates continuous, interval scores on depression with males and females (a dichotomous variable). A point-biserial correlation statistic is used by converting the dichotomous variable (males, females) into numerical scores by assigning males = 1 and females = 2. Using these numbers and the formula for ordinal data, the researcher calculates the point-biserial correlation coefficient that measures the degree and direction of association between males and females on depression.

A variation of this theme of using different types of scales in assessing the association between two variables is the phi coefficient. The **phi coefficient** is used to determine the degree and direction of association when *both* variable measures are dichotomous. In our example, males and females might be correlated with drug usage (no and yes). In this situation, the researcher also converts both dichotomous variables to numeric values (males = 1, females = 2; no to drugs = 1, yes to drugs = 2) and then uses the Pearson formula for converted scores.

What Is the Degree and Strength of Association?

Degree of association means that the association between two variables or sets of scores is a correlation coefficient of −1.00 to a +1.00, with 0.00 indicating no linear association at all. This association between two sets of scores reflects whether there is a consistent, predictable association between the scores (Gravetter & Wallnau, 2000).

Correlational researchers interpret the magnitude and direction of the correlations. With numbers indicating strength and valence signs indicating direction (+1.00 to −1.00), the statistic provides a measure of the magnitude of the relationship between two variables. Although the correlation measures the degree of relationship, many researchers prefer to square the correlation and use the resulting value to measure the strength of the relationship (Gravetter & Wallnau, 2000). In this procedure, researchers calculate the **coefficient of determination**, which assesses the proportion of variability in one variable that can be determined or explained by a second variable. For example, if you obtain $r = +.70$ (or $-.70$), squaring this value leads to $r^2 = .49$ (or 49%). This means that almost half (49%) of the variability in Y can be determined or explained by X. For example, we might say that parents' education level explains 49% of students' satisfaction with school ($r^2 = .49$).

Other standards for interpreting the strength of the association also exist. General guidelines indicate whether the size of the coefficient provides meaningful information about the strength of association between two variables. One such guide is available in Cohen and Manion (1994). Consider the following interpretations given the following size of coefficients:

- *.20–.35:* When correlations range from .20 to .35, there is only a slight relationship; this relationship may be slightly statistically significant for 100 or more participants. This size of a coefficient may be valuable to explore the interconnection of variables but of little value in prediction studies.
- *.35–.65:* When correlations are above .35, they are useful for limited prediction. They are the typical values used to identify variable membership in the statistical procedure of factor analysis (the intercorrelation of variables with a scale), and many correlation coefficients for bivariate relationships fall into this area.
- *.66–.85:* When correlations fall into this range, good prediction can result from one variable to the other. Coefficients in this range would be considered very good.
- *.86 and above:* Correlations in this range are typically achieved for studies of construct validity or test–retest reliability. In fact, researchers want their reliability and validity tests to be this high. When two or more variables are related, correlations this high are seldom achieved, and if they result, then two variables actually measure the same underlying trait and should probably be combined in data analysis.

Given a coefficient for the strength of the association between two variables, how do we know if the value is meaningful? One way to find out is to use significance testing. In hypothesis testing, we are selecting a sample and drawing inferences from the sample to the population. For correlational research, the null hypothesis would be that there is no association or relationship among the scores in the population. Testing this hypothesis involves setting a level of significance, calculating the test statistic, examining whether the correlation coefficient value falls into the region of rejection, and rejecting or failing to reject the null hypothesis (see chapter 7). In correlational research, the *r* squared expresses the magnitude of association between the two variables or sets of scores. As such, it represents the effect size (see chapter 7)—another means of assessing the magnitude of the relationship regardless of hypothesis testing.

Multiple Variable Analysis

In many correlation studies, researchers predict outcomes based on more than one predictor variable. Thus, they need to account for the impact of each variable. Two multiple variable analysis approaches are partial correlations and multiple regression.

Partial Correlations

In many research situations, we study three, four, or five variables as predictors of outcomes. Recall from chapter 5 the type of variable called a *mediating* or *intervening variable.* This variable, you may recall, "stands between" the independent and dependent variables and influences both of them. This variable is different from a control variable that influences the outcome in an experiment. We use **partial correlations** to determine the amount of variance that an intervening variable explains in *both* the independent and dependent variables.

A picture of two variables followed by the inclusion of a third can help explain partial correlations. Examine Figure 12.3, which shows a bivariate (two variable) correlation on the left-hand side and a partial (three variable) correlation analysis on the right-hand side. Assume that a researcher conducts a study correlating time-on-task with achievement for middle school children. After gathering the scores, our investigator calculates a

FIGURE 12.3

Common Variance Shared for Bivariate and Partial Correlations

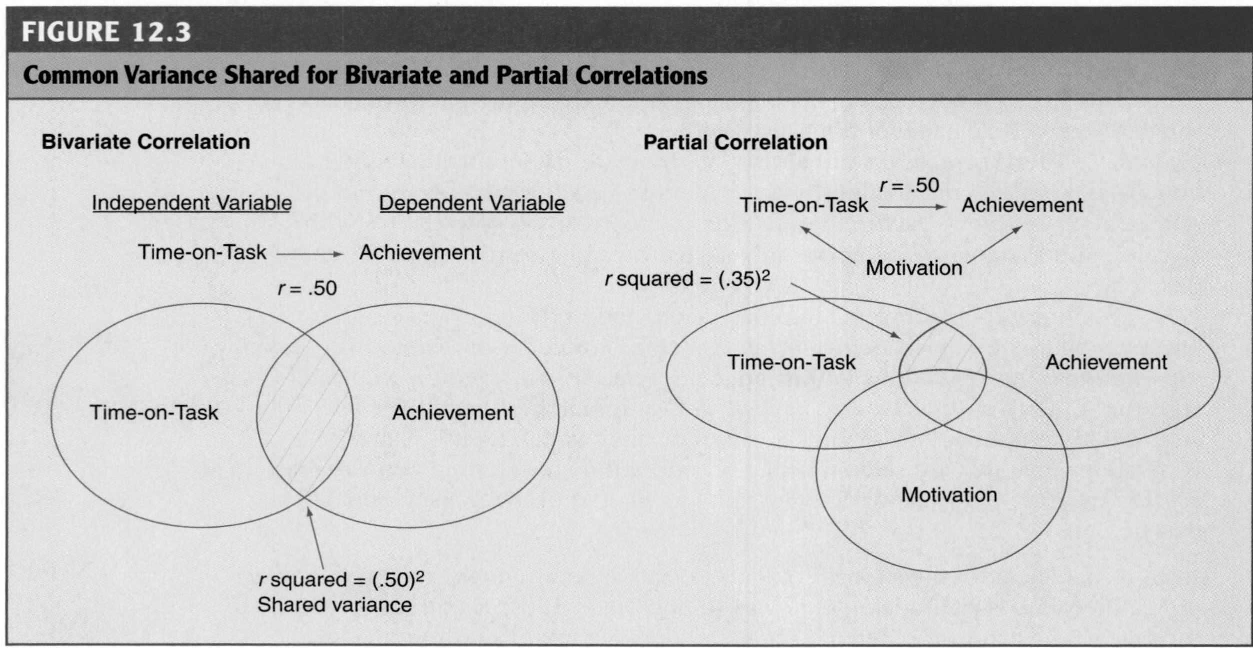

correlation coefficient with the results of $r = .50$. Figure 12.3 indicates this association as well as the r squared, or the proportion of common shared variance between the two variables. However, the situation is more complicated. Student motivation, a third variable, may also influence both the students' time-on-task as well as their achievement in class. The researcher identifies this third variable based on a literature review and a study of past theories that have shown factors likely to influence student achievement. In the design, motivation needs to be removed so that the relationship between time-on-task and achievement can be more clearly determined. A partial correlation statistical analysis is used that removes the shared variance in both time-on-task and achievement by motivation. The mathematical calculations for this coefficient are available in statistics books; it is based on the correlation coefficients among all three variables and their variances. The hatch-marked area indicates this shared variance left after removing the effects of motivation, and the r squared $= (.35)^2$ is now lower than the original correlation of $r = .50$.

Multiple Regression

Correlation researchers use the correlation statistic to predict future scores. To see what impact multiple variables have on an outcome, researchers use regression analysis. We will start with understanding a regression line and then move on to analysis using regression.

A **regression line** is a line of "best fit" for all of the points of scores on the graph. This line comes the closest to all of the points on the plot and it is calculated by drawing a line that minimizes the squared distance of the points from the line. Examine Figure 12.4, which is the same graph used in Figure 12.1, indicating the association between "hours of Internet use per week" and "depression scores" for middle school students. Figure 12.4 now contains additional information: more detail about the regression line. You can see how the line comes close to all of the points on the graph, and we draw it at a diagonal consistent with the positive correlation between Internet use and depression scores.

The calculation of this line holds value for predicting scores on the outcome (i.e., depression) with knowledge about the predictor (i.e., hours of Internet use per week).

FIGURE 12.4

Simple Regression Line

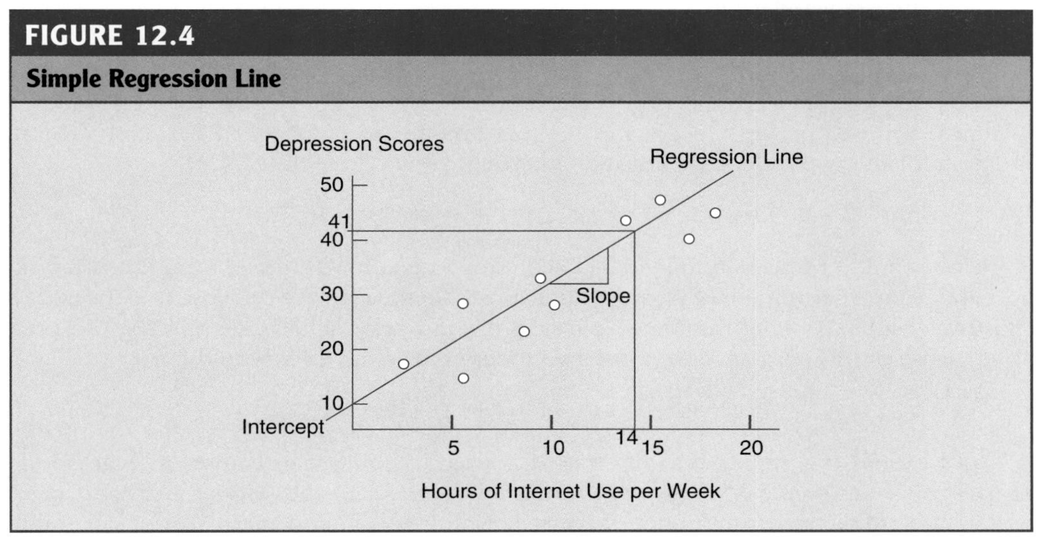

Based on a mathematical formula, a researcher can calculate an equation that expresses this line:

$$Y\text{(predicted)} = b(X) + a$$

where

Y = predicted score on depression
X = actual score on number of hours of Internet use
b = slope of the regression line (called the unstandardized regression coefficient)
a = the intercept or a constant, the value of the predicted Y (depression) score when $X = 0$.

We would expect an individual who uses the Internet 14 hours per week to have a depression score of 41. This score can be estimated by drawing a vertical line from the score for the X-axis variable up to the regression line and over to the Y-axis variable. Alternatively, using the regression formula,

$$\text{If } a = 6,\ b = 2.5, \text{ and } X = 14$$

$$\text{Then } Y\text{(predicted)} = 2.5(14) + 6 = 41$$

Consider a more complicated situation, where multiple independent variables may combine to correlate with a dependent variable. **Multiple regression** (or **multiple correlation**) is a statistical procedure for examining the combined relationship of *multiple* independent variables with a single dependent variable. In regression, the variation in the dependent variable is explained by the variance of each independent variable (the relative importance of each predictor), as well as the combined effect of all independent variables (the proportion of criterion variance explained by all predictors), designated by R^2 (Kline, 1998). Similar to the regression equation mentioned earlier, predicted scores on an outcome can be generated using an equation that is similar to the simple regression equation, but it includes additional predictors. The equation is:

$$Y\text{(predicted)} = b_1(X1) + b_2(X2) + a$$

where

Y = the predicted scores
b_1 = a constant for the slope of $X1$ (b_2, for $X2$)
a = the intercept

Assume that the slope for $b_1 = .24$ and $b_2 = .19$ and the intercept is 10.77. The prediction equation for the two independent variables would be:

$$Y\text{(predicted)} = .24(X1) + .19(X2) + 10.77$$

If we want to predict an individual's score on a quiz, for example, from time-on-task ($X1$) and prior achievement ($X2$), we would substitute their scores on these two measures into the formula. Assume that time-on-task is 10 and prior achievement is 70. The predicted score of this combination of the two independent variables would be:

$$Y\text{(predicted)} = .24(10) + .19(70) + 10.77$$

Let's extend our example to illustrate a couple of additional features of regression. Suppose that time-on-task, motivation, prior achievement in the subject area, and peer friends are predicted to influence student learning (or achievement) for at-risk high

TABLE 12.2

Sample Regression Table: Student Learning (Outcome Variable)

Predictor Variables	Beta
Time-on-task	.11
Motivation	.18
Prior achievement	.20*
Peer friend influence	.05

R = .38
R squared = .14
*$p < .05$
N = 90

school students. We may want to know how these variables *in combination* predict student learning. Knowing this information is probably more realistic than determining the correlation between time-on-task and achievement; it models the complex world in which high school students live. In short, a complicated situation exists, and we need to determine how each variable individually and in combination helps explain the variation in student learning. This information will help us isolate factors that can be changed in a high school or issues to be addressed with the students.

We can calculate regression coefficients for each variable, assess the combined influence of all variables, and provide a picture of the results. A **regression table** shows the overall amount of variance explained in a dependent variable by all independent variables, called R^2 (*R* squared). It also shows the regression weight—the amount of contribution of each variable controlling for the variance of all other variables, called beta—for each variable. Examine the regression table shown in Table 12.2. Here we see four predictor variables of student learning. The coefficients in the right column are the beta weights for each independent variable. A **beta weight** is a coefficient indicating the magnitude of prediction for a variable after removing the effects of all other predictors. The coefficient of a beta weight identifies the strength of the relationship of a predictor variable of the outcomes and enables a researcher to compare (in data with a normal distribution) the strength of one predictor variable with the strength of other predictors. Standardized regression coefficients are typically used for such purposes as choosing variables and assessing their relative importance (Bring, 1994). A beta weight is reported in standardized form (recall from chapter 7 that a *z* score standardizes the measures so that all variables can be compared) and is interpreted like a Pearson *r*, with a value typically from +1.00 to −1.00. Note that regression tables often report a *B* value (an unstandardized coefficient), but these values, while useful in a prediction formula, do not allow researchers to compare the relative strength of each independent variable as a predictor because the value may be scored in different units. For example, one variable may be scored on a 5-point scale and another one on a 3-point scale.

As seen in Table 12.2, the predictor "prior achievement" explains the most variance, followed by "motivation." Below the table we see the correlation of the combination of variables (the multiple correlation designated by *R*) of .38 and the proportion of variability explained in the dependent variables by all of the predictors (R^2) of .14. Recall that the value R^2, called the *coefficient of determination*, represents the proportion of variability explained by the independent variables in the dependent variable. In reporting results, correlational researchers should indicate not only the statistical significance of the test, but also the effect size variance, R^2.

HOW DO YOU CONDUCT A CORRELATIONAL STUDY?

From our discussion about the key characteristics of correlational research, we can begin to see steps emerge that you might use when planning or conducting a study. The following steps illustrate the process of conducting correlational research.

Step 1. Determine If a Correlational Study Best Addresses the Research Problem

A correlational study is used when a need exists to study a problem requiring the identification of the direction and degree of association between two sets of scores. It is useful for identifying the type of association, explaining complex relationships of multiple factors that explain an outcome, and predicting an outcome from one or more predictors. Correlational research does not "prove" a relationship; rather, it indicates an association between two or more variables.

Because you are not comparing groups in a correlational study, you use research questions rather than hypotheses. Sample questions in a correlational study might be:

- Is creativity related to IQ test scores for elementary children? (associating two variables)
- What factors explain a student teacher's ethical behavior during the student-teaching experience? (exploring a complex relationship)
- Does high school class rank predict a college student's grade point average in the first semester of college? (prediction)

Step 2. Identify Individuals to Study

Ideally, you should randomly select the individuals to generalize results to the population, and seek permissions to collect the data from responsible authorities and from the institutional review board. The group needs to be of adequate size for use of the correlational statistic, such as $N = 30$; larger sizes contribute to less error variance and better claims of representativeness. For instance, a researcher might study 100 high school athletes to correlate the extent of their participation in different sports and their use of tobacco. A narrow range of scores from a population may influence the strength of the correlation relationships. For example, if you look at the relationship between height of basketball players and number of baskets in a game, you might find a strong relationship among K–12th graders. But if you are selecting NBA players, this relationship may be significantly weaker.

Step 3. Identify Two or More Measures for Each Individual in the Study

Because the basic idea of correlational research is to compare participants in this single group on two or more characteristics, measures of variables in the research question need to be identified (e.g., literature search of past studies), and instruments that measure the variables need to be obtained. Ideally, these instruments should have proven validity and reliability. You can obtain permissions from publishers or authors to use the instruments. Typically one variable is measured on each instrument, but a single instrument might contain both variables being correlated in the study.

Step 4. Collect Data and Monitor Potential Threats

The next step is to administer the instruments and collect at least two sets of data from each individual. The actual research design is quite simple as a visual presentation. Two data scores are collected for each individual until you obtain scores from each person in the study. This is illustrated with three individuals as follows:

Participants:	Measures or Observations:	
Individual 1	01	02
Individual 2	01	02
Individual 3	01	02

This situation holds for describing the association between two variables or for predicting a single outcome from a single predictor variable. You collect multiple independent variables to understand complex relationships.

A small sample database for 10 college students is shown in Table 12.3. The investigator seeks to explain the variability in first-year grade point averages (GPAs) for these 10 graduate students in education. Assume that our investigator has identified these four predictors in a review of the literature. In past studies, these predictors have positively correlated with achievement in college. The researcher can obtain information for the predictor variables from the college admissions office. The criterion, GPA during the first year, is available from the registrar's office. In this regression study, the researcher seeks to identify which one factor or combination of factors best explains the variance in

TABLE 12.3

Example of Data Collected in a Regression Study

Student	College GPA	GRE Scores (Composite)	Strength of Recommendations (1–10 scale)	Fit to Program (1–10 scale)	First Semester GPA in Graduate School (4-point scale)
Lindsey	3.5	950	8	6	3.10
Palmira	3.6	1120	9	7	3.60
Benito	3.0	1000	9	8	3.10
Ren	3.8	1250	8	9	3.70
Lucy	3.2	1150	7	7	3.40
Kent	3.5	1000	8	8	3.10
Jason	3.2	900	6	6	3.00
Andrew	3.4	950	7	7	3.10
Dave	3.9	1200	9	9	3.80
Carlo	3.7	1140	8	8	3.70

first-year graduate-student GPAs. A review of this data shows that the scores varied on each variable, with more variation among GRE scores than among recommendation and fit-to-program scores. Also, it appears that higher college GPA and GRE scores are positively related to higher first-semester GPAs.

In this example, because the data were available from admissions offices, the researcher need not be overly concerned about procedures that threaten the validity of the scores. However, a potential for restricted range of scores—little variation in scores—certainly exists. Other factors that might affect the researcher's ability to draw valid inferences from the results are the lack of standard administration procedures, the conditions of the testing situation, and the expectations of participants.

Step 5. Analyze the Data and Represent the Results

The objective in correlational research is to describe the degree of association between two or more variables. The investigator looks for a pattern of responses and uses statistical procedures to determine the strength of the relationship as well as its direction. A statistically significant relationship, if found, does not imply causation (cause and effect) but merely an association between the variables. More rigorous procedures, such as those used in experiments, can provide better control than those used in a correlational study.

The analysis begins with coding the data and transferring it from the instruments into a computer file. Then the researcher needs to determine the appropriate statistic to use. An initial question is whether the data are linearly or curvilinearly related. A scatterplot of the scores (if a bivariate study) can help determine this question. Also, consider whether:

- Only one independent variable is being studied (Pearson's correlation coefficient)
- A mediating variable explains both the independent and dependent variables and needs to be controlled (partial correlation coefficient)
- More than one independent variable needs to be studied to explain the variability in a dependent variable (multiple regression coefficient)

Based on the most appropriate statistical test, the researcher next calculates whether the statistic is significant based on the scores. For example, a p value is obtained in a bivariate study by:

- Setting the alpha level
- Using the critical values of an r table, available in many statistics books
- Using degrees of freedom of $N = 2$ with this table
- Calculating the observed r coefficient and comparing it with the r-critical value
- Rejecting or failing to reject the null hypothesis at a specific significance level, such as $p < 0.05$

In addition, it is useful to also report effect size (r^2; as discussed in chapter 7). In correlational analysis, the effect size is the Pearson's correlation coefficient squared. In representing the results, the correlational researcher will present a correlation matrix of all variables as well as a statistical table (for a regression study) reporting the R and R^2 values and the beta weights for each variable.

Step 6. Interpret the Results

The final step in conducting a correlational study is interpreting the meaning of the results. This requires discussing the magnitude and the direction of the results in a correlational study, considering the impact of intervening variables in a partial correlation study, interpreting the regression weights of variables in a regression analysis, and developing a predictive equation for use in a prediction study.

In all of these steps, an overall concern is whether your data support the theory, the hypotheses, or questions. Further, the researcher considers whether the results confirm or disconfirm findings from other studies. Also, a reflection is made about whether some of the threats discussed above may have contributed to erroneous coefficients and the steps that might be taken by future researchers to address these concerns.

HOW DO YOU EVALUATE A CORRELATIONAL STUDY?

To evaluate and assess the quality of a correlational study, you might use the following criteria:

- Is the size of the sample adequate for hypothesis testing?
- Does the researcher adequately display the results in matrices or graphs?
- Is there an interpretation about the direction and magnitude of the association between two variables?
- Is there an assessment of the magnitude of the relationship based on the coefficient of determination, p values, effect size, or the size of the coefficient?
- Is the researcher concerned about the form of the relationship so that an appropriate statistic is chosen for analysis?
- Has the researcher identified the predictor and the criterion variables?
- If a visual model of the relationships is advanced, does the researcher indicate the expected direction of the relationships among variables? Or the predicted direction based on observed data?
- Are the statistical procedures clearly identified?

APPLYING WHAT YOU HAVE LEARNED: A CORRELATIONAL STUDY

To apply ideas in this chapter, read through the correlational study on page 378 by Ting (2000), noting the marginal annotations that identify the characteristics of both correlational *and* quantitative research. This article was chosen because it presents a prediction study using data from Asian Americans. It includes correlation analysis as well as the use of the advanced regression statistics. The predictors and the criterion variables were clearly identified in this study, and it contains useful, straightforward tables to present the data.

As you review this article, look for elements of the research process listed below:

- The research problem and the use of quantitative research
- The use of the literature
- The purpose statement and research questions or hypotheses
- Types and procedures of correlational data collection
- Types and procedures of correlational data analysis and interpretation
- The overall reporting structure

The Research Problem and Use of Quantitative Research

The research problem—see Paragraph 03

Characteristics of quantitative research—see the marginal annotations on the left side of the page

In the third paragraph, the author introduces the research problem—that Asian American college students continue to face problems such as racism, psychological and mental problems, loneliness, and isolation. This issue, plus the need for more studies about the psychosocial adjustment of Asian Americans (Paragraph 08), requires an examination of the predictors of academic success.

The article contains key characteristics of a quantitative study. It:

- Addresses a research problem focused on a need to predict factors that explain academic success and retention (Paragraph 03)
- Identifies predictors in the literature that influence success and retention (Paragraphs 04–08)
- Focuses the purpose statement on relating variables, specifically SAT and psychosocial variables to student GPA and retention (Paragraph 08)
- Collects numeric data (Paragraph 10) from a large number of students (Paragraph 09)
- Relies on instruments, such as the Noncognitive Questionnaire (NCQ), identified before the study began (Paragraph 10)
- Conducts statistical analysis (Paragraph 14) using descriptive statistics (Paragraph 15), correlations (Paragraph 18), multiple regression (Paragraph 18), and discriminant analysis (Paragraph 17)
- Analyzes the data by describing trends (Paragraph 15) and analyzing variables (Paragraph 18)
- Is written objectively, with the researcher in the background (e.g., Paragraph 15), and uses a standard approach to the structure (e.g., method, results, discussion; see headings throughout)
- Forms interpretations based on comparing results with predictions from past studies (e.g., Paragraphs 18–24)

Use of the Literature

Paragraphs 04–08

The literature at the beginning of the study helps to identify the predictors that potentially affect the academic success and retention of Asian Americans. One by one the author introduces these predictors and draws on specific studies. The author also introduces an instrument, the NCQ, that is used in the study.

The Purpose Statement and Research Questions

The purpose statement—Paragraph 08

Research questions—not stated

The author clearly identifies the purpose statement in Paragraph 08. This statement indicates that predictor variables will be examined in terms of two outcomes: GPA and retention. Research questions, however, are not stated, and perhaps the use of research questions is redundant with the purpose statement. Therefore, the author may not feel a need to include both questions and a purpose statement.

Types and Procedures of Correlational Data Collection

Paragraph 12

The data collection consists of administering an instrument to students at the new-student orientation. This instrument consists of the NCQ. In Paragraph 11, we learn about the validity and reliability of this instrument. The outcome measures related to GPA and retention are obtained later based on student consent (Paragraph 12), but we learn little about the process of accessing student records.

Types and Procedures of Correlational Data Analysis and Interpretation

Data analysis—Paragraph 14

Interpretation—Paragraphs 18–24

The author employs several data analysis procedures that are not discussed, such as descriptive statistics (Paragraph 14) and correlations (Paragraph 18). The discussion about data analysis consists of information about multiple regression analysis using SPSS and the procedures involved in this analysis. However, the author did present a correlation matrix (Paragraph 18) and provides an interpretation of the direction of the scores (Paragraph 15). The investigator uses the advanced statistics of regression analysis to examine the combined influence of the predictors on fall and spring GPAs (Paragraph 18). The regression formula enables the researcher to predict outcomes based on the combination of multiple factors.

In reporting the results, as well as the data analysis, the author does not check for the linear distribution of scores (although this procedure may have been done). In Paragraph 26, however, the author does mention the small sample size for multiple regression analysis, a factor that might have contributed to a nonnormal distribution of scores.

The Overall Reporting Structure

Objectivity—Paragraph 15 (as an example)

Structure—the headings throughout the report

The tone of this report is consistent with a quantitative study—the objective researcher reporting the results (e.g., see Paragraph 15). Also, the overall structure supports a quantitative study with headings that reflect methods, results, and discussion.

KEY IDEAS IN THE CHAPTER

In some educational situations, neither the treatment nor the ability to manipulate the conditions are conducive to an experiment. In this case, educators turn to a correlational design. In correlational research, investigators use a correlation statistical technique to describe and measure the degree of association (or relationship) between two or more variables or sets of scores. You use a correlational design to study the relationship between two or more variables or to predict outcome.

The history of correlational research draws on the themes of the origin and development of the correlation statistical test and the procedures for using and interpreting the statistical test. Statisticians first identified the procedures for calculating the correlation statistics in the late 19th century. In the late 1800s, Karl Pearson developed the familiar correlation formula we use today. Today, with the use of multiple statistical procedures such as factor analysis, reliability estimates, and regression, researchers can test elaborate models of variables using correlational statistical procedures.

Although a correlation is a statistic, its use in research has contributed to a specific research design called *correlational research*. This research has taken two primary forms of research design: explanation and prediction. An explanatory correlational design explains or clarifies the degree of association among two or more variables at one point in time. Researchers are interested in whether two variables co-vary, in which a change in one variable is reflected in changes in the other. An example is whether motivation is associated with academic performance. In the second form of design, a prediction design, the investigator identifies variables that will positively predict an outcome or criterion. In this form of research, the researcher uses one or more predictor variables and a criterion (or outcome) variable. A prediction permits us to forecast future performance, such as whether a student's GPA in college can be predicted from his or her high school performance.

Underlying both of these designs are key characteristics of correlational research. Researchers create displays of scores correlated for participants. These displays are scatterplots, a graphic representation of the data, and correlation matrices, a table that shows the correlation among all the variables. To interpret correlations, researchers examine the positive or negative direction of the correlation of scores, a plot of the distribution of scores to see if they are normally or nonnormally distributed, the degree of association between scores, and the strength of the association of the scores. When more than two variables are correlated, the researcher is interested in controlling for the effects of the third variable, and in examining a prediction equation of multiple variables that explains the outcome.

Steps in conducting a correlational study are to use the design for associating variables or making predictions, to identify individuals to study, to specify two or more measures for each individual, to collect data and monitor potential threats to the validity of the scores, to analyze the data using the correlation statistic for either continuous or categorical data, and to interpret the strength and the direction of the results.

Useful Information for Producers of Research

- Identify whether you plan to examine the association between or among variables or use correlational research to make predictions about an outcome.
- Plot on a graph the association between your variables so that you can determine the direction, form, and strength of the association.
- Use appropriate correlational statistics in your design based on whether the data are continuous or categorical and whether the form of the data is linear or nonlinear.
- Present a correlation matrix of the Pearson coefficients in your study.

Useful Information for Consumers of Research

- Recognize that a correlation study is not as rigorous as an experiment because the researcher can only control statistically for variables rather than physically manipulate variables. Correlational studies do not "prove" relationships; rather, they indicate an association between or among variables or sets of scores.
- Correlation studies are research in which the investigator seeks to explain the association or relationship among variables or to predict outcomes.
- Realize that all correlational studies, no matter how advanced the statistics, use a correlation coefficient as their base for analysis. Understanding the intent of this coefficient helps you determine the results in a correlational study.

Additional Resources You Might Examine

For additional detailed discussions about the correlation statistic and more advanced statistics, see:

Gravetter, F. J., & Wallnau, L. B. (2000). *Statistics for the behavioral sciences* (5th ed.). Belmont, CA: Wadsworth/Thomson Learning.

Salkind, N. J. (2000). *Statistics for people who (think they) hate statistics.* Thousand Oaks, CA: Sage.

For discussions about more advanced correlational procedures, especially regression analysis, see:

Pedhazur, E. J. (1997). *Multiple regression in behavioral research: Explanation and prediction* (3rd ed.) Ft. Worth, TX: Harcourt Brace College Publishers.

Go to our Companion Website at **www.prenhall.com/creswell** to:

- ◆ assess your understanding of chapter content with Multiple-Choice Questions,
- ◆ apply what you've learned with Essay Questions,
- ◆ practice your research skills with interactive Building Research Skills exercises, and
- ◆ broaden your knowledge of research with Web Links to research topics on the Internet.

Quantitative Characteristics

A quantitative research problem requires description or explanation.

Correlational Research Characteristics

Predicting Asian Americans' Academic Performance in the First Year of College: An Approach Combining SAT Scores and Noncognitive Variables

Siu-Man Raymond Ting

(01) *Factors related to academic performance and student retention of Asian American freshmen (N = 96) at a predominantly white university in the southeast were studied. In addition to SAT-mathematics score, three noncognitive variables were found to be significant predictors of GPA: realistic self-appraisal system, successful leadership experience, and demonstrated community service. Realistic self-appraisal and demonstrated community service were significant indicators of student retention. Implications for student affairs professionals and limitations of the study were discussed.*

(02) Asian Americans are the fastest growing minority group in universities in the United States (American Council on Education, 1998). Between 1976 and 1996, the number of Asian American college students tripled from 2% to 6% of the total undergraduate student population (Snyder, 1999). The current estimated population of Asian Americans is only 4% of the U.S. population (U.S. Census Bureau, 1999). These figures imply Asian Americans may be slightly overrepresented in universities. They also reflect an increase in recent Asian immigration to the United States and an emphasis on education among Asian cultures. This trend is likely to continue: by the year 2050, Asian Americans will constitute 10% of the U.S. population, primarily because of immigration (Atkinson, Morten, & Sue, 1993). To match the needs of this increasing population, student affairs professionals and other educators must gain more information about Asian Americans, including factors affecting their academic performance and retention in universities.

(03) Asian Americans are often portrayed as a model minority because of their hard work and educational achievements, and for earning family incomes close to White Americans (Kao, 1995; Okutsu, 1989; Taylor & Stern, 1997). Asian American students were found to spend significantly more time on homework and parents have higher educational expectations for their children than White Americans did (Mau, 1997). In spite of their accomplishments, Asian Americans continue to face problems such as a discrepancy between education and income (Atkinson et al., 1993), insufficient mastery of English (Sue & Sue, 1990), racism (Delucchi & Do, 1996; Leung, 1990; Tan, 1994), and psychosocial and mental problems such as loneliness, isolation, and anxiety (Solberg, Ritsma, Davis, Tata, & Jolly, 1994). Research studies show that, at colleges and universities, Asian Americans still face many challenges including inadequate services (Greene, 1987), challenge of affirmative action policy on admissions (Selingo, 1999), psychosocial problems when adjusting to universities (Abe & Zane, 1990), alcohol and substance abuse (Chi, Lubben, & Kitano, 1989), and less involvement than their White counterpart in student activities (Wang & Sedlacek, 1992). Many Asian Americans have expressed an interest in participating in student activities and also stated that they were not involved because of time constraints (Wang & Sedlacek, 1992). The resultant social isolation affects social well-being and student retention of ethnic

Reprinted with permission from *The Journal of College Student Development.*
Siu-Man Raymond Ting is Assistant Professor of Educational Research and Leadership and Counselor Education at North Carolina State University.

minorities in universities (Loo & Rolison, 1986). Asian Americans were found to experience difficulties in social adjustment and dissatisfaction with the campus services (Abe & Zane, 1990; Bennet & Okinaka, 1989; Sue & Zane, 1985). Similar to other ethnic minorities, Asian Americans who were dissatisfied about the quality of campus life and felt socially alienated were more likely to drop out (Bennet & Okinaka, 1989; Sue & Zane 1985).

(04) Owing to their minority status and cultural background, Asian American students face many challenges in universities. Nonetheless, little has been found explaining academic performance of Asian Americans. Traditional studies adopting standardized test scores and high school grade-point-average GPA to predict students' academic performance have produced low validity (Fuertes, Sedlacek, & Liu, 1994). In addition, more bias in the validity of using SAT scores and high school GPA to predict college first year GPA was found for ethnic minorities than in the majority group (Sedlacek, 1998; Stone, 1990). The U.S. Education Department also issued a guideline reminding universities not to use SAT scores as the sole admission criterion (Healy, 1999). Therefore, this guideline reflects the possibility that SAT does not accurately portray academic abilities of Asian Americans.

The quantitative literature plays a major role.

(05) Recent studies have shifted the focus to noncognitive or nontraditional factors. Astin (1993) found that student involvement in college, including physical and psychological energy devoted to college experience, affected learning and personal development. Tinto (1993) reported in his Student Departure Model that a student's decision to remain or leave a university campus is a function of the student's personal and academic background and how well she or he integrates into the academic and social life of the campus. Adopting attribution theory to explore student motivation for academic studies, Yan and Gaier (1994) found that all students attributed academic success first to their efforts, then to ability, strategies, and finally to luck. Gender differences were not found. They reported that Asian American students had less of a self-serving bias than White American students did. A self-serving bias refers to the tendency to take credit for success but denying responsibility for failure. Owing to cultural influences, Asian Americans attributed effort as equally important for success and failure or even more important for failure. Placing greater emphasis on individualism and autonomy, Yan and Gaier found that White Americans were significantly less likely than their Asian American colleagues to attribute failure to lack of effort. In summary, noncognitive factors were found to explain student academic performance and such factors may vary among different ethnic groups.

The quantitative literature justifies the research problem and provides direction for the study.

(06) Employing eight psychosocial variables in the Noncognitive Questionnaire (NCQ), Tracey and Sedlacek (1984, 1985, 1987) better predicted academic performance and student retention of Black and White students than using SAT scores. The Noncognitive Questionnaire (Tracey & Sedlacek, 1984, 1989) was designed to assess psychosocial aspects that influence college success: personal goals, college expectation, academic self-concept, self-appraisal system, leadership experience and community service in high school, knowledge acquired in a field, ability to understand and cope with racism, and availability of a strong support person.

(07) The NCQ was found to have effective predictability of academic performance and student retention for different student populations: Asian Americans (Fuertes et al., 1994), African Americans (Boyer & Sedlacek, 1988; Sedlacek & Adams-Gaston, 1992); Hispanics (Fuertes & Sedlacek, 1995), White Americans and African Americans (Ting & Robinson, 1998; Tracey & Sedlacek, 1984, 1985, 1987), specially admitted students (Ting, 1997; White & Sedlacek, 1986), and low-income and first-generation students (Ting, 1998). Correlations with college grades and retention were

significantly higher than the SAT scores alone when the noncognitive variables were used in conjunction with standardized test scores and earlier grades. In Fuertes et al.'s study, community service, realistic self-appraisal, and positive self-concept were found to be equally effective compared with SAT-math and SAT-verbal scores in predicting Asian Americans' first year GPAs. No significant predictors were found for student retention in the first year. In addition to confirming the predictive validity of Tracey and Sedlacek's (1984) psychosocial variables. Ting and Robinson (1998) also found that parent education level and need for financial aid were related to students' academic performance in the first year of college.

The quantitative purpose statement, research questions, or hypotheses are specific and narrow.

Correlational researchers seek the association or relationship between two variables or sets of scores.

(08) In summary, compared with other ethnic minorities, professional literature shows that Asian Americans are able to attain their educational goals although they experience challenges in college, particularly in the area of psychosocial adjustment. However, comparatively fewer studies were found studying how psychosocial adjustment may affect Asian Americans' academic performance and retention. Sedlacek (1998) suggested that each university should study psychosocial factors affecting student academic success. Although Fuertes et al. (1994) reported psychosocial predictors of academic success of Asian Americans, their study was based on a campus where Asian Americans comprised 9% of the student population, which may not be representative of U.S. population. Therefore, generalization of this study is somewhat limited. The purpose of the current study was to use SAT scores and Tracey and Sedlacek's psychosocial variables to predict Asian American students' GPA and retention in the first year of college.

The quantitative purpose statement, research questions, or hypotheses seek measurable, observable data on variables.

Correlation researchers use the correlation statistic to predict future scores.

Method

Participants

Quantitative data collection involves studying a large number of individuals.

(09) At a Southeastern public land-grant research university, 96 first-year Asian American students participated in the study in Fall 1996 as a part of the survey of the Noncognitive Variables Research Committee. This sample represents over 90% of the new Asian American freshmen at the university. The participants' mean age was 18.19. Fifty-nine of the participants were men and 37 were women.

Measures

Quantitative data collection is based on using instruments identified prior to the study.

Quantitative data collection involves gathering numeric data.

(10) *NCQ*. The NCQ was designed to assess psychosocial aspects that affect student success in college. It contains 23 items: 18 Likert-type, 2 multiple choice, and 3 open-ended. The NCQ's eight scales listed here (with the range of scores) are: (a) positive self-concept (7–27), (b) realistic self-appraisal system (4–14), (c) understanding and coping with racism (5–25), (d) preference of long-term goals (3–13), (e) a strong support person (3–15), (f) successful leadership experience (3–13), (g) demonstrated community service (2–8), and (h) acquired knowledge in a field (2–8). Tracey and Sedlacek (1984) reported a 2-week test-retest reliability of a range from .74 to .94, with a median of .85 for the NCQ scales. Interrater reliability on the three open-ended NCQ items ranged from .73 to 1.00. The NCQ appears to have promising content validity, and strong construct and predictive validity (Ting & Robinson, 1998).

(11) *Predictors*. Students' scores on the NCQ and the combined SAT score (verbal and mathematics) were the predictors.

(12) *Criterion Variables*. One criterion was academic performance during the freshmen year. This was measured by term GPA for the Fall and Spring semesters. The second criterion was retention at the end of Fall and Spring indicated by registration records. The students were categorized as being enrolled (coded as 1) or as having dropped out (coded as 0).

Procedure

(13) *Data Collection.* The data was collected as a part of the study of the all-university Noncognitive Variables Research Committee. At the new student orientation, each student received a packet that included the NCQ (Tracey & Sedlacek, 1984) and a demographic and personal background form. Over 90% of the new students attended the orientation where they met in small groups and were invited to participate voluntarily in the study completing the NCQ. Participants consented to access of their academic records. SAT scores and registration status in the first year were obtained from their university records.

Quantitative data analysis consists of statistical analysis.

(14) *Data Analysis.* College performance is defined here as students' GPA and continued enrollment. The author employed step-wise multiple regression analysis with the SPSS for windows (version 8.0) for the analysis. The author attempted to explore the relationships to noncognitive variables first before combining with SAT scores and background variables. Therefore, all NCQ variables were entered first in a step-wise procedure, then SAT scores. Such procedure was adopted for comparing two different measures in previous similar studies (Fuertes et al., 1994; Tracey & Sedlacek, 1981). Discriminant analysis was conducted to predict student retention.

Correlational researchers correlate two or more variables using the procedure of calculating the correlation statistic.

Results

Quantitative researchers take an objective and unbiased approach.

(15) Table 1 shows the means and standard deviations of the predictor and criterion variables. The noncognitive variable scores were similar to those in the Fuertes et al. (1994) study, except that the scores of preference for long-term goals and acquired knowledge in a field were smaller. Table 2 illustrates a correlation matrix between college first-year GPA and predictor variables. SAT-math score and realistic self-appraisal were positively related to students' GPA in Fall and Spring.

Correlational researchers use advanced statistics to control for variables and to examine the combination of factors that affect outcomes.

(16) Table 3 shows the prediction for GPA in Fall and Spring semesters. The multiple regression model explained 26.2% of the variance of Fall GPA. Realistic self-appraisal, successful leadership experience, and SAT-math scores

Quantitative data analysis consists of describing trends, comparing groups, or relating variables.

TABLE 1
Means and Standard Deviations of Predictors and Criterion Variables

	All Students	
Variable	***M***	***SD***
SAT-verbal	537.53	105.79
SAT-math	621.29	77.60
Positive self-concept	19.04	2.44
Realistic self-appraisal system	10.53	1.84
Coping with racism	18.60	2.36
Preference of long-term goals	8.40	1.70
Availability of a strong support person	13.51	1.44
Successful leadership experience	8.77	1.97
Demonstrated community service	5.21	1.44
Acquired knowledge in a field	3.63	1.12
Fall GPA	2.92	0.98
Spring GPA	2.88	.87

Note. Number of students in Fall = 93; Number of students in Spring = 80.

TABLE 2
Correlation Coefficients Between First-Year GPA and Predictor Variables

Correlational researchers present correlation coefficients in a matrix.

Variable	Fall GPA	Spring GPA
SAT-verbal scores	.06	.02
SAT-mathematics scores	.44**	.48**
Positive self-concept	.10	.15
Realistic self-appraisal system	.32*	.31*
Coping with racism	−.04	−.10
Preference of long-term goals	.01	−.09
Availability of a strong support person	.15	−.07
Successful leadership experience	−.18	.05
Demonstrated community service	.04	−.08
Acquired knowledge in a field	.08	.12

*$p < .01$. **$p < .001$.

TABLE 3
Multiple Regression Models Predicting Fall and Spring GPAs

		Standardized			
	Variable	*R*	R^2	Beta	*t*
Fall semester					
All students	Realistic self-appraisal system	.32	.10	.32	2.75*
	Successful leadership experience	.39	.15	−.23	3.85***
	SAT-math scores	.51	.26	.35	4.44***
Spring semester					
All students	Realistic self-appraisal system	.31	.10	.30	2.92**
	Demonstrated community service	.38	.15	−.24	−.21*
	SAT-math scores	.56	.31	.41	4.31***

*$p < .01$. **$p < .005$. ***$p < .001$.

In the Fall semester, $F = 10.267$; $p < .002$ for the regression model with realistic self-appraisal system; $F = 8.04$, $p < .001$ for the regression model with realistic self-appraisal system and successful leadership experience; $F = 10.54$; $p < .0001$ for the regression model with realistic self-appraisal system, successful leadership experience, and SAT-mathematics score.

In the Spring semester, $F = 8.52$; $p < .005$ for the regression model with realistic self-appraisal system; $F = 6.65$, $p < .002$ for the regression model with realistic self-appraisal system and demonstrated community service; $F = 11.55$; $p < .0001$ for the regression model with realistic self-appraisal system, demonstrated community service, and SAT-math score.

were significant predictors. In the Spring, the regression model accounted for 31.3% of the variance. Realistic self-appraisal, demonstrated community service, and SAT-math scores were significant indicators for Spring GPA.

(17) Employing discriminant analysis with stepwise procedure, realistic self-appraisal and demonstrated community service were the effective indicators for Fall student retention (Wilks's Lambda = .861, $\chi^2 = 13.36$, $df = 2$, and $p < .001$). In Spring, no variables were found to explain student retention.

Discussion

Quantitative interpretations compare results with predictions.

(18) The current study revealed both cognitive and noncognitive variables for academic success of Asian American students in the first year of college. SAT-math score and NCQ variables as a group appear to be similarly important indicating the students' GPA. Regarding SAT-math score, previous studies show similar findings for Asian Americans (Fuertes et al., 1994; Sue & Abe, 1988). SAT-verbal score was not a predictor, probably because being a land-grant institution, the studied university was popular for science and technology disciplines. Also, Asian Americans have a tendency to value applied science versus arts and social studies (Sue & Sue, 1990). In addition to their cultural values, Sue and Sue (1990) suggested that other reasons for such a tendency include choosing to study in better-paid fields and struggle with English even after a few generations in the United States; therefore most Asian American students studied in these majors.

(19) The noncognitive predictors in the current study explained a higher percentage of variance for student success than did Fuertes et al. (1994). In addition, a major difference between the two studies should be mentioned here. At the institution where the current study was conducted, Asian Americans comprised 3% of the student population, a closer representation of the current U.S. population than the institution where the earlier study was conducted.

(20) Realistic self-appraisal, successful leadership experience, and demonstrated community service were important predictors of the students' GPA. A realistic self-appraisal system was a consistent predictor for first-year GPA and retention. The need for self-understanding and proper self-evaluation is clear. In regard to a proper self-appraisal system, Asian American students need to understand their minority situation, recognize their level of academic performance and position and be able to cope with the social environment of the campus. They also need to be able to reward themselves appropriately for achievement as well as respond positively to failure or to obstacles such as racism. In Fuertes et al. (1994), a realistic self-appraisal system was also a factor related to first-year academic performance and continual enrollment beyond the sophomore year.

(21) Successful leadership experience reflects the ability to communicate, engage in a social group, establish relationships in social situations, organize, and complete a task in a team. Asian American students who had such experience would adjust better to a university campus than those who did not. In Fuertes et al.'s (1994) study, this factor was not found; however, a similar factor demonstrated community service was found to be an indicator for academic performance.

(22) Noncognitive variables were related to student retention probably because they helped students cope with reported psychosocial stresses including loneliness, isolation, and anxiety (Abe & Zane, 1990; Solberg et al., 1994; Sue & Zane, 1985) and racism (Delucchi & Do, 1996; Leung, 1990; Tan, 1994). Specifically, minority students who have a realistic self-appraisal system understand their minority situation, recognize the social environment of the campus, and understand ways to work through the existing system. Therefore, they are more likely to remain on the same campus.

(23) Demonstrated community service was another indicator for student retention and academic performance. Community service reflects the ability for the Asian American students to have a sense of belonging and establish a link to the community. Asian Americans were found to be the

most distant group from other ethnic minorities (Abe & Zane, 1990). They experienced problems adjusting to college life such as loneliness, anxiety, and depression (Abe & Zane, 1990; Loo & Rolison, 1986). Being an ethnic minority, Asian Americans need to integrate with the majority and other ethnic minority groups and contribute to the community in order to ease their adjustment and accomplish their academic goals (Sue & Sue, 1990).

(24) Professional literature reports academic support and student service programs that may enhance academic performance of Asian Americans (House & Wohlt, 1990; Mueller, 1993; Tan, 1995). An ethnic minority student in a predominantly White American campus may experience isolation and loneliness (Loo & Rolison, 1986). In the process of integrating to the campus community, they particularly need a person who can help them when they have problems. Mueller (1993) reported a mentor program for Asian Americans and other ethnic minorities that enhanced students' academic and psychosocial development in the first year of college. Tan (1995) found that such mentors could enhance minority student satisfaction about university life and academic performance. This mentor or role model can be a faculty member, a student affairs professional, or a peer. Therefore, Asian American students can benefit from student service by being both mentor or mentees. Tan (1995) also found that the Asian American and African American students did not feel their role models had to be from their own ethnic group.

(25) A tutoring program helped improve Asian American freshmen's cumulative GPA after they had participated in it for a semester (House & Wohlt, 1990). Therefore, faculty and student affairs professionals, particularly those who teach first-year seminars, should consider similar programs for Asian American students.

(26) A few methodological limitations should be noted. First, the current study was based on only one institution and the sample size was relatively small for multiple analyses. Regarding the number and type of analyses, the small sample size increased the risk of Type I error. However, the alpha for all major analyses was comparatively small, below .05 level. Also, the results for the current study seem to be compatible with other studies mentioned in the Discussion and Introduction sections. However, further study with a larger sample is needed to examine the validity of the current findings. Second, this is a 1-year study. Indicators of success for years beyond the freshman year should be explored in future research.

(27) In conclusion, the current results indicate that both SAT scores and selected noncognitive variables can predict academic performance of Asian American students. However, such information about variations among Asian American subgroups are still lacking. Student affairs professionals should continue to investigate this topic, including differences within Asian American populations. Other noncognitive variables unidentified in this study, yet related to Asian American's college academic performance over 4 years, included positive self-concept, preference of long-term goals, availability of a strong support person, acquired knowledge in a field, and

Quantitative research reports use standard, fixed structures and evaluation criteria.

Correspondence concerning this article should be addressed to Siu-Man Raymond Ting, Educational Research and Leadership and Counselor Education, North Carolina State University, 520 Poe Hall, Box 7801, Raleigh, NC 27695-7801: raymond_ring@ncsu.edu coping with racism (Fuertes et al., 1994). In this regard, longitudinal studies are needed to provide additional information about which noncognitive variables are important for Asian Americans' long-term persistence and success in colleges and universities.

References

Abe, J. S., & Zane, N. W. (1990). Psychological maladjustment among Asian and White American college students: Controlling for confounds. *Journal of Counseling Psychology, 37,* 437–444.

American Council on Education. (1998). *Minorities in higher education.* Washington, DC: Author.

Astin, A. W. (1993). *What matters in college? Four critical years revisited.* San Francisco: Jossey-Bass.

Atkinson, D. R., Morten, G., & Sue, D. W. (Eds.). (1993). *Counseling American minorities: A cross-cultural perspective* (5th ed.). Dubuque, IA: W. C. Brown.

Bennet, C., & Okinaka, A. M. (1989, March). *Factors related to persistence among Asian, Black, Hispanic, and White undergraduates at a predominantly White university: Compared between first-and fourth-year cohorts.* Paper presented at the annual meeting of the American Educational Research Association, San Francisco, CA.

Boyer, S. P., & Sedlacek, W. E. (1988). Noncognitive predictors of academic success for international students: A longitudinal study. *Journal of College Student Development, 29,* 218–222.

Chi, I., Lubben, J. E., & Kitano, H. H. (1989). Differences in drinking behavior among three Asian-American groups. *Journal of Studies on Alcohol, 50,* 15–23.

Delucchi, M., & Do., H. D. (1996). The model minority myth and perceptions of Asian Americans as victims of racial harassment. *College Student Journal, 30,* 411–414.

Fuertes, J. N., & Sedlacek, W. E. (1995). Using noncognitive variables to predict the grades and retention of Hispanic students. *College Student Affairs Journal, 14* (2), 30–36.

Fuertes, J. N., Sedlacek, W. E., & Liu, W. M. (1994). Using the SAT and noncognitive variables to predict the grades and retention of Asian-American university students. *Measurement and Evaluation in Counseling and Development, 27,* 74–84.

Greene. (1987, November 18). Asian-Americans find U.S. college insensitive, form campus organizations to fight bias. *The Chronicle of Higher Education,* p. A38–A40.

Healy, P. (1999, December 15). Education Department releases new draft guide to use of tests in admissions. *The Chronicle of Higher Education.* [on-line]. Available: http://www.chronicle.com/daily/99/12/99121501n.htm.

House, J. D., & Wohlt, V. (1990). The effect of tutoring program participation on the performance of academically underprepared college freshmen. *Journal of College Student Development, 31,* 365–370.

Kao, G. (1995). Asian-Americans as model minorities? A look at their academic performance. *American Journal of Education, 103,* 121–159.

Leung, P. (1990). Asian-Americans and psychology: Unresolved issues. *Journal of Training and Practice in Professional Psychology, 4* (1), 3–13.

Loo, C. M., & Rolison, G. (1986). Alienation of ethnic minority students at a predominantly White university. *Journal of Higher Education, 57,* 58–77.

Mau, W. C. (1997). Parental influences on high school students' academic achievement: A comparison of Asian immigrants, Asian-Americans, and White Americans. *Psychology in Schools, 34,* 267–277.

Mueller, M. K. (1993). *ALANA Intervention Program,* Port Huron, MI: Saint Clair County Community College. (ERIC Document Reproduction Service No. ED 361 043)

Okutsu, J. K. (1989). Pedagogic "hegemonicide" and the Asian-American student. *Amerasia Journal, 15,* 233–242.

Sedlacek, W. E. (1991). Using noncognitive variables in advising nontraditional students. *NACADA Journal, 11,* 75–82.

Sedlacek, W. E. (1998, Winter). Multiple choices for standardized tests. *Priorities, 10,* 1–15.

Sedlacek, W. E., & Adams-Gaston, J. (1992). Predicting the academic success of student-athletes using SAT and noncognitive variables. *Journal of Counseling and Development, 70*(6), 24–27.

Selingo, J. (1999, December 3). A quiet end to the use of race in college admissions in Florida. *The Chronicle of Higher Education,* p. A 31.

Snyder, T. (1999). *Digest of education statistics, 1998* [On-line]. Available: http://nces.ed.gov/pubsearch/pubsinfo.asp?pubid = 1999036.

Solberg, V. S., Ritsma, S., Davis, B. J., Tata, S. P., & Jolly, A. (1994). Asian American students' severity of problems and willingness to seek help from university counseling centers: Role of previous counseling experience, gender, and ethnicity. *Journal of Counseling Psychology, 41* 275–279.

Stone, B. (1990). Prediction of achievement by Asian-Americans and White children. *Journal of School Psychology, 30*(1), 91–99.

Sue, S., & Abe, J. (1988). *Predictors of academic achievement among Asian-American and White students.* (College Board Rep. No. 88–11). New York: College Entrance Examination Board.

Sue, S., & Zane, N. W. (1985). Academic achievement and socioemotional adjustment among Chinese university students. *Journal of Counseling Psychology, 32,* 570–579.

Sue, D. W., & Sue, D. (1990). *Counseling the culturally different: Theory and practice.* (2nd ed.). New York: Wiley.

Tan. D. L. (1994). Uniqueness of the Asian American experience in higher education. *College Student Journal, 28,* 412–421.

Tan, D. (1995). Perceived importance of role models and its relationship with minority student satisfaction and academic performance. *NACADA Journal, 15*(1), 48–51.

Taylor, C. R., & Stern, B. B. (1997). Asian-Americans: Television advertising and the "model minority" stereotype. *Journal of Advertising, 26,* 47–61.

Ting, S. R. (1997). The Excellence-Commitment-and-Effective-Learning (ExCEL) program: A group intervention for academically high-risk students. *NACADA Journal, 17,* 48–51.

Ting, S. R. (1998, Winter). Predicting first-year grades and retention of college students of first-generation and low-income families. *Journal of College Admission, 158,* 14–23.

Ting, S. R., & Robinson, T. L. (1998). First-year academic success: A prediction model combining cognitive and psychosocial variables: European- and African-Americans. *Journal of College Student Development, 39,* 599–610.

Tinto, V. (1993). *Leaving college: Rethinking the causes and cures of student attrition* (2nd ed.). Chicago: University of Chicago Press.

Tracey, T. J., & Sedlacek, W. E. (1981). Conducting student retention research. *National Association of Student Personnel Administrators Field Report, 5*(2), 5–6.

Tracey, T. J., & Sedlacek, W. E. (1984). Noncognitive variables in predicting academic success by race. *Measurement and Evaluation in Guidance, 16,* 171–178.

Tracey, T. J., & Sedlacek, W. E. (1985). The relationship of noncognitive variables to academic success: A longitudinal comparison by race. *Journal of College Student Personnel, 26,* 410.

Tracey, T. J., & Sedlacek, W. E. (1987). Predicting college graduation using noncognitive variables by race. *Measurement and Evaluation in Counseling and Development, 19,* 177–184.

Tracey, T. J., & Sedlacek, W. E. (1989). Factor structure of the noncognitive questionnaire: Revised across samples of Black and White college students. *Educational and Psychological Measurement, 49,* 637–648.

U.S. Census Bureau. (1999). *Resident population estimates of the United States by sex, race, and Hispanic origin: April 1, 1990 to August 1, 1999* [on-line]. Available: http://www.census.gov/pubsearcg/pubsinfo.asp?pubid = 1999036.

Wang, Y. Y., & Sedlacek, W. E. (1992). Asian-Americans and student organizations: Attitudes and participation. *Journal of College Student Development, 33,* 214–221.

White, T. J., & Sedlacek, W. E. (1986). Noncognitive predictors: Grades and retention of specially admitted students. *Journal of College Admissions, 3,* 20–23.

Yan, W., & Gaier, E. L. (1994). Causal attributions for college success and failure: An Asian-American comparison. *Journal of Cross-Cultural Psychology, 25,* 146–158.

CHAPTER 13

Survey Designs

Most people are familiar with surveys. We often receive surveys to record opinions as voters, to register approval of consumer products, and to measure opinions about electoral candidates. To many people, survey research is simply a "survey" instrument, such as a questionnaire or interview. Although we "survey" people using an instrument in educational research, the instrument is only one aspect of a broader procedure in survey designs. This chapter defines survey research, identifies when you use it, assesses the key characteristics of it, and advances the steps in conducting and evaluating this design.

By the end of this chapter, you should be able to:

- Identify the intent and the use of surveys.
- Describe the use of cross-sectional and longitudinal survey designs.
- Distinguish among the population, the target population, and the sample.
- Identify the types of interviews and questionnaires used in survey research.
- Identify the elements that go into writing good questions on a survey instrument.
- Describe the steps researchers take to develop a high return rate on a mailed questionnaire.
- Describe how to construct a good mailed questionnaire.
- Describe how to design and conduct an interview survey.
- List the steps in conducting survey research.
- Identify criteria useful for evaluating survey research.

Maria decides to use survey research for her graduate school research project. Her research question is "What factors explain why high school students hold positive attitudes toward possessing weapons in school?" By using a survey design to answer this question, Maria seeks to describe trends in students' thinking. Her approach provides an economical and efficient means of gathering a large amount of data from many students.

She randomly selects a sample of students, sends them a mailed questionnaire, analyzes the results, and draws conclusions about the population from her sample. She conducts survey research.

WHAT IS SURVEY RESEARCH?

With its many applications, survey research is a popular design in education. **Survey research designs** are procedures in quantitative research in which investigators administer a survey to a sample or to the entire population of people to describe the attitudes, opinions, behaviors, or characteristics of the population. In this procedure, survey researchers collect quantitative, numbered data using questionnaires (e.g., mailed questionnaires) or interviews (e.g., one-on-one interviews) and statistically analyze the data to describe trends about responses to questions and to test research questions or hypotheses. They also interpret the meaning of the data by relating results of the statistical test back to past research studies.

Survey designs differ from experimental research in that they do not involve a treatment given to participants by the researcher. Because survey researchers do not experimentally manipulate the conditions, they cannot explain cause and effect as well as experimental researchers can. Instead, survey studies describe trends in the data rather than offer rigorous explanations. Survey research has much in common with correlational designs. Survey researchers often correlate variables, but their focus is directed more toward learning about a population and less on relating variables or predicting outcomes, as is the focus in correlational research.

When Do You Use a Survey?

You use a survey to describe trends, such as community interests in school bond issues or state or national trends about mandatory student uniform policies. You also use a survey to determine individual opinions about policy issues, such as whether students need a choice of schools to attend. Surveys help identify important beliefs and attitudes of individuals, such as college students' beliefs about what constitutes abusive behaviors in dating relationships. They may be used to follow up with graduates 5, 10, or 15 years after college to learn about their present careers. Surveys provide useful information to evaluate programs in schools, such as the success of a robotics program in science education.

How Did Survey Research Develop?

Surveys have been widely used in education for many years. Early surveys date back to 1817, when Marc Antoine Jullien de Paris designed a 34-page international survey of national education systems (De Landsheere, 1988). In the 1890s, G. Stanley Hall surveyed children, and by 1907, the Pittsburgh Survey examined social problems, including educational issues ranging from educational planning for school buildings to issues of children in classrooms who are slow learners (Bogdan & Biklen, 1998).

During the period from World War I to World War II, the modern survey as we know it began to emerge. Factors that contributed to its development were improvements in sampling techniques and the development of different scales of measurement. Surveys found wide application in many social science fields, including marketing research, journalism, public opinion research, and organizations and charities (Neuman, 2000). By midcentury, efforts were under way to establish standardized questions through surveys at the U.S. Department of Agriculture. Scales improved through the development of the Likert scale (e.g., *strongly agree* to *strongly disagree*). Also, guidelines were written for writing clear questions, standardizing interviewing questions, training interviewers, and checking for consistency among interviewers (Fowler, 1988).

During World War II, surveys examined issues central to the war effort, such as the morale of soldiers, production capacity for weapons, and the effectiveness of bombing. Through these studies, survey researchers refined and developed their techniques of large-scale assessments, enabling the emergence of large social research organizations in American universities after the war. For example, investigators established social research centers at Berkeley (Survey Research Center), at the University of Chicago (National Opinion Research Center), and at the University of Michigan (Institute for Social Research). Also, opinion polling organizations, such as Gallup, Roper, and the Rand Corporation, furthered the understanding of large-scale data collection. The founding of polling and survey organizations, combined with the use of computers, the availability of data archives and storage, and funding from the federal government, helped to establish the popularity of surveys in education by midcentury (Neuman, 2000).

In recent years, both federal and state governments have funded national and state surveys such as the Youth Risk Behavior Survey developed by the U.S. Centers for Disease Control and Prevention (Valois & McKewon, 1998). Electronic surveys such as computer-assisted telephone interviewing (CATI), voice recognition (VR), touchtone data entry (TDE), and other approaches represent innovations in self-administered questionnaires that make use of the computer and telephone (Babbie, 1998). Individuals have increasingly used Web sites and the Internet to collect survey data. Survey researchers can now generate an e-mail survey, place questionnaires on computer disks in word processing formats, or create a hypertext file and place surveys on Web sites (Nesbary, 2000). Electronic surveys and communications will probably revolutionize the use and applications of survey research in the future.

WHAT ARE THE TYPES OF SURVEY DESIGNS?

Despite the many applications of surveys today, there are still only two basic types of research surveys: cross sectional and longitudinal. Figure 13.1 shows that each type serves a different purpose. Survey researchers use cross-sectional designs to collect data about current attitudes, opinions, or beliefs. Longitudinal designs are used to study individuals over time.

Cross-Sectional Survey Designs

The most popular form of survey design used in education is a cross-sectional survey design. In a **cross-sectional survey design**, the researcher collects data at one point in time. For example, when middle school children complete a survey about teasing, they are recording data about their present views. This design has the advantage of measuring current attitudes or practices. It also provides information in a short amount of time, such as the time required for administering the survey and collecting the information.

Cross-sectional designs are of several types. A cross-sectional study can *examine current attitudes, beliefs, opinions, or practices*. Attitudes, beliefs, and opinions are ways

FIGURE 13.1
Types of Cross-Sectional and Longitudinal Survey Designs

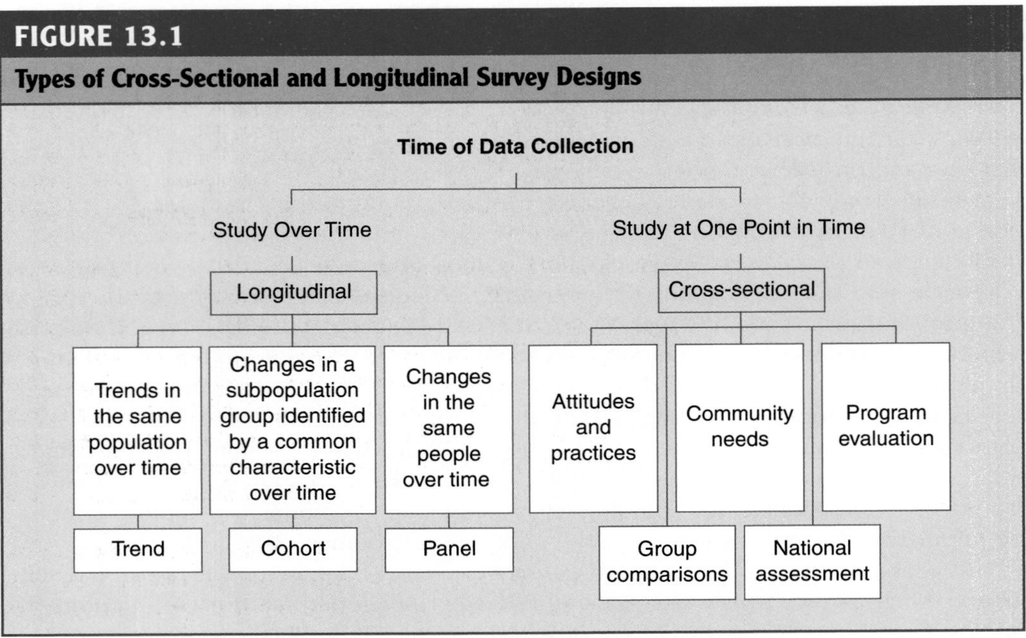

in which individuals think about issues, whereas practices are their actual behaviors. For example, three authors conducted a survey of the practices of reading teachers in elementary schools (Morrison, Jacobs, & Swinyard, 1999). The purpose of the study was to relate the personal, recreational reading of elementary teachers to their literacy instructional practices. Using a list of elementary teachers nationwide (obtained from a professional mailing list company), the researchers mailed 3,600 questionnaires to a probability sample. Of this sample, 52.3% responded to the four-page questionnaire consisting of 21 questions and several items asking for demographic information such as gender, age, and years of teaching experience. Overall, the authors concluded that teachers who saw themselves as readers were more likely than teachers who did not see themselves as readers to use recommended literacy instructional practices (e.g., "read aloud a picture book to your class," p. 88).

Another cross-sectional design *compares two or more educational groups* in terms of attitudes, beliefs, opinions, or practices. These group comparisons may compare students with students, students with teachers, students with parents, or they may compare other groups within educational and school settings. For example, one study compared 98 rural and urban secondary school teachers from 11 school systems in Georgia and North Carolina in terms of their sources of stress and symptoms of burnout (Abel & Sewell, 1999). This group consisted of 52 rural teachers and 46 urban teachers (a nonprobability sample) who volunteered to participate in the study. The researchers delivered packets that included two instruments, the Sources of Stress Questionnaire and the Maslach Burnout Inventory, to participating school districts. The teachers mailed the instruments back to the researchers. The statistical analysis of the data showed significantly greater self-reported stress for urban teachers than rural teachers because of poor working conditions and poor staff relations.

A cross-sectional design can *measure community needs* of educational services as they relate to programs, courses, school facilities projects, or involvement in the schools or in community planning. For example, community needs of Hispanic, Spanish-monolingual residents in Florida were studied by Batsche, Hernandez, and

Montenegro (1999). The authors felt that survey researchers used methods for reaching Hispanic residents that were more appropriate for non-Hispanic residents. To correct this problem, they designed procedures for an assessment interview survey for identifying needs and priorities for human service programs in the Tampa Bay, Florida, area. For example, they used the name "Hispanic" because the survey participants accepted this term. The instrument allowed individuals to identify themselves both by race and ethnicity. To identify the population to study, clubs and organizations were contacted by mail and asked to provide lists of individuals known to be Spanish-monolingual. The researchers first translated the instrument into Spanish and had it reviewed by the local Hispanic community, who translated it back into English to identify discrepancies. The researchers also conducted public meetings to explain the purpose and importance of the needs assessment. Further, the researchers scheduled the times of the interviews to avoid religious events and cultural holidays observed by the Hispanic residents.

Some cross-sectional designs *evaluate a program*, such as a survey that provides useful information to decision makers. In one study, students (and their parents) who had completed a suburban community college enrollment options program responded to surveys evaluating the program (Kiger & Johnson, 1997). This program provided opportunities for high school students to enroll in the community college. A 23-item survey asked the students and their parents their perceptions, such as whether the program helped "formulate long-term educational goals" (p. 691). An overall positive relationship resulted between student and parent perceptions, although their perceptions differed. Parents wanted the students to use the program as a "hands-on" career identification and planning tool, but students saw the program as an opportunity to "try out" the role of being a college student.

A final type of cross-sectional design is a large-scale assessment of students or teachers, such as a *statewide study or a national survey* involving thousands of participants. For example, the Higher Education Research Institute at the University of California at Los Angeles conducted a faculty survey in 1992–1993 of all operating institutions of higher education, which totaled 2,582 colleges and universities. The four-page instrument assessed many factors about faculty members and resulted in a sample of 29,771 full-time college and university faculty. Dey and Hurtado (1996) analyzed this national data to examine attitudes toward institutional attempts to regulate forms of on-campus speech. They found that the majority of faculty supported the prohibition of "hate speech" on campus but were much less likely to support the right of administrators to ban extreme speakers.

Longitudinal Survey Designs

An alternative to using a cross-sectional design is to collect data over time using a longitudinal survey design. A **longitudinal survey design** involves the survey procedure of collecting data about trends with the same population, changes in a cohort group or subpopulation, or changes in a panel group of the same individuals over time. Thus, in longitudinal designs, the participants may be different people or the same people. An example of the study of the same people would be research about high school graduates and their current occupation (e.g., student, food service worker, insurance agent) 1, 2, and 5 years after graduation. Another example of a longitudinal design would be a follow-up with graduates from a program or school to learn their views about their educational experiences. Several types of longitudinal designs are available to the educational researcher, including trend, cohort, and panel designs (Babbie, 1998).

Trend Studies

In some surveys, researchers aim to study changes within some general population over a period of time (Babbie, 1998). This form of longitudinal research is called a trend study. **Trend studies** are longitudinal survey designs that involve identifying a population and examining changes within that population over time. A popular example of this design is the Gallup Poll, which is used during elections to monitor trends in the population of voters from the primary to the final election. Applied to education, this type of study might focus on high school seniors (a population) and study the trends of their attitudes toward dating during the years 2001, 2002, and 2003. In this study, different seniors are studied each year, but they all represent the same population (high school seniors). The researcher can use this data to assess how trends change over time.

Cohort Studies

Rather than studying changing trends in a population, the researcher may be interested in identifying a subgroup in the population, called a *cohort*, that possesses a common defining characteristic. A **cohort study** is a longitudinal survey design in which a researcher identifies a subpopulation based on some specific characteristic and then studies that subpopulation over time. All members of the cohort must have the common characteristic, such as being 18 years old in the year 2001. If age is that characteristic, the researcher studies the group *as the group ages*. For example, a cohort group of 18-year-olds is studied in the year 2001. Five years later (in 2006), a group of 23-year-olds is studied. (They may or may not be the same individuals studied in 2001.) Five years after that (in 2011), a group of 28-year-olds is studied. While the individuals studied each time might be different, they must have been 18 years old in the year 2001 to qualify as representatives of the cohort group.

Panel Studies

A third type of longitudinal survey design is the panel study design. Distinct from both the trend and the cohort study, a **panel study** is a longitudinal survey design in which the researcher examines the same people over time. The high school seniors studied in 1998 will be the same people studied in 2000, 1 year after graduation, and again in 2002, 2 years after graduation. One disadvantage of a panel design is that individuals may be difficult to locate, especially 2 years after graduating from high school. The advantage to this type of study, however, is that the individuals studied will be the same each time, allowing the researcher to determine actual changes in specific individuals. Because of this, the panel study is the most rigorous of the three longitudinal designs.

Let's look at an actual study in which two authors used a longitudinal panel design to examine how adolescents with learning disabilities made the transition from vocational–technical schools to work (Shapiro & Lentz, 1991). The authors surveyed two groups of high school seniors: one with learning disabilities and one without learning disabilities. They were surveyed at graduation and at 6-, 12-, and 24-month intervals after graduation to learn about their occupational and living experiences. The surveys were sent to seniors who graduated in 1986 and 1987. At graduation, both groups held remarkably similar future plans. Only 50% of the individuals with learning disabilities, however, indicated they had specific future plans at graduation. The group with learning disabilities also had lower rates of enrollment in education after high school than the other group did. Further, only about half of all the students studied felt that their training in high school related to their work after graduation.

WHAT ARE THE KEY CHARACTERISTICS OF SURVEY RESEARCH?

Whether a survey design is longitudinal or cross sectional, there are key characteristics of both that will help you design a survey or read and evaluate a published survey study. Survey researchers engage in the processes of:

- Sampling from a population
- Collecting data through questionnaires or interviews
- Designing instruments for data collection
- Obtaining a high response rate

Sampling from a Population

Survey researchers typically select and study a sample from a population and generalize results from the sample to the population. We need to first define three terms: the population, the target population or sampling frame, and the sample. Figure 13.2 shows the differences among these three terms. At the broadest level is the *population*, in which a group of individuals possesses one characteristic that distinguishes them from other groups. For example, we might have a population made up of high school teachers, individuals who all teach in high schools, or school counselors, individuals who occupy counselor positions in all levels of educational schools. At a more specific level, researchers do not always study an entire population, either because they cannot identify the individuals or because they cannot obtain lists of names. (Lists are used when mailing out a questionnaire.) In practical, operational terms, researchers study a *target population* (sometimes called the *sampling frame*). This is the list or record of individuals in a population that a researcher *can* actually obtain. For example, researchers might obtain a list of all secondary high school teachers in one school district. This list constitutes the target population or sampling frame. From the target population, researchers choose a

FIGURE 13.2

Differences Between the Population, Target Population or Sampling Frame, and Sample

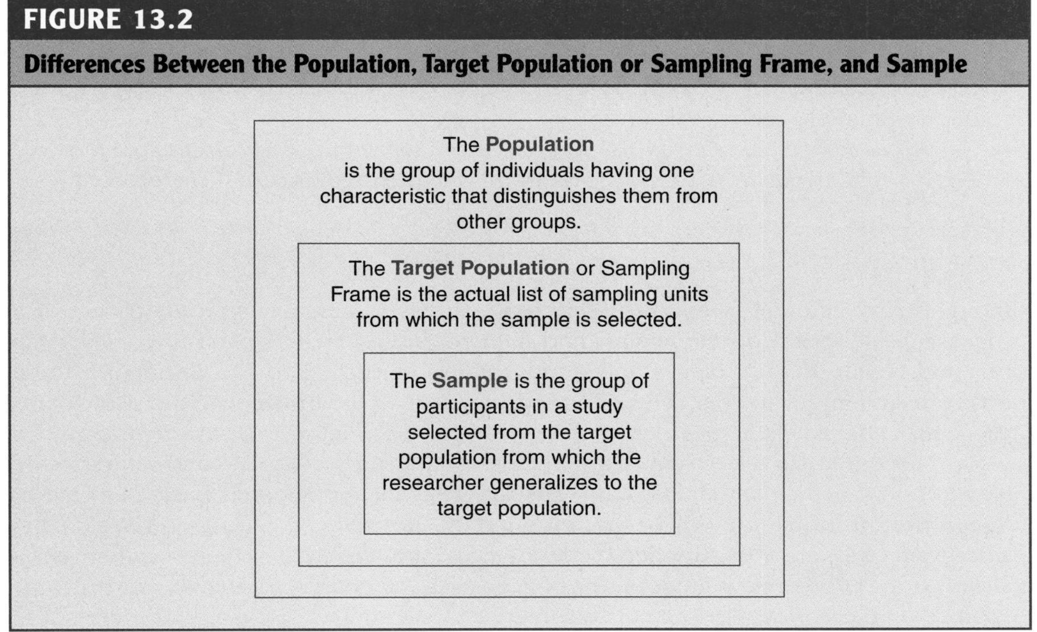

sample. At the most specific level, researchers select a *sample* from the target population. These individuals are actually studied.

The most rigorous form of sampling is to use random sampling by employing a procedure such as using a random numbers table. In this process, the researcher selects a sample representative of the population so that claims or inferences can be drawn from the sample to the population.

In survey research, it is important to select as large a sample as possible so that the sample will exhibit similar characteristics to the target population. Also, in survey studies, it is sometimes difficult to obtain a good list of the target population. For example, lists of individuals who belong to high school gangs or all left-handed individuals would not be easy to obtain. In many cases, however, the target population can be identified for study, and after several attempts, a good list of individuals for the target population can be compiled. It is also possible in survey research to study the entire population because it is small (e.g., members of literacy councils in a state) and can be easily identified. This type of survey study, sometimes called a *census study*, permits conclusions to be drawn about the entire population. Therefore, random sampling, hypothesis testing, and the use of inferential statistics are not necessary. For this type of study, survey researchers simply report descriptive statistics about the entire population.

When researchers select a sample from a population, however, certain factors may limit a survey researcher's ability to draw valid inference from the sample to the population. Salant and Dillman (1994) identified several factors in good survey research that may compromise drawing these inferences:

- *To reduce coverage error, have a good sampling frame list on which to select individuals.* When researchers use a good, complete list, their coverage of the population is adequate and not error prone.
- *To reduce sampling error, select as large a sample from the population as possible.* The larger the sample, the more the participants will be representative of the entire population and reflect attitudes, beliefs, practices, and trends of the population. Recognize that all samples selected will be only estimates of population values. Recall from chapter 6 that sampling errors occur in all surveys.
- *To reduce measurement error, use a good instrument, with clear, unambiguous questions and response options.* Such instruments will encourage individuals to respond and answer correctly. Later in this chapter, we discuss how to construct a questionnaire to reduce this error.
- *To reduce nonresponse error, use rigorous administration procedures to achieve as large a return rate as possible.* Later in this chapter, we discuss these procedures.

Questionnaires and Interviews

Although many different forms of surveys exist, survey researchers typically collect data using two basic forms: questionnaires and interviews. Researchers need to consider the forms and weigh the advantages and disadvantages of each. You can distinguish these forms by examining who completes or records the data on the instrument: the participants (called *respondents* or *interviewees*) or the researcher (see Figure 13.3). A **questionnaire** is a form used in a survey design that participants in a study complete and return to the researcher. The participant chooses answers to questions and supplies basic personal or demographic information. An **interview survey**, however, is a form on which the researcher records answers supplied by the participant in the study. The researcher asks a question from an interview guide, listens for answers or observes behavior, and records responses on the survey. The quantitative interview procedures, discussed here, are not to

FIGURE 13.3

Forms of Data Collection to Survey Research

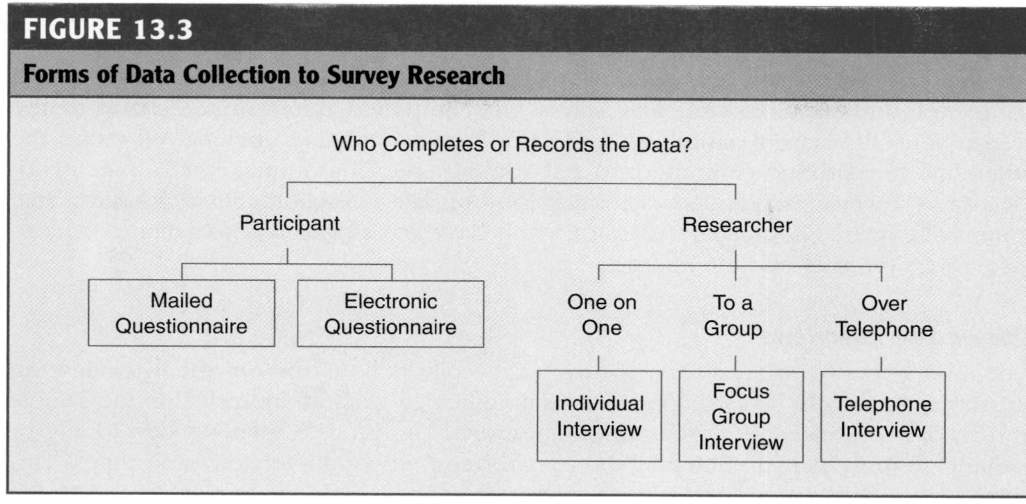

be confused with qualitative interviewing. In *quantitative survey interviews*, the investigator uses a structured or semistructured interview consisting of mostly closed-ended questions, provides response options to interviewees, and records their responses. In *qualitative survey interviews*, an interviewer asks open-ended questions without response options and listens to and records the comments of the interviewee.

Several different types of questionnaires and interviews are used in quantitative survey research. Here we will highlight the major types used in education:

- Mailed questionnaires
- Electronic questionnaires
- One-on-one interviews
- Focus group interviews
- Telephone interviews

Mailed Questionnaires

A **mailed questionnaire** is a form of data collection in survey research in which the investigator mails a questionnaire to members of the sample. Researchers might develop their own questionnaire, modify an existing one, or use one that they have located in the literature. The process consists of locating or developing a questionnaire, sending it out to the sample of the population, using repeated contacts with the sample to obtain a high response rate, checking for potential bias in responses, and analyzing the data. (These procedures are discussed later in this chapter.)

A mailed questionnaire is a convenient way to reach a geographically dispersed sample of a population. The mail facilitates quick data collection, often in as little time as 6 weeks from the first mailing to the conclusion of data collection. A mailed questionnaire is economical because it involves only duplication and mailing expenses. The disadvantage of mailed questionnaires is that individuals may lack any personal investment in the study and decide not to return the instrument. Also, because the researcher does not have a means for explaining questions, participants may misinterpret items on the survey.

Electronic Questionnaires

With increased use of Web sites and the Internet, electronic questionnaires are becoming popular. An **electronic questionnaire** is a survey instrument for collecting data that is available on the computer. Several variations exist, but a popular form is computer-assisted self-interviewing (Babbie, 1998). In this approach, the participant in a study logs onto a computer, uses the Internet or a Web site to locate and download a questionnaire, completes the questionnaire, and sends the completed questionnaire back to the researcher. Other approaches using electronic questionnaires include VR using the telephone keypad and computerized self-administered questionnaires (Babbie, 1998). Electronic surveys provide an easy, quick form of data collection, although their actual use may be limited because not all participants have access to computers or are comfortable using Web sites and the Internet.

One-on-One Interviews

One-on-one interviews are a form of survey data collection. In **one-on-one interviewing in survey research**, investigators conduct an interview with an individual in the sample and record responses to closed-ended questions. The process involves developing or locating an instrument and training the interviewer(s) in good interview procedures. This training consists of learning how to provide instructions during the interview, maintaining confidentiality about the interview, asking the exact question on the interview guide, completing the interview within the time allocated, being courteous, and not interjecting personal opinions into the interview. When multiple interviewers are used, researchers train all individuals to use the same procedure so that the procedures do not introduce bias into the study.

One-on-one interviews are useful for asking sensitive questions and enabling interviewees to ask questions or provide comments that go beyond the initial questions. Interviews lead to a high response rate because researchers schedule the interviews in advance and sample participants typically feel obligated to complete the interview. However, one-on-one interviews do not protect the anonymity of the participant as questionnaires do. Researchers may also prejudice participant answers, knowingly or unknowingly, through either comments or body language. Also, not all interviewees are comfortable disclosing information about themselves during the interview.

Focus Group Interviews

An alternative to a one-on-one interview is to administer a survey to a focus group. In quantitative **focus group interviews in survey research**, the researcher locates or develops a survey instrument, convenes a small group of people (typically a group of 4 to 6) who can answer the questions on the instrument, and records their comments on the instrument. For example, this group might consist of parents who evaluate a new math or science curriculum in a school. Alternatively, international students provide views about cultural integration into an American university setting. During processes such as these, researchers ask the group questions on an instrument and record or take notes on the group conversation.

Focus groups provide for interaction among interviewees, collection of extensive data, and participation by all individuals in a group (Krueger, 1994). A disadvantage of focus group interviews is that they require the researcher to find consensus on questions so one score can be marked for all individuals in the group. In addition, some individuals may dominate the conversation, leading to responses that do not reflect the consensus of the group.

Telephone Interviews

In **telephone interview surveys**, the researcher records the participants' comments to questions on instruments over the telephone. The researcher develops or locates an instrument, obtains the telephone numbers of participants in the sample, conducts the telephone calls, and asks the participants to answer questions on the instrument. Telephone interviews allow the researcher easy access to interviewees who are geographically dispersed. However, the researcher cannot see any nonverbal communication on the part of the participant, and people often dislike telephone contacts because of their prior personal experiences with calls from survey firms asking for information.

Assume that you advise Maria on the type of survey data collection she should use to study factors that explain why students hold positive attitudes toward weapon possession in the school. Should she use (a) a mailed questionnaire, (b) an electronic questionnaire, (c) one-on-one interviews, (d) focus group interviews, or (e) telephone interviews? Write down your answer and provide a rationale for your choice, then look at my answer below.

I would advise Maria to consider the sensitive nature of her study and realize that students need to have their anonymity protected. A mailed questionnaire would provide the greatest protection to students, and Maria could say that she will not identify individuals with survey responses in her report. To keep track of students who respond to the survey, she might enclose a postcard with a student identification number on it that the students return separately from their survey.

Instrument Design

Designing good survey instruments is a challenging and complex process. As mentioned in chapter 6, you should first consider whether a survey instrument is available to measure your variables. You might also consider modifying an existing instrument. If neither of these approaches will work, design your own instrument.

When survey researchers design an instrument for data collection, they typically perform the following steps:

1. *They write different types of questions.* These include personal, attitudinal, and behavioral questions; sensitive questions; and closed- and open-ended questions.
2. *They use strategies for good question construction.* This includes using clear language, making sure the answer options do not overlap, and posing questions that are applicable to all participants.
3. *They perform a pilot test of the questions.* This consists of administering the instrument to a small number of individuals and making changes based on their feedback.

Personal, Attitudinal, and Behavioral Questions

Consider the general forms of the types of *content* that questions might take on a survey instrument. There are three popular types. *Background questions* (or *demographic questions*) assess the personal characteristics of individuals in your sample. These questions can be easy to answer (i.e., gender) or difficult (i.e., level of income). Here are some examples of background questions:

What is your age? ___________
How many years of teaching have you completed? (end of school year) ___________

A second group of questions relates to obtaining individual *attitudes or opinions* from individuals in your sample. For example, you might ask:

How much do you agree or disagree with this statement:

Most days I am enthusiastic about being a student.
___________ Strongly agree
___________ Agree

___________ Neither agree or disagree
___________ Disagree
___________ Strongly disagree

A third group of questions can solicit information about the actual *behavior* of individuals in the sample. For example:

Did you take a semester off during any of your 4 years of college?
___________ Yes
___________ No

Sensitive Questions

Some surveys contain sensitive questions that must be developed and used with care. Sensitive questions might have to do with:

- Drug and alcohol use (e.g., use of cocaine)
- Mental health issues (e.g., paranoid behavior)

Depending on your topic, you may decide to use sensitive questions. If the questions are not tactfully stated, individuals may either over- or underrepresent their views, leading to bias in responses. Several strategies can be used to provide good questions (Neuman, 2000). You might include a sensitive question late in the survey, after the individual has "warmed up" by answering neutral questions and has established some rapport with the researcher. Also, prefatory comments can lead the respondent into the question:

Instead of: Have you ever used marijuana?
You might ask: In past surveys, many men have reported that at some point in their lives they have used marijuana. This could have happened before adolescence, during adolescence, or as an adult. Have you ever smoked marijuana?

Open- and Closed-Ended Questions

Surveys consist mainly of closed-ended questions. In **closed-ended questions in surveys**, the researcher poses a question and provides preset response options for the participant. A closed-ended question might be:

There are many reasons why adults wish to get more education. What is your most important reason for coming to adult basic education classes? (Check one.)
___________ To be able to help my children with their schoolwork
___________ To get a better job
___________ To improve myself
___________ To get a high school equivalency diploma

Here, the author provides a question followed by a limited number of response options. These options need to be mutually exclusive, or distinct from each other, and include the typical responses an individual might provide.

Closed-ended questions such as the example above are practical because all individuals will answer the question using the response options provided. This enables a researcher to conveniently compare responses. They are useful for sensitive questions because participants might feel more comfortable knowing the parameters of response options. Closed-ended questions also provide a means for coding responses or assigning a numeric value and statistically analyzing the data.

At times, however, you may want to probe a little deeper and explore the many possibilities that individuals might create for a question. In this case, open-ended questions are best. **Open-ended questions in a survey** are questions for which researchers do not provide the response options; the participants provide their own responses to questions. For example:

> Why are you attending adult education classes?
>
> ____
>
> ____
>
> ____

In an open-ended question, the participant supplies an answer. This question does not constrain individual responses. It is ideal when the researcher does not know the response possibilities and wants to explore the options. Further, an open-ended question allow participants to create responses within their cultural and social experiences instead of the researcher's experiences (Neuman, 2000).

However, open-ended questions have drawbacks of coding and analysis. The researcher needs to categorize the responses into themes, a process that may take considerable time. Open-ended responses require transforming word responses into numbers (e.g., participants mentioned "getting a better job" 15 times).

One further option is the use of **semi-closed-ended questions in a survey**. This type of question has all the advantages of open- and closed-ended questions. The technique is to ask a closed-ended question and then ask for additional responses in an open-ended question. For example:

> There are many reasons why adults wish to further their education. What is your most important reason for coming to adult basic education classes? (Check one.)
>
> ___________To be able to help my children with their schoolwork
> ___________To get a better job
> ___________To improve myself
> ___________To get a high school equivalency diploma
> ___________Other ___________
> ______________________

This question provides the typical response categories to the question, but it also allows respondents to write in answers that may not fit the response choices. While it also provides limited open-ended information to encourage responses, it does not overburden the researcher with information that needs to be coded.

Question Construction

As you select an instrument or develop one of your own, pay attention to the quality of the questions. Using good questions helps participants feel that they understand the question and can provide meaningful answers. Good questions are clear and unambiguous, and they do not confuse the participants. They also show respect for the participant by being sensitive to gender, class, and cultural needs of participants (see chapter 10 discussion on writing sensitively). For example, in the community needs survey mentioned earlier (Batsche et al., 1999), the researchers used the term *Hispanic* out of respect for what the Spanish-monolingual residents preferred to call themselves. By using good questions, you are encouraging the participant to complete the instrument.

When you construct questions for a survey questionnaire or interview, fit the questions to answers, include suitable response options, and do not overlap. These strategies for constructing good questions are identified in Table 13.1. First, read the poor question. Next, determine the problem. Then, read the improved question. When you write questions (or review those provided by others), you might assess them in terms of

TABLE 13.1

Common Problems in Item Construction in Survey Designs

Example of a Poor Question	Problem	Example of an Improved Question
Do you support gun control? _____ Yes _____ No _____ Don't know	Unclear question because of vague words	Do you believe that guns do not belong in schools? _____ Yes _____ No _____ Don't know
Do you believe that guns and knives do not belong in schools? _____ Yes _____ No _____ Don't know	Two or more questions	Do you believe that knives do not belong in schools? _____ Yes _____ No _____ Don't know
Whenever violence occurs in schools, weapons are typically found in school lockers. Do you believe that students should have guns in their lockers? _____ Yes _____ No _____ Don't know	Wordy or lengthy questions	Should students have guns in their lockers? _____ Yes _____ No _____ Don't know
Students should not carry weapons and not have them in their lockers. Do you agree? _____ Strongly agree _____ Agree _____ Undecided _____ Disagree _____ Strongly disagree	Question contains negatives	Should students have guns in their lockers? _____ Yes _____ No _____ Don't know
Should students pack a .45 at school? _____ Yes _____ No _____ Don't know	Question contains jargon	Should students carry a handgun at school? _____ Yes _____ No _____ Don't know
How many times have you seen a student carry a handgun? _____ 0 times _____ 1–2 times _____ 2–3 times _____ More than 3 times	Response categories overlap	How many times have you seen a student carry a handgun? _____ 0 times _____ 1–2 times _____ 3–4 times _____ More than 4 times
To what extent do you feel that handguns are a problem at your school? _____ A great extent _____ Some _____ Not very important _____ Not a problem	Unbalanced response options	To what extent do you feel that handguns are a problem at your school? _____ A great extent _____ Some extent _____ Little extent
To what extent do you feel that handguns are a problem at your school? _____ Very important _____ Important _____ Little importance	Mismatch between the question and the responses	To what extent do you feel that handguns are a problem at your school? _____ A great extent _____ Some extent _____ Little extent

TABLE 13.1

Continued

Example of a Poor Question	Problem	Example of an Improved Question
How often have you seen students carry semi-automatic weapons at school? _____ None _____ 1 time _____ 2 times _____ 3 or more times	Respondent does not have understanding to answer question	How often have you seen students carry a rifle at school? _____ None _____ 1 time _____ 2 times _____ 3 or more times
How many students have you seen carrying guns at school? _____ 1 student _____ 2 students _____ 3 students _____ More than 3 students	Not all respondents can answer the question—branching needed	Have you seen students carrying guns at school? _____ Yes _____ No → If Yes, how many students? _____ 1 student _____ 2 students _____ 3 students _____ More than 3 students

whether your question is clear, has a clear response, and whether your questions are within the participant's ability to answer. A review of these potential question construction problems and some solutions will provide guidance for survey development.

- *The question is unclear.* This usually occurs because words are vague or imprecise. Identify the unclear or vague words and replace them with words understood by participants in the study.
- *There are multiple questions.* Here, the question actually contains two or more questions, called a *double-* or *triple-barreled question.* Reduce the multiple questions to a single question.
- *The question is wordy.* When the question is too long, cut out unnecessary words to simplify and shorten the question. Look for excessive use of prepositions (e.g., more than three) or qualifying statements that lengthen the question.
- *The question is negatively worded or wordy.* If the question contains one or more negatives, such as "should not," the meaning becomes unclear. Also, reword the question if it leads the participants to one particular stance or another (e.g., using the words "pro-life"). Restate or reword the question to eliminate negative connotations or leading words.
- *The question includes jargon.* Jargon may not be familiar to all participants in a study. Eliminate the jargon and use words familiar to all participants.
- *There are overlapping responses.* This may lead to confusion when answering a question. Make sure that the response options do not overlap by creating distinct options.
- *There are unbalanced response options.* In this case, the responses may be unbalanced in terms of naturally occurring intervals. Response options may start with an "importance" word (e.g., "very important") and end with an "extent" word (e.g., "to a little extent"), rather than a matching adjective (e.g., "not important"). Decide on a single response option and use it consistently for all response categories for a question.

- *There is a mismatch between the question and the answers.* The responses may not match the "action" word used in the question. Identify the verb or adjective in the question that will be the basis for the response options and create options using this word. (E.g., if the question says "to what extent," the answer will say "a great extent.")
- *The question includes overly technical language.* When this occurs, the respondent may not have the level of understanding needed to respond to the question. Simplify the question so that all individuals will know the meaning of the words and can respond to the question.
- *Not all questions are applicable to all participants.* If some participants cannot answer the question, include "branching" or "contingency questions." These questions follow the original question and provide options to include all participants.

Pilot Testing the Questions

After good questions have been developed using principles of question construction, a researcher pilot tests the questions. This helps determine that the individuals in the sample are capable of completing the survey and that they can understand the questions. A **pilot test** of a questionnaire or interview survey is a procedure in which a researcher makes changes in an instrument based on feedback from a small number of individuals who complete and evaluate the instrument. The participants in the pilot test provide written comments directly on the survey, and the researcher modifies or changes the survey to reflect those concerns. Because the pilot group provides feedback on the questionnaire, you exclude them from the final sample for the study.

For example, a survey of 100 middle school students' attitudes toward school might begin with a pilot test of an instrument with 50 questions. In this pilot test, the researcher selects 15 students to complete the instrument. The investigator then asks them to mark any problems on the survey, such as poorly worded questions, responses that do not make sense, or if it takes an excessive amount of time to complete the instrument. Based on student feedback, the researcher then revises the instrument before sending it out to the sample in the study.

Response Rate

Survey researchers seek high response rates from participants in a study so that they can have confidence in generalizing the results to the population under study. When using interviews, the response rate is high because individuals interviewed typically consent to the interview in advance. However, when questionnaires are used, the number of responses returned (through mail or electronically) will vary. In either case, survey researchers place emphasis on obtaining a high response rate to their questionnaire or interview.

Response Rates for Mailed Questionnaires

As mentioned earlier, a high response rate creates a stronger claim in generalizing results from the sample to the population. A **response return rate** is the percentage of questionnaires that participants return to the researcher. Many survey studies in leading educational journals report a response rate of 50% or better. However, this rate will fluctuate depending on proper notification, adequate follow-up procedures, respondent interest in the study, the quality of the instrument, and use of incentives.

Researchers use several strategies to encourage high return rates. One is to *prenotify participants* that they will receive a questionnaire. Individuals receive an introductory

FIGURE 13.4

Three-Phase Survey Administration Procedure

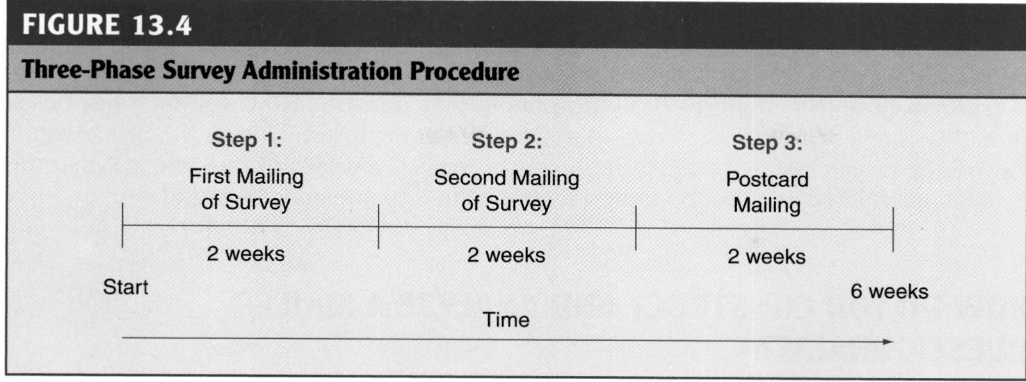

letter asking them to participate in the study and telling them that they will receive a survey in 2 weeks. Another strategy is to use *good follow-up procedures*. Figure 13.4 shows a three-step procedure that might be used.

1. Mail out the original questionnaire.
2. Follow it 2 weeks later with a second questionnaire to the individuals who have not responded (called *nonrespondents*).
3. After another 2 weeks, send a postcard to the nonrespondents, reminding them to complete the questionnaire.

Although you might take additional steps, this three-step process should help you attain a good return rate. The time for each notification will vary, of course, depending on the study. For most questionnaires mailed within the United States, however, this format should allow the researcher to conclude data collection in 6 weeks.

Another way to encourage a high response rate is to *study a problem of interest* to the population under study. If individuals in the sample are interested in the issue, they will be more apt to complete the survey. Also, *using a brief instrument* usually encourages a high return rate. Typically, a three-page instrument will take less than 15 minutes to complete.

A final strategy is to *consider the use of incentives* to encourage individuals to return the instrument. Studies show mixed results on the impact of incentives, even small ones like giving enough money for a cup of coffee (Babbie, 1998). As a researcher, you need to weigh the costs of incentives against their potential help with returns. In many cases, survey researchers combine many of the strategies mentioned so far—prenotification, follow-up procedures, and clear instrument constructions—with modest incentives to encourage high returns.

Response Bias

What do you do if your response rate is low? You might proceed with your study and report a limitation of a low response rate; extend the time to collect data to gather more responses; or report that your responses, although low, are representative of the sample (and population). This last option is response bias. With a low return rate, the key issue is not necessarily how many people returned an instrument, but whether bias exists in those who *did* return it. **Response bias** occurs in survey research when the responses do not accurately reflect the views of the sample and the population. For example, the individuals who return a questionnaire may be overly negative or positive. Thus, survey researchers monitor their returns to assess whether they display bias. We call this approach wave analysis. **Wave analysis** is a procedure to check for response bias in which investigators group returns by intervals (e.g., each week) and check to see if the answers to a few select questions change from the first week to the final week in a study, indicating response bias. Individuals responding in the final week of survey administration are as close to nonreturns or nonrespondents as possible. However, their responses should be similar (i.e., and not biased) to those returning instruments in the first week. If they differ, researchers report that the potential for bias exists, and the potential that the participants studied may not be representative of the sample and the population.

HOW DO YOU CONSTRUCT AND ANALYZE A MAILED QUESTIONNAIRE?

Because of the popularity of mailed questionnaires for student research projects, they deserve special attention. We will focus on three aspects of using mailed questionnaires:

- A cover letter to invite participants to complete the questionnaire
- The form and construction of the questionnaire
- Statistical procedures typically used to analyze data from a mailed questionnaire.

We use a mailed questionnaire from VanHorn-Grassmeyer (1998) as a specific example. VanHorn-Grassmeyer studied 119 individuals new to the field of student affairs (e.g., student activity leaders) in colleges and universities in the central United States and Canada. Her purpose was to explore the perceptions, attitudes, and behaviors of professionals regarding their professional practices. As one aspect of her data collection, she mailed a self-designed questionnaire to the participants. This instrument consisted of five parts:

1. A cover letter
2. Closed-ended questions asking participants about their background (i.e., demographic questions)
3. Closed-ended questions addressing practices or behaviors (e.g., "I claim responsibility when I've made a 'bad call' professionally") and attitudes (e.g., "I benefit from collaborative reflection with colleagues")
4. Open-ended questions permitting respondents to add their perceptions (e.g., "In your opinion, what defines a competent student affairs professional?")
5. Closing instructions thanking the participant for taking part in the study

This cover letter and mailed questionnaire comprised a five-page packet, which can be seen in Figures 13.5 and 13.6 as they were originally reported in VanHorn-Grassmeyer's dissertation. Inspecting these examples can provide useful ideas for designing your own cover letter and questionnaire.

The Cover Letter

A major component of a mailed questionnaire consists of a cover letter inviting the participant to take part in the study and to complete the instrument. When we inspect the cover letter in Figure 13.5, we find these major elements:

- *Importance of participant.* To encourage individuals to complete the questionnaire, they need to know why they have been sent the instrument. The first few sentences indicate the importance of recipients and the value of their response. It is often helpful to begin a cover letter with this statement, as illustrated in this example.

FIGURE 13.5

Sample Cover Letter

Cover Letter Components	July 10, 2004
	Dear Colleague,
Importance of participant	As a relative newcomer to the profession of student affairs, you undoubtedly have ways in which you enhance your practice. Graduate preparation programs, associations, and seasoned professionals must be aware of the strategies that are most useful to you and other professionals in order to help promote professional development, competency, and commitment to the field. Your response to this survey can greatly enhance our understanding.
Purpose of the study	I am conducting this research to explore how professionals new to the field of student affairs enhance their practice. I want to measure the extent to which new professionals use individual and collaborative (that is, in interaction with other professionals) strategies including reflection, and opportunities for development. I will also measure how new professionals view their own skills and knowledge. My population is new professionals in the west-central part of the United States and Canada.
Assurances Sponsorship	Your participation in this research is, of course, voluntary. Your confidentiality and anonymity are assured. Return of the survey to me is your consent for your responses to be compiled with others. Although the survey is coded to allow for follow-up with non-respondents, you will not be individually identified with your questionnaire or responses. Please understand that use of this data will be limited to this research, as authorized by the University of Nebraska at Lincoln, although results may ultimately (and hopefully!) be presented in formats other than the dissertation, such as journal articles or conference presentations. You also have the right to express concerns to me at the number below, my major professor Dr. John Creswell at the UNL Department of Educational Psychology address shown above, or the UNL Institutional Review Board.
Completion time Returns	I greatly appreciate your participation in this research. *The survey will take approximately 15–20 minutes to complete.* ***Please return the survey within two weeks (by July 25)*** *in the enclosed, self-addressed, stamped envelope.* This will save a follow-up mailing to you.
	If you have been in the field for more than five years, please note as much on survey item #1 and return the entire instrument to me.
	Thank you for your interest and participation in this study. I genuinely appreciate your time.
	Sincerely,
Sponsorship	Kimberly VanHorn-Grassmeyer Associate Director, Student Assistance Center University of Kansas, Lawrence KS 66045 913.864.4064; kgrassmeyer@ukans.edu

Source: Reprinted with permission from Kimberly VanHorn-Grassmeyer, Ph.D.

FIGURE 13.6

Sample Mailed Questionnaire

ENHANCING PRACTICE:
NEW PROFESSIONALS IN STUDENT AFFAIRS

I. DEMOGRAPHICS:

1. Years of employment in Student Affairs:
   ___ a. current Graduate Student
   ___ b. 0 up to 2 years
   ___ c. more than 2, up to 5 years
   ___ d. more than 5 years
   If d, do not complete remainder of survey. Return in envelope provided. Thank you.

2. Graduate program practical experiences *(check any of the following that apply to your experience):*
   ___ a. assistantship in student services (paid training experience)
   ___ b. practica in student services (unpaid training experience)
   ___ c. mentoring relationship with a mid- or senior-level administrator
   ___ d. peer group interactions such as case studies, problem-solving
   ___ e. peer group interactions more social in nature
   ___ f. other out-of-class experience: ____________________

3. National professional associations in which you are a member *(rank 1-3 in order of importance to you):*
   ___ a. AAHE ___ d. AERA ___ g. NASPA
   ___ b. ACPA ___ e. ASHE ___ h. NAWE / NAWDAC
   ___ c. ACUHO ___ f. NACA ___ i. Other: ____________

4. Gender: ___ a. female ___ b. male

II. PROFESSIONAL PRACTICE:

1. Indicate the amount of institutional funding you received in the past academic year for participation in professional development conferences and workshops off-site:
   ___ a. none ___ c. $101 to $250 ___ e. $501 to $1000
   ___ b. less than $100 ___ d. $251 to $500 ___ f. more than $1000

2. Indicate the amount of personal funds you spent in the past academic year for participation in professional development conferences and workshops off-site:
   ___ a. none ___ c. $101 to $250 ___ e. $501 to $1000
   ___ b. less than $100 ___ d. $251 to $500 ___ f. more than $1000

3. What professional development costs *(full or partial)* does your institution absorb for you? *(check any of the following that apply):*
   ___ a. association membership dues for more than one association
   ___ b. association membership dues for only one association
   ___ c. on-site seminars and workshops
   ___ d. staff retreats
   ___ e. subscriptions to professional journals and newsletters
   ___ f. release time for participation in programmed activities
   ___ g. release time for personal reflection and renewal
   ___ h. release time for courses related to my work
   ___ i. tuition assistance for courses related to my work

4. To what extent do you feel your graduate program prepared you for your work in student affairs?
   ACADEMICALLY: ___ a. not at all ___ b. a little bit ___ c. fairly well ___ d. very well
   EXPERIENTIALLY: ___ a. not at all ___ b. a little bit ___ c. fairly well ___ d. very well

Source: Reprinted with permission from Kimberly VanHorn-Grassmeyer, Ph.D.

FIGURE 13.6

Continued

Enhancing Practice Survey, p. 2

Using the following 1 - 5 scale, please indicate, by circling the most correct response, the degree to which you agree with the statements listed below:

1	2	3	4	5
strongly disagree	disagree	neutral	agree	strongly agree

1 2 3 4 5 5. I have a strong personal commitment to my professional growth and development.

6. Regarding my professional practice, I value the opinions of my:

1 2 3 4 5 a. colleagues
1 2 3 4 5 b. mentor(s)
1 2 3 4 5 c. graduate program peers

1 2 3 4 5 7. When I reflect on my practice, I know more than I'm really able to describe.

1 2 3 4 5 8. I believe my instincts compare favorably with colleagues I respect.

1 2 3 4 5 9. I have a responsibility to contribute to the development of other student affairs professionals.

1 2 3 4 5 10. My institution expects continued professional development of its staff.

1 2 3 4 5 11. I know that I need to consciously enhance my professional practice.

1 2 3 4 5 12. I like to talk with other professionals about my decision-making and professional practice.

1 2 3 4 5 13. I know most of what I will need to guide my practice.

1 2 3 4 5 14. I feel a sense of connection to the field of Student Affairs.

1 2 3 4 5 15. I have a professional responsibility to continue to learn and develop in my daily work.

1 2 3 4 5 16. I benefit from collaborative reflection with colleagues.

1 2 3 4 5 17. I believe my institution should ensure that I grow as a professional.

1 2 3 4 5 18. I consider myself to be a strong student affairs administrator.

1 2 3 4 5 19. I expect to continue working in student affairs for at least ten years.

20. I receive encouragement for continuing professional growth and development from:

1 2 3 4 5 a. institutional colleagues
1 2 3 4 5 b. my senior student affairs offficer

1 2 3 4 5 21. I still have a lot to learn from experience and practice.

22. I continue to learn a great deal from my:

1 2 3 4 5 a. colleagues
1 2 3 4 5 b. mentor(s)
1 2 3 4 5 c. graduate program peers

1 2 3 4 5 23. I have a sense of self-efficacy and confidence in my work.

FIGURE 13.6

Continued

Enhancing Practice Survey, p. 3

1	2	3	4	5
strongly disagree	disagree	neutral	agree	strongly agree

24. I maintain a strong network of or connection to:

1 2 3 4 5 a. professional colleagues
1 2 3 4 5 b. mentor(s)
1 2 3 4 5 c. graduate program peers

1 2 3 4 5 25. I believe my professional development is my responsibility.

1 2 3 4 5 26. I prefer close supervision over my activities at this point in my career.

1 2 3 4 5 27. I have learned about as much as I can of student development theory.

1 2 3 4 5 28. I am able to function autonomously in my professional role.

1 2 3 4 5 29. I have a professional responsibility to promote/advance the student affairs field.

Using the following 1 - 5 scale, please indicate by circling the most correct response, how regularly you practice the activities listed below:

1	2	3	4	5
never	rarely	sometimes	regularly	often

1 2 3 4 5 30. At least one of my institutional job performance measures (e.g., annual review, annual goals) includes an expectation for professional growth and development.

1 2 3 4 5 31. I read professional journals and periodicals to keep current in the field.

1 2 3 4 5 32. I make time for collaborative (with other professionals) reflection.

1 2 3 4 5 33. I claim responsibility when I've made a "bad call" professionally.

1 2 3 4 5 34. I consciously think back to and apply theory as I go about decision-making and professional practice.

1 2 3 4 5 35. I attend conferences even when I'm expected to personally absorb the majority of the cost of attendance.

36. I utilize the expertise of others (listed in a-b-c) to enhance my professional practice:

1 2 3 4 5 a. colleagues
1 2 3 4 5 b. mentor(s)
1 2 3 4 5 c. graduate program peers

1 2 3 4 5 37. After taking action or employing a strategy, I reflect to determine whether it was appropriate, and how I might respond differently next time.

1 2 3 4 5 38. I second-guess my actions in professional situations.

1 2 3 4 5 39. I seek out opportunities to share my professional knowledge and learning with other professionals.

Indicate how you have done so:

___ a. write for publication in professional journals, newsletters, etc.
___ b. present sessions at retreats, workshops and/or conferences
___ c. collaborate with others who seek advice and assistance
___ d. other methods: ____________________________________

FIGURE 13.6

Continued

Enhancing Practice Survey, p. 4

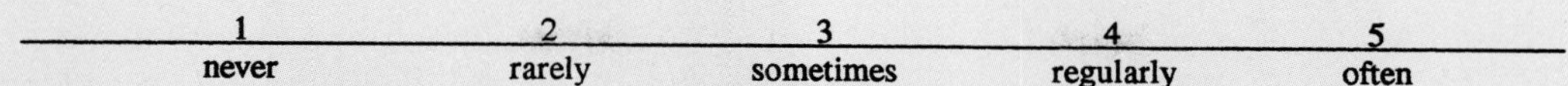

1 2 3 4 5 40. I serve on institution-wide committees, task forces, ad hoc groups, etc.

1 2 3 4 5 41. I seek out opportunities to enhance my professional knowledge and practice.

1 2 3 4 5 42. I attend professional association conferences (regional/state or national).
For this question only: 1=never, 2=rarely, 3=some years, 4=every year, 5=more than one each year

1 2 3 4 5 43. I feel confident when making particularly difficult professional decisions.

1 2 3 4 5 44. I record my thoughts about professional practice in a journal/diary.

1 2 3 4 5 45. I consciously think back to and apply personal experiences as I go about decision-making and professional practice.

1 2 3 4 5 46. I make time for individual professional reflection.

III. SHORT ANSWER QUESTIONS:

Please respond briefly to the following questions, ***using an additional sheet if necessary:***

47. Think back on one of the most difficult professional decisions you've made in your current position, one that involved a situation with others (colleagues, students, supervisees). Please describe how you reached that decision, what factors you considered, who, if anyone, you consulted with beforehand, and whether & how you processed it afterward.

48. In your opinion, what defines a competent student affairs professional? Would you describe yourself in those terms? Why or why not?

THANK YOU FOR YOUR PARTICIPATION AND CANDID RESPONSES.
Please return your survey in the enclosed stamped envelope before July 25.

- *Purpose of the study.* Include a statement indicating, succinctly, the intent or purpose of the study. This statement not only informs the participant about the nature of the study, but it also fulfills an important "informed consent" (see chapter 6) provision of identifying the purpose of the study for participants.
- *Assurances of confidentiality.* Also, to comply with informed consent and to be ethical, the investigator assures the individual of confidentiality (i.e., not identifying individuals specifically).
- *Sponsorship.* The cover letter includes the advisor's name as well as the institution where VanHorn-Grassmeyer works. In addition, write the letter on letterhead stationery to add additional sponsorship.
- *Completion time and returns.* Add to the letter an estimate of the amount of time the survey will take to be completed and the procedure for returning the instrument to the author.

Overall Questionnaire Construction

Examine Figure 13.6 to see a complete mailed questionnaire. This instrument contains features of good questionnaire construction. It is short and encourages a busy professional to return it. The instrument begins with demographic or personal questions that respondents can easily answer, and in the process of answering them, they become committed to completing the form. For variety, the author used different types of closed-ended questions, from checking the appropriate response (e.g., "years of employment") to an extent of agreement scale ("strongly disagree" to "strongly agree"), to a frequency scale ("never" to "often"). The questionnaire also contains open-ended items to encourage participants to elaborate on their experiences and definitions (e.g., "What defines a competent student affairs professional?"). It also contains a pleasing layout with much "white space" between the questions and the use of one scale (e.g., "strongly disagree" to "strongly agree") for multiple questions so that participants do not repeat responses.

Data Analysis of a Research Questionnaire

When researchers compare groups or relate variables, their statistical analysis of questionnaire data extends beyond simple descriptive analysis. Examine the steps identified in Figure 13.7. These steps describe the process typically used for analyzing mailed questionnaire data. The figure includes reporting response rate and checking for bias in responses. The researcher also descriptively reports aggregate responses to each item on the questionnaire. This process helps to discern general patterns of responses and variation (variance and standard deviation) in results. Typically, researchers using mailed questionnaires also correlate all of the questions (see chapter 12) and attempt to build scales that reflect multiple questions. As with all instruments, scores need to be reliable and valid, and statistical procedures such as internal consistency checks (e.g., the alpha reliability statistic) and validity (e.g., factor analysis) represent means for making these assessments. Finally, the researcher tests hypotheses or research questions using inferential statistics.

HOW DO YOU DESIGN AND CONDUCT AN INTERVIEW SURVEY?

Instead of a mailed survey, researchers might collect quantitative data using an interview survey instrument. In using this form of data collection, we need to know the stance of the interviewer, recognize the importance of training interviewers (if there is more than one),

FIGURE 13.7

Checklist for Analyzing Questionnaire Data

_____ Step 1. Identify response rate and response bias.

- _____ Develop table for percent of responses to the survey.
- _____ Develop table for the wave analysis response bias.

_____ Step 2. Descriptively analyze the data to identify general trends.

- _____ Calculate and present a table of descriptive statistics (mean, variance, and range) for each question on the instrument.
- _____ Analyze data to develop a demographic profile of the sample (analyze questions about personal factors).
- _____ Analyze data to provide answers to descriptive questions in the study (if any).

_____ Step 3. Write the report presenting the descriptive results or use advanced statistics.

- _____ Develop scales by combining questions on the instrument (i.e., correlate items using the statistical procedure of factor analysis).
- _____ Check for the reliability of the scores on the scales (i.e., use a coefficient of internal consistency).
- _____ Check for the validity of the scores on scales (or factors) (i.e., use factor analysis).
- _____ Analyze data using inferential statistics to address research questions or hypotheses (i.e., comparing groups, relating variables).

and know the general steps in administering this form of data collection. To understand this process, we will use a telephone interview as an example.

Stance of the Interviewer

Researchers use interview surveys less frequently than mailed questionnaires in educational research. Interview procedures often involve the need for the researcher to establish rapport with and gain the cooperation of the interviewee. Rapport builds through requests for an interview in the cover letter. During an interview, the researcher should remain neutral and should not share opinions (e.g., "I think that budget cutting is a good idea, too"). It is also important to use a positive tone of questioning and to have a neutral appearance.

Training of Interviewers

If more than one interviewer is involved in a research project, each person needs training. This training might consist of a role-playing demonstration by an experienced researcher and a practice interview by the individual researchers who will be conducting the interviews. It is important during this training for interviewers to become familiar with the questions so that they will know if the responses match the questions. Training also covers potential interruptions during interviews or questions interviewees might have about the interview. Problems can arise during an interview, such as when the interviewer:

- Does not ask the questions in order (e.g., Question 3 is asked before Question 2)
- Intentionally subverts the process because of disinterest in the topic (e.g., the interviewer does not take time to probe on questions)
- Brings certain expectations to the interview about how the individuals will answer (e.g., the interviewer prefaces the question with "I think you already know the answer to this. . . .")
- Dresses or appears inappropriately for the interview (e.g., wears shorts when the interviewee is dressed in a suit)
- Is disrespectful by not using names the interviewee wants to be called (e.g., referring to the individual as "Latino" instead of "Hispanic")

Steps in Interviewing

The steps in conducting an interview involve obtaining an interview survey to use and training individual interviewers (if more than one person will be conducting the interviews). Then the researcher gains access to the participants through a formal invitation, such as a cover letter, and establishes a time and place to conduct the interview. During the interview, the survey researcher asks questions, indicates the response options to questions, and records participant answers. The pace of the interview is set to be comfortable for the interviewee. When asking open-ended questions, the interviewer writes down answers to the questions (or tape-records them). The interview ends with the researcher thanking the individual for the interview and telling the participant what the next step will be in the study. After the interview, the researcher may want to write down comments that help explain the data, such as the demeanor of the interviewee or specifics about the situation (e.g., "It was so noisy I could hardly hear at times"). The interviewer might also record any personal feelings about the interview (e.g., "I felt uneasy during this interview and perhaps did not probe as much as I could have").

A Telephone Interview Guide

An example of a telephone interview guide is shown in Figure 13.8. This interview guide was for a telephone interview with 200 academic department chairpersons surveyed to understand how chairpersons assisted faculty in their units (Creswell et al., 1990). Consisting of 25 questions, each interview lasted, on average, about 45 minutes, and all interviews were audiotaped. Six interviewers assisted in the process of data collection, and their training consisted of a demonstration and a practice interview. The researchers constructed this guide to include:

- Introductory remarks to help establish rapport and direction for the interview (e.g., the amount of time required)
- Clearly marked boxes with instructions for each question in the interview so that each interviewer on the research team would ask the same question
- Closed-ended response options for each question, with space between questions permitting the interviewer to write in additional comments
- Numbers in parentheses to indicate the column number for coding the response into a data grid of a computer file for statistical analysis (see chapter 7 discussion on inputting data).

FIGURE 13.8

Sample Telephone Interview Guide

Structured Interview Schedule A

Interviewer's Code Sheet

Pre-Interview Information

Interviewer's ID ________ (1–2)
Institutional Code No. _________ (3–5)
Date of Interview _________ (6–10)
Discipline Code (Carnegie) for Interviewee ________ (11–12)
Gender of Interviewee (1) Female ______ (2) Male ______ (13)

[Note to interviewer: Mark # on your tape counter for potentially interesting quotes.]

Interview Information

Interviewer's Introduction

We appreciate your willingness to be interviewed today. As we indicated earlier, the purpose of our project is to interview department chairs (or their institutional equivalent) who are considered exceptional in assisting faculty on college and university campuses and to identify specific ways in which they enhance the professional growth and development of faculty in their units. This project is being sponsored by the Lilly Endowment and TIAA-CREF, and the information will be used in the preparation of a practical handbook.

The interview should last from 30 to 40 minutes. In our earlier communication with you, we described the nature of our interview questions. Should we go over the question areas at this time? (Pause for response.)

4. How were you selected? (25)
   (1) National search _____
   (2) Administrative appointment _____
   (3) Elected by faculty _____
   (4) Other _____

5. Please tell me some information about your appointment.

   Do you have a specific length of appointment in calendar years? (Probe: reappointed?)
   (1) Yes, # of years _____
   (2) No _____
   (3) Uncertain _____ (26–27)

   If yes, is this length typical on your campus?
   (1) Yes _____
   (2) No _____
   (3) Uncertain _____ (28)

   Do you serve at the pleasure of faculty in your unit or administrators?
   (1) Faculty _____
   (2) Administrators _____
   (3) Some combination _____ (29)

6. How long do you expect to stay in your current position?
   [Interviewer: Cite reasons where possible.]

   (1) Don't know _____
   (2) Certain number of years _____
   (3) Up to my dean _____
   (4) As long as I want _____
   (5) Up to the faculty _____

WHAT ARE THE STEPS IN CONDUCTING SURVEY RESEARCH?

The steps in the process of conducting survey research follow the general process of research identified in chapters 2 through 10. Survey steps, however, address primarily the procedures for collecting data, analyzing data, and writing the final report.

Step 1. Decide If a Survey Is the Best Design to Use

You need to decide whether survey research is the best design to use in the study. Surveys help describe the trends in a population or describe the relationship among variables or compare groups. Instances where surveys are most suitable are to assess trends or characteristics of a population; learn about individual attitudes, opinions, beliefs, and practices; evaluate the success or effectiveness of a program; or identify the needs of a community.

There are several advantages to using surveys. You can administer them in a short time, they are economical as a means of data collection, and they can reach a geographically dispersed population. Further, you can canvass the participants anonymously, without biasing their responses. However, survey data is self-reported information, reporting only what people think rather than what they do. Sometimes the response rates are low and researchers cannot make claims about the representativeness of the results to the population. As mentioned earlier, surveys do not control for many variables that might explain the relationship between the independent and dependent variables, and they do not provide participants flexibility in responding to questions (unless open-ended questions are included).

Step 2. Identify the Research Questions or Hypotheses

You can address both research questions and hypotheses in a survey design. Surveys lend themselves to hypothesis testing because you will be studying a sample to draw inferences to a population. Forms of research questions or hypotheses are those that:

- Describe the characteristics or trends of a population of people, such as the frequency of tobacco use among male high school students
- Compare groups in terms of specific attributes, such as a comparison of teachers and administrators about attitudes toward "inservice" learning days
- Relate two or more variables, such as a survey of teachers to relate "burnout" to number of years of teaching

Step 3. Identify the Population, the Sampling Frame, and the Sample

The process of survey research begins with identifying the population. This step requires defining the population, determining the number of people in it, and assessing whether you can obtain a list of names (i.e., the sampling frame) for the sample. Also, the population may need to be stratified before sampling, so select characteristics of the population (e.g., males and females) are represented in the sample.

Once you have identified the target population and compiled a list of its members, you can select the sample, preferably using random sampling procedures. You will need to identify an adequate sample size, using the sampling error formula in appendix B or the other recommendations advanced in chapter 6.

Step 4. Determine the Survey Design and Data-Collection Procedures

The researcher must also determine if the survey study will be cross sectional or longitudinal. The decision to use a longitudinal or cross-sectional design relates to the nature of the problem studied, access to participants, and the time available to the researchers for data collection. For example, learning about the longitudinal development of adolescent social skills in schools requires following adolescents over time and devoting extensive time to data collection. In contrast, examining parents' attitudes toward discipline in schools requires a cross-sectional study at one point in time to assess attitudes immediately and quickly.

Consider also whether data collection will be based on questionnaires (mailed or electronic) or interviews (individual, focus group, or telephone), and weigh the advantages and disadvantages of each form.

Step 5. Develop or Locate an Instrument

You need an instrument to collect or measure the variables in a study. Recall from chapter 6 that it is easier to locate an instrument than to develop one. Standards of reliability and construct validity need to be applied to scores from existing instruments. If a study addresses only a few variables, researchers can design their own instruments. A check for the reliability and validity of scores from this instrument during data analysis is most important.

Step 6. Administer the Instrument

This step is perhaps the most time-consuming phase of survey research. It involves seeking and obtaining permission to conduct the survey and using procedures for data gathering, such as training interviewers or preparing questionnaires for mailing. It requires continually following up to obtain a high response rate, checking for response bias if questionnaires are used, and preparing the data for analysis by coding the information from the instruments into a computer file.

Step 7. Analyze the Data to Address the Research Questions or Hypotheses

The data analysis procedures will reflect the types of research questions or hypotheses the researcher plans to address in the study. Analysis consists of noting response rates, checking for response bias, conducting descriptive analysis of all items, and then answering descriptive questions. It might also involve testing hypotheses or research questions using inferential statistics.

Step 8. Write the Report

You should write the survey study using a standard quantitative structure that consists of an introduction, the review of the literature, the methods, the results, and the discussion. Specify in the "Methods" section of the study detailed information about the survey procedures. Include in the "Discussion" section comments about the generalizability of the results to the population.

HOW DO YOU EVALUATE SURVEY RESEARCH?

Whether the research consists of interviews or mailed questionnaires, survey studies need to meet high standards of quality. If you plan to conduct a survey, you need to design and write a "Methods" section in your study that conveys the detailed survey research procedures. For educators who read and seek to use results from surveys, a checklist of elements to include in a survey design can provide basic information to look for in a published study. The following checklist, based on the key concepts introduced in this chapter and adapted from Fowler (1988) and Neuman (2000), provides one guide for educators to use.

- Did you describe and specify the target population or sampling frame?
- Did you specify the sampling procedures? If you did not use simple random sampling, did you explain the reason for other sampling procedures (e.g., nonprobability sampling, stratified sampling, and multistage cluster sampling)?
- Did you clearly identify the sample and the basis on which you chose it (e.g., size, use of a random numbers table, or the sampling error for the sample)?
- Did the type of survey (i.e., longitudinal or cross sectional) match your questions or hypotheses?
- Was it clear whether a questionnaire or an interview survey comprised your form of data collection? Did you identify the basis for selecting or developing the instrument?
- Did you report information on the reliability and validity of scores from past use of the questionnaire or interview?
- Did you mention the dates for administering the questionnaire or interview?
- Did you clearly identify the administration procedures?
- If you used a questionnaire, did you identify the procedures for obtaining responses? Did you identify follow-up procedures to ensure a high return rate?
- If you used an interview survey, did you identify the field procedures for collection of this information? Did you identify demographic characteristics, previous experience, training, and monitoring for the interviewer(s)?
- Did you provide a sample of the questionnaire items or the interview questions to help the reader determine if you used good item construction strategies?
- Did the data analysis match the research questions or hypotheses in the study?
- Did you write the study in an acceptable scientific and ethically sound way (i.e., you followed a standard structure, indicated a sensitivity to bias, were respectful to others and research sites)?

APPLYING WHAT YOU HAVE LEARNED: A SURVEY STUDY

To apply the ideas in this chapter, read the survey study on page 421 by Gallik (1999), noting the marginal annotations that identify characteristics of survey and quantitative research. The study is chosen because it demonstrates a high return rate (139 out of 151) based on an instrument given to students in classes, includes the actual survey instrument used, and presents detailed information about the use of the survey.

As you review this article, look for elements of the research process:

- The research problem and use of quantitative research
- Use of the literature
- The purpose statement and research questions
- Types and procedures of data collection

- Types and procedures of data analysis and interpretation
- The overall writing structure.

The Research Problem and Use of Quantitative Research

See Paragraph 02 and throughout the study

The author introduced the research problem in the second paragraph: the problem of students not reading well and the importance of reading as a cornerstone for success in school and life.

The study demonstrates a quantitative approach to research:

- A focus on a research problem of the need for students to read (Paragraph 02)
- A substantial literature review on reading skills at the beginning that foreshadows a need to examine the relationship between reading and achievement (Paragraphs 02–12)
- The relationship of variables related to reading, achievement, and group differences (Paragraphs 13–14)
- Data collection based on an instrument developed by the researcher (Paragraph 17) that gathers numeric data (Paragraph 17) from 151 students (Paragraph 16)
- Statistical data analysis (Paragraph 18), consisting of percentages, differences among groups (chi-square statistic), and the relationship among variables (Pearson correlations) (Paragraph 18)
- The analysis of results to each research question (Paragraphs 19–40) and the interpretation of the meaning of the results (paragraphs 44–45)
- A writing structure that begins with the problem, the methods, the results, and the discussion (see entire study) and reports "objective" results in terms of statistical findings, with the researcher in the background

Use of the Literature

See Paragraphs 02–12

In these paragraphs you find past studies reviewed about reading and other academic skills. Paragraph 09 focuses the study on the reading habits of college students, and Paragraph 11 relates reading achievement to nonacademic reading. Paragraph 13 indicates the gap in past research: None of the studies addressed the relationship between pleasure reading and academic achievement. In this way, by reviewing the literature, the author sets the stage for the purpose and research questions.

The Purpose Statement and Research Questions

See Paragraphs 01 and 13

The author states the purpose of the study initially in Paragraph 01 and then introduces four research questions in Paragraph 13. These questions show several types of quantitative questions: Questions 1 and 4 are descriptive; Question 2, a relationship; and Question 3, a comparison.

Survey Procedures in Data Collection

See Paragraphs 15–17

The author clearly specified this section on survey data collection. Rather than a simple random sample, the researcher selected a convenience sample of students in composition and writing classes. This means that claims about generalizing the results to all students is suspect, despite author comments about selecting courses that would yield a good cross section of students. The questionnaires were handed out to students, a procedure that contributes to a high return rate (139 out of 151). The author developed the instrument, although there was no explanation for the source of the questions. A copy of the instrument helps the reader understand the types of information collected and evaluate the quality of the questions. As this instrument shows (Paragraph 17), different types of scales were used, from closed-ended nominal (male–female) and ordinal (rarely/never, sometimes, frequently), to open-ended, fill-in-the-blank questions.

Survey Procedures of Data Analysis and Interpretation

See Paragraphs 19–41 for data analysis results

See Paragraphs 44–45 for interpretation

The data analysis in this study addressed the survey questions asking for descriptive, group comparisons, and relationship results. Percentages, Pearson product–moment correlations, and chi-square statistics are used. Tables reporting percentages portray the descriptive data.

You find the interpretation of the meaning of the results in the concluding paragraphs of the study. Knowing that reading is related to GPA facilitates making predictions about academic success (Paragraph 45), aids in understanding of students with superior academic skills (Paragraph 45), and suggests that reading improves attention and concentration (Paragraph 45). This last interpretation (Paragraph 45) and the suggestion that reading needs to be developed during the elementary years (Paragraph 44) do not seem to logically follow from the data in this study.

The Overall Writing Structure

This study follows a standard quantitative structure and the author logically develops the structure from the problem statement to the interpretation of results. The survey procedures are clearly delineated for the reader.

KEY IDEAS IN THE CHAPTER

This chapter provides an overview of survey research. Although broad in scope, survey research is a form of quantitative research in which the investigator identifies either the sample or the population, collects data through questionnaires or interviews, and draws conclusions or makes inferences about the population. It is a useful design to use when researchers seek to collect data quickly and economically, study attitudes and opinions, and survey geographically dispersed individuals. Surveys are also useful for assessing information at one point in time (a cross-sectional study) or over time (a longitudinal study). Survey researchers emphasize sample selection, collect data using questionnaires and interviews, administer well-tested instruments with good questions, and seek a high response rate from participants.

The steps in conducting a survey consist of determining if a survey design is the best design to use, forming questions or hypotheses, and identifying a population and a sample to study. Then the researcher identifies the type of survey to reach this sample or population, collects data to ensure a good rate of response and minimal response bias, and statistically analyzes the data to answer descriptive questions or to address relationship or comparison questions or hypotheses.

USEFUL INFORMATION FOR PRODUCERS OF RESEARCH

- Identify whether your study is cross sectional or longitudinal. Longitudinal surveys take more time to complete because you are studying individuals over time.
- In your research, distinguish between the population, the target population, and your sample. Choose a random sample so that you can generalize to your population. Consider the sources of error that may affect your ability to generalize findings or results to the population.
- Specify the type of data-collection instrument that you use, such as questionnaires or interviews.
- Conduct a pilot test of your questions, whatever your type of data collection instrument, so that it can provide useful information.
- Be aware of how you pose sensitive questions to participants. Realize that they may need some introductory comments before you ask participants to respond to sensitive questions.
- A number of potential problems arise when you create your own questions. Study Table 13.1 for a list of problems you should avoid when writing your own questions.
- A typical high response rate is above 50%, but check for response bias through wave analysis when you use a mailed questionnaire.
- Design a mailed questionnaire to include a cover letter, a clear layout of questions, and instructions to the participant. You should keep your instrument as short as possible.
- If you conduct an interview, adopt a neutral stance and record responses accurately. Follow the procedures advanced in this chapter.

USEFUL INFORMATION FOR CONSUMERS OF RESEARCH

- Surveys are used for many purposes in research. When evaluating a study, consider the intent of the author to describe trends, determine attitudes or opinions, describe characteristics of a population, identify practices, evaluate programs, or follow up on individuals over time.
- Mailed questionnaires are a popular form of data collection in educational research. However, these instruments need to be carefully designed. Determine whether the researcher used attitudinal, behavioral, or demographic questions in the instrument.
- A questionnaire response rate of 50% is considered adequate for most surveys. Examine the response rate of a survey study published in the literature and determine if it reaches this percentage. Also consider whether survey researchers addressed the question of response bias and checked to determine if their responses were biased.

Additional Resources You Might Examine

Several books provide an excellent introduction to survey research. An introduction to survey research is found in the "toolkit" series on survey research by Arlene Fink (1995). This nine-volume series by Fink and associates comprehensively addresses all aspects of survey development, from asking questions to writing reports. See:

Fink, A. (1995). *The survey handbook.* Thousand Oaks, CA: Sage.

An introductory book by Priscilla Salant and Don Dillman (1994) provides a non-technical overview to survey research, with a focus on survey instruments. Their information about errors common in surveys and the costs associated with survey administration offers useful guides for the beginning researcher. See:

Salant, P., & Dillman, D. A. (1994). *How to conduct your own survey.* New York: Wiley.

Also, examine the recent survey research book by Dillman (2007) on the use of mail and Internet surveys.

Dillman, D. A. (2007). *Mail and Internet surveys: The tailored design method* (2nd ed.) Hoboken, NJ: Wiley.

Floyd Fowler (1988) has issued a short book on survey research that is popular in introductory survey research courses. He focuses on sampling and design issues, as well as highlighting ethical issues and errors in survey designs. See:

Fowler, F. J. (1988). *Survey research methods.* Newbury Park, CA: Sage.

In a more advanced treatment of survey research, Earl Babbie has authored several books that provide a detailed, technical understanding (Babbie, 1990, 1998). His books broadly assess social research, but they are applicable to education. See:

Babbie, E. (1990). *Survey research methods.* Belmont, CA: Wadsworth.

Babbie, E. (2003). *The practice of social research* (9th ed.). Belmont, CA: Wadsworth.

Go to our Companion Website at **www.prenhall.com/creswell** to:

- assess your understanding of chapter content with Multiple-Choice Questions,
- apply what you've learned with Essay Questions,
- practice your research skills with interactive Building Research Skills exercises, and
- broaden your knowledge of research with Web Links to research topics on the Internet.

Quantitative Characteristics

Do They Read for Pleasure?: Recreational Reading Habits of College Students

Survey Research Characteristic

Jude D. Gallik

A quantitative research problem requires description or explanation.

(01) *Does a relationship exist between academic achievement and the time spent in recreational reading? A significant connection was found between achievement and the time these college students spent reading for pleasure during vacations.*

When my colleagues and I interview prospective students, we always seem to ask about their reading habits. "Do you read for pleasure?" we ask, hoping for the "yes" that we think will reveal an interest in matters academic and thereby portend future collegial success. We ask this question, over and over, year after year, because we assume that there is a relationship between reading and academic success: We believe that better students read more than poorer ones. Our assumption, however, has yet to be supported with scientific or statistical evidence. The purpose of this study was to reveal some evidence to either dispute or support our assumption that a positive relationship exists between the amount of time spent in recreational reading and academic achievement.

The quantitative literature justifies the research problem and provides direction for the study.

(02) Why do we think reading is so important? According to the Report of the Commission on Reading in the United States (Anderson, Hiebert, Scott, & Wilkinson, 1985), reading is a cornerstone for success, not just in school, but throughout life. The Commission noted, "Without the ability to read well, opportunities for personal fulfillment and job success will inevitably be lost" (p. 1). In their research with adult readers, Kirsch and Guthrie (1984) found that reading is a necessary aspect of job and career development, especially in responding to changes. They further reported that to the adults in their study, "reading is not an inconsequential aspect of life outside the classroom" (p. 230).

(03) Reading skills are important throughout the lifespan, and recreational reading has been found to improve reading comprehension, writing style, vocabulary, spelling, and grammatical development (Krashen, 1993). The effect of recreational reading on vocabulary development was demonstrated by Sarangi, Nation, and Meister (cited in Krashen, 1993). In their study readers learned the meaning of 45 invented words contained in the novel *A Clockwork Orange* (Burgess, 1987) simply by reading the novel, with no special instructions to attend to new words. In addition to improving reading skills, pleasure reading has been found to be associated with improved writing skills.

The quantitative literatue plays a major role.

(04) One study (Krashen, 1984) compared the pleasure-reading habits of college freshmen who wrote essays that were rated either highly competent or of low competence. Those writing highly competent essays reported more pleasure reading at all ages, especially in high school. No poor essay writer reported "a lot" of pleasure reading during high school. Another study (Applebee, 1978) found that outstanding high school writers (National Council of Teachers of English award winners) reported reading an average of 14 books for pleasure over summer vacation alone, significantly more than the average of 11 books per year reported elsewhere (Gallo in Applebee, 1978).*

---

*Jude D. Gallik is the director of Learning Support Services for Schreiner College, 2100 Memorial Blvd., Kerrville, Texas 78028, USA.

Gallik, Jude D. (1999, March). Do they read for pleasure?: Recreational reading habits of college students. *Journal of Adolescent & Adult Literacy, 42* (6), 480–488. Reprinted with permission of Jude D. Gallik and the International Reading Association.

(05) The relationship between reading and other academic skills becomes evident at the elementary level. Anderson, Wilson, and Fielding (1988) found that, for 5th graders, the amount of time spent reading books outside of school was the best predictor of reading comprehension, vocabulary, and speed. They also found that independent reading was associated with gains in reading achievement. Other studies found that one of the best predictors of leisure reading in 5th graders was reading achievement (Greaney, 1980; Greaney & Hegarty, 1987). Students in 4th, 8th, and 12th grade who reported more reading outside school were found to perform better on a test of reading comprehension (Foertsch, 1992). Taylor, Frye, and Maruyama (1990) found that reading as little as 15 minutes a day contributed significantly to gains in reading achievement for 5th and 6th graders.

(06) The relationship between gender and time spent in recreational reading is well established; girls consistently read more than boys at every age studied (Blackwood, Flowers, Rogers, & Staik, 1991; McCreath, 1975; Witty, 1961). Unfortunately, another consistent finding is that the amount of time spent in recreational reading declines in the middle school years (Clary, 1991; Greaney, 1980; McCoy, Larson, & Higginson, 1991).

(07) Although some people suggest that television viewing may reduce time spent in pleasure reading, studies over the last 30 years have consistently refuted this assumption. Witty (1961) found that the amount of time spent watching TV actually declined as the student progressed through school, with 12th graders watching an average of 3 hours less television per week than 9th graders. Greaney and Hegarty (1987) found no relationship between amount of time spent watching television and amount of time spent reading books. Libsch and Breslow (1996) also reported a decline in the amount of time spent watching television between 1976 and 1992.

(08) An overall decline in time spent reading may have occurred over the past few decades. In their study, Ross and Simone (1982) found that 10th, 11th, and 12th graders reported reading 1 hour or less outside of school, a slight decline from the 1.3 hours per day reported by Witty (1961) for the same grades. Declines in amount of time spent reading were also noted by Libsch and Breslow (1996) when they compared 1976–78 and 1992–94 data on high school seniors' recreational reading habits. During both periods, about half of all seniors reported reading one to five nonassigned books each year. Those reading six or more books decreased from 37% to 25%. Those reading no books increased from 14% to 22%. College-bound seniors in the study reported reading more than the noncollege bound, but the number of college bound who reported reading no books has doubled since 1976.

(09) The reading habits of college students have not received as much attention in the literature as those of younger students. McCreath (1975) reported on the reading habits and interests of 89 primarily African American students enrolled in a reading improvement course at an urban community college. While most of the students surveyed reported positive attitudes toward reading, only 38% said that they regularly or often read for pleasure, while 58% reported that they only sometimes or never read. However, the majority did report reading a newspaper regularly or often. McCreath (1975) also investigated relationships among reading habits, reading interests, and reading improvement, but found no statistically or practically significant relationships.

(10) Blackwood et al. (1991) studied the pleasure reading habits of 333 college seniors enrolled at a small, public, U.S. liberal arts university. In response to a survey, 88% reported reading for pleasure, primarily newspapers, and most reported spending more time reading during vacations

than when classes were in session. Both male and female students reported reading for pleasure about 2.5 hours each week while classes were in session, and slightly more during vacations. In this study, the researchers also considered the effect of parental encouragement, parental education, and parental occupation on the amount of reading reported by the students surveyed. None of these factors was found to be significantly related to amount of time spent reading.

(11) In another study, Sheorey and Mokhtari (1994) examined the reading habits of 85 college students enrolled in an elective developmental reading course at a large university in the midwestern United States. They reported that students read an average of 4.75 hours per week. Students who scored higher on a test of reading comprehension reported spending slightly more time on nonacademic reading, 5.85 hours per week, than those with lower reading ability, who reported spending an average of 3.65 hours per week, but this difference was not statistically significant.

(12) The study by Jeffries and Atkins (1996) focused primarily on reading interests of 261 college students enrolled in introductory media courses. They analyzed the responses by college major and found that humanities majors had the highest mean number of books read. Interestingly, the humanities majors did not differ from other majors in the average number of hours spent watching television, a finding consistent with those of Greaney and Witty mentioned previously.

Purpose of the Study

(13) While the studies with college students often examined time spent in pleasure reading, the type of reading the students did, and levels of reading achievement, none specifically examined the relationship between overall academic achievement and amount of time spent in pleasure reading.

The quantitative purpose statement, research questions, or hypotheses seek measurable, observable data on variables.

(14) The purpose of the present study was to find answers to the following questions:

1. How much time do college students spend in pleasure reading?
2. Is there a relationship between academic achievement in college (as measured by cumulative grade-point average) and the amount of time spent in pleasure reading?
3. Do significant differences exist between various groups (gender, age, student classification) in the amount of time spent pleasure reading?
4. What type of reading material(s) do the students prefer?

The quantitative purpose statement, research questions, or hypotheses are specific and narrow.

Conducting the Survey

Survey researchers select a sample from population.

(15) The sample consisted of students enrolled in four sections of first-year composition and three upper level writing classes at a small, church-affiliated, private liberal arts college located in central Texas, USA. These courses were selected because of the likelihood that they would yield the best cross-section of students, without being skewed toward any specific major. The composition courses are required of all first-year students, regardless of major. Students in all majors are required to take one of two upper level classes: Advanced Composition or Technical Writing. The third upper level class, Creative Writing, typically attracts students from a variety of majors. Both lower and upper level classes were included in order to provide additional variables (age and student classification) to consider when analyzing the data. Established classes were used to administer the surveys because it was likely to result in a much higher return than if the surveys were mailed to students.

Survey researchers see high response rates.

(16) A total of 151 surveys were administered in the English composition courses. In two of the courses, I administered them. In the remaining courses, the surveys were administered by the course instructors. Twelve

Quantitative data collection involves studying a large number of individuals.

surveys were not included in the data analysis due to one of two conditions: One or more of the questions were not answered or more than one answer was given to any question. Of the 139 usable surveys, 77 were completed by women and 62 were completed by men. The breakdown by student classification was as follows: 74 freshmen, 17 sophomores, 31 juniors, and 17 seniors. In terms of age, the sample consisted of 79 students in the 17–20 bracket, 41 students in the 21–24 bracket, 7 students in the 25–29 bracket, and 12 students age 30 or older.

Survey researchers develop or use instruments to collect data.

Quantitative data collection is based on using instruments identified prior to the study.

(17) A survey entitled "Recreational Reading Habits of College Students" was developed for this study (see figure on next page). It consisted of four demographic questions (age, gender, student classification, cumulative grade-point average), two questions about participation in special programs (Honors program for high-achieving students or comprehensive support program for students with learning disabilities) and two questions about recreational reading (time spent on recreational reading when classes are in session, and time spent on recreational reading during vacations). In addition, the survey elicited information about reading interest, asking whether the student would read more if more time were available and how frequently different types of material were read (e.g., novels, newspaper, poetry). Students who indicated that they read novels or nonfiction were asked to specify favorite authors or categories. Due to a design flaw in the survey, the information on frequency for nonfiction is incomplete.

Survey of Recreational Reading Habits

Quantitative data collection involves gathering numeric data.

Survey researchers Use questionnaires or interviews to collect data.

1. Please indicate your gender: Male ____ Female ____
2. Please indicate your student status:
   Freshman ____ Sophomore ____ Junior ____ Senior ____ Other (specify) ____
3. Please indicate your age: 17–20 ____ 21–24 ____ 25–29 ____ 30 or older ____
4. Please indicate your cumulative GPA:
   Less than 1.5 ____ 1.6 to 2.0 ____ 2.1 to 2.5 ____ 2.6 to 3.0 ____ Over 3.0 ____
5. Are you a current or former Learning Support Services (LSS) student? Yes ____ No ____
6. Are you in the Honors Program? Yes ____ No ____
7. Please indicate the amount of time you spend each week on recreational reading (not required for classes) when school is in session.
   Less than 1 hour ____ 1–2 hours ____ 3–5 hours ____ 6–10 hours ____ Over 10 hours ____
8. Please indicate the amount of time you spend each week on recreational reading (not required for classes) during vacations.
   Less than 1 hour ____ 1–2 hours ____ 3–5 hours ____ 6–10 hours ____ Over 10 hours ____
9. If you had more free time, would you read more? Yes ____ No ____
10. Please indicate how often you read each of the following:

	Rarely/never	Sometimes	Frequently
Newspaper	________	________	________
Magazines	________	________	________
Comic books	________	________	________
Poetry	________	________	________
Letters/e-mail/chat rooms	________	________	________
Internet	________	________	________
Novels	________	________	________
(Please specify preference: science fiction, mystery, etc., & favorite author)			
Nonfiction books	________	________	________
(Please specify preference: biography, self-help, religious, etc.)			

Quantitative data analysis consists of describing trends, comparing groups, or relating variables.

Quantitative data analysis consists of statistical analysis.

(18) The data regarding amount of time spent reading recreationally were summarized by category (e.g., less than 1 hour, 1 to 2 hours) and percentages of students for each category presented. Chi-square and Pearson product-moment correlations were used to determine whether significant differences existed between groups in the amount of time spent reading for pleasure. Data collected on types of reading materials preferred by students were summarized by category and the most and least preferred materials presented as percentages.

Time Spent Reading

Survey researchers analyze data to answer their research question hypotheses.

(19) Total responses for time spent in recreational reading each week while classes are in session are shown in Table 1. While classes are in session, 63% of the respondents report reading 2 hours or less each week. At the other end of the continuum, only 13% of students surveyed report 6 or more hours per week when classes are in session.

Quantitative researchers take an objective and unbiased approach.

TABLE 1
Time spent Reading Recreationally: Classes in Session

Hours per Week	Number of Students	Percentage of Students
Less than 1 hour	40	29
1–2 hours	47	34
3–5 hours	33	24
6–10 hours	12	8
More than 10 hours	7	5

TABLE 2
Time spent Reading Recreationally: During Vacation

Hours per Week	Number of Students	Percentage of Students
Less than 1 hour	29	21
1–2 hours	38	27
3–5 hours	38	27
6–10 hours	22	16
More than 10 hours	12	9

(20) Total responses for recreational reading each week when classes are not in session are shown in Table 2. Forty-eight percent of students reported reading 2 hours or less each week while on vacation, significantly less than the 63% who reported reading less than 2 hours each week when classes are in session, indicating that amount of time spent reading increases when classes are not in session. During vacations, 25% of students reported reading more than 6 hours each week, an increase over the 13% who reported doing so when classes are in session.

Relationship Between Academic Achievement and Recreational Reading

(21) Pearson product-moment correlations were performed to determine the relationship between reported cumulative grade-point average and amount of time spent reading for pleasure while classes were in session and during vacations. An insignificant correlation ($r = .08$) was found between cumulative grade-point average and pleasure reading while classes were in session. However, a weak but statistically significant correlation ($r = .275$, $p = .01$) was found between cumulative grade-point average and time spent reading for pleasure during vacations.

Group Differences in Pleasure Reading

(22) The data were analyzed using chi-square calculations to determine whether any significant differences in time spent pleasure reading existed between any groups. Group differences were calculated in terms of student classification, gender, age, participation in the college's Honors program, and participation in the college's support program for students with diagnosed learning disabilities.

(23) No statistically significant differences were found due to student classification. No gender differences were found between males and females for time spent reading while classes were in session; however, a difference between males and females that approached significant levels ($p = .08$) was found when amount of time spent reading during vacations was examined.

(24) The chi-square calculation indicated a statistically significant difference when age was compared to amount of reading during vacations. However, since more than one-fifth of the cells had a frequency of less than 5, the value may have been inflated, thereby making the significance suspect. A Pearson product-moment correlation was then conducted to compare the relationship between age and amount of reading during vacations, resulting in a weak but statistically significant difference ($r = .313$, $p = .01$).

(25) No statistically significant differences were found between students enrolled in the learning disabilities support program or students in the Honors program and the remaining students surveyed in the amount of time spent reading while classes were in session or during vacations.

Reading Interests

(26) Students were asked to indicate how frequently they engaged in eight different types of pleasure reading. Table 3 summarizes the responses. The survey instrument had spaces below the questions on novels and nonfiction reading where the students were asked to specify their preferences in those areas. Unfortunately, a number of the survey respondents misinterpreted the layout of the question about nonfiction books, and used the lines which were intended for indicating the frequency to indicate the type of reading they did. This design error resulted in only 84 of the students responding correctly to the question.

(27) Magazines were the most popular type of reading material, reported to be read frequently by 75% of the respondents. Letters, e-mail, and chat rooms were the next most popular, with 65% of students indicating frequent reading. Comic books were clearly the least popular reading material, with 88% of students reporting that they rarely or never read comic books.

TABLE 3
Reading Interests

	Rarely/Never	Sometimes	Frequently
Newspaper	21	64	54
Magazines	6	58	75
Comic books	123	15	1
Poetry	57	65	17
Letters/e-mail/chat rooms	28	46	65
Internet	42	42	55
Novels	42	51	46
Nonfiction books*	35	29	20

*Notification total does not equal sample total of 139. Design flaw in survey caused some students to respond incorrectly to the question.

(28) The survey provided a space for students to specify their preference for types of novels read. Only 49 of the students chose to indicate a preference in regard to novel reading. Of those responding, the most frequently mentioned categories were mysteries and horror, with Mary Higgins Clark, Stephen King, Dean Koontz, and John Grisham the most frequently mentioned authors. For nonfiction reading, 67 students reported preferences, with biographies, self-help, and religious/spiritual the most frequently listed.

(29) The survey question, "If you had more free time, would you read more?" could be considered an overall indicator of interest in reading. Seventy-six percent of all respondents answered yes. No statistically significant differences were found between any of the groups in their responses to this question; however, 80% of women answered yes, compared to 72% of men, which may be indicative of a general tendency for women to read more than men.

How Much Do They Read?

(30) The primary purposes for this study were to find out how much time students at this college spent reading for pleasure and to determine whether there was indeed a relationship between amount of recreational reading and academic achievement as indicated by cumulative grade-point average.

(31) The finding that 63% of students reported spending less than 2 hours per week reading for pleasure while classes are in session was not unexpected, considering that most students have a significant amount of required reading and other work for their classes. The amount of time reported by students spent on recreational reading (both on vacation and when classes are in session) is consistent with the average of 2.5 hours per week reported by Blackwood et al. (1996).

(32) However, both the present study and the Blackwood et al. study differ significantly from the findings of Sheorey and Mokhtari (1994) who reported an average of 4.75 hours per week of recreational reading. The fact that the Sheorey and Mokhtari study was conducted at a large university and the other two were at small colleges seems insufficient explanation for the difference. The reason for the disparate results in amount of time spent reading for pleasure most likely lies in the differences in the construction of the time categories from which students were to select and the way in which the data were analyzed. Sheorey and Mokhtari report that their subjects were provided with five categories of time frames: 0–4 hours, 5–9 hours, 10–14 hours, 15–19 hours, and 20 hours or more.

(33) In contrast, the current study provided time frames of less than 1 hour, 1–2 hours, 3–5 hours, 6–10 hours, and over 10 hours, while Blackwood et al. provided time frames of less than 1 hour, 1–2 hours, 3–4 hours, and over 4 hours. The much larger time frame provided by Sheorey and Mokhtari at the lower end of the scale, 0–4 hours, could therefore account for their report of an average of 4.75 hours per week spent in pleasure reading. Students who did not read at all, and those who read as many as 4 hours per week, were placed in the same category, whereas in the present study, this same group of students would have fallen into three different time frames. The use of this larger time frame could result in an inflated estimate of the amount of time spent on recreational reading, particularly when the data are presented as a mean.

(34) Sheorey and Mokhtari reported that their calculation for the mean amount of time spent on recreational reading was based upon the numerical value assigned to each category (i.e., 0–4 hours was considered category 1, 5–9 hours was category 2). A mean of 1.5 was reported, which represented

the mean of the assigned number of the category selected. This category mean was then converted to represent a specific number of hours, although it is unclear exactly how that conversion was accomplished. Calculating a mean in this fashion does not take into account the fact that all students selecting category 1 (0–4 hours) could have been reading only 2 hours or less each week or, conversely, all the students could have been reading for 4 hours each week. One would have to conclude that using a mean to report the number of hours of pleasure reading when such large time frame categories were used was inappropriate.

(35) Although students generally read more while on vacation than when classes are in session, almost half (48%) read only 2 hours or less per week even during vacations. This finding is somewhat surprising given that 76% of students indicated that they would read more if they had more time. One possible explanation for this response is that, while one might assume that being on vacation from school would give students more time, the students do not in fact have more time to read during vacations. It could be that many students work during school vacations, leaving no more time for leisure reading than when classes are in session. This contention may be supported by the fact that 14 respondents who answered yes to the question about reading more also indicated that they spent fewer hours in pleasure reading during vacations than when classes are in session. The finding that such a high percentage (76%) of students expressed a positive attitude toward reading (as measured by their interest in reading more) is, to an educator, reassuring.

(36) The statistically significant correlation between recreational reading during vacations and cumulative grade-point average ($r = .275$, $p = .01$) indicates that our favorite interview question, "Do you read for pleasure?" is a useful and relevant one. However, the answer should be weighed cautiously, since information about pleasure reading will only account for about 8% of the variation in cumulative grade-point average (the coefficient of determination is the square of the correlation coefficient). Pleasure reading in itself is not a strong predictor of achievement in college.

Who Reads the Most?

(37) Findings regarding group differences in amount of time spent reading for pleasure must be interpreted with consideration for the small number of subjects in some of the grouping categories. The finding that there was no significant difference in the amount of pleasure reading by students in the learning disabilities support program, when compared with those not in the program, was unexpected. Because many of the students in the learning disabilities support program have below-average levels of reading achievement, they were expected to spend less time reading for pleasure than non-learning-disabled students—considering the strong relationship that has been found between reading achievement and amount of time spent reading for pleasure (Foertsch, 1992; Sheorey & Mokhtari, 1994). However, the sample of 139 included only 19 students who were currently or formerly enrolled in the learning disabilities support program. This small number may have been insufficient to reveal any significant differences.

(38) Similarly, students enrolled in the Honors program were expected to report more time spent in recreational reading. Here, also, the small number of students who reported participation in the Honors program may have affected the results, which indicated that Honors students had reading habits no different than those of non-Honors students.

(39) The small sample size of some of the age groups may be responsible for the finding of a statistically significant relationship between age and amount of time spent reading for pleasure. The results indicated that older

students tended to read more. However, only 7 students were in the age 25–29 category, and 12 students were in the 30 or older category, so the findings would have to be considered suspect. Another confounding factor is the very specific nature of the sample. The older students in this study had chosen to enroll in a baccalaureate program at a nontraditional age. This fact makes them a very select group and limits the usefulness of the results.

(40) No significant differences were found between students of different classifications: Seniors didn't spend more time reading for pleasure than first-year students. This finding may indicate that reading habits are already well established by the time a student enters college, so that the experience of being a college student does not influence how much more time will be spent on reading recreationally if the student is not already so inclined. The finding may also simply reflect the fact that all college students, regardless of classification, spend the vast majority of their reading time and energy on academic pursuits, rather than recreational ones.

What Do They Read?

(41) In order to get a full and complete picture of reading interests, survey questions regarding the type of reading preferred by respondents would need to be much more detailed than the items included on the survey for this study. For example, the survey used by Blackwood et al. (1991) included 13 questions about which section of the newspapers were read, 10 questions about what type of magazines were read, and 14 categories about nonfiction books. Other studies of reading interest (Jeffries & Atkins, 1996; Ross & Simone, 1982) have included questions at a similar level of detail. Because determining areas of reading interest was not one of the primary purposes of this study, survey questions about the type of reading material and the frequency such material was read were of a more general nature. However, more specific information in this regard would provide a richer picture of the recreational reading habits of college students.

(42) The results of the present study were consistent with the results of the studies mentioned here in finding newspapers and magazines to be among the most preferred. The present study was the only one that allowed respondents a choice of "letters/e-mail/chat rooms" as a type of recreational reading. This option is significant because it was the second most popular type of pleasure reading selected, with 47% of students indicating frequent reading in that category. Because reading interests were of secondary importance, there was no analysis to determine whether any significant differences existed between groups in their interests.

(43) One limitation of this study has already been noted in regard to the limited number of survey questions about types of material read. Another limitation may lie in the use of the terms *academic achievement* and *recreational reading*. Consistent with the purposes of this study, these terms were defined rather broadly. Further research that defined these terms more narrowly could provide more detailed information about the relationship between recreational reading and academic achievement in college students.

Implications

Quantitative interpretations compare results with predictions.

(44) The results from this and other studies suggest that recreational reading habits are acquired fairly early in an individual's school life, probably in elementary school given that numerous studies show a decline in time spent reading that begins in middle school. If students are to have good reading skills and positive attitudes toward reading, these must be developed during the elementary years.

(45) The positive relationship that this study found between cumulative grade-point average and time spent in recreational reading has several implications. First, knowing about students' recreational reading habits is helpful in making predictions about their future academic success. Second, this relationship could indicate that students who spend more time reading have, in general, superior academic skills, and these skills help them achieve academic success. Finally, spending time in recreational reading could indicate that an individual has the ability for sustained attention and concentration necessary for academic success.

(46) One area for further study would be to compare reading achievement directly to cumulative grade-point average, so that achievement could be separated from time spent in recreational reading to determine its significance as a contributing factor in college success. Another area that warrants further attention is recreational reading habits over a lifetime. While we know that time spent reading declines during the middle school years, we do not know if the decline is permanent, or whether individuals may increase their time spent in pleasure reading at different times in their lives.

Quantitative research reports use standard, fixed structures and evaluation criteria.

References

Anderson, R. C., Hiebert, E. H., Scott, J. A., & Wilkinson, I. A. G. (1985). *Becoming a nation of readers: The report of the commission on reading*. Washington, DC: The National Institute of Education.

Anderson, R., Wilson, P., & Fielding, L (1988). Growth in reading and how children spend their time outside of school. *Reading Research Quarterly, 23,* 285–303.

Applebee, A. (1978). Teaching high achievement students: A survey of the winners of the 1977 NCTE achievement awards in writing. *Research in the Teaching of English, 1,* 41–53.

Blackwood, C., Flowers, S. S., Rogers, J. S., & Staik, I. M. (1996, November). *Pleasure reading by college students: Fact or fiction?* Paper presented at the annual meeting of the Mid-South Educational Research Association Conference, Lexington, KY.

Burgess, A. (1987). *A clockwork orange*. New York: W.W. Norton.

Clary, L. M. (1991). Getting adolescents to read. *Journal of Reading, 34,* 340–345.

Foertsch, M. (1992). *Reading in and out of school*. Washington, DC: U.S. Department of Education.

Greaney, V. (1980). Factors related to amount and type of leisure time reading. *Reading Research Quarterly, 15,* 337–357.

Greaney, V., & Hegarty, M. (1987). Correlates of leisure time reading. *Journal of Research in Reading, 10,* 3–20.

Jeffries, L., & Atkins, D. J. (1996). Dimensions of student interest in reading newspapers. *Journalism and Mass Communication Educator, 51,* 15–23.

Kirsch, I. S., & Guthrie, J. T. (1984). Adult reading practices for work and leisure. *Adult Education Quarterly, 34,* 213–232.

Krashen, S. (1984). *Writing: Research, theory and applications.* Torrence, CA: Laredo.

Krashen, S. (1993). *The power of reading: Insights from the research.* Englewood, CO: Libraries Unlimited.

Libsch, M. K., & Breslow, M. (1996). Trends in non-assigned reading by high school seniors. *NASSP Bulletin, 80,* 111–116.

McCoy, D., Larson, B., & Higginson, B. (1991, October). *Surveys of independent reading: Pinpointing the problems, seeking the solutions.* Paper presented at the annual meeting of the College Reading Association, Arlington, VA.

McCreath, E. E. (1975). An investigation of reading habits, reading interests, and their relationship to reading improvement of students at an urban open door junior college. In G. McNinch & W. Miller (Eds.), *Reading: Convention and inquiry* (pp. 100–106). Clemson, SC: National Reading Conference.

Ross, B., & Simone, N. (1982). *Reading interests of tenth, eleventh and twelfth grade students.* Unpublished master's thesis, Kean College of New Jersey, Union, NJ.

Sheorey, R., & Mokhtari, K. (1994). The reading habits of college students at different levels of reading proficiency. *Reading Improvement, 31,* 156–166.

Taylor, B., Frye, M., & Maruyama, K. (1990). Time spent reading and reading growth. *American Educational Research Journal, 27,* 351–362.

Witty, P. (1961). A study of pupil's interest, grades 9, 10, 11, 12. *Education, 82,* 100–110.

CHAPTER

14 Grounded Theory Designs

Grounded theory enables you to generate a broad theory about your qualitative central phenomenon "grounded" in the data. As a systematic procedure, it appeals to a wide range of educational researchers. This chapter defines grounded theory research, identifies when you use it, assesses the key characteristics of it, and advances the steps in conducting and evaluating this design.

By the end of this chapter, you should be able to:

- Define grounded theory and indicate when to use it in research.
- Distinguish among three types of grounded theory designs.
- Identify a process studied in grounded theory research.
- Illustrate how theoretical sampling works in grounded theory research.
- Describe the process of making a constant comparative data analysis.
- Identify a core category for a grounded theory model.
- Draw a theory generated from the data analysis.
- Explain the importance of memoing in grounded theory research.
- Describe how to conduct a grounded theory study.
- Evaluate the quality of a grounded theory study.

Maria designs a grounded theory study for her school committee and her graduate research project. Her research question is "What is the process involved in apprehending students for weapon possession in their high schools?" To study this question, she plans to explore a process, the process of apprehending students for carrying weapons. Study of this process will help her understand one aspect of carrying weapons in the school. She identifies 10 people to interview: 5 students who were actually caught and 5 teachers or administrators who were involved in the apprehensions. After interviewing these individuals, Maria analyzes the data for themes (or categories). She arranges these categories into a visual model of the process. She develops a theory of the process of "being apprehended" for weapon possession in the hope that this theory will provide an explanation that school officials might use to identify early-warning signs for students who may be prone to possess weapons in high schools. Maria has constructed a grounded theory qualitative study.

WHAT IS GROUNDED THEORY RESEARCH?

A **grounded theory design** is a systematic, qualitative procedure used to generate a theory that explains, at a broad conceptual level, a process, an action, or an interaction about a substantive topic. In grounded theory research, this theory is a "process" theory—it explains an educational process of events, activities, actions, and interactions that occur over time. Also, grounded theorists proceed through systematic procedures of collecting data, identifying categories (used synonymously with themes), connecting these categories, and forming a theory that explains the process.

When Do You Use Grounded Theory?

You use grounded theory when you need a broad theory or explanation of a process. Grounded theory *generates* a theory when existing theories do not address your problem or the participants that you plan to study. Because a theory is "grounded" in the data, it provides a better explanation than a theory borrowed "off the shelf," because it fits the situation, actually works in practice, is sensitive to individuals in a setting, and may represent all of the complexities actually found in the process. For instance, in the study of certain educational populations (e.g., children with attention disorders), existing theories may have little applicability to special populations.

You also use grounded theory when you wish to study some process, such as how students develop as writers (Neff, 1998) or how high-achieving African American and Caucasian women's careers develop (Richie, Fassinger, Linn, & Johnson, 1997). It also is used to explain an action of people, such as the process of participating in an adult education class (Courtney, Jha, & Babchuk, 1994), or an interaction among people, such as the support department chairs provide for faculty researchers (Creswell & Brown, 1992).

For the beginning qualitative researcher, grounded theory offers a step-by-step, systematic procedure for analyzing data. Having this procedure available may be helpful to students when they defend qualitative studies before faculty committees. As a systematic process, grounded theory exhibits the rigor quantitative researchers like to see in an educational study. As part of this process, grounded theory has features that contain a self-correction nature. Based on analyzing one set of data, the researcher obtains direction from the analysis for the next set of data (Charmaz, 2000). Also, in data analysis, the researcher builds categories systematically from incident to incident and from incident to category. In this way, the researcher stays close to the data at all times in the analysis.

How Did Grounded Theory Develop?

Two sociologists, Barney G. Glaser and the late Anselm L. Strauss, developed grounded theory in the late 1960s. It evolved out of their work at the University of California San Francisco Medical Center with patients who were terminally ill. In studying these patients, Glaser and Strauss recorded and publicized their methods of research. This led to many individuals contacting Glaser and Strauss to learn more about their research methods. In response, Glaser and Strauss developed a pioneering book that expounded in detail on their grounded theory procedures, *The Discovery of Grounded Theory* (1967). This book laid the foundation for the major ideas of grounded theory used today, and it became a procedural guide for numerous dissertations and research reports. In *Discovery,* Glaser and Strauss took the position that the current theory in sociology overly stressed verifying and testing theories rather than discovering the concepts (variables) and hypotheses based on actual field data from participants. A theory discovered during data collection will "fit the situation being researched and will work when put into use" (Glaser & Strauss, 1967, p. 3) better than a theory identified before a study begins.

The ideas in *Discovery* reflected the background of both authors. Glaser trained in quantitative research at Columbia University, with noted researchers who were interested in the inductive development of theory using quantitative and qualitative data. This inductive perspective led him to embrace the importance of generating theory from the perspective of participants in a study. Strauss, however, came to grounded theory from the University of Chicago, with a strong history and tradition in qualitative field research. This background led Strauss to emphasize the importance of field research, that is, going to individuals and listening closely to participants' ideas.

In the years following *Discovery,* both Glaser and Strauss independently authored several books that refined and explained their early methods (Glaser, 1978, 1992; Strauss, 1987). In 1990 and again in 1998, Strauss teamed with a community nursing health researcher, Juliet Corbin, to take the techniques and procedures of grounded theory to new levels. They introduced a more prescriptive form of grounded theory, with predetermined categories and with concerns about validity and reliability.

Their systematic approach, although embraced by new qualitative researchers (Charmaz, 2000), provoked a critical response from Glaser (1992), which he detailed in a book to "set researchers using grounded theory on a correct path" (p. 3). Glaser was primarily concerned about how Strauss used preconceived categories and frameworks that did not allow theory to emerge during the process of research. He also took issue with what he saw as an emphasis on simply describing acts rather than actively conceptualizing patterns or connections in the data that would lead to theory.

"So who's got the real grounded theory?" asks Charmaz (2000, p. 513). Her question was more than rhetorical; she answered it by advancing her own approach to grounded theory, the "constructivist" method (Charmaz, 2006). Charmaz felt that both Glaser and Strauss (and Strauss and Corbin) were much too systematic in their procedures. Grounded theorists needed to stress flexible strategies, emphasize the meaning participants ascribe to situations, acknowledge the roles of the researcher and the individuals being researched, and expand philosophically beyond a quantitative orientation to research.

TYPES OF GROUNDED THEORY DESIGNS

We can see that perspectives about conducting grounded theory research have differed depending on the advocate for a particular approach. However, three dominant designs are discernible: the systematic procedure allied with Strauss and Corbin (1998); the emerging design, associated with Glaser (1992); and the constructivist approach espoused by Charmaz (1990, 2000, 2006).

The Systematic Design

The systematic design for grounded theory is widely used in educational research, and it is associated with the detailed, rigorous procedures that Strauss and Corbin identified in 1990 and elaborated in their second edition on techniques and procedures for developing grounded theory (1998). It is much more prescribed than the original conceptualization of grounded theory in 1967 (Glaser & Strauss, 1967). A **systematic design in grounded theory** emphasizes the use of data analysis steps of open, axial, and selective coding, and the development of a logic paradigm or a visual picture of the theory generated. In this definition, three phases of coding exist.

In the first phase, **open coding**, the grounded theorist forms initial categories of information about the phenomenon being studied by segmenting information. The researcher bases categories on all data collected, such as interviews, observations, and researcher's memos or notes. Typically, researchers identify categories and subcategories, as is seen in the grounded theory study by Knapp (1995). She examined the career development of 27 educational trainers in career development. In interviews with these trainers, she learned about their adaptability and resilience. One page from her study, shown in Figure 14.1, portrays several categories that Knapp identified from her data, such as specialization, transferable skills, finding a focus, and on-the-job learning. In this coding presentation, we find that Knapp also indicates the sources of information that support the categories, such as interviews, focus groups, journals, memos, and observations.

To consider another example of open coding, see Figure 14.2, which displays the coding for a study of 33 academic chairpersons in colleges and universities and their roles in enhancing faculty research (Creswell & Brown, 1992). The authors organized their presentation of open coding differently than Knapp and included broad categories, properties, and dimensionalized examples, and followed the systematic procedures of Strauss and Corbin (1998). The major features of this table are the seven categories of roles: provider, enabler, advocate, mentor, encourager, collaborator, and challenger. However, the authors introduce two new ideas into our understanding of open coding. **Properties** are subcategories in grounded theory of open codes that serve to provide more detail about each category. Each property, in turn, is dimensionalized in grounded theory. A **dimensionalized property** means that the researcher views the property on a continuum and locates, in the data, examples representing extremes on this continuum. For example, the chair, as a provider (category), engages in funding faculty (a property), which consists of possibilities on a continuum of extent of funds ranging from long-term start-up seed money to short-term travel money (dimensionalized property).

In the second phase, **axial coding**, the grounded theorist selects one open coding category, positions it at the center of the process being explored (as the core phenomenon), and then relates other categories to it. These other categories are the causal conditions (factors that influence the core phenomenon), strategies (actions taken in response to the core phenomenon), contextual and intervening conditions (specific and general situational factors that influence the strategies), and consequences (outcomes from using the strategies). This phase involves drawing a diagram, called a **coding paradigm**, which portrays the interrelationship of causal conditions, strategies, contextual and intervening conditions, and consequences.

To illustrate this process, first examine Figure 14.3. In this figure, we see the open coding categories on the left and the axial coding paradigm on the right. A grounded theory researcher identifies one of the open coding categories as the core category that is central to a theory (we review the criteria for selecting this core category later). Then, this

FIGURE 14.1

An Example of Coding Categories in Grounded Theory

Categories	Coding Sources
Specialization	
definition	1, 2, 5, 6, 7, 10, 12, 13, 14, 15, 16, 17, 18, 19, 20, 21, 25, 26
generalist	1, 5, 7, 10, 12, 14, 15, 16, 19, 21, 23, 24
change agent	13, 17, J
Transferable skills	
previous job experience	CO2, 1, 3, 4, 5, 6, 8, 9, 11, 12, 13, 14, 15, 17, 19, 20, 22, 23, 24, 25, 26
cross training in another department	7, 8, 12, 17, 18, 19, 22, 23, 24, 25
Finding a focus	
entering field serendipitously	5, 6, 8, 9, 10, 11, 13, 15, 16, 19, 20, 22, 23, 24, J, M
occupational fit	2, 3, 4, 5, 6, 7, 8, 10, 11, 12, 13, 14, 15, 16, 17, 18, 19, 20, 21, 22, 23, 25, 26, J
turn down promotions	2, 12, 18, 23
understanding self	3, 6, 16, 17, 18, 19, 21, 22, 23, 24, 25
having a personal mission	3, 14, 16, 17, 18, 19
personally well grounded	2, 6, 13, 14, 19
other centered	CO2, 3, 8, 11, 13, 14, 15, 16, 17, 18, 19, 20, 21, 22, 24
Learning On-the-Job	
wandering around in the dark	CO2, 15, 22, M
trial and error	CO2, 2, 15, 16, 23, 24
gradual development	1, 4, 5, 6, 7, 8, 9, 17, 20, 22
facilitating training	1, 8, 11, 17, 20, 21, 24, 26
keeping current	CO2, 1, 2, 4, 5, 6, 8, 10, 11, 12, 15, 16, 17, 20, 21, 24, 26
learning environment	CO2, 18, 24, 26, F

KEY	
#	Interview
CO#	Pilot
F	Focus groups
J	Journal
M	Memo
O	Observation

Source: Reprinted with permission from Sharon Knapp, Ph. D.

FIGURE 14.2

An Example of Coding Categories in Grounded Theory With Properties and Dimensionalized Properties

Table 1
Open Coding of Chairperson's Role

Broad Categories*	Category	Properties	Dimensionalized Examples	
Administrative role	Provider	With funding	Start-up seed money	Short-term travel
		With nonfinancial aid	Laboratory equipment	Student personnel
	Enabler	With more money	Faculty committees	Long-term sabbatical
		With more visibility	Faculty committees	Administrative assignments
External role	Advocate	For resources	Short-term funds	Long-term facilities
		For interaction	With faculty	With students
		To assist politically	With dean	With faculty
Interpersonal role	Mentor	By role modeling	Time management	Working with others
		By sharing expertise	About research topics	About specific journals
		By reviewing and critiquing	Before manuscript submission	After manuscript submission
	Encourager	By hands off	No pressure	Choice belongs to professor
		By recognition and appreciation	Private communication	Public communication
		By general support	Personal friendship	Professional collegiality
		By task-specific encouragement	Supporting ideas	Encouraging specific book or article
	Collaborator	By jointly setting goals	Informal discussion	Formal performance reviews
		By working together on projects	Writing grant proposals	Writing journal articles
	Challenger	By prodding	Gentle reminder	Direct formal conversation
		By inspiring	Discussing general possibilities	Discussing specific examples
		By evaluating and monitoring	Biweekly conferences	Annual review

Source: Creswell & Brown, 1992.

*Strauss and Corbin (1990) define a category as "a classification of concepts." Concepts are conceptual labels placed on discrete happenings, events, and other phenomena, while properties are "attributes or characteristics pertaining to a category," and dimensions are "location of properties along a continuum" (p. 61).

FIGURE 14.3

Grounded Theory Coding from Open Coding to the Axial Coding Paradigm

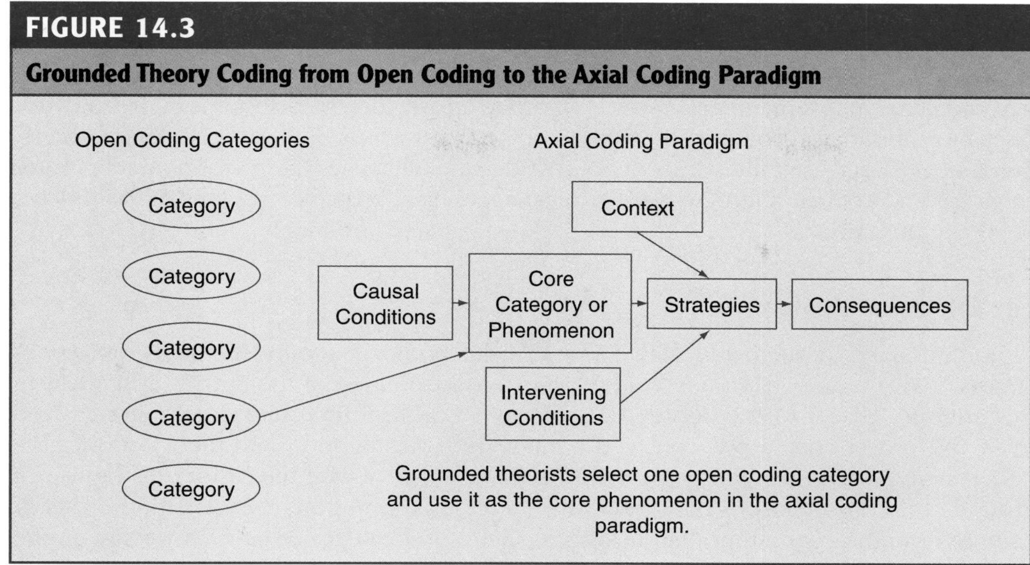

core category becomes the centerpoint of the axial coding paradigm. Examining this paradigm, you can see that there are six boxes (or categories) of information:

1. *Causal conditions*—categories of conditions that influence the core category
2. *Context*—the specific conditions that influence the strategies
3. *Core category*—the idea of phenomenon central to the process
4. *Intervening conditions*—the general contextual conditions that influence strategies
5. *Strategies*—the specific actions or interactions that result from the core phenomenon
6. *Consequences*—the outcomes of employing the strategies

In addition, viewing this coding paradigm from left to right, we see that the causal conditions influence the core phenomenon, the core phenomenon and the context and intervening conditions influence the strategies, and the strategies influence the consequences.

The third phase of coding consists of selective coding. In **selective coding** the grounded theorist writes a theory from the interrelationship of the categories in the axial coding model. At a basic level, this theory provides an abstract explanation for the process being studied in the research. It is the process of integrating and refining the theory (Strauss & Corbin, 1998) through such techniques as writing out the story line that interconnects the categories and sorting through personal memos about theoretical ideas (see discussion on memos later in the chapter). In a story line, a researcher might examine how certain factors influence the phenomenon leading to the use of specific strategies with certain outcomes.

Use of these three coding procedures means that grounded theorists use set procedures to develop their theory. They rely on analyzing their data for specific types of categories in axial coding and use diagrams to present their theories. A grounded theory study using this approach might end with hypotheses (called *propositions* by Strauss & Corbin, 1998) that make explicit the relationship among categories in the axial coding paradigm.

A study of the process of coping by 11 women who survived childhood sexual abuse illustrates this systematic procedure (Morrow & Smith, 1995). In this study we learn that the women felt threatened, helpless, and powerless, but that they survived and coped by managing their feelings (e.g., avoiding or escaping feelings, not remembering experiences). They also address their feelings of hopelessness and powerlessness using strategies such as seeking control in other areas of their life, reframing abuse to give the illusion of control, or simply rejecting power issues. As an example of the systematic procedure associated with Strauss and Corbin (1990, 1998), the authors include the process of open coding, axial coding, and generating a theoretical model. They had clearly identified sections in the study for discussion about each component of axial coding (e.g., causes of feelings and helplessness, the strategies used, and the consequences). A diagram illustrates the "theoretical model" for surviving and coping, and they discuss this diagram as a sequence of steps in the process of coping behavior.

The Emerging Design

Although Glaser participated with Strauss in the book on grounded theory (Glaser & Strauss, 1967), Glaser has since written an extensive critique of the Strauss approach. In this critique, Glaser (1992) felt that Strauss and Corbin (1990) had overly emphasized rules and procedures, a preconceived framework for categories, and theory verification rather than theory generation. (Babchuk [1996, 1997] reviewed the history of the use of grounded theory.) Glaser (1992), however, stresses the importance of letting a theory emerge from the data rather than using specific, preset categories such as we saw in the axial coding paradigm (e.g., causal conditions, content, intervening condition, strategies, and consequences). Moreover, for Glaser, the objective of a grounded theory study is for the author to explain a "basic social process." This explanation involves the constant comparative coding procedures of comparing incident to incident, incident to category, and category to category. The focus is on connecting categories and emerging theory, not on simply describing categories. In the end, the researcher builds a theory and discusses the relationship among categories without reference to a diagram or picture.

The more flexible, less prescribed form of grounded theory research as advanced by Glaser (1992) consists of several major ideas:

1. Grounded theory exists at the most abstract conceptual level rather than the least abstract level as found in visual data presentations such as a coding paradigm.
2. A theory is grounded in the data and it is not forced into categories.
3. A good grounded theory must meet four central criteria: fit, work, relevance, and modifiability. By carefully inducing the theory from a substantive area, it will fit the realities in the eyes of participants, practitioners, and researchers. If a grounded theory works, it will explain the variations in behavior of participants. If the theory fits and works, it has relevance. The theory should not be "written in stone" (Glaser, 1992, p. 15) and should be modified when new data are present.

Larson's (1997) study portrayed a grounded theory study consistent with Glaser's approach. The goal for Larson was to write a "theory-in-process" (p. 118) for high school social studies teachers' conception of discussion in their classrooms. This example of an emerging design takes the reader through six conceptions that emerged in the data: discussion as recitation, as a teacher-directed conversation, as an open-ended conversation, as posing challenging questions, as guided transfer of knowledge to the world outside the classroom, and as practice of verbal interaction. Larson also identified factors that influenced these conceptions, such as student diversity and lesson objectives.

In this emerging grounded theory approach, Larson's attention was on developing an explanation for discussion in high school social studies classrooms. His procedure was to generate categories by examining the data, refining the categories into fewer and fewer categories, comparing data with emerging categories, and writing a theory of several processes involved in classroom discussions. Larson developed categories but did not present a diagram of his theory.

The Constructivist Design

The constructivist approach has been articulated by Kathy Charmaz (1990, 2000, 2006) as a philosophical position between the more positivist (i.e., more quantitative) stance of Glaser and Strauss and Corbin and postmodern researchers (i.e., those who challenge the importance of methods). Overall, her focus is on the meanings ascribed by participants in a study. She is more interested in the views, values, beliefs, feelings, assumptions, and ideologies of individuals than in gathering facts and describing acts. Charmaz (2000, 2006) suggested that any aspects that obscure experiences, such as complex terms or jargon, diagrams, or conceptual maps, detract from grounded theory and represent an attempt to gain power in their use. Using active codes, such as "recasting life," best captures the experiences of individuals. Moreover, a grounded theory procedure does not minimize the role of the researcher in the process. The researcher makes decisions about the categories throughout the process (Charmaz, 1990). The researcher brings certain questions to the data, along with a "store of sociological concepts" (p. 1165). The researcher also brings values, experiences, and priorities. Any conclusions developed are suggestive, incomplete, and inconclusive.

In applying this approach, a grounded theorist explains the feelings of individuals as they experience a phenomenon or process. The constructivist study mentions the beliefs and values of the researcher and eschews predetermined categories, such as those found in axial coding. The narrative is written to be more explanatory, more discursive, and more probing of the assumptions and meanings for individuals in the study.

Charmaz illustrated the central elements of this approach to grounded theory. In a study of the processes involved in the experiences of 20 men with chronic illnesses (e.g., multiple sclerosis, renal failure, diabetes), Charmaz (1994) explored how and in what way their illnesses precipitated a personal identity dilemma. She contended that chronic illness threatens men's "taken-for-granted" masculine identities. Her findings explored several dilemmas, such as risking activity versus forced passivity, remaining independent versus becoming dependent, maintaining dominance versus becoming subordinate, and preserving a public persona versus acknowledging private feelings. These dilemmas clustered into several processes the men experienced—awakening to death, accommodating uncertainty, defining illness and disability, and preserving self.

Using a constructivist approach to grounded theory, she clearly articulated that her purpose was to understand "what it means to have a disease" (Charmaz, 1994, p. 284). She reported the feelings of the men, using active code labels such as *awakening, accommodating, defining,* and *preserving*. These codes signal basic processes the men were experiencing. Charmaz interrelated their experiences, their conditions, and their consequences in a narrative discussion without the use of diagrams or figures to summarize these processes. She ended with thoughts such as "What are the conditions that shape whether a man will reconstruct a positive identity or sink into depression?" (pp. 283–284), more suggestive and questioning of the data than conclusive.

Choosing Among the Designs

Choosing among the three approaches requires several considerations. As you consider conducting a grounded theory study, you need to weigh how strongly you want to emphasize procedures, use predetermined categories in analysis, position yourself as a researcher, and decide how to end the study, whether it is with tentative questions or hypotheses that are specific.

If you were Maria, seeking to generate a theory of the process of apprehending students for weapon possession, what design would you use? Because Maria is a beginning researcher, the more structured approach of the systematic design would be ideal. With the procedures clearly identified and the axial coding model specified in terms of types of categories to relate, the systematic procedure again would be best.

In selecting one of the three approaches, consider that the procedures advanced by Strauss and Corbin (1998) may lead to a premature commitment to a set of analytic categories (Robrecht, 1995) and a lack of conceptual depth (Becker, 1993). Also, in all types, grounded theory has a distinct language that some educators may view as jargon and, hence, in need of careful definition (e.g., constant comparative, open coding, axial coding). One criticism is that these terms are not always clearly defined (Charmaz, 2000), although Strauss and Corbin (1998) provided numerous definitions at the beginning of each chapter of their book. Finally, with the varied approaches to this design and the continual emergence of new perspectives, readers may become confused and not know which procedures would best produce a well-developed theory.

What Are the Key Characteristics of Grounded Theory Research?

Grounded theory can incorporate a systematic approach, a flexible emerging design, and the use of active codes to capture the experiences of participants. In the six characteristics that follow, you can find elements of the systematic, emerging, and constructivist approaches. Characteristics that grounded theory researchers use in their designs are:

- Process approach
- Theoretical sampling
- Constant comparative data analysis
- A core category
- Theory generation
- Memos

A Process Approach

Although grounded theorists might explore a single idea (e.g., leadership skills), they more frequently examine a process because the social world that we live in involves people interacting with other people. Grounded theorists generate an understanding of a process related to a substantive topic. A **process in grounded theory research** is a sequence of actions and interactions among people and events pertaining to a topic (Strauss & Corbin, 1998). The educational topic could be AIDS prevention, achievement assessment, or counseling between a school counselor and a student. In all of these topics, researchers can isolate and identify actions and interactions among people. Grounded theorists call these isolated aspects categories. **Categories in grounded theory designs** are themes of basic information identified in the data by the researcher and used to understand a process. A category for the process between a school counselor and student, for example, may be the student's understanding of "success" in the session.

As discussed in chapter 9, several types of labels or titles are used for themes or categories. In grounded theory research, a frequently used form is *in vivo* codes. **In vivo codes** are labels for categories (or themes) that are phrased in the exact words of participants, rather than in the words of the researcher or in social science or educational terms. Researchers identify these words by examining passages of transcripts or observational fieldnotes to locate phrases mentioned by participants that capture the intent of a category. For example, rather than use the social science concept "upward mobility," a participant might call this idea "goin' up the ladder." Using in vivo coding, the researcher would use the phrase "goin' up the ladder" to describe the category. Because categories

FIGURE 14.4

A Process and Categories Within the Flow of Research in Grounded Theory

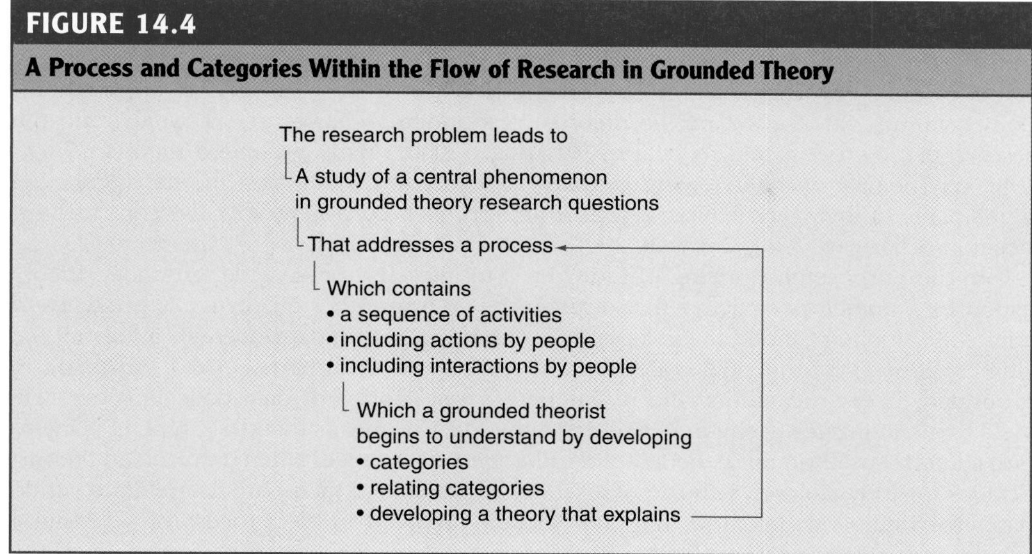

become major headings in research reports, this phrase would be the heading of the discussion about the open coding category "goin' up the ladder."

It is helpful to see how the two ideas of process and categories relate to activities that are typically applied by a grounded theorist. Examine the flow of activities as shown in Figure 14.4. A researcher begins with a research problem, such as the need to examine how academic chairpersons balance their work and personal lives. The central phenomenon, then, becomes a "balance of work and personal life." To study this central phenomenon, the grounded theorist frames it as a process, such as the "process by which chairs balance their work and personal lives" (alternatively, the process of "imbalance" might be explored). Whatever the process, it has a sequence of activities, actions by people, and interactions among people. The actions of the chair might include exercising early in the morning and visiting with faculty later in the morning about stressful situations in the department. Here we have several activities, organized into a sequence, exhibiting actions by people. As the grounded theorist studies chairs (e.g., through interviews or observations), an understanding of the process of balancing work and personal life slowly emerges. The researcher categorizes this information, drawing on evidence to support each category. This phase is the open coding phase. Then the researcher starts organizing the categories into a model (axial coding), and interrelating the categories to form a theory that explains the process of balancing work and personal life. In this example, the process emerges from the problem and the need to explore the central phenomenon, and the categories develop from data collection.

As grounded theorists conduct a study, they often use a phrase for the process starting with a gerund word (i.e., *ing* words; as recommended by Charmaz, 2000). As a phrase that appears in titles and purpose statements, it signals the action of the study. Listed below are titles for grounded theory studies in which we can see the use of gerund words, a key category of interest, and the broader topic being explored:

- "Educating Every Teacher, Every Year: The Public Schools and Parents of Children with ADHD" (Reid et al., 1996)—the process of educating teachers, the implied category of relations between parents and schools, the topic of children with ADHD
- "'Discovering' Chronic Illness: Using Grounded Theory" (Charmaz, 1990)—the process of patients discovering their illness, the category of chronic illness, and the implied topic of disease.

Theoretical Sampling

The data collected by grounded theorists to establish these processes includes many forms of qualitative information (see chapter 8). Researchers can collect observations, conversations, interviews, public records, respondents' diaries and journals, and the researcher's own personal reflections (Charmaz, 2000). Many grounded theorists, however, rely heavily on interviewing, perhaps as a way to capture best the experiences of participants in their own words, which is an approach consistent with the constructivist position (Charmaz, 2000; Creswell, 2007).

In the purposeful sampling of individuals to interview or observe, grounded theory espouses a unique perspective that distinguishes it from other qualitative approaches to data collection. Grounded theorists sample theoretically using a procedure involving the simultaneous and sequential collection and analysis of data. **Theoretical sampling** in grounded theory means that the researcher chooses forms of data collection that will yield text and images useful in generating a theory. This means that the sampling is intentional and focused on the generation of a theory. For instance, when a grounded theorist decides to study children's choice of a school, students and their parents are good candidates for interviews because they are actively involved in the process of selecting a school and can speak from firsthand experience. However, school personnel (e.g., the principal) may have useful information to inform this process, but they would be less central than the students and parents, who are making the choices. In this project, the grounded theorist would begin with students and their parents, who actually make the choice of schools.

Beyond sampling data for its theoretical value, grounded theorists also espouse the idea of using an emerging design. An **emerging design** in grounded theory research is the process in which the researcher collects data, analyzes it immediately rather than waiting until all data are collected, and then bases the decision about what data to collect next on this analysis. The image of a "zigzag" helps us to understand this procedure, as shown in Figure 14.5. As illustrated in this figure, the grounded theorist engages in initial data collection (e.g., the first collection of interview data), analyzes it for preliminary categories, and then looks for clues about what additional data to collect. These clues may be underdeveloped categories, missing information in the sequence of the study process, or new individuals who can provide insight into some aspect of the process. The

FIGURE 14.5

Zigzag Data Collection and Analysis to Achieve Saturation of Categories

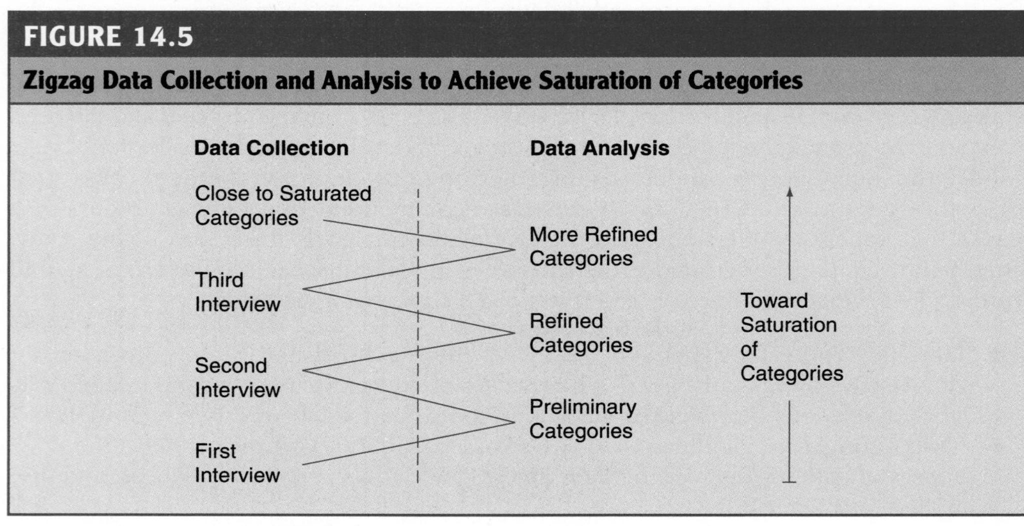

grounded theorist then returns to the field to gather this additional information. In this procedure, the inquirer refines, develops, and clarifies the meanings of categories for the theory. This process weaves back and forth between data collection and analysis, and it continues until the inquirer reaches saturation of a category. **Saturation** in grounded theory research is a state in which the researcher makes the subjective determination that new data will not provide any new information or insights for the developing categories.

Identifying this process in a published grounded theory study requires close examination of the data collection and analysis process to note whether the researcher seems to be recycling between data collection and data analysis. For example, in a study of the processes of men experiencing chronic illness, Charmaz (1990) carefully documented how she interviewed 7 of the 20 men in her study more than once to refine her emerging categories.

Constant Comparative Data Analysis

In grounded theory research, the inquirer engages in a process of gathering data, sorting it into categories, collecting additional information, and comparing the new information with emerging categories. This process of slowly developing categories of information is the constant comparative procedure. **Constant comparison** is an inductive (from specific to broad) data analysis procedure in grounded theory research of generating and connecting categories by comparing incidents in the data to other incidents, incidents to categories, and categories to other categories. The overall intent is to "ground" the categories in the data. As shown in Figure 14.6, raw data are formed into indicators (I; Glaser, 1978)—small segments of information that come from different people, different sources, or the same people over time. These indicators are, in turn, grouped into several codes (e.g., Code A, Code B, Code C), and then formed into more abstract categories (e.g., Category I, Category II). Throughout this process, the researcher is constantly comparing indicators to indicators, codes to codes, and categories to categories. This eliminates redundancy and develops evidence for categories. In addition, the grounded theorist compares the emerging scheme with the raw data to ground the categories in the information collected during the study.

In this process, the grounded theorist asks questions of the data. Glaser (1992), for example, suggested that the inquirer ask:

- What is the data a study of?
- What category or what property of what category does this incident indicate?

FIGURE 14.6

Constant Comparison Procedures in Grounded Theory

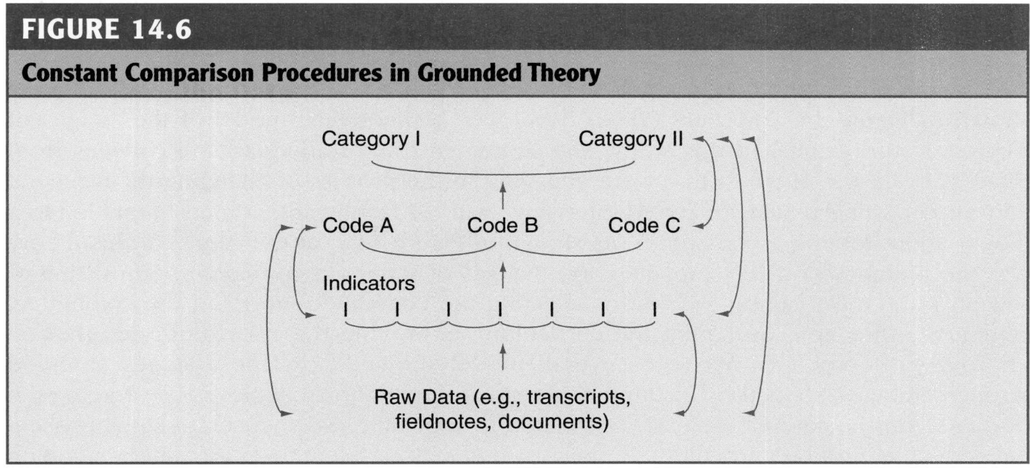

- What is actually happening in the data?
- What is the basic social psychological process or social structural process in the action scene? (p. 51)

In a grounded theory study of becoming an adult student in New Zealand, Cocklin (1996) collected observations, interviews, participant diary accounts, questionnaires, and documentary materials from teaching staff in one secondary school. In this study, Cocklin described the process of refining his categories (called themes) by returning to his data repeatedly as themes emerged. He commented:

> While doing this transcription and organization, and as an activity I undertook at weekends, statutory holidays, and term vacations, I also engaged in a continuous process of reflection and analysis which included placing interpretive comments alongside the transcribed data (see Figure 2). These comments, akin to the derivation of properties and hypotheses, I also subjected to ongoing analysis and development as the year progressed and data emerged. . . . (p. 97)

A Core Category

From among the major categories derived from the data, the grounded theorist selects a core category as the central phenomenon for the theory. After identifying several categories (say, 8 to 10 depending on the size of the database), the researcher selects a **core category** as the basis for writing the theory. (See Figure 14.3 for a visual of this process.) The researcher makes this selection based on several factors, such as its relationship to other categories, its frequency of occurrence, its quick and easy saturation, and its clear implications for development of theory (Glaser, 1978). It is a category that can "process out," in other words, be the center or main theme of the process (Glaser, 1978). Listed here are detailed criteria that Strauss and Corbin (1998) identified for choosing a central (or core) category:

1. It must be central; that is, all other major categories can relate to it.
2. It must appear frequently in the data. This means that within all or almost all cases, there are indicators pointing to that concept.
3. The explanation that evolves by relating the categories is logical and consistent. There is no forcing of data.
4. The name or phrase used to describe the central category should be sufficiently abstract.
5. As the concept is refined, the theory grows in depth and explanatory power.
6. When conditions vary, the explanation still holds, although the way in which a phenomenon is expressed might look somewhat different (p. 147).

We can illustrate a core category by turning to an actual grounded theory study. As shown in Figure 14.7, Mastera (1996) developed a theoretical model of the "stages of forging a curriculum." In this study, she examined three undergraduate colleges from three states in the Midwest that were engaging in the process of changing their general education curricula. Semistructured interviews with 34 faculty and administrators led to a theory about forging a curriculum. As shown in Figure 14.7, at the center of this theory was the phenomenon (or core category), "stages of forging a curriculum," consisting of several properties: calling for action, selecting the committee, norming the committee, setting the direction, designing the curriculum, approving the curriculum design, and approving the courses. Mastera's overall model showed how these stages emerged through changes, shaped by institutional context, that led to strategies for leveraging the discourse on the committees and contributed to specific consequences, such as revising the general education curriculum. In this process, Mastera identified early in open coding

FIGURE 14.7

Example of a "Core Category" in a Theoretical Model of "Stages of Forging a Curriculum"

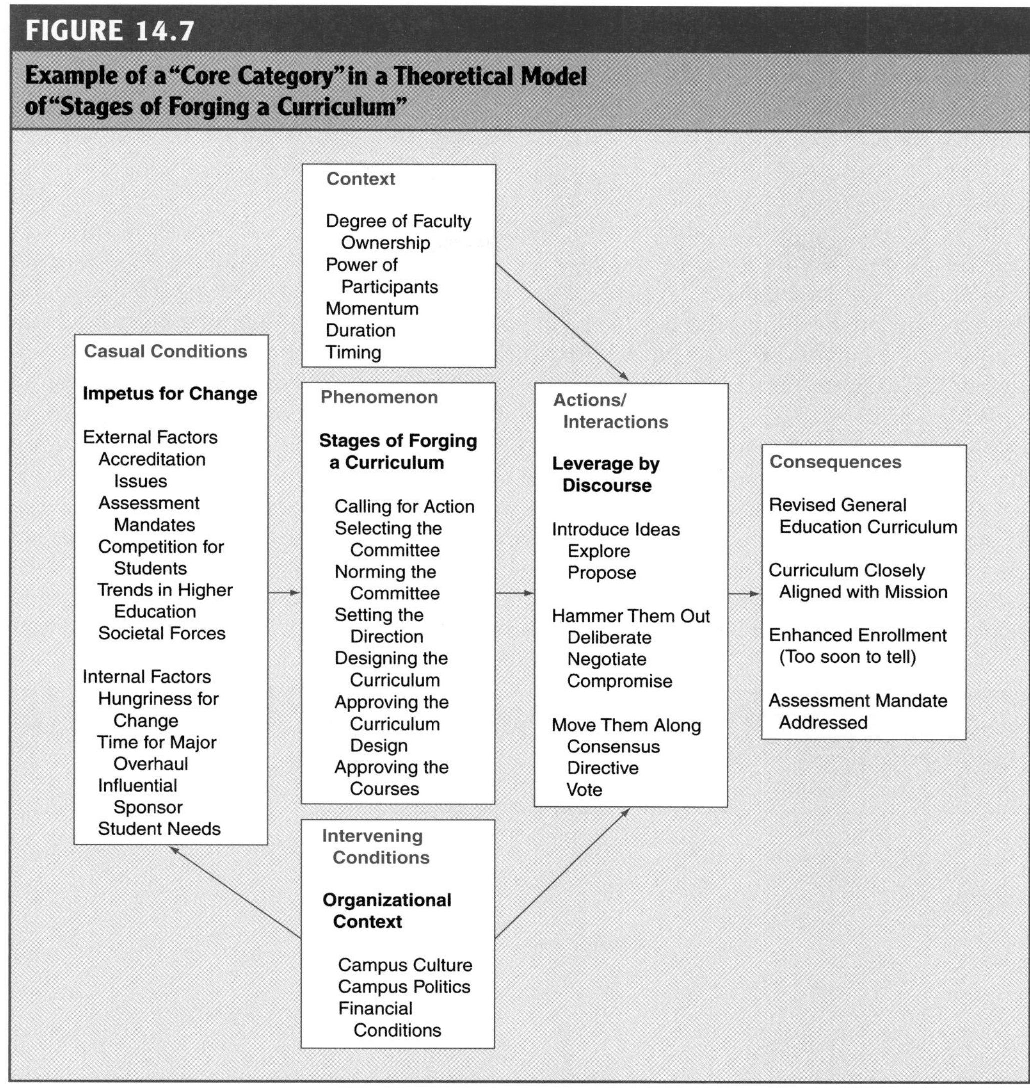

Source: Reprinted with permission from Georgianne Mastera, Ph.D.

the importance of her phenomenon or core category, "stages," although "selecting labels that captured this staged process proved to be more elusive" (p. 59).

Theory Generation

In identifying a core category and the process categories that explain it, grounded theorists have generated a middle-range theory. The entire procedure leads to generating a theory based on data collected by the researcher. This **theory in grounded theory research** is an abstract explanation or understanding of a process about a substantive topic grounded in the data. Because the theory is close to the data, it does not have wide applicability or scope, such as "grand" theories about human motivation that apply to many people and situations. Nor is it a "minor working hypothesis" (Glaser & Strauss, 1967, p. 33), such as an explanation for students in one school or classroom. Instead, the theory is "middle range" (Charmaz, 2000), drawn from multiple individuals or data sources, which provides an explanation for a substantive topic.

Consider how grounded theorists actually present their theory in three possible ways: as a visual coding paradigm, as a series of propositions (or hypotheses), or as a story written in narrative form.

Theory appears in studies as the visual coding model or coding paradigm discussed earlier in the systematic procedures of Strauss and Corbin (1998). We have viewed several of these coding paradigms already, but a slightly different version is seen in Brown's (1993) model of ethnic minority students' process of community building. As shown in Figure 14.8, Brown explored the process of community building among 23 black and Hispanic freshmen during the first 6 to 10 weeks at a private, predominantly white university in the Midwest. In this study, an inductively developed process of campus community building resulted from the data. The theory or model of this process is shown in Figure 14.8. Based largely on the predetermined, systematic categories of intervening conditions, strategies, causal conditions, and phenomena, Brown developed a picture of the process as the key theoretical description of the process.

Brown's (1993) study also illustrated a visual model and the use of theoretical propositions (or hypotheses) for conveying a theory. **Theoretical propositions** in grounded theory research are statements indicating the relationship among categories, such as in the systematic approach to axial coding that includes causal conditions, the core category or phenomenon, the context, intervening conditions, strategies, and consequences. After

FIGURE 14.8

Example of a Theory—A Model of Ethnic Minority Students Process of Community Building

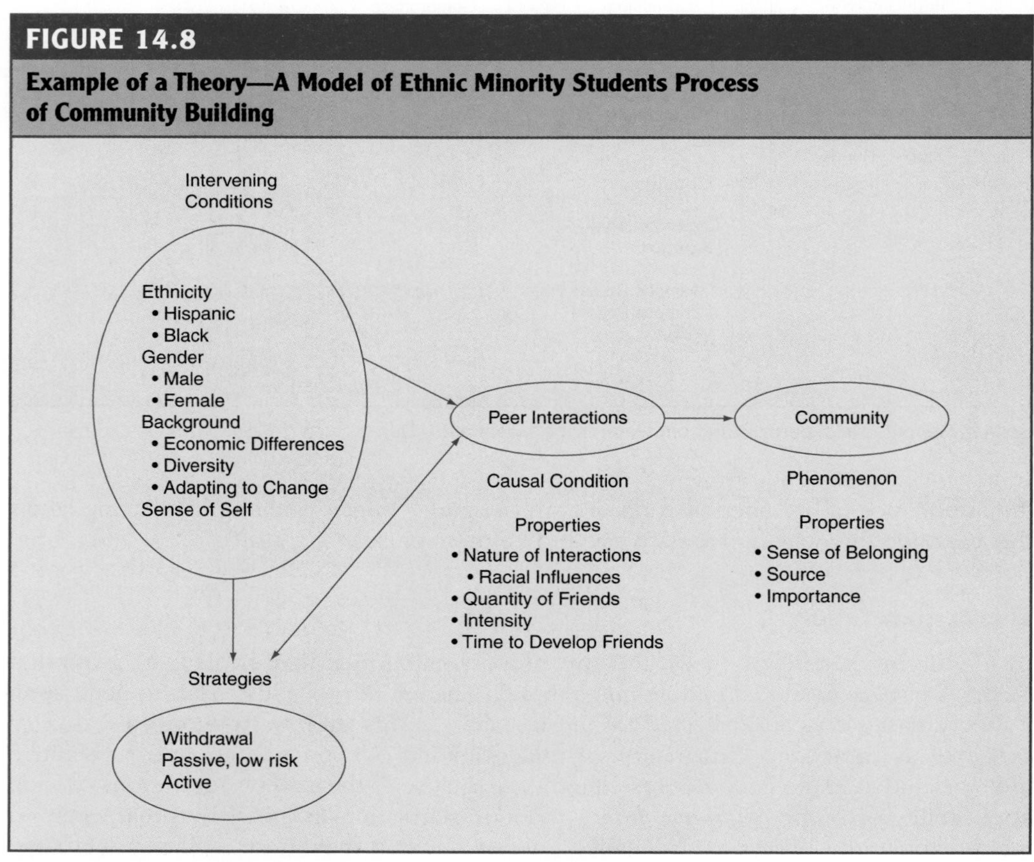

Source: Reprinted with permission from Martha L. Brown, Ph. D.

presenting her visual model, Brown identified propositions and subpropositions that relate her categories in the model:

1. Peer interactions influence community building among black and Hispanic college freshmen.
2. The more time students spend with peers, the greater their sense of community. The more their free time is spent alone, the greater the feelings of loneliness and alienation.
3. The more free time students spend on campus interacting with peers in the residence halls, the greater their sense of community.
4. Active involvement in small groups within the institutional setting (i.e., residence hall floors, freshmen seminar groups, intramural sports teams, clubs) will facilitate feelings of community.

Returning again to Figure 14.8, we can see that Brown is interrelating the causal conditions about interactions and friends in the proposition and subpropositions. In additional propositions in her study, Brown continued to identify propositions that interrelated other aspects of her model.

Although the "theory" may be easy to identify in a grounded theory study when the author presents it as a visual coding paradigm or as a series of propositions, a discussion written in the form of a story (Strauss & Corbin, 1998) may be less obvious to a reader. In the process of integrating the categories, grounded theorists develop a sense of what the research is all about and start writing a descriptive story about the process. Strauss and Corbin (1998) recommended that the researcher:

> . . . sit down and write a few descriptive sentences about "what seems to be going on here." It may take two, three, or even more starts to be able to articulate one's thoughts concisely. Eventually, the story emerges. (p. 148)

After refinement and reworking, grounded theorists include these stories in their research reports as a means for describing their theory of the process. A good example of this type of passage is a descriptive story about teen drug use cited by Strauss and Corbin (1998):

> What keeps striking us about these interviews is that, although many teens use drugs, few go on to become hard-core users. It seems to be a kind of teenage experimentation, a developmental phase in their lives that marks the passage from child to teen and from teen to adult. They learn about drugs and also themselves, gain acceptance from their peers, and challenge adult authority through using drugs. It is a very specific behavior that sets them apart from family, but, at the same time, makes them one of the teen group. (p. 149)

In this passage, the authors identify a causal condition (i.e., "developmental phase"). They also mention the outcomes (i.e., "marks the passage") and establish context (e.g., "sets them apart from family"). Through this descriptive story, the authors interrelate several categories of axial coding to form a theoretical discussion about the process of teen drug use—a third form for writing theory into a grounded theory project.

Memos

Throughout the grounded theory procedure, grounded theorists create memos about the data. Memo writing is a tool in grounded theory research that provides researchers with an ongoing dialogue with themselves about the emerging theory (Charmaz, 1990). **Memos** are notes the researcher writes throughout the research process to elaborate on ideas about the data and the coded categories. In memos, the researcher explores hunches, ideas, and thoughts, and then takes them apart, always searching for the broader explanations at work in the process. Memos help direct the inquirer toward new sources of data, shape which ideas to develop further, and prevent paralysis from mountains of data. However, grounded theory studies do not often report memoing, or if they do, they do not provide evidence of how it was used (Babchuck, 1997).

We can illustrate memoing in a study about the process of identity loss by individuals with Alzheimer's disease. Orona (1997) discussed how memoing helped her to:

1. Free associate and write whatever thoughts she became aware of
2. Unblock at times when she felt she could not quite describe in words what was occurring in the data
3. Begin conceptualizing by tracking ideas from raw data to coding and into categories

The memos can be short or long, more detailed and related to codes and categories or broader and more abstract. Here is an illustration of a short, detailed memo written by Charmaz (1994) during her study of patients who were terminally ill, and the "identifying moments" in the hospital when patients developed new insight into themselves.

> It became clear to me that how a particular chronically ill person was identified by others sometimes became revealed to them in the course of a moment's encounter or interaction. These moments gave the ill individual new reflections of self, often revealing that he (or she) is not the person he felt he was. . . . Negative identifying moments are those shrouded in embarrassment and devaluation. . . . One woman described a demeaning encounter with a social service agency when in the course of a moment, she saw herself as being defined as someone not worth helping. She said, "All I can do is dissolve in tears—there is nothing I can do. I just get immobilized. . . ." (pp. 110–111)

This passage illustrates how a grounded theorist can write a memo, use it in a study, highlight her own reflexive thoughts in a way consistent with qualitative research, and use the memo to highlight categories of information (i.e., "negative identifying moments").

WHAT ARE THE STEPS IN CONDUCTING GROUNDED THEORY RESEARCH?

With the different types of grounded theory procedures—systematic, emerging, and constructivist—researchers might engage in alternative procedures to conduct a grounded theory study. The approach taken here will be the systematic form of inquiry because it consists of easily identifiable steps, is frequently used for grounded theory research, and provides a procedure that beginning researchers will find useful.

Step 1. Decide If a Grounded Theory Design Best Addresses the Research Problem

A grounded theory design is appropriate when you want to develop or modify a theory, explain a process, and develop a general abstraction of the interaction and action of people. As such, it offers a macropicture of educational situations rather than a detailed microanalysis. Because of the generation of an abstract process, it seems suitable for sensitive topics, such as the coping process of women who have been sexually abused (Morrow & Smith, 1995), or any research problem situation in which individuals need their privacy protected. Grounded theory also seems applicable for those individuals who are trained in *quantitative* research but who want to explore a *qualitative* procedure that is rigorous and systematic. For example, in educational fields in which *qualitative* research has made slow inroads, such as counseling and school psychology, inquirers are turning to grounded theory as a useful procedure. (See one of many examples, such as Frontman & Kunkel's [1994] grounded theory study about how counselors construe success with clients.)

Step 2. Identify a Process to Study

Because the intent of grounded theory research is to explain a process, you need to identify early a tentative process to examine in your grounded theory study. This process may change and emerge during your study, but you need to have an idea of the process at this step. This process should naturally follow from the research problem and questions that you seek to answer. It needs to involve people who are acting or interacting with identifiable steps or sequence in their interactions. It is helpful to write down this process early in your plan for a study, such as "What is the process of coping for first-year teachers?" or "What is the process by which faculty develop into productive researchers?"

Step 3. Seek Approval and Access

As with all research studies, you need to obtain approval from the institutional review board. You also need access to individuals who can provide insight into the process that you plan to study. Like other studies, this step involves seeking approval to collect data, appraising individuals of the purpose of your study, and guaranteeing protection of the site and participants as you conduct the inquiry.

If you plan to use the zigzag approach to data collection and analysis, it is difficult to plan and receive approval for collecting data. This approach relies on collecting data, analyzing it, and using this information to determine the next step in data collection. Thus, as you seek permission to conduct a grounded theory study, it is helpful to apprise reviewers of this process and the tentative nature of the data-collection procedures at the beginning of the study.

Step 4. Conduct Theoretical Sampling

The key concept in grounded theory data collection is to gather information that can assist in your development of a theory (e.g., individuals who have experienced the process you are studying). Grounded theorists use many forms of data (such as those mentioned in chapter 8), but many researchers rely on interviews to best capture the experiences of individuals in their own words. A characteristic of grounded theory research, however, is that the inquirer collects data more than once and keeps returning to data sources for more information throughout a study until the categories are saturated and the theory is fully developed. There is no precise timeline for this process, and researchers need to make the decision as to when they have fully developed their categories and the theory. One rule of thumb in graduate student research and interviewing is to collect at least 20 to 30 interviews during data collection (Creswell, 1998). This general guideline, of course, may change if you collect multiple sources of data, such as observations, documents, and your own personal memos.

Step 5. Code the Data

The process of coding data occurs during data collection so that you can determine what data to collect next. It typically begins with the identification of open coding categories and using the constant comparative approach for saturation by comparing data with incident and incident with category. A reasonable number of 10 categories may suffice, although this number depends on the extent of your database and the complexity of the process you are exploring. McCaslin (1993), for example, conducted a grounded theory study of the complex question of leadership in rural communities. In exploring "What is leadership?" he identified 50 categories from observing and interviewing individuals participating in educational leadership development programs in six counties.

From open coding, you proceed to axial coding and the development of a coding paradigm. This involves the process identified in Figure 14.3 of selecting a core category from the open coding possibilities and positioning it at the center of the axial coding process as a core category. From here you will likely return to data collection or reanalyze your data to identify causal conditions, intervening and contextual categories, strategies, and consequences to develop the axial coding process. You can assemble this information in the form of a coding paradigm or visual picture of the process in which you indicate with arrows the direction of the process.

Step 6. Use Selective Coding and Develop the Theory

The final process of coding is selective coding, and it involves actually developing your theory. This procedure includes interrelating the categories in the coding paradigm. It may involve refining the axial coding paradigm and presenting it as a model or theory of the process. It may include writing propositions that provide testable ideas for further research. You can present your theory as a series of propositions or subpropositions. This stage may also involve writing a story or a narrative that describes the interrelationships among categories.

Step 7. Validate Your Theory

It is important to determine if your theoretical explanation makes sense to participants and is an accurate rendering of events and their sequence in the process. In grounded theory research, validation is an active part of the process of research (Creswell, 1998). For example, during the constant comparative procedure of open coding, the researcher triangulates data between the information and the emerging categories. The same process of checking data against categories occurs in the axial coding phase. The researcher poses questions that relate the categories, and then returns to the data and looks for evidence, incidents, and events—a process in grounded theory called **discriminant sampling**. After developing a theory, the grounded theorist validates the process by comparing it with existing processes found in the literature. Also, outside reviewers, such as participants in the project who judge the grounded theory using "canons" of good science, may substantiate the theory, including the validity and credibility of the data (Strauss & Corbin, 1998).

Step 8. Write a Grounded Theory Research Report

The structure of your grounded theory report will vary from a flexible structure in the emerging and constructivist design to a more quantitatively oriented structure in the systematic design. Compared with other qualitative designs, such as ethnography and narrative research, the structures of grounded theory studies are scientific and include a problem, methods, discussion, and results. In addition, the point of view of the writer in the systematic approach is sometimes third person and objective in tone. All grounded theory projects, however, end with the theory generated by the researcher reporting his or her abstraction of the process under examination.

HOW DO YOU EVALUATE GROUNDED THEORY RESEARCH?

Criteria for evaluating a grounded theory study rely on an assessment of the theory (Glaser, 1978, 1992) as well as the overall procedure used in generating it (Strauss & Corbin, 1990, 1998).

When evaluating the quality of a grounded theory study, ask about the theory itself:

- Is there an obvious connection or fit between the categories and the raw data?
- Is the theory useful as a conceptual explanation for the process being studied? In other words, does it work?
- Does the theory provide a relevant explanation of actual problems and a basic process?
- Is the theory modified as conditions change or the researcher collects additional data?

Next, ask about the process of research:

- Is a theoretical model developed or generated? Is the intent of this model to conceptualize a process, an action, or an interaction?
- Is there a central phenomenon (or core category) specified at the heart of this model?
- Does the model emerge through phases of coding (e.g., from initial codes to more theoretically oriented codes, or from open coding to axial coding to selective coding)?
- Does the researcher attempt to interrelate the categories (e.g., propositions, discussion, a model or diagram)?
- Does the researcher gather extensive data to develop a detailed conceptual theory well saturated in the data?
- Does the study show that the researcher validated the evolving theory by comparing it to data, examining how the theory supports or refutes existing theories in the literature, or checking the theory with participants?

Applying What You Have Learned: A Grounded Theory Study

To apply the ideas in this chapter, first read the grounded theory study on page 456 by Feen-Calligan (1999), noting marginal annotations that identify the characteristics of grounded theory research and qualitative research. This study was chosen because it focuses on a process (becoming enlightened during the recovery). It also employs solid grounded theory procedures consistent with the approach of Strauss and Corbin (1998), and it "educates" the reader about grounded theory by keeping the reader posted about each step in the process as it is taken. The article further uses a table to illustrate clearly the initial categories, and a diagram to show the interrelationship of categories. The study ends with propositions or hypotheses that make the connections among the categories and the emerging theory explicit. The author did not explicitly mention memoing, but she may have incorporated this procedure into her research activities.

As you review this article, look for elements of the research process:

- The research problem and the use of qualitative research
- Use of the literature
- The purpose statement and research questions
- Types and procedures of grounded theory data collection
- Types and procedures of grounded theory data analysis and interpretation
- The overall writing structure

After you read the article and reflect on these elements, read the following analysis of the study.

The Research Problem and Use of Qualitative Research

The research problem—see Paragraphs 02–04

Use of qualitative research—see the marginal annotations on the left side of the page

After an introductory paragraph summarizing the major aspects of the study, Paragraph 02 introduces the problem addressed in this study: the public health issue in our society of chemical addiction. Among the treatment options, one approach is art therapy, and the author suggests that no theory exists to explain the role of art therapy in treating chemical addictions.

This article has many key markings of qualitative research:

- ◆ It explores the process of the role of art therapy to help a person become enlightened in response to chemical dependency (Paragraph 04).
- ◆ The literature is used to focus the study on treatment for chemical dependency (Paragraph 03).
- ◆ The author uses self-reflection by including one of her own studies (Paragraph 03).
- ◆ The purpose of the study is identified in the first sentence of the article (Paragraph 01).
- ◆ Data are collected from a few individuals ($N = 19$; Paragraphs 06, 08).
- ◆ A collection is presented of words or text obtained through interviews (Paragraphs 08–09) and images are used (pictures of the patients; e.g., Figure 6.2 in Paragraph 27).
- ◆ The researcher uses her own forms rather than using existing instruments (Paragraph 09).
- ◆ The researcher analyzes the text through coding (Paragraphs 11–20).
- ◆ The author interprets the findings within the larger, more abstract value of art therapy and self-reflection and self-awareness (Paragraph 56).
- ◆ A flexible writing structure is used to reflect topics addressed in a grounded theory study (e.g., Paragraph 11 on open coding).

Use of the Literature

See Paragraph 02

With a couple of minor exceptions, the entire literature in this study is cited at the beginning, where it is used to describe the importance of the problem (addiction and the need for treatment). Consistent with qualitative inquiry, the literature plays a minor role and does not influence the questions being addressed by the researcher.

The Purpose Statement and Research Questions

Purpose statement—see Paragraph 01

Central question—see Paragraph 05

Interview questions—see Paragraph 09

The author opens with a statement about the intent of the study: to explore the role of art therapy in individuals' recovery from chemical addiction. The researcher might have identified the process more explicitly. You do not know whether the process being examined is the recovery or the use of art in therapy.

The central question in this study helps to clear up some of this mystery. The author asks, "What is the theory that explains the process of art therapy in addiction treatment?"

Generating a theory that explains this process is further supported by the specific interview questions aimed at understanding the role of art therapy, its outcomes, and the facility's treatment philosophy.

Types of Procedures of Grounded Theory Data Collection

See Paragraphs 06–10

Qualitative data were collected from a small number of individuals (N = 19), but these were people intentionally sampled because they could provide information for the generation of the theory. They experienced art therapy in therapist–client situations. Inconsistent with the zigzag approach, the author did not seem to make multiple trips to the field to collect data except for the second contact with therapists to obtain recommendations about patients who might participate in the study. The data collection consisted of interviewing and collecting pictures of art rather than using additional sources of information (e.g., personal journals by therapists and patients).

Types of Procedures of Grounded Theory Data Analysis and Interpretation

Data analysis—see Paragraphs 11–20
Interpretation—see Paragraphs 56–57

The author reports that she engaged in three forms of coding the data: open coding to generate initial categories, axial coding to form connections among the categories, and selective coding to help her develop a story that connected the categories. Consistent with grounded theory procedures, she identified her core category (central phenomenon) after initial coding. Specifically, from among the six categories listed in Table 6.1, she selected "self-expression" and "self-awareness" as the main theme and, using the words of participants in the study, called this core category "enlightenment." She then "processed out" this category in terms of categories related to it and drew a diagram of this process (see Figure 6.1, axial coding). She explained each of the categories in this diagram and made the relationships explicit through six hypotheses or propositions. In addition, to help the reader understand this core category, she introduced it in the title of the study and included it in the introduction (Paragraph 01). Feen-Calligan's open coding table and axial coding diagram provide useful models for representing findings in a grounded theory study.

Interpretation of the findings comes in the final section of the study, in which Feen-Calligan relates her finding about enlightenment to the value of art therapy and the self-awareness and self-reflection that aid individuals in recovery.

The Overall Writing Structure

See the headings used in the study

By examining the headings, you can see that this article closely resembles a scientific study. It begins with the literature and the problem, then proceeds to data collection and findings. The systematic procedures of coding discussed here (open, axial, and selective) give a strong procedural flavor to the study and emphasize rigor. The use of a diagram and tables also underscore the more scientific approach to this report.

KEY IDEAS IN THE CHAPTER

A grounded theory design is a set of procedures used to generate systematically a theory that explains, at a broad conceptual level, a process about a substantive topic. You use grounded theory when you seek to generate a theory because one is not available or suitable. It is also useful to study a process, an action, or an interaction. It offers a step-by-step, systematic procedure for the beginning researcher. In using grounded theory, a researcher can stay close to the data at all times in the analysis. This design was developed by sociologists Barney Glaser and Anselm Strauss at the University of California San Francisco in the late 1960s.

Grounded theory research consists of three types of designs. The systematic procedure of Strauss and Corbin (1998) involves using predetermined categories to interrelate the categories, visual diagrams, and specific propositions or hypotheses to make the connections explicit. The emergent design, consistent with Glaser's (1992) ideas, relies on exploring a basic social process without preset categories. The constructivist approach of Charmaz (2000) focuses on subjective meanings by participants, explicit researcher values and beliefs, and suggestive or tentative conclusions.

Despite these differences, six aspects characterize grounded theory. Grounded theorists employ this design to explore a process around a substantive topic. They theoretically sample using a procedure of simultaneous data collection and analysis. Grounded theorists analyze their data for increasing levels of abstraction by using constant comparative procedures and asking questions about their data. During analysis of the data for categories, grounded theorists identify a core category (or central phenomenon) that will "process out" (Strauss, 1987) into a theory. Grounded theorists explore this process to develop a theory. Throughout the grounded theory procedure, grounded theorists write memos to themselves.

USEFUL INFORMATION FOR PRODUCERS OF RESEARCH

- When planning a grounded theory study, use the steps for conducting a study advanced in this chapter.
- Consider whether your grounded theory study will be systematic, emergent, or constructivist. Make this decision based on reviewing the arguments for each design type and determining whether you prefer a more flexible or prescribed approach to grounded theory research.
- The visuals presented in this chapter can be adapted and used to display several processes and to create tables and diagrams, such as the zigzag data collection process and the constant comparative approach.
- Creating a visual diagram of your theory helps to clearly identify the categories and see their interrelationships.
- Validate your theory by using constant comparative procedures, triangulating during the research, and by employing member checking with participants in your study.

USEFUL INFORMATION FOR CONSUMERS OF RESEARCH

- Educators can use the criteria for evaluating a study and the six characteristics of a grounded research study to assess the quality of a published study.
- When examining a study to determine if it is a grounded theory project, you might look at the title to determine if the words "grounded theory" are included. Also, most grounded theory projects clearly include an exploration of a process, and the authors should identify this process in the purpose statement or research questions.

- A sign of grounded theory research is that the author employs multiple passes to the field to collect data. A well-refined theory (and categories) consists of saturation and zigzagging back and forth between data collection and analysis to build the categories and theory.
- Look for a visual model of the theory. This model is the centerpiece of the grounded theory study and represents the author's attempt to visualize the process under study.

ADDITIONAL RESOURCES YOU MIGHT EXAMINE

Several major books are available to provide the procedures used in grounded theory research. Examine the books by Strauss:

Strauss, A. (1987). *Qualitative analysis for social scientists.* New York: Cambridge University Press.

Strauss, A., & Corbin, J. (1998). *Basics of qualitative research: Techniques and procedures for developing grounded theory* (2nd ed.). Thousand Oaks, CA: Sage.

Examine the books by Glaser:

Glaser, B. G. (1978). *Theoretical sensitivity.* Mill Valley, CA: Sociology Press.

Glaser, B. G. (1992). *Basics of grounded theory analysis.* Mill Valley, CA: Sociology Press.

You might also consult the original book they developed together:

Glaser, B., & Strauss, A. (1967). *The discovery of grounded theory.* Chicago: Aldine.

For a recent perspective on grounded theory from a constructivist perspective, examine the book chapter by Charmaz (2000) and her recent book, Charmaz (2006), and look at her journal articles for applications of her approach:

Charmaz, K. (1990). "Discovering" chronic illness: Using grounded theory. *Social Science Medicine, 30,* 1161–1172.

Charmaz, K. (1994). Identity dilemmas of chronically ill men. *The Sociological Quarterly, 35,* 269–288.

Charmaz, K. (2000). Grounded theory: Objectivist and constructivist methods. In N. K. Denzin & Y. S. Lincoln (Eds.), *Handbook of qualitative research* (2nd ed., pp. 509–535). Thousand Oaks, CA: Sage.

Charmaz, K. (2006). *Constructing grounded theory.* London: Sage.

Go to our Companion Website at **www.prenhall.com/creswell** to:

- assess your understanding of chapter content with Multiple-Choice Questions,
- apply what you've learned with Essay Questions,
- practice your research skills with interactive Building Research Skills exercises, and
- broaden your knowledge of research with Web Links to research topics on the Internet.

Qualitative Characteristics

Enlightenment in Chemical Dependency Treatment Programs: A Grounded Theory

Grounded Theory Research Characteristics

Holly Feen-Calligan

The qualitative purpose statement and research questions are broad and general.

Introduction

Grounded theorists generated a theory.

(01) This chapter describes a study which explores the role of art therapy in recovery from chemical addiction. This study is "grounded" in the interview data of eleven art therapists, four psychiatrists, and five individuals in recovery. The grounded theory method used to analyze the data involves identifying a "central phenomenon" in the data. In this study, "enlightenment" emerged as the central phenomenon. It is hoped that the results will inform practice through contributing to the development of the theoretical basis of art therapy in recovery from addiction.

Grounded theorists study a process related to a substantive topic.

Grounded theorists select a core category of the central phenomenon.

Chemical Addiction

(02) Considered to be the largest and most serious public health problem facing our society, the cost of chemical addiction in health care, unemployment, poverty, and violence is immense (Chopra, 1997; Steele, 1997). Various approaches to treating chemical addiction, including Alcoholics Anonymous (AA), outpatient psychotherapy, and inpatient rehabilitation programs, have at best experienced mixed success (Miller, 1995). Employees of hospital-based rehabilitation programs are well aware of the high relapse rates among their patients. Among those who remain substance free, many fail to achieve recovery in the full sense of the word, leading dissatisfied or unfulfilled lives. Adding to the treatment dilemma are statistics showing an increasingly diverse patient population with more complicated medical problems (Craddock *et al.,* 1997) and reductions in health care funding available to treat the problem (Van Leit, 1995). Given this situation, alternative treatments need to be explored.

The qualitative literature justifies the research problem.

(03) One such alternative or complementary treatment is art therapy. The use of art in chemical dependency treatment programs has been documented since the 1950s (Ulman, 1953) and the benefits of art therapy have been addressed in the literature (Albert-Puleo & Osha, 1976–77; Allen, 1985; Devine, 1970; Foulke & Keller, 1976; Moore, 1983). Generally, art therapy is believed to help circumvent verbal defensiveness, often thought to be typical of addicts. Art therapy contributes to addicts' ability to get in touch with feelings numbed by chemicals and contributes to increased personal awareness of motivation for chemical use. Such personal awareness can be empowering and help to provide the self-confidence and strength necessary to pursue a life of sobriety "one day at a time." The process of mastering art processes and interpretation of art works parallels mastery of painful feelings. There is a reflective or even spiritual experience inherent to the creative process (Burke, 1985; Chickerneo, 1990) that seems to help individuals to trust spiritual concepts espoused in recovery programs such as "Let go and let God" (Feen-Calligan, 1995).

Qualitative researchers take a reflexive and biased approach.

A qualitative problem requires exploration and understanding.

(04) Because many benefits of art therapy were observed when patients were admitted for longer periods of stay than is typical in treatment programs today, it is less clear just how art therapy has been adapted for shortened hospital stays. No *theory* currently exists about the role of art therapy in chemical addiction treatment programs. In order to determine practical uses of art therapy in treatment programs given today's health care realities, it is important to develop a theory of how art therapy can be used with this population.

The qualitative purpose statement and research questions seek participants' experiences.

(05) The "grounded theory" tradition was selected as the method of data collection and analysis because of its potential to contribute to the development of theory. Grounded theory is a qualitative research method developed in the 1960s by two sociologists, Barney Glaser and Anselm Strauss (1967), that uses a systematic set of procedures to understand processes and interactions in order to develop theory about a particular phenomenon. The aim of this study is to generate theory about art therapy in recovery from addiction, 'grounded in,' or based upon the interviews of art therapists, psychiatrists, and individuals in recovery. The study sought to answer the following question: What is the theory that explains the process of art therapy in addiction treatment?

Data Collection and Analysis

Grounded theorists theoretically sample to best develop the theory.

Qualitative data collection involves studying a small number of individuals or sites.

(06) In the first phase of the study, eleven art therapists and four psychiatrists were interviewed about the process of using art with chemical dependency patients. A theoretical sampling procedure was used in which respondents were selected for what they could contribute to the evolving theory (Strauss & Corbin, 1990). The art therapists were selected from a list of members of the Art Therapy/Addiction Counselor (AT/AC) Network, a peer-support group formed by members of the American Art Therapy Association. Among the art therapists, nine worked with adults, two with adolescents. Four art therapists worked in outpatient settings, in programs of one month to one year duration. Four worked in hospitals in psychiatric inpatient, outpatient and day treatment programs, in programs ranging from three days to three weeks. Others practiced in settings including a residential substance abuse program for women and children, a domestic violence program, and a residential adolescent substance abuse program, with a range in length of stay from three to six months. One art therapist was a supervisor of a county-wide substance abuse program. All art therapists lived and worked in the United States, in Michigan, Ohio, Illinois, Kentucky, Massachusetts, South Carolina, and California.

(07) Psychiatrists were selected because of their work in addiction psychiatry, and all were associated with major medical centers and had outpatient practices. Consistent with grounded theory procedures (Conrad, 1978), psychiatrists were interviewed as a comparison group to help evaluate the conditions under which the art therapy model would hold. Although the focus of this research is upon adult medical settings, interviewing professionals in related settings helps the researcher "to be theoretically sensitive to the range of conditions that might bear upon the phenomenon under study" (Strauss & Corbin, 1990, p. 161). Furthermore, a formal theory must emerge from studying phenomena examined under many different types of situations.

Qualitative data collection involves gathering text or image data.

(08) In order to understand more about an individuals' first-hand experience with art therapy, the views of recovering individuals were solicited. The art therapists interviewed in the first phase were contacted a second time for recommendations of patients who might complete a questionnaire or consent to be interviewed. In the second phase of the study, four questionnaires were completed by individuals who, at the time, were patients in treatment programs. One individual in longer-term recovery was also interviewed. This individual had participated in an inpatient treatment program at the beginning of his recovery several years earlier, and had remained active in art. Although only one individual in longer-term recovery was interviewed, this person's experiences assist with relating conditions, actions/interactions, and consequences to the phenomenon being studied (Strauss & Corbin, 1990).

(09) Interviews were conducted both face-to-face, and over the phone when necessary. All interviews were audio taped and transcribed, verbatim.

Qualitative data collection is based on using protocols developed during the study.

Interviews ranged from 30 to 90 minutes in length. Interviews of psychiatrists and art therapists were open-ended and began by asking respondents to describe their work with patients, their view of the role of art therapy in the patient's recovery, how progress or successful outcome is assessed, and the facility's philosophy of treatment. Other questions covered descriptive information about their practices and any other information thought to be relevant. Individuals in recovery were asked to describe their experiences with art therapy or making art and the relationship between art making and recovery. They were asked whether a particular work of art created had special meaning for them, and what therapists should understand about someone in recovery.

(10) The transcribed interviews were mailed to the respondents for verification purposes, requesting clarification or additions when necessary. Additional verification was provided through triangulation. That is, the responses from the psychiatrists verified those of the art therapists with regard to the causal conditions of chemical addiction and strategies to address the problems. Rich description allows readers to make decisions about the transferability of the findings.

Open Coding

Qualitative data analysis consists of text analysis.

Grounded theorists use constant comparative analysis procedures for coding.

(11) The procedures for data analysis in grounded theory involve three types of coding procedures: open coding, axial coding, and selective coding. Open coding consists of naming and categorizing data. As interview transcriptions are reviewed, concepts or themes with similar properties are grouped together. The categories are arranged and rearranged until 'saturated;' that is, until I was satisfied that the concepts were similar and should be grouped together. Six major categories emerged in the open coding process. These categories were named using 'in vivo codes,' terms drawn directly from the data. The in vivo codes (six major categories) were named: (1) spectrum disease, (2) underlying turbulence, (3) type of treatment program, (4) art as healing, (5) waves of treatment, and (6) health care changes. In open coding, not only are categories grouped together, but properties of the categories are also examined as well as dimensions or ranges of the properties. Considering the properties of categories helps the researcher to know that the categories are properly grouped together, or are saturated.

Qualitative data analysis consists of describing information and developing themes.

(12) The first category, "spectrum disease," refers to the spectrum of problems an addicted person often has. There is a spectrum of severity and chronicity of problems experienced, and a range in ages of patients. Chemical addiction is a spectrum illness because it falls along a continuum of related disorders associated with it. Medical doctors often have great difficulty diagnosing the primary disorder, as substance abuse often is intertwined with a psychiatric disorder. Older chemically addicted patients also often have medical problems. Furthermore, there is a spectrum of treatment philosophies, ranging from addiction models (disease concept) to psychiatric models of treatment. Thus, one property of the spectrum disease is the diagnosis. The dimensions of diagnoses range from substance abuse as a primary disorder to a dual diagnosis coexisting with a psychiatric diagnosis. Table 1 lists the six categories, as well as their properties and dimensions.

(13) The second category, "underlying turbulence," reflects the addicts' motivation for use. Usually the motivation for use had to do with control. Controlling moods and feelings was commonplace, either to feel more high, or more low (in the case of bipolar, dually diagnosed individuals), or to numb out or fill an inner emptiness. Often there was a trauma, loss, or stressor that precipitated use. This was true of individuals coming from families with or without histories of chemical dependence.

(14)

TABLE 1
Open Coding of Art Therapy in Chemical Dependency Treatment Programs

Category	Properties	Dimensionalized examples	
Spectrum disease	Diagnosis	Primary substance abuse	Dual diagnosis
	Problem manifested	Biological/medical problems	Psycho-social problems
	Treatment philosophy	Addiction model (disease concept)	Psychiatry model
	Age of patient	Adolescent	Older adult
Underlying turbulence	Control feelings	Feel less depressed	Feel less anxious
	Painkiller	Numb painful feelings	Fill inner emptiness
	Reason for use	Psychic pain	Physical pain
		Genetic predisposition	Coping or learned behavior
Treatment program	Type of facility	Inpatient	Outpatient
	Treatment Type	Free Standing	General hospital
		Pharmacology	Psychotherapy
		Behavioral	Uncovering
		Group therapy	Individual
Art as healing	Benefits	Self-expression	Self-awareness
	Stages in art process	Resistant	Reflective
	Approaches	Structured/didactic	Unstructured/open studio
	Themes	Absence of self	Self-portraits
	Media	Pencils	Paint
	Art products	Colorless	Colorful
Waves of treatment	Process	Assessment	Ongoing evaluation
	Evidence of progress	Rough sea	Calm sea
		Patient statements	Patient behaviors
Health care changes	Shortened time in hospital	Days	Months
	Service	Less specialized	Generalized
	Job changes	Fewer staff	Increased responsibilities

(15) "Treatment programs" consisted of type of facility with which the respondents were affiliated—free standing or hospital based; inpatient or outpatient. This category includes type of treatment, other than art therapy, prescribed by the treatment program. Pharmacology, drug education, group or individual therapy, and activity therapy are types of treatment mentioned in the data. The treatment program category also includes the approach to treatment, encompassing behavioral through uncovering/analytic approaches.

(16) The category, "art as healing," represents the "benefits of art therapy," for example, art is beneficial to encouraging expression of feelings and increased self-awareness. Respondents were aware of stages experienced by the individual making art. Resistance to making art was common at first; however, as art was created, individuals became willing participants and reflective about their art. The healing in art often becomes evident in color use—from less to more color used, and from lack of human figures to inclusion of the self. Different approaches to art therapy were used with dimensions ranking between assigning art tasks through using open studio approaches. Art tasks mentioned by the respondents are listed in Table 2.

(17) The metaphor, "waves," was used by a psychiatrist to represent treatment progress, despite some temporary regression. In the course of treatment the waves become increasingly rough before they became calm again. Both professionals and individuals in recovery identified certain 'waves' in the treatment process, the violent rush of feelings followed by calm, experienced with a certain rhythm or expected regularity as treatment progressed.

(18) The last category, "health care changes," emphasized the increasingly shorter treatment periods and more generalized services offered by treatment programs.

Axial Coding

(19) Once major themes are identified, a second level coding procedure called axial coding was conducted. Axial coding puts the data back together in new ways by making connections between categories. Axial coding involves identifying a single category as the central phenomenon and exploring its relationship to the other categories. The central phenomenon is identified as well as the conditions that give rise to it, the context in which it is embedded, the action or interactional strategies by which it is handled, and the consequences of those strategies. In axial coding a paradigm model is created which visually portrays the relationship among the categories (Strauss & Corbin, 1990). Figure 1 represents the axial coding paradigm model.

Selective Coding

(20) The third set of coding procedures is selective coding, where the theory is developed. In selective coding, researchers build a story that connects the categories. A discursive set of propositions is generated and validated against the story (Strauss & Corbin, 1990).

The Experience of Enlightenment in Art Therapy

(21) The following sections describe the experience of enlightenment through the narratives of art therapists, psychiatrists, and people in recovery from addictions. Enlightenment is defined as self-awareness or insight, self-expression and a natural high. Being enlightened is critical to recovery from addiction.

(22) **FIGURE 1**
Axial Coding: Paradigm Model of Art Therapy in Chemical Addictions Treatment Programs

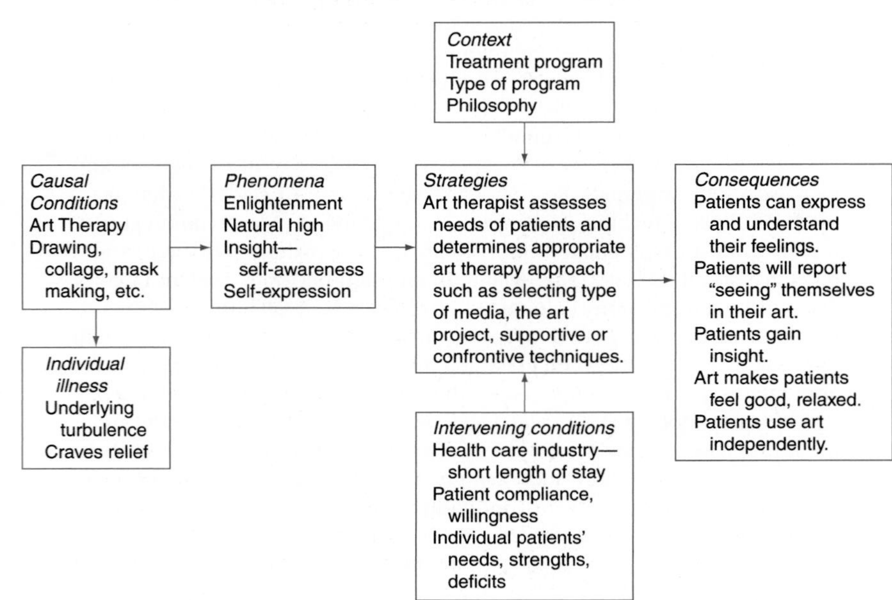

(23) The individuals about whom this chapter is written have chosen the path of recovery. They crave relief from the insanity of addiction. Initially, in treatment programs, art therapy provides relief. According to one recovering individual, "I find myself doodling and looking at [the doodles], it relieves pressure and is relaxing." An art therapist agrees, "Patients just want to do art so they don't have to think about all this other stuff . . . " Art provides a quiet refuge away from the chaos of life (Brezine, cited in Bailey, 1993). The hypnotic sketching sound of the pencil, back and forth, takes one away temporarily, and is comforting and soothing. "Artwork provides the environment of calmness that acts as a hearing aid for the heart" (Bailey, 1993, p. 39). A person who has been alienated from the true self may experience a new sense of being, in the quiet. According to one recovering person, "In a very simple and viable fashion the art therapy revealed the anxiety, frustration, pain, and hopelessness associated with my dependency in a gentle and fun process."

(24) Not only can an art group be quiet and relaxing, but it can be playful and fun. "I looked forward to art therapy because it gave me the opportunity to be a kid again . . . it allowed me to have fun during this earth shaking life change . . . " says one recovering individual. Everyone has a need for elation . . . for the cessation of pain . . . and to have an ecstatic dimension to our lives (Jung, cited in Segaller, 1989). Chickerneo (1990) connected the playful quality of art as facilitator of spirituality in recovering alcoholics. The sense of contented bliss in art and play mimics what is sought through drink. "The craving for alcohol was the equivalent on a low level of the spiritual thirst of our being for wholeness" (Jung, cited in Bauer, 1982). The playful handling of art materials, the energy mobilized in the process, and the contemplative nature of art at once soothes, relaxes, energizes, and lifts one up to a "natural high." Someone experiencing a natural high feels "en-lightened," or relieved, as if a load had been taken off one's shoulders.

(25) The enjoyment experienced through doing and working together with others in a room is reminiscent of a sewing circle or quilting bee. There is a feeling of belonging, of camaraderie, of pleasure, of fellowship. Says one recovering person, "It showed how well we can work with one another and how people see things different[ly] from others." The First Tradition of Alcoholics Anonymous states that most individuals cannot recover unless there is a group, and recovering individuals find that they cannot keep the gift of sobriety unless they give it away (Alcoholics Anonymous, 1988). A psychiatrist believes:

(26)
> If you provide a setting where the patient feels comfortable to begin their treatment, and start talking about their disorder, I think you've done 80 percent of the work. . . . If the patient feels comfortable, if they feel less need to use resistance . . . because you're sort of getting [therapy] to them in a way that they're not aware that . . . through art they're starting to talk about their issues . . . it's a unique process of its own.

(27) The benefits of play, quiet reflection and working together are directly experienced as individuals dabble with art media. Through direct experience, we learn, we gain insight, we become "enlightened." A psychiatrist explains, ". . . you can't learn how to swim by *talking* about swimming. The only way you learn how to swim is by walking into that pool with a swimming instructor, and beginning to swim." Considering the individuals who relapse because they didn't *do* their aftercare plans makes *doing* seem ever so important. As Harms (1973) suggests, many addicts experience a lack of impulse for any activity. Therefore, to do *any* activity reduces the tendency toward lethargy and repeating old habits.

(28) Self-expression is enlightening. One psychiatrist thought "patients have major needs to be able to express their view of their problems . . . many of

FIGURE 2

"This is my favorite because it is basically me. You go into a party and you want to be cool or want to look big or you want to be special and the only way you can do it is to do what the crowd says. It was me a couple of years ago."

them have limitations in their ability to identify problems." Self-expression implies the ability to find a voice for the feelings and words to represent the problems. Words are important because:

> . . . whatever words [people] use are where their feelings lie. Not *my* words—just like notes on a page come from the composer, so those notes are important to the composer. If I were using my notes, they wouldn't help. . . . (psychiatrist)

(29) Articulation of problems and feelings reduces their mystery and sense of being overwhelmed by them (Foulke & Keller, 1976). Traumatic events can be mastered in the art work because the patient is now taking an active role. The process of expressing feelings on paper can be encouraged in a way that patients achieve some mastery over their feelings. According to one recovering individual, "My recovery felt much more real and attainable as I pondered the picture I had created of what I thought my road to recovery would look like."

(30) One of the ways art therapy helps foster self-expression is its tendency to reveal the unexpected, and to connect with the emotional self the cognitive self may be blocking. An individual in recovery recalls, "We had to

draw ourselves on a rainy day. I drew just me—nothing or no one else around me and the raindrops were only around me. It made me aware of my self-centeredness." An art therapist had this to say:

> I had a woman in my office . . . and we went through an early recollection, and harvested the meaning out of it . . . we had not done the art work. She then took out a picture . . . she drew of the early recollection and it changed the meaning entirely. She started to cry when she was talking about it. She looked at the picture and said, "Oh, my gosh." The meaning had been about needing help from others, and she looked at the picture and . . . because her friend's arms were around her in this early recollection from childhood, and she was sturdy and strong and tall just like the friend, but the arms around her, she realized it was about intimacy—that it was important to her not so much because she needed the friend's help but because the friend was close and touching her. It was pretty powerful . . . we had come up with a script from the early recollection, and we changed the script, because of the art work.

(31) The potential of art to reveal the unexplained and the unexpected, to bring to conscious awareness inner desires and feelings means uncovering what addicts wanted to cover up by use of substances. Yet, there must be some uncovering to allow healing from within. Because,

> . . . just as with a burn wound, when you have a scab at the top, everything looks just fine, as if it were healing. We all know that unless you peel off those scabs and uncover the wound it can't heal from underneath, and won't. (psychiatrist)

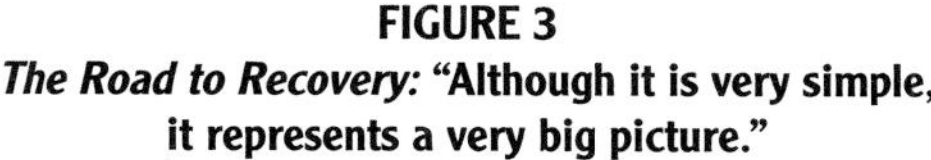

FIGURE 3
***The Road to Recovery:* "Although it is very simple, it represents a very big picture."**

(32) Recovering individuals may experience this sort of powerlessness over the symbolism that arises in their art work, yet ironically, they are empowered by the symbolism as well. Individuals learn to recognize their personal symbols, styles, and colors and learn what significance they have. Self-awareness is improved as the uniqueness of the individual is revealed, and patients become aware of personal strengths. "These classes brought a lot out of talent out of me I didn't even know I had," says one recovering individual. "It showed me the direction I need to stay focused on, the direction I need to go in."

(33) The "image" as concrete and permanent is important to this process. "Words come cheap in some ways, and I think the symbols, the art work gives it greater meaning and a little more impact," according to one art therapist. For example:

> One client . . . in therapy for three weeks . . . she is very focused and very involved in AA. She's got a sponsor. She says, "I'm going to do this right, no matter what." And I said to her, "you know, you've never put yourself in any of your drawings—Where are you in this recovery?" "I'm a spectator," is what she said. (art therapist)

(34) The art work can and does serve as concrete evidence of the individual's progress toward goals. Many programs used Step Books or workbooks wherein patients demonstrate through writing or drawing how they have made progress toward the Twelve Steps of AA.

> . . . [Clients] had to set five measurable goals . . . to accomplish within . . . two weeks, and then they came back to their counselor. So maybe someone would set a goal for their first step they would do an "inner-outer" [self] poster, for their second step they would do [a] "sanity-insanity" [drawing], so maybe they would take that back and show their counselor, and talk about what they learned from that. (art therapist)

Art Interventions

(35) In the beginning of treatment, the combination of biological, psychological, and social factors in the etiology and symptomology of the disease call for a thorough assessment on the part of the treatment program, necessary to understand all the factors in the individual's illness. "A part of any illness is pathology which is destructive behavior, and treatment involves altered behavior" (a psychiatrist). Recovery presumes abstinence, but recovery in the full sense of the word involves "understanding the stress that's resulted in the culmination of the addiction wherein there may have been predisposition, but without the stress may not have necessarily occurred" (a psychiatrist). Recovery involves understanding the alienation and emptiness that lead to use of substances in the first place.

(36) Certain interventions are used by art therapists, depending upon the needs of the patient, the philosophy of the treatment facility, the length of time someone might be in treatment, and other intervening conditions. Many art therapists design art experiences based on the theme or lecture presented in the treatment program. The art therapist may assign an art project responsive to patients' needs, and in conjunction with the treatment milieu. The art therapy approach often requires balancing addiction and psychiatric considerations simultaneously (Miller, 1995). A therapist might balance a disease concept focus (e.g., "Just for today . . . I will not drink/use") with a more insight-oriented understanding of the self and feelings. Therapists may facilitate enlightenment in terms of "a power greater than ourselves" or facilitate enlightenment through insight and personal awareness.

(37) Often, patients who first enter treatment are resistant to treatment and in denial. In these cases a therapist may use humor and play to encourage comfort with art making and engagement in therapy.

> I draw this little stick figure, and I show them and ask, "Can you draw better than that?" They say, "No." And I say "good, because otherwise I'd feel kind of intimidated if you did." And then they laugh, and it's kind of an ice breaker, and then we go from there. And I say, "The only thing I ask is that you put a little meat on that figure, because I'm not really into a lot of thin people, you know being full figured," and they kind of laugh, and so nine times out of ten, I get some wonderful things. (art therapist)

(38) The use of humor tends to deflect negative thinking that may prevent someone from participating in art. A therapist may assure patients "it is

best not to be an artist to do art therapy," to help individuals become comfortable with their art expression.

> I say stuff like, "everybody has a visual language. You had a visual language when you were little that was primary before you had a verbal language. When you dream you dream in your visual language . . . I'd like you just to trust yourself. If your little perfectionist pops up . . . put him out in the hallway so that you can be allowed to honor this part of yourself. I'd like you to just back off and give yourself, and whatever comes to your mind, I'd like you not to judge it . . . I'd like you to just draw with your non-dominant hand" . . . And then I say, "I'd like you to just try this once . . . and don't decide what it means, don't even think about what it means. We'll get into that after you do it. We'll talk about it, and if you just give it an opportunity and see . . . what comes out of it, you might find that it's useful for you." (art therapist)

(39) Some individuals have such low self-concept, they are afraid to succeed (an art therapist). They may say, "I can't draw, I can't do that." It is important that art therapists remember not everyone is quick or willing to try to put their thoughts and feelings in the form of art (a recovering individual).. . . According to one recovering person, "I think it's the word art that scares us. Remember we don't believe we can do anything right."

(40) As treatment progresses, some patients experience a period of darkness and pain. There is a confusing mix of emotions. Patients at once feel warmth, pain, closeness, and distance. There are waves of progress and regression, more progress, less regression.

> . . . the longer we go, the deeper and darker the [art] gets. And when they start really touching into those places that have been hidden and anesthetized for so long . . . all the things that are coming out. . . . It's almost like something's been festering. (art therapist)

(41) When there is obvious pain, therapists may use empathy, acceptance, validation, listening, and supporting. They may use metaphor to distance the pain. More fluid media such as oil pastels and paints foster freedom of expression, and to help individuals come to terms with painful areas in their lives. Verbal description of the art process and images depends upon what is sensed about the patient's needs and readiness to talk. Therapists may ask individuals to speak about some aspect of the art process they are comfortable to speak about. They may interpret certain issues as expressed in the art product; however, they may choose to wait to discuss them until the individual is able to face certain realities in their lives without being so overwhelmed they return to drinking and drugging. Artistic expression itself is one step toward objectifying subjective concerns, toward facing realities.

(42) A therapist may encourage continuing with art after discharge. Writing a journal may be used for increased self-exploration and to assist individuals in recognizing and drawing out triggers to relapse. Table 2 lists art tasks, or strategies mentioned by the respondents.

Intervening Conditions

(43) Intervening conditions are structural conditions that facilitate or constrain interventions offered (Strauss & Corbin, 1990). Certain intervening conditions facilitate art therapy—psychiatrists who believe in it, and recovering individuals willing to give it a try. Yet, conditions existing within the broader health care industry are considered constraints. According to one psychiatrist, in recent years inpatient treatment has dramatically changed. There is less time to work with someone, and the focus is primarily detoxification and getting patients into a less intense level of care.

> In outpatient oriented treatment programs a lot of the things we used to do . . . are not being done or they're being done in a very superficial, limited kind of way. In

(44)

TABLE 2
Art Tasks Mentioned by the Respondents
(Causal Conditions/Strategies)

Whole body outline drawn actual size, filled in with the effects of substances on the body
Round robin pass around drawings to create stress, and how the stress is dealt with
Draw what happens after you use substances
Group murals
Draw your addiction and what would it say?
Draw your feelings
Draw: Who I am/Who I was/Who I hope to be
Writing songs about addiction
Progressive relaxation/guided imagery
Find and illustrate a "power" symbol
Make a spirtual symbol: "What gives you faith?"
Inner and outer consequences of substance abuse
Mandalas
Family portraits
Draw your drinking history and where this leads
What does depression look like?
The Amusement Park Technique (Hrenko & Willis, 1996)
Draw: Who are you blaming?
Draw triggers to substance use
Likes and dislikes
Create a door of opportunity and a door of challenge
Bridge drawing (Hays & Lyons, 1981)
Draw yourself using/yourself sober
Create a group tree and leaves representing things you are thankful for and things you have lost
Masks
Media
Pastels, Collage, Colored pencils, Markers, Music, Creative writing, Paint, Charcoal, Crayons, Colored paper, Sandtray

> lots of instances they're just down to sort of a consultation, an analysis of what somebody needs and trying to arrange to get that done on an outpatient basis . . . . They're bumping everything down to the lowest level of cost . . . in a model that is very analogous to what the auto industry has gone through. If a robot can do it then you don't have to be doing it. If a human is necessary, but if you can train someone at five dollars an hour to do it versus somebody at nine dollars an hour to do it, then you're going to have the five dollars an hour person do it. I think that's the kind of shrinkage we're seeing in the entire system. (psychiatrist)

(45) An art therapist notes her job title change from art therapist to mental health worker/rehab coordinator, along with a change in job description—less art therapy and more of other kinds of case management services:

> We've been bought out by a company . . . they own a hundred or so hospitals across the nation. They have this model hospital . . . and they're trying to base their other hospitals on this model. It's . . . a way to save money . . . by lowering

> staff. About nineteen people got laid off in September, and the nursing-to patient ratio also decreased. I think it used to be 3 or 4 patients to one staff, now it's 5 to 1 . . . I think everyone across the board is feeling the stress of it. I guess we're supporting one another within our units . . . even though people get floated from unit to unit at times. We all talk about it and use humor a lot to get through it.

(46) Other art therapists describe programs designed to be three weeks, that are now one week in duration. Patients who thought they were to be admitted for a certain length of time were informed that day they were to be discharged, because the insurance wouldn't approve more time. One art therapist noticed that instead of one three-week stay, she might see someone for three one-week stays over the course of a year, losing a day of progress in each transition. Therapists who were accustomed to prescribing painting or other longer term projects found the length of time a patient stayed in the hospital did not allow for such involved projects. A therapist may have to balance creating art work, which involves time, against the time a patient is likely to be on the unit. This decrease in treatment time seemed to represent the greatest concern for art therapists.

(47) The issues and difficulties encountered by those attempting to treat clients or plan treatment strategies is complicated by the changing nature of drug treatment client populations. Clinicians in treatment programs have always struggled with patients not ready for recovery, who are in denial, have not "hit bottom," nor admitted powerlessness. Even patients who seem sincere in desiring recovery often relapse. Treatment programs today admit patients with multiple problems in addition to substance abuse that need to be addressed concurrently. "It is hard to deal with them in a chemical dependency model, when there were patients much more fragile" (an art therapist).

> Our age range will go from 19–86. When you get to that high end you get a lot of alcoholic dementia, and associated nutrition problems and neurological problems. . . . And then within the group, with the dual disorders, it could be alcohol, heroin or crack, or depression or schizophrenia. (art therapist)

Consequences

In spite of these conditions, many reported positive outcomes of art therapy.
(48) One art therapist believes:

> art therapy *can* be used well in conjunction with "brief therapy" or at least shorter-term therapy because of the ability to cut through the initial, more superficial stages of the therapeutic process, and move to the deeper content and emotional impact of particular issues at a quicker pace. Also, art therapy assignments can be given over the evenings/weekends between therapy sessions that can build on what has already been processed in group. Art therapy lends itself to self-empowerment and awareness, and as a client begins to pick up on his/her own symbols, color use, style, etc., it becomes more self-motivating, which may ultimately impact long-term outcome measures. Journaling, dream work, etc. are very good on-going techniques.

(49) When patients are progressively moving toward healthy awareness, there is increased insight: Something 'clicks.' Individuals begin sorting things out and taking responsibility for their recovery. '[In drawing] my personal solar system I realized where I stood with my family and where things in my life were' (a recovering individual). '[I drew a] bridge, a strong one, high above the water, with strong supports, guardrails, reaching the midpoint and now facing the reality that I am addicted. It's becoming easier' (an individual in recovery).

One art therapist noticed a transition in the colors used:

> (50) They would start moving away from the darker colors, the reds and the blacks. They would start to invest more in the art . . . and you would just see they would start using the projects to understand themselves, or they would use their journals . . . But the other thing . . . the symbol of the sun or a bright image in the

FIGURE 4
***Mike's Galaxy:* "With this I realized where I stood in my family and where things in my life were."**

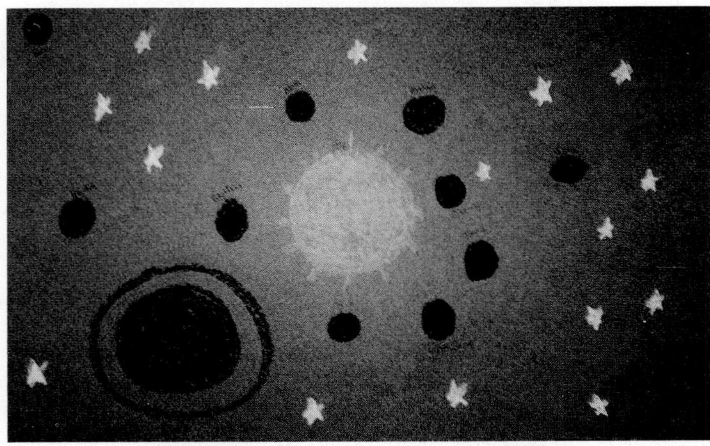

> center of something, usually in the beginning of treatment . . .: would be enveloped with darkness . . . the patients would show their addiction of something like the light being blocked, like there'd be a dark black circle around. At the end of the treatment there would be this opening.

(51) The individual in long term recovery interviewed paints all canvases in black first, then adds color on top:

> I never really know how to put really light colors together and match them really well. That's mainly why I always start with deep dark colors, and I put the light in as I go along. I got confused, I didn't know how to do it so I just painted all black and where these lines are, colors . . . . Everyone has a light and a dark side but they never admit the personalities they have.

(52) "The light bulb that clicks on," or "the light at the end of the tunnel," are common metaphors for enlightenment, for awareness or relief. In professional literature, Johnson (1990) discusses the transformation from darkness to light she found in adolescent and adult substance abuse patients' poetry and art work. She compares her findings with Whitfield's simplification of the Twelve Steps: 'struggle, confusion, surrender, seeing the light' (Whitfield, cited in Johnson, 1990, p. 301).

Propositions

(53) Co-founder of Alcoholics Anonymous W. B. Bill (1987) describes his experiences with recovery:

> Suddenly the room lit up with a great white light. It seemed to me, in the mind's eye, that I was on a mountain and that a wind not of air but of spirit was blowing. And then it burst upon me that I was a free man. Slowly the ecstasy subsided. I lay on the bed, but now for a time I was in another world, a new world of consciousness. All about me and through me there was a wonderful feeling of Presence, and I thought to myself, "So this is the God of the preachers!" (p. 2)

(54) Drawing from the story of enlightenment, the following propositions are offered.

1. The art experiences of recovering individuals in treatment programs contribute to a sense of enlightenment.
2. Individuals may experience one or more forms of enlightenment. Sometimes forms of enlightenment are experienced in succession, and

FIGURE 5

"This is my recovery picture. The guy at the bottom is stuck inside the crack pipe, which is his addiction. He wants to get out, but he doesn't know how. He is chained to drugs. On top is my recovery machine. You go into it addicted on whatever chemical you choose to use and then you come out punching your addiction. At the bottom I have a foot stomping alcoholism and drug addiction with an addict looking on who wants recovery."

sometimes simultaneously. Individuals may experience a natural high, a soothing, or playful sense of relief or a spiritual attunement. Self-expression is enlightening through sharing oneself and dividing problems. Last, self-awareness or insight is achieved through direct experiences with art.

3. Different interventions can be used by the therapist to encourage enlightenment, depending on the needs of patients, and the intervening conditions present. A therapist may foster enlightenment through recognizing the needs of the individual patients and responding to their needs through organizing the environment, the art materials, and the art directives and approach. Humor, education, and empathy are strategies employed. A therapist may match media with expressive needs—structured media may be used when individuals need support and containment. Fluid media may be used when individuals require assistance with uncovering and self-expression.

4. Certain conditions exist which impinge upon the success of an art therapy program: the decrease in the length or time, patients who are more ill, and patients who do not want to participate constrain the potential for enlightenment.

5. Art therapy works in conjunction with the two major philosophical approaches to chemical addiction—the disease concept and psychiatric models of treatment. Different forms of enlightenment promoted by art therapy parallel the two philosophies of treatment: The natural high/spiritual sense of enlightenment is akin to realizing a higher power that can restore sanity (Step 2)(AA, 1988). Enlightenment experienced through insight or personal awareness augments the psychiatric model of treatment.

6. Art therapy offers benefits to short-term care: art assignments given over weekends or in the evenings help bring consistency to the treatment, and bridges the treatment program and the home environment. One reason why art therapy works might be because it introduces how to work

independently through journaling and doing art work on one's own. It requires doing, and changing behavior.

Conclusion

(55) "Individuals who are relatively happy and who can live their lives without the use of drugs and alcohol," according to one psychiatrist, "are the desired outcome of chemical addiction treatment." However, as another psychiatrist noted, statistics show "a whole lot of people don't get better from getting an episode of treatment . . . [or] from multiple episodes of treatment, and part of that may not be the treatment, it may be the way that particular treatment is applied or utilized is less effective with that person. . . ." Finding the most effective treatment for each person is a challenge. Art therapy deserves consideration for its potential to contribute to the treatment, the relative happiness of each individual living life without drugs and alcohol. The benefits of art therapy in chemical dependency treatment are many, yet art therapy, like health care in general, feels the constraints of cost containment. This study offers little in the way of solutions, yet, hopefully greater awareness of the issues can lead to problem solving.

Qualitative interpretations situate findings within larger meanings.

(56) This study supports the value of art therapy in addiction recovery. The major finding concerns the phenomenon of enlightenment experienced in art therapy. Enlightenment in art therapy helps individuals to understand important concepts in recovery such as "letting go and letting God." It emphasizes the value of quiet, reflective time or play time. Self-reflection is viewed as empowering. Greater self-awareness helps individuals to understand and resolve the stress which precipitated the substance use in the first place. Enlightenment can mean the difference between abstinence and recovery in the full sense of the word.

(57) Although the art therapists expressed concern over the decreasing length of time patients were admitted to treatment, treatment strategies remained relatively unchanged over time. They may be fewer, or performed in shorter duration, yet the types of art interventions described in art therapy literature in years past are quite similar to those used today. It could be that no one has a better idea! Or, it could be that the interventions, despite the constraints upon them, are working to some extent, that they're trustworthy and not affected by the passing of time or the amount of time a patient is in treatment.

(58) Recommendations for further studies would be to continue to interview individuals who have had art therapy in treatment programs, both current patients or individuals in longer term recovery for whom art has been important. Exploring the role of art in recovering individuals who were not in treatment programs would also provide important information about the potential uses or consequences of art. Artists who are addicts (and/or recovering addicts) and continue to make art would help the researcher be theoretically sensitive to the range of conditions that impact art and recovery.

Qualitative research reports use flexible and emerging structures and evaluation criteria.

(59) It is my hope that this study helps to explain the theory of art therapy in recovery from chemical addiction. In the words of one psychiatrist, "Treatment is an art. Treatment is art therapy, that's what treatment is, if it's good treatment."

References

Albert-Puleo, N. and Osha, V. (1976–77) "Art therapy as an alcoholism treatment tool." *Alcohol Health and Research World,* Winter, 28–31.

Alcoholics Anonymous (1988) *Twelve Steps and Twelve Traditions* (37th printing). New York: AA.

Allen, P. B. (1985) "Integrating art therapy into an alcoholism treatment program." *American Journal of Art Therapy 24,* 10–12.

Bailey, J. (1993) "How art heals." *St. Anthony Messenger,* February, 36–41.

Bauer, J. (1982) *Alcoholism and Women.* Toronto: Inner City Books.

Bill, W. (1987) *As Bill Sees It.* New York: Alcoholics Anonymous World Services.

Burke, K. (1985) "When words aren't enough . . . a study of the use of art therapy in the treatment of chemically dependent adolescents with special focus upon the spiritual dimension." *Dissertation Abstracts International* 46, 08-A, p. 2166 (University Microfilms No. AAD85–23, 669).

Chickerneo, N. (1990) "New images, ancient paradigm: A study of the contribution of art to spirituality in addiction recovery." *Dissertation Abstracts International*. Order no. 9110801.

Chopra, D. (1997) *Overcoming Addictions*. New York: Harmony Books.

Conrad, C. (1978) "A grounded theory of academic change." *Sociology of Education 55,* 101–112.

Craddock, S. G., Rounds-Bryant, J. L., Flynn, P. M. and Hubbard, R. L. (1997) "Characteristics and pretreatment behaviors of clients entering drug abuse treatment: 1969 to 1993." *American Journal of Drug and Alcohol Abuse 23,* 1, 43–59.

Devine, D. (1970) "A preliminary investigation of paintings by alcoholic men." *American Journal of Art Therapy 9,* 115–128.

Feen-Calligan, H. (1995) "The use of art therapy in treatment programs to promote spiritual recovery from addiction." *Art Therapy: Journal of the American Art Therapy Association 12,* 46–50.

Foulke, W. E. and Keller, T. W. (1976). "The art experience in addict rehabilitation." *American Journal of Art Therapy 15,* 75–80.

Glaser, B. and Strauss, A. (1967) *The Discovery of Grounded Theory,* Chicago: Aldine.

Harms, E. (1973) "Art therapy for the drug addict." *Art Psychotherapy 1,* 55–59.

Hays, R. E. and Lyons, S. J. (1981) "The bridge drawing: A projection technique for assessment in art therapy." *The Arts in Psychotherapy 8,* 207–217.

Hrenko, K. D. and Willis, R. (1996) "The amusement park technique in the treatment of dually diagnosed, psychiatric inpatients." *Art Therapy: Journal of the American Art Therapy Association 13,* 261–264.

Johnson, L. (1990) "Creative therapies in the treatment of addictions: The art of transforming shame." *The Arts in Psychotherapy 17,* 299–308.

Miller, N. (1995) *Addiction Psychiatry: Current Diagnosis and Treatment*. New York: Wiley-Liss, Inc.

Moore, R. (1983) "Art therapy with substance abusers: A review of the literature." *The Arts in Psychotherapy 10,* 251–260.

Segaller, S. (Producer/Director)(1989) *The Wisdom of the Dream,* Vols. 1, 2, 3. [Film]. USA: Border Television.

Steele, C. (1997) "On the front lines: Fighting drugs in Dayton." *Community 2,* 2, 2–7.

Strauss, A. and Corbin, J. (1990) *Basics of Qualitative Research: Grounded Theory Procedures and Techniques*. Newbury Park, CA: Sage Publications.

Ulman, E. (1953) "Art therapy in an outpatient clinic." *Psychiatry 16,* 55–64.

Van Leit, B. (1995) "Managed mental health care: Reflections in a time of turmoil." *American Journal of Occupational Therapy 50,* 428–434.

Whitfield, C. (1987) *Healing the Child Within*. Deerfield Beach, FL: Health Communications, Inc.

Further Reading

Clemmens, M. C. (1997) *Getting Beyond Sobriety: Clinical Approaches to Long-Term Recovery*. San Francisco: Jossey Bass.

CHAPTER

15 Ethnographic Designs

The term ethnography *literally means "writing about groups of people." Using this qualitative design, you can identify a group of people; study them in their homes or workplaces; note how they behave, think, and talk; and develop a general portrait of the group. This chapter defines ethnographic research, identifies when you use it, assesses the key characteristics of it, and advances the steps in conducting and evaluating this design.*

By the end of this chapter, you should be able to:

- Define ethnographic research and identify when to use it.
- Distinguish among three types of ethnographic designs.
- Identify a cultural theme in an ethnographic study.
- List the characteristics of a culture-sharing group.
- Explain the types of shared patterns of behaviors, beliefs, and language studied in an ethnography.
- Describe several forms of ethnographic data collected during fieldwork.
- Describe the three components of description, themes, and interpretation in ethnography.
- Illustrate the aspects of context reported in ethnography.
- Identify approaches ethnographers might use to document their reflexivity.
- Identify steps in conducting an ethnography study.
- List criteria useful for evaluating an ethnographic research report.

Maria chooses to conduct a qualitative ethnography study for her graduate research project. Her school committee has been meeting throughout the year, and it has formed set ways in which it operates. As a member of this committee, Maria has a natural vantage point for observing how the committee works. She observes how people act, how they speak, and how they engage in practices such as starting promptly on time.

Maria conducts an ethnography. She asks this question: "What are the shared beliefs, values, and attitudes of the school committee on weapon possession in the school?" By answering this question, Maria will gain a deep understanding about how a school committee wrestles with the problem of weapons in the schools.

WHAT IS ETHNOGRAPHIC RESEARCH?

Ethnographic designs are qualitative research procedures for describing, analyzing, and interpreting a culture-sharing group's shared patterns of behavior, beliefs, and language that develop over time. Central to this definition is culture. A **culture** is "everything having to do with human behavior and belief" (LeCompte, Preissle, & Tesch, 1993, p. 5). It can include language, rituals, economic and political structures, life stages, interactions, and communication styles. To understand the patterns of a culture-sharing group, the ethnographer typically spends considerable time "in the field" interviewing, observing, and gathering documents about the group to understand their culture-sharing behaviors, beliefs, and language.

When Do You Conduct an Ethnography?

You conduct an ethnography when the study of a group provides understanding of a larger issue. You also conduct an ethnography when you have a culture-sharing group to study—one that has been together for some time and has developed shared values, beliefs, and language. You capture the "rules" of behavior, such as the informal relationships among teachers who congregate at favorite places to socialize (Pajak & Blasé, 1984). The culture-sharing group may be narrowly framed (e.g., teachers, students, or staff members) or broadly framed (e.g., entire schools and their success, innovation, or violence). The culture-sharing group may be a family, as in the ethnographic study of a 12-year-old child with Down syndrome and his family (Harry et al., 1998). The culture-sharing group may be representative or illustrative of some larger processes, events, or activities (e.g., participating in a graduate program). Fraternity settings are a site where men often exploit and victimize women. In a critical ethnography, Rhoads (1995) studied the culture of one fraternity and its practices that rendered women powerless and marginalized.

Ethnography can provide a detailed day-to-day picture of events, such as the thoughts and activities of a search committee hiring a new principal (Wolcott, 1974, 1994). You conduct an ethnography when you have long-term access to this culture-sharing group so that you can build a detailed record of their behaviors and beliefs over time. You may be a participant in the group or simply an observer, but you gather extensive fieldnotes, interview many people, and collect letters and documents to establish the record of the culture-sharing group.

How Did Ethnographic Research Develop?

Ethnography as practiced in education has been shaped by cultural anthropology, by an emphasis on the issues of writing about culture, and by how ethnographic reports need to be read and understood today. These factors lie at the heart of understanding current practices in ethnography (e.g., Bogdan & Biklen, 1998; Denzin, 1997; LeCompte et al., 1993; Wolcott, 1999).

The roots of educational ethnography lie in cultural anthropology. In the late 19th and early 20th centuries, anthropologists explored "primitive" cultures by visiting other countries and becoming immersed in their societies for extensive periods. They refrained from "going native" and identifying too closely with the people they were studying so that they could write an "objective" account of what they saw and heard. At times, these accounts compared distant cultures on other continents with the American way of life. For example, Margaret Mead, a well-known anthropologist, studied child rearing, adolescence, and the influence of culture on personality in Samoa (Mead, 1928).

Observations and interviews became standard procedures for collecting data "in the field." Also, under sociologists at the University of Chicago in the 1920s through the 1950s, research focused on the importance of studying a single case—whether that case was an individual, a group, a neighborhood, or a larger cultural unit. For example, Chicago sociologists conducted qualitative analyses of personal and public documents to construct a view of the life of Polish immigrants (Thomas & Znaniecki, 1927). With an emphasis on city life, they depicted ordinary life in U.S. cities: the Jewish ghetto, the taxi-dance hall, the professional thief, the hobo, and the delinquent (Bogdan & Biklen, 1998). In highlighting the lives of these individuals, they provided "insider" perspectives by reporting detailed accounts of individuals who are often marginalized in our society.

The infant interdisciplinary area of educational anthropology began to crystallize during the 1950s and continued to develop through the 1980s (LeCompte et al., 1993). Jules Henry depicted elementary school classrooms and high schools as tribes with rituals, culture, and social structure, and George and Louise Spindler examined educational decision making, curriculum content, and teaching (LeCompte et al., 1993). Educational anthropologists focused on subculture groups such as:

- Career and life histories or role analyses of individuals
- Microethnographies of small work and leisure groups within classrooms or schools
- Studies of single classrooms abstracted as small societies
- Studies of school facilities or school districts that approach these units as discrete communities (LeCompte et al., 1993, p. 14)

In studies such as these, educational ethnographers developed and refined procedures borrowed from anthropology and sociology. From the 1980s to the present, anthropologists and educational anthropologists have identified techniques for focusing on a cultural group, conducting observations, analyzing data, and writing up the research (e.g., Fetterman, 1998; Wolcott, 1992, 1994, 1999).

A watershed event in ethnography, according to Denzin (1997), was the publication of the book *Writing Culture* (Clifford & Marcus, 1986). Ethnographers have been "writing their way out" (Denzin, 1997, p. xvii) of this book ever since. Clifford and Marcus raised two issues that have commanded much attention in ethnography in general and within educational research. The first is the crisis of representation. This crisis consists of a reassessment of how ethnographers interpret the groups they are studying. Denzin argued that we can no longer view the researcher as an objective reporter who makes omnipresent pronouncements about the individuals being studied. Instead, the researcher is only one voice among many—individuals such as the reader, the participants, and the gatekeepers—who need to be heard. This has led to a second crisis: legitimacy. No longer do "canons" of validity, reliability, and objectivity of "normal science" represent the standards. Researchers need to evaluate each ethnographic study in terms of flexible standards embedded within the participants' lives; historical and cultural influences; and the interactive forces of race, gender, and class.

Viewed this way, ethnographies need to include perspectives drawn from feminist thought, racial views, sexual perspectives, and critical theory, and they need to be sensitive to race, class, and gender. Ethnographies today are now "messy" and find presentation in many forms, such as a performance, poem, play, novel, or a personal narrative (Denzin, 1997).

WHAT ARE THE TYPES OF ETHNOGRAPHIC DESIGNS?

With this development, eclecticism pervades educational ethnographies today. Table 15.1 illustrates the various types of ethnographies. For a researcher new to ethnography, the long list is less important than a focus on primary forms published in educational reports. Unquestionably, ethnographic research does not always fit cleanly into categories, but three forms are apparent:

- The realist ethnography
- The case study
- The critical ethnography

Realist Ethnographies

A realist ethnography is a popular approach used by cultural anthropologists. Characterized by Van Maanen (1988), it reflects a particular stance taken by the researcher toward the individuals being studied. A **realist ethnography** is an objective account of the situation, typically written in the third-person point of view, reporting objectively on the information learned from participants at a field site. In this ethnographic design:

- The realist ethnographer narrates the study in a third-person dispassionate voice and reports on observations of participants and their views. The ethnographer does not offer personal reflections in the research report and remains in the background as an omniscient reporter of the "facts."
- The researcher reports objective data in a measured style uncontaminated by personal bias, political goals, and judgment. The researcher may provide mundane

TABLE 15.1

Types of Ethnographies

- Realist ethnography—an objective scientifically written ethnography
- Confessional ethnography—a report of the ethnographer's fieldwork experiences
- Life history—a study of one individual situated within the cultural context of his or her life
- Autoethnography—a reflective self-examination by an individual set within his or her cultural context
- Microethnography—a study focused on a specific aspect of a cultural group and setting
- Ethnographic case study—a case analysis of a person, event, activity, or process set within a cultural perspective
- Critical ethnography—a study of the shared patterns of a marginalized group with the aim of advocacy
- Feminist ethnography—a study of women and the cultural practices that serve to disempower and oppress them
- Postmodern ethnography—an ethnography written to challenge the problems in our society that have emerged from a modern emphasis on progress and marginalizing individuals
- Ethnographic novels—a fictional work focused on cultural aspects of a group

Sources: Denzin, 1997; LeCompte et al., 1993; Van Maanan, 1988.

details of everyday life among the people studied. The ethnographer also uses standard categories for cultural description (e.g., family life, work life, social networks, and status systems).

- The ethnographer produces the participants' views through closely edited quotations and has the final word on the interpretation and presentation of the culture (Van Maanen, 1988).

This type of ethnography has a long tradition in cultural anthropology and education. For example, Wolcott (1974, 1994) used a realist approach to ethnography to study the activities of a committee appointed to select a principal. This study addressed the process a school selection committee experienced as they interviewed candidates. Wolcott started with Candidate Number 7, and discussed the committee's deliberation for each candidate (except one) until the final individual was identified. Following this description of the interviewing process, Wolcott interpreted the committee's actions in terms of a lack of professional knowledge, their "variety reducing" behavior, and the reluctance of schools to change.

As a realist ethnographer, Wolcott provided an account of committee deliberations as if he were looking in from the outside, reporting the procedures objectively, and including participants' views. The interpretation at the end presented Wolcott's view of the patterns he saw in the selection committee cultural group.

Case Studies

Writers often use the term *case study* in conjunction with ethnography (e.g., see LeCompte & Schensul, 1999). A case study is an important type of ethnography, although it differs from an ethnography in several important ways. Case study researchers may focus on a program, event, or activity involving individuals rather than a group per se (Stake, 1995). Also, when case study writers research a group, they may be more interested in describing the activities of the group instead of identifying shared patterns of behavior exhibited by the group. The ethnographer searches for the shared patterns that develop as a group interacts over time. Finally, case study researchers are less likely to identify a cultural theme to examine at the beginning of a study, especially one from anthropology; instead, they focus on an in-depth exploration of the actual "case."

Although some researchers identify "case" as an object of study (Stake, 1995), others consider it to be a procedure of inquiry (e.g., Merriam, 1998). A **case study** is an in-depth exploration of a bounded system (e.g., an activity, event, process, or individuals) based on extensive data collection (Creswell, 2007). *Bounded* means that the case is separated out for research in terms of time, place, or some physical boundaries.

It is useful to consider the types of cases that qualitative researchers often study:

- The "case" may be a single individual, several individuals separately or in a group, a program, events, or activities (e.g., a teacher, several teachers, or the implementation of a new math program).
- The "case" may represent a process consisting of a series of steps (e.g., a college curriculum process) that form a sequence of activities.
- As shown in Figure 15.1, a "case" may be selected for study because it is unusual and has merit in and of itself. When the case itself is of interest, it is called an **intrinsic case**. The study of a bilingual school illustrates this form of a case study (Stake, 2000). Alternatively, the focus of a qualitative study may be a specific issue, with a case (or cases) used to illustrate the issue. This type of case is called an **instrumental case**, because it serves the purpose of illuminating a particular issue. The gunman case study (Asmussen & Creswell, 1995) portrays an instrumental case of a campus to portray reactions to campus violence. Case studies may also include

FIGURE 15.1

Types of Qualitative Case Studies

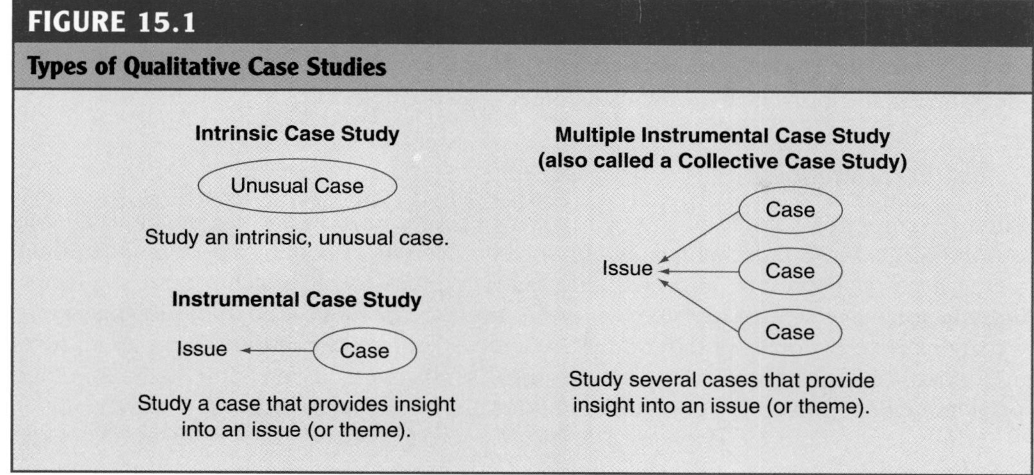

multiple cases, called a **collective case study** (Stake, 1995), in which multiple cases are described and compared to provide insight into an issue. A case study researcher might examine several schools to illustrate alternative approaches to school choice for students.

- The researcher seeks to develop an in-depth understanding of the case by collecting multiple forms of data (e.g., pictures, scrapbooks, videotapes, and e-mails). Providing this in-depth understanding requires that only a few cases be studied, because for each case examined, the researcher has less time to devote to exploring the depths of any one case.
- The researcher also locates the "case" or "cases" within their larger context, such as geographical, political, social, or economic settings (e.g., the family constellation consisting of grandparents, siblings, and "adopted" family members).

An example of a case study is the study by Kos (1991) of four middle school students who have reading disabilities. The study examined what factors contributed to the development of reading disabilities in adolescents. The author tutored the four students, observed their reading alone and reading in class, conducted interviews, and gathered school records on each student. All four students, who were between the ages of 13 and 15, were unable to read materials above the third-grade level. After describing each student, the author identified four themes that emerged about each student: reading behavior, negative and frustrating experiences with instruction, anxiety about reading, and histories about reading in kindergarten and first grade. From these individual case analyses, the author then compared the four individuals and found the students to be aware of their deficiencies, to display a connection between reading disability and stress, and to be unable to integrate various reading strategies.

This case study illustrates a study of four bounded systems—specific individuals—and an assessment of patterns of behavior for each individual and for all four students. The researcher focused on the issue of reading disabilities and conducted an in-depth examination of four cases to illustrate this issue. Multiple forms of data were collected, and the analysis consisted of both description and thematic development.

Another example is the case study by Padula and Miller (1999) of four women who had reentered the university as full-time doctoral students. In this case study, the authors questioned the students' decision to return to school, how they described their reentry experiences, and how the graduate experience changed their lives. Through interviewing and observing these women, the researchers found several themes about beliefs that these women held. For example, the women believed that their graduate experiences did not meet their needs, they compared themselves with younger students, and they felt a general need to finish their programs as quickly as possible.

Critical Ethnographies

When Denzin (1997) spoke of the twin crises of representation and legitimation, he was responding to profound changes in our society, such as becoming more multinational, joining a world economy, and changing demographics to include more racial groups. These factors have created a system of power, prestige, privilege, and authority that serves to marginalize individuals of different classes, races, and gender in our society. With roots in German thinking of the 1920s, the historical problems of domination, alienation, and social struggle are now playing out within educational and social science research.

Ethnography now incorporates a "critical" approach (Carspecken, 1995; Carspecken & Apple, 1992; Thomas, 1993) to include an advocacy perspective to ethnography. **Critical ethnographies** are a type of ethnographic research in which the author is interested in advocating for the emancipation of groups marginalized in our society (Thomas, 1993). Critical researchers are typically politically minded individuals who seek, through their research, to advocate against inequality and domination (Carspecken & Apple, 1992). For example, critical ethnographers might study schools that provide privileges to certain types of students, create inequitable situations among members of different social classes, and perpetuate boys "speaking up" and girls being silent participants in class.

The major components of a critical ethnography are summarized in Figure 15.2. These factors, such as a value-laden orientation, empowering people by giving them more authority, challenging the status quo, and a concern about power and control, play out in an ethnography in specific procedural characteristics, listed below:

- The critical ethnographer studies social issues of power, empowerment, inequality, inequity, dominance, repression, hegemony, and victimization.
- Researchers conduct critical ethnographies so that their studies do not further marginalize the individuals being studied. Thus, the inquirers collaborate, actively participate, negotiate the final written report, use care in entering and leaving a site, and reciprocate by giving back to study participants.

FIGURE 15.2

Characteristics of Critical Ethnography

- Critical researchers are usually politically minded people.
- Critical ethnographers speak to an audience on behalf of their participants as a means of empowering participants by giving them more authority.
- Critical ethnographers seek to change society.
- Critical ethnographers identify and celebrate their biases in research. They recognize that all research is value laden.
- Critical ethnographers challenge the status quo and ask why it is so.
- Critical researchers seek to connect the meaning of a situation to broader structures of social power and control.
- Critical researchers seek to create a literal dialogue with the participants they are studying.

Source: Adapted from Carspecken & Apple, 1992; Thomas, 1993.

- The critical ethnographer is self-conscious about his or her interpretation, recognizing that interpretations reflect our own history and culture. Interpretations can be only tentative and questioning and subject to how readers and participants will view them.
- Critical researchers position themselves in the text to be reflexive and self-aware of their role, and to be up front in the written research report. This means identifying biases and values; acknowledging views; and distinguishing among textual representations by the author, the participants, and the reader. No longer is the ethnographer an "objective" observer, as in the realist approach.
- This nonneutral position for the critical researcher also means that he or she will be an advocate for change to help transform our society so that people are less oppressed and marginalized.
- In the end, the critical ethnographic report will be a "messy, multilevel, multimethod" approach to inquiry, full of contradictions, imponderables, and tensions (Denzin, 1997).

The critical ethnographic study of one principal in an "inclusive" elementary school (Keyes, Hanley-Maxwell, & Capper, 1999) illustrated many of these features. The overall purpose was to describe and define the role of administrative leadership in an inclusive school for students with a high incidence of disability classifications (e.g., cognitive, emotional, learning, speech, and language). With the objective of generating a new theory that would empower individuals in the school, the authors began with a framework for empowering leadership: support, facilitation, and possibility.

Based on extensive fieldwork consisting of shadowing the principal (Marta), observing classrooms, conducting individual and focus group interviews, and reviewing weekly announcements, the researchers compiled a picture of Marta's leadership that included a personal belief system of spirituality. Marta's spirituality led him to value personal struggle, espouse the dignity of individuals, merge the professional and the personal, believe that people were doing their best, and emphasize the importance of listening and of dreams. In the end, Keyes et al. (1999) provided a "vision for equity nourished by spiritual beliefs" (p. 233) and posed the concluding questions "School reform for what?" and "Empowering leadership for whom?" (p. 234).

As an ethnography of a school that embraces a critical perspective, the project focused on the issue of empowerment felt by marginalized students and teachers in the school. The principal sought active collaborative participation through a shared dialogue with teachers and students. The researchers advocated for a change and highlighted the tensions that opened up new questions rather than closing down the conversation. Although the authors' views were not made explicit in the text, their interest in change and a new vision for leadership in schools for individuals with disabilities was clear.

WHAT ARE THE KEY CHARACTERISTICS OF AN ETHNOGRAPHIC DESTGN?

With the diverse approaches to ethnography identified in the realist, case study, and critical approaches, it is not easy to identify characteristics they have in common. However, for those learning about ethnographies, the following characteristics typically mark an ethnographic study:

- Cultural themes
- A culture-sharing group
- Shared patterns of behavior, belief, and language

- ◆ Fieldwork
- ◆ Description, themes, and interpretation
- ◆ Context or setting
- ◆ Researcher reflexivity

Cultural Themes

Ethnographers typically study cultural themes drawn from cultural anthropology. Ethnographers do not venture into the field looking haphazardly for anything they might see. Instead, they are interested in adding to the knowledge about culture and studying specific cultural themes. A **cultural theme** in ethnography is a general position, declared or implied, that is openly approved or promoted in a society or group (see Spradley, 1980b, for a discussion about cultural themes). As with all qualitative studies, this theme does not serve to narrow the study; instead, it becomes a broad lens that researchers use when they initially enter a field to study a group, and they look for manifestations of it. As Wolcott (1999) said, we can see "culture at work" (p. 125).

What are these cultural themes? They can be found in introductory texts in cultural anthropology. Wolcott (1999) mentioned introductory texts that discuss themes in cultural anthropology, such as those by Kessing (1958), Haviland (1993), or Howard (1996). They can also be found in dictionaries of concepts in cultural anthropology, such as Winthrop's (1991). Another approach is to locate the cultural theme in ethnographic studies in education. Authors announce them in titles or at the beginning of the study. You can see them in purpose statements in ethnographies or in research questions as a "central phenomenon" (see chapter 5). For example, here are several cultural themes explored by authors:

- ◆ *Persistence* in distance education courses (Garland, 1993)
- ◆ The "coming out" stages of gay *identity development* (Rhoads, 1997)
- ◆ Development of students' *social skills* in Japan (LeTendre, 1999)
- ◆ *Enculturation* in an early childhood program among the Maori in New Zealand (Bauermeister, 1998)

A Culture-Sharing Group

Ethnographers learn from studying a culture-sharing group at a single site. Less frequently authors examine single individuals, as in Wolcott's (1974, 1994) single case study of a principal. In the study of a group, ethnographers identify a single site (e.g., an elementary classroom), locate a group within it (e.g., a reading group), and gather data about the group (e.g., observe a reading period). This distinguishes ethnography from other forms of qualitative research (e.g., narrative research) that focus on individuals rather than groups of people. A **culture-sharing group** in ethnography is two or more individuals who have shared behaviors, beliefs, and language. For example, groups were studied in these ethnographies:

- ◆ 47 students in a distance education course in resource management and environmental subjects (Garland, 1993)
- ◆ 16 elementary education student teachers (Goodman & Adler, 1985)
- ◆ 40 college students in an organization who had identified themselves as either gay or bisexual (Rhoads, 1997)

Groups such as these typically possess certain characteristics, which are listed in Table 15.2. A group may vary in size, but the individuals in the group need to meet on a regular basis and interact over a period of time (e.g., more than 2 weeks up to 4 months) to develop

TABLE 15.2

The Study of a Culture-Sharing Group in a Third-Grade Elementary Classroom

Characteristics of a Culture-Sharing Group	An Example
The group consists of two or more individuals, and it may be small or large.	A small group—two readers in a classroom A larger group—six to ten readers in a classroom
The group interacts on a regular basis.	For a period three times a week, the group meets to discuss a reading.
The group has interacted for some time.	Since the beginning of September, the reading group has met three times a week for three periods.
The group is representative of some larger group.	The small reading group is representative of third-grade readers.
The group has adopted some shared patterns of behaving, thinking, or talking.	The group has certain rituals they perform as they begin to read, such as sitting on the floor, opening their book to the assigned page, and waiting to speak until the teacher calls on them to answer a question.

shared patterns of behaving, thinking, or talking. The group is often representative of a larger group, such as a reading group within a third-grade classroom.

Often, ethnographers study groups unfamiliar to them to be able to look at them in a "fresh and different way, as if they were exceptional and unique" (LeCompte et al., 1993, p. 3). Individuals sometimes mistake a cultural group with an ethnic group. Ethnic groups are self-identified individuals in a sociopolitical grouping that have a recognized public identity, such as Hispanics, Asian Pacific Islanders, and Arab Americans (LeCompte & Schensul, 1999). Using these ethnic labels can cause problems in an ethnography because the labels may not be terms used by the individuals themselves.

Shared Patterns of Behavior, Belief, and Language

Ethnographic researchers look for shared patterns of behavior, beliefs, and language that the culture-sharing group adopts over time. This characteristic has several elements to it. First, the culture-sharing group needs to have adopted shared patterns that the ethnographer can discern. A **shared pattern** in ethnography is a common social interaction that stabilizes as tacit rules and expectations of the group (Spindler & Spindler, 1992). Second, the group shares any one or a combination of behaviors, beliefs, and language.

- A **behavior** in an ethnography is an action taken by an individual in a cultural setting. For example, Wolcott (1974, 1994) studied how a principal's selection committee acted as they deliberated about selecting a candidate.
- A **belief** in an ethnography is how an individual thinks about or perceives things in a cultural setting. For example, Padula and Miller (1999) found that women doctoral students in psychology shared the concern that they were not able to invest much energy in their families.
- **Language** in an ethnography is how an individual talks to others in a cultural setting. In a study of life-history narratives of two African American women, Nelson (1990) analyzed code-switching (changing from standard English to Black English vernacular). Sara, for example, used the repetitive, parallel clause structure found in Black church tradition when she said, "It is pain, suffering, determination, perseverance" (p. 147).

These shared patterns raise several practical questions that ethnographers need to address in a study. How long does the group need to stay together to "share"? To answer this question, a specific study would have to be examined. Unquestionably, the longer the group is together, the more the individuals will adopt shared behaviors and ways of thinking and the easier it will be for an ethnographer to discern patterns. However, assessment techniques are available for gathering data quickly from a group that may be shared for a short period of time (LeCompte & Schensul, 1999). Fraternity members may form shared beliefs with new pledges quickly or school boards may develop common understandings through "board retreats" that allow an ethnographer to quickly assess patterns.

Another issue is whether the patterns are ideal (what *should* occur), actual (what *did* occur), or projective (what *might have* occurred). As an ethnographer observes or interviews, examples of all three patterns may emerge from the data. An ethnographer visiting a third-grade classroom might observe the reading group to see what did occur, interview the teacher to identify what might have occurred, and consult with the curriculum coordinator as to what the school district hoped should have occurred.

Fieldwork

Ethnographers collect data through spending time at participants' sites where they live, work, or play. To understand best the patterns of a cultural group, an ethnographer spends considerable time with the group. The patterns cannot be easily discerned through questionnaires or brief encounters. Instead, the ethnographer goes "to the field," lives with or frequently visits the people being studied, and slowly learns the cultural ways in which the group behaves or thinks. **Fieldwork** in ethnography means that the researcher gathers data in the setting where the participants are located and where their shared patterns can be studied. This data collection involves the following:

- **Emic data** is information supplied by participants in a study. *Emic* often refers to first-order concepts, such as local language, concepts, and ways of expression used by members in a cultural-sharing group (Schwandt, 2001). In an ethnographic study of a soup kitchen for the homeless, Miller, et al. (1998) interviewed and recorded "stories" supplied by Michael, Dan, Sarah, and Robert and used quotes from these individuals to construct their perspectives.
- **Etic data** is information representing the ethnographer's interpretation of the participants' perspectives. *Etic* typically refers to second-order concepts, such as the language used by the social scientist or educator to refer to the same phenomena mentioned by the participants (Schwandt, 2001). In the soup kitchen study (Miller et al., 1998), the authors formed themes as their interpretation of participants' data that represented how the soup kitchen worked.
- **Negotiation data** consist of information that the participant and the researcher agree to use in a study. Negotiation occurs at different stages in research, such as agreeing to entry procedures for a research site, mutually respecting individuals at the site, and developing a plan for giving back or reciprocating with the individuals. Again in the soup kitchen study (Miller et al., 1998), the authors sought out a gatekeeper to gain entry, helped advocate for the homeless with funding agencies, and participated in serving lunches on a regular basis.

During fieldwork, the ethnographer uses a variety of research techniques to gather data. Table 15.3, which is a composite list from LeCompte and Schensul (1999) and Wolcott (1999), displays mainly qualitative and a few quantitative forms of data collection. Of these possibilities, observation and unstructured interviewing are popular among ethnographers. To see the range of data collection that ethnographers gather in a single

TABLE 15.3

Popular Forms of Data Collected by Ethnographers

- Casual conversation
- Life history, life-cycle interview
- Key informant (participant) interview
- Semistructured interview
- Structured interview
- Survey
- Household census, ethnogenealogy
- Questionnaire (written and/or oral)
- Projective techniques
- Observations (nonparticipant to participant)
- Tests
- Content analysis of secondary text or visual material
- Focus group interview
- Elicitation techniques (e.g., looking at a scrapbook and talking about memories)
- Audiovisual material (e.g., audio or visual record, such as camera recording)
- Spatial mapping (e.g., recording ways data varies acros units, such as group and institution)
- Network analysis (e.g., describing networks in time and space)

Sources: Le Compte & Schensul, 1999; Wolcott, 1999.

study, examine the following forms used by Rhoads (1995) in his ethnographic study of fraternity life:

- 12 formal, structured interviews that lasted from 1 to 2 hours
- 18 less formal interviews recorded in handwritten notes
- Participation in both open fraternity parties and private rituals that were open to only a few outsiders
- Ongoing discussions with several key participants who explained the significance of various fraternity practices
- A review of numerous documents, including the university Greek handbook, minutes from chapter meetings, class papers, and the fraternity liability policy.

Description, Themes, and Interpretation

Ethnographic researchers describe and analyze the culture-sharing group and make an interpretation about the patterns seen and heard. During data collection, the ethnographer begins to forge a study. This consists of analyzing the data for a description of both the individuals and sites of the culture-sharing group; analyzing patterns of behavior, beliefs, and language; and reaching some conclusions about the meaning learned from studying the people and the site (Wolcott, 1994).

A **description in ethnography** is a detailed rendering of individuals and scenes to depict what is going on in the culture-sharing group. This description needs to be detailed and thick, and it needs to identify specifics. It serves to place the reader figuratively in the setting, to transport the reader to the actual scene, to make it real. This involves awakening the reader's senses through adjectives, nouns, and verbs that elicit sounds, sights, feelings, and smells. To do this, the researcher must single out some detail to include while excluding others. It means describing events, activities, and places without veering too far from the actual scene of attention and the people whose shared patterns need to be discerned. Passages from ethnographies that "describe" are long and detailed. Sometimes, ethnographers or case study writers provide a description from a general picture to the specific setting in which an event or events take place. For example, examine Figure 15.3, which maps the descriptive passage in the gunman incident case study (Asmussen & Creswell,

FIGURE 15.3

The Broad-to-Narrow Description in the Gunman Incident Case Study

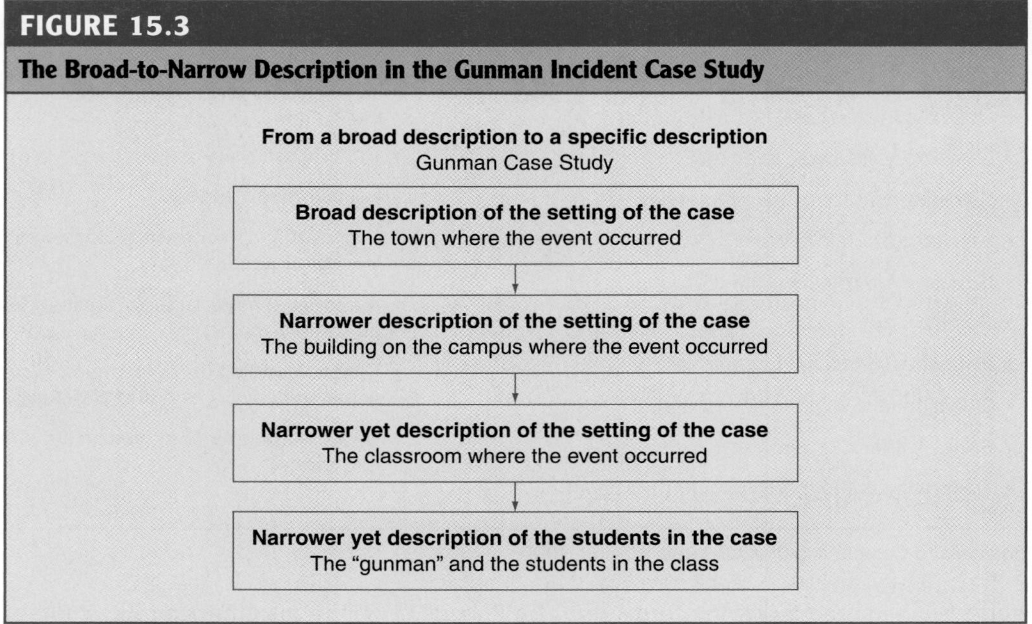

Source: Adapted from Asmussen & Creswell, 1995.

1995). The researchers began with describing the town, then narrowing the description to the campus, and finally focusing on the classroom in which the incident occurred.

In another example, Wolcott (1994) described a candidate for a principal's position who ended up "Mr. Fifth" in the competition:

> Committee members were cordial in their greetings and introductions when Mr. Fifth appeared for his interview. He was directed to choose one of the (few) comfortable chairs in the meeting room, prompting the personnel director to joke, "It won't be this comfortable again." After a folksy prelude, the director of elementary education asked, "What things have you been doing and how have you been involved?" (p. 129)

In this short descriptive passage, Wolcott conveys the feelings of propriety and anxiety, shares the appearance of the room, relates the language of the committee, and provides a sense of the feelings of the committee toward candidates.

The distinction between description and theme analysis is not always clear. Theme analysis moves away from reporting the "facts" to making an interpretation of people and activities. As part of making sense of the information, **thematic data analysis in ethnography** consists of distilling how things work and naming the essential features in themes in the cultural setting. Consistent with the process identified in chapter 9 about describing and developing themes from data, the ethnographer segments the text (or images), codes them, and formulates a small set of nonoverlapping themes. In an ethnography, however, these themes map the shared patterns of behavior, thinking, or talking. The difficulty is in reducing the themes down to a small set and providing adequate evidence for each. The themes are evident in the ethnographies described here:

- In an ethnographic study of conflict resolution between "typically developing" children and children with disabilities in an integrated preschool, Malloy and McMurray (1996) found several conflicts related to goals, oppositions, strategies, outcomes, and the teacher's role.
- A case study examined student teachers' perspectives toward social studies in elementary-level schools (Goodman & Adler, 1985). Student teachers viewed

social studies as a nonsubject, human relations, citizenship indoctrination, school knowledge, an integrative core of the elementary curriculum, and education for social action.

After description and analysis comes interpretation. In **interpretation in ethnography,** the ethnographer draws inferences and forms conclusions about what was learned. This phase of analysis is the most subjective. The researcher relates both the description and the themes back to a larger portrait of what was learned, which often reflects some combination of the researcher making a personal assessment, returning to the literature on the cultural theme, and raising further questions based on the data. It might also include addressing problems that arose during the fieldwork that render the account tentative and hypothetical, at best. In the ethnography of Raul, the 12-year-old child with disabilities, and his brothers, family, and friends (Harry et al., 1998), interpretation consisted of the authors' reflecting on the differences between exclusion in a nonfamily setting and unconditional acceptance in a family.

Context or Setting

Ethnographers present the description, themes, and interpretation within the context or setting of the culture-sharing group. The **context** for an ethnography is the setting, situation, or environment that surrounds the cultural group being studied. It is multilayered and interrelated, consisting of such factors as history, religion, politics, economy, and the environment (Fetterman, 1998). This context may be a physical location such as a description of the school, the state of the building, the color of the classroom walls, or the sounds coming down the hall. It may also be the historical context of individuals in the group, whether they have experienced suppression, domination, or are an emerging people who have arrived excited about their new land. It may be the social condition of the individuals, their longtime reunions to build kinship, their status as a profession, or their earnings and geographic mobility. The economic conditions may also include income levels, working-class or blue-collar background, or the systems of finance that keep the individuals below the poverty level.

Researcher Reflexivity

Ethnographic researchers make interpretations and write their report reflexively. **Reflexivity in ethnography** refers to the researcher being aware of and openly discussing his or her role in the study in a way that honors and respects the site and participants. Because ethnographic research involves a prolonged stay at a site, researchers are concerned about their impact on the site and the people. They negotiate entry with key individuals and plan to leave the site as undisturbed as they found it. As individuals who have a history and a cultural background themselves, they realize that their interpretation is only one possibility, and that their report does not have any privileged authority over other interpretations that readers, participants, and other researchers may have. It is important, therefore, for ethnographers to position themselves within their report and identify their standpoint or point of view (Denzin, 1997). They do this by talking about themselves, sharing their experiences, and mentioning how their interpretations shape their discussions about the sites and culture-sharing groups. One researcher, who studied identity development of adolescent females through reading teen magazines (Finders, 1996), documented her role as follows:

> I did not want to be viewed as a teacher or someone in authority. (p. 73)
>
> I gained their trust slowly and negotiated a relationship that did not fit their established patterns with significant adults. (p. 73)

> On several occasions, a girl would not allow me to see a note that she deemed "too obscene." I did not report such incidents as writing on a restroom wall or faking illness to avoid an exam. (p. 74)

Being reflexive also means that authors' conclusions are often tentative or inconclusive, leading to new questions to answer. The study might end with questions that beg for answers or multiple perspectives or viewpoints for the reader to consider.

WHAT ARE THE STEPS IN CONDUCTING AN ETHNOGRAPHY?

There are probably as many procedures for conducting an ethnography as there are ethnographers. From the early days in cultural anthropology when researchers were "sent" without guidance to remote islands or countries to conduct their ethnography, today we have procedures, albeit general procedures, to guide conduct of an ethnography. A highly structured approach can be found in Spradley (1980b), who has advanced a 12-stage "developmental research sequence" for conducting an ethnography. As shown in Figure 15.4, this sequence begins with the researcher's locating an informant (today we would call this person a "participant"; see chapter 10 on writing sensitively). Then the ethnographer cycles between collecting data and making analyses of various types, such as a taxonomy or a comparison table to explore relationships among ideas (see Spradley's componential analysis). Other authors besides Spradley have also suggested guidelines, such as Fetterman (1998), LeCompte and Schensul (1999), and Wolcott (1999).

Instead of Spradley's highly structured approach, we will consider a series of steps that represents a general template rather than a definitive procedure for conducting an ethnography. Moreover, the considerations of ethnographers and case study writers differ procedurally, and we will consider both similarities and differences among our three forms of ethnography: realist, case study, and critical. An overview of the steps used in each type of design is shown in Table 15.4.

Step 1. Identify Intent and the Type of Design, and Relate Intent to Your Research Problem

The first and most important steps in conducting research are to identify why you are undertaking a study, which form of design you plan to use, and how your intent relates to your research problem. These factors need to be identified in all three forms of ethnographies and case studies. The intent of your research and the type of problem you seek to study will differ significantly depending on if you plan to conduct a realist, case study, or critical ethnography.

For a realist ethnography, the focus is on understanding a culture-sharing group and using the group to develop a deeper understanding of a cultural theme. The culture-sharing group may be an entire school or a single classroom. The themes may include such topics as enculturation, acculturation, socialization, institutionalized education, learning and cognition, and child and adult development (LeCompte et al., 1993).

For a case study, the focus is on developing an in-depth understanding of a case, such as an event, activity, or process. In education, this often includes the study of an individual or several individuals, such as students or teachers. The important consideration is how you will use the case, such as to assess its intrinsic merit, to understand an issue, or to provide information to compare several cases.

In a critical ethnography, the intent changes dramatically from those used in a realist or case study project. A critical ethnographer seeks to address an inequity in society or

FIGURE 15.4

Spradley's Developmental Research Sequence

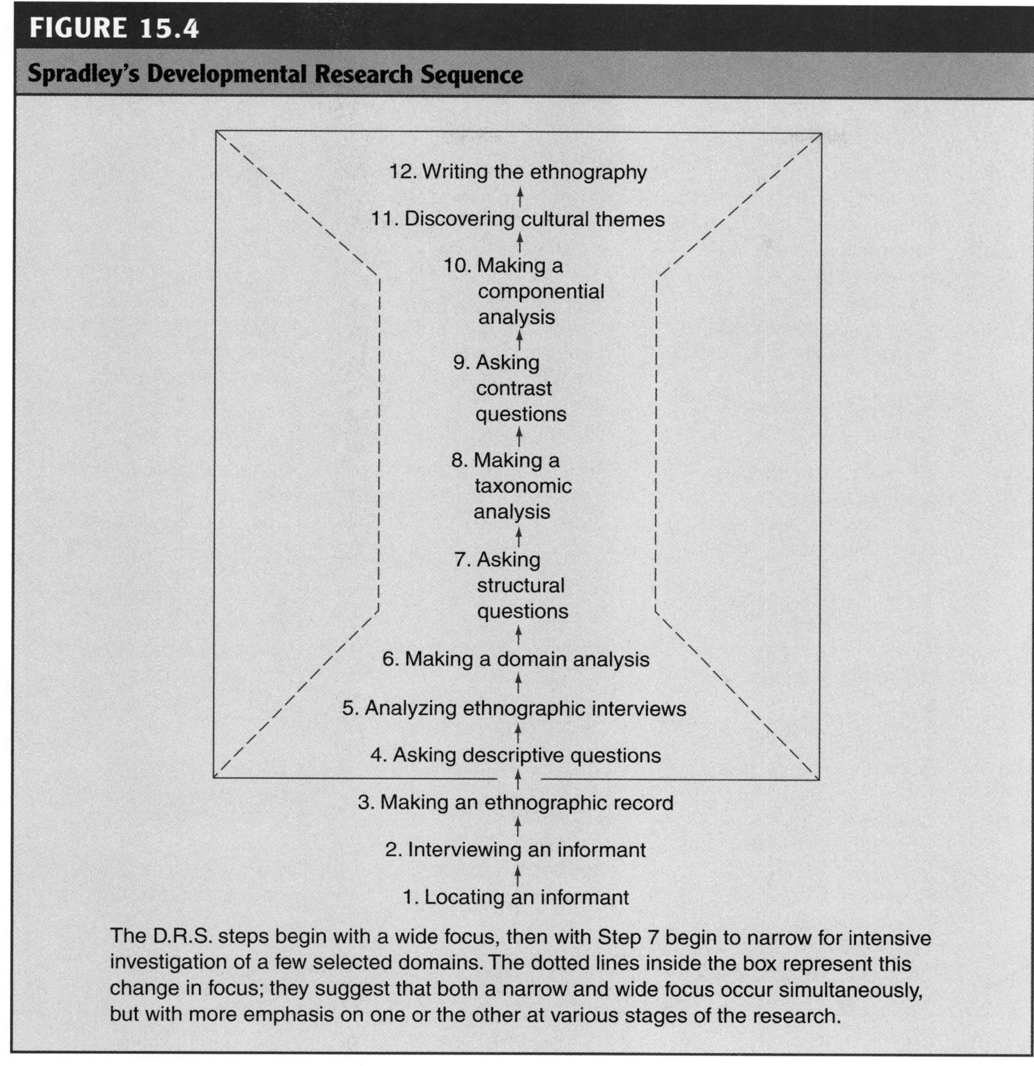

The D.R.S. steps begin with a wide focus, then with Step 7 begin to narrow for intensive investigation of a few selected domains. The dotted lines inside the box represent this change in focus; they suggest that both a narrow and wide focus occur simultaneously, but with more emphasis on one or the other at various stages of the research.

Source: From *The Ethnographic Interview* 1st edition by James P. Spradley. Copyright © 1979. Reprinted with permission of Wadsworth, a division of Thomson Learning: www.thomsonrights.com. Fax 800–730–2215.

schools, plans to use the research to advocate and call for changes, and typically identifies a specific issue (e.g., inequality, dominance, oppression, or empowerment) to study.

Step 2. Discuss Approval and Access Considerations

In this step, all three types of designs follow a similar procedure. You need to receive approval from the institutional review board (see chapter 6). You also need to identify the type of purposeful sampling that is available and that best answers your research questions. In this process, locate a site for your research and then identify a gatekeeper who can provide access to the site and participants for study. In all research, you need to guarantee provisions for respecting the site and actively design in the study how to reciprocate to the individuals at the site. This means that you will guarantee to disturb the site as little as possible and to follow good ethical practices such as guaranteeing privacy and anonymity, not deceiving individuals, and informing all participants of the purposes of your research.

TABLE 15.4

Procedures for Conducting a Realist Ethnography, a Case Study, and a Critical Ethnography

Procedures	Realist Ethnography	Case Study	Critical Ethnography
Identify your intent, the appropriate design, and how intent relates to your research problem.	The problem relates to a culture-sharing group and how it works. The problem requires detailed description of the daily lives of people. The problem relates to understanding a cultural theme. Identify your cultural theme.	The problem relates to developing an in-depth understanding of a "Case" or bounded system. The problem relates to understanding an event, activity, process, or one or more individuals. Identify the type of "case," such as intrinsic, instrumental, or collective.	The problem relates to a need to address inequities in our society or schools. The problem calls for action and advocacy. Identify the "critical" issue (e.g., inequality) that you wish to explore.
Discuss how you plan to receive approval and gain access to study sites and participants.	Receive approval from institutional review board. Locate a research site using purposeful sampling procedures. Identify a gatekeeper to provide access. Guarantee provisions for respecting the site.	Receive approval from institutional review board. Locate a research site using purposeful sampling procedures. Identify how many cases you plan to study. Identify a gatekeeper to provide access. Guarantee provisions for respecting the site.	Receive approval from institutional review board. Locate a research site using purposeful sampling procedures. Identify a gatekeeper to provide access. Guarantee provisions for respecting the site.
Collect appropriate data emphasizing time in the field, multiple sources of information, and collaboration.	Spend extensive time at the site and with the culture-sharing group. Enter the site slowly and build rapport. Plan to reciprocate for data provided. Emphasize observations and record fieldnotes.	Collect extensive data using multiple forms of data collection (observations, interviews, documents, audiovisual materials.)	Collaborate with participants by actively involving them in data collection. Collect multiple forms of data that individuals are willing to provide.

Step 3. Use Appropriate Data-Collection Procedures

We can see from Table 15.4 that the three designs have several common features, with an emphasis on extensive data collection, using multiple procedures for gathering data, and the active involvement of participants in the process.

In a realist ethnography, because you will likely spend considerable time with individuals in the field (e.g., up to 4 months or more), you need to enter the site slowly and as unobtrusively as possible. Building rapport with gatekeepers and key participants is essential for your long-term contacts. In many realist accounts, an emphasis is placed on taking fieldnotes and observing the "cultural scene." Interviews and artifacts such as drawings, relics, and symbols are also important forms of data. Any data that can help you develop an in-depth understanding of the shared patterns of the cultural group would be useful.

For a case study, the intent is to develop an in-depth understanding of a case or an issue, and researchers collect as many types of data as possible to develop this understanding. For example, in the gunman incident (Asmussen & Creswell, 1995), discussed in chapter 1, the authors provided a table in Paragraph 11 that showed 13 sources of information, including interviews, observations, documents, and audiovisual materials. The provision of a table specifically focused on data-collection sources emphasized the extent of data collection.

TABLE 15.4
(Continued)

Procedures	Realist Ethnography	Case Study	Critical Ethnography
Analyze and interpret your data within a design.	Read through data to develop an overall understanding of it. Develop a detailed description of the cultural setting to establish a context for the group being studied. Develop themes about the culture-sharing group. Make interpretations in view of the cultural theme you are studying.	Read through data to develop an overall understanding of it. Describe the case(s) in detail and establish a context for it. Develop issues or themes about the case(s). If more than one case is studied, consider a within-case analysis followed by a cross-case analysis.	Read through data to develop an overall understanding of it. Develop a detailed description of the cultural setting to establish a context for the group being studied. Develop themes that relate to the "critical" issues that are being explored in the ethnography. Identify changes that need to occur, advocate for specific changes, and advance a plan for change.
Write and report your research consistent with your design.	Report it as an objective study. As a researcher, remain in the background in the written report. Keep your biases out. Identify how your exploration of the cultural theme advances knowledge.	Report it based primarily on description of the case, or weigh description, analysis, and interpretation differently or equally. Choose to be objective or subjective in your reporting. Include your biases. Generalize to other cases.	Report it as a call to action to address that "critical" issue that you are studying. Include a specific plan of action for change based on your findings. Discuss how you, as well as those you studied, changed (be reflexive).

In a critical ethnography, the data collection is less focused on time in the field or on the extent of data and more on the active collaboration between the researcher and the participants during the study. Because the intent of a critical ethnography is to help bring about change that affects the lives of participants, the participants need to be involved in learning about themselves and what steps need to be taken to improve their equity, to provide empowerment, or to lessen their oppression. This collaboration may involve participants in the design of the study, the formulation of research questions, the collection of data, or the analysis of the data collected. It may also include having participants actively write the final research report with you.

Step 4. Analyze and Interpret Data Within a Design

In all ethnographic designs, you will engage in the general process of developing a description, analyzing your data for themes, and providing an interpretation of the meaning of your information. These are typical data analysis and interpretation procedures found in all qualitative studies. However, the different types of ethnographic designs vary in their approach to these procedures.

In a critical ethnography, you need to consider a balance among description, analysis, and interpretation so that each becomes an important element of your analysis. Moreover, you can discuss in your interpretation how you learned about the cultural theme, actively reflect back on what information existed in the literature, and advance how your study added to the understanding of the cultural theme. In a case study, again the analysis follows description, analysis, and interpretation, but the analysis procedures will vary depending on whether you are studying a single case or multiple cases. A typical case study procedure for multiple cases is to first analyze each case separately and then conduct a cross-case analysis (see Stake, 1995) to identify common and different themes among all of the cases.

In a critical ethnography, you shape the description, analysis, and interpretation to focus on the "critical" issue in your study. Specifically, you need to interpret your findings in view of the changes that need to occur and to advocate for improvements in the lives of your participants. Often, critical ethnographers will advance a plan for change with specific steps that need to occur. For example, in a study about improving the conditions for women's ice hockey teams in Canada, Theberge (1997) ended her study with an appeal for action. She calls for "a more fully transformative vision of hockey that would offer empowerment in a setting that rejects violence and the normalization of injury in favor of an ethic of care" (p. 85).

Step 5. Write the Report Consistent with Your Design

A realist ethnography is written as an objective report of information about the culture-sharing group. Your personal views and biases will be kept in the background, and a discussion at the end of the study should indicate how the research contributes to knowledge about the cultural theme based on understanding the shared patterns of behavior, thinking, or language of the culture-sharing group. However, a case study may emphasize the detailed description of the case. You can write entire case studies to focus on description rather than a thematic development, such as Stake's (1995) descriptive case study of "Harper School." Other case studies will balance description with themes, such as the gunman incident case study by Asmussen and Creswell (1995). One additional factor that sets case studies apart from other ethnographic designs is that the author may discuss generalizing the findings to other cases, especially if researchers examine multiple case studies. Although qualitative researchers are reluctant to generalize their findings, the use of multiple case studies provides some ability to identify findings that are common to all cases using cross-case analysis. When this occurs, case study writers may suggest that their findings are generalizable, but they make only modest claims in this direction.

In a critical ethnography, the researchers conclude their reports with the "critical" issue that initiated the study, and discuss how they as well as the participants have changed or benefited from the research. Included within a "call for action" by the critical ethnographer may be a reflection about changes they and the participants have experienced. Undoubtedly, in all forms of research, the investigators change, but critical ethnographers, as self-conscious researchers, emphasize how they and their participants have changed.

HOW DO YOU EVALUATE AN ETHNOGRAPHY?

The criteria for evaluating an ethnography begin with applying the standards used in qualitative research mentioned in chapter 10. Then, specific factors need to be considered within ethnography proper. Consider these questions as you read an ethnography or review a study you have conducted:

- ◆ Is the culture-sharing group or the case clearly identified and specified?
- ◆ Are patterns identified for the group or case?

- Is the group or the case described in detail?
- Do you learn about the context surrounding the group or the case?
- Does the author reflect on his or her role in the study?
- Is there a broader interpretation made of the meaning of the patterns or the case?
- Does the interpretation naturally flow from the description and the themes?
- From reading the ethnography, does the reader have a sense about how the culture works from the participant's or researcher's viewpoint?
- Has the author checked the accuracy of the study by using procedures such as triangulating among data sources or taking the study back to participants for review?

APPLYING WHAT YOU HAVE LEARNED: AN ETHNOGRAPHIC STUDY

To apply the ideas in this chapter, first read the ethnographic study on page 496 by Finders (1996), noting the marginal annotations that identify the key characteristics of an ethnography as addressed in this chapter, and the characteristics of qualitative research. The study was chosen because it follows sound ethnographic procedures (e.g., clearly defined group, understanding patterns of behavior, and observational data collection) and illustrates an example of critical ethnography with a focus on studying a gender issue and advocating for specific changes in our language arts classrooms.

As you review this article, look for elements of the research process:

- The research problem and use of qualitative research
- Use of the literature
- The purpose statement and research questions
- Types of procedures of ethnographic data collection
- Types of procedures of ethnographic data analysis and interpretation
- The overall writing structure.

The Research Problem and Use of Qualitative Research

See Paragraphs 02–03

The research problem or issue in this study is announced in Paragraph 02 when the author refers to the narrow topics and limited range of roles for females presented in teen magazines. Added to this is the problem that young female adolescents construct their sense of self through reading these magazines.

This study displays many key markings of a qualitative study:

- An exploration of a problem about how young female teens construct a sense of self (Paragraph 02)
- Minimal use of the literature and its application to discuss the problem at the beginning of the study (Paragraph 03)
- Open-ended and broad questions about adolescent females reading teen magazines (Paragraph 03)
- Collection of data from a small number of participants—four early-adolescent girls (Paragraph 04)
- The collection of words (text) from the adolescents and the use of the researcher's own forms of data collecting (Paragraph 06)
- The analysis of text by reporting words of the adolescents (e.g., see Paragraph 10)

- The description and analysis of themes about developmental issues, the queens reading "Zines," and reading "fluff" (Paragraphs 10–41)
- The interpretation of the findings within the larger meaning of teaching subliterature (Paragraphs 42–50).

Moreover, the study also displays characteristics of a critical ethnography:

- It examined the theoretical concept of social roles (Paragraph 03) and the issue of vulnerability of the adolescent readers (Paragraph 47).
- The researcher discussed her trust and negotiated a relationship with the teens that would not further marginalize them. In this way, the researcher openly discussed her position (Paragraph 07).
- The researcher was sensitive to the role of women in the social, political, and developmental context of schools and reading (e.g., see Paragraph 03).
- The researcher also became an advocate for the needs of teens by recommending changes for teaching subliterature (see Paragraphs 42–50).
- The author left the study with additional questions, such as what would happen to one of the teens, Cleo, because "there was no place for her" (Paragraph 50).

Use of the Literature

See Paragraph 03

As in most qualitative studies, the literature in this article played a minor role. It documented the reading of the literature by young girls and it set the "conversation" (Paragraph 03) to which this study was to add.

The Purpose Statement and Research Questions

See Paragraph 03

At the end of Paragraph 03 we find a general-purpose statement by the author that the study will add to the ongoing conversation about perspectives of adolescent females reading teen magazines and address how literacy shapes (and constrains) social roles. The author asks the question "How do early adolescent females read literature that falls outside the realm of fiction?" (Paragraph 03).

Types of Procedures of Ethnographic Data Collection

See Paragraphs 04, 06–08

Participant observation, interviews, and collecting written artifacts became the major forms of data collected. This process involved 1 year of data collection and consisted of participant observation, interviewing, and collecting of written artifacts from the participants both in and out of school.

Types of Procedures of Ethnographic Data Analysis and Interpretation

Data analysis—see Paragraphs 10–41

Interpretation—see Paragraphs 42–50

The author interwove both description and thematic development. This can be seen in Paragraph 16, for example, where the author first described the shared patterns of behavior by the adolescents, documenting a detailed description of the reading of the girls within the theme of "Crossing Developmental Boundaries: Zine Reading as a Rite of Passage." In this theme, we hear about the inclusion and exclusion of members from the "queens," and how the girls sought answers to their questions from the magazines. We meet Lauren, Angie, Tiffany, and Cleo.

An interpretation ends the study with the author reflecting on the larger meaning of teen magazines in teaching reading. The author believes these magazines need to come into the classroom and be examined as social scripts that shape the lives of teenage girls.

The Overall Writing Structure

In many ways, this study is traditionally structured to emphasize a problem, the data collection, the data analysis, and the interpretation and recommendations. What makes it unusual is the cultural concept—social roles—highlighted at the beginning of the study and the advocacy by the researcher for change emphasized at the end. These elements are clearly part of a critical approach to ethnography.

KEY IDEAS IN THE CHAPTER

An ethnography is a useful design for studying groups in education, their behaviors, beliefs, and language, and how they develop shared patterns of interacting over time. Ethnographic research is a qualitative design for describing, analyzing, and interpreting the patterns of a culture-sharing group. *Culture* is a broad term used to encompass all human behavior and beliefs. Typically, it includes a study of language, rituals, structures, life stages, interactions, and communication. Ethnographers visit the "field," collect extensive data through such procedures as observation and interviewing, and write up a cultural portrait of the group within its setting. Thus, ethnographers stress cultural concepts, and they study a group of individuals at a single site. The researcher examines shared patterns of behaviors, beliefs, and language that have developed over time by engaging in fieldwork such as observing and interviewing people where they live and work. The analysis begins with describing and analyzing the culture-sharing group and interpreting their patterns within the context of culture-at-work. Overall, the ethnographer employs a reflexive inquiry style of being self-conscious about the research and the writing and being respectful of participants.

The origins of this approach are found in anthropology; sociology; the application of anthropological methods to education, and postmodern, reflexive concerns about interpreting data and writing reports. These historical factors have led to three types of ethnographies: realist, case studies, and critical studies. The steps in conducting these ethnographies involve starting with an interest in studying a cultural theme, identifying a bounded site, and examining shared patterns for a group. The researcher poses general research questions to identify shared patterns of behavior, beliefs, or language and also collects extensive fieldwork data. From this data, a general portrait of how the culture-sharing group works is developed through description, analysis, and interpretation. The interpretation and writing are sensitive to the reflexivity of the researcher, and varied forms of writing structures are used.

Conducting an ethnography involves clarifying the intent of the study, selecting an appropriate design, and relating the design to the research problem in the study. Then the researcher needs to seek approval to conduct the study and obtain access to study sites and participants. Once this is accomplished, the ethnographer collects data using multiple sources of information and spending considerable time in the field. After gathering information, the analysis of data consists of describing, analyzing, and interpreting. Some researchers, when conducting a critical ethnography, will identify changes that need to occur and will actively advocate and plan for them. When writing the final research report, ethnographers and case study writers employ practices consistent with their designs, such as being objective, generalizing findings, and discussing how they and the participants changed during the research process.

Useful Information for Producers of Research

- Clarify the intent you have for your ethnographic research. Consider whether you plan to develop patterns and a portrait of a culture-sharing group, provide an in-depth description and analysis of a "case," or advocate for an issue based on studying a culture-sharing group.
- Recognize that many ethnographies today are written using a critical perspective. Read about these forms of ethnographies by consulting books such as Thomas (1993), Carspecken (1995), or Denzin (1997).
- If you conduct a case study, determine whether the issue (instrumental) or the case itself (intrinsic) is of primary interest for addressing your research problem.
- When conducting a realist ethnography, identify a cultural theme that you wish to explore. This cultural theme is the central phenomenon of your study.
- As you collect data in the field for a realist ethnography, look for shared patterns of behavior, beliefs, or language that develop over time.
- Engaging in fieldwork and collecting data involve negotiating relationships with participants and key gatekeepers at research sites. Be respectful of sites and individuals as you conduct your study.
- Consider in your ethnography how you will balance description of the culture-sharing group or case, analysis of themes about the group or case, and interpretation of the meaning of the description and analysis. Ideally, you should give them equal weight, but this would depend on the purposes and the research questions you plan to address in your study.
- Context is important in ethnographies and case studies. Include it in your description as well as in your themes.
- Authors write about how we interpret the "text," or written report, in ethnographic research. Recognize and discuss in your report your own position that affects your interpretation, and acknowledge that multiple interpretations exist in any report, such as those of readers and participants in the study.
- Consider the steps in the process of conducting an ethnography and make adjustments in them to reflect the type of design you use. See Table 15.4 as a guide.

Useful Information for Consumers of Research

- To identify the cultural theme in a realist ethnography, look at the purpose statement and the research question for the central phenomenon being examined.
- Recognize that the final ethnographic report or case study will vary in structure because of the differences among a realist ethnography, a case study, and a critical ethnography.
- Among several factors to use in evaluating an ethnography or case report, especially consider whether the author collects multiple forms of data and spends considerable time in the field gathering information.
- The information researchers may report in an ethnography or case study may be insights from examining a portrait of a culture-sharing group, contributions to understanding cultural themes, an in-depth exploration of a case that has not been examined before, or a plan for action to change or remedy inequities in education and in our society.

Additional Resources You Might Examine

A number of books, listed below, are available to expand your understanding of educational ethnographic research.

Harry Wolcott (1992, 1994, 1995, 1999) has authored four books that, taken as a series, introduce you to all facets of understanding and conducting ethnographic research. His conversational style illustrates good writing and serves as an accessible means for understanding ethnography. His 1999 book is perhaps the best overview of ethnographic practices and ideas available today. Examine Wolcott's books:

Wolcott, H. F. (1992). *Writing up qualitative research.* Newbury Park, CA: Sage.
Wolcott, H. F. (1994). *Transforming qualitative data: Description, analysis, and interpretation.* Thousand Oaks, CA: Sage.
Wolcott, H. F. (1995). *The art of fieldwork.* Walnut Creek, CA: AltaMira.
Wolcott, H. F. (1999). *Ethnography: A way of seeing.* Walnut Creek, CA: AltaMira.

Margaret LeCompte and Jean Schensul (1999) have authored a "toolkit" of seven short books that provides an excellent introduction to ethnography. See their introductory book as a guide to their toolkit:

LeCompte, M. D., & Schensul, J. J. (1999). *Designing and conducting ethnographic research* (Ethnographer's Toolkit No. 1). Walnut Creek, CA: AltaMira.

Another introductory text, now in its third edition, is the book on ethnography for educators by Robert Bogdan and Sari Biklen (1998). This book is a good introductory text to all facets of educational ethnography. See:

Bogdan, R. C., & Biklen, S. K. (1998). *Qualitative research for education: An introduction to theory and methods* (3rd ed.). Boston: Allyn & Bacon.

Practical step-by-step approaches to educational ethnography can be found in two books. David Fetterman's (1998) book, now in its second edition, is like a travelogue, identifying and discussing the major landmarks every ethnographer encounters. For steps and examples in writing fieldnotes in an ethnography, examine the book by Robert Emerson, Rachel Fretz, and Linda Shaw (1995). See:

Fetterman, D. M. (1998). *Ethnography: Step by step* (2nd Ed.). Thousand Oaks, CA: Sage.
Emerson, R. M., Fretz, R. I., & Shaw, L. L. (1995). *Writing ethnographic fieldnotes.* Chicago: University of Chicago Press.

Finally, two books to consult on case study research are Bob Stake's (1995) book on the art of case study research and Sharon Merriam's (1998) introduction to case studies. See:

Stake, R. E. (1995). *The art of case study research.* Thousand Oaks, CA: Sage.
Merriam, S. B. (1998). *Qualitative research and case study applications in education.* San Francisco: Jossey-Bass.

Go to our Companion Website at **www.prenhall.com/creswell** to:

- ◆ assess your understanding of chapter content with Multiple-Choice Questions,
- ◆ apply what you've learned with Essay Questions,
- ◆ practice your research skills with interactive Building Research Skills exercises, and
- ◆ broaden your knowledge of research with Web Links to research topics on the Internet.

Qualitative Charateristics

Queens and Teen Zines: Early Adolescent Females Reading Their Way toward Adulthood

Ethnography Research Characteristics

Margaret J. Finders
Purdue University

(01) *This article documents the reading of teen magazines by middle-class Euro-American seventh-grade girls. Examining the reading of teen zines as a literacy event provides an opportunity to explore how the girls perceive and construct their social roles and relationships as they enter a new cultural scene, the junior high school. Documenting this particular reading practice provides a window onto the complex social negotiations in operation as early adolescent females use literacy to shape emerging social roles. This study holds implications for literacy pedagogy that considers how textual representations serve to define and constrain social roles.*

A qualitative problem requires exploration and understanding.

Ethnographers start with cultural themes.

(02) Against a backdrop of feminist scholarship that emphasizes the social, political, and historical construction of gender (Biklen and Pollard 1993; Britzman 1993; Fine and Macpherson 1993; Griffin 1985; Hooks 1990), a growing body of research has begun to examine the contents of teen zines, magazines marketed for adolescent consumption, magazines marketed to serve adolescent females, in the words of the managing editor of *Seventeen,* "to inform, entertain and give teenage girls all the information they need to make sound choices in their lives" (Peirce 1990:496–497). While teen zines that target the adolescent female claim a focus on personal growth and self-improvement, scholars critique them, citing a narrowness of topics presented and a limited range of available roles for females. According to recent research, magazines such as *Sassy, Seventeen,* and *YM* constrain choices for the adolescent female to a traditional model of finding an adult place in society largely through men and commodities (Evans et al. 1991; Peirce 1990; Stretch 1991). Yet, as you will see, the adolescent females in this study demonstrated little ability to render such an ideology visible. One 12-year-old girl, for example, described her reason for reading teen zines in this way: "They tell you about woman stuff."

The qualitative literature justifies the research problem.

(03) Such "woman stuff" has been the focus of research studies that examine the social, political, and developmental nature of reading. Both school structure and popular adolescent literature have been criticized because they seem to constrict the roles available to young women and serve to reinscribe them into patriarchy (Apple 1986; Gilligan 1988; Stretch 1991). Furthermore, Christian-Smith argues that "through literacy, young women construct and reconstruct their desires and gender subjectivities, as well as their awareness of social differences and power relations" (1993: 1–2). In a study of women romance readers, Radway (1984) argues that reading was constructed as a "declaration of their independence." Following Radway's 1984 study, Willinsky and Hunniford conducted a parallel study of avid young adult romance readers. They report:

> The experience may be vicarious but not the pleasure. . . . With the young readers in this study, whom we found as given to these pleasures as Radway's adults, reading the romance this seriously, they appear on the verge of a total surrender on a number of fronts; they are, in effect, taking more from the books than the adults, more than many of us in education would want to ask. [1993:93]*

The qualitative literature plays a minor role.

The qualitative purpose statement and research questions are broad and general.

The qualitative purpose statement and research questions seek participants' experiences.

Willinsky and Hunniford argue that while Radway's readers cited a private pleasure and an escape from their daily responsibilities, the young romance readers' selection was based on a consistent concern with appearances, a new awareness of physical development, a desire to have a romance just like the heroine's, and a belief that they would live this way (1993:93). In another study of young adult readers, Cherland maintains that girls used reading "in order to exercise agency within approved social domains" (1994:173). She argues that such reading may serve as "combative" (as an escape from being good) and "compensatory" (as a way to feel more powerful). These studies examine fiction reading as it intertwines with an evolving sense of self. As scholars critique the limited subject positions available to adolescent females, the purpose of this article is to add to the ongoing conversation by including the perspective of the adolescent female reading teen magazines. How do early adolescent females read literature that falls outside the realm of fiction? Documenting the lived experiences of early adolescent females fills a gap in our understanding of adolescence by adding to our growing understanding of complex social negotiations in operation as early adolescent females use literacy to shape their social roles,[1] and in turn, how literate practices serve to define and constrain their social roles.

The Study

Qualitative data collection involves studying a small number of individuals or sites.

Ethnographers typically study a group of people.

(04) To more fully understand the perspective of the adolescent female, I undertook a yearlong ethnographic study at one midwestern junior high school during the 1992–93 school year (Finders, in press). This article is a slice of a much larger ethnographic study in which I followed four early adolescent girls (two sets of self-proclaimed best friends and their larger circle of friends) from May of their sixth-grade year through the completion of seventh grade. I focused on seventh graders because seventh grade marked the beginning of the secondary school experience within the district; within the larger culture, secondary school serves as a marker of entry into adolescence. Thus, by virtue of enrollment in a junior high school, focal students were at the threshold of adolescence, at a critical juncture in their academic as well as their social development. In September, they faced an unfamiliar cultural scene, the junior high school. They were just beginning to negotiate their way into this new adolescent arena, learning the social codes as they carved out a sense of shared identity within new groups. Through literate practices, I explore the rules and rituals that accompany entry into adolescence, documenting how adolescent girls perceive and negotiate their social roles and relationships.

Qualitative data collection is based on using protocols developed during the study.

Enthographers look for shared patterns of behaviors, beliefs, and language.

(05) Based upon a sociocultural theoretic framework,[2] emphasis was placed on documenting naturally occurring key incidents, specifically literacy events (Heath 1982).[3] Literacy events serve as a lens to bring into focus the competing expectations and assumptions that the early adolescent female must negotiate among in order to participate fully in each context. The goal of the larger project was to document how each event was framed from the point of view of key participants. By documenting who is present, where and when and for whom such events occurred, I attempt to make visible the tacit rules and demands that shape such events and ultimately shape available social roles within particular social networks. An examination of a group's literacy events will lead to a richer understanding of the dynamics of social networks. Such a focus demands an ethnographic approach (Erickson 1986; Spradley 1980).

Qualitative data collection involves gathering text or image data.

Ethnographers spend extensive time in fieldwork.

(06) Data were obtained by participant-observation (Spradley 1979, 1980) as well as interviewing and collecting written artifacts from participants. I spent 1 year documenting literate practices both in and out of school, tagging

along to athletic events and the mall, listening in on phone conversations, hanging out at slumber parties, and observing language arts classrooms.

(07) I was initially introduced to students in the language arts classrooms as someone from the university who was interested in learning about seventh graders' reading and writing practices. My presence in each classroom was for the most part nonparticipatory. I did not want to be viewed as a teacher or someone in authority; so I did not take on any of the teaching duties and tried not to interact with students during this time. Students gradually became aware that there were particular students that were the focus of my attention. Comments from students such as, "Oh, she's writing a book about girls," seemed to appease curious students. By meeting with focal students informally outside the school context, I gained their trust slowly and negotiated a relationship that did not fit their established patterns with significant adults. In October, for example, I overheard one focal student announcing, "That's not a teacher; that's Peg." I consciously chose dress to distinguish myself from school personnel, most often wearing jeans and tennis shoes.

Qualitative researchers take in a reflexive and biased approach.

(08) As seventh graders, the focal students had limited access to social outings outside the school context, and I occasionally drove them to a pizza parlor or to the mall. This allowed me the opportunity not only to observe them in induced natural contexts but to negotiate a relationship with them that did not position me as an authority figure. Early, there were moments in which I was tested by focal students. On several occasions, a girl would not allow me to see a note that she deemed "too obscene." I did not report such incidents as writing on a restroom wall or faking illness to avoid an exam. I avoided conveying any negative judgment, and as the study progressed, I slowly gained their trust and was permitted to receive literacies still deemed "too gross" for parents or teachers. As the year progressed, focal students began to see their roles as my teacher and wanted me to understand what being a teenager was really like. In order to, as they said, "get it right," I was soon being invited to their slumber parties and dances.

(09) As the study unfolded, teen zines became a central focus because, as will become clear, one group of girls used the zine as a marker, a yardstick to measure how one was progressing into womanhood, possession serving as a sign of one crossing the boundary from childhood into adolescence. As noted earlier, two distinct groups of girls were the centerpiece of the larger study. Teachers, administrators, and the girls themselves identified separate and clearly bounded friendship groups. Individual members carefully patrolled the borders between friendship groups. One group, those called tough cookies by one parent, did not report reading teen zines, and I never observed them carrying zines at school or home. For the other group of friends, those referred to as social queens by parents, reading and carrying a teen zine served, it seems, as a visible rite of passage, as a cultural practice to mark oneself as separate from children, as unlike those other "little kids" and ready to handle "woman stuff." It became increasingly clear that teen zines were used by this group, the social queens, to patrol the borders around their friendship network. Teen zines served as signs to make visible the boundaries between adolescents and children.

Qualitative data analysis consists of describing information and developing themes.

Crossing Developmental Boundaries: Zine Reading as Rite of Passage

(10) Lauren:[4] What do they [the "tough cookies"] read? They probably just read books. They have nothing better to do?

Angie: They probably don't even read these [*holds up a copy of* Sassy].

Tiffany: Did you guys see this? God, I'm gonna get some of these [*holds open a page from* YM *and points to a pair of pants*]. Isn't this so cool?

Qualitative data analysis consists of text analysis.

Angie: Way cool. My mom's gonna let me get some. Do you think I kinda look like her? [*Points to a model in* Sassy]
Lauren: Oh, yeah, right. Give me that. It's my copy. Give me that, you dork.
Angie: Give it to me. Who's the dork? Let me have it. Let me read you something.
Tiffany: Know what? I'm gonna get *YM*. My dad said he'd loan me the money. He'll forget, and I won't have to pay him back.
Angie: Did you take this best friend quiz?
Lauren: Did you see that article about who's in and who's out? I think he is so cool. He's a total babe. I mean B-A-B-E.

(11) After one year of documenting the reading and writing practices of early adolescent females, I regularly came to expect scenes like this one, played out like a well-rehearsed script, girls turning to the pages of teen zines, seeking answers to questions about their place in an adolescent world. The girls in this group turned to the models for advice on their appearance and action. They denied adult presence and most often consumed these magazines hidden behind closed doors, far outside the judgmental gaze of significant adults. Teen zines were most often read in private places such as bedrooms and school restrooms, places that might be considered safe havens from adults and boys.

Ethnographers describe the culture-sharing group.

Ethnographers describe the context of the culture-sharing group.

(12) While, of course, adults produce these magazines, the girls perceived zines as exclusively their own, as out-of-bounds for adults and beyond the reach of children. The girls never acknowledged any adult presence behind the youthful images, and most often considered the models to be the authors. When pushed by me to unpack the "they" that the early adolescents so often referred to in their talk about the magazines ("They tell you about boys and stuff," "They show you cool stuff," "They know what it's like to be a teenager today"), each focal student pointed to photographs of models within the magazines, and each denied adult presence behind the text.

(13) Looking to the models as older, more knowledgeable peers, the early adolescents sought their advice on hair care, fashion, friendships, entertainment, and sexual encounters. Regarding such topics as "woman stuff," the social queens were in a sense claiming for themselves adult positions. Yet at the same time they rejected this position. Searching for answers to questions about womanhood, the girls hid their concerns from adult women, arguing, "They don't understand." From their perspective, the models, in contrast to their mothers or teachers, "know what's it's like to be a teenager today."

(14) Their emerging sexuality, while clearly the central focus of such "woman stuff," was hidden from significant adults. From the queens' perspective, romance and sexuality were clearly aligned with appropriate adult behavior, yet regarded as taboo in the presence of adults. Conversations that surrounded the reading of teen zines were often labeled "too gross" for parents or teachers. The mature content was the stuff of an emerging sexual self. Caught between competing social roles, the queens negotiated topics that were deemed too obscene for an adult audience in the company of their peers.

(15) Distinguishing between adults and teens, girls in this social group reported with pride that their teachers and parents did not approve of such reading practices, making such comments as, "She [my mother] wants me to read books, but I read *Sassy*," "I put one [teen zine] in my notebook and read it during class, and Mr. T doesn't even know it," "My mom doesn't like them. I hide them in my science folder." Those who carried zines

were in a sense using literacy to make visible their entry into adolescence. Literacy served as an act of self-presentation. Not only were the queens documenting interest in what they considered mature content, but perhaps what is more important, they were demonstrating their defiance of adult authority by breaking the perceived rules of what constituted appropriate reading materials.

(16) The presence of zines was used to document one's passage into adolescence, and zine absence was noted as well. I, like many middle-class Euro-American adults, assumed that teen zines were the rave of all seventh-grade girls. Before I continue with a more detailed description of the reading practices of these seventh-grade girls, it must be noted that while the introductory scene is typical, it depicts only one part of the school population. It marks a boundary around one particular group of girls. The only girls who carried zines at school were the social queens, the group of friends who were active in extracurricular school activities and social events. While the queens regularly reported reading and buying zines, the other group denied reading them. Likewise, I saw no magazines in their homes.

(17) Lauren, a member of the social queens and one of the peer-reported "most popular" girls in the school, regularly referred to her friends as "normal teenagers" and as "regular teens" and often cited *Sassy* as a source of proof for appropriate teen dress and conduct. "See, this is cool," she reported, matching a magazine photograph of a pair of shorts with her own. Using teen zines as a way of borrowing authority, Lauren assessed her appearance and dress against the standards present in the magazine. On another occasion, after describing *YM* to me, Lauren asked, "What do the other girls [referring to Cleo and her friends, those girls who were considered by the queens to be "dogs" and "little kids"] read? They probably just read books. They don't have anything better to do. "Notice Lauren's distinction between friendship groups. From her perspective, zines were markers for adolescents who were no longer "girls" but now were defining themselves as teens. In contrast to appropriate girls' behavior to just "read books" because "they don't have anything better to do," teenagers, according to Lauren, were compelled by their newly acquired roles as adolescents to concern themselves with physical appearance and meeting zine standards of "cool." Queens used the teen zine as a way to document a rejection of the position of child.

(18) Angie, another of the social queens, wondered of Cleo's group, "Don't they care what they look like? They look like little kids. God, they wouldn't even know what to do with stuff like this," pointing to fashions in a current zine. The queens referred to those who did not read zines or adhere to their standards as "little kids" rather than "normal teenagers." Borrowing authority from the pages of the zines, the social queens measured status by the closeness of their match to zine fashions and used the zines to mark particular groups of early adolescent females as insiders.

(19) In contrast to Lauren's and Angie's embrace of zines, Cleo, one of the focal students who was a resident of a trailer park on the extreme eastern edge of town, was keenly aware that zines were not for her. Early in the year, one seventh-grade language arts teacher suggested that *Seventeen* magazine might be a possible publication source for some of her students' recent poems. Cleo told me privately, "That's not for me." Although her tone may have been intended to convey that she was far above this type of material, Cleo, at age 12, was already keenly aware of her place in the peer dynamic, her place in terms of socioeconomic status. Cleo's perception of zines as "not for me" matched the facts that she did not have the economic resources

necessary to participate in the social events surrounding the reading of zines, and zines were, in fact, used against her to mark her as deficient.

(20) Zine readings serve these adolescents at a very literal level. They created visible boundaries. On the social-sexual journey toward adulthood, they provided signposts to document progress. Zine readings serve adolescents to unite particular groups of peers and exclude others, serving as a powerful tool to mark insiders and outsiders.

(21) When one examines zines as a literacy event, it becomes quite apparent why Cleo would not be interested in them, why she could so matter of factly report that these magazines were "not for me," and why Lauren would turn to teen zines. Zines were marketed for one particular type of reader, the social queen, the middle-class female.

(22) So this becomes the story of the queens and the zines

Ethnographers analyze the culture-sharing group for themes.

Queens Reading Zines: Negotiating a Presentation of Self

(23) Angie: Hey, did you guys know that . . . [*and she begins to read from* Sassy, *one of the most popular teen zines*].

Lauren: Let me have that. [*She pulls the magazine from Angie's grasp. Angie attempts to continue reading by shoving up against Lauren's shoulder.*]

Tiffany: That really pisses me off. Mine never comes first. [*She rips the magazine out of her friend's hand. The girls laugh and wrestle over possession.*]

Angie: Do you know what it's got? [*Leaning across the library table, she grabs the magazine back, flips through the pages, searching for one article.*] It's got this really gross article about sleeping with *your* step-dad.

Lauren: God, that is gross. I wouldn't sleep with my step-dad. Can you even imagine you and Larry?

Tiffany: Gross.

Lauren: Gross.

(24) This brief exchange between seventh-grade girls typifies conversations that surround the reading of teen zines. After careful analysis of repeated occurrences of zine reading, three themes emerged from my data: (1) reading was an exclusive social event, (2) reading was used to ascribe special status, and (3) experiences reported in the magazines were appropriated by the girls as their own.

Reading as an Exclusive Social Event

(25) First, reading of these magazines was rarely a solitary act. While a sociocultural perspective focuses on literacy as socially based and culturally specific (Langer 1991), beyond learning meaning in culturally appropriate ways, the girls in this study quite literally read in groups. Zine reading was fiercely social. Groups of girls crowded together on a bed, in a large recliner, or in the corner of the school library to devour the cherished possession and negotiate a unified front as to their collective opinion of each article and advertisement. Often times, the arrival in the mail of a teen zine necessitated a "sleep over" to "hang together and look at our magazines." Social queens made arrangement to gather with the expressed purpose of "just hanging out and looking at magazines." These seventh-grade girls often bagged up back issues to cart to a Friday-night slumber party.

(26) I spent five hours at one such event. When I arrived at Angie's, her mother let me in and said, "Just follow the noise. They're already upstairs." I walked into Angie's bedroom, hairspray mist creating a

perfumed fog, music and giggles vibrating the glossy teen photographs and celebrated designer labels that had been carefully removed from clothing or torn from the pages of teen zines and taped to the walls. Once I settled in on a corner of the bed, the girls quit screaming and resumed their activities. Angie returned to her position, curling and spraying Tiffany's long auburn locks in front of a full-length mirror that was framed with images of adolescent beauty, snapshots of friends juxtaposed with the latest models trimmed from the pages of *Sassy* and *Seventeen*. Beside me, Lauren continued to flip through the pages of a zine, making a series of statements, "This is cool," "He is so cute," "This dress is so totally awesome." Such statements were regularly interrupted with a question, "Do you think he is cute?" "Do you think that's cool?" "God, she's pretty?" After each question, usually delivered with a tone that conveyed an assumed answer, Tiffany and Angie would turn from the mirror to glance momentarily at the picture in question and then together would answer "Yeah" or "Not."

(27) It was almost always a mutual agreement. The girls rarely disagreed, and when they did, they argued until a consensus was reached. Someone would have to give up on her opinion. Someone always did. No page was turned until the girls all agreed about fashion or face, beauty or body.

(28) These girls, it seems, were performing as members of what Goffman (1959) calls "performance teams," defined as "any set of individuals who co-operate in staging a single routine" (Goffman 1959:79). According to Goffman, individuals on a team work together backstage in order to present a unified front when they are on center stage. Scenes like this one, played out in the girls' bedrooms and in the school restrooms, match what Goffman described as backstage rehearsals for their more public performances. Goffman describes such private arenas as backstage regions defined in the following manner:

> Here costumes and other parts of personal front may be adjusted and scrutinized for flaws. Here the team can run through its performance, checking for offending expressions when no audience is present to be affronted by them; here poor members of the team, who are expressively inept, can be schooled or dropped from the performance. [Goffman 1959:112]

On this particular Friday night, these early adolescents were practicing their emerging adolescent roles, rehearsing their opinions with the help of a carefully constructed script, the teen zine. Allocated to backstage regions, the queens used zines to check and test ways of being adolescent. Those who were deemed in need of remediation were schooled by the others with the zine serving as an authoritative textbook. Queens made such remarks as, "Duh, you are so stupid. Look at this" (pointing to a page in *Sassy*), and "Geez, you should wear your hair like this" (pointing to a page in *YM*).

(29) At this developmental period, while much may have appeared unstable, zines provided solid guidelines. The girls often reported, "See, it shows you what's cool." At a time when all rules and rituals appear to be in flux, when even her body forsakes her, the early adolescent can turn to the pages of a teen zine for firm control. This illusion of stability provides a sense of power and control in a world that is often perceived as out of control. In entering the new social arena of adolescence, zines served as a handbook.

Reading as a Tool to Ascribe Special Status

(30) Second, the girls used teen zines to assign special status. At a literal level, there appeared to be two dimensions of status building: being first to possess the latest issue of a zine, and what is more important, ownership of

that copy. Note Tiffany's comment, "That really pisses me off. Mine never comes first." For these girls, it was very important to be first; copies borrowed from a friend or from the library carry much less clout. When a magazine was borrowed, one could not control the circulation as readily, and one could not control distribution of individual pages. The girl who arrived at school or at a slumber party first with the latest issue of a teen zine tucked under her arm wielded more power and prestige, controlling circulation of the latest important information about fashion, beauty, and entertainment.

(31) When a magazine arrived, the girls whom I talked to rushed to obtain that coveted position of being first by calling a best friend before the cover of the magazine has even been opened. As the phone was ringing, one hurried to find an article worthy of reading into the receiver in order to prove that one was indeed first. Being first merited clout because one's name became attached to the latest information. Comments such as "Lauren says that there is this awesome fingernail polish in *YM*," and "Lauren says that the Mall of America is bigger than a bunch of football fields" circulated around the junior high.

(32) On another level, status was achieved by possessing the closest match to the teens in the text. Although Angie had been the envy of two of her best friends since she began subscribing to *Sassy* in the middle of her sixth-grade year, she did not hold the powerful position of director. It is hardly surprising that that role was assigned to Lauren, who was claimed by all as "the prettiest" with "the best bod," and "she's the one with the most boyfriends." In other words, Lauren's physical features represented the closest match to those present on the pages of any zine. As director, Lauren regularly orchestrated the actions and opinions of the other girls. So whenever the girls got together to negotiate their collective opinions, Lauren most often held the magazine and held the final word.

Appropriating Reading Experiences

(33) A strong sense of community bridged from those present in the text to those present in the immediate context. The queens talked about the articles as if each carried an implicit command that one must follow in order to achieve high status. Their talk implied a powerful connectedness to the teens in the magazines. Following is one such incident in which the conversation weaves in and out from text to immediate bedroom scene, lacing them together in the present:

Angie: So what did Ronnie say about me?
Lauren: He said that you are fine. He goes, "She's a babe."
Tiffany: Come on, Lauren.
Angie: You know what? I just broke out in zits majorly.
Tiffany: Me too. It must be zit week or something.
Lauren: I know, I look in the mirror and, God. Did you take this kissing quiz [reference to a quiz in one of the teen zines]?
Tiffany: I was giving Sara the quiz on the phone. Do you have any sweats?
Angie: I don't have any sweats. I got some stretch pants you can wear.
Tiffany: Dang, this curling iron doesn't even work.
Lauren: Maybe I should get some of these [reference to jeans in advertisement]. When I get older, I'm gonna get braces so my teeth will look like this. [*Points to model in teen zine.*]
Angie: I want to try on those colored pocket pants of yours. Can I?
Lauren: Do it. Ouch! *Watch* where you sit.

Tiffany: Okay, here's this thing. [*She begins reading from a zine.*] "As my boyfriend and I are leaving my house to go to the game, my little sister had to come along [*inaudible, breaks into laughter*], and, and she asks me why I had put so many tissues in my bra."

Girls appropriated the experiences reported in the articles as their own. Just as Angie said, "sleeping with *your* step-dad," Lauren and Tiffany regularly used the pronouns "you" and "your" and directly made claims that the young women in the advertisements and articles were "just like me." In interviews, they said such things as "It [*Sassy*] tells the most embarrassing things of *your* life," and "I read it [*Sassy*] because I want to know about AIDS and stuff, and I want to know what happens to girls *just like me.*" In some ways the teens in the zines were just like them. A content analysis of the three top-selling teen magazines revealed those zines were populated in the following manner: Euro-American females, 65.2 percent; Euro-American males, 24.5 percent; non-Euro-American females, 7.7 percent; and non-Euro-American males, 2.6 percent; with adults of any color rare and limited to the even rarer educational career article (Evans et al. 1991:109).

(34) The invisibility of adults and the strong sense of sameness may have fostered a sense of seamless connection between their friends and experiences with those in the zines. Zines were often held up almost like a mirror and used, it seems, to reinforce cultural standards of adolescent beauty. Just as books provide mirrors for early adolescents (Willinsky and Hunniford 1993), the teen zine was held up as a looking glass to assess one's physical appearance. Social queens often pointed to teen zines and asked, "Do you think I look like her?" "Do you think my hair looks like this?" "Do you think these jeans would look good on me?"

(35) Lacking a critical distance that fiction creates, zines were received as truth: "They tell you about woman stuff" and "I want to know what happens to girls just like me." Similar to Bakhtin's (1981) suggestion that words come out of other people's mouths, the girls often quite literally lifted phrases directly from the pages to become part of the language of the social queens. When I asked the social queens to describe their best friends, their descriptions contained not only the rhythms and constructions but often times the exact words that fill the texts of the teen zines. According to Shuman, one may "appropriate another's voice as a means of borrowing authority" (1993:136). The girls in this study, it seems, borrowed authority from zine models. Here are some descriptions of their best friends: "She has her thick, dark, luxurious hair that you could die for and beautiful sky-blue eyes," "She has a perfect creamy complexion and a perfect posture," "Yeah, Angie is pretty. She has a perfect face, but her hips are too wide." In separate interviews, when asked to describe a best friend, the word "perfect" emerged in seven out of eight interviews and was repeated at least twice in three. As one listens in, one is struck by the emphasis upon perfection, on the singular standard that is so well established that a 13-year-old is marked because her hips are already "too wide" by an agreed upon standard that celebrates slimness. Certainly, this emphasis on physical perfection cannot be attributed solely to the reading of teen zines. Yet one cannot deny the power of the repeated occurrence of these girls' reading zines and asking, "Am I fatter than her?" "Do I kinda look like her?" One cannot deny the power of the representation of the singular model available to adolescent females in these magazines.

Reading Fluff: "You Don't Have to Think About It"

(36) In December of their seventh-grade year, Tiffany reported that she was "finally allowed to spend my own Christmas money to get *Sassy.*" She had

succeeded, in her own words, "by ragging my mom for about a year." Their disagreements over teen magazines became clear during my first visit to their home. Following is a bit of transcription from that evening.

M.F.: What else do you read? Do you read any magazines?
Tiffany: *YM.* [*She giggles and looks at her mother out of the corner of her eye.*]
M.F.: Do you get that at home?
Tiffany: I don't get them, but I get them at the library. [*She turns to plead for her mother to buy the magazine for her.*] But, Mom, get them. That's what I read.
Mother: [*Laughs and reaches over to the magazine rack to pick up a copy of* YM.] I'm not really comfortable with these teen magazines.
Tiffany: Mom!
Mother: She likes to read trash.
Tiffany: Yep!
Mother: Well, the advertisements are just too sensual.
Tiffany: [*Taking the copy from her mother, she slowly turns the pages, scrutinizing each one.*] What advertisements?
Mother: Maybe when she gets older she can get those magazines. I can't think that that reading experience will *broaden* your horizons. [*Her sarcastic tone and glance are directed toward Tiffany. She turns back to me.*] But she is reading.

One can sense the tensions in this parent. On the one hand she did not want her daughter to be exposed to such "sensual" materials, but on the other hand she acknowledged that such contents motivated her daughter's reading. She explained further about her daughter's time spent reading *YM.* "I know it's not wasted. It's still reading, but it's like fluff." Later in the conversation, this parent admitted that she, like her daughter, often enjoyed what she called "reading fluff." She said, "I do a lot of studying now, and I think I've got to find something that's just that [fluff]. When I pick something up, a *McCalls* or a newsstand-type magazine and read those things, you don't have to think about it. I suppose that's very similar to what you do, Tiff."

(37) Clearly, Tiffany's reading was very similar to her mother's account of reading as "fluff." What was missed in this discussion of "fluff reading" was Tiffany's misreading of the advertisements. In magazines that according to Evans et al. 1991 give 46 percent of their total space over to advertisements, it might seem remarkable that Tiffany was blind to it. On the following day at school, I asked Tiffany to explain about the advertisement in the magazines. She insisted, "There aren't any ads." And she proceeded to prove it to me. Pulling the latest issue of *Sassy* from her notebook, turning from ads to articles through full- and half-page ads, she argued, "This tells you about fingernail polish. This shows you about makeup. This is about zits and stuff. *See?*"

(38) Tiffany's emphasis on "See?" illustrates her use of these magazines as a kind of proof. She trusted the editors to do exactly what those at *Seventeen* had promised, "to provide her with all of the information she needed to make sound choices" (Peirce 1990:496–497). The seduction of these magazines is powerful. While it may appear that Tiffany was just extremely naive, the layout of teen zines is, in fact, quite seductive. Articles and advertisements look remarkably alike. Articles often times are presented as whole-page photos with a column on the left that details the dress complete with designer names and suggested retail prices.

(39) The social queens in this study used the articles and advertisements alike as criteria for establishing their own social roles and for judging those

of others. They pointed to the models in the pages to ask, "Am I fatter than her?" "Would that look good on me?" "Do you think that's cool?" "Do I look like her?" rehearsing their values and opinions with the assistance of these magazines marketed specifically for them. They measured their friends and foes alike by the singular standard that permeates the pages of *YM, Sassy, Teen,* and *Seventeen.* Queens called other girls "woof-woofs" and literally barked at those who they deemed did not measure up to standards of physical beauty.

(40) While some parents may label teen zines "fluff," they are neither benign nor neutral. They transport a powerful economic ideology into the lives of these early adolescents who are bathed in a set of societal norms for women. Teen zines echo the larger societal influences that constrict and enable particular gendered roles. Just as Tiffany's mother described this type of reading as reading in which "you don't have to think," the girls demonstrate little ability to render such an ideology conscious. The comment "What advertisements?" illustrates dramatically how these teens are lulled into accepting such a constrictive economic package. When one observes how readily these girls appropriate the words, experiences, and images as their own, one can hardly deny the impact of these texts upon the social construction of self. These teens accepted such images as a ruler by which adolescent girls measure their own successes as they try on more adult roles. Such messages, while quite overt to critical scholars, remain invisible to these early adolescents. These girls were left to their own devices to interpret, integrate, and mediate the images and text. These messages read over and over become scripts for the girls and will be impossible to revise unless they are made visible.

(41) Teen zines were generally consumed hidden behind closed doors, far outside the judgmental gaze of significant adults. Even within the pages themselves, there is a notable lack of adult images (Evans et al. 1991). By concealing any adult presence, teen zines were embraced by early adolescent females as their own; yet the layout and content are orchestrated by adults to make these early adolescents into a particular kind of female.

Teaching Subliterature: Implications for Pedagogy

Qualitative interpretations situate findings within larger meanings.

(42) These magazines, like their teen-romance-novel companions, are most often shunned by parents and teachers and cast into the category of subliterature. Considered lacking in literary qualities, these texts find no home in school curricula. I am not suggesting, however, that zines should be disregarded as trash reading or be censored. On the contrary, I wonder what might happen if some of the arguments made by feminists and researchers began to circulate in language arts classrooms? The consequence of allocating zines to the realms of subliterature is leaving the social scripts tacit and unexamined.

(43) Teachers that I talked with characterized magazines as "light reading, something they can do on their own," and they required novels read during reading time at school. One reported, "I want them to read novels. They can choose whatever they want, but it has to have a sustained story. That stuff [reference to magazines] they can read on their own time." Tiffany's mother explained that this kind of reading material was the kind of reading in which "you don't have to think." Teachers, as well, considered magazines to be "light reading," implying a lack of necessity for critical thinking.

(44) I advocate a pedagogy that cracks the veneer of this "light reading." I advocate a pedagogy that situates reading not simply as an aesthetic experience but a political act as well. Moss (1995) challenges existing assumptions about the relationships between texts and readers. She argues

Ethnographers interpret and write from a reflexive position.

that the assumptions that texts are potentially powerful in their effect rest upon a notion of vulnerable readers. Moss argues further:

> For what matters about texts is not the content alone, but the way that content can be mobilized and used by readers. And feminists would expect differences here to be governed, not by randomly individual choice, but by social and collective histories. In other words, we would expect there to be conflicting readings, which could not be settled by reference to the text alone. Rather than attempting to close things down by fixing once and for all what the text means, feminism would fore-ground the social strategies readers bring to the text. [1995:162]

(45) Moss advocates a pedagogical approach that calls for an ethnography of reading which would replace a personal response to reading and "stress the role diverse social and cultural practices play in shaping how texts get read" (1995:163). I strongly agree. In order to examine the seemingly homogeneous model that is presented to teens in such a slick package, the cultural assumptions beneath the images must be brought to the surface. What if the slim white models who populate the pages of teen zines found their way into an ethnography of reading? Provided with an arena for critical discussion, students might open up the possibilities for multiple perspectives.

(46) This, of course, is complicated by the very nature of the marketing of teen zines, perceived by the girls to be just outside the boundaries. The very facts that mothers and teachers grimaced and refused to buy or buy into them lead some teens straight to these sources. So by appropriating teen zines into a curriculum, by changing the perceived boundaries, any critique will lose some of its power by the very fact that placement within the context of the classroom has lessened the appeal and stolen exclusive ownership. What makes them so appealing is that they are "just for me," and they are perceived of as outside the control of adults. Like the girls in Cherland's (1994) study, this reading served as "combative" (as an escape from being good) and "compensatory" (as a way to feel more powerful). Rather than embrace the literacies that the school promotes, these teens were looking for unsanctioned literacies in order to stake their own claim, to mark their separation from the established authority. Such renegade reading served as a powerful tool to gain status and group solidarity. Like the Smithton women reading romances (Radway 1984), the social queens used zine reading as a "declaration of their independence." In order to move into adulthood, these early adolescents sought unsanctioned literacies to demonstrate independence. For them, the content of the curriculum constructed clear boundaries, dividing sanctioned from unsanctioned literacies. Using teen zines as curricular content devalues the keen sense of exclusive rights and diminishes the power of possession as a visible marker of adolescent control. Furthermore, classroom-based critiques of the zines will, of course, be social interactions in which the participants stand to gain and lose status among peers. How powerful can a pedagogy be if it counters critique by its very willingness to examine it? There are no simple answers.

(47) Yet how can one expect a critical stance when there is no suggestion of any alternative readings? The social queens were becoming exactly what marketers have trained them to be, consumers and competitors for men's desires. At age 12 and 13, they had few resources or experiences to resist such powerful images. They were, indeed, vulnerable readers. And a pedagogy must provide them with the tools to become critical readers and thinkers.

(48) I advocate a more explicit examination of the complexities that shape literacy learning, an unmasking of the ways in which textual representations construct social roles. I advocate a pedagogy that explicitly acknowledges

the political motivations that serve to define and limit available social roles. For example, examining the social, historical, and cultural motivations of particular roles available—in texts, classrooms, and the larger culture—will lead students to more critical awareness and thus, it is hoped, to the ability to revise those roles. A teacher might contrast *Sassy* with *Teen Voices* (an alternative magazine, published by Women's Express, Inc., that does not accept advertising), inviting students to ponder over the implications of advertising, pushing students toward more fully understanding how economics enable and constrain texts. Clearly, the girls' rejection of adult influence may blunt the power of any school-based critique of these popular texts. But if students learn to ask questions about the construction of social roles available in all texts and are taught to analyze the race, class, and gender relations as they are represented in texts, especially in other canonical works, students will learn to be critical consumers and producers of texts. Asking political questions about the social roles available in fiction, nonfiction, and the larger culture, teachers may begin to assist these early adolescents in adopting a critical stance. It becomes clearer in examining how these teens read zines that what is missing is the necessary addition of layers of critical reflection, an exploration of the ways in which particular texts situate individuals. Bringing a sociocultural pedagogy into the classroom is a necessary step. In addition to learning to ask about the aesthetic of any text, students need to learn to ask about its politics. Who is being privileged? Why are these stories being told at this particular historic moment? How might the woman's role be represented differently at a different historic period? Whose interests are being served? Teaching early adolescents to ask questions about the sociocultural construction of roles will lead students to a deeper understanding of how textual representations reflect and define the roles available in the larger culture.

(49) In looking for solid answers, in seeking stability in this new social arena, the queens turned to texts as authoritative. Just as Tiffany reported, "This tells you about fingernail polish. This shows you about makeup. This is about zits and stuff," zines served as a kind of proof. "See, they show you what's cool," Angie explained. For Angie and her friends, there was no awareness of how these texts served to constrain their lived experiences. For these teens, these texts were embraced with little sense of answering back, no critical doubt, no disruption, no tension. To these early adolescents, the zine was authoritative and monovocal. There appeared to be no sense of a text as dialogic (Bakhtin 1981). While according to Bakhtin (1981) there is a constant struggle between the authoritative and internally persuasive functions of discourse, no such struggle was evident in the reading of teen zines. How can one expect a critical stance when there is no awareness of the motivations that hide behind texts, where there has been no sense of negotiating, no answering back? I am suggesting that we open up classroom discussions to how texts situate us.

(50) As educators we might create a tiny tear in the seamless packaging of these zines. Rather than deny the power of such texts by allocating them to the realm of subliterature, I might suggest that we investigate, as Miller (1994) argues, how texts serve to define and limit lived experiences. If we deny our power as educators, we deny our students the opportunity to rewrite cultural and social scripts. We must teach skills in examining text as socially constructed for particular purposes. Unaware of alternative roles, the queens turned solely to teen zines to guide and measure their growth into womanhood. The other group, who for the most part were missing from this discussion, might appear to have resisted the singular role construction for the adolescent female, yet they hardly fared better.

Qualitative research reports use flexible and emerging structures and evaluation criteria.

With neither the economic resources nor the political clout to speak out, they remained silent as the queens wielded their borrowed power over them. While Lauren, Angie, and Tiffany rehearsed their roles to secure their place in society through romance and commodities, Cleo was reminded again and again that there was no place for her.

Notes

Acknowledgments. I appreciate the helpful commentary on earlier drafts of this article made by Julie Cheville, Carolyn Colvin, and Cynthia Lewis.

1. Social roles, as used here, are defined as performances assigned to a given status in a given context, as the enactment of rights and duties attached to a given status. Drawing extensively on Erving Goffman (1959, 1961), I use the term *social role* to suggest that one's role shifts depending on who is present and what the established expectations are of those present. In this manner, I argue that roles are not static but represent multiple and shifting selves.

2. This sociocultural framework is based on the theory that all utterances take place within a social situation; there is no such thing as an isolated speaker or text (Vygotsky 1962, 1978). Thought is mediated through language, which is a product of social interrelationships, a dialectic between self and community. Extending the theories of Vygotsky, Wertsch (1991) draws on Bakhtin (1981) to develop a more comprehensive understanding of voice as dialogic that emphasizes the dynamism of every text and the situatedness of the speaker within cultural, historical, and institutional settings.

3. Throughout this study, I maintained a focus on literacy events as defined by Heath as "a conceptual tool useful in examining within particular communities of modern society the actual forms and functions of oral and literate traditions and co-existing relationships between spoken and written language. A literacy event is any occasion in which a piece of writing is integral to the nature of participants' interactions and their interpretive processes" (1982:93).

4. All names used in this article are pseudonyms, required by the human-subjects protocol.

Margaret J. Finders is a assistant professor of English education at Purdue University, and author of *"Just Girls": The Literate Life and Underlife of Early Adolescent Girls,* in Press.

References Cited

Apple, Michael
1986 Teachers and Texts: A Political Economy of Class and Gender Relations in Education. New York: Routledge.
Bakhtin, Mikhail M.
1981 The Dialogic Imagination. Austin: University of Texas Press.
Biklen, Sari, and Diane Pollard
1993 Gender and Education: Ninety-Second Yearbook of the National Society for the Study of Education. Chicago: University of Chicago Press.
Britzman, Debra
1993 Beyond Rolling Models: Gender and Multicultural Education. *In* Gender and Education: Ninety-Second Yearbook of the National Society for the Study of Education. Sari Biklen and Diane Pollard, eds. pp. 25–42. Chicago: University of Chicago Press.
Cherland, Meredith
1994 Private Practices: Girls Reading Fiction and Constructing Identity. London: Taylor and Francis.
Christian-Smith, Linda
1993 Constituting and Reconstituting Desire: Fiction, Fantasy and Femininity. *In* Texts of Desire: Essays on Fiction, Feminity and Schooling. Linda Christian-Smith, ed. Pp. 1–8. London: Falmer Press.
Erickson, Frederick
1986 Qualitative Methods in Research on Teaching. *In* Handbook of Research on Teaching, 3rd edition. M. C. Wittrock, ed. Pp. 119–161. New York: Macmillan.
Evans, Ellis, Judith Rutberg, Carmela Sather, and Charli Turner
1991 Content Analysis of Contemporary Teen Magazines for Adolescent Females. Youth and Society 23(1):99–120.
Finders, Margaret
In press "Just Girls": The Literate Life and Underlife of Early Adolescent Girls. New York: Teachers College Press.

Fine, Michelle, and Pat Macpherson
1993 Over Dinner: Feminism and Adolescent Female Bodies. *In* Gender and Education: Ninety-Second Yearbook of the National Society for the Study of Education. Sari Biklen and Diane Pollard, eds. Pp. 126–154. Chicago: University of Chicago Press.
Gilligan, Carol
1988 Moral Voices: Adolescent Development and Secondary Education. Cambridge, MA: Harvard University Graduate School of Education.
Goffman, Erving
1959 The Presentation of Self in Everyday Life. New York: Doubleday & Company.
1961 Asylums: Essays on the Social Situation of Mental Patients and Other Inmates. Chicago: Aldine Publishing.
Griffin, Christine
1985 Typical Girls: Young Women from School to the Job Market. New York: Routledge and Kegan Paul Methuen.
Heath, Shirley Brice
1982 Protean Shapes in Literacy Events: Evershifting Oral and Literate Traditions. *In* Spoken and Written Language: Exploring Orality and Literacy. Deborah Tannen, ed. Advances in Discourse Processes, 9. Pp. 91–117. Norwood, NJ: Ablex.
Hooks, Bell
1990 Yearning: Race, Gender and Cultural Politics. Boston: South End Press.
Langer, Judith
1991 Literacy and Schooling: A Sociocognitive Perspective. *In* Literacy for a Diverse Society. Elfrieda Hiebert, ed. Pp. 9–27. New York: Teachers College Press.
Miller, Richard
1994 Fault Lines in the Contact Zone. College English 56(4):389–408.
Moss, Gemma
1995 Rewriting Reading. *In* Debates and Issues in Feminist Research and Pedagogy. Janet Holland and Maud Blair, eds. Pp. 157–168. Clevedon: Open University.
Peirce, Kate
1990 A Feminist Theoretical Perspective on the Socialization of Teenage Girls through Seventeen Magazine. Sex Roles 23(9/10):491–500.
Radway, Janice
1984 Reading the Romance: Women, Patriarchy and Popular Fiction. Chapel Hill: University of North Carolina Press.
Shuman, Amy
1993 "Get Outa My Face": Entitlement and Authoritative Discourse. *In* Responsibility and Evidence in Oral Discourse. S. Hill and J. Irvine, eds. Pp. 135–160. New York: Cambridge University Press.
Spradley, James
1979 The Ethnographic Interview. Fort Worth: Holt, Rinehart and Winston.
1980 Participant Observation. New York: Holt. Rinehart and Winston.
Stretch, Cynthia
1991 From Self-Awareness to Self-Mastery: Literacy and the Discourse of Body Consciousness in Teen Magazines. Unpublished manuscript.
Vygotsky, Lev
1962 Thought and Language. Cambridge, MA: Harvard University Press.
1978 Mind in Society. Cambridge, MA: Harvard University Press.
Wertsch, James
1991 Voices of the Mind: A Sociocultural Approach to Mediated Action. Cambridge, MA: Harvard University Press.
Willinsky, John, and R. Mark Hunniford
1993 Reading the Romance Younger: The Mirrors and Fears of a Preparatory Literature. *In* Texts of Desire; Essays on Fiction, Feminity and Schooling. Linda Christian-Smith, ed. Pp. 87–105. London: Falmer Press.

CHAPTER

16 Narrative Research Designs

People live storied lives. They tell stories to share their lives with others and to provide their personal accounts about classrooms, schools, educational issues, and the settings in which they work. When people tell stories to researchers, they feel listened to, and their information brings researchers closer to the actual practice of education. Thus, stories reported in qualitative narrative research enrich the lives of both the researcher and the participant. This chapter defines narrative research, identifies when you use it, assesses the key characteristics of it, and advances the steps in conducting and evaluating this design.

By the end of this chapter, you should be able to:

- Describe the major types of narrative studies.
- Define what it means to explore the experiences of an individual.
- Describe the type of information that goes into building a chronology of an individual's experiences.
- Identify the aspects of a "story" and the types of data used to report the "story."
- Describe the process of restorying in narrative research.
- Identify the use of themes in a narrative study.
- Define the setting or context that goes into a narrative study.
- Identify strategies for collaboration with participants in narrative research.
- Identify several types of issues that may arise in gathering narrative stories.
- Describe the steps used in conducting a narrative study.
- List criteria for evaluating a narrative study.

Maria chooses a narrative design for her research project studying the possession of weapons by high school students. Maria's teacher friend, Millie, has a story to tell about how she encountered a student in the high school who was hiding a weapon in his locker. Maria studies this question: "What is the story of a teacher who found a student hiding a weapon in her high school?" Maria interviews Millie and listens to her stories about her experiences with the student, with other teachers, and with the school principal. The story falls into an easy chronology from the initial incident to the follow-up discussions. To make the story as accurate as possible, Maria collaborates with Millie in writing the story, and she shares the written report as it unfolds. Maria engages in narrative research.

WHAT IS NARRATIVE RESEARCH?

The term *narrative* comes from the verb "to narrate" or "to tell (as a story) in detail" (Ehrlich, Flexner, Carruth, & Hawkins, 1980, p. 442). In **narrative research designs**, researchers describe the lives of individuals, collect and tell stories about people's lives, and write narratives of individual experiences (Connelly & Clandinin, 1990). As a distinct form of qualitative research, a narrative typically focuses on studying a single person, gathering data through the collection of stories, reporting individual experiences, and discussing the meaning of those experiences for the individual. With recent popularity, national research conferences have devoted sessions and papers to it, and educational journals have published stories reported by teachers, students, and other educators. New books are now available from publishers that provide essential information about the process of conducting this form of qualitative inquiry.

When Do You Use Narrative Research?

You use narrative research when you have individuals willing to tell their stories and you want to report their stories. For educators looking for personal experiences in actual school settings, narrative research offers practical, specific insights. By conducting narrative studies, researchers establish a close bond with the participants. This may help reduce a commonly held perception by practitioners in the field that research is distinct from practice and has little direct application. Additionally, for participants in a study, sharing their stories may make them feel that their stories are important and that they are heard. When they tell a story, it helps them understand topics that they need to process (McEwan & Egan, 1995). Telling stories is a natural part of life, and individuals all have stories about their experiences to tell others. In this way, narrative research captures an everyday, normal form of data that is familiar to individuals.

You use narrative research when the stories told to you follow a chronology of events. Narrative research is a literary form of qualitative research with strong ties to literature, and it provides a qualitative approach in which you can write in a persuasive, literary form. It focuses on the microanalytic picture—individual stories—rather than the broader picture of cultural norms, as in ethnography, or abstract theories, as in grounded theory research. As an example of this micropicture, consider the case of Ms. Meyer, who had two children in her fifth- and sixth-grade class write stories about their personal lives. Anthony, a 9-year-old who considered himself an inventor and writer, kept a scientific journal of his discoveries and wrote an expressive piece about his grandmother. Anita, an 11-year-old, wrote about the good times she had in a swimming pool, learning to play kickball, and being able to succeed at something (McCarthey, 1994).

How Did Narrative Research Develop?

Despite substantial interest in narrative research, its methods are still developing, and it is infrequently discussed in the literature (Errante, 2000). This has led to little agreement about its form. The "narrative turn," as Riessman (1993) called it, embraces all of the human sciences, so that this form of research is not the providence of any specific field of study. Writers in literature, history, anthropology, sociology, sociolinguistics, and education all lay claim to narrative and have developed discipline-specific procedures. Like the art and science of portraiture discussed recently in the social sciences, this design involves drawing portraits of individuals and documenting their voices and their visions within a social and cultural context (Lawrence-Lightfoot & Davis, 1997).

However, a comprehensive overview of this design of research in education emerged in 1990. Educators D. Jean Clandinin and Michael Connelly provided the first overview of narrative research for the field of education. In their informative, classic article, "Stories of Experience and Narrative Inquiry," published in the *Educational Researcher* (Connelly & Clandinin, 1990), they cited many social science applications of narrative, elaborated on the process of collecting narrative fieldnotes, and discussed the writing and structure of a narrative study. This article expanded their earlier discussion about narrative within the context of teaching and learning in classrooms (Connelly & Clandinin, 1988). More recently, these two authors expounded their ideas in a book titled *Narrative Inquiry* (Clandinin & Connelly, 2000), which openly espoused "what narrative researchers do" (p. 48).

Within the field of education, several trends influenced the development of narrative research. Cortazzi (1993) suggested three factors. First, there is currently an increased emphasis on teacher reflection. Second, more emphasis is being placed on teachers' knowledge—what they know, how they think, how they develop professionally, and how they make decisions in the classroom. Third, educators seek to bring teachers' voices to the forefront by empowering teachers to talk about their experiences. For example, "Our Own Stories," reported by Richard Meyer (1996), is a collection of stories about teachers sharing their experiences, whether they are sitting in the teachers' lounge at noon or after school. McEwan and Egan (1995) provided collections of stories about educators as teachers and curriculum developers. For women in general, as well as for female teachers, their stories to children, to adolescent girls, and to their own female associates often take on a feminine repertoire to serve their female audiences (Degh, 1995). Hearing these stories has encouraged educational studies using the narrative approach. In fact, within education recently, a special interest group in AERA has been formed to create an ongoing discussion about narrative research.

A growing number of interdisciplinary social scientists outside education have offered procedural guidance for narrative reports as a form of qualitative research (e.g., see the psychologists Lieblich, Tuval-Mashiach, & Zilber, 1998; the sociologist Cortazzi, 1993; and Riessman, 1993). Interdisciplinary efforts at narrative research have also been encouraged by the *Narrative Study of Lives* annual series that began in 1993 (e.g., Josselson & Lieblich, 1993).

WHAT ARE THE TYPES OF NARRATIVE DESIGNS?

Narrative research assumes multiple forms. If you plan to conduct a narrative study, you need to consider what *type* of narrative study to conduct. Narrative research is an overarching category for a variety of research practices (see Casey, 1995/1996), as shown in Figure 16.1. For individuals planning a narrative study, each type of narrative provides a structure for conducting the study and ready references for how to conduct the project that faculty, journal reviewers, and book publishers will recognize. For those reading narrative studies, it is less important to know what *type* of narrative is being used and more important

FIGURE 16.1

Examples of Types of Narrative Research Forms

- Autobiographies
- Biographies
- Life writing
- Personal accounts
- Personal narratives
- Narrative interviews
- Personal documents
- Documents of life
- Life stories and life histories
- Oral histories
- Ethnohistories
- Ethnobiographies
- Autoethnographies
- Ethnopsychologies
- Person-centered ethnographies
- Popular memories
- Latin American *testimonios*
- Polish memoirs

Source: Adapted from Casey, 1995/1996.

to recognize the essential *characteristics* of the types. The five questions discussed in the following subsections are helpful in determining your type of narrative study.

Who Writes or Records the Story?

Determining who will write and record the individual's story is a basic distinction in narrative research. A **biography** is a form of narrative study in which the researcher writes and records the experiences of another person's life. Typically, researchers construct biographies from records and archives (Angrosino, 1989), although researchers sometimes use other sources of information, such as interviews and photographs. In an **autobiography**, the individual who is the subject of the study writes the account. Although not a popular approach, you can find reports of autobiographical accounts of teachers as professionals (Connelly & Clandinin, 1990).

How Much of a Life Is Recorded and Presented?

This question introduces a second distinction among narrative studies. In anthropology, numerous examples exist of stories of an individual's entire life. A **life history** is a narrative story of the entire life experiences of a person. Anthropologists, for example, engage in life history research to learn about an individual's life within the context of a culture-sharing group. Often the focus includes turning points or significant events in the life of an individual (Angrosino, 1989). However, in education, narrative studies typically do not involve the account of an entire life but instead focus on an episode or single event in the individual's life. A **personal experience story** is a narrative study of an individual's personal experience found in single or multiple episodes, private situations, or communal folklore (Denzin, 1989). Clandinin and Connelly (2000) broadened the personal experience story to be both personal and social, and conveyed this stance as the essence of the experiences reported about teachers and teaching in schools.

Who Provides the Story?

A third approach for identifying the type of narrative is to examine closely who provides the story. This factor is especially relevant in education, where types of educators or learners have been the focus of many narrative studies. For example, **teachers' stories** are personal accounts by teachers of their own personal classroom experiences. As a popular form of narrative in education, researchers report teachers' stories to capture the lives of teachers as professionals and to examine learning in classrooms (e.g., Connelly & Clandinin, 1988). Other narrative studies focus on students in the classroom. In children's stories, narrative researchers ask the children in classrooms to present orally or in writing their own stories about their learning experiences (e.g., Ollerenshaw, 1998). Many different individuals in educational settings can provide stories, such as administrators, school board members, custodians, food service workers, and other educational personnel.

Is a Theoretical Lens Being Used?

Another question that shapes the character of a narrative is whether and to what extent the researcher uses a theoretical lens in developing the narrative. A **theoretical lens** in narrative research is a guiding perspective or ideology that provides structure for advocating for groups or individuals and writing the report. This lens may be to advocate for Latin Americans using *testimonios,* reporting the stories of women using a feminist lens (e.g., Personal Narratives Group, 1989), or collecting the stories of marginalized individuals. In all of these examples, the narrative researcher provides a voice for seldom-heard individuals in educational research.

Can Narrative Forms Be Combined?

In a narrative, it is possible to have the different elements listed above combined in the study. For example, a narrative study may be biographical because researchers write and report it about a participant in a study. This same study may focus on a personal study of a teacher. It may also address an event in the life of a teacher, such as a dismissal from a school (Huber & Whelan, 1999), resulting in a partial life story, or a personal narrative. In addition, if this individual is a woman, a researcher would use a theoretical lens to examine power and control issues in the school. This could lead to a feminist narrative. The final resulting narrative thus could be a combination of different elements: a biography, a personal story, a teacher's story, and a feminist perspective.

Given the many types of narrative studies, what type of narrative research should Maria conduct? As she gathers stories from Millie about her encounter with the student, does (a) Maria or Millie write the story? (b) Is Maria reporting on an entire life or a specific episode? (c) Who provides the story to Maria? (d) Should Maria advocate for weapon control in the school through her narrative study? Answer each of these questions and think through your rationale for answering them. What would you call Maria's narrative approach as she writes about it in her research study? She would probably use a personal narrative approach. How would you answer each of the questions above to arrive at this approach?

WHAT ARE THE KEY CHARACTERISTICS OF NARRATIVE DESIGNS?

Despite the many forms of narrative inquiry, they share several common characteristics. Before reviewing the key characteristics, we discuss them in general terms and relate them to the qualitative characteristics of research as developed in chapter 2.

As shown in Table 16.1, narrative researchers explore an educational research problem by understanding the experiences of an individual. As in most qualitative research, the literature review plays a minor role, especially in directing the research questions, and the inquirer emphasizes the importance of learning from participants in a setting. This learning occurs through stories told by individuals, such as teachers or students. The stories constitute

TABLE 16.1

The Research Process, Qualitative Characteristics, and Narrative Research Characteristics

The Research Process	Qualitative Characteristics (see Chapter 2)	Narrative Research Characteristics
Identify a research problem	• A qualitative problem requires exploration and understanding,	• Seeks to understand and represent experiences through the stories individual(s) live and tell.
Review the literature	• The qualitative literature plays a minor role. • The qualitative literature justifies the research problem.	• Seeks to minimize the use of literature and focus on the experiences of the individual(s).
Develop a purpose statement and research questions	• The qualitative purpose statement and research questions are broad and general. • The qualitative purpose statement and research questions seek participants' experiences.	• Seeks to explore the meaning of the individual's experiences as told through a story or stories.
Collect qualitative data	• Qualitative data collection is based on using protocols developed during the study. • Qualitative data collection involves gathering text or image data. • Qualitative data collection involves studying a small number of individuals or sites.	• Seeks to collect field texts that document the individual's story in his or her own words.
Analyze and interpret qualitative data	• Qualitative data analysis consists of text analysis. • Qualitative data analysis consists describing information and of developing themes. • Qualitative interpretations situate findings within larger meanings.	• Seeks to analyze the stories by retelling the individual's story. • Seeks to analyze the stories by identifying themes or categories of information. • Seeks to situate the story within its place or setting. • Seeks to analyze the story for chronological information about the individual's past, present, and future.
Write and evaluate a study	• Qualitative research reports use flexible and emerging structures and evaluation criteria. • Qualitative researchers take a reflexive and biased approach.	• Seeks to collaborate with the participant when writing the research study. • Seeks to write the study in a flexible storytelling mode. • Seeks to evaluate the study based on the depth, accuracy, persuasiveness, and realism of the account.

the data, and the researcher typically gathers it through interviews or informal conversations. These stories, called *field texts* (Clandinin & Connelly, 2000), provide the raw data for researchers to analyze as they retell the story based on narrative elements such as the problem, characters, setting, actions, and resolution (Ollerenshaw & Creswell, 2000). In this process, researchers narrate the story and often identify themes or categories that emerge. Thus, the qualitative data analysis may be both a description of the story and themes that emerge from it, as discussed in chapter 9. In addition, the researcher often writes into the reconstituted story a chronology of events describing the individual's past, present, and future experiences lodged within specific settings or contexts. Throughout this process of collecting and analyzing data, the researcher collaborates with the participant by checking the story and negotiating the meaning of the database. In addition, the researcher may interweave his or her personal story into the final report.

This brief overview of the process highlights specific characteristics of research often found in narrative reports. As shown in Figure 16.2, seven major characteristics are central to narrative research:

- Individual experiences
- Chronology of the experiences
- Collecting individual stories
- Restorying
- Coding for themes
- Context or setting
- Collaborating with participants

Individual Experiences

In narrative research, the inquirer often studies a single individual. Narrative researchers focus on the experiences of one or more individuals. In a study conducted about Stephanie, a primary school teacher, the researchers (Connelly & Clandinin, 1988) collected stories about her day-by-day planning of teaching and the planning done "on the fly." Although less frequent, researchers may study more than one individual (McCarthey, 1994).

In addition to the *study* of an individual, the researcher is most interested in *exploring the experiences* of that individual. For Clandinin and Connelly (2000), these **experiences** in narrative inquiry are both personal, what the individual experiences, and social, the individual interacting with others. This focus on experience draws on the

FIGURE 16.2

Major Characteristics of Narrative Research

- **Experiences of an individual**—social and personal interactions
- **Chronology of experiences**—past, present, and future experiences
- **Life stories**—first-person, oral accounts of actions obtained through field texts (data)
- **Restorying** (or retelling or developing a metastory) from the field texts
- Coding the field texts for **themes or categories**
- Incorporating the **context or place** into the story or themes
- **Collaboration** between the researcher and the participants in the study, such as negotiating field texts

Source: Adapted from Clandinin & Connelly, 2000; Lieblich et al., 1998; Riessman, 1993.

philosophical thoughts of John Dewey, who saw that individual experience was a central lens for understanding a person. One aspect of Dewey's thinking was to view experience as continuous (Clandinin & Connelly, 2000), where one experience led to another experience. Thus, narrative researchers focus on understanding individual history or past experiences and how it contributes to present and future experiences.

Chronology of the Experiences

Understanding the individual's past as well as the present and future is another key element in narrative research. Narrative researchers analyze and report a chronology of an individual's experiences. When researchers focus on understanding these experiences, they elicit information about a participant's past, present, and future. **Chronology** in narrative designs means that the researcher analyzes and writes about an individual life using a time sequence or chronology of events. Cortazzi (1993) suggested that the chronology of narrative research emphasizes a sequence, which sets narrative apart from other genres of research. For example, in a study about a teacher's use of computer technology in a high school classroom, the inquirer would include information about the teacher's introduction to computers, current computer use, and future goals and aspirations. The story reported by the researcher would include a discussion about the sequence of events for this teacher.

Collecting Individual Stories

To develop this chronological perspective of individual experiences, the narrative researcher asks the participant to tell a story (or stories) about his or her experiences. Narrative researchers place emphasis on collecting the stories told to them by individuals or gathered from a wide variety of field texts. These accounts might arise during informal group conversations (Huber & Whelan, 1999) or from one-on-one interviews. A **story in narrative research** is a first-person oral telling or retelling of an individual. Often these stories have a beginning, a middle, and an end. Similar to basic elements found in good novels, these aspects involve a predicament, conflict, or struggle; a protagonist or character; and a sequence with implied causality (a plot) during which the predicament is resolved in some fashion (Carter, 1993). In a more general sense, the story might include the elements typically found in novels, such as time, place, plot, and scene (Connelly & Clandinin, 1990). For those relating to narrative from a literary perspective, the sequence might be the development of the plot as it unfolds, the emergence of a crisis or turning point, and the conclusion or denouement. Narrative researchers hope to capture this story line as they listen to individuals tell their stories.

Narrative researchers collect stories from several data sources. **Field texts** represent information from different sources collected by researchers in a narrative design. Up to this point, our examples have illustrated collecting stories by using discussions, conversations, or interviews between a researcher and one individual. However, the stories might be autobiographical, with the researcher reflecting on his or her own story and interweaving that story with those of others. For example, in the sample study at the end of this chapter, Huber and Whelan (1999) discussed how their own stories interrelated with the stories of Naomi, a rural junior/senior high teacher, as she told about her decision to leave her position in the school district. Often the researcher's role in the inquiry process may be central, in which they find themselves in a "nested set of stories" (Clandinin & Connolly, 2000, p. 63). Journals are another form used for collecting stories, as are fieldnotes written by either the researcher or the participant. Letters provide useful data. These letters may be written back and forth between participants, research collaborators, or between the researchers and participants (Clandinin & Connelly, 2000). Family stories, photographs, and memory boxes—collections of items that trigger our memories—are other forms used for collecting stories in narrative research.

Restorying

After individuals tell a story about their experiences, narrative researchers retell (or restory or remap) the story in their own words. They do this to provide order and sequence to it. **Restorying** is the process in which the researcher gathers stories, analyzes them for key elements of the story (e.g., time, place, plot, and scene), and then rewrites the story to place it in a chronological sequence. When individuals tell a story, this sequence is often missing or not logically developed. By restorying, the researcher provides a causal link among ideas. There are several ways to restory the narrative.

Examine the transcript, shown in Table 16.2, from a narrative project addressing adolescent smoking behavior (Ollerenshaw & Creswell, 2000). This table displays the process of restorying interview data for a high school student who is attempting to quit smoking. The process involves three stages:

1. The researcher conducts the interview and transcribes the conversation from an audiotape. This transcription is shown in the first column as raw data.
2. Next the narrative researcher retranscribes the raw data by identifying the key elements of the story. This is shown in the second column. The key at the bottom of the table indicates the codes used by the researcher to identify the setting [s], characters [c], actions [a], problem [p], and resolution [r] in the student's transcript.
3. Finally, the narrative researcher restories the student's account by organizing the key codes into a sequence. The sequence presented in this passage is setting, characters, actions, problem, and resolution, although another narrative researcher might report these elements in another order. This restorying begins with the place (McDonald's), the characters (the student), and then the events (behaviors such as "shaky" and "hyper"). The researcher reworks the transcription to identify the elements of the story and restories the elements into a logical sequence of activities.

To clearly identify these elements, the researcher might organize them into a table similar to Table 16.3. This table describes five elements used in restorying (Ollerenshaw, 1998). The setting is the specific situation of the story, illustrated by such factors as time, locale, or year. The researcher may discuss characters in a story as archetypes or portray them through their personalities, behaviors, styles, or patterns. The actions are the movements of the individuals in the story, such as the specific thinking or behaving that occurs during the story. The problem represents the questions or concerns that arise during the story or the phenomena that need to be described or explained. The resolution is the outcome of addressing the problem: the answer to a question or the conclusion reached in the story. It may involve an explanation about what caused the character to change in the story.

The elements of setting, characters, actions, problem, and resolution illustrate only one example of the elements that narrative researchers look for as they restory an individual's experiences. They might also use the elements of the three-dimensional space narrative structure advanced by Clandinin and Connelly (2000). As shown in Table 16.4, the three dimensions of interaction, continuity, and situation create a "metaphorical" (p. 50) inquiry space that defines a narrative study. As researchers construct their story (either their own or someone else's), they would include information about the following:

TABLE 16.2

Retranscribing and Restorying a Transcript

Transcription of Audiotape (Raw Data)	Retranscription by the Researcher*	Restory by the Researcher
Well, I know it wasn't the first time but I remember this one most vividly. Almost. . . about a year ago, I had been trying to quit and I hadn't smoked for about, I'd say about a month or more, I think I just didn't want to do it anymore. There was this guy that I liked at McDonald's, but he didn't like me, he liked my best friend. We all worked at McDonald's after school until close. Oh, wow, I had nicotine fits a lot. Sometimes you get shaky. You get really high, you know, just like you need to go get some fresh air. You need to get a cigarette, just like, you know, you just get really hyper and start bouncing off the walls. I calmed down after a little bit, but . . . I was tempted to start again during the month I quit. Uhm, well my friends would be smoking outside by the tree, so it was like you know, you look at it and you're just like, it kind of looks like a cupcake or something good, you know. Just like you want, but then they ask you, "Hey, do you want to drive or something?" Just say, "No." So I'm trying to quit but I can't do it. They understand but then it's just like, "Okay. I gotta go home now" and I get to go to bed. Sometimes I just go back inside the school cause you can't smoke inside there, so . . . I might have slipped maybe one or two but I mean, I was upset, tense. This guy I liked started going out with my best friend and so then I got really upset and started just smoking again just like, you know. That's the one that I really remember. . . me and her were best friends no more.	about a year ago, [s] I [c] had been trying to quit and I hadn't smoked for about, I just didn't want to do it anymore [p] was this guy [c], that I liked [a] at McDonald's [s], but he didn't like me, he liked my best friend [c]. I had nicotine fits [a] a lot. You get shaky [a]. You get really high [a] You need to go get some fresh air. You need to get a cigarette [a]. You just get really hyper and start bouncing off the walls [a]. I calmed down after a little bit [a], friends [c] would be smoking outside by the tree [s]. It looks like a cupcake or something-good [a]. Hey, do you want to drive or something? [a] "No. I'm trying to quit [a]." I'd go to bed [a]. Sometimes I just go back inside the school [s] cause you can't smoke inside there, [a] I slipped maybe one or two but [a], I was upset, tense [a]. This guy I liked started going out with my best friend [a]. I got really upset and started just smoking again [a]. That's the one that I really remember . . . me and her were best friends no more [r].	• A year ago, I worked at McDonald's and I didn't buy cigarettes for about a month. • I had nicotine fits. • I got shaky. • I got high. • I got hyper. • I started bouncing off the walls. • I needed air. • I went outside. • Friends were smoking by the tree. • I wanted a cigarette because they looked good. • I wanted to drive. • I went inside the school. • I went home to bed. • I calmed down. • The guy I liked from McDonald's started dating my friend. • I got upset and tense. • I slipped one or two cigarettes. • I started smoking again. • We're not friends any more.

*Key to codes in the retranscription: setting [s], characters [c], actions [a], problem [p], and resolution [r].

Source: Adapted from Ollerenshaw & Creswell, 2000.

TABLE 16.3

Organizing the Story Elements into the Problem Solution Narrative Structure

Setting	Characters	Actions	Problem	Resolution
Context, environment, conditions, place, time, locale, year, and era	Individuals in the story described as archetypes, personalities, their behaviors, style, and patterns	Movements of individuals through the story illustrating the character's thinking or behaviors	Questions to be answered or phenomena to be described or explained	Answers to questions and explanations about what caused the character to change.

Source: Adapted from Ollerenshaw, 1998.

- *Interaction:* the personal interaction based on an individual's feelings, hopes, reactions, and dispositions as well as the social interaction to include other people and their intentions, purposes, assumptions, and points of view
- *Continuity:* a consideration of the past that is remembered; the present relating to experiences of an event; and the future, looking forward to possible experiences
- *Situation:* information about the context, time, and place within a physical setting, with boundaries and characters' intentions, purposes, and different points of view

Coding for Themes

As with all qualitative inquiry, the data can be segmented into themes (see chapter 9). Narrative researchers may code the data of the stories into themes or categories. The identification of themes provides the complexity of a story and adds depth to the insight about understanding individual experiences. As with all qualitative research, a small number of themes, such as five to seven, are identified by the researcher. Researchers incorporate these themes into the passages about the individual's story or include them as a separate section in a study. Narrative researchers typically present these themes after retelling the story.

TABLE 16.4

The Three-Dimensional Space Narrative Structure

Interaction		Continuity			Situation
Personal	**Social**	**Past**	**Present**	**Future**	**Place**
Look inward to internal conditions, feelings, hopes, aesthetic reactions, moral dispositions.	Look outward to existential conditions in the environment with other people and their intentions, purposes, assumptions, and points of view.	Look backward to remembered stories and experiences from earlier times.	Look at current stories and experiences relating to actions of an event.	Look forward to implied and possible experiences and plot lines.	Look at context, time, and place situated in a physical landscape or in a setting bounded by characters' intentions, purposes, and different points of view.

Source: Adapted from Clandinin & Connelly, 2000.

Context or Setting

Narrative researchers describe in detail the setting or context in which the individual experiences the central phenomenon. In the restorying of the participant's story and the telling of the themes, the narrative researcher includes rich detail about the setting or context of the participant's experiences. The **setting** in narrative research may be friends, family, workplace, home, social organization, or school—the place where a story physically occurs. In some narrative studies, the restoried accounts of an educator may actually begin with a description of the setting or context before the narrative researcher conveys the events or actions of the story. In other cases, information about the setting is woven throughout the story.

Collaborating with Participants

Throughout the process of research, narrative researchers collaborate with the study individuals. **Collaboration** in narrative research means that the inquirer actively involves the participant in the inquiry as it unfolds. This collaboration may include many steps in the research process, from formulating the central phenomenon to deciding which types of field texts will yield helpful information to writing the final restoried story of individual experiences. Collaboration involves negotiating relationships between the researcher and the participant to lessen the potential gap between the narrative told and the narrative reported (Clandinin & Connelly, 2000). It may also include explaining the purpose of the inquiry to the participant, negotiating transitions from gathering data to writing the story, and arranging ways to intermingle with participants in a study (Clandinin & Connelly, 2000). Collaboration often calls for a good working relationship between teachers and researchers, an idealized situation that takes time to develop as a mutually illuminating story between the researcher and the teacher (Elbaz-Luwisch, 1997).

WHAT ARE SOME POTENTIAL ISSUES IN GATHERING STORIES?

When gathering stories, narrative researchers need to be cautious about the stories. Is the story authentic? The participant may "fake the data" (Connelly & Clandinin, 1990, p. 10), providing a Pollyanna story or a story with a typical Hollywood ending, where the good guy or girl always wins. This distortion of the data may occur in any research study, and it presents an issue for narrative researchers in particular because they rely heavily on self-reported information from participants. The collection of multiple field texts, the triangulation of data, and member checking (as discussed in chapter 9) can help ensure that good data are collected.

Partcipants may not be able to tell the *real* story. This inability may arise when experiences are simply too horrific to report or too raw to recall (e.g., Holocaust victims, disaster victims). It may also occur when individuals fear sanctions against them if they report their story, such as in sexual harassment cases. The real story may also not emerge because individuals simply cannot recall it—the story is buried too deeply in the subconscious. It may also occur because individuals base their stories on events that happened years ago, leading to early memories that may distort events and provide inventions of past actions (Lieblich et al., 1998). Although distortion, fear of reprisal, and inability to tell may plague storytellers, narrative researchers remind us that stories are "truths of our experiences" (Riessman, 1993, p. 22) and that any story told has an element of truth in it.

The telling of the story by the participant also raises the issue of who *owns* the story. In reporting stories of individuals marginalized in our society, narrative researchers run the risk of reporting stories that they do not have permission to tell. At the minimum, narrative inquirers can obtain permission to report stories, and inform individuals of the purposes and use of the stories at the beginning of the project.

Along with the potential problem of ownership is also the issue about whether the participant's *voice is lost* in the final narrative report. For example, when restorying exists, it is possible for the report to reflect the researcher's story and not the participant's story. Using extensive participant quotes and the precise language of the participants, and carefully constructing the time and place for the story, may help to ameliorate this problem. A related issue is whether the researcher *gains* in the study at the expense of the participant. Careful attention to reciprocity or giving back to participants, such as serving as a volunteer in a classroom or providing an award for participating in the study, will maintain gains for both the researcher and the participant.

WHAT ARE THE STEPS IN CONDUCTING NARRATIVE RESEARCH?

Regardless of the type or form of narrative research, educators who conduct a narrative study proceed through similar steps, as shown in Figure 16.3. Seven major steps comprise the process typically undertaken during a narrative study. A visualization of the process as a circle shows that all steps are interconnected and not necessarily linear. The use of arrows to show the direction of steps is only a suggestion and is not prescripture of a process that you might use.

Step 1. Identify a Phenomenon to Explore That Addresses an Educational Problem

As with all research projects, the process begins by focusing on a research problem to study and identifying, in qualitative research, a central phenomenon to explore. Although the phenomenon of interest in narrative is the story (Connelly & Clandinin, 1990), you need to identify an issue or concern. For example, the issue for Huber (1999), in a narrative study of children in a classroom, consisted of stories about the difficulties that she and her student teacher, Shaun, had meeting the diverse needs of students. This included children excluding other children, using hurtful words with each other, and persistently using anger and aggression to solve problems. When exploring issues such as these, you seek to understand the personal or social experiences of an individual or individuals in an educational setting.

Step 2. Purposefully Select an Individual from Whom You Can Learn About the Phenomenon

You next find an individual or individuals who can provide an understanding of the phenomenon. The participant may be someone who is typical or someone who is critical to study because he or she has experienced a specific issue or situation. The study of Naomi was a critical case about the issue of teacher conflict between a special education junior/senior high teacher and a supervising teacher over the placement of a special needs student (Huber & Whelan, 1999). Other options for sampling, as introduced in chapter 8, are also available. Although many narrative studies examine only a single

FIGURE 16.3

Steps in Conducting Narrative Research

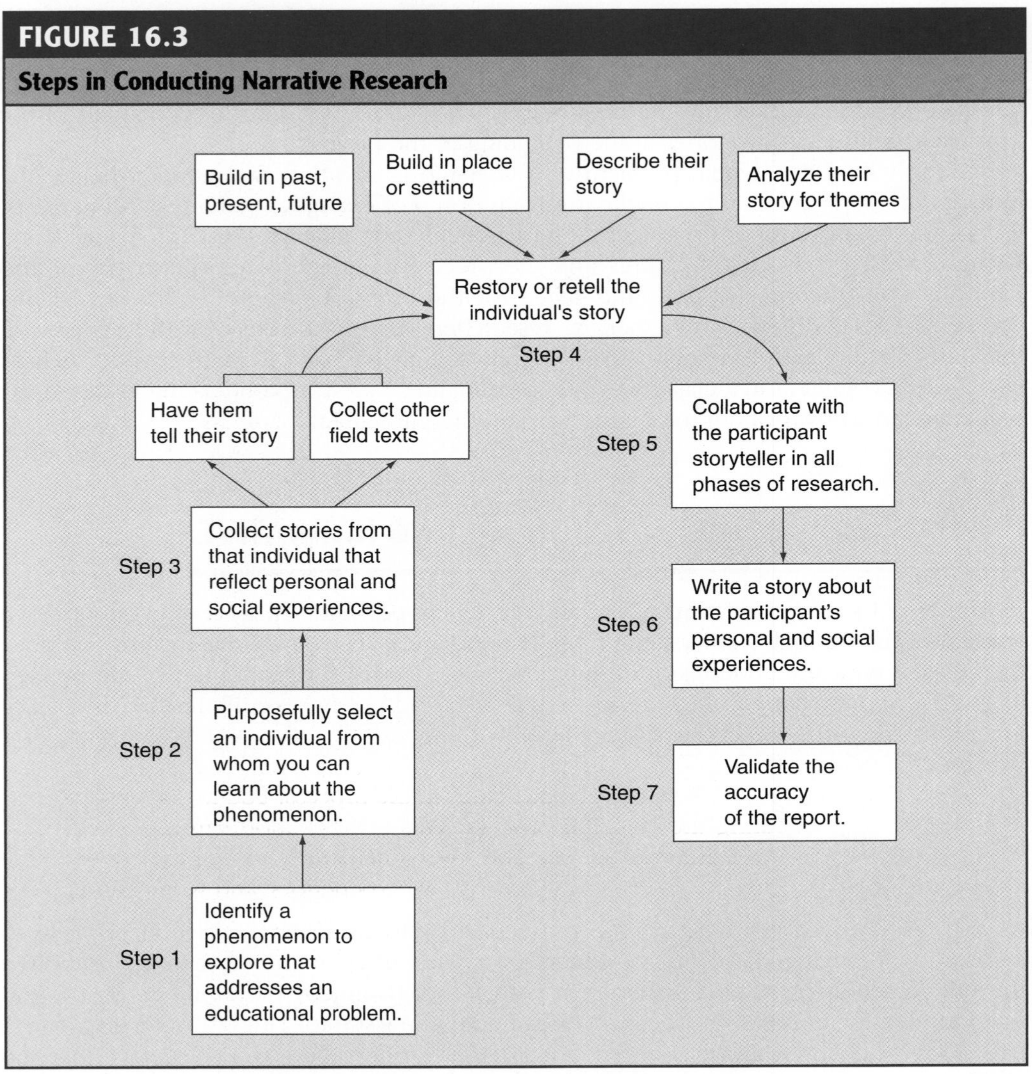

individual, you may study several individuals in a project, each with a different story that may conflict with or be supportive of each other.

Step 3. Collect the Story from That Individual

Your intent is to collect field texts that will provide the story of an individual's experiences. Perhaps the best way to gather the story is to have the individual tell about his or her experiences, through personal conversations or interviews. You can gather other field texts as well, such as these:

- Have the individual record his or her story in a journal or diary.
- Observe the individual and record fieldnotes.
- Collect letters sent by the individual.
- Assemble stories about the individual from family members.
- Gather documents such as memos or official correspondence about the individual.

- Obtain photographs, memory boxes, and other personal/family/social artifacts.
- Record the individual's life experiences (e.g., dance, theater, music, film, art, and literature; Clandinin & Connelly, 2000).

Step 4. Restory or Retell the Individual's Story

Next, review the data that contain the story and retell it. This process includes examining the raw data, identifying elements of a story in them, sequencing or organizing the story elements, and then presenting a retold story that conveys the individual's experiences. You use restorying because the listener and the reader will better understand the story told by the participant if you sequence it into a logical order.

What elements do you identify in the raw data for your story? How do you arrange these elements in *your* story? Narrative researchers differ about the elements to select, although in general you might mention the narrative elements found in a literary analysis of a novel. For example, time, place, plot, and scene are major elements located in stories by researchers (Connelly & Clandinin, 1990). Focusing on the plot, you might identify an abstract of the events or actions, orient the listener, convey the complicating action, evaluate its meaning, and resolve the action (Cortazzi, 1993). Another inquirer might examine the story for setting, characters, actions, problem, and resolution (Ollerenshaw & Creswell, 2000). Although several analytic strategies exist for locating and sequencing a story, all procedures order the story for the reader and listener using literary elements.

Step 5. Collaborate with the Participant–Storyteller

This step is one that interacts with all the other steps in the process. You actively collaborate with the participant during the research process. This collaboration can assume several forms, such as negotiating entry to the site and the participant, working closely with the participant to obtain field texts to capture the individual experiences, and writing and telling the individual's story in the researcher's words.

Step 6. Write a Story About the Participant's Experiences

The major step in the process of research is for the author to write and present the story of the individual's experiences. Although there is no single way to write the narrative report, it is helpful to include several features of narrative. Your restory certainly claims a central place in the narrative report. In addition, you might include an analysis to highlight specific themes that emerged during the story.

Typically, you do not include a specific literature section; instead, you incorporate the literature and research studies about the problem into the final sections of the study. Because readers are often not familiar with narrative, you might write a section about the importance of narrative research and the procedures involved in it so that you can inform readers about narrative research. As with all qualitative research, you are present in the narrative report, and you use the first-person pronoun to refer to yourself.

Step 7. Validate the Accuracy of the Report

You also need to validate the accuracy of your narrative account. When collaboration exists with participants, this validation may occur throughout the project. Several validation practices addressed in chapter 9, such as member checking, triangulating among data sources, and searching for disconfirming evidence, are useful to determine the accuracy and credibility of a narrative account.

HOW DO YOU EVALUATE NARRATIVE RESEARCH?

As a form of qualitative research, narrative needs to be consistent with the qualitative criteria identified in chapter 10. In addition, there are specific narrative aspects that people reading and evaluating a study might consider. Use the following list of questions to evaluate your own or someone else's narrative report:

- Does the researcher focus on individual experiences?
- Is there a focus on a single individual or a few individuals?
- Did the researcher collect the story of an individual's experience?
- Did the researcher restory the participant's story?
- In the restorying, was the participant's voice as well as the researcher's voice heard?
- Did the researcher identify themes that emerged from the story?
- Did the story include information about place or setting of the individual?
- Did the story have a temporal, chronological sequence including the past, present, and future?
- Is there evidence that the researcher collaborated with the participant?
- Does the story adequately address the purpose and questions of the researcher?

APPLYING WHAT YOU HAVE LEARNED: A NARRATIVE RESEARCH STUDY

To apply the ideas in this chapter, read the narrative study on page 532, by Huber and Whelan (1999), noting the marginal annotations that identify characteristics of qualitative research and narrative research. This article has interesting layers of meaning and useful insights for educators as we consider our own issues in the educational workplace. As a narrative design, the clearly told story of Naomi with people, contexts, a flow of events, and a denouement marks the article as useful reading for those learning narrative research. As a qualitative study filled with issues of power, marginalization, and boundary crossing, this study advances a qualitative study with an emancipatory and participatory perspective in which questions of agency, advocacy, powerlessness, and marginalization play a central role.

As you examine the study, locate the following parts of the research process:

- The research problem and use of qualitative research
- The use of the literature
- The purpose statement and research questions
- The types of procedures of narrative data collection
- The types of procedures of narrative data analysis and interpretation
- The writing structure

After you have read this article and noted the location and quality of each part (using the paragraph numbers), then turn to the analysis in the following sections and compare your analysis with mine.

The Research Problem and Use of Qualitative Research

See Paragraph 03 and throughout the article

In Paragraph 03, the author identifies the possibility of miseducation occurring in our schools when individuals struggle to understand and resist situations within their school context. Naomi experienced contradictions, gaps, and silences in her work in the school.

This article displays the following characteristics of a qualitative research study:

- The exploration and understanding of the complexity of one individual's experiences in the school (Paragraphs 08–17)
- A minimal use of literature and, when literature is mentioned, it reflects on the school landscape for professional teachers (e.g., Paragraph 02) or the research approach of narrative inquiry (Paragraph 04)
- A broad and general purpose of the study—to make sense of a teacher's story (Paragraph 03)
- A focus on the participant's experiences by exploring a storyteller/teacher who lived this experience (Paragraph 03)
- Collecting data (i.e., words) using procedures that involved conversations between a group of five teachers during an 18-month period (Paragraph 04)
- Studying only one individual (Paragraph 10)
- Analyzing the conversations and stories of Naomi by describing or retelling her story (Paragraphs 10–17)
- Interpreting the meaning of Naomi's story in a general sense about her power of resistance (Paragraphs 52–56)
- Using a flexible reporting structure that advances Naomi's story (Paragraphs 10–17) followed by classroom- and borders-related themes (Paragraphs 20–51)
- Reporting in a personal, reflexive style in which the authors identify how their own views changed as a result of listening to and reflecting on Naomi's story (Paragraphs 55–56)

The Use of the Literature

See Paragraphs 06, 52, and 53

As in most qualitative studies, the literature plays a minor role. In this study there is little literature, and when it appears, it documents the stories told on the professional knowledge landscape (Paragraph 05) or approaches to narrative research (Paragraph 04). Much of the literature used is methodological literature; that is, it informs or educates readers about the research design of narrative research rather than focusing on the content or topic of teachers in schools. This literature provides references, concepts, and language of narrative research. Also, there is no theory to test from the literature, an approach typically taken by authors in qualitative studies. By keeping the literature to a minimum, the researchers learn from and take direction from Naomi's experiences.

The Purpose Statement and Research Questions

See Paragraph 03

The authors indicate the purpose or intent of the study early, in Paragraph 03. They discuss making sense out of a teacher's story. This paragraph actually summarizes the entire study and indicates the central phenomenon of miseducation that is the focus of the study. No research questions are mentioned to provide specific direction for the study.

Types of Procedures of Narrative Data Collection

See Paragraph 04

As a qualitative study, this article reports text data—the words of Naomi, the teacher. However, the authors provide only minimal evidence about their data collection. We do learn that five teachers engaged in conversations over 18 months. These conversations were audiotaped and transcribed and represent the text data used in the study. The authors do not explicitly identify their sampling technique, but we assume that it was purposeful. Three of the five women are the authors and their advisor in this study, and the authors refer frequently to their own stories as well as Naomi's story. Although all five individuals participated in a conversation about their lives as teachers (Paragraph 08), this particular study focused on only one person, Naomi, who is seen as a coresearcher in the study.

Types and Procedures of Narrative Data Analysis and Interpretation

See Paragraphs 08–17 for the restory

See Paragraphs 18–51 for themes

See Paragraphs 52–56 for interpretations

In the passage on reconstructing Naomi's experiences, we find the first-level analysis of her story. This is the restorying of Naomi's story by the researchers. It includes contextual information (rural, junior/senior high school landscape), characters (Brian, Alicia, and Laura), specific events (tension in the relationship, intolerance, and silence), and the resolution or denouement (leaving the school). Following this restorying, the authors identify themes about the teacher landscape (in-classroom and out-of-classroom) and the borders (ownership, negotiations, home places, positional power, sameness, confrontation, arrogance, judgment, and silence). The analysis thus consists of a description of Naomi's situation (the restorying) and the identification of themes (classroom experiences and borders).

The authors develop the larger interpretation of Naomi's story in the final passage of the study. We learn about her caring for others (Paragraph 53) and the researchers' sense of the hopelessness of her story (Paragraph 54). After further reflection (and interpretation), the authors uncovered strong images of Naomi in her story. The researchers saw her resistance as a source of strength that she could use to help her live with the isolation she felt in her school (Paragraph 56).

The Overall Writing Structure

We see in this article a flexible, qualitative writing structure without a distinct review of the literature and a well-formed method discussion. The authors' use of references and comments about narrative research, throughout the article, add research interest to the study. For example, they emphasize early the importance of story for individuals to make meaning of their lives. They focus on the individual experiences of a single individual, and they include collaboration between the researcher and the participant. Throughout the story, they highlight the context of Naomi's workplace and use a temporal sequence, illustrated by the chronological presentation of her story. The authors' inclusion of strong method and research design content adds to the sophistication of this study. Although Naomi's voice might have been heard through more direct quotes, this study has many layers of meaning and insight for narrative researchers and those understanding the experiences of teachers in schools.

KEY IDEAS IN THE CHAPTER

Narrative research has emerged as a popular form of qualitative research. It has become a viable way to study teachers, students, and educators in educational settings. All of these individuals have stories to tell about their experiences. Narrative inquirers describe the lives of individuals, collect and tell stories about people's lives, and write narratives of individual experiences. These qualitative studies focus on identifying the experiences of a single individual or several individuals and understanding their past, present, and future experiences.

Narrative researchers collect stories from individuals and retell or restory the participants' stories into a framework such as a chronology of the characters, the setting, the problem, the actions, and a resolution of those actions. In addition, the inquirer may gather field texts and form them into themes or categories and describe, in detail, the setting or context in which the stories are told. Throughout the research process, the researcher emphasizes collaboration between the researcher and the participant.

The steps in conducting a narrative study are to identify a problem suited for narrative research and to select one or more participants to study. Researchers then collect stories from the participant about his or her life experiences and retell the story to form a chronology of events that may include the characters, setting, problem, actions, and resolution. Throughout this process, collaboration occurs with the participant, and the story composed by the researcher tells of the participant's life experiences.

USEFUL INFORMATION FOR PRODUCERS OF RESEARCH

- Individuals planning or conducting a narrative study can employ the steps in the process identified in this chapter.
- Consider the type of narrative design you plan to use. Ask yourself the following questions: Who writes or records the story? How much of a life is recorded and presented? Who provides the story? Is a theoretical lens being used? Can narrative forms be combined?
- The three steps used in restorying provide a structure for processing a transcript and developing a retelling of the participant's story.
- As you listen to a participant's story, consider some of the potential issues that may arise, such as whether the story is authentic, whether data are distorted, whether individuals can tell the story, and who owns the story.

USEFUL INFORMATION FOR CONSUMERS OF RESEARCH

- Consumers can review the steps in the research process in this chapter to determine how narrative inquirers conduct a study.
- The evaluation criteria discussed in this chapter can be used to assess the quality of a narrative study.

- ◆ When narrative researchers conduct an inquiry, they need to report that they have checked the accuracy of their findings. Look for reports about triangulating data, member checking, or providing disconfirming evidence for themes.
- ◆ The narrative journal article reported in this study provides one example of narrative research. It is used to identify the major characteristics of a narrative study and to model the composition of a narrative study.

ADDITIONAL RESOURCES YOU MIGHT EXAMINE

A major book to consult is the text on narrative inquiry by Clandinin and Connelly (2000). This text captures all aspects of narrative designs from learning to think narratively to constructing a story using the three-dimensional model to the types of field texts that narrative researchers collect. It also includes information about composing a narrative text and using the forms available in dissertations and books. See:

Clandinin, D. J., & Connelly, F. M. (2000). *Narrative inquiry: Experience and story in qualitative research*. San Francisco: Jossey-Bass.

Another useful book in education and teacher education is the book edited by McEwan and Egan (1995). This volume provides helpful examples of specific narrative studies in education. Examine:

McEwan, H., & Egan, K. (1995). *Narrative in teaching, learning, and research*. New York: Teachers College Press, Columbia University.

Several journals have published excellent overviews of narrative research as applied to the field of education. One article often cited is the Connelly and Clandinin (1990) discussion on "Stories of Experience and Narrative Inquiry" in the *Educational Researcher*. This article is especially good at identifying the procedures used in conducting a narrative study. Another article in the *Educational Researcher* is by Kathy Carter (1993) on "The Place of Story in the Study of Teaching and Teacher Education." This article presents the pros and cons of studying the stories of teachers, such as the political context of story and the issues of gender, power, ownership, and voice. A third article, by Kathleen Casey (1995/1996), titled "The New Narrative Research in Education," is found in the *Review of Research in Education*. This article addresses the history of narrative research and surveys many topics in narrative research, such as various types (e.g., autobiographical reflections), issues (e.g., plastic identities), and methodological concerns (e.g., nuanced discussions of emotions). See:

Connelly, F. M., & Clandinin, D. J. (1990). Stories of experience and narrative inquiry. *Educational Researcher, 19*(5), 2–14.

Carter, K. (1993). The place of a story in the study of teaching and teacher education. *Educational Researcher, 22*(1), 5–12, 18.

Casey, K. (1995/1996). The new narrative research in education. *Review of Research in Education, 21,* 211–253.

One entire issue of the journal *Teaching and Teacher Education* (Gudmundsdottir, 1997) addresses "Narrative Perspectives on Teaching and Teacher Education." Including major international writers on narrative research, this volume provides examples of specific narrative studies as well as thoughtful discussions about topics that critique as well as support narrative designs. See:

Gudmundsdottir, S. (1997). Introduction to the theme issue of "narrative perspectives on teaching and teacher education." *Teaching and Teacher Education, 13*(1), 1–3.

Outside the field of education, in the social sciences, are several books useful to understanding narrative designs. Riessman (1993) provided thoughtful procedures for analyzing and reporting narratives, Josselson and Lieblich (1993) provided a six-volume series on the study of narrative lives, and Cortazzi (1993) also included systematic approaches to narrative analysis. Examine:

Riessman, C. K. (1993). *Narrative analysis*. Newbury Park, CA: Sage.

Josselson, R., & Lieblich, A. (Eds.). (1993). *The narrative study of lives* (Vol. 1). Thousand Oaks, CA: Sage.

Cortazzi, M. (1993). *Narrative analysis*. London: Falmer Press.

Go to our Companion Website at **www.prenhall.com/creswell** to:

- assess your understanding of chapter content with Multiple-Choice Questions,
- apply what you've learned with Essay Questions,
- practice your research skills with interactive Building Research Skills exercises, and
- broaden your knowledge of research with Web Links to research topics on the Internet.

Qualitative Characteristics

Narrative Research Characteristics

A Marginal Story as a Place of Possibility: Negotiating Self on the Professional Knowledge Landscape

Janice Huber, Karen Whelan*
The Centre for Research for Teacher Education and Development, Faculty of Education, University of Alberta, Edmonton, Alberta, Canada

Abstract

(01) *Drawing on a two-year study focusing on teacher identity and marginalization within diverse school landscapes, we explore the educative and miseducative qualities of responses as told through one teacher's story. By reconstructing and making meaning of this story through the conceptual framework of the "professional knowledge landscape" [Clandinin, D. J.,& Connelly, F. M. (1995). Teacher's professional knowledge landscapes, New York: Teachers College Press], we consider how this teacher's identity—which we understand narratively as "story to live by"—shapes, and is shaped, within the in- and out-of-classroom places on her school landscape. Through a final retelling of this narrative, we pay close attention to the response which emerged from each of these fundamentally different places and we examine this teacher's negotiation of her story to live by in relation to a school story of inclusion. This focus enables us to name borders of power, judgment and silence, and "bordercrossings" [Anzaldúa, G. (Ed.). (1990). Making face, making soul = Haciendo caras: Creative and critical perspectives of feminists of color. San Francisco: Aunt Lute Books], which are shaped within "public homeplaces" [Belenky, M., Bond, L., & Weinstock, J. (1997). A tradition that has no name: Nurturing the development of people, families, and communities. New York: BasicBooks]. We believe that this story is a place of possibility—possibility for understanding the central role that presence to our narrative histories plays in enabling us to live and to sustain stories that run counter to those being scripted for us on school landscapes.*

(02) Storytellers are influenced by the telling of their own stories. Active construction and telling of a story is educative: The storyteller learns through the act of storytelling . . . [and] in their telling in relationship . . . It is an education that goes beyond writing for the self because it has a responsive audience, which makes possible both an imagined response and an actual response. These possibilities, the imagining of response and the response, are important for the storyteller. The possibilities are important in an educative way because the meaning of the story is reshaped and so, too, is the meaning of the world to which the story refers (Clandinin & Connelly, 1995, p. 155/56).

A qualitative problem requires exploration and understanding.

The qualitative purpose statement and research questions are broad and general.

Narrative researchers focus on the experiences of a single individual.

(03) This paper is about the storytelling to which Clandinin and Connelly refer. It is about telling stories to our selves and to others with whom we are in relationship. It is about how this telling, active construction, living out, and reconstruction of our stories influences our selves and those around us. Response and imagining of possibilities live at the centre of what this paper is about. The teacher's story we make sense of within this paper is a story of "miseducative" (Dewey, 1938) qualities, a story in which impossible contradictions, gaps, and silences are named. This story is

---

*Corresponding author. Tel.: +403-492-7770 fax: +403-492-0113

Reprinted from Huber, J., & Whelan, K. (1999). A marginal story as a place of possibility: Negotiating self on the professional knowledge landscape. *Teaching and Teacher Education*, 15, 381–396 with permission from Elsevier Science.

The qualitative purpose statement and research questions seek participants' experiences.

situated within one school context in which the storyteller/teacher who lived this experience uncovers her struggle to understand and to resist the response she received through negotiating her self within her professional surroundings. Located within a western Canadian province, in a large junior/senior high school, this story centres around issues of integrating students with special needs into "regular" programs. A context is described in which students with special needs are identified for individualized programming within a segregated setting in the school. Students who were labelled as "special needs" were selectively integrated into what is traditionally defined as "non-academic" courses, and were assigned classroom aides to assist with individualized programming.

The qualitative literature plays a minor role.

Qualitative researchers take a reflexive biased approach.

(04) This story was shared within the context of a narrative inquiry (Carr, 1986; Clandinin & Connelly, 1994; Connelly & Clandinin 1988, 1990) including eighteen months of taped and transcribed research conversations between a group of five teacher co-researchers who felt the need to construct a community away from our school landscapes, where our most vulnerable stories could be explored. The telling of this story was important for this particular teacher and for all of us as co-researchers-storytellers, storylisteners, and storyresponders in relationship with one another. The storytelling context, shaped by a responsive audience, was profoundly educative in that through the sharing of this story, the meaning of it was reshaped from beginning images of hopelessness to those of possibility.

(05) Our paper begins by situating this inquiry within a narrative conceptualization of teacher identity and the professional contexts in which teachers live and work. Our restructuring of the first meeting with the teacher co-researchers with whom we are in conversation provides an introduction to the methodological grounding which shapes our study. The introduction also provides an overview of the story we worked to understand in conversation within our teacher inquiry group and throughout this paper. Unpacking this story through the framework and narrative language developed by Clandinin and Connelly (1995) in their conceptualization of a "professional knowledge landscape" revealed the storied qualities of this school context and the central role response played within this storying. We conclude this paper by focusing on the ways in which response was continuously negotiated and lived out on this school landscape. Our purpose in this final exploration is to uncover the borders shaped out of response, as well as the possibilities for "bordercrossings" (Anzaldúa, 1987)—those hopeful meeting places where the retelling of our stories creates possibilities for imagining our selves in relation with others in new ways.

1. Understanding Identity as "Story to Live By"

The qualitative literature justifies the research problem.

(06) Our understanding of teacher identity is grounded within Connelly and Clandinin's (in press) narrative conceptualization of identity as a "story to live by." In their research into teacher knowledge and school contexts, they reveal how we tell storied compositions of our lives to "define who we are, what we do, and why . . . " (Connelly & Clandinin, 1999). A sense of fluidity shapes our story to live by as it is composed over time, recognizing the multiplicity of situations and experiences we embody. These multiple storylines interweave and interconnect, bearing upon one another and on how we come to understand our selves (Clandinin, 1997). We live, tell, retell, and relive our life stories (Clandinin & Connelly, 1998) as we negotiate our selves within and across various contexts. For example, within the context of our own

lives, we may draw upon our understanding of our selves as women to make meaning of a particular experience. Although this knowing will also be present as we make sense of our selves in other situations, it may dwell in the background while our self understanding of being elementary teachers may come more to the foreground as we make sense of another situation. As teachers, our story to live by is "both personal—reflecting a person's life history—and social—reflecting the milieu, the contexts in which teachers live" (Connelly & Clandinin, 1999).

Qualitative data collection involves studying a small number of individuals or sites.

(07) Understanding teacher identity as story to live by calls for a relational understanding between teachers and the contexts in which they work. In this way, teachers both shape and are shaped by their particular school landscapes. Considering schools as professional knowledge landscapes creates openings for exploring the storied nature of teacher identity while also challenging us to think about each school context from multiple vantage points. In the next section of this paper, we reconstruct a teacher's story, following the shifting nature of her story to live by as she composes her teaching life both inside and outside of her classroom context on the professional knowledge landscape of her school.

2. Reconstructing Naomi's[1] Experiences

Qualitative data collection is based on using protocols developed during the study.

Narrative researchers collaborate with participants.

Narrative researchers collect studies from individuals.

(08) It is our first time coming together with our group of teacher co-researchers. We are nervous and somewhat uncertain of how the evening will unfold, yet in the same moment, our sense of excitement and anticipation draws us to this conversation. We are a group of both strangers and acquaintances, gathering from various school landscapes. In the privacy of Janice's living room, we sit together, surrounded by candlelight, food, and wine. A common storyline joins us together—our lives as teachers.

Qualitative data collections involve gathering text or image data.

Narrative researchers retell the story.

Narrative researchers report a chronology of individual experiences.

(09) This common experience enables us, with ease, to pick up on the threads of our lives, connecting stories of where we last saw one another. After a few moments, the room becomes quiet, a sign that it is time to begin this new research conversation between us. Feeling a need to tell of our selves, as researchers positioned at the university, we (including our advisor, Jean Clandinin) each share stories of what has brought us to this exploration of a narrative understanding of teacher knowledge and identity. Our stories, centering around research themes of margins (Anzaldúa 1987, 1990) and positionings (Miller, 1994), create an opening for our co-researchers who are positioned as teachers on the landscape, to begin to share their stories. The circle of storytelling broadens as we go around the living room, listening to each teacher-coresearcher share of her life. When our storytelling has passed nearly full circle, there is one last pause, an invitation for Naomi, who has not yet spoken, to share her story.

Qualitative data analysis consists of describing information and developing themes.

(10) Naomi begins to tell the story of herself by situating her narrative within a rural junior/senior high school landscape. She describes her teaching assignment as very specialized, being the only teacher in this position within her school and school district over an eight-year period. Naomi's description speaks, to a certain degree, of the loneliness and isolation which surrounded her as she composed her teaching life, a context she describes in her own words when she states, "I really

---

[1]Because of the vulnerable nature of this story, pseudonyms have been assigned to the characters in order to protect their identities.

Qualitative data analysis consists of text analysis.

didn't have anyone that I could plan with." Having noted how this particular positioning shaped her life as a teacher on this school landscape, Naomi quickly emphasizes that her sense of marginalization was far more profound than her visible positioning on the landscape as the only teacher of a specialized program. She begins to describe this deeper sense of marginalization when she says, "Certainly when I started teaching there, I don't think I was on the margin at all. As time went on, though, I very much became an outsider." Naomi unpacks her knowledge of becoming an outsider by recounting how she came to recognize that she was not following the "status quo" story of her school. The magnitude of choosing to position herself in this way was expressed when she reflected, "I guess personally I made that choice but as a result of it, I quit my job because I couldn't be there anymore and agree." Naomi explained that in order for her to make sense of her experience and to continue to exist on this school landscape, she consciously chose to position herself outside the "school story"—a story shaped by a mandate of inclusion for students with special needs (Clandinin & Connelly, 1995, 1996). She reflected her deepening awareness of this story by saying, "I think I initially started to go there [outside the school story], maybe not consciously, but I think soon it was a conscious decision and I was not prepared to be there in any other way . . . , I think it was the only way that I could make sense. It was the only way that I could exist."

(11) Naomi's sharing in this first conversation speaks to us of her internal struggle, of her need to live in a space where she could "make sense" of her experiences in an "educative" (Dewey, 1938) way, constructively shaping her ongoing practice. In our second conversation as a research community, Naomi moves deeper into this story. She does this by unpacking experiences which led her to resign from her teaching position, leaving the school and her teaching community.

(12) Naomi began to speak of these experiences by introducing herself and "the special needs teacher" (who we named Brian) as two central characters in the story. In her first few words, Naomi positioned herself as living within her classroom on her school landscape. Through Naomi's eyes, Brian was positioned as someone who had influence in her program, yet lived distantly from the physical space of her classroom. At the outset, we learned from Naomi that Brian, alone, determined the placement of each special needs student. We also discovered that when a student with special needs (who we named Alicia) was placed in Naomi's room, a program aide (who we named Laura) was assigned to work with Alicia. Outlining the constraints of her timetable and teaching assignment, Naomi emphasized her struggle to negotiate a meaningful program for Alicia so that she would experience success.

(13) The tension in the relationship between Naomi and Brian became apparent at the first reporting period, and was heightened at each successive reporting period. At the centre of this tension was the confusion over who would be responsible for determining and assigning Alicia's grade. In the first reporting period Naomi both determined and assigned Alicia's grade. However, she was troubled by being prevented, by a school directive, from indicating to Alicia's parents that she was working on a program which had been modified to meet her particular learning needs. Through Naomi's telling, we learned that her desire for authentic dialogue with parents was in conflict with Brian, who lived a story of keeping parents happy at all costs.

(14) In the second reporting period, another special needs aide, with whom Naomi had little interaction, informed her that Brian would "do

the mark" for Alicia. Naomi was not involved in determining Alicia's grade, yet she discovered that her name was recorded beside the assigned grade on the report card which was sent home. In this situation, and in those following, Naomi attempted to understand this practice through conversation with Laura, the special needs program aide who was working in her classroom; the special needs teacher, Brian; her principal; her vice principal; and her colleagues on staff. As the plotline in this story developed, Naomi continued to question Brian's practice in "marking" the student's work. In Naomi's telling of the story, it appeared to her as though Brian deflected his responsibility onto others and eventually storied her as a teacher who simply did not understand how to mark students with special needs.

(15) As the story continued, a border began to appear between Naomi and Brian. Her intolerance over the absence of communication and understanding which was shaping their relationship led Naomi to request a meeting between Brian, Laura, and herself. Having Laura present at the meeting was responded to with resistance from Brian. However, Naomi insisted that Laura's voice be present because of her intimate understanding of Alicia and the classroom program. Following the meeting, Naomi learned that Brian storied the event as an upsetting exchange, as he felt Laura's questions had embarrassed him in front of Naomi. In response to their meeting, he requested that the school administrators "fire" Laura. Naomi countered his telling of this event to the administration with her own version of what happened, and Laura's position was maintained.

(16) Naomi described the aura of silence she experienced as the story continued to unfold into the second school year. At the edges of this silence, Naomi recalled witnessing "horrendous things" continuing to take place. Conversation in relation to the growing dilemma surrounding this school story begins to occur only in secrecy, when "nobody was in the vicinity." For Naomi, her school landscape became a place where there was an intolerance for tension. Because her story to live by necessitated exploring tension in relationship with others, her understanding of the complexities of her school landscape was pushed further to the margins.

(17) Naomi countered this push, continuing to resist the school story by challenging Brian's living out of it. Her principal responded to Naomi by consistently dismissing her concerns, eventually telling her that she must either support Brian or say nothing at all. Naomi's story closed with a profound sense of loss in the relationship she had lived with her principal. Her deeply felt sense of marginalization, shaped by the conflicting nature of the stories being lived and told on her school landscape, ultimately led her to leave her school community and to resign her position with the district. Finding no place for her story to "exist" on this school landscape, Naomi felt she was left with no choice but to leave.

3. Retelling Naomi's Story in Terms of the Professional Knowledge Landscape

Narrative researchers develop themes.

(18) While Naomi's recounting of her experience as a marginalized member of this school community was painful and troubling, her story holds educative promise for understanding school contexts and teachers' stories to live by. This promise led us to reconsider Naomi's story by focusing on the shaping nature of Naomi's school context on her story to live by as a teacher.

Narrative researchers describe the setting of context.

(19) We begin this exploration by drawing on Clandinin and Connelly's (1995) conceptual framework of the "professional knowledge landscape"[2] which enabled us to make meaning of Naomi's story through a focus on her story to live by and on her experience in "two fundamentally different places" on her school landscape— "the one behind the classroom door with students, and the other in professional places with others" (p. 5). When we discuss the physical space *inside* Naomi's classroom, we draw upon Clandinin and Connelly's (1995) metaphor by referring to this place on her school landscape as her "in-classroom" space. When we discuss Naomi's experience *outside* her classroom on this school landscape, we refer to these spaces as "out-of-classroom" places. Inquiring into Naomi's experience within each of these places, her in-classroom and her out-of-classroom places on this school landscape, allowed us to examine the unique qualities of these places and the differing ways in which Naomi authored her life within each.

4. Naomi's In-Classroom Place on the Professional Knowledge Landscape

(20) The conceptual framework of the professional knowledge landscape views teachers as actively engaged practitioners who are attempting to author meaningful lives, telling and retelling themselves through their classroom practice (Clandinin & Connelly, 1995) as they respond to the shifting policy expectations and social issues which surround their work, and to the specific needs of their students. From this vantage point, teachers are not viewed as empty vessels waiting to be filled by the ideas of others, but are understood as "holders and makers of knowledge" (Clandinin, 1997, p. 1).

(21) Within the in-classroom place on the professional knowledge landscape of schools, the moral authority for a teacher's understanding of her story to live by (Connelly & Clandinin, 1999) is self-authored, shaped by each teacher's particular narrative history and negotiated in relation with students. Because teachers position themselves within their classrooms

---

[2]An in-depth understanding of the term "professional knowledge landscape" is developed by Clandinin and Connelly (1995) in *Teachers' professional knowledge landscapes*. Our work in this paper draws upon Clandinin and Connelly's following description:

> A landscape metaphor . . . allows us to talk about space, place, and time. Furthermore, it has a sense of expansiveness and the possibility of being filled with diverse people, things, and events in different relationships. Understanding professional knowledge as comprising a landscape calls for a notion of professional knowledge as composed of a wide variety of components and influenced by a wide variety of people, places, and things. Because we see the professional knowledge landscape as composed of relationships among peoples, places, and things, we see it as both an intellectual and a moral landscape. (p. 4/5)

A central focus in this paper is toward understanding the relationship between one teacher's story of marginalization on her school landscape and her identity. Clandinin and Connelly's metaphor helped us uncover the multi-dimensional qualities of this teacher's context. Viewing her professional landscape from multiple vantage points provided insight into her knowledge context while also engaging us in questions of relationship—between this teacher and the shifting people, places, and things on her school landscape. Understanding this teacher's story from a place perspective, we were able to explore her differing experience in two very different places on her school landscape, her "in-classroom place" and the "out-of-classroom" places. The temporal qualities of this teacher's narrative created openings for us to inquire deeply into the ways the story of inclusive education was shaping her school landscape. By focusing on the personal history the teacher embodied as she negotiated her professional landscape, her knowing of her self in relation to a variety of diverse people, places, things, and events became visible.

around the story they embody of themselves as teachers, the in-classroom place on the professional knowledge landscape of schools is often characterized by a sense of safety and secrecy. While Clandinin and Connelly (1995) caution that this secrecy should not be glorified, they also note that it plays an important role in shaping the epistemological nature of the in-classroom place on the professional knowledge landscape as a space in which teachers feel "free from scrutiny . . . [and are able] to live stories of practice" (p. 13) which honour their embodied knowing. It is in this way that the in-classroom place on the professional knowledge landscape is epistemologically and morally grounded in narrative knowledge. This narrative grounding enables the in-classroom place to be educative for teachers, as their stories to live by can be negotiated without judgment framed by the "theoretical knowledge and the abstract rhetoric of conclusions found in the professional knowledge landscape outside the classroom" (p. 12).

(22) As we listened to Naomi tell stories of her in-classroom place on her school landscape, she shared telling images of how she viewed this space. Early in her storytelling, Naomi described her in-classroom place as "*my* space,"—an important image which awakened us to her strong sense of agency within this space. Beginning to describe her concerns about Brian's placement of Alicia into her classroom, Naomi explained, "Because he was special needs . . . he was involved in everybody else's program. And so you couldn't really just sort of say, "Well as long as you stay out of *my* space, I'll deal with this . . . because he was a part of your space." Naomi's description of her in-classroom place helped us to see that this was a space of belonging for Naomi, a secure place for her "self authorship" of her story to live by as teacher—one she felt determined to protect and uphold (Carr, 1986).

(23) We were also drawn to Naomi's images of herself as a teacher within her classroom space through her stories of experience with students. Naomi's understanding of her in-classroom place, and her ability to shape it, were evident when she discussed her struggle with the constraints of her teaching time-table. Recognizing the limitations this time-table placed upon her students and, in this particular story, upon Alicia, Naomi said,

> After I got to know my grade seven classes then [Alicia] was in one too where we met. Generally I had my students for a 40 minute class and an 80 minute class. Well, 40 minutes for all of my students was too short, for [Alicia] it was *really*, I mean she would just barely get her stuff out and get started and now it's time to finish . . . that class just really wasn't the type of setting that she should have been in. But my other two grade seven classes were a lot better, so finally after many discussions I got her moved into a different grade seven class that only had 80 minute blocks and so I'd see her twice one week and only once the next week, so that wasn't the best, but it was better than that 40 minute class and it was a much better environment. Plus she was in the biggest grade seven class and then afterwards she was in the smallest one.

(24) Naomi placed significance in this event and, as she told this story, we began to see that one of the threads woven into the story she was composing was that of working in close relationship with students. Naomi's focus on what was best for this particular student led her to the out-of-classroom place on her school landscape and into "many discussions" with colleagues. Within her recounting of this experience, there was a sense that the negotiation of Alicia's timetable on the out-of-classroom place may have been difficult. However, Naomi appeared to view the negotiation as morally necessary because, as she described, Alicia's first class placement "just . . . wasn't the type of setting that she should have been in." We were also left with the sense that, regardless of the difficulties Naomi experienced through this out-of-classroom negotiation, she eventually felt that she was able to successfully negotiate

a better situation for Alicia. In this way and in this particular instance, we felt as though the story she was authoring as teacher was honored, both within her in-classroom place and on the out-of-classroom places on the professional knowledge landscape of her school.

(25) Other qualities of Naomi's ability to negotiate her identity within her classroom were shared as she storied her relationship with Laura. We learned of the relationship which developed between Naomi and Laura when Naomi said, "I did have an aide and she was absolutely wonderful and she basically taught me how to modify and that type of thing, you know, meet that little girl's needs." By storying Laura as a co-teacher, Naomi made visible the deep sense of respect and validation she felt towards this woman. She described how their relationship enabled them to modify a program which made sense for Alicia. Through Naomi's telling of their relationship, we saw her recognition of Laura as a person who mattered in her life. Her words spoke to us of a relationship in which mutuality created openings for educative conversation, risk taking, and the imagining of possibilities for a student who had been defined as "special needs." It was being in relation which enabled them to work together in the best interests of Alicia.

(26) Naomi's story of Laura created an image of negotiation which occurred with authenticity. We wonder if the relationship they shared may have led Naomi to become more trusting of the out-of-classroom place on her school landscape with the intent of also engaging there "in conversations where stories can be told, reflected back, heard in different ways, retold, and relived in new ways" (Clandinin & Connelly, 1995, p. 13). Being in relationship was an overlapping thread in Naomi's story of both her students and Laura. This led us to believe that relational understanding of experience was the central plotline in Naomi's story to live by. These two stories of Naomi's in-classroom place on her school landscape also revealed that, within this space, Naomi was deeply engaged in living and retelling this story of herself in negotiation with those who shared the in-classroom space—the students and Laura.

(27) This was not the plotline which Naomi's telling took on as she continued to unpack more of her experience on this school landscape surrounding her work with Alicia and other students with special needs. Increasingly, Naomi's crossing of borders between the in- and out-of-classroom places on her school landscape created tensions for her. As Clandinin and Connelly's (1995) work highlights, "when teachers leave their classrooms and move into another place on the professional knowledge landscape, they leave the safe secrecy of the classroom and enter a public place on the landscape" (p. 14). These out-of-classroom places on the professional knowledge landscape are "dramatically different epistemological and moral place[s]" (p. 14). In the next section of this paper we explore numerous qualities of the out-of-classroom place on Naomi's school landscape and the ways they shaped her story to live by.

5. Naomi's Out-of-Classroom Place on the Professional Knowledge Landscape

(28) In contrast to the safety and self-authorship which shape the in-classroom place on the professional knowledge landscape, the out-of-classroom place is one largely defined by a sacred story of theory over practice (Clandinin & Connelly, 1995). In this out-of-classroom place, policies and prescriptions, holding "theoretical knowledge claims," are delivered from above via the conduit—the dominant communication pipeline which links teachers' lives to their school boards, governing agencies, and associations. This theoretical knowledge arrives into the lives of teachers in the form of new curriculum material, textbooks, and policy mandates. They

are scripted into teachers' lives, often with no substantive place for conversation about what is being "funneled down." Teachers are often left to make sense of these materials behind their classroom doors in secrecy and silence, negotiating these theories in relation to their story to live by.

(29) The sacred theory-practice story enters the school landscape with a "moral push," leaving teachers caught in what Clandinin and Connelly (1995) describe as a "split existence." Teachers begin to struggle with their own knowing—knowing that is grounded in their narrative histories and is embedded within their in-classroom practice—and their negotiation of a sacred knowing, a prescriptive "you should" kind of knowing which shares the out-of-classroom place on the professional knowledge landscape. It is this tension which causes teachers to experience the out-of-classroom place as abstract, a place that "floats untethered" with "policy prescriptions [that] . . . are torn out of their historical, narrative contexts" (Clandinin & Connelly, 1995, p. 11). On the out-of-classroom place, the self-authorship, which can be felt within the in-classroom place, becomes defined by an abstract "other," and the moral quality of the landscape becomes pre-scripted from outside. In this way, the out-of-classroom place can become a "de-personalized" and disconnected place for teachers to live their storied lives.

(30) In Naomi's story we are presented with an explicit example of the dilemmas and sense of split existence which become shaped by a teacher's movement between these two profoundly different places of knowing, defined by dramatically different moral qualities. The sacred story which arrived onto Naomi's landscape from some abstract place along the conduit appeared to be one of inclusion; a story loaded with moral implications for teachers. Naomi first faced this new school story when a student with special needs was placed in her classroom and, in her telling of the story, we sensed there was little discussion surrounding the placement—it was simply an expectation. Describing her understanding of this situation, Naomi said, "[Brian] picked which teacher they'd go in with." As Naomi recounted how the story of inclusion began to take hold on the professional knowledge landscape of her school, we began to see her story coming into conflict with the larger school story, and with those positioned distantly, outside of her classroom context: office support staff, other program aides, Brian, and the school administrators.

(31) Naomi faced her first moral dilemma on the out-of-classroom place when she was met with a prescriptive message from the office staff regarding the reporting process for students with special needs, such as Alicia. Naomi's intention was to communicate openly and honestly with the parents about Alicia's program. However, when she attempted to enter a conversation with the office staff about this process, offering her knowing and understanding of Alicia as she had lived it in her classroom, she came into direct conflict with the conduit and was told, "No, we want her [Alicia] to do the same as everybody else. . . . We're not going to do a different style of report card." Feeling strongly about this issue, Naomi countered this response with, "That's fine. I'll just type up a letter and tell her mom, explaining to her what we've been working on." She was met with, "No, you can't do that either." On the out-of-classroom place, as Clandinin and Connelly (1995) point out, "teachers are not, by and large, expected to personalize conduit materials by considering how materials fit their personality and teaching styles, classrooms, students, and so forth" (p. 11). Naomi was disturbed by the depersonalized message she received in this situation and the way in which she was forced to send home a mark in the report card which she felt "wasn't the truth." It was in this critical

moment of "self-sacrifice" that we saw Naomi's determination to live by what she knew. There was a sense of future possibility as she discussed her intention not to be constrained by the story of inclusion shaping the school landscape outside her classroom during the next reporting period.

(32) The impact of the out-of-classroom place on Naomi's story was felt again when she told of receiving another prescriptive message regarding the marking process, this time sent from Brian via his program aide. Naomi recalled the aide saying, "You're not supposed to do a mark for [Alicia], [Brian] is going to do all the marks for all the kids." The distance with which this message was delivered led us to wonder about the pervasive story which was shaping Naomi's school landscape—one in which spaces for authentic conversation were diminishing. By introducing a new character into the story, a "messenger" to deliver information, Brian reshaped the relational space between himself and Naomi, creating distance and separation. Naomi's response to this widening gap in their relational space was to seek out further conversation and connection so that she might better understand the marking process being implemented by Brian. As she recounted her story of this incident, Naomi recalled thinking to herself, "I'm sure he's going to come and have a meeting with me because he's never been in this classroom. He doesn't have any idea what [Alicia] is doing, so how could he possibly make a mark for her?" However, as Naomi remembered the unfolding events within this story, she shared that Brian did not come to speak with her and in the growing absence of conversation between them, a mark was entered into Alicia's report card, with Naomi's name placed beside it. The story, centering around inclusive practice, once again took on an abstract quality (Clandinin & Connelly, 1995) as the characters in this story lived out their practice in a distant, depersonalized, and disconnected manner.

(33) The embeddedness of this story within her school landscape became apparent as Naomi struggled to create openings for conversation with Brian. However, as she told the story, we came to see that these attempts ended in disappointment, creating further dilemmas for her. Clandinin and Connelly (1995) describe that in the absence of places for conversation on policies funneled down the conduit onto the school landscape, "discussion . . . is removed from matters of substance to matters of personality and power" (p. 11). Listening to Naomi's story, we heard how she experienced this shift from conversation to personality and power, as she described Brian's reaction to a meeting she had arranged between him, Laura, and herself. "I requested that [Laura] be there because, you know, she too works with [Alicia] so she should contribute to this. I mean she probably knows the most out of all of us how [Alicia] feels during all of those activities." Naomi was troubled when Brian responded to her request with resistance. Naomi said, "He didn't want [Laura] there and I just said, 'Well she, in my class, she works with [Alicia] in my classroom so, she's coming'." Brian's apparent devaluing of Laura's position on the school landscape came into direct conflict with the relational story Naomi lived by within her classroom, placing stress on the intended conversation which she had imagined would shape their meeting.

(34) Following this meeting, Naomi recalled how she felt Brian's final response was played out through personality, position, and power, "He wanted [Laura] fired because she asked him questions that embarrassed him in front of me." This dramatic and alarming response to what Naomi had imagined as a conversation to bridge their understanding between the in- and out-of-classroom places on the school landscape only served to create further distance between Naomi and Brian and their stories of one another.

(35) Personality and power become even more embedded in discussions outside Naomi's classroom context as the story Naomi was authoring eventually came into direct conflict with Brian's story. When Naomi questioned Brian about his positioning within the school story, she described him defining it as a "power-over" (Josselson, 1994) positioning in which he would "monitor" and "supervise" her practice, and the practice of others within the school. Naomi recalled,

> One day I got really angry at [Brian] and I said, 'Tell me what your job is here?' I said, 'You know, you just live off the sweat and tears of the other teachers here.' He told me that he had to be hired in our school to monitor the teachers because we weren't caring enough individuals and we were just cruel to the kids and he was there to save them.

(36) Unpacking how troubled she was by Brian's description of himself as being hired to monitor her because she was cruel to Alicia within her classroom, Naomi said, "He told me that one day, that he was hired to monitor me as well as the others and I said to him, 'So . . . do you view yourself as being my supervisor?' He responded by saying. 'Yeah' and I said, 'Well, that would be the day, and if you're ever in that position, it will certainly be the day that I cease to work here.' In Naomi's telling of this angry exchange between them, we sensed her struggle with this story. Caught between the borders of personalities and positions of power, shaped by the larger school story, we recognized her hopelessness in being able to enter into an educative conversation surrounding students with special needs in places outside her classroom on the landscape of her school.

(37) This critical absence of a space for conversation for Naomi reached its final, dramatic conclusion when she discovered that her principal, whom she respected, cared for, and trusted, attempted to silence her knowing in the face of the dominant school story. Describing two stories of the distance she began to experience between herself and her principal, Naomi recounted being "called down" to her principal's office after school to address the increasing tension between Brian and herself. As she told this story over the discussion of their confrontational exchange which had taken place between herself and Brian regarding his position in the school story in relation to her own, she said:

> As a result . . . my principal call[ed] me down and sa[id], 'Did you have a talk with [Brian] today?' 'Yup.' 'Well what happened? Did it get, you know, a little out of hand?' And I said, 'I don't know. I don't think it got out of hand, it was just very truthful.' 'Well did you tell him that you didn't think he did much at our school?' And I said, 'Yes, I told him exactly that. That's exactly how I feel and I would tell him that again because I haven't changed my opinion at all since.'

(38) The determination and conviction with which Naomi spoke about this exchange gave us insight into the strength of her story and her recurring need for "truthful" conversation. Naomi's sense of connection with Alicia and Laura created a moral space in which their knowing of one another shaped a relationship where care was central. In her telling of the story, we saw that Naomi was unwilling to compromise her "self positioning" as a teacher who cared about her students and Laura. However, we learned that, in her first meeting with her principal regarding this tension, the message Naomi received was, "You can't tell people stuff like that. . . ." In a second meeting with her principal, behind the closed doors of his office, Naomi's story to live by bumped up against the school story once again, and in this meeting as well, Naomi received a silencing response. "He said things like well, 'We do all kinds of things in our school, Naomi, graduation

and volleyball teams and na, na, na and we have special needs here.' And I'm kind of going, 'Oh yeah. How does a [special needs] program fit into extra curricular, you know?'." Her principal replied by saying, "We have to support those things and if we can't support them, then the least we can do is say nothing at all." It was at this moment in Naomi's storytelling that we were most profoundly struck by the shaping nature of the out-of-classroom place on Naomi's story to live by. Temporally casting her relationship with her principal in a past sense, Naomi shared, "I *did* really like my principal." We imagine Naomi's embodied knowing of this man may have been at least partially shaped by her recognition of his response, which seemed to honor her agency during the tension surrounding Laura's dismissal, resulting in her position being maintained. Naomi expressed her painful awakening to a different understanding of her principal as she began to realize that the person with whom she had always found a space for authentic conversation outside her classroom was also no longer able to hear her words. In one silencing instance Naomi was told to "say nothing at all," and, in another, she recalled her principal saying, "Look, I don't want to get involved with special needs. I know nothing about it, as long as everybody's quiet and happy. . . ."

(39) Reinforcing this message, we discovered that Naomi's vice principal would only enter into conversation with her in the hidden corridors of the school when, ". . . nobody was in the vicinity." In the face of the powerful school structures and prescriptive conduit story which was shaping the professional knowledge landscape of her school, Naomi's story was pushed aside, to a place of silence. As she continued to resist the "accepted school story," her story to live by became marginalized, moving further and further to the edges of what was defined as acceptable on her school landscape. Naomi described her outside positioning in our first conversation when she said, "I guess I went to the margins [of the "status quo" story of the school] because I wasn't willing to participate in some of the things that I saw happening [t]here. . . . You do live in that isolation. . . ." Ultimately the dilemmas which arose out of the abrasion between these two dramatically different moral spaces on the landscape—Naomi's in-classroom and out-of-classroom places—became too overwhelming for Naomi. It was at this point that she decided that she must leave the school.

6. Response on the Out-of-Classroom Place on Naomi's School Landscape

(40) By carefully following Naomi's story as it wove its way through both the in- and out-of-classroom places on the professional knowledge landscape of her school, we were struck by the essence of response as it developed in Naomi's story, both how it was given and the ways in which it was received. In this particular story, our challenge to more fully understand response was intensified as we learned of a school community, at least through the eyes of one teacher, where her story to live by came to live at the margins of the school story, surrounded by a profound sense of silence and isolation. The tensions which emerged between Naomi's story and the school story brought forward the significant gap formed as imagined and actual response came into conflict on the school landscape. The presence of this tension caused us to wonder about response—both how it is shaped by the school story and, in turn, how it shaped Naomi's story to live by. As we listened to, read, and re-read Naomi's story, we began to look more closely at response. Living with this story over time enabled us to see some of the ways that response shaped, and was shaped by, Naomi's story to live by, her relationships with her colleagues, and the larger school story of inclusion.

(41) Interweaving our previous unpacking of Naomi's story, through our focus on the in- and out-of-classroom places on her landscape, we continue this inquiry by exploring how the story of school, shaped through response, impacted Naomi's story to live by. Making meaning of Naomi's story, as lived out on a professional knowledge landscape, enabled us to illustrate that the teacher story Naomi was authoring was deeply grounded within her narrative knowing of herself as living in relationship with others. Such a view of Naomi's story revealed that as she crossed the border between her in- and out-of-classroom places on her school landscape, she consistently attempted to negotiate her relational story through conversation with various other characters with whom she interacted. It was both the actual and imagined response received by Naomi, as well as the response she gave in return, that uncovered the ways in which the borders on Naomi's school landscape were constructed and lived out.

(42) The dilemmas Naomi faced as she crossed these borders eventually drew forth her counterstory of resistance and insubordination (Nelson, 1995)—her story to live by which became a counterstory within her particular school landscape. Naomi named her "counterstory to live by" in our initial research conversation when she said, "I went to the margins . . . because I wasn't willing to participate in some of the things I saw happening there and as a result of that, I wasn't following the status quo of my school." Naomi's reconstruction of herself within her spoken text highlighted her determination to live her story in a way which she felt was educative. Even though this determination to stay with her story eventually led her to resign, there was a hopeful edge to her telling in that she came to see her resignation as an educative alternative to negotiating her story on a school landscape which she increasingly experienced as miseducative. In the final section of this paper, we return to Naomi's storytelling of her professional knowledge context, looking closely at the borders and border-crossings shaped out of the response on both the in- and out-of-classroom places on this school landscape. As we take a closer look at response by naming these borders and bordercrossings, we hope to gain further insight into the story Naomi authored as it was negotiated within and between borders shaped by the school story of inclusion.

Qualitative data analysis consists of describing information and developing themes.

7. Borders and Bordercrossings on the Professional Knowledge Landscape

7.1 Borders of Ownership

(43) The first border made present to us through the telling of this story, one of ownership, spoke to us of the significance of the in-classroom place in Naomi's life as a teacher. It is not surprising to us that this place, described with such passion by Naomi as "*my* space," was one she held sacred and was determined to protect. Looking carefully at this protective stance provided us insight into the nature of Naomi's response, where it came from, and the border that was shaped as a result. Naomi's classroom was a visible space on the landscape in which we were able to see her living her story in a meaningful and educative manner as highlighted through her telling of the relational story she composed alongside the students and Laura. We saw a shift in the safety of Naomi's classroom place, however, when the story of inclusion began to break through the protective border she had constructed around herself and her classroom. We believe the construction of this border was grounded within Naomi's narrative history with previous school stories imposed upon her, and was shaped along with her present response to a school story of inclusion she had little understanding of, and even less authority to negotiate as a member of this

school landscape. Faced with the threat this school story presented in relationship to her story, she struggled to protect the one place on the landscape she intimately understood, a place which made moral sense to her as she worked in relation with her students.

7.2 Negotiating Bordercrossings

(44) Naomi's understanding of the restrictive structures imposed from the out-of-classroom place on the school landscape was evident through her discussion of negotiating the school timetable to meet the needs of her students. In this context, the school timetable became symbolic of a "sacred story" (Crites, 1971) in the out-of-classroom place. These kinds of stories can confine students' and teachers' lives within predetermined frameworks and can become "internalized" and "absorbed" into a "taken-for-grantedness" (Greene, 1993, 1995) of experience. Naomi's knowledge of this sacredness made the crossing of this border even more significant. Her response, reflected through her re-negotiation of the school timetable, indicated her courage and conviction to stand up to this story of school even when this task seemed a challenge. Her success in addressing this challenge was a critical moment in Naomi's story. The response she received was a hopeful sign of possibility within the larger school landscape as it affirmed her knowing while also helping her to recognize that the story she was authoring could be honoured in places beyond the boundaries of her classroom. In this event, we saw a shift in Naomi's internal border of ownership. This shift enabled her to recognize the importance of her story to live by and the place it had in reshaping the borders constructed between her classroom and those outside her classroom.

(45) *7.2.1 Bordercrossings, within Public Homeplaces.* The response given and received in the relational space between Naomi and Laura was not evident within the telling of this story, yet this does not diminish its importance in Naomi's experience of living on this school landscape. Through Naomi's telling of the value of Laura to this program, a much different story of ownership and borders emerged, quite different from how Naomi storied the borders between herself and Brian. Naomi was open to the presence of Laura in her classroom and together they shaped a relational space, through response, which we imagine enabled both of them to live a story that made sense. As we read and reread Naomi's telling description of Laura, we were left with the image of "seamless" (Clandinin & Connelly, 1997), although continuously negotiated, bordercrossings in which the "self" was never placed in jeopardy, but rather, was enriched by seeing and being present to the other. In Buber's (1965) sense of "making present," Naomi was able to recognize herself through her relation to this other self, her program aide, Laura. The fluidity of distance and relation negotiated between them was ever-present. As Friedman (1965), referring to Buber, highlights:

> Making the other present means 'to imagine the real' to imagine quite concretely what another . . . is wishing, feeling, perceiving, and thinking . . . a bold swinging into the other which demands the intensest action of one's being. . . . One can only do this as a parntner, standing in a common situation with the other. (p. 29)

Naomi's deeply felt sense of Laura as a woman who embodied knowing of Alicia made visible Naomi's "bold swinging" into the story she perceived Laura was living. The "public homeplace" shaped between Naomi and Laura was the classroom, a safe place in which they could authentically enter into one another's presence (Belenky, Bond, & Weinstock, 1997).

7.3 Borders of Positional Power

(46) The borders of positional power emerged for Naomi when she recognized that the larger school story of inclusion being played out on her school landscape came to define Brian as someone who had direct power and influence within her in-classroom place. Naomi's tension with Brian centered around his positioning which allowed him to solely select the teachers with whom the students with special needs would be placed. Her understanding of the role Brian played within the school context drew forth an immediate border for Naomi, between herself and Brian. Naomi saw herself positioned on one side, with no voice in decision making, while Brian was positioned on the other side, with a powerful decision making voice. This border of power manifested itself in multiple ways through the response exchanged on the school landscape.

(47) *7.3.1 Sameness.* In the discussion surrounding the report card which took place at the school office, the border was shaped by response which dictated a message of unity in which, "We all must be the same"—a message common on school landscapes and one shaped by forces of power and control in out-of-classroom places. Naomi's challenging of this response was seen as a threat to the unified story of school. Unlike the response she received regarding the school timetable, this response restricted her story to live by and forced her into conflict with the school story of inclusion. In this social context, personal relation in favour of the elements of pure collectivity" (Friedman, 1965, p. 25) and Naomi's story to live by, with its central plotline of human relatedness, was placed at great risk.

(48) *7.3.2 Distance.* A border of distance became present in the story through the manner in which the second reporting period was addressed. The face to-face conflict which emerged through the response to "sameness" sent from the school office was reshaped to a more distant and evasive form of response as messages were delivered indirectly from those in positions of power on the school landscape. Naomi's telling of her expectation that Brian would come and meet with her regarding the marks he placed on Alicia's report card awakened us to a widening gap forming between the imagined and actual response which took place in this story, and how profoundly this response was being shaped by the larger school story. When Brian's actual response of not coming to engage in conversation with Naomi did not meet with her expectation, her tension over this distance between her imagined and his actual response was intensified and the space between solidified. As Friedman (in Buber, 1965) writes, "When [we] fail to enter into relation . . . the distance thickens and solidifies; instead of making room for relation it obstructs it" (p. 22). It became apparent to us that as the school story of inclusion thickened and reified itself on the school landscape, so too, did the relational story being lived out between Naomi and Brian. For Naomi, this distancing response came in conflict with her embodied knowing of living in relationship with others, pushing the story she was attempting to author into a vulnerable and isolating place on this school landscape.

(49) *7.3.3 Confrontation.* Naomi's need to confront the multiple borders, forming both within herself and between herself and others on the exterior landscape of her school, caused her story to live by to enter an even more fragile state as her experience and understanding of the story of inclusion became even more marginalized. Naomi's recognition of her more vulnerable place on this school landscape did not prevent her from attempting to create an opening through conversation with Brian regarding the report cards; however, in the process, she inadvertently strengthened the existing

borders between them, shaping additional ones as well. The relational story Naomi was determined to negotiate was "rapidly redefined on the landscape as [a] conflicting story" (Clandinin & Connelly, 1995).

(50) *7.3.4 Arrogance.* One of these additional borders appeared to be that of arrogance as Brian responded to Naomi's search for understanding by consciously separating himself from both Naomi and Laura, redefining his positioning to Naomi in terms of power over as her "supervisor" and "monitor." This new event in the space between brought forth an emotional response in Naomi which caused a shift in her image of Brian as well as her image of self (Josselson, 1992). This new border or arrogance hastened the solidification process of the school story and caused Naomi to rage against it as her story to live by struggled to survive. It was becoming, "more and more difficult to penetrate the increasingly tough layer which [had] settled down on . . . [her] being" (Buber, 1965, p. 78).

7.4 Borders of Judgment and Silence

(51) Naomi's conscious decision to live her story—one which ran counter to the school story—positioned her in a place of extreme vulnerability. This was powerfully illuminated through the silencing response she received from her school administrators regarding Brian and the school story of inclusion. The message of support and acceptance of the school story at any cost was uncovered for us in Buber's (1965) description of social contexts in which, "the life between person and person seems to retreat more and more before the advance of the collective" (p. 73). The response from both her principal and vice-principal created a border of secrecy and silence, pushing Naomi's story to live by to the far "ragged edges" (Greene, 1994) of the advancing school story. Living on that edge equated to living in isolation as the space for relatedness became more scarce on Naomi's school landscape. For Naomi, who understood her world through deep and connected relationship with others, this edge became too fragile a place on which to stand. Without the embeddedness of her relational story within this social context, Naomi had no "place" to "exist." Hope came through an ultimate act of resistance for Naomi—leaving her school. Like Bell Hooks (1996), who so knowingly describes this critical moment of self recovery, "standing on the edge of the cliff about to fall into the abyss, I remember who I am" (p. 182), we imagine that Naomi may have experienced a similar awakening. We have no way of knowing what Naomi's response of resistance may have done to reshape the school story of inclusion. However, we do know that Naomi's leaving moved her to an educative place in which she could be true to herself—one best described through her own words:

> I think that's very difficult to stand on the outside of things and say, 'Yes, I will fight for this.' I think that it's only really when you come into those places of 'there is an end to this' that you can make that choice. . . . I made the decision that if things weren't going to change there, then I was going to leave. . . . I made that decision, now I'm free to say what I want.

Qualitative interpretations situate findings within large meanings.

8. Imagining Possibilities

> Those who have been excluded by the mainstream, or who have chosen to live and/or learn apart from it, may be the very people to help us find particularly effective ways to learn in community—ways less skewed by conformity, less dominated by institutional aspirations; ways perhaps truer to the basic human needs we all . . . share—to first and foremost feel that we matter to those around us. (Heller, 1997, p. 160)

(52) There is no doubt that Naomi was profoundly influenced by telling and living her story of herself on this school landscape. Had she a choice in

living her story, she may not have eventually resigned from her position at this school. However, as Clandinin and Connelly (1995) have highlighted, "teachers must, of necessity, tell stories . . . because . . . [storytelling] is . . . the most basic way, that humans make meaning of their experience" (p. 154). Naomi's need to mediate her story to live by as she negotiated the school landscape shifted her experience of this professional context from educative to miseducative. This may not have occurred if she had continued to tell her story only within the confines of her in-classroom place on the school landscape. Unlike so many of the teachers with whom Clandinin and Connelly worked, who told "cover stories" of themselves as a way to manage their tensions between the in- and out-of-classroom places on the professional knowledge landscape, Naomi did not, even though doing so was at her own peril, pushing her to a marginalized and isolated place on her school landscape (p. 157). So what was it that drew Naomi to keep trying to tell her story on the out-of-classroom place on her school landscape even after she was told to be silent?

(53) We believe that Naomi's resistance to telling a cover story was grounded within her story to live by of "one-caring" for others (Noddings, 1984). It was this that enabled her to remain ever present to her embodied knowledge of herself. Because Naomi's embodied knowing of herself as a teacher was immersed in an "ethic of care," she could not take her gaze off her responsibility as the lived in caring relation with her students. It was this thread within Naomi's story that made it necessary for her to cross over the border between her in- and out-of-classroom places. However, radically different from the response she had experienced within her in-classroom place, the response on the out-of-classroom place was not grounded in relation but, instead, shifted to negotiating her story to live by through a conduit-delivered mandate on inclusive education. In the beginning fragments of her story, we sensed her hopefulness about this negotiation but as her story continued it seemed to become evident to Naomi that little, if anything, was negotiated on the out-of-classroom place. Although this moral dilemma caused tension for Naomi, she refused to deny her knowing or to fall into the plotline inscribed for her through the school story.

(54) Early on in our work, as Naomi shared her story of marginalization and again as we pulled it forward from the transcript, we felt a deep sense of hopelessness about the way in which we read her story as profoundly and miseducatively shaping her story to live by. We kept focusing on the conclusion of this story and Naomi's decision to leave her school landscape. What we could not see at such a distance from her telling were the possibilities which her story offered. Only as we began to explore the intricacies of Naomi's story did we begin to awaken to the educative ways in which the meaning of this story was reshaped. It was Naomi's resistance, lived out in this story, that became educative for each of the teacher co-researchers engaged in this inquiry.

(55) Our first awakening occurred as we tried to make sense of what drew Naomi to keep trying to tell her story on the out-of-classroom place on her school landscape even after she was told to be silent. We were drawn back to Naomi's introduction to her story where she described her sense of living outside the status quo story of her school. What could we learn from her story of choosing to position herself in such a marginal place on her school landscape? Returning to the literature where other writers had shared their experiences of such positionings, we began to reread Naomi's story in new ways.

(56) Were these marginal positionings not more hopeful than those positionings which shaped the living and telling of cover stories? Anzaldúa

(1990) helped us to think harder about what can happen to our sense of self as these masking roles exact a toll— "After years of wearing masks we may become just a series of roles, the constellated self limping along with its broken limbs" (p. xv). Naomi's story certainly did not present such an empty and debilitating image of herself. On the contrary, our continual rereading of Naomi's story led us to uncover stronger images of her personhood. Naomi's story was not one of internalized oppression imposed upon her from a distance. Instead, we saw Naomi as a woman who was intent on acquiring her own agency, of authoring her own story to live by. Unlike the school story which seemed disembodied, Naomi's story to live by was grounded in a narrative history which seemed to offer her the strength to sustain her isolated positioning in places on her school landscape outside her classroom. Drawing on Hurtado's (1996) notion of how we acquire and use "subjugated knowledge," we wondered if Naomi's deep sense of presence to her embodied knowing of self had enabled her to temporarily suspend or repress the "knowledge" pouring onto her school landscape through a sacred story of inclusive education. Was her alternative understanding of this story what enabled her to "resist structures of oppression and create interstices of rebellion and potential revolution" (p. 386)? Had it been her presence to her own knowing which had enabled her to dwell within an in-between positioning, gaining the courage to name the lack of spaces for differing ways of knowing to exist on her school landscape? We believe so. And, in this believing, we came to recognize Naomi's story as a place of possibility—possibility for understanding the central role that presence to our narrative histories plays in enabling us to live and to sustain stories that run counter to those being scripted for us on school landscapes.

Qualitative research reports use flexible and emerging structures and evaluation criteria.

Acknowledgments

We wish to express our gratitude to D. Jean Clandinin and F. Michael Connelly for their ongoing contributions to our work, and would also like to acknowledge the support of their grant through the Social Sciences and Humanities Research Council of Canada.

It is necessary for us to recognize the relational context in which this paper was written. Our knowing is a relational knowing that can never be reduced by a hierarchical ordering of names.

References

Anzaldúa, G. (Ed.). (1990). *Making faces, making soul = Haciendo caras: Creative and critical perspectives by feminists of color.* San Francisco: Aunt Lute Books.

Anzaldúa, G. (1987). *Borderlands: The new mestica = La frontera.* San Francisco: Aunt Lute Book Company.

Belenky, M., Bond, L., & Weinstock, J. (1997). *A tradition that has no name: Nurturing the development of people, families, and communities.* New York: BasicBooks.

Buber, M. (1965). *The knowledge of man.* (M. Friedman, & R. G. Smith, Trans.). London: George Allen and Unwin Ltd.

Carr, D. (1986). *Time, narrative, and history.* Bloomington, IN: Indiana University Press.

Clandinin, D. J. (1997). Authoring lives: stories to live by on the professional knowledge landscape. AERA address, April, 1997.

Clandinin, D. J., & Connelly, F. M. (1994). Personal experience methods. In N. K. Denzin & Y. S. Lincoln (Eds.), *Handbook of qualitative research* (pp. 413–427). London: Sage Publications.

Clandinin, D. J., & Connelly, F. M. (1995). *Teachers' professional knowledge landscapes.* New York: Teachers College Press.

Clandinin, D. J., & Connelly, F. M. (1996). Teachers' professional knowledge landscapes: Teacher stories—stories of teachers—school stories—stories of schools, *Educational Researcher, 25*(3), 24–30.

Clandinin, D. J., & Connelly, F. M. (1998). Asking questions about telling stories. In C. Kridel (Ed.), *Writing educational biography: Explorations in qualitative research* (pp. 202–209). New York: Garland.

Connelly, F. M., & Clandinin, D. J. (1988). *Teachers as curriculum planners: Narratives of experience.* Toronto, ON: The Ontario Institute for Studies in Education.

Connelly, F. M., & Clandinin, D. J. (1990). Stories of experience and narrative inquiry. *Educational Researcher, 19*(5), 2–14.

Connelly, F. M., & Clandinin, D. J. (1999). *Storied identities: Storied landscapes.* New York: Teachers College Press, in press.

Crites, S. (1971). The narrative quality of experience. *Journal of the American academy of religion, 39*(3), 291–311.

Dewey, J. (1938). *Experiences and education*. New York: Collier Books.
Greene, M. (1993). Diversity and inclusion: toward a curriculum for human beings, *Teachers College Record, 95*(2), 211–221.
Greene, M. (1994). Multiculturalism, community, and the arts. In A. Dyson & C. Genishi (Eds.), *The need for story: Cultural diversity in classroom and community* (pp. 11–27). New York: Teachers College Press.
Greene, M. (1995). *Releasing the imagination: Essays on education, the arts, and social change*. San Francisco: Jossey-Bass Inc.
Heller, C. (1997). *Until we are strong together: Women writers in the Tenderloin*. New York: Teachers College Press.
Hooks, B. (1996). *Bone black: Memories of girlhood*. New York: Henry Holt and Company.
Hurtado, A. (1996). Strategic suspensions: feminists of color theorize the production of knowledge. In N. Goldberger, J. Tarule, B. Clinchy, & M. Belenky (Eds.), *Knowledge, difference, and power: Essays inspired Women's Ways of Knowing* (pp. 372–388). New York: BasicBooks.
Josselson, R. (1994). *The space between us: Exploring the dimensions of human relationships*. San Francisco: Jossey-Bass Publishers.
Miller, J. (1994). "The surprise of a recognizable person" as troubling presence in educational research and writing, *Curriculum Inquiry, 24*(4), 503–512.
Nelson, N. (1995). Resistance and insubordination, *Hypatia, 10*(2), 23–40.
Noddings, N. (1984). *Caring: A feminine approach to ethics and moral education*. Los Angeles: University of California Press.

CHAPTER 17

Mixed Methods Designs

If you have access to both quantitative and qualitative data, you can use both forms of data to understand your research problem and answer your research questions. With qualitative research recognized and appreciated by more and more educators, and with quantitative research long established as an approach, mixed methods research has become popular as the newest development in research methods and in approaches to "mix" quantitative and qualitative research. This chapter defines mixed methods research, identifies when you use it, assesses the key characteristics of it, and advances the steps in conducting and evaluating this design.

By the end of this chapter, you should be able to:

- Define mixed methods research and identify when you use it.
- Distinguish among four types of mixed methods designs.
- Identify three reasons for conducting mixed methods research.
- List types of quantitative and qualitative data collected in a mixed methods study.
- Define priority of quantitative or qualitative research as a design decision in mixed methods research.
- Define sequence of qualitative or quantitative research as a design decision in mixed methods research.
- Describe the data analysis strategies for each of the types of mixed methods designs.
- Illustrate mixed methods procedures with a diagram.
- Describe steps in conducting a mixed methods study.
- List criteria useful in evaluating a mixed methods design.

Maria chooses to collect both quantitative and qualitative data. She decides to conduct a survey and then conduct follow-up interviews with a few students to explain the results of the survey. She views this research in two phases. For the first, quantitative phase, her research question is "What factors influence student attitudes toward weapon possession?" Later, in the follow-up, qualitative phase, her question is "When students mention 'peers' as a factor influencing student attitudes, what do they mean?" In this study, Maria collects quantitative survey data and then follows up with qualitative interview data to help explain the initial quantitative results. Maria conducts a study using mixed methods research.

WHAT IS MIXED METHODS RESEARCH?

A **mixed methods research design** is a procedure for collecting, analyzing, and "mixing" both quantitative and qualitative research and methods in a single study to understand a research problem (Creswell & Plano Clark, 2007). The basic assumption is that the use of both quantitative and qualitative methods, in combination, provides a better understanding of the research problem and questions than either method by itself. It is a "legitimate inquiry approach" (Brewer & Hunter, 1989, p. 28).

If you use this design, you need to understand *both* quantitative and qualitative research. Because audiences may not be familiar with this design, you often need to educate them about it. The procedures are time consuming, requiring extensive data collection and analysis (Bryman, 1988), and such time requirements may require that you participate in a research team when using it. Also, mixed methods research is not simply collecting two distinct "strands" of research – qualitative and quantitative. It consists of merging, integrating, linking, or embedding the two "strands." In short, the data are "mixed" in a mixed methods study.

When Do You Conduct a Mixed Methods Study?

There are several reasons for using a mixed methods design to conduct a study. In general, you conduct a mixed methods study when you have both quantitative and qualitative data and both types of data, together, provide a better understanding of your research problem than either type by itself. Mixed methods research is a good design to use if you seek to build on the strengths of both quantitative and qualitative data. Quantitative data, such as scores on instruments, yield specific numbers that can be statistically analyzed, can produce results to assess the frequency and magnitude of trends, and can provide useful information if you need to describe trends about a large number of people. However, qualitative data, such as open-ended interviews that provide actual words of people in the study, offer many different perspectives on the study topic and provide a complex picture of the situation. When one combines quantitative and qualitative data, "we have a very powerful mix" (Miles & Huberman, 1994, p. 42). For example, by assessing both outcomes of a study (i.e., quantitative) as well as the process (i.e., qualitative), we can develop "a complex" picture of social phenomenon (Greene & Caracelli, 1997, p. 7).

You also conduct a mixed methods study when one type of research (qualitative or quantiative) is not enough to address the research problem or answer the research questions. More data is needed to extend, elaborate on, or explain the first database. You may want to first explore the data qualitatively to develop an instrument or to identify variables to test in a later quantitative study. You engage in a mixed methods study when you want to follow up a quantitative study with a qualitative one to obtain more detailed, specific information than can be gained from the results of statistical tests.

You use mixed methods when you want to incorporate a qualitative component into an otherwise quantitative study. An example of this would be an experimental study in which the experiment yields useful information about outcomes, but the additional collection of qualitative data develops a more in-depth understanding of how the experimental intervention actually worked. Finally, on a practical level, you use mixed methods research for studies in graduate programs in which qualitative research has yet to be fully accepted and in which quantitative approaches are the norm. Although individuals in these programs may recognize the value of qualitative research, a mixed methods study is more acceptable than a "pure" qualitative study because there is still a component of quantitative research in the study.

How Did Mixed Methods Research Develop?

The historical development of mixed methods research has been outlined elsewhere (e.g., Creswell & Plano Clark, 2007; Datta, 1994; Tashakkori & Teddlie, 1998), and this review builds on these earlier discussions. We can trace this evolution through several phases.

Mixing Forms of Quantitative Data

Since the 1930s, educational and social science investigators have combined research methods of data collection in their studies (Sieber, 1973). However, when Campbell and Fiske (1959) introduced the multitrait, multimethod approach, they stimulated interest in employing multiple methods in a single study. Campbell and Fiske's interest was not in mixed methods research; rather, they sought to develop valid psychological traits. To develop these traits, they suggested a process whereby researchers would collect multiple measures of multiple traits and assess each measure by at least two methods. When they correlated scores and placed them into a matrix, a multimethod, multitrait matrix resulted. An investigator could determine if the trait was valid by examining this matrix and assessing whether the measures of the trait correlated higher with each other than they did with measures of different traits involving separate methods. Evidence from these correlations provided useful information about different forms of validity. At a broader level, the use of multiple methods to measure a trait encouraged other researchers to collect more than one type of data, even if this data was only quantitative, such as peer judgment scores and word association tests.

Expanding Use of Combined Quantitative and Qualitative Data

Soon others were collecting both quantitative and qualitative data. By 1973, Sieber suggested the combination of in-depth case studies with surveys, creating a "new style of research" and the "integration" of research techniques within a single study (p. 1337). A few years later, Jick (1979) used the combination of surveys, semistructured interviews, observations, and archival materials to provide a "rich and comprehensive picture" (p. 606) of anxiety and job insecurity during organizational mergers.

Jick's (1979) study was more than an examination of mergers; his article used the merger study to illustrate the procedure of triangulating data. *Triangulation,* a term drawn from naval military science, is the process where sailors use multiple reference points to locate an object's exact position at sea (Jick, 1979). Applied to research, it meant that investigators could improve their inquiries by collecting and converging (or integrating) different kinds of data bearing on the same phenomenon. The three points to the triangle are the two sources of the data and the phenomenon. This improvement in inquiries would come from blending the strengths of one type of method and neutralizing the weaknesses of the other. For example, in a study of middle school principal leadership, a researcher can augment qualitative observations of behavior with a quantitative survey that provides greater confidence in the generalizability of results. However, qualitative observations can provide the context in which this leadership is enacted and help clarify quantitative statistical relationships and numeric findings. To triangulate or converge data in a single study continues to be an attractive approach to mixed methods research today.

Questioning the Integration of Worldviews and Methods

Further developments on procedures, however, had to wait for several years. The paradigm debate developed that would question the legitimacy of mixed methods research (Reichardt & Cook, 1979). This debate was more than tension between those who embraced traditional quantitative research and those advocating for qualitative inquiry. The issue was whether a researcher who used certain methods also needed to use a specific worldview—the "compatibility" (Tashakkori & Teddlie, 1998) between worldviews and methods. Worldviews are the broad philosophical assumptions researchers use when they conduct studies. Although some researchers may not recognize it, they make assumptions about knowledge (e.g., math scores exist for seventh graders) and how it can be obtained (e.g., we can measure math ability using standardized achievement tests). Those who argued for "incompatibility" said that quantitative methods (e.g., student scores on an instrument) belonged to the quantitative worldview (e.g., an attempt to measure, objectively, student achievement), whereas qualitative methods (e.g., an observation of students) apply only to a qualitative worldview (e.g., the researcher assesses reality subjectively through his or her lens). The logic of this argument led to the conclusion that mixed methods research was untenable because a single worldview did not exist for the inquiry.

The worldview–method argument played out for several years, during the late 1980s and early 1990s, especially at national conferences such as the American Evaluation Association's annual meetings (Reichardt & Rallis, 1994). But it has largely diminished because of several factors. Some said that those who argued for the incompatibility of worldviews and methods created a false dichotomy (Reichardt & Cook, 1979) that does not hold under close inspection. For example, there is an "objective" reality (e.g., the classroom), but there is also a "subjective" reality (e.g., we see different things as we look at a classroom). Some methods are more closely associated with one worldview than the other, but to categorize them as "belonging" to one worldview more than another creates an unrealistic situation.

Others contended that mixed methods research has its own philosophical worldview: pragmatism. The pragmatists, for example, believe philosophically in using procedures that "work" for a particular research problem under study and that you should use many methods when understanding a research problem (e.g., see discussion by Tashakkori & Teddlie, 1998). Closely related to the pragmatist position is the *unity thesis,* which asserts that the idea of worldviews is mistaken and incoherent (Creswell, Goodchild, & Turner, 1996; Walker & Evers, 1988), thus opening the possibility for using mixed methods without substantial concern for philosophical underpinnings. In addition, the "dialectical" position, embraced by Greene and Caracelli (1997), recommends that researchers report the worldviews they hold—thus honoring worldviews as important—and also collect both quantitative and qualitative data.

Developing Procedures for Mixed Methods Studies

Another factor that quieted the debate was the increased interest in the procedural aspects of mixed methods research. Authors explored the "purposes" of mixed methods research, identified alternative designs to use, and specified a notation system and visual models for these designs.

The idea of triangulation had already introduced one purpose for mixing methods—to integrate multiple databases to understand a phenomenon and research problem (Rossman & Wilson, 1985). Other reasons soon emerged. You could collect quantitative

FIGURE 17.1

Notation System for a Mixed Methods Study

Study #1 QUAL + QUAN

Study #2 QUAN ⟶ qual

Notation Used:

+ indicates the simultaneous or concurrent collection of quantitative and qualitative data.

⟶ shows the sequential collection of quantitative and qualitative data.

Uppercase letters indicate a priority or increased weight for either the quantitative or qualitative data.

Lowercase letters indicate a lower priority or weight for either the quantitative or qualitative data.

Source: Adapted from Morse, 1991.

and qualitative data separately in two phases so that data from one source could enhance, elaborate, or complement data from the other source (Greene, Caracelli, & Graham, 1989; Rossman & Wilson, 1985). In more complicated designs, the data collection could extend from two to three phases (e.g., see Miles & Huberman, 1994) or be collected from multiple levels in an organization, such as the district, school, teacher, and student (e.g., see Tashakkori & Teddlie, 1998). You could also embed data, with one form of data becoming less important in a design emphasizing the other form of data (Creswell, 2003).

Central to this thinking about different models or designs has been the visualization of procedures and the use of a notation system designed by Morse (1991). This system, shown in Figure 17.1, is a way to portray the procedures in mixed methods designs. Shorthand labels for quantitative (quan) and qualitative (qual) simplify the terms.

Figure 17.1 also portrays two sample designs. As shown in Study #1, a researcher places an emphasis on both quantitative and qualitative data and integrates or combines the data in the study. In Study #2, the investigator emphasizes quantitative data in the first phase of a study, followed by a minor emphasis on qualitative data in the second phase of the study. Later in this chapter we consider names for these designs and explore several variations of them.

Advocating for a Distinct Design

With emerging procedures, a notation system, and specific designs, the discussion recently has turned to viewing mixed methods research as a separate and distinct design. To experiments, surveys, grounded theory, and others, we now add mixed methods research or we incorporate this form of research into these designs. Advocates for mixed methods research have written entire chapters and books on its use in the social and health sciences (Creswell, 2003; Creswell & Plano Clark, 2007; Greene & Caracelli, 1997; Reichardt & Rallis, 1994; Tashakkori & Teddlie, 1998, 2003). In addition, refinements continue in the process of integrating quantitative and qualitative data analysis (Caracelli & Greene, 1993), the use of computer programs for merging quantitative statistical programs with text analysis programs (Bazeley, 2000), and the identification and discussion of numerous mixed methods studies reported in the scholarly literature (e.g., Creswell et al., 1996; Datta, 1994; Greene et al., 1989).

WHAT ARE THE TYPES OF MIXED METHODS DESIGNS?

Although work has begun on identifying types of mixed methods designs, many models and approaches have been advanced in the literature. (To review the possibilities, see the helpful discussions by Creswell & Plano Clark, 2007; Greene et al., 1989; Morgan, 1998; Steckler, McLeroy, Goodman, Bird, & McCormick, 1992; Tashakkori & Teddlie, 1998.) The strategy authors have taken is to review published studies and classify them by type of design (e.g., Greene et al., 1989).

Before examining the types of designs, it might be helpful to reflect on useful strategies for identifying a mixed methods study reported in the published literature. One strategy is to ask the following questions to help you identify a study as mixed methods research:

- *Is there evidence in the title?* Look at the title to determine if it includes words such as *quantitative and qualitative, mixed methods,* or other related terms to signify the collection of both quantitative and qualitative data. Related terms might be *integrated, combined, triangulation, multimethod, mixed model,* or *mixed methodology* (Reichardt & Rallis, 1994; Tashakkori & Teddlie, 1998).
- *Is there evidence in the data-collection section?* Examine the "Methods" or "Procedure" section where the author addresses data collection and identify if researchers discuss forms of quantitative data (i.e., numbers reported) and qualitative data (i.e., words or images) as part of the data collection.
- *Is there evidence in the purpose statement or the research questions?* Examine the abstract or the introduction of the study to identify the purpose or research questions. Do these statements indicate that the researcher intends to collect both quantitative and qualitative data during the study?

Having identified the study as mixed methods, next determine the type of mixed methods design the author is using. You might ask the following questions:

1. *What priority or weight does the researcher give to the quantitative and qualitative data collection?* Priority or weight means that one form of data is given more attention or emphasis in the study; however, quantitative and qualitative data are sometimes treated equally.
2. *What is the sequence of collecting the quantitative and qualitative data?* Determine whether the qualitative data (or quantitative data) comes first and second in the data collection or whether they are collected concurrently.
3. *How does the researcher actually analyze the data?* Determine if the researchers combine the data in one analysis or keep the analyses separate.
4. *Where in the study does the researcher "mix" the data?* The two forms of data might be combined, linked, or mixed during data collection, between data collection and data analysis, during data analysis, or in the interpretation of a study.

Using these four questions, you can locate and identify most mixed methods designs commonly used in educational research. Figure 17.2 illustrates four of these designs: the triangulation design, the embedded design, the explanatory design, and the exploratory design (Creswell & Plano Clark, 2007).

FIGURE 17.2

Types of Mixed Methods Designs

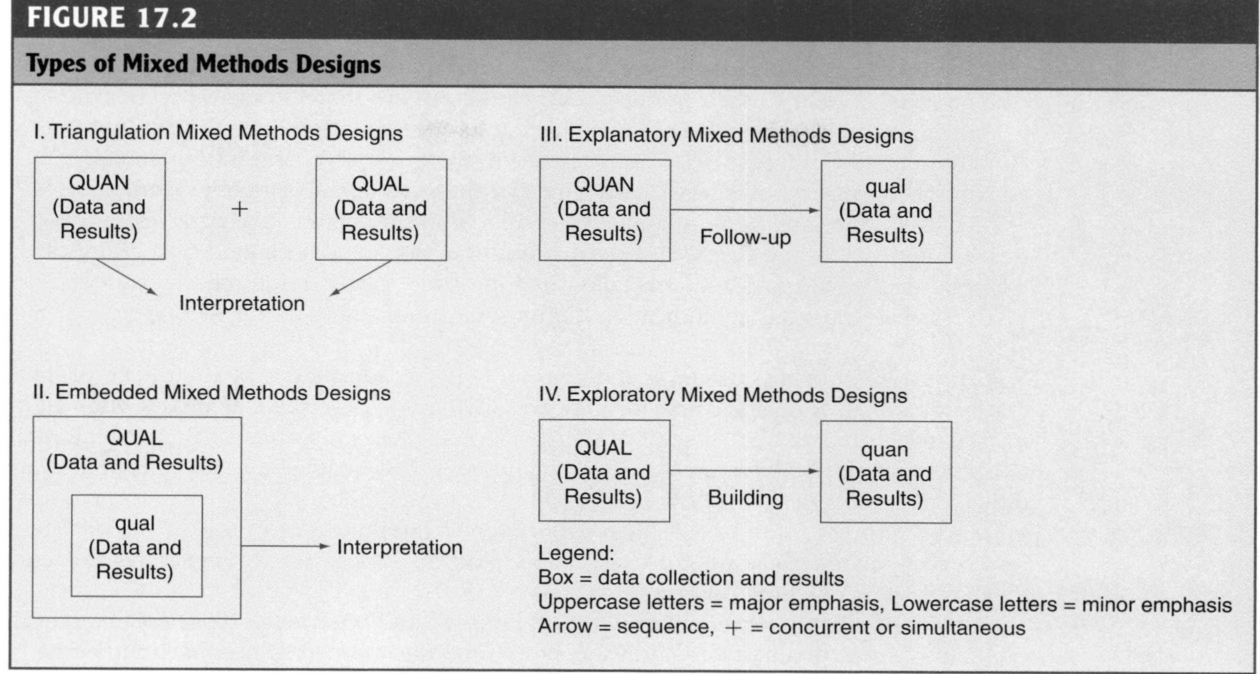

The Triangulation Design

From the historical sketch, you have already gained a familiarity with the triangulation design (Jick, 1979). The purpose of a **triangulation (or concurrent or parallel) mixed methods design** is to simultaneously collect both quantitative and qualitative data, merge the data, and use the results to understand a research problem. A basic rationale for this design is that one data-collection form supplies strengths to offset the weaknesses of the other form. For example, quantitative scores on an instrument from many individuals provide strengths to offset the weaknesses of qualitative documents from a few people. Alternatively, qualitative, in-depth observation of a few people offers strength to quantitative data that does not adequately provide detailed information about the context in which individuals provide information (e.g., the setting).

How does the process of a triangulation study work? The researcher gathers both quantitative and qualitative data, analyzes both datasets separately, compares the results from the analysis of both datasets, and makes an interpretation as to whether the results support or contradict each other. The direct comparison of the two data sets by the researcher provides a "triangulation" of data sources. As shown in Figure 17.2, in this design:

- *The mixed methods researcher often gives equal priority to both quantitative and qualitative data (see QUAN and QUAL).* The researcher values both quantitative and qualitative data and sees them as approximately equal sources of information in the study. For example, interview data are as important as the scores gathered on an instrument.
- *The mixed methods researcher collects both the quantitative and qualitative data concurrently or simultaneously during the study.* Qualitative documents about what the students learn in preschool are reviewed, for example, at the same time that the researcher collects quantitative observations on student behavior using a checklist.

- *The mixed methods researcher compares the results from quantitative and qualitative analyses to determine if the two databases yield similar or dissimilar results.* For instance, qualitative themes identified during interviews are "quantified" and given a score as to their frequency. These scores are then compared with scores from instruments measuring variables that address the same ideas as the themes. Alternatively, the researcher may transform the qualitative data into quantitative numbers (e.g., counts how many times participants talk about codes) and then compare them with the quantitative results from the quantitative database. For example, does the emphasis on safety in the school as determined by a count of the number of times students talk about the code, safety, reinforce the students' responses on a survey indicating the importance of safety in the school?

The strength of this design is that it combines the advantages of each form of data; that is, quantitative data provide for generalizability, whereas qualitative data offer information about the context or setting. This design enables a researcher to gather information that uses the best features of both quantitative and qualitative data collection. One difficulty with this design is how to transform one form of data into the other form to integrate and compare databases. Moreover, even if integration is possible, inconsistent results may emerge, making it necessary to collect additional data or revisit the collected databases to reconcile the differences.

In a triangulation mixed methods study, Russek and Weinberg (1993) collected both quantitative and qualitative data at the same time and used results from both forms to understand the implementation of technology in an elementary school. They sought to examine how 16 elementary school teachers implemented two sets of supplementary mathematics lessons, one utilizing the calculator and one utilizing the computer. To study this process, they conducted qualitative interviews with teachers and administrators, made informal classroom observations, examined school documents, and obtained teacher responses to open-ended questions on questionnaires. Quantitatively, they gathered classroom observation checklists and lesson and workshop evaluation forms, and collected two self-reported measures of teacher feelings, attitudes, and concerns (i.e., the self-evaluation questionnaire and the stages of concern questionnaire).

Russek and Wanberg's (1993) purpose in mixing methods was to provide a complete picture of the implementation process. They discussed how triangulated data could show convergence, inconsistency, and complementary results. For example, they compared results from teacher questionnaires with interview themes about using both the calculator and computers in the classroom. Finding inconsistencies in the results, they attributed this difference to the teachers' reluctance to put on paper what they revealed freely in their oral remarks. They also felt that the questionnaire was less valid because the teachers might have felt that the questionnaires would become part of their permanent personnel record.

The Embedded Design

A second form of mixed methods design is similar to the triangulation design, with some important exceptions. The purpose of the **embedded design** is to collect quantitative and qualitative data simultaneously but to have one form of data play a supportive role to the other form of data. The reason for collecting the second form of data is that it will augment or support the primary form of data. For example, during an experiment, the researcher may collect qualitative data during the trial to examine how participants in the treatment condition are experiencing the intervention. The primary aim of the study, in this case, is to examine the impact of the experimental conditions on the outcome, but the addition of qualitative data enables the researcher to also explore how participants are experiencing the process of the experiment. As another example, during a correlational study, the researcher may gather secondary qualitative data to help understand the reasons for the correlational results. In some embedded designs, the procedures are sequential, with the secondary form of data gathered before the experiment (or the correlational study) begins (e.g., to help determine the best means for recruiting participants) or after it concludes (e.g., to follow up and help explain the results).

How does the process of an embedded study work? The researcher collects both quantitative data and qualitative data during a single study (e.g., an experiment or a correlational study), the two data sets are analyzed separately, and they address different research questions. For example, the quantitative data will address whether the intervention had an impact on the outcomes, whereas the qualitative data will assess how the participants experienced the intervention. As shown in Figure 17.2, in this design:

- *The mixed methods researcher gives priority to the major form of data collection (e.g., often QUAN) and secondary status to the supportive form (e.g., often qual) of data collection.* The secondary form is used in the mixed methods study to support and provide additional information to the primary form.
- *The mixed methods researcher collects both the quantitative and qualitative data simultaneously.* Both forms of data are collected during the study at roughly the same time. The approach may be varied in some embedded designs, and the researcher may collect the secondary form of data prior to the study or after the study has concluded.
- *The mixed methods researcher uses the secondary form of data to augment or provide additional sources of information not provided by the primary source of data.* The augmentation is to gather information that typically addresses a different question than asked for by the primary form of data. For example, the collection of qualitative data during an experiment may be to understand the "process" the participants are going through, whereas the quantitative data assesses the impact of the treatment on the outcomes.

The strength of this design is that it combines the advantages of both quantitative and qualitative data. Quantitative data are more effective at recording outcomes of the experiment than identifying through qualitative data how individuals are experiencing the process. It also provides a type of mixed methods design in which the researcher can collect qualitative data, but the overall design still emphasizes quantitative approaches. In some fields new to qualitative research, this role of qualitative data helps to legitimize the use of such forms of data. The difficulty of using this design is that the two databases may not be easily compared because the data address different research questions. In addition, there is the possibility that introducing qualitative data collection during an experiment (or correlational study) will influence the outcomes. Strategies need to be put into place to minimize this effect (e.g., collecting qualitative data at the end of the experiment, having participants complete journals of their experience that are turned in after the experiment). Further, like the triangulation design, the simultaneous data collection of quantitative and qualitative data may be labor intensive for a single researcher.

Harrison's (2007) correlational study of an undergraduate mentoring program in teacher education illustrates the embedded mixed methods design. Using quantitative longitudinal analysis, she followed 18 undergraduates in a leadership program over 2 years as they learned how to forge mentor–mentee relationships in an undergraduate teacher education program. Harrison collected quantitative data on an instrument, the Working Alliance Inventory (WAI), during six administrations over a 2-year period. This quantitative information represented the major source of information during her study, and her correlation model suggested that a number of factors (e.g., number of times the mentors–mentees met) would influence the building of positive relationships. She also collected limited data in the form of three qualitative focus group interviews with the students. She plotted the longitudinal trends in relationship building using the WAI scores over time, and then used the secondary data, the focus group information, to help her understand why some mentor–mentees forged closer relationships, plateaued, or formed more distant relationships over time. Her study was a good example in education of an embedded design with a major quantitative correlational component and a smaller, supportive qualitative focus group component.

The Explanatory Design

Instead of collecting data at the same time, a mixed methods researcher might collect quantitative and qualitative information sequentially in two phases, with one form of data collection following the other. This design, also shown in Figure 17.2, is an explanatory mixed methods design, perhaps the most popular form of mixed methods design in educational research. An **explanatory mixed methods design** (also called a two-phase model; Creswell & Plano Clark, 2007) consists of first collecting quantitative data and then collecting qualitative data to help explain or elaborate on the quantitative results. The rationale for this approach is that the quantitative data and results provide a general picture of the research problem; more analysis, specifically through qualitative data collection, is needed to refine, extend, or explain the general picture. Referring back to Figure 17.2, you can see that in this design,

- *The mixed methods researcher places a priority on quantitative data (QUAN) collection and analysis.* This is done by introducing it first in the study and having it represent a major aspect of data collection. A small qualitative (qual) component follows in the second phase of the research.
- *The mixed methods researcher collects quantitative data first in the sequence.* This is followed by the secondary qualitative data collection. Researchers often present these studies in two phases, with each phase clearly identified in headings in the report.
- *The mixed methods researcher uses the qualitative data to refine the results from the quantitative data.* This refinement results in exploring a few typical cases, probing a key result in more detail, or following up with outlier or extreme cases.

This design has the advantage of clearly identified quantitative and qualitative parts, an advantage for readers as well as for those designing and conducting the study. Unlike the triangulation design, the researcher does not have to converge or integrate two different forms of data. This design also captures the best of both quantitative and qualitative data—to obtain quantitative results from a population in the first phase, and then refine or elaborate these findings through an in-depth qualitative exploration in the second phase. The difficulty in using this design, however, is that the researcher needs to determine what aspect of the quantitative results to use in the follow-up (e.g., a hypothesis that the researcher failed to reject?). Also, this design is labor intensive, and it requires both expertise and time to collect both quantitative and qualitative data.

A two-phase project by Blustein, Phillips, Jobin-David, Finkelberg, & Roarke (1997) is a good example of an explanatory design. Their research examined the school-to-work transition for 45 work-bound adults (ages 18 to 29) who had been out of high school for less than 10 years and who were neither college graduates nor current college students. The authors described their data collection and analysis strategy as follows: to "employ two initial quantitative methods to help focus and circumscribe our qualitative explorations" (p. 373). They gathered information from the 45 adults using a single interview protocol that contained closed- and open-ended questions. To this end, they first correlated two indexes to adaptive transition obtained from the closed-ended questions (i.e., job satisfaction and congruence). Isolating 14 variables for further analysis, they began the second phase, in which they identified participants with either notably high or low scores on each measure and examined passages in their interview transcription to learn more about their transition experiences.

The Exploratory Design

Rather than first analyzing or collecting *quantitative data* as is done in the explanatory design, the mixed methods researcher begins with *qualitative data* and then collects quantitative information. The purpose of an **exploratory mixed methods design** is the procedure of first gathering qualitative data to explore a phenomenon, and then collecting quantitative data to explain relationships found in the qualitative data. A popular application of this design is to explore a phenomenon, identify themes, design an instrument, and subsequently test it. Researchers use this design when existing instruments, variables, and measures may not be known or available for the population under study. Again refer to Figure 17.2. In this design,

- *The mixed methods researcher emphasizes the qualitative data (QUAL) more than the quantitative data (quan).* This emphasis may occur through presenting the overarching question as an open-ended question or discussing the qualitative results in more detail than the quantitative results.
- *The mixed methods researcher has a sequence to data collection that involves first collecting qualitative data followed by quantitative data.* Typically in these designs, the researcher presents the study in two phases, with the first phase involving qualitative data collection (e.g., interviews, observations) with a small number of individuals, followed by quantitative data collection (e.g., a survey) with a large, randomly selected number of participants.
- *The mixed methods researcher plans on the quantitative data to build on or explain the initial qualitative findings.* The intent of the researcher is for the quantitative data results to refine and extend the qualitative findings. The initial qualitative exploration leads to detailed, generalizable results through the second quantitative phase.

One advantage of this approach is that it allows the researcher to identify measures actually grounded in the data obtained from study participants. The researcher can initially explore views by listening to participants rather than approach a topic with a predetermined set of variables. However, it has the disadvantage of requiring extensive data collection as well as the time required for this process. The testing of an instrument adds considerably to the length of time this design requires to be implemented. It also requires researchers to make decisions about the most appropriate themes to measure in the follow-up, quantitative phase of the study.

In the exploratory mixed methods design by Holland, Chait, and Taylor (1989), the researchers used qualitative data to develop and test a quantitative instrument. They examined the effectiveness of boards of trustees in liberal arts and comprehensive colleges. The authors state that "the qualitative approach to this topic provided the basis for the development of a grounded theoretical framework that could subsequently be subjected to more rigorous quantitative specification and empirical testing" (p. 439). The qualitative first phase of the study consisted of interviews with 46 trustees at 10 colleges. From this data, the researchers identified six board competencies (e.g., understand institutional context, build capacity for learning). In the second phase of the study, the researchers identified 12 new sites, developed the competencies into a questionnaire, and gathered self-reported data from trustees. They also collected interviews and obtained institutional performance measures. A third phase was to test the instrument more broadly, with 357 trustees at the 12 sites used in the second phase.

When Maria starts with a survey and follows it up with an interview in her mixed methods study, what type of design does she have? What would be the possible priority and sequence for her design? What would be the reason for using this type of design?

WHAT ARE THE KEY CHARACTERISTICS OF MIXED METHODS DESIGNS?

All three types of mixed methods designs include basic characteristics that distinguish this design from others. In reviewing the following six characteristics, consider incorporating them into your plan for a study if you intend to conduct a mixed methods study. Also, look for them in a mixed methods study you might be reviewing or reading. They are:

- Rationale for the design
- Quantitative and qualitative forms of data
- Priority
- Sequence
- Data analysis matched to a design
- Diagram of the procedures

Rationale for the Design

Readers and those who review mixed methods studies need to know why you are mixing methods. Mixed methods researchers include a justification or rationale for their use of both quantitative and qualitative data. One justification is that collecting quantitative data in a second phase is important to test the qualitative explorations of the first phase of the study (i.e., exploratory design).

Alternatively, a reason for conducting a mixed methods study might be that you seek to explain in more detail through qualitative research the initial quantitative statistical results (i.e., explanatory design) or one form of data plays a supporting role to the other database (i.e., embedded design). Another justification results from combining the "best" of both quantitative and qualitative research (i.e., triangulation design). Quantitative provides the opportunity to gather data from a large number of people and generalize results, whereas qualitative permits an in-depth exploration of a few individuals. Whatever the rationale, mention this rationale early in a study, such as in the introduction.

Collecting Quantitative and Qualitative Data

In any mixed methods study, you should clearly indicate that you are collecting both quantitative and qualitative data. Methods of data collection are typically associated with either numbers or numeric data and words or text and image data. Mixed methods researchers collect both quantitative and qualitative data.

A broader picture of data forms, introduced earlier in chapters 6 and 8, is shown in Table 17.1. In this table, the columns show both methods and data. In practice, mixed methods researchers use different methods to collect different forms of data. In a mixed

TABLE 17.1

Quantitative and Qualitative Methods of Data Collection and Types of Data

Quantitative Research		**Qualitative Research**	
Methods of Data Collection	**Data**	**Methods of Data Collection**	**Data**
Instruments (e.g., questionnaire, closed-ended interview; closed-ended observation)	Numeric scores	Open-ended interviews	Text data from transcribed interviews
Documents (e.g., census, attendance records)	Numeric scores	Open-ended questions on questionnaires	Text data transcribed from questionnaires
		Open-ended observations	Fieldnotes (text) from researcher's notes
		Documents (e.g., private or public)	Text data optically scanned from diaries, journals, letters, or official documents
		Visual materials	Image data from pictures, photography, or audiotapes

methods study, researchers include specific forms of both quantitative and qualitative data and incorporate this discussion into the methods or procedure section of the study.

Priority

Mixed methods researchers advance the weight or priority to the collection of quantitative and qualitative data. Three options are available to the researcher for prioritizing data:

- Quantitative and qualitative data are of equal weight.
- Quantitative data is of greater weight than qualitative data.
- Qualitative data is of greater weight than quantitative data.

Weight or priority means that in a mixed methods design, the researcher places more emphasis on one type of data than on other types of data in the research and the written report. This emphasis may result from personal experience with data collection, the need to understand one form of data before proceeding to the next, or the audience reading the research. Whatever the reason, in examining a mixed methods study for the priority, ask the following questions:

- What do you emphasize more in the purpose statement—exploration or prediction of outcomes?
- Which data-collection process—quantitative or qualitative—do you give the most attention to (e.g., number of pages in a report) in the "Methods" and "Results" sections?
- Which data-collection process do you examine in the most depth (e.g., detailed statistical analysis or multiple-layered thematic analyses)?

Sequence

Mixed methods researchers advance the **sequence** of data collection using concurrent or sequential approaches. Again, several options exist for the sequencing of data collection:

- You collect both quantitative and qualitative data at the same time.
- You collect quantitative data first, followed by qualitative data.
- You collect qualitative data first, followed by quantitative data.

If the purpose of the study is to explain quantitative results further with qualitative data (i.e., explanatory design) or to develop an instrument from qualitative data (i.e., exploratory design), the procedures should clearly indicate this sequence. The data-collection procedures are independent of each other and typically presented as phases. If the intent of the study is to converge or triangulate the findings (i.e., triangulation design), then the data are collected at the same time, and the researcher is explicit about this process. This process involves two data-collection efforts that proceed simultaneously and are related to each other.

Data Analysis Matched to a Design

One of the most difficult challenges for the mixed methods researcher is how to analyze data collected from qualitative and quantitative research. This is more than simply being able to link or intersect data and numbers, although this connection does present some challenges. Several authors have begun the discussion about data analysis in mixed methods research (Caracelli & Greene, 1993; Tashakkori & Teddlie, 1998). To examine options for data analysis, reflect back on the type of design and the options for analysis within each design. An overview of these options is presented in Table 17.2. This list is not comprehensive and should not limit the creative potential of a mixed methods researcher; it is largely to focus the discussion and present typical analytic procedures discussed by writers and illustrated in mixed methods studies.

Triangulation Design Analysis

Of all of the designs, this analysis is perhaps the most difficult and controversial. The standard approach seems to be to converge or compare in some way quantitative data (e.g., scores) and qualitative data (e.g., text). One way is to provide a discussion about the themes emerging from the data and how they support or refute the statistical analysis. In a study conducted about controversial art on college campuses (e.g., a painting or novel), the researcher might collect questionnaires from campus constituents as well as interview data from administrators, faculty, and students. The researcher might then compare the two sources of data to determine if the interviews supported the questionnaire results.

Another approach is to combine the qualitative and quantitative data to arrive at new variables or new themes for further testing or exploration. In the controversial art case, the interview data and questionnaires' scores combine to produce a new variable, such as the sensitivity of campus constituents to some forms of art. This variable becomes information for further exploration.

Some mixed methods researchers quantify qualitative data to compare the data directly with statistical results. For instance, you could reduce interview data from campus personnel to themes and make counts of the occurrences of each theme. You could

TABLE 17.2

Type of Mixed Methods Designs and Data Analysis/Interpretation Procedures

Type of Mixed Methods Designs	Examples of Analytic and Interpretive Procedures
Triangulation (QUAN and QUAL data collected simultaneously)	• *Quantifying qualitative data:* Qualitative data are coded, codes are assigned numbers, and the number of times codes appear are recorded as numeric data. Quantitative data are descriptively analyzed for frequency of occurrence. The two data sets are compared. • *Qualifying quantitative data:* Quantitative data from questionnaires are factor analyzed. These factors then become themes that are compared with themes analyzed from qualitative data. • *Comparing results:* The results from qualitative data collection are directly compared with results from quantitative data collection. Statistical trends are supported by qualitative themes or vice versa. • *Consolidating data:* Qualitative data and quantitative data are combined to form new variables. Original quantitative variables are compared with qualitative themes to form new quantitative variables. (Caracelli & Greene, 1993)
Explanatory (QUAN followed by qual)	• *Following up on outliers or extreme cases:* Gather quantitative data and identify outlier or residual cases. Collect qualitative data to explore the characteristics of these cases. (Caracelli & Greene, 1993) • *Explaining results:* Conduct a quantitative survey to identify how two or more groups compare on a variable. Follow up with qualitative interviews to explore the reasons why these differences were found. • *Using a typology:* Conduct a quantitative survey and develop factors through a factor analysis. Use these factors as a typology to identify themes in qualitative data, such as observations or interviews. (Caracelli & Greene, 1993) • *Examining multilevels.* Conduct a survey at the student level. Gather qualitative data through interviews at the class level. Survey the entire school at the school level. Collect qualitative data at the district level. Information from each level builds to the next level. (Tashakkori & Teddlie, 1998)
Exploratory (QUAL followed by quan)	• *Locating an instrument:* Collect qualitative data and identify themes. Use these themes as a basis for locating instruments that use concepts parallel to the qualitative themes. • *Developing an instrument:* Obtain themes and specific statements from individuals that support the themes. In the next phase, use these themes and statements to create scales and items as a questionnaire. Alternatively, look for existing instruments that can be modified to fit the themes and statements found in the qualitative exploratory phase of the study. After developing the instrument, test it out with a sample of a population. • *Forming categorical data:* Site-level characteristics (e.g., different ethnic groups) gathered in an ethnography in the first phase of a study become a categorical variable in a second phase correlational or regression study. (Caracelli & Greene, 1993) • *Using extreme qualitative cases:* Qualitative data cases that are extreme in a comparative analysis are followed in a second phase by quantitative surveys. (Caracelli & Greene, 1993)

compare the frequency of these themes with the descriptive statistics about information from scales. Alternatively, the researcher might analyze the questionnaires, develop themes (or scales) that reflect issues surrounding campus art, and compare the themes to those generated by campus personnel during the qualitative interviews.

Embedded Design Analysis

In the embedded design analysis, the analyses of the quantitative and qualitative data are kept separate because the two data sets often reflect different questions. Thus, in an experiment, the outcome analysis is conducted for the quantitative data and the process qualitative data is analyzed for themes. In an embedded design for a correlational study (see Harrison, 2007), the analyses also proceed independently of each other. In both the experimental and the correlational examples, the two databases can be interpreted together—how one reinforces the other or complements the other. When a sequential design is used with the embedded design, researchers will use one form of analysis (e.g., qualitative data collected and analyzed before an experiment) to inform the quantitative phase or qualitative phase of the study.

Explanatory Design Analysis

Because you collect data in distinct phases, the analysis of an explanatory design is easier to see and conduct than in a triangulation design. A popular approach is to collect quantitative data and look for extreme cases to follow up in a qualitative phase. In a mixed methods study about the transition of adults from school to work, Blustein et al. (1997) first conducted a quantitative correlational analysis of transition measures (i.e., job satisfaction and congruence) and then employed the results to provide an "in-depth and focused approach to analyze the corresponding qualitative narratives" (p. 373). Specifically, they identified individuals with high and low scores (i.e., extreme cases) on the dependent measures and then conducted a qualitative, thematic analysis using interviews with these individuals.

Alternatively, within an explanatory design, the researcher might seek to explain the results in more depth in a qualitative phase of the study. This was the approach taken by Houtz (1995) in her study of attitudes and achievement of seventh- and eigth-grade science students. She first gathered survey data and found that her data on achievement and attitude were contradictory. Accordingly, in a follow-up qualitative phase, she interviewed science teachers, the school principal, and the university consultant.

Less frequently seen within the explanatory design is typology development through quantitative data collection and the use of this typology as a framework for identifying themes in a qualitative database. If Houtz (1995) had actually looked for themes based on her statistical results, she would have used this approach. Another procedure is to conduct a multilevel study, much like the quantitative procedures in multilevel modeling. The application of this approach would have been to study children's attitudes, teachers' attitudes, and organizational characteristics that support views toward science in a school. In this project, the survey of children might be followed by teacher interviews, and then by census or document data from organizational school records.

Exploratory Design Analysis

In this design, the substantial qualitative data collection becomes a means for developing or locating quantitative instruments; forming categorical information for later quantitative data collection; or developing generalizations from a few, initial qualitative cases. Perhaps the most popular use is to generate an instrument well grounded in the qualitative data from participants in a study. In the case of a researcher who studied first-year teachers in reservation-based, Native American elementary schools, the existing instruments were not sensitive enough to identify the cultural factors that affected this first-year experience. Thus, the researcher first conducted interviews with first-year teachers, identified themes and supporting statements, and developed an instrument to measure broadly the experiences of first-year teachers. As an alternative to this approach, the researcher might have identified the themes and located an instrument using the library resources mentioned in chapter 4.

In addition, you might combine categories of information from an exploratory qualitative data collection with continuous data in a statistical analysis. In the preceding example, the researcher would categorize experiences of the first-year teachers into their stages of development, such as "initiation," "apprentice," and "recruit," and use this categorization in a correlation or regression analysis. Unusual-or extreme-case individuals in these categories might serve as the basis for extensive analysis across a population. In this follow-up, the survey researcher might study Native American first-year teachers who saw themselves as in the "initiation" phase of development.

Diagram of the Procedures

Mixed methods researchers often provide a **visualization** or diagram of their design depicting the procedures. A visualization is a figure like the examples of Figure 17.2 that indicates the process of data collection. It consists of labeling the quantitative and qualitative data, indicating the sequence of activities (using arrows or plus signs), and emphasizing the priority (using lowercase or uppercase letters). By including this visualization, the researcher helps readers identify the sequence of data collection, an important aid when collecting multiple forms of data. The notation system by Morse (1991), described in Figure 17.1, can be useful in developing this visualization.

WHAT ARE THE STEPS IN CONDUCTING A MIXED METHODS STUDY?

Now that you have a basic understanding of mixed methods research, we can turn to specific steps typically undertaken by researchers when they use this design. These steps are not lockstep procedures; they provide a general guide to help you get started. See Figure 17.3 for an overview of this process.

Step 1. Determine If a Mixed Methods Study Is Feasible

The first step in the process is to assess the feasibility of using this design. You need skills in gathering both quantitative and qualitative data, time to collect extensive information, and a working knowledge of the different types of designs. Also important is whether audiences such as graduate committees, publishers, other researchers, and practitioners in educational settings will appreciate the complexity of your mixed methods study.

Step 2. Identify a Rationale for Mixing Methods

Assuming that a study is feasible, you need to consider why you are collecting both quantitative and qualitative data. The rationale for the four designs should provide a good starting point. Be explicit in this rationale, and include it early in your research plan or report. See the reasons for conducting mixed methods studies advanced earlier in this chapter.

FIGURE 17.3

Steps in the Process of Conducting a Mixed Methods Study

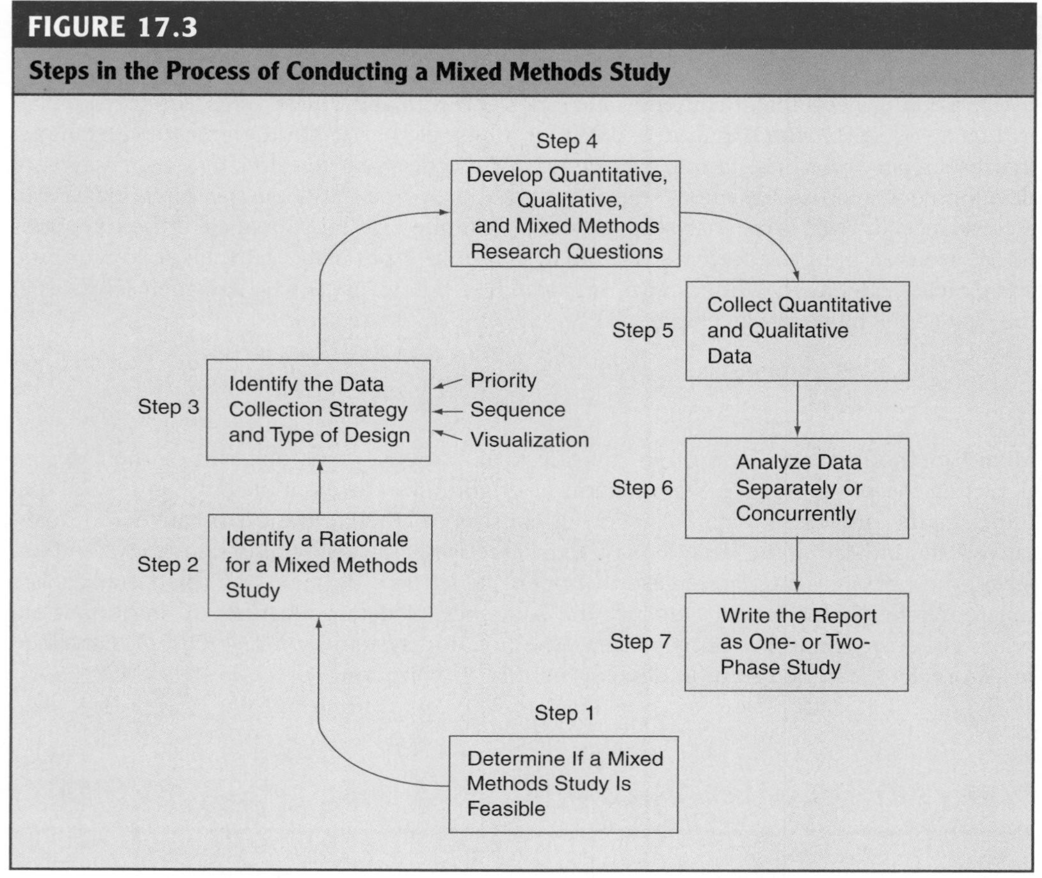

Step 3. Identify a Data-Collection Strategy

Identifying your rationale for the study will lead to planning your procedures for collecting data. You need to know:

- The priority you will give to quantitative and qualitative data
- The sequence of your data collection, if you do not plan to collect the data concurrently
- The specific forms of quantitative data (e.g., attendance records) and qualitative data (e.g., pictures) you will collect

Once you have made these decisions, create a visual diagram of the procedures. Use the notation system in Figure 17.1 and the models shown in Figure 17.2 to help you.

Step 4. Develop Quantitative, Qualitative, and Mixed Methods Questions

With the specific design in mind, next develop your research questions. Depending on the type of design, you can identify these questions prior to a study or they may emerge during the study. For instance, in a two-phase design, the questions for your second phase cannot be specifically identified early in the study—they will emerge as the study progresses. Alternatively, for a triangulation design, you can present the questions before data collection and specify them in detail.

If you can identify both quantitative and qualitative questions, pose both sets of questions. Typically, researchers present both exploratory questions and analytic-variable questions in a mixed methods study. As mentioned in chapter 5, quantitative questions specify the relationship among independent and dependent variables. They may be written in the null form but are typically written to convey an alternative directional form (e.g., the more mentoring, the greater the publications of faculty). Qualitative questions are open ended and nondirectional in nature and seek to describe the phenomenon. In addition, you might consider posing a mixed methods question. Most researchers are not familiar with this type of question. It is essentially a question that is to be answered by the mixed methods research design being used. For example, in a triangulation design, the mixed methods question could be "Do the two databases (quantitative and qualitative) converge and present consistent findings or diverge and show contradictory findings?" For an embedded design, the mixed methods question might be, "How does the supportive, secondary database help us better understand the primary database?" For an explanatory design, we might ask, "How does the qualitative follow up data help us to better understand the quantitative first phase results?" For an exploratory design, the question might be, "Is the instrument we develop in the second phase (as a result of exploring in the first phase) a better instrument that those available to measure the variables?"

Step 5. Collect Quantitative and Qualitative Data

Collecting data in a mixed methods study follows the procedures for data collection identified in chapters 6 and 8. For a mixed methods study, the sequence in which you collect the data will depend on the type of design. However, in all designs, this phase of the research will be lengthy and require good organization of the information. Statistical programs and text analysis programs, as discussed in chapters 7 and 9, can provide useful systems for storing, managing, and recording the data.

Step 6. Analyze Data Separately or Concurrently

The data analysis will also relate to the specific type of mixed methods design you are using. You can analyze quantitative data separately from qualitative data, as in the explanatory and exploratory designs, or integrate the data analysis, as in the triangulation design. Specific techniques have emerged for data analysis, as discussed in Table 17.2.

Step 7. Write the Report as a One- or Two-Phase Study

The final step in a mixed methods study is to write a scholarly report of the project. Some variations are seen in the writing structure of mixed methods studies, as outlined here:

- *The report is written in two phases.* The report contains one section to specify the problem and the literature. Then, the sections of data collection, analysis, and interpretation, two phases—one quantitative and one qualitative—are used for each section.
- *The report integrates the quantitative and qualitative phases of the study in each section.* The problem statement, for example, contains a need to explore (qualitative) and to predict or explain outcomes (quantitative). The research questions are posed as both quantitative and qualitative questions, and the data collection is in one section displaying an integration of quantitative and qualitative forms. The data analysis is an attempt to converge the two databases, and you form the results and

interpretation into information that sheds light on the research problem. This structure results in a triangulation design.

HOW DO YOU EVALUATE A MIXED METHODS STUDY?

An understanding of the basics of mixed methods research and a review of the steps in the process of conducting a study provide indicators for criteria that readers and study planners might use to evaluate a mixed methods study. Consider these questions as you design or review a study:

- Does the study employ at least one method associated with quantitative research and one method associated with qualitative research?
- Is it called a mixed methods (or a similar term) study?
- Is there a reason why the author intends to mix methods in a single study and is what you will gain in this process made clear?
- Does the author indicate the type of mixed methods study? Alternatively, can you identify the type from reading the rationale or from a visual figure depicting the flow of data-collection activities?
- Does the author mention the priority given to the quantitative and qualitative data and the sequence of their use in the study?
- Is the study feasible, given the amount of data to be collected and the monies, time, and expertise required?
- Has the author written research questions for the quantitative and the qualitative methods and the mixed methods procedures?
- Has the author clearly identified the quantitative and qualitative data-collection procedures?
- Is the procedure for data analysis consistent with the type of mixed methods study?
- Is the written structure of the study consistent with the type of mixed methods design?

APPLYING WHAT YOU HAVE LEARNED: A MIXED METHODS STUDY

To apply the ideas in this chapter, first read the mixed methods research study on page 576 by Way, Stauber, Nakkula, and London (1994), noting the marginal annotations that identify quantitative and qualitative characteristics as well as the five characteristics of a mixed methods study. This article was chosen because it includes the collection of both quantitative and qualitative data; provides an example of an explanatory design, a popular design in educational research; and has clearly identified quantitative and qualitative sections.

As you review this article, look for elements of the research process:

- The research problem and the type of design
- The use of the literature
- The purpose statement and research questions
- The types of procedures of mixed methods data collection
- The types of procedures of data analysis and interpretation
- The writing structure

The Research Problem

Paragraphs 01–04

The authors introduce the research problem early in the study, in the opening paragraph. They state that they need to understand the relationship between depression and substance use, controlling for gender, ethnicity, social class, and environment (see Paragraph 02). The authors base their evidence on past research studies. They might have drawn additional evidence from practice. For example, is substance use on the rise? Or is depression a major problem for adolescents?

This research problem passage also indicates a strong quantitative focus on the need to predict factors that explain the relationship between depression and substance use. Because the problem is stated as an examination of the relationship among variables (e.g., gender, ethnicity, social class, depression, and substance use), the authors are foreshadowing a quantitative framework (QUAN) for this study.

The Literature Review Paragraphs

Paragraphs 01–04

As seen in this article, the authors combine the literature review with the introduction/statement of the problem rather than presenting it as a distinct section in the study. From substantial references to the literature, the inclusion of variables, and a discussion of their relationships and differences, the literature indicates a strong quantitative orientation to the study.

The Purpose Statement and Rationale for Mixed Methods Research

Paragraphs 05–06, 27

The purpose statement ("In the present study . . . ") continues to emphasize a strong quantitative component to this study: the examination of a "relationship," the specification of variables, and the differences among schools. This statement also introduces the concept that both quantitative and qualitative methods will be used, indicating a mixed methods study. In addition, looking back at the title, we now see that it announces this study as a mixed methods design by indicating the inclusion of both quantitative and qualitative analysis.

In Paragraph 06, the authors introduce their reason for mixing methods. It is reintroduced in Paragraphs 27–28. We learn that the quantitative data provide a "context" for the qualitative data and that the qualitative data explore "possible explanations" for the quantitative findings about distinctions between the two schools in substance use. Specifically, we learn that depression by students who abused substances differed between the two high schools. Consequently, although not explicitly identified by name, the authors used an explanatory design with an initial quantitative first phase followed by a qualitative phase to explore the results about student depression in more detail. A visualization of the explanatory mixed methods design, such as the model shown in Figure 17.2, would have been most useful to help readers conceptualize the process of quantitative and qualitative data collection.

Collection of Mixed Methods Quantitative and Qualitative Data

Quantitative data collection—see Paragraphs 07–16

Qualitative data collection—see Paragraphs 27–33

The quantitative data collection is introduced first in this explanatory design. It consists of a large sample (N = 164), collection of scores or numeric data, a focus on instruments (i.e., Children's Depression Inventory and Substance Use), permissions, and data-collection procedures. Because the intent of this design was to conduct qualitative research to explain the quantitative results, the qualitative data collection followed the quantitative data collection. In the qualitative phase, the researchers examined their "most noteworthy" quantitative finding about depression among the students in both schools. They collected data from 19 students who were in the top 10% of depression scores from both the suburban and urban schools. They conducted interviews with these students, yielding text data for analysis.

The clear separation of the quantitative and qualitative data collection indicates a two-phase design, with the quantitative data collection preceding the qualitative data collection.

Analyzing and Interpreting Quantitative and Qualitative Data

Quantitative results—see Paragraphs 17–26

Qualitative results—see Paragraphs 34–47

Interpretation of quantitative and qualitative results—see Paragraphs 48–63

The authors report quantitative results using statistical analysis. They based this analysis on descriptive statistics about the two schools and then included inferential statistics that correlated and tested hypotheses (i.e., regressions) about the relationship among variables. In addition, gender differences and grade differences were also analyzed in terms of descriptive and inferential statistics about depression and substance use. This section displayed an increasingly detailed analysis from general trends and hypotheses to a more specific focus on gender and grade level.

The qualitative results reported three themes as indicated by headings: "Substance Use: Escape from Problems or Cause of Problems?" "Interpersonal Relationships and Substance Use," and "Peer Pressure and Substance Use." It also included multiple perspectives from students (e.g., Millie, Mara, Glen, and others), the frequent use of quotes to capture the voice of the participants, and the meaning that depressed youth ascribed to substance use.

The authors explain the meaning of the results in the "Summary and Discussion" section. Here we find a summary of the quantitative findings followed by a comparison of these findings with past literature and predictions from that literature (Paragraphs 48–58). Then the interpretation turns to the qualitative results, focusing on depressed students from both schools and reviewing the themes (Paragraphs 59–63).

The Overall Writing Structure

The clear separation of the quantitative phase from the qualitative phase makes this study easy to read and identify as a sequential, two-phase study. The authors might have identified more clearly their explanation for mixing methods, but the intent was to build on and extend a significant quantitative result about depression. The markings throughout this study—the title, the purpose statement, the separate data-collection analysis, the integration of results into an interpretation at the end of the project, the traditional quantitative structure, and the use of themes in the qualitative results—displayed many good elements of a mixed methods study.

KEY IDEAS IN THE CHAPTER

With a better understanding of qualitative research and the advantages of collecting both quantitative and qualitative data, mixed methods research designs are becoming popular in education. From initial multimethod quantitative studies, designs have emerged that incorporate quantitative data (e.g., scores from instruments, scores from observations, and census data) and qualitative data (e.g., open-ended interviews, observations, documents, and visual materials). Today, writers talk about a separate design in education—the mixed methods design—in which investigators collect and analyze at least one quantitative method of data and one qualitative method of data, with attention to sequence and priority. A mixed methods design involves the collection, analysis, and "mixing" of both quantitative and qualitative data to best understand a research problem.

Four major types of mixed methods designs exist. The triangulation design includes the collection of both quantitative and qualitative data simultaneously, with the purpose of converging or integrating the data. The embedded design includes collecting a primary form of data and then a secondary form of data that plays a supportive role in the study. Both forms of data are often collected simultaneously. The explanatory design begins with quantitative data collection and analysis followed by qualitative data collection and analysis. In this way, the researcher follows up on quantitative findings with qualitative explorations. The exploratory design reverses the data-collection procedure. The mixed methods researcher first gathers qualitative data and then builds on the analysis of it using quantitative data.

A major characteristic of mixed methods designs is a need to justify or provide a rationale for mixing methods. Researchers also collect both quantitative and qualitative data and provide a priority or weight and often a sequence to collecting both forms of data. Data analysis needs to relate to the type of design, and this analysis may involve transforming data, following up or explaining outlier or extreme cases, or using qualitative themes to develop a quantitative instrument.

The steps in conducting a mixed methods design involve assessing the feasibility of the study and presenting a rationale for mixing methods. They also involve making decisions about the priority and sequence of the analysis and developing research questions for the study. Researchers then collect both quantitative and qualitative data and analyze them together or separately, depending on the design. The final research report may present the study as one phase or as two phases, based on the research design chosen for the project.

USEFUL INFORMATION FOR PRODUCERS OF RESEARCH

- When presenting your mixed methods research to others, discuss your design as a distinct design in educational research.
- In the design of a mixed methods study, identify the advantages that will accrue from collecting both quantitative and qualitative data. Let these advantages point you toward the most appropriate design (e.g., triangulation, explanatory, exploratory) to study your research problem. In this chapter, the advantages of each design are specified.
- Of the three designs, recognize that it is easier to conduct a sequential explanatory or exploratory design than a triangulation design. With a triangulation design, you need to converge both quantitative and qualitative databases (e.g., numbers and text) and possibly collect additional data if the two databases are in conflict.

- Recognize that in selecting a mixed methods design you have taken on a challenging project. Mixed methods research involves extensive data collection and data analysis. Weigh the trade-off between drawbacks of time and resources and the advantages of collecting both quantitative and qualitative data to understand your research problem.
- Use the two factors, priority and sequence, to help you decide what mixed methods research design is appropriate for your study.
- To best present the procedures in your mixed methods design, create a diagram that portrays the steps in the process. Use the guidelines about notation, introduced in this chapter, to help you design this visual.

Useful Information for Consumers of Research

- Because researchers have only recently identified mixed methods as a specific design in educational research, authors of studies may not label their research as mixed methods. You might identify a mixed methods study by determining whether the researcher collects both quantitative and qualitative data to examine a research problem.
- When reading a mixed methods study, look for a diagram of the procedures to help you understand the flow of activities in the mixed methods research. If such a visual is not present, you may want to sketch out the sequence of activities, including the time sequence for collecting quantitative and qualitative data, how they were analyzed, and the intent for using both forms of data.
- Few discussions are available about how to evaluate a mixed methods study. But because both quantitative and qualitative data are being collected, you might judge a mixed method study on the basis of the quantitative and qualitative criteria introduced in Chapter 10. Also in this chapter are several standards that you might apply to help assess the quality of a mixed methods study.
- To locate useful information from mixed methods studies, look for the detailed picture that emerges from qualitative research and the generalizable results that emerge from quantitative research. This combined impact—the detail and the general—can help you best understand a research problem in education.

Additional Resources You Might Examine

A book available on mixed methods research is the *Handbook of Mixed Methods in the Social and Behavioral Research* edited by Tashakkori and Teddlie (2003). This handbook expands an earlier overview the authors provided (Tashakkori & Teddlie, 1998) and the research design text by Creswell (2003). The handbook covers many topics from the paradigms available as a philosophical foundation to the steps in data analysis and writing a mixed methods report. The 1998 book presents a history of mixed methods research, the various types of research designs, details about collecting both quantitative data and qualitative data, and various data analysis strategies for integrating text and numeric data. The Creswell book takes a reader through the steps of designing a study and compares qualitative, quantitative, and mixed methods approaches. A recent book (Creswell & Plano, 2007) provides an introduction to the design and conduct of mixed methods research and presents in detail the four designs mentioned in this chapter. See:

Creswell, J. W. (2003). *Research design: Quantitative, qualitative, and mixed method approaches* (2nd ed.). Thousand Oaks, CA: Sage.

Creswell, J. W., & Plano Clark, V. L. (2007). *Designing and conducting mixed methods research*. Thousand Oaks, CA: Sage.

Tashakkori, A., & Teddlie, C. (Eds.). (2003). *Handbook of mixed methods in social and behavioral research*. Thousand Oaks, CA: Sage.

Tashakkori, A., & Teddlie, C. (1998). *Mixed methodology: Combining qualitative and quantitative approaches*. Thousand Oaks, CA: Sage.

Another book is the Jossey-Bass sourcebook on evaluation by Greene and Caracelli (1997). Although aimed at the field of evaluation, this book provides a good overview of the types of mixed methods designs and illustrates the process of mixed methods research with numerous examples.

Examine:

Greene, J. C., & Caracelli, V. J. (Eds.). (1997). *Advances in mixed-method evaluation: The challenges and benefits of integrating diverse paradigms* (New Directions for Evaluation, No. 74). San Francisco: Jossey-Bass.

Another book on mixed methods research is the Jossey-Bass sourcebook on evaluation by Reichardt and Rallis (1994). This book discusses many topical issues related to mixed methods research and presents a good conceptual overview of the paradigm debate between quantitative and qualitative researchers. See:

Reichardt, C. S., & Rallis, S. E. (1994). *The qualitative–quantitative debate: New perspectives* (New Directions for Program Evaluation, No. 61). San Francisco: Jossey-Bass.

Three journal articles provide especially good introductions to mixed methods research. The article by Morgan (1998) provides the best example of decision areas, such as priority and sequencing, that go into determining the most appropriate mixed methods research design for you to use. A second article, by Morse (1991), pioneered the notation system we now use in mixed methods research, and Creswell (1999) also offers an overview of the history, the types of designs, and steps in the process of conducting a mixed methods study. Explore:

Creswell, J. W. (1999). Mixed-method research: Introduction and application. In G. J. Cizek (Ed.), *Handbook of educational policy* (pp. 455–472). San Diego, CA: Academic Press.

Morgan, D. L. (1998). Practical strategies for combining qualitative and quantitative methods: Applications to health research. *Qualitative Health Research, 3,* 362–376.

Morse, J. M. (1991). Approaches to qualitative–quantitative methodological triangulation. *Nursing Research, 40,* 120–123.

Go to our Companion Website at **www.prenhall.com/creswell** to:

- assess your understanding of chapter content with Multiple-Choice Questions,
- apply what you've learned with Essay Questions,
- practice your research skills with interactive Building Research Skills exercises, and
- broaden your knowledge of research with Web Links to research topics on the Internet.

Quantitative Characteristics
Qualitative Characteristics

Mixed Methods Research Characteristics

Depression and Substance Use in Two Divergent High School Cultures: A Quantitative and Qualitative Analysis

Niobe Way,[1] Helena Y. Stauber,[2] Michael J. Nakkula,[3] and Perry London[4]

*Research has generally concluded that adolescent depression and substance use are strongly interrelated, but has rarely considered how this relationship may vary across diverse populations. In this study, we used quantitative and qualitative methods to explore the relationships among depression and cigarette, alcohol, marijuana, and harder drug use across two culturally disparate environments: a suburban and an inner-city high school. Our sample included 164 suburban and 242 inner-city high school students. The students completed Kovacs' Children's Depression Inventory of 1985 and substance use measures derived from various sources. In-depth semistructured interviews were conducted with subjects who scored in the top 10% of the CDI (N = 19) from both schools. Our quantitative findings indicated a positive association between depression and cigarette, marijuana, and harder drug use among the suburban students, and no association between depression and the use of any substances for the urban students. There were no significant differences in levels of reported depression across samples. However, with the exception of marijuana use, suburban students reported greater involvement in substance use than urban students. Our qualitative analyses suggest that across-school differences in the relationships among depression and substance use may be related to the varied meanings of depression and substance use that are informed by cultural context.**

---

*Way, N., Stauber, H. Y., Nakkula, M. J., & London, P. (1994). Depression and substance use in two divergent high school cultures: A quantitative and qualitative analysis. *Journal of Youth and Adolescence*, 23(3), 331–357. Reprinted with permission of the author and Kluwer Academic/Plenum Publishers.
The research was funded by the National Institute of Drug Abuse (NIDA), Grant No. 1 R01 DA–06844, Perry London, principal investigator. The views, opinions, and findings contained in their article are not to be construed as NIDA's position or policy.

[1]Post-Doctoral Fellow, Psychology Department, Yale University. B.A. from University of California, Berkeley, and Ed.D. from the Graduate School of Education, Harvard University. Research interests include the phenomenology of high-risk behavior and social development among urban adolescents. To whom reprint requests should be addressed at Department of Psychology, Yale University, Box 208205, New Haven, Connecticut 06520.

[2]Doctoral student in Counseling and Consulting Psychology, Graduate School of Education, Harvard University. B.A. from Mount Holyoke College and Ed.M. from the Graduate School of Education, Harvard University. Research interests include the relationships among high-risk behavior, personality variables, and cultural context.

[3]Instructor in Human Development and Psychology, Graduate School of Education, Harvard University. B.A. from Michigan State University, M.A. from University of Minnesota—Duluth, and Ed.D. from Harvard Graduate School of Education. Research interests include integrating quantitative and qualitative methods in social science research and the phenomenology of high-risk behavior.

[4]Formerly Dean of the Graduate School of Applied and Professional Psychology, Rutgers University, and Professor of Education, Graduate School of Education, Harvard University, B.A. Yeshiva University, M.A. and Ph.D. Teachers College, Columbia University. Research interests included adolescent high-risk behavior and ethnic and religious identity development. Deceased June 1992.

Introduction

A quantitative research problem requires description or explanation.

(01) Over the past 30 years an abundance of research on adolescents and young adults has investigated the relationships among depression and substance use. The results of these studies suggest that adolescents or young adults who are heavy cigarette, drug, or alcohol users are more likely to show signs of depression than light or nonusers (Aneshensel and Huba, 1983; Braucht et al., 1973; Kaminer, 1991; Kaplan et al., 1980; Kaplan et al., 1984; Kennedy et al., 1987; Paton et al., 1977; Reinherz et al., 1991; Robins and Przybeck, 1985; Shiffman and Wills, 1985; Simons et al., 1991). Researchers and practitioners have typically concluded that there is a strong association between depression and substance use among adolescents (Blau et al., 1988; Kaplan et al., 1984; Reinherz et al., 1991; Simons et al., 1988).

The quantitative literature plays a major role.

(02) There has been little research, however, that has explored the effects of gender, ethnicity, social class, or environment (e.g., urban vs. suburban) on the relationships among depression and substance use. The few studies that have examined such sociodemographic differences have concluded that this type of investigation is critical (Dembo et al., 1979; Paton and Kandel, 1978; Prendergast, 1974; Siegel and Ehrlich, 1989). Paton and Kandel (1978) report widely disparate relationships between depression and substance use among different ethnic groups, and between males and females within selected ethnic groups. They found no relationship between depression and drug use among either black or Puerto Rican adolescents; however, this relationship was highly significant for white adolescents, with higher levels of depression associated with higher levels of drug use. Furthermore, the relationship between depression and drug use was significantly stronger for the white girls in the sample than for the white boys.

The quantitative literature justifies the research problem and provides direction for the study.

(03) Siegel and Ehrlich (1989) report socioeconomic status (SES) differences in levels of depression among adolescent substance abusers. The high SES, white adolescent substance abusers scored significantly higher on the depression scale (The Children's Depression Inventory) than the low SES, white adolescent substance abusers. Their findings suggest that the relationships among depression and substance use may vary across social class. Siegel and Ehrlich (1989) state that the low success rates among treatment programs for drug-abusing adolescents may be related to a failure to "take into account the possibility that adolescents from different ethnic or socioeconomic backgrounds may take drugs (and alcohol) for different reasons" (p. 925). Drug and alcohol use may not be related to depression for lower SES adolescents as it is for higher SES adolescents.

(04) While researchers have examined gender, ethnic, social class, or environmental (e.g., rural vs. urban) differences in levels of drug use (Kaplan et al., 1984; Kaplan et al., 1980; Siegel and Ehrlich, 1989), type of drug use (Hager et al., 1971; Harris, 1971; Siegel and Ehrlich, 1989; Smart and Fejer, 1969), and levels of depression (Baron and Perron, 1986: Doerfler et al., 1988; Kaplan et al., 1980; Siegel and Ehrlich, 1989), they rarely have looked for such sociodemographic differences in the relationships among depression and substance use.

The quantitative purpose statement, research questions, or hypotheses are specific and narrow.

Mixed methods researchers collect both quantitative and qualitative data.

(05) In the present study we used both quantitative and qualitative methods to explore the relationships among depression and cigarette, alcohol, marijuana, and harder drug use in two culturally divergent school environments: an inner-city public high school and a suburban public high school. The inner-city school and the suburban school are characterized by differences in racial and ethnic composition, social class, geographic location,

and educational and community resources. We assume that differences we may find between the two schools reflect a complex combination of these social class, racial, ethnic, and environmental factors. Rather than attempting to tease out the differential effects of such factors, as was done in the previously cited studies (e.g., Paton and Kandel, 1978), our analyses are conducted at a more macro level where individual contributions coalesce to form the distinct community of the school culture.

(06) We conducted an integrative analysis of quantitative and qualitative data in which quantitative results were used to select participants, generate questions, and provide a context for the qualitative analysis. Therefore, the paper is divided into two methods and results sections, one for the quantitative analysis and one for the contingent qualitative analysis. The two sets of findings are synthesized through a single discussion section.

Mixed methods researchers justify the use of mixing methods.

Mixed methods researchers can provide a visual picture of procedures.

Quantitative Analysis

Method

Subjects

Quantitative data collection involves studying a large number of individuals.

Mixed methods researchers sequence the quantitative and qualitative data collection.

(07) The sample included 164 students from a suburban high school (grades nine [N = 44], ten [N = 36], eleven [N = 35], and twelve [N = 49], 75 boys, 89 girls) and 242 students from an inner-city high school (grades nine [N = 45], ten [N = 33], eleven [N = 68], and twelve [N = 96], 108 boys and 134 girls). Both schools were located in the Greater Boston area. The students from the suburban high school primarily described themselves as Irish-American (26%), Italian-American (11%), Irish and Italian-American (5%), or white with no ethnicity specified (45%). The students from the inner-city high school primarily described themselves as African American (35%), Puerto Rican or Dominican (31%), Haitian (12%), white (7%), or American Indian (4%).

Quantitative researchers take an objective and unbiased approach.

(08) The suburban students came from predominantly middle- or working-class families, while the urban students came from predominantly working-class or poor families. These variations in social class were inferred from the parents' educational backgrounds, their current occupations, the families' housing situations, and the percentage of students who receive subsidized lunches (see Table 1).

(09) In addition to social class differences, the schools had substantially different dropout rates: It is projected that 32% of the freshman students in the urban school vs. 4% in the suburban school will not graduate. Due to this important distinction, our study does not attempt a broad description of the comparative experiences of inner-city and suburban youth. However, while the elevated dropout rate in the urban school restricts the generalizability of our findings, our inclusion of students from the four high school grade levels makes it possible to capture the experiences of numerous inner-city students who are potential dropouts. As such, while this study does not reflect the behavioral and emotional characteristics of students who have dropped out, neither does it provide a uniform picture of inner-city students who have fully circumvented risk for dropping out.

(10) In both schools, students were recruited for the study through presentations made to their classrooms by members of our research team. In the suburban school where tracking exists, equal numbers of required courses were targeted for presentation within each academic track, allowing us to reach a sample of students that was representative of the whole school population. In the urban school there is no tracking, but large numbers of students receive special education services. As such, we targeted proportional numbers of mainstream vs. special education classrooms for our presentations. Across all of the classrooms from which we recruited in both schools,

TABLE 1
Student Reports of Parent Job Type, Parent Education Levels, Family Housing, and School-Reported Percentages of Subsidized Lunches

	Parents' Jobs			
	Suburban School		Urban School	
	Mothers	Fathers	Mothers	Fathers
"Professional"	21%	40%	4%	4%
"Semiprofessional"	16	10	9	6
Business person	6	9	8	8
Own business	1	8	5	6
Blue-collar job	12	19	25	39
Office-clerical	22	3	4	0
Other	5	4	5	5
Unemployed	16	4	39	20
Don't know	0	1	4	13
	Parents' Education			
	Suburban School		Urban School	
	Mothers	Fathers	Mothers	Fathers
Graduate school	11%	16%	2%	2%
College grads	23	35	7	7
Some college	18	14	9	9
High school grads	25	12	21	16
Trade school	14	13	7	7
Less than twelfth grade	5	5	33	23
Don't know	4	5	23	35

	Housing	
	Suburban School	Urban School
Project housing	0%	19%
Two- or three-family homes	12	36
Apartments	4	28
Single-family homes	84	15
Rent home	12	71
Own home	82	27
	Students eligible for subsidized lunches	
	Suburban School	Urban School
	3%	80%

80–90% of the students agreed to participate. Of those students who agreed to participate, 98% in both schools agreed to *both* the questionnaire and the interview. Participants were paid five dollars for completing the questionnaire measures and five dollars to participate in a follow-up interview.

Questionnaires

(11) **Quantitative data collection is based on using instruments identified prior to the study.**

Children's Depression Inventory (CDI). All students completed the CDI (Kovacs, 1985), a 27-item questionnaire designed to assess the severity of depressive symptoms from mid-childhood through late adolescence. The scale, based on the BDI for adults, measures symptoms such as disturbances in mood, eating behaviors, self-esteem, and interpersonal behavior. For each item, students are asked to check one of three descriptions that best applies to them during the last 2 weeks (e.g., "I am sad all the time," "I am sad many times," "I am sad once in a while"). Responses to each item are scored on a 0–2 scale (from least depressed to most depressed). A total score of 19 or above, out of a maximum of 54 points, is considered a strong indicator of depression (Kovacs, 1982). According to Kovacs (1983), the CDI's "readability" is at the first grade level, thus increasing its accessibility to students in a high school population at various levels of literacy. The CDI has been used with urban and suburban samples and has typically indicated minor or no significant differences by grade, sex or race (Doerfler et al., 1988; Finch et al., 1985; Kovacs, 1980–1981). The CDI has shown high internal consistency ranging from .71 to .86, and test–retest reliability ranging from .38 to .87, depending on the length of time between tests and the population studied (Kovacs, 1983; Saylor et al., 1984). It has also been reported to be strongly related to other self-report measures of constructs associated with depression (e.g., self-concept, hopelessness, and anxiety; Doerfler et al., 1988; Kovacs, 1982; Way et al., 1990). In the present study, inter-item reliability, using Chronbach's α, was .80 for the urban school and .88 for the suburban school.

Quantitative data collection involves gathering numeric data.

(12) *Substance Use Scales.* Our substance use scales were derived from the Institute of Behavioral Science's Health Questionnaire (Donovan et al., 1985) and the California Substance Use Survey (Skager and Firth, 1988). Additional questions were developed in consultation with students from each school who advised us on the use of appropriate and accessible language for their age group and cultures.[5] Separate measures for cigarettes, alcohol, marijuana, and harder drugs (e.g., cocaine and LSD) employed Likert-type scales to assess the age at which the student started using the particular substance, the frequency of use, the amount of use at any one time, and when, where, and with whom the use typically occurs. Total scores for each measure included age of initiation, frequency, amount, and patterns of use.

(13) The alcohol use measure, for example, was comprised of nine equally weighted questions: 1 for age of initiation ("How old were you when you had your first drink?"), 2 for frequency of use (e.g., "How often do you drink alcohol?"), 2 for amount of use at any one time (e.g., "When you drink, how many whole drinks do you usually have at a time?"), and 4 for patterns of use (i.e., "When do you usually drink alcohol?" "What kind of alcohol do you drink most often?" "Have you ever gotten drunk during school?" "In the past year, have you ever been too drunk or hung over to stay at school?"). An overall alcohol score, is the summed total of the individual responses to each of these nine equally weighted questions. Rather than simply assessing frequency of use, the alcohol scale taps into other factors that contribute to the severity of alcohol-use problems. As a case in point, a student who reports drinking on average three beers at a time every week during the weekends, and has occasionally gotten drunk during school, would receive a higher score on the alcohol measure than a peer who reports drinking a six pack of beer at a time about once a month during the weekends, and has never gotten drunk during school. However, if this latter student has occasionally gotten drunk during school, then he or she would receive the same score as the former student. Scaling and scoring procedures were similar for each of the substance use measures.[6]

---

[5]These consultations with students, some with reading disabilities, allowed us to create measures that are accessible to students with diverse reading skills.

[6]Thoughout this paper, the phrase, "levels of substance use" or "levels of cigarette, alcohol, marijuana use or harder drug" are intended to describe patterns of use inclusive of but not limited to frequency of use.

(14) For the urban school, inter-item reliability for cigarettes was .82, for alcohol .86, for marijuana .78, and for harder drugs .73. For the suburban school, inter-item reliability for cigarettes was .86, for alcohol .84, for marijuana .82, and for harder drugs .92.

Procedure

(15) Parental consent forms were distributed and collected prior to questionnaire administration. Consent forms provided a brief description of the study and emphasized the confidentiality of student responses. In addition, prior to completing the questionnaires, all students were verbally assured of full confidentiality. Questionnaires were identified by number codes rather than student names. The researchers maintained a list with participants' names and corresponding code numbers for the purpose of identifying students for follow-up interviews.

(16) All 406 participants completed the questionnaires during one class period. To maximize the comfort of participants and the likelihood of honest responses, teachers were asked to leave the classroom during questionnaire administration. At least two research team members were present throughout the administrations to distribute and collect questionnaires, monitor student contact, and respond to students' questions and concerns. The use of simple language made the questionnaires accessible to most students. However, in a small number of case (N = 8) where reading deficiencies were profound, a team member read the questions aloud to students in a private setting.

Results

Comparisons Across Schools

Mixed methods researchers analyze data based on their design type.

Quantitative data analysis consists of statistical analysis.

(17) *Means Analysis.* The mean scores and standard deviations for depression and substance use, and a comparison of means across schools, are shown in Table 2. Levels of reported depression score did not differ significantly across schools. The mean depression score (9.2) and the range of scores (0–31) in the suburban school were very similar to the mean depression score (9.4) and range (0–29) in the urban school. There were significant differences between schools, however, in reported prevalence of students' drug and alcohol use. Suburban students reported using significantly more cigarettes, alcohol, and harder drugs than the urban students[7]. The average score for marijuana use was similar across schools (see Table 2).

TABLE 2
Mean Scores, Standard Deviations, and Comparisons of Means Across Schools[a]

	Suburban school	Urban school	*p* Value
Depression	9.2 (7.1)	9.4 (5.9)	NS
Cigarette smoking	5.5 (5.9)	3.7 (4.9)	.001
Alcohol use	16.8 (10.1)	11.7 (8.4)	.0001
Marijuana use	6.8 (6.7)	6.4 (5.9)	NS
Harder drug use	24.0 (6.0)	22.2 (1.1)	.001

[a]Standard deviations are in parentheses.

[7]For the urban students, relatively little harder drug use was reported, resulting in a non-normal distribution for this variable. Howver, harder drug use was normally distributed in the suburban sample. This discrepancy should be kept in mind when examining the results regarding harder drug use.

TABLE 3
Correlations Among Depression and Substance Use

	Suburban School				
	Depression	**Cigarette smoking**	**Alcohol use**	**Marijuana use**	**Harder drug use**
Depression	—	.33[a]	.14	.24[b]	.22[b]
Cigarette smoking		—	.58[a]	.65[a]	.41[a]
Alcohol use			—	.57[a]	.39[a]
Marijuana use				—	.72[a]
Harder drug use					—

	Urban school				
	Depression	**Cigarette smoking**	**Alcohol use**	**Marijuana use**	**Harder drug use**
Depression	—	.06	−.04	−.06	.07
Cigarette smoking		—	.53[a]	.42[a]	.22[a]
Alcohol use			—	.54[a]	.23[a]
Marijuana use				—	.26[a]
Harder drug use					—

[a]$p < .0001$.
[b]$p < .01$.

(18) *Correlation and Multiple Regression Analyses.* The results of analyses of correlation among depressiovn and different substances are shown in Table 3. In both schools, all forms of substance use were highly intercorrelated. Depression scores among the students in the suburban sample were positively correlated with cigarette use (r = 33, p < .0001), with marijuana use (r = 24, p < .0021), and with harder drug use (r = 22, p < .0037).

Quantitative data analysis consists of describing trends, comparing groups, or relating variables.

Depression and alcohol use was not significantly correlated (*r* = 14, p < .074); however, the nonsignificant correlation went in the same direction as the other significant correlations. A multiple regression analysis showed that substance use (the combined effect of cigarettes, alcohol, marijuana, and harder drugs) explained 16% of the variability (p < .001) in depression for the suburban sample. Depression, however, was not significantly correlated with any of these substances in the urban sample.

Comparisons Within Schools

Gender Differences

(19) *Means Analyses.* Means and standard deviations for depression and each substance, for boys and girls across both schools, are shown in Table 4. In the urban sample, males and females did not have significantly different depression scores, yet the girls were overrepresented in the top 10% of the sample, with 19 of the 24 highest depression scores.[8] The findings were similar for our suburban sample: males and females did not have significantly different depression scores, but again, the girls were overrepresented in the top 10% of the sample with 11 of the 16 highest depression scores.

(20) Females in the suburban sample used significantly less alcohol, marijuana, and harder drugs than males (see Table 4). There was no gender

[8]Six of these 19 were Haitian girls, revealing that a highly disproportionate percentage of very depressed girls were Haitian (only 12% of our sample were Haitian). The mean depression score for Haitian girls was 14.8, by far the highest mean in our sample.

TABLE 4
Means and Standard Deviations Across Gender Within Each School[a]

	Suburban school			Urban school		
	Girls	Boys	*p* Value	Girls	Boys	*p* Value
Depression	9.8 (7.7)	8.5 (6.4)	NS	10.1 (6.1)	8.6 (5.5)	NS
Cigarette smoking[b]	5.2 (6.0)	5.8 (5.8)	NS	4.2 (5.2)	3.1 (4.5)	NS
Alcohol use	14.5 (9.6)	19.4 (10.1)	.002	11.0 (8.2)	12.5 (8.8)	NS
Marijuana use	5.3 (4.6)	8.6 (8.3)	.004	5.9 (5.2)	7.1 (6.6)	NS
Harder drug use	22.8 (3.3)	25.4 (9.2)	.03	22.1 (1.1)	22.2 (1.2)	NS

[a]Standard deviations are in parentheses.
[b]Standard deviations are high relative to the means for cigarette smoking because the analyses include nonsmokers, which lowers the means. This results in a wide range of variation above each mean for smokers.

TABLE 5
Pearson Correlations Between Depression and Substance Use Across Gender Within Each School

	Urban		Suburban	
	Females	Males	Females	Males
	Depression	Depression	Depression	Depression
Cigarette smoking	.07	.07	.40[a]	.24[b]
Alcohol use	.01	–.10	.21[b]	.10
Marijuana use	–.04	–.05	.35[a]	.23[b]
Harder drug use	.07	.08	.36[a]	.26[b]

[a]$p < .001$.
[b]$p < .05$.

difference for cigarette use. Urban girls' scores on cigarettes, alcohol, marijuana, and harder drugs were not significantly different from boys' scores. However, when we looked at differences between girls and boys within the dominant ethnic groups in the urban school (African-American, Puerto Rican, and Haitian), we found that African-American girls, on average, scored significantly lower on the marijuana scale than African-American boys (means = 6.6 and 10.3, respectively, $p < .03$). No other statistically significant gender differences in substance use were found within or across ethnic groups.

(21) *Correlation and Multiple Regression Analyses.* The results of the correlation analyses for the depression and substance use scores for girls and boys can be seen in Table 5. Similar to the findings for the entire urban sample, data from urban girls alone and from urban boys alone revealed no significant correlation between depression and substance use of any kind.

(22) For the girls in the suburban sample, depression was correlated with the use of cigarettes ($r = .40$, $p < .0001$), alcohol ($r = .21$, $p < .05$), marijuana ($r = .36$, $p < .0006$), and harder drugs ($r = .36$, $p < .0006$). For the boys in the suburban sample, there were significant correlations between depression and the use of cigarettes ($r = .24$, $p < .03$), marijuana ($r = .22$, $p < .05$), and harder drugs ($r = .25$, $p < .03$), but not between depression and alcohol use.

(23) These correlational findings suggest that the relationship between depression and substance use may be stronger for girls than for boys in the suburban sample. To test this possibility, multiple regression models

were created using interaction effects of gender and each of the substances (separately) in the prediction of depression. These multiple regression models revealed that gender interacted significantly with marijuana and with harder drugs in the prediction of depression. Marijuana alone accounted for 5% of the variance in depression in the suburban school ($p < .002$). Although the main effect of gender ($p < .07$) did not significantly enhance the prediction of depression ($R^2 = .07$), the addition of the interaction variable for marijuana and gender ($p < .03$) to the model containing both main effects did significantly enhance the explained variance in depression ($R^2 = .10$). The picture was similar for harder drug use and gender. Harder drug use alone accounted for 5% of the variance in depression in the suburban school ($p < .003$). The addition of gender ($p < .09$) to the model was not significant ($R^2 = .06$); however, the addition of the interaction variable for harder drug use and gender ($p < .007$) to the model significantly enhanced the explained variance in depression ($R^2 = .11$). Gender did not interact significantly with alcohol or cigarettes in the prediction of depression.

(24) These multiple regression findings indicate that, as suggested by the correlational findings, there are significant gender differences in the relationship between depression and marijuana use, and between depression and harder drug use within the suburban sample. However, there are no significant gender differences in the relationship between depression and alcohol use or depression and cigarette use.

Grade Differences

(25) *Analysis of Variance.* The grade differences in reported levels of depression and cigarette, alcohol, marijuana, and harder drug use within the two schools are shown in Table 6. Within the suburban school, there were significant differences between grades in levels of cigarette ($p < .0005$), alcohol ($p < .0001$), and marijuana use ($p < .0001$). Students in the eleventh and twelfth grades reported greater alcohol use than did the ninth- and tenth-grade

TABLE 6
Mean Differences Across Grade for Depression and Substance Use

Suburban school

	Grades						
	9	**10**	**11**	**12**	***F* Value**	**Scheffé Contrasts**	***N***
Depression	9.9	7.5	9.2	9.8	.93	NS	163
Cigarette smoking	4.6	2.7	7.6	7.2	6.26[a]	10 < 11 and 12	160
Alcohol use	10.8	13.5	20.4	21.8	14.80[a]	9 and 10 < 11 and 12	162
Marijuana use	4.1	4.5	8.7	9.5	8.05[a]	9 and 10 < 12, 9 < 11	160
Hard drug use	22.4	22.2	25.2	25.9	3.29	NS	157

Urban school

	Grades						
	9	**10**	**11**	**12**	***F* Value**	**Scheffé Contrasts**	***N***
Depression	7.8	8.8	8.9	10.8	3.08	NS	231
Cigarette smoking	4.6	4.0	4.4	3.1	1.41	NS	230
Alcohol use	11.4	14.5	13.6	9.6	4.02[b]	12 < 11	224
Marijuana use	5.8	8.4	6.9	5.8	1.74	NS	225
Hard drug use	22.0	22.0	22.3	22.3	.87	NS	222

[a]$p < .001$.
[b]$p < .01$.

students, and greater cigarette use than the tenth-grade students. The twelfth graders also reported heavier patterns of marijuana use than the ninth and tenth graders, while the eleventh graders reported a heavier pattern of marijuana use than did the ninth graders. Within the urban school, grade differences were found only for alcohol use ($p < .01$). Eleventh graders reported greater alcohol use than did twelfth graders. No other grade differences were found in patterns of substance use in the urban school (see Table 6.)

(26) *Multiple Regression Analyses.* Interactions between grade level and substance use were examined to determine whether they predicted depression. No significant interaction effects were found in either school. For each grade, the relationships between depression and substance use of each type were similar to the overall relations (i.e., across all grades) between these variables in each school.

Qualitative Analysis

Method

A qualitative problem requires exploration and understanding.

(27) Perhaps our most noteworthy quantitative finding was the distinction between the two schools in patterns of substance use as predictors of depression. Depression was significantly correlated with cigarette, marijuana, and harder drug use in the suburban school, whereas in the urban school, depression was not significantly correlated with any type of substance use. As an initial step in exploring possible explanations for this finding, we analyzed interviews from the most depressed students (according to the CDI) in both schools.

The qualitative purpose statement and research questions seek participants' experiences.

(28) Our analyses focused on the following questions: (a) How might students with similarly high depression levels across the two schools differ in their perspectives on substance use? (b) How might these possible differences in perspectives begin to explain why depression and substance use are differentially related across the schools?

Subjects

Qualitative data collection involves studying a small number of individuals or sites.

(29) Our qualitative analyses were conducted on interview data from the 19 students across both schools who scored in the top 10% of our sample on the CDI, with depression scores ranging from 19 to 30. This range is consistent with the top 10% of scores reported by Kovacs (1985) in her large normative sample for the CDI. The 19 students comprise all of the subjects in the top 10% of the CDI scores who were interviewed.[9]

Qualitative data collection is based on using protocols developed during the study.

(30) The suburban sample included 10 students: four boys (1 ninth grader, 1 tenth grader, 1 eleventh grader, and 1 twelfth grader) and 6 girls (3 ninth graders, 1 tenth grader, 1 eleventh grader, and 1 twelfth grader). Nine of the students were white and one was African-American. Our urban sample included 9 students; 2 boys (a ninth grader and a twelfth grader) and seven girls (1 ninth grader, 2 tenth graders, 2 eleventh graders, and 2 twelfth graders). Of the 2 boys, 1 was Haitain and the other Puerto Rican; of the 7 girls, 3 were African-American, 2 were Puerto Rican, 1 was Haitian, and 1 was white.

---

[9]From the total sample in each school, interviews were conducted with 90 students in the suburban school and 85 students in the urban school. These students were randomly selected from each school sample (only 2 or 3 students in each school refused to be interviewed). The 19 students whose interviews were used for this qualitative analysis were all the students whose CDI scores were in the top 10% in the sample, and who were randomly selected to be interviewed from the total sample.

The Interview

(31) The interview is semi-structured, and designed to explore the extent, nature, and quality of the participants' thoughts and feelings about a range of personal, interpersonal, and behavioral phenomena. The interview process is guided by open-ended questions that lead into topical areas including substance use. Initial responses to interview questions (such as "How often do you drink?" "What is it that you like about drinking?" "Why don't you drink more than you do?") were probed by the interviewer to invite increasingly detailed and thoughtful reports of students' self-perspectives on their substance use or nonuse. These kinds of questions were asked for each substance (e.g., "Why do you think you haven't tried marijuana?" "Why do you smoke cigarettes?" etc.). The goal of the interview is to explore the meaning and attributions that the students assign to their behavior.

Qualitative data collection involves gathering text or image data.

Procedure

(32) Interviews were conducted by advanced doctoral students in counseling or developmental psychology. Participants were interviewed in one-on-one-meetings held in private rooms at the respective school sites. We assured all participating students of full confidentiality.

(33) Our interview analyses consisted of detailed readings of students' perspectives on substance use and their reasons for choosing to use or abstain from use. Typical of many qualitative approaches, our method involved a content analysis in which interview data were partitioned into content domains for the comparison of themes across individual cases (Strauss, 1987). Three trained readers independently read for common themes in students' descriptions of their substance use patterns. Themes were identified and compared within and across schools. Only those themes that were identified by all three readers *independently* were considered common themes in the interviews. The following results section describes the common themes detected from the interviews of the urban and suburban depressed sample by the three data analysts.

Results

Differences in Substance Use

(34) The interviews indicated that substance use was more pervasive among the depressed students in the suburban sample than among those in the inner-city sample. Seven of the 10 students in the suburban sample reported active substance use. Among the 7 current substance users, all reported smoking cigarettes, 6 reported drinking alcohol, 2 reported smoking marijuana, and 1 reported using harder drugs. In contrast to the students at the suburban school, only 3 of the 9 depressed inner-city teens reported active substance use. Of those 3, 2 claimed to smoke cigarettes and drink alcohol, and the third claimed only to drink alcohol. None of the depressed students in the inner-city sample reported current use of marijuana or experimentation (current or past) with drugs harder than marijuana.

Differences in Meaning

(35) The readers independently identified three common differences across the two schools in the ways that these depressed youth spoke about substance use.

(36) *Substance Use: Escape from Problems or Cause of Problems?* Five of the 10 depressed students at the suburban school spoke about cigarettes, alcohol, marijuana, and harder drugs as a way to "escape" problems or "relax," while only 1 out of 9 depressed students in the inner-city drew an association

between substance use and "escaping" or "relaxing." Among most of the depressed urban youth (8 out of 9), substance use was described as a cause of stress, rather than as an escape from it. In contrast, in the suburban school, only 4 out of 10 depressed students mentioned problems that have resulted or could result from using substances. While both ways of describing substance use (an escape from problems and a source of problems or stress) were almost equally evident (5 vs. 4) in the suburban school, in the urban school, the view that substance use causes problems was clearly predominant among the depressed students.

Qualitative data analysis consists of describing information and developing themes.

(37) Included among students' responses from the suburban school is that of Millie, a tenth grader with a history of "off-again-on-again" cigarette and marijuana use, who reports resuming smoking cigarettes after a breakup with her boyfriend: "I got mad and started smoking [cigarettes] again [and] I was smoking weed all the time because I wanted to escape." Janice, a ninth grader at the same high school, smokes about eight cigarettes a day and claims that "something about it relaxes me—if I had to quit now I'd probably get real tense." She also views alcohol as a way to relax, even though "it makes you tired afterwards." Nicole, another ninth grader who smokes about a pack of cigarettes a day, says "I just like the way it makes me feel—it relaxes me sometimes." Drinking for Nicole is one way to "laugh a lot and forget about my problems." Alex, a junior at the suburban high school who has been heavily involved in drugs for many years, claims that while he does not necessarily use drugs to "run away," he views them as "a good way to get away." He also states that he uses LSD and other drugs "not *just* as an escape but because I like it."

(38) In contrast, Roxie, a sophomore from the urban sample who occasionally drinks alcohol "but only a little bit," states that she sees no benefit to using, only costs:

Qualitative data analysis consists of text analysis.

> Smoke, I think it smells. . . . Why, why should you risk the point of drinking, you know? I see it as pointless, I guess, to get drunk and have a hangover the next morning. . . . I don't see what's the point in doing those things. It'll mess your head up.

Glen, a freshman at the inner-city school, who occasionally drinks alcohol, says he does not want to drink more than he does because he sees the bad health effects drinking has had on his father. He also says he does not want to use marijuana because he watches his friends smoke and realizes that it leads only to problems. When asked by the interviewer why he stays away from marijuana, he says:

> Just, you cut school, people use it in school, my friends, before school starts and they all be dazed and they got a headache and stuff like that. I don't want to get that.

Vera, a sophomore at the inner-city school who occasionally smokes cigarettes and drinks "sips" of alcohol, claims that she controls her use of these substances because she thinks using them often is "stupid" and pointless. She has decided to stop using marijuana because she had a bad experience with it and believes that using drugs just leads to trouble:

> Because to me I think that cigarettes are just like weed. Because I'm like, none of them. Cigarettes always gave me nothing. All weed gave me was that [a "bad trip" on marijuana]. You know, I could have died. . . . It was so scary. . . . So it's like dumb you know, why people do it. Now I think why do they do it? I mean they could die.

Mara, a senior, who does not use any substances, claims that she does not drink because:

> Sometimes when you get drunk you might react improperly, and then you might hit someone and hurt someone that you—that's close to you. So I don't want it to affect anyone.

With regard to drugs, she claims the following:

> Drugs can make people very, very, very—not unattractive, but they might look like someone who is sick and I don't want to look like someone—when people's on the diet and they never eat—they become skinny, skinny and you see bones only. . . . They look like that when they do drugs all the time and never stop.

Yolanda, a freshman in the urban school, claims that she does not use drugs because "I just hear too many people dying . . . of overdose . . . I don't want to be one of them."

(39) In short, substance use was depicted primarily as a cause of problems by the depressed students in the inner-city sample. In the depressed suburban sample, by contrast, substance use was described both as an escape and as a potential problem. It is important to note that the depressed students from each school who depicted substance use as a cause of problems included both substance users and nonusers.

(40) *Interpersonal Relationships and Substance Use.* Students from both the urban and suburban samples discussed the connection between substance use and relationships with family and friends. However, there were differences between the two samples in the way that relationships were reported to affect their substance use decisions. Six out of 10 of the depressed students from the suburban sample emphasized the fear of disappointing or angering someone important to them as a primary inhibitor of substance use, while only 1 out of 9 inner-city students mentioned these factors as reasons not to use. However, most of the depressed inner-city students (7 out of 9) cited examples of the negative impact drugs or alcohol has had on someone close to them and on people in the community, and stated that this influenced their decisions to abstain or use at low levels. Only 3 out of 10 depressed students from the suburban sample mentioned seeing the negative effects on others as a reason to abstain or modulate use.

(41) Alisann, a senior at the suburban school, stopped using LSD and cocaine because of disapproval from friends. Gaby, a junior at the suburban school, has decided not to drink more than two bottles of beer at a time "because like my parents, they're trusting me tonight, and look what I'm doing, they'll never be able to trust me again and I wouldn't drink that much, you know." And Terence, a suburban freshman, told the interviewer how he could possibly lose friends if he used drugs, and "I don't think my mother would like it either."

(42) Unlike these suburban teens, stories from the depressed, inner-city teens speak poignantly of the negative impact of substance use on people close to them. For example, Tara, a senior at the inner-city school, talks about earlier childhood memories of her mother's heavy use of marijuana and alcohol, recalling that "when she was high or drunk she was the meanest person in the world." Such memories, Tara says, make her want to prevent similar experiences for her own children:

> The reason why I don't do it [drugs], because my mother used to do it, and now because I got two kids. So I said I'm not even gonna—I mean, I don't want them to grow up the way I grew up. So I'm not even gonna do it.

(43) Glen, an urban freshman, says he does not want to drink because he sees the effects on his alcoholic father:

> I don't want to be like him, I don't want to drink that much. Because I think sometimes he's going to pass away because of his liver—because he drinks too much.

In addition, he says he does not use marijuana or cocaine because he has watched his ex-best friend and his uncle become heavily involved in drugs and destroy their lives. Similarly, Elena, an urban junior, has decided not to drink anymore because she has seen the negative impact of alcohol on a boy whom she liked.

(44) Relationships are mentioned among both the suburban and urban students as influencing their decision to abstain or modulate their use of substances. However, the specific effects of their relationships differed: At the suburban school, the majority of students cited a reluctance to disappoint others, whereas in the urban school, almost all of the teenagers stated that seeing the negative impact on others was one of their main reasons to modulate or abstain from use.

(45) *Peer Pressure and Substance Use.* Six of the 10 depressed students in the suburban sample reported succumbing to peer pressure to use substances, while none of the depressed students in the urban sample reported being influenced by peer pressure to use or not to use substances. Five of these urban students explicitly stated that they have avoided peer pressure, while none of the depressed suburban students spoke about avoiding peer pressure.

(46) A suburban sophomore, Millie, provided this telling account of peer pressure:

> I don't like drinking. I don't enjoy it, but everyone else was partying so what else is there to do. . . . I don't want to drink but I want to have a good time with everybody so I do.

Millie adds that when she is at a party drinking she is afraid that she would accept harder drugs if someone were to ask her. Blane, a suburban senior, says he has recently stopped drinking, and that doing so required his complete disassociation from all of his friends who drink. He said the pressure to drink when he was with them would have prevented his efforts toward abstinence. Terence, a suburban freshman, says that while he has not yet experienced pressure to use substances, he can imagine drinking to fit in at a party "but that hasn't happened yet." Alisann, a suburban senior, openly acknowledges that she began to smoke and drink because her friends were doing it. However, she said she eventually stopped because she switched friends and her current friends disapprove of her drinking and using drugs. MaryAnn, a suburban freshman, says that she has increased the number of cigarettes she smokes a day "not because of any reason—just because of the kids I've been hanging around with increased, so I've just increased and there's no reason why I have."

(47) In contrast, Elena, a junior at the inner-city school, stresses her independent stance with her friends:

> If my friends choose to do it, they do it. But they know me. They know me, I don't do it [use substances]. If I wanted to do it, I'd do it, but they have [no] control over me. . . . They know that I'll do what I want to do when I want to do it, and they can't tell me.

Mara, an inner-city senior, matter-of-factly states "I don't do drugs just because I don't want to do it." Glen, a freshman, claims that there is peer pressure to use marijuana but that he "just stays out of that." But, he adds, he feels pressure from his father to drink and he finds that kind of pressure harder to resist. Yolanda and Roxy, a freshman and sophomore, respectively, say that they are aware of peer pressure to use substances but that they have never felt it personally. Yolanda says the pressure has not affected her because nobody in her family or among her friends drinks or uses drugs. In sum, the suburban depressed students report being more influenced by peer pressure to use substances than their counterparts in the urban sample.

Summary and Discussion

(48) This comparative study of urban and suburban high school students found between-school similarities in levels of reported depression, differences in levels of reported substance use, and most importantly, differences in the *relationships* among depression and substance use. In addition, our qualitative analyses provide possible explanations for the quantitative differences revealed in the relationships among depression and substance use across the two schools.

(49) It is noteworthy, in our quantitative findings, that levels of depression were similar across the urban and suburban school samples. This finding stands in contrast to what one might expect given the relatively more stressful environment of the inner-city. It is possible that inner-city adolescents may develop psychological and emotional resilience in response to the extraordinary stresses of their social environment, resulting in levels of depression that do not exceed what might be expected in other populations of adolescents.

Quantitative interpretations compare results with predictions.

(50) While there were no significant gender differences in the mean level of depression within each school, girls were overrepresented in the top 10% of depression scores in both schools, suggesting gender differences in the severity, if not the overall prevalence, of depression. The lack of significant gender differences in mean depression scores on the CDI is consistent with previous findings in other large scale studies (Doerfler et al., 1988; Green, 1980; Kovacs 1983; Weissman et al., 1980). However, similar to our findings, studies that have looked beyond the mean scores on the depression scale have found, typically, that more girls score in the higher range of depression scores on the CDI than boys (McCauley et al., 1988; Reinherz et al., 1991; Worchel et al., 1987).

(51) Our failure to find grade differences in levels of depression within either school is consistent with previous findings on the relationship between age and depression among adolescents (Doerfler et al., 1988; Green, 1980; Kovacs, 1983; Weissman et al., 1980). The CDI has been administered to children and adolescents from varying backgrounds and has consistently revealed no significant relationship between the age of the respondent and the severity of self-rated depressive symptomatology (Doerfler et al., 1988; Weissman et al., 1980).

(52) The suburban school students in our study reported higher levels of cigarette, alcohol, and harder drug use than the inner-city school students, while there were equal levels of reported marijuana use in both schools. These findings are similar to related research that has found a lower rate of reported drug use among African-American youth when compared with other ethnic groups such as European-Americans (Darling and Brown, 1992; McCord, 1990). When interpreting our findings, however, one must consider the drop-out rates of public education. The inner-city school, which is quite typical of urban public schools, has a drop-out rate approximately eight times higher than that of the suburban school (32% vs. 4%,

respectively). Our school-based study, therefore, excludes those adolescents who have left school, perhaps as a result of substance use problems or other high-risk behaviors. It is important to remember, however, that not only were there equal levels of reported marijuana use across the two schools, but the distribution of cigarette, marijuana, and alcohol use was normal in both schools. Therefore, the exclusion of many of the urban dropouts did not lead to the exclusion of urban alcohol and drug users.[10]

(53) Levels of reported substance use differed by gender and by grade in the suburban school; in the urban school, alcohol use varied by grade, and marijuana use differed only by gender for the African-American youth. These findings are somewhat similar to those of other studies, which have found age and gender differences in levels of substance use among adolescents; younger adolescents and girls have reported less substance use than older adolescents and boys, respectively (Andrews et al., 1992). However, contrary to findings in previous studies, our data from the urban school indicate that younger adolescents were not less likely to use cigarettes, marijuana, or harder drugs than older adolescents, and with the exception of marijuana use among African-American youth, girls were not less likely to use substances than boys. The finding that African-American girls used significantly less marijuana than African-American boys is similar to the finding among Caucasian youth in the suburban school.

(54) A possible explanation for this lack of grade differences in the level of substance use in the urban sample is that drugs may be more accessible to adolescents not yet in high school in the inner-city than they are for their peers in the suburbs. Therefore, urban adolescents who decide to experiment with substances may begin at an earlier age (e.g., seventh or eighth grade) than their peers in the suburbs. Thus, when the relationship between age and substance use is examined in a high school population, transitions from not using to experimentation, or from experimentation to regular or heavy substance use, are not as readily apparent among inner-city students as among suburban students. Another equally plausible explanation for the lack of grade differences in substance use in the urban school is that the urban students who increase their use of substances during high school may be more likely to drop out than their peers in the suburban school. Therefore, the expected relationships among grade and substance use are not apparent in the urban sample because the older adolescents who may use more substances than the younger adolescents simply are not in school anymore.

(55) Our findings indicated gender and school differences in the relationships among substance use and depression. In the suburban sample, gender differences were detected specifically in the relationships between depression and marijuana use, and between depression and harder drug use. The relationships between depression and these substances, respectively, was greater for suburban girls than for suburban boys. This finding replicates previous findings regarding the differences between white girls and boys in the relationships among depression and substance use (Paton and Kandel, 1978; Reinherz et al., 1991). If suburban girls are more likely to be socially stigmatized for using drugs, such as marijuana or harder drugs, than

---

[10]This may not be the case for harder drug users. Since few students in the urban school reported using harder drugs, we believe the high dropout rate in the inner-city may have led to a very negatively skewed distribution of harder drug use in the urban school. Mensch and Kandel (1988) concluded, in their research on dropouts, that there is a strong positive association between heavy drug use and dropping out of school.

suburban boys (in middle class communities, at least, there may be more pressures for girls not to use drugs than boys), then perhaps the suburban girls who decide to engage in drug use (ignoring the social consequences) may be more likely to experience or be experiencing psychological difficulties (i.e., feeling depressed) than the suburban boys who engage in drug use. For suburban boys, drug use may be more commonly sanctioned and, therefore, suburban male substance users may be more psychologically or socially heterogeneous than their female counterparts (i.e., it may not only be the boys who are feeling depressed who choose to use drugs). Suburban boys may be also less likely to become depressed after using drugs because they may not be as socially stigmatized for using drugs as are suburban girls. Because of the possible social stigmatization for suburban girls who use drugs, those who decide to use drugs may be more likely to be on the "fringe" of their female peers. Those on the "fringe" may more likely be depressed or become depressed as a result of the social stigmatization of either using drugs or simply being on the "fringe."

(56) There were no gender differences, however, in the urban school with respect to the relationships among depression and substance use. There were no relationships among depression and substance use for either the boys or the girls. Given these findings, it is difficult to explain the apparent absence of gender differences in these relationships. It appears that the phenomena of substance use and depression are different among the urban students from those among the suburban students. These phenomena for urban adolescents must be explored further before hypotheses can be made concerning the lack of gender differences between depression and each of the substances.

(57) With regard to school differences, depression in the suburban school was positively correlated with the use of cigarettes, marijuana, and harder drugs, while in the urban school, depression was not correlated with the use of any substances. This finding lends support to Siegel and Ehrlich's (1989) and Paton and Kandel's (1978) contention that "adolescents from different ethnic [and] or socio-economic backgrounds may take drugs for different reasons" (Siegel and Ehrlich, 1989, p. 925). This finding also suggests that depression may be associated with different behaviors depending on the social context. Darling and Brown (1992) recently found that delinquency, including heavy drug use, and academic disengagement were related among adolescents in rural and suburban areas, but not in urban areas. They assert, along with Sutherland and Cressey (1978), that problem behaviors may cluster differently depending on the social context in which the child lives. With respect to the current study, depression may simply be a different type of phenomenon for urban youth than for suburban youth.

(58) However, it is important to remember that *both* schools revealed no significant correlations between alcohol use and depression (although the relationship was significant for suburban girls, there were no gender differences found in the interactional analyses). Given the prevalence and social acceptability of alcohol use among many high school students, one of the reasons for this finding may be that those students who do use alcohol to deal with their depression or become depressed after using alcohol may be outnumbered by those who use alcohol to have "fun" or "relax" with their peers in a socially acceptable way. This type of phenomenon could explain the nonsignificant correlation between depression and alcohol use in both schools.

(59) The qualitative analyses described in this paper focused on one major finding of this study, namely, the differential relationship between depression and substance use across the suburban and inner-city school samples. Analyses of interview data from the most depressed students in each school

elucidated possible reasons for this dissimilar relationship. First, the view that substance use is a vehicle for relaxation or "escape" may be a perspective unique to individuals living in relatively sheltered environments. Our interview data suggest that depressed children in the inner-city sample are markedly more in touch with the deleterious effects of substance use than are depressed students from the suburban school. The urban students commonly gave examples of the negative effects of drug and alcohol use on close family members or friends. The suburban depressed students rarely gave such responses; when they did speak about the negative aspects of substance use, these students primarily focused on their fears of disappointing others if they engaged in substance use. Since the urban students seem to be more acutely aware of the potential negative effects of substance use itself, perhaps these students may be less likely than the suburban students to use substances to cope with depression.

(60) Varying perspectives on depression may further explain school differences in the relationships among depression and substance use. For example, the belief that depressed or painful feelings are "treatable" (e.g., through the use of substances) may be more common among people living in relative privilege than among people for whom depression associated with life's difficulties may seem as endemic as the difficulties themselves.

(61) The aforementioned interpretations, however, assume depression to be a cause, rather than a consequence, of substance use. Given that our quantitative analyses highlight associations rather than directionality between the variables, no conclusions are being drawn about cause and effect between depression and substance use. However, if substance use is causing depression rather than vice versa, perhaps the social stigmatization that suburban substance users may feel leads them to become increasingly depressed. Social stigmatization may occur for suburban boys who are *heavily* involved with substances as opposed to suburban girls for whom it may occur at all levels of involvement with substances. There were stories in the interviews among the nondepressed girls and some of the nondepressed boys that conveyed a sense of disgust at their peers, girls or boys, whom they thought were heavily involved in drugs.[11]

(62) Finally, depressed students in the inner-city who are reporting less susceptibility to peer pressure and reporting a perspective that substance use augurs trouble rather than relief may be describing aspects of a need to preserve a measure of personal security that the urban environment cannot consistently provide for them. A commitment to avoid drugs in the interest of maintaining personal safety may prevail especially in the face of depression or despair when life may feel particularly out of one's control. In contrast, children raised in the suburbs may feel a greater personal freedom to take certain risks when they are feeling depressed, or to consciously experience depression when they are using substances, believing that the fundamental securities of their environment will nonetheless remain intact.

(63) Our qualitative study of depressed students' beliefs and attitudes about substance use suggests that depressed urban and suburban students may differ in their views about substance use. These different attitudes and beliefs may be centrally important to understanding why depression and substance use are differently related across schools. However, in future studies it would be important to examine beliefs and attitudes concerning substance use held by a broader population of students, including those

Qualitative interpretations situate findings within larger meanings.

[11]Given that our study assesses one point in time and does not include a control group, we were not able to determine causality among the variables.

reporting no, low, or moderate levels of depression. Such an examination could help determine whether the attitudes and beliefs revealed in our qualitative analyses are unique to depressed students (and somehow related to "being depressed") or whether these beliefs are typical of the larger student body in each school.

Implications

(64) Our finding concerning urban and suburban school differences in the relationship between substance use and depression has implications for future research, and potentially, for the goals of adolescent substance use treatment programs. First, subsequent research is needed to determine whether the apparent relationship between depression and substance use for suburban students, and the apparent absence of this relationship for urban students, is representative of the experiences of urban and suburban adolescents in other geographical areas. If, as suggested by our study and by previous research, the psychological correlates of substance use typically vary across urban and suburban populations of adolescents, then the effective treatment of adolescent substance use and abuse will necessarily rest upon a consideration and incorporation of these differences. Effective treatment for suburban adolescents, for example, should include a concurrent focus on the depression that may both motivate and ensue from substance use, particularly for adolescent girls. In addition, further research on the psychological correlates of urban adolescents' substance use is needed to enhance the efficacy of treatment programs for this population. Increasing evidence that the psychological diversity of adolescent substance users is informed by factors such as gender, ethnicity, and environmental context argues strongly for prevention and intervention efforts that are sensitive to the role of these differences in the etiology and psychological consequences of substance use.

Quantitative research reports use standard, fixed structures and evaluation criteria.

Qualitative research reports use flexible and emerging structures and evaluation criteria.

References

Andrews, J. A., Hops, H., Duncan, S. C., Tildesley, E., Ary, D., and Smolkowski, K. (1992, March). Long-term consequences of level of substance use in adolescence. Paper presented at the fourth biennial meetings of the Society for Research on Adolescence, Washington, DC.

Aneshensel, C. S., and Huba, G. J. (1983). Depression, alcohol use, and smoking over one year: A four wave longitudinal casual model. *J. Abnorm. Psychol.* 92: 134–150.

Blau, G., Gillespie, J., Felner, R. D., and Evans, E. G. (1988). Predispositic to drug use in rural adolescents: Preliminary relationships and methodological considerations. *J. Drug Educat.* 18: 13–22.

Braucht, G. N., Brakarsch, D., Follingstad, D., and Berry, K. L. (1973). Deviant drugs use in adolescence: A review of psychological correlates. *Psychol. Bull.* 79: 92–106.

Darling, N., and Brown, B. B. (1992, March). Patterning of academic performance and deviance among African-American and European-American youths in three communities. Paper presented at the biennial meetings of the Society for Research on Adolescence, Washington, DC.

Dembo, R., Burgos, W., Des Jarlais, D., and Schmeidler, J. (1979). Ethnicity and drug use among urban junior high school youths. *Intl. J. Addict.* 14: 557–568.

Doerfler, L., Felner, R., Rowlison, R., Raley, P., and Evans, E. (1988). Depression in children and adolescents: A comparative analysis of the utility and construct validity of two assessment measures. *J. Consult. Clin. Pscychol.* 56: 769–772.

Donovan, J., Costa, F., and Jessor, R. (1985). *Health Questionnaire.* University of Colorado, Institute of Behavioral Science.

Finch, A. J., Saylor, C. F., and Edwards, G. E., (1985). Children's Depression Inventory: Sex and grade norms for normal children. *J. Consult. Clin. Psychol.* 53: 424–425.

Green, B. J. (1980). Depression in early adolescence: An exploratory investigation of its frequency, intensity, and correlates (Doctoral dissertation. Pennsylvania State University). *Dissert. Abst. Int.* 41: 3890B.

Hager, D. L., Verner, A. M., and Stewart, C. S. (1971). Patterns of adolescent drug use in middle America. *J. Counsel. Psychol.* 18: 292–297.

Harris, E. M. (1971). Measurement of alienation of college students: Marijuana users and nonusers. *J. School Health* 41: 130–133.

Kaminer, Y. (1991). The magnitude of concurrent psychiatric disorders in hospitalized substance abusing adolescents. *Child Psychiat. Human Develop.* 22: 89–95.

Kaplan, S. L., Nussbaum, M., Skomorowsky, P., Shenker, R., and Ramsey, P. (1980). Health habits and depression in adolescence. *J. Youth Adolesc.* 9: 299–304.

Kaplan, S. L., Landa, B., Weinhold, C., and Shenker, R. (1984). Adverse health behaviors and depressive symptomatology in adolescents. *J. Am. Acad. Child Psychiat.* 23: 595–601.

Kennedy, B., Konstantareas, M., and Homatidis, S. (1987). A behavior profile of polydrug abusers. *J. Youth Adolesc.* 16: 115–117.

Kovacs, M. (1980–1981). Rating scales to assess depression in school-aged children. *Acta Paedopsychiat.* 46: 305–315.

Kovacs, M. (1982). The Children's Depression Inventory: A self-rated depression scale for school-aged youngsters. Unpublished manuscript, University of Pittsburgh.

Kovacs, M. (1983). Definition and assessment of childhood depressions. In Ricks, D. F., and Dohrenwend, B. S. (eds.), *Origins of*

Psychopathology: Problems in Research and Public Policy. Cambridge University Press. New York.

Kovacs, M. (1985). The Children's Depression Inventory. *Psychol. Bull.* 21: 995–998.

McCauley, E., Burke, P., Mitchell, J., and Moss, S. (1988). Cognitive attributes of depression in children and adolescents. *J. Consult. Clin. Psychol.* 56: 903–908.

McCord, J. (1990). Problems behaviors. In Feldman, S. S., and Elliot, G. R. (eds.), *At the Threshold: The Developing Adolescent.* Harvard University Press, Cambridge, MA.

Mensch, B. S., and Kandel, D. B. (1988). Dropping out of high school and drug involvement. *Social. Educat.* 61: 95–113.

Paton, S., and Kandel, D. B. (1978). Psychological factors and adolescent illicit drugs use: Ethnicity and sex differences. *Adolescence* 13: 187–199.

Paton, S., Kessler, R., and Kandel, D. (1977). Depressive mood and adolescent illicit drug use: A longitudinal analysis. *J. Genet. Psychol.* 131: 267–289.

Prendergast, T. J. (1974). Family characteristics associated with marijuana use among adolescents. *Int. J. Addict.* 12: 625–632.

Reinherz, H. Z., Frost, A. K., and Pakiz, B. (1991). Changing faces: Correlates of depressive symptoms in late adolescence. *Family Commun. Health* 14: 52–63.

Robins, L. N., & Przybeck, T. R. (1985). Age of onset of drug use as a factor in drug and other disorders. In Jones, C. L., and Battjes, R. J. (eds.), *Etiology of Drug Abuse: Implication for prevention.* National Institute of Drug Abuse, Rockville. MD.

Saylor, C. F., Finch, A. J., Spirito, A., and Bennett, B. (1984). The Children Depression Inventory: A systematic evaluation of psychometric properties. *J. Consult. Clin. Psychol.* 52: 955–967.

Shiffman, S., and Wills, T. A. (1985). *Coping and Substance Use,* Free Press, New York.

Siegel, R. A., and Ehrlich, A. (1989). A comparison of personality characteristics, family relationships, and drug-taking behavior in low and high socioeconomic status adolescents who are drug abusers. *Adolescence* 24: 925–936.

Simons, R., Conger, R. D., and Whitbeck, L. B., (1988). A multistage social learning model of the influences of family and peers upon adolescent, substance abuse. *J. Drug Issues* 18: 293–315.

Simons, R. L., Whitbeck, L. B., Conger, R. D., and Melby, J. N. (1991). The effects of social skills, values, peers, and depression on adolescent substance use. *J. Early Adoles.* 11: 466–481.

Skager, R., and Firth, S. L. (1988). *Identifying High Risk Substance Users in Grades 9 and 11: A Report Based on the 1987/1988 California Substance Abuse Survey.* Crime Prevention Center, Office of the Attorney General, Sacramento, CA.

Smart, R. G., and Fejer, D. (1969). Illicit drug users: Their social backgrounds, drug use and psychopathology. *J. Health Social. Behav.* 10: 297–308.

Strauss, A. (1987). *Qualitative Analysis for Social Scientists.* Cambridge University Press, New York.

Sutherland, E. W., and Cressey, D. R. (1978). *Criminology* (10th ed.). Lippincott, Philadelphia, PA.

Way, N., Stauber, H., and Nakkula, M. (1990). Hopelessness, depression, and substance use in two divergent cultures. Paper presented at the Society for Research on Child Development in Seattle, WA.

Weissman, M. M., Orvaschel, H., and Padian, N. (1980). Children's symptom and social functioning self-report scales: Comparison of mothers' and children's reports. *J. Nervous and Mental Dis.* 168: 736–740.

Worchel, F., Nolan, B., and Wilson, V. (1987). New perspectives on child and adolescent depression. *J. School Psychol.* 25: 411–414.

CHAPTER 18

Action Research Designs

Of all of the research designs, action research is the most applied, practical design. Action researchers explore a practical problem with an aim toward developing a solution to a problem. This chapter defines action research, identifies when you use it, assesses the key characteristics of it, and advances the steps in conducting and evaluating this design.

By the end of this chapter, you should be able to:

- Define the purpose and the uses of action research.
- Describe practical and participatory action research designs.
- Identify types of practical issues studied in action research.
- Define how action research is self-reflective.
- Describe collaboration in action research.
- Summarize the activities in the dynamic process used in action research.
- Identify the types of plans developed in action research.
- Describe typical audiences for sharing action research.
- Identify the steps in conducting an action research study.
- List the criteria for evaluating an action research report.

Maria chooses to conduct an action research study. Her school committee especially likes this approach because Maria will develop a practical solution to the problem of students carrying weapons in school. She asks this research question: "What steps can our school take to encourage students to be more concerned about the possession of weapons in the school?" Maria collects information from her students by asking them to complete a brief questionnaire (quantitative data) and by having them keep and write in a journal (qualitative data) for a couple of months about their experiences with other students who carry weapons to school. Maria also holds conversations with fellow teachers and obtains their reaction to the problem. From this data, Maria compiles a list of possible solutions and rank orders them based on how individuals rated them. She presents this list to her school committee, and they choose which solutions they can realistically implement. Maria has conducted an action research study.

WHAT IS ACTION RESEARCH?

Action research has an applied focus. Similar to mixed methods research, action research uses data collection based on either quantitative or qualitative methods or both. However, it differs in that action research addresses a specific, practical issue and seeks to obtain solutions to a problem. Thus, **action research designs** are systematic procedures done by teachers (or other individuals in an educational setting) to gather information about, and subsequently improve, the ways their particular educational setting operates, their teaching, and their student learning (Mills, 2000). Educators aim to improve the practice of education by studying issues or problems they face. Educators reflect about these problems, collect and analyze data, and implement changes based on their findings. In some cases, the research solves a local, practical problem, such as a classroom issue for a teacher. In other situations, the researcher seeks to empower, transform, and emancipate individuals from situations that constrain their self-development and self-determination.

When Do You Use Action Research?

You use action research when you have a specific educational problem to solve. This problem may be the difficulties facing part-time faculty (Watters, Christensen, Arcodia, Ryan, & Weeks, 1998), ascertaining whether problem-based learning is superior to the traditional lecture (Dods, 1997), or discovering how literacy in writing emerges for first-grade students (Ceprano & Garan, 1998). Action research provides an opportunity for educators to reflect on their own practices. Within the scope of a school, action research offers a means for staff development, for teachers' development as professionals, and for addressing schoolwide problems (Allen & Calhoun, 1998). In fact, the scope of action research provides a means for teachers or educators in the schools to improve their practices of taking *action* and to do so by participating in research.

How Did Action Research Develop?

Three stages mark the development of action research. The first stage consists of the identification of a process for addressing societal issues. The second stage turns toward practice and the need to involve practitioners, such as teachers, in the solution to their own problems. The third and most recent phase represents the participatory, emancipatory, or community action research approach in which groups assume responsibility for their own emancipation and change.

The social-psychologist Kurt Lewin coined the term action research in the 1930s (Mills, 2000). Lewin felt that social conditions in the 1940s—such as the shortage of meat, the need for aerial reconnaissance during World War II, and the improvement of intercultural group relations after the war—might be enhanced through the process of group discussions (Kemmis, 1994). These group processes consisted of four steps: planning, acting, observing, and reflecting. By focusing on group processes and identifying phases of action, Lewin's approach introduced many of the modern ideas of action research: a process of steps, participation, the democratic impulse of involvement, and the contribution to social change (Kemmis, 1994). Spreading from the social sector to education, Lewin's ideas were adopted at the Horace-Mann-Lincoln Institute at Teachers College, Columbia University, and in England at the Tavistock Institute.

This spread of action research slowed during the mid- to late 1950s. The growing gulf between theory and practice, the emphasis on research development in regional educational laboratories, and the emphasis on experiments and systematic research all contributed to this decline. Then, in the 1970s, action research projects in Great Britain, the United States, and Australia reemerged. For example, the Fort Teaching project in England focused on teachers studying their own practices. The Classroom Action Research Network at the Cambridge Institute of Education in Great Britain addresses practical issues between teachers and students. Team-based inquiry between researchers and the schools emerged at Columbia University in the United States. The emancipation of individuals in education based on the German writings of Habermas became the focus of inquiry by the Australian Stephen Kemmis and his colleagues (Kemmis & McTaggart, 2000).

Having teachers study their own classroom problems and issues has emerged as an important direction for school renewal today. As shown in Figure 18.1, the movement toward action research has evolved from the in-service days of the 1970s to the site-based plans for staff development during the 1980s to the present emphasis on educators reflecting on their own practices (Schmuck, 1997). Reasons cited today for the importance of action research reinforce these trends. Action research:

- Encourages change in the schools
- Fosters a democratic (i.e., involvement of many individuals) approach to education
- Empowers individuals through collaboration on projects
- Positions teachers and other educators as learners who seek to narrow the gap between practice and their vision of education
- Encourages educators to reflect on their practices
- Promotes a process of testing new ideas (Mills, 2000)

Although action research has gained support in education, it is not without critics, who are reluctant to view it as a legitimate form of inquiry (Stringer, 1999). Some view it as an informal process of research, conducted by teachers and other educators who are not formal academic researchers. The practical aspect of action research also suggests an applied orientation to this form of inquiry with a less than scientific approach. Action researchers typically report results of their studies not to scholarly journals in education,

FIGURE 18.1

Evolution of Action Research for Teachers and Schools

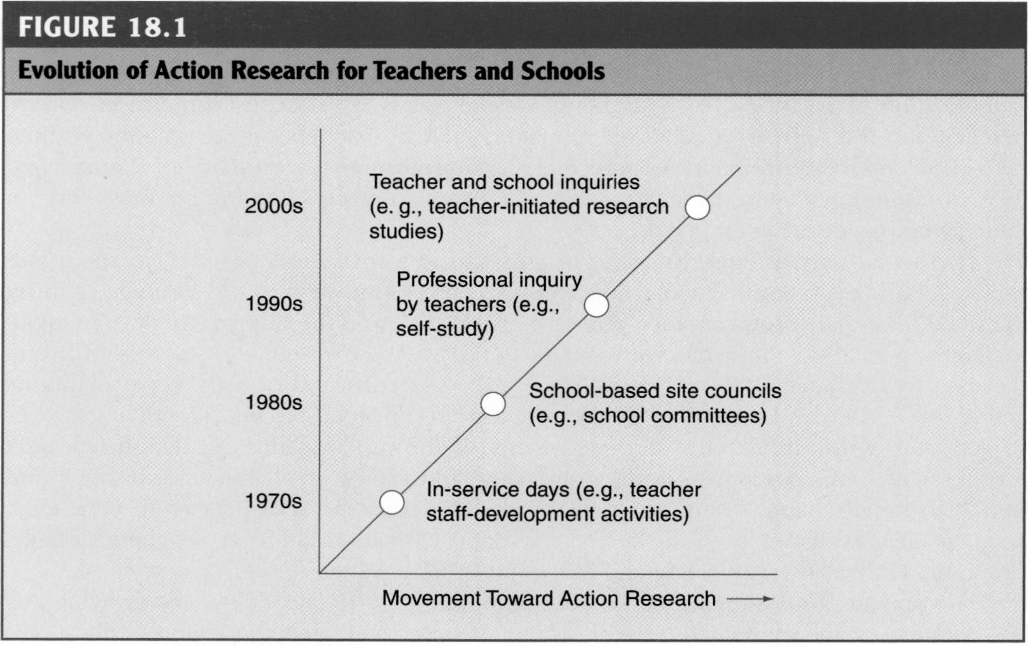

Source: Adapted from Schmuck, 1997.

but to online journals, Web sites, or local school groups. The methods are adapted and changed in response to the practitioners' objectives to understand a practical problem. Hence, the design may not have the rigor and systematic approach found in other designs.

Despite these concerns, action research fulfills an important role for the teacher–researcher and school-based teams formed to study local school issues. It also provides a design that encourages collaboration among school and community participants to help transform schools and educational practices.

WHAT ARE THE TYPES OF ACTION RESEARCH DESIGNS?

Action research means different things to different people, and some writers hold limited views as to what counts as action research (Watters et al., 1998). A review of the major writers in education, however, shows that the following two basic research designs are typically discussed (Mills, 2000):

- Practical action research
- Participatory action research

As you read about these two forms of action research, the overview of their differences shown in Figure 18.2 will help you distinguish between their major features.

Practical Action Research

Teachers seek to research problems in their own classrooms so that they can improve their students' learning and their own professional performance. Teams comprised of teachers, students, counselors, and administrators engage in action research to address common issues such as escalating violence in school. In these situations, educators seek to enhance the practice of education through the systematic study of a local problem. This form of action research is called **practical action research**, and its purpose is to

FIGURE 18.2

Two Types of Action Research Designs

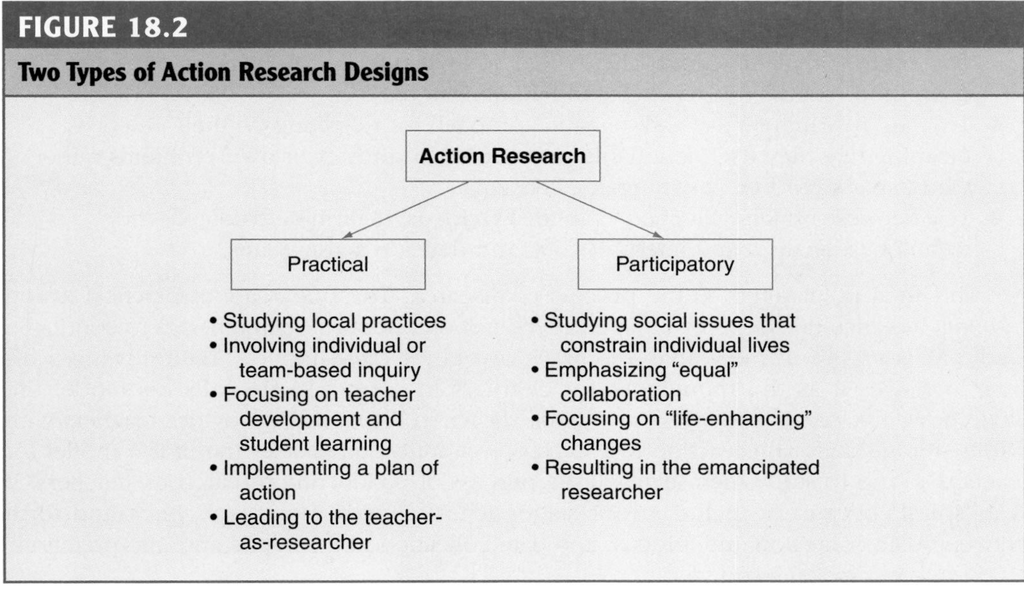

research a specific school situation with a view toward improving practice (Schmuck, 1997). Practical action research involves a small-scale research project, narrowly focuses on a specific problem or issue, and is undertaken by individual teachers or teams within a school or school district. Examples of practical action research studies include these:

- An elementary teacher studies the disruptive behavior of a child in her classroom.
- A team composed of students, teachers, and parents studies the results of implementing a new math program in the junior high.
- A community college instructor studies his professional development using technology in teaching.

In all of these examples, action research seeks to improve specific, local issues. It calls for educators to involve teachers in research to study concerns in their own schools or classrooms and to implement site-based councils or committees in schools to enhance research as an integral part of daily classes and education. In this spirit, educators can test their own theories and explanations about learning, examine the effects of their practices on students, and explore the impact of approaches on parents, colleagues, and administrators within their schools.

A drawback of this approach is that although teachers seek to improve their classroom practices, they have little time to engage in their own research. Although teachers may be good at what they do and familiar with teaching kids in classes, they may need assistance in becoming researchers. To this end, they can participate in graduate classes, which will help them renew or develop the requisite skills for inquiry required in an action research project (e.g., Hughes, 1999; Kosnik, 1996).

To understand practical action research, we need to review its major ideas or principles. As identified by Mills (2000), the following principles focus on assumptions about the role of teachers as learners, as reflective practitioners, and as individuals engaging in small-scale research projects:

- Teacher–researchers have decision-making authority to study an educational practice as part of their own ongoing professional development.
- Teacher–researchers are committed to continued professional development and school improvement, a core assumption for any teacher who decides to engage in action research.
- Teacher–researchers want to reflect on their practices. They reflect so that they can improve their practices. They reflect individually or in school-based teams composed of students, teachers, and administrators.
- Teacher–researchers use a systematic approach for reflecting on their practices, meaning that they use identifiable procedures to study their own problems rather than using a random, anything-goes design.
- Teacher–researchers will choose an area of focus, determine data-collection techniques, analyze and interpret data, and develop action plans.

This final point refers to the process of research. The books about practical action research advance detailed steps that teachers and other educators might use to conduct a study. Mills (2000), for example, discusses several of these models, then advances his own and uses it as the framework for chapters in his book. He calls his model the *dialectic action research spiral.* This model, shown in Figure 18.3, provides teachers with a four-step guide for their action research project. Mills emphasizes that it is a model for teachers to use to study themselves, not a process of conducting research *on* teachers. It is a "spiral" because it includes four stages where investigators cycle back and forth between data collection and a focus, and data collection and analysis and interpretation.

FIGURE 18.3

Mills (2000) Dialectic Action Research Spiral

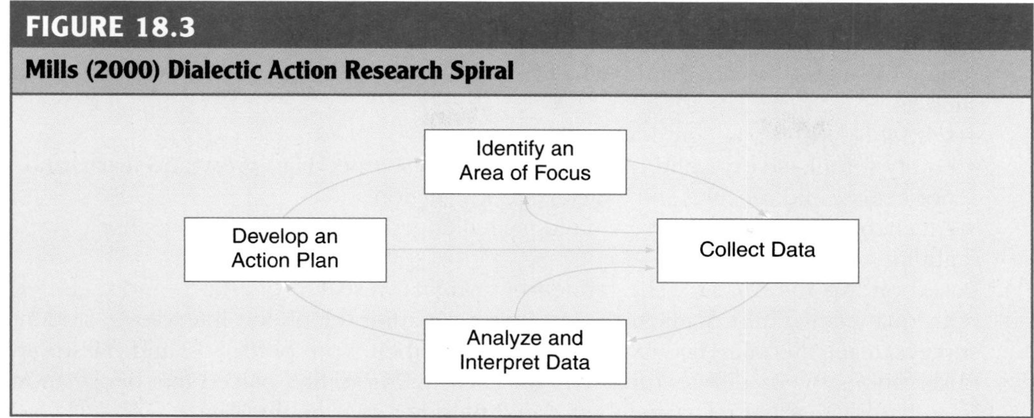

Source: Action Research by Mills © 2000. Reprinted by permission of Pearson Education, Inc. Upper Saddle River, NJ 07458.

In this procedure, the teacher–researcher identifies an area of focus. This process involves defining an area of focus, doing reconnaissance (self-reflection and description), reviewing the literature, and writing an action plan to guide the research. Then the teacher–researcher collects data by gathering multiple sources of data (quantitative and qualitative) and by using a variety of inquiry tools, such as interviews, questionnaires, or attitude scales. Data collection also consists of attending to issues of validity, reliability, and ethics, such as provisions for informed consent.

The action researcher follows this phase with analysis and interpretation. The process includes identifying themes; coding surveys, interviews, and questionnaires; asking key questions; doing an organizational review; engaging in concept mapping (i.e., visualizing the relationship of ideas); analyzing antecedents and consequences; and displaying findings. Interpretation involves extending the analysis by raising questions, connecting findings to personal experiences, seeking the advice of critical friends, and contextualizing the findings in literature and theory.

In the final stage, the teacher–researcher finally completes an action plan or chart. This chart includes a summary of findings, recommended actions, and the identification of individuals responsible for action and individuals who need to be consulted and informed. The chart also indicates who will monitor and collect the data, the timeline for data collection, and the resources needed to carry out the action.

Overall, this process emphasizes practical action research centered around studying a local problem, engaging in inquiry by an individual teacher (teacher-as-researcher) or a team, and focusing on teacher development. A review of an actual study can illustrate this practical approach to action research.

Hughes (1999) was a fourth-grade teacher in a small country-suburban K–8 district school. She begins by describing her class and the problem of not having in-class support for high-ability students in her room. The gifted students were pulled out of her classroom daily during math instruction to work on special science projects. In view of this, she wondered whether she was meeting the needs of these high-ability students, and she initiated an action research study. Here were the steps she took:

1. She first reviewed the published literature on her issue (e.g., pull-out programs, inclusion of gifted in the classroom, and meeting the needs of the gifted).
2. In addition, she interviewed colleagues from her school and neighboring elementary schools for their perspectives.

3. From the literature review and her interviews, she identified four themes—school reform, enrichment versus acceleration, pull-out versus in-class, and new educational strategies—and developed a flowchart listing the factors that surfaced for each theme, such as:
   - school reform-movement ideas
   - equity for all—every child receives what he or she needs to grow and learn, and not every child receives the exact same instruction
   - excellence for all where every child is challenged to the limit of his or her abilities (Hughes, 1999, p. 284).
4. Based on this information, she refined her original research questions and collected both quantitative and qualitative data through parent telephone interviews, student surveys, teacher conferences with students about their work portfolios, and classroom observations by six different teachers for each question. She placed this information in a chart so that her team members could help her analyze the data.
5. She enlisted six other elementary teachers from her building to create a team to help with the process of data analysis.
6. The team first skimmed the data to obtain a clear picture of it and then sorted all of the data under four themes about how to incorporate gifted children into the class (in-class flexible groups, differentiated instruction, enrichment, and acceleration).
7. She turned these themes into four major activities for the teacher to try in her classroom.
8. Next she put the findings into an *action plan*, resulting in specific activities (e.g., continue to self-evaluate and find ways to incorporate differentiated instruction and assessment in the classroom).
9. She shared her findings with others, to "make a difference on a larger scale" (Hughes, 1999, p. 295). This included sharing her study with other fourth-grade teachers, her principal, and a district committee.
10. The study ended with Hughes reflecting on future questions that she needed answered, such as "Which is better, pull-out programs, in-class programs, or a combination?"

These 10 steps illustrate a good practical action research study in which a teacher collaborates to study a local problem, develops as a professional, uses a systematic approach to inquiry (e.g., gathering and analyzing data), and implements a plan of action.

Participatory Action Research

Participatory action research (PAR) has a long history in social inquiry involving communities, industries and corporations, and other organizations outside of education (e.g., Whyte, 1991). Rather than a focus on individual teachers solving immediate classroom problems or schools addressing internal issues, PAR has a social and community orientation and an emphasis on research that contributes to emancipation or change in our society. Drawing on the work of the South American Paulo Freire, the German critical theorist Jurgen Habermas, and more recently Australians Stephen Kemmis and Ernest Stringer (Schmuck, 1997), this approach has emerged as an action-oriented, advocacy means of inquiry. Often PAR includes qualitative data collection, but it may also involve quantitative data collection.

Individuals refer to participatory action research by different names, such as *community-based inquiry* (Stringer, 1999, p. 9), *collaborative action research or participatory research* (Kemmis & McTaggart, 2000, p. 567), or *critical action research* (Mills, 2000, p. 7). To acknowledge the collaborative nature of this type of inquiry, this chapter uses the term *participatory action research.*

The purpose of **participatory action research** is to improve the quality of people's organizations, communities, and family lives (Stringer, 1999). Although espousing many of the ideas of teacher and school-based practical action research, it differs by incorporating an emancipatory aim of improving and empowering individuals and organizations in educational (and other) settings. Applied to education, the focus is on improving and empowering individuals in schools, systems of education, and school communities. PAR also has a distinct ideological foundation that shapes the direction of the process of inquiry in the type of issue that commands attention of the action researcher; in the procedures of research, especially data collection; and in the intent and outcomes of the inquiry.

For example, participatory action researchers study issues that relate to a need to address social problems that constrain and repress the lives of students and educators. For example, consider these issues that address social, economic, political, and class problems in our society that may be the focus of a PAR study:

- Tests that label and stereotype students
- Texts that omit important historical persons or events of cultural and ethnic groups
- Assessments that serve to confirm student failure rather than learning
- K–12 classroom interactions that silence or quiet the voices of minority students.

In addition to studying these sensitive issues, the participatory action researcher also engages in a process of research that promotes egalitarian and democratic aims. Participatory action researchers strive for an open, broad-based involvement of participants in their studies by collaborating in decisions as consensual partners and engaging participants as equals to ensure their well-being. For example, in their inquiries, researchers emphasize the importance of establishing contacts, identifying stakeholder groups, identifying key people, negotiating the researcher's role, and building a preliminary picture of the field context of the study (Stringer, 1999). The social values of liberation and life-enhancing changes also are important, and action researchers seek to bring about a new vision for schools, community agencies, youth clubs, and ethnic groups within schools.

Kemmis and Wilkinson (1998) summarized six central features of PAR:

1. *PAR is a social process in which the researcher deliberately explores the relationship between the individual and other people.* The object is to understand how social interaction forms and re-forms individuals. Applied to education, participatory action researchers might explore teachers working together in teams.
2. *This form of inquiry is participatory.* This means that individuals conduct studies *on* themselves. During this process, people examine how their own understandings, skills, values, and present knowledge both frame and constrain their actions. Teachers, for example, would study themselves to gain a better understanding of their practices and how this knowledge shapes (and constrains) their work with students.
3. *This form of research is practical and collaborative.* It is collaborative because it is inquiry completed *with* others. It is practical because researchers typically explore acts of communication, the production of knowledge, and the structure of social organization to reduce irrational, unproductive, unjust, or unsatisfying interactions. Teachers, for example, might collaborate with other teachers to reduce the unproductive and unsatisfying levels of bureaucracy in a school that might inhibit classroom innovations.
4. *PAR is emancipatory in that it helps unshackle people from the constraints of irrational and unjust structures that limit self-development and self-determination.* The intent of a study, for example, might be to change the bureaucratic procedures for teachers in schools so that they can better facilitate student learning.
5. *One intent of PAR research is to help individuals free themselves from constraints found in the media, in language, in work procedures, and in the relationships of power in*

FIGURE 18.4

Stringer's (1999) Action Research Interacting Spiral

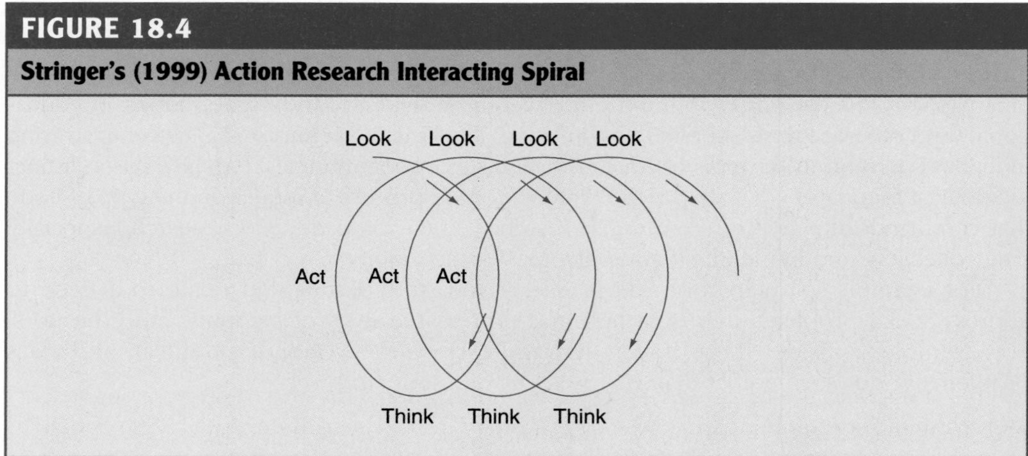

Source: Stringer, E. T. *Action Research*, p. 19, copyright © 1999 by Sage Publications. Reprinted by permission of Sage Publications, Inc.

educational settings. For instance, teachers may be constrained by a subservient role in the school district so that they do not feel empowered in their classrooms.

6. *PAR is recursive (reflexive or dialectical) and focused on bringing about change in practices*. This occurs through spirals of reflection and action. When teachers reflect on their roles in schools, they will try one action and then another, always returning to the central question of what they learned and accomplished because of their actions.

A spiral of looking, thinking, and action best reflects the action research process. This process, called the interacting spiral by Stringer (1999), is shown in Figure 18.4. This model contains three phases: look, think, and act. The spiral of this model conveys that action research is not neat, orderly, and linear, but is a process of repeating and revising procedures and interpretations.

Let's examine more closely the components of the action research process for looking, thinking, and acting. The detailed analysis of the three phases is shown in Figure 18.5. In this model, Stringer (1999) placed emphasis on the importance of "looking" to build a picture to help stakeholders understand issues they are experiencing. The "look" phase consists of collecting data (e.g., through interviews, observation, and documents), recording and analyzing the information, and constructing and reporting to stakeholders about the issue. The "think" phase then moves into interpreting the issues in greater depth and identifying priorities for action. In the final phase, the researcher identifies the "act" phase: devising practical solutions to the problems. This involves devising a plan and setting direction, such as objectives, tasks, and persons to carry out the objectives and secure needed resources. It also means implementing the plan, encouraging people to carry it out, and evaluating it in terms of its effect and achievements.

Let's examine a PAR study to see this process at work. Stanulis and Jeffers (1995) studied the mentoring relationship between a fifth-grade classroom teacher (Lynn), her student teacher (Shawna), and a university coordinator (Randi). Called critical action research, the authors described Lynn's mentoring of Shawna. Randi, as the coordinator of field experiences and a university mentor, worked with Lynn to compile data to assess her mentoring of the student teacher. They collected three sets of data to explore this mentoring:

- Five videotaped conferences were recorded between the student teacher and the classroom teacher every other week during a 10-week period.

- Weekly personal journal entries of the classroom teacher and the student teacher were reviewed.
- Five interviews were conducted by the university coordinator with the classroom teacher and the student teacher using the method of individual stimulated recall, a procedure of viewing the videotapes and answering interview questions (e.g., "Was there a point in the conference that you chose not to say something?").

Based on this data, the university coordinator and the classroom teacher identified four themes: (a) the process in which the student teacher gained the students' respect, (b) how the student teacher learned about the children as a learning community (e.g., their family backgrounds, their interests), (c) the mentoring relationship between the student teacher and the classroom teacher, and (d) ideas learned from action research.

Consistent with participatory action research, the authors mentioned that the student teacher brought to the classroom issues of knowledge and authority. The mentoring teacher viewed authority, embedded within the structure of the student-teaching experience, as shifting and changing during the course of the experience. The mentoring began as a springboard where the teacher told and shared how to teach the children and shifted to the mentor teacher serving as someone to listen and help clarify the student's ideas. The semester ended with the student teacher and mentor teacher viewing each other as colleagues, sharing ideas, and, in the process, loosening the constraints of teacher authority lodged within a student-teaching experience. They changed and transformed the mentoring relationship during this work together—a result consistent with PAR. Also, in the student teacher–teacher conferences, the opportunity to reflect on each individual's approach to teaching provided collaboration and reflection before action. Each individual, as well, learned about himself or herself and became sensitive to changes in the teacher–student relationship.

As you think back on Maria's action research project where she addresses the question "What steps can our school take to encourage students to be more concerned about the possession of weapons in the school?" should she use practical action research or PAR as her approach? Please provide three reasons for your choice.

WHAT ARE THE KEY CHARACTERISTICS OF ACTION RESEARCH?

Despite differences between practical action research and PAR, both types of designs have common characteristics found in action research. Understanding these characteristics will help you better design your own study or read, evaluate, and use an action research study published in the literature. These characteristics are:

- A practical focus
- The educator–researcher's own practices
- Collaboration
- A dynamic process
- A plan of action
- Sharing research

A Practical Focus

The aim of action research is to address an actual problem in an educational setting. Thus, action researchers study **practical issues** that will have immediate benefits for education. These issues may be a concern of a single teacher in a classroom or a problem involving many educators in a building. It may be a school–community issue, an issue with a school

FIGURE 18.5

Detailed Steps in Stringer's (1999) Action Research Model

Look: Building the Picture	Think: Interpreting and Analyzing	Act: Resolving Problems
PURPOSE: To assist stakeholding groups to build a picture that leads to: Understanding — What and how events occur Clarity — A detailed picture of the context Insight — An extended understanding of the issue **PROCESS:** **Gather information** Interviews — Key people from each stakeholding group Observation — Significant settings, events, and/or activities Review — Documents, records, and materials **Record information** Notes — A written record of what people said and/or did Audiotapes — Audio record of interviews Videotapes — Video record of events, people, places, etc. Photographs — Photographs of events, people, places, etc. **Analyze information** Identify key elements — Identify significant items of information Formulate categories — Group similar items Formulate themes — Group similar categories	**PURPOSE:** To use interpretive processes to extend and clarify people's understanding of the issue and identify priorities for action **PROCESS:** **Extend participants' understanding: Frameworks for interpretation** **Interpretive questions:** Why, what, how, who, where, when **Organizational review:** vision, mission, structure, operation, problems **Concept mapping:** Issue, concepts/influences, links **Problem analysis:** Problem, antecedents, consequences **Group processes for interpreting issues** **Meet** with representatives of all stakeholding groups **Set the agenda:** Clarify the purpose of the meeting **Review descriptive information:** Identify key elements of experience **Distill the information:** Analyze by sorting elements into categories **Extend understanding of issues:** Enact interpretive activities described in a "Framework for Interpretation" **Identify priorities for action** **Formulate follow-up activities:** Identify next steps; formulate working party	**PURPOSE:** To formulate practical solutions to problems that have been the focus of research **PROCESS:** **Plan** **Priorities:** Arrange projected actions in order of importance **Goals:** State the broad actions required to resolve prioritized issues **Objectives:** List actions required to accomplish goal(s) **Tasks:** Stipulate the sequence of tasks required to accomplish each action **Persons:** Specify those who will carry out the tasks **Time:** Determine time frame within which each task will be completed **Resources:** Calculate materials, equipment, and funds required to complete tasks **Implement** **Communicate:** Inform people of each other's activities **Nurture:** Praise people's efforts **Reflect:** Assist participants in reflecting on problems and progress **Assist:** Actively assist people when difficulties hinder progress **Model:** Apply working principles in all activities **Link:** Connect people in a mutually supportive network

Construct reports
Using themes as headings, categories as subheadings, and key elements as content, construct an account for each stakeholding group that describes

Research activities	Who has done what, where, when, and why
The situation/context	Group members' descriptions
The issue	Group members' experiences and perspectives

Communicate
Inform people of research activities by distributing reports as

Meeting minutes	For meeting participants
Bulletins	For stakeholding groups
Interim reports	For key stakeholders

Construct joint reports
Working party: Organize meeting of stakeholder representatives
Review materials: Identify key elements from previous activities
Formulate structure of report: Arrange in appropriate sequence of headings
Write report: Write draft, obtain feedback, write final manuscript

Evaluate
Review the plan
Assess the effect of activities
Revise the plan if needed
Prioritize unresolved issues
Celebrate achievements

Source: Stringer, E.T. *Action Research,* p. 134. copyright © 1999 by Sage Publications. Reprinted by permission of Sage Publications, Inc.

policy or structure that constrains individual freedom and action, or a concern of individuals in towns and cities. Action researchers do not undertake this form of research to advance knowledge for knowledge's sake, but to solve an immediate, applied problem.

The Teacher–Researcher's Own Practices

When action researchers engage in a study, they are interested in examining their own practices rather than studying someone else's practices. In this sense, action researchers engage in **participatory or self-reflective research** in which they turn the lens on their own educational classroom, school, or practices. As they study their own situation, they reflect on what they have learned—a form of self-development—as well as what they can do to improve their educational practices. Action researchers deliberately experiment with their own practices, monitor the actions and circumstances in which they occur, and then retrospectively reconstruct an interpretation of the action as a basis for future action. In this reflection, action researchers weigh different solutions to their problems and learn from testing ideas. Action research has been called "a spiral of self-reflection" (Kemmis, 1994, p. 46).

Collaboration

Action researchers **collaborate with others**, often involving coparticipants in the research. These coparticipants may be individuals within a school or outside personnel such as university researchers or professional association groups. This does not mean that outsiders should co-opt practitioners by gathering data that serve only their needs. So that this co-opting will not occur, outsiders need to negotiate their entry to a site with participants and be sensitive to the involvement of participants in the project (Stringer, 1999). It involves establishing acceptable and cooperative relationships, communicating in a manner that is sincere and appropriate, and including all individuals, groups, and issues. As shown in Figure 18.6, many individuals and groups may participate in an action research project. Individuals may review results of findings with the researcher, help collect data, or assist in the presentation of the final report. Many aspects of the research process are open to collaboration in an action research project. During this collaboration, roles may vary and be negotiated, but the concept of interacting is central to understanding one's practices.

FIGURE 18.6

Collaborative Teams in Action Research

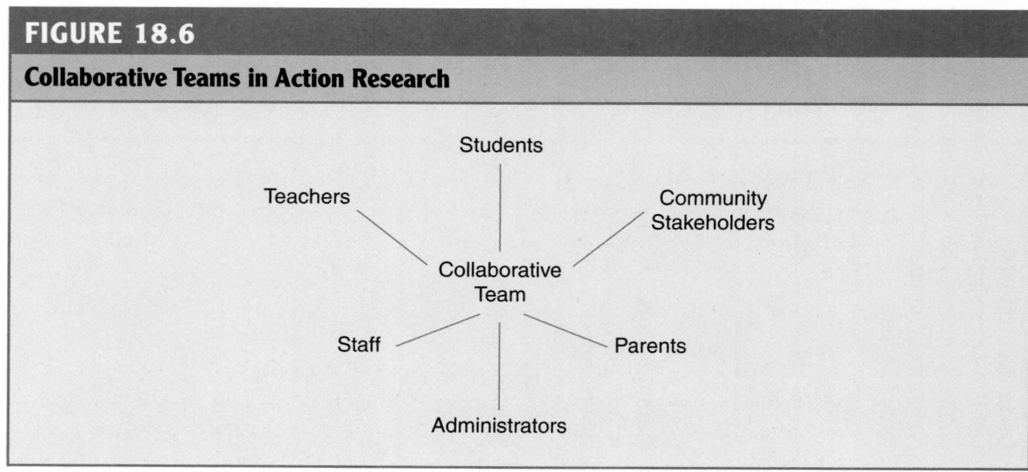

A Dynamic Process

Action researchers engage in a **dynamic process** involving iterations of activities, such as a "spiral" of activities. The key idea is that the researcher "spirals" back and forth between reflection about a problem, data collection, and action. A school-based team, for example, may try several actions after reflecting on the best time for high school classes to begin. Reflecting, collecting data, trying a solution, and spiraling back to reflection are all part of the process of action research. The process does not follow a linear pattern or a causal sequence from problem to action.

A Plan of Action

The next step is to identify a **plan of action**. At some point in the process, the action researcher formulates an action plan in response to the problem. This plan may be simply presenting the data to important stakeholders, establishing a pilot program, starting several competing programs, or implementing an ongoing research agenda to explore new practices (Stringer, 1999). It may be a formal written plan or an informal discussion about how to proceed, and it may engage a few individuals (e.g., students in a classroom) or involve an entire community (e.g., in a participatory research study).

Sharing Research

Unlike traditional research that investigators report in journal and book publications, action researchers report their research to educators, who can then immediately use the results. Action researchers often engage in **sharing reports** with local school, community, and educational personnel. Although action researchers publish in scholarly journals, they are typically more interested in sharing the information locally with individuals who can promote change or enact plans within their classroom or building. Action researchers share results with teachers, the building principal, school district personnel, and parent associations (e.g., Hughes, 1999). In addition, online journals (both with and without standards for inclusion), Web sites, and Listservs (online computer discussion groups typically hosted by a university computer system) provide opportunities for action researchers to publicize their studies (see Mills, 2000). Innovative forums also exist for performance texts where the researchers perform what they have learned through action research (see Denzin, 1997). These performances might be a play, a poem, a reading of text, slides, or music.

WHAT ARE THE STEPS IN CONDUCTING AN ACTION RESEARCH STUDY?

In the steps that follow, remember that action research is a dynamic, flexible process and that no blueprint exists for how to proceed. However, several steps in the process can illustrate a general approach for your use.

Step 1. Determine If Action Research Is the Best Design to Use

Action research is an applied form of inquiry and it is useful in many situations. You might use it to address a problem, typically one in your work situation or community. It requires that you have the time to collect and analyze data and to experiment with different options for solving the problem. To help with the process of reflection, you ideally need collaborators with whom to share findings and who can potentially serve as coresearchers on the project. Action research also requires a broad understanding of the many types of quantitative and qualitative data collection to gather information to devise a plan of action.

Step 2. Identify a Problem to Study

The most important factor in action research is that you need to solve a practical problem. This problem may be one that you face in your own practice or in your community (Kemmis & Wilkinson, 1998). After reflection, you write down the problem or phrase it as a question to answer.

The research problem is only one place that you might begin your study. In addition to starting with solving a problem, you might enter action research at other points (Schmuck, 1997). Action researchers may begin with collecting data, evaluating existing information, or even planning an action to try. Figure 18.7 shows these multiple entry points to start an action research study. Viewing action research as a spiral of activities introduces several points in the spiral in which you might begin your action research study.

Step 3. Locate Resources to Help Address the Problem

Explore several resources to help study the problem. Literature and existing data may help you formulate a plan of action. You may need to review the literature and determine what others have learned about solving the issue. Asking colleagues for advice helps initiate a study. Teaming with university personnel or knowledgeable people in the community provides a resource base for an action research project. Individuals who have conducted action research projects can also help you during your research study.

Step 4. Identify Information You Will Need

Plan a strategy for gathering data. This means that you need to decide who can provide data, how many people you will study, your access to individuals, and the rapport and support you can expect to obtain from them. You may need to file a proposal for data collection with the institutional review board if you plan to use the research for your graduate research project.

FIGURE 18.7

Points of Entry into an Action Research Project

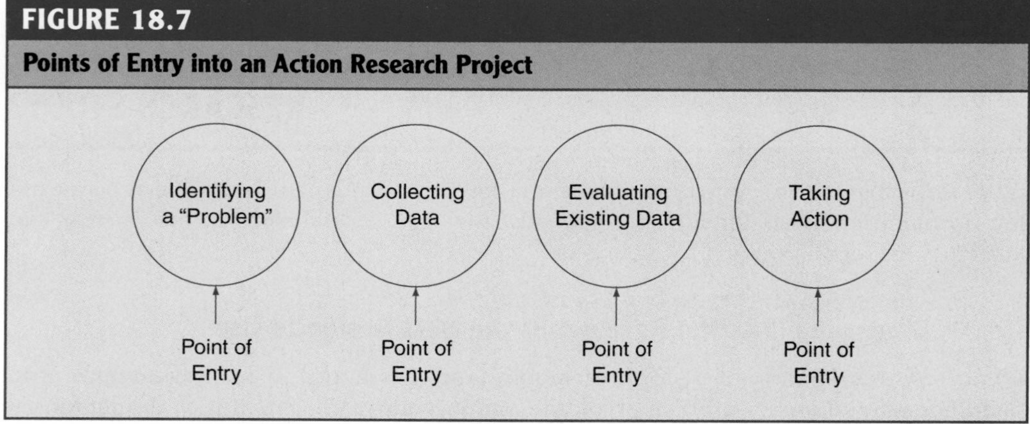

Source: Action Research by Mills © 2000. Reprinted by permission of Pearson Education, Inc. Upper Saddle River, NJ 07458.

FIGURE 18.8

A Taxonomy of Action Research Data Collection Techniques

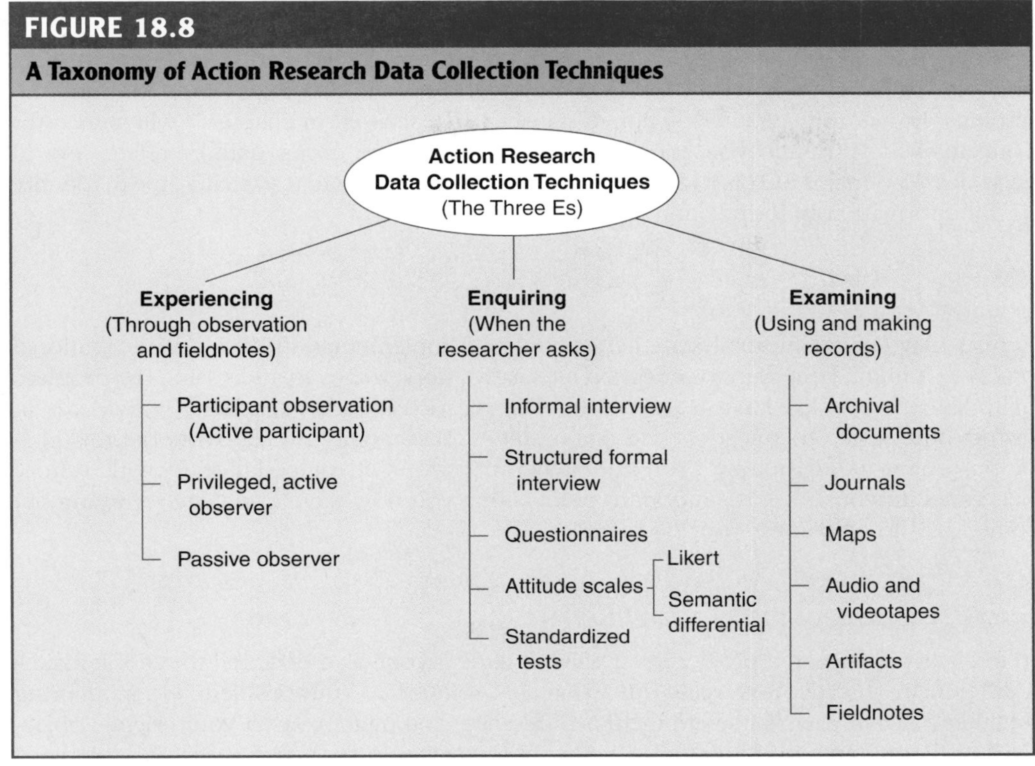

Source: Mills, 2000.

Another consideration is what type of data you need to collect. Your choices are to collect quantitative or qualitative data or both. It is helpful to understand the possibilities that exist for both forms of data. Mills (2000), for example, has organized quantitative and qualitative sources, as shown in Figure 18.8, into three dimensions:

- *Experiencing*—observing and taking fieldnotes
- *Enquiring*—asking people for information
- *Examining*—using and making records

The choice of data sources depends on the questions, time and resources, availability of individuals, and sources of information. In general, the more sources used and the more triangulation among them (Sagor, 2000), the more you will be able to understand the problem and develop viable action plans. It is probably wise to limit data collection in your first action research study so that you have a manageable amount of information to analyze. For example, as noted in chapter 9, qualitative interviews involve labor-intensive work.

Step 5. Implement the Data Collection

Implementing data collection takes time, especially if you gather multiple sources of information. In addition, your participants may have limited time to complete instruments or engage in interviews. Keeping an accurate record of the information collected, organizing it into data files for numeric or theme analysis, and examining the quality of the information are important data-collection steps.

Step 6. Analyze the Data

You may decide to analyze the data yourself or enlist the help of other educators or data analysts. You might show your results to others to find out how they would interpret the findings. In most situations, descriptive statistics as discussed in chapter 7 will suffice for your analysis, although you may want to compare some group data or relate several variables. The major idea is to keep the data analysis manageable so that you can identify useful information in formulating a plan of action.

Step 7. Develop a Plan for Action

A plan may be an informal statement about the implementation of a new educational practice. It might be a plan to reflect on alternative approaches to addressing the problem or to share what you have learned with others, such as other teachers, individuals in district offices, or other schools and communities. You might formally write out this plan or present it as an outline. You can develop it yourself or collaborate with school personnel in writing it. The important point is that you now have a strategy for trying out some ideas to help solve your problem.

Step 8. Implement the Plan and Reflect

In many action research projects, you will implement your plan of action to see if it makes a difference. This involves trying out a potential solution to your problem and monitoring whether it has impact. To determine this difference, you might consult your original objectives or the research question that you sought to answer in the action research project.

You also need to reflect on what you have learned from implementing your plan and sharing it with others. You may need to share it broadly with school colleagues, school committees, university researchers, or policy makers. In some cases, you will not achieve an adequate solution, and you will need to try out another idea and see if it makes a difference. In this way, one action research project often leads to another.

HOW DO YOU EVALUATE AN ACTION RESEARCH STUDY?

To evaluate an action research study, consider using the following criteria to assess its quality. These criteria are applicable to both practical action research and PAR (e.g., see Kemmis & Wilkinson, 1998; Mills, 2000):

- Does the project clearly address a problem or issue in practice that needs to be solved?
- Did the action researcher collect sufficient data to help address the problem?
- Did the action researcher collaborate with others during the study? Was there respect for all collaborators?
- Did the plan of action advanced by the researcher build logically from the data?
- Is there evidence that the plan of action contributed to the researcher's reflection as a professional?
- Has the research enhanced the lives of participants by empowering them, changing them, or providing them with new understandings?
- Did the action research actually lead to a change or did a solution to a problem make a difference?
- Did the author report the action research to audiences who might use the information?

APPLYING WHAT YOU HAVE LEARNED: AN ACTION RESEARCH STUDY

To apply ideas in this chapter, read through the action research study on page 618 by Dicker (1990), noting the marginal annotations that identify the characteristics of action research and the characteristics of quantitative and qualitative research. This study was chosen because it involves a reflective teacher who sought to improve learning for students by trying out different practices. As a practical action research study, it signifies the elements of teacher development, the improvement of student learning, and the collaborative research. In this classroom project, we see the major elements of action research. It focuses on a practical classroom problem: teaching a new course without the requisite skills. The teacher reflects on her experiences and participates with another former teacher of English. Throughout the study, a dynamic process unfolds, with this teacher trying out an idea, making adjustments, and exploring another idea. A series of miniplans ensues as this author shares her personal frustrations and successes in teaching an unfamiliar subject in a high school.

The Research Problem and Qualitative Approach to Research

Problem—see Paragraphs 01 and 04

Qualitative approach—throughout the article

At the beginning of the study, Dicker shares her anger about her assignment to teach a communications course after teaching mathematics and drama at her high school for several years (Paragraph 01). She also reflects (Paragraph 04) on how teachers often face the problem of limited resources after being assigned new courses outside their teaching area. It is not difficult to identify the research problem in this study—Dicker's teaching dilemma—and how it is consistent with action research.

Dicker's approach is to use qualitative research, and she displays this approach with the following characteristics:

- *Exploring a process.* The problem requires the author to understand and explore her own experiences in the process of teaching a new course (Paragraphs 01 and 04).
- *Minimal use of literature.* The literature does not shape the questions asked in this study. Rather, the questions evolve out of the author's personal reflection. The literature, when presented (Paragraph 05), describes the research procedure of action research, but it does not reflect on the topic (i.e., teaching a new course) presented in this study. In fact, this article shows minimal use of literature in a study based on the personal experiences of the author–researcher.
- *A focus on a single phenomenon.* In Paragraph 04, Dicker states that the purpose of her study is to understand her own questions (e.g., "How do teachers cope in such situations?"). The object of the study, then, was for Dicker to understand her own questions related to how to teach outside her area.
- *Collecting text data from a small number of people.* Dicker considers data collected from a small number of individuals, including her personal reflections in journal entries (text data), to be the most important source of information (Paragraphs 06–10).
- *Analysis of text.* She performs an informal analysis of data from her own journals, the student journals, conversations with a friend, and tape recordings. Her analysis, as shown by a continuous return to reflections from her journal (e.g., Paragraphs 17 and 20), informs the strategy that she will try next as she adjusts to the class.

- *Analysis by description.* Dicker's data analysis reflects how she analyzed her information to build a description. This process emerges (as is consistent with qualitative research) and consists of trying out practices from drama and mathematics (Paragraph 11), reflecting on this practice, adopting a new practice using a textbook (Paragraph 21), and then returning to the drama teaching style (Paragraph 27).
- *Interpretation based on the larger, more abstract meaning.* At the end of the article (Paragraph 38), Dicker interprets the larger meaning of her experience: knowledge of various teaching styles, a willingness to try them out, a continual monitoring process, and learning along with students.
- *Reporting research flexibly and reflexively.* The qualitative writing style is personal, informal, and in a storytelling form. The presence of the author is apparent throughout the study.

Use of the Literature

Paragraph 05

The only literature found in this personal, reflective study is when Dicker reviews studies about action research to inform the reader about this type of design.

The Purpose Statement and Research Questions

Paragraph 04

This study does not contain a specific purpose statement. Instead, the author relies on research questions to carry the major intent of the study. A purpose statement might have strengthened the direction of the project and focused the reader's attention on the teacher's emerging understanding. For example, the author could have described the purpose as a practical action research study to reflect and make adjustments in teaching an unfamiliar course at one high school in Canada. The action researcher is also the participant in his or her own study, and this author seeks to answer her own questions using her personal reflections (Paragraph 06).

Types of Procedures of Action Research Data Collection

Paragraphs 06–10

The data collection is described well and we learn that the author used four sources of data in this project: her own journals (the major source), student journals, comments from a former teacher, and tape recordings. The inclusion of students and a former teacher indicates the use of coparticipants in the project (e.g., Paragraphs 07 and 09).

Types of Procedures of Action Research Data Analysis and Interpretation

Analysis—not specifically mentioned

Interpretation—see Paragraphs 36–39

The author does not formally mention her data analysis: how she analyzed the tape recordings or the student journals. From quotes in this article, however, we see that she used her own journal entries to reflect on specific changes or ideas that would inform her practice. From a close reading of the study, we must conclude that her analysis is informal and addresses her specific classroom problem (changing from mathematics and drama teaching to only the drama teaching style). This exhibits an iterative, dynamic process found in action research (e.g., see Paragraph 27).

The author articulates interpretive insights in the final paragraphs of the study. We find that she reflects on her years as a teacher to draw conclusions about the importance of action research and her professional development. In the final paragraph (Paragraph 39), she discusses how she took action research to the final step of sharing her results with the principal and expressing a desire not to teach the course again.

The Overall Writing Structure

The reporting structure was informal through a storytelling approach to qualitative research. We learn much about the author–researcher as she reflected on her progress in teaching the new course and about her planning and monitoring of changes (e.g., Paragraph 38). Without knowing the elements of action research, a reader might dismiss this study as less than scientific, but the researcher includes all major elements of an action research project and illustrates the practical form of inquiry that full-time teachers might conduct to understand pressing problems in their classrooms.

KEY IDEAS IN THE CHAPTER

The purpose of action research is to improve the practice of education, with researchers studying their own problems or issues in a school or educational setting. Educators engage in reflection about these problems, collect and analyze data, and implement changes or a plan of action based on their findings. In some cases, the research solves a local, practical problem, such as a classroom issue for a teacher. In other situations, the research seeks ideological aims, such as to empower, transform, and emancipate individuals.

Action research developed in the 1930s with citizen group processes. After a short time, it resurfaced in the 1970s with projects in Great Britain, the United States, and Australia. These projects focused on teachers studying their own practices, educators working with schools, and researchers helping individuals emancipate themselves from social issues in educational settings. Today, action research has grown in importance as a means for enhancing school renewal, promoting teacher development, and testing new ideas.

Action research is an informal process of research in which educators engage in a study of their own practices. Individual teachers, teams within a school or district, or school–community inquiry groups undertake this form of inquiry. Two types of action research designs exist. The first design, practical action research, is an approach that involves educators examining a school situation with a view toward improving practice. Rather than a focus on individual teachers solving immediate classroom problems or schools addressing internal issues, a second design, PAR, has a social and community orientation and places emphasis on research that contributes to emancipation or change in our society. The PAR approach seeks to improve the quality of organizations, community, and family lives. It espouses an objective of improving and empowering individuals and organizations in educational settings. Both the practical and the participatory forms of action research have basic principles and models for conducting research.

Action researchers use a process of inquiry, regardless of design. The teacher or educator becomes the researcher. As the researcher, the practitioner becomes self-reflective about the process. Action researchers often engage others collaboratively in the process as coparticipants and enact a dynamic model of inquiry involving iterations of activities, cycling back and forth between identifying a problem, trying a solution, reflecting on information learned, and trying new solutions. During this process, they use a plan of action to guide the use of a new practice. They base this plan on what they learned about the research problem, and they share it with others, such as in informal reports to colleagues, school officials, school boards, and community members.

USEFUL INFORMATION FOR PRODUCERS OF RESEARCH

- Design an action research project that matches your time and resources.
- Recognize that the process of conducting an action research study is like a spiral with phases that repeat, such as looking, thinking, and acting, as in the Stringer (1999) model.
- Remember that in action research, you will be the participant in your own research project. You are not studying someone else; instead, you are examining your own practices.
- It is useful to collaborate with others in action research. Consider university personnel, other colleagues, or individuals familiar with action research. They may have insight or be able to draw conclusions that you cannot.
- Collect data and analyze it so that it will be understandable to the applied audience for action research studies in your school, district, or other educational unit.
- Consider the full array of data-collection types for your action research, such as quantitative and qualitative data.
- Decide on the point of entry into your study that best fits your present understanding of the problem. This point may be at several phases in a research project.
- Construct a plan of action that you can realistically carry out in your school or educational setting.

USEFUL INFORMATION FOR CONSUMERS OF RESEARCH

- Recognize the differences between practical action research and PAR. The former has the intent of addressing a practical problem in education, whereas the latter has a social or community orientation and emphasizes emancipation or change in our society.
- Action researchers study their own situation and attempt to develop solutions to practical (or community) problems. When you review a study, identify the intent of the researcher and look for how the study addresses some issue in which the researcher is involved.
- Action research studies are applied and the results should be action oriented and easy to understand.
- Evaluate whether the action research study made a difference or changed the situation presented in the research problem.

ADDITIONAL RESOURCES YOU MIGHT EXAMINE

A number of useful books can help expand your understanding of action research:

Geoffrey Mills (2003) authored an excellent guide for the teacher–researcher who seeks to engage in action research. Mills provided a good discussion of both practical and critical action research perspectives and reviewed the primary process models available for conducting this form of inquiry. His discussion about online electronic journals, Web sites, and Listservs to connect with other action researchers is a unique, timely contribution. See:

Mills, G. E. (2003). *Action research: A guide for the teacher researcher* (2nd ed.). Upper Saddle River, NJ: Merrill/Prentice Hall.

Sagor (2000) has authored a "practical" action research guide to help teachers become action researchers. This guide provides a useful, readable approach to practical action research with a focus on teachers collaborating with other teachers. Published by the Association for Supervision and Curriculum Development, this guide takes the reader through the many aspects of action research. Examine:

Sagor, R. (2000). *Guiding school improvement with action research.* Alexandria, VA: Association for Supervision and Curriculum Development.

Another book on practical action research by Schmuck (1997) is for teachers, curriculum specialists, counselors, psychologists, school administrators, parents, and students who want to form groups and conduct action research studies. This book contains many exercises, step-by-step guides, and useful visuals to help you understand action research. A book on practical action research is by Calhoun (1994), from the Association for Supervision and Curriculum Development. It focuses on inquiry for educators to assist in our renewal of American schools. See:

Schmuck, R. A. (1997). *Practical action research for change.* Arlington Heights, IL: IRI/SkyLight Training and Publishing.

Calhoun, E. F. (1994). *How to use action research in the self-renewing school.* Alexandria, VA: Association for Supervision and Curriculum Development.

Turning to participatory action research, Stringer's (1999) book provides an excellent guide to the principles of community-based action research (e.g., relationships, communication, participation, and inclusion) as well as how to negotiate entry to a research site. An entire chapter addresses writing formal reports, theses, and dissertations, an invaluable guide to students who plan to undertake their own action research studies within a critical, emancipatory, and participatory framework. Examine:

Stringer, E. T. (1999). *Action research* (2nd ed.). Thousand Oaks, CA: Sage.

Another participatory perspective is available in the works by Kemmis (e.g., Kemmis & McTaggart, 1988). Atweh, Kemmis and Weeks (1998) have edited a book of readings about PAR in education. This book offers numerous examples of action research projects based on projects included in the Participatory Action Research for the Advancement of Practice in Education and Teaching at the Queensland University of Technology in Australia. Especially valuable in this volume is the chapter by Kemmis and Wilkinson (1998), which advances the central features of participatory action research and its interface with the study of practice in education. See:

Kemmis, S., & McTaggart, R. (1988). *The action research planner.* Geelong, Victoria, Australia: Deakin University Press.

Kemmis, S., & Wilkinson, M. (1998). Participatory action research and the study of practice. In B. Atweh, S. Kemmis, and P. Weeks (Eds.), *Action research in practice: Partnerships for social justice in education* (pp. 21–36). London and New York: Routledge.

Go to our Companion Website at **www.prenhall.com/creswell** to:

- assess your understanding of chapter content with Multiple-Choice Questions,
- apply what you've learned with Essay Questions,
- practice your research skills with interactive Building Research Skills exercises, and
- broaden your knowledge of research with Web Links to research topics on the Internet.

Qualitative Characteristics

Using Action Research to Navigate an Unfamiliar Teaching Assignment

Action Research Characteristics

Mary Dicker

(01) It was the last week of June, just before the summer holidays, that I learned about the change in my teaching assignment for the following year. I was teaching five mathematics courses and two drama courses in a secondary school in Burns Lake, British Columbia. Proud of my achievement in both of these areas, I assumed that this situation would continue the following year. A casual check of the next year's timetable in the principal's office, however, stopped me in my tracks. My 11th-grade drama course (Acting 11) had been cut from the schedule and in its place I had been assigned an 11th-grade English course, Communications 11. I was both angry and apprehensive—angry that my hard won victory establishing drama in our school program was so short lived and apprehensive that the course I was being assigned was in an area in which I had no professional expertise or experience.

Action researchers study practical issues.

(02) Communications 11 was a new course developed by the ministry of education to replace an 11th-grade English course called Minimum Essentials, a course intended for students with weak English skills. The new course, aimed at the same audience, was to be implemented for the first time the following year. I was given the assignment despite the fact that I had no formal training or expertise in the teaching of English.

(03) My anxiety increased when I learned that the only materials available from the ministry prior to September were a thin curriculum guide summarizing the learning outcomes expected in reading, writing, listening, and speaking and two writing textbooks, one of which was a reference communications handbook. It was expected that teachers would rely largely on their own knowledge of and training in the subject. The difficulties of my situations were compounded by the fact that there were not enough textbooks for each student in the class. I expressed my feelings on the matter to the administration and was assured that, although I was not qualified to teach English as such, my general professional skills combined with a knowledge base in drama would enable me to teach the new course.

(04) Many teachers have been placed in similar predicaments, being faced with new courses outside their teaching area and limited resource materials with which to teach them. How do teachers cope in such a situation? How do they utilize their own knowledge and organize their teaching so that the learning situation becomes a viable one for their students in spite of the circumstances? Assuming the role of teacher researcher, I decided to undertake an action research project to answer these questions.

A qualitative problem requires exploration and understanding.

The qualitative purpose statement and research questions seek participants' experiences.

(05) Action research is a form of self-reflective inquiry that can be utilized by teachers in order to improve the rationality and justice of (a) their own practices, (b) their understanding of these practices, and (c) the situations in which these practices are carried out (Carr & Kemmis, 1983, p. 152). It seemed an appropriate choice of inquiry for my situation. Therefore, applying the four components of the action research cycle, planning, acting, monitoring, and reflecting (Kemmis & McTaggart, 1982, p. 7), I examined the knowledge I used in teaching Communications 11 and how I used this knowledge.[1*]

Qualitative researchers take a reflexive and biased approach.

---

*From Dicker, M. (1990). Using action research to navigate an unfamiliar teaching assignment. *Theory into Practice*, 29, 203–208.

Examining My Knowledge

Action researchers study their own practices.

Qualitative data collection involves gathering text or image data.

(06) The examination of my knowledge base took place over approximately 3 months from the first day of classes in September to the beginning of December. Following the recommendations of Kemmis and McTaggart (1982), the major data collection device was my own reflective journal or diary, written each evening following a class period. The journal had two purposes: to shed a focused light on the previous lesson and to clarify plans for the following lesson. It was in fact a record of my thinking, revealing my practical knowledge and the particular way it was held and used. A further reflection was written each weekend in order to extend and deepen the reflections on the week's work and to develop a sufficiently thick description for the study.

Qualitative data collection involves studying a small number of individuals or sites.

(07) As a second source of data, students wrote journals during the last 10 minutes of each class or for homework. Not only did this deepen the students' thinking about their work but it provided me with a different perspective on the events that were happening in the class. Anticipating that students might need some assistance in writing the journal, I posed several questions for them to answer.[2] Using the daily journal as a basis, the students wrote a longer reflection for homework every 2 weeks. Again they were asked to respond to specific questions.[3]

(08) The students' journal writing was not only educationally valid as an assignment that encouraged writing skills as they reflected on their experiences in the class and organized their thoughts, but it also provided a basis for my future planning. The knowledge gained from my reading and reflection on the student journals became an integral part of my own journal as I commented on student writings.

Action researchers often collaborate with coparticipants.

(09) A third source of data for the study of my practical knowledge use was a former teacher of English who took the role of "critical friend." In this role she read my journal and asked questions that helped me reveal the thinking that was not always fully expressed in the journal. This critical friend was an important part of the study. As I developed insights during the progress of the study, the validity of these interpretations were checked by this independent critic.

Qualitative data analysis consists of text analysis.

(10) A final monitoring technique was the tape recording of the first and final lessons of the period under study and occasional other discussions, brainstorming lessons, and oral work. Not only did the tapes capture the "teacher-in-action" but, like the student journals, they also provided a student perspective. The tape recordings were a valuable check on the accuracy of my interpretations as I analyzed my journal.[4]

My Teaching Styles

(11) The journal analysis and other monitoring devices made it clear that I had used two major teaching styles while teaching the course. As teachers gain experience in the art of teaching they inevitably develop a style reflecting a basic philosophy about how a particular subject should be taught. My two different teaching styles reflect my philosophy in each of my teaching areas, mathematics and drama. I regard mathematics as a formal and logical subject that requires a formal, ordered approach. Although students can work together to achieve understanding, the test of student mastery is their ability to solve problems individually. In my view, the British Columbia mathematics curriculum is process oriented,[5] with a correct answer for each problem. The underlying question is, "Which process has to be used in order to get the correct result?" Even if one can take several routes to solve the problem, the student is still looking for the "right" answer.

Qualitative data analysis consists of describing information and developing themes.

(12) In order to achieve individual mastery of mathematical processes, I use a traditional, teacher-directed approach. I follow the curriculum by adhering to the textbook and supplementing this with worksheets. The students sit in rows facing the chalkboard. I explain, the students learn, and I check their understanding with questions, quizzes, and tests. The premise in my math teaching is that I know the correct processes and the correct answers. My job is to show the student these processes so they can find the correct answers. In addition to my own evaluation of student progress, the benchmark of my success in covering the prescribed courses is the evaluation tests the ministry gives at the end of grade 10 and the provincial exam at the end of grade 12.

(13) My view of educational drama, however, is that it should encourage students' creative thinking by inviting them to solve problems through the drama mode. Student learning is a group process rather than an individual one. In my drama classroom, I encourage students to share ideas and possible solutions, for the problems are open ended with no one "correct" answer. The "solution" is usually the consensus of the group. Even this solution is not always the final one, but is changed and modified as circumstances require.

(14) I also encourage students to make their own improvements to the work in progress. For the initial brainstorming sessions we are usually seated in a circle to allow all ideas to be considered equally. As the work progresses I question the students to make them think a little deeper about their work. It is a probing rather than a deliberate attempt to get at a "right" answer. Presentation is not my primary goal, although the work is frequently presented to an audience. Of most concern is the development of the work and the learning inherent in this development. The personal growth of each student is not easily evaluated. Their input is necessary to judge this, in addition to my own observations.

(15) Thus, in my two different teaching areas, I have two different teaching styles. These teaching styles reflect not only the nature of the subjects being taught but my philosophy of how each one should be taught. Both styles were used in implementing Communications 11 but I was not aware of this while I was teaching. It was not until I had reflected on and analyzed my data that I realized that I possessed two teaching styles and that they both had had a strong impact on the progress of the course. The following description of what took place in my classroom is the result of my reflection on and analysis of the data collected. It reveals the knowledge I used when teaching Communications 11 and how I used this knowledge.

Knowledge from Drama

(16) In teaching Communications 11 I was forced to examine what strategies I had for coping with my situation. From the outset I had felt that the only way I could cope with teaching this course was by using my background knowledge in drama. If I could interpret "communication" in its broadest sense, I could teach a quasi-acting course by disguising it as Communications 11. In this way I could combat two problems. I would have an acting class and would also be on familiar ground even though the subject area itself was unfamiliar.

(17) As the work progressed I discovered I had chosen an approach that not only could be adapted to the course but that also allowed the course to be adapted to it. As in my drama courses, I wanted the students to be actively involved in their own learning in the course. I wanted to explore communication *with* the students instead of trying to instruct them directly. Note the journal entry made in preparation for the first lesson:

> I want to find out what students think Communications 11 means. *Discussion*—round the table—different format might help the students to

> think differently—they're weak students—I want to encourage their ideas and let them see I *listen* to *them*.

(18) I was able to start the course by using a previous drama lesson plan. I observed in my journal, "Today's lesson was almost identical to the first lesson in Acting 11 last year. I changed 'teenage interests and problems' to 'communication' but method the same." The ability to adapt materials and ideas from other sources is an integral part of the art of teaching. I had embarked on my quasi-acting course with a familiar strategy that I knew would be successful.

(19) The first idea that was contributed by the students and which could be used in developing the course was a list of the different ways people communicate. They developed the list through their own discussion. I wrote in my journal,

> I didn't make nearly enough of their lists which had good ideas—I want to make up for this by using the lists next lesson somehow. . . . Interesting to see that the students are coming up with the wider view of "communication"—more along my conception.

Using the lists was important not only for the ideas. It was a way of demonstrating my acceptance and approval of students' suggestions. What they had to offer was worthwhile, and I wanted them to know that I thought so. We expanded the lists the next day and used the dramatic technique of "tableaux" (frozen action pictures created by students) to depict the means of communication contained in the lists. Their view of communication was even broader than mine, including such areas as sign language, Braille, Morse code, and even smoke signals. I felt my concept for the course had been justified, and I believe the "meeting of minds" enhanced students' confidence and developed rapport.

(20) By continually being aware of and recording the general reactions of the students, I think I became more sensitive to their needs. I was ready to make adjustments if I thought them necessary. By reading the "pulse" of the class I was brought closer to them and this, in a subtle way, helped in further establishing the rapport. A few lessons later I commented,

> A nice atmosphere—relaxed. I felt this lesson was an important one. I was able to talk to all the students individually or in small groups. There was an atmosphere similar to my drama class last year. I was very pleased to be able to praise their work.

The use of my knowledge from drama appeared to be working well, and as I confidently developed lessons around themes taken from the initial communications lists, I inevitably pushed the drama mode further. As time went on, however, a change occurred in my teaching style. I slipped out of the drama mode and into the formality of my mathematics style of teaching. It was at this time that my knowledge of class control stood me in good stead.

A Loss of Focus

(21) Twice it happened that my teaching lost focus and direction and seemed to flounder, but my control of the class did not. I was able to continue teaching and I doubt if the students were aware of the change. In both instances the loss of focus came after active periods of group work using drama techniques. There was a need for a change of pace, a need to "settle down" for a while. It seemed to me that this was probably a good time to start using the textbook. The favorable impression I had formed about the text is recorded in my journal.

> I've been looking at the text, *Writing Sense* [Potter, 1981]. I like the way it's written and presented—pictures, activities, common-sense down-to-earth style. Emphasis seems to be on writing flow rather than grammar. The first four chapters contain ideas I have emphasized with the students—honesty in writing—reading aloud to improve writing.

(22) Philosophically it seemed the perfect book for me to use. It also appeared to be suitable for use by students weak in English as the chapters were short and easy to read. What I did not realize at the time was that each short chapter is on a different topic with no real link between chapters. This deficiency may not create difficulties for a qualified English specialist, but for someone in my position it created an unforeseen problem that I will say more about later.

(23) I had the feeling that I ought to use the text at some point in the course so that I could say I was following the curriculum. My instincts seemed justified when I was told that I was to be evaluated for my teaching report. This knowledge prompted me to write in my journal, "I'm wondering if I have enough marks for the class at the present time—I think I'll have to make specific parts of my lessons markable. The type of work I've been doing is difficult to mark." Not only was the text the prescribed one for the course but it also had exercises in it that were markable.

(24) I used the next two lessons in a row to encourage a feeling of continuity. The actual lessons themselves, however, were not linked as each chapter was on a different topic. My reflection for the lessons shows that the students were not enthusiastic.

> The reading was fine but they did not really apply themselves to the questions—a few of the girls did. The reporting back was not successful—students didn't listen so I eventually abandoned this and got them down to write. . . . I did not have them read aloud as I had planned because of the previous lack of concentration. Instead I had them proof-read each other's work to themselves.

The desks went back in rows as this seemed the appropriate arrangement for students who had to concentrate on individual writing assignments. I think perhaps this was one of the subtle ways in which I was influenced by the textbook. The formality of using the text demanded the formality that I used in math class.

(25) Because each lesson was on a different topic, it meant I was planning one lesson at a time. I wrote, "I'm beginning to feel the need for a little longer planning—one day at a time is difficult." As I limped from lesson to lesson a feeling of desperation began to creep into my journal.

> I am now beginning to get a "swamped" feeling. I am not having enough time to plan and organize because of the work in other classes. I have marking to do all the time. I also feel I am losing my efficiency which is compounding the problem. I am needing help from colleagues. I think I have passed the "going it alone" stage. What are they actually *learning* at the moment—I am beginning to wonder. . . . I am not sure what to do about the books they are reading—do I have them write a report?—or does that kill the enjoyment of the book? Could they communicate the ideas in the book another way? Should I give a deadline by which the book should be read? Better ask my colleagues these questions.

(26) By turning to the textbook I inadvertently moved into a series of short, teacher-directed lessons more like math teaching than drama teaching. This teacher-directed style worked well in math, where I was knowledgeable; in Communications 11, it took me into an area where my knowledge of the subject was at its weakest. I lost my original focus and although my experience as a teacher enabled me to continue teaching without a loss of control or rapport, I was not pleased with the work I was doing.

Back to a Drama Teaching Mode

Action researchers engage in an iterative, dynamic process.

(27) Toward the end of October a resource book for the course appeared in my box in the office. I found that it contained some philosophical ideas that supported my approach to the course. It emphasized the value of student based literature content and the importance of finding situations in which students want to learn and can find success. Reading the resource book prepared the ground for the development of a new focus and a return to my drama teaching style.

(28) I noticed in the section on short stories a story about nuclear war. Initially I asked the department head for advice on reading the story. He suggested I read it aloud, with the students following in their own books. In my journal I commented, "I thought this would be too similar to them listening to the record, but the fact that they are reading along silently will be sufficiently different." The unfamiliarity of the subject was prompting me to assume I always had to be doing a new activity or slightly varying the activity. Yet I often repeated activities when teaching in my own subject areas.

(29) The reading of the story aloud was not only a natural progression from the silent reading I was doing with the students each lesson but also encouraged me to abandon desks in rows and place them in a circle again. I began to feel the pull of my drama background again and this was evidenced in the first lesson on the new topic of nuclear war. Having read the story to them, we did an activity used by drama teachers called "hot-seat." Several students volunteered to be characters from the story and, in role ourselves, we all asked them questions. This was quite successful and a positive end to the lesson. I was back in my drama mode with a focus that lasted nearly 3 weeks.

(30) Unfortunately, at the end of the 3 weeks, as I again sensed the need to vary the pace, I repeated my previous mistake of using the textbook. By the third lesson I was caught in the one-lesson-at-a-time trap and had returned to the traditional teaching style of my math classes, which included arranging the desks in rows. When I tried to conduct a discussion on phobias without changing the desks, my journal records,

> The discussion tended to be "patchy." Groups would take part but often the others didn't really listen—I had to do my "policeman act."

Again I felt the need to control students' behavior, using body language, direct looks, and spoken admonitions. I was aware that part of the trouble was because of the struggle to think of what to do each lesson. I talked to my husband and he suggested that I follow the example of the head of the English department and give them a project that would last 2 weeks (survival tactics!).

(31) Even though I had done several longer units and knew this was the answer, I needed this reminder. Teaching an unfamiliar subject seems to make a person react in a similar way to being in unfamiliar situations—thinking is thrown off balance and one can miss the obvious. A project had the advantage that, once the parameters had been established, the students would work for several lessons without the teacher having to prepare new lessons. Each lesson would be spent helping the students develop their ideas in the project. I had done many a project with eighth-grade drama students.

(32) Teachers frequently utilize the year's calendar when planning their work. Seasons and specific dates become a meaningful focus for a variety of educational activities. As it was less than 3 weeks to the Christmas holidays I decided to devise a project on the Christmas theme that applied specifically to the course. I felt some intellectual satisfaction in arriving at

an idea that would tie together the work done in the term. In groups of about four, the students would make presentations on the theme of Christmas utilizing all the means of communication used in their term's work. In my journal I described how I started the project:

> We then sat in the circle again and I started the discussion on Christmas—why we have it, themes associated with it, etc. We then established a list of the forms of communication used so far. They made the major suggestions in both parts of the discussion with some minor prompting from me. . . . They then split up into their groups and started to discuss the project. They seemed interested and enthusiastic.

All the elements I had hoped for at the beginning of the course and had partially lost at two stages during the term combined to make this project a satisfying one for both me and the class. The students were making a positive contribution of their own ideas. They were involved in their own learning and making their own decisions in a relaxed atmosphere under my guidance, not my direction.

(33) A few new developments also occurred during the project. The students started to search out suitable poetry to be part of their presentation—an area we had not explored as yet in the course. Kathy,[6] who had refused to speak in front of the class during the oral presentation on music because of her shyness, read aloud with Wilma during their presentation. One group read a poem as a radio play and Don learned his part by heart. Another group unified all means of communications into an effective dramatic presentation.

(34) The written components also showed that students had thought about their work. Wilma, Sonja, and Kathy based their writing on a dictionary exercise we had done. They thought of a long list of words associated with Christmas and gave definitions for each. Ron's group researched Christmas customs in other countries. The satisfaction I had as a teacher was in seeing how much the class had progressed as a whole, and how individuals had demonstrated a personal growth.

(35) Knowing that one has taught and the students have learned is essential for any teacher, but it is particularly important for teachers working in a subject area outside their specialty. I did not have teaching knowledge of specific English skills. However, I do believe my own knowledge of how to teach contributed to students' ability to communicate and think clearly.

Conclusions

(36) Teaching Communications 11 was a professional development activity that contained as much learning for me as for the students. By reflecting on my teaching decisions through action research, I was able to cope with teaching a course in a subject area that was unfamiliar. Teaching a new course outside one's own area forces teachers to examine the strategies that are available to them. My reflection made me aware that I was using the two teaching styles with which I was already familiar, and that one of these styles was more appropriate for this circumstance than the other.

(37) My 15 years experience as a teacher has given me practical knowledge that has been constructed through time by the actions taken (Connelly & Elbaz, 1982, p. 117). An important element in my practical knowledge was the ability to maintain a disciplined learning environment. While this knowledge gave me confidence in my ability in dealing with students, it was not sufficient. During the time I was using my more traditional teaching style, the monitoring techniques of action research enabled me to see that while the situation was under control, it was not the learning atmosphere I wanted to create.

Qualitative interpretations situate findings within larger meanings.

(38) As Fullan (1982) has stated, one dimension of educational change is the possible use of new teaching approaches. For teachers faced with assignments outside their areas, the need for a new approach, or at least a modification, is highly probable. In order to cope with unfamiliar assignments teachers require not only knowledge of various teaching styles but a willingness to try them out. Action research provides the opportunity of trying out a new approach while monitoring what is occurring. Through the use of journals, tape recordings, and discussions with other educators, I was able to become a learner along with my students. Action research created the possibility for perpetual, self-generated, professional development.

Action researchers implement an action plan in response to the research.

(39) I learned a lot from Communications 11, but I did not want my professional development to continue through this course for another year. My goal was to reinstate Acting 11 on the timetable and work to improve it. So I tackled the principal early in spring and elicited a firm commitment on the matter. While I do not want to repeat the experience of teaching a course for which I am unprepared, the experience of coping with new subject matter materials using action research techniques has probably made me a better teacher.

Qualitative research reports use flexible and emerging structures and evaluation criteria.

Action researchers share results of their studies with other practitioners.

Notes

1. This article is based on a longer study undertaken as part of a M.Ed. degree in curriculum studies at the University of Victoria, British Columbia, 1986–87.
2. Examples of questions posed:
   - How did *you* practice communication today?
   - Did you feel your communication was successful? Why or why not?
   - How well did your group work together?
   - What were your thoughts when you showed your work to the class?
3. Examples of questions posed:
   - What do you feel you have learned so far in this course?
   - Which activities have you enjoyed the most, and why?
   - Which activities have you not enjoyed, and why?
   - What other activities do you think we should do?
4. See Kemmis & McTaggart (1982, pp. 39–42) for a full list of techniques to use as possible monitoring devices.
5. Since the writing of the original M.Ed. study on which this article is based, a new math curriculum has been implemented in British Columbia which is less process oriented. Considerable emphasis is now placed on the development of problem-solving skills.
6. The student names used here are not their real names.

References

Carr, W., & Kemmis, S. (1983). *Becoming critical: Knowing through action research.* Geelong, Victoria, Australia: Deakin University.

Connelly, F. M., & Elbaz, F. (1982). Conceptual bases for curriculum thought: A teacher's perspective. In A. W. Foshey (Ed.), *Considered action for curriculum improvement* (pp. 95–119). Alexandria, VA: Association for Supervision and Curriculum Development.

Fullan, M. (1982). *The meaning of educational change.* Toronto: Ontario Institute for Studies in Education.

Kemmis, S., & McTaggart, R. (1982). *The action research planner* (2nd ed.) Geelong, Victoria, Australia: Deakin University.

Potter, R. (1981). *Writing sense.* Toronto: Globe/Modern Curriculum Press.

Appendix A

Answers to the Chapter Study Questions

Chapter 1

1. Three advantages you might identify are that research contributes to knowledge, that it helps with practice, and that it provides information to policy makers. Three disadvantages might be that results are vague, are contradictory, and may be based on inaccurate data.
2. If I were Maria, I would first clearly identify the issue that needed to be studied by visiting with a member or two of the committee. Second, I would go to the university library and begin to locate studies on the issue. Third, I would write down the central question that I would like answered.
3. Ethical issues that Maria might encounter are the need to respect the rights of the students and to obtain permission from them and their parents to participate in a research study. Maria also needs to respect the learning process going on in her school and not gather information that might disrupt the learning process in the classrooms.

Chapter 2

1. If the parent involvement study were qualitative instead of quantitative, the authors would have sought the views of the parents on the question of their involvement with their adolescents in school and at home. They may have asked the parents open-ended questions and explored their different perspectives. Instead, the authors chose to test whether four factors would help explain parental involvement. If the gunman case study were quantitative rather than qualitative, the authors would have set up an experiment to test whether one group of people (e.g., students) differed from others (e.g., teachers) in their responses to the gunman incident. The authors might also have surveyed people on campus to obtain their attitudes toward the gunman incident. But, as a qualitative study, the authors were interested in exploring the campus reaction and mapping a detailed understanding of how campus personnel reacted.

   There are several reasons why the authors chose a quantitative approach (in the case of Deslandes and Bertrand) and a qualitative approach (in the case of Asmussen and Creswell). The authors of the quantitative approach felt that their problem was best studied using quantitative procedures. They sought to explain the impact of the four factors on parent involvement. They also were writing for a journal that most likely embraced quantitative research, and their own training was probably in quantitative research. Asmussen and Creswell, on the other hand, felt that views of personnel on campus could describe the campus reaction. The journal they published their study in had published qualitative studies in the past, and both authors were trained in qualitative procedures.
2. The current historical era in quantitative research is one of sophisticated statistical tests, accountability in terms of assessment of children's knowledge, and the use of increasingly powerful and sensitive experiments. In qualitative research, the era is one in which researchers explore the contradictions among worldviews, differentiate among the types of research designs, and often employ participatory and advocacy procedures in inquiry.

Chapter 3

1. The parent involvement study narrative hook is fair. It is a reference to another article in which the author makes the case for the importance of parent involvement. It points to the many studies that have documented parent involvement as a problem worth studying. It is, in short, a literature-based hook, but it would be of more interest to academics and other researchers than to educational personnel in the schools or to parents. It lacks emotion and numbers to back up the stance. The gunman case study narrative hook suffers from similar weaknesses. It does identify a problem with which many people can identify. It does not use numeric information or cause a particular emotional or attitudinal response.

It represents a literature research statement that may or may not draw readers into the study.

2. The problem in the parent involvement study discusses the importance of learning how the four constructs influence parent involvement. *Explaining* the relationship among variables is a key element in quantitative research. In the gunman case study, however, the authors seek to develop an *understanding* of campus reaction to a gunman incident. Explanation is a central characteristic of quantitative research, whereas understanding is a characteristic of qualitative research.
3. The parent involvement study contributes to knowledge by helping to fill a void in the existing literature. The gunman case study contributes to knowledge by studying a problem (how campuses react to a gun incident) that researchers have not examined.
4. A justification based on personal experience would require that the researchers talk about their personal experiences with adolescents, with parenting, and with the schools of their children (if they have them). The gunman case study authors would relate their own personal experiences with campus violence (such as one author did reveal in the epilogue).
5. If we compare the introductions to the two studies, the authors of the parent involvement study cite more references to the literature than do the authors of the gunman case study. The authors of the parent involvement study used extensive references because their primary justification for studying the problem was based on findings from prior research.
6. Answers will vary.

Chapter 4

1. The key terms would be *teens, high schools,* and *pregnancies*. I would need to see if these terms are those used in the ERIC system or use the *Thesaurus* to see what terms would be appropriate to use when running my ERIC search.
2. I would first examine recent articles, say, those articles published in the last 2 to 3 years. Because they are all journal articles, they represent a good place to start. I may not be familiar with the quality or stature of the journals, but they all seem like national, review-based journals. This leaves me with scanning the titles. Some titles seem to convey content broader than others. I would begin with the broader articles first (e.g., "Violence-related attitudes and behaviors of high school students" rather than "Response of African American adolescents . . .").
3. The reference might look might look like this:

Kingery, P. M., Coggeshall, M. B., & Alford, A. A. (1998). Violence at school: Recent evidence from four national surveys. *Psychology in the Schools, 35*(3), 247–258.

Chapter 5

1a. Independent variable = parental involvement; dependent variable = student reading performance.
1b. Independent variable = students' knowledge of accountability; dependent variable = changes in attitudes toward learning.
1c. Independent variables = mutuality, comprehensiveness, gender sensitivity, congruence; dependent variable = functional mentoring relationships.
2a. Central phenomenon = conceptions of reading.
2b. Central phenomenon = aspects of sorority life.
2c. Central phenomenon = academic change (sources and processes).
3a. Directional hypothesis
3b. Null hypothesis

Chapter 6

1. Cronbach's alpha is a measure of reliability and, more specifically, internal consistency. A coefficient of .93 is a high coefficient; .6 is an acceptable level for determining whether the scale has internal consistency. With a .72 reliability coefficient, the reliability is satisfactory for the scores.
2. Permissions should have been obtained from (a) the administrator in the school district responsible for permitting researchers to enter schools and conduct research, (b) possibly the building principal, (c) the teachers in the classrooms of the parents' students, and (d) the campus institutional review board at the authors' institution.
3. Steps in locating this instrument: (a) Run an ERIC search and examine the references netted in this search. (b) Next look in the Buros Institute indices, TIP, or MYY, to see if there are any instruments that measure this variable. (c) Look for published research journal articles that contain this variable. See if the authors cite an instrument that they may have used to measure the variable. (d) Ask your advisor or a specialist in the field who may have studied this variable. Find out if this person knows of an instrument that you might use.
4. Maria needs to make these decisions: Who will she study? She needs to decide whether she will study students in high schools, teachers, administrators, or other personnel. She also needs to determine how she will select these individuals. A random sampling procedure would be ideal. Also, she needs to identify how many individuals she needs for her sample using the rough guide in the section on "Sample Size." Next, based on the questions she plans to answer, she needs to determine what kinds of data she will collect. For example, she may collect attitudinal data or public school document data. With this decision, she will next look for instruments to use in collecting this information and perhaps conduct a search of the literature for existing

instruments. These instruments need to be of high quality, reliable, and valid. The procedure for data collection needs to fit the individuals who will provide the data, and the scales need to conform to standard types of interval, ordinal, or nominal scales. Finally, with an instrument identified, she will collect data using standardized procedures for all participants and ethical practices.

Chapter 7

1. Is the hypothesis a comparison of groups or the relationship of variables? It is a comparison of three groups.

   How many independent variables do you have? Dependent variables? One independent variable with three groups; one dependent variable, math scores.
   Are there any covariates being controlled? No.
   Is the independent variable categorical or continuous? Categorical.
   Is the dependent variable categorical or continuous? Continuous.
   Statistical test of choice: Analysis of variance (ANOVA).

2. You fix the responses that are out of range (e.g., 6 and 8).
3. In this statement:

   What does F stand for? ANOVA, the statistical test.
   What is (1, 110)? The degrees of freedom.
   What is 6.81? The calculated value using the ANOVA formula.
   What does $p = .001$ mean? The p value or the significance level of the calculated value; the groups differ statistically at the alpha level of .001.

Chapter 8

1. The purposeful sampling strategy would be *critical sampling* because the authors interviewed students who knew something about the incident and may have experienced the incident (but were no longer in therapy). Granted, more sampling occurred after the study started (i.e., the psychologist interviewed who talked about "retriggering"), but the strategy prior to the study was critical sampling.
2. Ethical issues: They might have mentioned how they conveyed the purpose of the study to the participants prior to the interviews, they might have addressed whether some participants had declined participation in the study, they might have highlighted information they obtained that contradicted the themes they presented, they might have spoken to whether their presence at the site might have disrupted the educational process (e.g., classes, students' attention to their studies).
3. Collecting observations would yield specific information about behaviors, whereas interviews would net people's attitudes and reactions. Documents provide a written record of events and evidence for the themes.
4. To encourage participants to participate in a 30-minute interview, I would (a) set a time that is convenient for their schedule, (b) offer an incentive (e.g., a coffee coupon), (c) convey to them that their anonymity will be protected by combining all student data and assigning an alias when I mention their quotes, and (d) set the location so that it is least disruptive of their school routine.

Chapter 9

1. The passages of description were included under the heading "The Incident and Response," Paragraphs 04–10. They provided detail about the gunman, the actual incident in the classroom, and the specific activities of campus offices immediately following the incident (e.g., EAP office).
2. That one theme would be something about the community because from this passage, we learn (a) that it was close-knit, (b) about its health, (c) about its values, and (d) a description of its people.
3. We would expect the themes of denial, fear, and safety. Less expected would be retriggering and the need for a campus plan.
4. The interpretation is based mainly on the literature, which seems to provide a framework for grouping the themes in the case into a larger meaning. They document these levels as emerging in the literature.

5–9. Answers will vary.

Chapter 10

1. The standards might be those used (a) in assessing past students in the program, (b) by the individual faculty member, and (c) by the college or university.
2. Correct the discriminatory language:
   a. **Poor** (level of specificity problem): Teachers under 25 adopt an open learning environment for students.
   Improved: Teachers in their first 2 years out of teacher education adopt an open learning environment for students.
   b. **Poor** (insensitive to labels): The at-risk students scored below the average in math.
   Improved: The students who have been identified as at risk scored below the average in math.
   c. **Poor** (fails to acknowledge participation of individuals with specific cultural identification): The homeless used the school shelter at night.
   Improved: The adults who do not have a permanent residence used the school shelter at night.

3. It was more of a quantitative approach. It had a structure much like a quantitative study: introduction, methods, results, and discussion.
4. The bulleted points that I would include would address the key results for each of the four research questions. I might pose each question and then provide the results to the question in nonstatistical terms. I would strongly emphasize the results and the implications of the study.

5–9. Answers will vary.

Appendix B

Determine Size Using Sample Size Tables

In the process of collecting data, researchers need to determine the number of participants to use in their studies. Several options are available. They can make an educated guess as to how many people are needed, such as 10% of the population. They can ask as many people to participate as possible within the resources and time that both researchers and participants can provide. They can select a number that satisfies different types of statistical procedures, such as approximately 30 scores for each variable in a correlational analysis.

A more rigorous approach than any of these is to systematically identify the number of participants based on sample size tables available in published texts. To understand these tables, you need to understand the fundamentals of the formulas used. Two formulas will be explained here: the sampling error formula and the power analysis formula.

This discussion about the two formulas builds on earlier comments about the importance of systematically calculating sample size using formulas in quantitative research. This importance was introduced in chapter 6 in the "Sample Size" section and reinforced in chapter 11 on experimental designs under "Step 3. Select an Experimental Unit and Identify Study Participants." It was also mentioned in chapter 12 on correlational designs, although sample size is often dictated by the required size for making assumptions about normality of the distribution of scores. (See chapter 12 discussion about size in correlation studies in "Step 2. Identify Individuals to Study.") However, a sampling error formula may be used when the intent of the correlational study is to generalize from a sample to a population. Using a formula was also encouraged again in chapter 13 on survey designs in "Step 3. Identify the Population, the Sampling Frame, and the Sample." Here we will explore the calculations involved in the sample size formulas and present tables that simplify the process of making the calculations.

SAMPLING ERROR FORMULA

A sampling error formula is often used in survey or correlational research (see Fink & Kosekoff, 1985; Fowler, 1988) when investigators seek to generalize results from a sample to a population. A **sampling error formula** is a calculation for determining size of a sample based on the chance (or proportion) that the sample will be evenly divided on a question, sampling error, and a confidence interval.

The formula is based on the proportion of the sample that will have the desired characteristic that you are trying to estimate. For example, when parents are polled to determine whether they would vote "yes" or "no" on a school bond issue, there is a 50/50 chance that they will vote "yes." Selecting a proportion of 50/50 means that the population will be evenly split, and this proportion yields the largest size for your sample.

The sampling error formula is also based on stating the amount of sampling error you are willing to tolerate. Recall that sampling error (stated as a percent, such as from 4% of the time) is the difference between your sample mean and the true population mean. This error results because samples are randomly selected from the population and may not represent the true characteristics of the population (see chapter 6). Finally, the formula also includes identifying a confidence interval, such as a 95% confidence interval. Recall that a confidence interval indicates the upper and lower values that are likely to contain the actual population mean (see chapter 7).

Understanding these three factors helps you interpret a sample size formula table, such as Table B.1 by Fowler (1988, p. 42). The first row in this table shows the percentage of the sample with the desired characteristic, ranging from 5/95 (small chance) to 50/50 (equally split chance). To maximally divide the sample, researchers typically select 50/50 as the proportion of the sample with the characteristic

TABLE B.1

Fowler's (1988, p. 42) Sample Size Table: Confidence Ranges for Variability Due to Sampling*

	Percentage of Sample with Characteristic				
Sample Size	**5/95**	**10/90**	**20/80**	**30/70**	**50/50**
35	7	10	14	15	17
50	6	8	11	13	14
75	5	7	9	11	12
100	4	6	8	9	10
200	3	4	6	6	7
300	3	3	5	5	6
500	2	3	4	4	4
1000	1	2	3	3	3
1500	1	2	2	2	2

Note: Chances are 95 in 100 that the real population figure lies in the range defined by +/− number indicated in table, given percentage of sample reporting characteristics and number of sample cases on which the percentage is based.

*This table describes variability due to sampling. Errors due to nonresponse or reporting errors are not reflected in this table. In addition, this table assumes simple random sample. Estimates may be subject to more variability than this table indicates due to the sample design or the influence of interviewers on the answers they obtained; stratification might reduce the sampling errors below those indicated here.

Source: Fowler, F. J. *Survey Research Methods,* p. 42. Copyright © 1988. Reprinted by permission of Sage Publications, Inc.

they are trying to estimate. In terms of the confidence interval, this table reports only a 95% confidence interval (default), which means that 95 out of 100 times the sample mean will fall within the upper and lower limits, or range, of the population mean. This is a rigorous standard to use. In the columns under the heading "Percentage of Sample with Characteristic," we see values, such as 17, 14, and 12, under the 50/50 column. These values are the amount of sampling error we are willing to tolerate. Typically, researchers set a small error that they are willing to tolerate, such as 4% or 6%. This means that only 4% or 6% of the time the sample mean will differ from the true population mean. Finally, in the left column we see the sample size recommendation that you would use as a guide to the minimum sample size for the sample in your study.

Let's apply information from this table to a study to see how it works. Assume that you need to determine the size of your sample in a study of Native American students in a school district. You want to survey students in high schools in a large metropolitan district to determine if students plan to enroll in advanced placement courses ("yes" they plan to enroll "no" they do not plan to enroll). The procedure needs to be as rigorous as possible, so you decide to use Fowler's (1988) table to calculate the sample size for your study.

A given in Fowler's (1988) table is that you will use a rigorous confidence interval standard—a 95% confidence interval (95 out of 100 times your sample value will fall within the range of the population mean). You assume that students have a 50/50 chance of participating in these courses. Based on this information, you select the column 50/50. Further, you want a low error rate—a small percentage of the time your sample mean will differ from the population mean. You select an error of 4% (4 out of 100 times).

To identify the appropriate sample size you need in your study, you look at the last column (50/50), go down the column to "4" (4%), and then look across the row and find that the ideal sample size is 500 Native American students. This number, based on the sample size formula, will ensure that 95 out of 100 times (95% confidence interval) your sample mean will have an equal chance (50/50 split) of differentiating among the students 96% of the time (or an error of 4%)

POWER ANALYSIS FORMULA

In many experiments, the size of the overall number of participants (and participants per group) is dictated by practical issues related to the number of volunteers who enroll for the study or the individuals who are available to the researcher. Researchers can also use statistics to analyze the data, and these statistics call for minimum numbers of participants for each group when group comparisons are made.

A rigorous, systematic approach is to use a power analysis. A **power analysis** is a means of identifying appropriate sample size for group comparisons by taking into consideration the level of statistical significance (alpha), the amount of power desired in a study, and the effect size. By determining these three factors, you can look up the adequate size for each comparison group in an experiment and use tables available in published texts (e.g., Lipsey, 1990). The process works this way as shown in Table B.2:

- First identify the statistical level of significance to use in testing your group comparison hypothesis, typically set at $p = .05$ or $p = .01$. (See chapter 7 discussions on hypothesis testing.)
- Next identify the power needed to reject the hypothesis when it is false, typically set at .80. (See chapter 7 discussions on types of outcomes of hypothesis testing.)
- Determine the effect size, which is the expected difference in the means between the control and experimental groups expressed in standard deviation units. This effect size is often based on expectations drawn from past research and is typically set at .5 for much educational research (Murphy & Myors, 1998). (See chapter 7.)
- Go to a table for calculating the size of the sample given these parameters, and identify the size of each group in the experiment. This size becomes the number of participants you need for each group in your sample. The approximate sample size per experimental group with an alpha set at .05 is given in Table B.2 (Lipsey, 1990, p. 137).

Let's take an example to apply the power formula and Lipsey's table. Assume that elementary education children identified as gifted in a school district are assigned to one of two groups. One group receives an enrichment program (the experimental group), and the other group receives traditional instruction (the control group). At the end of the semester both groups are tested for creativity. How many gifted students are needed for both the experimental and control groups? We might use the number of students available and equally assign them to groups. Although such an experiment could be made, we want a sufficient number of students in our groups so that we can be confident in our hypothesis test of no differences between the control and experimental groups.

In other words, we need an experiment with sufficient size to have power (see Table 7.8 on possible outcomes in hypothesis testing). We turn to Lipsey's (1990) power analysis table for assistance in determining the appropriate sample size for our experimental and control groups. This table will indicate the size needed given a confidence level, the amount of power desired, and the effect size. Examining Lipsey's table, we find that the significance level for the table is set at an alpha = .05.

We use a rigorous standard for power, such as .80 (80% of the time we will reject the null when it is false), and select the column ".80." Then we look at the column for effect size and choose ".50" as the standard for differences in the means (in standard deviation units) that we will expect between the two groups. Using this information, and going down the column of .80 to the row .50, we find that 65 students are needed for each of our two groups, the experimental and control groups, in our study of gifted children.

TABLE B.2

Lipsey's (1990, p. 137) Sample Size Table: Approximate Sample Size per Experimental Group Needed to Attain Various Criterion Levels of Power for a Range of Effect Sizes at Alpha = .05

	Power Criterion		
Effect size	**.80**	**.90**	**.95**
.10	1570	2100	2600
.20	395	525	650
.30	175	235	290
.40	100	130	165
.50	65	85	105
.60	45	60	75
.70	35	45	55
.80	25	35	45
.90	20	30	35
1.00	20	25	30

Source: Lipsey, M. W. *Design Sensitivity: Statistical Power for Experimental Research,* p. 137.

Appendix C

Nonnormal Distribution

We cannot collect sample after sample of individuals to study (e.g., collect their depression scores), but we can plot the scores of our sample and see what shape the distribution of their scores might be. On the one hand, they may reflect a normal curve. On the other hand, they may not be normal. Examine Figure C.1. Here we see a **nonnormal distribution** of scores in which the actual shape of a frequency distribution of scores may be negatively skewed to the right, positively skewed to the left, concentrated around the mean (negative kurtosis), or resemble a flat picture (positive kurtosis). In a **skewed distribution**, the scores tend to pile up toward one end of the scale and then taper off slowly at the other end (Gravetter & Wallnau, 2000). In a **kurtosis distribution**, the scores pile up at the middle or spread out to the sides. Most distributions are not normal and will exhibit some skewness or kurtosis. Whether the distribution of scores from your sample are normal or nonnormal is one factor that determines what statistical test you will use to analyze your comparative or relationship questions or hypotheses.

FIGURE C.1

Skewness and Kurtosis

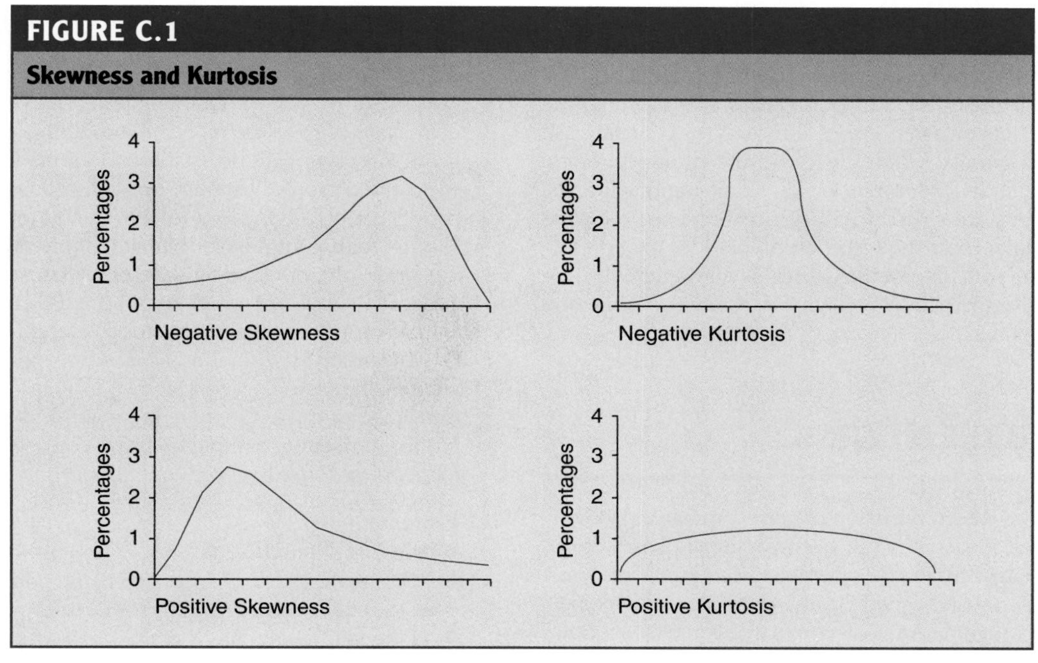

Appendix D

Strategies for Defending a Research Proposal

In doctoral programs and in many master's programs, students are required to complete a formal research study as part of their requirements for graduation. This requirement is included in programs so students can demonstrate their knowledge and application of research. As a first step in preparing the formal research study, a student develops a proposal or plan for the study. The proposal is distributed to the student's faculty. Then, a short time later, the student presents the proposal to the faculty in a meeting called a *proposal defense*. The intent of this meeting is for faculty to have a chance to react and provide constructive comments about the study before the student begins the project. It also serves to provide an opportunity for the student to carefully review the entire project, practice giving an oral presentation of research, and improve the study based on faculty feedback.

The proposal defense meeting varies in length. A typical meeting might last about 1 hour. During this meeting, the student presents an overview of the study, and faculty ask questions that arose when they read the proposal. Some defense meetings are open to all faculty and students, whereas others are closed to all participants except for the student's faculty committee. To best prepare for this meeting and to leave with productive ideas, several strategies are identified here that students might use before, during, and after the meeting.

PRIOR TO THE MEETING

- Look over the composition of your committee. Do you have individuals who can assist you in all phases of your research? Can you substitute faculty on your committee to obtain needed faculty resources at this point in your program? An ideal committee consists of a statistician or research methodologist who can help with the technical aspects of a study, an editor who can help you shape your writing, a content specialist who knows the literature about your topic, and a supporter who can give positive feedback throughout the process.
- Talk with your advisor about the degree of formality required during the meeting. A formal meeting consists of a brief, organized presentation by the student followed by faculty questions. It may also include a slide presentation to present the proposal for the research study. An informal meeting may be a discussion or conversation about your proposed project without the use of a slide presentation or an organized, formal presentation.
- If possible, attend proposal defenses held by other students so that you can gain some experience with the procedures of this meeting.
- Visit with your faculty committee members before the meeting to gauge their feedback. They will likely have suggestions for improving the study before the defense meeting.
- Consider how you will build rapport with your faculty committee prior to the meeting and during your program. Rapport might be established informally through social interaction or formally through collaboration on projects or by serving as a teacher's assistant.
- Discuss with your advisor her or his role during the meeting. Advisors assume different roles, such as advocate, supporter, arbitrator, and adversary. The better you understand his or her role, the better you can anticipate how your advisor will respond during a defense meeting.
- Anticipate questions that faculty will ask during a proposal meeting. Sample questions during a meeting for a *quantitative* proposal might be:

Research design questions:

- Is the problem trivial?
- What is the research question being addressed?
- Is the theory a good predictor to use?
- Is the study internally valid?

Data collection and analysis questions:

- Are the methods detailed?
- Is the best data collection approach used?
- Was the most appropriate statistic chosen?

- Are the constructs valid?
- Do items on the instrument need refinement?
- Was a good instrument chosen to be used in the study?

- Sample questions during a meeting for a *qualitative* study will likely range from research design to the legitimacy of the design as compared with quantitative research.

Design questions:

- Why did you choose a qualitative study (instead of a quantitative study)?
- What is the type of design you are using (e.g., ethnography, grounded theory)?
- Is the study valid?

Quantitative-type questions that require knowledge about qualitative research:

- How can you generalize from this study?
- Are your variables measurable and valid?
- Do you plan to use theory in this study?
- Why did you conduct a brief literature review?

Legitimacy questions:

- Are there journals that will publish this type of research?
- Is this type of research rigorous enough?
- Will your involvement in the study influence the findings?

DURING THE MEETING

- Keep your presentation brief—15 minutes or less.
- Be open, negotiable, and responsive to faculty questions.
- Restate questions in your own words to indicate that you have correctly heard them.
- Be willing to admit that you have not considered the question being raised.
- Have your advisor intercede if the questions become unfair or unrelated to your topic.
- Listen for constructive suggestions for improving your project. Keep notes of these suggestions or have your advisor take notes for you so that later there will not be any question about changes needed.

AFTER THE MEETING

- Review the events of the meeting with your advisor.
- Note suggestions that need to be made to improve or change your study. Negotiate with your advisor about what committee suggestions need to be implemented and what suggestions need to be revisited with members of the committee.
- Visit with faculty on your committee, if needed, to clarify their suggestions for improvement.
- Talk with your advisor about the next step in the process—what chapters you should begin to write and when.

Glossary

A/B designs are single-subject studies in experimental research that consist of observing and measuring behavior during a trial period (*A*), administering an intervention, and observing and measuring the behavior after the intervention (*B*).
abstracts are summaries of the major aspects of a study or article, conveyed in a concise way (for this purpose, often no more than 350 words) and inclusive of specific components that describe the study.
action research designs are systematic procedures used by teachers (or other individuals in an educational setting) to gather quantitative, qualitative (or both) data about—and subsequently improve—the ways their particular setting operates, how they teach, and how well their students learn (Mills, 2000).
adding to knowledge means that educators undertake research for it to contribute to existing information about issues.
alternate forms and test–retest reliability is an approach to reliability in which the researcher administers the test twice and also uses an alternate form of the test from the first administration to the second.
alternating treatment designs are a type of single-subject design in which the researcher examines the relative effects of two or more interventions and determines which intervention is the more effective treatment on the outcome.
alternative forms reliability involves using two instruments, both measuring the same variables and relating (or correlating) the scores for the same group of individuals to the two instruments.
analyzing and interpreting the data indicates that researchers analyze the data; represent it in tables, figures, and pictures; and explain it to come up with answers to research questions and statements asked in the research.
attitudinal measures seek to assess affect or feelings toward educational topics (e.g., assessing positive or negative attitudes toward giving students a choice of school to attend).
audience consists of individuals who will read and potentially use information provided in a research study. Audiences will vary depending on the nature of the study, but several often considered by educators include researchers, practitioners, policy makers, and individuals participating in the studies.
audiovisual materials consist of images or sounds that are collected by the qualitative researcher to help understand the central phenomenon under study. Photographs, videotapes, digital images, paintings and pictures, and physical traces of images (e.g., footsteps in the snow) are all sources of information for qualitative inquiry.
autobiography is a narrative account written and recorded by the individual who is the subject of the study.
axial coding is when the grounded theorist selects one open-coding category, positions it at the center of the process being explored (as the core phenomenon), and then relates other categories to it.
bar charts depict trends and distributions of data.
behavior in ethnography is an action taken by an individual in a cultural setting.
behavioral observations consist of selecting an instrument to record a behavior, observing individuals for that behavior, and checking points on a scale that reflect the behavior (e.g., behavioral checklists).
belief in ethnography is how an individual thinks about or perceives things in a cultural setting.
beta weights are coefficients indicating the magnitude of prediction for a variable after removing the effects of all other predictors.
between-group designs are those in which the researcher compares results between different groups in terms of outcome scores.
biography is a form of narrative study in which the researcher writes and records the experiences of another person's life.
blocking variable is a variable in an experiment that the researcher controls before the experiment starts by dividing (or "blocking") the participants into subgroups (or categories) and analyzing the impact of each subgroup on the outcome.
case study is a variation of an ethnography in that the researcher provides an in-depth exploration of a bounded system (e.g., an activity, an event, a process, or an individual) based on extensive data collection (Creswell, 2007).
categories in grounded theory designs are themes of basic information identified in the data by the researcher and used to understand a process.
central phenomenon is an issue or process explored in qualitative research.

central question is the overarching question being asked in a qualitative study. It is the attempt by the researcher to ask the most general question that can be addressed in a study.

changing observational role is one in which researchers adapt their role to the situation, such as entering a site and observing as a nonparticipant and then later becoming a participant.

charts portray the complex relationships among variables in correlational research designs.

children's stories in educational research are narrative studies in which children in classrooms are asked to present orally, or in writing, their own stories about their learnings.

chronology in narrative designs means that the researcher analyzes and writes about an individual's life using a time sequence or chronology of events.

cleaning the data is the process of visually inspecting the data for scores (or values) that are outside the accepted range of scores.

closed-ended questions in surveys consist of questions posed by the researcher in which the participant responds to preset response options.

codebooks are lists of variables or questions that indicate how the researcher will code or score responses from instruments or checklists.

codes are labels used to describe a segment of text or an image.

coding paradigm is a diagram that portrays the interrelationship of causal conditions, strategies, contextual and intervening conditions, and consequences in grounded theory research.

coding process is a qualitative research process in which the researcher makes sense out of text data, divides it into text or image segments, labels the segments, examines codes for overlap and redundancy, and collapses these codes into themes.

coefficient alpha is a measure of the internal consistency of items on an instrument when the items are scored as continuous variables (e.g., *strongly agree* to *strongly disagree*).

coefficient of determination assesses the proportion of variability in one variable that can be determined or explained by a second variable.

cohort studies are longitudinal survey designs in which a researcher identifies a subpopulation, based on some specific characteristic, and studies that subpopulation over time.

collaborate with others this is often central to action research, and it involves actively participating with others in research. These coparticipants may be "inside" individuals in a school or "outside" personnel, such as university researchers or professional association groups.

collaboration in narrative research means that the inquirer actively involves the participant in the inquiry as it unfolds. This collaboration may include many steps in the research process, from formulating the central phenomena to be examined to the types of field texts that will yield helpful information to the final written "restoried" rendition of the individual's experiences by the researcher.

collecting data means identifying and selecting individuals for a study, obtaining their permission to be studied, and gathering information by administering instruments through asking people questions or observing their behaviors.

collective case studies are case studies in which multiple cases are described and compared to provide insight into an issue.

comparison question addresses how two or more groups differ in terms of one or more outcome variables. A comparison question is typically used in an experiment, and the researcher provides some intervention to one group and withholds it from the second group.

compensatory equalization is a potential threat to internal validity when only the experimental group receives a treatment and an inequality exists that may affect the experiment.

compensatory rivalry is a potential threat to internal validity when rivalry develops between the groups because the control group feels that it is the "underdog."

computer analysis of qualitative data means that researchers use a qualitative computer program to facilitate the process of storing, analyzing, and making sense of the data.

conference papers are research reports presented to an audience at a state, regional, national, or international conference typically sponsored by professional associations (e.g., AERA, American Association of Teacher Educators).

conference proposals are short summaries of a study, typically about three pages, that reviewers use to determine whether research studies should be presented at conferences.

confidence intervals are the range of upper and lower sample statistical values that are consistent with observed data and are likely to contain the actual population mean.

confirming and disconfirming sampling is a purposeful strategy used during a qualitative study to follow up on specific cases to test out or explore further specific findings.

confounding variables (sometimes called *spurious variables*) are attributes or characteristics that the researcher cannot directly measure because their effects cannot be easily separated from other variables, even though they may influence the relationship between the independent and the dependent variable.

constant comparison is an inductive (from specific to broad) data analysis procedure in grounded theory research of generating and connecting categories by comparing incidents in the data to other incidents, incidents to categories, and categories to other categories.

construct is an attribute or characteristic expressed in an abstract, general way, whereas a variable is an attribute or characteristic stated in a specific, applied way.

construct validity is a determination of the significance, meaning, purpose, and use of scores from an instrument.
content validity is the extent to which the questions on the instrument and the scores from these questions are representative of all the possible questions that could be asked about the content or skills.
context in ethnography is the setting, situation, or environment that surrounds the cultural-sharing group being studied.
contrary evidence is information that does not support or confirm the themes and provides contradictory evidence for a theme.
control variable is a variable that the researcher does not want to measure directly but is important to consider and "neutralize" because it potentially influences the dependent variable. Typically, control variables are personal, demographic attributes or characteristics.
convenience sampling is a quantitative sampling procedure in which the researcher selects participants because they are willing and available to be studied.
core category in grounded theory research is the central category around which the theory is written.
correlation is defined as a statistical test to determine the tendency or pattern for two (or more) variables or two sets of data to vary consistently.
correlation matrix is a visual display of the correlation coefficients for all variables in a study.
correlational research designs are quantitative designs in which investigators use a correlation statistical technique to describe and measure the degree of association (or relationship) between two or more variables or sets of scores.
covariates are variables that the researcher controls for using statistics and that relate to the dependent variable but do not relate to the independent variable.
co-vary means that a score can be predicted on one variable with knowledge about the individual's score on another variable.
criterion variable is the outcome variable being predicted in correlational research.
criterion-related validity refers to whether scores from an instrument are a good predictor of some outcome (or criterion) they are expected to predict.
critical ethnographies are a type of ethnographic research in which the author has an interest in advocating for the emancipation of groups marginalized in our society (Thomas, 1993).
critical region is the area on the normal curve for low probability values if the null hypothesis is true.
critical sampling is a qualitative purposeful sampling strategy in which the researcher selects an exceptionally vivid case for learning about a phenomenon.
cross-sectional survey design is a design in which the researcher collects data at one point in time.
cultural theme in ethnography is a general position, declared or implied, that is opened, approved, or promoted in a society or group (Spradley, 1980).
culture is "everything having to do with human behavior and belief" (LeCompte, Preissle, & Tesch, 1993, p. 5). It can include language, rituals, economic and political structures, life stages, interactions, and communication styles.
culture-sharing group in ethnography is two or more individuals that have shared behaviors, beliefs, and language.
curvilinear or non-linear relationship is a U-shaped distribution in scores on a graph.
data recording protocols are forms designed and used by qualitative researchers to record information during observations and interviews.
deficiencies in the evidence refer to a situation in which the past literature or practical experiences of the researchers do not adequately address the research problem. In the "Statement of the Problem" the researcher summarizes the ways the literature or experiences are deficient.
degree of association means the association between two variables or sets of scores with a correlation coefficient of −1.00 to +1.00, with .00 indicating no linear association at all.
degrees of freedom (*df*) indicate to the researcher how much data was used to calculate a particular statistic; usually one less than the number of scores.
dependent variable is an attribute or characteristic that is influenced by the independent variable. Dependent variables are dependent or influenced by independent variables.
describing and developing themes from the data in qualitative research consists of answering the major research questions and developing an in-depth understanding of the central phenomenon.
description in ethnography is a detailed rendering of individuals and scenes to depict what is going on in the culture-sharing group.
descriptive fieldnotes record a description of the events, activities, and people (e.g., what happened).
descriptive question identifies participants' responses to a single variable or question in quantitative research.
descriptive statistics present information that helps a researcher describe responses to each question in a database as well as determine overall trends and the distribution of the data.
dictionaries and glossaries contain terms with which researchers must be familiar when studying a particular topic.
diffusion of treatments is a potential threat to internal validity when the experimental and control groups can communicate with each other and the control group may learn from the experimental group information about the treatment.
dimensionalized properties are when the grounded theory researcher views the property on a continuum and locates, in the data, examples representing extremes on this continuum.
directional alternative hypotheses predict a certain direction for the relationship between the independent

variable and the dependent variable. This prediction is typically based on prior research conducted by the investigator or reported by others in the literature.

discriminant sampling in grounded theory is when the researcher poses questions that relate the categories and then returns to the data and looks for evidence, incidents, and events to develop a theory.

dissertation or thesis proposals are plans for a research report, initiated and developed prior to the actual conduct of research.

dissertations and theses are the doctoral and master's research reports prepared by students for faculty and graduate committees.

documents consist of public and private records that qualitative researchers can obtain about a site or participants in a study, such as newspapers, minutes of meetings, personal journals, or diaries.

dynamic process in action research involves iterations of activities, such as a "spiral" of activities. The key idea is that the researcher "spirals" back and forth between reflection about a problem and data collection and action.

educational topic is the broad subject matter area that a researcher wishes to address in a study.

effect size is a means for identifying the strength of the conclusions about group differences or about the relationship among variables in a quantitative study. The calculation of this coefficient differs for statistical tests (e.g., R^2, eta^2, omega^2, phi, Cohen's *D;* American Psychological Association, 2001).

electronic questionnaire is a survey instrument for collecting data that is available on the computer.

e-mail interviews consist of collecting open-ended data through interviews from individuals using the technology of Web sites or the Internet.

embedded mixed design in mixed methods research consists of presenting a study with a primary data source of quantitative or qualitative data, and a secondary data source of qualitative or quantitative data that plays a supportive auxiliary role in the study. Examples would include a quantitative experiment with a supportive qualitative data component or a correlational study with a smaller qualitative component to help explain the quantitative correlational results.

emerging design in grounded theory research is the process in which the researcher collects data, immediately analyzes it rather than waiting until all data are collected, and then bases the decision about what data to collect next on this analysis. The image of a "zigzag" helps explain this procedure.

emerging process indicates that the intent or purpose of a qualitative study and the questions asked by the researcher may change during the process of inquiry based on feedback or participants' views.

emic data is information supplied by participants in a study. It often refers to first-order concepts such as local language, concepts, and ways of expression used by members in a cultural-sharing group (Schwandt, 2001).

encoding is the intentional use, by an author, of specific terms to convey ideas, such as using research terms.

encyclopedias provide information about a lot of broad topics and are a good starting place for someone who knows little about a certain topic.

end-of-text references are references listed at the end of a research report.

equating the groups means that the researcher randomly assigns individuals to groups equally and equally distributes any variability of individuals between or among the groups or conditions in the experiment.

equivalent time series design is an experimental design in which the investigator alternates a treatment with a posttest measure. The data analysis then consists of comparing posttest measures or plotting them to discern patterns, over time, in the data.

ERIC database is a database of educational information that contains information about journal articles and documents addressing educational topics, broadly construed.

ethical issues in qualitative research include issues such as informing participants of the purpose of the study, refraining from deceptive practices, sharing information with participants (including your role as a researcher), being respectful of the research site, reciprocity, using ethical interview practices, maintaining confidentiality, and collaborating with participants.

ethnographic designs are qualitative procedures for describing, analyzing, and interpreting a cultural group's shared patterns of behavior, beliefs, and language that develop over time.

etic data is information representing the ethnographer's interpretation of the participant's perspective. *Etic* typically refers to second-order concepts such as the language used by the social scientist or educator to refer to the same phenomena mentioned by the participants (Schwandt, 2001).

evaluating research involves making an assessment of the quality of a study using standards advanced by individuals in education.

experiences in narrative research are both personal, what the individual experiences, as well as social, the individual's interacting with others (Clandinin & Connelly, 2000).

experimental group is a group in an experiment that receives the treatment (e.g., the activity or procedure) that the researcher would like to test.

experimental treatment is when the researcher physically intervenes to alter the conditions experienced by the experimental unit.

experimental unit of analysis is the smallest unit treated by the researcher during an experiment.

experiments are used by researchers to test activities, practices, or procedures to determine whether they influence an outcome or dependent variable.

explanatory mixed methods design (also called a *two-phase model;* Creswell & Plano Clark, 2007) consists of first, collecting quantitative data, and then collecting qualitative data to help explain or elaborate on the quantitative results.

explanatory research design is a type of correlational research in which the researcher is interested in the extent to which two variables (or more) co-vary, where variance or change in one variable is reflected in variance or change in the other.

exploratory mixed methods design consists of first, gathering qualitative data to explore a phenomenon, and then collecting quantitative data to test relationships found in the qualitative data.

external audit in qualitative research is when a researcher hires or obtains the services of an individual outside the study to review many aspects of the research. This auditor reviews the project and writes or communicates an evaluation of the study.

extraneous factors are any influences in the selection of participants, procedures, statistics, or design likely to affect the outcome and provide an alternative explanation for the results than what was expected.

extreme case sampling is a form of purposeful sampling in which the researcher studies an outlier case or one that displays extreme characteristics.

factorial designs represent a modification of the between-group design in which the researcher studies two or more categorical, independent variables, each examined at two or more levels (Vogt, 1999).

factual information or personal documents consist of numeric data in public records of individuals. This data can include grade reports, school attendance records, student demographic data, and census information.

field texts represent information from different sources collected by researchers in a narrative design.

fieldnotes are text (or words) recorded by the researcher during an observation in a qualitative study.

fieldwork in ethnography means that the researcher gathers data in the setting where the participants are located and where their shared patterns can be studied.

figures are summaries of quantitative information presented as a chart, graph, or picture that shows relations among scores or variables.

focus group interviews in survey research involve the researcher locating or developing a survey instrument, convening a small group of people—typically a group of four to six people—who can answer the questions asked on the instrument, and recording their comments about the questions on the instrument.

future research directions are suggestions made by the researcher about additional studies that need to be conducted based on the results of the present research.

gatekeepers are individuals who have an official or unofficial role at the site, provide entrance to a site, help researchers locate people, and assist in the identification of places to study.

grounded theory designs are systematic, qualitative procedures that researchers use to generate a theory that explains, at a broad conceptual level, a process, action, or interaction about a substantive topic.

group comparison is an analytic process in experiments of obtaining scores for individuals or groups on the dependent variable and making comparisons of their means and variance both within the group and between the groups.

hand analysis of qualitative data means that researchers read the data and mark it by hand and divide the data into parts. Traditionally, hand analyzing of text data involves color coding parts of the text or cutting and pasting sentences onto cards.

handbooks are concise reference books on a specific topic.

history is a potential threat to internal validity in an experiment in which time passes between the beginning of the experiment and the end, and events may occur during that time that affect the outcome of the experiment.

homogeneous samples are individuals in an experiment who vary little in their personal characteristics.

homogeneous sampling is a purposeful sampling strategy in which the researcher samples individuals or sites based on membership in a subgroup with defining characteristics.

hypotheses are declarative statements in quantitative research in which the investigator makes a prediction or a conjecture about the outcomes of a relationship.

hypothesis testing is a procedure for making decisions about results by comparing an observed value with a population value to determine if no difference or relationship exists between the values.

identifying a research problem consists of specifying an issue to study, developing a justification for studying it, and suggesting the importance of the study for select audiences that will read the report.

implications in a study are those suggestions for the importance of the study for different audiences. They elaborate on the significance for audiences presented initially in the statement of the problem.

in vivo codes are labels for categories (or themes) that are phrased in the exact words of participants rather than in the words of the researcher or in social science or educational terms.

independent variable is an attribute or characteristic that influences or affects an outcome or dependent variable.

inferential statistics enable a researcher to draw conclusions, inferences, or generalizations from a sample to a population of participants.

informed consent form is a statement that participants sign before they participate in research. This form includes language that will guarantee them certain rights. When they sign the form, they agree to be involved in the study and acknowledge that their rights are protected.

inputting the data means that the researcher transfers the data from the responses on instruments to a computer file for analysis.

institutional review board is a committee of faculty who reviews and approves research so that the rights of humans are protected.

instrumental case is a type of qualitative case study in which the researcher studies a particular issue and finds one or more cases that illuminates the issue.

instrumentation is a potential threat to validity in an experiment when the instrument changes during a pretest and a posttest.

instruments are tools for measuring, observing, or documenting quantitative data. Researchers identify these instruments before they collect data, and they may include a test, a questionnaire, a tally sheet, a log, an observational checklist, an inventory, or an assessment instrument.

interaction effects exist when the influence on one independent variable depends on (or co-varies with) the other independent variable in an experiment.

interaction of history and treatment is a threat to external validity in an experiment that arises when the researcher tries to generalize findings to past and future situations.

interaction of selection and treatment is a threat to external validity in an experiment that involves the inability to generalize beyond the groups in the experiment, such as to other racial, social, geographical, age, gender, or personality groups.

interaction of setting and treatment is a threat to external validity in an experiment that arises from the inability to generalize from one setting, where the experiment occurred, to another setting.

interactions with selection may pose a potential threat to internal validity in an experiment. Threats may interact with selection of participants, such as individuals selected may mature at different rates (e.g., 16-year-old boys and girls may mature at different rates during the study), historical events may interact with selection because individuals in different groups come from different settings, or the selection of participants may also influence the instrument scores, especially when different groups score at different mean positions on a test whose intervals are not equal.

interconnecting themes means that the researcher connects the themes to display a chronology or sequence of events, such as when qualitative researchers generate a theoretical and conceptual model or report stories of individuals.

internally consistent means that scores from an instrument are reliable and accurate if they are consistent across the items on the instrument.

interpretation in ethnography is the process in qualitative ethnographic research in which the inquirer assesses how, overall, the culture-sharing group works.

interpretation in qualitative research means that the researcher steps back and forms some larger meaning about the phenomenon based on personal views, comparisons with past studies, or both.

interrater reliability means that two or more individuals observe an individual's behavior and record scores, and then the scores of the observers are compared to determine whether they are similar.

interrupted time series design consists of experimental procedures for studying one group, obtaining multiple pretest measures, administering an intervention (or interrupting the activities), and then measuring outcomes (or posttests) several times.

interval (or rating) scales provide "continuous" response options to questions that have presumably equal distances between options.

intervening variable is an attribute or characteristic that "stands between" the independent and dependent variables and exercises an influence on the dependent variable apart from the independent variable. Intervening variables transmit (or mediate) the effects of the independent variable on the dependent variable.

interventes (or manipulates) in an experiment are ways a researcher physically intervenes with one or more conditions so that individuals experience something different in the experimental conditions than what is experienced in the control conditions.

interview protocol is a form designed by the researcher that contains instructions for the process of the interview, the questions to be asked, and space to take notes on responses from the interviewee.

interview surveys are forms on which the researcher records answers supplied by the participant in the study. The researcher asks a question from an interview guide, listens for answers or observes behavior, and records responses on the survey.

interviews occur when researchers ask one or more participants general, open-ended questions and record their answers.

intrinsic case is a type of qualitative case study in which the researcher studies the case itself because it is of exceptional interest.

issue subquestions are questions that narrow the focus of the central question into specific topics the researcher seeks to learn from participants in a qualitative study.

journal articles are polished, short research reports that have been sent to an editor of a journal, accepted for inclusion, and published in a volume of the journal.

justifying a research problem means that the researcher presents reasons for the importance of studying the issue or concern.

Kuder–Richardson split half test (K-R 20, K-R 21) is a formula for calculating reliability of scores when items on an instrument are (a) scored right or wrong as categorical scores, (b) the responses are not influenced by speed, and (c) the items measure a common factor.

kurtosis distribution is a distribution of scores that pile up at the middle or spread out to the sides.

language in ethnography is how an individual talks to others in a cultural setting.

layering the analysis (also called *first-* and *second-order abstractions*) in qualitative research means representing the data using interconnected levels of themes.

lean coding is the assignment of only a few codes the first time a researcher goes through a manuscript.

levels in an experiment are categories of a treatment variable.

levels of headings in a scholarly study and literature review provide logical subdivisions of the text.

life history is a narrative study of an individual's entire life experiences.

limitations are potential weaknesses or problems in quantitative research that are identified by the researcher. In quantitative research, these weaknesses are enumerated one by one, and they often relate to inadequate measures of variables, loss or lack of participants, small sample sizes, errors in measurement, and other factors typically related to data collection and analysis.

line graphs display the interaction between two variables in an experiment.

linking devices in writing are words or phrases that tie together sections of a research report.

literature map is a figure or drawing that displays the research literature (e.g., studies, essays, books, chapters, and summaries) on a topic.

literature review is a written summary of articles, books, and other documents that describe the past and current state of knowledge about a topic.

longitudinal survey design is a design in which the researcher collects data about trends with the same population, changes in a cohort group or subpopulation, or changes in a panel group of the same individuals over time.

mailed questionnaires are forms of data collection in survey research in which the investigator mails a questionnaire to members of the sample.

main effects are the influence of each independent variable (e.g., type of instruction or extent of depression) on the outcome (e.g., the dependent variable, rate of smoking) in an experiment.

matching is the process of identifying one or more personal characteristics that influence the outcome and assigning individuals to the experimental and control groups equally matched on that characteristic.

maturation is a potential threat to internal validity in an experiment in which individuals develop or change during the experiment (i.e., become older, wiser, stronger, and more experienced). These changes may affect their scores between the pretest and the posttest.

maximal variation sampling is a purposeful sampling strategy in which the researcher samples cases or individuals who differ on some characteristic.

mean (*M*) is the total of the scores divided by the number of scores.

measured variable is an independent variable that is measured or observed by the researcher and consists of a range of continuous or categorical scores for variables.

measurement means that the researcher records information from individuals by asking them to answer questions on an instrument (e.g., a student completes questions on a survey asking about self-esteem) or by observing an individual and recording scores on an instrument (e.g., a researcher watches a student playing basketball).

measures of central tendency are summary numbers that represent a single value in a distribution of scores (Vogt, 1999).

measures of relative standing are statistics that describe one score relative to a group of scores. Two frequently used statistics are the *z* score and the percentile rank.

measures of variability indicate the spread of the scores in a distribution. Variance, standard deviation, and range all indicate the amount of variability in a distribution of scores.

median is the term given to the score that divides the scores, rank ordered from top to bottom, in half.

member checking is a qualitative process during which the researcher asks one or more participants in the study to check the accuracy of the account.

memos are notes the researcher writes throughout the research process to elaborate on ideas about the data and the coded categories.

meta-analysis is a type of research report in which the author integrates the findings of many (primary source) research studies.

missing data is information that is not supplied by participants to specific questions or items. This information may be lost, individuals may skip questions, participants may be absent when observational data is collected, or persons may actually refuse to complete a sensitive question.

mixed methods research designs are procedures for collecting both quantitative and qualitative data in a single study, and for analyzing and reporting this data based on a priority and sequence of the information.

mode is the term given to the score that appears most frequently in a list of scores.

moderating variables are new variables constructed by the researcher by taking one variable times another to determine the joint impact of both variables together.

modifying an instrument means locating an existing instrument, obtaining permission to change it, and making changes in it to fit the participants.

mortality is a potential threat to internal validity in an experiment when individuals drop out during the experiment for any number of reasons (e.g., time, interest, money, friends, or parents who do not want them to participate).

multiple baseline designs are single-subject studies in experimental research consisting of procedures in which the participant receives an experimental treatment at a different time (hence, multiple baselines exist) so that treatment diffusion will not occur among participants.

multiple perspectives in qualitative research refer to evidence for a theme that is based on several viewpoints from different individuals and sources of data.

multiple regression (or multiple correlation) is a statistical procedure for examining the combined relationship of multiple independent variables on a single dependent variable.

multistage cluster sampling is a quantitative sampling procedure in which the researcher chooses a sample in two or more stages because the populations cannot be easily identified or they are extremely large.

narrative discussion is a written passage in a qualitative study in which authors summarize, in detail, the findings from their data analysis.

narrative hooks are the first sentences in a research report that draw readers into a study; cause readers to pay attention; elicit an emotional or attitudinal response from readers; and encourage readers to continue reading.

narrative research designs are qualitative procedures in which researchers describe the lives of individuals, collect and tell stories about these individuals' lives, and write narratives about their experiences (Connelly & Clandinin, 1990).

negative correlations (indicated by a "−" correlation coefficient) are when the points move in the opposite direction—when *X* increases, *Y* decreases and when *X* decreases, *Y* increases.

negative linear relationship results when low scores (or high scores) on one variable relate to high scores (or low scores) on the other variable.

negotiation data consists of information that the participant and the researcher agree to use in a study.

net or difference scores are scores in a quantitative study in which the researcher develops a score that represents a difference or change for each individual.

nominal (or categorical) scales provide response options where participants check one or more categories that describe their traits, attributes, or characteristics.

nondirectional alternative hypotheses predict a difference between groups on the dependent variable but do not indicate the direction of this prediction (e.g., positive or negative).

nonnormal distributions of scores result in frequency distributions that may be negatively skewed to the right, positively skewed to the left, concentrated around the mean (negative kurtosis), or resemble a flat picture (positive kurtosis).

nonparticipant observer is an observational role adopted by researchers when they visit a site and record notes without becoming involved in the activities of the participants.

nonprobability sampling is a quantitative sampling procedure in which the researcher chooses participants because they are available, convenient, and represent some characteristic the investigator seeks to study.

normal distribution or normal probability curve is a distribution of scores by participants that can be represented by a graph that approximates a bell-shaped curve.

null hypotheses make predictions that there will be no statistically significant difference between the independent variable and the dependent variable.

observation is the process of gathering firsthand information by observing people and places at a research site.

observational protocol is a form designed by the researcher, before data collection, that is used for taking fieldnotes during an observation.

one-on-one interviewing in survey research consists of investigators conducting an interview with an individual in the sample and recording responses to questions.

one-on-one interviews are the-data collection processes in which the researcher asks questions to and records answers from only one participant in the study at a time.

one-tailed tests of significance are when the region for rejection of the null hypothesis is placed only at one end of the distribution.

open coding is the process used by the grounded theorist to form initial categories of information about the phenomenon being studied.

open-ended questions in surveys consist of questions posed by the researcher in which the participant provides her or his own responses to questions.

open-ended responses to a question allow the participant to create the options for responding.

operational definitions are the specification of how variables will be defined and measured (or assessed) in a study.

opportunistic sampling is purposeful sampling undertaken after the research begins, to take advantage of unfolding events.

ordinal (or ranking) scales are response options in which participants rank order from best, or most important, to worst, or least important, some trait, attribute, or characteristic.

outcomes (or *responses, criteria,* or *posttests*) are the dependent variables in an experiment that are the presumed effect of the treatment variables. They are also the effects predicted in a hypothesis in the cause-and-effect equation.

panel studies are longitudinal survey designs in which a researcher examines the same people over time.

partial correlations are used to determine the amount of variance that an intervening variable explains in both the independent and dependent variables.

participant observer is an observational role adopted by researchers in which they take part in activities in the setting they observe.

participatory action research (PAR) is a design in action research aimed at improving the quality of people's organization, community, and family lives (Stringer, 1999). Although espousing many of the ideas of teacher- and school-based practical action research, it differs by incorporating an emancipatory aim of improving and empowering individuals and organizations in educational (and other) settings.

participatory or self-reflective research means that the researchers are self-reflective and study their own classrooms, schools, or practices.

percentile rank of a particular score is the percentage of participants in the distribution with scores at or below a particular score.

performance measures assess an individual's ability to perform on an achievement test, an intelligence test, an aptitude test, an interest inventory, or a personality assessment inventory.

personal documents in quantitative research consist of numeric, individual data available in public records such as grade reports or school attendance records.

personal experience story is a narrative study of an individual's personal experience found in single or multiple episodes, private situations, or communal folklore (Denzin, 1989).

phi coefficient is the correlation statistic used to determine the degree and direction of association when *both* variables being related are dichotomous measures.

physical structure of a study is the underlying organization of topics that form a structure for a research report.

pilot test of a questionnaire or interview survey is a procedure in which a researcher makes changes in an instrument based on feedback from a small number of individuals who complete and evaluate the instrument.

plan of action in action research is where the researcher formulates an action plan in response to a problem. This plan may be presenting the data to important stakeholders, establishing a pilot program, starting several competing programs, or implementing an ongoing research agenda to explore new practices (Stringer, 1999).

point-biserial correlation is the correlation statistic used when one variable is measured as an interval or ratio scale and the other has two different values (a dichotomous scale).

population is a group of individuals who comprise the same characteristics. For example, all teachers would make up the population of teachers, and all high school administrators in a school district would make up the population of administrators.

positive correlations (indicated by a "+" correlation coefficient) are when the points move in the same direction—when *X* increases, so does *Y*, or alternatively, if *X* decreases, so does *Y*.

positive linear relationship means that low (or high) scores on one variable relate to low (or high) scores on a second variable.

posttest in an experiment measures some attribute or characteristic that is assessed for participants after a treatment.

power in quantitative hypothesis testing is the probability of correctly rejecting a false null hypothesis.

power analysis is a means of identifying appropriate sample size for group comparisons by taking into consideration the level of statistical significance (alpha), the amount of power desired in a study, and the effect size.

practical action research is a design in action research in which educators study a specific school situation with a view toward improving practice (Schmuck, 1997). This form of action research focuses on a small-scale research project, narrowly focused on a specific problem or issue and undertaken by individual teachers or teams within a school or school district.

practical issues are often the focus of action research. These issues are concerns or problems that teachers or other school officials have in their educational setting.

practical research problems are those that arise from the setting and activities of educators.

prediction research design is a type of correlational research in which the researcher identifies variables that will positively predict an outcome or criterion.

predictor variable is the variable the researcher uses to make a forecast about an outcome in correlational research.

preliminary exploratory analysis in qualitative research consists of obtaining a general sense of the data, memoing ideas, thinking about the organization of the data, and considering whether more data are needed.

preparing and organizing data for analysis in quantitative research consists of assembling all data, transforming it into numeric scores, creating a data file for computer or hand tabulation, and selecting a computer program to use in performing statistical tests on the data.

presentation of results in quantitative research is where the investigator presents detailed information about the specific results of the descriptive and inferential statistical analyses.

pretest in an experiment measures some attribute or characteristic that is assessed for participants before they receive a treatment.

primary source literature is literature reported by the individual or individuals who actually conducted the research or who originated the ideas.

probability sampling is a quantitative sampling procedure in which the researcher selects individuals from the population so that each person has an equal probability of being selected from the population.

probable causation means that researchers attempt to establish a likely cause-and-effect relationship between variables, rather than *prove* the relationship.

probes are subquestions under each question that the researcher asks to elicit more information. These probes vary from exploring the content in more depth (elaborating) to asking the interviewee to explain her or his answer in more detail (clarifying).

procedural subquestions indicate the steps in analyzing the data to be used in a qualitative study. This form of writing subquestions is less frequently used than issue questions.

process in grounded theory research is a sequence of actions and interactions among people and events pertaining to a topic (Strauss & Corbin, 1998).

process of research consists of a series of six steps used by researchers when they conduct a study. They are identifying a research problem, reviewing the literature, specifying a purpose and research questions or hypotheses, collecting data, analyzing and interpreting the data, and reporting and evaluating research.

product–moment correlation coefficient is called the *bivariate correlation*, the *zero-order correlation*, or simply the *Pearson r*, and it is indicated with an "*r*" for its notation. The statistic is calculated for two variables (r_{xy}) by multiplying the z scores on X and Y for each case and then dividing by the number of cases minus 1 (e.g., see the detailed steps in Vockell & Asher, 1995).

properties are subcategories in grounded theory of open codes that serve to provide more detail about each category.

purpose for research consists of identifying the major intent or objective for a study and narrowing it into specific research questions or hypotheses.

purpose statement is a declarative statement that advances the overall direction or focus of a study. Researchers describe the purpose in one or more succinctly formed sentences. It is used both in quantitative and qualitative research and it is typically found in the introduction or beginning section of research.

purpose statement in qualitative research indicates the need to explore or understand the central phenomenon with specific individuals at a certain research site.

purposeful sampling is a qualitative sampling procedure in which researchers intentionally select individuals and sites to learn or understand the central phenomenon.

purposes of a proposal are to help an investigator think through all aspects of the study and anticipate problems.

***p* values** are the probability (p) that a result could have been produced by chance if the null hypothesis were really true.

qualitative data analysis computer programs are programs that store and organize qualitative data (i.e., text, such as transcribed interviews or typed fieldnotes) and facilitate the process of analyzing data.

qualitative research is an inquiry approach useful for exploring and understanding a central phenomenon. To learn about this phenomenon, the inquirer asks participants broad, general questions, collects the detailed views of participants in the form of words or images, and analyzes the information for description and themes. From this data, the researcher interprets the meaning of the information, drawing on personal reflections and past research. The final structure of the final report is flexible, and it displays the researcher's biases and thoughts.

qualitative research questions are open-ended, general questions that the researcher would like answered during the study.

qualitative scientific structure of a research report includes detailed procedures of inquiry and follows a traditional form for reporting research to include the introduction, the procedures, the findings, and a discussion.

qualitative storytelling structure is a flexible approach to writing a qualitative report. The meaning of the study unfolds through descriptions, an author's reflection on the meaning of the data, a larger understanding of the phenomenon, and a return to the author's stance on the topic.

quantitative purpose statement identifies the variables, their relationship, and the participants and site for research.

quantitative research is an inquiry approach useful for describing trends and explaining the relationship among variables found in the literature. To conduct this inquiry, the investigator specifies narrow questions, locates or develops instruments to gather data to answer the questions, and analyzes numbers from the instruments, using statistics. From the results of these analyses, the researcher interprets the data using prior predictions and research studies. The final report, presented in a standard format, displays researcher objectivity and lack of bias.

quasi-experiments are experimental situations in which the researcher assigns, but not randomly, participants to groups because the experimenter cannot artificially create groups for the experiment.

questionnaires are forms used in a survey design that participants in a study complete and return to the researcher. Participants mark answers to questions and supply basic personal or demographic information about themselves.

random assignment is the process of assigning individuals at random to groups or to different conditions of a group in an experiment. It is a characteristic of a true experiment in research.

random selection is the process of selecting individuals so each individual has an equal chance of being selected.

range of scores is the difference between the highest and the lowest scores for items on an instrument.

ratio (or true zero) scale is a response scale in which participants check a response option with a true zero and equal distances between units.

realist ethnography is a type of ethnographic design in which the researcher provides an objective account of the situation, typically written in the third-person point of view, reporting on the information learned from participants at a field site.

reflective fieldnotes record personal thoughts that researchers have that relate to their insights, hunches, or broad ideas or themes that emerge during an observation.

reflexivity means that the researchers reflect on their own biases, values, and assumptions and actively write them into their research.

reflexivity in ethnography means that the researcher is aware of and openly discusses his or her role in a study in a way that honors and respects the site and the people being studied.

regression is a potential threat to internal validity in an experiment in which the researchers select individuals for a group based on extreme scores, and because they will naturally do better (or worse) on a posttest than on the pretest regardless of the treatment, they will threaten the validity of the outcomes.

regression line in correlation research is a line of "best fit" for all of the points of scores on a graph. This line comes the closest to all of the points on the plot and it is calculated by drawing a line that minimizes the squared distance of the points from the line.

regression tables show the overall amount of variance explained in a dependent variable by all independent variables, called R^2 (*R* squared).

relationship questions seek to answer the degree and magnitude of the relationship between two or more variables. These questions often relate different types of variables in a study, such as independent variables to independent variables or dependent variables to control variables.

reliability means that individual scores from an instrument should be nearly the same or stable on repeated administrations of the instrument and that they should be free from sources of measurement error and consistent.

repeated measures design is an experimental design in which all participants in a single group participate in all experimental treatments. Each group becomes its own control. The researcher compares a group's performance under one experimental treatment with their performance under another experimental treatment.

reporting research involves deciding on audiences, structuring the report in a format acceptable to these audiences, and then writing the report in a manner that is sensitive to all readers.

representative refers to the selection of individuals from a sample of a population such that the individuals selected are typical of the population under study, enabling the researcher to draw conclusions from the sample about the population as a whole.

research is a cyclical process of steps that typically begins with identifying a research problem or issue of study. It then involves reviewing the literature, specifying a purpose for the study, collecting and analyzing data, and forming an interpretation of the information. This process culminates in a report, disseminated to audiences, that is evaluated and used in the educational community.

research designs are procedures for collecting, analyzing, and reporting research in quantitative and qualitative research.

research objective is a statement of intent for the study that declares specific goals that the investigator plans to achieve in a study.

research problems are the educational issues, controversies, or concerns studied by researchers.

research questions are interrogative statements that narrow the purpose statement to specific questions that researchers seek to answer in their studies.

research report is a study that reports an investigation or exploration of a problem; identifies questions to be addressed; and includes data collected, analyzed, and interpreted by the researcher.

research-based research problems are problems that need further research because a gap in the research exists or because the research needs to be extended into other areas.

resentful demoralization is a potential threat to internal validity when a control group is used and individuals in this group feel resentful and demoralized because they perceive that they receive a less desirable treatment than other groups.

response bias occurs in survey research when the responses do not accurately reflect the views of the sample and the population.

response return rate is the percentage of questionnaires that are returned from the participants to the researcher.

restorying is the process in which the researcher gathers stories, analyzes them for key elements of the story (e.g., time, place, plot, and scene), and then rewrites the story to place it in a chronological sequence.

reviewing the literature means locating summaries, books, journals, and indexed publications on a topic; selectively choosing which literature is relevant; and then writing a report that summarizes that literature.

reviews and syntheses provide summaries on various topics.

sample is a subgroup of the target population that the researcher plans to study for the purpose of making generalizations about the target population.

sample size formulas provide formulas, based on several parameters, that can be used to calculate the size of the sample.

sampling error is the difference between the sample estimate and the true population score.

sampling error formula is a calculation for determining the size of a sample based on the chance (or proportion) that the sample will be evenly divided on a question, sampling error, and a confidence interval.

saturation in qualitative research is a state in which the researcher makes the subjective determination that new data will not provide any new information or insights for the developing categories.

scales of measurement are response options to questions that measure (or observe) variables in nominal, ordinal, or interval/ratio units.

scatterplot (or scatter diagram) is a pictorial image of two sets of scores for participants on a graph.

scoring means that the researcher assigns a numeric score (or value) to each response category for each question on the instruments used to collect data.

scoring data means that the researcher assigns a numeric score (or value) to each response category for each question on the instruments used to collect data.

secondary source literature summarizes primary sources, and it does not represent material published by the original researchers or the creators of the idea.

selection is a potential threat to internal validity in an experiment in which "people factors" may introduce threats that influence the outcome, such as selecting individuals who are brighter, more receptive to a treatment, or more familiar with a treatment.

selective coding is the process in which the grounded theorist writes a theory based on the interrelationship of the categories in the axial coding model.

semi-closed-ended questions in a survey consist of questions that include both closed-ended and open-ended questions.

sequence in mixed methods designs means that the researcher collects data using concurrent or sequential procedures.
setting in narrative research may be friends, family, workplace, home, social organization, or school—the place in which a story physically occurs.
shared pattern in ethnography is a common social interaction that stabilizes, as tacit, rules and expectations of the group (Spindler & Spindler, 1992).
sharing reports in action research means that the inquirer shares the action research study locally with individuals who can promote change or enact plans within their classroom or building. Action researchers share results with teachers, the building principal, school district personnel, and parent associations (e.g., Hughes, 1999).
significance (or alpha) level is a probability level that reflects the maximum risk you are willing to take that any observed differences are due to chance. It is called the *alpha level* and is typically set at .01 (1 out of 100 times the sample statistic fall will be due to chance) or .05 (5 out of 100 times it will be due to chance).
simple random sampling is a quantitative sampling procedure in which the researcher selects participants (or units, such as schools) for the sample so that any sample of size N has an equal probability of being selected from the population. The intent of simple random sampling is to choose units to be sampled that will be representative of the population.
single-item scores are individual scores to each question for each participant in your study.
single-subject research (also called *N = 1 research, behavior analysis,* or *within-subjects research*) involves the study of single individuals, their observation over a baseline period, and the administration of an intervention. This is followed by another observation after the intervention to determine if the treatment affects the outcome.
skewed distribution is a distribution of scores that tends to pile up toward one end of the scale and taper off slowly at the other end (Gravetter & Wallnau, 2000).
snowball quantitative sampling is a sampling procedure in which the researcher asks participants to identify other participants to become members of the sample.
snowball qualitative sampling is a form of qualitative purposeful sampling that typically proceeds after a study begins in which the researcher asks participants to recommend individuals to study.
Spearman–Brown formula is a formula for calculating the reliability of scores using all questions on an instrument. Because the split half test relies on information from only half of the test, a modification in this procedure is to use this formula to estimate full-length test reliability.
Spearman rho (r_s) is the correlation statistic used for nonlinear data when the data are measured on ordinal scales (rank-ordered scales).
standard deviation (*SD*) is the square root of the variance.
standard scores are calculated scores that enable a researcher to compare scores from different scales.
statement of the problem is a section in a research report that contains the topic for the study, the research problem within this topic, a justification for the problem based on past research and practice, deficiencies or shortcomings of past research or practical knowledge, and the importance of addressing the problem for diverse audiences.
statistical indexes report trends that are useful for research.
statistical significance is when the observed values (e.g., before and after a treatment in an experiment, the difference between mean scores for two or more groups or the relationship between two variables) provide a statistical value (p value) that exceeds the predetermined alpha level set by the researcher.
statistics are the numbers derived from formulas to measure aspects of a set of data.
story in narrative research is a first-person oral telling or retelling of events related to the personal or social experiences of an individual. Often these stories have a beginning, a middle, and an end.
stratified sampling is a quantitative sampling procedure in which researchers stratify the population on some specific characteristic (e.g., gender) and then sample, using simple random sampling, from each stratum of the population.
study-by-study review of the literature is a detailed summary of each study grouped under a broad theme.
style manuals provide a structure for citing references, labeling headings, and constructing tables and figures for a scholarly research report.
subquestions in qualitative research refine the central question into subtopics or indicate the processes to be used in research. These subquestions contain the same elements as in central questions (e.g., they are open ended, emerging, neutral in language, and few in number), but they provide greater specificity to the questions in the study. They are of two types: issue and procedural subquestions.
summaries provide overviews of the literature and research on timely issues in education.
summed scores are scores of an individual added over several questions that measure the same variable.
survey research designs are procedures in quantitative research in which investigators administer a survey or questionnaire to a sample or to the entire population of people to describe the attitudes, opinions, behaviors, or characteristics of the population.
systematic design in grounded theory emphasizes the use of data analysis steps of open, axial, and selective coding, and the development of a logic paradigm or a visual picture of the theory generated.
systematic sampling is a quantitative sampling procedure in which the researcher chooses every "*n*th" individual or site in the population until the desired sample size is achieved.

tables are summaries of quantitative data organized into rows and columns.

target population (sometimes called the *sampling frame*) is a group of individuals with some common defining characteristic that the researcher can identify with a list or set of names.

teachers' stories are narrative research, personal accounts by teachers of their own personal classroom experiences.

telephone interview surveys are interviews in which the researcher records comments by participants to questions on instruments over the telephone.

telephone interviews are used to gather data using the telephone and asking a small number of general questions.

testing is a potential threat to validity in an experiment when participants become familiar with the outcome measures and remember responses for later testing.

test–retest reliability examines the extent to which scores from one sample are stable over time from one test administration to another.

text segments are sentences or paragraphs that all relate to a single code in qualitative research.

thematic data analysis in ethnography consists of distilling how things work and naming the essential features in these in the cultural setting.

thematic review of the literature includes a theme and supporting literature found by the researcher to document the theme.

themes in qualitative research are similar codes aggregated together to form a major idea in the database.

theoretical lens in narrative research is a guiding perspective or ideology that provides a structure for advocating for groups or individuals and writing the report.

theoretical propositions in grounded theory research are statements indicating the relationship among categories, such as in the systematic approach to axial coding that includes causal conditions, the core category or phenomenon, the context, intervening conditions, strategies, and consequences.

theoretical sampling in grounded theory means that the researcher chooses forms of data collection that will yield text and images useful in generating a theory.

theory or concept sampling is a purposeful sampling strategy in which individuals or sites are sampled because they can help the researcher generate or discover a theory or specific concept within the theory.

theory in grounded theory research is an abstract explanation or understanding of a process about a substantive topic "grounded" in the data. The theory is "middle-range" (Charmaz, 2000), drawn from multiple individuals or data sources that provide an explanation for a substantive topic.

theory in quantitative research explains and predicts the relationship between independent and dependent variables. They are called the *outcome, effect, criterion,* or *consequence variables.*

threats to external validity are problems in experiments that threaten drawing correct inferences from the sample data to persons, settings, and past and future situations.

threats to internal validity are potential problems that threaten drawing correct inferences that arise because of the experimental procedures or the experiences of participants.

threats to validity refer to statistical and design issues that may threaten the experiment so that the conclusions reached from data may provide a false reading about probable causality—the relationship between the treatment and the outcome.

time series is an experimental design consisting of studying one group, over time, with multiple pretest and posttest measures or observations made by the researcher.

transcription is the process of converting audiotape recordings or fieldnotes into text data.

treatment variable is an independent variable that the researcher manipulates to determine the effect it will have on an outcome. It is always a categorically scored variable measuring two or more groups or levels.

trend studies are longitudinal survey designs that involve identifying a population and examining changes within that population over time.

triangulation is the process of corroborating evidence from different individuals (e.g., a principal and a student), types of data (e.g., observational fieldnotes and interviews), or methods of data collection (e.g., documents and interviews) in descriptions and themes in qualitative research.

triangulation mixed methods design consists of simultaneously collecting both quantitative and qualitative data, merging the data, and using the results to best understand a research problem.

true experiments are experimental situations in which the researcher randomly assigns participants to different conditions (or levels) of the experimental variable.

two-tailed tests of significance are when the critical region for rejection of the null hypothesis is divided into two areas at the ends of the sampling distribution (Vogt, 1999).

type I error occurs when the null hypothesis is rejected by the researcher when it is actually true. The probability of this error rate is "alpha."

type II error occurs when the researcher fails to reject the null hypothesis when an effect actually occurs in the population. The probability of this error rate is called "beta."

typical sampling is a form of purposeful sampling in which the researcher studies a person or site that is "typical" to those unfamiliar with the situation.

uncorrelated relationship of scores means that the scores in the distribution are independent of each other.

unit of analysis refers to the unit (e.g., individual, family, school, school district) the researcher uses to gather the data.

validating findings in qualitative research means that the researcher determines the accuracy or credibility of the findings through strategies such as member checking or triangulation.

validity means that researchers can draw meaningful and justifiable inferences from scores about a sample or population.

values are scores assigned to response options for questions.

variable is a characteristic or attribute of an individual or an organization that can be (a) measured or observed by the researcher and that (b) varies among individuals or organizations studied.

variables measured in categories are variables measured by the researcher as a small number of groups or categories.

variables measured as continuous are variables measured by the researcher on a point along a continuum of scores, from low to high.

variance means that scores will assume different values depending on the type of variable being measured.

visualization in mixed methods research consists of a figure or drawing displaying the procedures of a study.

wave analysis is a survey research procedure to check for response bias in which investigators group returns by intervals (e.g., by week) and check to see if the answers to a few select questions change from the first week to the final week in a study.

weight or priority in mixed methods designs means that the researcher places more emphasis on one type of data than another in the research and the written report.

within-group experimental design is an experiment design in which the researcher studies only one group of individuals, such as time series or repeated measure designs.

within-individual design is an experimental design in which the researcher studies single individuals, such as single-subject designs.

within-text references are references cited in a brief format within the body of the text to provide credit to authors.

***z* scores** have a mean of 0 and a standard deviation of 1 and enable the researcher to compare scores from one instrument to scores from another instrument.

References

Abel, M., & Sewell, J. (1999). Stress and burnout in rural and urban secondary school teachers. *Journal of Educational Research, 92,* 287–293.

Abelson, R. P. (1995). *Statistics as principled argument.* Hillsdale, NJ: Erlbaum.

Agar, M. H. (1980). *The professional stranger: An informal introduction to ethnography.* San Diego, CA: Academic Press.

Alkin, M. C. (Ed.). (1992). *Encyclopedia of educational research* (6th ed.). New York: Macmillan.

Allen, L., & Calhoun, E. F. (1998). Schoolwide action research: Findings from six years of study. *Phi Delta Kappan, 79*(9), 706–710.

American Anthropological Association. (1998). *Code of ethics of the American Anthropological Association.* Arlington, VA: Author.

American Educational Research Association. (1999). American Educational Research Association 2000 Annual Meeting call for proposals. *Educational Research, 28,* 33.

American Educational Research Association, American Psychological Association, National Council on Measurement in Education. (1999). *Standards for educational and psychological testing.* Washington, DC: American Educational Research Association.

American Psychological Association. (1927–). *Psychological abstracts.* Washington, DC: Author.

American Psychological Association. (2001). *Publication manual of the American Psychological Association* (5th ed.). Washington, DC: Author.

American Psychological Association. (2003). *Ethical principles of psychologists and code of conduct.* Washington, DC: Author.

Anderson, E. S., & Keith, T. Z. (1997). A longitudinal test of a model of academic success for at-risk high school students. *Journal of Educational Research, 90,* 259–266.

Angrosino, M. V. (1989). *Documents of interaction: Biography, autobiography, and life history in social science perspective.* Gainesville: University of Florida Press.

Annual review of psychology. (1950–). Stanford, CA: Annual Reviews.

Asmussen, K. J., & Creswell, J. W. (1995). Campus response to a student gunman. *Journal of Higher Education, 66,* 575–591.

Atweh, B., Kemmis, S., & Weeks, P. (1998). *Action research in practice: Partnerships for social justice in education.* London and New York: Routledge.

Babbie, E. (1990). *Survey research methods.* Belmont, CA: Wadsworth.

Babbie, E. (1998). *The practice of social research* (8th ed.). Belmont, CA: Wadsworth.

Babbie, E. (2003). *The practice of social research* (9th ed.). Belmont, CA: Wadsworth.

Babchuk, W. A. (1996). *Glaser or Strauss?: Grounded theory and adult education.* Paper presented at the Midwest Research-to-Practice Conference in Adult, Continuing and Community Education, University of Nebraska–Lincoln.

Babchuk, W. A. (1997). *The rediscovery of grounded theory: Strategies for qualitative research in adult education.* Unpublished doctoral dissertation, University of Nebraska–Lincoln.

Baker, R. W., & Siryk, B. (1989). *Student adaptation to college questionnaire (SACQ).* Los Angeles: Western Psychological Services.

Banks, J. A., & Banks, C. A. (1995). *Handbook of research on multicultural education.* New York: Macmillan.

Barzun, J., & Graff, H. G. (1985). *The modern researcher* (4th ed.). New York: Harcourt Brace & World.

Batsche, C., Hernandez, M., & Montenegro, M. C. (1999). Community needs assessment with Hispanic, Spanish-monolingual residents. *Evaluation and Program Planning, 22,* 13–20.

Bauermeister, M. L. (1998). *The child of the mist: Enculturation in a New Zealand Kohanga Reo.* Unpublished doctoral dissertation, University of Nebraska–Lincoln.

Bausell, R. B. (1994). *Conducting meaningful experiments.* Thousand Oaks, CA: Sage.

Bazeley, P. (2000). *Mixed methods data analysis using NUD*IST/Nvivo with table based software and/or a statistics program.* Paper presented at the American Educational Research Association Annual Meeting, New Orleans, LA.

Becker, P. H. (1993). Common pitfalls in published grounded theory research. *Qualitative Health Research, 3,* 254–260.

Benson, J., & Clark, F. (1983). A guide for instrument development and validation. *The American Journal of Occupational Therapy, 36,* 790–801.

Bickman, L., & Rog, D. J. (2000). (Eds.). *Handbook of applied social research methods.* Thousand Oaks, CA: Sage.

Blaikie, N. (2003). *Analysing quantitative data: From description to explanation.* London: Sage.

Blustein, D. L., Phillips, S. D., Jobin-David, K., Finkelberg, S. L., & Roarke, A. E. (1997). A theory-building investigation of the school-to-work transition. *The Counseling Psychologist, 25,* 364–402.

Bogdan, R. C., & Biklen, S. K. (1982). *Qualitative research for education: An introduction to theory and methods.* Boston: Allyn & Bacon.

Bogdan, R. C., & Biklen, S. K. (1998). *Qualitative research for education: An introduction to theory and methods* (3rd ed.). Boston: Allyn & Bacon.

Boruch, R. F. (1998). Randomized controlled experiments for evaluation and planning. In L. Bickman & D. J. Rog (Eds.), *Handbook of applied social research methods* (pp. 161–191). Thousand Oaks, CA: Sage.

Bracht, G. H., & Glass, G. V. (1968). The external validity of experiments. *American Educational Research Journal, 4,* 73–81.

Brewer, J., & Hunter, A. (1989). *Multimethod research: A synthesis of styles.* Newbury Park, CA: Sage.

Brickhouse, N., & Bodner, G. M. (1992). The beginning science teacher: Classroom narratives of convictions and constraints. *Journal of Research in Science Teaching, 29,* 471–485.

Bring, J. (1994). How to standardize regression coefficients. *The American Statistician, 48*(3), 209–213.

Brown, M. L. (1993). *Ethnic minority student's process of community building on a predominantly white campus.* Unpublished doctoral dissertation, University of Nebraska–Lincoln.

Brown, R. (1998). *Theory about the process of community-building in distance learning courses.* Unpublished dissertation proposal, University of Nebraska–Lincoln.

Brown, S. P., Parham, T. A., & Yonker, R. (1996). Influence of a cross-cultural training course on racial identity attitudes of white women and men: Preliminary perspectives. *Journal of Counseling & Development, 74*(5), 510–516.

Bryman, A. (1988). *Quantity and quality in social science research.* London and New York: Routledge.

Budnitz, J. (2000). Flush. In M. Cunningham, P. Houston, & G. Saunders (Eds.), *Prize stories 2000.* New York: Random House.

Calhoun, E. F. (1994). *How to use action research in the self-renewing school.* Alexandria, VA: Association for Supervision and Curriculum Development.

Campbell, D. T., & Fiske, D. W. (1959). Convergent and discriminant validation by the multitrait–multimethod matrix. *Psychological Bulletin, 56,* 81–105.

Campbell, D. T., & Stanley, J. C. (1963). Experimental and quasi-experimental designs for research. In N. L. Gage (Ed.), *Handbook on research in teaching* (pp. 1–80). Chicago: Rand-McNally.

Campbell, W. G., Ballou, S. V., & Slade, C. (1990). *Form and style: Theses, reports, and term papers* (8th ed.). Boston: Houghton Mifflin.

Caracelli, V. J., & Greene, J. C. (1993). Data analysis strategies for mixed-method evaluation designs. *Educational Evaluation and Policy Analysis, 15*(2), 195–207.

Carspecken, P. F. (1995). *Critical ethnography in educational research: A theoretical and practical guide.* London: Routledge.

Carspecken, P. F., & Apple, M. (1992). Critical qualitative research: Theory, methodology, and practice. In M. D. LeCompte, W. L. Millroy, & J. Preissle (Eds.), *The handbook of qualitative research in education* (pp. 507–553). San Diego: Academic Press.

Carter, K. (1993). The place of a story in the study of teaching and teacher education. *Educational Researcher, 22*(1), 5–12, 18.

Casey, K. (1995/1996). The new narrative research in education. *Review of Research in Education, 21,* 211–253.

Ceprano, M. A., & Garan, E. M. (1998). Emerging voices in a university pen-pal project: Layers of discovery in action research. *Reading Research and Instruction, 38*(1), 31–56.

Charmaz, K. (1990). "Discovering" chronic illness: Using grounded theory. *Social Science Medicine, 30,* 1161–1172.

Charmaz, K. (1994). Identity dilemmas of chronically ill men. *The Sociological Quarterly, 35,* 269–288.

Charmaz, K. (2000). Grounded theory: Objectivist and constructivist methods. In N. K. Denzin & Y. S. Lincoln (Eds.), *Handbook of qualitative research* (2nd ed., pp. 509–535). Thousand Oaks, CA: Sage.

Charmaz, K. (2006). *Constructing grounded theory.* London: Sage.

Clandinin, D. J., & Connelly, F. M. (2000). *Narrative inquiry: Experience and story in qualitative research.* San Francisco: Jossey-Bass.

Clifford, J., & Marcus, G. E. (Eds.). (1986). *Writing culture.* Berkeley: University of California Press.

Cocklin, B. (1996). Applying qualitative research to adult education: Reflections upon analytic processes. *Studies in the Education of Adults, 28,* 88–116.

Cohen, J. (1977). *Statistical power analysis for the behavioral sciences* (rev. ed.). New York: Academic Press.

Cohen, L., & Manion, L. (1994). *Research methods in education* (4th ed.). London and New York: Routledge.

Congressional Information Service. (1973–). *American statistics index.* Washington, DC: Author.

Connelly, F. M., & Clandinin, D. J. (1988). *Teachers as curriculum planners: Narratives of experience.* New York: Teachers College Press.

Connelly, F. M., & Clandinin, D. J. (1990). Stories of experience and narrative inquiry. *Educational Researcher, 19*(5), 2–14.

Connelly, F. M., Dukacz, A. S., & Quinlan, F. (1980). *Curriculum planning for the classroom.* Toronto, Canada: OISE Press.

Cook, T. D., & Campbell, D. T. (1979). *Quasi-experimentation: Design and analysis issues for field settings.* Boston: Houghton Mifflin.

Cooper, H. (1984). *The integrated research review: A systematic approach.* Beverly Hills, CA: Sage.

Cooper, H. M., & Lindsay, J. J. (1998). Research synthesis and meta-analysis. In L. Bickman & D. J. Rog (Eds.), *Handbook of applied social research methods* (pp. 315–337). Thousand Oaks, CA: Sage.

Cooper, J. O., Heron, T. E., & Heward, W. L. (1987). *Applied behavior analysis.* Columbus, OH: Merrill/Prentice Hall.

Cortazzi, M. (1993). *Narrative analysis.* London: Falmer Press.

Courtney, S., Jha, L. R., & Babchuk, W. A. (1994). Like school?: A grounded theory of life in an ABE/GED classroom. *Adult Basic Education, 4,* 172–195.

Cowles, M. (1989). *Statistics in psychology: A historical perspective.* Hillsdale, NJ: Erlbaum.

Creswell, J. W. (1998). *Qualitative inquiry and research design: Choosing among five traditions.* Thousand Oaks, CA: Sage.

Creswell, J. W. (1999). Mixed-method research: Introduction and application. In G. J. Cizek (Ed.), *Handbook of educational policy* (pp. 455–472). San Diego: Academic Press.

Creswell, J. W. (2003). *Research design: Qualitative, quantitative, and mixed methods approaches* (2nd ed.). Thousand Oaks, CA: Sage.

Creswell, J. W. (2007). *Qualitative inquiry and research design: Choosing among five approaches* (2nd ed.). Thousand Oaks, CA: Sage.

Creswell, J. W., & Brown, M. L. (1992). How chairpersons enhance faculty research: A grounded theory study. *The Review of Higher Education, 16*(1), 41–62.

Creswell, J. W., Goodchild, L. F., & Turner, P. (1996). Integrated qualitative and quantitative research: Epistemology, history, and designs. In J. Smart (Ed.), *Higher education: Handbook of theory and research* (Vol. XI, pp. 455–471). New York: Agathon Press.

Creswell, J. W., & Maietta, R. C. (2002). Qualitative research. In D. C. Miller & N. J. Salkind (Eds.), *Handbook of social research* (pp. 143–184). Thousand Oaks, CA: Sage.

Creswell, J. W., & Miller, D. M. (2000). Determining validity in qualitative inquiry. *Theory into Practice XXXIX*(3), 124–130.

Creswell, J. W., & Plano Clark, V. L. (2007). *Designing and conducting mixed methods research*. Thousand Oaks, CA: Sage.

Creswell, J. W., Tashakkori, A., Jensen, K., & Shapley, K. (2003). Teaching mixed methods research: Practice, dilemmas and challenges. In A. Tashakkori & C. Teddlie (Eds.), *Handbook of mixed methods in the behavioral and social sciences*. Thousand Oaks, CA: Sage.

Creswell, J. W., Wheeler, D. W., Seagren, A. T., Egly, N. J., & Beyer, K. D. (1990). *The academic chairperson's handbook*. Lincoln and London: University of Nebraska Press.

Cronbach, L. J. (1984). *Essentials of psychological testing* (4th ed.). New York: Harper & Row.

Csikszentmihalyi, M., Rathunde, K., Whalen, S., & Wong, M. (1993). *Talented teenagers: The roots of success and failure*. New York: Cambridge University Press.

Dahmus, S., Bernardin, H. J., & Bernardin, K. (1992). Test review: Student adaptation to college questionnaire. *Measurement and evaluation in counseling and development, 25,* 139–142.

Datta, L. (1994). Paradigm wars: A basis for peaceful coexistence and beyond. In C. S. Reichardt & S. F. Rallis (Eds.), *The qualitative-quantitative debate: New perspectives* (New Directions for Program Evaluation, No. 61, pp. 53–70). San Francisco: Jossey-Bass.

Davis, T. C., Arnold, C., Nandy, I., Bocchini, J. A., Gottlief, A., George, R., et al. (1997). Tobacco use among male high school athletes. *Journal of Adolescent Health, 21,* 97–101.

De Landsheere, G. (1988). History of educational research. In J. P. Keeves (Ed.), *Educational research, methodology, and measurement: An international handbook* (pp. 9–16). Oxford: Pergamon Press.

Degh, L. (1995). *Narratives in society: A performer-centered study of narration*. Helsinki, Norway: Suomalainen Tiedeakatemia, Academia Scientiarum Fennica.

Delgado, R., & Stefancic, J. (Eds.). (1997). *Critical white studies: Looking behind the mirror*. Philadelphia: Temple University Press.

Denzin, N. (1989). *Interpretative biography*. Newbury Park, CA: Sage.

Denzin, N. K. (1997). *Interpretive ethnography: Ethnographic practices for the 21st century*. Thousand Oaks, CA: Sage.

Denzin, N. K., & Lincoln, Y. S. (1994). Introduction: Entering the field of qualitative research. In N. K. Denzin & Y. S. Lincoln (Eds.), *Handbook of qualitative research* (pp. 1–17). Thousand Oaks, CA: Sage.

Denzin, N. K., & Lincoln, Y. S. (Eds.). (2005). *The Sage handbook of qualitative research* (3rd ed.). Thousand Oaks, CA: Sage.

Deslandes, R., & Bertrand, R. (2005). Motivation of parent involvement in secondary-level schooling. *The Journal of Educational Research, 98*(33), 164–175.

Dey, E. L., & Hurtado, S. (1996). Faculty attitudes toward regulating speech on college campuses. *The Review of Higher Education, 20,* 15–32.

Dey, I. (1993). *Qualitative data analysis: A user-friendly guide for social scientists*. London: Routledge.

Dicker, M. (1990). Using action research to navigate an unfamiliar teaching assignment. *Theory into Practice, XXIX,* 203–208.

Dillman, D. A. (2007). *Mail and internet surveys (electronic resource): The tailored design method*. Hoboken, NJ: Wiley.

Dods, R. F. (1997). An action research study of the effectiveness of problem-based learning in promoting the acquisition and retention of knowledge. *Journal for the Education of the Gifted, 20*(4), 423–437.

Educational Resources Information Center (U.S.). (1966–). *Resources in education*. Washington, DC: Author.

Educational Resources Information Center (U.S.). (1969–). *Current index to journals in education*. New York: Macmillan.

Educational Resources Information Center (U.S.). (1991). *ERIC directory of education-related information centers*. Washington, DC: Author.

Ehrlich, E., Flexner, S. B., Carruth, G., & Hawkins, J. M. (1980). *Oxford American dictionary*. New York and Oxford: Oxford University Press.

Elbaz-Luwisch, F. (1997). Narrative research: Political issues and implications. *Teaching and Teacher Education, 13*(1), 75–83.

Emerson, R. M., Fretz, R. I., & Shaw, L. L. (1995). *Writing ethnographic fieldnotes*. Chicago: University of Chicago Press.

Epper, R. M. (1997). Coordination and competition in postsecondary distance education. *Journal of Higher Education, 68*(5), 551–587.

Errante, A. (2000). But sometimes you're not part of the story: Oral histories and ways of remembering and telling. *Educational Researcher, 29,* 16–27.

Feen-Calligan, H. (1999). Enlightenment in chemical dependency treatment programs: A grounded theory. In C. A. Malchiodi (Ed.), *Medical art therapy with adults* (pp. 147–161). London: Jessica Kingsley.

Ferguson, C. D., & Bunge, C. A. (1997, May). The shape of services to come: Values-based reference service for the largely digital library. *College and Research Libraries, 58*(3), 252–265.

Fetterman, D. M. (1998). *Ethnography: Step by step* (2nd ed.). Thousand Oaks, CA: Sage.

Finch, S., Cumming, G., & Thomason, N. (2001). Reporting of statistical inference in the *Journal of Applied Psychology:* Little evidence of reform. *Educational and Psychological Measurement, 61*(1), 181–210.

Finders, M. J. (1996). Queens and teen zines: Early adolescent females reading their way toward adulthood. *Anthropology and Education Quarterly, 27,* 71–89.

Fink, A. (1995). *The survey handbook*. Thousand Oaks, CA: Sage.

Fink, A., & Kosekoff, J. (1985). *How to conduct surveys: A step-by-step guide*. Newbury Park, CA: Sage.

Firestone, W. A. (1987). Meaning in method: The rhetoric of quantitative and qualitative research. *Educational Researcher, 16*(7), 16–21.

Fisher, R. A. (1935). *The design of experiments*. London: Oliver & Boyd.

Fisher, R. A. (1936). *Statistical methods for research workers*. London: Oliver & Boyd.

Fowler, F. J. (1988). *Survey research methods* (2nd ed.). Newbury Park, CA: Sage.

Fraenkel, J. R., & Wallen, N. E. (2000). *How to design and evaluate research in education* (4th ed.). Boston: McGraw-Hill.

Frontman, K. C., & Kunkel, M. A. (1994). A grounded theory of counselors' construal of success in the initial session. *Journal of Counseling Psychology, 41,* 492–499.

Gall, M. D., Borg, W. R., & Gall, J. P. (1996). *Educational research* (6th ed.). White Plains, NY: Longman.

Gallik, J. D. (1999). Do they read for pleasure? Recreational reading habits of college students. *Journal of Adolescent and Adult Literacy, 42,* 480–488.

Garland, M. (1993). Ethnography penetrates the "I didn't have time" rationale to elucidate higher order reasons for distance education withdrawal. *Research in Distance Education, 5,* 6–10.

Gay, L. R., & Airasian, P. (2003). *Educational research: Competencies for analysis and application* (7th ed.). Upper Saddle River, NJ: Merrill/Prentice Hall.

George, D., & Mallery, P. (2001). *SPSS for Windows: Step by step. A simple guide and reference 10.0 update.* Boston: Allyn & Bacon.

Gettinger, M. (1993). Effects of error correction on third graders' spelling. *Journal of Educational Research, 87,* 39–45.

Glaser, B. G. (1978). *Theoretical sensitivity.* Mill Valley, CA: Sociology Press.

Glaser, B. G. (1992). *Basics of grounded theory analysis.* Mill Valley, CA: Sociology Press.

Glaser, B., & Strauss, A. (1967). *The discovery of grounded theory.* Chicago: Aldine.

Glesne, C., & Peshkin, A. (1992). *Becoming qualitative researchers: An introduction.* White Plains, NY: Longman.

Goldberg, N. (2000). *Thunder and lightning: Cracking open the writer's craft.* New York: Bantam Books.

Goodman, J., & Adler, S. (1985). Becoming an elementary social studies teacher: A study of perspectives. *Theory and Research in Social Education, 15,* 1–20.

Gravetter, F. J., & Wallnau, L. B. (2000). *Statistics for the behavioral science* (5th ed.). Belmont, CA: Wadsworth/Thomson Learning.

Gravetter, F. J., & Wallnau, L. B. (2007). *Statistics for the behavioral sciences* (7th ed.). Belmont, CA: Thomson Learning.

Greene, J. C., & Caracelli, V. J. (Eds.). (1997). *Advances in mixed-method evaluation: The challenges and benefits of integrating diverse paradigms* (New Directions for Evaluation, No. 74). San Francisco: Jossey-Bass.

Greene, J. C., Caracelli, V. J., & Graham, W. F. (1989). Toward a conceptual framework for mixed-method evaluation designs. *Educational Evaluation and Policy Analysis, 11*(3), 255–274.

Guba, E. G. (1978). *Toward a methodology of naturalistic inquiry in educational evaluation* (Monograph 8). Los Angeles: UCLA Center for the Study of Evaluation.

Guba, E. G., & Lincoln, Y. S. (1988). Do inquiry paradigms imply inquiry methodologies? In D. M. Fetterman (Ed.), *Qualitative approaches to evaluation in education* (pp. 89–115). New York: Praeger.

Gudmundsdottir, S. (1997). Introduction to the theme issue of "narrative perspectives on teaching and teacher education." *Teaching and Teacher Education, 13*(1), 1–3.

Guthrie, J. T., Wigfield, A., Humenick, N. M., Perencevich, K. C., Taboada, A., & Barbosa, P. (2006). Influences of stimulating tasks on reading motivation and comprehension. *The Journal of Educational Research, 99*(4), 232–245.

Hall, B. W., Ward, A. W., & Comer, C. B. (1988). Published educational research: An empirical study of its quality. *Journal of Educational Research, 81,* 182–189.

Hammersley, M., & Atkinson, P. (1995). *Ethnography: Principles in practice* (2nd ed.). New York: Routledge.

Harrison, A. (2007). *Relationship-building in an undergraduate leadership program in teacher education.* An unpublished doctoral dissertation, University of Nebraska–Lincoln.

Harry, B., Day, M., & Quist, F. (1998). "He can't really play": An ethnographic study of sibling acceptance and interaction. *Journal for the Association of the Severely Handicapped (JASH), 23*(4), 289–299.

Hatch, J. A. (2002). *Doing qualitative research in education settings.* Albany: State University of New York Press.

Haviland, W. A. (1993). *Cultural anthropology* (7th ed.). Forth Worth, TX: Harcourt Brace.

Hesse-Bieber, S. N., & Leavy, P. (2006). *The practice of qualitative research.* Thousand Oaks, CA: Sage.

Holland, T. P., Chait, R. P., & Taylor, B. E. (1989). Board effectiveness: Identifying and measuring trustee competencies. *Research in Higher Education, 30,* 435–453.

Houston, W. R., Haberman, M., & Sikula, J. P. (1990). *Handbook of research on teacher education.* New York: Macmillan.

Houtz, L. (1995). Instructional strategy change and the attitude and achievement of seventh- and eighth-grade science students. *Journal of Research in Science Teaching, 32*(6), 629–648.

Hovater, S. E. (2000). *Preparing culturally responsive teachers through preservice teaching programs.* Unpublished manuscript, University of Nebraska–Lincoln.

Howard, M. C. (1996). *Contemporary cultural anthropology* (5th ed.). New York: HarperCollins College Publishers.

Howe, K. R., & Dougherty, K. C. (1993). Ethics, institutional review boards, and the changing face of educational research. *Educational Researcher, 22,* 16–21.

Huber, J. (1999). Listening to children on the landscape. In F. M. Connelly & D. J. Clandinin (Eds.), *Shaping a professional identity: Stories of educational practice* (pp. 9–19). New York and London: Teachers College Press.

Huber, J., & Whelan, K. (1999). A marginal story as a place of possibility: Negotiating self on the professional knowledge landscape. *Teaching and Teacher Education, 15,* 381–396.

Huberty, C. J. (1993). Historical origins of statistical testing practices: The treatment of Fisher versus Neyman-Pearson views in textbooks. *Journal of Experimental Education, 61,* 317–333.

Hubley, A. M., & Zumbo, B. D. (1996). A dialectic on validity: Where we have been and where we are going. *The Journal of General Psychology, 123,* 207–215.

Hughes, L. (1999). Action research and practical inquiry: How can I meet the needs of the high-ability student within my regular educational classroom? *Journal for the Education of the Gifted, 22,* 282–297.

Husen, T., & Postlethwaite, T. N. (Eds.). (1994). *The international encyclopedia of education* (2nd ed.). Tarrytown, NY: Elsevier Science.

Impara, J. C., & Plake, B. S. (Eds.). (1999). *The thirteenth mental measurements yearbook.* Lincoln: Buros Institute of Mental Measurements, University of Nebraska–Lincoln.

Institute for Scientific Information. (1969–). *Social sciences citation index*. Philadelphia: Author.

Institute for Scientific Information. (1989–). *Social sciences citation index* (Compact disc ed.). Philadelphia: Author.

Jaccard, J., & Wan, C. K. (1996). *Lisrel approaches to interaction effects in multiple regression*. Thousand Oaks, CA: Sage.

Jamieson, S. (2004). Likert scales: How to (ab)use them. *Medical Education, 38,* 1212–1218.

Jeffries, R. B. (1993). To go or not to go: Rural African-American students' perspective about their education. *Journal of Negro Education, 62*(4), 427–432.

Jick, T. D. (1979). Mixing qualitative and quantitative methods: Triangulation in action. *Administrative Science Quarterly, 24,* 602–611.

Joint Committee on Standards for Educational Evaluation. (1995). *Program evaluation standards*. Kalamazoo: Evaluation Center, Western Michigan University.

Jones, J. (1999). *The process of structuring a community-based curriculum in a rural school setting: A grounded theory study*. Unpublished doctoral dissertation, University of Nebraska–Lincoln.

Josselson, R., & Lieblich, A. (Eds.). (1993). *The narrative study of lives* (Vol. 1). Thousand Oaks, CA: Sage.

Keeves, J. P. (Ed.). (1988). *Educational research, methodology, and measurement: An international handbook*. Oxford: Pergamon.

Kellogg, J. M. (1997). A study of the effectiveness of self-monitoring as a learning strategy for increasing on-task behavior. Unpublished master's thesis, Western Illinois University, Macomb.

Kemmis, S. (1994). Action research. In T. Husen & T. N. Postlethwaite (Eds.), *International encyclopedia of education* (2nd ed., pp. 42–49). Oxford and New York: Pergamon and Elsevier Science.

Kemmis, S., & McTaggart, R. (1988). *The action research planner*. Geelong, Victoria, Australia: Deakin University Press.

Kemmis, S., & McTaggart, R. (2000). Participatory action research. In N. K. Denzin & Y. S. Lincoln (Eds.), *Handbook of qualitative research* (2nd ed., pp. 567–605). Thousand Oaks, CA: Sage.

Kemmis, S., & Wilkinson, M. (1998). Participatory action research and the study of practice. In B. Atweh, S. Kemmis, & P. Weeks (Eds.), *Action research in practice: Partnerships for social justice in education* (pp. 21–36). London and New York: Routledge.

Keppel, G. (1991). *Design and analysis: A researcher's handbook*. Upper Saddle River, NJ: Prentice Hall.

Kerlinger, F. N. (1964). *Foundations of behavioral research*. New York: Holt, Rinehart and Winston.

Kerlinger, F. N. (1972). *Behavioral research: A conceptual approach*. New York: Holt, Rinehart and Winston.

Kessing, F. (1958). *Cultural anthropology: The science of custom*. New York: Rinehart and Company.

Kester, V. M. (1994). Factors that affect African-American students' bonding to middle school. *The Elementary School Journal, 95*(1), 63–73.

Ketner, C. S., Smith, K. E., & Parnell, M. K. (1997). Relationship between teacher theoretical orientation to reading and endorsement of developmentally appropriate practice. *Journal of Educational Research, 90,* 212–220.

Keyes, M. W., Hanley-Maxwell, C., & Capper, C. A. (1999). "Spirituality? It's the core of my leadership": Empowering leadership in an inclusive elementary school. *Educational Administration Quarterly, 35,* 203–237.

Kiger, D. M., & Johnson, J. A. (1997). Marketing the perceptions of a community college's postsecondary enrollment options program. *Community College Journal of Research and Practice, 21,* 687–693.

Kline, R. B. (1998). *Principles and practice of structural equation modeling*. New York: Guilford Press.

Knapp, S. (1995). *Reframing paradox: A grounded theory of career development in HRD*. Unpublished doctoral dissertation, University of Nebraska–Lincoln.

Kos, R. (1991). Persistence of reading disabilities: The voices of four middle school students. *American Educational Research Journal, 28*(4), 875–895.

Kosnik, C. (1996). *The effects of action research on a teacher education community*. Paper presented at the American Educational Research Association Conference, New York.

Kramer, J. J., & Conoley, J. C. (Eds.). (1992). *The eleventh mental measurements yearbook*. Lincoln: Buros Institute of Mental Measurements, University of Nebraska–Lincoln.

Krueger, R. A. (1994). *Focus groups: A practical guide for applied research* (2nd ed.). Thousand Oaks, CA: Sage.

Larson, B. W. (1997). Social studies teachers' conceptions of discussion: A grounded theory study. *Theory and Research in Social Education, 25,* 114–146.

Lather, P. (1991). *Getting smart: Feminist research and pedagogy with/in the postmodern*. New York and London: Routledge.

Laursen, B., Coy, K. C., & Collins, W. A. (1998). Reconsidering changes in parent–child conflict across adolescence. *Child Development, 69*(3), 817–832.

Lawrence-Lightfoot, S., & Davis, J. H. (1997). *The art and science of portraiture*. San Francisco: Jossey-Bass.

LeCompte, M. D., Millroy, W. L., & Preissle, J. (1992). *The handbook of qualitative research in education*. San Diego: Academic Press.

LeCompte, M. D., Preissle, J., & Tesch, R. (1993). *Ethnography and qualitative design in educational research* (2nd ed.). San Diego: Academic Press.

LeCompte, M. D., & Schensul, J. J. (1999). *Designing and conducting ethnographic research* (Ethnographer's Toolkit, No. 1). Walnut Creek, CA: AltaMira.

Leedy, P. D., & Ormrod, J. E. (2001). *Practical research: Planning and design* (7th ed.). Upper Saddle River, NJ: Prentice Hall.

LeTendre, G. K. (1999). Community-building activities in Japanese schools: Alternative paradigms of the democratic school. *Comparative Education Review, 43,* 283–310.

Libutti, P. O., & Blandy, S. G. (1995). *Teaching information retrieval and evaluation skills to education students and practitioners: A casebook of applications*. Chicago: Association of College and Research Libraries.

Lieblich, A., Tuval-Mashiach, R., & Zilber, T. (1998). *Narrative research: Reading, analysis, and interpretation*. Thousand Oaks, CA: Sage.

Lincoln, Y. S. (1995). Emerging criteria for quality in qualitative and interpretive research. *Qualitative Inquiry, 1,* 275–289.

Lincoln, Y. S., & Guba, E. G. (1985). *Naturalistic inquiry*. Newbury Park, CA: Sage.

Lincoln Public Schools. (n.d.) *Guidelines for conducting external research in the Lincoln public schools*. Retrieved November 21, 2006, from http://misc.lps.org.

Lipsey, M. W. (1990). *Design sensitivity: Statistical power for experimental research*. Newbury Park, CA: Sage.

Lipsey, M. W. (1998). Design sensitivity: Statistical power for applied experimental research. In L. Bickman & D. J. Rog (Eds.), *Handbook of applied social research methods* (pp. 39–68). Thousand Oaks, CA: Sage.

Locke, L. F., Spirduso, W. W., & Silverman, S. J. (1999). *Proposals that work: A guide for planning dissertations and grant proposals* (4th ed.). Thousand Oaks, CA: Sage.

Lofland, J., & Lofland, L. H. (1995). *Analyzing social settings: A guide to qualitative observation and analysis* (3rd ed.). Belmont, CA: Wadsworth.

Maggio, R. (1991). *The bias-free word finder: A dictionary of nondiscriminatory language*. Boston: Beacon Press.

Malloy, H. L., & McMurray, P. (1996). Conflict strategies and resolutions: Peer conflict in an integrated early childhood classroom. *Early Childhood Research Quarterly, 11,* 185–206.

Marshall, C., & Rossman, G. B. (1989). *Designing qualitative research*. Newbury Park, CA: Sage.

Marshall, C., & Rossman, G. B. (1999). *Designing qualitative research* (3rd ed.). Thousand Oaks, CA: Sage.

Mastera, G. (1996). *The process of revising general education curricula in three private baccalaureate colleges: A grounded theory study*. Unpublished doctoral dissertation, University of Nebraska–Lincoln.

Maxwell, J. (1996). *Qualitative research design: An interactive approach*. Thousand Oaks, CA: Sage.

McAllister, G., & Irvine, J. J. (2000). Cross cultural competency and multicultural teacher education. *Review of Educational Research, 70*(1), 3–24.

McCall, W. A., & Crabbs, L. M. (1925). *Manual of directions for the Standard test lessons in reading*. New York, N.Y.: [s.n.].

McCarthey, S. J. (1994). Opportunities and risks of writing from personal experience. *Language Arts, 71,* 182–191.

McCaslin, M. L. (1993). *The nature of leadership within rural communities: A grounded theory*. Unpublished dissertation, University of Nebraska–Lincoln.

McEwan, H., & Egan, K. (1995). *Narrative in teaching, learning, and research*. New York: Teachers College Press.

Mead, M. (1928). *Coming of age in Samoa: A psychological study of primitive youth for Western civilization*. New York: Morrow.

Merriam, S. B. (1998). *Qualitative research and case study applications in education*. San Francisco: Jossey-Bass.

Mertens, D. (2005). *Research and evaluation in education and psychology: Integrating diversity with quantitative, qualitative, and mixed methods*. Thousand Oaks, CA: Sage.

Mertler, C. A. (2001). *Lessons learned from the administration of a Web-based survey*. (ERIC Document Reproduction Service No. ED 458278)

Messick, S. (1980). Test validity and the ethics of assessment. *American Psychologist, 35,* 1012–1027.

Metzner, B. (1989). Perceived quality of academic advising: The effect on freshman attrition. *American Educational Research Journal, 26*(3), 422–442.

Meyer, R. C. (1996). *Stories from the heart*. Mahwah, NJ: Erlbaum.

Miles, M. B., & Huberman, A. M. (1984). *Qualitative data analysis: A sourcebook for new methods*. Thousand Oaks, CA: Sage.

Miles, M. B., & Huberman, A. M. (1994). *Qualitative data analysis: A sourcebook for new methods* (2nd ed.). Thousand Oaks, CA: Sage.

Miller, D. L. (1992). *The experiences of a first-year college president: An ethnography*. Unpublished doctoral dissertation, University of Nebraska–Lincoln.

Miller, D. L., Creswell, J. W., & Olander, L. S. (1998). Writing and retelling multiple ethnographic tales of a soup kitchen for the homeless. *Qualitative Inquiry, 4,* 469–491.

Mills, G. E. (2000). *Action research: A guide for the teacher researcher*. Upper Saddle River, NJ: Merrill/Prentice Hall.

Mills, G. E. (2003). *Action research: A guide for the teacher researcher* (2nd ed.). Upper Saddle River, NJ: Merrill/Prentice Hall.

Morgan, D. L. (1998). Practical strategies for combining qualitative and quantitative methods: Applications to health research. *Qualitative Health Research, 3,* 362–376.

Morrison, T. G., Jacobs, J. S., & Swinyard, W. R. (1999). Do teachers who read personally use recommended literacy practices in their classrooms? *Reading Research and Instruction, 38,* 81–100.

Morrow, S. L., & Smith, M. L. (1995). Constructions of survival and coping by women who have survived childhood sexual abuse. *Journal of Counseling Psychology, 42,* 24–33.

Morse, J. M. (1991). Approaches to qualitative-quantitative methodological triangulation. *Nursing Research, 40,* 120–123.

Muffo, J. A. (1986). The impact of faculty research on state and federal policy. In J. W. Creswell (Ed.), *Measuring faculty research performance* (New Directions for Institutional Research, No. 50, pp. 75–85). San Francisco: Jossey-Bass.

Murphy, K. R., & Myors, B. (1998). *Statistical power analysis: A simple and general model for traditional and modern hypothesis tests*. Mahwah, NJ: Erlbaum.

Murphy, L. L., Impara, J. C., & Plake, B. S. (Eds.). (1999). *Tests in print V*. Lincoln: Buros Institute of Mental Measurements, University of Nebraska–Lincoln.

National Center for Educational Statistics. (1997). *Digest of educational statistics 1997*. Washington, DC: U.S. Department of Education, Office of Educational Research and Improvement.

Neff, J. M. (1998). From a distance: Teaching writing on interactive television. *Research in the Teaching of English, 33,* 146–157.

Nelson, L. W. (1990). Code-switching in the oral life narratives of African-American women: Challenges to linguistic hegemony. *Journal of Education, 172*(3), 142–155.

Nesbary, D. K. (2000). *Survey research and the World Wide Web*. Boston: Allyn & Bacon.

Neuman, S. G., & McCormick, S. (Eds.). (1995). *Single-subject experimental research: Applications for literacy*. Newark, DE: International Reading Association.

Neuman, W. L. (2000). *Social research methods: Qualitative and quantitative approaches* (4th ed.). Boston: Allyn & Bacon.

O'Brien, N. P., & Fabiano, E. (Eds.). (1990). *Core list of books and journals in education*. Phoenix, AZ: Oryn.

Ollerenshaw, J. A. (1998). *A study of the impact of a supplemental storytelling (oral narrative) strategy on fourth grade students' understanding of the physics of sound*. Unpublished doctoral dissertation, University of Iowa, Iowa City.

Ollerenshaw, J. A., & Creswell, J. W. (2000). *Data analysis in narrative research: A comparison of two "restorying" approaches*. Paper presented at the Annual American Educational Research Association, New Orleans, LA.

Orona, C. J. (1997). Temporality and identity loss due to Alzheimer's disease. In A. Strauss & J. Corbin (Eds.),

Grounded theory in practice (pp. 171–196). Thousand Oaks, CA: Sage.

Pachnowski, L. M., Newman, I., & Jurczyk, J. P. (1997). *Immediate data: The World Wide Web as a resource for teaching research methods.* (ERIC Document Reproduction Service No. ED409361)

Padula, M. A., & Miller, D. L. (1999). Understanding graduate women's reentry experiences. *Psychology of Women Quarterly, 23,* 327–343.

Pajak, E. F., & Blasé, J. J. (1984). Teachers in bars: From professional to personal self. *Sociology of Education, 57,* 164–173.

Patton, M. Q. (1990). *Qualitative evaluation and research methods* (2nd ed.). Newbury Park, CA: Sage.

Patton, M. Q. (2002). *Qualitative research and evaluation methods* (3rd ed.). Thousand Oaks, CA: Sage.

Pedhazur, E. J. (1997). *Multiple regression in behavioral research: Explanation and prediction* (3rd ed.). Fort Worth, TX: Harcourt Brace College Publishers.

Perrine, R. M., Lisle, J., & Tucker, D. L. (1996). Effects of a syllabus offer of help, student age, and class size on college students' willingness to seek support from faculty. *Journal of Experimental Education, 64*(1), 41–52.

Persichitte, K. A., Young, S., & Tharp, D. D. (1997). *Conducting research on the Internet: Strategies for electronic interviewing.* (ERIC Document Reproduction Service No. ED409860)

Personal Narratives Group. (1989). *Interpreting women's lives.* Bloomington: Indiana University Press.

Plano Clark, V. L., Miller, D. L., Creswell, J. W., McVea, K., McEntarffer, R., Mickelson, W. T. (2001). In conversation: High school students talk to students about tobacco use and prevention strategies. *Qualitative Health Research, 12*(9), 1264–1283.

Poling, A., & Grosset, D. (1986). Basic research designs in applied behavior analysis. In A. Poling & R. Fuque (Eds.), *Research methods in applied behavior analysis: Issues and advances.* New York: Plenum, pp. 7–27.

Punch, K. F. (1998). *Introduction to social research: Quantitative and qualitative approaches.* London: Sage.

Reichardt, C. S., & Cook, T. D. (1979). Beyond qualitative versus quantitative methods. In T. D. Cook & C. S. Reichardt (Eds.), *Qualitative and quantitative methods in evaluation research* (pp. 7–32). Beverly Hills, CA: Sage.

Reichardt, C. S., & Mark, M. M. (1998). Quasi-experimentation. In L. Bickman & D. J. Rog (Eds.), *Handbook of applied social research methods* (pp. 193–228). Thousand Oaks, CA: Sage.

Reichardt, C. S., & Rallis, S. E. (1994). *The qualitative-quantitative debate: New perspectives* (New Directions for Program Evaluation, No. 61; pp. 5–11). San Francisco: Jossey-Bass.

Reid, R., Hertzog, M., & Snyder, M. (1996). Educating every teacher, every year: The public schools and parents of children with ADHD. *Seminars in Speech and Language, 17,* 73–90.

Review of Educational Research. (1931–). Washington, DC: American Educational Research Association.

Rhoads, R. A. (1995). Whales tales, dog piles, and beer goggles: An ethnographic case study of fraternity life. *Anthropology and Education Quarterly, 26,* 306–323.

Rhoads, R. A. (1997). Implications of the growing visibility of gay and bisexual male students on campus. *NASPA Journal, 34,* 275–286.

Richardson, L. (2000). Writing: A method of inquiry. In N. K. Denzin & Y. S. Lincoln (Eds.), *Handbook of qualitative research* (2nd ed.). Thousand Oaks, CA: Sage.

Richie, B. S., Fassinger, R. E., Linn, S. G., & Johnson, J. (1997). Persistence, connection, and passion: A qualitative study of the career development of highly achieving African American-Black and White women. *Journal of Counseling Psychology, 44,* 143–148.

Riessman, C. K. (1993). *Narrative analysis.* Newbury Park, CA: Sage.

Robrecht, L. C. (1995). Grounded theory: Evolving methods. *Qualitative Health Research, 5,* 169–177.

Rosenau, P. M. (1992). *Post-modernism and the social sciences: Insights, inroads, and intrusions.* Princeton, NJ: Princeton University Press.

Ross-Larson, B. (2003). *Writing for the information age: Light, layered, and linked.* New York: W. W. Norton.

Rossman, G. B., & Wilson, B. L. (1985). Number and words: Combining quantitative and qualitative methods in a single large-scale evaluation study. *Evaluation Review, 9*(5), 627–643.

Royal, M. A., & Rossi, R. J. (1999). Predictors of within-school differences in teachers' sense of community. *The Journal of Educational Research, 92*(5), 259–265.

Rudestam, K. E., & Newton, R. R. (1992). *Surviving your dissertation.* Newbury Park, CA: Sage.

Rudner, L. M. (1993). Test evaluation [Online]. Available at www.ericae.net.

Russek, B. E., & Weinberg, S. L. (1993). Mixed methods in a study of implementation of technology-based materials in the elementary classroom. *Evaluation and Program Planning, 16,* 131–142.

Sagor, R. (2000). *Guiding school improvement with action research.* Alexandria, VA: Association for Supervision and Curriculum Development.

Salant, P., & Dillman, D. A. (1994). *How to conduct your own survey.* New York: Wiley.

Salkind, N. J. (2000). *Statistics for people who (think they) hate statistics.* Thousand Oaks, CA: Sage.

Schmuck, R. A. (1997). *Practical action research for change.* Arlington Heights, IL: IRI/SkyLight Training and Publishing.

Schwandt, T. A. (2001). *Qualitative inquiry: A dictionary of terms* (2nd ed.). Thousand Oaks, CA: Sage.

Schwandt, T. A., & Halpern, E. S. (1988). *Linking auditing and metaevaluation: Enhancing quality in applied research.* Newbury Park, CA: Sage.

Shapiro, E. S., & Lentz, F. E. (1991). Vocational-technical programs: Follow-up of students with learning disabilities. *Exceptional Children, 58,* 47–59.

Sieber, S. (1973). Integration of fieldwork and survey methods. *American Journal of Sociology (AJS), 78,* 1335–1359.

SilverPlatter Information Services. (1974/86–). *Sociofile.* Wellesley Hills, MA: Author.

SilverPlatter Information Services. (1986). *PsycLIT.* Wellesley Hills, MA: Author.

Sleeter, C. (1996). *Multicultural education as social activism.* Albany: State University of New York Press.

Smetana, J. G., & Asquith, P. (1994). Adolescents' and parents' conceptions of parental authority and personal autonomy. *Child Development, 65,* 1147–1162.

Smith, J. K. (1983, March). Quantitative versus qualitative research: An attempt to clarify the issue. *Educational Research, 12*(3) 6–13.

Society for Research in Child Development. (1945–). *Child development abstracts and bibliography*. Washington, DC: Committee on Child Development, National Research Council.

Sociological Abstracts, Inc. (1953–). *Sociological abstracts*. San Diego: Author.

Solomon, D. J. (2001). Conducting Web-based surveys. *Practical Assessment, Research & Evaluation, 7*(19), 1–6.

Spindler, G., & Spindler, L. (1992). Cultural process and ethnography: An anthropological perspective. In M. D. LeCompte, W. L. Millroy, & J. Preissle (Eds.), *The handbook of qualitative research in education* (pp. 53–92). San Diego: Academic Press.

Spradley, J. P. (1979). *The ethnographic interview*. Fort Worth, TX: Harcourt Brace Jovanovich College Publishers.

Spradley, J. P. (1980). *Participant observation*. New York: Holt, Rinehart and Winston.

Stake, R. E. (1995). *The art of case study research*. Thousand Oaks, CA: Sage.

Stake, R. E. (2000). Case studies. In N. K. Denzin & Y. S. Lincoln (Eds.), *Handbook of qualitative research* (2nd ed., pp. 435–454). Thousand Oaks, CA: Sage.

Stanulis, R. N., & Jeffers, L. (1995). Action research as a way of learning about teaching in a mentor/student teacher relationship. *Action in Teacher Education, XVI*(4), 14–24.

Steckler, A., McLeroy, K. R., Goodman, R. M., Bird, S. T., & McCormick, L. (1992). Toward integrating qualitative and quantitative methods: An introduction. *Health Education Quarterly, 19*(1), 1–8.

Strauss, A. (1987). *Qualitative analysis for social scientists*. New York: Cambridge University Press.

Strauss, A., & Corbin, J. (1990). *Basics of qualitative research: Grounded theory procedures and techniques*. Newbury Park, CA: Sage.

Strauss, A., & Corbin, J. (1998). *Basics of qualitative research: Techniques and procedures for developing grounded theory* (2nd ed.). Thousand Oaks, CA: Sage.

Strike, K. A., Anderson, M. S., Curren, R., Geel, T. V., Pritchard, I., & Robertson, E. (2002). *Ethical standards of the American Educational Research Association: Cases and commentary*. Washington, DC: American Educational Research Association.

Stringer, E. T. (1999). *Action research* (2nd ed.). Thousand Oaks, CA: Sage.

Subject guide to books in print. (1957–). New York: R. R. Bowker.

Tashakkori, A., & Teddlie, C. (1998). *Mixed methodology: Combining qualitative and quantitative approaches*. Thousand Oaks, CA: Sage.

Tashakkori, A., & Teddlie, C. (Eds.). (2003). *Handbook of mixed methods in social and behavioral research*. Thousand Oaks, CA: Sage.

Tesch, R. (1990). *Qualitative research: Analysis types and software tools*. Bristol, PA: Falmer Press.

Theberge, N. (1997). "It's part of the game": Physicality and the production of gender in women's hockey. *Gender & Society, 11*(1), 69–87.

Thomas, J. (1993). *Doing critical ethnography*. Newbury Park, CA: Sage.

Thomas, W. I., & Znaniecki, F. (1927). *The Polish peasant in Europe and America*. New York: Knopf.

Thorndike, R. M. (1997a). Correlational procedures in data analysis. In T. Husen & T. N. Postlethwaite (Eds.), *International encyclopedia of education* (2nd ed., pp. 1107–1117). Oxford and New York: Pergamon and Elsevier Science.

Thorndike, R. M. (1997b). *Measurement and evaluation in psychology and education* (6th ed.). Upper Saddle River, NJ: Macmillan/Prentice Hall.

Thorndike, R. M. (2005). *Measurement and evaluation in psychology and education* (7th ed.). Upper Saddle River, NJ: Pearson Education.

Tierney, W. (1997). *Academic outlaws: Queer theory and cultural studies in the academy*. Thousand Oaks, CA: Sage.

Tierney, W. G. (1993). *Building communities of difference: Higher education in the twenty-first century*. Westport, CT: Bergin & Garvey.

Ting, S. R. (2000). Predicting Asian-Americans' academic performance in the first year of college: An approach combining SAT scores and noncognitive variables. *Journal of College Student Development, 41*, 442–449.

Travers, R. M. W. (1992). History of educational research. In M. C. Alkin (Ed.), *Encyclopedia of educational research* (6th ed., pp. 384–389). New York: Macmillan.

Tuckman, B. W. (1999). *Conducting educational research* (5th ed.). Fort Worth, TX: Harcourt Brace College Publishers.

Turabian, K. L. (1996). *A manual for writers of term papers, theses, and dissertations* (6th ed.). Chicago: University of Chicago Press.

Unger, H. G. (1996). *Encyclopedia of American education*. New York: Facts on File, Inc.

University Council for Educational Administration. (1966–). *Educational administration abstracts*. Columbus, OH: Author.

University of Chicago Press. (2003). *The Chicago manual of style* (15th ed.). Chicago: Author.

University Microfilms International. (1938–1965/66). *Dissertation abstracts*. Ann Arbor, MI: Author.

University Microfilms International. (1987–). *Dissertation abstracts ondisc* (computer file). Ann Arbor, MI: Author.

University of Nebraska at Lincoln. (1997, January). *Institutional review board guidelines for the protection of human subjects in research studies*. Lincoln: Author.

Valois, R. F., & McKewon, R. E. (1998). Frequency and correlates of fighting and carrying weapons among public school adolescents. *American Journal of Health Behavior, 22*, 8–17.

Van Maanen, J. (1988). *Tales of the field: On writing ethnography*. Chicago: University of Chicago Press.

VanHorn-Grassmeyer, K. (1998). *Enhancing practice: New professional in student affairs*. Unpublished doctoral dissertation, University of Nebraska–Lincoln.

Viadero, D. (1999). What is (and isn't) research? *Education Week, XVIII*(41), 33, 34–36.

Vockell, E. L., & Asher, J. W. (1995). *Educational research* (2nd ed.). Upper Saddle River, NJ: Prentice Hall.

Vogt, W. P. (1999). *Dictionary of statistics and methodology: A nontechnical guide for the social sciences* (2nd ed.). Thousand Oaks, CA: Sage.

Vogt, W. P. (2005). *Dictionary of statistics and methodology: A nontechnical guide for the social sciences* (3rd ed.). Thousand Oaks, CA: Sage.

Walker, J. C., & Evers, C. W. (1988). The epistemological unit of educational research. In J. P. Keeves (Ed.), *Educational research, methodology, and measurement: An international handbook*. New York: Pergamon Press.

Wang, J., & Staver, J. R. (1997). An empirical study of gender differences in Chinese students' science achievement. *Journal of Educational Research, 90,* 252–255.

Ward, P. (1999). Chapter 3: Design of the Saber-Tooth project. *Journal of Teaching in Physical Education, 18,* 403–416.

Ward, P., Barrett, T. M., Evans, S. A., Doutis, P., Nguyen, P. T., & Johnson, M. K. (1999). Chapter 5: Curriculum effects in eighth-grade lacrosse. *Journal of Teaching in Physical Education, 18,* 428–443.

Watters, J. J., Christensen, C., Arcodia, C., Ryan, Y., & Weeks, P. (1998). Occasional visits to the kingdom. In B. Atweh, S. Kemmis, & P. Weeks (Eds.), *Action research in practice: Partnerships for social justice in education* (pp. 250–279). London and New York: Routledge.

Way, N., Stauber, H., Nakkula, M. J., & London, P. (1994). Depression and substance use in two divergent high school cultures: A qualitative and quantitative analysis. *Journal of Youth and Adolescence, 23*(3), 331–357.

Webb, E. J. (1966). *Unobtrusive measures: Nonreactive research in the social sciences*. Chicago: Rand-McNally.

Weitzman, E. A., & Miles, M. B. (1995). *Computer programs for qualitative data analysis*. Thousand Oaks, CA: Sage.

Whyte, W. F. (Ed.). (1991). *Participatory action research*. Newbury Park, CA: Sage.

Wilkinson, L., and the Task Force on Statistical Inference. (1999). Statistical methods in psychology journals. *American Psychologist, 54*(8), 594–604.

Wilson, H. W. (1929/32–). *Education index*. New York: H. W. Wilson.

Winthrop, R. H. (1991). *Dictionary of concepts in cultural anthropology*. Westport, CT: Greenwood.

Wolcott, H. F. (1974). The elementary school principal: Notes from a field study. In G. Spindler (Ed.), *Education and cultural process: Toward an anthropology of education* (pp. 176–204). New York: Holt, Rinehart and Winston.

Wolcott, H. F. (1983). Adequate schools and inadequate education: The life history of a sneaky kid. *Anthropology and Education Quarterly, 14,* 3–32.

Wolcott, H. F. (1992). *Writing up qualitative research*. Newbury Park, CA: Sage.

Wolcott, H. F. (1994). *Transforming qualitative data: Description, analysis, and interpretation*. Thousand Oaks, CA: Sage.

Wolcott, H. F. (1995). *The art of fieldwork*. Walnut Creek, CA: AltaMira.

Wolcott, H. F. (1999). *Ethnography: A way of seeing*. Walnut Creek, CA: AltaMira.

Wright, D. B. (1997). *Understanding statistics: An introduction for the social sciences*. London: Sage.

Zeichner, K. (1999). The new scholarship in teacher education. *Educational Researcher, 28*(9), 4–15.

Ziller, R. C. (1990). *Photographing the self: Methods for observing personal orientation*. Newbury Park, CA: Sage.

Author Index

Subject Index